Homelessness an

eleventh edition

Andrew Arden QC is a barrister and member of Arden Chambers, which he founded in 1993 to provide a centre for specialist practice primarily in the area of housing law and local government. He has appeared in many of the leading cases in housing law over the past 40 years. He is author or editor of the principal practitioner texts on housing law, including the *Encyclopaedia of Housing Law, Housing Law Reports, Journal of Housing Law, Arden & Partington's Housing Law, Local Government Constitutional and Administrative Law* (all Sweet & Maxwell), *Manual of Housing Law* and *Quiet Enjoyment: protection from rogue landlords* (LAG).

Justin Bates is a barrister and member of Arden Chambers. His practice covers all aspects of housing, property and local government law. Justin is the deputy general editor of the *Encyclopaedia of Housing Law*, a contributing editor to *Arden & Partington's Housing Law* and *Local Government Constitutional and Administrative Law* (all Sweet & Maxwell) and co-author of *Leasehold Disputes* (LAG).

Toby Vanhegan is a barrister and member of Arden Chambers specialising in housing law particularly homelessness, immigration and asylum, human rights and EU law. He has a particular knowledge and expertise in issues of eligibility, especially in the context of housing. Toby has written articles for *Journal of Housing Law* and *Legal Action* concerning freedom of movement of persons within the EU. He speaks regularly at conferences and provides legal training courses.

The purpose of the Legal Action Group is to promote equal access to justice for all members of society who are socially, economically or otherwise disadvantaged. To this end, it seeks to improve law and practice, the administration of justice and legal services.

Homelessness and Allocations

A guide to the Housing Act 1996 Parts 6 and 7 and the Housing (Wales) Act 2014 Part 2

ELEVENTH EDITION

Andrew Arden QC, Justin Bates and Toby Vanhegan

Editorial assistant: Brooke Lyne, barrister of Arden Chambers

Legal Action Group
2018

Eleventh edition published in Great Britain 2018
by LAG Education and Service Trust Limited
National Pro Bono Centre, 48 Chancery Lane, London WC2A 1JF
www.lag.org.uk

First edition 1982 as *The Homeless Persons Act* by Andrew Arden
Second edition 1986 as *Homeless Persons* by Andrew Arden
Third edition 1988 as *Homeless Persons* by Andrew Arden
Fourth edition 1992 as *Homeless Persons* by Caroline Hunter and Siobhan McGrath
Fifth edition 1997 as *Homelessness & Allocations* by Andrew Arden QC and Caroline Hunter
Sixth edition 2002 by Andrew Arden QC and Caroline Hunter
Revised sixth edition 2003 by Andrew Arden QC and Caroline Hunter
Seventh edition 2006 by Andrew Arden QC and Caroline Hunter
Eighth edition 2010 by Andrew Arden QC, Emily Orme and Toby Vanhegan
Ninth edition 2012 by Andrew Arden QC, Emily Orme and Toby Vanhegan
Tenth edition 2017 by Andrew Arden QC, Justin Bates and Toby Vanhegan

British Library Cataloguing in Publication Data.
A CIP catalogue record for this book is available from the British Library.

print ISBN: 978 1 912273 02 7
ebook ISBN: 978 1 912273 03 4

Typeset by RefineCatch Limited, Bungay, Suffolk
Printed in Great Britain by Hobbs the Printer, Totton, Hampshire

Contents

Table of cases

Table of statutes

Table of statutory instruments

Immigration Act 2016 (Commencement No 7 and Transitional Provisions) Regulations 2017 SI No 1241–	
reg 2	13.53
Immigration and Asylum (Provision of Accommodation to Failed Asylum-Seekers) Regulations 2005 SI No 930	13.53
reg 3(2)	13.54
Local Authorities (Contracting Out of Allocation of Housing and Homelessness Functions) Order 1996 SI No 3205	9.5, 9.7, 9.211, 12.57
art 3	9.5, 9.6
Sch 2	9.5, 9.6
Local Authorities (Executive Arrangements) (Functions and Responsibilities) (Wales) Regulations 2007 SI No 399 (W 45)	12.59
Sch 2 para 2	12.61
Local Authorities (Functions and Responsibilities) (England) Regulations 2000 SI No 2853	9.206, 12.59
reg 3(1)	12.61
Sch 2 para 2	12.61
Local Authorities' Plans and Strategies (Disapplication) (England) Order 2005 SI No 157	14.3
Local Government and Public Involvement in Health Act 2007 (Commencement No 5 and Transitional, Saving and Transitory Provision) Order 2008 SI No 917–	
reg 2(1)(i)	12.270
Local Government Changes for England Regulations 1994 SI No 867	2.17, 2.19
Local Housing Authorities (Prescribed Principles for Allocation Schemes) (Wales) Regulations 1997 SI No 45–	
reg 3	11.127, 11.128
Sch para 1	11.128
Sch para 2	11.127
Localism Act 2011 (Commencement No 2 and Transitional and Saving Provision) Order 2012 SI No 57	11.158
Localism Act 2011 (Commencement No 2 and Transitional Provisions) (England) Order 2012 SI No 2599–	
art 2	4.23, 4.61, 4.142, 5.1, 7.19, 9.25, 9.195, 10.15, 10.210, 10.211, 10.215, 10.217, 10.228, 10.231, 10.241, 10.251

Table of European legislation

Treaties etc

Regulations

Directives

Table of international conventions

European Convention on the Protection of Human Rights and Fundamental Freedoms (ECHR) 1950 Protocol 1—	
Art 2	10.193
Hague Convention on the Civil Aspects of International Child Abduction 1980	13.121, 13.122
Refugee Convention (United Nations Convention relating to the Status of Refugees 1951)	3.155, 3.163, 13.44
Art 1	3.155
Art 32	3.6

Abbreviations

AC(IWA) Regs 2013	Accession of Croatia (Immigration and Worker Authorisation) Regulations 2013 SI No 1460
ADR	alternative dispute resolution
AH(W) Regs 2003	Allocation of Housing (Wales) Regulations 2003 SI No 239
AIA 1996	Asylum and Immigration Act 1996
AIAA 1993	Asylum and Immigration Appeals Act 1993
A(IWA) Regs 2006	Accession (Immigration and Worker Authorisation) Regulations 2006 SI No 3317
A(IWR) Regs 2004	Accession (Immigration and Worker Registration) Regulations 2004 SI No 1219
ARC	application registration card
AS Regs 2000	Asylum Support Regulations 2000 SI No 704
ASBCPA 2014	Anti-social Behaviour, Crime and Policing Act 2014
A(WAWR)(A) Regs 2007	Accession (Worker Authorisation and Worker Registration) (Amendment) Regulations 2007 SI No 3012
A(WAWR)(A) Regs 2009	Accession (Worker Authorisation and Worker Registration) (Amendment) Regulations 2009 SI No 2426
BIA	Border and Immigration Agency
BNA 1981	British Nationality Act 1981
CA 1989	Children Act 1989
CA 2004	Children Act 2004
CA 2014	Care Act 2014
CACA 1985	Child Abduction and Custody Act 1985
CFA 2014	Children and Families Act 2014
CJA 1982	Criminal Justice Act 1982
CJA 1991	Criminal Justice Act 1991
CJEU	Court of Justice of the European Union
CLG Select Committee	Communities and Local Government Select Committee
CoSLA	Convention of Scottish Local Authorities
COT	Certificate of Travel
CPR	Civil Procedure Rules
CUKC	Citizen of the United Kingdom and Colonies

DCLG	Department for Communities and Local Government
DETR	Department of the Environment, Transport and the Regions
DHP	discretionary housing payment
DHSS	Department of Health and Social Security
DoE	Department of the Environment
DTLR	Department of Transport, Local Government and Regions
DWP	Department for Work and Pensions
EA 1996	Education Act 1996
EC	European Community
ECHR	European Convention on Human Rights
ECJ	European Court of Justice
ECtHR	European Court of Human Rights
EEA	European Economic Area
EEA Regs 2006	Immigration (European Economic Area) Regulations 2006 SI No 1003
EEA Regs 2016	Immigration (European Economic Area) Regulations 2016 SI No 1052
EEU	Evidence and Enquiries Unit
EFTA	European Free Trade Association
Eligibility Regs 2006	Allocation of Housing and Homelessness (Eligibility) (England) Regulations 2006 SI No 1294
Eligibility (Amendment) Regs 2012	Allocation of Housing and Homelessness (Eligibility) (England) (Amendment) Regulations 2012 SI No 2588
Eligibility (Amendment) Regs 2016	Allocation of Housing and Homelessness (Eligibility) (England) (Amendment) Regulations 2016 SI No 965
Eligibility (Wales) Regs 2014	Allocation of Housing and Homelessness (Eligibility) (Wales) Regulations 2014 SI No 2603
ELR	exceptional leave to remain
English Review Procedure Regs 1999	Allocation of Housing and Homelessness (Review Procedures) Regulations 1999 SI No 71
English Review Procedure Regs 2018	Homelessness (Review Procedures etc) Regulations 2018 SI No 223
EqA 2010	Equality Act 2010
EU	European Union
H&RA 2008	Housing and Regeneration Act 2008
HA	Housing Act
HCA	Homes and Communities Agency
H(HP)A 1977	Housing (Homeless Persons) Act 1977
HMO	house in multiple occupation
HOS	Housing Ombudsman Service
HP	humanitarian protection
HPA 1986	Housing and Planning Act 1986

HRA 1998	Human Rights Act 1998
HRA 2017	Homelessness Reduction Act 2017
H(W) Regs 2006	Homelessness (Wales) Regulations 2006 SI No 2646
H(W)A 2014	Housing (Wales) Act 2014
IA 1971	Immigration Act 1971
IA 1988	Immigration Act 1998
IA 2014	Immigration Act 2014
IAA 1999	Immigration and Asylum Act 1999
IA(PAFAS) Regs 2005	Immigration and Asylum (Provision of Accommodation to Failed Asylum Seekers) Regulations 2005 SI No 930
ILR	indefinite leave to remain
IND	Immigration and Nationality Directorate
ISD	Immigration Status Document
LA 2011	Localism Act 2011
LASPO 2012	Legal Aid, Sentencing and Punishment of Offenders Act 2012
LGA	Local Government Association
LGA 1972	Local Government Act 1972
LGA 1974	Local Government Act 1974
LGA 1985	Local Government Act 1985
LGA 2000	Local Government Act 2000
LG(MP)A 1982	Local Government (Miscellaneous Provisions) Act 1982
MHCLG	Ministry of Housing, Communities and Local Government
NAA 1948	National Assistance Act 1948
NAB	National Assistance Board
NAM	New Asylum Model
NASS	National Asylum Support Service
NHS	National Health Service
NHSCCA 1990	National Health Service and Community Care Act 1990
NIAA 2002	Nationality, Immigration and Asylum Act 2002
NIHE	Northern Ireland Housing Executive
ODPM	Office of the Deputy Prime Minister
PD	Practice Direction
PEA 1977	Protection from Eviction Act 1977
PRP	private registered provider of social housing
PSO(W)A 2005	Public Services Ombudsman (Wales) Act 2005
RA 1977	Rent Act 1977
R(A)A 1976	Rent (Agriculture) Act 1976
RSL	registered social landlord
SSWB(W)A 2014	Social Services and Well-being (Wales) Act 2014
TFEU	Treaty on the Functioning of the European Union
TSA	Tenant Services Authority
UKBA	UK Border Agency

UKRP	UK Residence Permit
UKVI	UK Visas and Immigration
UN	United Nations
Welsh Review Procedure Regs 2015	Homelessness (Review Procedure) (Wales) Regulations 2015 SI No 1266
WLGA	Welsh Local Government Association
WRS	Worker Registration Scheme

CHAPTER 1

The history and policy of the provisions

continued

Introduction

1.1 This chapter outlines the history of the law on homelessness and allocations, from before the Housing (Homeless Persons) Act (H(HP)A) 1977 through Housing Act (HA) 1996 Parts 6 and 7 – the present, principal Acts in England – and Homelessness Act 2002 to changes in England under the Localism Act (LA) 2011 followed by major changes to assist the homeless in Wales under Housing (Wales) Act (H(W)A) 2014 Part 2 and the adoption of some of these in England by the Homeless Reduction Act (HRA) 2017.

1.2 Although HA 1996 Parts 6 and 7 comprise free-standing legislation – in the sense that they are neither consolidation nor amendment – and it is unnecessary always to approach them by reference to their evolution, both Parts are nonetheless best understood historically not least because of the adoption by Part 7 of the well-litigated, critical definitions introduced by H(HP)A 1977 which had and subsequently been consolidated into Housing Act (HA) 1985 Part 3.

1.3 Thus, the then Minister for Local Government, Housing and Urban Regeneration (Mr Curry) said of the changes to homelessness law to be made by the HA 1996:

> We shall not go back to pre-1977 days. We shall keep the 1977 Act concepts of entitlement, homelessness, priority need, intentionality and local connection. Essentially, what we are changing is the way in which the duty is to be discharged.[1]

1.4 That discharge was closely interwoven with the allocation of local authority housing – Part 6 was the first major conceptual change in allocations law since 1935, when the concept of 'reasonable preference' for certain categories of housing need was introduced: in practice, however, allocations policy (and certainly its practice) had been dominated by the homeless since H(HP)A 1977.

1.5 Since HA 1996, the Homelessness Act 2002 again changed the shape of the law, introducing a new 'strategic' duty to formulate a response to homelessness and reshaping HA 1996 Part 6 to seek to include 'choice-based letting' within allocations law. Further changes have been made by regulations. Subsequently, LA 2011 reversed some of the effects of the Homelessness Act 2002 both by placing more emphasis on the use of private sector accommodation, and by introducing much greater freedom for authorities in England to

1 *Hansard*, Standing Committee G, 12 March 1996, col 587.

determine their own criteria as to whom they will house in their own accommodation (although, as will be seen in chapter 11, the case-law has rather limited this apparent freedom, see paras 11.61–11.62).

1.6 Wales subsequently led the way for further change in H(W)A 2014, including: extension of the period during which a person is threatened with homelessness from 28 to 56 days; assessment of those who need help to retain or obtain accommodation and help to prevent them becoming homeless; and, a power for authorities in conjunction with Welsh Ministers to jettison intentional homelessness (the most controversial of all of the homelessness provisions). The first two of these reforms were then adopted in England through what appropriately started life as a private member's bill,[2] the HRA 2017.

1.7 In this chapter, homelessness and allocations policy as embodied in law are approached as follows:

a) National Assistance Act (NAA) 1948 Part 3;
b) H(HP)A 1977; HA 1985 Part 3;
c) *Re Puhlhofer*;[3]
d) Housing and Planning Act (HPA) 1986;
e) Asylum and Immigration Appeals Act (AIAA) 1993;
f) *ex p Awua*;[4]
g) HA 1996 Parts 6 and 7;
h) between Acts;
i) Homelessness Act 2002;
j) changes following the Homelessness Act 2002;
k) LA 2011;
l) H(W)A 2014; and
m) HRA 2017.

National Assistance Act 1948

1.8 The provisions of NAA 1948 s21(1) placed local authorities under a duty to provide:

> . . . residential accommodation for persons who by reason of age, infirmity or any other circumstances are in need of care and attention which is not otherwise available to them, [and] temporary

2 H(HP)A 1977 was itself a private member's bill.

3 *R v Hillingdon LBC ex p Puhlhofer* [1986] AC 484, (1986) 18 HLR 158, HL.

4 *R v Brent LBC ex p Awua* [1996] AC 55, (1995) 27 HLR 453, HL.

accommodation for persons who are in urgent need thereof, being need arising in circumstances which could not reasonably have been foreseen or in such other circumstances as the authority may in any particular case determine.

1.9 Homelessness law – starting with H(HP)A 1977 – replaces only the second limb of that duty, ie the duty to provide temporary accommodation in urgent need.[5] (The first limb was replaced in England by Care Act 2014, and in Wales by Social Services and Well-being (Wales) Act 2014.)

1.10 The NAA 1948 duty extended to people ordinarily resident in a local authority's area.[6] Where satisfied that such a person was in urgent need of accommodation, the National Assistance Board (NAB) (later the Supplementary Benefits Commission) had power to require an authority to provide it. The local authority was under a further duty to protect the property of a person to whom it provided assistance under these provisions.[7]

1.11 Local authority duties under NAA 1948 were exercised under the general guidance of the minister: for these purposes, the Minister of Health.[8]

1.12 This legal structure fell far short of imposing a duty on local authorities to protect all homeless people, let alone to provide permanent accommodation. Rather, it provided for emergencies, especially unforeseeable emergencies.[9] The duration of accommodation was a matter for the authority. It probably meant no more than for so long as the authority considered appropriate or necessary;[10] urgent need for temporary accommodation was not to be equated with a vital but continuing need for permanent accommodation.[11]

1.13 The discretionary and temporary nature of this provision was the principal problem. Another problem was that of deciding 'ordinary residence' in an area. Reminiscent of the Poor Laws which the NAA 1948 had repealed and replaced, authorities 'shuttled' homeless

5 H(HP)A 1977 s20 and Schedule, repealing this part of NAA 1948 s21.

6 NAA 1948 s24.

7 NAA 1948 s24.

8 NAA 1948 s33, subsequently Local Authority Social Services Act 1970 s7.

9 *Southwark LBC v Williams* [1971] Ch 734, CA; see also Ministry of Health Circular 87/48 illustrating 'urgent and unforeseen need' as homelessness arising as a result of 'fire, flood or eviction'.

10 *Bristol Corporation v Stockford* (1973), reported in Carnwath, *A guide to the Housing (Homeless Persons) Act 1977*, Knight's Annotated Acts, 1978.

11 *Roberts v Dorset CC* (1976) 75 LGR 462.

people between areas, asserting that they were ordinarily resident in another authority's area which should take responsibility for them.

1.14 Even more problematic was the division of responsibilities between different authorities within a single geographical area: homelessness provision was to be found in NAA 1948 and was regarded as a social services problem; the duty to provide housing in any area lay, however, with the authority having responsibility under the Housing Acts.[12]

1.15 This problem was exacerbated by the re-organisation effected by the Local Government Act (LGA) 1972 with effect from 1 April 1974. From that date, social services outside London, and in non-metropolitan areas, became the responsibility of county councils, while housing was the responsibility of the district council.[13] Even in London and the metropolitan areas, where social services and housing remained the responsibility of the same authority, different departments would usually handle the different responsibilities. In either event, this brought with it a different kind of shuttling, not in this case between different geographical areas, but between different authorities or different departments carrying out different functions in the same locality.

1.16 This was an unsatisfactory division. Popular perception was changing – homelessness was no longer readily regarded as a symptom of personal or social inadequacy, but had come to be recognised as part of the continuing severe housing problem (whether a crude shortage of housing or a shortage of adequate housing where it was needed).[14]

1.17 The fact that children were commonly taken into care for no reason other than their parents' want of accommodation was itself a significant factor in the changing attitudes which produced the climate for H(HP)A 1977.

1.18 There are two other points to make concerning the pre-H(HP)A 1977 position, both of them occurring in 1974. The first is largely technical. The LGA 1972 contained an amendment to the NAA

12 Formerly HA 1957 Part 5, now HA 1985 Part 2.

13 Formerly HA 1957 s1, as amended by LGA 1972 s193 and Sch 22, now HA 1985 s1.

14 Significant contributions to this rise in awareness included those of J Sandford and K Loach, *Cathy come home*, 'The Wednesday Play', 1966 television film; J Greve et al, *Homelessness in London*, Scottish Academic Press, 1971; Bryan Glastonbury, *Homeless near a thousand homes*, Allen & Unwin, 1971; F Berry, *Housing – the great British failure*, Charles Knight, 1974. Of less popular, but greater official, influence was the Cullingworth Report, *Council housing – purposes, procedures and priorities*, 9th report of Housing Management Sub-committee of the Central Housing Advisory Committee, 1969.

1948, additional to the redistribution of responsibilities in non-metropolitan areas. The amendment reduced to a mere power what had previously been a duty.[15] The secretary of state, however, was empowered to re-impose the duty by directive, and, following an outcry by voluntary and welfare workers, lawyers and others concerned with the homeless,[16] did so in February 1974.

1.19 Second, and of more significance, was the circular issued in February 1974, which came to be known as the 'Joint Circular',[17] directed both to social services departments and authorities, and to housing departments and authorities.

1.20 The Joint Circular had two main aims: first, it urged the transfer to housing authorities or departments of such stock as was held by social services authorities and social services departments for the purpose of discharging their responsibilities towards the homeless; second, it identified what it described as 'priority groups' who were intended to enjoy a claim on local authority stock.

1.21 The definition of 'priority groups' in the Joint Circular closely resembled the definition of 'priority need' that was adopted in H(HP)A 1977 s2, subsequently in HA 1985 s59 and now to be found in HA 1996 s189 and H(W)A 2014 s70:

> The Priority Groups comprise families with dependent children living with them or in care; and adult families or people living alone who either become homeless in an emergency such as fire or flooding or are vulnerable because of old age, disability, pregnancy or other special reasons. For these priority groups, the issue is not whether, but by what means, local authorities should provide accommodation themselves or help those concerned to obtain accommodation in the private sector . . .
>
> Where a family has children there is no acceptable alternative to accommodation in which the family can be together as a family. The social cost, personal hardship, the long-term damage to children, as well as the expense involved in receiving a child into care rules this out as an acceptable course, other than in the exceptional case when professional social work advice is that there are compelling reasons apart from homelessness for separating children from their family. The provision of shelter from which the husband is excluded is also not acceptable unless there are sound social reasons, as, for example, where a wife is seeking temporary refuge following matrimonial

15 LGA 1972 s195, Sch 23.

16 See Partington, *Housing (Homeless Persons) Act 1977*, Sweet & Maxwell, 1978, introductory notes.

17 Department of Environment (DoE) Circular 18/74; Department of Health and Social Security (DHSS) Circular 4/74.

dispute and it is undesirable that she should be under pressure to return home.[18]

1.22 Notwithstanding this advice, many authorities failed to transfer responsibility from social services to housing, or to give the priority groups preference over their own, local priorities.[19] Accordingly, when a Liberal MP, Stephen Ross, was successful in the ballot for private members' bills, the government of the day supported him in introducing a Homeless Persons Bill and the opposition announced that it, too, would broadly support the measure. The bill was introduced and became law as the H(HP)A 1977.

Housing (Homeless Persons) Act 1977; Housing Act 1985 Part 3

Overview

1.23 These two Acts are taken together, as the HA 1985 was an exercise of consolidation of housing law – as such, save so far as there were recommendations of the Law Commission (Cmnd 9515) to effect explicit changes (of which there were none relevant to the policy of the legislation), no substantive change in homelessness law was intended or achieved.

1.24 One clear aim of H(HP)A 1977 was to place responsibility for the homeless on district councils and London borough councils.[20] Provision was made to transfer staff and stock from social services to housing: the Secretary of State for the Environment enjoyed power to compel the transfer of property and staff from one authority to another, not merely between London borough councils and district councils, but as between all 'relevant authorities', defined to include social service authorities.[21]

1.25 Another aim was to provide a uniform and national definition of, or criteria for, the circumstances in which one authority could shift on to another responsibility for a homeless person, so as to end

18 DoE Circular 18/74 paras 10–12.
19 *Hansard* HC Debs, 15 December 1975, Vol 902 cols 473–475.
20 H(HP)A 1977 s19.
21 H(HP)A 1977 s14; Housing (Consequential Provisions) Act 1985 s5 and Sch 4 para 8.

shuttling. These 'local connection' provisions included a positive link between employment and housing.[22]

1.26 The local connection provisions operated not so much to permit an authority to shift the burden of housing a homeless person on to another authority, as to prevent it from doing so once the applicant was shown to have a local connection with the area of the authority to which he or she had applied. Thus, the authority for the area in which an applicant had only an employment connection had to house the applicant, even though the applicant might have had no other connections with that area, for example, family or residence.

1.27 The most important provision of H(HP)A 1977, however, was the establishment of a national criterion which required local authorities to accommodate, or to secure accommodation for, those who:

a) were homeless;
b) were in priority need of accommodation; and
c) did not become homeless intentionally.

1.28 Leaving aside the resolution of responsibility embodied in the local connection provisions, the three key questions, therefore, became:

d) what was homelessness?
e) who was in priority need? and
f) when was homelessness intentional?

Homelessness

1.29 Defining homelessness is not easy, either as a matter of law or as a matter of policy.[23] The most literal approach is to deal with those without a roof over their heads. This is not only difficult to estimate, but is likely to exclude those with children as, commonly, some form of accommodation, however inadequate, is found for them.

1.30 The most radical approach, advocated by Shelter, the National Campaign for the Homeless, was that a person was homeless if the person lived 'in conditions so bad that a civilised family life is impossible': this was homelessness 'in the true sense of the word'.[24]

1.31 Another approach is to consider those families who have no home where they can live together. This excludes both single people and

22 H(HP)A 1977 s18; HA 1985 s61.

23 This and the next paragraph are based largely on Partington, *Housing (Homeless Persons) Act 1977*, Sweet & Maxwell, 1978, introductory notes, subheading 'Definitions of homelessness and extent of homelessness'.

24 *The grief report*, Shelter, 1972.

childless couples, but it was at the core of the definition which was adopted.

1.32 Under H(HP)A 1977, Parliament started with legal rights of occupation: a person was homeless if there was no accommodation which he or she could occupy by virtue of an interest or estate, or contract, together with anyone else who usually resided with him or her either as a member of the family, or in circumstances in which it was reasonable for that person to do so.[25]

1.33 A person was also not to be regarded as homeless if he or she was in occupation in circumstances in which a court order was required for eviction – for example, tenants whose tenancies had been determined. A person was homeless, however, if the person had been locked out of accommodation, had to leave accommodation because of domestic violence or, in the case of mobile homes and houseboats, if there was nowhere to park/moor accommodation and to live in it.[26]

Priority need

1.34 The definition of homelessness did not create any substantive housing rights on its own. It had to be read together with the definition of 'priority need'.

1.35 Only homeless people with a priority need for accommodation received housing assistance under H(HP)A 1977 and HA 1985:

a) those with children who were residing, or who might reasonably be expected to reside, with either the applicant or with anyone with whom the applicant might be expected to reside;
b) those who were residing, or who might reasonably be expected to reside, with someone who had become homeless as a result of an emergency;
c) those who were residing, or who might reasonably be expected to reside, with someone who was vulnerable on account of age, handicap or other special reason; and
d) a person who was residing, or who might reasonably be expected to reside, with someone who was a pregnant woman.[27]

1.36 The important point to note was this: in determining whether or not there was a priority need, not only the applicant but anyone who might reasonably be expected to reside with the applicant, regardless

25 H(HP)A 1977 s1; HA 1985 s58.
26 H(HP)A 1977 s1; HA 1985 s58.
27 H(HP)A 1977 s2; HA 1985 s59; cf para 1.21.

of whether he or she had hitherto lived together, had to be taken into account.

Intentional homelessness

1.37 Homeless people in priority need thus acquired a prima facie right to accommodation. To have become homeless, however, did not necessarily mean that someone had been evicted: the person might have quit of his or her own accord.

1.38 This provoked a hostile local authority reaction to H(HP)A 1977 as a bill and, in turn, led to the inclusion of 'intentional homelessness' provisions which had not been in the original bill.

1.39 Infamously, the bill was described as a charter for 'scroungers and scrimshankers'.[28]

1.40 Mr G Cunningham acquired a notoriety that in earlier editions of this book was described as 'unenviable' when he suggested that women would become pregnant in order to acquire a priority need and then terminate their pregnancies once housing had been secured.[29] 'Families who have hesitated in the past to make themselves homeless [as opposed to finding themselves homeless] need have no such reluctance now . . .' 'It will mean chaos.' 'Fifty per cent of alleged claims of homelessness are "try-ons".'[30]

1.41 Mr Cunningham's observation was nonetheless given a degree of judicial sanction by the House of Lords decision in *R v Brent LBC ex p Awua*,[31] in which Lord Hoffmann, delivering the only substantive speech, suggested that local authorities could decide to provide only temporary accommodation to a pregnant woman and 'wait and see' whether or not the child is placed for adoption.

1.42 Parliament did not wholly give in to these fears. Under H(HP)A 1977, and then HA 1985, not everyone who voluntarily quit accommodation was considered to be homeless intentionally, from which it followed that some could quit and yet be entitled to assistance from a local authority. It is when this class is considered – those who could quit of their own accord yet not be deemed homeless intentionally – that the remit of H(HP)A 1977 and HA 1985 is finally defined.

28 Per Mr W R Rees-Davies, *Hansard* HC Debs, 18 February 1977, Vol 926 col 905.

29 *Hansard* HC Debs, 8 July 1977, Vol 934 col 1689.

30 Quotes to be found in Widdowson, *Intentional homelessness*, Shelter, 1981, p6.

31 [1996] AC 55, (1995) 27 HLR 453, HL.

1.43 For an authority to find that someone had become homeless intentionally – and, thus, had forfeited his or her right to assistance – required satisfaction by the authority as to four conditions:

a) the applicant had to have ceased to occupy accommodation – so that those who had never had accommodation or last had it so long ago that it could not properly be taken into account, could not be homeless intentionally;
b) the applicant had to have ceased to occupy accommodation in consequence of a deliberate act or omission – an act or omission in good faith, in ignorance of a material fact (for example, ignorance of security of tenure or financial assistance towards housing costs), was not to be considered deliberate;
c) the accommodation had to have been such that it was reasonable to continue to occupy it, although those who left bad physical conditions were faced with the qualification that, in determining whether or not it was reasonable to remain in occupation, a housing authority could take into account housing conditions in its area generally; and
d) the accommodation which had been quit had to have been 'available for the occupation' of the applicant.[32] Accommodation was only 'available for occupation' if it was available both for the homeless person and for anyone who might reasonably be expected to reside with him or her.[33] In determining who might reasonably be expected to live together, no account was to be taken of want of accommodation.[34]

1.44 It followed that people who had never been able to live together but who were reasonably to be expected to do so – for example, the young couple who had to live apart for want of accommodation – and who acquired a priority need (for example, through pregnancy), could not be found to be intentionally homeless should one or other or both of them leave the separate accommodations in which they had hitherto been living. Only those who had quit accommodation which was available both for themselves and for those with whom they might reasonably be expected to live could be deemed homeless intentionally.

32 H(HP)A 1977 s17; HA 1985 s60.
33 H(HP)A 1977 s16; HA 1985 s75.
34 *Re Islam* [1983] 1 AC 688, (1981) 1 HLR 107, HL.

Discharge

1.45 Homeless people, then, for whom it was the policy of H(HP)A 1977 to ensure that any authority with which there was a local connection provided substantive assistance, were those: who had no accommodation as defined; who were in priority need of accommodation, which most commonly meant that they had children; and, who did not quit accommodation which was available for themselves and for the whole of their family unit.

1.46 The right which such applicants acquired was not, however, the legal right to council housing itself. Rather, the authority's duty was to ensure that accommodation was made available for the applicant (and for those who might reasonably be expected to reside with him or her). The authority might discharge this duty in any of the following ways:

a) by making available accommodation held by it under what is now HA 1985 Part 2 (ie, the principal part of that Act under which council housing is held)[35] or under any other enactment (for example, housing acquired in the exercise of other functions, such as education, highways, etc); or
b) by securing that the applicant obtained accommodation from some other person; or
c) by giving such advice and assistance as would secure that accommodation was obtained from some other person.[36]

1.47 The principal burden was in practice, however, bound to be placed on the local authority's own stock. Since 1935,[37] local authorities had been under an obligation to 'secure that in the selection of their tenants a reasonable preference is given to persons who were occupying insanitary or overcrowded houses, had large families or were living under unsatisfactory housing conditions';[38] subject to this somewhat loose 'reasonable preference' obligation, they were free to determine their own priorities. To this there was now added a new group: those to whom authorities owed a duty under the homeless legislation.[39]

1.48 In principle, this did no more than require authorities to treat the homeless on the same footing as others, which in law was largely a

35 Formerly HA 1957 Part 5.
36 H(HP)A 1977 s6(1); HA 1985 s69(1).
37 HA 1935 s51.
38 As consolidated in HA 1936 s85(2).
39 H(HP)A 1977 s6(2), amending HA 1957 s113(2), subsequently HA 1985 s22.

matter of local choice. In practice, however, provision for the homeless was bound to make a significant impact – especially as no added money was made available to authorities under the H(HP)A 1977.[40] Exacerbating the problem, public spending powers were severely restricted from 1980 onwards.[41] In addition, the introduction of security of tenure and the right to buy under the HA 1980 Part 1[42] meant that the stock of new housing available to local authorities was in decline. Inevitably, therefore, an increasing proportion of allocations went to homeless people.

Re Puhlhofer

1.49 With so much at stake for individuals, and with authorities unable – and in some cases unwilling – to fulfil the hope that H(HP)A 1977 appeared to hold out, it was inevitable that the courts would come to broker the interests of these two main parties. Because of the structure of the rights and duties created by the legislation – and following a period during which it had been considered that challenges to authorities' decisions might be mounted by way of an ordinary civil claim (in the county court or the High Court)[43] – it was held that this was a role which could only be fulfilled by way of judicial review in the High Court,[44] a process with which many practitioners were unfamiliar and which was – to put it mildly – a process which most of the homeless found opaque.

1.50 In time, practitioners adjusted and a very substantial number of cases in what has subsequently become the Administrative Court[45] came to hear judicial review applications at first instance.[46] Any

40 A point made by Lord Brightman in *R v Hillingdon LBC ex p Puhlhofer* [1986] AC 484, (1986) 18 HLR 158, HL.

41 Local Government, Planning and Land Act 1980; subsequently, see Local Government and Housing Act 1989. See now, the somewhat more liberal regime of Local Government Act 2003 Part 1. The financial crisis of 1976 had, in any event, led to stringent controls effectively imposed by the International Monetary Fund.

42 See now HA 1985 Parts 4, 5.

43 But see, now, chapter 12, for appeal to the county court on a point of law under HA 1996 s204.

44 Under RSC Order 53, now CPR 54; *Cocks v Thanet DC* [1983] AC 286, (1983) 6 HLR 15, HL.

45 Formerly, the Crown Office List of the High Court.

46 By 1991, almost 20 per cent of all cases in the Crown Office list were homelessness cases, second only to immigration: Bridges, Meszaros and Sunkin, *Judicial review in perspective*, Public Law Project, 1995.

analysis runs the risk of being subjective, but there was a popular perception that the High Court (and, on appeal, the Court of Appeal), far from maintaining a bias against the homeless, were not uncommonly helpful in their interpretation of the legislation – a perception which derives much support from many of the earlier decisions referred to in the body of this book.

1.51 One body of this judge-made law developed the obviously sensible notion that if a person was occupying accommodation so poor that it could be quit without a finding of intentionality, the person ought to be treated as if already homeless. This in effect wrote into the definition of homelessness itself – with its reliance on rights of occupation[47] – a minimum standard below which any accommodation should be entirely disregarded, even if there was a right to occupy it.[48]

1.52 Another, related, body of judge-made law introduced the concept of 'settled accommodation'.[49] Only departure from settled accommodation could constitute intentionality, whether because of its condition, terms of occupation or temporary quality. Conversely, only acquisition of settled accommodation would, in normal circumstances, break a period of intentional homelessness and entitle an applicant to re-apply.

1.53 Sympathy – while on occasion expressed – was rarely to be seen in action, however, at the highest level, the House of Lords. Of the nine cases under the 1977/1985 legislation which reached the House of Lords,[50] the homeless were successful in only two of them.[51]

47 See para 1.32.

48 See *R v South Herefordshire DC ex p Miles* (1983) 17 HLR 82, QBD; *City of Gloucester v Miles* (1985) 17 HLR 292, CA; *R v Dinefwr BC ex p Marshall* (1984) 17 HLR 310, QBD; see also the judgment of Ackner LJ in *Re Puhlhofer* at the Court of Appeal (1985) 17 HLR 558.

49 The phrase was coined by Ackner LJ in *Din v Wandsworth LBC* at the Court of Appeal: [1983] 1 AC 657, (1983) 1 HLR 73, HL; see also *Dyson v Kerrier DC* [1980] 1 WLR 1205, CA. See chapter 6.

50 *Re Islam* [1983] 1 AC 688, (1981) 1 HLR 107, HL; *Din v Wandsworth LBC* [1983] 1 AC 657, (1983) 1 HLR 73; *Re Betts* [1983] 2 AC 613, (1983) 10 HLR 97; *Cocks v Thanet DC* [1983] 2 AC 286, (1983) 6 HLR 15, HL; *Eastleigh BC v Walsh* [1985] 1 WLR 525, (1985) 17 HLR 392; *R v Hillingdon LBC ex p Puhlhofer* [1986] AC 484, (1986) 18 HLR 158, HL; *R v Oldham BC ex p G, R v Bexley LBC ex p Bentum, R v Tower Hamlets LBC ex p Begum* [1993] AC 509, (1983) 25 HLR 319; *R v Northavon DC ex p Smith* [1994] 2 AC 402, (1984) 26 HLR 659; *R v Brent LBC ex p Awua* [1996] AC 55, (1995) 27 HLR 453, HL.

51 *Re Islam and Eastleigh BC v Walsh*, above. Of these, *Walsh* was part of a wider issue – the distinction between tenancy and licence – which was contemporaneously being reviewed (and recast) by the House of Lords: see *Street v Mountford* [1985] AC 809, (1985) 17 HLR 402.

1.54 One of those nine cases was *Re Puhlhofer*,[52] in which the equiparation of homelessness and want of intentionality[53] was firmly rejected. No words such as 'appropriate' or 'reasonable' were to be imported into the term 'accommodation' in H(HP)A 1977 s1 / HA 1985 s58 (definition of homelessness), as Parliament had 'plainly and wisely' determined. The only example of what would not comprise accommodation was that of Diogenes' tub.

1.55 The House of Lords also took the opportunity forcefully to express its concern about the 'prolific' use of judicial review in this area: great restraint should be exercised when giving leave to proceed by way of judicial review; the courts should be used to monitor the actions of local authorities under the legislation only in exceptional cases. The speech of Lord Brightman, in particular, expressed the hope that there would be a lessening in the number of challenges under the legislation.[54]

> My Lords, I am troubled at the prolific use of judicial review for the purpose of challenging the performance by local authorities of their functions under the Act of 1977. Parliament intended the local authority to be the judge of fact. The Act abounds with the formula when, or if the housing authority are satisfied as to this, or that, or have reason to believe this, or that. Although the action or inaction of a local authority is clearly susceptible to judicial review where they have misconstrued the Act, or abused their powers or otherwise acted perversely, I think that great restraint should be exercised in giving leave to proceed by judicial review. The plight of the homeless is a desperate one, and the plight of the applicants in the present case commands the deepest sympathy. But it is not, in my opinion, appropriate that the remedy of judicial review, which is a discretionary remedy, should be made use of to monitor the actions of local authorities under the Act save in the exceptional case. The ground upon which the courts will review the exercise of an administrative discretion is abuse of power – eg bad faith, a mistake in construing the limits of the power, a procedural irregularity, or unreasonableness in the *Wednesbury* sense – unreasonableness verging on an absurdity: see the speech of Lord Scarman in *R v Secretary of State for the Environment, ex p Nottinghamshire CC*.[55] Where the existence or non-existence of a fact is left to the judgment and discretion of a public body and that fact involves a broad spectrum ranging from the obvious to the debatable to the just conceivable, it is the duty of the

52 *R v Hillingdon LBC ex p Puhlhofer* [1986] AC 484, (1986) 18 HLR 158, HL.
53 See para 1.54.
54 [1986] AC 484 at 518.
55 [1986] AC 240, 247–248 – see para 12.25.

> court to leave the decision of that fact to the public body to whom Parliament has entrusted the decision-making power save in a case where it is obvious that the public body, consciously or unconsciously, are acting perversely.
>
> . . . I express the hope that there will be a lessening in the number of challenges which are mounted against local authorities who are endeavouring, in extremely difficult circumstances, to perform their duties under the Homeless Persons Act with due regard for all their other housing problems.

1.56 Save for a relatively brief period, however, there was no appearance of any such reduction, or indeed of a lower rate of success on the part of the homeless.

Housing and Planning Act 1986

1.57 In 1986, in direct response to *Puhlhofer*,[56] Parliament reacted to the judgment that it had been 'wise'[57] not to qualify the accommodation the absence of which rendered a person homeless by amending the principal definition of 'homelessness' to do precisely that, in substance to harmonise the criteria of homelessness and intentionality: the homeless were now those who, even if enjoying one of the qualifying rights of occupation, occupied accommodation of which it would not be reasonable to remain in occupation (having regard to the general housing circumstances of their area).[58]

1.58 This, in substance, preferred the High Court approach[59] to that of the House of Lords, although it did not go quite so far because the amendment did not require that the accommodation of which the person was in occupation was also available for his or her occupation in the statutory sense, ie available for himself or herself together with anyone who might reasonably be expected to reside with him or her.[60] In practical or applied terms, it tended towards treating as homeless a person without settled accommodation.[61]

56 Above.

57 See para 1.54.

58 HPA 1986 s14(2), amending HA 1985 s58. In Scotland, the equivalent amendment treated as already homeless those who were overcrowded under Scots law and in such circumstances that their health was endangered: Housing (Scotland) Act 1986 s21(2), amending H(HP)A 1977 s1(2).

59 See para 1.50.

60 See para 1.43.

61 See para 1.52.

1.59 The HPA 1986 also amended HA 1985 to ensure that accommodation provided under Part 3 met broadly the same minimum criterion, likewise rejecting critical observations by Lord Brightman in *Re Puhlhofer* in relation to what had not otherwise proved to be controversial.[62] In practice, it was now accepted that the accommodation to be provided had to be settled.

1.60 It may be said that at this point homelessness law had reached its greatest coherence or cohesiveness – the lower courts had taken the parliamentary framework and, reinforced by HPA 1986, fleshed it out to identify a level of accommodation to which all those in priority need were entitled, below which they could quit without being intentionally homeless or else they continued to be homeless; and, they were entitled to the benefit of rehousing assistance under the Act, including priority in the allocation of local authority stock, to the same level.

Asylum and Immigration Appeals Act 1993

1.61 For a period, homelessness and allocations law enjoyed a period of statutory stability. Complaints of unfairness towards others awaiting public sector accommodation, or of an unduly liberal approach to intentionality, were met with revisions to the Code of Guidance issued by the Secretary of State for the Environment,[63] but neither achieved – nor sought to achieve – any substantive differences in effect.

1.62 During the 1990s, however, there was growing antagonism towards asylum-seekers, many of whom remained in the UK for years before a final decision on a claim was reached. As persons lawfully in the country pending that decision, they had at all times fallen within the protection of the legislation.[64] Under the AIAA 1993, however, they were now placed on a different footing from other homeless people. Until the final determination of a claim for

62 In two cases, without drawing the same link that had been drawn between homelessness and non-intentionality, it had been held that accommodation to be provided had to be appropriate or suitable or habitable (having regard to the applicant and those to reside with him or her): *Parr v Wyre BC* (1982) 2 HLR 71, CA (disapproved in *Re Puhlhofer*); and *R v Ryedale DC ex p Smith* (1983) 16 HLR 66.

63 Under HA 1985 s71; see now HA 1996 s182 and H(W)A 2014 s98.

64 *R v Hillingdon LBC ex p Streeting (No 2)* [1980] 1 WLR 1425, CA; *R v Westminster City Council ex p Castelli, Same ex p Tristram-Garcia* (1996) 28 HLR 616, CA.

asylum, when authorities were bound to reach a new decision,[65] there would be no duty towards any asylum-seeker who had the benefit of some accommodation, however temporary. Likewise, the accommodation to be provided did not have to be more than temporary.[66] In effect, therefore, for the duration of their period as such, asylum-seekers did not have a right to settled accommodation.

Ex p Awua

1.63 Leaving aside the policy of the AIAA 1993, as a matter of legal structure, that Act acknowledged what the courts, and the HPA 1986, had achieved in terms of quality of accommodation;[67] that was what asylum-seekers were to be deprived of, not rights under the legislation altogether.

1.64 This did not stop the House of Lords taking another crack at minimum standards. In *R v Brent LBC ex p Awua*,[68] rejecting the idea that 'accommodation' in both HA 1985 s58(1) (definition of homelessness) and s60(1) (definition of intentionality) had to be 'settled', still less 'permanent': notwithstanding the HPA 1986 amendments, the provisions meant no more than a place which could fairly be described as accommodation which it would be reasonable, having regard to general housing conditions in the local housing authority's district, for the person in question to continue to occupy.

1.65 The same was held to be true of the accommodation which a local housing authority had to make available to an unintentionally homeless person under HA 1985 s65(2); the accommodation had to be 'suitable', but there was no requirement of permanence.

1.66 Temporary accommodation was accordingly not, per se, unsuitable. If the tenure was so precarious that the person was likely to have to leave within 28 days without any alternative accommodation being available, then he or she remained threatened with homelessness[69] and the authority would not have discharged its duty. Otherwise, the period for which the accommodation was provided was a matter for the authority to decide.

65 AIAA 1993 s4(4).
66 AIAA 1993 s4(4).
67 See paras 1.57–1.60.
68 [1996] AC 55, (1995) 27 HLR 453, HL.
69 HA 1985 s58(4); see now HA 1996 s175(4).

1.67 The decision despatched the concept of settled accommodation save for the purpose of defining what class of accommodation an intentionally homeless applicant would need to have secured for himself or herself before being entitled to re-apply.[70] It was no longer to be used to identify accommodation which a person could quit without being found intentionally homeless or as the class of accommodation to which a qualifying applicant was entitled.

1.68 The committee was not referred to – and did not refer to – the AIAA 1993,[71] although it is unlikely that this would have rendered the decision per incuriam, as it is unlikely that it would have led the committee to a different result. Given the thrust of the decision, it seems more likely that the committee would have brushed it aside as an error into which the lower courts had led Parliament.

Housing Act 1996 Parts 6 and 7

Policy

1.69 The decision in *Awua*:

> . . . caught most people in the housing world somewhat by surprise. It said that a housing authority's duty could be discharged in as little as 28 days. The legal landscape . . . has, therefore, changed.

This was how the Minister for Local Government, Housing and Urban Regeneration described the decision, noting that HA 1996 was neither introduced because of the *Awua* case nor was a response to it.[72]

1.70 Indeed, the minister suggested that it went further than the government intended, by removing the safety net of immediate help that it was its new policy to provide,[73] in order to reduce the (increasing) proportion of (decreasing) local authority accommodation that was then being allocated to the homeless.

70 See para 1.52.

71 See para 1.61.

72 *Hansard*, Standing Committee G, 19 March 1996, col 691.

73 *Hansard*, Standing Committee G, 21 March 1996, col 776. The minister was aware of the implications of *Pepper v Hart* [1993] AC 593, HL, even if none too accurately, when he remarked, at col 769: 'The Hon Gentleman should also know that what Ministers say during the passage of a Bill is taken into consideration in legal proceedings'.

1.71 HA 1996 was foreshadowed by a consultation paper – *Access to local authority and housing association tenancies* – in January 1994, which described:

> . . . two main methods of acquiring a local authority or housing association tenancy – by making a direct application to the landlord concerned (and usually going on the relevant waiting list until a suitable property becomes available), or by being accepted as statutorily 'homeless' by a local authority . . .[74]

1.72 Government research[75] published contemporaneously:

> . . . shows that people rehoused from the waiting list are in many important respects (such as income, employment status and previous tenure) similar to households through the homelessness route . . . But statutorily homeless households receive automatic priority over others . . . As a result, in some areas – particularly in parts of London – it is almost impossible for any applicant ever to be rehoused from the waiting list . . . Of those who did manage to get rehoused, people using the waiting list route had to wait nearly twice as long . . . as people housed under the homelessness legislation . . .[76]
>
> By giving the local authority a greater responsibility towards those who can demonstrate 'homelessness' than towards anyone else in housing need, the current legislation creates a perverse incentive for people to have themselves accepted by a local authority as homeless . . . In the great majority of cases, someone accepted as homeless is in fact occupying accommodation of some sort at the time he or she approached the authority. Indeed, the largest single category of households accepted as statutorily homeless are people living as licensees of parents, relatives or friends who are no longer willing or able to accommodate them . . . There is a growing belief that the homelessness provisions are frequently used as a quick route into a separate home . . .[77]
>
> Against this background, the government is proposing measures to ensure fairer access to all parts of the rented housing sector. These include measures to prevent homelessness, to remove the distorting effect that the present provisions have on the allocation of housing, and to ensure that subsidised housing is equally available to all who genuinely need it, particularly couples seeking to establish a good home in which to start and raise a family.[78]

74 January 1994 Consultation Paper, para 2.5.

75 *Routes into local authority housing*, DoE Housing Research Summary No 16, 1994.

76 January 1994 Consultation Paper, para 2.6.

77 January 1994 Consultation Paper, para 2.8.

78 January 1994 Consultation Paper, para 3.1.

1.73 The proposals were threefold:

a) to limit the extent of an authority's duties to the homeless;
b) to limit local authority housing allocation to the homeless; and
c) to encourage more advisory activity to help people find other accommodation.[79]

1.74 The idea was to provide an immediate safety net, while longer-term allocation to homeless people would be considered alongside others seeking council housing.[80] This would be achieved by new constraints on allocation, subject to 'broad principles' to be laid down by central government.[81]

1.75 The white paper on which HA 1996 was based, *Our future homes*,[82] pursued the theme that homelessness was:

> . . . usually a short term crisis . . . We are committed to maintaining an immediate safety net, but this should be separate from a fair system of allocating long-term accommodation in a house or flat owned by a local authority or housing association . . .[83]
>
> Local authorities will continue to have an immediate duty to secure accommodation for families and vulnerable individuals who have nowhere to go. Where such people are found to have no alternative available accommodation, the local housing authority will have to secure suitable accommodation for not less than twelve months.[84] The authority may continue to secure accommodation for longer than that, although after two years it must check that the household's housing circumstances have not changed . . . These arrangements are intended to tide people over the immediate crisis of homelessness, and to give them time to find longer-term accommodation . . .[85]

1.76 The white paper was followed in January 1996 by a linked consultation paper, *Allocation of housing accommodation by local authorities*. This introduced the ideas that were to become Part 6 of HA 1996, governing the waiting list. It identified changes proposed to HA 1985

79 January 1994 Consultation Paper, para 3.2.
80 January 1994 Consultation Paper, para 3.4.
81 January 1994 Consultation Paper, paras 20.2, 22.1.
82 Cm 2901, HMSO, June 1995.
83 *Our future homes* (see footnote 82, above), p36, claiming that over 40 per cent of local authority new tenancies – over 80 per cent in some London authorities – and over 25 per cent of allocations of housing association tenancies were going to those accepted under the homelessness legislation.
84 Later changed to two years: see HA 1996 s193(2). See also *Hansard*, Standing Committee G, 21 March 1996, col 776 – reflecting a concern that, even if renewable, one year would not provide sufficient security.
85 White paper, *Our future homes*, p37.

s22,[86] designed to 'create a single route into social housing',[87] in accordance with the policy[88] of putting '*all* those with long-term housing needs on the same footing, while providing a safety net for emergency and pressing needs' (emphasis in original). It will be 'the only route into social housing allocated by local authorities; it will be dynamic, and will focus on basic underlying need rather than immediate emergency'.[89]

1.77 The consultation paper proposed to retain the long-established categories of those occupying insanitary or overcrowded housing, or living in unsatisfactory housing conditions,[90] to which it would add:

a) those living in conditions of temporary or insecure tenure (including those at risk of losing accommodation, for example, tied accommodation);
b) families with dependent children or who are expecting a child ('recognising the importance of a stable home environment to children's development');
c) households containing a person with an identified need for settled accommodation (for example, those who give or need to receive care or other personal circumstances); and
d) those households with limited opportunities to secure settled accommodation (for example, low income), bearing in mind longer-term prospects.[91]

1.78 The principal policy change – to minimise the priority call of homeless people on local authority stock – may be addressed under its two heads: principal homelessness changes and allocation changes. In addition, there was a number of other discrete changes.

Principal homelessness changes

1.79 The principal homelessness changes[92] were:

86 See paras 1.47 and 1.48.

87 *Hansard* (HC), Standing Committee G, 16th Sitting, 12 March 1996, Minister for Local Government, Housing and Urban Regeneration (Mr Curry), col 614.

88 White paper, *Our future homes*, chapter 6.

89 *Hansard* (HC), Standing Committee G, 15th Sitting, 12 March 1996, Minister for Local Government, Housing and Urban Regeneration (Mr Curry), col 588.

90 See para 1.47.

91 January 1996 Consultation Paper (see para 1.75), paras 26, 27, 28–31, 33.

92 The exclusion of those subject to immigration control, introduced in 1993 (paras 1.61–1.62).

a) persons subject to immigration control under the Asylum and Immigration Act (AIA) 1996, unless of a class prescribed by the secretary of state, were no longer eligible under HA 1996 Part 7;[93] nor were others within any class prescribed by the secretary of state; nor were such persons to be taken into consideration when determining whether someone else was homeless, threatened with homelessness or had a priority need for accommodation;[94]
b) where the authority was satisfied that there was other suitable accommodation available in its area, the duty was limited to giving 'such advice and assistance as the authority consider is reasonably required to enable' the applicant to secure such accommodation;[95]
c) in cases where such suitable accommodation was not available, the duty to secure that accommodation was made available to the applicant was limited to two years (although could be continued in defined circumstances following a review, and – in default – a new application could otherwise be made);[96]
d) unless and until the authority could make an offer from its waiting list, the authority was prohibited from providing its own accommodation in discharge of functions under HA 1996 Part 7 for more than two years out of any three (whether continuously or in aggregate), unless it was hostel accommodation or accommodation privately leased by the authority from a private landlord.[97]

Allocations

1.80 Meanwhile, HA 1996 Part 6 provided that:

a) local authorities were bound to comply with Part 6 when making any allocation decision, including the selection of their own tenants and nominations to a registered social landlord,[98] but not including, among others, transfers;[99]

93 HA 1996 s185.
94 HA 1996 s185(4).
95 HA 1996 s197.
96 HA 1996 ss193, 194.
97 HA 1996 s207; this included housing associations or, as they and other similar bodies were known by HA 1996 Part 1, registered social landlords.
98 HA 1996 s159.
99 HA 1996 s159(9).

b) allocation could also[100] only be to persons qualified on the housing register which they were bound to maintain,[101] which could not include a person subject to immigration control under the AIA 1996, unless of a class prescribed by the secretary of state, nor could it include others within any class prescribed by the secretary of state; qualification was otherwise within the discretion of the authority;[102]
c) authorities had to adopt an allocation scheme for determining priority between applicants, including by whom decisions could be taken.

1.81 Subject to this, the scheme had to be framed to secure a reasonable preference not for the homeless to whom duties were owed per se,[103] but for:

a) those occupying insanitary or overcrowded housing, or otherwise living in insanitary conditions;
b) those living in temporary accommodation or on insecure terms;
c) families with dependent children;
d) households consisting of or including someone who was expecting a child;
e) households consisting of or including someone with a particular need for settled accommodation on medical or welfare grounds, with added preference under this heading to those who could not reasonably be expected to find their own settled accommodation in the near future; and
f) households whose social or economic circumstances were such that they had difficulty in securing settled accommodation.[104]

Other changes

1.82 HA 1996 Part 6 included a number of ancillary provisions, including notification of entry on and removal from the register, review of entries and review of decisions. Part 7 also effected a number of changes to homelessness law, of which the most significant were

100 See para 1.80.
101 HA 1996 s162.
102 HA 1996 s161.
103 Though plainly many of the homeless would qualify within the classes to be given a reasonable preference.
104 HA 1996 s167(2).

the introduction of a right to internal review and subsequent appeal to the county court.[105]

Between 1996 and 2002 Acts

Restoration of priority to homeless people

1.83 HA 1996 Parts 6 and 7 had been in force for only a relatively short period of time when the general election of 1997 brought in a new government. One of its first acts was to restore priority to homeless people under HA 1996 Part 6. Using a power[106] to specify further descriptions of people to whom a preference should be given, the Allocation of Housing (Reasonable and Additional Preference) Regulations 1997[107] re-instated[108] a reasonable preference for the unintentionally homeless towards whom a duty was owed under HA 1996 Part 7 or its predecessor provisions in the HA 1985.

Asylum-seekers

1.84 The Immigration and Asylum Act 1999 set up an entirely separate national service – the National Asylum Support Service (NASS) – to deal with destitute asylum-seekers.[109] As a result, all asylum-seekers whose claims were made on or after 3 April 2000 were taken out of HA 1996 Part 7.

A decent home for all

1.85 These changes were followed, in April 2000, by 'the first comprehensive review of housing policy for 23 years' – the green paper, *Quality and choice: a decent home for all*,[110] which set out aims for

105 HA 1996 ss202, 204.
106 HA 1996 s167(3).
107 SI No 1902.
108 Cf para 1.47.
109 Those who made their first asylum claim on or after 5 March 2007 were dealt with under the New Asylum Model (NAM) – see chapter 3; earlier applicants are known as 'legacy' cases and should have their asylum and support claims dealt with by the Casework Resolution Directorate. NAM was replaced by the UK Border Agency (UKBA) Local Authority Team and this, in turn, was replaced by the Home Office's UK Visa and Immigration Centre: see para 3.137.
110 Department of the Environment, Transport and the Regions (DETR), 2000.

reform in relation to both homelessness and allocations. The changes to the allocations provisions were subject to an overall aim of encouraging 'social landlords to see themselves more as providers of a lettings service which is responsive to the needs and wishes of individuals rather than purely as housing "allocators"'.[111]

1.86 The aims were to ensure that lettings and transfer services:

a) meet the long-term housing requirements of those who need social housing most, in a way which is sustainable both for individuals and the community;
b) adopt a simple and customer-centred approach, empowering first-time applicants and existing tenants to make decisions in choosing housing which meets their requirements;
c) make better use of the national housing stock, by widening the scope for lettings and transfers across local authority boundaries, and between local authorities and registered social landlords; and
d) give local authorities more flexibility to build sustainable communities within the national context of extreme variations in local housing markets.[112]

1.87 The green paper's proposals for the reform of homelessness policy were intended to:

a) ensure that unintentionally homeless people in priority need were provided with temporary accommodation until they obtained settled accommodation (in either the public or private sector);
b) broaden the definition of priority need to ensure that the most vulnerable citizens were protected by the homelessness safety net;
c) enable local authorities to use their own housing stock to provide temporary accommodation, without the restriction that it could only be provided for two years in any three;[113]
d) give those housed in temporary accommodation a reasonable period in which they could exercise the same degree of customer choice of settled accommodation as available to other people with urgent housing needs waiting on the housing register;
e) allow local authorities greater flexibility to assist non-priority homeless households, particularly in areas of low demand; and
f) encourage a more strategic approach to the prevention of homelessness and the rehousing of homeless households.[114]

111 *Quality and choice: a decent home for all*, para 9.3.
112 *Quality and choice: a decent home for all*, para 9.4.
113 See para 1.79.
114 *Quality and choice: a decent home for all*, para 9.42.

1.88 Following consultation, the government published *Quality and choice: a decent home for all – The way forward*,[115] explaining how it was 'taking the agenda forward'.[116] 'The principle of choice in lettings was broadly welcomed.'[117] Indeed, the move towards choice-based lettings was already being facilitated within the existing legal framework of HA 1996 Part 6, through a series of government-funded pilot schemes.[118] In relation to the homelessness proposals, 'there was almost unanimous support, from those who responded'.[119] Legislation was promised.

1.89 This legislation originally formed part of the Homes Bill 2001, which also included provisions to improve the process of buying and selling homes through a requirement for a 'home-buyers pack'. The bill fell at committee stage in the House of Lords, as a result of the general election in May 2001. Following re-election, the government decided not to proceed immediately with the provisions relating to home-buying, but re-introduced those relating to homelessness and allocation, in the Homelessness Bill.

Priority need categories

1.90 Not all the elements of the green paper proposals required primary legislation, however. In particular, the paper had proposed extending the categories of priority need[120] to those leaving an institutional or care background, those fleeing domestic violence, and 16- and 17-year-olds. This could be achieved by statutory instrument, under HA 1996 s189(2).

1.91 An amendment to this effect was made by the National Assembly for Wales on 1 March 2001.[121] In England, there was consultation on a draft statutory instrument during 2001, and it was not until 2002 that the changes were made, to coincide with the coming into force of most of the homelessness provisions in the Homelessness Act 2002.[122]

115 DETR, December 2000.
116 *The way forward*, p4.
117 *The way forward*, para 6.2.
118 *The way forward*, para 6.5.
119 *The way forward*, para 7.3.
120 *Quality and choice: a decent home for all*, paras 9.55, 9.56.
121 Homeless Persons (Priority Need) (Wales) Order 2001 SI No 607.
122 See the Homelessness (Priority Need for Accommodation) (England) Order 2002 SI No 2051.

1.92 The Welsh and English provisions are not worded identically, illustrating an increasing divergence in housing policy following devolution. In particular, while the Welsh identified certain applicants as being in priority need,[123] the English provisions identified certain applicants as being in priority need but only if vulnerable,[124] leaving a measure of room for manoeuvre for recalcitrant authorities.

Homelessness Act 2002

Strategies

1.93 The green paper had emphasised the need for authorities to develop a more strategic approach to the prevention and redress of homelessness. This was embodied in Homelessness Act 2002 ss1–4, by a duty requiring each local housing authority to undertake a review of homelessness and to formulate an effective strategy to deal with it, in consultation with both social services (whether of the same authority or another) and other organisations.

Duties

1.94 One of the main changes of HA 1996 had been to limit the initial duty to house homeless people to a period of two years.[125] This limit was repealed by the Homelessness Act 2002, along with the prohibition[126] on use of an authority's stock to house the homeless.[127] Also repealed was the provision of HA 1996 s197 which allowed the main duties to be avoided[128] if other suitable accommodation was available.[129]

1.95 Nonetheless, the duty was not intended to last indefinitely, and the circumstances which bring an authority's duty to an end under HA 1996 s193 were accordingly widened to allow more reliance on

123 See now H(W)A 2014 s70.

124 Homelessness (Priority Need for Accommodation) (England) Order 2002 SI No 2051.

125 See para 1.79.

126 See para 1.79.

127 Homelessness Act 2002 s6.

128 See para 1.79.

129 Homelessness Act 2002 s9.

assured tenancies, and – in certain circumstances – even assured shorthold tenancies.[130]

Non-priority need applicants

1.96 Homelessness Act 2002 s5 also gave local authorities power to house the unintentionally homeless under HA 1996 Part 7, even where not in priority need.

Other changes

1.97 Further changes were made to the definitions of 'homelessness' and 'intentionality', to ensure that any kind of violence – not only domestic violence – would mean that it is not reasonable to continue to occupy accommodation.[131] This helps, for example, those fleeing racial harassment or intimidation.

1.98 In addition, there was an extension in the jurisdiction of the county court to allow an applicant who appeals against an authority's decision also to appeal to that court against a refusal by the authority to provide the applicant with interim accommodation pending the outcome of the appeal process.[132]

1.99 The Homelessness Act 2002 made two other amendments to the review process: applicants are allowed both to accept an offer of accommodation and to challenge its suitability by way of review;[133] and, the county court may itself extend the 21-day time limit for appealing.[134]

Allocations

1.100 The amendments to HA 1996 Part 6 almost all reflected the government's aim of bringing greater choice to the allocation process by local authorities.

1.101 One change was to bring transfer applications[135] (whether within the stock of a single landlord or between the stocks of more than one landlord) into the ambit of HA 1996 Part 6.[136] This ensured both that

130 Homelessness Act 2002 s7.
131 Homelessness Act 2002 s10.
132 Homelessness Act 2002 s11.
133 Homelessness Act 2002 s8(2).
134 Homelessness Act 2002 Sch 1 para 17.
135 Cf para 1.80.
136 Homelessness Act 2002 s13.

existing tenants are dealt with on the same basis as new applicants and that their qualification for rehousing is not limited.[137]

1.102 The HA 1996 requirement to keep a housing register was abolished:[138]

> Removing the requirement to have a register is an important step in facilitating the development by local authorities of choice-based letting schemes that put the applicant at the centre of the decision-making process. We want to encourage authorities to move away from the rigid formulas of an often artificial points-based system, which typically becomes associated with allocation schemes based on the housing register.[139]

1.103 The government retained the ineligibility of persons from abroad for an allocation.[140] In addition, the Homelessness Act 2002 (as had the green paper) reflected a widespread concern about anti-social behaviour, and the Act therefore contained provisions allowing those guilty of 'unacceptable behaviour serious enough to make him or her unsuitable to be a tenant' to be excluded from social housing.[141]

1.104 The requirement that allocation schemes reflect housing need in some way was not abandoned and the Homelessness Act 2002 retained the concept of the 'reasonable preference' to be given to certain groups, albeit subject to some changes.[142] Authorities' schemes were explicitly allowed to take into account financial resources, behaviour and local connection when determining preference and, even where those guilty of seriously unacceptable behaviour were not excluded from the allocation scheme altogether, they could be accorded no preference.

1.105 Changes were made to the ancillary provisions on notification and internal review to allow an applicant to seek an internal review in relation to any decision about the facts of the applicant's case, including a decision that the applicant is to be excluded or given no preference because of unacceptable behaviour.[143]

137 See *Quality and choice: a decent home for all*, DETR, 2000, para 9.8.

138 See para 1.80.

139 Standing Committee A, 12 July 2001, col 81, per Dr Alan Whitehead, Parliamentary Under-Secretary for Transport, Local Government and the Regions.

140 See para 1.80.

141 Homelessness Act 2002 s16.

142 Including giving preference to all homeless people, whether in priority need or not, and whether or not intentionally homeless: HA 1996 s167(2)(a) as amended by HA 2002 s16(3).

143 Homelessness Act 2002 s14.

1.106 The Homelessness Act 2002 provisions still did not comprise a tightly-prescriptive framework and there remained considerable room for local variation.

> We believe the right way forward is for local authorities and registered social landlords to decide in the light of local circumstances, and drawing on the experiences of the pilot studies, the ways in which they should amend or develop their existing arrangements.[144]

Between 2002 and 2011 Acts

1.107 Devolution is an issue that goes well beyond this book. It may be said, however, that by the transfer of powers[145] it has brought benefits (in terms of this book) not only to the people of Wales but also to those of England, by introducing new approaches and otherwise leading the way towards a markedly less harsh approach, albeit at the cost of some added length to any description of the subject which sets out to cover both, increasingly divergent systems.

1.108 Leaving this aside, the focus of Westminster government policy following the Homelessness Act 2002 and prior to the change of administration in 2010 was primarily on implementation. One particular area of attack was on use of bed and breakfast accommodation: in 2003, secondary legislation made it unlawful in England for local authorities to place families in bed and breakfast accommodation for more than six weeks.[146]

1.109 Other key changes governed immigration and asylum. While it has already been noted that asylum-seekers were taken outside the existing statutory provisions in April 2000 by the establishment of

144 *The way forward*, para 6.4.

145 In Wales, ministerial functions in many areas of activity (including housing) were transferred to the National Assembly for Wales by Government of Wales Act 1998 s22, Sch 2 para 9; National Assembly for Wales (Transfer of Functions) Order 1999 SI No 672. The Government of Wales Act 2006 then transferred those functions from the Assembly to the Welsh Ministers (ss58, 161, Sch 11 para 30). The National Assembly for Wales was not granted legislative competence over housing matters but, by Government of Wales Act 2006 s95, could be given such competence by Order in Council. To date, two relevant Orders have been made: the National Assembly for Wales (Legislative Competence) (Housing) (Fire Safety) Order 2010 SI No 1210 and the National Assembly for Wales (Legislative Competence) (Housing and Local Government) Order 2010 SI No 1838.

146 Homelessness (Suitability of Accommodation) (England) Order 2003 SI No 3326. Similar (although not identical) limitations were introduced in Wales in 2006.

NASS,[147] the question arose whether accommodation provided by NASS gave rise to a local connection under HA 1996 Part 7 if and when asylum-seekers achieved refugee status and were thus able to apply under Part 7. The House of Lords initially answered this question in the negative.[148] The government, concerned that refugees would overwhelmingly apply to areas of greatest housing stress in London and the south-east, reversed this decision by amendments to HA 1996 s199 contained in Asylum and Immigration (Treatment of Claimants, etc) Act 2004 s11.

1.110 Another immigration-related statutory change followed from the exclusion of ineligible persons when considering whether an applicant for HA 1996 Part 7 assistance was homeless, threatened with homelessness or in priority need.[149] This was held to be incompatible with the family life provisions of Article 8 of the European Convention on Human Rights (ECHR).[150] As a result, the Housing and Regeneration Act (H&RA) 2008 amended HA 1996 s185(4) so as to take such persons into account, except in those cases where, although eligible, the applicant[151] is subject to immigration control;[152] such an application would, however, be known as a 'restricted case' to whom the authority owes a – somewhat lesser – duty by way of making a 'private accommodation offer',[153] and by exclusion from the reasonable preference afforded to the homeless under HA 1996 Part 6.[154]

1.111 The H&RA 2008 also made changes to the local connection provisions, so as to include employment in the armed forces and residence during such service as grounds for a local connection, where they had formerly been excluded.[155]

147 See para 1.84.

148 *Al-ameri v Kensington and Chelsea RLBC; Osmani v Harrow LBC* [2004] UKHL 4, [2004] HLR 20.

149 See para 1.79.

150 *R (Morris) v Westminster City Council (No 3)* [2005] EWCA Civ 1184, [2006] 1 WLR 505, [2006] HLR 8. In *Bah v UK* App No 56328/07, [2012] HLR 2, however, the European Court of Human Rights held that it was not in contravention.

151 Not being a European Economic Area (EEA) or Swiss national, who are fully eligible: see paras 3.140–3.152.

152 Ie, asylum-seekers, those with indefinite leave to remain: see paras 3.154–3.176.

153 H&RA 2008 s314 and Sch 15 Part 1; now called a 'private rented sector offer'. The details of what this duty entails may be seen at paras 5.8–5.11.

154 HA 1996 s167(2ZA), inserted by H&RA 2008 s314 and Sch 15 Part 1.

155 See para 7.37.

1.112 No case-law,[156] however, had the seminal effect of a *Puhlhofer*[157] or *Awua*,[158] with the possible exception of the HA 1996 Part 6 decision in *R (Ahmad) v Newham LBC*,[159] in which shades of Lord Brightman's speech in *Puhlhofer*[160] to be found in the speech of Lord Neuberger,[161] albeit on a reasoned basis.

> [A]s a general proposition, it is undesirable for the courts to get involved in questions of how priorities are accorded in housing allocation policies. Of course, there will be cases where the court has a duty to interfere, for instance if a policy does not comply with statutory requirements, or if it is plainly irrational. It seems unlikely, however, that the legislature can have intended that Judges should embark on the exercise of telling authorities how to decide on priorities as between applicants in need of rehousing, save in relatively rare and extreme circumstances. Housing allocation policy is a difficult exercise which requires not only social and political sensitivity and judgment, but also local expertise and knowledge.
>
> In relation to the provision of accommodation under the National Assistance Act 1948, my noble and learned friend, Baroness Hale of Richmond, then Hale LJ, said in *R (Wahid) v Tower Hamlets LBC*,[162] para 33, '[n]eed is a relative concept, which trained and experienced social workers are much better equipped to assess than are lawyers and courts, provided that they act rationally'. Precisely the same is true of relative housing needs under Part 6 of the 1996 Act, and trained and experienced local authority housing officers.

Localism Act 2011

1.113 The 'coalition government' which followed the general election in 2010 made a number of changes to housing, including changes to

156 Other important decisions include *Holmes-Moorhouse v Richmond upon Thames LBC* [2009] UKHL 7, [2009] HLR 34 (see para 5.30) rejecting the proposition that if a court in family proceedings makes a shared residence order, both parents are in priority need, and *Birmingham City Council v Ali, Moran v Manchester City Council* [2009] UKHL 36, [2009] 1 WLR 1506 (see paras 4.13 and 4.70) opening the way to the practice of treating people as 'homeless at home', ie without loss of preference. The first has also been much relied on by authorities for its relatively relaxed approach to the wording of decision-letters (see paras 12.91–12.92).

157 See paras 1.49–1.56.

158 See paras 1.63–1.68.

159 [2009] UKHL 14, [2009] HLR 31.

160 See para 1.55.

161 At [46]–[47].

162 [2002] EWCA Civ 287, [2003] HLR 13.

both the homelessness and allocation provisions of HA 1996 Part 6 (as amended by the Homelessness Act 2002).

1.114 The consultation paper which preceded the Act – *Local decisions: a fairer future for social housing*[163] – was reminiscent of the policy which preceded the HA 1996.[164]

1.115 Thus, on homelessness:

> 6.7 Under the current legislation, although local authorities have considerable flexibility in how to meet the immediate housing needs of people owed the main homelessness duty, they are very restricted in the way they can bring the duty to an end. Suitable accommodation in the private rented sector can be offered as a settled home that ends the duty, but applicants can refuse such offers without good reason, and the duty continues to be owed . . .
>
> 6.8 People owed the main homelessness duty can therefore effectively insist on being provided with temporary accommodation until offered social housing (and under housing allocation legislation, they must be given reasonable preference for social housing). We believe this encourages some households to apply as homeless in order to secure reasonable preference and an effective guarantee of being offered social housing . . .
>
> . . .
>
> 6.12 We intend to give authorities the discretion to decide in any particular case whether a person owed the homelessness duty needs social housing or whether their needs could be met with suitable accommodation in the private rented sector . . .

1.116 Likewise, on allocations:

> 4.6 The requirement to maintain open waiting lists, coupled with the introduction of choice-based lettings, may also have encouraged a commonly held – but mistaken – perception that anyone will be able to get into social housing if they wait long enough. Open waiting lists may be acceptable – should even perhaps be encouraged – where there is low demand for social housing. Where there is not enough housing, even for those who really need it, continuing to operate an open waiting list raises false expectations and is likely to fuel the belief that the allocation system is unfair.
>
> . . .
>
> 4.9 We take the view that it should be for local authorities to put in place arrangements which suit the particular needs of their local

163 Consultation paper, Department for Communities and Local Government (DCLG), November 2010, para 6.8. See www.gov.uk/government/consultations/a-fairer-future-for-social-housing.

164 See paras 1.69–1.77.

area. Some local authorities might restrict social housing to those in housing need (e.g. homeless households and overcrowded families). Other local authorities might impose residency criteria or exclude applicants with a poor tenancy record or those with sufficient financial resources to rent or buy privately. Others may decide to continue with open waiting lists. If, having taken into account the views of their local community, local authorities decide that there are benefits in maintaining open waiting lists (for example, to stimulate demand for social housing), we believe they should be able to do so.

1.117 In relation to homelessness, the principal change was designed to allow authorities more use of the private sector, so that even the offer of an assured shorthold tenancy – without the consent of the applicant – could be used to discharge the full duty, subject to a right to a further offer within two years (even if not by then in priority need).[165] In substance, even if not in form, this reinstated the original HA 1996 s197 power to by-pass Part 7 where there was other suitable accommodation available in the authority's area,[166] which had been repealed by Homelessness Act 2002.[167]

1.118 In relation to allocations, the principal change – applicable only in England – was to allow authorities, subject to any overriding regulations, to define classes of 'qualifying' applicant,[168] ie to abandon 'open' waiting lists in favour of an authority's own criteria, no longer confined to the exclusion of the anti-social.[169] In addition, transfer applicants were removed from the allocation provisions, likewise effectively reinstating the HA 1996 as unamended,[170] otherwise than where (in effect) the tenant has applied for a transfer and qualifies for a reasonable preference.[171]

1.119 The purpose was to restore authorities' historical discretion over to whom they allocate housing from what was something closer to a national code of preferences. This apparent freedom was, however, significantly undermined by the Court of Appeal in *Jakimaviciute*[172] (see para 11.50), in which it was held that the qualification criteria

165 HA 1996 s195A.

166 See para 1.79.

167 See para 1.94.

168 HA 1996 s160ZA.

169 See para 1.103.

170 HA 1996 s159(5), cf paras 1.80, 1.101.

171 HA 1996 s159(4A), (4B). Cf para 1.101.

172 *R (Jakimaviciute) v Hammersmith and Fulham LBC* [2014] EWCA Civ 1438, [2015] HLR 5.

adopted by an authority are subject to the reasonable preference duty, so that an authority is not able to adopt qualification criteria which exclude a person entitled to a reasonable preference. This was a conclusion that, however welcome to the homeless, plainly conflicted with the policy intention.

Housing (Wales) Act 2014

1.120 In 2009, the Welsh Assembly Government published a Ten Year Homelessness Plan for Wales. It expressed concern that there were inconsistencies around decision-making, interpretation and implementation of the legislation, with too little attention being paid to the needs of the vulnerable. There was an undertaking to 'review . . . key areas of homelessness legislation and the duties placed on Local Authorities, especially around the areas of priority need, intentionality, local connection and the discharge of duty into the private rented sector'.[173]

1.121 As part of this process, Dr Peter Mackie[174] was commissioned to carry out a 'review of homelessness legislation in Wales in order to explore whether and how the existing legislative framework might be changed to minimise homelessness'.[175] The review concluded that the priority need categories were 'used to ration limited housing resources'[176] and that applicants found it painful and upsetting to have to 'prove' that they were vulnerable.[177] While homelessness prevention techniques were generally thought to be successful, both in terms of assisting a wide range of households and in exploring a broader range of solutions, there was concern that such prevention techniques sat uncomfortably with statutory duties.[178] Moreover, there was only limited support provided for those who became homeless after leaving care or other institutional accommodation.[179]

173 Ten Year Homelessness Plan for Wales, p26.

174 Dr Peter Mackie, Ian Thomas, Kate Hodgson *Impact analysis of existing homelessness legislation in Wales*, January 2012.

175 *Impact analysis of existing homelessness legislation in Wales*, p3.

176 *Impact analysis of existing homelessness legislation in Wales*, para 7.2.2.

177 *Impact analysis of existing homelessness legislation in Wales*, para 7.2.14.

178 *Impact analysis of existing homelessness legislation in Wales*, p44, second bullet point.

179 *Impact analysis of existing homelessness legislation in Wales*, para 7.3.6.

1.122 That report was followed, in May 2012, by the Welsh Government's white paper *Homes for Wales*. Chapter 8 noted that, as a result of economic decline and welfare reform, homelessness was rising in Wales. The priority of the Welsh Government was to prevent homelessness and, in the long term, eliminate it completely.

1.123 The white paper promised a 'radical shift from existing legislation' with greater focus on duties designed to prevent homelessness.[180] The period of time in which a person was considered to be 'threatened with homelessness' would be increased from 28 to 56 days, but the intention of the new legislative model would be that people should approach authorities for assistance as early as possible once they experienced a housing problem.[181] A new duty would be introduced which would require authorities to take 'all reasonable steps to achieve a suitable housing solution for all [eligible] households which are homeless or threatened with homelessness'.[182]

1.124 Although the existing law on intentional homelessness would be re-enacted, authorities would be given a power to disapply the intentionality test; in time, the Welsh Government planned to prevent any consideration of intentionality where the household included children.[183] The Welsh Government also intended to 'gradually phase out' the priority need test.[184]

1.125 Save for the last of these, the proposals were introduced in the H(W)A 2014 Part 2. The majority of that Part re-enacted provisions already found in HA 1996 Part 7 and subordinate legislation, but new provisions included:

a) extending the time within which a person may be threatened with homelessness to 56 days;[185]
b) a requirement to ensure that information and advice about prevention, securing accommodation and other help is provided, in particular, to people leaving prison, youth detention, hospital

180 *Homes for Wales*, para 8.40.
181 *Homes for Wales*, para 8.43.
182 *Homes for Wales*, para 8.44.
183 *Homes for Wales*, para 8.53.
184 *Homes for Wales*, para 8.55–8.56, see also *Life on the Streets: Preventing and tackling rough sleeping, in Wales*, Welsh Assembly: April 2018. In Scotland, see Homelessness (Abolition of Priority Need Test) (Scotland) Order 2012 SI No 330.
185 H(W)A 2014 s55(4).

after treatment for a mental disorder and young people leaving care;[186]

c) a new requirement to assess the needs of those who need help in retaining or obtaining accommodation[187] and to help to prevent an applicant from becoming homeless;[188]
d) power for the authorities, in conjunction with the Welsh Ministers, to resolve not to apply the intentionality test to specified categories of applicant.[189]

Homelessness Reduction Act 2017

1.126 The period from 2008 has been one of significant reduction of public funding, particularly for local authorities.[190] One consequence of this which practitioners were acutely aware was an increase in efforts by some local authorities to minimise their HA 1996 Part 7 duties, by way of tactics generically referred to as 'gate-keeping', including measures to divert applicants to other sources of accommodation without ever getting a foot on the Part 7 ladder. In addition, homelessness was statistically and visibly on the rise.[191]

1.127 In December 2015, the Communities and Local Government (CLG) Select Committee launched an inquiry into homelessness in England. The Committee was concerned both that homelessness, particularly rough sleeping, was increasing and that government

186 See paras 14.11, 14.21 and H(W)A 2014 s60.

187 H(W)A 2014 s62.

188 H(W)A 2014 s66.

189 H(W)A 2014 s78; para 6.3.

190 Figures vary wildly, but no one doubts that they have been very significant indeed.

191 To use more recent statistics, by Autumn 2017 there were 4,751 people sleeping rough in England (a 15 per cent rise from 2016 and up from a low of 1,768 people in 2010); in the third quarter of 2017, 79,190 households were in temporary accommodation, of which 61,090 were households with children, giving a total of 121,360 children in temporary accommodation, the highest figures since 2007: *Live tables on homelessness*, February 2018.

data was not robust enough to provide an accurate picture.[192] The final report praised the 'prevention' elements of the H(W)A 2014, particularly the duty to help to prevent an applicant from becoming homeless and the extension of time within which a person is threatened with homelessness to 56 days.[193]

1.128 During the inquiry, a member of the Committee (Bob Blackman MP) drew second place in the private members' bill ballot and announced that he would introduce a Homelessness Reduction Bill. The government subsequently announced that it would support the bill. The general election in June 2017 affected the timetable, but it came into force on 3 April 2018.[194]

1.129 The key provisions of the HRA 2017 are as follows.

a) Section 1 extended the period of time within which a person is threatened with homelessness from 28 to 56 days. It also provides that a person is threatened with homelessness if he or she has been served with a valid notice under HA 1988 s21 expiring within 56 days in respect of their only home.[195]
b) Section 3 created a new HA 1996 s189A, introducing an assessment duty in England. Where an applicant is homeless (or threatened with homelessness) and eligible for assistance, the authority must assess the applicant's housing needs and consider what support it can provide to ensure that the applicant has or retains suitable accommodation. The authority and applicant must try to agree a written list of the actions that each will take: if they cannot agree, the authority must produce a record of the reasons for the disagreement and specify what steps the authority will take and those that it expects of the applicant.

192 A National Audit Office report, *Homelessness* (September 2017) was also critical: it concluded that the DCLG does not achieve value for money in the administration of homelessness policy, noting that it costs the public sector in excess of £1b per annum and concluding that the rise in the number of homeless people and households had been driven, at least in part, by restrictions and caps on welfare benefit payments, the effect of which changes the government had taken no steps to evaluate; the DCLG had provided only a 'light touch' approach to working with local authorities with which the report found it 'difficult to understand why the Department' had 'persisted . . . in the face of such a visibly growing problem'.

193 CLG Select Committee, Homelessness, HC40, August 2016.

194 Homelessness Reduction Act 2017 (Commencement and Transitional and Savings Provisions) Regulations 2018 SI No 167 reg 3, only applicable to applications made and reviews sought on or after that date – see reg 4.

195 Ie notice of seeking possession in respect of an assured shorthold tenancy.

c) Section 4 amended HA 1996 s195 so that, where an applicant is threatened with homelessness and eligible for assistance, the authority will have to take reasonable steps to help the applicant secure that accommodation does not cease to be available for his or her occupation, having regard to the assessment under HA 1996 s189A.

d) Section 5 introduced new HA 1996 s189B, requiring the authority to take reasonable steps for 56 days to help the applicant try to secure suitable accommodation for a minimum period of six months, regardless of whether the applicant is in priority need or intentionally homeless, known as the initial help duty.

1.130 The government initially indicated that it would make £35.4m available in 2017/18 and £12.1m in 2018/19 to assist with the likely costs authorities will incur in respect of the new Act, but that no funding would be provided beyond that.[196] This was subsequently increased to £61m over the same period.[197] None of these figures takes into account any increase in legal costs[198] flowing from additional judicial review claims or HA 1996 s204 appeals. There is much concern as to whether this will be sufficient.[199]

1.131 It is too early to tell how the HRA 2017 will perform. While well-intentioned, a sceptic – bearing in mind the tension recognised by Dr Mackie and his colleagues[200] between prevention techniques and statutory housing duties – might fear that the Act would institutionalise gate-keeping.

1.132 Whether or not this is a well-founded fear, there is no doubt at all that it will serve to continue the emphasis on private sector housing that has been the bi-partisan hallmark of all the homelessness legislation since 1996.

196 House of Commons Written Statement 17 January 2017 (HCWS418). There is also the possibility of the government making 'available a small amount of further funding for local authorities in high-pressure areas to manage the transition to the new duties'.

197 House of Commons Written Statement, 15 March 2017 (HCWS538).

198 Whether to authorities or to the legal aid fund.

199 In submissions to the CLG Select Committee, Bedford BC suggested that the new duties would add c£1m pa to its homelessness costs; Kensington and Chelsea RLBC put its figure at closer to £3.5m and Redbridge BC considered that its costs (including additional staffing) could eventually reach £4.3m. The Association of Housing Advice Services put the costs in London alone at £161m. On 12 December 2017, Clive Betts MP, Chair of the Communities and Local Government Committee, wrote to the government to express concern that, in London alone, there was a funding gap of £67m pa.

200 See para 1.121.

CHAPTER 2

The provisions in outline

continued

Introduction

2.1 In this chapter, the provisions of the Housing Act (HA) 1996 Parts 6 and 7, as amended by the Homelessness Act 2002, the Localism Act (LA) 2011 and the Homelessness Reduction Act (HRA) 2017, will be considered. The Housing (Wales) Act (H(W)A) 2014 largely follows the structure of Part 7 and incorporates much of what is to be found in HRA 2017.

2.2 HA 1996 Part 6 extends to England and Wales, but with differences between them. HA 1996 Part 7 now only applies in England; in Wales, it is replaced by H(W)A 2014 Part 2.[1] The provisions of the Housing (Homeless Persons) Act (H(HP)A) 1977 were consolidated in the Housing (Scotland) Act 1987 and, subject to amendment,[2] so remain; they are not considered here, but provision is made to ensure that homelessness applications in England allow for connections with Scottish authorities and for referrals by Scottish authorities.[3] In Northern Ireland, duties towards the homeless and those threatened with homelessness are imposed on the Northern Ireland Housing Executive (NIHE) by the Housing (Northern Ireland) Order 1988;[4] these duties are likewise not considered here.

2.3 The provisions are considered on their face, uncluttered by case-law, codes or other commentaries. Regular amendment has diminished the benefit of such an overview; some of the detail has therefore been left to be considered in later chapters.

2.4 Despite this, the chapter continues the practice of not cross-referring to the details in other chapters. Hopefully, each chapter is sufficiently clear in itself to allow the reader to find the detail without

1 For applications made on or after 27 April 2015; otherwise, HA 1996 Part 7 remains applicable: Housing (Wales) Act 2014 (Commencement No 3 and Transitory, Transitional and Saving Provisions) Order 2015 SI No 1272.

2 The Housing (Scotland) Act 1987 was amended by the Housing (Scotland) Act 2001. A major review of homelessness in Scotland (Scottish Executive *Homelessness task force final report* (2002)) led to further legislation in the Homelessness etc (Scotland) Act 2003. There has been increasing divergence between the law in Scotland and that in the rest of the UK. The 2003 Act provided for the eventual abolition of categories of priority need, so that a duty will be owed to all homeless persons. That reform came into force on 31 December 2012 (see the Homelessness (Abolition of Priority Need Test) (Scotland) Order 2012 SI No 330). The 2003 Act also provides for continuing duties towards the intentionally homeless.

3 HA 1996 ss201, 217.

4 SI No 1990 (NI 23). The order was amended to bring it more in line with HA 1996 Part 7 by the Housing (Northern Ireland) Order 2003 SI No 412 (NI 2). See also NIHE *Homelessness strategy for Northern Ireland 2012–2017.*

difficulty. Cross-references are made within this chapter in order to avoid unnecessary duplication of material and otherwise only where necessary to understand the text.

Chapter outline

2.5 HA 1996 Part 7 and H(W)A 2014 Part 2 place obligations on local housing authorities to assess applications by those who are homeless or threatened with homelessness, to seek to help those threatened with homelessness to avoid it, to afford initial help to the homeless who are eligible for assistance, and to secure that suitable accommodation is made available for a person:

a) who is homeless;
b) who is in priority need of accommodation;
c) who did not become homeless intentionally,[5]
d) subject to the local connection provisions which allow one authority to pass responsibility to another.[6]

2.6 The housing obligation is the peak duty under HA 1996 Part 7 or H(W)A 2014 Part 2. Where, however, discharge is to be by way of the allocation of a secure or introductory tenancy of an authority's own accommodation or nomination to such a tenancy of another authority or to an assured tenancy from a private registered provider of social housing or a registered social landlord, it is subject to the allocation provisions of HA 1996 Part 6.

2.7 Certain persons are ineligible for assistance on immigration grounds.[7] Special provision is made for those who, while eligible for assistance, are only homeless or in priority need by reference to others with whom they reside or might reasonably be expected to reside who are themselves ineligible.

2.8 There are also specific obligations in respect of those:

a) who are not yet homeless;
b) who do not have a priority need;
c) who have a priority need but become homeless intentionally; and

5 In Wales, authorities have power to disapply the intentionality test: H(W)A 2014 s78.

6 HA 1996 ss193(2), 198(1); H(W)A 2014 ss80, 81.

7 HA 1996 s185; H(W)A 2014 s61. The detail is set out in regulations. For England, see the Allocation of Housing and Homelessness (Eligibility) (England) Regulations 2006 SI No 1294 and, in Wales, see Allocation of Housing and Homelessness (Eligibility) (Wales) Regulations 2014 SI No 2603.

d) who are considered to be subject to the local connection provisions, pending determination of ultimate responsibility.

2.9 In addition, authorities have duties:

a) to make enquiries;
b) to notify the applicant of their decisions and the reasons for them;
c) to protect the property of the homeless;
d) to assess applications in order to identify steps which applicants can take to ensure that they have and retain accommodation; and
e) to take reasonable steps to help applicants secure accommodation for themselves for a limited period, by way of an initial help duty.

2.10 There are ancillary provisions governing deception. There is provision for the funding of voluntary agencies. There is also provision for the internal review of decisions, and appeal to the county court on a point of law.

2.11 The approach adopted here is, first, to define the key concepts contained in HA 1996 Part 7 and H(W)A 2014 Part 2, before matching them to the duties which Part 7 and Part 2 impose, considering separately and under their own headings the ancillary provisions, review and appeal, and allocation under HA 1996 Part 6.

2.12 The key definitions which must be considered are:

a) 'authorities';
b) 'eligibility for assistance';
c) 'homelessness';
d) 'priority need';
e) 'intentional homelessness'; and
f) 'local connection'.

2.13 Duties are considered under two heads:

a) preliminary duties; and
b) principal duties.

2.14 Further matters which must be considered are:

a) protection of property;
b) homelessness strategies;
c) advice, information and voluntary organisations;
d) Code of Guidance;
e) Code of Practice;
f) review and appeal;
g) criminal offences;
h) co-operation between authorities; and
i) allocation.

Definitions

Administration

Central government

2.15 HA 1996 falls within the responsibilities of the Ministry of Housing, Communities and Local Government (MHCLG),[8] and its secretary of state; in Wales, legislative competence over housing is now enjoyed by the National Assembly while ministerial functions are exercised by the Welsh Ministers.[9]

Local government

2.16 HA 1996 Part 7 (s217) and H(W)A 2014 Part 2 (s99) refers to three classes of authority:

a) local housing authorities;
b) relevant authorities; and
c) social services authorities.

Local housing authority

2.17 'Local housing authority' means a district council except in London where it means the London borough council or the Common Council of the City of London,[10] and in Wales where it means the county or county borough council (HA 1985 s1, as amended).[11] Unitary authorities under the Local Government Act 1992 or Local Government and Public Involvement in Health Act 2007, if not already local housing authorities, will invariably be housing authorities.[12]

8 Formerly the Department of Communities and Local Government (DCLG) from 2006–2018, formerly the Office of the Deputy Prime Minister (ODPM) from 2002–2006, formerly the Department of Transport, Local Government and the Regions (DTLR) from 2001–2002, formerly the Department of the Environment, Transport and the Regions (DETR) from 1997–2001, formerly the Department of the Environment (DoE).

9 See Government of Wales Act 1998 s22, Sch 2 para 9; National Assembly for Wales (Transfer of Functions) Order 1999 SI No 672; Government of Wales Act 2006 ss58, 161, Sch 11 para 30; Government of Wales Act 2006 s95; National Assembly for Wales (Legislative Competence) (Housing and Local Government) Order 2010 SI No 1838.

10 HA 1996 s230; HA 1985 s1.

11 H(W)A 2014 s99. See also Local Government (Wales) Act 1994 s17.

12 Local Government Changes for England Regulations 1994 SI No 867.

Relevant and specified authority

2.18 'Relevant authority' means, in England and Wales, a local housing authority and a social services authority.[13] The secretary of state has power to specify public authorities on whom is place a duty to refer to a local housing authority someone in relation to whom it exercises functions whom it considers may be homeless or threatened with homelessness.[14]

Social services authority

2.19 'Social services authority' means a non-metropolitan county council, a metropolitan district council, a London borough council or the Common Council of the City of London, and in Wales a county or county borough council.[15] Unitary authorities will also be social services authorities, if not already social services authorities.[16]

Eligibility for assistance

2.20 Persons from abroad are ineligible for assistance if they are persons who are subject to immigration control under the Asylum and Immigration Act (AIA) 1996, who have not been re-qualified by regulations.[17] No person who is excluded from entitlement to housing benefit by Immigration and Asylum Act (IAA) 1999 s115 may be re-included by such regulations.[18]

2.21 The secretary of state may, by regulation, add categories of people who are to be treated as persons from abroad for these purposes.[19] Asylum-seekers, whose position was formerly governed separately by HA 1996 s186, are now governed by the regulations, as are other immigrants. Ineligible asylum-seekers may, however, be able to access accommodation from the UK Visa and Immigration (UKVI) (formerly through the National Asylum Support Service (NASS));

13 HA 1996 s217; H(W)A 2014 s80. Where appropriate, it may include a Scottish housing or social services authority: HA 1996 s217.

14 HA 1996 s213B.

15 HA 1996 s217; Local Authority Social Services Act 1970 s1; and, in Wales, Social Services and Well-being (Wales) Act 2014.

16 Local Government Changes for England Regulations 1994 SI No 867.

17 HA 1996 s185(1), (2); H(W)A 2014 s61.

18 HA 1996 s185(2A); H(W)A 2014 Sch 2 para 1(3). Allocation of Housing and Homelessness (Eligibility) (England) Regulations (Eligibility Regs) 2006 SI No 1294 and Allocation of Housing and Homelessness (Eligibility) (Wales) Regulations (Welsh Eligibility Regs) 2014 SI No 2603.

19 HA 1996 s185(3); H(W)A 2014 Sch 2 para 1(2). See Eligibility Regs 2006 and Welsh Eligibility Regs 2014, above.

and children in need – including those of ineligible persons from abroad – may be able to obtain assistance under local authority social service powers.

2.22 When deciding whether an eligible applicant is homeless or in priority need, provision is made governing whether to take account of persons who are themselves ineligible and subject to immigration control, and who either do not have leave to enter or remain in the UK or have leave subject to a condition of no recourse to public funds.[20] Such persons are not taken into account if (but only if) the applicant is him or herself subject to immigration control (not including European Economic Area (EEA) and Swiss nationals for this purpose);[21] where reliance by an applicant is placed on such an ineligible member of his or her household, the case is known as a 'restricted case' and there are discrete provisions governing how a duty is to be discharged.[22]

Information

2.23 In order to reach a decision on the issue of eligibility, a local housing authority may seek such information as it requires from the secretary of state, who is bound to provide it (and, whether or not the original request for information was in writing, to provide it in writing if the authority, in writing, asks for it so to be provided).[23]

2.24 The secretary of state is under an additional duty to notify the authority in writing if it subsequently appears to him or her that any application, decision or other change of circumstance has affected the status of a person about whom he or she had previously provided information.[24]

Notifications

2.25 In a number of cases, the legislation requires notification to be made to an applicant, of a decision or other matter, eg a written record. In all cases, the notice or other matter must be in writing and, if not received by the applicant, is treated as having been given if made available at the authority's office for a reasonable period for collection

20 HA 1996 s185(7); H(W)A 2014 s63.
21 HA 1996 s185(5); H(W)A 2014 s63.
22 HA 1996 s193(7AA); H(W)A 2014 s76.
23 HA 1996 s187(1), (2); H(W)A 2014 Sch 2 para 3.
24 HA 1996 s187(3); H(W)A 2014 Sch 2 para 3.

by the applicant or on his or her behalf; where there is a right to review, the notice will invariably need to say so and specify the time (21 days or such longer period as may be allowed) with which the review must be sought.[25] In some cases, the secretary of state or Welsh Ministers may make provision by regulations as to the procedure to be followed in connection with notices.[26]

Homelessness

2.26 A person is homeless for the purposes of HA 1996 Part 7 or H(W)A 2014 Part 2 if he or she has no accommodation in the UK or elsewhere in the world, which is available for his or her occupation,[27] and which he or she is:

a) entitled to occupy by virtue of an interest in it (for example, as tenant or owner or under an equitable interest); or
b) entitled to occupy by virtue of a court order (for example, in the course of domestic proceedings); or
c) entitled to occupy by virtue of an express or implied licence (for example, friendly or family arrangement, contractual licence); or
d) actually occupying as a residence, 'by virtue of any enactment or rule of law giving him the right to remain in occupation or restricting the right of any other person to recover possession of it' (for example, between termination of tenancy and order for possession).[28]

Available for occupation

2.27 Accommodation is only available for an applicant's occupation if it is available for the applicant, together with any other person who normally resides with the applicant as a member of his or her family and any other person who might reasonably be expected to reside with the applicant.[29]

25 HA 1996 ss184(5), (6), 189A(12), 193B(3), (7), (8), 195(7), (9), 199A(3), (7), 200(6), 202(1), (3), 203(8); H(W)A 2014 ss84(1), (3), (4), 85(5), 86.
26 HA 1996 s193B(7).
27 HA 1996 s175(1); H(W)A 2014 s55.
28 HA 1996 s175(1); H(W)A 2014 s55.
29 HA 1996 s176; H(W)A 2014 s56.

Reasonable to continue to occupy

2.28 Accommodation is disregarded if it is not accommodation which it would be reasonable to continue to occupy it.[30] When deciding whether or not it would be reasonable for a person to remain in occupation, an authority to which application has been made may take into account the general housing circumstances prevailing in its area.[31]

Violence/abuse

2.29 It is not reasonable to continue to occupy accommodation if it is probable that to do so will lead to 'violence' (domestic or otherwise) – or, in Wales, 'abuse' – against the applicant, or against someone who normally resides with the applicant as a member of his or her family, or against anyone else who might reasonably be expected to reside with the applicant.[32]

2.30 'Violence' means violence from another person, or threats of violence from another person which are likely to be carried out.[33] 'Abuse' means physical violence, threatening or intimidating behaviour and any other form of abuse which, directly or indirectly, may give rise to the risk of harm.[34]

Domestic violence/abuse

2.31 Violence and abuse are 'domestic' if from a person who is 'associated' with the victim.[35] 'Associated persons' includes those who are or have been married, civil partners, cohabitants, specified relatives, those in the same household, those who have agreed to marry or enter into a civil partnership, persons with parental responsibility for a child, certain adoptive relations; and, in Wales, those living together in an enduring family relationship (whether of different sexes or the same) or who have or have had an intimate personal relationship with each other which is or was of significant duration.[36]

30 HA 1996 s175(3); H(W)A 2014 s57.
31 HA 1996 s177(2); H(W)A 2014 s57.
32 HA 1996 s177(1); H(W)A 2014 s58.
33 HA 1996 s177(1A).
34 H(W)A 2014 s58(1).
35 HA 1996 s177(1A); see H(W)A 2014 s58(1).
36 HA 1996 s178; H(W)A 2014 s58.

Unusable accommodation

2.32 A person is homeless if he or she has accommodation which he or she occupies or is entitled to occupy, and which is available for his or her occupation and reasonable to continue to occupy, but he or she cannot secure entry to it or the accommodation consists of a movable structure, vehicle or vessel, designed or adapted for living in, and there is no place where he or she is entitled or permitted both to place it and to reside in it.[37]

Threatened with homelessness

2.33 A person is threatened with homelessness if it is likely that the person will become homeless within 56 days.[38] In addition, in England, an assured shorthold tenant served with a valid notice under HA 1988 s21, in respect of the only accommodation which he or she has which is available for his or her occupation, and which will expire within 56 days, is also threatened with homelessness.[39]

Priority need

2.34 A person has a priority need for accommodation if the authority is satisfied that:

a) the person has dependent children who are residing with, or who might reasonably be expected to reside with, the person; or
b) the person is homeless or threatened with homelessness as a result of any emergency such as flood, fire or any other disaster; or
c) the person, or any person who resides or who might reasonably be expected to reside with the person, is vulnerable – in England, this is vulnerability because of old age, mental illness, handicap or physical disability or other special reason; in Wales it is because of some special reason of which those causes are illustrative; or
d) she is pregnant, or is a person who resides or might reasonably be expected to reside with a pregnant woman.[40]

2.35 In England, the secretary of state may specify further classes of person as having a priority need for accommodation, or amend or

37 HA 1996 s175(2); H(W)A 2014 s55.
38 HA 1996 s175(4); H(W)A 2014 s55.
39 HA 1996 s175(5).
40 HA 1996 s189(1); H(W)A 2014 s70(1)(a)–(d). Vulnerability has its own statutory definition in Wales: H(W)A 2014 s71.

repeal any of the present classes.[41] A number of additional classes have been specified, including all 16- and 17-year-olds, save those for whom social service provision is or has been made under the Children Act (CA) 1989, those aged 18 to 20, who were subject to subject provision under CA 1989 other than certain students, those who are vulnerable because they have previously been looked after, accommodated or fostered or as a result of service in Her Majesty's regular armed forces or of having served a custodial sentence, having been committed for contempt of court or having been remanded in custody, and those who have had to cease to occupy accommodation because of violence.[42]

2.36 In Wales, while there is power for the Welsh Ministers to add categories,[43] the legislation specifies additional categories of priority need, including:

- those homeless as a result of domestic abuse;
- a person aged 16 or 17 when application is made;
- a person who has attained the age of 18 when application is made (but not the age of 21) who is at particular risk of sexual or financial exploitation;
- a person who has attained the age of 18 when application is made, but not the age of 21, who was looked after, accommodated or fostered at any time while under the age of 18;
- a person who has served in the regular armed forces of the Crown who has been homeless since leaving; and
- a person who has a local connection with the area of the local housing authority who is vulnerable as a result of having served a custodial sentence, having been remanded in or committed to custody by an order of a court, or having been remanded to youth detention accommodation.[44]

Intentional homelessness

2.37 A person becomes intentionally homeless if the person deliberately does or fails to do anything in consequence of which he or she ceases

41 HA 1996 s189(2).

42 Homelessness (Priority Need for Accommodation) (England) Order 2002 SI No 2051.

43 H(W)A 2014 s72.

44 H(W)A 2014 s70(1)(e)–(j).

to occupy accommodation which is available for occupation, and which it would have been reasonable to continue to occupy.[45]

2.38 A person becomes threatened with homelessness intentionally if the person deliberately does or fails to do anything, the likely result of which is that he or she will be forced to leave accommodation which is available for occupation, and which it would have been reasonable to continue to occupy.[46]

2.39 These definitions incorporate a number of elements:

a) there must be a deliberate act or failure to act;
b) the act or omission must have a consequence;
c) the consequence must be that accommodation ceases or will cease to be occupied;
d) that accommodation must be or have been, 'accommodation available for [the] occupation' of the homeless person; and
e) it must have been reasonable to continue in occupation of that accommodation.

2.40 An act or omission in good faith, on the part of a person who was unaware of any relevant fact, is not to be treated as deliberate for these purposes.[47] In Wales, local housing authorities must decide whether to apply the intentionality test at all in their areas and it can only be applied once the authority have notified the Welsh Government that the test will apply and have published a notice to this effect.[48] The test may only be applied to categories of applicant specified by the Welsh Ministers.[49]

Collusive arrangements

2.41 A person becomes homeless intentionally or threatened with homelessness intentionally if he or she enters into an arrangement under which he or she is required to cease to occupy accommodation, which it would have been reasonable for him or her to continue to occupy, the purpose of which arrangement is to enable the person to qualify for assistance under HA 1996 Part 7 or H(W)A 2014 Part 2, and there

45 HA 1996 s191(1); H(W)A 2014 s77(2).
46 HA 1996 s196(1).
47 HA 1996 ss191(2) and 196(2); H(W)A 2014 s77(3).
48 H(W)A 2014 s78.
49 Homelessness (Intentionality) (Specified Categories) (Wales) Regulations 2015 SI No 1265. Currently all priority need categories are so specified.

is no other, or independent, good reason for the actual or threatened homelessness.[50]

Local connection

2.42 A person has a 'local connection' with an area if:

a) the person is or was as a matter of choice normally resident in it; or
b) the person is employed in the area; or
c) the person has family associations with the area; or
d) there are other special circumstances which result in a local connection with the area.[51]

2.43 Since 3 April 2018,[52] there are in England additional provisions applicable to those towards whom a social services authority in England has a duty under CA 1989 s23C, as a former relevant child.[53] If the authority is a local housing authority as well as a social services authority, the former relevant child is deemed to have a local connection with its area; if the authority is not a local housing authority, the deemed connection is with every district in its area.

2.44 Likewise, since 3 April 2018,[54] where accommodation for a child in care has been provided under CA 1989 s22A, so that the child is normally resident in the district of a local housing authority for a continuous period of at least two years, some or all of which falls before he or she turns 16, he or she is likewise deemed to have a local connection with that district,[55] although ceases to do so once he or she turns 21 (unless a local connection can be established on any of the other grounds for it).[56]

Residence of choice

2.45 Residence is not 'of choice' for these purposes if the person:[57]

50 HA 1996 ss191(3), 196(3); H(W)A 2014 s77(4).
51 HA 1996 s199(1); H(W)A 2014 s81.
52 The provision does not apply to an application made or a review sought before this date: see Homelessness Reduction Act 2017 (Commencement and Transitional and Savings Provisions) Regulations 2018 SI No 167 reg 4.
53 HA 1996 s199(8).
54 See footnote 52, above.
55 HA 1996 s199(9).
56 HA 1996 s199(10).
57 Residence arising from service in the armed forces was formerly also excluded, which remains the case for applications made before 1 December 2008.

a) became resident in it because the person or any person who might reasonably be expected to reside with him or her was detained under the authority of any Act of Parliament (for example, prison or mental hospital); or
b) became resident in it in such other circumstances as the secretary of state or the Welsh Ministers may specify.[58]

Employment

2.46 A person is not employed in an area if[59] the person falls within such other circumstances as the secretary of state or Welsh Ministers may specify.[60]

Former asylum-seekers

2.47 A person has a local connection with an area if the person was at any time provided with accommodation in that area under IAA 1999 s95, unless either the person was subsequently provided with accommodation in another local housing authority area under section 95, or else the accommodation was provided in an accommodation centre under Nationality, Immigration and Asylum Act (NIAA) 2002 s22.[61]

Preliminary duties

2.48 The preliminary duties arise where a person applies to a housing authority for accommodation, or for assistance in obtaining it,[62] and the authority has reason to believe that he or she may be homeless or threatened with homelessness.[63]

2.49 There is no requirement for any particular form of application, or even that the application should be in writing.

2.50 The main preliminary duties are:

a) to make enquiries into the application and reach a decision on it;
b) to carry out an assessment of the applicant's case; and

58 HA 1996 s199(3), (5); H(W)A 2014 s81(3), (4).

59 Employment in the armed forces was formerly also excluded, which remains the case for applications made before 1 December 2008.

60 HA 1996 s199(5); H(W)A 2014 s81(4)(a). This power has not been exercised to date.

61 HA 1996 s199(6), (7). Note that NIAA 2002 s22 has not yet been brought into effect.

62 In Wales, help in retaining or obtaining accommodation: H(W)A 2014 s62.

63 HA 1996 s184(1).

c) in the case of an eligible homeless person in priority need,[64] to provide interim accommodation during enquiries and notification of its decision.

England

Enquiry and decision

2.51 Where an English authority has reason to believe that there may be actual or threatened homelessness, then it must make enquiries:

a) such as are necessary to satisfy it whether the applicant is eligible for assistance; and

b) if so, whether any, and what, duties are owed to the person under HA 1996 Part 7.[65]

2.52 The authority may also make further enquiries as to whether there is a local connection with the district of another authority.[66]

2.53 If the authority is not satisfied as to eligibility, it need not proceed to make any further enquiries. If it does make further enquiries, then the authority must, on completion, notify the applicant of its decision and 'so far as any issue is decided against [the applicant's] interests' inform the applicant of the reasons for it.[67]

2.54 If the decision is to notify another authority under the local connection provisions, the applicant must also be notified of this decision and its reasons.[68]

2.55 If the decision is that a duty is owed, or after the end of the initial help duty would be owed, but only because of the presence of a restricted person in the applicant's household, the notification must provide prescribed additional information.[69]

64 In some circumstances, an English authority's duty to provide interim accommodation pending a decision also arises even if there is no apparent priority need, where the authority has reason to believe that the application is a 'second application', following a previous application in the preceding two years which resulted in an assured shorthold tenancy which has come to an end, provided that the applicant is still eligible, and did not become homeless intentionally: HA 1996 s188A. This only arises on one re-application: HA 1996 s195A(6).

65 HA 1996 s184(1).

66 HA 1996 s184(2).

67 HA 1996 s184(3).

68 HA 1996 s184(4).

69 HA 1996 s184(3A).

Assessment and plan

2.56 If the authority is satisfied that the applicant is homeless or threatened with homelessness and eligible, it will be under a duty to assess the applicant's case:[70] accordingly, this will usually be once it reaches its decision on the application, although these issues may be determined at an earlier stage.

2.57 The assessment must include an assessment of the circumstances which resulted in the applicant's homelessness or being threatened with homelessness, his or her housing needs, and his or her needs for support[71] in order to be able to have and retain suitable accommodation.[72] The authority must notify the applicant in writing of its assessment.[73]

2.58 The authority must try to agree with the applicant what steps he or she is to be required to take in order to secure that he or she[74] has and is able to retain suitable accommodation, and what steps the authority is to take under HA 1996 Part 7 for those purposes.[75] If the authority and the applicant reach such an agreement, the authority must record it in writing.[76]

2.59 If they cannot agree, the authority must record in writing why, what steps it considers it would be reasonable to require the applicant to take, and what steps the authority is to take under Part 7 for those purposes.[77]

2.60 Either class of record can include any advice the authority considers appropriate, including as to steps which the authority thinks it would be 'a good idea for the applicant to take', albeit that he or she is not to be required to take.[78] The authority must give the applicant a copy of the written record.[79]

2.61 Until the authority decides that it owes the applicant no duty under any of the remaining provisions of Part 7, the authority has to

70 HA 1996 s189A(1).

71 Together with those of anyone with whom he or she resides or might reasonably be expected to reside.

72 HA 1996 s189A(2).

73 HA 1996 s189A(3).

74 Together with anyone with whom he or she resides or might reasonably be expected to reside.

75 HA 1996 s189A(4).

76 HA 1996 s189A(5).

77 HA 1996 s189A(6).

78 HA 1996 s189A(7).

79 HA 1996 s189A(8).

keep the assessment under review, together with the appropriateness of any agreement reached or steps recorded.[80]

2.62 If the assessment of the mandatory considerations[81] changes, the authority must notify the applicant, in writing, of how its assessment has changed (whether by providing a revised written assessment or otherwise); the same applies if the authority's assessment otherwise changes in a way that it considers it appropriate to notify the applicant.[82]

2.63 If the authority considers that any agreement reached or any step recorded under is no longer appropriate, it must so notify the applicant in writing to this effect and that any subsequent failure to take a step that was agreed or recorded is to be disregarded.[83]

Wales

Assessment

2.64 If it appears to a Welsh authority that an applicant may be homeless or threatened with homelessness, it must carry out an assessment of his or her case.[84] There is no such duty if the applicant has previously been assessed by a Welsh local authority under this provision and the authority is satisfied that his or her circumstances have not changed materially since that assessment and that there is no new information which materially affects that assessment.[85]

2.65 The assessment must consider whether the applicant is eligible.[86] If the applicant is eligible, the assessment must address how the applicant has become homeless or threatened with homelessness, his or her housing needs,[87] the support required to meet those needs and whether or not the authority has any duty towards the applicant under H(W)A 2014 Part 2.[88]

2.66 The assessment must seek to identify what the applicant wishes to achieve with the authority's help and the authority must consider

80 HA 1996 s189A(9).
81 Para 2.57.
82 HA 1996 s189A(10).
83 HA 1996 s189A(11).
84 H(W)A 2014 s62(1), (4), (5).
85 H(W)A 2014 s62(1)(c), (2).
86 H(W)A 2014 s62(3).
87 Together with anyone with whom he or she resides or might reasonably be expected to reside.
88 H(W)A 2014 s62(5).

whether the exercise of any of its powers under Part 2 can contribute to that outcome.[89] The assessment must be kept under review.[90]

2.67 Once the assessment is complete, the authority must notify the applicant of its outcome (and of any review of the assessment) and, insofar as any issue is decided against his or her interests, give reasons for the decision.[91]

2.68 Where the authority has notified or intends to notify another authority under the local connection provisions, the notification must inform the applicant why the authority has done so or intends to do so.[92]

2.69 Additional notification duties apply where a duty under H(W)A 2014 s75 is owed only because of a restricted person.[93]

Interim accommodation during enquiries

2.70 A duty to secure that accommodation is made available pending a decision arises if the authority has reason to believe that the applicant may be homeless, and eligible for assistance, and in priority need.[94]

2.71 From commencement of LA 2011 s149 in England,[95] an English authority's duty to house pending a decision also arises – even if there is no apparent priority need – if the authority has reason to believe that the application is a second application, following a previous application in the preceding two years which resulted in an assured shorthold tenancy which has come to an end, provided that the applicant is still eligible, and did not become homeless intentionally.[96]

2.72 The obligation to secure accommodation pending a decision is imposed on the authority to which the application has been made, whether or not the applicant may have a local connection with another authority.[97]

2.73 The accommodation must be made available for the applicant and for any other family member who normally resides with, or

89 H(W)A 2014 s62(6).
90 H(W)A 2014 s62(8), (9).
91 H(W)A 2014 s63(1).
92 H(W)A 2014 s63(3).
93 H(W)A 2014 s63(2).
94 HA 1996 s188(1); H(W)A 2014 s68.
95 9 November 2012.
96 HA 1996 s188(1A). This right only arises on one re-application: HA 1996 s195A(6).
97 HA 1996 s188(2); H(W)A 2014 s68(4).

anyone else who might reasonably be expected to reside with, the applicant.[98]

Accommodation following decision

England

2.74 If the authority decides that there is no priority need and that no initial help duty arises, the duty ends once the applicant is notified of that decision; if no priority need but the initial help duty does arise, it comes to an end when the authority notifies the applicant that no duty is owed under s190 (intentional homelessness) or the principal housing duty (s193).[99]

2.75 Where there is a priority need, the duty ends on the later of the date when the initial help duty comes to an end or the authority notifies the applicant that it has decided that it does not owe such a duty, and of the date when the authority notifies the applicant what other duty (if any) it owes him or her under the principal provisions of Part 7 on the coming to an end of the initial help duty.[100]

2.76 If the applicant seeks a review of a decision as to a final accommodation offer or a final Part 6 offer as defined in s193A, the duty does not come to an end until the decision on the review has been notified.[101] A review on any other ground does not extend the date when the duty terminates,[102] but the authority has power to house pending the review.[103]

Wales

2.77 The duty ends if the authority notifies the applicant that it has no initial help duty because it is not satisfied that the applicant is homeless and eligible.[104] In the case of an applicant towards whom such a duty is owed, the accommodation duty ends when the authority notifies the applicant that the initial help duty has come to an end and that a duty is or is not owed to the applicant under H(W)A 2014 s75.[105]

98 HA 1996 ss176, 188(1); H(W)A 2014 s56.
99 HA 1996 s188(1ZA).
100 HA 1996 s188(1ZB).
101 HA 1996 s188(2A).
102 HA 1996 s188(3).
103 HA 1996 s188 (3).
104 H(W)A 2014 s69(2).
105 H(W)A 2014 s69(3).

2.78 The duty also ends if the applicant, having been notified of the possible consequences, refused an offer of suitable interim accommodation, or became homeless intentionally from that accommodation, or voluntarily ceased to occupy such accommodation as his or her only or principal home.[106]

2.79 The duty does not come to an end, however, if the authority has decided that there is no duty under H(W)A 2014 s75 either on the ground that the applicant became homeless intentionally (in the circumstances which gave rise to the application) or on the ground that it had previously secured accommodation to the applicant following a previous application for help within five years before the day on which the applicant is notified that a duty is not owed to him or her.[107]

2.80 In either case, the accommodation duty continues until the authority is satisfied that the period of accommodation has been sufficient to allow the applicant a reasonable opportunity of securing his or her own accommodation,[108] not being less than the 56 days for which the initial help duty was applicable.[109]

2.81 The duty comes to an end even if a review is sought; the authority has a discretion to continue to secure suitable accommodation pending a decision on the review.[110]

2.82 The duty also comes to an end if the authority is no longer satisfied that the applicant is eligible, or is satisfied that a mistake of fact led to the decision that the duty was owed at all, or is satisfied that the applicant has withdrawn his or her application, or is satisfied that the applicant is unreasonably failing to co-operate with it in connection with the exercise of its homelessness functions which relate to him or her.[111]

Principal duties

2.83 The extent of an authority's duty depends on its decision. Duties may be considered as:

a) limited duties; and
b) full duties.

106 H(W)A 2014 s69(7)–(9).
107 H(W)A 2014 s69(4), (5).
108 H(W)A 2014 s69(5).
109 H(W)A 2014 s69(6).
110 H(W)A 2014 s69(10), (11).
111 H(W)A 2014 ss69(12), 79.

Limited duties

Duties to those threatened with homelessness

England

2.84 In all cases where the authority is satisfied that an applicant is threatened with homelessness and eligible for assistance,[112] it has, since commencement of HRA 2017,[113] been under a duty to take reasonable steps to help the applicant to secure that accommodation does not cease to be available for his or her occupation.[114] In deciding what steps to take, the authority has to have regard to its assessment of the applicant's case.[115]

2.85 The obligation is without prejudice to the authority's right to recover possession of any accommodation.[116]

2.86 The authority may give notice to bring this duty to an end when it is satisfied that any one of a number of circumstances is applicable:[117]

a) The applicant has suitable accommodation which is available for his or her occupation and there is a reasonable prospect of him or her having such available for at least six months from the date of the notice.
b) The authority has complied with the duty to take reasonable steps and the period of 56 days beginning with the day that the authority is first satisfied that the applicant is threatened with homeless and eligible has ended (whether or not he or she is still threatened with homelessness).
c) The applicant has become homeless.
d) The applicant has refused an offer of suitable accommodation and, on the date of refusal, there was a reasonable prospect that suitable accommodation would be available for occupation by the applicant for at least six months.[118]
e) The applicant has become homeless intentionally from any accommodation that has been made available to him or her.
f) The applicant is no longer eligible for assistance.

112 HA 1996 s195(1).
113 3 April 2018: see Homelessness Reduction Act 2017 (Commencement and Transitional and Savings Provisions) Regulations 2018 SI No 167 reg 3.
114 HA 1996 s195(2).
115 HA 1996 s195(3).
116 HA 1996 s195(4).
117 HA 1996 s195(5), (8).
118 Or such longer period as may be prescribed.

g) The applicant has withdrawn the application for accommodation or assistance in obtaining it.

2.87 The notice must specify which of the circumstances applies.[119]

2.88 The duty can also be brought to an end if the authority considers that the applicant has deliberately and unreasonably refused to take any step that was agreed to be taken under s89A(4) or that was recorded under s89A(6)(b)[120] although this does not end a right to accommodation for an applicant who is threatened with homelessness, eligible, in priority need and not threatened with homelessness intentionally, to whom a duty to secure suitable accommodation will still be owed,[121] instead of the principal duty[122] to secure housing.[123]

2.89 No notice may be given without a prior 'relevant warning' notice[124] and a reasonable period must have elapsed since it was given.[125] Detailed provisions govern what must be contained in a notice to this effect.[126]

2.90 The housing duty which arises will itself cease if the applicant ceases to be eligible, or becomes homeless intentionally from accommodation made available for the applicant, accepts an offer of an assured tenancy from a private landlord or otherwise voluntarily ceases to the accommodation made available as his or her only or principal home.[127] It also ceases[128] if the applicant, having been warned of the consequences of refusal or acceptance, and of his or her right to request a review of the suitability of the accommodation, refuses or accepts a final accommodation offer, or a final Part 6 offer. These provisions are considered below.[129]

119 HA 1996 s195(7).
120 HA 1996 ss195(10), 189B(2).
121 HA 1996 s193C(3).
122 Under HA 1996 s193.
123 HA 1996 s193C(4).
124 This is a notice given by the authority after the refusal to take the agreed or recorded step, which warns the applicant that, if he or she continues deliberately and unreasonably to refuse to take the step after receiving the notice, the authority intends to give the notice which will bring the duty to an end, and which explains the consequences of that notice: HA 1996 s193B(5).
125 HA 1996 s193B(4).
126 HA 1996 s193B(1), (2).
127 HA 1996 s193C(5).
128 HA 1996 s193C(6).
129 Paras 2.126–2.146.

Wales

2.91 If the authority is satisfied that an applicant is eligible and threatened with homelessness, it is under a duty help to secure that accommodation does not cease to be available to the applicant.[130] The duty cannot be used to prevent the authority obtaining vacant possession of any accommodation.[131]

2.92 The duty requires the authority to take reasonable steps to help.[132] It does not require the authority to offer accommodation, whether under HA 1996 Part 6 or otherwise.[133] The authority can help to secure that suitable accommodation does not cease to be available either by providing some form of assistance itself or arranging for someone else to provide it.[134] The H(W)A 2014 gives examples of what may be provided or arranged, including mediation, grants, guarantees, support in management of arrears, security for applicants at risk of abuse, accommodation, information and advice, and other services, goods or facilities.[135]

2.93 The authority can give notice bringing this duty to an end if the authority is satisfied[136] that:[137]

a) the applicant has become homeless;[138]
b) the applicant is no longer threatened with homelessness and suitable accommodation is likely to remain available for his or her occupation for at least another six months;[139]
c) the applicant refuses an offer of accommodation from any person, having been notified in writing of the possible consequences of refusal or acceptance of the offer, provided that the authority is satisfied that the accommodation was suitable for the applicant and was likely to be available for at least the next[140] six months;[141]

130 H(W)A 2014 s66(1).
131 H(W)A 2014 s66(2).
132 H(W)A 2014 s65(a): the authority must (among other things) have regard to the need to make the best use of its resources.
133 H(W)A 2014 s65(b)–(c).
134 H(W)A 2014 s64(1).
135 H(W)A 2014 s64(2).
136 Whether or not as a result of the steps the authority has taken.
137 H(W)A 2014 s67.
138 H(W)A 2014 s67(2).
139 H(W)A 2014 s67(3).
140 Beginning with the day of notification: H(W)A 2014 s67(5).
141 H(W)A 2014 s67(4).

d) the applicant ceases to be eligible;[142]
e) a mistake of fact led to authority to notify the applicant that it owed him or her a duty to help to secure accommodation for the applicant;[143]
f) the applicant has withdrawn the application;[144] or
g) the applicant is unreasonably failing to co-operate with the authority.[145]

Initial help duty

England

2.94 An authority which is satisfied that an applicant is homeless and eligible for assistance[146] has, since commencement of HRA 2017,[147] been under a duty is to take reasonable steps to help the applicant to secure that suitable accommodation becomes available for his or her occupation for at least six months or such longer period[148] as may be prescribed.[149] In deciding what steps to take, the authority must have regard to its assessment of the applicant's case.[150] The duty will not arise where the authority refers the application to another local housing authority in England under the local connection provisions.[151]

2.95 Where the authority is satisfied that the applicant has a priority need and is not satisfied that the applicant became homeless intentionally, the duty comes to an end 56 days following the day the authority was first satisfied that the applicant was homeless and eligible.[152] The authority may also give notice bringing the duty to an end when it is satisfied that any one of certain circumstances is

142 H(W)A 2014 s79(2).
143 H(W)A 2014 s79(3).
144 H(W)A 2014 s79(4).
145 H(W)A 2014 s79(5).
146 HA 1996 s189B(1).
147 3 April 2018: see Homelessness Reduction Act 2017 (Commencement and Transitional and Savings Provisions) Regulations 2018 SI No 167 reg 3. The initial help duties do not apply to applications made or reviews sought before 3 April 2018: reg 4.
148 Not exceeding 12 months.
149 HA 1996 s189B(2).
150 HA 1996 s189B(3).
151 HA 1996 s189B(2). This may accordingly be before it has reached decisions on priority need and intentionality.
152 HA 1996 s189B(4).

applicable.[153] The circumstances are[154] identical[155] to those which allowed an authority to bring to an end the duty it owes to a person threatened with homelessness, described above.[156] The notice must specify which of the circumstances applies.[157]

2.96 As with the duty to those threatened with homelessness,[158] the initial help duty can also be brought to an end if the authority considers that the applicant has deliberately and unreasonably refused to take any step that was agreed to be taken under HA 1996 s89A(4) or that was recorded under s89A(6)(b),[159] although this does not end a right to accommodation for an applicant who is homeless, eligible, in priority need and not threatened with homelessness intentionally,[160] to whom a duty to secure suitable accommodation will still be owed,[161] instead of the principal duty[162] to secure housing.[163] The warning notice provisions[164] also apply. The housing duty which arises can be brought to an end[165] in the same circumstances as for those threatened with homelessness.[166]

2.97 The initial help duty can also be brought to an end under its own provisions,[167] if a final accommodation offer or a final Part 6 offer is refused.[168] The provisions are considered below.[169]

Wales

2.98 In Wales, the initial help duty to be found in H(W)A 2014 s73. The duty does not arise if there is a local connection referral to another authority in England or Wales.[170]

153 HA 1996 s189B(5).
154 HA 1996 s189B(7).
155 Save that the applicant is already homeless.
156 Para 2.86.
157 HA 1996 s189B(6).
158 Para 2.84.
159 HA 1996 s189B(2), (10).
160 HA 1996 s193C(3), (4).
161 HA 1996 s193C(3).
162 Under HA 1996 s193.
163 HA 1996 s193C(4).
164 Para 2.89.
165 HA 1996 s189B(9)
166 Para 2.89.
167 HA 1996 ss189B(9), 193A.
168 HA 1996 s193A(1).
169 Paras 2.141–2.146.
170 H(W)A 2014 s80(1).

2.99 If an authority is satisfied that an applicant is homeless and eligible for assistance, whether or not he or she has a priority need or may be homeless intentionally, it must help to secure that accommodation is available for the applicant.[171] The duty requires the authority to take reasonable steps to help, having regard to (among other things) the need to make the best use of its resources.[172] It does not require the authority to offer accommodation, whether under HA 1996 Part 6 or otherwise.[173]

2.100 The duty lasts only for 56 days[174] although the authority can decide on a shorter period if reasonable steps to secure accommodation for the applicant have been taken.[175]

2.101 The duty will come to an end[176] before the end of that period in the same circumstances[177] as for the duty towards those threatened with homelessness.[178] Once the duty comes to an end, the main housing duty will apply to those who do not have suitable accommodation available and likely to be available for at least six months, who are eligible and in priority need and, if having regard to intentionality,[179] not homeless intentionally:[180] this is considered further below.[181]

2.102 Where the authority decides that its duty has come to an end, it must so notify the applicant and include notification of its reasons for that conclusion, of the right to request a review and of the time within such a request must be made.[182] If the decision is because the 56-day or shorter period has expired, the notice must also identify the steps taken by the authority to help secure suitable accommodation for the applicant.[183]

171 H(W)A 2014 s73.
172 H(W)A 2014 s65(a).
173 H(W)A 2014 s65(b)–(c).
174 H(W)A 2014 s74(2).
175 H(W)A 2014 s74(3).
176 H(W)A 2014 ss74(4), (5), 79(2), (3), (4), (5).
177 Para 2.93.
178 Save that becoming homeless or ceasing to be threatened with homelessness are inapplicable.
179 Para 2.108.
180 Or if, having regard to intentionality, the applicant falls within the specified categories who are entitled in any event to accommodation: paras 2.111–2.112.
181 Paras 2.111–2.113.
182 H(W)A 2014 s84(1).
183 H(W)A 2014 s84(2).

Other duties without priority need

2.103 If an authority in England is satisfied that an applicant is homeless – whether intentionally[184] or unintentionally[185] – or threatened with homelessness (intentionally or not),[186] and eligible for assistance, but it is also satisfied that the applicant is not in priority need, it owes an advice and appropriate assistance duty to the applicant.[187]

2.104 The duty requires the authority to assess the applicant's housing needs and provide him or her (or secure that he or she is provided) with advice and assistance,[188] which must include information about the likely availability in the authority's area of types of accommodation appropriate to the applicant's housing needs, including the location and sources of such types of accommodation.[189]

2.105 In Wales, the assessment and initial help duties include power to provide advice and assistance.[190]

2.106 From commencement of LA 2011 s149,[191] an English authority also owes a full duty to secure accommodation, even if there is no priority need, if the application is a renewed application, following a previous application which resulted in an assured shorthold tenancy in the preceding two years, provided that the applicant is still eligible, and did not become homeless intentionally.[192]

2.107 If the authority is satisfied that the applicant is unintentionally homeless although not in priority need, then although there is no duty to secure that accommodation is made available for occupation by the applicant, there is power to do so.[193]

Other duties to the intentionally homeless

England

2.108 Once an English authority's initial help duty has come to an end, if satisfied that an applicant is homeless, and in priority need of accommodation, but the authority is also satisfied that the applicant became

184 HA 1996 s190(3).
185 HA 1996 s192.
186 HA 1996 s195(5)(a).
187 HA 1996 s190(2)(b), (4).
188 HA 1996 s190(2)(b), (4).
189 HA 1996 s190(5).
190 H(W)A 2014 s64(2)(h).
191 9 November 2012.
192 HA 1996 s195A(1). This right only arises on one re-application: HA 1996 s195A(6).
193 HA 1996 s192(3).

homeless intentionally, it must secure that suitable[194] accommodation is made available for the applicant's occupation[195] for such period as it considers will give the applicant a reasonable opportunity of himself or herself securing accommodation for his or her own occupation.[196]

2.109 If the authority provides its own accommodation, it will not be secure unless and until the authority notifies the applicant otherwise,[197] which it may not do except in accordance with HA 1996 Part 6 (allocation).

2.110 If the authority secures accommodation through a landlord whose tenants are not secure, then the accommodation will not be within any statutory protection for a year from when the authority first gave notification of its decision, or – if there is a review (or an appeal) – from its final determination, unless the tenant is notified by the landlord that it is to be regarded either as an assured shorthold or a fully assured tenancy.[198]

Wales

2.111 In Wales, the position is somewhat different. [199] The authority may have decided not to apply the intentionality provisions at all. If those provisions are being applied, then a duty to accommodate under H(W)A 2014 s75 will arise either i) if the authority is not satisfied that the applicant is homeless intentionally or ii) if the applicant, even though homeless intentionally, is:

a) a pregnant woman or a person with whom she resides or might reasonably be expected to reside;
b) a person with whom a dependent child resides or might reasonably be expected to reside;
c) a person who had not attained the age of 21 when the application was made or a person with whom such a person resides or might reasonably be expected to reside; or
d) a person who had attained the age of 21, but not the age of 25, when the application was made and who was looked after, accommodated or fostered at any time while under the age of 18, or a

194 See HA 1996 ss205, 206; H(W)A 2014 s59.
195 HA 1996 s176.
196 HA 1996 s190(2)(a).
197 HA 1985 Sch 1 para 4.
198 HA 1996 s209(2).
199 H(W)A 2014 s56.

person with whom such a person resides or might reasonably be expected to reside.[200]

2.112 In these circumstances, the duty will arise despite the intentionality if:

a) the applicant has no suitable accommodation available for occupation, or suitable accommodation which it is not likely will be available for occupation for at least six months starting on the day on which the applicant is notified[201] that the full duty will not apply;
b) the applicant is eligible for help and has a priority need for accommodation; and
c) the authority has not previously secured an offer of accommodation to the applicant under these provisions following a previous application for help, at any time within the period of five years before the day on which the applicant is notified that a duty is owed to him or her under them.

2.113 If the duty does not arise for any of these reasons, or because the applicant is not within the H(W)A 2014 s75(3) class,[202] then the initial duty to help is all that applies: it is limited to 56 days.[203]

Duties where local connection referral

2.114 The local connection provisions allow one housing authority to shift to another the burdens of the initial help duty and of making accommodation available. The provisions apply when the authority is satisfied that the applicant is homeless (not merely threatened with homelessness); in priority need; not homeless intentionally; and either:

a) in England, the applicant was placed in accommodation in its area by another authority, in pursuance of HA 1996 Part 7 functions, within such period as may be prescribed[204] for this purpose;[205] or

200 H(W)A 2014 s75(3).
201 Under H(W)A 2014 s84.
202 Para 2.111.
203 H(W)A 2014 s74(2).
204 By the secretary of state under HA 1996 s215. The relevant period is five years from the date of the placement together with the time between the date the application was initially made and the time the placement first became available: Allocation of Housing and Homelessness (Miscellaneous Provisions) (England) Regulations 2006 SI No 2527.
205 HA 1996 s198(4).

b) in England and Wales, the authority considers that all of the following conditions apply:
   i) neither the applicant nor anyone who might reasonably be expected to reside with him or her has a local connection with its area; and
   ii) the applicant or a person who might reasonably be expected to reside with the applicant does have a local connection with the area of another housing authority; and
   iii) neither the applicant nor any person who might reasonably be expected to reside with the applicant will run the risk of domestic violence[206] in the area of the other authority.[207]

2.115 From commencement of LA 2011 s149 in England,[208] the provisions also apply[209] if the application is made to an English authority within the period of two years beginning with the date on which the applicant accepted an offer from the other authority under HA 1996 s193(7AC) (private rented sector offer), and neither the applicant nor any person who might reasonably be expected to reside with the applicant will run the risk of domestic violence in the district of the other authority.[210]

2.116 A local connection referral may not be made where the applicant or any person who might reasonably be expected to reside with the applicant has suffered non-domestic violence in the area of the other authority and it is probable that the return to that area of the victim will lead to further violence of a similar kind against him or her.[211]

Violence and domestic violence

2.117 Violence and domestic violence are defined in the same terms as when determining whether or not it is reasonable to remain in occupation.[212]

Passing and retaining responsibility

2.118 The initial help and housing duties can be passed to the other authority if the conditions for referral are met; if so, the applicant is treated as having made an application to the notified authority on the date on

206 In Wales, domestic abuse.
207 HA 1996 s198(1), (2); H(W)A 2014 s80(1)–(3).
208 9 November 2012.
209 Assuming homelessness, priority need and no intentionality.
210 HA 1996 s198(2ZA).
211 HA 1996 s198(2A); H(W)A 2014 s84.
212 HA 1996 s198(3); H(W)A 2014 s58.

which he or she is given notification of this decision.[213] The notified authority's obligations are to provide initial help[214] and to house under HA 1996 s193.[215] If the conditions are not met, the initial help and housing duties under HA 1996 s193 remain with the authority to which the application was made.[216]

Interim accommodation and notification

2.119 Pending determination of final responsibility, the authority to which the application is made must provide temporary accommodation.[217]

2.120 Once the issue has been decided, it is for the authority to notify the applicant of the decision and of the reasons for it, as well as of the applicant's right to request a review (and the time within which it must be requested).[218] The temporary housing duty ceases when the notification is given, even if a review is requested, although the authority may continue to provide it pending review.[219]

Arbitration

2.121 HA 1996 Part 7 and the H(W)A 2014 provide elaborate machinery for the determination of disputes between authorities, by agreement or, if necessary, by reference to an independent arbitrator.[220]

2.122 An arbitration decision can itself be the subject of internal review, and thence appeal to the county court.[221]

Cross-border referrals

2.123 When a reference is made by an authority in Wales to an English authority, and the final duty lies with the English authority, the English authority will owe a duty to house under HA 1996 s193;[222] otherwise, the application continues to be dealt with under the Welsh legislation.[223] Where the reference is by an English authority to one in Wales, with which the final duty is agreed or held to lie, it is the

213 HA 1996 s199(5); H(W)A 2014 s82.
214 HA 1996 s189A(5).
215 The same provisions apply under HA 1996 s200(5) as to continuation of accommodation pending review as apply if the case is referred to the other authority: H(W)A 2014 s82.
216 HA 1996 s199A(4); H(W)A 2014 s82.
217 HA 1996 s199A; H(W)A 2014 s82.
218 HA 1996 s199(3); H(W)A 2014 s82.
219 HA 1996 s199(6); H(W)A 2014 s69(11).
220 HA 1996 s198(5); H(W)A 2014 s80(5).
221 HA 1996 ss198(5), 202(1)(d), (e); H(W)A 2014 ss85, 88.
222 HA 1996 s201A.
223 HA 1996 s201A; H(W)A 2014 s80.

Welsh provisions which will apply;[224] otherwise, the application remains with the English authority.[225]

2.124 An English authority cannot seek to transfer the initial help duty to an authority in Wales.[226] Once the duty to secure housing is transferred, the Welsh authority will still be subject to that duty, albeit in its Welsh form.[227] In the reverse case, a Welsh authority is under no initial help duty if it refers the application to another authority,[228] including an English authority, but it can only refer an application where the applicant is in priority need and unintentionally homeless.[229]

2.125 Scottish authorities may refer an applicant to an English or Welsh authority in the circumstances set out in Housing (Scotland) Act 1987 s33. Where such a reference is made, and agreed or upheld, the provisions which relate to England are applicable.[230] There is no corresponding provision in the Welsh legislation governing referrals between Scotland and Wales.

Full duties

2.126 If the authority is satisfied that the applicant is homeless, eligible for assistance, in priority need and not intentionally homeless, then (subject to the possibility of referral to another authority) its duty is to secure that accommodation is made available for the applicant's occupation (and, therefore, for any other family member who normally resides with, or anyone else who might reasonably be expected to reside with, the applicant).[231]

2.127 From commencement of LA 2011 s149 in England,[232] an English authority also owes a full duty, even if there is no priority need, if the application is a renewed application, following a previous application which resulted in an assured shorthold tenancy in the preceding two years, provided that the applicant is still eligible, and did not become homeless intentionally.[233]

224 H(W)A 2014 s83.
225 HA 1996 s200; H(W)A 2014 s83.
226 HA 1996 s198(A1).
227 H(W)A 2014 s83(2).
228 H(W)A 2014 s73(2).
229 H(W)A 2014 s80(1)(a).
230 HA 1996 s201.
231 HA 1996 s193(2); H(W)A 2014 s75.
232 9 November 2012.
233 HA 1996 s195A(1). This right only arises on one re-application: HA 1996 s195A(6).

2.128 In addition, an English authority must give the applicant a copy of the statement included in its allocation policy on offering choice to people allocated housing accommodation under HA 1996 Part 6.[234]

Securing accommodation

2.129 The duty to secure that accommodation is made available for the applicant's occupation can be discharged by:

a) making available suitable accommodation held by the authority under HA 1985 Part 2, or under any other powers; or
b) securing that the applicant obtains suitable accommodation from some other person; or
c) giving the applicant such advice and assistance as will secure that the applicant obtains suitable accommodation from some other person.[235]

2.130 In deciding whether accommodation is suitable, the authority must have regard to the provisions of the HAs 1985 and 2004 which govern hazardous housing, overcrowding and houses in multiple occupation (HMOs);[236] the secretary of state has power to specify circumstances in which accommodation is, or is not, to be regarded as suitable, and as to the matters which the authority must take into account or disregard when deciding suitability.[237]

Charges

2.131 Authorities have a general power to make reasonable charges for the provision of their own accommodation under HA 1985 Part 2.[238] HA 1996 Part 7 and H(W)A 2014 Part 2 entitle them to make charges to a homeless person for accommodation which they provide, or for or towards accommodation which they arrange for some other person to provide, under HA 1996 Part 7 or H(W)A 2014 Part 2.[239]

234 HA 1996 s193(3A).
235 HA 1996 s206(1); H(W)A 2014 s76.
236 HA 1996 s210(1); H(W)A 2014 s59.
237 HA 1996 s210(2). A number of statutory instruments have been made under this power – see: Homelessness (Suitability of Accommodation) Order 1996 SI No 3204; Homelessness (Suitability of Accommodation) (England) Order 2003 SI No 3326; and Homelessness (Suitability of Accommodation) (England) Order 2012 SI No 2601. In Wales, the same power is given to the Welsh Ministers: H(W)A 2014 s59(3).
238 HA 1985 s24.
239 HA 1996 s206(2); H(W)A 2014 s90.

Out-of-area accommodation

2.132 So far as reasonably practicable, authorities are bound to secure accommodation within their own area.[240] If the authority places an applicant in another area, it must give notice to the local housing authority with responsibility for that area, stating:

a) the name of the applicant;
b) the number and description of other members of the applicant's family normally residing with him or her, or of anyone else who might reasonably to be expected to reside with him or her;
c) the address;
d) the date on which the accommodation was made available to the applicant; and
e) what HA 1996 Part 7 function the authority was discharging when securing the accommodation for the applicant.[241]

2.133 The notice must be given in writing within two weeks from when the accommodation was made available.[242]

Security

2.134 Where an authority provides its own accommodation in discharge of the full duty, it is not secure.[243]

Discharge of duty (England pre-LA 2011; Wales pre-H(W)A 2014)

2.135 In relation to applications in England made before commencement of LA 2011 s148(3)[244] in respect of which the duty to secure accommodation had arisen but had not ceased by that date,[245] and continuing in Wales for applications made prior to 27 April 2015,[246] the duty to secure accommodation is owed to an applicant until it is brought to an end in any of the circumstances set out in HA 1996 s193.[247]

240 HA 1996 s208(1); H(W)A 2014 s91.
241 HA 1996 s208(2), (3); H(W)A 2014 s91(3).
242 HA 1996 s208(4); H(W)A 2014 s91(4).
243 HA 1985 Sch 1 para 4.
244 9 November 2012.
245 Localism Act 2011 (Commencement No 2 and Transitional Provisions) (England) Order 2012 SI No 2599 art 3.
246 For applications made on or after that date, H(W)A 2014 applies: see Housing (Wales) Act 2014 (Commencement No 3 and Transitory, Transitional and Saving Provisions) Order 2015 SI No 1272 art 7.
247 HA 1996 s193(3).

2.136 Those circumstances are as follows.

a) if the applicant refuses an offer under HA 1996 Part 7, which the authority is satisfied is suitable for him or her, and the authority has informed the applicant of the possible consequences of refusal, of his or her right to a review of the suitability of the accommodation and that it will regard itself as having discharged the duty;[248]
b) if the applicant ceases to be eligible for assistance;[249]
c) if the applicant becomes homeless intentionally from HA 1996 Part 7 accommodation;[250]
d) if the applicant accepts an allocation under HA 1996 Part 6;[251]
e) if the applicant accepts an offer of an assured tenancy (other than an assured shorthold tenancy) from a private landlord, ie, one whose tenants are not secure;[252]
f) if the applicant voluntarily ceases to occupy HA 1996 Part 7 accommodation as an only or principal home;[253]
g) if the applicant, having been informed:
   i) of the possible consequences of refusal; and
   ii) of his or her right to request a review of the suitability of accommodation refused,

   refuses a written final offer of HA 1996 Part 6 allocation, and the authority is satisfied that:
   A) the accommodation was suitable for the applicant; and
   B) that it was reasonable for the applicant to accept it.

   An applicant may for this purpose reasonably be considered to accept an offer even though the applicant is under a contractual or other obligation in respect of his or her existing accommodation, if (but only if) he or she can bring that other obligation to an end before he or she has to take up the offer;[254]
h) if the applicant accepts a qualifying offer of an assured shorthold tenancy from a private landlord.[255] Again, the applicant must be able to bring any obligation in respect of the applicant's existing

248 HA 1996 s193(5).
249 HA 1996 s193(6)(a).
250 HA 1996 s193(6)(b).
251 HA 1996 s193(6)(c).
252 HA 1996 s193(6)(cc).
253 HA 1996 s193(6)(d).
254 HA 1996 s193(8).
255 HA 1996 s193(7B).

accommodation to an end before he or she has to take up the offer.[256] An offer qualifies if:

i) it is made with the approval of the authority, in pursuance of arrangements made by the authority with the landlord with a view to bringing the duty towards the applicant to an end;
ii) it is of a fixed-term tenancy; and
iii) it is accompanied by a statement in writing, which states the term of the tenancy being offered and explains in ordinary language that there is no obligation on the applicant to accept it but that if it is accepted the authority will cease to be under a duty to the applicant.[257]

2.137 Acceptance of a qualifying offer is only effective if the applicant signs a statement acknowledging that he or she has understood the authority's statement.[258] An authority may not make a qualifying offer unless satisfied that the accommodation is suitable for the applicant and that it is reasonable for the applicant to accept the offer.[259] The applicant is free to reject a qualifying offer without affecting the duty owed to him or her under this section by the authority.[260]

Discharge of duty (England post-LA 2011; Wales post-H(W)A 2014)

2.138 From commencement of LA 2011 s148[261] in England and H(W)A 2014 in Wales,[262] the circumstances in which the duty to secure accommodation is brought to an end are as follows:

a) if the applicant refuses an offer under HA 1996 Part 7 or H(W)A 2014 Part 2, which is not an offer under Part 6 (below, item g)) or a private rented sector offer (below, item h)), which the authority is satisfied is suitable for the applicant, and the authority has informed the applicant of the possible consequences of refusal or acceptance, of his or her right to a review of the suitability of the accommodation and that it will regard itself as having discharged the duty;[263]

256 HA 1996 s193(8).
257 HA 1996 s193(7D).
258 HA 1996 s193(7E).
259 HA 1996 s193(7F).
260 HA 1996 s193(7C).
261 9 November 2012.
262 27 April 2015.
263 HA 1996 s193(5); H(W)A 2014 s76(3).

b),[264] c),[265] d),[266] e),[267] f)[268] – these are the same[269] as above;[270]

g) if the applicant, having been informed:
   i) of the possible consequences of refusal or acceptance; and
   ii) of his or her right to request a review of the suitability of accommodation refused,

   refuses a written final offer of HA 1996 Part 6 allocation, and the authority is satisfied that:
   A) the accommodation was suitable for the applicant; and
   B) (in England only) the applicant was not under any contractual or other obligations in respect of his or her existing accommodation which he or she could not bring to an end before having to take up the HA 1996 Part 6 offer;[271]

h) if the applicant accepts or refuses a private rented sector offer, having been informed in writing:
   i) of the possible consequence of refusal or acceptance of the offer;
   ii) that the applicant has the right to request a review of the suitability of the accommodation;[272] and
   iii) (in a case which is not a restricted case and in England only) of the effect under HA 1996 s195A of a further application to a local housing authority within two years of acceptance of the offer.

   A private rented sector offer means:
   i) an offer of an assured shorthold tenancy made by a private landlord to the applicant in relation to any accommodation which is, or may become, available for the applicant's occupation;
   ii) made, with the approval of the authority, in pursuance of arrangements made by the authority with the landlord with a view to bringing the authority's duty under this section to an end;

264 H(W)A 2014 ss76(8), 79(2).
265 HA 1996 s193(6)(b); H(W)A 2014 s76(6).
266 HA 1996 s193(6)(c); H(W)A 2014 s76(2)(a).
267 HA 1996 s193(6)(cc); H(W)A 2014 s76(2)(b).
268 HA 1996 s193(6)(d); H(W)A 2014 s76(7).
269 Save that in Wales, (f) refers to ceasing to occupy H(W)A 2014 Part 2 accommodation.
270 Para 2.136.
271 HA 1996 s193(7), (7A), (7F); H(W)A 2014 s76(3)(c).
272 H(W)A 2014 ss76(3), 84.

iii) which is a fixed-term tenancy for a period of at least 12[273] months.[274]

The authority may not approve such an offer unless it is satisfied that:

i) the accommodation was suitable for the applicant; and
ii) (in England only) the applicant was not under any contractual or other obligations in respect of his or her existing accommodation which he or she could not bring to an end before having to take up the offer.[275]

2.139 In Wales only, the duty to secure accommodation may also be brought to an end if the authority is satisfied that that a mistake of fact led to the applicant being notified that the duty was owed, or that the applicant has withdrawn his or her application, or that the applicant is unreasonable failing to co-operate with the authority in connection with its exercise of functions under these provisions in relation to his or her case.[276]

Restricted cases

2.140 Where the duty arises by reference to a household member who is a restricted person, the authority must, so far reasonably practicable, bring the full housing duty to an end by arranging for a private rented sector offer to be made.[277]

England post-Homelessness Reduction Act 2017

2.141 From commencement of the HRA 2017 in England,[278] the full duty will not arise if a final accommodation or HA 1996 Part 6 offer was refused in the course of the authority's discharge of the initial help duty.[279]

2.142 A final accommodation offer is an offer of an assured shorthold tenancy made by a private landlord – including a private registered provider of social housing (England) or a registered social landlord

273 In Wales, six months: see H(W)A 2014 s76(4)(c).

274 The secretary of state has power to increase the minimum term, other than in a restricted case: HA 1996 s193(10)–(12).

275 HA 1996 s193(7AA)–(7AC), (7F), (8).

276 H(W)A 2014 ss76(8), 79(3)–(5).

277 HA 1996 s193(7AD); H(W)A 2014 s76(5).

278 3 April 2018: see Homelessness Reduction Act 2017 (Commencement and Transitional and Savings Provisions) Regulations 2018 SI No 167 reg 3. The provisions do not apply to applications made or reviews sought on or after that date: reg 4.

279 HA 1996 s193A(1), (2).

(Wales) – in relation to any accommodation which is, or may become, available for the applicant's occupation, made, with the approval of the authority, in pursuance of arrangements made by the authority in discharge of the HA 1996 s189B(2) duty, which is a fixed-term tenancy for a period of at least six months.[280] A 'final Part 6 offer' is an offer of accommodation under HA 1996 Part 6 made in writing in discharge of the authority's HA 1996 s189B duty, which states that it is a final offer for that purpose.[281]

2.143 As in other cases, the applicant must be warned of the consequences of refusal and of his or her right to seek a review of the suitability of the offer.[282] The authority cannot approve a final accommodation offer or make a final Part 6 offer unless it is satisfied that it is suitable for the applicant;[283] nor can it approve or make such an offer if the applicant is under contractual or other obligations in respect of his or her existing accommodation, which he or she is not able to bring to an end before he or she would have to take up the offer.[284]

2.144 An authority may also serve notice bringing both the initial help duty under HA 1996 s189B and the duty to help those threatened with homelessness under HA 1996 s195 to an end on account of the applicant's deliberate and unreasonable refusal to co-operate.[285]

2.145 In such cases, HA 1996 s193 does not apply,[286] but if the applicant is homeless, eligible for assistance, in priority need for accommodation and did not become homeless intentionally, a similar duty will arise under section 193C.[287] The duty is to secure that accommodation is available for occupation by the applicant.[288] The duty will cease if the applicant:

a) ceases to be eligible for assistance;
b) becomes homeless intentionally from accommodation made available for his or her occupation;
c) accepts an offer of an assured tenancy from a private landlord; or

280 HA 1996 s193A(4).
281 HA 1996 s193A(5).
282 HA 1996 s193A(1).
283 HA 1996 s193A(6).
284 HA 1996 s193A(7).
285 HA 1996 s193B(1), (2).
286 HA 1996 s193C(4).
287 HA 1996 s193C(3).
288 HA 1996 s193C(4).

d) otherwise voluntarily ceases to occupy, as his or her only or principal home, the accommodation made available for his or her occupation.[289]

2.146 The duty will also cease if the applicant, having been informed of the possible consequences of refusal or acceptance and of his or her right to request a review of the suitability of the accommodation, refuses or accepts a final accommodation offer,[290] or a final HA 1996 Part 6[291] offer.[292] These are defined[293] in the same terms, and are subject[294] to the same requirements as to suitability and obligations in respect of existing accommodation as above.[295]

Protection of property

Duty

2.147 An authority may be under a duty to take reasonable steps to prevent the loss of an applicant's property, or prevent or mitigate damage to it,[296] if it is or has been under a duty under HA 1996 s188, s190, s193, s195 or s200; or H(W)A 2014 s66, s68, s75 or s82. Since 3 April 2018,[297] the duty is also owed where an English authority has become subject to the initial duty to help under HA 1996 s189B.[298]

289 HA 1996 s193C(5).

290 An offer of an assured shorthold tenancy made by a private landlord – including a private registered provider of social housing (England) or a registered social landlord (Wales) – in relation to any accommodation which is, or may become, available for the applicant's occupation, made, with the approval of the authority, in pursuance of arrangements made by the authority in discharge of the HA 1996 s193C duty, which is a fixed-term tenancy for a period of at least six months: HA 1996 s193C(7).

291 An offer of accommodation under HA 1996 Part 6 made in writing in discharge of the authority's the HA 1996 s193C duty, which states that it is a final offer for that purpose: HA 1996 s193C(8).

292 HA 1996 s193C(6).

293 HA 1996 s193C(7), (8).

294 HA 1996 s193C(9), (10).

295 Para 2.129–2.137.

296 HA 1996 s211(2); H(W)A 2014 s93(2).

297 Commencement of HRA 2017: see Homelessness Reduction Act 2017 (Commencement and Transitional and Savings Provisions) Regulations 2018 SI No 167 reg 3.

298 HA 1996 s211(2).

2.148 For these purposes, an applicant's personal property includes the personal property of any person reasonably expected to reside with him or her.[299]

2.149 The duty arises if the authority has reason to believe:

a) that there is a danger of loss of or damage to property because of the applicant's inability to protect or deal with it; and
b) that no other suitable arrangements have been or are being made.[300]

Power

2.150 If the authority is or has not been under one of these duties, but has reason to believe that a relevant danger to property exists, for which there are no arrangements, it has power to protect property.[301]

Charges and terms

2.151 The authority can, however, decline to take action under these provisions other than on such conditions as it considers appropriate, including as to reasonable charges and the disposal of property.[302]

Power of entry

2.152 In connection with these provisions, the authority has power, at all reasonable times, to enter any premises which are or were the usual or last usual place of residence of the applicant, and to deal with the applicant's property in any way that is reasonably necessary, including by way of storage.[303]

Choice of storage

2.153 If the applicant asks the authority to move the property to a nominated location and the authority considers the request to be reasonable, the authority may discharge its responsibilities under these provisions by complying and, therefore, treating its responsibilities as being ended.[304]

299 HA 1996 s211(5); H(W)A 2014 s93(6).
300 HA 1996 s211(1); H(W)A 2014 s93(1).
301 HA 1996 s211(3); H(W)A 2914 s93(5).
302 HA 1996 s211(4); H(W)A 2014 s93(4).
303 HA 1996 s212(1); H(W)A 2014 s94(1).
304 HA 1996 s212(2); H(W)A 2014 s94(4).

Termination

2.154 Otherwise, the responsibilities end when the authority considers that there is no longer any danger of loss or damage by reason of the applicant's inability to protect or deal with the applicant's personal property, although, if the authority has provided storage, it may continue to do so.[305]

2.155 When the authority's responsibilities end, it must notify the applicant that they have done so, and of the reasons why.[306] Notification may be given by delivery, or by leaving it or sending it to the applicant's last known address.[307]

Review

2.156 These provisions are not subject to internal review or appeal to the county court.

Homelessness strategies

2.157 The Homelessness Act 2002 imposed a new duty on local housing authorities to carry out a homelessness review in their areas and formulate and publish a homelessness strategy based on its results.[308]

2.158 The first strategy had to be published within 12 months of Homelessness Act 2002 s1 coming into force[309] and, thereafter, a new one has to be published at least every five years.[310] Since 1 December 2014, the position in Wales has been governed by H(W)A 2014 s50. A Welsh authority must carry out a homelessness review for its area, and formulate and adopt a homelessness strategy based on the results of that review.[311] The strategy must be adopted in 2018, with a new strategy every fourth year thereafter.[312]

305 HA 1996 s212(3); H(W)A 2014 s94(6), (7).
306 HA 1996 s212(4); H(W)A 2014 s94(8).
307 HA 1996 s212(5); H(W)A 2014 s94(9).
308 Homelessness Act 2002 s1(1).
309 31 July 2003 (see the Homelessness Act 2002 (Commencement No 1) (England) Order 2002 SI No 1799 art 2) and 30 September 2003 (see the Homelessness Act 2002 (Commencement) (Wales) Order 2002 SI No 1736 art 2).
310 Homelessness Act 2002 s1(3) and (4).
311 H(W)A 2014 s50(1). The strategy can form part of the Well-being Plan under the Well-being of Future Generations (Wales) Act 2015, Welsh Code para 5.4.
312 H(W)A 2014 s50(2). The Welsh Code of Guidance notes that the strategy should reflect the Welsh Government's *Ten year homeless plan* (July 2009), para 5.7.

Authorities

2.159 Where it is a different authority, the social services authority for the area of the authority must afford such assistance in the review and in the formulation of the strategy as the housing authority may reasonably require.[313] The strategy must be taken into account by both the local housing authority and the social services authority in the exercise of their functions.[314] In Wales, the strategy must be taken into account by the authority when exercising any of its functions.[315]

Homelessness review

2.160 For these purposes, a homelessness review means a review of:

a) the level, and likely future levels, of homelessness in the authority's area;
b) the activities which are carried out in the area to:
    i) prevent homelessness in the authority's area;
    ii) secure that accommodation is or will be available for people in the area who are or may become homeless; and
    iii) provide support for people in the area who are or may become homeless or who have been homeless and need support to prevent it happening again; and
c) the resources available to the authority, the social services authority, other public authorities, voluntary organisations and other persons for such activities.[316]

2.161 On completion of the review, the authority must arrange for the results to be available for inspection at its principal office, at all reasonable hours, without charge, and provide (on payment of a reasonable charge, if required) a copy of the results.[317]

Homelessness strategy

2.162 A homelessness strategy means one formulated for:

a) preventing homelessness in the authority's area;

313 Homelessness Act 2002 s1(2). In Wales there is no requirement that the exercise be carried out with the assistance of the local social services authority as all Welsh authorities are unitary, ie have both housing and social service functions.

314 Homelessness Act 2002 s1(5) and (6).

315 H(W)A 2014 s50(4).

316 Homelessness Act 2002 s2(1), (2); H(W)A 2014 s51.

317 Homelessness Act 2002 s2(3); H(W)A 2014 s51(2) – in Wales, the results must also be published on the authority's website, if it has one.

b) securing that sufficient accommodation is and will be available for people in the area who are or may become homeless; and
c) securing that there is satisfactory provision of support for people in the area who are or who may become homeless or who have become homeless and need support to prevent them becoming homeless again.[318]

2.163 The strategy may include specific objectives to be pursued, and specific action planned to be taken in the course of the exercise of the authority's housing functions, and also of the functions of the social services authority for the district.[319] In Wales, the strategy must include details of both general and specific actions planned by the authority, including actions expected to be taken by other public authorities and voluntary organisations, in relation to those who may be in particular need of support if they are or may become homeless, in particular:

a) people leaving prison or youth detention accommodation;
b) young people leaving care;
c) people leaving the regular armed forces of the Crown;
d) people leaving hospital after medical treatment for mental disorder as an inpatient; and
e) people receiving mental health services in the community.[320]

2.164 The strategy may also include specific action which the authority expects to be taken by any other public authority, voluntary organisation or other person, which or who can contribute to the objectives of the strategy, albeit only with the approval of the body or person in question.[321] The authority must consider how far the objectives of the strategy can be met by joint action between itself, the social services authority or any other body or persons.[322]

2.165 The strategy must be kept under review and may be modified.[323] Any modification must be published and, before adopting or modifying the strategy, the authority must consult such public or local authorities, voluntary organisations or other persons as it considers appropriate.[324]

318 Homelessness Act 2002 s3(1); H(W)A 2014 s52.
319 Homelessness Act 2002 s3(2); H(W)A 2014 s52(2).
320 H(W)A 2014 s52(6).
321 Homelessness Act 2002 s3(3), (4); H(W)A 2014 s52(3), (4).
322 Homelessness Act 2002 s3(5); H(W)A 2014 s52(5).
323 Homelessness Act 2002 s3(6); H(W)A 2014 s52(7).
324 Homelessness Act 2002 s3(7), (8); H(W)A 2014 s52(8).

2.166 A copy of the strategy must be available at the authority's principal office for inspection at all reasonable hours, free of charge, and be provided to members of the public on request, on payment (if required) of a reasonable charge.[325]

Advice, information and voluntary organisations

England

2.167 HA 1996 Part 7 makes provision for English authorities to give grants, loans, premises or goods in kind to voluntary organisations concerned with the homeless.[326]

2.168 Since commencement of the HRA 2017,[327] English housing authorities have been under a duty to provide or secure the provision of a service, to be available free of charge to any person in its district, providing information and advice on:

a) preventing homelessness;
b) securing accommodation when homeless;
c) the rights of persons who are homeless or threatened with homelessness, and the duties of the authority, under HA 1996 Part 7;
d) any help that is available from the authority or anyone else, whether under Part 7 or otherwise, for persons in the district who are homeless or may become homeless (whether or not they are threatened with homelessness); and
e) how to access that help.[328]

2.169 The service must be designed to meet the needs of persons in the authority's district including, in particular, the needs of:

a) people released from prison or youth detention accommodation;
b) care leavers;
c) former members of the regular armed forces;
d) victims of domestic abuse;
e) people leaving hospital;
f) people suffering from a mental illness or impairment; and

325 Homelessness Act 2002 s3(8); H(W)A 2014 s52(9).

326 HA 1996 ss180, 181.

327 3 April 2018: see Homelessness Reduction Act 2017 (Commencement and Transitional and Savings Provisions) Regulations 2018 SI No 167 reg 3. The initial help duties do not apply to applications made or reviews sought before 3 April 2018: reg 4.

328 HA 1996 s179(1).

g) any other group which the authority identifies as being at particular risk of homelessness in its district.[329]

2.170 The authority may provide grants or loans to someone providing the service on its behalf.[330]

Wales

2.171 In Wales, authorities have an obligation to ensure that advice and assistance about homelessness and its prevention are available to any person in their area, free of charge.[331]

2.172 The advice and information must include details about how the homelessness service operates in the authority's area, other help which might be available and how to access it.[332] Whether or not someone is threatened with homelessness, assistance must be provided to access help to prevent him or her becoming homeless.[333]

2.173 The authority must work with other public authorities, voluntary organisations and others to ensure that the service is designed to meet the needs of groups at particular risk of homelessness, including in particular:

a) people leaving prison or youth detention accommodation;
b) young people leaving care;
c) people leaving the regular armed forces of the Crown;
d) people leaving hospital after medical treatment for mental disorder as an inpatient; and
e) people receiving mental health services in the community.[334]

2.174 Two or more authorities may provide the service jointly.[335]

Code of Guidance

2.175 In the exercise of their functions under HA 1996 Part 7 or H(W)A 2014 Part 2, authorities are bound to have regard to such guidance as may from time to time be given by the secretary of state or the Welsh

329 HA 1996 s179(2).
330 HA 1996 s179(3). Assistance may also be given by way of the use of premises, furniture or other goods and even the services of staff: HA 1996 s179(4).
331 HA H(W)A 2014 s60(1).
332 H(W)A 2014 s60(2).
333 H(W)A 2014 s60(3).
334 H(W)A 2014 s60(4).
335 H(W)A 2014 s60(5).

Ministers.[336] Under these provisions, there have been issued Codes of Guidance for England[337] and for Wales.[338]

Code of Practice

2.176 Since the commencement of the HRA 2017,[339] in England the secretary of state has had power to issue Codes of Practice relating to homelessness or homelessness prevention to local housing authorities,[340] in particular concerning the exercise by a local housing authority of functions under Part 7, staff training relating to the exercise of those functions and monitoring by the authority of the exercise of those functions.[341]

2.177 A code may apply to all local housing authorities or to a local housing authority specified or described in the code, and may contain different provision for different kinds of local housing authority.[342] A local housing authority must have regard to a Code of Practice in exercising its functions.[343]

Review and appeal

Review

2.178 Applicants have a statutory right to request an internal review of what, if any, duty is owed under HA 1996 ss190–193 and 195–196; or H(W)A 2014 s66, s68, s73 or s75.[344] This expressly encompasses whether or not the applicant is eligible for assistance, in priority need, intentionally homeless, whether a duty has ceased, and whether an applicant is threatened with homelessness or threatened with homelessness intentionally; it includes the full range of questions

336 HA 1996 s182; H(W)A 2014 s98.

337 See appendix C. The English code is available both as a downloadable PDF and as a series of webpages. The government regards the webpages as the definitive version and does not guarantee to update the PDF (see version control sheet on PDF).

338 The present version (2016) is reproduced in full in the ebook version of *Homelessness and allocations*. The first Welsh Code was in 2015.

339 3 April 2018: see Homelessness Reduction Act 2017 (Commencement and Transitional and Savings Provisions) Regulations 2018 SI No 167 reg 3.

340 HA 1996 s214A(1).

341 HA 1996 s214A(2).

342 HA 1996 s214A(3).

343 HA 1996 s214A(12).

344 HA 1996 s202; H(W)A 2014 s85.

involved in local connection referrals, issues of suitability and a range of subsidiary issues.[345]

2.179 Since the HRA 2017 came into force,[346] the decisions which may be the subject of review in England include decisions under the new initial duty to help, and the new duties to those threatened with homelessness, along with the corresponding provisions governing cessation of those new duties by reference to final offers and deliberate and unreasonable refusal to co-operate.[347]

2.180 An applicant may seek a review of whether accommodation offered in discharge of a duty is suitable and, where applicable, whether it is reasonable to accept it, whether or not the applicant has accepted the offer of accommodation.[348] The right of review does not, however, entitle the applicant to a review of an earlier review.[349]

Accommodation pending review

2.181 Pending the outcome of the review, the authority may – but is not under a duty to – provide accommodation for the applicant.[350]

Request for review

2.182 A request for a review must be made within 21 days of notification of decision, or such longer period as the authority may in writing allow.[351]

345 There is a small amount of doubt about whether there is a review from a decision as to which authority has responsibility under HA 1996 s199A if a referral is made at the initial duty stage: see the discussion at para 7.104.

346 3 April 2018: see Homelessness Reduction Act 2017 (Commencement and Transitional and Savings Provisions) Regulations 2018 SI No 167 reg 3. The assessment and initial help duties do not apply to applications made or reviews sought before 3 April 2018: reg 4.

347 HA 1996 s202(1).

348 HA 1996 s202(1A); H(W)A 2014 s85(3).

349 HA 1996 s202(2); H(W)A 2014 s85(4).

350 HA 1996 s188(3); H(W)A 2014 s69(11). In local connection review cases, where an English authority notifies an applicant that it intends to notify or has notified another local housing authority in England under section 198(A1) of its opinion that the conditions are met for referral of the applicant's case to the notified authority, the notifying authority ceases to be subject to any duty under section 188, but, if it has reason to believe that the applicant may have a priority need, must secure that accommodation is available for occupation by the applicant until the applicant is notified of the decision as to whether the conditions for referral of the applicant's case are met under section 199A(2). In Wales, see H(W)A 2014 s84 to like effect.

351 HA 1996 s202(3); H(W)A 2014 s85(2).

Review procedure

2.183 The secretary of state and the Welsh Ministers have power to regulate review procedure, including power to require that the review be conducted by a person of 'appropriate seniority . . . not involved in the original decision', and to prescribe the 'circumstances in which the applicant is entitled to an oral hearing, and whether and by whom [the applicant] may be represented at such a hearing'.[352]

Notification

2.184 The authority has to notify the applicant of the outcome of the review and, if it is adverse to the applicant's interests or confirms a local connection referral, of the reasons for it.[353] The authority must also notify the applicant of the right of appeal to the county court on a point of law.[354] If either of these requirements is not fulfilled, the notification is treated as not having been given.[355] The review may also need to be carried out, and notification given, within a period to be prescribed by the regulations.[356]

Appeal

2.185 An appeal lies to the county court if the applicant either:

a) is dissatisfied with the outcome of the review; or
b) has not been notified of the outcome within any time that may be prescribed.[357]

2.186 Appeal lies only on a point of law, whether it arises from the original decision or from the decision on review.[358]

Time for appeal

2.187 The appeal must be brought within 21 days of notification, or of when the applicant ought to have been notified of the outcome.[359] The court may give permission to appeal out of time where there is

352 HA 1996 s203; H(W)A 2014 s86.
353 HA 1996 s203(4); H(W)A 2014 s86(4).
354 HA 1996 s203(5); H(W)A 2014 s86(5).
355 HA 1996 s203(6); H(W)A 2014 s86(6).
356 HA 1996 s203(7); H(W)A 2014 s86(2)(c).
357 HA 1996 s204(1); H(W)A 2014 s88.
358 HA 1996 s204(1); H(W)A 2014 s88.
359 HA 1996 s204(2); H(W)A 2014 s88.

good reason for the applicant being unable to bring the appeal within the 21-day limit.[360]

Powers of court

2.188 The court may make such order as it thinks fit, confirming, quashing or varying the decision.[361]

Accommodation pending appeal

2.189 Pending an appeal (and any further appeal), the authority may, but is not obliged to, provide accommodation.[362] If the authority refuses to do so, the applicant may appeal that decision to the county court[363] and the court may order that accommodation is made available pending the outcome of the appeal (or such earlier time as it may specify), and may confirm or quash the decision of the authority not to provide accommodation.[364]

2.190 In considering whether to confirm or quash the decision, the court must apply the principles applied by the High Court on an application for judicial review.[365]

2.191 If the court quashes the decision, it may order the authority to exercise the power to accommodate pending appeal in the applicant's case for such period as it specifies.[366] Such an order may, however, only be made if the court is satisfied that failure to exercise the accommodation power in accordance with its order would substantially prejudice the applicant's ability to pursue his or her substantive appeal.[367]

Criminal offences

2.192 It is a criminal offence knowingly or recklessly to make a statement which is false in a material particular, or knowingly to withhold information which an authority has reasonably required in connection with the exercise of its functions under HA 1996 Part 7 or H(W)A 2014 Part 2, with intent to induce an authority to believe that

360 HA 1996 s204(2A); H(W)A 2014 s88(3).
361 HA 1996 s204(3); H(W)A 2014 s88(4).
362 HA 1996 s204(4); H(W)A 2014 s88(5).
363 HA 1996 s204A; H(W)A 2014 s89.
364 HA 1996 s204A(4)(a), (b); H(W)A 2014 s89(4).
365 HA 1996 s204A(4); H(W)A 2014 s89(5).
366 HA 1996 s204A(5); H(W)A 2014 s89(6).
367 HA 1996 s204A(6)(a); H(W)A 2014 s89(7).

the person making the statement, or any other person, is entitled to accommodation or assistance (or accommodation or assistance of a particular kind).[368]

2.193 The offence is punishable on summary conviction in England by a fine of up to level 5, and in Wales by a fine of up to level 4 on the standard scale,[369] ie, the standard scale for the time being under Criminal Justice Act (CJA) 1982 s37.[370]

2.194 An applicant has a duty to notify an authority as soon as possible of any material change of facts material to his or her case, which occurs before the applicant receives the notification of the authority's decision on his or her application.[371]

2.195 The authority is under a corresponding obligation to explain to an applicant, in ordinary language, the nature of this duty and the effect of the defence to a charge of non-compliance.[372] The defence is that no such explanation was given or that, although such an explanation was given, there is some other reasonable excuse for non-compliance.[373]

2.196 In the absence of such a defence, it is a criminal offence to fail to comply with the duty to notify the authority of material changes, punishable on summary conviction at levels 5 and 4 on the standard scale.[374]

Co-operation between authorities

Co-operation

2.197 In the discharge of its functions under HA 1996 Part 7, a local housing authority in England may request assistance from another local housing authority (in England, Wales or Scotland), a private registered provider of social housing, a registered social landlord or a housing action trust, or a development corporation, registered housing association or Scottish Homes.[375]

368 HA 1996 s214(1); H(W)A 2014 s97(1).
369 HA 1996 s214(4); H(W)A 2014 s97.
370 Level 5 is presently unlimited (see CJA 1982 s37 and Legal Aid, Sentencing and Punishment of Offenders Act (LASPO) 2012 s85); level 4 is currently £2,500 (CJA 1982 s37).
371 HA 1996 s214(2); H(W)A 2014 s97(2).
372 HA 1996 s214(2); H(W)A 2014 s97(3), (4).
373 HA 1996 s214(3); H(W)A 2014 s97(3), (5).
374 HA 1996 s214(4); H(W)A 2014 s97(6); see above.
375 HA 1996 s213(1)(a), (2).

2.198 The other authority (or body) must co-operate with the housing authority by rendering such assistance as is reasonable in the circumstances.[376] The provisions also apply when a Scottish local authority seeks assistance from an English authority under Housing (Scotland) Act 1987 s38.[377]

2.199 The secretary of state in England has power to specify public authorities[378] on whom is placed a duty[379] to seek to refer to a local housing authority someone in relation to whom it exercises functions whom it considers may be homeless or threatened with homelessness;[380] the referral must be made if the person agrees to the specified authority notifying a housing authority of its opinion and of his or her contact information.[381]

2.200 In Wales, where all authorities are unitary and therefore have both housing and social services functions, the corresponding provisions require each authority to make arrangements to promote co-operation between those of its officers who exercise its social services functions and those who exercise its functions as the local housing authority, with a view to achieving the following objectives in its area:

a) the prevention of homelessness;
b) that suitable accommodation is or will be available for people who are or may become homeless;
c) that satisfactory support is available for people who are or may become homeless; and
d) the effective discharge of its functions under H(W)A 2014 Part 2.[382]

2.201 In addition, the authority may request the co-operation of the following persons (whether in Wales or England): a local housing authority; a social services authority; a registered social landlord; a private registered provider of social housing; or a housing action trust.[383]

376 HA 1996 s213(1).
377 HA 1996 s213(3).
378 A body other than a local authority with functions of a public nature: HA 1996 s213B(5).
379 Since commencement of the HRA 2017: 3 April 2017 – see Homelessness Reduction Act 2017 (Commencement and Transitional and Savings Provisions) Regulations 2018 SI No 167 reg 3.
380 HA 1996 s213B(1), (2), (4).
381 HA 1996 s213B(2), (3).
382 H(W)A 2014 s95(1).
383 H(W)A 2014 s95(5). The Welsh Ministers may add or omit persons from this list, other than a Minister of the Crown: s95(6), (7).

2.202 The body is bound to comply with the request unless it considers that doing so would be incompatible with its own duties, or would otherwise have an adverse effect on the exercise of its functions.[384] If the authority seeks information from the body, it must likewise comply unless it considers that doing so would be incompatible with its own duties or would otherwise have an adverse effect on the exercise of the person's functions.[385] In either case, a body which decides not to comply with the request must give the local housing authority who made the request written reasons for its decision.[386]

Referral

England

2.203 In addition, where an English local housing authority has reason to believe that an applicant with whom children reside, or usually reside, may be ineligible for assistance, may be homeless or may have become so intentionally, or may be threatened with homelessness intentionally, it must make arrangements for ensuring that the applicant is invited to consent to the referral of his or her case to the social services authority (or department in the case of a unitary authority) and, if consent is given, must make the social services authority/department aware of the essential facts of the case and the subsequent decision in relation to it.[387]

2.204 Following such a referral, the social services authority/department may request that the housing authority provide it with advice and assistance in the exercise of its functions under the CA 1989 Part 3 and the housing authority must provide it with such advice and assistance as is reasonable in all the circumstances.[388]

Wales

2.205 The corresponding provisions in Wales apply where the authority has reason to believe that an applicant with whom a person under the age of 18 normally resides, or might reasonably be expected to reside, may be ineligible for help, may be homeless but that a duty under H(W)A 2014 s68, s73 or s75 is not likely to apply, or may

384 H(W)A 2014 s95(2).
385 H(W)A 2014 s95(3).
386 H(W)A 2014 s95(4).
387 HA 1996 s213A(1), (2).
388 HA 1996 s213A(5), (6).

be threatened with homelessness and that a duty under section 66 is not likely to apply.[389]

2.206 The authority must make arrangements for ensuring that the applicant is invited to consent to the referral to its social services department of the essential facts of his or her case, and, if he or she has given that consent, that the social services department is made aware of those facts and of the subsequent decision in respect of his or her case.[390] The authority must also make arrangements to ensure that where it makes a decision that an applicant is ineligible for help, became homeless intentionally or became threatened with homelessness intentionally, its housing department provides the social services department with such advice and assistance as the social services department reasonably requests.[391]

Allocation

2.207 When allocating housing, local housing authorities in England and Wales are obliged to comply with the provisions of HA 1996 Part 6.[392]

Meaning of allocation

2.208 For these purposes, 'allocation' means:

a) selecting a secure[393] or introductory tenant[394] for the authority's own accommodation. This includes notifying an existing tenant or licensee that his or her tenancy is to be secure,[395] for example, under HA 1985 Sch 1 para 2 (employment-related accommodation), para 5 (temporary accommodation for people taking up employment) or para 10 (student accommodation), as amended;
b) nominating a person to be a secure or introductory tenant of another (nomination includes formal and informal arrangements);[396]

389 H(W)A 2014 s96(1).
390 H(W)A 2014 s96(2).
391 H(W)A 2014 s96(4).
392 HA 1996 s159(1).
393 HA 1985 Part 4.
394 HA 1996 Part 5 Chapter 1.
395 HA 1996 s159(3).
396 HA 1996 s159(4).

c) nominating (in the same sense as above) a person to be an assured tenant[397] of a registered provider of social housing or a registered social landlord.[398]

Excluded allocations

2.209 Allocations to existing secure or introductory tenants are excluded, unless the allocation involves a transfer of housing accommodation for that tenant, and the transfer is made on the tenant's application.[399]

2.210 From the commencement of LA 2011 s145, this exclusion applies only in Wales. In England, the corresponding exclusion is an allocation to a person who is already a secure or introductory tenant, or an assured tenant of housing accommodation held by a private registered provider of social housing or a registered social landlord, unless the allocation involves a transfer of housing accommodation for that person, the application for the transfer is made by that person, and the authority is satisfied that the person is to be given a reasonable preference,[400] ie under HA 1996 s166A.

2.211 There is a number of other cases which are not treated as an allocation:

a) succession and devolution on death, or assignment to a potential successor;
b) assignment by way of exchange;
c) vesting under a number of family or domestic law provisions; and
d) other cases as may be prescribed by regulations.[401]

Eligibility

2.212 Any person may be allocated housing, provided that he or she is not ineligible under HA 1996 s160ZA (England) or s160A (Wales).[402] An allocation may not be made to two or more persons jointly if one of them is ineligible.[403]

397 HA 1988 Part 1.
398 HA 1996 Part 1, s159(2).
399 HA 1996 s159(5).
400 HA 1996 s159(4A), (4B).
401 HA 1996 s160.
402 HA 1996 ss160ZA(1), 160A(1), (2).
403 HA 1996 ss160ZA(1)(b), 160A(1)(c).

Persons from abroad

2.213 Persons subject to immigration control under the AIA 1996 are ineligible unless re-included by regulations.[404] The secretary of state may not include in regulations any person who is excluded from entitlement to housing benefit by IAA 1999 s115.[405] The secretary of state may prescribe other persons from abroad who are ineligible, either in relation to local housing authorities generally or any particular local housing authority.[406]

2.214 In Wales, these provisions do not affect the eligibility of someone who is already a secure or introductory tenant or an assured tenant of housing accommodation allocated to him or her by a local housing authority.[407] In England, the disqualification does not affect the eligibility of someone who is already a secure or introductory tenant or an assured tenant of housing accommodation held by a private registered provider of social housing or a registered social landlord, if the allocation involves a transfer of housing accommodation for that person, the application for the transfer is made by that person, and the authority is satisfied that the person is to be given a reasonable preference,[408] ie under HA 1996 s166A.

Unacceptable behaviour

2.215 A local authority in Wales may decide that an applicant is to be treated as ineligible if it is satisfied that:

a) the applicant or a member of the applicant's household has been guilty of unacceptable behaviour serious enough to make the applicant unsuitable to be a tenant of the authority; and
b) by reason of the circumstances at the time that the applicant's application is considered, he or she is unsuitable to be a tenant of the authority by reason of that behaviour.[409]

2.216 'Unacceptable behaviour' is that which would (if the applicant was a secure tenant of the authority) entitle the authority to a possession order under HA 1985 s84 on any of grounds 1–7 of Schedule 2 to that Act or under the absolute ground for possession, or behaviour by a member of the applicant's household, which would (if he or she were

404 HA 1996 ss160ZA(2), 160A(3).
405 HA 1996 ss160ZA(3), 160A(4).
406 HA 1996 ss160ZA(4), 160A(5).
407 HA 1996 s160A(6).
408 HA 1996 ss159(4B), 160ZA(5).
409 HA 1996 s160A(7).

a person residing with a secure tenant of the authority) entitle the authority to such a possession order.[410]

Re-application

2.217 An applicant who is treated as ineligible because of unacceptable behaviour may (if the applicant considers that he or she should no longer be so treated) make a fresh application.[411]

Notification

2.218 If the authority decides that the applicant is ineligible for an allocation, it must notify the applicant of that decision and the ground(s) for it.[412] Notification must be given in writing and, if not received by the applicant, shall be treated as having been given if it is made available at the authority's office for a reasonable period for collection by the applicant or on the applicant's behalf.[413] There is a right to a review of such a decision.[414]

Localism Act 2011

2.219 Since the commencement of LA 2011 s145,[415] the anti-social behaviour provisions[416] have only been applicable in Wales.[417] In England, the authority may determine for itself whom it will treat as a person qualifying for an allocation,[418] subject to the prohibition on persons ineligible for immigration reasons,[419] and to the power of the secretary of state by regulations to prescribe classes of person who are or who are not to be treated as qualifying, and/or to prescribe criteria that may not be used by authorities in determining who is not to qualify.[420] In the case of joint tenants, at least one of them must be a qualifying person.[421] There are analogous duties relating to

410 HA 1996 s160A(8).
411 HA 1996 s160A(11).
412 HA 1996 s160A(9).
413 HA 1996 s160A(10).
414 HA 1996 s167(4A).
415 15 January 2012.
416 Paras 2.215–2.216.
417 LA 2011 s146(1).
418 HA 1996 s160ZA(6), (7).
419 HA 1996 s160ZA(7).
420 HA 1996 s160ZA(8).
421 HA 1996 s160ZA(6).

notification in writing with reasons,[422] and to review,[423] and the right of re-application on the part of someone who considers that he or she should be treated as a qualifying person.[424]

Applications

2.220 Authorities must ensure that there is free advice and information available in their areas about the right to make an application for an allocation of housing.[425]

2.221 Authorities must also ensure that any necessary assistance in making an application is available free of charge to those who are likely to have difficulty in doing so without assistance.[426]

2.222 Authorities must also ensure that applicants are aware of their right to request information about the likely availability of accommodation.[427]

2.223 Every application for an allocation of housing made in accordance with the procedural requirements of the authority's allocation scheme must be considered by the authority.[428] The fact that a person is an applicant for an allocation must not be divulged by the authority to any member of the public without the applicant's consent.[429]

Priorities and procedures

2.224 An authority must maintain an allocation 'scheme' governing both priorities and procedures (including all aspects of the allocation procedure, including by whom decisions may be made).[430] An authority may not allocate accommodation otherwise than in accordance with its scheme.[431]

422 HA 1996 s160ZA(9), (10). If the notification is not received by the applicant, it is to be treated as having been received if it is made available at the authority's office for a reasonable period for collection by or on his or her behalf: HA 1996 s160ZA(10).

423 HA 1996 s166A(9).

424 HA 1996 s160ZA(11).

425 HA 1996 s166(1)(a).

426 HA 1996 s166(1)(b).

427 HA 1996 s166(1A) (England); s166(2) (Wales).

428 HA 1996 s166(3).

429 HA 1996 s166(4).

430 HA 1996 s166A(1) (England); s167(1) (Wales).

431 HA 1996 s166A(14) (England); s167(8) (Wales).

Procedure

2.225 The scheme must be framed so as to give an applicant the right to request general information that will enable the applicant to assess:

a) how his or her application is likely to be treated under the scheme (including whether the applicant is likely to be regarded as in one of the reasonable preference categories); and
b) whether accommodation appropriate to the applicant's needs is likely to be made available to the applicant and, if so, how long it is likely to be before such accommodation becomes available for allocation to him or her.[432]

Regulations

2.226 The secretary of state or the Welsh Ministers may require that the procedures are framed in accordance with such principles as he or she may prescribe.[433]

Choice policy

2.227 The scheme must include a statement of the authority's policy on offering people who are to be allocated housing:

a) a choice of housing accommodation; or
b) the opportunity to express preference about the housing accommodation to be allocated to them.[434]

Priority

2.228 The scheme must be framed so as to ensure that a reasonable preference is given to the following:

a) people who are homeless;[435]
b) people who are owed a duty by an local housing authority under HA 1996 s190(2), s193(2) or s195(2) (or under HA 1985 s65(2) or s68(2)) or who are occupying accommodation secured by any such authority under HA 1996 s192(3) or, in Wales, those owed a duty under H(W)A 2014 s66, s73 or s75;[436]

432 HA 1996 s166A(9) (England); s167(4A)(a) (Wales).
433 HA 1996 s166A(10) (England); s167(5) (Wales).
434 HA 1996 s166A(2) (England); s167(1A) (Wales).
435 This does not apply if the only reason someone is homeless is because of a restricted person: HA 1996 s167(2ZA).
436 As last footnote.

c) people occupying insanitary or overcrowded housing or otherwise living in unsatisfactory housing conditions;
d) people who need to move on medical or welfare grounds (including grounds relating to disability); and
e) people who need to move to a particular locality in the authority's area, where failure to meet that need would cause hardship to themselves or to others.[437]

2.229 The scheme may also be framed so as to give additional preference to those within these categories who have an urgent housing need.[438]

2.230 The scheme may also include provision for determining priorities between those in the reasonable preference categories, taking into account:

a) the financial resources available to a person to meet his or her housing costs;
b) any behaviour of a person (or a member of the person's household) which affects his or her suitability to be a tenant;
c) any local connection which exists between a person and the authority's area.[439]

Unacceptable behaviour

2.231 In Wales,[440] the scheme does not have to provide for any preference to be given to an applicant where the authority is satisfied that:

a) the applicant, or a member of his or her household, has been guilty of unacceptable behaviour serious enough to make him or her unsuitable to be a tenant of the authority; and
b) in the circumstances at the time that the applicant's case is considered, he or she deserves by reason of that behaviour not to be treated as a member of one of the groups to whom a reasonable preference is to be given.[441]

437 HA 1996 s166A(3) (England); s167(2) (Wales).
438 HA 1996 s166A(3) (England); s167(2) (Wales).
439 HA 1996 s166A(5) (England); s167(2A) (Wales).
440 This provision was considered unnecessary after changes made by LA 2011 meant that English authorities could decide for themselves who qualifies for an allocation (HA 1996 s160ZA(7)), although subsequent case-law instead means that English authorities have simply been deprived of this right.
441 HA 1996 s167(2B)–(2D).

Regulations

2.232 The secretary of state and Welsh Ministers have power to add to, amend or repeal any part of the list of those to whom a reasonable preference is to be accorded.[442] They also have power to specify factors which are not to be taken into account when allocating housing.[443]

Other allocations

2.233 Subject to the reasonable preference categories, the scheme may contain provisions about the allocation of particular accommodation to a person who makes a specific application for it and to people of a particular description, whether or not they are within the reasonable preference categories.[444]

Notification

2.234 The scheme must be framed so that an applicant is notified:

a) in Wales only, in writing of any decision that he or she is a person being given no preference because of a decision as to behaviour under HA 1996 s167(2C); and
b) in England and Wales, of the right to request the authority to inform him or her about the facts of his or her case which are likely to be, or have been, taken into account in considering whether to allocate housing accommodation to the applicant.[445]

Review

2.235 The scheme must include the right for an applicant to request a review of a decision as to any decision about the facts of his or her case, whether he or she is a person who is ineligible under HA 1996 s160ZA(9) (England) or s160A (Wales), or whether (in Wales) he or she is to be given no preference under s167(2C).[446]

Change and consultation

2.236 Priorities and procedures are otherwise in the discretion of the authority.[447] Before adopting or making any major policy change to a scheme,

442 HA 1996 s167(3).
443 HA 1996 s166A(8) (England); s167(4) (Wales).
444 HA 1996 s166A(6) (England); s167(2E) (Wales).
445 HA 1996 s166A(9)(b) (England); s167(4A)(b), (c) (Wales).
446 HA 1996 s166A(9)(c) (England); s167(4A)(d) (Wales).
447 HA 1996 s166A(11) (England); s167(6) (Wales).

the authority must send a copy of it in draft to every private registered provider and every registered social landlord with which they have nomination arrangements, and afford them a reasonable opportunity to comment.[448] When preparing or modifying its allocation scheme, an English authority must have regard to its strategy under the Homelessness Act 2002, to its current tenancy strategy under LA 2011 s150, and, if a London borough, to the London housing strategy.[449]

Code of Guidance

2.237 The secretary of state may issue guidance to which authorities must have regard.[450]

Co-operation

2.238 When an authority asks it to offer accommodation to people with priority under the authority's allocation scheme, a private registered provider of social housing or a registered social landlord is bound to co-operate to such extent as is reasonable in the circumstances.[451]

Information

2.239 An authority must publish a summary of its scheme and provide a copy of it, free of charge, to any member of the public who asks for it.[452] The full scheme must be made available for inspection at the authority's principal office and a copy must be made available to any member of the public who asks for it, on payment of a reasonable fee.[453]

2.240 When the authority makes a major policy alteration to its scheme, it has to take such steps as it considers reasonable to bring the effect of the alteration to the attention of those likely to be affected by it.[454]

Criminal offences

2.241 It is a criminal offence knowingly or recklessly to make a statement – in connection with the exercise by an authority of its functions under HA 1996 Part 6 – which is false in a material particular, or

448 HA 1996 s166A(13) (England); s167(7) (Wales).
449 HA 1996 s166A(12).
450 HA 1996 s169.
451 HA 1996 s170.
452 HA 1996 s168(1).
453 HA 1996 s168(2).
454 HA 1996 s168(3).

knowingly to withhold information which an authority has reasonably required in connection with the exercise of its functions under HA 1996 Part 6.[455]

2.242 The offence is punishable on summary conviction by a fine of up to level 5 on the standard scale,[456] ie the standard scale for the time being under CJA 1982 s37.[457]

455 HA 1996 s171(1).
456 HA 1996 s171(2).
457 Level 5 is a fine of up to an unlimited amount: see CJA 1982 s37 and LASPO 2012 s85.

CHAPTER 3

Immigration

Introduction

3.1 Immigration status is a key topic in relation to both homelessness and allocations. In each case, it is determinative of eligibility, excluding certain applicants in England from the protection of Housing Act (HA) 1996 Part 7 and in Wales from the Housing (Wales) Act (H(W)A) 2014 Part 2, and, in both England and Wales, from the prospect of an allocation under the HA 1996 Part 6.

3.2 That does not mean that no assistance will ever be available from a local authority to someone thus disqualified: there remains the possibility of assistance in England under the Care Act 2014, and in Wales under the equivalent provision which is now the Social Services and Well-being (Wales) Act (SSWB(W)A) 2014, where an applicant is in need of care and attention (otherwise than as a result of destitution) – this is dealt with below.[1] In addition, some immigrants who are asylum-seekers disqualified from local authority assistance may be able to obtain housing help through the Home Office.[2]

3.3 Moreover, local authorities in England[3] and Wales[4] may have to afford assistance to children in need, even though they or their parents are disqualified from housing under HA 1996 Parts 6 and 7 or H(W)A 2014 Part 2.[5] There are also other powers – 'general power of competence' in England, under the Localism Act (LA) 2011; and 'well-being powers' in Wales, under the Local Government Act (LGA) 2000 Part 1, which may be exercisable in some circumstances.[6]

3.4 Even if an applicant is not ineligible for assistance under HA 1996 Part 7, there are, however, additional provisions which apply in England only, which may exclude the applicant from temporary accommodation under some of the interim duties in Part 7; the same classes will also be excluded from assistance under the provisions mentioned in the last paragraph, ie, under the Care Act 2014 or the SSWB(W)A 2014, through the Home Office, under the Children

1 See paras 13.23–13.56.
2 See paras 3.136, 13.40–13.56.
3 Under CA 1989.
4 Under SSWB(W)A 2014.
5 See paras 13.57–13.113.
6 See paras 13.113–13.120.

Act (CA) 1989 or under LGA 2000[7] or under LA 2011. These classes are described in this chapter below.[8]

3.5 Even if an applicant is not ineligible for assistance under HA 1996 Part 7 or H(W)A 2014 Part 2, if qualification for assistance relies on family or household members who would themselves be ineligible, it may affect the duty placed on the authority: this is also dealt with below.[9] Likewise, it will affect priority in the allocation of housing under HA 1996 Part 6.[10]

3.6 Historically, the Housing (Homeless Persons) Act (H(HP)A) 1977 did not contain a test of eligibility. On the face of the Act, anyone could make an application. The Court of Appeal, however, expressed the view that duties were owed only to a person lawfully in the country.[11]

3.7 The consolidating HA 1985 Part 3, which replaced H(HP)A 1977, likewise did not limit who could apply, but the Court of Appeal interpreted the provisions to mean an authority owed no duty to an applicant for housing who was an illegal entrant.[12] It was also held that where – as a result of enquiries – the authority suspected that an

7 LA 2011 ss1 and 2 and Sch 1, which came into force on 28 March 2012, and 6 April 2012 by operation of the Localism Act 2011 (Consequential Amendments) Order 2012 SI No 961, repealed the well-being power in LGA 2000 s2 in England, and replaced it with a general power of competence. Nationality, Immigration and Asylum Act (NIAA) 2002 Sch 3 has yet to be amended to include the general power of competence. The position in Wales is unaffected by these changes.

8 See para 3.188.

9 See paras 3.143–3.152.

10 See paras 3.198–3.208.

11 *R v Hillingdon LBC ex p Streeting (No 2)* [1980] 1 WLR 1425, CA. Following *R v Westminster City Council ex p Castelli* (1996) 28 HLR 616, this would seem to include a European Economic Area (EEA) national who is not exercising a right to reside in the UK and has no leave to enter or remain because the Court of Appeal held that such a person was not unlawfully in the country. In *R (ST (Eritrea)) v Secretary of State for the Home Department* [2012] UKSC 12, [2012] 2 AC 135, however, the Supreme Court held that a person who had been granted temporary admission to the UK for the purposes of determining her claim for asylum, but had not yet been granted leave to enter or remain, was not lawfully in the UK within the meaning of Article 32 of the Geneva Convention relating to the Status of Refugees (Refugee Convention) and was thus not entitled to the protection of that Article.

12 *Tower Hamlets LBC v Secretary of State for the Environment* [1993] QB 632, (1993) 25 HLR 524, CA.

applicant was an illegal entrant, it had a duty to inform the immigration authorities of its suspicion.[13]

3.8 The Asylum and Immigration Appeals Act (AIAA) 1993 was the first legislative provision explicitly to limit the rights of immigrants to housing assistance. The effect of its sections 4 and 5 was that authorities owed no duty to an asylum-seeker and the asylum-seeker's dependants if he or she had accommodation that was available for the asylum-seeker's occupation, however temporary, and which it would be reasonable for him or her to occupy. Asylum and Immigration Act (AIA) 1996 s9 additionally provided that an authority should not, so far as practicable, grant a tenancy or licence of housing accommodation to a person subject to immigration control, unless he or she is of a prescribed class.

3.9 These limitations were reproduced in HA 1996 Part 7, ss185 and 186, and in H(W)A 2014 Sch 2 para 1, defining 'eligibility for assistance'. Subject to qualification and exception, excluded persons from abroad under HA 1996 s185,[14] and asylum-seekers under HA 1996 s186,[15] were not eligible for assistance. A person ineligible for assistance could not receive 'the benefit of any function under ... Part [7] relating to accommodation or assistance in obtaining accommodation',[16] although he or she could receive advice and assistance from any advisory service provided by the authority under its HA 1996 s179 duty.[17]

3.10 Eligibility requirements were also introduced in HA 1996 Part 6 for allocations,[18] which, so far as concerns immigration, matched those for homelessness.

3.11 In this chapter, eligibility is considered for both homelessness and allocations. Before addressing each of these, in turn, below, it is first necessary to consider the detailed rules governing the relevant classes of the various immigration statuses which may be enjoyed by – or which may limit the rights of – applicants under either HA 1996 Part 6 or Part 7 or H(W)A 2014 Part 2.

13 See *Tower Hamlets LBC v Secretary of State for the Environment*, above.

14 In Wales, the equivalent provision is H(W)A 2014 Sch 2 para 1. Whether a person who was born in the UK but who is not a British citizen can be a 'person from abroad' is a point of law of general importance on which there is as yet no definitive answer: *Ismail v Newham LBC* [2018] EWCA Civ 665 (where the issue was raised but had become academic owing to a change in the immigration status of the appellant so that the appeal was not allowed to proceed).

15 This has effect in Wales until repealed, see H(W)A 2014 Sch 2 para 2.

16 HA 1996 s183(2).

17 HA 1996 s183(3); see chapter 14.

18 See now HA 1996 s160A(1)–(6), as amended by the Homelessness Act 2002.

3.12 Qualification as an applicant who is eligible for assistance is set out in secondary legislation in both England[19] and Wales.[20] In summary, applicants who are subject to immigration control are eligible if they come within one of the prescribed classes, and applicants who are not subject to immigration control are generally eligible, though jobseekers and those with an initial right to reside are excluded from eligibility for homelessness assistance and an allocation and certain applicants are also required to be habitually resident in the UK.

Immigration control

3.13 People in the UK are divided into two classes: persons who are subject to immigration control; and persons who are not subject to immigration control. The latter group includes all persons who have a right to reside in the UK.

Persons subject to immigration control

3.14 The term 'persons subject to immigration control' as used in both HA 1996 Parts 6[21] and 7[22] and H(W)A 2014 Sch 2 para 1, is based on immigration legislation[23] and means a person who, under the Immigration Act (IA) 1971, requires leave to enter or remain in the UK (whether or not such leave has been given). Generally speaking, this means anyone who requires a visa to come to the UK. It primarily applies to non-EEA (European Economic Area) nationals, but EEA nationals who are not exercising a right to reside in the UK are

19 Allocation of Housing and Homelessness (Eligibility) (England) Regulations (Eligibility Regs) 2006 SI No 1294, as amended by the Allocation of Housing and Homelessness (Eligibility) (England) (Amendment) Regulations (Eligibility (Amendment) Regs) 2012 SI No 2588 with effect from 8 November 2012, though the amendments do not affect an application for an allocation of housing or for homelessness assistance which was made before that date.

20 For allocation and homelessness applications see the Allocation of Housing and Homelessness (Eligibility) (Wales) Regulations (Eligibility (Wales) Regs) 2014 SI No 2603 which came into force on 31 October 2014 and apply to all applications for an allocation or homelessness assistance made on or after that date.

21 HA 1996 s160A(3).

22 HA 1996 s185(2).

23 AIA 1996 s13.

also subject to immigration control[24] (even though they are legally present).[25]

Persons not subject to immigration control

Overview

3.15 Persons not subject to immigration control form two groups.

3.16 The first group consists of those who are *exempt from the requirement to have* leave to enter or remain in the UK.[26] This group is relatively unimportant for eligibility purposes, and comprises three main classes:

a) diplomats and certain staff of embassies and high commissions and their families who form part of their household;[27]
b) members of UK armed forces, members of a Commonwealth or similar force undergoing training in the UK with the UK armed forces, and members of a visiting force coming to the UK at the invitation of the government;[28] and
c) members of the crew of a ship or aircraft, hired or under orders to depart as part of that ship's crew or to depart on the same or another aircraft within seven days of arrival in the UK.[29]

3.17 The second group is those who *do not require* leave to enter or remain in the UK. They include:

a) British citizens;
b) Commonwealth citizens with the right of abode in the UK;
c) EEA nationals who have a right to reside in the UK.

The IA 1971 expressly excludes a) and b) from the requirement to have leave to enter or remain in the UK;[30] c) was a later addition to the group to reflect the evolving nature of the EU.[31]

24 *Abdi v Barnet LBC and First Secretary of State; Ismail v Barnet LBC and First Secretary of State* [2006] EWCA Civ 383, [2006] HLR 23. See para 3.20. See footnote 54, below, for members of the EEA.

25 *Abdirahman v Secretary of State for Work and Pensions* [2007] EWCA Civ 657, [2008] 1 WLR 254, [2007] 4 All ER 882. A person who has temporary admission to the UK is also lawfully present: see *Szoma v Secretary of State for Work and Pensions* [2005] UKHL 64, [2006] 1 AC 564.

26 IA 1971 s8.

27 IA 1971 ss3, 3A.

28 IA 1971 s8(4), (6).

29 IA 1971 s8(1).

30 IA 1971 s1(1).

31 IA 1988 s7(1).

British citizenship

3.18 British citizenship was created by the British Nationality Act (BNA) 1981.[32] It came into force on 1 January 1983. Prior to that date, the most beneficial form of national status was to be a 'citizen of the United Kingdom and colonies' (CUKC) with the right of abode in the UK.[33] A person can become a British citizen in a variety of ways, which include the following:

a) a person who, on 31 December 1982, was a CUKC with the right of abode in the UK because of his or her birth, adoption, naturalisation or registration in the UK, or because he or she has a parent or grandparent who was born, adopted, naturalised or registered in the UK;[34]
b) a person who, on 31 December 1982, had been ordinarily resident in the UK for five years;[35]
c) a person born in the UK after 1 January 1983 is a British citizen if at the time of the birth, the person's father or mother was a British citizen or settled in the UK;[36] in this context, 'settled' means that he or she has indefinite leave to remain or permanent residence in the UK;
d) a person born in the UK after 1 January 1983 is entitled to be registered as a British citizen if, while the person is a minor, his or her father or mother becomes a British citizen or becomes settled in the UK;[37]
e) otherwise, a person born in the UK after 1 January 1983 can apply for registration as a British citizen after the person is ten years old, providing that he or she has not been absent from the UK for more than 90 days a year;[38]
f) a person born outside the UK after 1 January 1983 will be a British citizen if at the time of the birth, his or her father or mother was a British citizen who was born in the UK;[39]

32 This has been the subject of numerous amendments including by the Borders, Citizenship and Immigration Act 2009.
33 IA 1971 s2 as it was then in force.
34 BNA 1981 s11(1).
35 IA 1971 s2(1)(c) as it was in force on 31 December 1982.
36 BNA 1981 s1(1).
37 BNA 1981 s1(3).
38 BNA 1981 s1(4).
39 BNA 1981 s2.

g) a person may also apply for naturalisation[40] as a British citizen so long as the person fulfils certain requirements set out in the BNA 1981.[41]

Commonwealth citizens with the right of abode in the UK

3.19 Since the coming into force of the BNA 1981,[42] the following now have the right of abode in the UK:

a) persons who automatically became British citizens[43] on the coming into force of the BNA 1981:[44] These will include all the former citizens of the UK and Colonies who had a right of abode because they were 'patrials', ie, citizens of the UK and colonies born, adopted, registered or naturalised in the UK, those with the necessary ancestral connections with the UK, and those who were ordinarily resident here for five years free of immigration restrictions;[45]
b) Commonwealth citizens[46] who, immediately before commencement, had the right of abode by virtue of having a parent who was born in the UK under the now revoked IA 1971 s2(1)(d);
c) female Commonwealth citizens who, immediately before commencement, had a right of abode under the now revoked IA 1971 s2(2) by virtue of their marriage to a patrial.[47]

EEA nationals with the right to reside in the UK

Overview

3.20 The right to reside in the UK for EEA nationals now derives from the Treaty on the Functioning of the European Union (TFEU).[48] It is not

40 BNA 1981 s6.
41 BNA 1981 Sch 1.
42 On 1 January 1983.
43 See para 3.18.
44 BNA 1981 s11.
45 IA 1971 s2(1)(c) before amendment.
46 Commonwealth citizens are all those who are citizens of the countries set out in BNA 1981 Sch 3.
47 IA 1971 s2 before amendment. Patriality was conferred on certain citizens of the UK and Colonies and certain other Commonwealth citizens.
48 This came into force on 1 December 2009.

an unconditional right.[49] The requirements to be met are principally[50] set out in Directive 2004/38/EC[51] ('the Directive') which has been enacted into domestic law by the Immigration (European Economic Area) Regulations (EEA Regs) 2016.[52] The EEA Regs 2016 are not simply a repetition of the Directive: where the Directive gives a right to reside and the EEA Regs 2016 do not, an applicant is entitled to rely on the Directive.[53] Conversely, if the Directive does not give a right to reside but the EEA Regs 2016 do so, then an applicant can rely on those more favourable provisions.

3.21 There are two ways in which a person can have a right to reside in the UK. These are either

a) as an EEA[54] national who satisfies the relevant conditions,[55] known as a 'qualified person'[56] in the EEA Regs 2016; or
b) as a family member of an EEA national who either has, or has had, a right to reside.

3.22 The right to reside exists independently of any residence documentation: the latter is merely evidence of the right,[57] although a person who is in possession of such documentation may be able to rely on

49 TFEU Article 21; *Minister voor Vreemdelingenzaken en Integratie v RNG Eind*, Case C-291/05 at [28]; *Trojani v Centre public d'aide sociale de Bruxelles (CPAS)*, Case C-456/02, [2004] ECR I-7573 at paras [31] and [32]; *Zhu and Chen v Secretary of State for the Home Department*, Case C-200/02, [2004] ECR I-9925 at para [26]; *Ali v Secretary of State for the Home Department* [2006] EWCA Civ 484, [2006] 3 CMLR 10 at para [20].

50 Some rights of residence exist outside the scope of the Directive, see paras 3.99–3.116.

51 Of the European Parliament and of the Council of 29 April 2004, which came into force on 30 April 2004.

52 SI No 1052, which came into force on 1 February 2017.

53 IA 1988 s7(1).

54 The EEA consists of the EU plus Norway, Iceland and Liechtenstein. The EU consists of the EU15: Austria, Belgium, Denmark, Finland, France, Germany, Greece, Ireland, Italy, Luxembourg, the Netherlands, Portugal, Spain, Sweden and the UK, plus the countries which acceded on 1 May 2004, which are Cyprus, the Czech Republic, Estonia, Hungary, Latvia, Lithuania, Malta, Poland, Slovakia, Slovenia, plus the countries which acceded on 1 January 2007 (the A2), which are Bulgaria and Romania and Croatia which acceded on 1 July 2013 pursuant to the Accession Treaty signed on 9 December 2011.

55 These are either set out in the Directive or the EEA Regs 2016.

56 EEA Regs 2016 reg 6(1).

57 *Mario Lopes da Veiga v Staatssecretaris van Justitie*, Case 9/88; *Echternach and Moritz v Minister van Onderwijs en Wetenschappen*, Cases 389/87 and 390/87, at para [25]; *Secretary of State for Work and Pensions v Maria Dias*, Case C-325/09 at para [48].

Article 18 of the TFEU in order to be granted social assistance:[58] in *Sanneh*,[59] however, the Court of Appeal held that the ability to rely on Article 18 only applied to EU citizens in possession of a residence permit.[60] This seems consistent with the judgment of the Court of Justice of the European Union (CJEU) in *Ahmed*,[61] which concerned an Algerian national with a right under domestic law to be present in Belgium, which was not enough to enable her to claim social assistance under EU law.[62]

3.23 There are three categories of the EEA national right to reside:

a) initial right to reside;
b) extended right to reside;
c) permanent right to reside.

Initial right to reside

3.24 An EEA national must be admitted to the UK if he or she produces on arrival a valid national identity card or passport issued by an EEA state.[63] A person who is not an EEA national must produce on arrival a valid passport and an EEA family permit, a residence card or a permanent residence card.[64] An EEA family permit acts as a sort of entry clearance or visa for non-EEA nationals and its issue cannot be made subject to conditions that are more restrictive than those set out in the Directive.[65]

3.25 The initial right to reside lasts for no longer than three months and is on condition that the EEA national or his or her family member does not become an unreasonable burden on the social assistance system of the UK.[66] The phrase 'unreasonable burden' may be thought to imply that a temporary or short-term reliance on social assistance does not deprive a person of an initial right to reside.

58 *Trojani v Centre public d'aide sociale de Bruxelles (CPAS)*, Case C-456/02, [2004] ECR I-7573 at para [43].

59 *Sanneh v Secretary of State for Work and Pensions* [2015] EWCA Civ 49, [2015] HLR 27.

60 *Sanneh* at [110].

61 *Office national d'allocations familiales pour travailleurs salaries (ONAFTS) v Ahmed*, Case C-45/12.

62 *Ahmed* at [40] and [41].

63 Directive 2004/38/EC Article 5(1); EEA Regs 2016 reg 11(1).

64 EEA Regs 2016 reg 11(2); see also Directive 2004/38/EC Article 5(2).

65 *Metock v Minister for Justice, Equality and Law Reform*, Case C-127/08.

66 Directive 2004/38/EC Article 14(1); EEA Regs 2016 reg 13.

3.26 The term 'social assistance' is not defined in the Directive, or elsewhere in EU legislation, but has been considered by the CJEU, which has held that the grant of such assistance must essentially depend on need and not be linked to employment or contributions.[67] This is therefore likely to include social housing.[68] In England, a person who has an initial right to reside is ineligible under HA 1996 Parts 6[69] and 7.[70] In Wales, such a person is also ineligible under HA 1996 Part 6[71] and H(W)A 2014 Part 2.[72]

Extended right to reside

3.27 There are five ways in which an EEA national may have an extended right to reside in the UK.[73] These are as:

a) a jobseeker;
b) a worker;
c) a self-employed person;
d) a self-sufficient person; or
e) a student.

A jobseeker

3.28 A jobseeker is a person who:

a) entered the UK in order to seek employment; or
b) is present in the UK seeking employment, after having previously had a right to reside;

and in either case:

c) provides evidence of seeking employment and having a genuine chance of being engaged.

3.29 A person can retain the status of jobseeker for as long as he or she provides compelling evidence of continuing to seek employment and of having a genuine chance of being engaged.[74] The CJEU has held

67 *Frilli v Belgium* Case 1/72, [1972] ECR 457, [1973] CMLR 386.

68 By analogy, for the purposes of immigration law, the term 'public funds' is defined (Immigration Rules (HC 395) para 6) as including housing under HA 1996 Part 6 or Part 7 and HA 1985 Part 2.

69 Eligibility Regs 2006 reg 4(1)(b)(ii).

70 Eligibility Regs 2006 reg 6(1)(b)(ii).

71 Eligibility (Wales) Regs 2014 reg 4(1)(b)(ii).

72 Eligibility (Wales) Regs 2014 reg 6(1)(b)(ii).

73 EEA Regs 2016 reg 6(1)(a)–(e).

74 EEA Regs 2016 reg 6(1).

that, after six months, a jobseeker must provide evidence that he or she is continuing to seek employment and has genuine chances of being engaged.[75]

3.30 In English law, jobseekers are expressly excluded from eligibility under HA 1996 Parts 6[76] and 7.[77] In Wales, jobseekers are ineligible under HA 1996 Part 6[78] and H(W)A 2014 Part 2.[79]

A worker

3.31 There are three essential criteria which determine whether a person is a worker for the purposes of Article 45 of the TFEU.

3.32 First, the person must perform services of some economic value.[80] The activity must be real and genuine, to the exclusion of activity on such a small scale as to be marginal and ancillary.[81]

3.33 Second, the performance of such services must be for and under the direction of another person. Any activity performed outside a relationship of subordination must be classified as an activity pursued in a self-employed capacity.[82]

3.34 Third, the person concerned must receive remuneration.[83] Neither the origin of the funds from which the remuneration is paid nor the limited amount of that remuneration can have any consequences with regard to whether or not the person is a worker.[84] The fact that the income from employment is lower than the minimum required for subsistence does not prevent the person from being regarded as a worker,[85] even if he or she seeks

75 *R v Immigration Appeal Tribunal ex p Antonissen*, Case C-292/98, [1991] ECR I 745.

76 Eligibility Regs 2006 reg 4(1)(b)(i).

77 Eligibility Regs 2006 reg 6(1)(b)(i).

78 Eligibility (Wales) Regs 2014 reg 4(1)(b)(i).

79 Eligibility (Wales) Regs 2014 reg 6(1)(b)(i).

80 *Lawrie-Blum v Land Baden Wurttemberg*, Case 66/85, [1986] ECR 2121; in *Bristol City Council v FV* [2011] UKUT 494 (AAC) (21 December 2011), the Upper Tribunal held that sellers of the *Big Issue* can be considered self-employed. The opposite decision was reached in *DV v Secretary of State for Work and Pensions* [2017] UKUT 155 (AAC).

81 *Vatsouras and Koupatantze v Arbeitgemeinschaft (ARGE) Nurnberg 900*, Cases C-22/08 and C-23/08; *Lawrie Blum*, above.

82 *Jany v Staatssecretaris van Justitie*, Case C-268/99 at [34].

83 *Vatsouras*, above, at para [25]; and *Lawrie-Blum*, above.

84 *Vatsouras*, above, at para [27].

85 *Levin v Staatssecretaris van Justitie*, Case 53/81.

to supplement that remuneration by other means of subsistence such as financial assistance drawn from the public funds[86] of the host member state.[87]

3.35 The fact that the employment is of short duration does not, of itself, prevent the employee from being a worker.[88]

3.36 A person who is no longer working does *not* cease to be a worker if:[89]

a) the person is temporarily[90] unable to work as the result of an illness or accident;
b) the person is in duly recorded involuntary unemployment[91] after having been employed in the UK for at least one year, provided that he or she has registered as a jobseeker with the relevant

86 For the purposes of UK immigration law, the term 'public funds' is defined in the Immigration Rules (HC 395) para 6 as including housing under HA 1996 Part 6 or Part 7 and HA 1985 Part 2. The Immigration Rules have not been updated to reflect the H(W)A 2014.

87 *Kempf v Staatssecretaris van Justitie*, Case 139/85, [1986] ECR 1741.

88 *Vatsouras*, above, at para [29]; *Ninni Orasche v Bundesminister für Wissenschaft, Verkehr und Kunst*, Case C-413/01; *Barry v Southwark LBC* [2008] EWCA Civ 1140, [2009] HLR 30.

89 EEA Regs 2016 reg 6(2).

90 In *Secretary of State for the Home Department v FB* [2010] UKUT 447 (IAC), it was held that temporary means not permanent, see paras [23]–[26], followed by the Court of Appeal in *Aurelio de Brito and Lizette de Noronha v Secretary of State for the Home Department* [2012] EWCA Civ 709, [2012] 3 CMLR 24 at [30]–[35], where it was held that the test is objective and that a temporary condition could become permanent and a permanent condition could become temporary depending upon the facts of the case, such as a successful medical intervention. In *Konodyba v Royal Borough of Kensington and Chelsea* [2012] EWCA Civ 982, [2013] PTSR 13 at [22] and [23], the Court of Appeal held that whether a homeless applicant is temporarily unable to work or unlikely to be able to work in the foreseeable future is a question of fact. These decisions were followed in *Samin v Westminster City Council* [2012] EWCA Civ 1468, [2013] 2 CMLR 6, [2013] HLR 7 where the Court of Appeal held that the question is one of fact in every case and that it will generally be helpful to ask whether there is or is not a realistic prospect of a return to work. This case has now been the subject of an appeal to the Supreme Court, [2016] UKSC 1, [2016] HLR 7, but this aspect of the case was unaffected by its judgment: see para 3.178.

91 In decisions of the Social Security Commissioner CH/3314/2005 and CIS/3315/2005, it was held that this phrase is concerned with why the worker is not working at the date of the decision, not with why the worker ceased to be employed, though this may also be relevant: see para [11].

employment office,[92] and satisfies conditions A and B (below); such status cannot be retained for longer than six months without providing compelling evidence[93] of continuing to seek employment and having a genuine chance of being engaged;

c) the person is in duly recorded involuntary unemployment after having been employed in the UK for less than one year, provided he or she has registered as a jobseeker with the relevant employment office, and satisfies conditions A and B, but he or she can only retain worker status for a maximum of six months under this provision;[94]

d) the person is involuntarily unemployed and has embarked on vocational training; or

e) the person has voluntarily ceased working and embarked on vocational training that is related to his or her previous employment.

3.37 Condition A is that the person entered the UK in order to seek employment, or is present in the UK seeking employment, immediately after enjoying a right to reside other than as a jobseeker.[95] Condition B is that the person provides evidence of seeking employment and of having a genuine chance of being engaged.[96]

92 *Elmi v Secretary of State for Work and Pensions* [2011] EWCA Civ 1403, [2012] PTSR 780 concerned an EU citizen who had become involuntarily unemployed and then claimed income support at Jobcentre Plus. She ticked the box on the relevant form stating that she was looking for work. The Court of Appeal held that she had registered with the employment office as a jobseeker, even though she was in receipt of income support and not jobseeker's allowance, and had therefore retained her worker status.

93 In *KS v Secretary of State for Work and Pensions* [2016] UKUT 269 (AAC), it was held that this means no more than the requirement for evidence to establish on a balance of probabilities that the claimant is continuing to seek employment and has genuine chances of being engaged. To interpret the phrase as meaning a higher standard of proof would be contrary to EU law. See also *Secretary of State for Work and Pensions v MB (JSA)* [2016] UKUT 372 (AAC), where it was held that the fact that a claimant has been looking for work for six months is only one factor in determining whether he or she has a genuine chance of being engaged; 'compelling' evidence does not mean more than chances that are founded on something objective and which offer real prospects of employment within a reasonable period. Given that evaluating a 'chance' necessitates a degree of looking forward, events likely to occur in the near future may be relevant to a claimant's genuine chance of being engaged. The government's guidance, the *Decision makers' guide volume 2: International subjects: staff guide*, para 073099 suggests an approach that is much higher than a mere balance of probabilities and may therefore not be correct.

94 EEA Regs 2016 reg 6(3).

95 EEA Regs 2016 reg 6(5).

96 EEA Regs 2016 reg 6(6).

3.38 If a woman is incapable of working due to pregnancy, this does not constitute an illness or accident within point a) above unless there is an actual associated illness.[97] In *JS* the Court of Appeal adopted a similar approach to a woman who ceased working as a nursery school teacher because the demands of the job were too great for her because of her pregnancy, although it had not been found that she could not work because of the pregnancy:[98] it was held that the term 'worker' could not be construed to include a person who has no contract of employment and is not therefore on maternity leave, although the issue of whether this amounted to unlawful sex discrimination was left open because it did not arise on the evidence.[99]

3.39 *JS*[100] was the subject of a reference to the CJEU as *St Prix*,[101] where it was held that a woman who had temporarily given up work because of the late stages of her pregnancy and aftermath of childbirth could not be regarded as a person temporarily unable to work as the result of an illness, but that she nevertheless retained the status of worker provided that she returned to work or found another job within a reasonable time after the birth of her child; in order to determine whether the period was reasonable, the national court should take account of all the specific circumstances of the case and the applicable national rules on the duration of maternity leave.[102]

3.40 In a decision of the Upper Tribunal[103] it was held that it will be unusual for the reasonable period to be other than 52-weeks.[104] This is consistent with the concession made by the secretary of state in the

97 *Adrian John Dalton* [2009] UKUT 71 (AAC), decided in the context of a benefits appeal and *Webb v EMO Air Cargo (UK) Ltd*, Case C-32/93, [1994] ECR I-3567.

98 *JS v Secretary of State for Work and Pensions* [2011] EWCA Civ 806. The case is now the subject of a reference to the ECJ, see [2012] UKSC 49.

99 *JS* at paras [19] and [27].

100 See para 3.38 and the last two footnotes.

101 *St Prix v Secretary of State for Work and Pensions*, Case C-507/12, [2014] PTSR 1448.

102 *St Prix* at [29], [47] and [48].

103 *Secretary of State for Work and Pensions v SFF* [2015] UKUT 0502 (AAC) and *Weldemichael and Obulor v Secretary of State for the Home Department* [2015] UKUT 540 (IAC) at [59], a determination in relation to an immigration case, where it was held, as a general proposition, that a woman will retain worker status where maternity leave did not commence more than 11 weeks before the expected date of birth, she did not have more than 52 weeks off and she returned to work after that period.

104 *Secretary of State for Work and Pensions v SFF* at [35].

Court of Appeal in *Dias*, that a woman on maternity leave retains her status as a worker, which the court assumed was correct.[105]

A self-employed person

3.41 A self-employed person is a person who establishes himself or herself in another EU state in order to pursue activity as a self-employed person in accordance with Article 49 of the TFEU.[106] Essentially, this means someone who is working outside a relationship of subordination.[107]

3.42 The EEA Regs 2016 provide that a person who is no longer in self-employment shall *not* cease to be treated as a self-employed person if he or she is temporarily unable to pursue his or her activity as the result of an illness or accident.[108] This is much narrower than the provisions of the Directive,[109] which allow a self-employed person to retain that status in the same way as a worker who is no longer working.

3.43 In *Tilianu*, the Court of Appeal applied this differential treatment and held that unless a self-employed person is temporarily unable to pursue his or her activity because of illness or accident, a person who is not working is not self-employed.[110] This means that the self-employed have fewer rights than workers, because there are fewer circumstances in which they can retain that status when they are not working.[111] This is arguably discriminatory under Article 18 of the TFEU, unless there is some justification for the differential treatment.

3.44 The decision of the Court of Appeal in *Tilianu* was distinguished in a benefits appeal,[112] where the Upper Tribunal held that a self-employed person does not necessarily cease to be self-employed just because he or she does not have any contract work at a particular time. If the person is actively seeking self-employed work, then he or she can still be held to be self-employed and therefore continue to have a right to reside. The basis of the distinction was that the Court of Appeal had not considered whether self-employed status had been retained.

105 *Secretary of State for Work and Pensions v Dias* [2009] EWCA Civ 807, [2010] 1 CMLR 4 at para [18].
106 EEA Regs 2016 reg 4(1)(b).
107 See *Jany*, above.
108 EEA Regs 2016 reg 6(4).
109 Directive 2004/38/EC Article 7(3).
110 *R (Tilianu) v Secretary of State for Work and Pensions* [2010] EWCA Civ 1397, [2011] PTSR 781.
111 See paras 3.41–3.44.
112 *Secretary of State for Work and Pensions v AL* [2010] UKUT 451 (AAC).

A self-sufficient person

3.45 A self-sufficient person is a person who has sufficient resources not to become a burden on the social assistance system of the UK during his or her period of residence, and who has comprehensive sickness insurance cover in the UK.[113]

3.46 The requirement not to become a burden on the social assistance system of the UK is not qualified (as in the case of a person who has an initial right to reside, which only requires that the person is not to be an 'unreasonable' burden).[114]

3.47 A self-sufficient person is most unlikely to be eligible in England under HA 1996 Parts 6 and 7, and in Wales under HA 1996 Part 6 and H(W)A 2014 Part 2, because the need for social housing will mean that he or she has become a burden on the social assistance system of the UK and therefore cannot have a right to reside on the basis of self-sufficiency.[115]

3.48 The Commission of the European Communities has published[116] guidance on the interpretation of the Directive. This states that any insurance cover, private or public, contracted in the host member state or elsewhere, is acceptable in principle, so long as it provides comprehensive coverage and does not create a burden on the public finances of the host member state.[117]

3.49 This could suggest that private health insurance may not be necessary, and raised the possibility that NHS cover would be sufficient.[118] In *Ahmad*,[119] however, the Court of Appeal held that access to NHS treatment did not count as comprehensive sickness

113 EEA Regs 2016 reg 4(1)(c).

114 Directive 2004/38/EC Article 14(1); EEA Regs 2016 reg 13; see paras 3.24–3.26.

115 By analogy, for the purposes of immigration law, 'public funds' is defined (Immigration Rules (HC 395) para 6) as including housing under HA 1996 Part 6 or Part 7 and HA 1985 Part 2; the rules have not yet been amended to reflect the introduction of H(W)A 2014 Part 2.

116 On 2 July 2009.

117 At para 2.3.2.

118 In *Secretary of State for Work and Pensions v SW* [2011] UKUT 508 (AAC), 15 December 2011 at [20], the Upper Tribunal stated that a person could be self-sufficient by virtue of being entitled to treatment under the NHS by satisfying the residence and presence conditions under domestic law. In *Secretary of State for Work and Pensions v Czop*, C-147/11 at [38], the UK government conceded that the claimant was self-sufficient even though she did not have private health insurance.

119 *Ahmad v Secretary of State for the Home Department* [2014] EWCA Civ 988, [2015] 1 WLR 593.

insurance. The court followed its previous decision in *W (China)*,[120] in which use of free state medical services was held to create a burden on the host state and that contributions towards it were not a proxy for insurance designed to remove the burden of providing health care.

3.50 In a benefits appeal,[121] a Polish national who was receiving an invalidity pension from Sweden was held to have comprehensive sickness cover by virtue of Regulation (EEC) No 1408/71,[122] because these provisions allowed the UK to claim back the cost of her NHS care from Sweden. She did not, however, have sufficient resources, taking into account her housing needs and the fact that her stay in the UK was intended to be permanent.

A student

3.51 A student is a person who:

a) is enrolled, for the principal purpose of following a course of study (including vocational training), at a private or public establishment which is financed from public funds or otherwise recognised by the secretary of state as an establishment which has been accredited for the purpose of providing such courses or training within the law or administrative practice of the part of the UK in which the establishment is located;
b) has comprehensive sickness insurance cover in the UK; and
c) assures the secretary of state by means of a declaration or by such equivalent means as he or she may choose that he or she has sufficient resources not to become a burden on the social assistance system of the UK during his or her period of residence.[123]

3.52 This means that a person can have a right to reside as a student even if he or she subsequently becomes a burden on the social assistance system of the UK, ie if his or her circumstances change. If a student can have a right of residence despite having a need for social housing, then the student is likely to be eligible in England under

120 *W (China) v Secretary of State for the Home Department* [2006] EWCA Civ 1494, [2007] 1 WLR 1514.
121 *SG v Tameside MBC* [2010] UKUT 243 (AAC).
122 This has now been replaced by Regulation (EC) No 883/04.
123 Directive 2004/38/EC Article 7(1)(c); EEA Regs 2016 reg 4(1)(d).

both HA 1996 Parts 6[124] and 7,[125] and in Wales under HA 1996 Part 6 and H(W)A 2014 Part 2, so long as he or she is habitually resident in the UK.

Permanent right to reside

3.53 An EEA national who has resided in the UK for a continuous period of five years has a permanent right to reside.[126] The CJEU has held that periods of imprisonment cannot be taken into account, so that they interrupt continuity of residence for this purpose.[127] Family members who are not EEA nationals but who have resided with the EEA national for a continuous period of five years also obtain the right.[128]

3.54 Workers or self-employed persons who have stopped working (and their family members) also have a permanent right of residence.[129] The worker or self-employed person must have resided in the UK continuously for more than three years, must have worked for the last one of those years and then stopped working at an age when he or she is entitled to a state pension or, in the case of an employed person, has ceased work in order to take early retirement.[130]

3.55 The definition also applies to a person who has stopped working as a result of a permanent incapacity who either resided in the UK continuously for more than two years prior to the termination, or whose incapacity is the result of an accident at work or an occupational disease that entitles him or her to a pension payable in full or in part by an institution in the UK.[131]

3.56 The Court of Appeal has held that a non-EU national[132] is entitled to a permanent right to reside under Directive 2004/38/EC Article 17(3) on marrying an EU worker who has stopped working due to a permanent incapacity and who had lived in the UK for two years

124 In England, Eligibility Regs 2006 reg 4(1); in Wales, Eligibility (Wales) Regs 2014 reg 4(1).

125 In England, Eligibility Regs 2006 reg 6(1); in Wales, Eligibility (Wales) Regs 2014 reg 6(1).

126 Directive 2004/38/EC Article 16(1); EEA Regs 2016 reg 15(1).

127 *Onuekwere v Secretary of State for the Home Department*, *Secretary of State for the Home Department v MG*, Cases C-378/12 and C-400/12.

128 Directive 2004/38/EC Article 16(1); EEA Regs 2016 reg 15(1)(b).

129 Directive 2004/38/EC Article 17; EEA Regs 2016 reg 15(1)(c) and (d).

130 Directive 2004/38/EC Article 17; EEA Regs 2016 reg 5(2).

131 Directive 2004/38/EC Article 17; EEA Regs 2016 reg 5(3).

132 Sometimes known as a third country national.

prior to that time; it was not necessary for her to have been a family member before, or as at the date of, her husband's acquisition of permanent residence.[133]

3.57 In *Lassal*,[134] the European Court of Justice (ECJ) noted that the permanent right to reside did not appear in previous EU legislation;[135] it held that continuous periods of five years' residence completed before the Directive came into force on 30 April 2006, in accordance with the previous legislation, had to be taken into account for the purposes of the acquisition of the right. It also held that absences from the host member state of less than two consecutive years, which occurred before 30 April 2006 but after a continuous period of five years' legal residence completed before that date, did not affect acquisition of the right of permanent residence.

3.58 In *Dias*,[136] the ECJ held that time spent in the UK before 30 April 2006, when Ms Dias had no right to reside but was in possession of a residence permit granted by the national authorities, did not constitute legal residence and therefore could not count towards the five years required for permanent residence. It was, however, also held that such time would not, so long as it amounted to less than two consecutive years, affect any right of permanent residence which had already been acquired.

3.59 This does not seem to rule out the argument that the holder of a valid residence permit is entitled to social assistance; otherwise, there would be discrimination contrary to Article 18 of the TFEU.[137] This, however, seems only to apply to EU citizens, by virtue of what

133 *RM (Zimbabwe) v Secretary of State for the Home Department* [2013] EWCA Civ 775, [2014] 1 WLR 2259.

134 *Secretary of State for Work and Pensions v Lassal and Child Poverty Action Group (intervener)*, Case C-162/09, [2011] 1 CMLR 31.

135 Directives 64/221/EEC, 68/360/EEC, 72/194/EEC, 73/148/EEC, 75/34/EEC, 75/35/EEC, 90/364/EEC, 90/365/EEC and 93/96/EEC all of which were repealed by the Directive, and Regulation (EEC) No 1612/68 which was amended by the Directive.

136 *Secretary of State for Work and Pensions v Maria Dias*, Case C-325/09, [2011] 3 CMLR 40.

137 *Trojani v Centre public d'aide sociale de Bruxelles (CPAS)*, Case C-456/02, [2004] ECR1–7573, ECJ at paras [43]–[46], which was followed in *R (Bidar) v Ealing LBC and Secretary of State for Education and Skills*, Case C-209/03, at para [37].

was said in *Sanneh*[138] (after consideration of what was said in *Ahmed*[139] by the CJEU).[140]

3.60 In *Clauder*,[141] the European Free Trade Association (EFTA)[142] Court held that, although Article 16 of the Directive does not confer an autonomous right of residence on the family members of an EEA national with a permanent right to reside, it does grant them a derivative right to live with the holder of permanent residence. The admission and residence of the family members in such cases is not subject to a condition of sufficient resources, because the holder of a permanent right of residence is not subject to any such requirement and his or her enjoyment of that right would be impaired and deprived of its full effectiveness if he or she were prevented from founding a family on the basis of insufficient resources. Family members will only obtain permanent residence when they have fulfilled five years' residence.

3.61 In *Ziolkowski*,[143] the ECJ held that Article 16 of the Directive means that an EU citizen who has been resident for more than five years in a host member state on the sole basis of the national law of that state, and without a right of residence pursuant to Article 7(1) of the Directive, cannot be regarded as having acquired permanent residence.

3.62 In the same case, it also held that periods of residence completed by a national of a non-member state in the territory of a member state before its accession to the EU must, in the absence of specific provisions in the Act of Accession, count towards the period required to obtain permanent residence, provided they were completed in accordance with Article 7(1) of the Directive.

138 *Sanneh v Secretary of State for Work and Pensions* [2015] EWCA Civ 49, [2015] HLR 27 at [110].

139 *ONAFTS v Ahmed*, C-45/12 at [40] and [41].

140 See para 3.22.

141 Case E-4/11, 26 July 2011.

142 This was not a decision of the CJEU because it concerned a retired German citizen living in Liechtenstein which is not a member of the EU and therefore not subject to the jurisdiction of the CJEU. Liechtenstein, along with Iceland and Norway, are part of the EEA and therefore their references go to the EFTA Court instead.

143 *Ziolkowski and Szeja v Land Berlin*, Cases C-424/10 and C-425/10.

Residence documentation

3.63 An EEA national who has a right to reside in the UK is entitled to a registration certificate or derivative[144] residence card.[145] A non-EEA national who has a right to reside in the UK is entitled to a residence card or derivative residence card.[146] A person with a permanent right of residence is entitled to a permanent residence document.[147]

Family members of EEA nationals

3.64 The EEA Regs 2016[148] define a 'family member' as:

a) a spouse[149] or civil partner;
b) direct descendants,[150] including those of a spouse or civil partner, who are:

144 A derivative residence card is granted to a person whose right to reside in the UK is dependent upon another person's right to reside; see paras 3.64–3.74.

145 Directive 2004/38/EC Article 8; EEA Regs 2016 regs 17 and 20; the right to reside exists independently of any residence documentation which is merely evidence of the right, see *da Veiga v Staatssecretaris van Justitie*, Case 9/88; *Echternach and Moritz v Minister van Onderwijs en Wetenschappen*, Cases 389/87 and 390/87, at para [25]; *Secretary of State for Work and Pensions v Dias*, Case C-325/09 at para [48]; a person who is in possession of such documentation may, however, rely on EC Treaty Article 12 in order to be granted social assistance, see *Trojani v Centre public d'aide sociale de Bruxelles (CPAS)*, Case C-456/02, [2004] ECR I-7573, at para [43].

146 Directive 2004/38/EC Article 10; EEA Regs 2016 regs 18 and 20.

147 Directive 2004/38/EC Articles 19 and 20; EEA Regs 2016 reg 19.

148 EEA Regs 2016 reg 7(1).

149 EEA Regs 2016 reg 7(1)(a). In *Diatta v Land Berlin* [1985] EUECJ R 267/83, the CJEU held that a marital relationship continues until terminated by the competent authority and is not affected by the fact that the spouses live separately, even where they intend to divorce at a later date. Note EEA Regs 2016 reg 2(1) states that a spouse does not include: a) a party to a marriage of convenience; or b) the spouse of a person who already has a spouse, civil partner or durable partner in the UK.

150 In *SM (Algeria) v Entry Clearance Officer* [2018] UKSC 9, it was held that direct descendants refers to consanguineous children, grandchildren and other blood descendants in the direct line, which may include step descendants, and those descendants who had been lawfully adopted in accordance with the requirements of the host country. The case concerned a child who had become the subject of guardianship under the kefalah system in Algeria. The Supreme Court referred to the CJEU the question whether the child was a direct descendant in those circumstances. It did, however, decide that if the child was not a direct descendant under Article 2(2)(c) of the Directive, then it would be another family member under Article 3(2)(a).

i) under 21; or
ii) their dependants;[151]

c) dependent[152] direct[153] relatives in the person's ascending line (ie, parents or grandparents) or those of the person's spouse or civil partner; or
d) extended family members[154] who have been issued with an EEA family permit, a registration certificate or a residence card and who satisfy the conditions in EEA Regs 2016 reg 8.

3.65 In *Jia*,[155] the CJEU defined 'dependency' to mean that the family member needs the material support of the EEA national or his or her spouse in order to meet his or her essential needs in the country of origin. Proof to establish such material support may be adduced by any appropriate means and is not confined to financial dependency.[156]

3.66 This decision has been distinguished by the Court of Appeal,[157] which has held that Article 2(2) of the Directive did not specify when the dependency had to have arisen, nor did it require that the relative had to be dependent in the country of origin. It was further held that Article 2(2), taken together with Article 8(5)(d), suggested that dependency in the state of origin need not be proved for family members and that it was sufficient for the dependency to have arisen in the host member state: such an interpretation reflected the policy of the Directive to strengthen and simplify the realisation of realistic

151 In *Reyes v Migrationsverket*, Case C-423/12, the CJEU held that a member state cannot require a direct descendent who is 21 years old or over to have tried to obtain employment or subsistence support from his or her home state before he or she can be treated as a dependant under the Directive Article 2(2)(c). In *Lim v Entry Clearance Officer Manila* [2015] EWCA Civ 1383 per Elias LJ at [32], it was held that the critical question is whether the claimant is in fact in a position to support himself which is an issue of fact. If he can support himself, there is no dependency, even if he is given financial material support by the EU citizen. If he cannot, the court will not ask why, except where there is an abuse of rights. The fact that he chooses not to get a job and become self-supporting is irrelevant.

152 EEA Regs 2016 reg 7(1)(c).

153 *PG and VG* [2007] UKAIT 19, where it was held that 'direct' is not confined to the first generation but can include grandchildren, although it does not include nieces, nephews, uncles and aunts. This approach was assumed to be correct in *Bigia and others v Entry Clearance Officer* [2009] EWCA Civ 79 at [4].

154 See para 3.70.

155 *Jia v Migrationsverket*, Case C-1/05, [2007] QB 545.

156 *Jia* at para [43].

157 *Pedro v Secretary of State for Work and Pensions* [2009] EWCA Civ 1358, [2010] PTSR 1504.

free movement rights of EU citizens compatibly with their family rights; accordingly, proof of dependency by the claimant on her son in the UK sufficed.

3.67 In *Metock*,[158] the CJEU held that, in order to benefit from the free movement rights set out in the Directive, it was contrary to the Directive for a member state to enact legislation which requires a non-EEA national, who is the spouse of an EU citizen residing in that member state but not possessing its nationality, to have previously been lawfully resident in another member state before arriving in the host member state.

3.68 It was also held that Article 3(1) must be interpreted to mean that a non-EEA national who is the spouse of an EU citizen residing in a member state whose nationality he or she does not possess, and who accompanies or joins that EU citizen, benefits from the provisions of the Directive, irrespective of when and where the marriage took place and of how the national of a non-member country entered the host member state.

3.69 The EEA Regs 2006 were amended[159] to reflect this judgment, which change has been carried across to the EEA Regs 2016, so that the family member who is accompanying the EEA national to the UK, or joining the EEA national here, no longer has to be lawfully resident in an EEA state or meet the requirements of the Immigration Rules.

3.70 An extended family member[160] is treated as the family member of the relevant EEA national for so long as he or she holds a valid EEA family permit, a registration certificate or a residence card,[161] and is one of the following:[162]

a) a relative of an EEA national, residing in a country other than the UK who is dependent on the EEA national or is a member of the EEA national's household and who either is accompanying the EEA national to the UK or wants to join him or her in the UK, or who has joined the EEA national in the UK and continues to be dependent upon him or her, or to be a member of the EEA national's household;[163]

158 *Metock and others v Minister for Justice, Equality and Law Reform*, Case C-127/08.

159 Immigration (European Economic Area) (Amendment) Regulations 2011 SI No 1247.

160 See para 3.64(d).

161 EEA Regs 2016 reg 7(3).

162 EEA Regs 2016 reg 8.

163 EEA Regs 2016 reg 8(2).

b) a relative of an EEA national or his or her spouse or civil partner, who strictly requires his or her personal care on serious health grounds;[164]
c) a relative of an EEA national who would meet the requirements for indefinite leave to enter or remain in the UK as a dependent relative of the EEA national;[165]
d) a partner of an EEA national who can prove that he or she is in a durable[166] relationship with the EEA national.[167]

3.71 A number of questions about extended family members have been referred[168] to the CJEU. The CJEU has held that member states have a wide discretion in setting criteria for extended family members: Article 3(2) of the Directive does not provide a direct right to reside for such persons, and states can impose requirements in their own domestic legislation.[169] This is consistent with domestic cases which have held that extended family members have no right to reside unless they have residence documentation.[170]

3.72 Subsequent to the decision of the CJEU in *Rahman*,[171] the Court of Appeal has approved its approach and held that Article 3(2) requires an extended family member to show dependence that existed in the country from which the family member comes; accordingly, and in contrast to the position of non-extended family members,[172] there is a requirement that the necessary relationship of dependency or membership of the household must have existed in another country as well as in the host state.[173]

3.73 A family member has a right to reside in the UK for so long as he or she remains the family member of an EEA national who has a

164 EEA Regs 2016 reg 8(3).
165 EEA Regs 2016 reg 8(4).
166 Home Office policy suggests that a period of two years' cohabitation is required. EEA Regs 2016 reg 2(1) defines a durable partner as not including a party to a durable partnership of convenience, or the durable partner (D) of a person (P) where a spouse, civil partner or durable partner of D or P is already present in the UK which marriage, civil partnership or durable relationship is subsisting.
167 EEA Regs 2016 reg 8(5).
168 *MR (Bangladesh) and others* [2010] UKUT 449 (IAC).
169 *Secretary of State for the Home Department v Rahman and others*, Case C-83/11 at [26].
170 *SS v Secretary of State for Work and Pensions (ESA)* [2011] UKUT 8 (AAC).
171 *Secretary of State for the Home Department v Rahman and others*, Case C-83/11.
172 See para 3.64.
173 *Oboh and others v Secretary of State for the Home Department* [2013] EWCA Civ 1525, [2014] 1 WLR 1680.

right to reside in the UK.[174] The Directive provides that EEA nationals who are family members of an EEA national retain the right to reside on the death or departure of the EEA national from the host member state[175] or where there has been a divorce, annulment of marriage or termination of the registered partnership between the family member and the EEA national.[176] Under the Directive, family members who are not EEA nationals may also retain their right to reside.[177]

3.74 The EEA Regs 2016 provide that family members who are not EEA nationals may retain a right to reside in the following circumstances,[178] which are more restrictive than the Directive:

a) if the qualified person has died and the family member has resided in the UK for at least a year before the death and, if he or she were an EEA national, would be a worker, a self-employed person or a self-sufficient person or the family member of such a person;[179]
b) if the family member is the direct descendant of a qualified person who has died or left the UK, or is a direct descendant of that person's spouse or civil partner, and he or she was attending an educational course in the UK immediately before the qualified person died or left the UK, and continues to attend such a course;[180]
c) if the family member is the parent with actual custody of a child who satisfies b) above;[181]
d) if the family member ceased to be such because he or she is divorced from the qualified person[182] or their civil partnership has

174 EEA Regs 2016 reg 14(2).
175 Directive 2004/38/EC Article 12(1).
176 Directive 2004/38/EC Article 13(1).
177 Directive 2004/38/EC Articles 12(2), (3), 13(2).
178 EEA Regs 2016 reg 10.
179 EEA Regs 2016 reg 10(2).
180 EEA Regs 2016 reg 10(3).
181 EEA Regs 2016 reg 10(4).
182 In *Singh and others v Minister for Justice and Equality and Immigrant Council of Ireland*, Case C-218/14, [2016] QB 208, the ECJ held that a third country national, divorced from an EU citizen, whose marriage had lasted for at least three years before the commencement of divorce proceedings, including at least one year in the host member state, cannot retain a right of residence in that member state where the commencement of the divorce proceedings is preceded by the departure from that member state of the spouse who is the EU citizen. This decision was followed and applied by the CJEU in the later case of *Secretary of State for the Home Department v NA (Pakistan)*, Case C-115/15, [2017] QB 109.

been terminated, he or she is not an EEA national but if he or she were, he or she would be a worker,[183] a self-employed person or self-sufficient person or the family member of such a person, and either:

i) the marriage or civil partnership lasted for at least three years, and the couple resided in the UK for at least one year during its duration;[184] or
ii) the former spouse or civil partner has custody of a child of the qualified person; or
iii) the former spouse or civil partner has the right of access to a child under the age of 18, and a court has ordered that such access must take place in the UK; or
iv) the continued right of residence in the UK of the person is warranted by particularly difficult circumstances,[185] eg, he or she or another family member has been a victim of domestic violence while the marriage or civil partnership was subsisting.[186]

A8 nationals

3.75 The Accession Treaty signed in Athens on 16 April 2003 provided that ten countries[187] would accede to the EU on 1 May 2004. The treaty provides that existing member states can, as a derogation from the usual position under EU law, regulate access to their labour markets by nationals of the accession states, other than nationals of

183 In *Ahmed v Secretary of State for the Home Department* [2017] EWCA Civ 99, per Arden LJ at [14]–[19], the Court of Appeal held that the non-EU national former spouse must have been working at the date of the decree absolute in the divorce proceedings and that the non-EU national former spouse will not retain a right of residence if he or she only started working after that date. Both *Singh* and *NA (Pakistan)* – see last footnote – were followed and applied; the court did not consider that there was sufficient lack of clarity on the issue to justify a reference to the CJEU.

184 EEA Regs 2016 reg 10(5)(d)(i).

185 In *Secretary of State for the Home Department v NA (Pakistan)*, Case C-115/15, [2017] QB 109, CJEU, the former non-EU national spouse of an EU national claimed a derivative right of residence because of domestic violence, even though her former spouse had left the UK before the divorce proceedings began. The CJEU held that she did not retain any right of residence and that a non-EU national spouse of an EU national had a derivative right of residence in a member state only if the EU national spouse was resident in that member state at the start of the divorce proceedings.

186 EEA Regs 2016 reg 10(5).

187 Cyprus, the Czech Republic, Estonia, Hungary, Latvia, Lithuania, Malta, Poland, Slovakia and Slovenia.

Cyprus and Malta. The states to which this derogation applies are known as the 'A8' countries.

3.76 The derogation could be applied for a transitional period of five years from 1 May 2004, with a provision for a further two years in the case of disturbances to the labour market of the member state. In England and Wales, the derogation was extended until 30 April 2011,[188] but ended from midnight on that date.[189]

3.77 The secondary legislation which abolished the derogation introduced a new regulation (reg 7A) into the EEA Regs 2006, the effect of which was that an A8 national could retain worker status if he or she became unable to work, became unemployed or ceased to work, as the case may be, on or after 1 May 2011, or if on 30 April 2011 he or she had ceased working for an authorised employer in the circumstances mentioned in EEA Regs 2006 reg 6(2), during the first month of his or her employment and was still within that first month.

3.78 The treaty was given domestic effect by the European Union (Accessions) Act 2003[190] which gives the secretary of state the power to enact regulations to permit the derogation. This resulted in the Accession (Immigration and Worker Registration) Regulations (A(IWR) Regs) 2004[191] the legality of which has been unsuccessfully challenged.[192]

3.79 In certain respects, A8 nationals were worse off than nationals of the original EEA states. A8 nationals who were subject to the Worker Registration Scheme (WRS) had no right to reside in the UK as work-seekers unless they were self-sufficient.[193] A8 nationals who were subject to the WRS only had a right to reside in the UK as a worker if their employment was in accordance with the requirements of the scheme.[194] A8 nationals who were subject to the WRS and who

188 Accession (Immigration and Worker Registration) (Amendment) Regulations 2009 SI No 892, which came into force on 29 April 2009.

189 By operation of the Accession (Immigration and Worker Registration) (Revocation, Savings and Consequential Provisions) Regulations 2011 SI No 544 which came into force on 1 May 2011.

190 It received royal assent on 13 November 2003.

191 SI No 1219.

192 *Zalewska v Department for Social Development (Northern Ireland)* [2008] UKHL 67, [2008] 1 WLR 2602, HL (NI); *Putans v Tower Hamlets LBC* [2006] EWHC 1634 (Ch), [2007] HLR 10.

193 A(IWR) Regs 2004 reg 4(2) and (3). See paras 3.45–3.50.

194 A(IWR) Regs 2004 reg 5(2).

ceased to work in accordance with the requirements of the scheme ceased to have a right to reside in the UK as a worker.[195]

3.80 If they ceased to work within one month of the commencement of their employment with an authorised employer, they retained the right to reside as a worker until the end of that month. A8 nationals who were subject to the WRS were not entitled to the issue of registration certificates and could not entitle non-EEA nationals to the issue of residence cards.[196]

The Worker Registration Scheme

3.81 Most A8 nationals were only able to work as employed persons in the UK if they complied with the requirements of the WRS. The following exemptions applied:

a) Self-employed people were exempt from the WRS.[197]
b) A8 nationals were not subject to the WRS if on 30 April 2004 they had leave to enter or remain in the UK which was not subject to any condition restricting employment.[198]
c) The WRS did not apply to A8 nationals who had worked legally in the UK without interruption for a period of 12 months up to and including 30 April 2004.[199] This could include up to 30 days during which the A8 national was not working legally in the UK.
d) A8 nationals who worked legally in the UK without interruption for a period of 12 months which ended after 30 April 2004 ceased to be subject to the WRS.[200] This could also include up to 30 days during which the A8 national was not working legally in the UK.
e) A8 nationals were not subject to the WRS during any period in which they were members of a diplomatic mission or the family member of such a person.[201]
f) A8 nationals were exempt from the WRS if their employer was not based in the UK but they had been sent here to work on that employer's behalf.[202]

195 A(IWR) Regs 2004 reg 5(3), (4).

196 A(IWR) Regs 2004 reg 5(5).

197 A(IWR) Regs 2004 regs 1(2)(k), 2(1). See paras 3.41–3.44.

198 A(IWR) Regs 2004 reg 2(2).

199 A(IWR) Regs 2004 reg 2(3), (8).

200 A(IWR) Regs 2004 reg 2(4), (8).

201 A(IWR) Regs 2004 reg 2(5A), inserted by Accession (Worker Authorisation and Worker Registration) (Amendment) Regulations (A(WAWR)(A) Regs) 2007 SI No 3012 reg 3(a), from 19 November 2007.

202 A(IWR) Regs 2004 reg 2(6)(a), (9)(b).

g) A8 nationals were exempt from the WRS if they were also UK nationals, Swiss nationals or nationals of another EEA state except Bulgaria and Romania.[203]
h) A8 nationals were also exempt from the WRS if they were the spouse, civil partner or child under 18 of a person who had leave to enter or remain in the UK that allowed that person to work.[204]
i) A family member of a Swiss national or EEA national who had a right to reside in the UK was also exempt from the WRS. This did not include family members of nationals of the A8 or Bulgaria and Romania who were subject to the relevant scheme and who only had an initial right to reside under reg 13 of the EEA Regs 2006.[205]

3.82 A8 nationals who were not exempt had to comply with the WRS. Their employment gave them a right to reside in the UK as a worker in any of the following circumstances:

a) they were working legally for an employer on 30 April 2004 and had not ceased working for that employer;[206]
b) they applied for a registration certificate[207] authorising their work within one month of starting work for an employer and had not received a valid certificate, notice of refusal or ceased working for that employer;[208]
c) they had received a valid registration certificate authorising work for that employer and the certificate is still valid;[209] or
d) they were within the first month of their employment.[210]

203 A(IWR) Regs 2004 reg 2(5), as amended by Accession (Immigration and Worker Authorisation) Regulations (A(IWA) Regs) 2006 SI No 3317 reg 1(3), Sch 2 para 1(1), (2)(a), from 1 January 2007.

204 A(IWR) Regs 2004 reg 2(5A), inserted by Accession (Worker Authorisation and Worker Registration) (Amendment) Regulations (A(WAWR)(A) Regs) 2009 SI No 2426 regs 1, 3(a), from 2 October 2009.

205 A(IWR) Regs 2004 reg 2(6)(b), substituted by A(WAWR)(A) Regs 2009 regs 1, 3(b), from 2 October 2009.

206 A(IWR) Regs 2004 reg 7(2)(a).

207 In *Szpak v Secretary of State for Work and Pensions* [2013] EWCA Civ 46, the Court of Appeal held that a registration certificate did not operate retrospectively; where the claimant had not applied for the certificate within the first month of employment, his work was therefore not registered until the certificate had been issued.

208 A(IWR) Regs 2004 reg 7(2)(b).

209 A(IWR) Regs 2004 reg 7(2)(c).

210 A(IWR) Regs 2004 reg 7(3).

A2 nationals

3.83 The Treaty of Accession for Bulgaria and Romania was signed in Luxembourg on 25 April 2005. It provided for the accession of Bulgaria and Romania ('the A2') to the EU on 1 January 2007. During a transitional period of five years from 1 January 2007 to 31 December 2011, the existing member states could regulate access to their labour markets by A2 workers and restrict their rights of residence.[211] There are also provisions for member states to continue to maintain restrictions for a further two years in the case of disturbances to their labour markets.

3.84 The treaty was given domestic effect by the European Union (Accessions) Act 2006. This gave the secretary of state the power to enact regulations to permit the derogation from the provisions of EU law relating to workers. The detail of the derogation is contained in the Accession (Immigration and Worker Authorisation) Regulations (A(IWA) Regs) 2006.[212] On 23 November 2011, the government decided to extend the derogation for a further two years from 31 December 2011.

3.85 A2 nationals were worse off than nationals of other EEA states. A2 nationals who were subject to worker authorisation had no right to reside in the UK as jobseekers,[213] and only had a right to reside as a worker when working in accordance with an accession worker authorisation document.[214] A2 nationals subject to worker authorisation did not retain a right to reside as a worker if they ceased to work.[215] A2 nationals who were subject to worker authorisation were not entitled to the issue of registration certificates and could not entitle non-EEA nationals to the issue of residence cards.[216]

3.86 This did not apply to a highly skilled person who was seeking employment in the UK who was entitled to a registration certificate which stated that he or she had unconditional access to the UK labour market. A 'highly skilled person' is defined as someone who meets the requirements of the Highly Skilled Migrant Programme or holds a certain type of qualification.[217]

211 Annexes VI and VII of the Treaty of Accession.
212 SI No 3317, which came into force on 1 January 2007.
213 A(IWA) Regs 2006 reg 6(2). See para 3.31.
214 A(IWA) Regs 2006 reg 6(1).
215 A(IWA) Regs 2006 reg 6(3).
216 A(IWA) Regs 2006 reg 7(1).
217 A(IWA) Regs 2006 regs 4, 7(2).

Worker authorisation

3.87 Certain A2 nationals were classified as 'subject to worker authorisation' and thereby restricted to authorised categories of employment.[218] The following exemptions applied:

a) Self-employed people were exempt.[219]
b) A2 nationals were not subject to worker authorisation if on 31 December 2006 they had leave to enter or remain in the UK which was not subject to any condition restricting employment.[220]
c) Worker authorisation did not apply to A2 nationals who worked legally in the UK without interruption throughout 2006.[221] This included up to 30 days during which the A2 national was not working legally in the UK.
d) A2 nationals who worked legally in the UK without interruption for a period of 12 months which ended after 31 December 2006 ceased to be subject to worker authorisation.[222] This could also include up to 30 days during which the A2 national was not working legally in the UK.
e) A2 nationals were not subject to worker authorisation during any period in which they were members of a diplomatic mission or the family member of such a person.[223]
f) A2 nationals were also exempt if their employer was not based in the UK but they had been sent here to work on that employer's behalf.[224]
g) A2 nationals were not subject to worker authorisation if they were also nationals of the UK or an EEA state other than an A2 state. They were also exempt if they had a right of permanent residence.[225] This also applied if they were the spouse or civil partner of a national of the UK or of a person settled in the UK.[226]

218 A(IWA) Regs 2006 reg 1(2)(f); these are the categories of employment listed in the first column of the table in Sch 1.
219 A(IWA) Regs 2006 reg 1(2)(t); see paras 3.41–3.45.
220 A(IWA) Regs 2006 reg 2(2), as amended by Accession (Immigration and Worker Authorisation) (Amendment) Regulations 2007 SI No 475 reg 2(1), (2)(a), from 16 March 2007.
221 A(IWA) Regs 2006 reg 2(3).
222 A(IWA) Regs 2006 reg 2(4), (12)(c).
223 A(IWA) Regs 2006 reg 2(6A), inserted by A(WAWR)(A) Regs 2007 reg 2(1), (2)(a), from 19 November 2007.
224 A(IWA) Regs 2006 reg 2(11), (13)(a).
225 A(IWA) Regs 2006 reg 2(5), (7).
226 A(IWA) Regs 2006 reg 2(6).

h) A2 nationals were not subject to worker authorisation if they were the spouse, civil partner or child under 18 of a person who had leave to enter or remain in the UK which allowed that person to work.[227]

i) A2 nationals were not subject to worker authorisation if they were family members of an EEA national who had a right to reside in the UK. This did not include family members of A2 nationals who were subject to worker authorisation. Neither did it include family members of a person who was exempt from worker authorisation because he or she was the family member of a self-employed person, a self-sufficient person or a student. A2 nationals were nevertheless exempt if they were family members of a person who was self-employed, self-sufficient or a student.[228]

j) A2 nationals were not subject to worker authorisation if they were the spouse, civil partner or descendant of an A2 national who was working in accordance with the scheme, provided that the descendant was under 21 or dependent on the A2 worker.[229]

k) A2 nationals were not subject to worker authorisation if they were highly skilled persons and held a registration certificate which stated that they had unconditional access to the UK labour market.[230]

l) A2 nationals were not subject to worker authorisation if they were students, held a registration certificate that permitted employment for no more than 20 hours a week (unless the work was vocational training or vacation work), and complied with that condition. This exemption was retained for four months after the end of the course of study.[231]

3.88 A2 nationals who were subject to worker authorisation had to hold an accession worker authorisation document and work in

227 A(IWA) Regs 2006 reg 2(5A), inserted by A(WAWR)(A) Regs 2009 regs 1, 2(2)(a), from 2 October 2009.

228 A(IWA) Regs 2006 reg 2(8), substituted by the A(WAWR)(A) Regs 2007 reg 2(1), (2)(b), from 19 November 2007, and amended by A(WAWR)(A) Regs 2009 regs 1, 2(2)(b), from 2 October 2009.

229 A(IWA) Regs 2006 reg 2(8A), inserted by A(WAWR)(A) Regs 2009 regs 1, 2(2)(c), from 2 October 2009.

230 A(IWA) Regs 2006 reg 2(9).

231 A(IWA) Regs 2006 reg 2(10), (10A), (10B), substituted by the Accession (Immigration and Worker Authorisation) (Amendment) Regulations 2007 SI No 475 reg 2(1), (2)(c), from 16 March 2007.

accordance with the conditions set out in that document. Such a document had to be:[232]

a) a passport or other travel document containing a visa which gave the holder the right to carry out a particular type of employment;
b) a seasonal agricultural card; or
c) an accession worker card.

3.89 An application for an A2 accession worker card could be made in two circumstances. First, if the applicant could prove that the employment concerned was within an authorised category of employment.[233] Second, an application could be made by an authorised family member, in which case there was no restriction on the type of employment.[234] An authorised family member was a family member of an A2 national who was working in accordance with the scheme, unless the worker was only authorised to work by virtue of holding an accession worker card as an authorised family member, or the family member was the spouse or civil partner of the worker or his or her descendant who was under 21 or dependent.[235]

Croatians

3.90 On 1 July 2013, the Republic of Croatia acceded to the EU. Annex V to the Treaty of Accession, signed at Brussels on 9 December 2011, permits member states to derogate from various provisions concerning freedom of movement under EU law which relate to access to their labour markets by Croatian nationals during the accession period from 1 July 2013 to 30 June 2018.

3.91 The UK has chosen to take advantage of this right and, in exercise of the powers conferred under the European Union (Croatian Accession and Irish Protocol) Act 2013,[236] the secretary of state made the Accession of Croatia (Immigration and Worker Authorisation) Regulations (AC(IWA) Regs) 2013[237] which came into force on 1 July 2013. The effect of the AC(IWA) Regs 2013 is to create a worker authorisation scheme for Croatian nationals which is almost identical

232 A(IWA) Regs 2006 reg 9(2).
233 A(IWA) Regs 2006 reg 10(1)(a).
234 A(IWA) Regs 2006 reg 10(1)(b).
235 A(IWA) Regs 2006 reg 3, substituted by A(WAWR)(A) Regs 2009 regs 1, 2(3), from 2 October 2009.
236 Section 4.
237 SI No. 1460.

to that which was in place for A2 nationals,[238] and which will last until 30 June 2018.

3.92 The accession also necessitated an amendment to the Eligibility Regs 2006 on 1 July 2013[239] to exempt from the habitual residence test nationals of Croatia subject to the worker authorisation scheme and who are treated as workers pursuant to that scheme.

3.93 Croatian nationals are worse off than nationals of other EEA states. Croatian nationals who are subject to worker authorisation have no right to reside in the UK as jobseekers,[240] and will only have a right to right as a worker when working in accordance with the scheme, if they hold an accession worker authorisation document and if they are working in accordance with the conditions set out in that document.[241] Croatian nationals subject to worker authorisation will not retain a right to reside as a worker if they cease to work.[242] Not all Croatian nationals are, however, subject to worker authorisation.

Worker authorisation

3.94 Certain Croatian nationals are classified as 'subject to worker authorisation' and thereby restricted to authorised categories of employment, which means:

a) employment for which a sponsor has issued the applicant with a valid certificate of sponsorship under Tier 2 or Tier 5 of the Points Based System;[243] or
b) employment as:
   i) a representative of an overseas business;
   ii) a postgraduate doctor or dentist; or
   iii) a domestic worker in a private household.[244]

3.95 The following Croatian nationals are exempt from worker authorisation:[245]

238 Paras 3.83–3.90.

239 Allocation of Housing and Homelessness (Eligibility) (England) (Amendment) Regulations 2013 SI No 1467 which came into force on 1 July 2013.

240 AC(IWA) Regs 2013 reg 5.

241 AC(IWA) Regs 2013 reg 5.

242 AC(IWA) Regs 2013 reg 4.

243 The system set out in the Immigration Rules which regulates entry to the UK for work and study.

244 AC(IWA) Regs 2013 reg 1(2).

245 AC(IWA) Regs 2013 reg 2.

a) a Croatian national who on or after 30 June 2013 was granted leave to enter or remain in the UK not subject to any condition restricting his or her employment;[246]
b) a Croatian national who was working legally in the UK on 30 June 2013 and had been working legally in the UK for the 12 months prior to that date;[247]
c) a Croatian national who legally works in the UK without interruption for a period of 12 months which ended after 30 June 2013 ceased to be subject to the scheme at the end of the 12 months;[248]
d) a Croatian national who is also a national of the UK, or an EEA state other than Croatia – but this does not include an A2 national subject to worker authorisation;[249]
e) a Croatian national who is also an A2 national and is working in accordance with that worker authorisation scheme;[250]
f) a Croatian national who is the spouse, civil partner, unmarried or same-sex partner, or child under 18, of a person who has leave to enter or remain in the UK which leave allows him or her to work in the UK;[251]
g) a Croatian national who is the spouse, civil partner, unmarried or same sex partner of a national of the UK, or a person who is settled[252] in the UK;[253]
h) a Croatian national who is a member of a diplomatic mission;[254]
i) a Croatian national who is exempt from the requirement to have leave to enter and remain in the UK;[255]
j) a Croatian national who has a permanent right of residence under the EEA Regs 2006 reg 15;[256]
k) a Croatian national who is a family member of an EEA national who has a right to reside in the UK, although where the EEA national is a Croatian or A2 national subject to worker authorisa-

246 AC(IWA) Regs 2013 reg 2(2).
247 AC(IWA) Regs 2013 reg 2(3), the period of 12 months cannot be interrupted by more than 30 days.
248 AC(IWA) Regs 2013 reg 2(4), the period of 12 months cannot be interrupted by more than 30 days.
249 AC(IWA) Regs 2013 reg 2(6).
250 AC(IWA) Regs 2013 reg 2(7).
251 AC(IWA) Regs 2013 reg 2(8).
252 IA 1971 s33(2A).
253 AC(IWA) Regs 2013 reg 2(9).
254 AC(IWA) Regs 2013 reg 2(10) and IA 1971 s8(3) and (3A).
255 AC(IWA) Regs 2013 reg 2(11) and IA 1971 s8(2).
256 AC(IWA) Regs 2013 reg 2(12).

tion, he or she must be the spouse or civil partner, unmarried or same-sex partner or a direct descendant, of the EEA national, the EEA national's spouse or civil partner and, if he or she is a direct descendant, he or she must be under 21 or a dependant of the EEA national, or the EEA national's civil partner or spouse;[257]

l) a Croatian national who is a highly skilled person[258] and holds an EEA registration certificate issued in accordance with reg 7 that includes a statement that he or she has unconditional access to the UK labour market;[259]

m) a Croatian national who is in the UK as a student and either holds an EEA registration certificate which includes a statement that he or she may work[260] or he or she has leave to enter or remain as a student and works in accordance with any conditions attached to that leave;[261]

n) a Croatian national who ceases to be a student, but only for the four months after the end of his or her course and provided he or she holds an EEA registration certificate that was issued before the end of the course and includes a statement that he or she may work during that period;[262]

o) a Croatian national who is a posted[263] worker;[264]

p) a Croatian national who is self-employed.[265]

3.96 A Croatian national subject to worker authorisation is only authorised to work in the UK during the accession period if he or she holds an accession worker authorisation document and is working in accordance with the conditions set out in that document.[266] An accession worker authorisation document means a passport or a worker authorisation registration certificate endorsed with a condition

257 AC(IWA) Regs 2013 reg 2(13) and 2(14).
258 AC(IWA) Regs 2013 reg 3.
259 AC(IWA) Regs 2013 reg 2(15).
260 AC(IWA) Regs 2013 reg 2(17), this means he or she may not work for more than 20 hours each week.
261 AC(IWA) Regs 2013 reg 2(16).
262 AC(IWA) Regs 2013 reg 2(18).
263 AC(IWA) Regs 2013 reg 2(20). A 'posted worker' means a worker who is sent to work in the UK within the meaning of Article 1(3) of Directive 96/71/EC, ie by his or her employer.
264 AC(IWA) Regs 2013 reg 2(19).
265 AC(IWA) Regs 2013 reg 1(2) and the European Union (Croatian Accession and Irish Protocol) Act 2013 s4(11).
266 AC(IWA) Regs 2013 reg 8(1).

restricting the holder's employment to a particular employer and authorised category of employment.[267]

3.97 The latter document ceases to be valid if the holder stops working for more than 30 days.[268] The document must be applied for in writing to the secretary of state.[269]

3.98 A Croatian national who works in breach of the authorisation scheme is liable to a penalty and commits an offence;[270] the same is true of an employer who breaches the scheme.[271]

Other rights of residence

Self-sufficient families

3.99 Rights of residence can exist outside the scope of the Directive. In *Chen*,[272] Mrs Chen and her husband were both Chinese nationals and worked for a company established in China but, for the purposes of work, Mr Chen travelled frequently to various member states of the EU, in particular the UK.[273] Their daughter was born in Belfast and had Irish nationality.[274] The child was dependent both emotionally and financially on her mother, Mrs Chen, who was her primary carer, and she received private medical and childcare services in the UK.[275]

3.100 The CJEU held that Article 18 of the EC Treaty and Council Directive 90/364/EEC[276] confer on a minor who is himself or herself an EEA national a right to reside for an indefinite period in a host member state, where that minor is covered by appropriate sickness insurance and is in the care of a parent who is not an EEA national but who has sufficient resources for that minor not to become a burden on the public finances of the host member state; in such circumstances, the parent who is the primary carer is also entitled to reside with the child in the host member state.[277]

267 AC(IWA) Regs 2013 reg 8(2).
268 AC(IWA) Regs 2013 reg 8(4).
269 AC(IWA) Regs 2013 reg 9.
270 AC(IWA) Regs 2013 reg 16.
271 AC(IWA) Regs 2013 regs 11, 15.
272 *Zhu and Chen v Secretary of State for the Home Department*, Case C-200/02, [2004] ECR I-9925.
273 *Zhu* at [7].
274 *Zhu* at [8].
275 *Zhu* at [12]–[14].
276 Of 28 June 1990.
277 *Zhu* at [41], [46], [47].

3.101 The Court of Appeal[278] has held that the requirements to have both comprehensive sickness insurance and sufficient resources such as to avoid becoming a burden on the social assistance system of the host member state applied to the parents and the child, and must exist before any right of residence can arise. It has also been held that the right to reside in such circumstances is directly effective and exists independently of the terms of the EEA Regs 2016 and the Immigration Rules which must, in any event, be interpreted compatibly with EU law where it is possible to do so.[279]

Primary carers[280] of children in education

3.102 The CJEU has also derived a right of residence from Article 12 of Regulation (EEC) No 1612/68[281] which has now been repealed and replaced by Article 10 of Regulation (EU) No 492/2011.[282] This provides that the child of a national of a member state who is or has been employed in the territory of another member state is to be admitted to that state's general educational, apprenticeship and vocational training courses on the same conditions as nationals of that state, if the child is residing in its territory.

3.103 In *Baumbast and R v Secretary of State for the Home Department*,[283] the CJEU held that children of an EU citizen who have installed themselves in a member state during the exercise by their parent of rights of residence as a migrant worker are entitled to reside there in order to attend general educational courses.

3.104 The CJEU also held that Article 12 must be interpreted as entitling the parent who is the primary carer of those children, irrespective of nationality, to reside with them in order to facilitate the

278 *W (China) and another v Secretary of State for the Home Department* [2006] EWCA Civ 1494, [2007] 1 WLR 1514.

279 *ECO (Dubai) v M (Ivory Coast)* [2010] UKUT 277 (IAC).

280 EEA Regs 2016 reg 16(8) defines a 'primary carer' as a person who is a direct relative or legal guardian of another person (AP), and either the person has primary responsibility for AP's care, or shares equally the responsibility for AP's care with one other person who is not an exempt person. An exempt person is a person who has a right to reside under the EEA Regs 2016, or who has a right of abode under IA 1971 s2, or to whom IA 1971 s8 applies, or in respect of whom an order has been made under IA 1971 s8(2), or who has indefinite leave to enter or remain in the UK.

281 Of 15 October 1968.

282 Of 5 April 2011. This right was recognised as a derivative right of residence in EEA Regs 2006 reg 15A as inserted by Immigration (European Economic Area) (Amendment) Regulations 2012 SI No 1547 Sch 1 para 9 with effect from 16 July 2012. This is now EEA Regs 2016 reg 16.

283 Case C-413/99, [2002] ECR I-7091, [2002] 3 CMLR 23.

exercise of their right. It did not matter that the parents had divorced or that the parent who was an EU citizen had ceased to be a migrant worker in the host member state.[284]

3.105 *Baumbast* was reconsidered by the CJEU in *Ibrahim*[285] and *Teixeira*,[286] two homelessness appeals referred by the Court of Appeal[287] to the CJEU, which were heard together.

3.106 Ms Ibrahim was a Somali national, married to but separated from Mr Yusuf, a Danish citizen. They had four children, who were Danish. The two eldest were at school in the UK. Initially, Mr Yusuf worked but he then ceased to enjoy a right to reside as a worker and left to live in Eastern Europe. Although he returned to live in the UK, he never regained a right to reside. Ms Ibrahim did not work, was entirely reliant on means-tested benefits and had no medical insurance. She applied with her children for homelessness assistance under HA 1996 Part 7, but was refused on the basis that she had no right to reside under EU law.

3.107 Ms Teixeira was a Portuguese national. She came to the UK in 1989 with her husband, from whom she subsequently divorced. Her daughter was born in 1991. Ms Teixeira worked from 1989 to 1991, after which time she had intermittent periods of employment. She last worked in early 2005. The daughter entered education in the UK at a time when Ms Teixeira was not a worker; in November 2006, she enrolled in a child-care course and, in March 2007, she went to live with her mother. In April 2007, Ms Teixeira applied under HA 1996 Part 7, but was refused on the basis that she had no right to reside.

3.108 On both references, the ECJ held that where a child of an EU citizen is in education in a member state in which that citizen is or has been employed as a migrant worker, the parent who is the child's primary carer enjoys a right of residence in the host state, derived from Article 12.[288] The child also has a right to reside in those circumstances.

3.109 The right of residence of the parent is not subject to a requirement that the parent should have sufficient resources and comprehensive

284 *Baumbast*, at [63] and [75].
285 Case C-310/08, [2010] HLR 31.
286 Case C-480/08, [2010] HLR 32.
287 *Harrow LBC and Secretary of State for the Home Department v Ibrahim* [2008] EWCA Civ 386, [2009] HLR 2; and *Teixeira v Lambeth LBC and Secretary of State for the Home Department* [2008] EWCA Civ 1088, [2009] HLR 9.
288 Now Article 10 of Regulation (EU) No 492/2011.

sickness insurance cover, nor is it subject to a requirement that the parent should have been employed as a migrant worker in the host state when the child first started education.

3.110 It is sufficient for the child to have been installed in the host state during the exercise by a parent of rights of residence as a migrant worker in that state. The right of residence of the parent ends when the child reaches the age of 18, unless the child continues to need the presence and care of that parent in order to be able to pursue and complete his or her education in the host member state.

3.111 The right to reside as the primary carer of a child in education who is the child of a migrant worker can apply to an A8 national, even where he or she has not completed 12 months of such work pursuant to the WRS.[289] A former self-employed worker who is the primary carer of a dependent child who is in education in the host state, does not have a right to reside.[290] In *Hrabkova,*[291] the Court of Appeal approved and followed this principle.

3.112 It has been held that education for children, at least in England, starts for these purposes at around the age of five when compulsory education begins.[292] The term 'child' in Article 12 of Regulation (EEC) No 1612/68[293] should be read as including 'stepchild' as well.[294] This is consistent with the decision of the CJEU in *Depesme,*[295] that 'child' includes not only a 'child' in a child–parent relationship with a worker, but also a child of the spouse or registered

289 *Secretary of State for Work and Pensions v JS (IS)* [2010] UKUT 347 (AAC) which was approved in *Secretary of State for Work and Pensions v MP (IS)* [2011] UKUT 109 (AAC) at para [32]. See paras 3.79–3.82 as to the WRS in respect of A8 nationals and their families.

290 *Czop*, Case C-147/11; and *Punakova*, Case C-148/11, at [33], [40].

291 *Hrabkova v Secretary of State for Work and Pensions* [2017] EWCA Civ 794.

292 *Secretary of State for Work and Pensions v IM* [2011] UKUT 231 (AAC). This is reflected in the EEA Regs 2016 reg 16(7)(a) which states that education excludes nursery education but does not exclude education received before the compulsory school age where that education is equivalent to the education received at or after compulsory school age.

293 Now repealed and replaced by Article 10 of Regulation (EU) No 492/2011.

294 *Alarape and another (Article 12, EC Reg 1612/68) Nigeria* [2011] UKUT 413 (IAC) which was the subject of a reference to the ECJ, see *Alarape and Tijani v Secretary of State for the Home Department and AIRE Centre*, C-529/11.

295 *Depesme, Kerrou, Kauffmann and Lefort v Ministre de l'Enseignement superieur et de la Recherche*, Cases C-401/15 to C-403/15.

partner of that worker, where that worker supports the child in question.[296]

3.113 The Court of Appeal has held that Article 12 of Regulation (EEC) No 1612/68[297] does not provide a qualifying right for permanent residence under Article 16 of the Directive,[298] which is in conflict with the decision of the ECJ in *Lassal*,[299] where it was held that continuous periods of five years' residence completed before the Directive came into force on 30 April 2006, in accordance with earlier legislation, had to be taken into account for the purposes of the acquisition of the right of permanent residence.

3.114 In *Alarape*,[300] however, the CJEU held that the primary carer's right to reside under what was then Article 12 continued even after the child reached the age of 18, if that child remains in need of the presence and care of that parent in order to be able to continue and to complete his or her education, which it is for the referring court to assess, taking into account all the circumstances of the case. It was also held that periods of residence completed solely on the basis of Article 12, could not be counted for the purpose of acquiring permanent residence.

3.115 In *Ahmed*,[301] the CJEU held that a third country national mother could not rely on Article 12, where she was not married to the EU worker, they were merely cohabiting and the child was not the EU worker's biological child, because the daughter could not be regarded as the child of the spouse of a migrant worker or former migrant worker.

296 *Depesme* at [64] and [65], which concerned the meaning of child of a frontier worker under TFEU Article 45 and Regulation (EU) No 492/2011 Article 7(2). A 'frontier worker' is a worker or self-employed person who, after three years of continuous employment and residence in the host member state, works in an employed or self-employed capacity in another member state, while retaining his or her place of residence in the host member state, to which he or she returns, as a rule, each day or at least once a week.

297 Now repealed and replaced by Article 10 of Regulation (EU) No 492/2011.

298 *Okafor and others v Secretary of State for the Home Department* [2011] EWCA Civ 499, [2011] 1 WLR 3071. This was reflected in the EEA Regs 2006 reg 15(1A) inserted by Immigration (European Economic Area) (Amendment) Regulations 2012 SI No 1547 Sch 1 para 8(a), with effect from 16 July 2012. This is now contained in the EEA Regs 2016 reg 15(2).

299 *Secretary of State for Work and Pensions v Lassal and Child Poverty Action Group (intervener)*, Case C-162/09, [2011] 1 CMLR 31, CJEU.

300 *Alarape and Tijani v Secretary of State for the Home Department and AIRE Centre*, Case C-529/11.

301 *ONAFTS v Ahmed*, Case C-45/12.

3.116 In *NA*,[302] the CJEU held that the right under Article 12 of Regulation (EEC) No 1612/68 is a right both to commence or continue education in the host member state and, as a consequence, confers a right of residence. Whether the parent, the former migrant worker, did or did not reside in the host member state on the date when that child began to attend school, is of no relevance.[303]

British citizens and their families[304]

3.117 In *McCarthy*,[305] the applicant had both British and Irish nationality but was born and had always lived in England. She married a Jamaican national and argued that he had a right to reside in the UK as her spouse. The CJEU held that an EU citizen cannot have a right to reside in circumstances where he or she has never exercised a right of free movement, and where he or she has always resided in a member state of which he or she is a national, even though he or she is also a national of another member state, provided that the circumstances do not include the application of measures by a member state which would deprive him or her of the genuine enjoyment of the substance of the rights conferred by virtue of his or her status as an EU citizen nor would impede the exercise of her or his right of free movement and residence within the territory of the member states.

3.118 In *Zambrano*,[306] the CJEU held that Article 20 of the TFEU is to be interpreted as precluding a member state from refusing a third country national upon whom his or her minor children, who are EU citizens, are dependent, a right of residence in the member state of

302 *Secretary of State for the Home Department v NA (Pakistan)*, Case C-115/15, [2017] QB 109, CJEU.

303 *Secretary of State for the Home Department v NA* at [63].

304 The Immigration (European Economic Area) (Amendment) (No 2) Regulations 2012 SI No 2560 amended the EEA Regs 2006 by inserting a new reg 15A(4A) which recognised a derivative right to reside for a person who is the primary carer of a British citizen, where the relevant British citizen is residing in the UK and would be unable to reside in the UK or in another EEA state if the person were refused a right of residence. The Eligibility (Amendment) Regs 2012 have amended the Eligibility Regs 2006 with effect from 8 November 2012 so that such a person is ineligible for an allocation of housing and for homelessness assistance. In *Pryce v Southwark LBC* [2013] EWCA Civ 1572, [2013] HLR 10, the Court of Appeal held, on a concession made by the local authority and the government, that such a person has a right to reside and, at least in respect of applications made before 8 November 2012, is eligible for homelessness assistance.

305 *McCarthy v Secretary of State for the Home Department*, Case C-434/09.

306 *Zambrano v Office national de l'emploi (ONEm)*, Case C-34/09, [2012] QB 265.

residence and nationality of those children, insofar as such decisions deprive those children of the genuine enjoyment of the substance of the rights attaching to the status of an EU citizen. In that case, Mr Zambrano and his wife were Colombian citizens, but their children were Belgian citizens who had been born in and never moved from Belgium. *McCarthy* was distinguished on the basis that Mrs McCarthy was not obliged to leave the territory of the EU. The *Zambrano* decision has been considered by the Upper Tribunal in both benefits appeals[307] and immigration appeals.[308]

3.119 In *Dereci*,[309] the *Zambrano* principle was applied in a number of cases where there was no risk that the EU citizens concerned would be deprived of their means of subsistence.[310] It was held that EU law allows a member state to refuse to allow a third country national to reside in its territory, where that third country national wishes to reside with a member of his or her family who is a citizen of the host member state who has never exercised his or her right to freedom of movement. Such a refusal may not, however, cause the EU citizen to be denied the genuine enjoyment of the substance of the rights conferred by virtue of his or her status as a citizen of the EU. Whether this test is met is a matter for the referring court to verify.

3.120 These cases led to the Immigration (European Economic Area) (Amendment) (No 2) Regulations 2012 which amended the EEA Regs 2006 so as to recognise, in domestic law, a derivative right to reside for a person who is the primary carer of a British citizen who is residing in the UK, which citizen would be unable to reside in the UK or in another EEA state if the carer was refused a right of residence.

3.121 The Eligibility Regs 2006 were, however, amended[311] so as specifically to exclude such persons from eligibility under HA 1996 Parts 6 and 7. The changes came into force on 8 November 2012, but only applied to applications under Parts 6 and 7 made on or after that date. In Wales, the equivalent changes were not made until the coming into force of the Eligibility (Wales) Regs 2014 on 31 October 2014.

307 For example, *Secretary of State for Work and Pensions v RR (IS)* [2011] UKUT 451 (AAC), though the tribunal has now set aside this determination so it is no longer good law.

308 For example, *Sanade and others v Secretary of State for the Home Department* [2012] UKUT 48 (IAC).

309 *Dereci and others v Bundesministerium fur Inneres*, Case C-256/11.

310 *Dereci*, at para [32].

311 By operation of Eligibility (Amendment) Regs 2012 with effect from 8 November 2012.

3.122 The *Zambrano* principle has been applied by the CJEU in *Iida*,[312] *O and S*[313] and *Ymeraga*,[314] In *CS*,[315] however, the CJEU held that a decision to expel a third country national who was the sole carer of minors who were citizens of the EU could be consistent with EU law where it was founded on the existence of a genuine, present and sufficiently serious threat to the requirements of public policy or of public security, provided account was taken of fundamental rights, in particular the right to respect for private and family life.

3.123 In *Pryce*,[316] based on concessions made by the local authority and the secretary of state, the Court of Appeal held that an applicant with a *Zambrano* right to reside was not subject to immigration control and was therefore eligible for homelessness assistance. The amended eligibility regulations did not apply because of the date of the application, and the court therefore did not consider their lawfulness.

3.124 In *Harrison*,[317] the Court of Appeal held that the *Zambrano* principle does not extend to cover anything short of a situation where the EU citizen is forced to leave the territory of the EU;[318] the fact that the right to family life is adversely affected, or that the presence of the non EU national is desirable for economic reasons, will not of themselves constitute factors capable of triggering the *Zambrano* principle.

3.125 In *Ahmed*,[319] the Upper Tribunal held that *Zambrano* only arises where a refusal decision would lead to an EU citizen child having to leave the EU, and only applies in exceptional circumstances.[320] *Zambrano* does, however, potentially apply even where the children are not citizens of the host member state but are nevertheless, EU citizens.[321]

312 *Iida v Stadt Ulm*, Case C-40/11, [2013] Fam 203, CJEU.

313 *O and S v Maahanmuuttovirasto*, Cases C-356/11 and C-357/11, [2013] CMLR 33, CJEU.

314 *Ymeraga and others v Ministre du Travail, de l'emploi et de l'immigration*, Case C-87/12.

315 *Secretary of State for the Home Department v Rendon Marin*, Case C-165/14; *Secretary of State for the Home Department v CS*, Case C-304/14, [2017] QB 558, CJEU. See also *Robinson v Secretary of State for the Home Department* [2018] EWCA Civ 85, summarising and applying *CS*.

316 *Pryce v Southwark LBC* [2013] EWCA Civ 1572, [2013] HLR 10.

317 *Harrison (Jamaica) and AB (Morocco) v Secretary of State for the Home Department* [2012] EWCA Civ 1736, [2013] 2 CMLR 23.

318 *Harrison* at [63].

319 *Ahmed v Secretary of State for the Home Department* [2013] UKUT 89 (IAC).

320 *Ahmed* at [67].

321 *Ahmed* at [68].

3.126 In a case where the child had a parent who was a national of the host member state, the CJEU held[322] that the fact that the EU national parent may be able to look after the child does not necessarily mean that the child would not be compelled to leave the EU if the non-EU parent could not remain there. The ability and willingness of the EU parent is a relevant factor, but an assessment of all of the child's circumstances must be carried out, taking into account Articles 7 and 24(2) of the Charter of Fundamental Rights of the EU. This requires consideration of the best interests of the child, all the specific circumstances, including age and physical and emotional development, extent of emotional ties to both parents and the risks which separation from the third country parent might entail for the child's equilibrium.[323]

3.127 In *Hines*,[324] the Court of Appeal held that where a *Zambrano* carer has applied for homelessness assistance, the authority must consider the welfare of the British citizen child and the extent to which the quality or standard of his life will be impaired if the non-EU citizen is required to leave. This is for the purpose of answering the question whether the child would, as a matter of practicality, be unable to remain in the UK. This requires a consideration, among other things, of the impact which the removal of the primary carer would have on the child, and the child's available alternative care.[325]

3.128 In *R (HC)*,[326] the Supreme Court considered that the *Zambrano* right is exceptional; it only arises if the child would have to leave the EU if the right was not granted to the child's carer; the right is not concerned with the desirability of keeping a family together on economic or other grounds but is merely a right to reside in the EU not a right to a particular quality of life or to any particular standard of living.[327] It was held that the exclusion of *Zambrano* carers from homelessness assistance, allocations and most forms of welfare benefits, was not contrary to Article 21 of the EU Charter of Fundamental Rights because the Charter had no application because of Article 51. Nor was the exclusion a breach of Article 14 of the

322 *Chavez-Vilchez and others v Raad van Bestuur van de Sociale Verzekeringsbank and others*, Case C-133/15.

323 See [72].

324 *Hines v Lambeth LBC* [2014] EWCA Civ 660, [2014] HLR 32.

325 *Hines* at [6], [23].

326 *R (HC) v Secretary of State for Work and Pensions* [2017] UKSC 73, [2018] HLR 6.

327 See [11], [15].

European Convention on Human Rights (ECHR) because its purpose was within the wide margin of discretion allowed to national governments in this field.[328]

3.129 In *Lounes*,[329] the Grand Chamber of the CJEU again considered the position of British citizens under EU law. Mr Lounes had married a Spanish national who had become a British citizen after exercising a right to reside in the UK. This distinguished his case from that of *McCarthy*[330] who had dual nationality but had never exercised a right of free movement.[331] It was held that Mr Lounes had no right under the Directive[332] but did have a derivative right to reside under Article 21(1) of the TFEU:[333] it would be contrary to the underlying logic of gradual integration that informs that article to hold that such citizens, who have acquired rights under that provision as a result of having exercised their freedom of movement, must forego those rights because they have sought, by becoming naturalised in that member state, to become more deeply integrated in the society of that state.[334]

Habitual residence

3.130 The test of habitual residence applies to all persons from abroad who are not subject to immigration control and are returning to the UK. This can therefore include British citizens.

3.131 Two basic requirements need to be fulfilled to establish habitual residence. The first is that an appreciable period of time must elapse before a person can be considered habitually resident. The second is that the person concerned must have a settled intention to reside in the UK.[335]

3.132 Whether a person is habitually resident is a question of fact to be decided by reference to all the circumstances of the particular case.[336] The requirement for an appreciable period of time is not

328 See [32].
329 *Lounes v Secretary of State for the Home Department*, Case C 165/16.
330 Para 3.118.
331 See [23].
332 See [37].
333 See [58].
334 See [58], [62], [63].
335 *R (Paul-Coker) v Southwark LBC* [2006] EWHC 497 (Admin), [2006] HLR 32 at [19]–[28].
336 *Re J* [1990] 2 AC 562, HL per Lord Brandon at 578F–G.

for a fixed period and may be short.[337] A month can be an appreciable period of time.[338] Where the person concerned is not coming to the UK for the first time, but resuming a previous habitual residence, which frequently occurs with British citizens, no appreciable period of time is required.[339] In the context of a benefits appeal, it has been held that, in the general run of cases, the period required to establish habitual residence will lie between one and three months.[340]

3.133 The second requirement for habitual residence is settled intention. For this, there must be a degree of settled purpose; what is necessary is that the purpose of living where one does has a sufficient degree of continuity to be properly described as settled.[341]

3.134 The English Code of Guidance states that if an applicant who was previously habitually resident in the UK is returning after a period spent abroad, and it can be established that he or she is returning to resume his or her former period of habitual residence, he or she will be immediately habitually resident.[342] The English Code recommends that applicants who have been resident continuously for a two-year period[343] prior to their housing application will be habitually resident but enquiries will need to be conducted where an applicant has less than two years' continuous residence.[344]

3.135 A useful definition of habitual residence is also to be found in EU law, which focuses on where the centre of interest of the person concerned is to be found, based on an overall assessment of all available information relating to relevant facts, which may include, as appropriate:

a) the duration and continuity of presence; and
b) the person's situation, including the nature and the specific characteristics of any activity pursued; his or her family status and ties; the exercise of any non-remunerated activity; in the case of a student, the source of his or her income; his or her housing

337 *Nessa v Chief Adjudication Officer* [1998] 2 All ER 728 per Lord Slynn at 682–683.
338 *Re S* [1998] AC 750 at 763A; *Re F* [1994] FLR 548 at 555.
339 *Lewis v Lewis* [1956] 1 WLR 200; *Swaddling v Adjudication Officer*, Case C-90/97, [1999] All ER (EC) 217.
340 CIS/4474/2003.
341 *Shah v Barnet LBC* [1983] 2 AC 309, HL, at 344D.
342 English Code of Guidance annex 1 para 7; Welsh Code of Guidance annex 6 para 7.
343 A period of about six months appears to be applied more regularly in practice.
344 English Code of Guidance para 7.19; Welsh Code of Guidance annex 6 para 1.

situation and in particular how permanent it is; and the member state in which the person is deemed to reside for taxation purposes.[345]

Provision of information

3.136 If there are doubts about an applicant's immigration status, an authority can contact the Home Office to obtain relevant information. When a request is made, in England HA 1996 s187 and in Wales H(W)A 2014 Sch 2 para 3, place a duty on the secretary of state to provide the authority with such information as it may require to enable it to determine whether a person is eligible for assistance in England under HA 1996 Part 7 and in Wales under H(W)A 2014 Part 2, respectively.

3.137 The English Code of Guidance no longer explains how to contact the relevant immigration authorities. By contrast, the Welsh Code explains that contact should be made with the Home Office's UK Visa and Immigration Centre (UKVI).[346] Enquiries are dealt with by the Evidence and Enquiries Unit (EEU).

3.138 The EEU's Local Authorities' Team will only assist once the authority has registered. This requires:

a) the name of the enquiring housing authority on headed paper;
b) the job title/status of the officer registering on behalf of the local housing authority; and
c) the names of officers, and their job titles, who will be making the enquiries.

3.139 Once registered, enquiries can be made by letter or fax, or by email,[347] but replies will be returned by post. If the authority makes a written request, the secretary of state must confirm the information in writing.[348] The secretary of state is under a duty to update an authority in respect of any change in information that has been provided. Such a correction must be in writing, detail the change, the date on

345 Regulation (EC) No 987/2009 Article 11, but note that this is in the context of eligibility for social security and therefore not directly applicable to housing assistance.

346 See annex 5 of the Welsh Code. UKVI can be found by following the links on www.gov.uk.

347 In non-asylum cases, the email address is EvidenceandEnquiry@homeoffice.gsi.gov.uk.; Welsh Code of Guidance annex 5 para 2.

348 In England, HA 1996 s187(2); in Wales, H(W)A 2014 Sch 2 para 3(2).

which the previous information became inaccurate and the reason why the information changed.[349]

Eligibility – homelessness: Housing Act 1996 Part 7 and Housing (Wales) Act 2014 Part 2

Introduction

Applicants

3.140 In England under HA 1996 Part 7 and in Wales under H(W)A 2014 Part 2, eligibility must be determined whenever an authority has reason to believe that an applicant may be homeless or threatened with homelessness.[350] The date for establishing whether an applicant is eligible is the date of the decision and not the date of application.[351] Where there is a review, it is the date of the review decision that is key.[352]

3.141 While an authority is entitled to reach its own decision as to an applicant's immigration status, any such decision is only for housing purposes and will be subject to any contrary decision by the immigration authorities.[353] An authority is entitled to take an immigration decision of the Home Office at face value and is not required to carry out its own further investigations to determine eligibility.[354]

3.142 Where a full housing duty has been accepted in England under HA 1996 s193(2),[355] or in Wales under H(W)A 2014 s66, s68, s73 or s75, an authority may revisit the issue of eligibility and will cease to be subject to the duty if an applicant ceases to be eligible.[356]

349 In England, HA 1996 s187(3); in Wales, H(W)A 2014 Sch 2 para 3(3).

350 In England, HA 1996 s184(1)(a); in Wales, H(W)A 2014 s62(4).

351 *R v Southwark LBC ex p Bediako* (1997) 30 HLR 22, QBD.

352 *Mohamed v Hammersmith and Fulham LBC* [2001] UKHL 57, [2002] 1 AC 547, [2002] HLR 7.

353 *R v Westminster City Council ex p Castelli and Tristan-Garcia* (1996) 28 HLR 617, CA; *Tower Hamlets LBC v Secretary of State for the Environment* [1993] QB 632, (1993) 25 HLR 524, CA.

354 *R (Burns) v Southwark LBC* [2004] EWHC 1901 (Admin), [2004] NPC 127.

355 See paras 10.118–10.204.

356 In England, HA 1996 s193(6)(a); in Wales, H(W)A 2014 s79(2).

Other members of the household

3.143 In England, HA 1996 s185(4), and in Wales, H(W)A 2014 Sch 2 para 1(5), require authorities also to consider the eligibility of household members.

3.144 The section formerly required[357] authorities to disregard ineligible household members[358] when determining whether an eligible applicant was homeless or had a priority need. The provision was, however, declared incompatible with Article 14 (prohibition of discrimination) when read with Article 8 (right to respect for one's private and family life) of the ECHR, to the extent that it required a dependent child or pregnant spouse of a British citizen, habitually resident in the UK but subject to immigration control, to be disregarded when determining whether the British citizen had a priority need for accommodation.[359]

3.145 The section was accordingly amended[360] so that it now[361] applies only to eligible applicants who are themselves subject to immigration control (except for EEA and Swiss nationals) – for example, those granted refugee status, indefinite leave to remain or humanitarian protection.[362] In Wales, the same approach has been followed.[363] When considering an application from such an applicant, authorities must continue to disregard any dependants or other household members who are ineligible for assistance for any reason, for the purpose of deciding whether the applicant is homeless or has a priority need[364] but, otherwise (ie, when the applicant is not himself or

357 In respect of all applications for accommodation or assistance in obtaining accommodation, within the meaning of HA 1996 s183, made before 2 March 2009.

358 For example, in *Ehiabor v Kensington and Chelsea RLBC* [2008] EWCA Civ 1074, the applicant could not rely on the dependent child to establish a priority need because the child, although born in the UK, was not a British citizen and therefore required leave to remain under IA 1971 s1(2) and was subject to immigration control. See also *Ismail v Newham LBC* [2018] EWCA Civ 665 at footnote 14.

359 *R (Morris) v Westminster City Council (No 3)* [2005] EWCA Civ 1184, [2006] 1 WLR 505, [2006] HLR 8.

360 By operation of the Housing and Regeneration Act 2008 s314 and Sch 15 Part 1.

361 In respect of all applications for accommodation or assistance in obtaining accommodation, within the meaning of HA 1996 s183, made on or after 2 March 2009.

362 See paras 3.154–3.176.

363 H(W)A 2014 Sch 2 para 1(6).

364 See the letter from the Department for Communities and Local Government (DCLG) to Chief Housing Officers dated 16 February 2009 and the accompanying guidance note.

herself a person subject to immigration control[365]), they are to be taken into account.

3.146 The Court of Appeal granted permission for a challenge to the lawfulness of the restricted cases regime but the issue was not pursued in the substantive appeal because the appeal did not in fact involve a restricted case.[366]

3.147 It follows that applicants who are not subject to immigration control, plus EEA and Swiss nationals, will now be able to rely on ineligible household members to qualify as homeless or in priority need, and to confer an entitlement to be secured suitable accommodation in England under HA 1996 s193(2) and in Wales a duty under H(W)A 2014 s66, s68, s73 or s75. Typically, ineligible household members who could confer priority need in this way are likely to be dependent children and pregnant women who have been granted leave with a condition of no recourse to public funds.[367]

3.148 This does not, however, give such applicants the same rights as others. An application pursuant to which the authority would not be satisfied that the applicant had a priority need but for what is termed a 'restricted person' is called a 'restricted case'.[368]

3.149 A restricted person is a person who is ineligible and subject to immigration control,[369] who either does not have leave to enter or remain in the UK[370] or who has leave subject to a condition of no recourse to public funds.[371] In a restricted case, in both England and Wales, a local housing authority must, so far as reasonably practicable, bring its duty to an end by securing a private rented sector offer.[372]

3.150 The discharge provisions governing restricted cases are considered in chapter 10 below,[373] both before and after the commencement of the LA 2011.

365 See paras 3.15–3.139.

366 *Lekpo-Bozua v Hackney LBC* [2010] EWCA Civ 909, [2010] HLR 46.

367 For the purposes of UK immigration law, the term 'public funds' is defined in Immigration Rules (HC 395) para 6 as including housing under HA 1996 Part 6 or Part 7 and HA 1985 Part 2. The Immigration Rules have not yet been updated to reflect the position under the H(W)A 2014 Part 2, but there seems little doubt that the phrase will be interpreted the same way.

368 In England, HA 1996 s193(3B); in Wales, H(W)A 2014 s76(5).

369 See paras 3.14 and 3.154–3.176.

370 See paras 3.164–3.166.

371 In England, HA 1996 s184(7); in Wales, H(W)A 2014 s63(5).

372 In England, HA 1996 s193(7AD); in Wales, H(W)A 2014 s76(5).

373 See paras 10.241–10.250.

3.151 It may be noted that the European Court of Human Rights[374] (ECtHR) did not follow *Morris*,[375] but has instead held that the immigration status of the child which resulted in his mother's differential treatment was reasonably and objectively justified by the need to allocate, as fairly as possible, the scarce stock of social housing available in the UK and the legitimacy, in so allocating, of having regard to the immigration status of those who are in need of housing.

3.152 Accordingly, there was no violation of Article 14, when taken in conjunction with Article 8 of the ECHR. The court expressly stated, however, that it was not ruling on the discriminatory effect of the amendments.[376]

Homelessness assistance

Generally

3.153 The division into persons subject and not subject to immigration control[377] applies in both England and Wales. Eligibility for both homelessness assistance and for an allocation is the same in England and Wales for all persons, whether or not subject to immigration control.[378]

Persons subject to immigration control

3.154 For a person subject to immigration control to be eligible for assistance, the person must fall within one of the prescribed classes.

Class A

3.155 Class A[379] is a person who is recorded by the secretary of state as a refugee within the definition set out in Article 1 of the Refugee Convention[380] and who has leave to enter or remain in the UK.

374 *Bah v UK*, App No 56328/07, 27 September 2011.

375 See para 3.144.

376 See para 3.144.

377 Above, paras 3.13–3.15.

378 Eligibility Regs 2006 regs 3, 4. 5 and 6 are the same as the Eligibility (Wales) Regs 2014 regs 3, 4 5 and 6. There were minor differences prior to 22 June 2017, ie prior to the amendments made by the Allocation of Housing and Homelessness (Eligibility) (Wales) (Amendment) Regulations 2017 SI No 698 (W 164), as described in the 10th edition of this book.

379 Eligibility Regs 2006 reg 5(1)(a) and Eligibility (Wales) Regs 2014 reg 5(1)(a).

380 The Convention relating to the Status of Refugees was adopted by a Conference of Plenipotentiaries of the United Nations (UN) on 28 July 1951 and entered into force on 21 April 1954.

3.156 A refugee is any person:

a) who, owing to a well-founded fear of being persecuted for reasons of race, religion, nationality, membership of a particular social group or political opinion, is outside the country of his or her nationality and is unable or, owing to such fear, unwilling to avail himself or herself of the protection of that country; or
b) who, not having a nationality and being outside the country of his or her former habitual residence as a result of such events, is unable or, owing to such fear, unwilling to return to it.

3.157 A decision whether or not to recognise a person as a refugee must be taken in accordance with Council Directive 2004/83/EC[381] which lays down minimum standards for the qualification and status of third-country nationals or stateless persons as refugees or as persons who otherwise need international protection and for the protection granted. Such a decision is made by the Home Office.

3.158 Recognition as a refugee almost inevitably leads to a grant of leave to remain. Prior to 30 August 2005, refugees were granted indefinite leave to remain (ILR). From that date, the grant is normally five years' leave to remain.

3.159 During the limited five-year period, refugee status can be reviewed and removed, eg, if there has been a change in circumstances in the refugee's country of origin, or he or she has returned there. There is normally no review at the end of the five-year period but one can be triggered if there is evidence of criminality or if an application for settlement is made after the initial period of leave has expired. At the end of the five-year period, the refugee qualifies for indefinite leave to remain in the UK.

3.160 From early 2002, application registration cards (ARCs) have been issued to asylum-seekers and their dependants during the asylum screening process. The ARC is a credit card sized form of identity. If an application for asylum is successful, the applicant will be given a letter by the Home Office which explains the applicant's position as a refugee and some of his or her rights in the UK.

3.161 A refugee's national passport is not stamped, because the refugee cannot use it without forfeiting his or her refugee status. Instead, the refugee will be issued with an Immigration Status Document (ISD). These were phased in during late 2003 and early 2004 and are an A4 sheet of paper, folded into four, confirming the immigration status of

381 Of 29 April 2004, which entered into force on 20 October 2004.

the holder. An ISD is also designed to hold a UK Residence Permit (UKRP).

3.162 Since late 2003, the ink stamps that used to be endorsed in passports and travel documents have been progressively replaced by UKRPs which are issued to those granted more than six months' leave to enter or remain in the UK. The UKRP takes the form of a credit card sized sticker or vignette. It was introduced in accordance with Regulation (EC) No 1030/2002 which requires EU countries which have opted in to this regulation to issue uniform format vignettes to all non-EEA nationals granted more than six months' leave to enter or remain. They are a security measure.

3.163 Refugees may apply for a refugee travel document, which looks like a passport. This is issued by the Home Office under the United Nations Convention relating to the Status of Refugees and the applicant's leave will be endorsed in the document on a UKRP vignette.

Class B

3.164 Class B[382] is a person who has exceptional leave to enter or remain in the UK granted outside the provisions of the Immigration Rules, whose leave to enter or remain is not subject to a condition requiring the person to maintain and accommodate himself or herself and any person who is dependent on him or her without recourse to public funds, which includes housing and assistance under HA 1985 Part 2 or HA 1996 Parts 6 and 7.[383]

3.165 Exceptional leave to enter or remain was abolished from 1 April 2003 so that only a dwindling group now has this status. Exceptional leave to remain (ELR) describes the leave granted to applicants who were not found to be refugees but whom the Home Office, for humanitarian or compassionate reasons, determined it would not be right to require to return to their country of origin.

3.166 Persons with ELR should have a letter from the Home Office, sometimes known as a 'grant letter', explaining that they have been granted ELR. They should also have their status stamped in their national passport. If they do not have a national passport, they will have been issued with an ISD containing a UKRP vignette. If such persons wish to travel but do not have a national passport, they may apply to the UKBA for a travel document known as a Certificate of Travel (COT).

382 Eligibility Regs 2006 reg 5(1)(b) and Eligibility (Wales) Regs 2014 reg 5(1)(b).
383 Immigration Rules (HC 395) para 6.

Class C

3.167 Class C[384] applies to a person who is habitually resident in the UK, the Channel Islands, the Isle of Man or the Republic of Ireland and whose leave to enter or remain in the UK is not subject to any limitation or condition, other than a person:

a) who has been given leave to enter or remain in the UK upon an undertaking given by his or her sponsor;
b) who has been resident in the UK, the Channel Islands, the Isle of Man or the Republic of Ireland for less than five years beginning on the date of entry or the date on which his or her sponsor gave the undertaking in respect of him or her, whichever date is the later; and
c) whose sponsor or, where there is more than one sponsor, at least one of whose sponsors, is still alive.

3.168 This class applies to any person with indefinite leave to remain in the UK unless that leave was granted on an undertaking by a sponsor less than five years ago and the sponsor is still alive.

3.169 Such a person should have a grant letter[385] from the Home Office, explaining that he or she has been granted indefinite leave to remain. He or she should have a stamp or UKRP in his or her national passport which shows that he or she has ILR. He or she may also have an ISD or a COT with a UKRP vignette which shows his or her status.

Class D

3.170 Class D applies to a person who has humanitarian protection granted under the Immigration Rules.[386]

3.171 From 1 April 2003, the Home Office abolished ELR and replaced it with humanitarian protection (HP) and discretionary leave (DL). HP is granted to someone who, if removed, would face a serious risk to life or person arising from capital punishment, unlawful killing or torture or inhuman or degrading treatment or punishment in the country of return.[387] Although not qualifying for refugee status, such persons would be at risk of treatment in violation of Articles 2 or 3 of

384 Eligibility Regs 2006 reg 5(1)(c) and Eligibility (Wales) Regs 2014 reg 5(1)(c).

385 See para 3.166.

386 Eligibility Regs 2006 reg 5(1)(d), substituted by Allocation of Housing and Homelessness (Miscellaneous Provisions) (England) Regulations 2006 SI No 2527 reg 2(1) and (3), from 9 October 2006 and Eligibility (Wales) Regs 2014 reg 5(1)(d).

387 Immigration Rules para 339C.

the ECHR (right to life; and prohibition of torture, and inhuman or degrading treatment or punishment, respectively). The requirements in relation to HP can now be found in the Immigration Rules.[388]

3.172 From 30 August 2005, if someone is granted HP, he or she is also granted leave to remain for five years, after which an application can be made for settlement, at which point there is an automatic review of whether there is a continuing protection need.

3.173 Those with HP should have a grant letter[389] from the Home Office, explaining that they have been granted HL. Their ISD or national passport will contain a UKRP vignette granting leave for a period of five years. If they do not have a national passport, they may apply for a travel document or COT which, if issued, will contain the UKRP vignette.

Class E

3.174 Class E[390] has been repealed in England, and, from 22 June 2017, in Wales.[391] It applied to certain asylum-seekers whose claims for asylum had been recorded by the secretary of state as having been made before 3 April 2000.

Class F

3.175 Class F[392] applies to a person who is habitually resident in the UK, the Channel Islands, the Isle of Man or the Republic of Ireland and who has limited leave to enter the UK as a relevant Afghan citizen under para 276BA(1) of the Immigration Rules.[393]

Class G

3.176 Class G[394] applies to a person who has limited leave to enter or remain in the UK on family or private life grounds under Article 8 of

388 Immigration Rules para 339C.
389 See para 3.166.
390 Eligibility Regs 2006 reg 5(1)(e).
391 Allocation of Housing and Homelessness (Eligibility) (Wales) (Amendment) Regulations 2017 SI No 698 (W 164) reg 2(4)(a), which repealed class E in Wales.
392 Added by the Allocation of Housing and Homelessness (Eligibility) (England) (Amendment) Regulations 2014 SI No 435 reg 2(5)(c) with effect from 31 March 2014.
393 Eligibility Regs 2006 reg 5(1)(f) and Eligibility (Wales) Regs 2014 reg 5(1)(f).
394 Eligibility Regs 2006 reg 5(1)(g) added by Eligibility (Amendment) Regs 2016 reg 2(4)(c) with effect from 30 October 2016 and Eligibility (Wales) Regs 2014 reg 5(1)(g) inserted by and by Allocation of Housing and Homelessness (Eligibility) (Wales) (Amendment) Regulations 2017 reg 2(4)(c) with effect from 22 June 2017.

the ECHR, which leave has been granted under para 276BE(1), para 276DG or Appendix FM of the Immigration Rules[395] and is not subject to a condition requiring him or her to maintain and accommodate himself or herself and his or her dependants without recourse to public funds.[396]

Persons not subject to immigration control

3.177 A person who is not subject to immigration control will be eligible if he or she a) has the right to reside and b) is habitually resident in the UK. Certain rights of residence are, however, excluded, and certain applicants are exempt from the habitual resident test.

The right to reside

3.178 Those with the right to reside have been identified above.[397] In *Mirga and Samin,*[398] the Supreme Court rejected a submission that it could only be applied subject to 'proportionality':[399] it would severely undermine the thrust and purpose of European Union (EU) free movement law if proportionality could be invoked to entitle a person to have the right of residence and social assistance in another member state, save perhaps in extreme circumstances; it would place a substantial burden on a host member state if it had to carry out a proportionality exercise in every case where the right of residence, or a right against discrimination, was invoked.[400]

3.179 The decision was consistent with its earlier decision in *Patmalniece,*[401] in which it was held that while the right to reside test is indirectly discriminatory, the discrimination is justified because its purpose is to protect the resources of the UK against 'benefit tourism'

395 This covers persons with leave to enter or remain in the UK on the basis of their family life with a person who is a British citizen, is settled in the UK, or is in the UK with limited leave as a refugee or person granted humanitarian protection, and reflects the requirements of Article 8 of the ECHR.

396 Eligibility Regs 2006 reg 5(1)(g) and Eligibility (Wales) Regs 2014 reg 5(1)(g).

397 Paras 3.20–3.62.

398 *Mirga v Secretary of State for Work and Pensions; Samin v Westminster City Council* [2016] UKSC 1, [2016] HLR 7.

399 Ie that there needed to be consideration of the proportionality of refusing each of the claimants social assistance given their personal circumstances and the limited burden that they would place on the UK if they were to be accorded the social assistance which they sought.

400 *Mirga* at [69].

401 *Patmalniece v Secretary of State for Work and Pensions* [2011] UKSC 11, [2011] 1 WLR 783.

by persons who are not economically or socially integrated; accordingly, the application of the test does not give rise to unlawful discrimination on the grounds of nationality.[402]

3.180 This approach is also consistent with the jurisprudence of the Court of Justice of the European Union (CJEU). In *Commission v UK*[403] the court agreed with the UK's submission that the legality of the claimant's residence in its territory is a substantive condition which economically inactive persons must meet in order to be eligible for the social benefits at issue; accordingly, the 'right to reside' test did not amount to unlawful discrimination.[404] In *Dano,*[405] the court held that member states are allowed to enact legislation which excludes economically inactive nationals of other member states from entitlement to state benefits if they do not comply with the conditions for residence set down in EU law.[406]

3.181 In *Alimanovic,*[407] the CJEU also held that a member state can enact legislation which excluded entitlement to certain special non-contributory cash benefits, even though those benefits are granted to nationals of the member state concerned who are in the same situation.[408]

3.182 In *Brey,*[409] however, it held that national legislation could not automatically bar the grant of a benefit to a national of another member state who is not economically active. Austria had refused Mr Brey a benefit on the ground that, although he had a certificate of residence, he did not in fact have a right to reside. The automatic bar was unlawful because it prevented the host member state from carrying out an overall assessment of the specific burden which granting that benefit would place on its social assistance system by reference to the personal circumstances of the person concerned.[410] There is accordingly a tension between *Mirga* and *Samin* on the one hand, and *Brey* on the other.

402 *Patmalniece* at [46], [48], [53], [61].

403 *European Commission v United Kingdom of Great Britain and Northern Ireland,* Case C-308/14.

404 *Commission v UK* at [72] and [86].

405 *Dano v Jobcenter Leipzig,* Case C-333/13, [2015] 1 WLR 2519, CJEU.

406 *Dano* at [60], [61].

407 *Jobcenter Berlin Neukolin v Alimanovic,* Case C-67/14, [2016] 2 WLR 208, CJEU.

408 *Alimanovic* at [46], [63], [64].

409 *Pensionsversicherungsanstalt v Brey,* Case C-140/12, [2014] 1 WLR 1080, CJEU.

410 *Brey* at [77], [80], [81].

3.183 A person who is not subject to immigration control with the right to reside is, however, ineligible if:[411]

a) he or she is not habitually resident in the UK, the Channel Islands, the Isle of Man or the Republic of Ireland;[412]
b) his or her only right to reside in the UK:
   i) is derived from his or her status as a jobseeker or as the family member of a jobseeker;[413] or
   ii) is an initial right to reside for a period not exceeding three months;[414] or
   iii) is a derivative right to reside to which he or she is entitled under EEA Regs 2006 reg 15A(1), but only in a case where the right exists under that regulation because the applicant satisfies the criteria in reg 15A(4A);[415] or
   iv) is derived from Article 20 of the TFEU in a case where the right to reside arises because a British citizen would otherwise be deprived of the genuine enjoyment of the substance of the rights attaching to the status of EU citizen;[416] or
c) his or her only right to reside in the Channel Islands, the Isle of Man or the Republic of Ireland:
   i) is a right equivalent to one of those mentioned in b) above which is derived from the TFEU;[417] or
   ii) is derived from Article 20 of the TFEU in a case where the right to reside
      A) in the Republic of Ireland arises because an Irish citizen, or
      B) in the Channel Islands or the Isle of Man arises because a British citizen,

411 Eligibility Regs 2006 reg 6(1), as amended by Eligibility (Amendment) Regs 2012, which inserted a new reg 6(1)(b)(iii) and (iv) and a new reg 6(1)(c), with effect from 8 November 2012, though the amendments do not have effect in relation to an application for an allocation of housing under HA 1996 Part 6 or for housing assistance under Part 7 which was made before that date. See para 3.12 above. Eligibility (Wales) Regs 2014 reg 6(1).

412 Eligibility Regs 2006 reg 6(1)(a); Eligibility (Wales) Regs 2014 reg 6(1)(a).

413 Eligibility Regs 2006 reg 6(1)(b)(i); Eligibility (Wales) Regs 2014 reg 6(1)(b)(i).

414 Eligibility Regs 2006 reg 6(1)(b)(ii); Eligibility (Wales) Regs 2014 reg 6(1)(b)(ii).

415 Eligibility Regs 2006 reg 6(1)(b)(iii); Eligibility (Wales) Regs 2014 reg 6(1)(b)(iii).

416 Eligibility Regs 2006 reg 6(1)(b)(iv); Eligibility (Wales) Regs 2014 reg 6(1)(b)(iv).

417 Eligibility Regs 2006 reg 6(1)(c)(i); Eligibility (Wales) Regs 2014 reg 6(1)(c)(i).

also entitled to reside there would otherwise be deprived of the genuine enjoyment of the substance of his or her rights as an EU citizen.[418]

Habitual residence

3.184 Habitual residence has been considered above.[419] A person who is not subject to immigration control is exempt from the test if he or she is:[420]

a) a worker;[421]
b) a self-employed person;[422]
c) a person who is a Croatian national who has a right to reside under the Croatian Accession Regulations;[423]
d) a person who is the family member of a person specified in a) to c) above;[424]
e) a person with a right to reside permanently in the UK by virtue of reg 15(1)(c), (d) or (e) of the EEA Regs 2006;[425]
f) (now repealed)[426] a person who left the territory of Montserrat after 1 November 1995 because of the effect on that territory of a volcanic eruption;
g) a person who is in the UK as a result of his/her deportation, expulsion or other removal by compulsion of law from another country to the UK.[427]

418 Eligibility Regs 2006 reg 6(1)(c)(ii); Eligibility (Wales) Regs 2014 reg 6(1)(c)(ii).
419 Paras 3.130–3.135.
420 Eligibility Regs 2006 reg 6(2); Eligibility (Wales) Regs 2014 reg 6(2).
421 Eligibility Regs 2006 reg 6(2)(a); Eligibility (Wales) Regs 2014 reg 6(2)(a).
422 Eligibility Regs 2006 reg 6(2)(b); Eligibility (Wales) Regs 2014 reg 6(2)(b).
423 Accession of Croatia (Immigration and Worker Authorisation) Regulations 2013 SI No 1460 reg 5; Eligibility Regs 2006 reg 6(2)(c); see paras 3.12–3.18. Eligibility (Wales) Regs 2014 reg 6(2)(c).
424 Eligibility Regs 2006 reg 6(2)(d); Eligibility (Wales) Regs 2014 reg 6(2)(d).
425 Eligibility Regs 2006 reg 6(2)(e); Eligibility (Wales) Regs 2014 reg 6(2)(e). This refers to workers or self-employed persons who have ceased activity, or their family members, who have, as a result, acquired acquiring permanent residence, or workers or self-employed persons who have passed away in circumstances which mean that their family members have acquired permanent residence (see para 3.53–3.62).
426 Revoked by the Allocation of Housing and Homelessness (Eligibility) (England) (Amendment) Regulations 2014 SI No 435 reg 2(6)(c), with effect from 31 March 2014.
427 Eligibility Regs 2006 reg 6(2)(g); Eligibility (Wales) Regs 2014 reg 6(2)(f).

Interim accommodation

Ineligibility

3.185 Notwithstanding prima facie eligibility for homelessness assistance as set out above,[428] the provisions of Nationality, Immigration and Asylum Act (NIAA) 2002 Sch 3 nonetheless disqualify certain classes of immigrant in England from two types of interim accommodation.

3.186 These exclusions do not apply to British citizens or to those who are under 18.[429] They also do not apply in Wales, because the two statutory provisions no longer have effect there, having been replaced by the H(W)A 2014.[430] The two types of interim accommodation excluded are:

a) HA 1996 s188(3) accommodation pending review;[431]
b) HA 1996 s204(4) accommodation pending appeal to the county court.[432]

3.187 These classes are also disqualified from assistance under other statutory powers which are considered below in chapter 13, which include:

a) Care Act 2014 Part 1;[433]
b) SSWB(W)A 2014 Part 4 and ss105–116;[434]
c) CA 1989 ss17, 23C, 23CA,[435] 24A and 24B;[436]
d) IAA 1999;[437]

428 Paras 3.140–3.184.
429 NIAA 2002 Sch 3 para 2(1)(a), (b).
430 NIAA 2002 Sch 3 para 1(1)(j) has not been amended to take account of the fact that the HA 1996 ss188(3) and 204(4) no longer apply in Wales, from the coming into force of the H(W)A 2014. Accordingly, certain homelessness applicants in Wales are still ineligible under HA 1996 ss188(3) and 204(4) even though those provisions have no effect in Wales. The five classes of ineligible applicant (in para 3.188) are the same as in England and are set out in NIAA 2002 Sch 3 paras 4–7A.
431 NIAA 2002 Sch 3 para 1(1)(j). See paras 10.49–10.57
432 NIAA 2002 Sch 3 para 1(1)(j). See paras 12.238–12.247.
433 NIAA 2002 Sch 3 para 1(1)(n): the Act applies only in England. See paras 13.9–13.39.
434 NIAA 2002 Sch 3 para 1(1)(o): the Act applies only in Wales.
435 Inserted by Children and Young Persons Act 2008 s22(6). See paras 13.57–3.107.
436 NIAA 2002 Sch 3 para 1(1)(g). See paras 13.57–3.107.
437 NIAA 2002 Sch 3 para 1(1)(l). See paras 13.40–13.56.

e) LA 2011 s1;[438] and
f) LGA 2000 s2.[439]

3.188 NIAA 2003 Sch 3 excludes the following five classes of persons from eligibility:

a) someone who has been recognised as a refugee by a European Economic Area (EEA) state other than the UK; this class also applies to a person who is the dependant of a person who is in the UK and who has such status;[440]
b) someone who has the nationality of an EEA state other than the UK, or who is the dependant of such a person;[441]
c) someone who was, but is no longer, an asylum-seeker and who is not co-operating with removal directions; it also applies to the dependant of such a person;[442]
d) someone who is in the UK in breach of NIAA 2002 s11 and who is not an asylum-seeker.[443] In summary, this means anyone who is in the UK in breach of immigration laws, ie, who does not have a right to reside under EU law, does not have leave to enter or remain, does not have a right of abode, etc;
e) someone who, although his or her asylum claim has been rejected, continues to be treated as an asylum-seeker and accommodated by the UKBA because he or she has dependent children,[444] but the Home Secretary has certified that he or she has, without reasonable excuse, not taken reasonable steps to leave the UK voluntarily or place himself or herself in a position in which he or she is able to leave the UK voluntarily. He or she must have received the certificate and have been given 14 days to act. This class also applies to his or her dependants.[445]

438 NIAA 2002 Sch 3 para 1(1)(ka): the Act applies only in England.
439 NIAA 2002 Sch 3 para 1(1)(k): this part of the Act applies only in Wales. See paras 13.114–13.120.
440 NIAA 2002 Sch 3 para 4.
441 NIAA 2002 Sch 3 para 5.
442 NIAA 2002 Sch 3 para 6.
443 NIAA 2002 Sch 3 para 7.
444 See paras 13.47–13.52.
445 NIAA 2002 Sch 3 para 7A, inserted by Asylum and Immigration (Treatment of Claimants, etc) Act 2004 s9 with effect from 1 December 2004, see Asylum and Immigration (Treatment of Claimants, etc) Act 2004 (Commencement No 2) Order 2004 SI No 2999.

Exceptions to ineligibility

3.189 A person who falls within one of these classes will not, however, be ineligible if the exercise of a power or the performance of a duty is necessary for the purpose of avoiding a breach of:

a) a person's rights under the ECHR;[446] or
b) a person's rights under the Community Treaties.[447]

3.190 The ECtHR has been sympathetic to arguments based on ECHR Article 8 (right to respect for one's private and family life).[448] It has held that the right to family life includes the right of a parent and child mutually to enjoy each other's company,[449] and has found a violation of that Article where the deportation of an applicant from the Netherlands would interrupt his intermittent contact with his daughter there.[450]

3.191 Conversely, the Court of Appeal has held that neither Article 8 nor Article 3[451] (prohibition of torture and inhuman or degrading treatment or punishment) imposes a duty on the UK to provide support to foreign nationals who are in a position freely to return to their country of origin.[452]

3.192 This proposition was also applied in a case where the claimant had an undetermined human rights claim.[453] It has been held that the making of a purported fresh claim either for asylum or under Article 3, by a claimant whose original claim had been rejected, did not always make it necessary for support to be provided in order to avoid a breach of the ECHR. In considering the issue, the authority had to have regard to all the relevant circumstances, including where appropriate the matters which were alleged to constitute a fresh claim. It was necessary to proceed on a case-by-case basis considering the facts of each case with care.[454]

446 See, generally, paras 12.114–12.128.
447 NIAA 2002 Sch 3 para 3.
448 See paras 12.123–12.125.
449 *Olsson v Sweden* (1989) 11 EHRR 259.
450 *Ciliz v Netherlands* [2000] 2 FLR 469.
451 See paras 12.114–12.128.
452 *R (K) v Lambeth LBC* [2003] EWCA Civ 1150, [2004] 1 WLR 272, [2004] HLR 15.
453 *R (Blackburn-Smith) v Lambeth LBC* [2007] EWHC 767 (Admin), (2007) 10 CCLR 352.
454 *R (AW) v Croydon LBC* [2005] EWHC 2950 (QB), (2005) 9 CCLR 252.

3.193 In *Clue*,[455] the Court of Appeal held that, when applying NIAA 2002 Sch 3, the authority should not consider the merits of an outstanding application for leave to remain unless satisfied that it was obviously hopeless or abusive. Otherwise, the authority should not refuse assistance if to do so would have the effect of requiring the person to leave the UK and thereby forfeiting the claim. In that case, the authority's decision to refuse assistance was unlawful because its assessment had not taken account of the application for leave to remain, nor had it stated that it was abusive or hopeless; moreover, the court was of the view that the application did have merits under ECHR Article 8.

3.194 Nevertheless, an authority does have the power to fund the costs of returning an applicant and his or her family to their country of origin.[456] It would, however, be unlawful to offer to fund the cost of return travel if this is not a viable option.[457] An authority must closely scrutinise any argument that a return to the country of origin would give rise to a breach of ECHR rights.[458] It is important to take into account the potential effect of removal on each relevant family member and the impact on other family members. An authority should also take into account any relevant Home Office policy that concerns the issue of whether or not the claimant and his or her family will be able to remain in the UK.[459]

3.195 *R (De Alemeida)* is an example of where the claimant's circumstances were so dire that not providing accommodation would have breached his rights under Article 3 of the ECHR:[460] the case concerned a Portuguese man who was terminally ill with HIV.

455 *R (Clue) v Birmingham City Council* [2010] EWCA Civ 460, [2011] 1 WLR 99.

456 *R (Grant) v Lambeth LBC* [2005] 1 WLR 1781, [2005] HLR 27, decided under LGA 2000 Part 1 (well-being) – which continues to apply in Wales – but it would seem likely that the same would apply to exercise of the general power of competence now available in England, under LA 2011 Part 1 Chapter 1.

457 *R (J) v Enfield LBC* [2002] EWHC 432 (Admin); likewise under LGA 2000, but see chapter 13, footnote 277 on the LA 2011.

458 *R (PB) v Haringey LBC and others* [2006] EWHC 2255 (Admin), [2007] HLR 13, (2007) 10 CCLR 99; this was likewise under LGA 2000, but see para 13.120 on the LA 2011.

459 *Clue*, above.

460 *R (De Almeida) v Royal Borough of Kensington and Chelsea* [2012] EWHC 1082 (Admin).

3.196 In *Paposhvili*,[461] the ECtHR qualified a previous decision, *N*,[462] in order to hold that Article 3 should be understood to prevent the removal of a seriously ill person in which substantial grounds have been shown for believing that he or she, although not at the end of his or her life, would face a real risk, on account of the absence of appropriate treatment in the receiving country or the lack of access to such treatment, of being exposed to a serious, rapid and irreversible decline in his or her state of health resulting in intense suffering; the benchmark is not, however, the health care system in the returning state and the focus should be on the individual's suffering instead. It is not decisive that the person is to be returned to a country which is a party to the ECHR (see also *MSS*[463] and *Tarakhel*[464] to the same effect as *Paposhvili*).

3.197 The exception governing EU Treaty rights[465] has also been interpreted narrowly. It appears not to apply for the benefit of work seekers[466] but probably does assist workers.[467]

Eligibility – allocations: Housing Act 1996 Part 6

Introduction

3.198 The operation of HA 1996 Part 6 is the subject of chapter 11. This section is accordingly only concerned with its application in the immigration context.

3.199 The constraints considered here, which are applicable to both England and Wales,[468] do not apply to a person who is already a secure or introductory tenant, or an assured tenant of housing accommodation allocated to him or her by a local housing authority.[469]

461 *Paposhvili v Belgium*, App No 41738/10, in particular at [181].
462 *N v UK*, App No 26565/05, (2008) 47 EHRR 39, ECtHR.
463 *MSS v Belgium and Greece*, App No 30696/09, (2011) 53 EHRR 2, ECtHR.
464 *Tarakhel v Switzerland*, App No 29217/12, (2015) 60 EHRR 28, ECtHR.
465 See para 3.189.
466 *R (Mohamed) v Harrow LBC* [2005] EWHC 3194 (Admin), [2006] HLR 18. As to work-seekers, see paras 3.28–3.31.
467 *R (Conde) v Lambeth LBC* [2005] EWHC 62 (Admin), [2005] HLR 29.
468 Eligibility (Wales) Regs 2014 regs 3 and 4 as amended by the Allocation of Housing and Homelessness (Eligibility) (Wales) (Amendment) Regulations 2017 with effect from 22 June 2017.
469 HA 1996 s159(5) as amended by Homelessness Act 2002 s13.

3.200 Under the legislation preceding the HA 1996, when immigration was not explicitly addressed in either homelessness or allocations law,[470] it was held that a tenancy granted to a person unlawfully in the UK was not void for that reason.[471] The same applies under Part 6: notwithstanding the prohibition in HA 1996 s167(8), it has been held that the grant of a tenancy, even though contrary to Part 6, is itself valid.[472]

3.201 The immigration status of members of the household of an applicant for an allocation under Part 6 is relevant, in particular when determining the size of the property to be allocated. It has long been said that Parliament cannot have intended to require authorities to house those who enter the country unlawfully.[473] Similarly, in *Akinbolu*,[474] it was held that it was proper to refuse to provide public sector housing to applicants who are illegal immigrants or overstayers.

3.202 In *Ariemuguvbe*,[475] the appellant lived in a three-bedroom property with her husband, her five adult children who had come to the UK from Nigeria but who had overstayed their visitor's visas and three grandchildren. She contended that she was entitled to additional points under the authority's allocation scheme to take account of the five adult children.[476]

3.203 The authority was held to be entitled to conclude that it was not appropriate to allocate a larger property to the appellant, because the five children were all independent adults, some having families of their own, who should have been able to make their own housing arrangements and also because they were subject to immigration control[477] in circumstances where providing accommodation for

470 See paras 3.6–3.8.
471 *Akinbolu v Hackney LBC* (1996) 29 HLR 259, CA.
472 See *Birmingham City Council v Qasim* [2009] EWCA Civ 1080, [2010] HLR 19.
473 *Tower Hamlets LBC v Secretary of State for the Environment* [1993] QB 632, per Sir Thomas Bingham at p632, (1993) 25 HLR 524, CA; see also *R v Hillingdon LBC ex p Streeting (No 2)* [1980] 1 WLR 1425, CA.
474 *Akinbolu v Hackney LBC* (1996) 29 HLR 259, CA, at 269.
475 *R (Ariemuguvbe) v Islington LBC* [2009] EWCA Civ 1308. The Court of Appeal overruled the decision in *R (Kimvono) v Tower Hamlets LBC* (2001) 33 HLR 78, QBD, in which neither *Tower Hamlets* nor *Akinbolu* had been cited and in which it had been held that the immigration status of the applicant's dependent child was irrelevant to the authority's duties under HA 1996 Part 6.
476 *Ariemuguvbe* at [2] and [3].
477 See paras 3.154–3.176.

them would amount to them having recourse to public funds in breach of their conditions of entry to the UK.[478]

3.204 Restricted cases are considered in chapter 10.[479] If the authority only owes a full housing duty to the applicant because of the restricted person, then, so far as reasonably practicable, it must bring the duty to an end by making a private accommodation offer;[480] where it is not reasonably practicable to do so, the authority may discharge its duty under the other provisions of HA 1996 s193 but should continue to try to bring the duty to an end with a private accommodation offer.[481] Consequently, if considering an allocation under Part 6, the authority will need to take particular care to ensure that it is in accordance with the priorities of its published allocation scheme.[482]

3.205 Authorities must consider eligibility at the point at which an applicant is considered for an allocation.[483] Authorities are, however, advised to consider applicants' eligibility both at the time of the initial application and again when considering making an allocation to them, especially where a substantial amount of time has elapsed since the original application.[484]

3.206 Eligibility for an allocation of housing depends on whether the applicant is a person subject to immigration control[485] or not subject to immigration control.[486]

Persons subject to immigration control

3.207 For a person subject to immigration control to be eligible, he or she must fall within one of the prescribed classes A–D, F or G described

478 *Ariemuguvbe* at [19].

479 Paras 10.241–10.250.

480 HA 1996 s193(7AD).

481 Department of Communities and Local Government (DCLG) Guidance Note, 16 February 2009, para 14.

482 See para 17 of the guidance note that accompanied the DCLG letter dated 16 February 2009.

483 HA 1996 s160A.

484 DCLG, *Allocation of accommodation: guidance for local housing authorities in England*, 2012, para 3.2; available at www.communities.gov.uk/publications/housing/allocationaccommodationguide.

485 Eligibility Regs 2006 reg 3.

486 Eligibility Regs 2006 reg 4.

above at paras 3.155–3.176.[487] For the purposes of an allocation, however, class F is known as class E,[488] and class G as class F.[489]

Persons not subject to immigration control

3.208 Eligibility for an allocation of housing on the part of persons who are not subject to immigration control,[490] is the same as eligibility under Part 7 of the HA 1996.[491]

487 Eligibility Regs 2006 reg 3(a)–(f) and the Eligibility (Wales) Regs 2014 reg 3(a)–(f). Reg 3(f) was inserted by the Allocation of Housing and Homelessness (Eligibility) (Wales) (Amendment) Regulations 2017 reg 2(3)(c) from 22 June 2017.

488 Eligibility Regs 2006 reg 3(e) as amended by the Eligibility (Amendment) Regs 2016 reg 2(3)(b)(i), with effect from 30 October 2016. Eligibility (Wales) Regs 2014 reg 3(e).

489 Eligibility Regs 2006 reg 3(f) inserted by the Eligibility (Amendment) Regs 2016 reg 2(3)(c) with effect from 30 October 2016. Eligibility (Wales) Regs 2014 reg 3(f).

490 Eligibility Regs 2006 reg 4, as amended by Eligibility (Amendment) Regs 2012, which inserted a new reg 4(1)(b)(iii) and (iv) and a new reg 4(1)(c), with effect from 8 November 2012, though the amendments do not have effect in relation to an application for an allocation of housing which was made before that date.

491 See paras 3.177–3.197.

CHAPTER 4

Homelessness

continued

Introduction

4.1 This chapter considers the statutory definitions of 'homelessness' and of being 'threatened with homelessness'.

4.2 'Homelessness' is defined by Housing Act (HA) 1996 s175 and Housing (Wales) Act (H(W)A) 2014 s55 as:

a) accommodation, which is
b) available for the applicant's occupation, to which
c) there are rights of occupation (subsection (1)),
d) entry to or use of which is not restricted (subsection (2)), and which
e) it is reasonable for the applicant to continue to occupy (subsection (3)).[1]

4.3 The same terms also apply to:

f) what is meant by being threatened with homelessness (subsection (4)).

Accommodation

Location

4.4 Under HA 1985, only accommodation in England, Wales or Scotland was to be taken into account. This had not been stated explicitly in the original legislation – the Housing (Homeless Persons) Act 1977 – but had been accepted, albeit obiter, in *Streeting*[2] and was expressly enacted in HA 1985.

4.5 As departure from accommodation abroad can, however, qualify as intentional homelessness,[3] this does not mean that accommodation abroad is irrelevant: HA 1996 s175(1) and H(W)A 2014 s55(1) now refer to accommodation in the UK 'or elsewhere'.[4]

1 See *Nipa Begum v Tower Hamlets LBC* (1999) 32 HLR 445, CA, for a discussion of the interaction of these different subsections.

2 *R v Hillingdon LBC ex p Streeting* [1980] 1 WLR 1425, CA.

3 See *de Falco, Silvestri v Crawley BC* [1980] QB 460, CA, and other cases considered at paras 6.138, 6.146–6.148.

4 See, eg, *Nipa Begum v Tower Hamlets LBC* (1999) 32 HLR 445, CA, where the accommodation in question was situated in Bangladesh.

Nature

4.6 The term 'accommodation' has proved one of the most controversial under the homelessness legislation, not so much as between applicant and authority, but between, on the one hand, the lower courts and the House of Lords, and, on the other, the House of Lords and Parliament.

Settled accommodation

4.7 Between 1977 and 1986, there was a growing tendency on the part of the courts – High Court and Court of Appeal – to equiparate a want of accommodation with accommodation of such poor quality that it could be quit without a finding of intentionality. In this context, a distinction was drawn for both purposes (and arguably for the purpose of defining the duties owed by authorities) between 'settled' and 'unsettled' accommodation.

4.8 Both applications of this approach were firmly rejected by the House of Lords, first in *Puhlhofer*,[5] and, later, in *Awua*.[6] The first of these led to further legislation in the Housing and Planning Act 1986 reversing the view of the House of Lords, and, to an extent, also under HA 1996 Part 7 itself.

4.9 In the second of these cases,[7] the House of Lords held that the only gloss on the word 'accommodation' which can properly be imported, other than pursuant to the statute itself (ie, availability and reasonableness to continue in occupation),[8] is that it must mean 'a place which can fairly be described as accommodation'.[9]

Non-qualifying accommodation

4.10 As an example of shelter which would have failed this test, Lord Brightman in *Puhlhofer* instanced Diogenes' tub.

4.11 In *Awua*, the modern equivalent was said to be the night shelter in *R v Waveney DC ex p Bowers*,[10] in which the applicant could have a

5 *R v Hillingdon LBC ex p Puhlhofer* [1986] AC 484, (1986) 18 HLR 158, HL.

6 *R v Brent LBC ex p Awua* [1996] AC 55, (1995) 27 HLR 453, HL.

7 *Awua*, above.

8 See paras 4.16–4.38 and 4.69–4.140.

9 *R v Brent LBC ex p Awua*, above, per Lord Hoffmann at 461.

10 (1982) *Times* 25 May, QBD. Not cross-appealed on this point – see further [1983] QB 238, (1983) 4 HLR 118, CA.

bed if one was available but where he could not remain by day so that he had to walk the streets.[11]

4.12 In *Sidhu*,[12] it was held that a women's refuge was not accommodation: a woman who left her violent partner and found temporary shelter in a refuge was still homeless while residing there.[13]

4.13 In *Ali* and *Moran*,[14] however, the House of Lords concluded that *Sidhu* could probably not survive the decisions in *Puhlhofer*[15] and *Awua*[16] as a theoretical proposition, although the effect of the decision was preserved by reference to HA 1996 ss175(3) and 177, ie it would not normally be reasonable to continue to occupy accommodation in a women's refuge.[17] (The House of Lords declined to comment on whether a prison cell or a hospital ward could amount to accommodation.)[18]

4.14 An applicant who occupies interim accommodation provided to him or her pending enquiries, review or appeal under HA 1996 s188 or s204(4) is nevertheless homeless for the purpose of section 175(1), because to find otherwise would create the absurd result that a homeless person who is temporarily accommodated would not be entitled to benefit from Part 7.[19]

11 *R v Brent LBC ex p Awua*, above, at 459.

12 *R v Ealing LBC ex p Sidhu* (1982) 2 HLR 45, QBD.

13 *Sidhu* followed a county court decision, *Williams v Cynon Valley Council*, January 1980 *LAG Bulletin* 16, CC. In addition to *Bowers* (see para 4.11 and footnote 10, above), other cases to consider the meaning of accommodation within the definition of homelessness before *Puhlhofer* and *Awua* were: *Parr v Wyre BC* (1982) 2 HLR 71, CA; *R v South Herefordshire DC ex p Miles* (1983) 17 HLR 82; *R v Preseli DC ex p Fisher* (1984) 17 HLR 147, QBD; and *R v Dinefwr BC ex p Marshall* (1984) 17 HLR 310, QBD.

14 *Birmingham City Council v Ali; Moran v Manchester City Council (Secretary of State for Communities and Local Government and another intervening)* [2009] UKHL 36, [2009] 1 WLR 1506 at [56].

15 *R v Hillingdon LBC ex p Puhlhofer* [1986] AC 484, (1986) 18 HLR 158, HL.

16 *R v Brent LBC ex p Awua* [1996] AC 55, (1995) 27 HLR 453, HL.

17 See para 4.72.

18 *Stewart v Lambeth LBC* [2002] HLR 747; *R (B) v Southwark LBC* [2004] HLR 40.

19 *R (Alam) v Tower Hamlets LBC* [2009] EWHC 44 (Admin), [2009] JHL D47. Approved by the House of Lords in *Ali* at [54]. See, to like effect, H(W)A 2014 ss68(1), 69(11) and 88(5). Likewise, where an authority has concluded that a person is owed the full housing duty under HA 1996 s193(2), but has not identified any specific property in which he could live, there is therefore no accommodation available for his occupation: *Johnston v Westminster City Council* [2015] EWCA Civ 554, [2015] HLR 35.

4.15 Reference may also be made to *Miles*,[20] in which it was held that accommodation within the definition of homelessness means 'habitable'. This decision was followed by the majority in the Court of Appeal in *Puhlhofer*,[21] which was upheld by the House of Lords without reference to *Miles*; nor was the case mentioned in *Awua*.

Accommodation available for occupation

Preconditions

4.16 The requirement that accommodation is 'available for occupation' requires consideration of a number of elements:

a) whether accommodation allows occupation 'together with' others;
b) practical accessibility; and
c) for whom the accommodation must be available.

4.17 The requirement of availability means that the accommodation must be available to occupy 'together with' other members of the applicant's household: HA 1996 s176 and H(W)A 2014 s56. This can be satisfied by a single unit of accommodation in which a family can live together, but may also be satisfied by two units of accommodation if they are so located that they enable the family to live 'together' in practical terms; it does not require shared living space.[22]

4.18 To be practically accessible and accordingly available to an applicant, it must be possible for the applicant physically to access the accommodation, a question which includes whether an applicant can afford to return to accommodation overseas which is otherwise available.[23]

4.19 Accommodation will not be available if the applicant is not legally entitled to live in the country in which the accommodation is situated.

20 *City of Gloucester v Miles* (1985) 17 HLR 292, CA.

21 See (1985) 17 HLR 588.

22 *Sharif v Camden LBC* [2013] UKSC 10, [2013] HLR 16.

23 See *Nipa Begum v Tower Hamlets LBC* (1999) 32 HLR 445, CA. Although the authority had failed to consider this issue in the case, the Court of Appeal refused to quash the decision since the applicant had not raised the issue, and the authority was accordingly not required to investigate the matter (see para 9.125).

Accommodation for whom?

4.20 By HA 1996 s176 and H(W)A 2014 s256, accommodation is only 'available' if it is available for the applicant together[24] with:

a) any person who usually resides with the applicant as a member of his or her family; or
b) any other person who might reasonably be expected to do so.

Immigration

4.21 HA 1996 s185(4) formerly[25] required local housing authorities in England and Wales to disregard household members (including dependent children) who were ineligible[26] for housing assistance when considering whether an eligible housing applicant was homeless. This provision was[27] amended so that it applies only to an eligible applicant who is himself or herself a person subject to immigration control[28] – for example, those granted refugee status,[29] indefinite leave to remain[30] or humanitarian protection.[31] Accordingly, when deciding whether an applicant who is a person subject to immigration control (excluding for this purpose a European Economic Area (EEA) or Swiss national)[32] and who is eligible for assistance, is homeless, a local authority must continue to disregard any dependants or other household members who are ineligible for assistance.

4.22 The effect is that HA 1996 s185(4) no longer applies to eligible[33] applicants who are not subject to immigration control[34] – for example, a British citizen,[35] a Commonwealth citizen with a right of abode in the UK[36] or an EEA or Swiss national with a right to reside in the

24 Cf para 4.17.
25 In respect of all applications for accommodation or assistance in obtaining accommodation within the meaning of HA 1996 s183, made before 2 March 2009.
26 See chapter 3.
27 By Housing and Regeneration Act 2008 s314 and Sch 15 Part 1, in respect of all applications for accommodation or assistance in obtaining accommodation within the meaning of HA 1996 s183, made on or after 2 March 2009.
28 See para 3.154.
29 See paras 3.155–3.163.
30 See paras 3.167–3.169.
31 See paras 3.170–3.173.
32 See para 3.154.
33 See chapter 3.
34 See paras 5.8–5.11.
35 See para 3.18.
36 See para 3.19.

UK.[37] This group of eligible applicants will be able to rely on ineligible household members, known as 'restricted persons', to establish homelessness.[38]

4.23 If, however, the authority can be satisfied that the applicant is homeless only by taking into account the restricted person, the application is known as a 'restricted case'.[39] In these circumstances, the authority must, so far as reasonably practical, bring any HA 1996 s193(2) duty to an end by arranging for an offer of an assured shorthold tenancy to be made to the applicant by a private landlord.[40] This is known as a 'private accommodation offer'.[41]

4.24 In Wales, the substantive position is the same, as the provisions of HA 1996 ss185 and 186 are deemed to apply to the H(W)A 2014.[42] It follows that, as in England, a duty owed to a restricted person must, so far as is reasonably practicable, be brought to an end by securing an offer of accommodation from a private sector landlord.[43]

Family

4.25 'Member of the family' is not defined. Both the English and Welsh Codes of Guidance say that the expression will 'include those with close blood or marital relationships and cohabiting partners'.[44]

4.26 Both Codes also suggest that 'any other person' (who normally resides with the applicant as a member of the family) might cover a companion for an elderly or disabled person, or children being fostered by the applicant or by a member of his or her family.[45]

4.27 The English and Welsh Codes conclude:

37 See paras 3.20 onwards.

38 HA 1996 s184(7): someone who is not eligible for assistance under Part 7, who is subject to immigration control and who either does not have leave to enter or remain in the UK or who has leave subject to a condition of no recourse to public funds.

39 HA 1996 s193(3B).

40 HA 1996 s193(7AD). See further paras 10.241–10.250.

41 HA 1996 s193(7AC). See para 10.244. From 9 November 2012, when the Localism Act (LA) 2011 s148 came into force in England, a new offer by an English authority has been known as a 'private rented sector offer': Localism Act 2011 (Commencement No 2 and Transitional Provisions) (England) Order 2012 SI No 2599 art 2.

42 H(W)A 2014 Sch 2 para 2.

43 H(W)A 2014 s76.

44 English Code of Guidance para 6.7; Welsh Code paras 8.6–8.8; the Welsh Code goes on to say that the expression will include 'same sex partners, adopted or foster children and legal guardianship'.

45 English Code of Guidance para 6.8; Welsh Code paras 8.6–8.8.

Persons who normally live with the applicant but who are unable to do so because there is no accommodation in which they can all live together should be included in the assessment.[46]

4.28 This approach echoes the decision of the House of Lords in *Islam*,[47] where the applicant lost his right to a shared room as a result of the arrival of his wife and four children from Bangladesh. A finding of intentionality was quashed by the House of Lords on the basis that what had been lost was not accommodation 'available for his occupation', meaning that of the applicant *and* his family.[48]

4.29 Accordingly, a family which has never enjoyed accommodation in which there were rights of occupation for all of its members will at all times have been homeless. For example, a couple without a home of their own, each still living with his and her parents, will be able to assert an effective right to assistance under Part 7 or Part 2 as soon as a priority need is acquired. An authority wishing to resist the claim cannot resort to intentional homelessness based on the pregnancy itself, as this is precluded by *Islam*.[49]

4.30 Note, however, that an unborn child will not be a person with whom the applicant would be expected to reside. Accordingly, the future housing needs of the unborn child need not be considered by the authority when determining homelessness,[50] save to the extent to which it had otherwise rendered the mother's accommodation unavailable in her own right.

4.31 That does not make the pregnancy irrelevant. In *Rouf*,[51] it was held that an authority could not jump to the conclusion that accommodation would continue to be available to an applicant with an increasing family. See also *Ali*,[52] in which the court found the proposition that a single, small room was 'available' for a large family (applicant, wife and five children) 'quite extraordinary'.

46 English Code of Guidance para 6.9; Welsh Code para 8.8.

47 *Re Islam* [1983] 1 AC 688, (1981) 1 HLR 107, HL.

48 The argument in the Court of Appeal that Mr Islam had made the accommodation unavailable by bringing his family over was dismissed as 'circular . . . because that lack is the very circumstance which section 16 [of the Housing (Homeless Persons) Act 1977, subsequently HA 1985 s75, now s176] and the Act are designed to relieve'.

49 In *R v Eastleigh BC ex p Beattie (No 1)* (1983) 10 HLR 134, QBD, the court rejected out of hand a suggestion that pregnancy causing accommodation to cease to be reasonable to occupy could amount to intentionality.

50 See *R v Newham LBC ex p Dada* (1995) 27 HLR 502, CA.

51 *R v Tower Hamlets LBC ex p Rouf* (1989) 21 HLR 294, QBD.

52 *R v Westminster City Council ex p Ali* (1983) 11 HLR 83, QBD.

4.32 In other cases, hopelessly inadequate accommodation has been held not to be accommodation which it was reasonable to continue to occupy.[53]

4.33 A member of the family who usually resides with the applicant need not also be shown to do so reasonably.[54] On the other hand, where children who were not reasonably to be expected to reside with the applicant came to live with him in a single room, he was (to that point) occupying accommodation that was available for him, so that he could be held intentionally homeless for allowing them to come and live with him (which made the accommodation unavailable).[55]

Others

4.34 The question of who is reasonably to be expected to reside with an applicant is a matter for the authority, challengeable on conventional grounds of public law,[56] rather than a question of fact which a court can decide for itself: see *Ly*.[57] Cases turn quite largely on their own facts.

4.35 In *Carr*,[58] it was held that the authority had erred in law in failing to consider whether the applicant's boyfriend – the father of her child – was a person with whom she might reasonably be expected to reside. The authority had wrongly reached its decision solely on the basis that they had not lived together at the applicant's last settled accommodation.

4.36 In *Okuneye*,[59] however, the fact that two people were intending or expecting to reside together did not mean that – when each departed from his and her separate accommodation – they were necessarily reasonably to be expected to reside together at that time. The authority was accordingly entitled to conclude that each had become homeless intentionally for ceasing to occupy available accommodation.

53 See paras 4.103–4.113.

54 Compare *R v Hillingdon Homeless Persons Panel ex p Islam* (1980) *Times*, February 10, QBD, not cross-appealed on the proposition, as it relates to priority need.

55 *Oxford City Council v Bull* [2011] EWCA Civ 609, [2011] HLR 35.

56 See chapter 12.

57 *R v Lambeth LBC ex p Ly* (1986) 19 HLR 51, QBD. Compare *R v Newham LBC ex p Khan and Hussain* (2001) 33 HLR 29, QBD, where a decision that a grandmother, her two daughters and their respective husbands and children did not usually reside together was quashed as *Wednesbury* unreasonable.

58 *R v Peterborough City Council ex p Carr* (1990) 22 HLR 207, CA.

59 *R v Barking and Dagenham LBC ex p Okuneye* (1995) 28 HLR 174, QBD.

4.37 In *Ryder*,[60] the authority approached the question of whether a carer could reasonably be expected to reside with a disabled applicant by reference to whether the applicant was eligible for Disability Living Allowance. As the test for such an allowance was more stringent – and different – from what is now HA 1996 s176 (H(W)A 2014 s56), the decision was quashed. Similarly, the authority in *Tonnicodi*[61] was wrong to apply the test whether the applicant needed a live-in carer rather than whether the carer was a person who might reasonably be expected to reside with the applicant.

4.38 In *Curtis*,[62] the applicant was occupying her former matrimonial home under a separation agreement which contained a cohabitation clause to the effect that if she cohabited or remarried the property would be sold. The applicant started to cohabit and her husband enforced the power of sale. The authority found the applicant to be homeless intentionally, a decision that was quashed because it had not considered availability in the statutory sense, ie whether, if it was reasonable for her and her cohabitant to live together, the property was available to both of them (which it was not).

Rights of occupation

4.39 It is only accommodation occupied under one of three categories of right which will preclude a finding of homelessness (HA 1996 s175(1); H(W)A 2014 s55(1)):

a) occupation under interest or order;
b) occupation under express or implied licence; or
c) occupation by enactment or restriction.

4.40 It has been held that accommodation in a prison does not fall within any of these rights of occupation, as the prisoner has no enforceable right to occupy the cell;[63] this question was, however, reserved by the House of Lords.[64]

60 *R v Southwark LBC ex p Ryder* (1996) 28 HLR 56, QBD.
61 *R v Hackney LBC ex p Tonnicodi* (1997) 30 HLR 916, QBD.
62 *R v Wimborne DC ex p Curtis* (1985) 18 HLR 79, QBD.
63 *R (B) v Southwark LBC* [2003] EWHC 1678 (Admin), [2004] HLR 3; see further para 4.132.
64 *Birmingham City Council v Ali; Moran v Manchester City Council (Secretary of State for Communities and Local Government and another intervening)* [2009] UKHL 36, [2009] 1 WLR 1506; see para 4.13.

Occupation under interest or order

4.41 The right of occupation may be by virtue of an 'interest' in the accommodation: this would seem to mean a legal or equitable interest.

4.42 Those with a legal interest will include both owner-occupiers and tenants, whether under long leases or on short, periodic tenancies, and whether under an initially agreed contractual period or under the contract as statutorily extended by HA 1985 and HA 1988 (secure tenants and assured tenants). If one of a pair of joint tenants unilaterally terminates the joint tenancy, regardless of the concurrence or knowledge of the other, the remaining joint tenant no longer has an interest in the property and therefore cannot be said to have a right of occupation as a tenant.[65]

4.43 Those with an equitable interest commonly include the spouse of an owner-occupier. Spouses and civil partners, whether of owner-occupiers or of tenants, may also be given a right to occupy under an 'order of the court', ie under family legislation.[66]

Occupation under express or implied licence

4.44 Where spouses or other partners are living together, and only one has a right of occupation (such as ownership or tenancy) the other is his or her licensee.[67] Lodgers will usually be licensees rather than tenants; flat-sharers may be only licensees rather than joint tenants; a child in the home of his or her parents will be a licensee rather than a tenant or sub-tenant,[68] except in the most exceptional circumstances.[69]

65 *Fletcher v Brent LBC* [2006] EWCA Civ 960, [2007] HLR 12; see further para 4.45.

66 See, in particular, Family Law Act 1996 Part 4. The powers can also be applied to cohabitants and former cohabitants.

67 *Hemans & Hemans v Windsor and Maidenhead BC* [2011] EWCA Civ 374, [2011] HLR 25.

68 On the distinction between tenant and licensee, see the decisions in *Street v Mountford* [1985] AC 809, (1985) 17 HLR 402, HL; and *AG Securities v Vaughan; Antoniades v Villiers* [1990] AC 417, (1988) 21 HLR 79, HL. See also English Code of Guidance paras 6.12–6.16 and Welsh Code paras 8.11–8.12 on applicants asked to leave accommodation by family or friends. See also Arden & Dymond, *Manual of housing law*, 10th edn, LAG, 2017, paras 1.22–1.58.

69 For example, where the house has been subdivided into two flats (self-contained or not), for one of which the parents are charging rent and there are no other criteria which lean against tenancy (such as sharing utilities).

4.45 Where the authority claims that an applicant has a licence to occupy accommodation, it must determine its precise nature. In *Fletcher*,[70] the applicant's wife terminated their joint tenancy by service of a notice to quit. The local authority nonetheless concluded that the applicant was not homeless. On appeal to the county court, the judge held that the applicant had some form of licence to occupy the property – the nature of which she decided that it was unnecessary for her to determine – and was therefore not homeless. The Court of Appeal, allowing a further appeal, remitted the case to the authority to determine whether a licence existed and, if so, on what terms.

Tied accommodation

4.46 Where the applicant's licence is as a service occupier and contingent on the contract of employment, there cannot be said to be a licence to occupy once the contract of employment has been terminated.

4.47 Even where the employer of a live-in housekeeper, having terminated the contract of employment, said that the applicant could return to occupy her room, the local authority was in error in concluding that she had a licence to occupy. The licence was dependent on a contract for employment which no longer existed.[71]

Occupation by enactment or restriction

4.48 The final category of 'right of occupation' is occupation as a residence by virtue of any enactment or rule of law giving the applicant the right to remain in occupation, or restricting the right of any other person to recover possession of it.

Actual occupation v right to occupy

4.49 This category predicates actual occupation, as distinct from a right to occupy, so that a person who walks out of accommodation occupied on this basis will be homeless, albeit at risk of a finding of intentionality.[72] In contrast, a person who walks out of a house in which he or she has an interest will, presuming it is available for his or her occupation,[73] not be homeless until such time as he or she divests

70 *Fletcher v Brent LBC* [2006] EWCA Civ 960, [2007] HLR 12.

71 See *R v Kensington and Chelsea RLBC ex p Minton* (1988) 20 HLR 648, QBD and *Norris v Checksfield* (1991) 23 HLR 425, CA.

72 But see further 'Reasonable to continue to occupy' at para 4.69 onwards.

73 See paras 4.16–4.38.

himself or herself of that interest, for example, by release or sale, at which point the question of intentionality may arise.

Protection from Eviction Act 1977

4.50 The definition closely follows the wording of Protection from Eviction Act (PEA) 1977 s1(1).

Rent Act protection

4.51 A tenant within the protection of the Rent Act (RA) 1977 will occupy by virtue of an interest until the determination of the tenancy; thereafter, the person is a statutory tenant. A statutory tenancy is not an interest in land.[74] It is, however, a right of occupation by virtue of an enactment or rule of law, as well as one which gives the tenant the right to remain in occupation and which restricts the right of another to recover possession.

Secure/assured protection

4.52 The same approach was not taken for secure and assured tenants under HAs 1985 and 1988. Rather, there is a restriction on the landlord's right to determine the tenancy itself save by order of the court. Accordingly, the tenancy continues and, as such, occupation is under that interest.

Tied accommodation

4.53 An agricultural worker in tied accommodation, enjoying the benefit of the Rent (Agriculture) Act (R(A)A) 1976,[75] will usually occupy by virtue of a licence before its determination, and thereafter in the same way as a Rent Act statutory tenant. Those whose rights were granted after commencement of HA 1988 Part 1 may have assured agricultural occupancies[76] which – as with assured tenancies[77] – can only be terminated by an order of the court. Those in tied accommodation who do not enjoy the benefit of R(A)A 1976 or HA 1988 derive some temporary benefits under PEA 1977.[78]

74 *Keeves v Dean* [1924] 1 KB 685, CA.
75 There are conditions which apply before the protection is available.
76 As last footnote.
77 See para 4.52.
78 See PEA 1977 s8(2) applying provisions of that Act to 'a person who, under the terms of his employment, had exclusive possession of any premises other than as a tenant'.

Former long leaseholders

4.54 Long leaseholders usually continue to occupy beyond what would otherwise contractually be the termination of their interests by virtue of a statutorily extended tenancy, which is thus still an interest. They will subsequently become either statutory tenants under RA 1977 or assured tenants under HA 1988.[79]

Other tenants and licensees

4.55 PEA 1977 s3 itself prohibits the eviction – otherwise than by court proceedings – of former unprotected tenants and licensees,[80] those who had licences granted on or after 28 November 1980 which qualify as restricted contracts within RA 1977 s19, as well as certain service occupiers. All these people will occupy either by virtue of an interest or a licence until determination, and subsequently by virtue of an enactment restricting the right of another to recover possession.[81]

Spouses, civil partners and cohabitants

4.56 Even where the applicant is not the tenant, Family Law Act 1996 Part 4[82] protects spouses, civil partners and some cohabitants (including those living together as civil partners) by giving them a right to remain in occupation, or restricting the right of another to recover possession.[83]

Non-qualifying persons

4.57 Those who are left outside the definition altogether are:

a) those who have been trespassers from the outset and remain so; and

79 Landlord and Tenant Act 1954 Part 1; Local Government and Housing Act 1989 Sch 10.

80 Other than excluded tenants and licensees: see PEA 1977 s3(2B). Note that, by judicial extension, temporary accommodation provided under a licence pursuant to what is now HA 1996 ss188(1), (3), 190(2), 200(1) and 204(4) is incapable of qualifying under PEA 1977 s3: see *R (ZH and CN) v Newham LBC and Lewisham LBC* [2014] UKSC 62, [2015] HLR 6. See also *Mohamed v Manek* (1995) 27 HLR 439, CA and *Desnousse v Newham LBC* [2006] EWCA Civ 547, [2006] HLR 38. It is, however, unclear whether this proposition applies (as it was said in *Manek* to apply) to both tenancies and licences so provided, or only to licences (a difference expressly raised and left open by the court in *Desnousse*).

81 PEA 1977 ss2, 3, as amended by HA 1980 s69(1) and HA 1988 s30.

82 As amended by the Civil Partnership Act 2004.

83 *Abdullah v Westminster City Council* [2011] EWCA Civ 1171, [2012] HLR 5.

b) those who have excluded tenancies and licences which have been brought to an end;[84] or who are otherwise excluded from PEA 1977.[85]

4.58 It follows that 'squatters' properly so-called, as distinct from those to whom a licence to occupy has been granted,[86] are statutorily homeless even though no possession order may yet have been made against them – for, even though they may have the benefit of a roof over their heads, they have no accommodation within any of the classes specified.

4.59 As noted above,[87] an applicant who occupies interim accommodation provided to him or her pending enquiries, review or appeal under HA 1996 s188 or s204(4) is nevertheless homeless for the purpose of section 175(1).

Timing

4.60 The right not to be evicted otherwise than by court proceedings in PEA 1977 s3 confers protection until execution of a possession order by the court bailiff in accordance with the relevant court rules.[88]

4.61 In *Sacupima*,[89] it was held that the same applied under the Civil Procedure Rules (CPR) and, therefore, under HA 1996 s175(1)(c).[90] Accordingly, an assured tenant[91] does not become homeless for the purposes of s175(1)(c) until the warrant for possession against him or her is executed.[92] Note, however, that from 9 November 2012 when Localism Act (LA) 2011 s149 came into force,[93] an applicant who makes a fresh application to an English authority within two years of a previous application which had resulted in the offer and acceptance

84 *R v Blankley* [1979] Crim LR 166 and see PEA 1977 s3(2B).

85 Cf footnote 80.

86 Ie a short-life occupation agreement, usually pending redevelopment.

87 Para 4.14.

88 *Hanniff v Robinson* [1993] QB 419, CA. The relevant county court rules are found in CPR Part 83.

89 *R v Newham LBC ex p Sacupima* (2001) 33 HLR 1, QBD. See also *R v Newham LBC ex p Khan* (2001) 33 HLR 29, QBD.

90 HA 1996 s230 defines 'enactment' as including subordinate legislation.

91 Entitled to remain in occupation under HA 1988 s5 until a court order is made. The same argument will apply to secure tenancies: see HA 1985 s82.

92 In these circumstances, however, the applicant will be threatened with homelessness: see para 4.141 onwards.

93 Localism Act 2011 (Commencement No 2 and Transitional Provisions) (England) Order 2012 SI No 2599 art 2.

of an assured shorthold tenancy,[94] in respect of which notice has been given under HA 1988 s21,[95] is entitled to be treated as homeless from the expiry of that notice, so that he or she need not await proceedings for eviction.[96] This does not apply where the application was made before – and the duty to secure accommodation was still in existence at – that date.[97]

Restriction on entry or use

Entry prevented

4.62 A person is also homeless if he or she 'cannot secure entry to' his or her accommodation.[98]

4.63 This provision is primarily intended to benefit the illegally evicted tenant or occupier, but covers anyone else who for some reason cannot immediately be restored to occupation of a home to which he or she has a legal entitlement – for example, because of occupation by squatters.[99]

4.64 This provision has not proved to be of as much practical use as was intended, because authorities have tended to consider that unless the applicant uses available legal remedies to re-enter, he or she will be considered intentionally homeless, albeit possibly provided with temporary assistance until an order from the court is obtained.

4.65 Authorities should, however, have no rigid policy to this effect:[100] there may be circumstances in which, even though legal redress exists, both the benefits to be gained from using it and the circumstances generally suggest that it would be inappropriate, for example, illegal eviction by a resident landlord who will shortly

94 See Arden & Dymond, *Manual of housing law*, 10th edn, LAG, 2017, para 1.248.

95 See Arden & Dymond, *Manual of housing law*, 10th edn, LAG, 2017, para 2.203.

96 HA 1996 s195A(2). This right only arises on one re-application: HA 1996 s195A(6).

97 Localism Act 2011 (Commencement No 2 and Transitional Provisions) (England) Order 2012 SI No 2599 art 3.

98 HA 1996 s175(2)(a); H(W)A 2014 s55(2)(a).

99 English Code of Guidance paras 6.20–6.21; Welsh Code para 8.16. It does not include where an applicant cannot travel to accommodation (which is otherwise available): *Nipa Begum v Tower Hamlets LBC* (1999) 32 HLR 445, CA.

100 See, eg, *British Oxygen Co Ltd v Minister of Technology* [1971] AC 610, HL; *Re Betts* [1983] 2 AC 613, 10 HLR 97, HL; *Attorney-General ex rel Tilley v Wandsworth LBC* [1981] 1 WLR 854, CA; *R v Warwickshire CC ex p Williams* [1995] COD 182, QBD; *R v North Yorkshire CC ex p Hargreaves* (1997) 96 LGR 39, QBD.

recover possession in any event, where tensions are such that it is impracticable for the tenant to remain in the property.[101]

Moveable structures

4.66 A person is also homeless if his or her accommodation consists of a moveable structure, vehicle or vessel designed or adapted for human habitation, and there is no place where the applicant is entitled or permitted both to place it and to reside in it – for example, a mobile home, caravan or house-boat.[102]

4.67 In *Roberts*,[103] travelling showmen were considered to be neither homeless nor threatened with homelessness while moving between fairgrounds during the fairground season, residing at each ground in caravans on a temporary basis. 'Reside' does not require permanence: it means 'live' or 'occupy'.

4.68 In *Smith v Wokingham DC*,[104] a county court held that a caravan parked on land belonging to a county council, without express permission but in which the applicant and his family had lived for two-and-a-half years, had been the subject of acquiescence sufficient to constitute permission for the purpose of what is now HA 1996 s175(2)(b).

Reasonable to continue to occupy

4.69 A person is homeless if his or her accommodation is such that it is not reasonable to continue to occupy it.[105] There is a relationship between reasonableness to continue to occupy and suitability of accommodation.[106] Therefore, case-law on one of these issues may be relevant to the other.[107]

101 This could in any event mean that it was not reasonable to continue to occupy the accommodation: see paras 4.69–4.140.

102 HA 1996 s175(2)(b); H(W)A 2014 s55(2)(b).

103 *R v Chiltern DC ex p Roberts et al* (1990) 23 HLR 387, QBD.

104 April 1980 *LAG Bulletin* 92, CC. See also *Higgs v Brighton and Hove City Council* [2003] EWCA Civ 895, [2004] HLR 2.

105 HA 1996 s175(3); H(W)A 2014 s55(3).

106 See para 4.71; see further paras 10.162–10.204.

107 *Harouki v Kensington and Chelsea RLBC* [2007] EWCA Civ 1000, [2008] HLR 16. This is also implicit in *Birmingham City Council v Ali; Moran v Manchester City Council (Secretary of State for Communities and Local Government)* [2009] UKHL 36, [2009] 1 WLR 1506 where the House of Lords came close to eliding the two concepts.

4.70 The test is satisfied only if it is reasonable for the applicant to occupy the accommodation indefinitely, or at least for as long as the applicant otherwise would do so if the authority did not intervene to rehouse him or her: *Ali* and *Moran*.[108] Thus, an applicant may be homeless long before the situation becomes so bad that it is not reasonable for him or her to occupy the accommodation for another night.[109] What this recognises is that accommodation which it may be unreasonable for a person to occupy for a long period, may nonetheless be reasonable to occupy for a short period.[110]

4.71 The test is linked to 'suitability':[111] accommodation which is not reasonable for an applicant to continue to occupy may nevertheless be suitable for the time being; there are degrees of suitability and what is suitable for occupation in the short term may not be suitable in the longer term.[112] The point in time at which accommodation which it is not reasonable for an applicant to continue to occupy becomes unsuitable is primarily for the authority to decide, and involves taking into account matters such as the severe constraints on the authority's budgets and personnel and the very limited number of satisfactory properties for large families.[113]

4.72 A woman who has left her home because of domestic or other violence[114] normally remains homeless even if she has found a temporary haven in a women's refuge[115] because it would usually not be reasonable for her to continue to occupy her place in the refuge indefinitely,[116] ie for as long as she would have to occupy it if the authority did not intervene to rehouse her.[117]

4.73 The test of reasonableness to continue to occupy does not apply only to accommodation which is actually occupied: continuation refers to the entitlement rather than the occupation. Accordingly, a person is homeless if it is – or if it would not be – reasonable to occupy the accommodation, whether or not in prior occupation of it,

108 *Birmingham City Council v Ali; Moran v Manchester City Council (Secretary of State for Communities and Local Government)*, above, at [37].

109 *Ali* and *Moran* at [40].

110 *Ali* and *Moran* at [42].

111 See paras 10.162–10.204.

112 *Ali* and *Moran* at [47]. See also *R (Edwards) v Birmingham City Council* [2016] EWHC 173 (Admin), [2016] HLR 11.

113 *Ali* and *Moran* at [50].

114 See paras 4.82–4.92.

115 *Ali* and *Moran* at [65].

116 *Ali* and *Moran* at [52].

117 *Ali* and *Moran* at [46].

or in occupation of it at the time of the application or decision. Any other approach would mean that if the circumstances were so bad that the applicant had left, he or she might (in theory at least) be found not to be homeless,[118] though he or she would be found homeless if, although unreasonable to continue to occupy the accommodation, they were not so bad that the applicant had actually left it. Such a result could not have been intended: *Maloba*.[119]

4.74 Whether it would have been reasonable for an applicant to continue to occupy accommodation for the purposes of HA 1996 s191(1) is to be determined at a time before the deliberate acts or omissions which led to the loss of that accommodation. In answering this question, an authority must ignore those acts or omissions: *Denton*.[120]

4.75 The term 'reasonable to continue to occupy' is governed by HA 1996 s177 or H(W)A 2014 s57, as to both:

a) violence (HA 1996 s177(1), (1A)) or abuse (H(W)A 2014 s57(1)); and
b) the general housing circumstances of the area (HA 1996 s177(2); H(W)A 2014 s57(3)).

4.76 The secretary of state and the Welsh Ministers have power to specify other circumstances in which it is or is not to be regarded as reasonable to continue to occupy accommodation, and matters (other than the general housing circumstances of the area) which are to be taken into account when determining whether or not it is reasonable to continue in occupation (HA 1996 s177(3); H(W)A 2014 s57(4)).[121]

4.77 The statutory considerations are not exhaustive of matters to be taken into account in determining whether or not it is reasonable to continue in occupation: *Duro-Rama*.[122] Nor is the question limited to consideration of size, structural quality and amenities of accommodation.[123] It follows that, in addition to violence and the general housing circumstances of the area and any other considerations that

118 In *Nipa Begum v Tower Hamlets LBC* (1999) 32 HLR 445, CA, at [41], while taking a contrary view of the statutory provisions, it was said that no reasonable authority could reach such a decision.

119 *Waltham Forest LBC v Maloba* [2007] EWCA Civ 1281, [2008] HLR 26, rejecting the majority obiter conclusion in *Nipa Begum*, in favour of the minority view.

120 *Denton v Southwark LBC* [2007] EWCA Civ 623, [2008] HLR 11.

121 See para 4.122 as to the regulations which have been issued.

122 *R v Hammersmith and Fulham LBC ex p Duro-Rama* (1983) 9 HLR 71, QBD.

123 *Waltham Forest LBC v Maloba* [2007] EWCA Civ 1281, [2008] HLR 26.

may be specified, there is a wide range of other matters which may affect the issue.

4.78 Subject to the provisions of HA 1996 s177(2) and H(W)A 2014 s57(3), allowing the authority to have regard to the general housing circumstances of the area, the question whether it is reasonable to continue to occupy has been described as subjective, and not susceptible to a generalised or objective standard: *McManus*.[124] This does not mean wholly subjective in the view of the applicant, but means that the issue has to be determined on all the facts of the case – not, on the one hand, determined simply by reference to local conditions or the local authority's policy, nor, on the other, looked at from the perspective of the applicant alone, so that the role of other persons or factors is ignored.[125]

4.79 The question is not, however, whether it is reasonable to leave accommodation, but whether or not it is reasonable to continue to occupy it.[126] The distinction is significant: it will commonly be reasonable (ie not unreasonable) to leave somewhere; what has to be sustained is the proposition that it is positively not reasonable to stay.

4.80 There is no presumption that an applicant's current accommodation is unsuitable, such as to impose a burden on the authority to rebut it: *McCarthy*.[127]

4.81 Whether or not it is reasonable to continue to occupy accommodation relates not only to the applicant but also to any other person who might reasonably be expected to reside with him or her: *Bishop*.[128] This must be as true of a person residing with the applicant as a member of the family.

124 *R v Brent LBC ex p McManus* (1993) 25 HLR 643, QBD.

125 *Denton v Southwark LBC* [2007] EWCA Civ 623, [2008] HLR 11, at [13], [30] and [31]. This approach is consistent with *Ahmed v Leicester City Council* [2007] EWCA Civ 843, [2008] HLR 6, which concerned HA 1996 s193(7F) (para 10.224), in which it was held that an applicant's genuine belief that it was not reasonable to accept an offer of accommodation was not conclusive of whether it was reasonable to do so; if the authority has evidence which entitles it to consider that the belief was not objectively reasonable, even if that evidence was not available to the applicant at the time of the refusal, the authority may decide that it was reasonable for the applicant to accept the offer. It would seem that a similar approach may therefore be available in relation to HA 1996 s177.

126 See *R v Kensington and Chelsea RLBC ex p Bayani* (1990) 22 HLR 406, CA; see also *R v Gravesham BC ex p Winchester* (1986) 18 HLR 208, QBD.

127 *R v Sedgemoor DC ex p McCarthy* (1996) 28 HLR 608, QBD.

128 *R v Westminster City Council ex p Bishop* (1993) 25 HLR 459, CA.

Violence and abuse

4.82 It is not reasonable to continue to occupy accommodation if, even though there may be a legal entitlement to do so, it is 'probable' that occupation of it will lead to domestic or other abuse (in Wales)[129] or violence or threats of violence which are likely to be carried out (in England):

a) against the applicant; or
b) against any person who usually resides with the applicant, or against any person who might reasonably be expected to reside with the applicant.[130]

4.83 In *Danesh*[131] a narrow definition of 'violence' was adopted, meaning actual physical violence, not including threats of violence or acts or gestures which lead a person to fear physical violence. In *Yemshaw*,[132] the Supreme Court adopted a much broader view which, it held, was consistent with the purpose of the legislative scheme – accordingly, it included physical violence, threats, intimidating behaviour and any other form of abuse which, directly or indirectly, may give rise to a risk of harm.[133] This wider definition was subsequently incorporated into statutory guidance[134] and, in *Waltham Forest LBC v Hussein*,[135] it was held that, although *Danesh* had not been expressly overruled by *Yemshaw*, it was clear that much of the reasoning was disapproved; the wider approach in *Yemshaw* should be followed.

4.84 It is not necessary to show an actual history of violence. The test may be satisfied by the lower standard, ie, threats by someone likely to carry them out. Many authorities fail to observe this important distinction, and require a high standard of proof of actual past violence as evidence of both probability and likelihood. As this section draws a careful distinction, so also must authorities.

129 'Abuse' means physical violence, threatening or intimidating behaviour and any other form of abuse which, directly or indirectly, may give rise to the risk of harm: H(W)A 2014 s58(1). Given the decision in *Yemshaw* (below), the terms violence and abuse appear to be synonymous.

130 HA 1996 s177(1), (1A); H(W)A 2014 s57(1).

131 *Danesh v Kensington and Chelsea RLBC* [2006] EWCA Civ 1404, [2007] HLR 17.

132 *Yemshaw v Hounslow LBC* [2011] UKSC 3, [2011] HLR 16; see also H(W)A 2014 s58.

133 The wider view had also been adopted in the 2006 edition of the English Code of Guidance para 8.21 which *Danesh* had criticised.

134 Originally *Supplementary guidance on domestic abuse and homelessness*: CLG, November 2014, but now English Code of Guidance chapter 21.

135 [2015] EWCA Civ 14, [2015] HLR 16.

4.85 The position is not on all fours with failure to use legal redress in connection with 'entry prevented'.[136] Authorities are not to concern themselves with what steps to prevent the violence applicants should (in the authority's view) take or could have taken: *Bond*.[137]

4.86 Accordingly, when determining whether it is reasonable to continue to occupy under HA 1996 s177, an authority may consider only whether it was probable that continued occupation of the property would lead to violence or the threat of violence.[138] Whether a victim of violence had failed to take measures to prevent the violence (such as contacting the police or taking out an injunction) is irrelevant: if, however, the victim does take preventative measures which it is considered will probably prove effective in preventing actual or threatened violence, the level of risk may factually be reduced below probability. Those are the questions which an authority must ask itself; it may not assume that such measures will be taken or, if taken, that they will be effective.[139]

Threats

4.87 The only test that an authority may apply to establish whether threats are likely to be carried out is likewise what is probable: see *Bond*.[140] See also English Code of Guidance:[141]

> . . . an assessment of the likelihood of a threat of violence being carried out should not be based on whether there has been actual violence in the past.

136 See para 4.62.

137 *Bond v Leicester City Council* [2001] EWCA Civ 1544, [2002] HLR 6. See also English Code of Guidance para 6.21; Welsh Code para 8.23. Compare the earlier decisions of *R v Eastleigh BC ex p Evans* (1984) 17 HLR 515, QBD; *R v Purbeck DC ex p Cadney* (1985) 17 HLR 534; and *R v Wandsworth LBC ex p Nimako-Boateng* (1984) 11 HLR 95, QBD.

138 *Bond v Leicester City Council* [2001] EWCA Civ 1544, [2002] HLR 6.

139 *Bond v Leicester City Council* [2001] EWCA Civ 1544, [2002] HLR 6. The earlier decision in *R v Wandsworth LBC ex p Nimako-Boateng*, above, in which it had been held that an authority could conclude that it would be reasonable for a woman to continue to occupy accommodation – notwithstanding domestic violence – by reference to the remedies otherwise available to her for her protection, was decided under HA 1985 s58, now HA 1996 s175(3), at a time when the question of reasonableness was at large, rather than statutorily defined. *Nimako-Boateng* was accordingly distinguished in *Bond*, as was the decision to like effect in *R v Purbeck DC ex p Cadney* (1985) 17 HLR 534.

140 *Bond v Leicester City Council* [2001] EWCA Civ 1544, [2002] HLR 6.

141 Para 21.20. See Welsh Code para 8.22 to the same effect.

Residing with applicant

4.88 The violence need not be against the applicant, but could be against any person who usually resides with him or her, or against any person who might reasonably be expected to do so. See 'Accommodation available for occupation' at paras 4.16–4.38, and note that the person to whom the violence is shown need not be residing with the applicant as a member of the applicant's family, so that, eg, violence against a carer could qualify.

Domestic violence/abuse

4.89 Domestic violence or abuse is not confined to that between spouses or cohabitants. It may come from any person with whom the applicant or other person who is the subject of it is associated.[142] The English Code of Guidance[143] suggests that 'domestic violence' should be understood to include threatening behaviour, violence or abuse (psychological, physical, sexual, financial or emotional), controlling or coercive behaviour or 'so-called honour based abuse' between associated persons.

4.90 People are associated if:

a) they are or have been married to each other;
b) they are or have been civil partners of each other;
c) they are cohabitants or former cohabitants[144] or, in Wales, they live or have lived together in an enduring family relationship (whether they are of different sexes or the same sex);
d) they live or have lived in the same household;
e) they are relatives;[145]
f) they have agreed to marry (whether or not that agreement has been terminated);
g) they have entered into a civil partnership agreement between them (whether or not that agreement has been terminated);

142 HA 1996 s177(1A); H(W)A 2014 s58(2).

143 English Code of Guidance paras 21.4–21.7; see also Welsh Code para 8.21 and Violence Against Women, Domestic Abuse and Sexual Violence (Wales) Act 2015 s24.

144 A man and a woman who are or were living together without being married to one another, or two people of the same sex who are or were living together without being civil partners.

145 i) Parent, step-parent, child, stepchild, grandparent or grandchild of a person or of that person's spouse, civil partner, former spouse or former civil partner; ii) sibling, aunt or uncle, niece or nephew of a person or that person's spouse, civil partner, former spouse or former civil partner, whether of full- or half-blood, or by marriage or civil partnership.

h) in relation to a child, each of the persons is a parent of the child, or has or has had parental responsibility for the child;[146]
i) in relation to a child who has been adopted (or subsequently freed from adoption), if one person is a natural parent or natural parent of a natural parent, and the other is the child, or is a person who has become a parent by adoption, or who has applied for an adoption order, or with whom the child was at any time placed for adoption;[147] and
j) in Wales, people who have or have had an intimate personal relationship with each other which is or was of significant duration.[148]

4.91 HA 1996 s178(2) and (2A) and H(W)A 2014 s58(3) and (4) contain detailed provisions governing association arising out of adoptions.

Other violence

4.92 The Homelessness Act 2002 extended the application of HA 1996 s177 to 'other violence', ie, from someone not associated with the victim – covering, for example, those suffering from violent racial harassment or witnesses in trials who have been intimidated by violence or threats of violence.[149] This is a significant extension. Formerly, violence from non-associated persons was only relevant to the question of reasonableness 'at large'.[150] An authority considering reasonableness at large could therefore take into account whether an applicant could obtain protection from violence through the courts or by seeking a transfer.[151] Incorporation into HA 1996 s177 means that the proper approach to the availability of alternative remedies will be the same as set out in *Bond*.[152]

General housing circumstances of area

4.93 The comparison between accommodation occupied and the general circumstances prevailing in relation to housing accommodation in the district of the authority to which an application has been made[153]

146 Within Children Act (CA) 1989.
147 HA 1996 s178; H(W)A 2014 s58.
148 H(W)A 2014 s58(2)(h).
149 In Wales, the extension is found in H(W)A 2014 s58(1) in respect of 'abuse'.
150 *R v Hillingdon LBC ex p H* (1988) 20 HLR 554, QBD.
151 See, eg, *R v Newham LBC ex p McIlroy* (1991) 23 HLR 570, QBD.
152 See para 4.85.
153 HA 1996 s177(2); H(W)A 2014 s57(3).

is one of the central concepts of homelessness law, albeit that most of it was developed in relation to intentionality.

4.94 Initially, it bore not at all on the definition of homelessness, although it was in practice being applied by the courts at the point in the evolution of the law[154] at which an there was an equiparation between being homeless and occupation of accommodation so poor that it could be left without a finding of intentionality.

4.95 *Awua*[155] notwithstanding, it is plain that Parliament intended the importation of an identical criterion when it adopted the exact same phraseology for use in the definition (HA 1985 s58) of homelessness as had long existed in relation to intentionality (HA 1985 s60), ie whether or not it was reasonable to continue to occupy, subject to the general housing conditions of the area.[156]

4.96 The comparison is between current accommodation, wherever situated, and conditions in the area of the authority to which application is made.[157]

4.97 HA 1996 s177(2) requires the authority to carry out a balancing act between the housing conditions in the authority's area and the accommodation quit, although whether or not it is reasonable to continue to occupy accommodation involves other questions, such as the pattern of life followed by the applicant: *Monaf*.[158] Such comparisons should only be made, however, where relevant to an application.[159]

4.98 The decision in *Tickner v Mole Valley DC*,[160] in which the applicants were evicted from a caravan site because they refused to pay increased rents which they thought excessive in view of the conditions on the site, turned on what is now HA 1996 s177(2), albeit in the context of intentionality:

154 See para 4.7 in relation to accommodation.

155 *R v Brent LBC ex p Awua* [1996] AC 55, (1995) 27 HLR 453, HL.

156 Housing and Planning Act 1986 s14(2); see also para 4.75. See also *R v Wandsworth LBC ex p Wingrove*, and *R v Wandsworth LBC ex p Mansoor* [1996] 3 All ER 913, (1997) 29 HLR 801, CA. See also *Nipa Begum v Tower Hamlets LBC* (1999) 32 HLR 445, CA, at p319/H ('[T]he plain intention of Parliament was to enable a local authority to determine the question of homelessness . . . without having to go on to the corresponding question in the test of intentional homelessness') and at p326/A–B.

157 *R v Tower Hamlets LBC ex p Monaf* (1988) 20 HLR 529, CA.

158 See para 4.78. See also *R v Newham LBC ex p Ajayi* (1994) 28 HLR 25, QBD, referring to matters 'of social history and national status', such as where children were born and how long a person has lived somewhere.

159 *R v Newham LBC ex p Tower Hamlets LBC* (1990) 23 HLR 62, CA.

160 August 1980 *LAG Bulletin* 187, CA.

> That is what influenced this authority here. They had long waiting lists for housing. On those lists there were young couples waiting to be married: or young married couples sometimes staying with their in-laws: or people in poor accommodation. All those people were on the housing waiting lists – people who had been waiting for housing for years. The council thought it would be extremely unfair to all those on the waiting lists if these caravan dwellers – by coming in in this way – jumped the queue, when they were well able to pay the rent for the caravans and stay on. Those were perfectly legitimate considerations for the local authority to consider.[161]

4.99 In order to rely on this provision, the authority need not consider in great detail all the information on housing conditions in its area, but may have regard to 'the generally prevailing standard of accommodation in their area, with which people have to be satisfied'.[162]

Other reasons

4.100 There are potentially as many reasons why people may not wish to remain in accommodation as there are applicants; accordingly, there is no simple test of reasonableness.[163]

Location

4.101 The question is not confined to the accommodation in itself, but can extend to its location: *Homes*.[164]

Permanence

4.102 The fact that the accommodation is not permanent is not, however, relevant to whether or not it is reasonable to continue the occupation: *Nipa Begum*.[165]

Physical conditions

4.103 Physical conditions may produce circumstances in which it is not reasonable to continue to occupy accommodation.

161 *Per* Lord Denning MR. In *de Falco, Silvestri v Crawley BC* [1980] QB 460, CA, he described the provision as a 'ray of hope', allowing the authority to say: 'You ought to have stayed where you were before. You ought not to have landed yourself on us when it would have been reasonable for you to stay where you were.'

162 *Tickner*, para 4.98.

163 See English Code of Guidance paras 6.39–6.40; Welsh Code para 8.20.

164 *R v Wycombe DC ex p Homes* (1988) 22 HLR 150, QBD.

165 *Nipa Begum v Tower Hamlets LBC* (1999) 32 HLR 445, CA.

4.104 Accommodation will have to be very poor indeed before an applicant can claim with confidence that it would not be reasonable to continue to occupy it on the ground of its physical condition, although in some cases (for example, a wheelchair user) the physical characteristics of the accommodation may make it per se unsuitable for the particular applicant.[166]

4.105 In *Miles*,[167] a hut approximately 20 feet by ten feet, with two rooms, infested by rats, and with no mains services (although services were available in a nearby caravan occupied by relatives), was held to constitute accommodation of which an authority could consider it reasonable for the applicant to continue in occupation, at a time when there were two adults and two children living in it, albeit that it was on the 'borderline' of what was reasonable and would cross the borderline into what no authority could consider reasonable on the birth of a third child.

4.106 In *Fisher*,[168] the applicant and her children had been living in temporary accommodation. For a period they lived in a caravan. Immediately before her application, they lived on a boat, without bath, shower, WC, electricity, hot water system or kitchen with a sink. There was one cabin, which was kitchen, living room and bedroom combined, and the applicant occupied it with her children and two friends. It was held that this was not accommodation of which it was reasonable to continue in occupation.

4.107 In *Winchester*,[169] the applicant and his family had left accommodation in Alderney. Among the reasons for leaving was that the accommodation was in an appalling state of disrepair, suffering from damp and a dangerous outside staircase and balcony. The family was found to be intentionally homeless. The decision of the local authority that it would have been reasonable to remain was not considered to be unreasonable or perverse.

4.108 In *Dee*,[170] a decision that it would have been reasonable for a young woman and her new baby to occupy a pre-fabricated beach bungalow which suffered severe damp problems was quashed because the authority had given too much weight to the fact that the property was not considered to be unfit for human habitation

166 English Code of Guidance para 6.39; Welsh Code para 8.27.
167 *R v South Herefordshire DC ex p Miles* (1983) 17 HLR 82, QBD.
168 *R v Preseli DC ex p Fisher* (1984) 17 HLR 147, QBD.
169 *R v Gravesham BC ex p Winchester* (1986) 18 HLR 208, QBD.
170 *R v Medina BC ex p Dee* (1992) 24 HLR 562, QBD.

and too little to the medical advice which had been given to the applicant.[171]

4.109 In *Ben-El-Mabrouk*,[172] the want of adequate means of escape from fire did not necessarily mean that it was not reasonable for a couple with a small baby to stay in occupation of a fifth-floor flat in a house in multiple occupation (HMO), although a delay in rehousing the family under the provisions of the Land Compensation Act 1973[173] might itself (in the absence of an explanation from the authority) have been challengeable.

4.110 In *Puhlhofer* at the Court of Appeal,[174] Ackner LJ's view as to whether or not the applicants had any accommodation (within the meaning of the legislation) at all[175] was based in part on the question whether or not it would have been reasonable to continue to occupy it. He considered that accommodation for the applicant, his wife and two children in one room in a guesthouse, with no cooking or laundry facilities, could have been reasonable to continue to occupy in the light of the authority's evidence that there were at least 44 families on the council's waiting list for two-bedroomed accommodation considered to be of higher priority.

Overcrowding

4.111 Overcrowding is a relevant consideration: *Beattie (No 1)*.[176] An authority cannot refuse to consider an application simply because the accommodation is not statutorily overcrowded: *Alouat*.[177] The authority is, however, entitled to take into account the fact that the

171 See also the discussion of *Shala v Birmingham City Council* [2007] EWCA Civ 624, [2008] HLR 8 at para 5.49, the principle of which must apply in the same way to issues of suitability having regard to medical conditions.

172 *R v Kensington and Chelsea RLBC ex p Youssef Ben-El-Mabrouk* (1995) 27 HLR 564, CA.

173 Land Compensation Act 1973 s39 requires an authority to re-house residential occupiers displaced from their accommodation as a result of specified enforcement action taken by the authority under (now) HA 2004 Part 1, previously under HA 1985 Part 10.

174 (1985) 17 HLR 588, CA.

175 See para 4.8.

176 *R v Eastleigh BC ex p Beattie (No 1)* (1983) 10 HLR 134, QBD.

177 *R v Westminster City Council ex p Alouat* (1989) 21 HLR 477, QBD. See also English Code of Guidance para 6.27. The Welsh Code para 8.27 says that: 'Although statutory overcrowding, by itself, is not sufficient to determine whether it is unreasonable for the applicant to continue to live in accommodation, it can be a key factor which suggests unreasonableness.'

property is not statutorily overcrowded: *Beattie (No 2)*.[178] Even if it is, this does not prevent it being reasonable for an applicant to continue to occupy the accommodation.[179]

4.112 In *Ali*,[180] even if accommodation had been 'available', it was said:

> . . . that anyone should regard it as reasonable that a family of that size should live in one room 10ft x 12ft in size, or thereabouts, is something which I find astonishing. However, the matter has to be seen in the light of s17(4) [now HA 1996 s177(2)] which requires that reasonableness must take account of the general circumstances prevailing in relation to housing in the area. No evidence has been placed before me that accommodation in the area of the Westminster City Council is so desperately short that it is reasonable to accept overcrowding of this degree. In the absence of such evidence I am driven to the conclusion that this question could not properly have been determined against the applicant.[181]

4.113 In *Osei*,[182] it was held that, even if the applicant's flat in Madrid had been overcrowded when he surrendered his tenancy, it was open to the authority to conclude that it was reasonable for him and his family to continue to occupy it until he had secured alternative accommodation for his family in London.

Legal conditions

4.114 The fact that accommodation had been obtained by deception meant that it would not have been reasonable to remain in occupation of it: *Gliddon*.[183]

4.115 In *Knight*,[184] and in *Li*,[185] once service occupancies had been ended and there could be no defence to an action for possession, the

178 *R v Eastleigh BC ex p Beattie (No 2)* (1984) 17 HLR 168, QBD. See also, on overcrowding, *Krishnan v Hillingdon LBC* January 1981 *LAG Bulletin* 137, QBD; *R v Tower Hamlets LBC ex p Ojo* (1991) 23 HLR 488, QBD; and *R v Tower Hamlets LBC ex p Bibi* (1991) 23 HLR 500, QBD.

179 *Harouki v Kensington and Chelsea RLBC* [2007] EWCA Civ 1000, [2008] HLR 16.

180 *R v Westminster City Council ex p Ali* (1983) 11 HLR 83, QBD.

181 The applicant had left a shared single room to return to Bangladesh; he returned with his wife and four children. The observations were made both in relation to the shared single room, which put it on a par with *Re Islam* [1983] 1 AC 688, (1981) 1 HLR 107, HL, para 4.28, and to a notional single room for the family.

182 *Osei v Southwark LBC* [2007] EWCA Civ 787, [2008] HLR 15.

183 *R v Exeter City Council ex p Gliddon* (1984) 14 HLR 103, QBD; *Chishimba v Kensington and Chelsea RLBC* [2013] EWCA Civ 786, [2013] HLR 34.

184 *R v Portsmouth City Council ex p Knight* (1983) 10 HLR 115, QBD.

185 *R v Surrey Heath BC ex p Li* (1984) 16 HLR 79, QBD.

authorities were not able to consider that occupiers should reasonably have remained in occupation pending proceedings.

4.116 These decisions can be difficult to reconcile with the definition of rights of occupation (including the right to remain in occupation under an enactment),[186] although it is not hard to see the common sense in discouraging authorities from requiring possession orders where there would be no defence. The Codes of Guidance have long made clear that authorities should not require tenants to fight possession proceedings where the landlord has a strong prospect of success.[187] In *Ugbo*,[188] the authority's failure to consider such guidance (and the implications of the fact that that applicant was only an assured shorthold tenant rather than fully assured) invalidated its decision on this issue.

4.117 The current Codes[189] suggest that where the applicant is an assured shorthold tenant who has received proper notice (under HA 1988 s21)[190] that the tenancy is to be terminated and the landlord intends to seek possession, that further efforts from the housing authority to resolve the situation and persuade the landlord to allow the tenant to remain in the property are unlikely to be successful, and that there is no defence to the possession proceedings, it is unlikely to be reasonable for the applicant to occupy the accommodation beyond the date given in the section 21 notice, unless he or she is taking steps to persuade the landlord to withdraw the notice.

186 See paras 4.48–4.61.

187 See English Code para 6.33; Welsh Code paras 8.14, 8.31. The concept appears to have first been stated in para A1.3 of the 2nd edn of the Code, although has been strengthened and developed in subsequent editions.

188 *R v Newham LBC ex p Ugbo* (1993) 26 HLR 263, QBD, a case on para 10.12 of the 3rd edn of the Code: 'Local authorities should not require tenants to fight a possession action where the landlord has a certain prospect of success, such as an action for recovery of property let on an assured shorthold tenant, on the ground that the fixed term of the tenancy has ended. Authorities need only be satisfied that proper notice had been served with the intention to proceed.'

189 English Code of Guidance para 6.35; Welsh Code para 8.31. See also the letter from the secretary of state to English Local Authority CEOs (Department for Communities and Local Government, June 2016) reminding authorities that they 'should not adopt a general policy of accepting – or refusing to accept – applicants as homeless or threatened with homelessness when they are threatened with eviction but a court has not yet made an order for possession or issued a warrant of execution'; see, to the same effect, English Code paras 6.33, 6.36–6.37

190 See Arden & Dymond, *Manual of housing law*, 10th edn, LAG, 2017, para 2.203.

4.118 *Ugbo* must be compared with *Jarvis*,[191] where the authority had considered the Code but was held still to be entitled to reach the conclusion that it was reasonable to continue to occupy pending a court order following termination of an assured shorthold tenancy.[192]

4.119 In *Minnett*,[193] the authority should have disregarded departure one day before the date specified in a consent order for possession. Given the decision in *Khan and Hussain*[194] that a tenant who is subject to a possession order only becomes homeless when that order is executed, authorities should also consider cases where the applicant leaves between the possession order and physical eviction by the court bailiffs, even though – on that analysis – the applicant will not yet be homeless.[195]

4.120 Since commencement of the Homelessness Reduction Act (HRA) 2017,[196] authorities have been under a set of new duties to assess applications and provide help to postpone homelessness or to secure accommodation for a period of time.[197] In certain circumstances, an authority may end its duty to help postpone homelessness for those threatened with homelessness,[198] one of which is that it has taken reasonable steps to secure that accommodation does not cease to be available, that the applicant has suitable accommodation, and that a period of 56 days has elapsed since it was first satisfied that the applicant was threatened with homelessness and eligible for assistance.[199] No such notice may, however, be given if the applicant has been given a valid notice under HA 1988 s21 to terminate an assured shorthold tenancy, in respect of the only accommodation available to the applicant and which has expired or will expire within 56 days.[200] This provides support for the proposition that it is not

191 *R v Croydon LBC ex p Jarvis* (1993) 26 HLR 194, QBD; see also *R v Bradford City Council ex p Parveen* (1996) 28 HLR 681, QBD.

192 The 2nd edn of the Code at para 1.3 read: 'Where it is clear from the facts that tenants have no defence . . . to an application for possession, authorities should not insist that an order is obtained, and a date for eviction set, before agreeing to help the tenant.'

193 *R v Mole Valley DC ex p Minnett* (1983) 12 HLR 49, QBD.

194 *R v Newham LBC ex p Khan and Hussain* (2001) 33 HLR 29, QBD.

195 *R v Newham LBC ex p Sacupima* (2001) 33 HLR 1, QBD.

196 3 April 2018: see Homelessness Reduction Act 2017 (Commencement and Transitional and Savings Provisions) Regulations 2018 SI No 167 reg 3.

197 See, generally, chapters 2 and 10.

198 Paras 4.141–4.148.

199 HA 1996 s195(1), (2), (5), (8).

200 HA 1996 s195(6). See also para 4.143 as to the definition of threatened with homelessness when a section 21 notice has been served.

reasonable to continue to occupy accommodation in the face of court proceedings to which there will be no defence.

Financial conditions

4.121 Financial considerations raise the question of 'affordability': see *Hawthorne*,[201] in which the authority had to consider whether the applicant's failure to pay rent had been caused by the inadequacy of her financial resources.

4.122 Authorities in England are required to take affordability into account when determining whether or not it is reasonable to continue to occupy accommodation: Homelessness (Suitability of Accommodation) Order 1996.[202]

4.123 In reaching this decision, the authority must consider the financial resources available to a person, including, but not limited to: the costs of the accommodation; payments being made under a court order to a spouse or former spouse; any payments made to support children; whether under a court order or under the Child Support Act 1991; and the applicant's other reasonable living expenses.[203]

4.124 The order also contains a detailed list of deductible accommodation costs,[204] although authorities are not limited to consideration of these.[205]

4.125 In determining the amount that an applicant requires for residual living costs, the English Code of Guidance[206] suggests that authorities may wish to be guided by Universal Credit standard allowances when assessing the income that an applicant will require to meet essential needs aside from housing costs, but should ensure that the wishes, needs and circumstances of the applicant and his or her household are taken into account. Both the English and Welsh

201 *R v Wandsworth LBC ex p Hawthorne* (1994) 27 HLR 59, CA.

202 SI No 3204 (see appendix B). In Wales, see H(W)A 2014 s59(2), to the same effect. When deciding issues of affordability, all forms of income should be considered: *Samuels v Birmingham City Council* [2015] EWCA Civ 1051, [2015] HLR 47 (rejecting an argument that all welfare benefits other than housing benefit should be left out of account). Permission to appeal to the Supreme Court has been granted.

203 1996 Order art 2(a).

204 1996 Order art 2(b).

205 Unlike under the 1996 Order in England, in Wales H(W)A 2014 s59(2) provides no further details. The Welsh Code requires consideration of the 'financial resources available to the applicant; the costs in respect of the accommodation; maintenance payments (in respect of ex-family members); and the applicant's other reasonable living expenses': see para 8.29; see also para 19.26.

206 English Code of Guidance para 17.45.

Codes[207] make it clear that affordability is always an issue which must be considered.[208]

4.126 This is consistent with case-law. In *Duro-Rama,*[209] the availability of benefits was held to be a relevant consideration which the authority had ignored[210] by confining itself to the matters set out in HA 1985 s60(4) (now HA 1996 s177(2)).

4.127 In *Griffiths,*[211] it was said that it cannot be assumed that income support is sufficient to meet housing costs.

4.128 Inadequacy of financial resources goes not merely to ability to pay the rent, but also to funding the necessities of life, including food: *Bibi,*[212] following *Tinn.*[213]

4.129 It is, however, for the authority, not the court, to assess whether or not accommodation is affordable: *Grossett.*[214]

Employment

4.130 In *Duro-Rama,*[215] it was also said that the issue of employment was a relevant considerations which the authority had ignored. This reflects the comment of Lord Lowry in *Islam,*[216] that:

> There will, of course, and in the interests of mobility of labour ought to be, cases where the housing authority will . . . accept that it would

207 English Code of Guidance para 6.28; Welsh Code para 8.29.

208 Welsh Code para 19.28 is more prescriptive: accommodation is not to be considered affordable if the applicant 'would be left with a residual income which would be significantly less than the level of income support or income-based Jobseekers allowance or Universal Credit that is applicable in respect of the applicant, or would be applicable if he or she was entitled to claim such benefit . . . Local authorities will need to consider whether the applicant can afford the housing costs without being deprived of basic essentials such as food, clothing, heating, transport and other essentials'.

209 *R v Hammersmith and Fulham LBC ex p Duro-Rama* (1983) 9 HLR 71, QBD.

210 When considering the applicants' reasons for departing their previous accommodation.

211 *R v Shrewsbury BC ex p Griffiths* (1993) 25 HLR 613, QBD. See further *R v Hillingdon LBC ex p Tinn* (1988) 20 HLR 206, QBD; and *R v Camden LBC ex p Aranda* (1996) 28 HLR 672, QBD. Cf *R v Westminster City Council ex p Moklis Ali* (1996) 29 HLR 580, QBD.

212 *R v Islington LBC ex p Bibi* (1996) 29 HLR 498, QBD.

213 *R v Hillingdon LBC ex p Tinn* (1988) 20 HLR 206, QBD.

214 *R v Brent LBC ex p Grossett* (1994) 28 HLR 9, CA. See too *R v Brent LBC ex p Baruwa* (1997) 29 HLR 915, CA and *Bernard v Enfield LBC* [2001] EWCA Civ 1831, CA.

215 *R v Hammersmith and Fulham LBC ex p Duro-Rama* (1983) 9 HLR 71, QBD.

216 *Re Islam* [1983] 1 AC 688, (1981) 1 HLR 107, HL.

not have been reasonable in the circumstances for the applicant to continue to occupy the accommodation which he has left.

4.131 In *Ashton*,[217] to the same effect, it was held that no reasonable authority would have allowed the provisions of what is now HA 1996 s177(2) to have led to a decision on intentionality where a middle-aged woman who had been unemployed for six years, and who had chronic active hepatitis, left settled accommodation to take up work in another area.

Type of accommodation

4.132 It has been held that accommodation in a prison cell is not accommodation which it is reasonable for the applicant to continue to occupy (where the applicant has the opportunity to obtain early release under a tagging scheme): *B*.[218]

4.133 Both the English and Welsh Codes[219] suggest that some types of accommodation – for example, women's refuges; direct access hostels; and night shelters intended to provide very short-term temporary accommodation in a crisis – should not be regarded as reasonable for someone to continue to occupy in the medium and longer term. It may be that in some circumstances such accommodation should not be considered reasonable to occupy at all.[220]

Other considerations

4.134 In *Bassett*,[221] the court held that a woman who had followed her husband to Canada, notwithstanding the uncertainties of their prospects there, could not reasonably have remained in occupation of their secure council accommodation, when going to join him was her only chance of saving their marriage.

217 *R v Winchester City Council ex p Ashton* (1991) 24 HLR 520, CA.

218 *R (B) v Southwark LBC* [2003] EWHC 1678 (Admin), [2004] HLR 3. But see *Birmingham City Council v Ali; Moran v Manchester City Council (Secretary of State for Communities and Local Government and another intervening)* [2009] UKHL 36, [2009] 1 WLR 1506, and para 4.13, where the House of Lords expressly reserved the issue of whether prison could comprise accommodation at all.

219 English Code para 6.39; Welsh Code para 8.27.

220 See now *Birmingham City Council v Ali; Moran v Manchester City Council (Secretary of State for Communities and Local Government and another intervening)*, para 4.13.

221 *R v Basingstoke and Deane BC ex p Bassett* (1983) 10 HLR 125, QBD.

4.135 It would be wrong, however, to view this as anything more than an illustration of the proposition that it is the particular circumstances of applicant and household which are relevant.[222]

4.136 In *Hearn*,[223] the applicant's sense of isolation was held to be a factor relevant to deciding whether it was reasonable for her to continue to occupy premises.

4.137 In *Healiss*,[224] the authority failed to consider the applicant's reasons for leaving accommodation of which she was a secure tenant, including repeated break-ins to empty flats in her block, two burglaries of her own flat, harassment involving strangers knocking at the door, stones thrown at windows, and shouting up to her windows at all hours of the day and night; in addition, gangs of youths congregated on the stairway smoking what was assumed to be drugs, the first-floor landing was used as a latrine and smelled as such, and the applicant was too frightened to allow her child to play in the block and gardens.

4.138 In *Nimako-Boateng*,[225] however, the court upheld the decision of the authority that a woman could reasonably have remained in occupation of the matrimonial home in Ghana, even though her relationship with her husband had broken down. (The court noted that it had been given no information about Ghanaian family law, and assumed that the woman's rights would have been the same as under English law. There was no complaint of domestic violence.)[226] *Nimako-Boateng* was followed in *Evans*.[227]

4.139 In *Moncada*,[228] the applicant was divorced from his wife and had custody of his two sons. The court refused to interfere with a finding that, given the shortage of accommodation in London, it was reasonable for him to continue to live in the four-bedroomed matrimonial home, even though his ex-wife and daughter were also still living in it.

222 Cf, above, *R v Brent LBC ex p McManus* (1993) 25 HLR 643, QBD; and *R v Shrewsbury BC ex p Griffiths* (1993) 25 HLR 613, QBD.

223 *R v Swansea City Council ex p Hearn* (1990) 23 HLR 372, QBD.

224 *R v Sefton MBC ex p Healiss* (1994) 27 HLR 34, QBD.

225 *R v Wandsworth LBC ex p Nimako-Boateng* (1983) 11 HLR 95, QBD.

226 On the issue of domestic violence, as distinct from matrimonial breakdown, see now, however, *Bond*, para 4.85.

227 *R v Eastleigh BC ex p Evans* (1984) 17 HLR 515, QBD.

228 *R v Kensington and Chelsea RLBC ex p Moncada* (1996) 29 HLR 289, QBD.

4.140 All violence and threats of violence, whatever their source, will now fall to be considered under HA 1996 s177[229] rather than – as previously – under s175(2).[230]

Threatened with homelessness

4.141 A person is 'threatened with homelessness' for the purposes of HA 1996 Part 7 if it is likely that he or she will become homeless within 56 days.[231]

4.142 Since 9 November 2012, when LA 2011 s149 came fully into force in England,[232] an applicant who makes a fresh application to an English authority within two years of a previous application which had resulted in the offer and acceptance of an assured shorthold tenancy,[233] in respect of which notice has been given under HA 1988 s21,[234] is entitled to be treated as threatened with homelessness from when the notice is given.[235] This does not apply where the application was made before – and the duty to secure accommodation was still in existence at – that date.[236]

4.143 Since 3 April 2018 when the HRA 2017 came into force,[237] an assured shorthold tenant[238] served with a valid notice under HA 1988

229 See paras 4.82–4.92.

230 See, for example, *R v Hillingdon LBC ex p H* (1988) 20 HLR 559, QBD; *R v Northampton BC ex p Clarkson* (1992) 24 HLR 529, QBD; *R v Croydon LBC ex p Toth* (1987) 20 HLR 576, CA; and *R v Newham LBC ex p McIlroy and McIlroy* (1991) 23 HLR 570, QBD.

231 HA 1996 s175(4), H(W)A 2014 s55(4).

232 Localism Act 2011 (Commencement No 2 and Transitional Provisions) (England) Order 2012 SI No 2599 art 2.

233 See Arden & Dymond, *Manual of housing law*, 10th edn, LAG, 2017, para 1.246.

234 See Arden & Dymond, *Manual of housing law*, 10th edn, LAG, 2017, para 2.203.

235 HA 1996 s195A(4). This right only arises on one re-application: HA 1996 s195A(6). See also the letter in June 2016, from the secretary of state to all local authority chief executives reminding them that authorities 'should not adopt a general policy of accepting – or refusing to accept – applicants as homeless or threatened with homelessness when they are threatened with eviction but a court has not yet made an order for possession or issued a warrant of execution'.

236 Localism Act 2011 (Commencement No 2 and Transitional Provisions) (England) Order 2012 SI No 2599 art 3.

237 Homelessness Reduction Act 2017 (Commencement and Transitional and Savings Provisions) Regulations 2018 SI No 167 reg 3, only applicable to applications made and reviews sought on or after that date – see reg.4.

238 See Arden & Dymond, *Manual of housing law*, 10th edn, LAG, 2017, para 1.246.

s21,[239] in respect of the only accommodation which that person has[240] which is available for his or her occupation,[241] and which will expire within 56 days, is also threatened with homelessness.[242]

4.144 Until the HRA 2017 in England, and H(W)A 2014 in Wales, the period was 28 days; it was originally referable to the 'normal' period granted by a court before a possession order would take effect. Since 3 October 1980, however, courts have been obliged to make orders to take effect within 14 days, save where exceptional hardship would be caused: see HA 1980 s89, although this is applicable only where the court has no other discretion to suspend, for example, under the RA 1977, HA 1985 or HA 1988.

4.145 Even once the date for possession has passed, the applicant will not be homeless until the warrant for possession is executed.[243] During this period, the applicant will, however, be threatened with homelessness.

4.146 There is no reason to draw any distinction of principle between the definitions of 'homelessness' and 'threatened with homelessness', other than the 56-day criterion: *Dyson*.[244] This seems to be based on a concession by counsel, but must surely be correct.

4.147 Once faced with an applicant who is threatened with homelessness, the authority must start making appropriate enquiries under HA 1996 s184 or H(W)A 2014 s60.[245] The duty cannot be postponed until the applicant is actually homeless: *Khan and Hussain*.[246]

4.148 If enquiries are made before the 56 days, they will be non-statutory: *Hunt*.[247]

239 See Arden & Dymond, *Manual of housing law*, 10th edn, LAG, 2017, para 2.203.

240 For a tenancy to be assured – including assured shorthold – it must be occupied as an only or principal home; accordingly, a tenant could have a principal home with a second home elsewhere, eg used for weekends or holidays; such a tenant will therefore not benefit from this extension. See, generally, Arden & Dymond, *Manual of housing law*, 10th edn, LAG, 2017, chapter 1.

241 This will be interpreted in the usual way: paras 4.16–4.38.

242 HA 1996 s175(5).

243 See *R v Newham LBC ex p Sacupima* (2001) 33 HLR 1, QBD.

244 *Dyson v Kerrier DC* [1980] 1 WLR 1206, CA, at p1212.

245 See chapter 9.

246 *R v Newham LBC ex p Khan and Hussain* (2001) 33 HLR 29, QBD.

247 *R v Rugby BC ex p Hunt* (1992) 26 HLR 1, QBD.

CHAPTER 5

Priority need

continued

Introduction

Overview

5.1 There are – normally[1] – no substantive housing rights or duties under either Housing Act (HA) 1996 Part 7 or Housing (Wales) Act (H(W)A) 2014 Part 2[2] unless the applicant has a 'priority need for accommodation'.

5.2 In England, a homeless person or a person threatened with homelessness has a priority need for accommodation if the person is within one of the following categories:[3]

a) she is a pregnant woman, or a person with whom a pregnant woman resides or might reasonably be expected to reside;
b) he or she is a person with whom dependent children reside or might reasonably be expected to reside;
c) he or she is vulnerable as a result of old age, mental illness or handicap or physical disability or other special reason, or is someone with whom such a person resides or might reasonably be expected to reside;
d) he or she is homeless or threatened with homelessness as a result of an emergency such as flood, fire or other disaster.

5.3 These categories closely follow those formerly described in Department of the Environment (DoE) Circular 18/74 as the 'priority groups' who were to have the first claim on resources available:

1 Since 9 November 2012, however, when the Localism Act (LA) 2011 s149 came into force in England (see Localism Act 2011 (Commencement No 2 and Transitional Provisions) (England) Order 2012 SI No 2599 art 2), an applicant who makes a fresh application to an English authority within two years of a previous application which resulted in an assured shorthold tenancy, will – if still eligible (see chapter 3) and not homeless intentionally (see chapter 6) – be entitled to assistance if homeless (defined as arising when the notice expires: see para 4.61) or threatened with homelessness (defined as arising when the notice is given: see para 4.141) regardless of whether or not the applicant is still in priority need: HA 1996 s195A(1), (3). This right only arises on one re-application: HA 1996 s195A(6). It only arises where the new duty to secure accommodation has arisen and had not ceased before the relevant date (Localism Act 2011 (Commencement No 2 and Transitional Provisions) (England) Order 2012 SI No 2599 art 3).

2 But see paras 10.58–10.66.

3 HA 1996 s189(1).

> The Priority Groups comprise families with dependent children living with them, or in care; and adult families or people living alone who either become homeless in an emergency such as fire or flooding or are vulnerable because of old age, disability, pregnancy or other special reasons.[4]

5.4 In England, the secretary of state[5] may add to these categories, which power has been exercised in the Homelessness (Priority Need for Accommodation) (England) Order 2002[6] and is discussed below.[7]

5.5 In Wales, the position is similar but not identical. The English priority need categories in HA 1996 s189 and the 2002 Order are largely mirrored in H(W)A 2014 s70. Differences are discussed in the relevant subheadings below. As in England, there is a power to add to these categories, although this has not yet been exercised.[8]

5.6 Whether in England or Wales, a local authority cannot fetter its discretion by pre-determining that people within specified groups – for example, the single or childless homeless – should never be considered 'vulnerable' within category c) in para 5.2 above.[9]

Time of priority need

5.7 Authorities must, when reaching decisions, take into account all material factors up to the date of the decision and, if there is a review, up to the date of the review: *Mohamed v Hammersmith and Fulham LBC*.[10] Accordingly, a priority need can be acquired after application but before decision, or after decision but before review, eg pregnancy; thus, where children were accommodated with an applicant pending

4 DoE Circular 18/74 para 10; see para 1.21.

5 HA 1996 s189(2). See also para 2.15.

6 SI No 2051.

7 See further paras 5.71–5.72.

8 H(W)A 2014 s72. Unlike in England, there is an additional power for the Welsh Ministers to remove any condition that a local housing authority must have reason to believe or be satisfied that an applicant is in priority need for accommodation before any power or duty to secure accommodation arises, which would allow a court to decide that issue for itself, instead of being confined to principles of public law intervention: see paras 12.19–12.128. It is, accordingly, a power of great potential significance. No plans to exercise this power have yet been announced.

9 See also paras 12.54–12.55.

10 [2001] UKHL 57, [2002] HLR 7. See para 9.219.

the authority's enquiries, who would not otherwise have been able to live with him or her, the applicant was still in priority need.[11]

Immigration

5.8 HA 1996 s185(4) formerly[12] required local housing authorities in England and Wales to disregard household members (including dependent children) who were ineligible[13] for housing assistance, when considering whether any eligible housing applicant was in priority need. This provision was amended[14] so that:

a) it only applies on its face in England (but see para 5.11); and
b) it applies only to an eligible applicant who is himself or herself a person subject to immigration control,[15] other than a European Economic Area (EEA) or Swiss national[16], for example, those granted refugee status,[17] indefinite leave to remain[18] or humanitarian protection.

Thus, the ineligible dependants or other household members of those who are not subject to immigration control, or who – though subject to immigration control – are EEA or Swiss nationals, are to be taken into account when deciding whether the applicant is in priority need; while those who are still subject to the requirement are to be disregarded when deciding that question if they are themselves ineligible for assistance.

11 *Oxford City Council v Bull* [2011] EWCA Civ 609, [2011] HLR 35.
12 In respect of all applications for accommodation or assistance in obtaining accommodation within the meaning of HA 1996 s183, made before 2 March 2009.
13 See paras 3.143–3.152. For example, in *Ehiabor v Kensington and Chelsea RLBC* [2008] EWCA Civ 1074, the applicant could not rely on the dependent child to establish a priority need because the child, although born in the UK, was not a British citizen and therefore required leave to remain under the Immigration Act 1971 s1(2) and was subject to immigration control. The restriction was declared incompatible with Article 14 when read with Article 8 of the European Convention on Human Rights (ECHR) in *R (Morris) v Westminster City Council (No 3)* [2005] EWCA Civ 1184, [2006] HLR 8. Cf the different approach taken by the European Court of Human Rights (ECtHR) in *Bah v UK*, App No 56328/07, [2012] HLR 2.
14 By Housing and Regeneration Act 2008 s314 and Sch 15 Part 1, in respect of all applications for accommodation or assistance in obtaining accommodation within the meaning of HA 1996 s183, made on or after 2 March 2009.
15 See paras 3.14 and 3.154–3.176.
16 See paras 3.20 onwards.
17 See paras 3.155–3.163.
18 See paras 3.167–3.169.

5.9 These ineligible household members on whom – since the amendment – reliance can be placed when deciding whether or not the applicant is in priority need are known as 'restricted persons':[19] they are persons who are not themselves eligible for assistance under HA 1996 Part 7, who are subject to immigration control, and who either do not have leave to enter or remain in the UK or who have leave subject to a condition of no recourse to public funds.[20]

5.10 If the authority is only satisfied that the applicant is in priority need by taking into account the restricted person, the application is known as a 'restricted case'.[21] In these circumstances, the authority must, so far as reasonably practical, bring any HA 1996 s193(2) duty to an end by arranging for an offer of an assured shorthold tenancy to be made to the applicant by a private landlord.[22] This is known as a 'private rented sector offer'.[23]

5.11 In Wales, the substantive position is the same: the provisions of HA 1996 ss185 and 186 are deemed to apply to the H(W)A 2014.[24] It follows that, as in England, a duty owed to a restricted person must, so far as is reasonably practicable, be brought to an end by securing an offer of accommodation from a private sector landlord.[25]

Pregnancy[26]

5.12 Any stage of pregnancy qualifies as priority need. One of the objects of the Housing (Homeless Persons) Act 1977 was to eliminate the practice of some authorities, who refused to consider a woman's pregnancy as a factor until a given stage of pregnancy. Once the pregnancy is established, there is priority need.[27]

19 HA 1996 s184(7).
20 See *Lekpo-Bozua v Hackney LBC* [2010] EWCA Civ 909, [2010] HLR 46.
21 HA 1996 s193(3B). See also para 3.149.
22 HA 1996 s193(7AD). See further paras 10.241–10.250.
23 HA 1996 s193.
24 H(W)A 2014 Sch 2 para 2.
25 H(W)A 2014 s76.
26 HA 1996 s189(1)(a); H(W)A 2014 s70(1)(a).
27 See also para 5.7. Both the English and the Welsh Codes consider that the 'normal letter of confirmation of pregnancy from the medical services issued to pregnant women or a midwife's letter' should be adequate evidence of pregnancy (English Code para 8.5; Welsh Code para 16.5). They note that, if the woman suffers a miscarriage, the authority may need to consider whether she nonetheless remains in priority need because she is vulnerable for another special reason (English Code para 8.5; Welsh Code para 16.5).

Dependent children[28]

Generally

5.13 Dependent children do not qualify in priority need in their own right; nor will they qualify as vulnerable either because of their youth or because of any disability: *ex p G*.[29] Dependent children are expected to be provided for (with assistance where appropriate, including under HA 1996 Part 7 or H(W)A 2014 Part 2) by those on whom they are dependent.

5.14 The notion of a dependent child connotes a relationship akin to that of parent–child:[30] an applicant with a 17-year-old wife could not claim to be in priority need under this category on the basis of her dependency on him.[31] The same is likely to be held in relation to siblings, eg an 18-year-old applicant with a 17-year-old sibling. A greater age difference between siblings, however, giving rise to a truly dependent relationship more akin to that of parent–child, could still give rise to a priority need.[32]

5.15 Children must be 'residing' with an applicant, not merely 'staying' – that is to say that some degree of permanence or regularity must exist.[33]

Alternative tests

5.16 The tests are alternative. In *Islam*,[34] not cross-appealed on this point,[35] the authority unsuccessfully contended that, where reliance is placed by an applicant on dependent children living with the applicant, it is also necessary to show that such children might reasonably be expected to reside with the applicant. This is not correct: if there are

28 HA 1996 s189(1)(b); H(W)A 2014 s70(1)(b).

29 *R v Oldham BC ex p G; R v Bexley LBC ex p B; R v Tower Hamlets LBC ex p Begum* [1993] AC 509, (1993) 25 HLR 319, HL; and see para 9.20.

30 See English Code of Guidance para 8.8; Welsh Code para 16.6.

31 *Hackney LBC v Ekinci* [2001] EWCA Civ 776, [2002] HLR 2.

32 *R (Lusamba) v Islington LBC* [2008] EWHC 1149 (Admin), [2008] JHL D89.

33 See also *R v Lewisham LBC ex p Creppy* (1991) 24 HLR 121, CA and *R v Lambeth LBC ex p Bodunrin* (1992) 24 HLR 647, QBD. This may, however, have started while in interim accommodation provided by the authority pending enquiries, ie it need not pre-date the application; this is consistent with the normal approach to time of priority need: para 5.7.

34 *R v Hillingdon Homeless Persons Panel ex p Islam* (1980) *Times* 10 February, QBD.

35 *Re Islam* [1983] 1 AC 688, (1981) 1 HLR 107, HL.

dependent children actually residing with the applicant at the date of the authority's decision (not the date of application),[36] it is not relevant to consider whether or not they are reasonably expected to do so.

5.17 In *Sidhu*,[37] the applicant and her children were living in a women's refuge.[38] The applicant had obtained an interim custody order from the county court, but the authority contended that it was entitled not to consider her to be in priority need until a full custody order was granted. The court rejected this argument: the full order was irrelevant (nor could the authority defer its decision in order to have time to assure itself that no change would take place in the future[39] – in that case, the prospective change was the remote prospect of the applicant losing custody at full hearing). The same may now be said of child arrangement orders.[40]

5.18 An order of a court will, however, be relevant where an applicant's children are not currently residing with the applicant, but reliance is placed on a claim that they are reasonably to be expected to do so – for example, where the applicant has won custody but cannot in practice take care of the children for want of accommodation.

Dependence on applicant

5.19 There must be dependence on the applicant: an applicant is not in priority need where children who reside with him or her are dependent on someone else.[41]

5.20 'Dependent' is not defined in HA 1996 Part 7 or in H(W)A 2014 Part 2. In *Amarfio*,[42] the Court of Appeal considered the Code of Guidance under HA 1985 Part 3 (reproduced so far as relevant in the current Codes),[43] which referred to children under the age of 16 as dependent, together with those under the age of 19 either receiving full-time education or training or otherwise unable to support themselves. It was held that once a child has gone into full-time

36 See para 9.171.
37 *R v Ealing LBC ex p Sidhu* (1982) 2 HLR 45, QBD.
38 See paras 4.12–4.13.
39 A proposition approved in *Robinson v Hammersmith and Fulham LBC* [2006] EWCA Civ 1122, [2006] 1 WLR 3295, [2006] HLR 7. See para 9.133.
40 Under Children Act 1989 s8.
41 See *R v Westminster City Council ex p Bishop* (1997) 29 HLR 546, QBD. See also *R v Camden LBC ex p Hersi* (2001) 33 HLR 52, QBD.
42 *R v Kensington and Chelsea RLBC ex p Amarfio* (1995) 27 HLR 543, CA.
43 English Code of Guidance para 8.7; Welsh Code para 16.6.

employment, the child could not be dependant: a young person on a youth training scheme was considered to be in gainful employment by way of training and therefore to be regarded as being in full-time employment.

5.21 The court did, however, recognise that there may be circumstances where a 16- or 17-year-old, even though not financially dependent on his or her parents, is sufficiently dependent on them in other respects to fall within the subsection.[44]

5.22 In *Miah v Newham LBC*,[45] the authority had treated the Code of Guidance as limited to children up to their 18th birthday. The Court of Appeal held that the Code addressed children under 19 years old (who are in full-time education or training or otherwise unable to support themselves): the Code had therefore been misinterpreted by the authority.

Separated parents

5.23 Where parents are separated, a child may divide his or her time between parents or others.[46] Three separate issues arise:

a) whether the child is dependent on the applicant;
b) whether the child resides with the applicant; and
c) if the child is not currently residing with the applicant, whether the child may reasonably be expected to do so.

Dependence on applicant

5.24 In *Vagliviello*,[47] the authority erred by applying a 'wholly and exclusively dependent' test. For the purposes of HA 1985 s59, now HA 1996 s189, it is possible for a child to reside with and be dependent

44 This accords with the conclusion in *Shortt v Secretary of State for Communities and Local Government and Tewkesbury BC* [2015] EWCA Civ 1192, [2016] 1 P&CR 15 in which the differing views expressed in the non-homelessness decision of *Fawcett Properties Ltd v Buckingham CC* [1961] AC 636, HL were considered in relation to a planning condition imposed by a local authority, the effect of which was to limit occupation of a property to persons employed in agricultural activities and their dependants: it was held that dependency was not confined to financial dependency; 'dependant' was an ordinary word, capable of referring to relationships involving non-financial dependency.

45 [2001] EWCA Civ 487.

46 See English Code of Guidance paras 8.6–8.12; Welsh Code para 16.8.

47 *R v Lambeth LBC ex p Vagliviello* (1990) 22 HLR 392, CA.

on more than one person, only one of whom may be applying for assistance.[48]

5.25 In *Bishop*,[49] parents had agreed that the children should split their time between each of them; the authority was nonetheless entitled to conclude that the children were not dependent on one of them, the father. In reaching this decision, it took into account that the children were adequately housed with the mother, that she received income support and child benefit for them, and that the applicant, who was unemployed, did not have the financial means of supporting them.

Residing with applicant

5.26 In *Smith-Morse*,[50] the authority erred because it applied a 'main' residence test; it also failed to consider the future as well as present arrangements for the child. On the other hand, in *McCarthy*,[51] the parents were divorced and, though there was a joint custody order, care and control had been given to the mother. Although it had been agreed that the children should spend three days per week with their father, this sort of 'staying access' did not equate to residence. It would only be in very exceptional circumstances that a child might reside with both parents living apart: this type of arrangement has become much more common since the Children Act (CA) 1989 came into force.[52]

5.27 The question is to be determined at the date of the decision.[53] Where the decision is made while the applicant is still only threatened with homelessness,[54] at which point the applicant may still be residing with children, for example, before leaving the family home, the applicant will only be in priority need if the children will be residing with the applicant once he or she is actually

48 But see *Holmes-Moorhouse v Richmond upon Thames LBC* [2009] UKHL 7, [2009] HLR 34, para 5.30.

49 *R v Westminster City Council ex p Bishop* (1997) 29 HLR 546, QBD.

50 *R v Kingswood BC ex p Smith-Morse* (1994) *Times*, December 8, QBD.

51 *R v Port Talbot BC ex p McCarthy* (1990) 23 HLR 208, CA.

52 See also *Holmes-Moorhouse v Richmond upon Thames LBC* [2009] UKHL 7, [2009] HLR 34. It was recognised that shared residence orders (now 'child arrangement orders') are much more common now. The policy reasons for a local authority not providing a family that previously lived under one roof with a second home are, however, considered to be overwhelming.

53 See para 5.7.

54 See paras 4.141–4.148.

homeless, which may not be the case if the authority provides no accommodation.[55]

Reasonably expected to reside

5.28 *McCarthy*[56] also held that, while not bound to do so, the authority could conclude that children are usually reasonably to be expected to reside with the parent who has care and control.

5.29 A child arrangement order[57] does not, however, mean that the children are reasonably to be expected to reside with both parents. In *Doyle*,[58] four children were to spend half the week with each parent under such an order. The father applied to the authority as homeless. The authority took the joint residence order into account but could still decide that the children were not reasonably expected to reside with the applicant. In reaching this decision, the authority was entitled to take into account the shortage of housing stock in its area and the under-occupation for part of each week that would result.

5.30 In *Holmes-Moorhouse v Richmond upon Thames LBC*,[59] the separated parents of four children agreed to a shared residence order pursuant to which the three youngest children would spend alternate weeks and half of each school holiday with the father. The father then applied to the local authority relying on the order to demonstrate priority need. The House of Lords held that, although such an order is part of the material to which an authority should have regard when making its decision, whether children are reasonably expected to reside with an applicant is a matter for the local authority to decide and cannot be dictated by a residence order.[60]

5.31 The question that the local authority should ask is whether it is reasonably to be expected, *in the context of a scheme for housing the homeless*, that children who already have a home with their mother should be able also to reside with their father, ie, asking that question in the context of a scheme for the allocation of a scarce

55 *Holmes-Moorhouse v Richmond upon Thames LBC*, above, at [20].

56 See para 5.26.

57 Under CA 1989 s8, known as a 'residence order' or 'shared/joint residence order' prior to 22 April 2014.

58 *R v Oxford City Council ex p Doyle* (1997) 30 HLR 506, QBD.

59 [2009] UKHL 7, [2009] HLR 34.

60 [2009] UKHL 7, [2009] HLR 34 at [17].

resource.[61] Only in exceptional circumstances[62] will it be reasonable to expect a child who has a home with one parent to be provided under HA 1996 Part 7[63] with another so that the child can reside with both parents.

5.32 The reference to exceptional circumstances is not a gloss on the statutory scheme, but an observation as to the probable result in the majority of cases involving separated parents.[64]

Children in social services care

5.33 The alternative limbs – 'are residing, or might reasonably be expected to reside' – avoid the difficulties which might otherwise arise where children are in temporary accommodation.

5.34 Where children are being looked after by the local social services authority, they may still be dependent on their parents and liaison with social services will be essential. 'Joint consideration with social services will ensure that the best interests of the applicant and the children are served.'[65]

Vulnerability[66]

Generally

England

5.35 The question in England is whether a person is vulnerable as a result of old age, mental illness or handicap or physical disability or other special reason. Much of the litigation in this area has focused

61 [2009] UKHL 7, [2009] HLR 34 at [9] and [14]–[16].

62 [2009] UKHL 7, [2009] HLR 34 at [21]: 'It seems to me that the likely needs of the children will have to be exceptional before a housing authority will decide that it is reasonable to expect an applicant to be provided with accommodation for them which will stand empty for at least half the time. I do not say that there may not be such a case; for example, if there is a child suffering from a disability which makes it imperative for care to be shared between separated parents. But such cases, in which that child (but not necessarily any sibling) might reasonably be expected to reside with both parents, will be unusual.'

63 Or H(W)A 2014 Part 2.

64 *El Goure v Kensington and Chelsea RLBC* [2012] EWCA Civ 670, [2012] HLR 36, in which it was stressed that the question of reasonableness is primarily one for the authority.

65 English Code of Guidance para 8.12; Welsh Code para 16.10.

66 HA 1996 s189(1)(c); H(W)A 2014 s70(1)(c).

on the meaning of 'vulnerable'. The 2015 Supreme Court decision in *Hotak v Southwark LBC and other appeals*[67] represented a change in approach, but it is easiest understood in the light the law as it stood previously.

5.36 It had formerly been held that vulnerability meant that someone was 'less able to fend for himself than an ordinary homeless person so that injury or detriment to him will result where a less vulnerable man will be able to cope without harmful effects': *Pereira*.[68]

5.37 Detriment might include a significantly increased risk of suicide or of developing a serious ailment, but it did not have to be measured in percentage terms.[69] The authority was not obliged to identify precisely the attributes of the ordinary homeless person against whom the applicant was being compared;[70] it made no difference whether the authority expressed its conclusions in terms of the

67 *Hotak v Southwark LBC; Kanu v Southwark LBC; Johnson v Solihull MBC* [2015] UKSC 30, [2015] HLR 23.

68 *R v Camden LBC ex p Pereira* (1998) 31 HLR 317, CA at 330, applying *Bowers* (above), overruling *R v Reigate and Banstead BC ex p Di Domenico* (1987) 20 HLR 153, QBD and *Ortiz v Westminster City Council* (1993) 27 HLR 364, CA. These cases had added the gloss – amounting to a two-part test – that in addition to being less able to fend when homeless, there had to be a lessened ability to find and keep accommodation. In *R v Kensington and Chelsea RLBC, Hammersmith and Fulham LBC, Westminster City Council, and Islington LBC ex p Kihara and others* (1996) 29 HLR 147, CA, however, Simon Brown LJ doubted his own proposition to this effect in *Ortiz* (although not the outcome on the facts), which he had not intended to comprise a new statement of principle, and *Pereira* disposed of it. The issue at this stage of the law's development was whether the applicant was less able to fend with the consequences of homelessness than a less vulnerable person, without a risk of injury or detriment. The cases of *R v Bath City Council ex p Sangermano* (1984) 17 HLR 94, QBD (approved in *R v Wandsworth LBC ex p Banbury* (1986) 19 HLR 76) and *R v Lambeth LBC ex p Carroll* (1987) 20 HLR 142, QBD, which had referred to vulnerability as being 'loosely in housing terms or the context of housing', while not overruled, were not to be taken to suggest anything other than assessment of ability to cope without the risk of injury or detriment: *Pereira* at 330. See also *Osmani v Camden LBC* [2004] EWCA Civ 1706, [2005] HLR 22.

69 *Griffin v Westminster City Council* [2004] EWCA Civ 108, [2004] HLR 32. In *Ajilore v Hackney LBC* [2014] EWCA Civ 1273, [2014] HLR 46, the applicant's depression and suicidal ideation did not make him vulnerable as statistics showed that significant numbers of homeless people had similar conditions; an appeal was unsuccessful: even though the reviewing officer had misunderstood the statistics, it did not undermine the thrust of the decision. The decision was overtaken by *Hotak* and other appeals.

70 *Tetteh v Kingston upon Thames RLBC* [2004] EWCA Civ 1775, [2005] HLR 21. Cf *Hall v Wandsworth LBC; Carter v Wandsworth LBC* [2004] EWCA Civ 1740, [2005] HLR 23, where the authority posed the wrong question.

applicant being at no greater risk of injury or detriment than the ordinary homeless person, or in terms of the applicant being no less able to fend for himself or herself than the ordinary homeless person: they were considered to be no more than two ways of saying the same thing.[71]

5.38 The *Periera* test was considered and approved in *Osmani*,[72] although it was stressed that it was a judicial guide, not a statutory formulation. It was said to involve a necessarily imprecise exercise in comparison between the applicant and the 'ordinary homeless person'.

> Given that each authority is charged with local application of a national scheme of priorities but against its own burden of homeless persons and finite resources, such decisions are often likely to be highly judgmental. In the context of balancing the priorities of such persons a local housing authority is likely to be better placed in most instances for making such a judgment.[73]

5.39 The authority was required to be careful to assess and apply the test on the assumption that an applicant had become or would become street homeless, not on the applicant's ability to fend for himself or herself while still housed.[74]

5.40 This was the context in which *Hotak and other appeals* settled a new approach,[75] more clearly focused on the individual applicant: when assessing whether an applicant is vulnerable, an authority must pay close attention to his or her particular circumstances rather than to a statistical analysis of the homeless population; expressions such as 'street homeless' and 'fend for oneself' are not found in HA 1996 and should be avoided; whether a person is considered to be 'vulnerable' requires comparison between the ordinary person who is homeless, not the ordinary homeless person; '"vulnerable" . . .

71 *Bellouti v Wandsworth LBC* [2005] EWCA Civ 602, [2005] HLR 46.

72 *Osmani v Camden LBC* [2004] EWCA Civ 1706, [2005] HLR 22. The judgment of Auld LJ in *Osmani* was described by Jonathon Parker LJ in *Bellouti v Wandsworth LBC* [2005] EWCA Civ 602, [2005] HLR 46 at [57] as saying 'all that (at least for present purposes) need be said or can be said on the matter' of deciding whether an applicant is vulnerable.

73 Per Auld LJ at [38].

74 *Osmani*, above, per Auld LJ at [38].

75 In *Hemley v Croydon LBC* [2018] HLR 1, the Court of Appeal considered that *Hotak* had so substantially modified the previous test that where the review officer had applied the *Pereira* test, it could not be certain that he would have reached the same conclusion had he applied the *Hotak* test; his decision was therefore quashed.

connotes "significantly more vulnerable than ordinarily vulnerable" as a result of being rendered homeless'[76].[77]

5.41 An applicant who would otherwise be vulnerable might not be so, however, if – when homeless – he or she would be provided with support and care by a third party; whether a particular applicant will in fact receive support and, if so, what support, is a case-specific question, to which the answer must be based on evidence; even if very substantial support is provided, it does not necessarily mean that an applicant is not vulnerable.[78]

5.42 Moreover, Equality Act 2010 s149 is complementary to the authority's duties under HA 1996 Part 7, and requires the authority to focus on: i) whether the applicant is under a disability (or has another relevant protected characteristic); ii) the extent of such disability; iii) the likely effect of the disability, when taken together with any other features, on the applicant if and when homeless; and, iv) whether the applicant is, as a result, vulnerable.[79]

5.43 Before *Hotak*, there had been some discussion about the relationship between vulnerability and the statutory causes:[80] it was held to be a composite question, rather than two separate stages,[81] ie, not

76 Lord Neuberger in *Hotak* at [53]; see also English Code of Guidance para 8.15.

77 In *Panayiotou v Waltham Forest LBC; Smith v Haringey LBC* [2017] EWCA Civ 1624, it was held that this gave rise to a qualitative test rather than setting a quantitative threshold: 'In other words, the question to be asked is whether, when compared to an ordinary person if made homeless, the applicant, in consequence of a characteristic within section 189(1)(c), would suffer or be at risk of suffering harm or detriment which the ordinary person would not suffer or be at risk of suffering such that the harm or detriment would make a noticeable difference to his ability to deal with the consequences of homelessness': at [64]. The authority does not need explicitly to spell out the comparison, provided that it can be discerned that it has approached the issue correctly: see *Rother DC v Freeman-Roach* [2018] EWCA Civ 368 where it was sufficient for the review officer to have correctly set out the *Hotak* test and given reasons why he did not consider the applicant's health conditions (osteoarthritis and two strokes) made him more vulnerable than an ordinary person who was homeless.

78 English Code of Guidance para 8.16.

79 This was considered and expanded in *Hackney LBC v Haque* [2017] EWCA Civ 4, [2017] HLR 14: see para 9.92. See also English Code of Guidance para 8.17.

80 Old age, mental illness or handicap or physical disability or other special reason.

81 *R v Kensington and Chelsea RLBC, Hammersmith and Fulham LBC, Westminster City Council, and Islington LBC ex p Kihara and others* (1996) 29 HLR 147, CA.

asking separately whether there is vulnerability at all and, discretely, whether it was attributable to any of the factors.[82]

5.44 On this aspect, *Hotak* largely disagreed as a matter of theory, although may be thought to have ended up making not much difference.[83]

> [T]he cases reveal a disagreement as to whether section 189(1)(c) gives rise to a two-stage test – (i) whether the applicant is 'vulnerable', and (ii) whether it is as a result of 'old age, mental illness or handicap or physical disability or other special reason' – or whether there is a single, composite test. This is a somewhat arid argument, and I am unconvinced that it is sensible to force housing authorities and reviewing officers into a straitjacket on this sort of issue. In any event, the correct answer may depend on the facts of the particular case. However, given the reference to 'other special reason', and given the fact that in many cases there will be a mixture of reasons as to why an applicant is said to be vulnerable, I suspect that the one-stage test will probably be more practical in most cases.

Wales

5.45 The position is slightly different in Wales. The sole question is whether a person is vulnerable as a result of some special reason.[84] The H(W)A 2014 then illustrates special reason in terms of 'old age, physical or mental illness or physical or mental disability'. The H(W)A 2014 preceded *Hotak*; it defines someone as 'vulnerable' if, having regard to all the circumstances, he or she is less able to fend for himself or herself if he or she were to become street homeless[85] than would an ordinary homeless person who became street homeless,

82 As the court had suggested in *R v Waveney DC ex p Bowers* [1983] QB 238, (1982) 4 HLR 118, CA. *Bowers* was not overruled by *Kihara*, but it was thought that the two-stage test was capable of causing confusion, which the composite approach would not. The composite approach was approved in *Osmani v Camden LBC* [2004] EWCA Civ 1706, [2005] HLR 22 and said to have been correctly applied in *Bellouti v Wandsworth LBC* [2005] EWCA Civ 602, [2005] HLR 46. See also *Crossley v Westminster City Council* [2006] EWCA Civ 140, [2006] HLR 26.

83 At [46].

84 H(W)A 2014 s70(1)(c).

85 'Street homelessness' means that the applicant has no accommodation available for his or her occupation in the UK or elsewhere, which he or she is entitled to occupy by virtue of an interest in it or by virtue of an order of a court, has an express or implied licence to occupy, or occupies as a residence by virtue of any enactment or rule of law giving the person the right to remain in occupation or restricting the right of another person to recover possession (see paras 4.39–4.61): H(W)A 2014 s71(2).

and this would lead to the person suffering more harm than would be suffered by the ordinary homeless person.[86] Although this was plainly a codification of the *Pereira* test[87] effectively rejected by *Hotak*, the Welsh Code of Guidance[88] nonetheless recommends that authorities adopt *Hotak*.

Old age[89]

5.46 The English Code suggests that authorities should consider whether old age makes the applicant significantly more vulnerable than an ordinary person would be if homeless; the Welsh Code refers to it as a factor which may make it harder for an applicant to fend for him or herself; both Codes stress the need to consider each case on its individual circumstances.[90]

Mental illness or handicap or physical disability[91]

5.47 In considering vulnerability due to mental or physical illness or disability, both the English and Welsh Codes[92] suggest that authorities should have regard to medical advice and – where appropriate – seek social services advice. It is for the local authority to decide whether to obtain its own advice in respect of medical reports relied on by a homeless applicant; there is no absolute requirement to refer an applicant's medical reports for evaluation by a medical adviser in every case; it depends on the facts.[93] Local authorities are not, however, expected to make their own critical evaluation of an applicant's medical evidence and should have access to specialist advice where necessary.[94]

5.48 Where the authority does decide to refer the applicant's medical reports to an adviser for specialist advice, it must take care not to

86 H(W)A 2014 s71.

87 See *Panayiotou v Waltham Forest LBC; Smith v Haringey LBC* [2017] EWCA Civ 1624: 'The *Pereira* test has been given statutory force in Wales (Housing (Wales) Act 2014, section 71)': at [4]. See also *Hemley v Croydon LBC* [2018] HLR 1: 'in Wales the test laid down by *Pereira* has been given statutory force by s.71 of the Housing (Wales) Act 2014': at [9].

88 Para 16.71 and following.

89 HA 1996 s189(1)(c); H(W)A 2014 s70(1)(c).

90 English Code of Guidance para 8.24; Welsh Code para 16.20.

91 HA 1996 s189(1)(c); H(W)A 2014 s70(1)(c).

92 English Code of Guidance paras 8.25–8.27; Welsh Code para 16.21.

93 *Simms v Islington LBC* [2008] EWCA Civ 1083, [2009] HLR 20.

94 *Shala v Birmingham City Council* [2007] EWCA Civ 624, [2008] HLR 8.

appear to be using the opinion of the medical adviser to provide or support the authority's reasons for not finding a priority on medical grounds.

5.49 In *Shala v Birmingham City Council*,[95] the applicant relied on a medical report from a psychiatrist. The local authority referred that report to its own medical adviser who, although a qualified medical practitioner, was not a qualified psychiatrist. Nor did the medical adviser examine the applicant in person. When evaluating the applicant's vulnerability on the grounds of mental illness, the authority nonetheless chose the opinion of the medical adviser over that of the applicant's psychiatrist.

5.50 The Court of Appeal held that – although the local authority had done nothing wrong in obtaining medical advice – it had fallen into the trap of thinking that it was comparing like with like when looking at the medical opinions. The function of the medical adviser was to assist the authority in understanding the medical issues and to evaluate the applicant's expert evidence. In the absence of an examination of the patient, the medical adviser's evidence could not itself ordinarily constitute expert evidence. The review officer had failed to take the lack of examination by the medical adviser into account when considering the medical evidence.

5.51 The local authority should also consider the nature and extent of the illness or disability; the relationship between the illness or disability and the individual's housing difficulties; and the relationship between the illness or disability and other factors such as drug/alcohol misuse, offending behaviour, challenging behaviours, age and personality disorder.[96] In *Osmani*,[97] Auld LJ said that authorities should have regard to the particular debilitating effects of depressive disorders and the fragility of those suffering from them if suddenly deprived of the prop of their own home.

5.52 Particular reference is made in both the English and Welsh Codes[98] to those with mental health problems who have been

95 [2007] EWCA Civ 624, [2008] HLR 8.

96 English Code of Guidance para 8.25; Welsh Code para 14.16.

97 *Osmani v Camden LBC*, above, at [38] referring to the observations of Brooke LJ in *R v Newham LBC ex p Lumley* (2001) 33 HLR 111, QBD at [63]. Cf *R (Yeter) v Enfield LBC* [2002] EWHC 2185 (Admin), [2003] JHL D19, where a decision that an applicant suffering from depression was not vulnerable – on the basis that an ordinary homeless person can be expected to suffer from depression so that the applicant was no more vulnerable than an ordinary homeless person – was upheld; this would not now survive the approach in *Hotak* and other cases (paras 5.35–5.44).

98 English Code of Guidance para 8.26; Welsh Code para 16.26.

discharged from psychiatric hospitals. The need for effective liaison between housing, social services and health authorities is stressed. Authorities should also be sensitive to direct approaches from homeless discharged patients.

5.53 Cases of vulnerability due solely to the problems of drink will not usually be attributable to one of the specified causes,[99] although an extreme case may amount to a mental or physical handicap or disability. While in some cases vulnerability may be a medical question only, it may also be a question of housing and social welfare.[100] In all cases, the question must be determined by the local authority; it cannot merely 'rubber stamp' a decision of its medical experts.[101]

5.54 In *Banbury*,[102] whether epilepsy amounted to vulnerability was said to be a question of fact and degree, which would be established if attacks occurred with intense regularity. In *Leek*,[103] a decision on the vulnerability of an epileptic – comprising refusal to reconsider an earlier decision – was quashed on the ground that the position of any particular sufferer may need to be re-assessed from time to time.

5.55 A delusional condition which rendered the applicant unable to manage his own financial affairs made him vulnerable in *Dukic*.[104]

5.56 In *Sangermano*,[105] the court distinguished between mental illness that is psychotic and mental handicap. The latter is not concerned with illness, but with subnormality or severe subnormality, although not all subnormality will necessarily amount to vulnerability; where medical evidence of subnormality is put before an authority, the authority ought either to accept it or make its own further enquiries.[106]

99 *R v Waveney DC ex p Bowers* [1983] QB 238, (1982) 4 HLR 118, CA.

100 *R v Lambeth LBC ex p Carroll* (1987) 20 HLR 142, QBD.

101 *R v Wandsworth LBC ex p Banbury* (1986) 19 HLR 76, QBD and *Osmani v Camden LBC* [2004] EWCA Civ 1706, [2005] HLR 22. Note, however, the comments of Auld LJ at [38] in *Osmani* stressing the need to look for and pay close regard to medical evidence submitted in support of applicants' claims of vulnerability on account of mental illness or handicap. Compare *Hall v Wandsworth LBC; Carter v Wandsworth LBC* [2004] EWCA Civ 1740, [2005] HLR 23, where the medical officer was entitled to advise that no further enquiries or specialist advice was required and *R v Newham LBC ex p Lumley* (2001) 33 HLR 11, QBD, where the medical officer failed to carry out adequate enquiries (see para 9.130).

102 *R v Wandsworth LBC ex p Banbury*, above.

103 *R v Sheffield City Council ex p Leek* (1993) 26 HLR 669, CA.

104 *R v Greenwich LBC ex p Dukic* (1996) 29 HLR 87, QBD.

105 *R v Bath City Council ex p Sangermano* (1984) 17 HLR 94.

106 Furthermore, when determining priority need, the applicant's earlier rent arrears had been a wholly irrelevant consideration.

5.57 The Welsh Code also refers to those who are chronically sick.[107] It suggests that while some chronically sick people may have progressed to the point of physical or mental disability, they may also be vulnerable 'because the manifestations or effects of their illness, or common attitudes to it, make it very difficult for them to find stable or suitable accommodation'.

Other special reason[108]

5.58 In *Kihara*,[109] the court rejected an approach to 'other special reason' which would mean that it had to be of the same order as the specific causes so that it would be limited to the mental or physical characteristics of an applicant: the category is free-standing, untrammelled by any notion of physical or mental weakness other than is inherent in the word 'vulnerable'. It can comprise a combination of circumstances.[110]

5.59 The word 'special' imports the requirement that the housing difficulties faced by an applicant are to an unusual degree of gravity, enough to differentiate the applicant from others. This does not include impecuniosity by itself, because an absence of means alone does not mark out one case from the generality of cases to a sufficient degree to render it 'special', but, eg, would include someone peculiarly in need of housing because of the risk of physical harm run from continuing homelessness.[111]

5.60 The expression 'other special reason' requires examination of all the personal circumstances of an applicant, including physical or mental characteristics or disabilities, but is not limited to those. Accordingly, impecuniosity may still be relevant as will be opportunities to raise money (for example, whether or not a person[112] is prohibited from employment), or whether or not an applicant has family and friends and familiarity with the language, or – put another way – is subject to 'utter poverty and resourcelessness'.[113]

107 Welsh Code para 16.27.

108 HA 1996 s189(1)(c); H(W)A 2014 s70(1)(c); see English Code of Guidance paras 8.38–8.42 and chapters 21, 25 for suggestions as to groups who might fall within this category; Welsh Code paras 16.28–16.33.

109 *R v Kensington and Chelsea RLBC, Hammersmith and Fulham LBC, Westminster City Council, and Islington LBC ex p Kihara and others* (1996) 29 HLR 147, CA.

110 *R v Waveney DC ex p Bowers* [1983] QB 238, (1982) 4 HLR 118, CA.

111 *R v Kensington and Chelsea RLBC, Hammersmith and Fulham LBC, Westminster City Council, and Islington LBC ex p Kihara and others*, above.

112 By reason of immigration status.

113 *Kihara*, above, at 159.

5.61 In *Sangermano*,[114] the court considered that language difficulties on their own would not amount to a 'special reason' within what is now HA 1996 s189(1)(c). Drug addiction alone does not amount to a 'special reason', but a likelihood of relapse into such addiction may do so.[115]

5.62 The English Code also draws attention to the position of young homeless people, noting that they may be vulnerable and have a priority need for a variety of reasons. It also draws attention to the plight of applicants who are the victims of harassment and people trafficking/modern slavery.[116]

Multiple causes

5.63 In *Crossley*,[117] the applicant, as well as being a drug addict at risk of relapse and accordingly – it was contended – vulnerable for a 'special reason', had also been in care between the ages of three and 17. It was while in care that he had become a drug addict. The authority had failed to consider whether his vulnerability had arisen from the period in care. The court stated:[118]

> This appeal has not needed to address the question of how the decision-maker should deal with a case involving two of the prescribed causes of vulnerability – here, if the claimant is right, having been in care and some other special reason. We would nevertheless observe that where two such causes have produced a single set of effects, it would not seem consistent with Parliament's intention that the effects should be artificially distributed between the causes in arriving at a decision on the critical question of vulnerability.[119]

Emergency[120]

5.64 This covers homelessness caused by an emergency such as flood, fire or other disaster. HA 1996 Part 7 and H(W)A 2014 Part 2 are in the same form: each requires that the event which causes the

114 *R v Bath City Council ex p Sangermano*, above.
115 *Crossley v Westminster City Council* [2006] EWCA Civ 140, [2006] HLR 26.
116 English Code of Guidance paras 8.40–8.42.
117 *Crossley v Westminster City Council*, above.
118 At [31].
119 This is consistent with *Hotak* and other cases, at [46], see paras 5.35–5.44.
120 HA 1996 s189(1)(d); H(W)A 2014 s70(1)(d).

homelessness and the priority need must be both an emergency and a disaster.[121]

5.65 Fire and flood are not the only qualifying disasters. In *Noble v South Herefordshire DC*,[122] the words 'or any other disaster' (in Housing (Homeless Persons) Act 1977 s2(1)(b)) were held to mean another disaster similar to flood or fire. The omission of the word 'any' in HA 1996 s189(1)(d) would not seem to affect this.

5.66 *Noble* was concerned with a demolition order under what is now HA 1985 Part 9. This was not considered to comprise a disaster similar to flood or fire, although the facts were unhelpful to the argument insofar as the occupiers had moved in after the demolition order had been made and it is therefore distinguishable in the case of a dangerous structure notice under Building Act 1984 s77, or analogous urgency powers, imposed without any real forewarning.[123] Where a demolition order under HA 1985 was imposed, however, its procedural provisions suggested that it would not qualify as an emergency, and an occupier will in any event usually be entitled to rehousing under Land Compensation Act 1973 s39;[124] the modern equivalents[125] are to be found in HA 2004 Part 1.[126]

5.67 The words 'other disaster' as of the same order as fire or floor.[127] Accordingly, a person who has been unlawfully evicted from his or her home is not in priority need within the subsection: it is not an emergency similar to flood or fire – *Bradic*. The subsection is not

121 The need for the emergency to have caused the homelessness was illustrated in *Higgs v Brighton and Hove City Council* [2003] EWCA Civ 895, [2004] HLR 2: although the loss of the applicant's caravan was an emergency (see para 5.68) it had not caused his homelessness; he was already homeless – prior to the loss – because the caravan was illegally sited (see para 4.69).

122 *Noble v South Herefordshire DC* (1983) 17 HLR 80, CA.

123 But compare the provisions of Greater London Council (General Powers) Act 1984 s39, para 5.69. If these were considered both to need, and to justify, deeming emergencies, it may be implied by the courts that other provisions of a like quality do not have the same effect.

124 See also *R v Kensington and Chelsea RLBC ex p Ben-El-Mabrouk* (1995) 27 HLR 564, CA (para 4.109), in which accommodation subject to action for want of means of escape from fire could reasonably continue to be occupied pending rehousing under the Land Compensation Act 1973. The perceived need for Greater London Council (General Powers) Act 1984 s39 (para 5.69) tends to support this result (where that Act does not apply).

125 Prohibition and demolition orders.

126 See generally Arden & Dymond, *Manual of housing law*, 10th edn, LAG, 2017, chapter 12.

127 *R v Bristol City Council ex p Bradic* (1995) 27 HLR 584, CA (following *Noble v South Herefordshire DC*, above).

confined to emergencies amounting to force majeure, however, but embraces all emergencies consisting of physical damage: *Bradic.*

5.68 Where the applicant occupies a moving structure, such as a caravan, as his or her home, the disappearance of that structure is an emergency within the subsection because it involves the sudden and unexpected loss of the applicant's home in circumstances outside his or her control: *Higgs.*[128]

5.69 The following are statutorily deemed to have become homeless or threatened with homelessness as a result of emergency such as flood, fire or other disaster:[129]

a) a person who resides in a building in outer London in respect of which an order has been made by a magistrates' court under the Greater London Council (General Powers) Act 1984 s37 that the occupants are to be removed because of its dangerous state;
b) a person who resides in a building in inner or outer London whose occupants are in danger by reason of its proximity to a dangerous structure or building, within Greater London Council (General Powers) Act 1984 s38(1), in respect of which an order has been made by the magistrates' court under section 38(2).

Other categories

Introduction

5.70 The secretary of state and, in Wales, the Welsh Ministers[130] can add further categories of priority need, or alter or remove existing categories,[131] after consultation with such associations representing authorities and such other persons as the secretary of state considers or Welsh Ministers consider appropriate.[132]

5.71 In England, the categories have been supplemented so as to reflect concerns about homelessness among young people, those leaving care, those leaving institutional settings, such as prison and the armed forces, and those fleeing violence. These additional

128 *Higgs v Brighton and Hove City Council* [2003] EWCA Civ 895, [2004] HLR 2.

129 Greater London Council (General Powers) Act 1984 s39, as amended by HA 1996 Sch 17.

130 HA 1996 s189(2); H(W)A 2014 s72.

131 HA 1996 s189(2); H(W)A 2014 s72.

132 HA 1996 s189(3); H(W)A 2014 s72(3).

categories have largely been mirrored in Wales, where they are incorporated in H(W)A 2014 s70.

5.72 In England, the Homelessness (Priority Need for Accommodation) (England) Order 2002[133] came into force on 31 July 2002. It has six additional categories of priority need.[134] See also English Code of Guidance paras 8.19–8.23 and 8.28–8.37. These six categories are also relevant in Wales as they are largely adopted into H(W)A 2014 s70, although there are differences, noted in the text and footnotes. These six categories are:

a) 16- and 17-year-olds;
b) 18- to 20-year-old care leavers;
c) vulnerable care leavers;
d) former members of the armed forces;
e) vulnerable former prisoners;
f) persons fleeing violence.

Wales also has one additional category:

g) young person at risk of exploitation.

16- and 17-year-olds

England

5.73 All 16- and 17-year-olds are in priority need provided they are not classified as a relevant child[135] or its Welsh equivalent[136] (who will therefore remain the responsibility of the social services authority) nor are owed a duty by a local authority under CA 1989 s20[137] or its Welsh equivalent.[138]

5.74 Whether a 16- or 17-year-old is a child in need for the purposes of CA 1989, and accordingly owed a duty under section 20, is a mixed question of law and fact for the local authority to decide: *M*.[139]

133 SI No 2051.
134 SI No 2051 art 3.
135 As defined by CA 1989 s23A, ie a child who has left care having been an eligible child. Eligible children are those in care who have been looked after for a prescribed period of time, ie 13 weeks (see Care Leavers (England) Regulations 2010 SI No 2571 reg 3).
136 A 'category 2' young person, see Social Services and Well-being (Wales) Act (SSWB(W)A) 2014 s104(2).
137 *R (S) v Sutton LBC* [2007] EWCA Civ 790. See further para 13.67.
138 SSWB(W)A 2014 s76.
139 *R (M) v Hammersmith and Fulham LBC* [2008] UKHL 14, [2008] 1 WLR 535, (2008) 4 All ER 271, HL, per Baroness Hale at [29].

5.75 When considering whether to house a 16- or 17-year-old applicant under HA 1996 s188 pending enquiries,[140] a housing officer is not required to assess whether the applicant is a child in need, but – if the young person is eligible and is (or may be) homeless – the authority should provide interim accommodation while an assessment is carried out by social services,[141] to whom the child should be referred.[142] It is unlawful for a social services department to sidestep its responsibilities under section 20 by assuming that a child in need can be suitably accommodated as a homeless person.[143]

5.76 If an authority's normal enquiry time would mean that an applicant will have turned 18 by the time of the decision, the authority cannot take the view that the applicant will not be in priority need and refuse all assistance, or simply provide accommodation until the birthday, even though, if enquiries in fact take the applicant to 18, the applicant will not be in priority need at the time of the decision.[144]

5.77 Nor may the authority postpone its decision to that date.[145] Nor can an authority take the benefit of an invalid decision which forces the applicant into a review, by which time the applicant has turned 18: the principle in *Mohamed v Hammersmith and Fulham LBC*,[146] that the reviewer takes into account all facts to the date of the review,[147] cannot apply in this way, for:

140 See chapter 10.

141 *Prevention of homelessness and provision of accommodation for 16 and 17 year old young people who may be homeless and/or require accommodation*, Ministry of Housing, Communities and Local Government (MHCLG) / Department for Education, April 2018, para 4.5.

142 See also *R (M) v Hammersmith and Fulham LBC*, above, at [33], [36] and [42].

143 *R (S) v Sutton LBC* [2007] EWCA Civ 790. See also *R (M) v Hammersmith and Fulham LBC*, above, HL, per Baroness Hale at [33] and [42]. Although there was no evidence of a deliberate policy in that case, to seek 'to avoid its responsibilities under the 1989 Act by shifting them on to the housing department . . . would be unlawful'. The observation was made in connection with *any* duty under the CA 1989, not section 20 alone. Social services authorities may, however, enter into an arrangement with another authority for assistance in discharge of the section 20 duty: *R (G) v Southwark LBC* [2009] UKHL 26, [2009] 1 WLR 1299.

144 *Robinson v Hammersmith and Fulham LBC* [2006] EWCA Civ 1122, [2006] 1 WLR 3295, [2007] HLR 7.

145 *Robinson v Hammersmith and Fulham LBC*, above, even for a short period.

146 [2001] UKHL 57, [2002] HLR 7.

147 See paras 5.7 and 9.229.

> If the original decision was unlawful . . . the review decision maker should have so held and made a decision that would have restored to the appellant the rights she would have had if the decision had been lawful.[148]

5.78 The April 2018 guidance[149] suggests that for some young homeless applicants the most appropriate solution may be reconciliation with their families so that they can return home. It recognises that in some cases, however, relationships may have broken down irretrievably, and in others that it may not be safe for a young person to return to the family home. Accordingly, any mediation or reconciliation will need careful brokering, and social services should be involved.[150] Temporary accommodation may need to be provided while the process takes place.[151]

5.79 If mediation would take an applicant beyond his or her 18th birthday, however, the authority is bound to reach its decision without awaiting the outcome, as – if unsuccessful – the effect would otherwise be to deprive the applicant of his or her right to a full duty.[152] Mediation and enquiries are separate processes:

> The two processes may of course proceed in parallel; and if mediation is successful while the section 184 inquiry process is still on foot, then of course there will be no need for the latter process to continue any further. On the other hand, a local housing authority has . . . no power to defer making inquiries pursuant to section 184 on the ground that there is a pending mediation.[153]

148 *Robinson v Hammersmith and Fulham LBC*, above, per Waller LJ at [32].

149 *Prevention and homelessness and provision of accommodation for 16 and 17 year old young people who may be homeless and/or require accommodation*, MHCLG / Department for Education, April 2018, chapter 2; Welsh Code para 14.39 simply suggests that this should be considered for 16- and 17-year-olds.

150 See also the comments of Baroness Hale who approved the 'wisdom of this guidance' in *R (M) v Hammersmith and Fulham LBC* [2008] UKHL 14, [2008] 1 WLR 535, [2008] 4 All ER 271, HL at [27].

151 Such matters may form part of a joint protocol between the housing and children's services departments: *Prevention and homelessness and provision of accommodation for 16 and 17 year old young people who may be homeless and/or require accommodation*, MHCLG / Department for Education, April 2018, chapter 6. It should not be in an 'all-ages night shelter provision, even in an emergency' (para 5.12).

152 *Robinson v Hammersmith and Fulham LBC*, above.

153 *Robinson*, above, at [42], per Jonathan Parker LJ. See also per Jacob LJ at [45], who additionally relied on the HA 1996 s179 duty (para 14.20) to provide advice and information: 'A near–18-year-old who came to the authority could obviously not be properly be advised to mediate if the effect of mediation would be to delay the actual s184 decision past the 18th birthday.'

Wales

5.80 Any child who is aged 16 or 17 when he or she applies to a local housing authority for accommodation or help in obtaining or retaining accommodation is in priority need.[154]

18- to 20-year-old care leavers

England

5.81 Any person who is aged 18 to 20 (other than a relevant student)[155] who at any time after reaching the age of 16, but while under 18, was, but is no longer, looked after, accommodated or fostered[156] is in priority need.

Wales

5.82 Any person who is aged 18 to 20 who was looked after, accommodated or fostered at any time while under the age of 18 is in priority need.[157]

154 H(W)A 2014 s70(1)(f). The Welsh Code similarly stresses that it is in the best interests of most 16- and 17-year-olds to live in the family home unless this is unsafe or it is unsuitable for them because of risk of violence or abuse; in recognition of this, authorities are encouraged to consider the possibility of reconciliation through mediation: para 16.44.

155 'Relevant student' is defined by the CA 1989 as a care leaver under 24 to whom CA 1989 s24B(3) applies, who is in full-time further or higher education and whose term time accommodation is not available to him or her during a vacation. Relevant students remain the responsibility of social services authorities.

156 As defined by CA 1989 s22, ie, looked after by a local authority (ie, has been subject to a care order or voluntarily accommodated); accommodated by or on behalf of a voluntary organisation; accommodated in a private children's home; accommodated for a consecutive period of at least three months by a health authority, special health authority, primary care trust or local education authority or in any care home or independent hospital or in any accommodation provided by the National Health Service Trust; or, privately fostered. See para 13.69.

157 H(W)A 2014 s70(1)(h). 'Looked after' within the meaning of SSWB(W)A 2014 s74 or CA 1989 s22, accommodated by or on behalf of a voluntary organisation; accommodated in a private children's home; accommodated for a continuous period of at least three months by a local health board, special health authority, primary care trust or local education authority, or in any care home or independent hospital or in any accommodation provided by the National Health Service Trust; or, privately fostered: Welsh Code para 16.49. See also *Provision of accommodation for 16 and 17 year old young people who may be homeless* (Welsh Assembly Government, September 2010) and Welsh Code paras 16.41–16.43.

Vulnerable care leavers

England

5.83 Where a person has previously been looked after, accommodated or fostered,[158] the person will be in priority need no matter what his or her age, if this has resulted in the person being vulnerable.[159]

Wales

5.84 There is no equivalent in Wales. The Welsh Code does, however, stress that care leavers who are over 20 are 'likely to be vulnerable as a result of being in care' and so in priority need in their own right.[160]

Former members of the armed forces

England

5.85 Those who have been members of Her Majesty's regular armed forces[161] are in priority need, but only if they are vulnerable[162] as a result of that service.

Wales

5.86 A person who has served in the regular armed forces of the Crown who has been homeless since leaving those forces is in priority need (ie, there is no need for the applicant also to be vulnerable).[163]

Vulnerable former prisoners

England

5.87 A person who is vulnerable[164] as a result of having served a custodial sentence,[165] having been committed for contempt of court or having been remanded in custody[166] is also in priority need.

158 See footnote 156, above.
159 As to whether someone is vulnerable, see paras 5.35–5.63. See also *Crossley v Westminster City Council* [2006] EWCA Civ 140, [2006] HLR 26.
160 Welsh Code para 16.52.
161 See HA 1996 s199(4); para 7.41.
162 As to whether someone is vulnerable, see paras 5.35–5.63.
163 H(W)A 2014 s70(1)(i).
164 It is not to be assumed that a person released from prison will always be vulnerable: *Johnson v Solihull MBC* [2013] EWCA Civ 752, [2013] HLR 39 (not considered on appeal: [2015] UKSC 30, [2015] HLR 23).
165 Within the meaning of Powers of Criminal Courts (Sentencing) Act 2000 s76.
166 Within the meaning of Criminal Justice Act 2003 s242(2).

Wales

5.88 The position is the same, save that the prisoner must also have a local connection with the area of the local authority.[167]

Persons fleeing violence

England

5.89 If an applicant has had to cease to occupy accommodation because of violence[168] or threats of violence which are likely to be carried out, the applicant will be in priority need if he or she is vulnerable[169] as a result.

Wales

5.90 If an applicant is homeless as a result of being subject to domestic abuse,[170] he or she will be in priority need, ie, there is no need that he or she also be vulnerable.[171]

Young person at risk of exploitation

Wales only

5.91 A person aged between 18 and 21 who requires help in obtaining or retaining accommodation and who is at particular risk of sexual or financial exploitation, is in priority need.[172]

167 H(W)A 2014 s70(1)(j); as to local connection, see chapter 7.

168 See the definition of violence in HA 1996 s177(1), paras 4.82–4.92.

169 As to whether someone is vulnerable, see paras 5.35–5.63.

170 'Abuse' is probably synonymous with 'violence' (see H(W)A 2014 s58, *Yemshaw v Hounslow LBC* [2011] UKSC 3, [2011] HLR 16 and *Waltham Forest LBC v Hussein* [2015] EWCA Civ 14, [2015] HLR 16.

171 H(W)A 2014 s70(1)(e).

172 H(W)A 2014 s70(1)(g); Welsh Code para 16.48. If a person turns 21 while still being assessed, this category of vulnerability remains applicable: Welsh Code para 16.46.

CHAPTER 6

Intentional homelessness

continued

Introduction

6.1 This chapter concerns the provision which at one time attracted most attention and controversy in homelessness law, intentional homelessness – although with so many issues related to it fairly well settled in law, more recent attention passed to the definition of vulnerability in relation to priority need,[1] and otherwise to the suitability of accommodation.[2] The issue nonetheless remains of considerable importance as, where a person is homeless intentionally, the authority's housing duty[3] is limited to temporary accommodation only for as long as it thinks is reasonable for the applicant to get his or her own accommodation.[4]

6.2 The principal definition of intentionality is the same under both the Housing Act (HA) 1996 and the Housing (Wales) Act (H(W)A) 2014 as it was under HA 1985. It was extended by HA 1996 to include arrangements under which an applicant is required to cease to occupy accommodation which it would have been reasonable for the applicant to continue to occupy, being an arrangement entered into so as to entitle the applicant to assistance under HA 1996 Part 7, where there is no other good reason for the applicant to be homeless.[5] The same extension is to be found in the H(W)A 2014.[6]

6.3 In Wales there is, however, this critical distinction: local housing authorities must decide whether to apply the intentionality test at all in their areas;[7] and it can only be applied once the authority has notified the Welsh Government that the test will apply and has published a notice to this effect.[8]

6.4 Moreover, the test may only be applied to categories of applicant specified by the Welsh Ministers, although currently all the priority

1 See paras 5.35–5.63.

2 See paras 4.71 and 10.162–10.204.

3 There are other duties which apply, including assessment, initial help and advice and assistance: see chapters 2 and 10.

4 See chapter 10.

5 HA 1996 s191(3). A further extension – to include persons to whom advice and assistance had been given under HA 1996 s197 (where the authority was satisfied that other suitable accommodation was available for the applicant's occupation in its area) but who failed to secure accommodation in circumstances where it was reasonable to be expected to do so (section 191(4)) – was repealed by the Homelessness Act 2002.

6 H(W)A 2014 s77(4).

7 H(W)A 2014 s78.

8 H(W)A 2014 s78(3).

need categories are specified.[9] An authority may choose to adopt none, some, or all of the specified categories.[10] The Welsh Government does not appear to publish a centralised list of decisions made by authorities, and it is accordingly necessary to check the website of each.

Principal definition

Overview

6.5 A person is 'homeless intentionally' if he or she has deliberately done or failed to do something, in consequence of which he or she ceases to occupy accommodation which is available for his or her occupation, and which it would have been reasonable for him or her to continue to occupy.[11]

6.6 A person is 'threatened with' homelessness intentionally if the person has deliberately done or failed to do something, the likely result of which is that the person will be forced to leave accommodation, which is available for his or her occupation, and which it would have been reasonable for him or her to continue to occupy.[12] There is no reason for drawing any distinction of principle between the operation of the two definitions.[13]

6.7 Before an applicant can be considered homeless intentionally, the authority must satisfy itself that *all* the elements of this definition apply: for example, if the applicant left accommodation that was not available for the applicant's occupation, there can be no finding of intentionality.[14]

Elements of principal definition

6.8 The elements of the principal definition are:

9 Homelessness (Intentionality) (Specified Categories) (Wales) Regulations 2015 SI No 1265.

10 Welsh Code paras 17.6–17.11.

11 HA 1996 s191(1); H(W)A 2014 s77(2).

12 HA 1996 s196(1); there is no direct equivalent in Wales, but see H(W)A 2014 s55 which defines 'threatened with homelessness'.

13 *Dyson v Kerrier DC* [1980] 1 WLR 1205, CA, at 1212. This seems to be based on a concession by counsel, but must surely be correct.

14 *Re Islam* [1983] 1 AC 688, (1981) 1 HLR 107, HL; see also, eg, *R v Eastleigh BC ex p Beattie (No 1)* (1983) 10 HLR 134, QBD.

a) the applicant must deliberately have done something or failed to do something;
b) the loss of accommodation must be in consequence of the act or omission;
c) there must be a cessation of occupation, as distinct from a failure to take up accommodation;
d) the accommodation must have been available for the occupation of the homeless person; and
e) it must have been reasonable for the homeless person to continue to occupy the accommodation.

6.9 Each of these elements, some of which are subject to further statutory definition or qualification, must be considered carefully and in the light of the case-law.

6.10 Before turning to these questions, there is one preliminary issue which requires discussion: that is, when an application is by or on behalf of more than one person, the question of *whose conduct* is to be taken into account.

Whose conduct?

Generally

6.11 A number of cases have considered how an authority should treat an application where one of the applicants, or a member of the applicant's household, has either already been adjudged homeless intentionally, or is susceptible to a finding of intentionality. The point tends to arouse strong views for, as will be seen below,[15] the duty to a homeless person is also owed to anyone who might reasonably be expected to reside with him or her, which may well include the putatively intentionally homeless member of the household.[16]

6.12 The question was first considered in *Lewis*,[17] where a man quit his employment and lost his tied accommodation. He applied to the authority, which held that he had become homeless intentionally.[18] Thereupon, the woman with whom he lived applied in her own name. The court rejected the authority's argument that it need only

15 See para 10.27.
16 See also the English Code of Guidance para 9.5; Welsh Code para 17.3.
17 *R v North Devon DC ex p Lewis* [1981] 1 WLR 328, QBD.
18 See further paras 6.76–6.85.

consider one application for the family unit as a whole: each applicant was entitled to individual consideration.[19]

6.13 The court nonetheless upheld the authority's argument that, in considering whether or not the women had become homeless intentionally, it could take into account conduct to which she had been a party or in which she had acquiesced:

> In my view, the fact that the Act requires consideration of the family unit as a whole indicates that it would be perfectly proper in the ordinary case for the housing authority to look at the family as a whole and assume, in the absence of material which indicates to the contrary, where the conduct of one member of the family was such that he should be regarded as having become homeless intentionally, that was conduct to which the other members of the family were a party . . .
>
> If, however, at the end of the day because of material put before the housing authority by the wife, the housing authority are not satisfied that she was a party to the decision, they would have to regard her as not having become homeless intentionally. In argument the housing authority drew my attention to the difficulties which could arise in cases where the husband spent the rent on drink. If the wife acquiesced to his doing this then it seems to me it would be proper to regard her, as well as him, as having become homeless intentionally. If, on the other hand, she had done what she could to prevent the husband spending his money on drink instead of rent then she had not failed to do anything (the likely result of which would be that she would be forced to leave the accommodation) and it would not be right to regard her as having become homeless intentionally.

6.14 See also *Caine*,[20] in which the Court of Appeal held that the authority was entitled to look at the family as a whole, to infer that the applicant was aware that her partner had been withholding rent, and – even though there was no direct evidence that they had done so – to infer that the couple would have discussed the matter. The authority could not be criticised for proceeding on the basis that what it was considering was a normal family/couple in which such information would be shared.

Burden

6.15 This creates something of a shift in the normal burden lying on an authority to make enquiries, because it imposes on an applicant who

19 See paras 9.45–9.46.

20 *R v Nottingham City Council ex p Caine* (1995) 28 HLR 374, CA. See too *R v Hillingdon LBC ex p Thomas* (1987) 19 HLR 196, QBD.

wants to avail himself or herself of the principle of non-acquiescence something of a positive obligation to show why acquiescence should not be presumed.[21]

Non-acquiescent applicants

6.16 *Lewis* was applied to the benefit of the applicant in *Sidhu*,[22] where the authority additionally[23] sought to rely on an earlier finding of intentionality relating to rent arrears which had occurred while the applicant was still living with her husband, even though the couple had since separated.

6.17 *Lewis* was also applied to the applicant's benefit in *Beattie (No 2)*,[24] a case of non-payment of mortgage arrears,[25] even though the applicants were still living together as a couple; and in *Phillips*,[26] a case of rent arrears caused by the husband's drinking, likewise even though the applicants were still living together as a couple.

6.18 In *Trevena*,[27] a wife – the sole tenant of a flat – surrendered the tenancy in order to move in with another man in another town, leaving her husband in (unlawful) occupation. Possession proceedings had to be taken for his eviction. Subsequently, the couple were reconciled and he was able to rely on his lack of acquiescence in (indeed, opposition to) the surrender.

6.19 An attempt to raise a finding of intentionality against a wife for her husband's conduct, dating from before she even met him, was (unsurprisingly) rejected by the court in *Puhlhofer*.[28]

Findings of acquiescence

6.20 In *Thomas*,[29] however, Woolf J (who had decided *Lewis*), while restating the principle, upheld 'acquiescence' on the part of a male joint tenant whose cohabitant had caused the loss of their council tenancy by nuisance and annoyance, even though he had been in prison both

21 See chapter 9.
22 *R v Ealing LBC ex p Sidhu* (1982) 2 HLR 45, QBD.
23 See paras 4.12 and 5.17.
24 *R v Eastleigh BC ex p Beattie (No 2)* (1984) 17 HLR 168, QBD.
25 See further, paras 6.63–6.66.
26 *R v West Dorset DC ex p Phillips* (1984) 17 HLR 336, QBD.
27 *R v Penwith DC ex p Trevena* (1984) 17 HLR 526, QBD.
28 *R v Hillingdon LBC ex p Puhlhofer* (1985) 17 HLR 278, QBD, not appealed on this point; cf [1986] AC 484, CA and HL, (1985) 17 HLR 588, CA, (1986) 18 HLR 158, HL.
29 *R v Swansea City Council ex p Thomas* (1983) 9 HLR 64, QBD.

at the time of the conduct and at the time of the proceedings for possession.

6.21 The factors which influenced the court were:

a) that the man had been offered, but had declined, an opportunity to attend the hearing; and
b) that there was no evidence of attempts by him to persuade the woman to desist in the conduct, which had persisted up until the hearing.

6.22 In *Khatun*,[30] it was unsuccessfully argued on behalf of a Bangladeshi wife that she had not acquiesced in her husband's conduct in leaving accommodation which it would have been reasonable to continue to occupy, on the basis that – as a matter of culture and practice – she had no choice but to abide by her husband's decision. Dismissing her appeal, the court held that, as she had been content to leave decisions to her spouse and to co-operate in implementing those decisions, she could properly be regarded as having acquiesced.

Rent arrears

6.23 It may be the case, particularly in arrears cases, that the spouse has found out too late to be able to do anything about rent arrears. So, for example, arrears may be so substantial when the spouse discovers them that simple awareness of the debt before homelessness cannot be said to amount to acquiescence: see *Spruce*.[31]

6.24 On the other hand, in *O'Connor*[32] the authority was entitled to conclude that there had been acquiescence, and in *Salmons*[33] the authority had addressed the critical question of whether it was entitled to conclude that the applicant must have known about, or at least turned a blind eye to, the arrears, and was accordingly entitled to reach the view that the applicant had either not been honest about his knowledge of the arrears, or that he had at the least been reckless about the true situation.

Non-cohabitants

6.25 The acquiescence point is not confined to cohabitants. In *Smith v Bristol City Council*,[34] a woman was held responsible for acts of

30 *R v Tower Hamlets LBC ex p Khatun* (1993) 27 HLR 344, CA.
31 *R v East Northamptonshire DC ex p Spruce* (1988) 20 HLR 508, QBD.
32 *R v Barnet LBC ex p O'Connor* (1990) 22 HLR 486, QBD.
33 *R v Ealing LBC ex p Salmons* (1990) 23 HLR 272, QBD.
34 See discussion at December 1981 *LAG Bulletin* 287.

nuisance caused by her son and lodgers, which resulted in her eviction. Similarly, the basis for the order for possession which resulted[35] in a finding of intentionality in *Devenport*[36] was conduct by the children of the family; conduct by children was included in the reasons for the finding of intentionality in *Ward*.[37]

6.26 In *Bannon*,[38] acquiescence was upheld in relation to nuisance by the family as a whole, to which the applicant had either been a party or else which she had done nothing to prevent. In *John*,[39] nuisance and annoyance by a lodger caused the eviction of the tenant even though it occurred only when she was out of the flat, and the lodger was both younger and considerably stronger than she, so that she was unable to control his behaviour. Her 'acquiescence' was the failure to evict him.[40]

6.27 An attempt to use the principle of non-acquiescence on behalf of child applicants failed on the basis that the children were not in priority need in their own right: *ex p G*.[41]

Deliberate act or omission

General principles

6.28 The issue is not whether a person deliberately became homeless, but whether he or she deliberately did (or failed to do) something as a result of which he or she became homeless: the word 'deliberate'

35 But see para 6.28.

36 *Devenport v Salford City Council* (1983) 8 HLR 54, CA.

37 *R v Southampton City Council ex p Ward* (1984) 14 HLR 114, QBD.

38 *R v East Hertfordshire DC ex p Bannon* (1986) 18 HLR 515, QBD.

39 *R v Swansea City Council ex p John* (1982) 9 HLR 56, QBD.

40 In *Darlington BC v Sterling* (1997) 29 HLR 309, CA, it was taken for granted that eviction on the grounds of nuisance and annoyance by – in that case – the tenant's son was capable of giving rise to a finding of intentionality (which should not, it was held, have prevented an order for possession being made against the tenant).

41 *R v Oldham MBC ex p G; R v Bexley LBC ex p B* (1993) 25 HLR 319, HL, see para 5.13. See also *R v Camden LBC ex p Hersi* (2001) 33 HLR 52, CA. On the applicability of the Children Act 1989 in such cases, see paras 13.57–13.107. Children Act 2004 s11 (duty on authorities to have regard to the need to safeguard and promote the welfare of children when discharging any functions) adds nothing to the assessment of whether someone is intentionally homeless: *Huzrat v Hounslow LBC* [2013] EWCA Civ 1865, [2014] HLR 17. The correct forum for deploying arguments about section 11 is at the application and/or review stage: *Mohamoud v Kensington and Chelsea RLBC; Saleem v Wandsworth LBC* [2015] EWCA Civ 780, [2015] HLR 38.

only governs the act or omission – *Devenport.*[42] The link between the act and the homelessness must be judged objectively: *Robinson v Torbay BC.*[43]

Good faith

6.29 That said, 'an act or omission in good faith on the part of a person who was unaware of any relevant fact shall not be treated as deliberate' for the purposes of establishing intentional homelessness.[44] This statutory qualification introduces a subjective element into the issue.[45] Subsections HA 1996 191(1) and (2) pose 'serial questions': whether an act is in good faith *and* in ignorance of relevant facts must be considered separately – *O'Connor,*[46] in which the authority had wrongly merged the two subsections and obscured the critical, good faith question.

6.30 If it is established that the applicant was unaware of a relevant fact, the question is not whether the ignorance was reasonable, but whether it was in good faith.[47] Good faith can include cases where the applicant's ignorance of a relevant fact was due to his or her own unreasonable conduct[48] and where the applicant could be said to have been foolish or imprudent.[49] The good faith requirement will not, however, be satisfied where an applicant has shut his or her eyes to the obvious, or has acted with wilful ignorance or on little more than a wing and a prayer.[50]

6.31 Want of 'good faith' carries the connotation of some kind of impropriety, or an element of misuse or abuse of the legislation.[51] Dishonesty will not constitute good faith.[52] Whether or not an act is

42 *Devenport v Salford City Council*, above. Cf the obiter comments of the Master of the Rolls in *R v Slough BC ex p Ealing LBC* [1981] QB 801, CA.

43 *Robinson v Torbay BC* [1982] 1 All ER 726, QBD.

44 HA 1996 ss191(2) and 196(2); H(W)A 2014 s77(3).

45 *R v Exeter City Council ex p Tranckle* (1993) 26 HLR 244, CA. See the examples in the English Code of Guidance para 9.26; Welsh Code para 17.26.

46 *O'Connor v Kensington and Chelsea RLBC* [2004] EWCA Civ 394, [2004] HLR 37.

47 *F v Birmingham City Council* [2006] EWCA Civ 1427, [2007] HLR 18 at [17].

48 *F*, above, at [17].

49 *Ugiagbe v Southwark LBC* [2009] EWCA Civ 31, [2009] HLR 35 at [26].

50 *F*, above, at [17].

51 *Ugiagbe*, above, at [27].

52 *Ugiagbe*, above, at [27].

laudable or done for good motives has no bearing on whether it is in good faith.[53]

Ignorance of facts

6.32 An applicant's failure properly to appreciate his or her prospects (or lack of prospects) of future housing can be treated as 'awareness of a relevant fact' for the purposes of HA 1996 s191(2),[54] provided that it is sufficiently specific and based on a degree of genuine investigation, not mere aspiration.[55] If the prospect of future housing rests on next to nothing but hope, not applying section 191(2) in the applicant's favour is not an error of law;[56] in such a case, the subsection is a non-starter and no specific reference to it is needed.[57]

6.33 In *Ugiagbe*,[58] the applicant was unaware of a relevant fact because she did not know that she could not be required to leave without a court order.[59] It is, however, ignorance of a relevant fact which must not have been deliberate, not ignorance of the legal consequences.[60]

6.34 Where an applicant temporarily went to live with her mother while at college but was warned by her father that she would not be allowed to return, the authority misdirected itself in disregarding her genuine belief that he did not mean it, ie, that she would be able to go back. The father's state of mind was a relevant fact and so his daughter's action – taken in genuine ignorance of her father's

53 In *Alfonso-da-Trinade v Hackney LBC* [2017] EWCA Civ 942, the appellant had come to the UK in order to seek better medical provision for her disabled child; whilst that was laudable, good faith did not turn on motivation; the applicant had left her settled accommodation with a reckless disregard for her housing prospects in the UK.

54 *F v Birmingham City Council*, above, at [17].

55 *R v Westminster City Council ex p Obeid* (1996) 29 HLR 389, QBD at 398; *Aw-Aden v Birmingham City Council* [2005] EWCA Civ 1834 at [10] and [11].

56 *Aw-Aden*, above, at [11].

57 *Aw-Aden*, above, at [12].

58 *Ugiagbe v Southwark LBC* [2009] EWCA Civ 31, [2009] HLR 35 at [8].

59 For the facts, see further para 6.44.

60 *R v Eastleigh BC ex p Beattie (No 2)* (1984) 17 HLR 168, QBD; *R v Croydon LBC ex p Toth* (1988) 20 HLR 576, CA; cf *R v Mole Valley DC ex p Burton* (1988) 20 HLR 479, QBD, where the applicant's belief in assurances by her husband that they would be rehoused under a union agreement was held to be a belief of fact, not of law. See also *Alfonso-da-Trinade v Hackney LBC* [2017] EWCA Civ 942, in which the authority had been entitled to find that the appellant's ignorance of the possibility that her sister could be evicted was not ignorance of a relevant fact but of a possible future event.

true intent – could not be classified as deliberate: *Wincentzen v Monklands DC*.[61]

6.35 It was a relevant fact of which the applicant was ignorant where a person was misled as to business prospects, which caused him to move abroad: *Lusi*.[62]

6.36 In *Sukhija*,[63] a distinction was drawn between a mistake of fact (which could be within the good faith defence) and a mere unfulfilled hope (which was not). The decision that the applicant – who had come to England in the mistaken belief that she would be able to find employment and a home – was intentionally homeless was accordingly upheld.

6.37 See also *Khatun*,[64] in which the applicant was described as having no more than an expectation of being able to live temporarily with her parents-in-law on her return to the UK: it was not a fact to which the good faith defence could be applied.

6.38 In *Ashton*,[65] a middle-aged woman moved from her home in Tunbridge Wells to take up a temporary job in Winchester, where the authority provided her with a one-year tenancy subject to the exception in HA 1985 Sch 1 para 5.[66] After a year, the authority obtained possession of the premises. A finding that the applicant was intentionally homeless was quashed on the basis, inter alia, that, in leaving Tunbridge Wells, the applicant had acted in good faith because she was unaware that she would be unable to find either housing or employment after the initial year. Accordingly, her action in surrendering the tenancy at Tunbridge Wells should not have been treated as deliberate.

6.39 In *Conway*,[67] a woman erroneously but genuinely believed that she had a further period of a year in which to decide whether or

61 *Wincentzen v Monklands DC* (1988) SLT (Court of Session) 259, September 1988 *LAG Bulletin* 13.
62 *R v Hammersmith and Fulham RLBC ex p Lusi* (1991) 23 HLR 460, QBD.
63 *R v Ealing LBC ex p Sukhija* (1994) 26 HLR 726, QBD.
64 *R v Tower Hamlets LBC ex p Khatun* (1994) 27 HLR 465, CA.
65 *R v Winchester City Council ex p Ashton* (1991) 24 HLR 48, QBD. The decision of Kennedy J was upheld by the Court of Appeal (see (1991) 24 HLR 520) on the additional basis that, although the authority had stated that they had had regard to the general circumstances prevailing in relation to housing in their area (H(HP)A 1977 s60, now HA 1996 s177), they had failed to balance that against the 'quite exceptional circumstances' of the applicant (ie that she had left her previous accommodation in Tunbridge Wells in order to take up employment in Winchester after six years of involuntary unemployment).
66 Temporary accommodation for people taking up employment.
67 *R v Christchurch BC ex p Conway* (1987) 19 HLR 238, QBD.

not to extend her existing shorthold tenancy. This was ignorance of a material fact, ie, the time remaining in which to make her decision.

6.40 In *Rose*,[68] the applicant had been born in the UK but when her parents separated, she had gone to live with her mother in Jamaica. Subsequently, her siblings came to England, to live with their father, who paid their fares and accommodated them; when the applicant asked her father if she, and her daughter, could also come to England, her father was unable to pay her fare but otherwise confirmed that she could come to England, which the applicant understood to mean that he would have adequate accommodation for them, though she made no specific inquiries as to for how long they would be able to stay with him. There was no accommodation for them and her father asked them to leave after a week. The authority's decision that she had become homeless intentionally was quashed: it had failed to take into account a material consideration, ie her unawareness of the lack of accommodation with her father; it was not entitled to assume without further inquiry that because she had made no specific inquiries, she had acted other than in good faith in ignorance of a relevant fact.

6.41 In *Obeid*,[69] the applicant had taken private-sector accommodation in the belief that her rent would be covered by housing benefit, in ignorance of (and without making enquiries about) the provisions of the (then) Housing Benefit (General) Regulations 1987[70] which could limit her benefit to a proportion of her rent. This was capable of constituting ignorance of a relevant fact. Carnwath J, considering, among other things, the decisions in *Lusi*[71] and *Sukhija*,[72] said that:

> The effect of those judgments, as I understand them, is that an applicant's appreciation of the prospects of future housing or future employment can be treated as 'awareness of a relevant fact' for the purposes of this subsection, provided it is sufficiently specific (that is related to specific employment or specific housing opportunities) and provided it is based on some genuine investigation and not mere 'aspiration'.[73]

68 *R v Wandsworth LBC ex p Rose* (1983) 11 HLR 105, QBD.

69 *R v Westminster City Council ex p Obeid* (1996) 29 HLR 389, QBD.

70 SI No 1971.

71 *R v Hammersmith and Fulham LBC ex p Lusi*, above; see para 6.35.

72 *R v Ealing LBC ex p Sukhija*, above, at 398; see para 6.36.

73 This statement was approved in *Aw-Aden v Birmingham City Council* [2005] EWCA Civ 1834, where the applicant's unfulfilled hope of finding employment in this country was insufficiently specific; rather, it was a mere aspiration.

6.42 Leaving settled accommodation to move into unsettled accommodation may form part of the circumstances amounting to intentional homelessness, under the HA 1996 extended definition of intentionality governing 'collusive arrangements' – see further below.[74] Ignorance of the unsettled quality of intended accommodation would, however, amount to ignorance of a relevant fact and as such should mean that a move is not caught, because 'the purpose of the arrangement' implies an element of intention ('to enable [the applicant] to become entitled to assistance').[75]

Carelessness v deliberate conduct

6.43 In deciding whether the ignorance is in good faith, an authority must distinguish between honest blundering or carelessness on the one hand, which can amount to good faith conduct; and dishonesty, where there can be no question of good faith: *Lusi*;[76] *Ali and Bibi*.[77] The question is whether the action is taken in good faith, not whether it was reasonable.

6.44 In *Ugiagbe*,[78] the applicant was asked by her landlord to leave; she went to her local authority's 'One-Stop Shop' and was told to go to the Homeless Persons' Unit (HPU) to get temporary accommodation; as she did not want to be treated as homeless, she returned to the property. Eventually, her landlord again asked her to leave, which she did, and she applied for homelessness assistance. Her omission to follow the advice to go to the HPU could be described as foolish or imprudent, yet it was the opposite of bad faith because her subjective motivation in not doing so was because she had been led to believe that she would be treated as homeless, which was the last thing she wanted.[79]

6.45 In *F*,[80] the applicant surrendered a secure tenancy of a two-bedroom flat, ignoring advice from her social worker that she risked being found intentionally homeless, and took a tenancy of a three-bedroom house, from which she was evicted for arrears which accrued because she did not receive housing benefit. She was found, at best, to have proceeded on a wing and a prayer; her conduct was

74 See paras 6.163–6.168.
75 HA 1996 s191(4)(b).
76 *R v Hammersmith and Fulham LBC ex p Lusi* (1991) 23 HLR 460, QBD.
77 *R v Westminster City Council ex p Ali and Bibi* (1992) 25 HLR 109, QBD.
78 *Ugiagbe v Southwark LBC* [2009] EWCA Civ 31, [2009] HLR 35 at [3].
79 *Ugiagbe*, above, at [25], [26] and [28].
80 *F v Birmingham City Council* [2006] EWCA Civ 1427, [2007] HLR 18 at [9].

described as wilful ignorance or shutting her eyes to the obvious which could not satisfy the good faith test; HA 1996 s191(2) did not arise for consideration.[81]

6.46 In *Rouf*,[82] a finding of intentionality against an applicant who returned to a flat that had been repossessed after an absence of three years, but who nonetheless had believed it would still be available to him, was quashed. The authority had failed to consider whether the belief was genuine, wrongly approaching the question as one of the reasonableness of his conduct.

6.47 In *Onwudiwe*,[83] however, an unemployed applicant's conduct in taking on large mortgage commitments in order to fund a business for which there had been no market-testing, took the case beyond the stage of honest incompetence and provided material on which it could be said that he was deliberately putting his house at risk.

6.48 In *Beattie (No 2)*,[84] persistent failure to pay mortgage arrears was deliberate, notwithstanding that the applicant had been advised by his solicitors that it would not be.

6.49 On the other hand, in *White*,[85] the applicant believed that the then Department of Health and Social Security (DHSS) was, or ought to be, paying the whole of the interest element on the mortgage instalments by direct deduction from his benefit. In fact, his supplementary benefit entitlement was so low that it did not cover the full amount of the interest, so that arrears continued to mount. The court held that – for most of the period in question – the applicant was under a genuine misapprehension as to a relevant fact,[86] and that he had acted in good faith in failing to make the payments himself. There was, accordingly, no deliberate omission and, in consequence, no intentional homelessness.

6.50 In *O'Connor v Kensington and Chelsea RLBC*,[87] the applicant husband and wife believed that a friend, who was staying at their flat while they were visiting Ireland for a funeral and while the husband recovered from depression, was paying the rent. He was not in fact doing so; a suspended possession order was obtained in their absence and subsequently enforced after their return. The Court of Appeal

81 *F*, above, at [19].

82 *R v Tower Hamlets LBC ex p Rouf* (1991) 23 HLR 460, QBD.

83 *R v Wandsworth LBC ex p Onwudiwe* (1994) 26 HLR 302, CA.

84 *R v Eastleigh BC ex p Beattie (No 2)* (1984) 17 HLR 168, QBD.

85 *White v Exeter City Council*, December 1981 *LAG Bulletin* 287, QBD.

86 Whether or not the DHSS was paying the whole of the interest payments.

87 *O'Connor v Kensington and Chelsea RLBC* [2004] EWCA Civ 394, [2004] HLR 37.

held that it is not necessary for the ignorance of the relevant fact to be reasonable before an omission qualifies as non-deliberate; a person's ignorance may well be due to unreasonable behaviour, yet what the person does in consequence may still be in good faith. The dividing line is not at the point where an applicant's ignorance of a relevant fact is due to the applicant's own unreasonable conduct but at the point where, by shutting his or her eyes to the obvious, the applicant cannot be said to have acted in good faith.

Act causing loss of accommodation

6.51 The act of good faith referred to in HA 1996 s191(2) is the act or omission causing homelessness; this is the act which must be considered under section 191(1).[88]

6.52 In *Stewart*,[89] the authority found that the deliberate act which caused the homelessness was the commission of a criminal act by the applicant, following which he was imprisoned and a warrant executed (without notice) on the basis of an earlier possession order for arrears. The authority accepted that, after his imprisonment, the applicant had made an arrangement with his sister to maintain the tenancy, but no rent was in fact paid under it. He argued that the deliberate act or omission was the failure to pay the rent, which was an act in good faith because he had been unaware of a relevant fact, ie, his sister's failure to keep to the arrangement. The Court of Appeal held that, given a proper finding that the deliberate act which caused the homelessness was the offence, the subsequent acts in good faith were irrelevant and the authority was not obliged to investigate them.

6.53 Where the cause of homelessness was an applicant's inability to meet mortgage repayments as a result of a severe downturn in business, the homelessness was intentional because the mortgage itself had been obtained as a result of the applicant's fraudulent misrepresentation of her income: *Rughooputh*.[90]

6.54 In *Chishimba v Kensington and Chelsea RLBC*,[91] however, the appellant used a counterfeit passport to secure assistance under HA 1996 Part 7; she was granted a tenancy by the authority but, when it was discovered that she had not been eligible for assistance, the

88 Which is why it is important correctly to identify the date when the (putatively intentional) homelessness began – cf *O'Connor v Kensington and Chelsea RLBC*, above. See also *Ugiagbe v Southwark LBC*, above at [6].

89 *Stewart v Lambeth LBC* [2002] EWCA Civ 753, [2002] HLR 40.

90 *R v Barnet LBC ex p Rughooputh* (1993) 25 HLR 607, CA.

91 [2013] EWCA Civ 786, [2013] HLR 34.

authority sought possession. After being granted leave to remain, the appellant re-applied, following which she was evicted from the flat. The authority held that she was homeless intentionally, as the cause of her homelessness was her use of the counterfeit passport.

6.55 The Court of Appeal accepted that the immediate cause of the appellant's homelessness was the discovery that she had obtained her tenancy by deception; proceeding back in time from that immediate cause, however, the effective cause of her homelessness was that she had been ineligible for assistance, so that she was not intentionally homeless as it could not have been reasonable for her to continue to occupy accommodation to which she never had any lawful right.

6.56 In *Tranckle*,[92] the applicant entered into an imprudent financial arrangement in good faith, unaware of the (un)reality of the prospects of success for the public house which she was purchasing, which had been concealed from her by the brewery; her decision to purchase the pub was in good faith.

6.57 In *Watchman*,[93] the applicant was a secure tenant who exercised the right to buy with the aid of a mortgage on which the repayments were significantly higher than the rent she had previously been paying in respect of which there was a history of arrears. Her husband subsequently lost his job but, although he found another at a lower salary, mortgage arrears built up and the mortgagee repossessed the property. The authority decided that the applicant was intentionally homeless by taking on the mortgage when it was inevitable that she would get into severe financial difficulties within a short time; her husband's employment problems had not caused the repossession but merely accelerated the inevitable eviction.[94]

6.58 Upholding that decision, it was held that – when deciding whether an applicant is intentionally homeless where there are several potential causes of the homelessness – the authority must make a careful judgment on the particular facts in order to decide whether the homelessness is a likely consequence of a deliberate act on the part of the applicant, bearing in mind that it is the applicant's responsibility for the homelessness that is in question.[95] While the authority

92 *R v Exeter City Council ex p Tranckle* (1993) 26 HLR 244, CA.

93 *Watchman v Ipswich BC* [2007] EWCA Civ 348, [2007] HLR 33 at [6].

94 *Watchman*, above, at [9].

95 *Watchman*, above, at [22]; see also *Carthew v Exeter City Council* [2012] EWCA Civ 1913, [2013] HLR 19, in which the authority failed to consider why the appellant had transferred her interest in a property to her former partner.

has to consider the time when the applicant in fact became homeless,[96] it is entitled to take account of events prior to that date.[97]

6.59 Ironically, in some cases a person who takes the trouble to find out relevant facts, and reaches a decision on them, will be more vulnerable to a finding of intentionality than a person who has omitted to make any enquiries at all.[98]

Bad faith

6.60 Where bad faith is suspected, it has been suggested that it may not invariably be necessary to put the matter to the applicant (*Hobbs v Sutton LBC*)[99] – but see *Moozary-Oraky*,[100] in which good faith relative to awareness of housing benefit was considered to be a question of jurisdictional fact, without which no reasonable authority could reach a conclusion on intentionality, into which the authority was accordingly required to make explicit enquiry of the applicant.[101]

6.61 In *Joyce*,[102] the authority did not even ask the applicant why mortgage arrears had arisen. This failure was fatal to its decision, as it had omitted to take something relevant into account,[103] ie, the applicant's explanation or answer.

Illustrations

6.62 There is much guidance and a large number of cases on intentionality, which can conveniently be approached under a series of headings – but it is essential to remember that the cases are all illustrative of the operation of the provisions rather than precedents on their facts, and that guidance is not binding.[104]

96 *Din v Wandsworth LBC* [1983] 1 AC 657, HL.
97 *Watchman* at [23].
98 *R v Westminster City Council ex p Obeid* (1996) 29 HLR 389, QBD.
99 (1993) 26 HLR 132, CA.
100 *R v Westminster City Council ex p Moozary-Oraky* (1993) 26 HLR 214, QBD.
101 As to whether or not the applicant had seen a letter informing her that her benefit had been stopped.
102 *R v Wyre BC ex p Joyce* (1983) 11 HLR 73, QBD.
103 See para 12.48.
104 As to departing from guidance, see *De Falco v Crawley* BC [1980] QB 460, CA, at 478; see also the recent summary of authorities in relation to departing from statutory guidance in *R (X) v Tower Hamlets LBC* [2013] EWHC 480 (Admin), at [27]–[35]: see generally paras 12.49–12.51.

Rent/mortgage arrears

6.63 The English Code gives as an example of homelessness which should not be treated as deliberate:

> An applicant's actions would not amount to intentional homelessness where they have lost their home, or were obliged to sell it, because of rent or mortgage arrears resulting from significant financial difficulties, and the applicant was genuinely unable to keep up the rent or mortgage payments even after claiming benefits, and no further financial help was available.[105]

6.64 This is to be contrasted with cases where an applicant:

a) chooses to sell his or her home in circumstances where is the applicant is under no risk of losing it;
b) has lost his or her home because of wilful and persistent refusal to pay rent or mortgage payments.[106]

6.65 The Code issued under HA 1985 Part 3 was in similar terms. In *Hawthorne*,[107] it was considered not to misstate the law. In *Bryant*,[108] it was said that the Code drew a distinction 'between those who can, or could reasonably be expected to, pay mortgage payments or rent but do not do so, and those who in reality cannot pay because of real financial difficulties'. It was a question of fact for the authority to decide into which category an applicant fell, open only to challenge on usual public law principles.[109]

6.66 The English Code also considers that authorities should not find an applicant to be intentionally homeless where the non-payment of rent or mortgage costs arose from financial difficulties which were beyond the applicant's control or which were the result of housing benefit or universal credit delays.[110]

6.67 By way of further example, in *Noel v Hillingdon LBC*,[111] the applicant had taken a tenancy which he could not afford; his partner and child then moved in and he failed to apply for an increase in his

105 English Code of Guidance para 9.18; see Welsh Code para 17.18 to like effect.
106 English Code of Guidance para 9.20; Welsh Code para 17.23.
107 *R v Wandsworth LBC ex p Hawthorne* (1994) 27 HLR 59, CA. See also *Ekwuru v Westminster City Council* [2003] EWCA Civ 1293, [2004] HLR 14, where arrears arose because of a housing benefit cap.
108 *R v Warrington BC ex p Bryant* (2001) JHL D5, QBD.
109 As to which, see chapter 12. See also *William v Wandsworth LBC; Bellamy v Hounslow LBC* [2006] EWCA Civ 535, on failure to make mortgage payments after taking out a further loan.
110 English Code, para 9.17(a).
111 [2013] EWCA Civ 1602, [2014] HLR 10.

housing benefit. Both the decision to take an unaffordable tenancy and the failure to apply for an increase in housing benefit were held to amount to intentional homelessness.

6.68 In *Viackiene v Tower Hamlets LBC*,[112] a failure to seek a joint tenant who could have assisted with paying the rent – as suggested by the landlord – was held to amount to intentional homelessness.

Nuisance and annoyance

6.69 Nuisance and annoyance can clearly be considered 'deliberate' for this purpose.[113] In *ex p P*,[114] a finding of intentionality was upheld in relation to alleged criminal and anti-social behaviour[115] (confirmed by the authority's own enquiries) which had led to threats from the IRA that the applicants would be killed if they did not leave their accommodation.

6.70 In *Bell*,[116] a possession order was obtained against the applicant on the grounds of nuisance and annoyance. She was accepted by Wirral MBC as having a priority need because of the state of her mental health. Applying a test to be found in the Code of Guidance under HA 1985 Part 3 – which referred to capacity to manage affairs[117] – the authority nonetheless found that she had become homeless intentionally. Her application for judicial review was dismissed. It was said to be one thing to be less able to fend for oneself (for the purpose of establishing vulnerability),[118] and another

112 [2013] EWCA Civ 1764, [2014] HLR 13.

113 *Devenport v Salford City Council* (1983) 8 HLR 54, CA; *R v Swansea City Council ex p John* (1982) 9 HLR 56, QBD; and *R v East Hertfordshire DC ex p Bannon* (1986) 18 HLR 515, QBD. See also English Code of Guidance para 9.20; Welsh Code para 17.23.

114 *R v Hammersmith and Fulham LBC ex p P* (1989) 22 HLR 21, QBD.

115 In *Bristol City Council v Mousah* (1997) 30 HLR 32, CA, allowing premises to be used in connection with the sale of drugs, even though the tenant was himself absent and was not charged, appears to have been presumed to be capable of giving rise to a finding of intentionality (which it was held should not have prevented the making of an order for possession on the basis of 'reasonableness'; compare also the details of *Darlington BC v Sterling* (1997) 29 HLR 309, CA, summarised above at footnote 40).

116 *R v Wirral MBC ex p Bell* (1994) 27 HLR 234, QBD.

117 The 2018 English Code refers to persons who are 'incapable of managing their affairs, for example, by reason of age, mental Illness or disability' and those with 'limited mental capacity; or a temporary aberration or aberrations caused by mental illness, frailty, or an assessed substance misuse problem': paras 9.17(b), (c). There is no equivalent in the Welsh Code.

118 See paras 5.35–5.63.

to be incapable of managing one's own affairs (for the purpose of intentionality); the two findings were accordingly not inconsistent.

6.71 In *Denton*,[119] the applicant's mother asked him to leave the family home because of his behaviour. The authority found that he had become homeless intentionally, a decision upheld by the Court of Appeal: when people live together, they must show appropriate respect for each other's needs and follow reasonable requests; there had been nothing inappropriate about the rules the mother had laid down.[120] It was relevant that what the applicant had lost was a family home rather than rented accommodation, because a child has no enforceable right to remain in his or her family home and therefore has to obey the house rules.[121] Accordingly, when deciding the issue of intentionality, the reasonableness of those rules should be considered.

Pregnancy

6.72 A person does not become homeless intentionally by becoming pregnant,[122] for example, because accommodation is lost (on account of size or for other reasons, such as terms of accommodation), or because it is the family home and the family reject the pregnant woman.

Failure to use other remedies

6.73 Two common examples of omission alleged to amount to intentional homelessness are:

a) failure by an evicted private tenant to take civil proceedings to secure re-entry; and
b) failure by a cohabitant or spouse to use domestic remedies.

Each of these examples merits closer consideration.

6.74 Under HA 1996 s175(2), 'a person is also homeless if he has accommodation but . . . he cannot secure entry to it'.[123] This defines as homeless a person who has been locked out of his or her home, and is generally taken to refer to the illegally evicted occupier.[124] While it is open to an authority to treat an occupier who does not use his or her civil remedies as intentionally homeless, it

119 *Denton v Southwark LBC* [2007] EWCA Civ 623, [2008] HLR 11 at [1].
120 *Denton*, above, at [21].
121 *Denton*, above, at [14].
122 *R v Eastleigh BC ex p Beattie (No 1)* (1983) 10 HLR 134, QBD.
123 In Wales, H(W)A 2014 s55(2); see paras 4.62–4.65.
124 English Code of Guidance para 6.20; Welsh Code para 8.16.

would be unlawful to adopt a blanket policy that all such occupiers must do so.[125]

6.75 Detailed provision is now made for cases of domestic and non-domestic violence,[126] and – since the decision in *Bond*[127] – it is clear that authorities cannot require an applicant to use civil remedies. A person who knows what can be done to prevent violence but deliberately fails to do it has not caused the probability of the domestic violence which makes the continued occupation of that accommodation unreasonable.[128] The probability of violence is to be assessed objectively, by the person carrying out the assessment.[129]

Loss of tied accommodation

6.76 Another common example is loss of tied accommodation.[130] It was not merely accepted in the High Court in *Lewis*[131] that the man's departure from his job, and consequent loss of accommodation, qualified as intentional, but an earlier challenge[132] to that decision had been, albeit reluctantly, dismissed. Loss of tied accommodation also amounted to intentionality in *Goddard*[133] and *Jennings*,[134] but the cases were determined on the meaning of 'in consequence' and are, as such, considered below.

6.77 Detailed consideration was given to this problem in *Williams*.[135] The manager of a public house was dismissed for stock and profit irregularities, which he denied. In the course of an appeals procedure,

125 See para 4.65; see also paras 12.54–12.55.

126 See paras 4.82–4.92.

127 *Bond v Leicester City Council* [2001] EWCA Civ 1544, (2002) HLR 6. On domestic abuse, see also English Code chapter 12.

128 *Bond*, above, at [33].

129 *Danesh v Kensington and Chelsea RLBC* [2006] EWCA Civ 1404, [2007] HLR 17.

130 See English Code of Guidance para 9.20(g); Welsh Code para 17.23. Note, however, English Code of Guidance para 24.11, which states that the secretary of state considers that service personnel required to vacate service quarters as a result of taking up an option to give notice to leave the service should not be considered to have become homeless intentionally. There is no direct equivalent in the Welsh Code.

131 See para 6.12.

132 Unreported.

133 *Goddard v Torridge DC* January 1982 *LAG Bulletin* 9, QBD.

134 *Jennings v Northavon DC* January 1982 *LAG Bulletin* 9, QBD.

135 *R v Thurrock DC ex p Williams* (1981) 1 HLR 128, QBD.

which he pursued with the assistance of his union representative, his employers offered him the choice of resigning or dismissal. He resigned and, while threatened with homelessness, applied to the local authority for accommodation.

6.78 The authority made enquiries of the former employers and concluded:

> My understanding of the circumstances of your resignation lead me to the conclusion that, had you not resigned, the end result would be the same, ie, that events leading up to your appeal against dismissal would be regarded as something 'the likely result of which is that you will be forced to leave accommodation which is available for your occupation and which it would have been reasonable for you to continue to occupy'.

6.79 The court interpreted this as:

> . . . saying it was intentional because he resigned. It also seems to go on to say that in any event 'even if you had not resigned you would have been dismissed because of your own faults.' In either event, it would have been an intentional homelessness.

6.80 During the course of the judgment, the court likened the position of the applicant to that of a person who had been constructively dismissed for the purposes of employment law:

> Had he gone to an industrial tribunal and complained that he had been unfairly dismissed, it would not have been open to the employers to say by way of answer . . . you resigned, because he would have been able to reply that he resigned only because he had been told that if he did not do so, he would be dismissed.

6.81 This may be a basis for distinguishing a resignation from dismissal, but what the authority was seeking to do was to say: either the applicant resigned (intentional homelessness) or he was dismissed (intentional homelessness), and it ignored the 'grey area' of dispute, which had led to the compromise.

6.82 The court analysed the case in stages. It asked:

a) why the applicant was homeless (because there had been a possession order against him);
b) why a possession order was made (because his contract of employment came to an end);
c) why did it end (because he resigned);
d) why did he resign (because if he did not do so, he would be dismissed);
e) why would he have been dismissed, was it his fault (this was in dispute).

The authority was therefore bound to reach a view as to fault, however hard it was for it to do so.

6.83 The court approved the authority's initial approach to 'job loss cases'. An act the consequences of which can be construed as a deliberate departure can qualify within the provisions; but someone who loses his or her job for incompetence, which will usually comprise a course of conduct spread over a period of time, cannot be said to be carrying out a deliberate act. This would seem to be because the person would lack the necessary intention, or state of mind, in the absence of clear proof that a course of incompetent conduct had been adopted in order to provoke dismissal.

6.84 *Reeve*[136] was also a case on loss of tied accommodation, although it was as much on the meaning of 'in consequence' as 'deliberate'. A woman worked as a receptionist for a car hire firm and lived above the office. She was living with a man. She told her employers that he was not disqualified from driving, although he was. When the employers found out, they dismissed her. The authority found that she lost her accommodation because of the misconduct leading to loss of employment, which misconduct was the statement made to the employers.

6.85 This allegation was, at the time of dismissal and indeed at the time of the local authority's decision and of the hearing at the High Court, disputed. Nonetheless, the authority had investigated, and it had concluded that the dismissal was 'for that deliberate act of misconduct'. This was the crucial point of distinction from *Williams* (above):

> Some acts which a person does will lead indirectly to their becoming homeless . . . Other acts will be sufficiently proximate to render the person within the category of those who become homeless intentionally . . . [T] his case probably comes close to the border-line. For it to fall on the right side so far as the local authority are concerned it seems to me that the termination of the employment . . . must be lawful. It must be some conduct on the part of the applicant which justifies the employer treating the contract as at an end . . .

Sale of jointly owned home

6.86 In *Bellamy*,[137] the applicant was the joint owner of a property with her mother. She applied as homeless when the property was sold,

136 *R v Thanet DC ex p Reeve* (1981) 6 HLR 31, QBD.

137 *William v Wandsworth LBC; Bellamy v Hounslow LBC* [2006] EWCA Civ 535, [2006] HLR 42.

having waived all rights to any of the proceeds of sale in favour of her mother. The authority found her intentionally homeless. On review, the authority rejected the applicant's assertion that she had intended her mother to be the sole owner of the property and concluded that the she had been aware that she had the right to object to the sale and had also been aware that – as a beneficial owner – she had a right to an interest in the property: her failure to object to the sale constituted a deliberate act which caused her to become homeless.

6.87 The decision was quashed at first instance, but restored by the Court of Appeal: the authority had been entitled, on the basis of the evidence before it, to conclude that the appellant was a joint legal owner of the property with rights over it, including the right to object to the sale under Trusts of Land and Appointment of Trustees Act 1996 ss14 and 15. The question for the judge had not been what the appellant and the mother intended when jointly purchasing the property, but whether the authority had been obviously wrong in its understanding of that intention.

Overlap with 'reasonable to continue to occupy'

6.88 The question whether there has been a deliberate act or omission frequently overlaps with the question whether it was reasonable for the applicant to continue to occupy the accommodation.[138] Whether accommodation is accommodation which it would have been reasonable for an applicant to continue to occupy must be determined at a time before – and without regard to – the deliberate acts or omissions which led to the loss of that accommodation.[139]

6.89 In *Tinn*,[140] Kennedy J expressed the view that, as a matter of common sense, it cannot be reasonable for someone to continue to occupy accommodation when he or she can no longer discharge the financial obligations in relation to it without so straining his or her resources as to deprive himself or herself of the ordinary necessities of life.

6.90 Likewise, in *Hawthorne*,[141] the authority's omission to consider whether the applicant's failure to pay rent was caused by the inadequacy of her financial resources allowed her to succeed in her

138 See paras 4.69–4.140, and, in particular, now the Homelessness (Suitability of Accommodation) Order 1996 SI No 3204: see para 4.122, 6.156–6.162.

139 *Denton v Southwark LBC* [2007] EWCA Civ 623, [2008] HLR 11 at [2], [25].

140 *R v Hillingdon LBC ex p Tinn* (1988) 20 HLR 305, QBD.

141 *R v Wandsworth LBC ex p Hawthorne* (1994) 27 HLR 59, CA.

application to quash a finding of intentionality: it was a question the authority was bound to address.

6.91 See also *Griffiths*,[142] in which the authority was held to have failed to have regard to the family's particular circumstances; and *Bibi*,[143] where the authority had failed to make a finding whether the applicant could reasonably have continued to occupy accommodation, in the light of her stated financial inability to feed her family.

6.92 On the other hand, in *Khan*,[144] the authority was entitled to reach the view that the applicants had not been forced to sell their previous home by reason of financial pressure; and in *Baruwa*[145] it was said that deciding what are the necessities of life for any particular family affords a substantial 'margin of appreciation' to authorities: the authority was entitled to be satisfied that the applicant had sufficient income, given that – although no longer in work – she was spending £954 on a university course for herself and over £50 per week on nursery education for her child. In *Samuels*,[146] the argument that only housing benefit should be taken into account when deciding whether a property was affordable for the applicant was rejected; all household income should be taken into account.

In consequence

Overview

6.93 The homelessness must be 'in consequence of' the deliberate act or omission. This is a question of 'cause and effect'.[147] The principal issue which has arisen is the attribution of present homelessness to past act or omission. That is to say, there is commonly an act which has or could have been the subject of a finding of intentionality, and the argument becomes whether or not that act or omission is the cause of this homelessness.

142 *R v Shrewsbury and Atcham BC ex p Griffiths* (1993) 25 HLR 613, QBD.

143 *R v Islington LBC ex p Bibi* (1996) 29 HLR 498, QBD.

144 *R v Westminster City Council ex p Khan* (1991) 23 HLR 230, QBD. See also *R v Leeds City Council ex p Adamiec* (1991) 24 HLR 138, QBD; and *R v Westminster City Council ex p Moklis Ali* (1996) 29 HLR 580, QBD.

145 *R v Brent LBC ex p Baruwa* (1997) 29 HLR 915, CA.

146 *Samuels v Birmingham City Council* [2015] EWCA Civ 1051, [2015] HLR 47. Permission has been granted to appeal to the Supreme Court.

147 *Dyson v Kerrier DC* [1980] 1 WLR 1205, CA; *Din v Wandsworth LBC* [1983] 1 AC 657, (1981) 1 HLR 73, HL.

6.94 See also *Bashir Hassan*,[148] where the authority wrongly sought to rely on events which post-dated the onset of homelessness. See also, generally, above, under the heading 'Act causing loss of accommodation' at para 6.51.[149]

Cause and effect

6.95 A causal link may continue to subsist following the act of intentionality even though the applicant ceases to be homeless in the interim – for example, because he or she finds some temporary accommodation which is subsequently lost: *Awua*.[150]

6.96 The authority must look back to the original cause of the homelessness and determine whether it was intentional.[151] This follows from the wording of the provisions and the distinction between tenses within what is now HA 1996 s191(1) – 'is' homeless, but 'became' homeless intentionally; see also HA 1996 s189(2) – 'has' a priority need', and s191 'is homeless . . . and has a priority need, and did not become homeless intentionally'.

6.97 Thus, in *Bull*,[152] the applicant allowed his children to come to live with him in a single room (rather than continuing to live with their mother in a property with sufficient rooms for them), from which they were then evicted: the authority having provided accommodation pending enquiries for them all, he was in priority need (at the date of decision), regardless of whether the children were reasonably to be expected to reside with him,[153] but because the accommodation had been available for him when he allowed them to join him,[154] he was homeless intentionally for allowing them to reside with him when they were not reasonably to be expected to do so – allowing them to come to live with him had caused his homelessness.

6.98 In *Reeve*,[155] Woolf J said:

> It seems to me that the answer to the question of whether or not the council were entitled to take the view which they did of the applicant's

148 *R v Islington LBC ex p Bashir Hassan* (1995) 27 HLR 485, although compare *R v Newham LBC ex p Campbell* (1993) 26 HLR 183, QBD.

149 Paras 6.51–6.59.

150 *R v Brent LBC ex p Awua* [1996] AC 55, (1995) 27 HLR 453, HL. See also *Bratton v Croydon LBC* [2002] EWCA Civ 1494, [2002] All ER (D) 404.

151 *Din v Wandsworth LBC*, above.

152 *Oxford City Council v Bull* [2011] EWCA Civ 609, [2011] HLR 35.

153 See para 5.28.

154 See para 4.33.

155 *R v Thanet DC ex p Reeve* (1981) 6 HLR 31, QBD.

> conduct depends on the proper interpretation of s17(1) [now HA 1996 s191(1)]. It appears to me that the use of the words 'in consequence' in that subsection does raise problems of causation. Really, what is involved in deciding whether or not the applicant is right is a decision as to remoteness . . .

6.99 In *ex p P*,[156] Schiemann J commented that causation was a notorious minefield in jurisprudence and philosophy. The authority was entitled to conclude that the misbehaviour of the applicants – resulting in threats from the IRA causing them to have to leave their home – was something 'in consequence of which' the applicants had ceased to occupy accommodation.

6.100 In *Hinds*,[157] the applicant undertook to leave the matrimonial home to avoid an ouster order; this led to termination of the secure tenancy. The authority's conclusion that his violence towards his wife had caused the loss of accommodation was upheld.

6.101 In *Aranda*,[158] the judge applied a 'but for' test.[159] The applicant and her husband received a grant of £20,000 from the authority to give up a secure tenancy. That money was used to partially fund the purchase of a family home in Colombia. Shortly after the family arrived in Colombia, the marriage failed. The house was transferred to a relative and the applicant and her children returned to the UK, where she applied as homeless. The authority concluded that she was intentionally homeless. The matters relied on by the authority, including the grant, were matters 'but for' which she might never have gone to Colombia at all, rather than matters but for which the applicant would have continued in occupation of the property in Colombia. Accordingly, they could not be considered deliberate acts which had caused the applicant's loss of (the Colombian) accommodation.

6.102 In *Robinson v Torbay BC*,[160] it was said that the loss of the home must be the 'reasonable result' of the deliberate act. This approach was adopted in *Reid*.[161]

6.103 In *R v Hounslow LBC ex p R*,[162] the applicant had terminated his tenancy when he was sentenced to seven years' imprisonment for

156 *R v Hammersmith and Fulham LBC ex p P* (1989) 22 HLR 21, QBD.

157 *R v Islington LBC ex p Hinds* (1995) 28 HLR 302, CA.

158 *R v Camden LBC ex p Aranda* (1996) 28 HLR 672, QBD.

159 See now *Haile v Waltham Forest LBC* [2015] UKSC 34, [2015] AC 1471, [2015] HLR 24 at paras 6.143–6.145.

160 [1982] 1 All ER 726, QBD.

161 *R v Westminster City Council ex p Reid* (1994) 26 HLR 691, QBD.

162 (1997) 29 HLR 939, QBD.

indecent assault, as he could no longer pay his rent. In considering whether he was intentionally homeless, the test correctly applied was whether ceasing to occupy the accommodation would reasonably have been regarded at the time as a likely consequence of the deliberate conduct.[163]

6.104 *Ex p R* was approved in *Stewart v Lambeth LBC*,[164] where the applicant lost his home after being convicted of drug dealing. In *Goodger v Ealing LBC*,[165] the Court of Appeal described the decision of a review panel that an applicant had become homeless intentionally by breaching a prohibition in his tenancy agreement against drug dealing from the property – which had led to a term of six years' imprisonment – as being the only decision possible in the circumstances, so much so that what might otherwise have been the procedural unfairness[166] of failing to disclose his housing file until a few days before the review hearing was irrelevant.

6.105 The decision in *City of Gloucester v Miles*[167] may also be considered to turn on cause and effect. The applicant had left her home for a period of time, but had not clearly or certainly quit it. During her absence, her estranged husband returned and caused damage which rendered the property entirely uninhabitable. As she was not a party to the vandalism, she had done nothing that could be classed as intentional, even though she might subsequently have lost the property either through failing to resume residence or because arrears had accrued and there was a threat of proceedings.

6.106 The authority must act reasonably in regarding present homelessness as being caused by a departure from earlier accommodation. In *Krishnan*,[168] Birmingham City Council was putting pressure on owner-occupiers to reduce overcrowding in their premises. A family of relatives sharing the home were offered accommodation by another relative in Uxbridge until such time as they could afford to buy their own house. At the same time, there was a possibility of promotion if the family moved to London. Subsequently, the

163 Which, on the facts, it was.

164 *Stewart v Lambeth LBC* [2002] EWCA Civ 753, [2002] HLR 40.

165 [2002] EWCA Civ 751, [2003] HLR 6.

166 See paras 12.66–12.70.

167 (1985) 17 HLR 292, CA, referred to in the Court of Appeal in *Puhlhofer* (1985) 17 HLR 558, CA, but not criticised either in that case at the House of Lords ([1986] AC 484, 18 HLR 158) or in *R v Brent LBC ex p Awua* [1996] AC 55, (1995) 27 HLR 453, HL.

168 *Krishnan v Hillingdon LBC* January 1981 *LAG Bulletin* 137, QBD.

Uxbridge relative decided to sell his house and move to Canada, at which point the family became homeless.

6.107 The authority wrongly considered that the family could reasonably have gone on occupying the Birmingham property and wrongly took the view that the Uxbridge arrangement was only temporary:[169]

> I also hold that the Council's officers made insufficient enquiry as to the state of knowledge and expectations of the Plaintiff with regard to the availability of his accommodation at Uxbridge at the time when he moved here. Mrs Bates states in her note . . . that the Plaintiff did not deny that his accommodation at [Uxbridge] was temporary. That, however, was not the point. The word 'temporary' can aptly cover a considerable period. Thus, accommodation held on a tenancy for a year or more can rightly be described as temporary.
>
> As I have already indicated, the Plaintiff's expectation at the time when he moved . . . was that the accommodation there would be available for him for at least a year. It follows as it seems to me that if the Council's officers had been aware of that fact they might well have taken the view that the Plaintiff became homeless not because he moved to [Uxbridge] from . . . Birmingham, but because the Plaintiff's cousin changed his mind about the length of time for which he was willing to accommodate the Plaintiff and his family . . .

6.108 Similarly, in *Rose,*[170] although decided on the meaning of 'deliberate',[171] the point may as easily be made that an earlier departure had not caused the homelessness: what had caused the homelessness was the loss of the intervening, temporary accommodation, which the applicant had not appreciated was – or was likely to be – temporary.

6.109 In *Gliddon,*[172] the applicants quit private-sector accommodation. Initially, they had been granted a tenancy. The landlord alleged that they had obtained it by deception and compelled them to enter into a licence agreement in substitution. It was the loss of accommodation under licence which was the immediate cause of the homelessness.

6.110 At first, the authority advised the applicants to await court proceedings for determination of their status; the court held that this was a valid approach.[173] On the applicants' failure to follow this advice, however, the authority reached a new decision, based on the deception

169 Ie, unsettled; cf para 6.113.

170 *R v Wandsworth LBC ex p Rose* (1983) 11 HLR 105, QBD.

171 Para 6.40.

172 *R v Exeter City Council ex p Gliddon* (1984) 14 HLR 103, QBD.

173 See para 6.157.

pursuant to which the accommodation had been obtained, and concluded that it had therefore been lost by the applicants' own fault. In the light of this finding of fact by the authority, however, the authority could no longer conclude that the applicants could reasonably have remained in occupation. Accordingly, the accommodation obtained by deception ought to have been ignored and the authority was obliged to look back instead to the loss of the applicants' previous accommodation.

Breaking the chain of causation

6.111 The question, then, becomes one of how the chain of causation between an act causing homelessness and current homelessness may be broken.

6.112 Where the applicant has enjoyed a period of 'settled accommodation'[174] or 'other than temporary accommodation',[175] this will break the chain.[176] There is no reverse corollary: acquisition and loss of settled accommodation is not the only means of breaking the chain; the fact that what has been lost is unsettled does not mean that the applicant is still homeless intentionally.[177]

Settled accommodation

6.113 The concept of settled accommodation was developed by the judiciary – under the Housing (Homeless Persons) Act 1977 and under HA 1985 Part 3 – and was used in a number of different contexts:

a) HA 1985 s58(1) – definition of homelessness;
b) HA 1985 s60(1) – intentionality: whether what was quit could give rise to a finding of intentionality/whether there had been a break in a period of intentionality;
c) HA 1985 s65(2) – discharge of duty in relation to unintentionally homeless.

Following the decision in *Awua*,[178] however, the distinction between settled and unsettled accommodation is now only

174 *Din v Wandsworth LBC* [1983] 1 AC 657, (1981) 1 HLR 73, HL, per Lord Wilberforce, adopting Ackner LJ in the Court of Appeal.

175 *Din*, above, per Lord Lowry.

176 *R v Brent LBC ex p Awua*, above. See also *Mohammed v Westminster City Council* [2005] EWCA Civ 796, [2005] HLR 47.

177 See paras 6.131–6.145.

178 *R v Brent LBC ex p Awua*, above.

relevant to the question of whether the chain of causation has been broken.[179]

6.114 In *Din*, in which the concept of settled accommodation first emerged, it was said to be a question of 'fact and degree'.

6.115 Different circumstances may lead to accommodation being found to be unsettled. One circumstance relates to the physical conditions in the property; another, to the security of tenure which an applicant had, which is often linked to how long the applicant has occupied the accommodation.

Physical conditions

6.116 If physical conditions are so poor as to be unfit for human habitation,[180] or otherwise in such a condition that no reasonable person could consider it to be capable of amounting to accommodation,[181] the accommodation should not be treated as settled.[182] In *Mohammed*,[183] one of the reasons why accommodation occupied by the applicant was not settled was because it was severely overcrowded.

Security/temporal conditions

6.117 Most of the cases have turned on security.

6.118 *Ruffle*[184] concerned a family who had earlier applied to the authority and been found intentionally homeless. That decision was not contested. The applicants subsequently moved into the flat of a

179 See paras 1.63, 4.8, 6.95, 6.113. As *Awua* preserved this use of the concept of settled accommodation, albeit only for the purpose of determining whether the chain of causation has been broken, it is appropriate to consider pre-*Awua* cases alongside subsequent decisions.

180 As it was put in *R v South Herefordshire DC ex p Miles* (1983) 17 HLR 82, QBD. *City of Gloucester v Miles* (1985) 17 HLR 292, CA, to the same effect, asked whether the property was 'uninhabitable'. It is doubtful, however, that this test would be met simply because a property does not meet the *statutory* definition of unfitness (Landlord and Tenant Act 1985 s8) as distinct from a common sense view of it, or if the causes of the unfitness are such as to qualify as hazards which the local authority could require to be remedied under HA 2004 Part 1.

181 (1983) 17 HLR 82, QBD.

182 See the early cases of *R v South Herefordshire DC ex p Miles* (1983) 17 HLR 82, QBD; *City of Gloucester v Miles* (1985) 17 HLR 292, CA; *R v Dinefwr BC ex p Marshall* (1984) 17 HLR 310, which – notwithstanding their disapproval in *R v Hillingdon LBC ex p Puhlhofer* [1986] AC 484, HL, on the question of whether the accommodation was so physically poor that the applicant was already homeless – remain illustrative of when the physical condition of a property is so bad that it cannot be considered settled.

183 *Mohammed v Westminster City Council*, above. See para 6.129.

184 *R v Merton LBC ex p Ruffle* (1989) 21 HLR 361, QBD.

council tenant under an arrangement which was intended to be permanent but which broke down after a few months through no fault of their own. The family returned to the authority, which decided that they were still intentionally homeless because the intervening period had not 'been one in settled occupation which would give rise to a new cause of homelessness'.

6.119 The applicants argued that the authority had asked the wrong question: it should have asked not whether the intervening accommodation was settled, but whether it was obviously temporary. There was a spectrum of accommodation of which 'settled' and 'obviously temporary' were only the extremes. The applicants contended that they needed only to have secured something more than the least secure type of accommodation in order to have ended homelessness and broken the chain, not the most secure.

6.120 The judge disagreed:[185]

> I think that one or the other term encompasses all states of accommodation. Thus, it is correct to contrast, as the various cases do, settled or permanent accommodation on the one hand with less than secure accommodation, variously described as precarious or temporary or transient on the other . . . [For] the authority to ask themselves . . . has the intervening period been one of settled accommodation occupation, involves asking the same question as whether the accommodation was only temporary. These questions are merely the opposite sides of the same coin.[186]

6.121 In *Evans*,[187] a couple left a secure tenancy for larger premises in the private sector, purportedly on a bed and breakfast basis. There was, however, a strong argument that they had full protection under the Rent Act 1977. Following threats of – and actual – violence from their landlord, the couple left the new accommodation. The authority's decision that they were intentionally homeless was quashed because the authority had failed to consider whether the new accommodation, with security, had been settled.

6.122 Authorities are not bound to accept the applicant's view as to whether accommodation was settled. In *Cadney*,[188] a woman sought

185 *Ruffle*, above, at 366.

186 Simon Brown J contemplated an alternative analysis, which he considered contains possible tensions, of three possible types of accommodation: one so tenuous that it is discounted altogether; one which is sufficient to preclude homelessness; and a further type, 'settled' accommodation, which is required to break the chain of intentionality.

187 *R v Swansea City Council ex p Evans* (1990) 22 HLR 467, CA.

188 *R v Purbeck DC ex p Cadney* (1985) 17 HLR 534, QBD.

to rely on a period of three months during which she had moved out of the matrimonial home and into the home of another man. Their relationship was not successful and she left. She sought to rely on this as a period of intervening accommodation, because she had intended to stay with him permanently. The court considered this too subjective an approach. The authority had been entitled to take the view that it was a transient or precarious arrangement, ie that an objective test could be applied.[189]

6.123 In *Ashton*,[190] the authority's decision that occupation of premises under a tenancy falling within the exception in HA 1985 Sch 1 para 5[191] was not occupation of settled accommodation was upheld, entitling the authority to look back to the previous accommodation.

6.124 Length of time will be important in establishing whether accommodation is settled: see *Easom*,[192] in which it was open to the authority to conclude that accommodation was not settled – over several years – because the applicants had at all times been illegal immigrants to Australia who might have been deported at any moment.

6.125 In *Ajayi*,[193] Dyson J reiterated that whether accommodation was settled is a question of fact and degree. The applicant had lived with family friends (in the first instance for a period of 20 months, and in the second for some nine months) since leaving her family home in Nigeria. The authority concluded that neither accommodation had been settled. The term 'settled accommodation' was an ordinary English expression, not a term of art. Although when the applicant moved in with her friends the duration of the accommodation had been uncertain, the authority was entitled – having regard to the circumstances – to conclude that it had been precarious.

6.126 The fact and degree test was re-stated in *Knight*,[194] where the question was whether occupation of a property under a six-month assured shorthold tenancy could amount to settled accommodation for the purpose of breaking the chain of causation. Although the Court of Appeal accepted that such occupation was capable of

189 See also *R v Merton LBC ex p Ruffle*, above.

190 *R v Winchester City Council ex p Ashton* (1991) 24 HLR 48, QBD, (1991) 24 HLR 520, CA.

191 Temporary accommodation for persons taking up employment.

192 *R v Croydon LBC ex p Easom* (1992) 25 HLR 262, QBD.

193 *R v Hackney LBC ex p Ajayi* (1997) 30 HLR 473, QBD.

194 *Knight v Vale Royal BC* [2003] EWCA Civ 1258, [2004] HLR 9.

constituting settled accommodation, it did not as a matter of law always do so.[195] The question remained one of fact and degree to be determined by the authority. In the circumstances of the particular case, it was open to the authority to find that the accommodation was not settled, because the applicant had known from the outset that the tenancy was only for six months and would not be renewed.

6.127 In *Huda*[196] the applicant had been provided with temporary accommodation by the authority under a licence agreement with a third party. He was subsequently found to be intentionally homeless but, due to an administrative oversight, no steps were taken to evict him. After four years he re-applied for assistance, contending that his lengthy occupation of the temporary accommodation amounted to settled accommodation. The authority decided that it was not settled accommodation as it had been due to administrative error and was of a precarious nature with no security of tenure; the Court of Appeal repeated that settled accommodation was a matter of fact and degree and held that the decision was one the authority were entitled to reach.

6.128 In *Doka*[197] the applicant was evicted for rent arrears. For the subsequent two years, he rented a room in the house of his former employer, but had to vacate the room for short periods from time to time when the son of the former employer came home from university. The authority was entitled to conclude that this was not settled accommodation as it had been too precarious; what was required was a real prospect of the accommodation continuing for a significant or indefinite period of time.

Combination of factors

6.129 The applicant in *Mohammed*[198] also took an assured shorthold tenancy. She was evicted after 12 months because of a shortfall in housing benefit leading to arrears of rent. The authority on

195 It was suggested at [25] that, where accommodation is let on an assured shorthold tenancy, it is normally a significant pointer to it being settled. Given that this is one of the ways in which an authority can discharge a duty to house under HA 1996 s193 (see paras 10.142–10.145), there would seem to need to be some discrete factor to suggest that it is not settled and that in the ordinary case it will be.

196 *Huda v Redbridge LBC* [2016] EWCA Civ 709, [2016] HLR 30.

197 *Doka v Southwark LBC* [2017] EWCA Civ 1532.

198 *Mohammed v Westminster City Council* [2005] EWCA Civ 796, [2005] HLR 47.

review considered that the accommodation was not settled for three reasons:

a) the applicant had obtained the accommodation with a view to making a second application to the authority as homeless;[199]
b) she could not afford the rent for the accommodation; and
c) the accommodation was overcrowded.

The Court of Appeal held that the reviewing officer was entitled to have regard to all these matters in reaching his decision.

Prison

6.130 An argument that a period of imprisonment could amount to settled accommodation was rejected in *Stewart.*[200]

Breaking the chain by other means

6.131 Whether acquisition of settled accommodation is the only means of breaking the causal link was expressly reserved in *Awua.*[201] The question was considered by the Court of Appeal in *Fahia.*[202] The applicant had been found intentionally homeless by the authority and housed temporarily in a guest house. She remained in the guest house for over a year, her rent paid by housing benefit. A subsequent review of her housing benefit led to payments being cut and she was, in consequence, evicted from the guest house.

6.132 The authority decided that it had no new duty towards the applicant because the accommodation at the guest house did not constitute intervening settled accommodation such as to break the causal link with the applicant's original intentional homelessness.

6.133 The Court of Appeal rejected this approach and decided that events other than securing settled accommodation could break the chain; it remitted the case to the authority to decide whether the change in housing benefit had constituted such an event.

6.134 The court expressly approved the earlier decision in *Bassett*[203] as an example of a break in the chain of causation otherwise than by settled accommodation. In that case, temporary accommodation was lost not because of its temporary quality but because the applicant

199 See now para 6.163.
200 *Stewart v Lambeth LBC* [2002] EWCA Civ 753, [2002] HLR 40.
201 *Stewart v Lambeth LBC*, above.
202 *R v Harrow LBC ex p Fahia* (1997) 29 HLR 974, CA (not overruled by the House of Lords on this point, see [1998] 1 WLR 1396, (1998) 30 HLR 1124).
203 *R v Basingstoke and Deane BC ex p Bassett* (1983) 10 HLR 125, QBD; see para 4.134.

had been staying with her sister-in-law and had to leave when she separated from her husband.

6.135 Although *Fahia* went to the House of Lords, the authority abandoned its appeal on this aspect.[204]

6.136 In subsequent cases, following *Fahia* at the Court of Appeal (and its approval of *Bassett*), it has been held that the subsequent event must be unconnected to the temporary nature of the accommodation.

6.137 Thus, in *Harvey*,[205] the applicant was evicted from his home for noise nuisance and he moved in with a friend. After four months, the friend was taken into hospital and the applicant had to move out. The loss of the friend's accommodation did not break the chain of causation because it could not be said to be unconnected with the temporary or unsettled nature of the accommodation the applicant had been occupying.[206]

6.138 Likewise, in *Ajayi*,[207] the applicant left accommodation in Nigeria and moved to London, where she stayed with various friends and acquaintances. She moved in with one friend in January 1996, at the same time as she discovered she was pregnant and, on the birth of the baby, was asked to leave. The chain of causation had not been broken. The real and effective cause of her homelessness was not the pregnancy but leaving her accommodation in Nigeria.

6.139 A term of imprisonment cannot amount to a supervening event which breaks the chain of causation.[208]

6.140 A slightly different question was posed in *Din*[209] – whether an act which at its inception was one causing intentional homelessness can cease to qualify as such merely through the passage of time, ie, whether it can become 'spent'?

6.141 In that case, a family were living in accommodation under extremely trying circumstances, and would ultimately have had to

204 *R v Harrow LBC ex p Fahia*, above, at p1130.

205 *R v Brighton BC ex p Harvey* (1997) 30 HLR 670, QBD.

206 For instance, because the hospitalisation was no different from being asked to leave, which could have happened at any time due to the temporary nature of the accommodation: *Harvey*, above, at 678.

207 *R v Hackney LBC ex p Ajayi* (1997) 30 HLR 473, QBD.

208 *Stewart v Lambeth LBC*, above. See also para 6.119 – prison is not settled accommodation. In *Birmingham City Council v Ali; Moran v Manchester City Council (Secretary of State for Communities and Local Government and another intervening)* [2009] UKHL 36, [2009] 1 WLR 1506, the House of Lords expressly reserved the issue of whether prison could comprise accommodation at all.

209 *Din v Wandsworth LBC* [1983] 1 AC 657, (1981) 1 HLR 73, HL.

leave, but they were advised by the authority to remain in occupation until a court order was made.[210] It was common ground, at least on appeal, that if an application had been made immediately after the departure, the authority could have found the family to be homeless intentionally, because at that date it would have been reasonable to remain in occupation (see further below), whereas, on application at a later date, it was conceded by the authority that the family would by then have become homeless in any event, and not intentionally so.[211]

6.142 During the interim period, the family had stayed with relatives and it was not argued that there had, on that account, been a break in the homelessness. Rather, it was argued that the original cause of homelessness had ceased to be effective because the family would have become homeless unintentionally by the time of application. This argument was upheld in the county court, but dismissed on appeal. The question was whether the present period of homelessness had, at its inception, been intentional. The fact that the applicants would have become homeless unintentionally by the date of application was held to be irrelevant.[212]

6.143 *Din* was re-considered in *Haile*.[213] While stating that *Din* remained good law, the Supreme Court held that, when considering whether an applicant is intentionally homeless, the authority must look at the conduct which caused the present homelessness unless a later event (which is not itself an act of voluntary homelessness) supersedes the earlier conduct, so that it cannot reasonably be said that 'but for' that earlier conduct, the applicant would not have become homeless, in which case the causal connection between current homelessness and earlier conduct will have been interrupted.

6.144 In the absence of any such event, the question is whether the proximate cause of the homelessness is an event which is unconnected to the earlier conduct. The question may be approached in two stages: first, was the homelessness intentional at its inception; second, has it been superseded by a later (unconnected) event which means that the authority must ignore the origins of the homelessness because the applicant would have been homeless in any event. The connection between the initial event and the immediate cause is therefore a critical element in the analysis.

210 Paras 6.156–6.157.

211 There was no defence to the landlord's proposed proceedings for possession and the order would have already taken effect.

212 See also *R v Brent LBC ex p Yusuf* (1995) 29 HLR 48, QBD.

213 *Haile v Waltham Forest LBC* [2015] UKSC 34, [2015] AC 1471, [2015] HLR 24.

6.145 It is not easy to square this decision with *Din*:[214] in particular, it is extremely difficult – if even possible – to distinguish the reasoning adopted in *Haile* from the homeless person's submissions which were rejected in *Din*.[215]

Cessation of occupation

Accommodation abroad

6.146 The accommodation which has been lost can be accommodation abroad and the act causing its loss can be an act abroad.

6.147 In *de Falco*,[216] the reason given by the authority for finding intentional homelessness was that the family in question had come to the UK without arranging permanent accommodation.

6.148 That reason was patently bad on its face. It was upheld by the Court of Appeal, however, by expanding it – against the factual background – to refer to a departure from accommodation in Italy. That this approach had been devised by the Court of Appeal was made clear in *Paris*,[217] where the authority used the same wording as in *de Falco* but had erred because it had failed actually to consider the accommodation which had been quit and the circumstances of departure from it.

Short-term accommodation

6.149 Where the authority is providing temporary housing pending a permanent allocation, its loss may lead to a finding of intentionality: *Hunt*.[218]

214 Lord Carnwath in the minority commented that the majority had engaged in a re-analysis of *Din* that had not been contended for by the appellant. Moreover, it is extremely difficult – if even possible – to distinguish the reasoning adopted in *Haile* from the homeless person's argument which was rejected in *Din*.

215 See, in particular, pp658/F–661/B, and, at 660/A and 661/A, the reliance in *Din* on precisely the 'but for' approach that is at the heart of the majority decision in *Haile*.

216 *De Falco, Silvestri v Crawley BC* [1980] QB 460, CA.

217 *R v Reigate and Banstead BC ex p Paris* (1984) 17 HLR 103, QBD.

218 *R v East Hertfordshire DC ex p Hunt* (1985) 18 HLR 51, QBD. The basis for the decision was politely criticised (described as 'heroic') in *Awua*, but the outcome remains correct. In any event, in such circumstances the authority will now be considered to have discharged its duty to the applicant: see HA 1996 s193(6)(b) – para 10.152.

6.150 In *Conway*,[219] the applicant failed to renew a protected shorthold tenancy. It was held that this could amount to a deliberate omission (although on the facts, it had not been).[220]

Notional occupation

6.151 In *Islam*,[221] at the Court of Appeal, it was argued that the accommodation lost had not been available for the occupation of the applicant and his family (who had recently arrived from Bangladesh).[222] One of the grounds advanced for upholding the decision in the Court of Appeal was that the applicant – while living in a shared single room in Uxbridge – had at all material times nonetheless been in 'notional occupation' of the family home in Bangladesh, through his wife and children. Another suggestion was that the accommodation available for, and occupied by, the family was made up of the family home in Bangladesh and the room in Uxbridge.

6.152 The House of Lords rejected both of these approaches:

> The Master of the Rolls was . . . using the word occupation in an artificial sense, which . . . is quite inconsistent with its ordinary meaning and with the probably narrower sense in which it is used in the Act. When it speaks of occupying accommodation, the Act has in contemplation people who are residing in that accommodation . . .

6.153 It has been held, however, that an applicant may be occupying accommodation even though not physically residing in it. Thus, in *Khan*,[223] the applicants represented to immigration authorities that they would be living in a house which the first applicant subsequently sold. The applicants never occupied the house, although the first applicant's family had done so. This was held to be sufficient occupation for the purposes of intentionality so that, on sale of the house, the applicants could be considered to have ceased to occupy it.

6.154 In *Lee-Lawrence*,[224] the applicant had to leave his home because it became uninhabitable following an arson attack. He accepted the offer of a tenancy elsewhere, on which he claimed housing benefit, but, when he subsequently applied as homeless, he asserted that he had never in fact occupied the new property. The Court of Appeal

219 *R v Christchurch BC ex p Conway* (1987) 19 HLR 238, QBD.

220 See para 6.28.

221 *Re Islam* [1983] 1 AC 688, (1981) 1 HLR 107, HL.

222 See para 4.28.

223 *R v Westminster City Council ex p Khan* (1991) 23 HLR 230, QBD.

224 *Lee-Lawrence v Penwith DC* [2006] EWCA Civ 1672.

held that the fact that a person had a legal right to possession or held the keys was not, of itself, sufficient to establish occupation; nonetheless, those factors combined with the claim for housing benefit and other representations by the applicant that he had been resident in the premises, were sufficient to support a finding of occupancy.

Available for occupation

6.155 This has been considered in chapter 4.[225]

Reasonable to continue to occupy

6.156 It must have been reasonable to continue to occupy the accommodation which has been lost. This has also been considered in chapter 4,[226] to which reference should be made, but there are circumstances which are particular to findings of intentionality which merit mention. This is particularly so where advice has been given to the applicant by the authority prior to departure from the accommodation.[227]

6.157 In *Hughes*,[228] it appeared that an alleged winter letting might not fall within the provisions of Rent Act 1977 Sch 15 case 13, so that there would be no mandatory ground for possession available to the landlord. The occupier was accordingly advised to await the outcome of proceedings but did not do so:

> The important point which this application raises . . . is the question as to what extent an authority exercising its powers under [the] Act is entitled to say to a person . . . 'You should remain in accommodation which you at present occupy and not leave that accommodation until there is a court order made against you requiring you to vacate . . .'
>
> [W]here there is a situation which is doubtful or difficult, it is reasonable for the authority to give advice to a person who is a prospective candidate for assistance under the . . . Act . . . that they should not vacate the accommodation which they are at present occupying without the order of the court because otherwise they may be regarded as persons intentionally homeless.

225 See paras 4.16–4.38.

226 See paras 4.69–4.140.

227 See also *F v Birmingham City Council* [2006] EWCA Civ 1427, [2007] HLR 18, para 6.45; and *Ugiagbe v Southwark LBC* [2009] EWCA Civ 31, [2009] HLR 35, para 6.44.

228 *R v Penwith DC ex p Hughes* August 1980 *LAG Bulletin* 187, QBD.

6.158 In *Adamiec*,[229] the failure of an applicant to heed advice not to sell his home resulted in a finding of intentionality which was upheld as, although he might ultimately have been forced to sell because of his financial circumstances, that was a stage he had not yet reached.

6.159 Whether it is reasonable for an applicant to continue to occupy accommodation is to be judged at the time that the conduct in consequence of which the accommodation was lost took place, not at some later date when the applicant actually left: *ex p P*.[230]

6.160 Whether it is reasonable to continue to occupy may be affected by whether alternative accommodation will be available if the applicants remain in their present accommodation in the short term.[231] See also *McIlory*,[232] in which Catholic applicants left accommodation in Northern Ireland after being subjected to several years of harassment by Protestant factions, culminating in a shooting incident. A finding of intentionality was upheld on the ground that they had failed to wait and see whether they would be rehoused by the Northern Ireland Housing Executive.

6.161 This may be contrasted with *McManus*,[233] where the applicant lived in a house in Belfast just off a road which was the dividing line between the two main religious groups and the scene of much sectarian violence. The applicant left her home and went to London where she applied for homelessness assistance; the authority found her to have become homeless intentionally. Her challenge was successful: the authority should have examined the effect of the situation in Belfast on the applicant and her daughter and focused on the particular area of Belfast where they lived, which the evidence suggested was particularly prone to the worst sectarian violence in the city.[234]

6.162 In *Wilson*,[235] the court, albeit with some hesitation, held that it had not been reasonable for a woman to remain in accommodation in Australia because: a) she had no legal permission to remain; and b) she was pregnant and would shortly have reached the stage of pregnancy when she would not have been able to fly back to the UK.

229 *R v Leeds City Council ex p Adamiec* (1991) 24 HLR 138, QBD. See also *R v Westminster City Council ex p Moklis Ali* (1996) 29 HLR 580, QBD.

230 *R v Hammersmith and Fulham LBC ex p P* (1989) 22 HLR 21, QBD. See also *Denton v Southwark LBC* [2007] EWCA Civ 623, [2008] HLR 11.

231 *R v Hammersmith and Fulham LBC ex p P* (1989) 22 HLR 21, QBD.

232 *R v Newham LBC ex p McIlroy* (1991) 23 HLR 570, QBD.

233 *R v Brent LBC ex p McManus* (1993) 25 HLR 643, QBD at 645, 646.

234 *McManus*, above, at 648.

235 *R v Hillingdon LBC ex p Wilson* (1983) 12 HLR 61, QBD.

Extended definition – collusive arrangements

6.163 HA 1996 s191(3) and H(W)A 2014 s77(4) contain extended definitions of intentionality under which a person is to be treated as intentionally homeless if he or she enters into an arrangement pursuant to which he or she has to cease to occupy accommodation, which it would have been reasonable to continue to occupy,[236] and the purpose of the arrangement is to enable him or her to become entitled to assistance under HA 1996 Part 7 or H(W)A 2014 Part 2, and there is no other good reason why the applicant is homeless.

6.164 This provision is aimed at arrangements designed to give the impression of being obliged to leave accommodation[237] which would have been reasonable to continue to occupy, so as to create an apparent right to assistance under HA 1996 Part 7 or H(W)A 2014 Part 2.

6.165 If it would not have been accommodation which it was reasonable to continue to occupy in any event, the arrangement may be disregarded, although this would not prevent the authority looking back to the loss of any previous accommodation which may properly be considered to be the cause of the present homelessness.

6.166 The English Code[238] suggests that collusion is not confined to those staying with friends or relatives, but can also arise between landlords and tenants:

> Housing authorities, while relying on experience, nonetheless need to be satisfied that collusion exists, and must not merely rely on hearsay or unfounded suspicions.[239]

6.167 Even if the subsection is prima facie applicable, there must also be no other 'good reason' for the homelessness. Examples of 'other good reasons' include overcrowding, or an obvious breakdown in relationship between the applicant and the 'host' household or landlord.[240]

6.168 Authorities do not frequently find collusive arrangements. A rare example is to be found in *Lomotey v Enfield LBC*,[241] where the claimant surrendered her joint interest in a property to her brother, who then evicted her.

236 See paras 4.69–4.140, 6.156–6.162.

237 Note that it does not also have to have been 'available for . . . occupation'.

238 English Code of Guidance para 9.28; Welsh Code para 17.30 is in similar terms.

239 This is true for all decision-making (see chapter 9) but may be a particular problem in reaching decisions on collusion given the connotation of discreditable conduct.

240 English Code of Guidance para 9.29; Welsh Code para 17.30.

241 [2004] EWCA Civ 627, [2004] HLR 45.

CHAPTER 7

Local connection

continued

Introduction

7.1 The local connection provisions of Housing Act (HA) 1996 Part 7 and Housing (Wales) Act (H(W)A) 2014 Part 2 allow one authority to pass on to another the burden of providing initial help duty and of securing permanent accommodation for an applicant.

7.2 This chapter represents something of a turning-point in this book. The previous three chapters have been purely definitional; save in passing, nothing about the duties to which the definitions relate is discussed – it has been all about what the terms mean. The local connections provisions cannot, however, properly be understood in the abstract: they represent a mixture of substance and procedure, and of binding law and voluntary agreement. Accordingly, this chapter describes not only the concept of local connection but also its operation. The chapter is therefore both the last to describe key concepts and the first in a series of chapters describing duties.

7.3 The local connection provisions operate only in specified circumstances. It was one of the principal aims of the Housing (Homeless Persons) Act (H(HP)A) 1977 to end 'shuttling' homeless people between different local authorities, each alleging there was a 'greater' connection with the other.[1] The original provisions were described[2] as 'curiously reminiscent of one of the features of the old Poor Law 1601, whereby paupers could be sent back to the parishes where they had a settlement'.

7.4 Reference will be made in this chapter not only to HA 1996 Part 7 and H(W)A 2014 Part 2, and the Codes of Guidance (see appendix C), but also to the document known as the Local Authority Agreement[3] and to the statutory instrument governing arbitration of disputes between authorities,[4] as well as operation of the review regime.

7.5 At the core of the provisions are the local connection 'conditions for referral': if they apply, an authority to which application has been made (the 'notifying' authority) may be exempt both from the initial help duty under HA 1996 s189B(2),[5] and/or the duty to

1 See chapter 1.
2 *R v Slough BC ex p Ealing LBC* [1981] QB 801, CA, per Lord Denning MR.
3 See English Code of Guidance annex 2 in appendix C, below.
4 Homelessness (Decisions on Referrals) Order 1998 SI No 1578.
5 HA 1996 199A(1); H(W)A 2014 s73.

secure that accommodation is made available under HA 1996 s193[6] or H(W)A 2014 ss68 and 73.[7] These duties will pass to the 'notified' authority.[8]

7.6 At a number of stages, there are obligations to notify applicants; there are also rights to review; there is provision for accommodation pending resolution of which authority has final responsibility for an applicant; and for protection of his or her property. The position governing cross-boundary referrals – ie between England, Wales and Scotland – also needs consideration. While overlapping with the content of later chapters, these topics are all considered in this chapter.

7.7 The matters which must be considered are:

a) what are the conditions for referral?
b) what is a local connection?
c) when are the local connection provisions applicable?
d) initial help duty;
e) duty to secure housing;
f) resolution of disputes;
g) cross-border referrals;
h) notification duties;
i) rights to review;
j) accommodation pending resolution and protection of property.

Conditions for referral

Generally

7.8 The conditions for referral are that:

a) neither the applicant nor any person who might reasonably be expected to reside with him or her, has a local connection with the area of the authority to which application is made; and
b) the applicant or a person who might reasonably be expected to reside with the applicant, does have a local connection with the area of another housing authority; and

6 HA 1996 s200(1); H(W)A 2014 s83(1).
7 H(W)A 2014 s82(1).
8 HA 1996 ss199A(5), 200(4); H(W)A 2014 ss82(4), 83(2). See also *Johnston v City of Westminster* [2015] EWCA Civ 554, [2015] HLR 35.

c) neither the applicant nor any person who might reasonably be expected to reside with the applicant, will run the risk of domestic violence[9] in that other authority's area.[10]

7.9 All three conditions must usually be fulfilled before the local connection provisions can be relied on. The procedure is unavailable if there is a local connection with the area to which application has been made, but the authority is of the opinion that the applicant has a greater or closer local connection elsewhere.[11]

Violence/abuse

7.10 The referral conditions are not met, however, if the applicant or any person who might reasonably be expected to reside with the applicant has suffered non-domestic violence (in Wales, non-domestic abuse) in the area of another authority, and it is probable that return to the area will lead to further violence (or abuse) of a similar kind against the victim.[12]

7.11 For the purposes of HA 1996 s198, 'violence' is not confined to actual physical violence but can include physical violence, threats, intimidating behaviour and any other form of abuse which, directly or indirectly, may give rise to a risk of harm.[13] For the purposes of H(W)A 2014 s80, 'abuse' is similarly defined to include physical violence, threatening or intimidating behaviour and any other form of abuse which, directly or indirectly, may give rise to the risk of harm.[14]

9 In Wales, 'domestic abuse' rather than 'violence': H(W)A 2014 s80(3)(c). Given the definition of 'abuse' in H(W)A 2014 s58 and the decisions in *Yemshaw v Hounslow* LBC [2011] UKSC 3, [2011] HLR 16 and *Waltham Forest LBC v Hussein* [2015] EWCA Civ 14, [2015] HLR 16, the two terms appear to be synonymous.

10 HA 1996 s198(2); H(W)A 2014 s80(3). On the meaning of 'domestic violence' see *Supplementary guidance on domestic abuse and homelessness*, Department for Communities and Local Government (DCLG), November 2014, endorsing the broad approach taken in *Yemshaw v Hounslow* LBC, above.

11 See *Re Betts* [1983] 2 AC 613, (1983) 10 HLR 97, HL; the House of Lords did not overrule the Court of Appeal on this point. See also Welsh Code para 18.10.

12 HA 1996 s198(2A); H(W)A 2014 s80(4).

13 *Yemshaw v Hounslow LBC* [2011] UKSC 3, [2011] HLR 16 and *Waltham Forest LBC v Hussein* [2015] EWCA Civ 14, [2015] HLR 16, overruling *Danesh v Kensington and Chelsea RLBC* [2006] EWCA Civ 1404, [2007] HLR 17. See para 4.83.

14 H(W)A 2014 s56; Welsh Code paras 18.20–18.21.

7.12 The circumstances in which a person runs the risk of either domestic violence or non-domestic violence are the same as those considered in relation to whether or not it would have been reasonable – on this ground – to continue to occupy accommodation, pursuant to HA 1996 s177.[15] The authority is under a positive duty to enquire whether the applicant is subject to such a risk.[16]

7.13 One point which may be made here relates to the interaction with intentional homelessness. It is not uncommon for someone not merely to leave home on account of domestic violence, but to want to leave the area. Some authorities who find that a person is not homeless intentionally on account of domestic violence or abuse will nonetheless seek to refer him or her back. While there is no necessary conflict between finding that someone is homeless (perhaps on account of the domestic violence) and finding that he or she will not run the risk of domestic violence in the area from which he or she has fled, this represents a relatively fine distinction, for which there needs to be a material basis.[17]

7.14 In *Browne*,[18] which for these purposes and on this issue may be treated as if a local connection case,[19] the authority had not found intentional homelessness, but appeared to have addressed itself expressly to the point made in the last paragraph. In *Adigun*,[20] it was stressed that the task of determining whether or not there was a risk of domestic violence is one for the local authority: so long as there was material on which it could base its decision, the court would not intervene.

No connections

7.15 If a person has no local connection with *any* housing authority in England, Wales or Scotland, he or she will be entitled to help and housing from the authority to which the application has been made.[21]

15 HA 1996 s198(3); H(W)A 2014 s57; see paras 4.82–4.92.

16 *Patterson v Greenwich LBC* (1993) 26 HLR 159, CA.

17 Eg that although the applicant left because of violence, the risk no longer subsists.

18 *R v Bristol City Council ex p Browne* [1979] 1 WLR 1437, DC.

19 See para 10.144.

20 *R v Islington LBC ex p Adigun* (1986) 20 HLR 600, QBD. See also *R v Newham LBC ex p Smith* (1996) 29 HLR 213, QBD.

21 *R v Hillingdon LBC ex p Streeting (No 2)* [1980] 1 WLR 1425, CA. Although note the limitations in relation to former asylum-seekers at paras 7.22–7.25.

Time for determining connection

7.16 When seeking to establish whether an applicant has a local connection with a particular area, the authority must look at the facts at the time of the decision. If there is a review of the decision,[22] it is the facts at the date of the review which must be considered.[23] An applicant may not have a local connection with an authority at the date of application, but may acquire one subsequently, either prior to a decision or between decision and review – for example, by obtaining permanent employment or through normal residence in the area.[24]

England: additional application of provisions

Placement by another authority

7.17 By HA 1996 s198(4), the conditions for referral are deemed to be fulfilled – regardless, therefore, of local connection with the authority to which the application was made (on any of the foregoing grounds), and regardless of risk of domestic or other violence – if:

a) the applicant was placed by another authority[25] in accommodation in the area of the authority to which the application has been made;
b) in discharge of its functions under HA 1996 Part 7 or H(W)A 2014 Part 2;
c) within such period as may be prescribed.

7.18 The relevant period is five years from the date of the placement, plus the time between the date the application was initially made to the time of the first placement in the area of the authority to which the application has now been made.[26]

7.19 From 9 November 2012, when Localism Act (LA) 2011 s149(6) came into force in England,[27] the conditions for referral are also met (in England) if the applicant had accepted a private sector offer of accommodation[28] from another authority in the area of the authority

22 See paras 7.104–7.107.
23 *Mohamed v Hammersmith and Fulham LBC* [2001] UKHL 57, [2002] HLR 7.
24 See further para 9.129.
25 Including a Welsh authority, see HA 1996 s198(4A).
26 Allocation of Housing and Homelessness (Miscellaneous Provisions) (England) Regulations 2006 SI No 2527.
27 Localism Act 2011 (Commencement No 2 and Transitional Provisions) (England) Order 2012 SI No 2599 art 2.
28 See paras 10.231–10.240.

to which the application has now been made within the previous two years, and neither the applicant nor anyone who might reasonably be expected to reside with the applicant runs the risk of domestic violence in the district of that other authority.[29]

7.20 As this only applies where the private sector offer had been made before – and the duty to secure accommodation was still in existence at – that date,[30] it can now only apply to an application made before 9 November 2014 which is still undetermined.

Eligible asylum-seekers

7.21 In relation to eligible asylum-seekers[31] in England, the provisions permit a referral in any case where another authority has agreed to accept the referral and there is no risk of violence,[32] even if there is no local connection with that other area.

Former asylum-seekers

7.22 In *Al-ameri*,[33] the House of Lords held that a former asylum-seeker who subsequently applied as homeless did not have a local connection with the area in which he had been provided with accommodation by the National Asylum Support Service (NASS),[34] because residence in that accommodation was not 'of choice'.[35] HA 1996 Part 7 was amended by Asylum and Immigration (Treatment of Claimants, etc) Act 2004 s11 to reverse this.[36] The H(W)A 2014 adopted the same approach.[37]

29 HA 1996 s198(2ZA).

30 Localism Act 2011 (Commencement No 2 and Transitional Provisions) (England) Order 2012 SI No 2599 art 3.

31 See para 3.174.

32 Homelessness (Asylum-seekers) (Interim Period) (England) Order 1999 SI No 3126.

33 *Al-ameri v Kensington and Chelsea RLBC; Osmani v Harrow LBC* [2004] UKHL 4, [2004] HLR 20.

34 Now UKVI, as it has been since 2013. Between 2008 and 2013, the UK Border Agency (UKBA) dealt with such matters. Asylum support was previously administered by the NASS which was part of the Home Office.

35 See paras 7.36–7.38.

36 Given the statutory amendment, the absence of support from family and friends in the area in which an asylum-seeker has been housed by UKVI does not provide sufficient reason for an authority to decide against making a referral which it is otherwise entitled to make: *Ozbek v Ispwich BC* [2006] EWCA Civ 534, [2006] HLR 41.

37 H(W)A 2014 s81(5), (6), in the same terms as HA 1996 s199(6), (7); Welsh Code paras 18.16–18.18.

7.23 By HA 1996 s199(6), (7) and H(W)A 2014 s81(5), (6), a person has a local connection with an authority's district if he or she was at any time provided with accommodation in that district under Immigration and Asylum Act 1999 s95[38] unless:

a) the applicant was subsequently provided with accommodation under section 95 in another authority's district; or
b) the accommodation was provided in an accommodation centre under Nationality, Immigration and Asylum Act 2002 s22.[39]

7.24 The amendments apply only to accommodation provided by UK Visas and Immigration (UKVI) in England or Wales.[40] Accordingly, a former asylum-seeker who has been housed by UKVI in Scotland will not have a local connection in the district where the accommodation was provided.

7.25 Where a former asylum-seeker who has been housed by UKVI in Scotland[41] applies to an authority in England,[42] and has no local connection with the authority to which he or she has applied nor any with an authority in Scotland, the principal housing duty under HA 1996 s193[43] is, however, disapplied.[44] Instead, the local authority has a discretion to secure accommodation for a reasonable period and may provide advice and assistance.[45]

38 See further paras 13.40–13.56, on the provision of accommodation by UKVI under this section.

39 This provision has not yet been brought into force.

40 See paras 13.40–13.56.

41 Other than in an accommodation centre under Nationality, Immigration and Asylum Act 2002 s22. This provision has not yet been brought into force.

42 The position appears to be different in Wales. The Asylum and Immigration (Treatment of Claimants, etc) Act 2004 s11 has not been amended in the light of the H(W)A 2014, so that the disapplication provisions do not apply to Wales, with the effect that a former asylum-seeker who was housed in Scotland is potentially entitled to the full range of services and support if he or she applies to a Welsh local housing authority.

43 See paras 10.118–10.204.

44 Asylum and Immigration (Treatment of Claimants, etc) Act 2004 s11(2), (3)(a).

45 Asylum and Immigration (Treatment of Claimants, etc) Act 2004 s11(3)(b). This discretion is framed in the same terms as the duty towards the intentionally homeless; see paras 10.98–10.112.

Children Act 1989 cases

7.26 From 3 April 2018, when Homelessness Reduction Act (HRA) 2017 came into force,[46] there are additional provisions governing those towards whom a social services authority[47] in England has a duty under Children Act (CA) 1989 s23C,[48] as a former relevant child.[49] So long as an authority in England has such a duty, then, if the authority is a local housing authority as well as a social services authority,[50] the former relevant child is deemed to have a local connection with its area; if the authority is not a local housing authority,[51] the former relevant child is deemed to have a local connection with every district in the area of the social services authority.

7.27 Furthermore, where accommodation for a child in care has been provided under CA 1989 s22A,[52] so that the child is normally resident in the district of a local housing authority for a continuous period of at all least two years, some or all of which falls before he or she turns 16, he or she is likewise deemed to have a local connection with that district,[53] although ceases to do so once he or she turns 21 unless a local connection can be established on any of the other grounds for it.[54]

What is a local connection?

Overview

7.28 The term 'local connection' is defined in HA 1996 s199 and H(W)A 2014 s81.[55] A person may have a local connection with

46 Homelessness Reduction Act 2017 (Commencement and Transitional and Savings Provisions) Regulations 2018 SI No 167 reg 3. This does not apply to applications made or sought before 3 April 2018: reg 4. For the position before this date, see the 10th edition of this work.
47 See para 13.7.
48 See paras 13.97–13.107.
49 HA 1996 s199(8).
50 Which will mean all London Boroughs and the Common Council of the City of London, all unitary authorities and all district councils in metropolitan areas.
51 Ie county council in non-metropolitan areas.
52 See para 13.83.
53 HA 1996 s199(9).
54 HA 1996 s199(10).
55 It may be noted that the provisions do not apply in relation to the Isles of Scilly, where there is a requirement of residence of two years and six months during the previous three years: Homelessness (Isles of Scilly) Order 1997 SI No 797.

the district of a local housing authority[56] based on one of four grounds:

a) because the person is, or in the past was, normally *resident* in it, and the person's residence is or was of his or her own choice;
b) because the person is *employed* in it;
c) because of *family associations*; and
d) because of any *special circumstances*.[57]

In addition, special provisions apply to applicants who have previously been housed by UKVI.[58] There are also additional provisions applicable in England.[59]

7.29 It is important not to pay so much attention to the four grounds that insufficient regard is had to the governing phrase 'local connection' itself: see *Re Betts*.[60] In that case, the applicant was living with his family in the area of Blaby DC between 1978 and 1980. In August 1980, he got a job in Southampton, and moved into a houseboat in the area, where he was joined by his family. In October 1980, he was given a house by Eastleigh BC. Soon after, he lost his job through no fault of his own, fell into arrears with his rent and was evicted. In February 1981, shortly before the order for possession expired, he applied under H(HP)A 1977. Eastleigh BC referred the application to Blaby DC on the basis that the family had lived in Eastleigh BC's district for less than six months, and, accordingly, was not normally resident in its area.[61] The applicant challenged this decision.

7.30 The Court of Appeal allowed the challenge.[62] The only reason for the finding that the family was not normally resident in the area was that the family had lived in the area for less than six months, which decision had been reached by rigid application of the Local Authority

56 For these purposes, this includes a local authority within the meaning of the Housing (Scotland) Act 1988: HA 1996 ss201, 217.

57 HA 1996 s199(1); H(W)A 2014 s81(1).It is possible for a person to have no local connection with any authority (eg if he or she has just arrived in the country), in which case these provisions will not be applicable and the applicant will be the responsibility of the authority to whom he or she applied: see English Code para 10.35; Welsh Code para 18.19.

58 As it has been since 2013. Between 2008 and 2013, the UKBA dealt with such matters. Asylum support was previously administered by the National Asylum Support Service (NASS) which was part of the Home Office. See paras 7.22–7.25; see further paras 13.40–13.56.

59 Paras 7.17–7.20. There are no equivalent provisions in Wales.

60 *Re Betts* [1983] 2 AC 613, (1983) 10 HLR 97, HL.

61 This is the time used in the Local Authority Agreement – see paras 7.32, 7.33 and 7.75–7.81.

62 *Betts v Eastleigh BC* [1983] 1 WLR 774, (1983) 8 HLR 28, CA.

Agreement.[63] Normal residence was where a person intended to settle, not necessarily permanently or indefinitely, and a person may have more than one normal residence at different times. It requires consideration of many features, not merely the application of a six-month, or any other arbitrary, period.

7.31 Allowing the authority's appeal, the House of Lords held that the fundamental question was whether or not the applicant had a local connection with the area. This meant more than 'normal residence'. Normal residence, and the other specified grounds of local connection, are subsidiary components of the formula to be applied. The formula is governed by the proposition that residence of any sort will be irrelevant unless and until it is such as to establish a local connection.[64]

7.32 The House of Lords did not dissent from the Court of Appeal's analysis of 'residence'.[65] Nor did it dissent from the proposition that rigid application of the Local Authority Agreement would constitute a fetter on the authority's discretion.[66] The Agreement could certainly be taken into account and applied as a guideline, provided an authority does not shut out the particular facts of the individual case, ie, provided its *application* is given individual consideration.[67] The House of Lords found that the authority had not misdirected itself in this respect.

Residence

7.33 The Local Authority Agreement suggests a working (or extended) definition of 'normal residence' as six months in an area during the previous 12 months, or not less than three years during the previous five-year period.[68] In *Re Betts*, this was described as 'eminently sensible and proper to have been included in the agreement'.

7.34 In *Smith and Hay*,[69] a period of a few months, some ten years before application, during which one of the spouses had been

63 See paras 7.75–7.81. See also Welsh Code para 18.8.

64 This approach was taken in *R v Islington LBC ex p Adigun* (1986) 20 HLR 600, QBD and *R v Westminster City Council ex p Benniche* (1996) 29 HLR 230, CA.

65 It was based on *R v Barnet LBC ex p Shah* [1983] 2 AC 309, HL under the Education Act 1962.

66 See paras 12.54–12.55.

67 In *Ozbek v Ispwich BC* [2006] EWCA Civ 534, [2006] HLR 41, at [39], Chadwick LJ stated that the need for a common basis of decision-making meant that there was an 'imperative for all authorities to apply the guidelines generally to all applications which come before them'. This must be read in the light of *Betts*.

68 Local Authority Agreement para 4.3(i).

69 *R v Vale of White Horse DC ex p Smith and Hay* (1984) 17 HLR 160, QBD.

employed – and therefore resident – in an area, was considered too short necessarily to have established a local connection.

7.35 Compare, however, *Hughes*,[70] where the applicant had moved into the area to set up a permanent home with the man by whom she became pregnant. The relationship broke down owing to domestic violence after only two months, and the applicant applied as homeless. A decision made some months later – during which the applicant had resided in a local women's aid refuge – that the applicant did not have a local connection with the area, was quashed as one to which no reasonable authority could have come.

7.36 Residence must be 'of choice'.[71] There is no residence of choice if the applicant, or a person who might reasonably be expected to reside with the applicant, is detained under the authority of any Act of Parliament.[72] Thus, prisoners (whether or not convicted) and those detained under the Mental Health Act 1983 will not acquire a local connection with the area in which the prison or hospital is situated. The secretary of state has power to specify further circumstances in which residence is not to be considered 'of choice',[73] although this power has not been exercised. In Wales, the Welsh Ministers have the same power, which has likewise not been exercised.[74]

7.37 Prior to 1 December 2008, residence resulting from service in the armed forces did not constitute residence 'of choice' for serving members of the armed forces.[75] This still applies to applications

70 *R v Southwark LBC ex p Hughes* (1998) 30 HLR 1082, QBD.

71 HA 1996 s199(1)(a); H(W)A 2014 s81(2)(a). See *Wandsworth LBC v NJ* [2013] EWCA Civ 1373, [2014] HLR 6 as to whether accommodation in a refuge is 'of choice'.

72 HA 1996 s199(3); H(W)A 2014 s81(3) and Welsh Code para 18.14.

73 HA 1996 s199(5).

74 H(W)A 2014 s81(4)(b).

75 The armed forces were defined as the Royal Navy, the regular armed forces as defined by Army Act 1955 s225, and the regular air forces as defined by Air Force Act 1955 s223: HA 1996 s199(4). From 31 October 2009, the armed forces are defined as Royal Navy, the Royal Marines, the regular army or the Royal Air Force: Armed Forces Act 2006 s374. The repealed provision was addressed in *R v Vale of White Horse DC ex p Smith and Hay* (1984) 17 HLR 160, QBD, two cases heard together which considered the usual practice of the armed forces to allow a period of time after the termination of service before recovering possession of married quarters. It was held that the exclusion of residence as a result of service in the armed forces referred to the time residence commenced; a fresh residence after leaving the armed forces could be established, even in the same premises, but would not usually be established merely by holding over after the right to occupy married quarters had come to an end.

made before 1 December 2008.[76] For applications made on or after that date, residence resulting from service in the armed forces is to be treated as 'of choice' for the purposes of HA 1996 s199 or H(W)A 2014 s82.[77]

7.38 In *Mohamed*,[78] the House of Lords concluded that occupation of interim accommodation provided[79] by a local authority during enquiries and pending review could amount to normal residence:

> . . . the prima facie meaning of normal residence is a place where at the relevant time the person in fact resides. That therefore is the question to be asked . . . So long as that place where he eats and sleeps is voluntarily accepted by him, the reason why he is there rather than somewhere else does not prevent that place from being his normal residence. He may not like it, he may prefer some other place, but that place is for the relevant time the place where he normally resides . . . Where he is given interim accommodation by a local housing authority even more clearly is that the place where for the time being he is normally resident. The fact that it is provided subject to statutory duty does not . . . prevent it from being such.

Employment

7.39 The Local Authority Agreement suggests that an authority should seek confirmation from the employer both of the employment and that it is not of a casual nature.[80] This implies that 'employment' is to be given a restrictive meaning, ie, one in the employ of another – but neither HA 1996 Part 7 nor H(W)A 2014 suggests that self-employed people should be excluded, or that employment need be full-time.

76 While now long ago, someone may have remained in housing provided under HA 1996 Part 7, without cessation of the duty under section 193, whether by a final offer of accommodation or otherwise.

77 HA 1996 s199(2) repealed with effect from 1 December 2008. See also Circular 04/2009 *Housing allocations – members of the armed forces* from the DCLG; and English Code para 10.21 and chapter 24. No such restriction was included in H(W)A 2014; see Welsh Code para 18.11.

78 *Mohamed v Hammersmith and Fulham LBC*, above. Cf *Al-ameri v Kensington and Chelsea RLBC; Osmani v Harrow LBC* [2004] UKHL 4, [2004] HLR 20 where accommodation provided by NASS to asylum-seekers was not residence of choice. The effect of this latter decision has now been statutorily overturned: see para 7.22.

79 Usually under HA 1996 s188(1) but also potentially under s200(1) or s188(3) or s200(5) pending the review.

80 Local Authority Agreement para 4.3(ii).

7.40 Given that employment is a subsidiary consideration, and merely one of the grounds for establishing a local connection,[81] it is clearly open to an authority to exclude casual work, but not, it is submitted, self-employment. In *Smith and Hay* (above), the same few months' employment, some ten years before the application, was described as limited and of short duration and the authority did not err in finding that it did not give rise to a local connection, but – especially in this day and age when employment relationships are markedly more diverse than traditional – to suggest, say, that someone who has been a self-employed trader (eg a local builder) for a period of time long enough to be considered a connection is not employed in an area would not only be a gloss on the legislation but would fly in its face.

7.41 A person was not formerly regarded as employed in an area either if he or she was serving in the regular armed forces,[82] or in such other circumstance as the secretary of state or Welsh Ministers[83] may by order specify.[84] (This power has not been exercised.) For applications made on or after 1 December 2008, a person serving as a member of the regular armed forces is regarded as employed so as to give rise to a local connection.[85]

Family associations

7.42 There is no statutory definition of the phrase 'family associations'. The English Code of Guidance[86] suggests that, in addition to partners, parents, adult children or siblings, it may include associations with family members such as step-parents, grandparents, grandchildren, aunts or uncles 'provided there are sufficiently close links in the form of frequent contact, commitment or dependency'. This goes further than the Local Authority Agreement, which suggests that it arises where an applicant or a member of the applicant's household

81 See also paras 7.28–7.34.

82 HA 1996 s199(2). This subsection was repealed with effect from 1 December 2008: Housing and Regeneration Act 2008 ss315(a), 321(1) and Sch 16, and Housing and Regeneration Act 2008 (Commencement No 2 and Transitional, Saving and Transitory Provisions) Order 2008 SI No 3068.

83 See H(W)A 2014 s81(4)(a).

84 HA 1996 s199(5).

85 Housing and Regeneration Act 2008 ss315(a), 321(1) and Sch 16 and Housing and Regeneration Act 2008 (Commencement No 2 and Transitional, Saving and Transitory Provisions) Order 2008 SI No 3068. See also para 7.39. See Welsh Code para 18.11.

86 English Code para 10.9. The Welsh Code does not comment on this matter.

has parents, adult children, brothers or sisters currently residing in the area in question.[87]

7.43 In *Avdic*,[88] a claim based on a first-cousin-once-removed was insufficient. The decision is not, however, to be interpreted as limiting family associations to those mentioned in the Agreement: see *Ozbek*,[89] where it was said that the character of the family association was at least as relevant – if not more so – than the degree of consanguinity.[90]

7.44 In that case, the applicants sought to establish their local connection with the borough to which they had applied through brothers who had lived in the area for only 18 months, and cousins and other extended family members who had lived there for over five years. The relevant question for the authority in these circumstance was 'whether, in the particular circumstances of the individual case, the bond between the applicant and one or more members of the extended family was of such a nature that it would be appropriate to regard those members of the extended family as "near relatives" in the sense in which that concept is recognised in [the Local Authority Agreement]'.[91] The authority had correctly asked itself this question in reaching its conclusion that there was no local connection.

7.45 The Local Authority Agreement suggests that relatives must have been resident for a period of at least five years and that the applicant must indicate a wish to be near them.[92] It also says that an applicant who objects to being referred to an area on account of family associations should not be so referred.[93]

7.46 Once family association has been raised by the applicant, the authority should address the issue. A decision letter which failed to

87 Local Authority Agreement para 4.3(iii). It continues that 'only in exceptional circumstances would the residence of relatives other than those listed above be taken to establish a local connection'.

88 *R v Hammersmith and Fulham LBC ex p Avdic* (1996) 28 HLR 897, QBD; (1998) 30 HLR 1, CA.

89 *Ozbek v Ispwich BC* [2006] EWCA Civ 534, [2006] HLR 41. This is now reflected in the English Code of Guidance, see previous paragraph. See also the first instance decision of *Munting v Hamnersmith and Fulham LBC* [1998] JHL D91, where the authority had wrongly concluded that a step-father could not be a close relative.

90 At [64].

91 At [49].

92 Local Authority Agreement para 4.3(iii).

93 Local Authority Agreement para 4.1(ii), but compare, *R v McCall and others ex p Eastbourne BC*, unreported, but referred to at (1981) 8 HLR 48, QBD, in which it was observed that though the applicant's wishes are relevant, where other factors are equally balanced, they cannot override the words of the statute.

do so after the issue had been raised was held to be defective in *Khan*,[94] as it appeared from the letter that only residence had been addressed.

Other special circumstances

7.47 'Other special circumstances' is a phrase likewise left undefined in HA 1996 Part 7 or H(W)A 2014 Part 2. The English Code[95] suggests, by way of example, the need to be near medical or support services which are only available in a particular district. The Welsh Code suggests that young adults leaving the care system should be considered to have a local connection either to their original area of residence or to the area where they were placed.[96]

7.48 The Local Authority Agreement mentions[97] those who have been in prison or in hospital or who wish to return to an area where they were brought up or had lived for a considerable length of time in the past. It stresses that an authority must exercise its discretion when considering whether special circumstances apply.

7.49 In *Smith and Hay*,[98] one of the families attempted to place some reliance on membership of an evangelical church, around which their lives revolved. Following *Betts* (see para 7.29) – which held that the fundamental test is whether or not there is a local connection – the authority had not erred in concluding as a matter of fact that this did not amount to a special circumstance giving rise to a local connection in their case. Nor does a mere desire not to return to an area with which the applicant has a local connection amount to a special circumstance giving rise to a local connection with a different area: *Adigun*.[99]

7.50 It has been suggested that family associations too weak to qualify under HA 1996 s199(1)(c) cannot amount to a special circumstance under this subsection: see *Khan* and *Avdic*.[100] This also seems too

94 *R v Slough BC ex p Khan* (1995) 27 HLR 492, QBD.

95 English Code of Guidance para 10.11; the Welsh Code does not comment on this.

96 Welsh Code para 18.9, perhaps akin to the position in England, see paras 7.26–7.27.

97 Local Authority Agreement para 4.3(iv).

98 *R v Vale of White Horse DC ex p Smith and Hay* (1984) 17 HLR 160, QBD. See also *R v Westminster City Council ex p Benniche* (1996) 29 HLR 230, CA.

99 *R v Islington LBC ex p Adigun* (1986) 20 HLR 600, QBD.

100 *R v Slough BC ex p Khan* (1995) 27 HLR 492, QBD; *R v Hammersmith and Fulham LBC ex p Avdic* (1996) 28 HLR 897, QBD; (1998) 30 HLR 1, CA.

rigid. If a connection of importance exists, which could be based on what might also be described as a weak family association, it cannot automatically rule out qualification as a special circumstance.

When are the local connection provisions applicable?

Generally

7.51 The principal application of the local connection provisions is when the conditions for referral – actual or deemed[101] – exist so that the authority to which application has been made may be exempt from the initial help duty under HA 1996 ss189B(2),[102] and/or the duty to secure that accommodation is made available under HA 1996 s193[103] or H(W)A 2014 ss68 and 73,[104] and these duties will pass instead to the 'notified' authority.[105]

Threatened with homelessness

7.52 It has been held that the local connection provisions are not applicable when the authority's duty arises because of threatened homelessness under HA 1996 s195(2).[106] In *Williams v Exeter City Council*,[107] a woman was occupying army property let to her husband, a serviceman, in the Exeter area. As such, she had[108] no connection with Exeter on the basis of residence of choice,[109] nor on any other ground. The Ministry of Defence secured an order for possession against her and, before it was executed, she applied to the authority.

7.53 The authority agreed that she was threatened with homelessness, but referred her case to East Devon DC. The applicant challenged this decision: it was held that the local connection provisions

101 See paras 7.8–7.9, 7.17.
102 HA 1996 199A(1); H(W)A 2014 s73.
103 HA 1996 s200(1); H(W)A 2014 s83(1).
104 H(W)A 2014 s82(1).
105 HA 1996 s199A(5); H(W)A 2014 ss82(4), 83(2). See also *Johnston v City of Westminster* [2015] EWCA Civ 554, [2015] HLR 35.
106 As enacted.
107 *Williams v Exeter City Council* September 1981 *LAG Bulletin* 211.
108 At that time: see now para 7.41.
109 Under the provisions at that time: see now paras 7.36–7.38.

applied only once the duty arose under HA 1985 s65(2) (now HA 1996 s193), not under s195(2), ie once she was actually homeless.

Discretion

7.54 The decision to make enquiries into local connection, and, therefore, whether or not to refer, is discretionary and, as such, may be vulnerable to challenge if exercised unreasonably.[110] Given the discretionary nature of the exercise, however, authorities are under no obligation to investigate local connection, even where the applicant indicates that he or she wishes to live in another area.[111]

7.55 In *Tower Hamlets*,[112] a decision by Newham LBC to refer an applicant to Tower Hamlets LBC was quashed. The referral concerned a Bangladeshi man who had originally applied to Tower Hamlets LBC for housing but was found to be intentionally homeless. He subsequently applied to Newham LBC, who found him not to be intentionally homeless. In reaching its decision, Newham LBC wrongly made a comparison between the housing conditions in Bangladesh and housing conditions in its own area, rather than to the general circumstances prevailing in relation to housing in Tower Hamlets LBC.[113] Tower Hamlets challenged the referral.

7.56 While the decision on intentionality was for the notifying authority, the Court of Appeal held that: 'Whilst its decision cannot be appealed, that decision cannot found a referral if it is flawed to an extent and in respects which, in appropriate judicial review proceedings, would lead to its being quashed'.[114] In effect, Newham's exercise of its discretion was flawed and could be treated as such.[115] It has been held that the decision does not allow the notified authority to disregard the decision to refer without taking judicial

110 HA 1996 s184(2). *R v Newham LBC ex p Tower Hamlets LBC* (1990) 23 HLR 62, CA; *Ozbek v Ispwich BC* [2006] EWCA Civ 534, [2006] HLR 41. See also *R v East Devon DC ex p Robb* (1997) 30 HLR 922, QBD, where the authority failed to consider whether it had a discretion to refer the applicant.

111 *Hackney LBC v Sareen* [2003] EWCA Civ 351, [2003] HLR 54.

112 *R v Newham LBC ex p Tower Hamlets LBC*, above, CA. See also Local Authority Agreement para 3.7, advising on this decision.

113 See paras 4.93–4.99.

114 At para 12.140.

115 The decision was also flawed in that it failed to take account of the applicant's prospects of obtaining employment in the UK and to ascertain and consider Tower Hamlets' reasons for holding that Mr. Ullah had become homeless intentionally.

review proceedings,[116] although the language used does suggest that it could be.[117]

7.57 Although it is lawful for an authority to have a policy about how it proposes to exercise its discretion, it cannot decide in advance that every applicant who qualifies for referral should be referred: *Carter*.[118]

Enquiries

7.58 The duty to make all preliminary enquiries initially lies on the authority to which application is made, culminating in a duty to notify the applicant what, if any, duty is owed him or her under Part 7.[119] The latter obligation may be fulfilled even if, as it is entitled to do,[120] the authority elects at some point during its enquiries – or contemporaneously with its conclusion – to make a local connection referral without determining all the key issues, provided it is satisfied that the applicant is eligible for assistance and homeless.[121] If it takes this course, and the referral is successful in the sense of transferring the duty, then it is the notified authority which will need to determine the questions of priority need and intentionality.[122]

7.59 In England, if the notifying authority does not refer the case before its initial duty has arisen, it may not do so until the initial duty has come to an end.[123] This may be on a number of grounds, including that it has complied with the duty for 56 days.[124] This means that

116 *R (Bantamagbari) v Westminster City Council* [2003] EWHC 1350 (Admin), [2003] JHL D70, transcript at [21].

117 Whether and when a decision can be treated as void without being quashed is a difficult area of law: see paras 12.20–12.21 where it is touched on briefly. In the homelessness context, it will invariably be best practice to obtain an order; it is unattractive for one public authority simply to treat the decision of another as void; in *Bantamagbari*, above, the court adopted counsel's submission 'it would lead to anarchy'.

118 *R v Harrow LBC ex p Carter* (1992) 26 HLR 32, QBD.

119 HA 1996 s184(1); H(W)A 2014 s82(1); Welsh Code para 18.3.

120 HA 1996 ss189B(1), 198(A1); H(W)A 2014 s73(2).

121 HA 1996 ss189B(1), 198(1A); H(W)A 2014 s80(1)(b).

122 See paras 7.58–7.59 where the notifying authority has determined the issue of intentionality.

123 HA 1996 s200(1A). There is no statutory equivalent in Wales. The Welsh Code of Guidance envisages the referral taking place before the initial duty has arisen (para 18.3). If the referral is accepted, then the notified authority will be subject to the initial help duty (H(W)A 2014 s82(4)); if the referral is rejected, then the initial help duty is imposed on the notifying authority (H(W)A 2014 s82(3)).

124 HA 1996 s189B(7)(b): para 10.84. For the position in Wales, see last footnote.

an authority cannot accept the initial help duty and then change its mind, eg because it finds it more difficult than it had anticipated to secure accommodation for at least six months.[125]

7.60 It follows that the initial help duty will have been discharged by the notifying authority: hence, there is no such duty on the notified authority when the reference is made later. Such a reference can, however, only be made provided not only that the notifying authority is satisfied that the applicant is eligible for assistance and homeless, but also that he or she is in priority need and not homeless intentionally.[126] If the reference is successful – in the sense that it is agreed or decided that the conditions for referral are present – the obligation to secure housing passes to the notified authority.[127]

7.61 Assuming a successful reference, the notified authority is bound by the decisions of the notifying authority on the issues of eligibility, homelessness, priority need and intentionality, unless the decision on those issues is so flawed that it can be quashed in judicial review proceedings:[128] there is no statutory power[129] permitting the notified authority to reach its own decisions on these questions; nor is there a deemed new application.[130]

7.62 This leads to what has been described as a 'merry-go-round',[131] in which a person may apply to authority A, be found homeless intentionally, move across to the area of authority B, make a new application, be found homeless unintentionally and then be referred back for permanent housing to authority A.[132] This is less likely to occur since the HRA 2017 came into force,[133] as authority B may well refer the applicant back before the initial duty arises, in which case decisions on intentionality will be for authority A.[134]

125 HA 1996 s189B(2)(a): paras 10.76–10.96. For the position in Wales, see footnote 123.

126 HA 1996 s193(1) and s198(1). For the position in Wales, see footnote 122.

127 Which may include a Welsh local authority – see HA 1996 s201A and H(W)A 2015 s83 – or a Scottish local authority: under Housing (Scotland) Act 1987: HA 1996 ss201, 217.

128 See the discussion at para 7.56.

129 Cf HA 1996 s199A(5)(c), where the reference is before the initial duty has arisen: see para 7.67. There is no equivalent provision in H(W)A 2014.

130 Again, cf HA 1996 s199A(5)(a) where the reference is before the initial duty arises: see para 7.67. There is no equivalent provision in H(W)A 2014.

131 *R v Slough BC ex p Ealing LBC*, above.

132 *R v Slough BC ex p Ealing LBC*, above.

133 3 April 2018: see Homelessness Reduction Act 2017 (Commencement and Transitional and Savings Provisions) Regulations 2018 SI No 167 reg 3.

134 See para 7.67.

Initial help duty

Overview

7.63 From 3 April 2018, when the HRA 2017 came into force in England,[135] a new initial help duty was introduced for the homeless who are eligible for assistance (regardless of priority need or intentionality).[136] The provisions are similar to those which were already in force in Wales in the H(W)A 2014.[137]

7.64 If the authority to which application is made would be subject to the initial help duty, but considers that the conditions for referral are met, it will not be subject to the initial help duty,[138] but may instead notify the other authority of its opinion. If it does so, it ceases to be under any HA 1996 s188 preliminary duty[139] for applicants whom the authority has reason to believe may be in priority need,[140] but is instead subject to an identical duty under HA 1996 s199A(2) to secure that accommodation is available until the applicant is notified[141] of the decision whether the conditions for referral are met;[142] that duty ends even if there is a request for a review, although the authority has a discretion to continue it pending the decision on review.[143]

7.65 If it is decided that the conditions for referral are not met, the notifying authority is subject to the initial help duty[144] and, if it has reason to believe that the applicant has a priority need, it must continue to secure that accommodation is available for occupation by the applicant until the later of when the HA 1996 s189B duty itself comes to an end[145] or when the authority decides what (if any) other duty it owes the applicant

135 Homelessness Reduction Act 2017 (Commencement and Transitional and Savings Provisions) Regulations 2018 SI No 167 reg 3, only applicable to applications made and reviews sought on or after that date – see reg 4. For the position before this date, see the 10th edition of this work.

136 See paras 10.76–10.96.

137 H(W)A 2014 s73, and see paras 10.92–10.96.

138 HA 1996 ss189B(2), 199A(1); in Wales, H(W)A 2014 s73.

139 See paras 10.11–10.48.

140 HA 1996 s198(A1); in Wales, H(W)A 2014 s73(2).

141 Paras 7.108–7.111.

142 HA 1996 s199A(2); in Wales, H(W)A 2014 s82(1).

143 HA 1996 s199A(6); in Wales, H(W)A 2014 s82(6).

144 HA 1996 s199A(4). The references in HA 1996 s189B(4) and (7) – in the context of the duty being brought to an end – to dates when the authority is first satisfied as to the s189B criteria (paras 10.76–10.96) are to be read as references to the day on which notice is given under HA 1996 s199A(3). In Wales, see H(W)A 2014 s82(3).

145 Paras 10.76–10.96.

under HA 1996 Part 7 following the duty under section 189B;[146] the duty ends even if there is a request for a review, although the authority has a discretion to continue it pending the decision on review.[147]

7.66 If it is decided that the conditions for referral are met, then the applicant is treated as having made an application to the notified authority on the date on which he or she is given notice of the decision,[148] thus imposing on it the initial help duty (among others).[149] From that date, the notifying authority owes no duties under HA 1996 Part 7.[150] The notifying authority must give the notified authority copies of any notifications that it gave the applicant as to its assessment of his or her case.[151]

Initial help duty or housing duty

7.67 As the initial help duty arises once the authority is satisfied that an applicant is eligible for assistance and homeless,[152] without necessarily deciding the issues of priority need and intentionality[153] or issuing a decision under HA 2006 s184,[154] these provisions allow the authority to avoid the initial help duty altogether. If, however, the authority does start to discharge the initial help duty, then – as noted[155] – it will not be able to invoke the local connection provisions until it has brought the initial help duty to an end.[156]

Decision on intentional homelessness

7.68 It may be, however, that the notifying authority has also reached a decision on intentionality: if so, then under these new, statutory provisions the notified authority is now allowed to come to a different decision[157] but only if it is satisfied that the applicant's circumstances

146 HA 1996 s199A(4); H(W)A 2014 s82(3). For the position in Wales, see para 10.94 for the circumstances in which the initial help duty may be brought to an end.
147 HA 1996 s199A(6).
148 Paras 7.100–7.103.
149 Including the duty to secure interim housing under HA 1996 s188.
150 HA 1996 s199A(5)(a), (b); H(W)A 2014 s82(4).
151 See paras 10.10, 10.58. HA 1996 s199A(5); there is no equivalent in Wales.
152 HA 1996 s189B(1).
153 See paras 10.76–10.96.
154 See para 9.177.
155 Para 7.59.
156 HA 1996 s200(1A).
157 Cf para 7.68.

have changed, or that further information has come to light, since the notifying authority came to that decision, and that the change in circumstances or further information justifies coming to a different decision.[158]

Decision on priority need

7.69 There is no equivalent statutory provision governing priority need: if the notifying authority has also reached a decision on priority need, the previous position applies, that the notified authority is normally bound[159] by the decision of the notifying authority.[160]

Duty to secure housing

7.70 If the referral takes place after the initial help duty has been discharged, it will be under HA 1996 s198 or H(W)A 2014 s80. Such a referral gives rise to a new HA 1996 s193 or H(W)A 2014 s73 housing duty, so that if an applicant applies to authority A, is not found homeless intentionally but rejects its offer of accommodation, and then applies to authority B which refers the applicant back to authority A, authority A cannot rely on its earlier offer.[161]

7.71 An authority which finds an applicant homeless intentionally but wrongly refers the applicant to another authority, is not bound by its error; the erroneous reference may simply be ignored: merely because the local connection provisions do not apply to the duty to secure housing if there is intentionality, it does not follow that the erroneous referral in some way nullifies the intentionality decision.[162]

Resolution of disputes

Overview

7.72 In the event of a dispute between the two (or more) authorities, the first stage in both England and Wales will be to try to resolve it by

158 HA 1996 s199A(5)(c).
159 See the discussion at paras 7.68–7.69.
160 Below, paras 9.177–9.178.
161 *R v Tower Hamlets LBC ex p Ali; R v Tower Hamlets LBC ex p Bibi* (1992) 25 HLR 158, CA (overruling *R v Hammersmith and Fulham LBC ex p O'Brian* (1985) 17 HLR 471, QBD on this point).
162 This is consistent with the approach and decision in *Crawley BC v B* (2000) 32 HLR 636, CA: see paras 9.157–9.158.

reference to the Local Authority Agreement.[163] In default of agreement, the matter must be referred to arbitration.[164] Pending the resolution of the dispute, principal responsibility[165] for the homeless person or family continues to rest with the authority to which application was initially made, ie, the notifying authority.[166]

7.73 The question whether the conditions for referral of an application[167] are satisfied is to be determined by agreement between the notifying authority and the notified authority or, in default of agreement, in accordance with such arrangements as the secretary of state or Welsh Ministers may order by statutory instrument.[168] 'Arrangements' are those agreed by the authorities, or by associations of authorities, or in default of agreement such as appears to the secretary of state and/or Welsh Ministers to be suitable, after consultation with the local authority associations and such other persons as he or she thinks appropriate.[169]

7.74 The current arrangements are to be found in the Homelessness (Decisions on Referrals) Order 1998[170] and the agreement reached by the Association of London Government, the Convention of Scottish Local Authorities (CoSLA), the Local Government Association (LGA) and the Welsh Local Government Association (WLGA) in 2006 – the Local Authority Agreement.

163 HA 1996 s198(5); H(W)A 2014 s80(5). The Local Government Association consulted on the agreement in early 2018; it was subsequently included in the English Code of Guidance as annex 2. The consultation paper made clear that the LGA was not aware of problems with the previous edition, but it considered that it needed updating in the light of the HRA 2017, H(W)A 2014 and the Homelessness etc (Scotland) Act 2003: see *Procedures for referrals of homeless applicants to another local authority: consultation*, Local Government Association, February 2018.

164 HA 1996 s198(5); H(W)A 2014 s80(5).

165 Including protection of property: HA 1996 s211(2): see chapter 8.

166 HA 1996 s200(1); H(W)A 2014 s82(1). See, eg, *R (Tanushi) v (1) Westminster City Council (2) Hillingdon LBC*, CO/156/2016, High Court (QBD), 22 January 2016, in which Westminster sought to refer the application to Hillingdon, who had not accepted it; Ms Tanushi was granted interim relief requiring Westminster to continue to provide her with accommodation.

167 See para 7.8.

168 HA 1996 s198(5), (5A); H(W)A 2014 s80(5). This applies only to disputes about whether the applicant has a local connection. If an authority wishes to challenge a referral, eg because it believes the applicant should have been found intentionally homeless, it should do so by judicial review: see the discussion at para 7.56.

169 HA 1996 s198(6); H(W)A 2014 s80(6).

170 SI No 1578.

Local Authority Agreement

7.75 Some of the substantive provisions of the Local Authority Agreement in relation to the four grounds for local connections have been noted above.

7.76 The authority to which application has been made is urged to investigate all circumstances with the same thoroughness that it would use if it did not have it in mind to refer the application to another authority. These enquiries may be of another authority, one to which it may be making a referral, and such enquiries should be made as soon as possible.[171]

7.77 Where an applicant has a local connection with a number of authorities, the English Code of Guidance[172] suggests that the wishes of the applicant should be taken into account in deciding which authority to notify.

7.78 In *McCall*,[173] it was held that, although an arbitrator[174] will not – without the consent of the authorities – usually be entitled to apply the criteria set out in the Local Authority Agreement, it is proper for him or her to have regard to the wishes of the applicant if issues are evenly balanced. Indeed, where all other considerations give no indication one way or another, the court described it as 'perfectly reasonable and perfectly sensible, and within the spirit of the statutory provisions', to have regard to the wishes of the family.

7.79 Under the terms of the Local Authority Agreement, each authority should nominate one person to receive notifications of referral from other authorities.[175] Unless it has clear evidence to the contrary, the notified authority should accept all statements of the facts of the case as stated by the notifying authority.[176]

7.80 If the notified authority provides new information which causes the notifying authority to want to reconsider questions of homelessness, priority need or intentionality, the position will be the same as in other reconsideration cases.[177] The Local Authority Agreement

171 Local Authority Agreement para 5.1.

172 English Code of Guidance para 10.344.

173 *R v McCall and others ex p Eastbourne BC*, unreported, but referred to at (1981) 8 HLR 48, QBD, in which it was observed that though the applicant's wishes are relevant, where other factors are equally balanced, they cannot override the words of the statute.

174 See paras 7.86–7.89.

175 Local Authority Agreement para 6.2.

176 Local Authority Agreement para 6.3.

177 See paras 9.153–9.160.

stresses that the disputes procedures should be used only where there is a disagreement over the existence of a local connection, not for resolving disagreement on any other matter; and that – once enquiries have been completed – a challenge to the notifying authority's decision that the applicant is eligible, homeless, in priority need and not intentionally homeless can only be made by judicial review.[178]

7.81 If the issue is resolved through the Local Authority Agreement, then the notified authority should, if it has accepted responsibility, provide accommodation for the applicant and the applicant's family immediately. Once the notified authority has accepted responsibility, it is liable to repay the notifying authority for expenses incurred in the provision of temporary accommodation, although if the notifying authority has delayed unduly[179] the notified authority need only reimburse it for expenses incurred since notification of the referral was received.[180]

Arbitration

7.82 Where a notified authority disputes the referral, it should set out its reasons in full within ten days.[181] If there is still no agreement, the authorities must seek, within 21 days of receipt of the referral, to agree on an arbitrator who will make the decision.[182] The LGA maintains an independent panel of persons – generally known as referees – for this purpose.[183] In default of agreement as to the referee, the authorities must jointly request the chairman of the LGA or his or her nominee (the proper officer) to appoint a person from the panel.[184] If an arbitrator has not been appointed within six weeks of the date of notification, the notifying authority must request the proper officer to appoint a referee from the panel.[185]

178 Local Authority Agreement para 5.6. See paras 7.56 and 7.61.
179 Usually a period of more than 30 days from the date of initial application: Local Authority Agreement para 7.4.
180 Local Authority Agreement para 7.4.
181 Local Authority Agreement para 10.1.
182 Homelessness (Decisions on Referrals) Order ('Homelessness Order') 1998 SI No 1578 Schedule paras 1 and 2; Local Authority Agreement para 10.3.
183 Homelessness Order 1998 Schedule para 3; Local Authority Agreement para 10.3.
184 Homelessness Order 1998 Schedule para 4(1); Local Authority Agreement para 10.5.
185 Homelessness Order 1998 Schedule para 4(2); Local Authority Agreement para 10.6.

7.83 The referee must invite written representations from both the notifying and the notified authority.[186] The referee may also invite further written representations from the authorities, written representations from any other person[187] and oral representations from any person.[188]

7.84 The Local Authority Agreement suggests[189] that, where an oral hearing is necessary or more convenient (for example, where the applicant is illiterate, where English is not the applicant's first language or where further information is necessary to resolve the dispute), the notifying authority should be invited to present its case first, followed by the notified authority and any other persons whom the referee wishes to hear.

7.85 It is for the referee to arrange the venue, although it is suggested that the offices of the notifying authority will often be the most convenient location.[190] Where a person has made oral representations, the referee may direct that reasonable travelling expenses are paid by either or both authorities.[191]

7.86 It is no part of the referee's duties to enquire into matters preceding a local connection reference: homelessness, eligibility, priority need or intentional homelessness.[192]

7.87 The referee must notify both authorities of his or her decision and the reasons for it.[193] The Local Authority Agreement[194] suggests a target of one month for the decision, from receipt of the authorities' written submissions. There is no obligation on the referee to notify the applicant of his or her decision – that is the notifying authority's duty.[195]

186 Homelessness Order 1998 Schedule para 5(2); Local Authority Agreement para 14.2.

187 Most obviously the applicant, who the Local Authority Agreement suggests (paras 14.3–14.4), should be supplied with copies of the authorities' submissions. Representations may be made by someone, whether or not legally qualified, acting on behalf of the person invited to submit them: Homelessness Order 1998 Schedule para 5(4).

188 Homelessness Order 1998 Schedule para 5(3).

189 Local Authority Agreement para 15.1.

190 Local Authority Agreement para 15.2.

191 Homelessness Order 1998 Schedule para 7(2); Local Authority Agreement para 15.3.

192 *R v Slough BC ex p Ealing LBC* [1981] QB 801, CA.

193 Homelessness Order 1998 Schedule para 6.

194 Local Authority Agreement para 14.5.

195 HA 1996 s200(2); H(W)A 2014 s82(2).

7.88 The previous regulations[196] specifically provided that the decision of the referee was final and binding on the authorities. No such provision is included in the current regulations, but the Local Authority Agreement states[197] that it is binding on the participating authorities, subject to the applicant's right to review.[198] Once a referee has made the determination, the referee should not reopen the case, even though facts may be presented to him or her, unless it is to rectify an error arising from a mistake or omission.[199] The proviso that the decision is final and binding on the authority does not, however, prevent challenge on the grounds that the decision is wrong in law.[200]

7.89 The notifying and notified authorities pay their own costs of the determination.[201] Unlike the 1978 Order,[202] there is no explicit discretion for the referee to make a costs order against either party. The Local Authority Agreement suggests,[203] however, that the referee's fees and expenses, and any third party costs, would usually be recovered from the unsuccessful party to the dispute, although the referee may choose to apportion expenses between the authorities if the referee considers it warranted.

Post-resolution procedure

7.90 If the burden of providing housing does not shift to the notified authority, it will remain with the notifying authority[204] and the principal housing duty under HA 1996 s193[205] will apply.[206]

7.91 The mere fact that an authority has unsuccessfully sought to shift the burden on to another authority is not a basis on which to alter the original decision that the applicant has not become homeless intentionally. If the duty does pass to the notified authority, it will (in the

196 Housing (Homeless Persons) (Appropriate Arrangements) Order 1978 SI No 69.

197 Local Authority Agreement para 16.1.

198 See para 9.186.

199 Local Authority Agreement para 20.1.

200 See chapter 12.

201 Homelessness Order 1998 Schedule para 7(1).

202 Housing (Homeless Persons) (Appropriate Arrangements) Order 1978 SI No 69.

203 Local Authority Agreement para 19.3.

204 HA 1996 s200(3); H(W)A 2014 s82(3).

205 In Wales, H(W)A 2014 s73.

206 See chapter 10.

case of an English authority) be a HA 1996 s193 duty and (in Wales) be a duty under either H(W)A 2014 s68 or s73.[207]

Cross-border referrals

Wales

7.92 The local connection provisions governing referral are largely the same in Wales as in England.[208] Duties are, however, different: see chapter 10.

7.93 When a reference is made by an authority in Wales to an English authority, and the final duty lies with the English authority, the English authority will owe a duty to house[209] under HA 1996 s193;[210] otherwise, the application continues to be dealt with under the Welsh legislation.[211] Where the reference is by an English authority to one in Wales, with which the final duty is agreed or held to lie, it is the Welsh provisions which will apply;[212] otherwise, the application remains with the English authority.[213]

7.94 Although an English authority can normally seek to transfer the initial help duty to another authority,[214] this is not so if the other authority is in Wales.[215] Accordingly, it is only the duty to secure housing, ie the final duty, which is transferable. Nonetheless, even though the English authority will have been under, and brought to an end, its initial help duty, the Welsh authority will also still be subject to that duty, albeit in its Welsh[216] form.[217]

7.95 In the reverse case, ie where a Welsh authority seeks to refer the application to an English authority, a Welsh authority is under no

207 Where an English authority refers to another English authority, see HA 1996 s200(4); where an English authority refers to a Welsh authority, see H(W)A 2014 s83; where a Welsh authority refers to an English authority, see HA 1996 s201A; and, where a Welsh authority refers to another Welsh authority, see H(W)A 2014 s82(4).

208 And sources have been provided accordingly.

209 Paras 7.108–7.111.

210 HA 1996 s201A.

211 HA 1996 s201A; H(W)A 2014 s80.

212 H(W)A 2014 s83.

213 HA 1996 s200; H(W)A 2014 s83.

214 Paras 10.76–10.96.

215 HA 1996 s198(A1).

216 Paras 10.92–10.96.

217 H(W)A 2014 s83(2).

initial help duty if it refers the application to another authority,[218] including an English authority, but it can only refer an application where the applicant is in priority need and unintentionally homeless.[219] It would seem, therefore, that where the Welsh authority considers that there is the prospect of a referral, it will proceed to reach a full decision on all the key elements and[220] such an applicant will at no time benefit from the initial help duty but will proceed directly to the full duty imposed by HA 1996 s193.

Scotland

7.96 Scottish authorities may refer an applicant to an English or Welsh authority in the circumstances set out in Housing (Scotland) Act 1987 s33.[221] Where such a reference is made, and agreed or upheld, the provisions which relate to England are applicable.[222]

7.97 There is no corresponding provision in the Welsh legislation governing referrals between Scotland and Wales; it remains open for consideration, therefore, whether HA 1996 s201 – which was originally applicable to Wales before the homelessness provisions of HA 1996 Part 7 were replaced by those of Part 2 H(W)A 2014 – continues to apply in such a case, ie whether section 201 can be construed as filling the gap.

Resolution of disputes

7.98 It has been noted that the CoSLA and the WLGA were parties to the Local Authority Agreement in 2006.[223]

7.99 Disputes between an English and a Welsh authority may be decided by agreement between them.[224] In default, the Homelessness (Decisions on Referrals) Order 1998[225] applied to Wales and, as it has not been repealed or replaced by any legislation made by the Welsh Ministers, continues to apply in Wales,[226] although there is power for the English secretary of state and the Welsh Ministers to make a

218 H(W)A 2014 s73(2).
219 H(W)A 2014 s80(1)(a).
220 Premising that the referral is agreed or upheld.
221 Scottish law is beyond the scope of this book, but it may be said that the circumstances are very similar indeed to those in England and Wales.
222 HA 1996 s201.
223 Para 7.75.
224 HA 1996 s198(5A).
225 SI No 1578.
226 Welsh Code para 18.30.

joint order in its place.[227] There is no order that directly deals with referrals to Scotland.[228]

Notification duties

7.100 The power to refer an application to another authority begins, in relation both to a referral designed to transfer the initial help duty and one after that duty has come to an end which is designed to transfer the duty to secure housing, with notification to the applicant.[229] The notification must inform the applicant of the referral and of the authority's reasons.[230] The notification must inform the applicant of his or her right to seek a review, and the time with which the request must be made.[231]

7.101 Only a decision to notify in relation to the duty to secure housing is – apparently – subject to review.[232]

7.102 Once it has been agreed or decided[233] whether the conditions for referral are met, likewise in relation to either duty, the notifying authority must give the applicant notice of the decision and the reasons for it, and must inform the applicant of his or her right to request a review of the decision and of the time within which such a request must be made.[234]

7.103 Notices must be in writing and, if not received by the applicant, are treated as given if made available at the authority's office for a reasonable period for collection by the applicant or on his or her behalf.[235]

Reviews

7.104 The detailed provisions governing reviews generally are considered in chapter 9.[236] As noted, review may be sought of a decision to refer

227 HA 1996 s198(5A).

228 See the Homelessness (Decisions on Referrals) (Scotland) Order 1998 SI No 1603, made under Housing (Scotland) Act 1987 s33, for the provisions applicable there.

229 HA 1996 s198(A1), (1).

230 HA 1996 s184(4); H(W)A 2014 s84.

231 HA 1996 s184(5); H(W)A 2014 s84(1).

232 HA 1996 s202(1)(c). This appears to be an oversight: see further para 7.106 for discussion of whether it is nonetheless possible to seek a review of a decision to seek to transfer the initial help duty. H(W)A 2014 s85(1)(c).

233 Ie by arbitration: paras 7.82–7.89.

234 HA 1996 ss199A(3), 200(2); in Wales, H(W)A 2014 ss82(2) and 84.

235 HA 1996 ss184(6), 199A(7), 200(6); H(W)A 2014 s84(3), (4).

236 Paras 9.186–9.250.

to another authority, at least when it is sought to transfer the duty to secure housing,[237] and when it is decided which authority has responsibility for securing housing under these provisions.[238] It seems clear that a review can encompass the 'decision' of the arbitrator.[239] Thus, an applicant has two opportunities to challenge a referral: on the decision to refer and on the outcome of the referral. There is, however, no review of a decision not to make a local connection referral.[240]

7.105 A decision that the conditions of referral are met may be reached either as a result of an agreement between the authorities, or as the result of an arbitration between them.[241] It may at first glance seem somewhat surprising to find provision for review of a decision that the conditions for referral are met when it is statutorily provided that this is to be a matter for agreement or approved arbitration arrangements.[242] It needs to be remembered, however, that the applicant is himself or herself party to neither agreement nor arbitration: this is accordingly the applicant's opportunity to dispute the outcome.

7.106 Notwithstanding the references to reviews in HA 1996 s199A(6) (referral of initial help duty) which explicitly applies to s199A(2)[243] and (4)(c),[244] HA 1996 s202(1)[245] as amended by HRA 2017 does not specify a decision that no further duty is owed under s199A as one of those of which a review may be sought.[246] This appears to be an oversight and the courts may decide that the express references to review in s199A(6) are sufficient to conclude that there is a right.

237 Para 7.70.

238 Paras 7.72–7.92.

239 HA 1996 s202(1)(d) explicitly conferring such a right in relation to a decision under section 189(5) whether the conditions are met *not* involving a referral to a Welsh authority, not limited to a decision by an authority (cf other provisions in section 202(1)). It is not so clear that it is available where the referral is by an English authority to a Welsh authority: there is no reference in section 202(1) to a decision under section 189(5A); on the other hand, there can be a review of a decision under section 200(3), (4) – where it is decided that the conditions for referral are met so that the duty passes to the notified authority – which explicitly includes referrals to a Welsh authority.

240 *Hackney LBC v Sareen* [2003] EWCA Civ 351, [2003] HLR 54.

241 See paras 7.72–7.92.

242 See paras 7.72–7.92.

243 Interim duty to housing pending outcome of referral: paras 7.108–7.111.

244 Duty on notifying authority if conditions not met: para 7.67.

245 Which specifies when a review lies: see paras 9.186–9.250.

246 In contrast, it does so when the local connection referral is under HA 1996 s198(1): see s202(1)(e).

7.107 Decisions on how the duty is to be discharged may themselves also be reviewed. This includes discharge, both where the local connection referral conditions are met[247] and where they are not.[248]

Accommodation pending resolution and protection of property

7.108 Until it is decided whether or not the conditions for referral mean that a duty[249] will transfer, it is the duty of the notifying authority to secure that accommodation is available for an applicant in priority need until he or she is notified of the outcome of the referral.[250] It will continue to be under such a duty if it is decided that the conditions for referral are not met.[251] The duty ends even if there is a request for a review, although the authority has a discretion to continue it pending the decision on review.[252]

7.109 So long as it remains under a duty towards the applicant, whether to accommodate pending enquiries or pending resolution of a local connection referral, the notifying authority also has duties in relation to the protection of the applicant's property.[253]

7.110 The law applicable to the provision of temporary accommodation under other provisions of HA 1996 Part 7 is considered in chapter 10, and will be applicable to interim accommodation for those potentially or actually to be referred to another authority: see the observations on quality[254] and termination made in relation to interim accommodation,[255] those on availability,[256] payment[257] and security,[258]

247 HA 1996 s200(4).
248 HA 1996 s200(3).
249 Whether initial help or to secure housing.
250 HA 1996 s199A(2); H(WA) 2014 s82(1). It is not wholly clear that in Wales this is confined to applicants in priority need, as section 82(1) does not include this requirement; on the other hand, section 82(1) is directed to what follows interim accommodation under section 68, which is so confined. The Welsh Code assumes that the applicant must be in priority need: paras 18.2–18.3.
251 HA 1996 s199A(4); H(W)A 2014 s82(3).
252 HA 1996 s199A(6); H(W)A 2014 s82(5), (6).
253 HA 1996 s211(2); H(W)A 2014 s93; see chapter 8.
254 Paras 10.37–10.46.
255 Paras10.42–10.46.
256 Para 10.27.
257 Paras 10.31–10.32.
258 Paras 10.33–10.36.

exclusion from Protection from Eviction Act 1977[259] and defences on eviction.[260]

7.111 How accommodation may be provided,[261] suitability[262] and the constraints on out-of-area placements,[263] which are all considered in chapter 10 in relation to the principal housing duty under HA 1996 s193 and H(W)A 2014 s75, also apply to discharge under this section.

259 Para 10.47.
260 Para 10.47.
261 See para 10.135.
262 See paras 10.162–10.204.
263 See para 10.147–10.161.

CHAPTER 8

Protection of property

Introduction

8.1 Both Housing Act (HA) 1996 Part 7 and Housing (Wales) Act (H(W)A) 2014 Part 2 make provision for local housing authorities to take steps to protect the property of homeless people. These provisions – which appeared in the Housing (Homeless Persons) Act 1977 and the HA 1985 – are of considerable practical importance. Failure to take steps to protect the belongings of those who are homeless or threatened with homelessness can only have the effect of prolonging or worsening their economic position.

8.2 HA 1996 Part 7 and H(W)A 2014 Part 2 each contain:

a) a duty to protect property in some circumstances; and
b) a power to do so in others.

The discharge of this duty and the power[1] are not co-extensive with the discharge of housing duties and it is necessary, therefore, to consider these property provisions in their own right. Authorities do not necessarily have to discharge duties themselves, but can contract them out – this is discussed at the start of chapter 9.

To whom is a duty owed?

8.3 In England, the duty is owed[2] to an applicant towards whom the authority has become subject to a duty under one of the following provisions of the HA 1996:

a) section 188 – interim accommodation;
b) section 190 – temporary accommodation for the intentionally homeless in priority need;
c) section 193 – full duty;
d) section 195 – accommodation for those threatened with homelessness, in priority need and not so threatened intentionally; and
e) section 200 – accommodation for those who are or have been the subject of a local connection issue.

In addition, the duty is owed to someone who is reasonably to be expected to reside with the applicant, ie, for whom housing must also be provided.[3] Since the Homelessness Reduction Act (HRA) 2017

1 Both of which may be contracted out; see para 9.5.
2 HA 1996 s211(2).
3 HA 1996 s211(5).

came into force on 3 April 2018,[4] the property duty is also owed where the authority has become subject to the initial duty to help under HA 1996 s189B (paras 10.66–10.74).[5]

8.4 In Wales, the duty is owed[6] to an applicant towards whom the authority has become subject to a duty under one of the following provisions of the H(W)A 2014:

a) section 66 – duty to prevent an applicant who is in priority need from becoming homeless;
b) section 68 – interim accommodation;
c) section 75 – full duty; and
d) section 82 – accommodation for those who are or have been the subject of a local connection issue.

In addition, the duty is owed to someone who might reasonably be expected to reside with the applicant.[7]

When is the duty owed?

8.5 The duty is owed when the authority has reason to believe that:

a) by reason of the applicant's inability to protect or deal with it, there is a danger of loss of, or damage to, any personal property of the applicant or other person to whom the duty is owed; and
b) no other suitable arrangements have been or are being made.[8]

'Danger' of loss or damage means a likelihood of harm, not merely a possibility.[9]

8.6 The duty continues until the authority is of the opinion that there is no longer any reason to believe that there is a danger of loss of, or damage to, that property by reason of the applicant's inability to protect or deal with it, or that of someone else to whom the duty is owed.[10]

4 Homelessness Reduction Act 2017 (Commencement and Transitional and Savings Provisions) Regulations 2018 SI No 167 reg 3, only applicable to applications made and reviews sought on or after that date – see reg 4.
5 HA 1996 s211(2).
6 H(W)A 2014 s93(2).
7 H(W)A 2014 s93(6).
8 HA 1996 s211(1); H(W)A 2014 s93(1).
9 *Deadman v Southwark LBC* (2001) 33 HLR 75, CA.
10 HA 1996 s212(3); H(W)A 2014 s94(6).

8.7 The duty is owed not only when the authority is subject to one of the prescribed duties, but also when it has been.[11] For example, a person may be evicted from accommodation and subsequently be held to be homeless intentionally. The former landlord may have been willing to hold on to the person's property for a period of time. That period may be no longer than the period for which accommodation has been provided under HA 1996 s190(2)(a). If, after the expiry of section 190(2)(a) accommodation, the property duty has not expired, application may yet be made for assistance under section 211 and, if the relevant conditions are fulfilled, the authority will be obliged to provide it.

8.8 Even when the property duty has expired, because the authority has formed the view that there is no further danger of loss of or damage to the property, or that the applicant is no longer unable to protect or deal with it, the authority has power to continue to protect that property.[12] Property may be kept in store; the conditions on which it was taken into store will continue to have effect, with any necessary modifications.[13]

8.9 Both the English and Welsh Codes of Guidance illustrate inability to protect property with the example of a person who is ill or who cannot afford to have his or her property placed in store.[14] The English Code also suggests that a person could be deemed capable of taking back responsibility if he or she is no longer ill, or has obtained accommodation, or is able to afford the cost of storage.[15]

What is the duty?

8.10 The duty is to take reasonable steps to prevent loss or prevent or mitigate damage to the property.[16] In order to discharge the duty, the authority has power of entry on to private property.[17] At all reasonable times, it may enter any premises which are 'the usual

11 HA 1996 s211(2); H(W)A 2014 s93(3).
12 HA 1996 s212(3); H(W)A 2014 s94(7).
13 HA 1996 s212(3); H(W)A 2014 s94(7).
14 English Code of Guidance para 20.6; Welsh Code para 11.16.
15 English Code of Guidance para 20.11; there is no equivalent example in the Welsh Code.
16 HA 1996 s211(2); H(W)A 2014 s93(1).
17 HA 1996 s212(1); H(W)A 2014 s94(1). Such provisions were also to be found in the National Assistance Act 1948 s48.

place of residence of the applicant or which were his last usual place of residence', and deal with the applicant's property in any way that is reasonably necessary, including by storing or arranging to store the property.[18]

8.11 The duty is owed in respect of 'personal property'. In *Roberts*,[19] there are dicta that suggest that this would not extend to equipment used by an applicant in his or her business, at any rate where the business is conducted other than at the accommodation.

8.12 The authority generally has responsibility for arranging storage. It may, however, refuse to exercise the duty except on appropriate conditions.[20] This means such conditions as it considers appropriate in a particular case, and can include conditions empowering it:

a) to charge for discharge of the duty; and
b) to dispose of the property in respect of which it discharged the duty, in such circumstances as may be specified.[21]

8.13 Both the English and the Welsh Codes suggest[22] that the authority might dispose of the property if it loses touch with the person concerned and is unable to trace him or her after a specified period. Whether or not a charge is made or a duty to store exists, the authority must, as bailee of the property, take reasonable care of it, and deliver it up when reasonably requested to do so. Failure to do this will render the authority liable to damages, even if the failure to deliver up is accidental, albeit a negligent accident.[23] The standard of care is high; the burden of disproving negligence when damage has resulted from an accident lies on the authority, as bailee.[24]

8.14 The position set out in the above paragraphs may, however, need to be considered in the light of Local Government (Miscellaneous

18 HA 1996 s212(1); H(W)A 2014 s94(1).Under H(W)A 2014 s94(2), where the authority proposes to exercise a power of entry, the officer it authorises to do so must, on request, produce valid documentation setting out the authorisation. A person who without reasonable excuse obstructs the exercise of the power of entry commits an offence and, on summary conviction, is liable for a fine not exceeding level 4 on the standard scale (currently £2,500) (H(W)A 2014 s94(3)). There is no equivalent to either of these provisions in England.

19 *R v Chiltern DC ex p Roberts* (1990) 23 HLR 387, QBD.

20 HA 1996 s211(4); H(W)A 2014 s93(4).

21 HA 1996 s211(4); H(W)A 2014 s93(4).

22 English Code of Guidance para 20.10; Welsh Code para 11.19.

23 *Mitchell v Ealing LBC* [1979] QB 1.

24 *Port Swettenham Authority v TW Wu & Co* [1979] AC 580, PC (Malaysia).

Provisions) Act (LG(MP)A) 1982 s41. That section applies wherever property comes into the possession of a local authority, after being found on premises owned or managed by it, or property has been deposited with the local authority and is not collected from it in accordance with the terms on which it was deposited.

8.15 LG(MP)A 1982 s41 entitles the authority to give the owner or depositor of the property notice in writing that it requires him or her to collect the property by a date specified in the notice, and that if he or she does not do so the property will vest in the authority as from that date. If the person notified then fails to comply with the notice, the property vests in the authority on that date.

8.16 The date to be specified has to be not less than one month from the date of the notice. When an authority finds property, as distinct from when property is deposited with it, and it appears to it that it is impossible to serve a notice, the property vests in it one month from the date when it found the property. In any other case, including deposit, if the authority is satisfied after reasonable enquiry that it is impossible to serve notice, the property vests in it six months after the property was deposited with it or six months from the date when the period from which the property was deposited with it expired, whichever is the later.

8.17 Perishable property, and property which would involve the authority in unreasonable expense or inconvenience storing, may, in any event, be sold or otherwise disposed of by the authority as it thinks fit. In such a case, the proceeds of sale vest in the authority on the same date as the property itself would have done were it not perishable or too inconvenient or expensive to store. If property is claimed by its owner prior to the date when it vests in the authority, the owner can collect it on payment to the authority of its costs in storing the property, and in making enquiries or carrying out any of the other steps referred to in this section.

8.18 There is no express reference in the LG(MP)A 1982 to the provisions of the Housing (Homeless Persons) Act 1977, nor (by way of amendment) to the HA 1985 nor HA 1996 Part 7 nor H(W)A 2014 Part 2. The courts may therefore take the view that references to the LG(MP)A 1982 to 'property deposited' with the authority do not include property taken into safe-keeping under HA 1996 s211 or H(W)A 2014 s93. If so, the HA 1996 Part 7 (or H(W)A 2014 Part 2) provisions only will apply. Otherwise, the LG(MP)A 1982 makes it somewhat easier for authorities to limit the impact of their HA 1996 s211 or H(W)A 2014 s93 duties.

The power to protect property

8.19 The authority has power to take the identical steps to prevent loss of property, or to prevent or mitigate damage to it, as it is obliged to take under the duty described above, in any case where there is no duty to do so.[25] This power might benefit those not in priority need of accommodation or those who, though in priority need, are only threatened with homelessness, and in respect of whom no decision on intentionality has yet been taken.

8.20 Where the authority exercises this power, it has the same ancillary powers as in relation to the duty – ie, entry into premises, imposing conditions, etc.

Notification of cessation of responsibility

8.21 When the authority considers that it no longer has a duty or a power to protect property, it is obliged to notify the person towards whom it was subject to the duty, or in relation to whose property it has exercised the power:

a) that it has ceased to be subject to the duty, or to enjoy the power; and
b) why it is of the opinion that the duty or power has come to an end.[26]

The notification must be by personal delivery to the person to be notified or by leaving it or sending it by post to his or her last known address.[27]

25 HA 1996 s211(3); H(W)A 2014 s93(5).
26 HA 1996 s212(4); H(W)A 2014 s94(8).
27 HA 1996 s212(5); H(W)A 2014 s94(9).

CHAPTER 9

Homelessness decisions

continued

Introduction

Overview

9.1 The previous chapters have addressed the elements of entitlement as homeless. This and the following chapters are concerned with:

- the procedure by which an applicant applies as homeless;
- the procedures to be followed by an authority on receipt of the application;
- the formal requirements concerning the decision-making process;
- the right to request an internal review of an adverse decision; and
- the method by which the duty (if any) is discharged.

9.2 The next chapter is concerned with the discharge of duty – this chapter is therefore concerned with the steps from application to decision and (if any) to review. This process involves a number of steps:

a) application;
b) enquiry into the application;
c) initial decision;
d) request for a review;
e) further enquiries on review;
f) 'minded to find' letter where necessary;
g) review decision.

Preliminary points

Changes in law

9.3 A number of points may be made at the outset. First, it is to be remembered that the body of homelessness law is organic and develops over time, whether court-led, by the introduction of new legislation and/or through the relationship between housing and other areas of public law.[1]

Decision-making

9.4 The second point of general significance is the question of who may discharge the various duties under Housing Act (HA) 1996 Part 7 or Housing (Wales) Act (H(W)A) 2014. It is common for decision-making in relation to homelessness to be delegated to an individual

1 Including the impact of immigration law and European law on the issue of eligibility (chapter 3) and of human rights law on the extent of housing duties. See generally chapter 12.

officer; the reviewing function – which in England[2] must in any event be conducted by a person senior to the person carrying out the initial decision – is sometimes reserved to a panel rather than an individual, whether a panel of members, officers or both.

9.5 Under the Local Authorities (Contracting Out of Allocation of Housing and Homelessness Functions) Order 1996,[3] an authority may 'contract out' all or part[4] of its homelessness functions (including, for example, enquiries or reviews),[5] save for functions relating to:[6] the provision of advisory services;[7] assistance for voluntary organisations;[8] and the duty to co-operate with relevant housing authorities and bodies.[9]

9.6 A contract may be for a period of up to ten years, but 'may be revoked at any time' by the authority.[10]

9.7 The 1996 Order continues to apply in Wales, even after the commencement of the H(W)A 2014.[11]

Relationship between decision and review

9.8 A third point should be made in relation to enquiries. Authorities are under obligations to conduct all relevant enquiries when an application is received – it would nonetheless be wrong to proceed on the basis that a failure to do so (or that there is a defect in the enquiries process) is sufficient immediately to vitiate the decision-making process.

2 But not in Wales, where regulations only require that the reviewing officer be someone who was not involved in the original decision, see Homelessness (Review Procedure) (Wales) Regulations 2015 SI No 1266 reg 3; see also Welsh Code para 20.9.

3 SI No 3205. See further para 12.57.

4 Deregulation and Contracting Out Act 1994 ss70(4) and 69(5).

5 The 'public sector equality duty' imposed on authorities by Equality Act (EqA) 2010 s149 does not prevent contracting out: first, the decisions of the contractor are treated as the decision of the authority by Deregulation and Contracting Out Act 1994 s72; in any event, the contractor is performing a public function and, as such, is bound by the same duty under section 149(2) – see *Panayiotou v Waltham Forest LBC; Smith v Haringey LBC* [2017] EWCA Civ 1624, [2017] HLR 48.

6 SI No 3205 art 3 and Sch 2.

7 See para 14.20.

8 See para 14.29.

9 See para 9.71.

10 Local Authorities (Contracting Out of Allocation of Housing and Homelessness Functions) Order 1996 art 3 and Sch 2.

11 See Housing (Wales) Act 2014 (Consequential Amendments) Regulations 2015 SI No 752, amending the 1996 Order.

9.9 The availability of a review of a decision affords an applicant an opportunity to remedy any perceived failure to conduct enquiries; it goes further than this, because it can be said positively to require the applicant to draw to the authority's attention all matters that the applicant wishes to be considered or in relation to which he or she believes there to be a need for enquiries.[12] In this sense, the review process serves to remedy any failures in the initial enquiry process, without necessarily vitiating it.

9.10 Otherwise, although the substance of the duties on enquiries is discussed below in relation to the application itself,[13] the same principles as apply to enquiries are as relevant on review.

Decision and discretion

9.11 A final preliminary point may be made in relation to the nature of decisions. While there are some elements of discretion in the provisions, decisions on the key issues – eg homelessness, priority need, intentionality and whether there is a local connection – involve consideration and determination of the facts and the correct application to them of the law: this is not 'discretionary decision-making' in the way that term is otherwise used and understood.[14]

Applications

Who can apply?

Generally

9.12 Applications as homeless may in principle be made by any person who is lawfully in the country. 'Lawfully' in this context means 'not unlawfully', ie, someone who is not an offender under Immigration Act 1971 s14 – see *Castelli and Tristran-Garcia, Tower Hamlets* and *Streeting*.[15]

12 See *Bellouti v Wandsworth LBC* [2005] EWCA Civ 602, [2005] HLR 46.

13 Under HA 1996 s184(1).

14 *Tachie v Welwyn Hatfield BC* [2013] EWHC 3972 (QB), [26–27], approved in *Panayiotou v Waltham Forest LBC; Smith v Haringey LBC* [2017] EWCA Civ 1624, [2017] HLR 48, [81]–[84].

15 *R v Westminster City Council ex p Castelli and Tristran-Garcia* (1996) 28 HLR 617, CA; *R v Secretary of State for the Environment ex p Tower Hamlets LBC* [1993] QB 632, 25 HLR 524, CA; *R v Hillingdon LBC ex p Streeting (No 2)* [1980] 1 WLR 1425, CA. A person is lawfully here even where the person has only been given temporary permission to enter, eg, as an asylum-seeker: *Szoma v Secretary of State for Work and Pensions* [2005] UKHL 64, [2006] 1 All ER 1.

9.13 Accordingly, 'applicant' under HA 1996 Part 7 means any person who applies to a local housing authority for accommodation, or for assistance in obtaining accommodation, whom the authority has reason to believe is or may be homeless, or threatened with homelessness.[16]

9.14 In Wales, 'applicant' means any person who applies to a local housing authority for accommodation or help in *retaining or obtaining* accommodation, and whom it appears to the authority may be homeless or threatened with homelessness.[17] If the person has previously been assessed for assistance under H(W)A 2014 Part 2, then there must have been a material change in circumstances since the previous assessment or new information which materially affects the assessment must have come to light, before he or she will be considered an applicant again.[18]

9.15 Subject to these qualifications, it follows that anyone – regardless of whether he or she has a local connection with the authority (or any other authority in the UK)[19] – is entitled to make an application, and refusal to permit him or her to do so is a breach of duty. This bald proposition does, however, merit a number of qualifications.

Qualifications

Immigrants

9.16 As noted,[20] a person unlawfully in the UK will not be permitted to make an application. An authority is entitled to reach its own decision as to whether or not an applicant for assistance is disqualified as such an illegal immigrant, albeit:

a) only for its own purposes; and
b) subject to a contrary decision by the Home Secretary.[21]

9.17 If, after the housing authority has decided the issue against an applicant, the immigration authorities later determine the issue of legality in the applicant's favour, or else decide not to take immigration action against the applicant, he or she will cease to be an illegal immigrant for the purposes of HA 1996 Part 7 (or H(W)A 2014 Part 2), and will

16 HA 1996 s183(1), (2); See *R (Edwards and others) v Birmingham City Council* [2016] EWHC 173 (Admin), [2016] HLR 11.
17 H(W)A 2014 s62(1).
18 H(W)A 2014 s62(2).
19 *R v Hillingdon LBC ex p Streeting (No 2)*, above.
20 See para 9.12.
21 See *Castelli and Tristran-Garcia* and *ex p Tower Hamlets LBC*, above.

be entitled to apply. The question of more detailed immigration status will then govern the question of eligibility.[22]

9.18 If a person has already been granted accommodation by the authority, questions of status do not deprive the person of his or her rights under the accommodation agreement: see *Akinbolu v Hackney LBC*.[23]

9.19 In *Tower Hamlets*,[24] it was held – by concession – that, in addition to making enquiries of the immigration authorities and providing them with information, the authority was under a positive duty to report suspected illegal immigrants to the immigration authorities.

Dependent children

9.20 A dependent child cannot apply in his or her own right: see *Garlick* and *Bentum*.[25] Children are expected to be provided for by those on whom they are dependent (with – where appropriate and qualifying – assistance under HA 1996 Part 7 or H(W)A 2014 Part 2).

9.21 The emphasis here is on 'dependent' children. The statutory scheme itself envisages the possibility of minors – 16- or 17-year-olds – applying as homeless.[26] It may be that subsequent enquiries disclose a family home to which the minor can return, but the absence of such at the date of the application is sufficient to require an application to be received and considered.

Capacity

9.22 A person must be capable of accepting or rejecting an offer of accommodation or assistance in order to qualify as an applicant: see *Begum*.[27] Persons so disabled that they have neither the capacity themselves to

22 See chapter 3.

23 (1996) 29 HLR 259, CA.

24 *R v Secretary of State for the Environment ex p Tower Hamlets LBC*, above.

25 *R v Oldham MBC ex p Garlick; R v Bexley LBC ex p Bentum; R v Tower Hamlets LBC ex p Begum* [1993] AC 509, (1993) 25 HLR 319, HL.

26 See Homelessness (Priority Need for Accommodation) (England) Order 2002 SI No 2051 arts 3, 4; and H(W)A 2014 s70(1)(f); see paras 5.73–5.80.

27 *R v Tower Hamlets LBC ex p Begum* [1993] AC 509, (1993) 25 HLR 319, HL. This remains good law notwithstanding Article 14 of the European Convention on Human Rights (which has been applied to disability, even though not specifically mentioned in it: see *AM (Somalia) v Entry Clearance Officer* [2009] EWCA Civ 634, [2009] UKHRR 1073): see *R (MT, by his father as litigation friend) v Oxford City Council* [2015] EWHC 795 (Admin). Where a deputy is appointed under the Mental Capacity Act 2005, who has been given power to make decisions about where a person should live or whether they should acquire property, he or she may apply on the person's behalf for homelessness assistance: *WB (by her litigation friend, the Official Solicitor) v W District Council* [2018] EWCA Civ 982.

apply nor to authorise an agent on their behalf do not qualify unless a deputy is appointed to make decisions under the Mental Capacity Act 2005. There must otherwise be the capacity to understand and respond to the offer, and to undertake its responsibilities; whether or not a person so qualifies is a matter for the authority.

Transfers

9.23 In *Pattinson*,[28] it was suggested that an application for housing by an existing tenant of the authority is usually to be presumed to be an application for transfer, rather than for assistance under HA 1996 Part 7. That approach was, however, rejected in *ex p B*,[29] in which it was noted than an application for a transfer could overlap with what may on its facts require to be treated as an application as a homeless person. Although the point was not taken in it, the latter approach may be considered to have been put beyond doubt by the decision (and its factual basis) in *Ali*.[30]

9.24 The question in each case is whether the conditions are satisfied. Even if an existing tenant is accepted as homeless, however, an authority may nonetheless continue to consider his or her transfer application and may resolve the homelessness by that means.[31]

Renewed applications

9.25 From 9 November 2012 when Localism Act (LA) 2011 s149 came fully into force in England,[32] an applicant who makes a fresh application[33] within two years of a previous application to an English authority, which resulted in discharge by means of an assured shorthold tenancy, in respect of which tenancy notice has been given under HA 1988 s21, is

a) homeless from the expiry of that notice;[34]

28 *R v Lambeth LBC ex p Pattinson* (1985) 28 HLR 214, QBD.
29 *R v Islington LBC ex p B* (1997) 30 HLR 706, QBD.
30 *Birmingham City Council v Ali; Moran v Manchester City Council (Secretary of State for Communities and Local Government and another intervening)* [2009] UKHL 36, [2009] HLR 41 at [56].
31 *Ali* and *Moran*, at para 4.70; and see also *R (Bilverstone) v Oxford City Council* [2003] EWHC 2434 (Admin), [2004] JHL D12.
32 Localism Act 2011 (Commencement No 2 and Transitional Provisions) (England) Order 2012 SI No 2599 art 2.
33 Provided that the authority's duty to secure accommodation had not ceased before that date: Localism Act 2011 (Commencement No 2 and Transitional Provisions) (England) Order 2012 SI No 2599 art 3.
34 HA 1996 s195A(2), cf the normal position (which usually means when actual eviction occurs) at para 4.61 above.

b) entitled to further assistance by way of accommodation provided that the applicant is still eligible and did not become homeless intentionally, even if no longer in priority need;[35] and
c) entitled to interim accommodation if there is reason to believe that the applicant may qualify under this provision.[36]

Repeat applications

9.26 This is an area which has attracted much litigation. Where an applicant who was refused assistance in the past, or in respect of whom a duty has been discharged because the applicant abandoned accommodation offered by the authority following a previous application, applies again to the authority for assistance, there is a conflict between:

a) the absolute right of a person to make an application as homeless and the fact that the HA 1996 'does not place any express limitation on who can make an application or as to how many applications can be made';[37] and
b) the need to prevent repetitive applications on the same grounds which serve only to waste the authority's resources, which entitle the applicant to temporary accommodation[38] pending the authority's enquiries,[39] and which may have arisen as a result of the applicant's own actions – for example, because the applicant refused accommodation previously offered to him or her by the authority.[40]

9.27 In many cases, an authority will have to accept a repeat application. A number of separate questions arise:

a) Who may make a repeat application?
b) What needs to have occurred before an applicant can re-apply?
c) Where one member of a household has, or may be treated as having, become homeless intentionally, but another member seeks 'separate treatment',[41] does he or she have to make a separate

35 HA 1996 s195A(1).
36 HA 1996 s188(1A). This right only arises on one re-application: HA 1996 s195A(6).
37 *R v North Devon DC ex p Lewis* [1981] 1 WLR 328, QBD, under HA 1985 Part 3.
38 See para 10.11 onwards.
39 *Delahaye v Oswestry BC* (1980) *Times* 29 July, QBD.
40 *R v Westminster City Council ex p Chambers* (1982) 6 HLR 24, QBD.
41 See para 6.11 onwards.

application, or does a duty to consider this issue arise whoever makes the application?

d) What is the position when there are applications to different authorities?

Who may make a repeat application?

9.28 In England, a person who has become homeless intentionally[42] from accommodation provided under HA 1996 s193 or who loses its benefits for some other reason, has a statutory right to re-apply.[43] Other applicants, including those in respect of whom the authority has previously refused assistance and those who have previously refused assistance offered by the authority under HA 1996 Part 7, are not governed by statutory provisions and must therefore be considered in the light of the case-law.

9.29 The position is, on the face of it, different in Wales: a person has a right to apply for assistance (and the authority must carry out an assessment).[44] The duty to assess does not arise, however, if a person has previously been assessed and there has been no material change in his or her circumstances and no new material information.[45] This is something of a codification of the case-law, and it may be thought that the cases still serve to illustrate what this provision means.

What needs to have occurred before an applicant can re-apply?

9.30 Until the decision of the House of Lords in *Fahia,*[46] it had been held that what was needed before an applicant could make a repeat application was a material change of circumstances.[47]

9.31 In *Fahia*, the applicant, who had one year previously been found intentionally homeless, made a new application for assistance, after being evicted from the bed and breakfast accommodation in which she had initially been placed by the authority and in which she had remained. There had been no intervening settled accommodation.[48] The application was refused by the authority.

42 See chapter 6.

43 HA 1996 s193(9).

44 H(W)A 2014 s62(1).

45 H(W)A 2014 s62(2).

46 *R v Harrow LBC ex p Fahia* [1998] 1 WLR 1396, (1998) 30 HLR 1124, HL.

47 See *R v Westminster City Council ex p Chambers* (1982) 6 HLR 24, QBD; *R v Ealing LBC ex p McBain* [1985] 1 WLR 1351, (1985) 18 HLR 59, CA; *R v Southwark LBC ex p Campisi* (1998) 31 HLR 560, CA.

48 See paras 6.111–6.130.

9.32 In the House of Lords it was decided that, if it has reason to believe that an applicant is homeless, the authority is bound to accept the application and make necessary enquiries.

> [W]hen an applicant has been given temporary accommodation . . . and is then found to be intentionally homeless, he cannot then make a further application based on exactly the same facts as his earlier application . . . But those are very special cases when it is possible to say that there is no application before the local authority and therefore the mandatory duty under [HA 1996 s184] has not arisen. But in the present case there is no doubt that when Mrs Fahia made her further application for accommodation she was threatened with homelessness. Moreover in my judgment her application could not be treated as identical with the earlier 1994 application. She was relying on her eviction from the guesthouse which, for one year, she had been occupying as the direct licensee of the guesthouse proprietor, paying the rent for that accommodation . . . It is impossible to say that there has been no relevant change in circumstances at all.[49]

This introduced a test of whether the application is 'identical', but begged the question of how that was to be approached – change of *circumstances* or change of *facts*.

9.33 In the post-*Fahia* case of *J*,[50] the applicant was living with a friend who had asked her to leave. She was found not to be threatened with homelessness. More than a year later, when possession proceedings were issued against the friend, she re-applied. The authority refused to conduct any enquiries, contending that there had been no material change in circumstances. The decision was quashed. *Fahia* was authority for the proposition that an authority is not under a duty to make enquiries in relation to an application based on exactly the same *facts* as an earlier application but it did not entitle an authority to refuse to make enquiries where there had been a material change of *circumstances*. There had clearly been a material change in circumstances: possession proceedings against the friend were imminent.

9.34 In *Rikha Begum*,[51] the applicant, who had been living with her parents when she initially applied as homeless, refused an offer of accommodation made under HA 1996 s193 and the authority decided that it had discharged its duty towards her. She returned to live with her family. Nearly two years later, she re-applied. She claimed there

49 At WLR 1402/D–E, HLR 1130. *Delahaye v Oswestry BC* (1980) *Times*, July 29, QBD, which appeared to have decided to the contrary was distinguished on the basis of the requirement for a change in the facts.

50 *R (J) v Waltham Forest LBC* [2002] EWHC 487 (Admin), [2002] JHL D38.

51 *Rikha Begum v Tower Hamlets LBC* [2005] EWCA Civ 340, [2005] HLR 34.

had been a change in circumstances since her first application, because she had given birth to a second child[52] and other family members had come to live at her parents' home so that it was now overcrowded. The authority decided there had been no material change of circumstances and refused to accept an application. It was held that this was the wrong test: the authority ought to have asked whether the application was based on exactly the same *facts* as the previous application, not whether there had been a material change in *circumstances*.

9.35 These decisions raise as many questions as they resolve – for example, what constitutes a change of fact and when must the change have occurred. Most importantly, they could have re-opened the flood-gates to repeat applications, which could not be summarily dismissed, regardless of how insignificant the factual change was.

9.36 To address those concerns, the Court of Appeal in *Rikha Begum* offered guidance in identifying when an application may be refused on the ground that it is not on exactly the same facts:

a) while it is for the applicant to identify in any subsequent application the facts which he or she contends render the application different from prior applications, it is for the authority to assess whether the circumstances of the two applications are exactly the same;
b) if a subsequent application for assistance purports to reveal new facts but those facts are, to the authority's knowledge (and without the need for further enquiry), not new, or else they are fanciful or trivial, the authority may reject the application as 'incompetent'; and
c) if a subsequent application reveals new facts which, in the light of the information then available to the authority, are neither fanciful nor trivial, the authority must accept the application; it is not open to the authority to investigate the accuracy of the alleged new facts before deciding whether to treat the application as valid, even if it suspects (but does not know) that the new facts are inaccurate.

9.37 While there plainly is a difference, at least in theory and occasionally in practice, between a change of circumstances and new facts, the reality is that the distinction will rarely be one on which an authority

52 The child had been born between the previous application and the refusal of an offer, and the decision by the authority that it had discharged its duty.

can rely with any confidence as a basis for refusing to entertain a new application, unless it falls within the second limb of this guidance.

9.38 Thus, in *Gardiner v Haringey LBC*,[53] the applicant was a British national living in Colombia, where she had a house. Her daughter suffered from autism and needed care and support – including educational support – that was not available in Colombia. She came to the UK and applied to the authority as homeless. That authority refused the application because it was considered reasonable for the applicant to continue to occupy the house in Colombia, and she was accordingly not homeless.

9.39 Almost a year later, the applicant made another application to the authority and provided new information about her daughter's special needs and an updated medical report in support of the application. The new information included a statement that since the daughter had been in the UK she had demonstrated 'considerable and dramatic improvements'.

9.40 The authority sought to rely on *Rikha Begum* and refused to accept the application on the ground that there had been no change in the facts since the previous application. The claimant successfully applied for judicial review: the new information amounted to new facts which rendered it different from the earlier application.

9.41 To determine whether a subsequent application is based on exactly the same facts as an earlier application, the comparison is not between the facts as they existed at the time of the original application, and those existing at the time of the second application. Rather, it is between the circumstances as they were at the time of the authority's original decision (or review if there was one) on the earlier application, and the circumstances revealed by the subsequent application.[54]

9.42 See also *R (Hoyte) v Southwark LBC*[55] in which the applicant had attempted suicide between the first and second applications. See also *R (Abdulrahman) v Hillingdon LBC*[56] in which the new facts were that the applicant's husband had left her and three of her nine children no longer lived with her.

9.43 There is a mild discrepancy within *Rikha Begum*: although reference is made to 'the date of the authority's *decision*'[57] as the appropriate

53 *R (Gardiner) v Haringey LBC* [2009] EWHC 2699 (Admin).

54 *Rikha Begum* at [43].

55 [2016] EWHC 1665 (Admin), [2016] HLR 35.

56 [2016] EWHC 2647 (Admin), [2017] HLR 1.

57 *Rikha Begum* at [43].

date for comparison, there is also reference to 'the circumstances as they were known to be when the earlier application was *disposed of*' as the appropriate date for comparison;[58] and, when disposing of the appeal,[59] there is reference to the facts at the date of *discharge* of the original decision.

9.44 This might seem to suggest that – where the original application was determined by way of discharge by the authority of its duty by means of an offer that was not accepted – the time for comparison is the date of discharge rather than that of the authority's decision. That theory draws some support from *Griffin*,[60] in which a new application was properly held to have been based on the same facts: the change – relationship breakdown – had been known to the authority and taken into account at the time when the earlier offer of accommodation had been made, but had occurred subsequently to the decision on the original application.

Applications by other family members

9.45 There is no bar to a family member of an unsuccessful applicant making a fresh application in his or her own name. This not uncommonly occurs where an applicant is found intentionally homeless and a member of the applicant's family claims not to have acquiesced in the act which gave rise to the intentionality.[61]

9.46 An application by another member of the family cannot, however, be used to circumvent a decision that the authority has discharged its duty towards the family: it is considered irrelevant that the member of the family making the new application did not acquiesce in or agree to the refusal of accommodation which led to the decision that the duty had been discharged.[62]

Applications to other authorities

9.47 In *R v Slough BC ex p Ealing LBC*,[63] two applicants were found homeless intentionally in Slough. One moved and applied to Ealing, the other to Hillingdon; both authorities concluded that the applicants were not homeless intentionally. In each case, however, the local connection provisions entitled them to refer the applicants back to

58 *Rikha Begum* at [44].

59 *Rikha Begum* at [54].

60 *R (Griffin) v Southwark LBC* [2004] EWHC 2463 (Admin), [2005] HLR 12.

61 *R v North Devon DC ex p Lewis* [1981] 1 WLR 328, QBD. See also paras 6.12–6.19.

62 *R v Camden LBC ex p Hersi* (2001) 33 HLR 52, CA.

63 *R v Slough BC ex p Ealing LBC* [1981] QB 801, CA.

Slough.[64] It was held that Slough BC was bound by the unintentionally decisions of Ealing and Hillingdon.

9.48 There is therefore nothing in principle to stop an applicant moving around until he or she finds an authority which concludes that he or she is not homeless intentionally, and – unless the second authority's decision can be vitiated as a matter of public law[65] – there is no way in which the authority fixed with final responsibility for the applicant can defeat the decision, even though it conflicts with its own finding.[66]

9.49 *Ex p Ealing LBC* was applied in *ex p Camden LBC*,[67] which was on like facts. In its discretion, however, the court refused judicial review to quash the original authority's refusal to accept the referral, because the referring authority had failed to make adequate enquiries either of the applicant or of the other authority to resolve certain factual discrepancies between the applicant's statements to the two authorities. Authorities should therefore examine with care applications by people who have been declared homeless intentionally elsewhere. They should afford the first authority to which application was made (and which will bear the burden if a second application is successful) an opportunity to comment on any discrepancies between the applications.

9.50 The Court of Appeal went somewhat further in *ex p Tower Hamlets LBC*:[68] where an application is made to a second authority, that authority's enquiries should extend to examination of the reasons for the first authority's refusal to assist, and should take into account the general housing circumstances prevailing in the first authority's district, just as it may take into account the housing circumstances in its own.[69]

9.51 In *Ali and Bibi*,[70] it was held that, when the duty to house an applicant on a first application was discharged by reference to another

64 The case is a reminder that different authorities can reach different conclusions on the same question.

65 See paras 12.23–12.128.

66 See the discussion of *R v Newham LBC ex p Tower Hamlets LBC* (1990) 23 HLR 62, CA and *R (Bantamagbari) v Westminster City Council* [2003] EWHC 1350 (Admin), [2003] JHL D70 at para 7.56 as to whether this means that the new decision has to be quashed by proceedings for judicial review.

67 *R v Tower Hamlets LBC ex p Camden LBC* (1988) 21 HLR 197, QBD.

68 *R v Newham LBC ex p Tower Hamlets LBC* (1990) 23 HLR 62, QBD.

69 See para 4.93.

70 *R v Tower Hamlets LBC ex p Ali; R v Tower Hamlets LBC ex p Bibi* (1992) 25 HLR 158, CA, overruling *R v Hammersmith and Fulham LBC ex p O'Brian* (1985) 17 HLR 471, QBD.

authority under what is now HA 1996 s198, there was no discharge of duty (by the first authority) under what is now section 193. Accordingly, assuming there had been no take-up of an accommodation offer from the other authority, the acquisition of a local connection with the area of the first authority entitled an applicant to re-apply. This was consistent with the early decision in *Wyness v Poole BC*,[71] in which the family declined to accept a reference to another authority, but 'made do' until one of its members had acquired employment and – thence – a local connection.

9.52 It has recently been explicitly determined that the principle derived from *ex p Ealing LBC*[72] applies where the application to the second authority is made even when the first authority had accepted a duty and made an offer.[73]

9.53 In practice, both *Ali and Bibi* and *Wyness* are overtaken by – and absorbed into – the post-*Fahia* position:[74] *Wyness* was decided on the basis of 'change of circumstance' but it was also a change of facts and *Ali and Bibi*, while on a somewhat different point (whether there had been any previous discharge such as to prevent a new application) becomes somewhat redundant.

How to apply

9.54 Authorities have a duty to hear and adjudicate on applications[75] made by people who are potentially homeless, and they must therefore

71 *Wyness v Poole DC* July 1979 *LAG Bulletin* 166, CC.

72 See para 9.47.

73 *R (Kensington and Chelsea RLBC) v Ealing LBC* [2017] EWHC 24 (Admin), [2017] HLR 13.

74 Paras 9.30–9.44.

75 The English Code of Guidance (para 18.5) suggests that applications can be made 'to any department of the local authority', but it is submitted that this in wrong. It is inconsistent with paras 18.2–18.4, all of which envisage (leaving aside out-of-hours provision) a dedicated and expert service with sole responsibility for accepting and processing applications; taken literally, it would also mean that applications could be made at a library or a school, the leisure department or even the waste collection department. Such departments are manifestly unsuitable for dealing with such an application, could not arrange interim accommodation where necessary and may not even recognise that an application is being made at all, for which failure an authority should surely not be held to be legally in default. It is submitted that the correct position is that an application is not made until there is an approach to a suitable or appropriate department or service which a homeless person could reasonably think might be able to help: this does not necessarily mean a *housing* department or service, but would include, eg, a general help-line or an out-of-hours emergency service for all the functions of the authority.

make provision to receive applications. In heavily populated areas, reasonable provision would be expected to comprise some form of 24-hour cover.[76]

9.55 There is no requirement that applications be in writing or in any particular form, and an authority is therefore not at liberty to refuse an application on that basis.[77] Once the authority has enough information to comprise reason to believe[78] that the applicant may be homeless or threatened with homelessness, its duties arise,[79] although circumstances – including action taken by the authority – may mean that the applicant is no longer homeless or threatened with homelessness by the time a decision is taken on the application.[80]

Provision of accommodation on application

9.56 Once an application has been received and accepted, the preliminary consideration for any local authority is whether it must provide accommodation pending the decision on the application, because the applicant appears to it to be eligible for assistance and in priority need.[81] This is considered in chapter 10.[82]

76 *R v Camden LBC ex p Gillan* (1988) 21 HLR 114, QBD.

77 *R v Chiltern DC ex p Roberts* (1990) 23 HLR 387, QBD. See also *R (Aweys) v Birmingham City Council* [2007] EWHC 52 (Admin), [2007] HLR 27 (point not taken in Court of Appeal or House of Lords – see *Birmingham City Council v Aweys and others* [2008] EWCA Civ 48, [2008] HLR 32 and *Birmingham City Council v Ali and others; Moran v Manchester City Council* [2009] UKHL 36, [2009] HLR 41).

78 Whether this standard is met is a matter for the authority, subject to challenge on conventional *Wednesbury* grounds: see *R (Edwards and others) v Birmingham City Council* [2016] EWHC 173 (Admin), [2016] HLR 11.

79 Thus, in *Bury MBC v Gibbons* [2010] EWCA Civ 327, [2010] HLR 33, an approach to the authority asking for assistance when the applicant had been given notice meant that he was threatened with homelessness, and the authority should at that stage have treated the approach as an application under HA 1996 Part 7. See also *R (Edwards and others) v Birmingham City Council* [2016] EWHC 173 (Admin), [2016] HLR 11: an authority is entitled to question an applicant to clarify whether, in fact, there is reason to believe that any accommodation presently occupied is such that it may not be reasonable to continue to occupy it; it is not the case that every complaint about the condition is sufficient to meet the 'reason to believe' threshold.

80 See paras 9.161–9.164.

81 HA 1996 s188(1); H(W)A 2014 s68. Priority need is not a precondition in the case of a first renewed application (ie within two years of acceptance of a private sector offer on a previous application, see HA 1996 s195A(6)): see para 9.25.

82 Paras 10.11–10.49.

Enquiries

9.57 Once an application has been received, in England, the next stage in the application process is for the authority to make enquiries into the application to determine what (if any) duty is owed: the duty arises when the authority considers that an applicant is or may be homeless or threatened with homelessness.

9.58 In Wales, this first-stage duty has been replaced by a duty to make an assessment of the applicant's housing needs,[83] a duty which now also applies in England[84] but only at a later stage when the authority is satisfied that the applicant is homeless or threatened with homelessness and eligible for assistance, albeit that the authority may not yet have reached a determination on priority need, intentionality or local connection.

9.59 The assessment duties are considered in chapter 10,[85] although there is a considerable overlap with the enquiry duty and frequent references are accordingly made to the assessment duty in this chapter: it is, however, not clear how far the court will treat the assessment duty as impacting on the enquiry duty, especially where the enquiry is into eligibility or homelessness or threatened with homelessness and the assessment duty does not arise until after the authority is satisfied on these points.

The duty to make enquiries

9.60 The duty to make enquiries arises in England if the authority:

a) receives an application for accommodation or for assistance in obtaining accommodation; and
b) has 'reason to believe' that the applicant may be homeless or threatened with homelessness.[86]

83 H(W)A 2014 s62.

84 HA 1996 s189A with effect from 3 April 2018: see Homelessness Reduction Act (HRA) 2017 (Commencement and Transitional and Savings Provisions) Regulations 2018 SI No 167 reg 3, but only applicable to applications made and reviews sought on or after that date – see reg 4.

85 Paras 10.58–10.66.

86 Note also the possibility that an assured shorthold applicant in England may be threatened with homelessness as a result of service of a valid HA 1988 s21 notice which will expire within 56 days: HA 1996 s175(5) with effect from 3 April 2018, commencement of HRA 2017: see Homelessness Reduction Act 2017 (Commencement and Transitional and Savings Provisions) Regulations 2018 SI No 167 reg 3, only applicable to applications made and reviews sought on or after that date – see reg 4. See paras 4.141–4.148.

9.61 These conditions arise relatively easily: the authority need only 'have reason to believe'[87] that the applicant 'may' be homeless or threatened with homelessness.[88]

9.62 Since commencement of the HRA 2017,[89] certain specified English public authorities[90] have notification duties under HA 1996 s213B: these arise when the authority considers that a person in relation to whom it exercises any functions is or may be homeless or threatened with homelessness. The duty only exists if the person agrees to the notification and identifies a local housing authority in England which he or she would like to be notified of the public authority's opinion.[91]

9.63 It is arguable that this will activate the housing authority's enquiry duty, at least if the notification asserts, in whatever terms, that the individual is applying to the housing authority for accommodation or assistance in obtaining it,[92] ie that it will give the housing authority reason to believe that the person may be homeless or threatened with homelessness.[93]

9.64 Indeed, if any other public authority, or anyone whom the housing authority considers a credible source of information, provides the

87 HA 1996 s184(1). See also *R (Edwards and others) v Birmingham City Council* [2016] EWHC 173 (Admin), [2016] HLR 11: the authority is entitled to question an applicant to clarify whether, in fact, there is reason to believe that any accommodation presently occupied is such that it may be reasonable to continue to occupy it; it is not the case that every complaint about the condition is sufficient to meet the 'reason to believe' threshold. Note the different dates when the application is a first renewed application (see HA 1996 s195A(6)), ie following an earlier application which resulted in a private sector letting; if an assured shorthold, homelessness arises once notice under HA 1988 s21 has expired, and the applicant is threatened with homelessness once it has been served – see para 9.25.

88 HA 1996 s184(1).

89 3 April 2018: see Homelessness Reduction Act 2017 (Commencement and Transitional and Savings Provisions) Regulations 2018 SI No 167 reg 3.

90 See para 13.90–13.93.

91 HA 1996 s213B; contact details must also be notified.

92 See generally para 13.84.

93 The English Code of Guidance puts it this way (paras 4.19–4.20): 'A referral made by a public authority to the housing authority under section 213B will not in itself constitute an application for assistance under Part 7, but housing authorities should always respond to any referral received . . . If the housing authority's subsequent contact with the individual following receipt of the referral reveals details that provide the housing authority with reason to believe that they might be homeless or threatened with homelessness and the individual indicates they would like assistance it will trigger an application for assistance under Part 7.'

appropriate information, that condition would appear to be fulfilled regardless of whether they are under any duty to do so.

9.65 In neither case, however, is the *first* condition on its face fulfilled by a notification – statutory or voluntary – unless it *also* asserts, in whatever terms, that the individual is applying to the housing authority for accommodation or assistance in obtaining it, although this could, depending on the circumstances, be implied. In the case of a statutory notification under HA 1996 s213B, however, it is strongly arguable that this is the intention of section 213B and that section 184 should be construed commensurately with it; it is difficult to see what other purpose section 213B could have sought to achieve.

9.66 Failure to undertake the necessary enquiries does not, however, give rise to an action in damages: *Palmer*.[94]

9.67 Where there is no reason to believe that an applicant is yet threatened with homelessness, the duty to make enquiries has not been triggered and the authority cannot make a decision whether or not an applicant is threatened with homelessness intentionally: *Hunt*.[95]

9.68 In *Jarvis*,[96] notice that possession would be required of premises let on an assured shorthold tenancy was not of itself sufficient to trigger a duty under HA 1996 s184.[97]

9.69 The enquiries must be sufficient to satisfy the authority whether the applicant is eligible for assistance and if so what (if any) duty is owed to the applicant under HA 1996 Part 7 or H(W)A 2014 Part 2.

9.70 The subject of enquiries into local connection has been considered in chapter 7.[98] The authority can start local connection enquiries without awaiting the conclusion of its other enquiries, but the issue has to be determined as at the date of the decision,[99] and it may therefore become necessary to reconsider a decision to refer on local connection grounds if other enquiries are prolonged,[100] as the connection itself may be based on factors arising during the enquiries.[101]

94 *R v Northavon DC ex p Palmer* (1995) 27 HLR 576, CA.

95 *R v Rugby BC ex p Hunt* (1992) 26 HLR 1, QBD.

96 *R v Croydon LBC ex p Jarvis* (1993) 26 HLR 194, QBD.

97 But see now HA 1996 s175(4): a person is homeless if given a valid notice seeking possession under HA 1988 s21 in respect of the only accommodation the person has that is available for his or her occupation and the notice will expire within 56 days.

98 Paras 7.58–7.62.

99 *Mohamed v Hammersmith and Fulham LBC* [2001] UKHL 57, [2002] HLR 7.

100 *R v Newham LBC ex p Smith* (1996) 29 HLR 213, QBD.

101 See *Mohamed*, above.

Who must make the enquiries?

9.71 The burden of making enquiries rests with the authority to whom the application was made. In the absence of a contracting out agreement,[102] the duty to enquire may not be delegated to another organisation although the authority may ask another housing authority or relevant body,[103] or a social services authority,[104] to assist in discharging the enquiry duty, which body is obliged to co-operate in the discharge of the function to which the request relates, to the extent that is reasonable in the circumstances.[105]

9.72 In *Gerrard*,[106] the authority had transferred all of its housing stock to a registered housing association,[107] and had reached an agreement pursuant to which the association was to carry out the enquiries under what is now HA 1996 s184, on the basis of which enquiries the authority would make its decisions. Quashing the authority's decision that the applicant was not homeless, it was held that, although entitled under what is now HA 1996 s213 to enlist assistance from it in making its enquiries, the authority must nonetheless take an active and dominant role in the investigative process.

9.73 On the other hand, in *Woolgar*[108] it was held that it is only the decision-making function which is exclusive to the authority (absent a contracting-out arrangement), so that the investigative function involved in making enquiries could properly be delegated to an outside body (at least, one recognised by statute, such as what is now a private registered provider or, in Wales, registered social landlord).[109]

9.74 The cases are not irreconcilable: as a matter of law, authorities are not bound to carry out all their functions through employees but may

102 See para 9.5.

103 Registered provider (in Wales, registered social landlord) or housing action trust, or in Scotland a local authority, development corporation, registered housing association or Scottish Homes: HA 1996 s213(2); H(W)A 2014 s95(5).

104 In the case of 16- and 17-year-olds, the English Code of Guidance (para 18.8) recognises that such a child may apply under HA 1996 Part 7 but requires an assessment under Children Act 1989 to be completed (Welsh Code para 11.10). See also *R (M) v Hammersmith and Fulham LBC* [2008] UKHL 14, [2008] 1 WLR 535, [2008] 4 All ER 271.

105 HA 1996 s213; H(W)A 2014 s95. In Wales, there are additional provisions with which the other body must comply: see para 13.94–13.96.

106 *R v West Dorset DC, West Dorset HA ex p Gerrard* (1994) 27 HLR 150, QBD. Both this and *Woolgar*, below, preceded the contracting out power: see para 9.5.

107 Now, private registered proprietors of social housing.

108 *R v Hertsmere BC ex p Woolgar* (1995) 27 HLR 703, QBD.

109 HA 1996 s213(2)(a).

retain outside contractors; if it can be said, however, that the contractor has determined what enquiries need to be made, and takes them to such a point that the decision is 'all but' made before the authority exercises its decision-making function, the authority will improperly have delegated rather than properly used an outside service in order to lay the ground for its decision.

Conduct of enquiries

9.75 It is for the authority, not the courts, to determine how the necessary enquiries are made, including who should conduct interviews and what questions should be asked.[110] Enquiries should nonetheless be carried out in a sympathetic way:[111] *Phillips*.[112]

9.76 Whether an interview is necessary is likewise primarily for the authority to decide,[113] although the new assessment duty now makes it all but inevitable.[114] In *Tetteh*,[115] the applicant had set out his position in correspondence and there was nothing which required the

110 Subject to *Wednesbury* review: see *R (IA) v Westminster City Council* [2013] EWHC 1273 (QB) where a short interview with the applicant was considered insufficient, leading to 'irrational and, indeed, perverse' conclusions.

111 See English Code para 11.9, which, although in the context of the new assessment duty (HA 1996 s189A), must be of relevance more generally: 'Applicants should be encouraged to share information without fear that this will reduce their chances of receiving support, and questions should be asked in a sensitive way and with an awareness that the applicant may be reluctant to disclose personal details if they lack confidence that their circumstances will be understood and considered sympathetically. Housing authorities should ensure staff have sufficient skills and training to conduct assessments of applicants who may find it difficult to disclose their circumstances, including people at risk of domestic abuse, violence or hate crime.'

See also chapters 21, 22, 23, 24 and 25 of the English Code for advice on how to deal with applications by victims of domestic abuse; care leavers; people with an offending history; former members of the armed forces; and victims of modern slavery and people trafficking.

112 *R v West Dorset DC ex p Phillips* (1984) 17 HLR 336, QBD. See also comments in the decision in *R v Camden LBC ex p Gillan* (1988) 21 HLR 114, QBD. The change to the English Code (see footnote 111, above) does not appear to derogate from these cases; the same conclusion would probably have been reached by the courts in any event, as a matter of construction of HA 1996 and its purposes.

113 If an interview is needed, the interviewer must speak fluent English: see Immigration Act 2016 s77(1) and the Code of Practice (English Language Requirements for Public Sector Workers) Regulations 2016 SI No 1157.

114 See paras 10.58–10.66.

115 *Tetteh v Kingston upon Thames RLBC* [2004] EWCA Civ 1775, [2005] HLR 21.

authority to interview him; failure to do so could therefore not be seen to be a breach of the principles of natural justice.[116]

9.77 A number of authorities – and/or contractors – carry out interviews by telephone, and it may be thought that some will seek to carry out assessments the same way.[117] While this may be proper where all that is involved is to establish or check facts, it is submitted that this will nonetheless not be sufficient where the matter under consideration calls for a face-to-face interview,[118] for example, vulnerability.[119]

9.78 Thus, many people find it difficult to express themselves on the telephone, whether because of language difficulties or mental ability or through unease at being asked to talk about potentially sensitive issues without forewarning, as is often the case on receipt of a telephone call.

9.79 Likewise, the interviewer is deprived of the ability to assess 'body language', a concept that may be difficult to describe but that is well-recognised and that is essential to the overall evaluative exercise in which the interviewer is engaged. It may be observed that the interviewee, too, is deprived of the element of 'reading' the interviewer that is likewise central to comprehension (and to assessing reactions).[120]

9.80 Furthermore, the interviewee may, without the knowledge of the interviewer, be distracted by other people or events;[121] indeed, the interviewee may be temporarily impaired, for example, through drink or drugs.[122] Nor is it impossible for someone else to be

116 See paras 12.66–12.70.

117 There is nothing in HA 1996 s189A which prohibits this, though it may be thought to be far from consonant with the spirit of the exercise.

118 In *R v Camden LBC ex p Gillan* (1988) 21 HLR 114, QBD, the Divisional Court referred to the expectation of a 'face-to-face' opportunity to explain an applicant's situation, in contrast to a telephone-based system, and criticised the authority's 'cavalier treatment' of applicants who were required to explain their circumstances by telephone. See also the position on review, para 9.238.

119 An authority must approach vulnerability with 'great care' – see *Crossley v Westminster City Council* [2006] EWCA Civ 140, [2006] HLR 26, at [30].

120 An interviewee may – is likely to – wish to appear co-operative, and/or may be suggestible, at least to a point; in a telephone interview, an interviewee cannot gauge how his or her answers are impacting on the interviewer.

121 Particularly if the interview is with someone in a hostel, taking the call on a telephone in the common parts.

122 It is not impossible, including in cases such as those referred to in the previous footnotes, for there to be a mistake in identity, whether by misunderstanding or even deliberate conduct by a third party.

answering questions, eg in a hostel or house in multiple occupation (HMO), whether maliciously or through mistake: such conversations are ripe for misunderstanding.

9.81 Even in person, inconsistencies will frequently be found when someone's native language is not English: *Li*.[123] Previous editions of the Code recommended that authorities secure access to competent interpreters for the community languages of their area, but that recommendation is not found in either the current English Code or the Welsh Code.[124]

9.82 Where there is doubt about the competence of an interpreter, the test is whether it has been shown that the interpreter is not – to the knowledge of the authority – competent to conduct the interview: *Jalika Begum*.[125] In *Khatun*,[126] interviews with an applicant (without the applicant's own independent adviser or counsellor) were not inherently flawed on the basis that they had been conducted by an employee of the council who would be inclined to protect the employer's limited resources.[127]

Ambit of enquiries

Generally

9.83 The burden of making enquiries is squarely on the authority.[128] Even without the duty to assess the applicant's case, which carries with it a number of specific matters to be included,[129] inquiries have to cover

123 *R v Surrey Heath BC ex p Li* (1984) 16 HLR 79, QBD.

124 The English Code does, however, suggest that 'translated information and interpreting services should be made available to applicants for who[m] English is not a first language, and the availability of these services publicised to residents and community organisations': para 18.4. The Welsh Code also recommends that consideration be given to producing Information in minority languages: see Welsh Code para 7.17.

125 *R v Tower Hamlets LBC ex p Begum* (1990) 24 HLR 188, QBD.

126 *R v Tower Hamlets LBC ex p Khatun* (1994) 27 HLR 465, CA.

127 Cf the 'fairness' discussions in *Runa Begum v Tower Hamlets LBC* [2003] UKHL 5, [2003] 2 AC 430, [2003] HLR 32; *Feld v Barnet LBC* [2005] EWCA Civ 1307, [2005] HLR 9 (see also see paras 9.140–9.151); *De-Winter Heald and others v Brent LBC* [2009] EWCA Civ 930, [2010] HLR 8. See para 12.76.

128 *R v Woodspring DC ex p Walters* (1984) 16 HLR 73, QBD; *R v Reigate and Banstead DC ex p Paris* (1984) 17 HLR 103, QBD; *R v Barnet LBC ex p Babalola* (1995) 28 HLR 196, QBD; *R v Wandsworth LBC ex p Dodia* (1997) 30 HLR 562, QBD.

129 HA 1996 s189A(2); see paras 10.58–10.66.

all the relevant factors – for example, priority need,[130] or risk of domestic violence in another area.[131]

9.84 Enquiries need not, however, amount to 'CID-type' enquiries.[132] The approach is summarised in *Winchester*:[133]

> The burden lies upon the local authority to make appropriate enquiries . . . in a caring and sympathetic way . . . These enquiries should be pursued rigorously and fairly albeit the authority are not under a duty to conduct detailed CID-type enquiries . . . The applicant must be given an opportunity to explain matters which the local authority is minded to regard as weighing substantially against him . . .

9.85 It follows that there may be some limited circumstances where a local housing authority need not make enquiries into some matters, although the new assessment duty requires the authority to consider 'the circumstances that caused the applicant to become homeless or threatened with homelessness',[134] which will certainly affect the ambit of the enquiries. Nonetheless, there are some limits.

9.86 For example, in *Green v Croydon LBC*[135] the applicant had been evicted from a privately rented property for rent arrears; when she applied as homeless, the authority decided that she was intentionally homeless. She contended that the possession order was wrongly made as they had proceeded on the basis of a monthly rent of £700, whereas the true rent was only £650 per month. It was held that the authority did not have to make enquiries of the landlord, applicant or district judge but were entitled to rely on the possession order which was only consistent with a rent of £700 per month. It is unlikely that this would be different today, notwithstanding the assessment duty.

9.87 In most cases where accommodation has been lost as a result of rent (or mortgage) arrears, the authority will need to make enquiries about the applicant's financial affairs, if only to be satisfied whether

130 *R v Ryedale DC ex p Smith* (1983) 16 HLR 66, QBD.

131 *Patterson v Greenwich LBC* (1993) 26 HLR 159, CA.

132 *Lally v Kensington and Chelsea RLBC* (1980) *Times*, March 27, QBD. They must, however, address obviously relevant factors, see *Wandsworth LBC v NJ* [2013] EWCA Civ 1373, [2014] HLR 6, in which the authority failed to make any enquiries into the possibility that a violent man would be able to locate his ex-partner (the applicant), despite clear evidence that he was attempting to do so.

133 *R v Gravesham BC ex p Winchester* (1986) 18 HLR 208, QBD, at 214–215.

134 HA 1996 s189A(2)(a); see paras 10.58–10.66.

135 [2007] EWCA Civ 1367, [2008] HLR 28.

the accommodation that was lost was affordable,[136] although it has been held that when considering whether an applicant has been occupying what was asserted by her to be settled accommodation, an authority does not necessarily have to enquire into its legal character,[137] which again might not be different even subject to the assessment duty.

9.88 In *Gilby v Westminster City Council*,[138] the applicant occupied accommodation either as an unlawful subtenant or as a bare licensee. The question was whether the occupation constituted settled accommodation, for which purpose the relevant question was whether the applicant had the basis for a reasonable expectation of continued occupation: the difference between bare license and unlawful subtenancy was irrelevant to that question; the authority had been entitled to determine that the accommodation was not settled either way.

9.89 Enquiries may extend to other departments within the authority – for example, the housing department (referable to an earlier tenancy): *Adair*.[139] Where an application is made by an occupier of property owned by the authority, the duty to make enquiries does not, however, fetter any decision to recover possession, nor is it likely to be fettered by the assessment duty: in *Grumbridge*,[140] a trespasser sought judicial review of the authority's decision to evict him before determining his application for housing: it was held that there was no requirement or statutory obligation on the authority to determine whether a person is either homeless or in priority need or, indeed, as to any of the other matters under (then) HA 1985 Part 3 (now HA 1996 Part 7), before deciding whether to obtain possession of property.

9.90 Where the facts relating to an application are fairly placed before the applicant for the applicant to agree, dispute or supplement, and the applicant agrees them, it is not unfair for the decision-maker or the reviewing officer to proceed on the basis that the agreed facts

136 As to which, see the Homelessness (Suitability of Accommodation) Order 1996 SI No 3204 and H(W)A 2014 s59(2). See further English Code paras 9.17–9.20, 17.44–17.45; Welsh Code paras 8.29–8.30, 17.18–17.19.

137 *Gilby v Westminster City Council* [2008] EWCA Civ 604, [2008] HLR 7.

138 [2007] EWCA Civ 604, [2008] HLR 7.

139 *R v Camden LBC ex p Adair* (1996) 29 HLR 236, QBD.

140 *R v Barnet LBC ex p Grumbridge* (1992) 24 HLR 433, QBD.

are accurate,[141] bearing particularly in mind that the burden is normally on the applicant to put forward the matters and evidence which he or she wishes to be taken into account: see *Cramp*.[142]

9.91 Note, however, that if reliance is placed on a disability, (EqA 2010 s149 – the public sector equality duty)[143] – may[144] oblige the authority to carry out further inquiries if some feature of the evidence presents a real possibility that an applicant is within it.[145]

141 *Rowley v Rugby BC* [2007] EWCA Civ 483, [2007] HLR 40. See para 9.141. See also *R (Lynch) v Lambeth LBC* [2007] HLR 15 at [32]: 'All the medical evidence was accepted, and the housing authority did not consider, either before the s184 or the review, that any further inquiries were necessary. No suggestion was made by the claimant or her advisers that further information should be sought, nor was any more offered. No response was made to the minded to find letter of the reviewing officer. In line with the decision of the *Cramp* case, . . . the Housing Authority were not unreasonable in failing to make further inquiries. It is difficult to envisage what other inquiries needed to be made, given the wealth of information with the original application.'

142 *Cramp v Hastings BC; Phillips v Camden LBC* [2005] EWCA Civ 1005, [2005] HLR 48, see para 9.90. See also *Mohamoud v Kensington and Chelsea RLBC; Saleem v Wandsworth LBC* [2015] EWCA Civ 780, [2015] HLR 38: where an applicant seeks to rely on Children Act 2004 s11 (duty on authorities to safeguard and promote the welfare of children when discharging any functions), he or she must notify the authority of any relevant matters relating to the child on which he or she wishes to rely.

143 In the exercise of functions, to have due regard to the need to eliminate unlawful discrimination, harassment and victimisation and to advance equality of opportunity and foster good relations between persons with protected characteristics (age, disability, gender reassignment, pregnancy or maternity, race, sex, sexual orientation, religion or belief) and other persons.

144 In *Wilson v Birmingham City Council* [2016] EWCA Civ 1137, [2017] HLR 4, it was held that a review officer was entitled to expect the appellant to bring forward any information which might be relevant to show that her children had a disability; the absence of any response from the appellant to invitations to submit information meant that the officer had been entitled to conclude that any problems experienced by the children were not such as to engage the EqA 2010.

145 *Pieretti v Enfield LBC* [2010] EWCA Civ 1104, [2011] HLR 3, rejecting arguments a) that the predecessor provisions of Disability Discrimination Act 1995 s49A had no application to homelessness applications, but only to the formulation of policy; b) that HA 1996 Part 7 was a complete code that comprehensively addressed the rights and needs of disabled people so that section 49A added nothing; c) that a determination under Part 7 was not a 'function' within the meaning of section 49A; and d) that neither the original decision-maker nor the review officer had been asked to consider section 49A.

9.92 In *Hackney LBC v Haque*,[146] it was held, in the context of a suitability review, that EqA 2010 s149 required the authority:

a) to recognise that the appellant had a disability;
b) to focus on specific aspects of his impairments to the extent that they were relevant to the suitability of the accommodation;
c) to focus on the disadvantages he might suffer when compared to a person without those impairments;
d) to focus on his accommodation needs arising from those impairments and the extent to which the accommodation met those needs;
e) to recognise that the appellant's particular needs might require him to be treated more favourably than a person without a disability; and
f) to review the suitability of the accommodation, paying due regard to those matters.[147]

Whose circumstances?

9.93 HA 1996 s183(2) – governing applications – refers to 'a person making . . . an application', and enquiries under section 184[148] are whether 'he is' eligible for assistance, or whether 'he has a local connection' with another authority. The wording might therefore be said to suggest that it is only the applicant who is to be considered.[149]

9.94 On the other hand, enquiries into the local connection of the applicant alone would not suffice, for the local connections of a person reasonably to be expected to reside with the applicant are relevant,[150] and priority need may likewise arise by reference to non-applicants.[151] The circumstances of a person reasonably to be

146 [2017] EWCA Civ 4, [2017] HLR 14.

147 There is no need to refer in terms to EqA 2010 s149, what matters is whether the substance has been complied with: *Haque*, above, *Poshteh v Kensington and Chelsea RLBC* [2015] EWCA Civ 711, [2015] HLR 36, *Poshteh* went on appeal to the Supreme Court ([2017] UKSC 36, [2017] HLR 28) where there was no substantive discussion of the nature of the duty under EqA 2010 s149 and the argument that it had not been considered by the review officer was dismissed as an example of the 'over-zealous linguistic analysis' deprecated in *Holmes-Moorhouse v Richmond-upon-Thames LBC* [2009] UKHL 7, [2009] HLR 34.

148 See para 9.57.

149 In Wales, the H(W)A 2014 speaks of an assessment of 'a person's case': s62. Likewise, the assessment duty in HA 1996 s189A talks of 'an assessment of the applicant's case'.

150 See para 7.58.

151 See para 5.2.

expected to reside with the applicant may also affect the issue of intentionality – for example, if those circumstances meant that the accommodation which has been quit was not available or reasonable to continue to be occupied;[152] likewise, that person is explicitly relevant to an assessment of the applicant's housing needs.[153] The suitability of accommodation offered will also require regard to be had to those reasonably to be expected to reside with the applicant.[154]

9.95 It would introduce a surprising – and inconsistent – degree of legality or formality into HA 1996 Part 7 and H(W)A 2014 Part 2 if anything turned on who actually approaches the authority or signs an application form.

9.96 It seems clear, therefore, that any person whose circumstances will, under HA 1996 Part 7 (or H(W)A 2014 Part 2), necessarily be taken into consideration in determining either eligibility for assistance or the level of that assistance, should be considered within the ambit of an application and its enquiries.[155]

Burden of proof

9.97 It is not for the applicant to 'prove' his or her homelessness. In *Walters*,[156] the applicant's solicitor gave the authority information which, if confirmed, would have led to a finding that the applicant was homeless; the authority said that she had not established that she was homeless. This wrongly treated the burden as being on the applicant to prove homelessness. The assessment duty in HA 1996 s189A is, in any event, inquisitorial in nature.[157]

Relevant matters

9.98 It is a trite proposition that enquiries must cover all relevant matters; this means more than merely 'touching on' relevant matters: an

152 See paras 6.88, 6.156.

153 HA 1996 s189A(2)(b); para 10.58.

154 See para 10.173.

155 In turn, this could lead to a finding that there had not been intentional homelessness – where one member is or could be held to have become homeless intentionally but another is or could not be. At that point, assuming that there is at least a minimal degree of knowledge that the 'second' person is asking the authority for housing assistance, there is in substance an 'application', and that person is entitled to his or her separate consideration: see para 9.93.

156 *R v Woodspring DC ex p Walters* (1984) 16 HLR 73, QBD.

157 HA 1996 s189A(1) –'The authority must make an assessment of the applicant's case': see para 10.58.

authority must engage with the issues that are germane to the application.[158]

9.99 A relevant matter may evolve from the factual background provided by the applicant or of the authority's own motion. In *Paris*,[159] it was held that enquiries into matters relevant to a finding of intentionality have to be made whether or not the applicant provides information which suggests that there may be something to follow up – for example, whether or not the last accommodation occupied was available and whether it was reasonable to continue in occupation of it.

9.100 Thus, in *Silchenstedt*,[160] the applicant was asked to leave accommodation consisting of two bedrooms on the ground of rent arrears, but was offered alternative accommodation by the same landlord, which the applicant refused on the ground that it was not suitable. The authority found the applicant intentionally homeless and that the *alternative* accommodation was available for him and reasonable for him to occupy.[161] The applicant successfully challenged the decision on the basis that the authority had not conducted sufficient enquiries into the size and nature of the accommodation which the applicant had refused.

9.101 By way of contrast, in *de Falco*[162] the applicants gave their reason for leaving Italy as unemployment and did not put forward any material from which it might have been inferred that the accommodation that they had left was not accommodation which had been

158 See *Islington LBC v Mohammed* [2013] EWCA Civ 739, [2013] HLR 41 (not engaged with whether applicant would be vulnerable because fainting attacks more likely if street homeless). See also *Farah v Hillingdon LBC* [2014] EWCA Civ 359, [2014] HLR 24 (intentional homelessness because of arrears which could have been avoided by unnecessary expenditure, including taxis: authority had not engaged with whether the applicant's argument that some of the fares were necessary expenditure because of her mobility difficulties). See further paras 12.10, 12.48–12.51.

159 *R v Reigate and Banstead BC ex p Paris* (1984) 17 HLR 103, QBD.

160 *R v Kensington and Chelsea RLBC ex p Silchenstedt* (1996) 29 HLR 728, QBD.

161 For reasons that are not apparent on the face of the report, the argument (described as 'legalistic, although it may be a perfectly proper, approach') that the applicant could not be homeless intentionally as a result of a failure to take up accommodation 'has not been pressed in this application before me': *Silchenstedt*, at 731.

162 *De Falco, Silvestri v Crawley BC* [1980] QB 460, CA.

reasonable to continue to occupy.[163] The authority was held not to have erred in drawing the inference that what they had left had been suitable,[164] even though it had made no express enquiry to this effect. *De Falco* was, however, an interlocutory application and was treated as such in *Paris*.[165] On this aspect, it is somewhat out of harmony with subsequent decisions.

9.102 In *Fisher*,[166] it was held that intentionality enquiries may have to go back over several years, to the last accommodation occupied by the applicant (if any) which was available and reasonable. See also *Iqbal*,[167] where insufficient enquiries were made into the applicant's claim that he was a political refugee.

Adequacy of enquiries

9.103 The requirement to enquire into all relevant matters does not, however, mean that a failure to enquire into every matter raised will necessarily make the enquiry[168] process flawed. What is relevant will be different in every case. The duty to make enquiries means enquiries appropriate to the facts known to the authority, or of which it ought reasonably to have been aware;[169] the applicant should normally put forward the matters and evidence which he or she wishes to be taken into account.[170]

9.104 Enquiries can only be attacked as inadequate if they are enquiries that no reasonable authority could have failed to make; the court should not intervene merely because further enquiries would have been sensible or desirable, only if they were such that no reasonable authority could be satisfied had been sufficient – see *Costello*,[171]

163 Although Bridge LJ considered the reason for leaving Italy to be 'not their lack of suitable accommodation, but their lack of employment' (at 482F; a phrase then picked up by the headnote writer), the correct test was reasonable to continue to occupy, as is recognised later in the same paragraph.

164 Ie reasonable for them to continue to occupy, see last footnote.

165 *R v Reigate and Banstead BC ex p Paris* (1984) 17 HLR 103, QBD.

166 *R v Preseli DC ex p Fisher* (1984) 17 HLR 147, QBD.

167 *R v Westminster City Council ex p Iqbal* (1988) 22 HLR 215, QBD.

168 Or assessment.

169 *R v Sedgemoor DC ex p McCarthy* (1996) 28 HLR 608, QBD.

170 *Cramp v Hastings BC; Phillips v Camden LBC* [2005] EWCA Civ 1005, [2005] HLR 48; see para 9.90.

171 *R v Nottingham City Council ex p Costello* (1989) 21 HLR 301, QBD.

Bayani[172] and *Kassam.*[173] The existing examples will need to be reconsidered in light of the assessment duty in HA 1996 s189A,[174] but it is likely that many of them would be decided the same way nonetheless.

Examples – unsuccessful challenge

9.105 In *Adamiec,*[175] where the applicant alleged that he had been constrained to sell his home because of financial circumstances, the court refused to quash the decision that he was intentionally homeless either on the basis that a reasonable authority would have further tested the financial material before it or that a reasonable authority would have made further enquiries; this is a decision which, even before the assessment duty came into force, would probably not have survived more modern approaches.

9.106 On the other hand, in *Baruwa,*[176] where the applicant claimed that she could not afford her rent because of other necessary outgoings, the Court of Appeal held that it was not necessary for the authority to investigate every detail and every inconsistency in the income and expenditure figures provided by the applicant before reaching its decision,[177] which is likely to remain an approach which would still be taken.

9.107 In *Bariise,*[178] the applicant complained that insufficient enquiries had been made into her allegations that those she had shared a house with had stolen her food and had scolded her children, making them cry. All the allegations were, however, known to the authority; there were no further enquiries which it could usefully have made. This would probably be decided the same way today.

9.108 In *McDonagh,*[179] a failure to enquire into the applicant's British nationality could not be criticised, as the applicant had informed the authority that his family was a large Irish travelling family just arrived

172 *R v Kensington and Chelsea RLBC ex p Bayani* (1990) 22 HLR 406, CA.

173 *R v Kensington and Chelsea RLBC ex p Kassam* (1993) 26 HLR 455, QBD. See also *R v Nottingham City Council ex p Edwards* (1998) 31 HLR 33, QBD.

174 Paras 10.58–10.66.

175 *R v Leeds City Council ex p Adamiec* (1991) 24 HLR 138, QBD.

176 *R v Brent LBC ex p Baruwa* (1997) 29 HLR 915, CA.

177 Contrast *R v Tower Hamlets LBC ex p Ullah* (1992) 24 HLR 680, QBD, where further enquiries were held to have been necessary on very similar facts to *Baruwa.*

178 *R v Brent LBC ex p Bariise* (1998) 31 HLR 50, CA.

179 *R (McDonagh) v Hounslow LBC* [2004] EWHC 511 (Admin), [2004] JHL D61.

from Dublin, and only claimed to be British after the decision that he was intentionally homeless had been made.

9.109 In *Augustin*,[180] it could not be said – on the material before it – that the authority could not have been satisfied that the applicant was homeless intentionally. In the circumstances, it could not be said that it had not made necessary enquiries.

Examples – successful challenge

9.110 In *Beattie (No 2)*,[181] affidavit evidence in earlier proceedings was considered to be material which the authority ought to have taken into account, even though it had not expressly been referred to during the course of a further application.

9.111 In *Krishnan v Hillingdon LBC*,[182] the authority had made inadequate enquiries when it failed to chase up its letter to another authority, or to follow up the applicant's own description of pressure on him to leave his earlier accommodation because of overcrowding.

9.112 In *Phillips*,[183] the applicant burst out at her husband during their interview that she had always told him his drinking would get them into trouble. This was said not to be capable of being construed as acquiescence,[184] even by the most hard-hearted of officers; it was astonishing that the officer had not made further enquiries. If he had, for example, of social services, it would inevitably have led to the conclusion that the applicant could not be blamed.

9.113 In *Ajayi*,[185] the authority had failed to enquire into 'important matters of social history and national status' – such as for how long the applicant had been away from the UK and where her children were born – which failure led the authority to consider that the applicant was an immigrant, whereas she had actually been born in the UK.

9.114 In *Tickner v Mole Valley DC*,[186] Lord Denning MR criticised the enquiries made as to whether or not the applicants were actually homeless. The applicants, while living in mobile homes, had given permanent addresses to the site manager, on which the authority based its conclusion that they were not homeless:

180 *R v Westminster City Council ex p Augustin* (1993) 25 HLR 281, CA.
181 *R v Eastleigh BC ex p Beattie (No 2)* (1984) 17 HLR 168, QBD.
182 *Krishnan v Hillingdon LBC* June 1981 *LAG Bulletin* 137, QBD.
183 *R v West Dorset DC ex p Phillips* (1984) 17 HLR 336, QBD.
184 See para 6.16.
185 *R v Newham LBC ex p Ajayi* (1994) 28 HLR 25, QBD.
186 *Tickner v Mole Valley DC* August 1980 *LAG Bulletin* 187, CA.

> They made that finding because each couple gave their permanent address elsewhere. One gave a mother-in-law's address. Another gave a divorced husband's address. I think that was not sufficient. Enquiries should have been made at the addresses given as permanent addresses. If the mother-in-law was asked – or if the divorced husband was asked – the answer would have been: 'We are not going to have that person back.' So Mole Council should have found these couples were homeless.

9.115 As foreshadowed above,[187] the right to review is likely to cure any deficiency or failure to conduct adequate enquiries. In *Cramp*,[188] Brooke LJ said:[189]

> Given the full-scale nature of the review, a court whose powers are limited to considering points of law should now be even more hesitant than the High Court was encouraged to be at the time of *ex p Bayani*[190] if the appellant's ground of appeal relates to a matter which the reviewing officer was never invited to consider, and which was not an obvious matter he should have considered.

9.116 Although *Cramp* undoubtedly raised the bar which an applicant must cross in order to establish illegality on the grounds of the adequacy of enquiries, that is not to say that the issue can no longer be raised. Challenges are frequently pursued on the basis of failure to make enquiries and the obligation to do so remains extant and, if a failure to make an enquiry remains uncorrected on review, the right to challenge remains available. The inquisitorial nature of the assessment duty in HA 1996 s189A[191] may be thought to have helped in this respect.

9.117 In *Pieretti v Enfield LBC*,[192] it was said that the dictum of Brooke LJ requires qualification where the applicant is a disabled[193] person; even where a decision-maker (whether under HA 1996 s184 or s202)

187 See para 9.9.

188 *Cramp v Hastings BC; Phillips v Camden LBC*, above.

189 *Cramp* at [14].

190 *R v Kensington and Chelsea RLBC ex p Bayani* (1990) 22 HLR 406, CA.

191 Paras 10.58–10.66.

192 [2010] EWCA Civ 1104, [2011] HLR 3.

193 *Pieretti* concerned Disability Discrimination Act 1995 s49A; this has been replaced with the broader 'public sector equality duty' in EqA 2010 s149 and, as such, the full range of 'protected characteristics' should be considered, ie age, disability, gender reassignment; pregnancy or maternity, race, sex, sexual orientation, religion or belief.

is not expressly invited to consider a putative[194] disability, he or she must still have due regard to the need to take steps to take account of it.

9.118 The pre-*Cramp* case-law still provides useful guidance as to the matters which will influence the court's decision. It should, however, be read with the limitations of *Cramp* in mind.

Reliance on particular circumstances

9.119 If reliance is sought to be placed on some eventuality which is not to be taken for granted – eg some idiosyncratic or uncommon circumstance which would alter the decision – of which not even a suspicion has come to the authority's attention, it is much harder to complain of its failure to ask a relevant question.[195]

9.120 Note, however, the possibility that EqA 2010 s149 – the public sector equality duty – may oblige the authority to carry out further inquiries if some feature of the evidence presents a real possibility that an applicant is within its provisions,[196] as may the assessment duty.

9.121 Advisers should nonetheless always try to put all relevant matters before an authority. An authority will not be criticised for failing to make enquiries of someone they have no reason to believe will provide relevant information – for example, a doctor or a school where health or education did not appear to be in issue – especially if an experienced adviser has not raised the point.

9.122 In *Holland*,[197] a couple applied as homeless. They had been living at a series of temporary addresses since leaving a caravan site, which the authority was satisfied had been quit in circumstances which amounted to intentional homelessness. At the Court of Appeal, the couple sought to rely on a suggestion that the man had enjoyed an intervening period of what would have been permanent accommodation in a boarding-house (because he and his wife had at that time separated), but which he had lost for reasons beyond his control, so that he could not be treated as being intentionally homeless. This argument was rejected: the authority had been given no reason to

194 The decision-maker is, however, entitled to ask for evidence of an alleged disability and, if none is provided, may conclude that there is no disability: *Birmingham City Council v Wilson* [2016] EWCA Civ 1137, [2017] HLR 4.

195 See *Cramp*. See also *Bellouti v Wandsworth LBC* [2005] EWCA Civ 602, [2005] HLR 46.

196 *Pieretti v Enfield LBC* [2010] EWCA Civ 1104, [2011] HLR 3.

197 *R v Harrow LBC ex p Holland* (1982) 4 HLR 108, CA.

suspect that the accommodation might have been permanent or acceptable to the man, whose separation from his wife had never been mentioned.

9.123 In *Henderson*,[198] the applicants contended that they were unaware of material facts when they agreed to an order for possession being made against them. The authority could not, however, be faulted for failing to make appropriate enquiries when, on the facts available to it (including what it had been told by the applicants), it had no reason to be aware of this.

9.124 See also *Mahsood*,[199] in which it was held that the authority had no reason to be aware of the applicant's ignorance of housing benefit entitlement during a period of absence.[200] See further *Cunha*,[201] where there had been little or no reference to the illness of the applicant's child as a reason for her return from Brazil; in contrast, see *Ajayi*,[202] where the authority had failed to enquire into 'important matters of social history and national status', such as for how long the applicant had been away from the UK and where her children were born, which failure led to an error in the way in which the application was considered

9.125 In *Nipa Begum*,[203] although relevant to consider whether an applicant could afford to travel to accommodation when deciding whether it was available to her,[204] the challenge failed because the applicant had not raised the issue, nor was it evident from any of the information before the authority that it was an issue. The authority was accordingly entitled to conclude without further enquiries that she could return to it.

Medical evidence

9.126 In cases where vulnerability is claimed for medical reasons, it will be both proper and a necessary part of an authority's enquiries to consider a medical opinion. The authority must, however, still decide the question of vulnerability for itself: *Carroll*.[205]

198 *R v Wandsworth LBC ex p Henderson* (1986) 18 HLR 522, QBD.

199 *R v Wycombe DC ex p Mahsood* (1988) 20 HLR 683, QBD.

200 This could surely not survive the duty to assess the circumstances that caused the applicant's homelessness in HA 1996 s189A(2)(a).

201 *R v Kensington and Chelsea RLBC ex p Cunha* (1988) 21 HLR 16, QBD.

202 *R v Newham LBC ex p Ajayi* (1994) 28 HLR 25, QBD.

203 *Nipa Begum v Tower Hamlets LBC* (1999) 32 HLR 445, CA.

204 See para 4.18.

205 *R v Lambeth LBC ex p Carroll* (1987) 20 HLR 142, QBD; *Osmani v Camden LBC* [2004] EWCA Civ 1706, [2004] HLR 22.

9.127 A medical report obtained in pursuance of enquiries is not necessarily required to be disclosed to an applicant. In *R (Lynch) v Lambeth LBC*,[206] the authority made reference to extracts of its medical officer's report within the 'minded to find' letter sent in compliance with the Allocation of Housing and Homelessness (Review Procedures) Regulations 1999.[207] The applicant had the opportunity to make representations in response to the letter on any matter with which she disagreed, including the references to the medical officer's report. She did not do so. The failure by the authority to provide the applicant with a copy of the medical report was therefore 'not conclusive of any error of public law'.[208]

9.128 In *Sangermano*,[209] the authority ought either to have accepted medical evidence which was submitted by the applicant's advisers, or to have made its own further enquiries. Once medical evidence has been provided to an authority and properly considered, however, it is open to the authority to reject it.[210]

9.129 Medical evidence may also be rejected if it does not relate to a relevant time. In *Hijazi*,[211] a psychiatrist's opinion was rejected because it did not relate to the applicant's condition at the material time of his eviction.

9.130 In *Lumley*,[212] the authority was provided with a questionnaire completed by the applicant's GP which confirmed that the applicant suffered from severe depression for which he was on medication. The information was passed to the authority's medical officer, who was not qualified in psychiatric medicine, and who neither saw the applicant nor made any further enquiries. He concluded, without giving any reasons, that the applicant was not vulnerable on medical grounds. The enquiries made by the medical officer were held to be inadequate.

9.131 In *Kacar*,[213] however, the applicant claimed that it was not reasonable for him to continue to live away from London because of his wife's depression and phobia of being alone. His wife was not receiving any medical treatment, nor had she consulted her GP, nor had she spoken to her social worker. There were no further enquiries

206 [2006] EWHC 2737 (Admin), [2007] HLR 15.
207 SI No 71. See paras 9.219–9.227.
208 *R (Lynch) v Lambeth LBC* [2006] EWHC 2737 (Admin), [2007] HLR 15, at [33].
209 *R v Bath City Council ex p Sangermano* (1984) 17 HLR 94, QBD.
210 *Noh v Hammersmith and Fulham LBC* [2001] JHL D54, CA.
211 *Hijazi v Kensington and Chelsea RLBC* [2003] EWCA Civ 692, [2003] HLR 73.
212 *R v Newham LBC ex p Lumley* (2001) 33 HLR 11, QBD.
213 *Kacar v Enfield LBC* (2001) 33 HLR 5, CA.

which a reasonable authority could have been expected to make; it had sufficient information to assess the seriousness of the wife's depression.

9.132 In *Shala v Birmingham City Council*,[214] the applicants – a husband and wife – applied as homeless and asserted that the wife had mental health issues which meant that she had a priority need. Information was provided from a GP setting out the diagnosis and treatment of post-traumatic stress disorder and depression. The authority concluded that the wife was not in priority need. The couple asked for a review and obtained medical evidence from a psychiatrist stating that the wife was 'very depressed'.

9.133 The local authority referred this to a medical adviser who provided an opinion that 'there was no particular assertion of severity' and no suggestion of admission to a psychiatric hospital or of other significant treatment being necessary. The medical adviser did not carry out any examination of the wife. Further information was subsequently provided as to the wife's vulnerability from the psychiatrist and the GP. None of that information was referred to the medical adviser. The authority upheld the original decision that there was no priority need.

9.134 On appeal, quashing the authority's decision, it was said that:

a) where an authority's medical expert lacks parity of qualification with the appellant's expert (as here the authority's medical adviser did not have the qualifications of the psychiatrist), the authority 'must not fall into the trap of thinking that it is comparing like with like';[215] and
b) if one medical expert advises on the implications of another expert's report without examining the patient, 'his advice cannot itself ordinarily constitute expert evidence of the applicant's condition'; and, if he or she does advise without examination, 'the decision-maker needs to take the absence of an examination into account'.[216]

Blanket policies

9.135 A decision reached without proper enquiries will be invalid. A decision reached pursuant to a policy to treat all those evicted for arrears as homeless intentionally will be plainly void as a failure to

214 *Shala v Birmingham City Council* [2007] EWCA Civ 624, [2008] HLR 8. See also para 5.49.

215 *Shala* at [22].

216 *Shala* at [22]–[23].

exercise properly the duty to reach an individual decision: *Williams v Cynon Valley Council*.[217] Nor may an authority automatically or invariably treat as homeless intentionally all those who have been evicted from premises on grounds which reflect tenant default (for example, nuisance and annoyance) – the authority must take the reasons for the eviction into account and look at the circumstances giving rise to the order.[218]

9.136 An authority must also bear in mind that some possession orders are within the discretion of the county court judge, who may have taken into account matters for which the applicant has no responsibility. In *Stubbs v Slough BC*,[219] a county court ordered the authority to reconsider its finding of intentionality because an element in the decision to order possession on the ground of nuisance had been the proximity of landlord and tenant, and their relationship, over which the tenant had no control.

Loss of employment

9.137 If the cause of an application is loss of employment, the authority must enquire why the job was lost: *Williams*.[220] Consider also *Cosmo*,[221] where there was a successful challenge on the ground that the authority had failed to make enquiries into whether the loss of accommodation was due to the failure of the applicant's business.

9.138 In *Cunha*,[222] however, the claimant sought to require the authority to consider the difficulties in sustaining employment in Brazil before deciding that she had become intentionally homeless when she had left employment there to come to the UK; it was held that there was no requirement for the authority to enquire into local employment conditions in Brazil.

9.139 Likewise in *Bayani*,[223] the failure of the local authority to make full enquiries into the applicant's employment situation in the Philippines was not fatal to its finding of intentionality.

217 January 1980 *LAG Bulletin* 16, CC.

218 *Devenport v Salford City Council* (1983) 8 HLR 54, CA; *R v Cardiff City Council ex p John* (1982) 9 HLR 56, QBD.

219 January 1980 *LAG Bulletin* 16, CC.

220 *R v Thurrock DC ex p Williams* (1981) 1 HLR 128, QBD; see para 6.77.

221 *R v Camden LBC ex p Cosmo* (1997) 30 HLR 817, QBD.

222 *R v Kensington and Chelsea RLBC ex p Cunha* (1988) 21 HLR 16, QBD.

223 *R v Kensington and Chelsea RLBC ex p Bayani* (1990) 22 HLR 406, CA.

Fairness

9.140 It is a trite proposition that fairness calls for all basic issues (that may be decided adversely to the applicant) to be put to an applicant. When conducting enquiries fairly, authorities are not bound to treat the issue as if in a court of law: *Ward.*[224] They act reasonably if they act on responsible material from responsible people who might reasonably be expected to provide a reliable account. An authority can rely on hearsay, in the sense that it is not obliged to confine itself to direct evidence – for example, where an authority relied on evidence from a social worker's supervisor, rather than the social worker himself or herself.[225]

9.141 In *Goddard v Torridge DC,*[226] the authority discussed with the applicant's former employers the circumstances in which he had quit his job and, accordingly, had lost his tied accommodation, and went into these matters fully with the applicant on three separate occasions, which was sufficient for these purposes.

9.142 In the Divisional Court hearing in *Islam,*[227] an allegation of want of natural justice failed because – by the time of the decision – the authority had given the applicant the benefit of no fewer than six interviews. The judgment nonetheless takes for granted that a want of natural justice would be fatal to an authority's decision.

9.143 The authority is, however, not obliged to put every detail to an applicant, although the applicant must have an opportunity to deal with at least the generality of material which will adversely affect him or her; this will usually include matters of factual detail.[228] Where facts are agreed by an applicant, however, which facts form the basis of the decision, the decision-maker is entitled to take the applicant's acceptance of the facts at face value.[229]

9.144 A failure to ask why the applicant fell into mortgage arrears,[230] or a failure to enquire into the applicant's state of mind when she quit her previous accommodation, ie, what she had believed about the accommodation that she was coming to (which turned out to be less

224 *R v Southampton City Council ex p Ward* (1984) 14 HLR 114, QBD.

225 *Ward,* above. See also *R v Nottingham City Council ex p Costello* (1989) 21 HLR 301, QBD.

226 January 1982 *LAG Bulletin* 9, QBD.

227 *R v Hillingdon Homeless Panel ex p Islam* (1980) *Times,* February 10, QBD (not forming part of the subsequent appeals – see [1983] 1 AC 688, CA and HL, (1981) 1 HLR 107, HL).

228 On the requirements of fairness, see paras 12.66–12.70.

229 *Rowley v Rugby BC* [2007] EWCA Civ 483, [2007] HLR 40.

230 *R v Wyre BC ex p Joyce* (1983) 11 HLR 73, QBD.

than settled),[231] have both been held to have been errors on the part of an authority and would now fall within the assessment duty in any event.[232]

9.145 Where matters are put, they must be put to the applicant himself or herself[233] and, if during interview, a record of the interview should be kept: *Brown*.[234]

9.146 All matters that are ultimately decided against the applicant should be put to the applicant,[235] whether related to an admission by the applicant of which he or she is aware[236] (regardless of whether it was provided on a 'confidential' basis)[237] or where the authority obtains information from a third party on which it intends to rely, such as a bank,[238] or information from the applicant's GP which is inconsistent with that which the applicant has himself or herself provided.[239]

9.147 The duty is not, however, absolute. A finding of intentionality was upheld in *Reynolds*,[240] even though important but ultimately not decisive issues had not been put directly to the applicant, who had refused both a home visit and an interview and who had requested that all communication be made through her solicitors.

9.148 Nor, in *Jaafer*,[241] was the authority required to put to the applicant its conclusion that her husband and child were illegal immigrants, as it had given her every opportunity to offer her version of events in an interview.

9.149 Where the facts are uncontested, there is no general obligation to inform each and every applicant in advance of any negative decision; this would place an unrealistically heavy burden on authorities: *Tetteh*.[242]

231 *R v Wandsworth LBC ex p Rose* (1983) 11 HLR 105, QBD.

232 HA 1996 s189(12)(a); see paras 10.58–10.66.

233 *R v Tower Hamlets LBC ex p Saber* (1992) 24 HLR 611, QBD.

234 *R v Dacorum BC ex p Brown* (1989) 21 HLR 405, QBD. If part of the assessment, written records of certain matters need to be kept in any event: see para 10.10.

235 *R v Tower Hamlets LBC ex p Rouf* (1989) 21 HLR 294, QBD.

236 *Robinson v Brent LBC* (1998) 31 HLR 1015, CA. See also *R v Wandsworth LBC ex p Dodia* (1997) 30 HLR 562, QBD and *R v Camden LBC ex p Mohammed* (1998) 30 HLR 315, QBD on inconsistent statements given by applicants.

237 *R v Poole BC ex p Cooper* (1995) 27 HLR 605, QBD.

238 *R v Shrewsbury and Atcham BC ex p Griffiths* (1993) 25 HLR 613, QBD. See also *R v Brent LBC ex p McManus* (1993) 25 HLR 643, QBD and *R v Hackney LBC ex p Decordova* (1994) 27 HLR 108, QBD.

239 *R (Begum) v Tower Hamlets LBC* [2002] EWHC 633 (Admin), [2003] HLR 8.

240 *R v Sevenoaks DC ex p Reynolds* (1989) 22 HLR 250, CA.

241 *R v Westminster City Council ex p Jaafer* (1997) 30 HLR 698, QBD.

242 *Tetteh v Kingston upon Thames RLBC* [2004] EWCA Civ 1775, [2005] HLR 21.

9.150 Nor is there an obligation to give the applicant the last word in every case. Whether or not it is unfair not to do so depends on the facts of the particular case.

9.151 Thus, in *Bellouti*,[243] medical evidence from the applicant's GP was submitted to the authority's medical adviser, who advised that it did not make the applicant vulnerable. Taking into account the evidence and the views of the medical adviser, a decision that the applicant was not vulnerable was upheld on review and appeal. The views of the medical adviser did not have to be put to the applicant because they were not factual material obtained from a third party; all the authority had done was to refer material on which the applicant relied to its own medical adviser for comment. There was no unfairness in the comments not being shown to the applicant.

Doubt

9.152 If enquiries suggest that the applicant may have become homeless intentionally, but any doubt or uncertainty remains, the issue must be resolved in favour of the applicant.[244]

Further enquiries and reconsideration

9.153 Once a decision has been made, there is no statutory power to make further enquiries unless application is made for a review[245] or on a new application.[246] The local authority is entitled to take as its starting point the matters which the applicant has specifically raised on review.[247] If a decision taken has been adverse to an applicant, the authority can nonetheless re-open its enquiries of its own motion if it receives new information.[248] This will cure any defects in its earlier procedure, for example, failure to consider relevant matters.

9.154 If the authority has power to reopen enquiries of its own motion, then it is hard to see how any reasonable authority could refuse to

243 *Bellouti v Wandsworth LBC* [2005] EWCA Civ 602, [2005] HLR 46. See also *Hall v Wandsworth LBC; Carter v Wandsworth LBC* [2004] EWCA Civ 1740, [2005] HLR 23.

244 *R v North Devon DC ex p Lewis* [1981] 1 WLR 328, QBD; see also *R v Thurrock BC ex p Williams* (1982) 1 HLR 71, QBD and *R v Gravesham BC ex p Winchester* (1986) 18 HLR 208, QBD.

245 *Mohamed v Hammersmith and Fulham LBC* [2001] UKHL 57, [2002] HLR 7, HL.

246 *R v Lambeth LBC ex p Miah* (1994) 27 HLR 21, QBD.

247 *Williams v Birmingham City Council* [2007] EWCA Civ 691, [2008] HLR 4.

248 Consider *R v Hambleton DC ex p Geoghan* [1985] JPL 394, QBD.

exercise it, ie, at the request of a disappointed applicant, provided that the new information has some degree of credibility and could (if accepted) affect the decision. If an authority refuses to do so, however, the correct course is not to seek judicial review but to appeal the original decision.[249]

9.155 In *Walsh*,[250] further enquiries led the authority to the conclusion that an earlier account of being locked out of accommodation was entirely false: while there was no general right to make a new decision on the same facts, the authority could do so if there was a material change, including new facts or the ascertained falsity of former facts.

9.156 In *Dagou*,[251] however, it was suggested that only fraud and deception would entitle the authority to re-open enquiries once its decision had been reached, although new information might still be relevant to the accommodation which was to be provided.

9.157 In *Crawley BC v B*,[252] the authority decided initially that an applicant was not in priority need and had so notified her (without reaching a decision on intentionality). Subsequently, during an appeal, it changed the priority need decision. It was still entitled to go on to consider whether the applicant had become intentionally homeless. This was, however, not so much a case of revising a decision as completing it. Some dicta in the case do, however, suggest that an authority may revisit a decision whenever, on public law grounds, it would be reasonable to do so.[253]

9.158 *Crawley* was distinguished in *Sadiq*.[254] Once a duty had been accepted under HA 1996 s193,[255] the section provides a complete code of when an authority ceases to be subject to its requirements, so that, for example, loss of priority need after acceptance of a section 193 duty does not entitle the authority to make a new decision that no further duty is owed.

9.159 Nonetheless, in *Porteous*,[256] the authority was permitted to change its decision even after a duty had been accepted under section 193.

249 *Demetri v Westminster City Council* (2000) 32 HLR 470, CA; and see para 9.201.
250 *R v Dacorum BC ex p Walsh* (1991) 24 HLR 401, QBD. Under HA 1985, there was no statutory review process.
251 *R v Southwark LBC ex p Dagou* (1995) 28 HLR 72, QBD.
252 (2000) 32 HLR 636, CA.
253 See per Buxton LJ at 645.
254 *R v Brent LBC ex p Sadiq* (2000) 33 HLR 47, QBD.
255 See paras 10.118–10.263.
256 *Porteous v West Dorset DC* [2004] EWCA Civ 244, [2004] HLR 30.

Rejecting the proposition in *Dagou*[257] – that decisions could only be re-opened in cases of fraud or deception – it was held that they could also be revisited where the original decision was based on a fundamental mistake of fact.[258]

9.160 Likewise, in *Slaiman*,[259] the return of an applicant to her husband following domestic violence was held to go to the existence or non-existence of the original allegation of domestic violence, rather than comprising a change of circumstances arising after acceptance of a full duty, so that the authority was entitled to reconsider.

Time-scales

9.161 There is no statutory requirement that enquiries be carried out within any specific time; in Wales, where the enquiry and assessment duties are fully assimilated,[260] there is a target of ten days, although 'The priority is that the assessment and the decision are correct'.[261]

257 *R v Southwark LBC ex p Dagou* (1995) 28 HLR 72, QBD; see para 9.156.

258 Both applicant and authority had operated under a fundamental mistake of fact relating to a tenancy which neither had realised the applicant still held. See also *R (Sambotin) v Brent LBC* [2017] EWHC 1190 (Admin); [2017] HLR 31, in which it was held that a decision could be revisited in the event of fraud or deception (*Dagou*) or if there were a fundamental mistake of fact (*Porteous*). In *Sambotin*, neither was present. The claimant had provided correct information about his immigration status, including an earlier decision letter from a different authority which had concluded that he was not eligible for assistance. If there was any error, it would have been a failure on Brent's part properly to apply the eligibility criteria to those facts, something which Brent did not suggest entitled it to reach a new decision; moreover, Brent was under a duty to give reasons for reaching a second decision, with which duty it had failed to comply (see also para 12.78, n169); permission to appeal was granted in *Sambotin* – the appeal is listed for July 2018.

259 *R (Slaiman) v Richmond upon Thames LBC* [2006] EWHC 329 (Admin), [2006] HLR 20.

260 See paras 10.63–10.66.

261 See Welsh Code para 10.54: 'The Welsh Government recommends where the eligibility and housing status has been determined the decision on which duty is owed if any can be relayed to the customer as soon as possible and the remaining elements of the assessment can be concluded within the 10 working days'. There is no equivalent in the English Code, in fairly stark contrast with the previous Code at para 6.16 which said that authorities should deal with enquiries as quickly as possible and suggested that authorities should aim to achieve interview and initial assessment of eligibility on the day of application with enquiries and notification within 33 working days of accepting the duty to make enquiries.

9.162 An authority may not avoid the enquiry duty on the basis that it will owe no duty to a person whose priority need will be lost by the time they are completed, eg where a young person with an automatic priority need because he or she is 16 or 17 years old[262] will turn 18 during that period.[263]

Decisions

Postponement

9.163 Although the obligation to reach a decision is not spelled out in the section, it is implicit: *Sidhu*.[264] An authority may not defer the obligation in the hope or expectation of a change in circumstances such as might reduce its duties, for example, by loss of priority need.[265]

9.164 Nor can an authority seek to use mediation (eg to reconcile a 17-year-old with his or her family) to prolong the decision-making process, so that the child turns 18 and loses his or her automatic priority need. Where mediation cannot take place without depriving the child of a right he or she would otherwise have had, the authority must perform its full duty – although it may be able to use mediation in order to fulfil that duty.[266] Mediation and enquiries are entirely independent processes.[267]

262 See paras 5.73–5.80.

263 *Robinson v Hammersmith and Fulham LBC* [2006] EWCA Civ 1122, [2006] 1 WLR 3295, [2007] HLR 7 at [35].

264 *R v Ealing LBC ex p Sidhu* (1982) 2 HLR 45, QBD, approved in *Robinson v Hammersmith and Fulham LBC*, above, at [36].

265 *R v Ealing LBC ex p Sidhu* (1982) 2 HLR 45, QBD. A suggestion in the *Encyclopaedia of housing law and practice* (Sweet & Maxwell) that in an appropriate case, a de minimis deferral, perhaps a few days, may be permissible where there is a substantive basis (as distinct from speculation or a remote chance) for the authority to anticipate a material change was not disapproved, but 'in the case of a 17 year old child, it would not seem to me to be lawful for a local authority to postpone the taking of a decision even for a short period on the basis that by postponing that decision the child will have reached the age of 18 before the decision is taken': per Waller LJ in *Robinson v Hammersmith and Fulham LBC* at [38]. The effect would seem to be that the proposition will not apply if it will cause loss of the priority need (as where priority need will, absent other grounds, be lost on reaching 18, see paras 5.76–5.79).

266 *Robinson v Hammersmith and Fulham LBC*, above, per Waller LJ at [41].

267 *Robinson v Hammersmith and Fulham LBC*, above, at [42] and [45].

9.165 If the issue is eligibility for accommodation,[268] there would in any event be no point in deferring because the authority's housing duty under HA 1996 Part 7 ceases if the applicant's eligibility ends.[269]

Gatekeeping

9.166 An authority's decision on completion of its enquiries is taken on the basis of the information known to it at the time it is reached. It follows that changed circumstances – including those generated by the authority itself – may lead to a different finding than might have been taken had the decision immediately followed the application.

9.167 This, in turn, opens the way for authorities to engage in forms of 'gatekeeping', ie action which obviates homelessness by ensuring that the applicant finds accommodation otherwise than through HA 1996 Part 7 or H(W)A 2014 Part 2.

9.168 There is a number of reasons why authorities may engage in this, eg: to help to ensure that targets are achieved for the purposes of audit or performance criteria and/or in the interests of returns to central government; for local presentational purposes; and to avoid the need to comply with ancillary provisions, including written decision with reasons, right to review and a reasonable preference in relation to allocations.

9.169 In *Hanton-Rhouila*,[270] a challenge based on failure to advise the applicant of the implications of accepting private accommodation[271] without completing the HA 1996 Part 7 process failed on the facts, and the review officer had been entitled to conclude that the applicant was no longer homeless.

9.170 The new help duties – towards those threatened with homelessness[272] and towards the homeless[273] – mean that authorities are now bound to take steps to obviate homelessness within Parts 7 and 2, but it is not certain that this will mean an end to practices outside the legislation.

268 See chapter 3.

269 HA 1996 s193(6)(a).

270 *Hanton-Rhouila v Westminster City Council* [2010] EWCA Civ 1334, [2011] HLR 12.

271 An assured shorthold tenancy arranged by the authority's Private Sector Housing Initiatives team under its Finders Payment Scheme (a discretionary scheme for helping people find suitable accommodation in the private sector).

272 Paras 10.67–10.75.

273 Paras 10.76–10.96.

Material to be taken into account

9.171 An authority must always take into account all that is relevant up to the date of its decision. An applicant cannot complain of a decision which failed to take into account a matter which only came to the knowledge of the authority after it had made its final decision: *Islam*.[274]

9.172 If material comes to light after the initial decision, but before the review, it must be taken into account on the review.[275] If it comes to light after the review, the technically proper course would appear to be to put the further information before the authority for it to re-open its enquiries and to consider judicial review of a refusal to do so,[276] although in practice, if the information and request are included in a pre-action protocol letter before appeal, it would be very difficult indeed for an authority to resist the appeal if the information was decisive.

9.173 It may even be that the power to raise an ECHR Article 8 issue on appeal[277] could be used as a legal basis for the court to have regard to the information if none other is available.

9.174 In *Crossley*,[278] the decision was so at odds with the evidence put before the authority that the authority must have failed to take it into account. As the court put it:[279]

> . . . there were also stark facts, or appraisals of fact, pointing towards vulnerability for a statutorily recognised reason; and these the decision-maker had an obligation to acknowledge, take into account and evaluate along with everything else.

9.175 An authority must consider those matters which sensibly arise on the facts of a case. In *F*,[280] the applicant took a tenancy of a property that she could not afford and contended that she had made appropriate enquiries with the housing benefit department before doing so. The authority found that she had not acted in good faith when

274 *R v Hillingdon Homeless Panel ex p Islam* (1981) *Times*, February 24, QBD (not forming part of the subsequent appeals [1983] 1 AC 688, [1981] 1 HLR 107, HL).

275 See para 9.229.

276 See para 12.154.

277 See paras 12.123–12.125.

278 *Crossley v Westminster City Council* [2006] EWCA Civ 140, [2006] HLR 26.

279 At [28].

280 *F v Birmingham City Council* [2006] EWCA Civ 1427, [2007] HLR 18.

accepting the tenancy.[281] Although it had not explicitly been invited to consider whether the applicant had acted in good faith, the court held that it was a matter that was sensibly capable of arising on the facts and therefore required consideration by the authority – which, however, the authority had undertaken.

9.176 In *Elrify*,[282] the applicant applied as homeless by reason of overcrowding. Both in its original decision and on review, the authority had applied only one part of the statutory test for overcrowding under HA 1985 Part 10. The review decision was accordingly flawed because the authority had failed properly to apply the statutory test and had therefore miscalculated the level of statutory overcrowding in the applicant's flat.

Own decision

9.177 The authority must reach its own decision. Even though other authorities from which an authority requests assistance must co-operate,[283] one authority cannot simply 'rubber-stamp' the decision of another: *Miles*.[284] There may, for example, be information about what has occurred between the two applications, such as a separation which means that intervening accommodation was 'settled' for the purposes of the separated parts of a family.[285]

9.178 This principle applies even to decisions of a court[286] – thus, while an authority must take into consideration decisions by family courts relating to with whom children are to live, the authority is not bound by them but must reach its own decision in the context of its own duties in the (different) legislative context in which they arise: *Holmes-Moorhouse*.[287]

281 Within the meaning of HA 1996 s191(2); see paras 6.29–6.31.

282 *Elrify v Westminster City Council* [2007] EWCA Civ 332, [2007] HLR 36.

283 HA 1996 s213.

284 *R v South Herefordshire DC ex p Miles* (1983) 17 HLR 82, QBD. See also *Eren v Haringey LBC* [2007] EWCA Civ 409.

285 See para 6.113.

286 Otherwise than so far as they are decisions of a court directly relating to the decision, ie, appeal against it or on judicial review.

287 *Holmes-Moorhouse v Richmond upon Thames LBC* [2009] UKHL 7, [2009] HLR 34.

Notification

Reasons

9.179 Once the authority has reached its decision, it must notify the applicant.[288] While there will generally be no reason to distinguish between when the decision is made and notification of reasons, these do not necessarily occur on the same date: ascertaining the date of the decision is essentially a question of fact.[289] If the authority decides an issue – relating either to eligibility or to level of duty – adversely to an applicant, it must also notify the applicant of its reasons.[290]

Local connection

9.180 A decision to refer an application to another authority under the local connection provisions, and the reasons for doing so, must likewise be notified.[291]

Review

9.181 Notifications must inform applicants of the right to request a review of a decision and of the time within which the request must be made.[292]

Relationship of notification duty and substantive duty

9.182 Duties to notify and to give reasons for decisions arise independently of the substantive duties to which they refer: *R v Beverley BC ex p McPhee*.[293] It is not open to an authority to claim that it has no duty under, for example, HA 1996 s193[294] or s200,[295] on the basis that it has not yet given notice of its decision; that would be to allow an authority to rely on its own wrong, ie its failure to provide notice 'on completion' of enquiries.

288 HA 1996 s184(3); H(W)A 2014 s63.

289 *Robinson v Hammersmith and Fulham LBC* [2006] EWCA Civ 1122, [2006] 1 WLR 3295, [2007] HLR 7, at [25], referring (at [24]) to *R v Beverley BC ex p McPhee* (1978) *Times* 27 October, QBD.

290 *Robinson v Hammersmith and Fulham LBC*, above. And see para 9.231.

291 HA 1996 s184(4); H(W)A 2014 s82(2).

292 HA 1996 s184(5); H(W)A 2014 s84; see further below.

293 (1978) *Times* 27 October, QBD.

294 See para 10.118.

295 See para 7.51.

Written notification

9.183 Notification, and reasons, must be given in writing; if not received by the applicant, notification will be treated as having been given only if made available at the authority's office for a reasonable time for collection by the applicant or on the applicant's behalf.[296] This appears to be so even if a copy of the notice is sent by registered post to one of the authority's own hostels or other property.[297]

Restricted cases[298]

9.184 If the authority decides that a duty is, or[299] after the end of its initial help duty under HA 1996 s189B(2)[300] would be, owed under HA 1996 s193(2), or H(W)A 2014 s75,[301] but only because of a restricted person, the notification is subject to additional requirements.[302] It must inform the applicant that the decision was reached on this basis, include the name of the restricted person, explain why the person is a restricted person, and explain the effect of HA 1996 s193(7AD)[303] or, in Wales, H(W)A 2014 s76(5).

Oral explanation

9.185 In cases where the applicant may have difficulty understanding the implications of a decision, authorities may need to arrange for a member of staff to provide and explain the notification in person.[304]

296 HA 1996 s184(6); H(W)A 2014 s84.

297 There was no express requirement for writing in the Housing (Homeless Persons) Act 1977; it was added to HA 1985 pursuant to Law Commission Recommendations (Cmnd 9515), No 5.

298 See para 3.149.

299 Since commencement of HRA 2017 on 3 April 2018: see Homelessness Reduction Act 2017 (Commencement and Transitional and Savings Provisions) Regulations 2018 SI No 167 reg 3, only applicable to applications made and reviews sought on or after that date – see reg 4.

300 See paras 10.76–10.96.

301 See para 10.118.

302 HA 1996 s184(3A); H(W)A 2014 s63(2).

303 See paras 10.211–10.216.

304 Although this is no longer recommended (see previous English Code para 6.23) by the English Code of Guidance, it may be that the authority is required to take such steps if, eg, the applicant has a learning disability which engages the EqA 2010, in order to avoid unlawful discrimination. See also Welsh Code para 15.95.

Review

9.186 Neither the Housing (Homeless Persons) Act 1977 nor HA 1985 Part 3 made any provision for an applicant to seek an internal review of the authority's decision. The third edition of the Code of Guidance issued under HA 1985 Part 3 had, however, recommended[305] that authorities 'should have in place arrangements to review decisions on homelessness cases where an applicant wishes to appeal against the decision'. That recommendation is now a statutory requirement.[306] An applicant is statutorily entitled to request a review, provided that the decision complained of falls within those specified in HA 1996 s202 or H(W)A 2014 s85.

9.187 The request for a review should be interpreted generously. In *Nzamy*,[307] the authority informed the applicant that if he did not accept an offer of alternative accommodation, it would treat its duty as discharged:[308] a request for a review of the suitability of the offer, in the course of which the applicant made clear that the family was willing to remain in their current temporary accommodation pending a permanent offer, should also have been treated as a request for a review of the discharge decision.

9.188 The right to request a review arises in relation to the following decisions.

Eligibility[309]

9.189 A decision on eligibility may be reviewed.[310] This includes whether or not the applicant is a person subject to immigration control.[311]

Duties[312]

9.190 An applicant may also seek review of any decision on what, if any, duty is owed under HA 1996 ss190, 193 and 195–196 or H(W)A 2014 ss66, 68, 73 or 75.[313] This expressly encompasses whether or not the

305 Code of Guidance para 9.6.
306 HA 1996 s202(4); H(W)A 2014 s85.
307 *Nzamy v Brent LBC* [2011] EWCA (Civ) 283, [2011] HLR 20.
308 See paras 10.135–10.137.
309 See generally chapter 3.
310 HA 1996 s202(1)(a); H(W)A 2014 s85(1).
311 See paras 3.154–3.176.
312 See generally chapter 10.
313 HA 1996 s202(1)(b); in Wales, see H(W)A 2014 s85(1)(b), (c).

applicant is in priority need,[314] whether intentionally homeless,[315] and whether a duty has ceased under HA 1996 s193(6) or (7).[316]

9.191 A review may be sought of an authority's decision to bring its duty to those threatened with homelessness or its initial help duty to an end,[317] along with the corresponding provisions of HA 1996 ss193A–193C governing cessation of those new duties by reference to final offers (para 10.70) or deliberate and unreasonable refusal to co-operate (para 10.88).[318]

9.192 Whether an authority has complied with the requirement to notify the applicant of the consequences of refusal and the right to request a review under HA 1996 s193(7) and (7A)[319] is itself also subject to review under this provision.[320]

Local connection

9.193 The review provisions governing local connection referrals have been considered in chapter 7.[321]

314 HA 1996 s190(3). See also H(W)A 2014 ss70, 71.

315 HA 1996 s190(1); H(W)A 2014 s77.

316 HA 1996 s193 encompasses a decision that a duty, once owed, is no longer owed: *Warsame v Hounslow LBC* (1999) 32 HLR 335, CA, affirmed notwithstanding intervening legislative changes under Homelessness Act 2002 in *Ravichandran v Lewisham LBC* [2010] EWCA Civ 755, [2010] HLR 42 (discussed below). In Wales, see H(W)A 2014 s85(1)(c).

317 HA 1996 s189B(6), 195(7); H(W)A 2014 s85.

318 HA 1996 s202(1).

319 See para 10.229.

320 *Tower Hamlets LBC v Rahanara Begum* [2005] EWCA Civ 116, [2006] HLR 9. The applicant had failed to seek an internal review and the matter could not be raised as a defence to eviction proceedings being brought against her. Cf *R (Zaher) v Westminster City Council* [2003] EWHC 101 (Admin), where the failure of the authority to inform the applicant of his right to review entitled the applicant to challenge the decision on suitability by judicial review. In Wales, the equivalent to HA 1996 s193(7) and (7A) is now H(W)A 2014 s76(3)(c) and it is likely that the cases cited in this footnote will apply equally.

321 Paras 7.104–7.107.

Suitability and availability of offers

9.194 An applicant may seek a review of whether accommodation offered in discharge of duty under HA 1996 s190, s193[322] or s200 is 'suitable'[323] and, where applicable,[324] whether it is reasonable to accept it.

9.195 An applicant may seek a review of a decision of an authority as to the suitability of accommodation offered by way of a private accommodation offer,[325] ie, in a restricted case;[326] from the commencement of LA 2011 s148,[327] there is likewise a right to seek a review of a decision as to the suitability of a private rented sector offer,[328] in a restricted case or otherwise.[329]

9.196 It had formerly been held that, where an applicant accepted an offer of accommodation, the applicant could not also seek a review as to its suitability: *Alghile*.[330] The result of this was that an applicant to whom an unsatisfactory offer of accommodation had been made had to face 'an unwholesome opportunity to gamble',[331] either to refuse – which gave rise to the risk that, if unsuccessful on the review, the applicant would end up with nowhere to live – or to accept, which meant putting up with accommodation that the applicant considered unsatisfactory.[332]

322 Including expressly HA 1996 s193(7) (see para 10.217) to clear up any residual doubt following the decision in *Warsame v Hounslow LBC* (1999) 32 HLR 335, CA, which had the effect of confining application of HA 1996 s202(1)(f) to the question of the suitability of an offer under section 193(6). In Wales, see H(W)A 2014 s85(1)(c).

323 HA 1996 s202(1)(f); H(W)A 2014 s59.

324 HA 1996 s193(7F). See, in particular, *Ravichandran v Lewisham LBC* [2010] EWCA Civ 755, [2010] HLR 42, where the authority had considered suitability at a previous review, but at no time had considered whether it was reasonable for the applicant to accept it, for which reason its decision could not stand.

325 HA 1996 s202(1)(g); H(W)A 2014 s76(2) requires all private rented sector offers to be suitable, ie the position in Wales is the same as the post-Localism Act (LA) 2011 position in England.

326 See above, paras 3.149 and 9.184; see paras 10.241–10.250.

327 Localism Act 2011 (Commencement No 2 and Transitional Provisions) (England) Order 2012 SI No 2599 art 2.

328 Provided that the authority's duty to secure accommodation has not ceased before that date: Localism Act 2011 (Commencement No 2 and Transitional Provisions) (England) Order 2012 SI No 2599 art 3.

329 See paras 10.241–10.250.

330 *Alghile v Westminster City Council* (2001) 33 HLR 57, CA, overruling *R v Kensington and Chelsea RLBC ex p Byfield* (1997) 31 HLR 913, QBD.

331 *Alghile v Westminster City Council* [2001] EWCA Civ 363, (2001) 33 HLR 57 per Tuckey LJ at [28].

332 This contrasts with the outcome in *R v Wycombe DC ex p Hazeltine* (1993) 25 HLR 313, CA; see para 10.259.

9.197 There is now a right to seek an internal review of the suitability of accommodation offered under HA 1996 s193(5) or (7), whether or not the applicant has accepted the offer of accommodation.[333]

9.198 The date at which suitability of accommodation should be considered on a review will differ depending whether the accommodation was accepted or refused. If an offer of accommodation was accepted, then the authority should consider the facts at the date of review because the accommodation is still available.[334]

9.199 Conversely, where an offer of accommodation has been refused, then the council has taken the decision that it has fulfilled its duty and the property will no longer be available; in those circumstances, the issue has to be tested by reference to the circumstances as they existed at the date of the decision that the duty had been discharged.[335]

Further review

9.200 There is no right to request a review of a decision reached on an earlier review.[336]

9.201 Although HA 1996 s202(2) does not prevent an authority from further reconsidering a decision if asked and willing to do so, a refusal to exercise the discretion to reconsider has been held not to be judicially reviewable.[337] The correct forum for challenge remains by way of appeal to the county court of the original review decision.[338]

333 HA 1996 s202(1A); H(W)A 2014 s85(3).

334 *Omar v Westminster City Council* [2008] EWCA Civ 421, [2008] HLR 36.

335 *Omar*, above, per Waller LJ at [25].

336 HA 1996 s202(2); H(W)A 2014 s85(4).

337 *R v Westminster City Council ex p Ellioua* (1998) 31 HLR 440, CA. See also *R (C) v Lewisham LBC* [2003] EWCA Civ 927, [2004] HLR 4.

338 See *Demetri v Westminster City Council* (2000) 32 HLR 470, CA as to the effects of reconsideration on time limits to appeal to the county court, discussed at paras 12.203–12.207.

Review procedure

9.202 A request for a review should be made within 21 days of notification of a decision under HA 1996 s184.[339] The applicant must be told about the right to request a review in the decision notification;[340] if the notification does not do so, time cannot be considered to have started to run.

9.203 If the notification does inform the applicant of the right to review, the applicant who fails to exercise it in time will on the face of it lose it. The authority has power to extend time.[341] This discretion must be exercised in furtherance of its statutory purpose, which is to establish procedures and time limits necessary to enable the authority to manage its housing stock in an orderly way, and – where appropriate – to grant an indulgence to an applicant where the merits of the applicant's claim for review are deserving enough to override the failure to request a review in time. Accordingly, the authority is entitled but not bound to take into account the prospect of the review's success.[342]

9.204 The secretary of state has power to make regulations as to the procedure to be followed in connection with a review:[343] see the Homelessness (Review Procedures etc) Regulations (English Review Procedure Regs) 2018.[344] In Wales, the Welsh Ministers have the same power: see Homelessness (Review Procedure) (Wales) Regulations (Welsh Review Procedure Regs) 2015.[345]

339 HA 1996 s202(3); H(W)A 2014 s85(5). The wording need not be followed slavishly – thus, saying that the appeal 'must be made within 21 days of the date of this letter' rather than of when the applicant was notified of the decision did not vitiate the letter in *Dharmaraj v Hounslow LBC* [2011] EWCA Civ 312, [2011] HLR 18.

340 HA 1996 s202(3); H(W)A 2015 s85(5). Notification to an applicant's solicitor suffices: *Dharmaraj v Hounslow LBC*, above. See also *Dragic v Wandsworth LBC* [2011] JHL D59.

341 HA 1996 s202(3); H(W)A 2014 s85(5).

342 *R (C) v Lewisham LBC* [2003] EWCA Civ 927, [2004] HLR 4. See also *R (Slaiman) v Richmond upon Thames LBC* [2006] EWHC 329 (Admin), [2006] HLR 20.

343 HA 1996 s203(1); in Wales, the Welsh Ministers have the same power, see H(W)A 2014 s86 and Homelessness (Review Procedure) (Wales) Regulations 2015 SI No 1266.

344 SI No 223. For reviews requested prior to 3 April 2018, see the Allocation of Housing and Homelessness (Review Procedures) Regulations 1999 SI No 71 and the 10th edition of this work.

345 See H(W)A 2014 s86 and SI No 1266.

Identity of the reviewer

9.205 Both sets of regulations may require that the decision on review be made by a person of appropriate seniority who was not involved in the original decision.[346] The Welsh regulations do not do so; they only require that the review officer be someone who was not involved in the original decision.[347]

9.206 The English regulations,[348] however, do require that, when the original decision was made by an officer of the authority[349] and the review is also to be carried out by an officer of the authority, the latter must be someone who was not involved in the original decision and who is senior to the original decision-maker:

> Seniority for these purposes means seniority in rank within the authority's organisational structure.[350]

9.207 The officer who is undertaking the review may nonetheless enlist the assistance of a more junior officer, even where that junior officer made the original decision.[351] A view expressed by a more senior officer about the type of allocation for which an applicant qualified under the authority's HA 1996 Part 6 allocation scheme was not a decision for the purposes of the (then) English Review Procedure Regs 1999 reg 2, nor could it be subject to a HA 1996 s202 review, nor therefore did it disqualify a more junior officer from conducting the review: *Feld*.[352]

9.208 If elected members are involved in the review process,[353] neither the English nor the Welsh regulations set any particular requirements.

9.209 There may be more than one review on a single application, for example, following a successful county court appeal or where – following a finding that an original offer of accommodation was unsuitable – the applicant seeks to challenge a further offer. The fact

346 HA 1996 s203(2)(a); H(W)A 2014 s86(2)(a).

347 Welsh Review Procedure Regs 2015 reg 3; see also Welsh Code para 20.9.

348 English Review Procedure Regs 2018 reg 8.

349 The decision must be made by the authority by its executive (single member, committee, sub-committee or officer) to whom the function is delegated: see Local Government Act 2000 ss13–15 and Local Authorities (Functions and Responsibilities) (England) Regulations 2000 SI No 2853.

350 English Code of Guidance para 19.9; see also Welsh Code para 20.9.

351 *Butler v Fareham BC* May 2001 *Legal Action* 24, CA.

352 *Feld v Barnet LBC; Pour v Westminster City Council* [2004] EWCA Civ 1307, [2005] HLR 9.

353 These will have to be members of the executive: see footnote 349, above.

that a review officer has conducted an earlier review does not prevent him or her conducting a second review; there is no apparent bias and any actual unfairness can be cured on appeal to the county court: *Feld*.[354]

9.210 There is nothing in HA 1996 Part 7 or H(W)A 2014 Part 2 that requires a decision as to whether or not to secure interim accommodation under HA 1996 s188(3) or H(W)A 2014 s85[355] pending a review[356] to be made by an officer who is senior to the officer who made the original decision on the application; nor is there anything necessarily objectionable in the same officer who made the decision under review also making the decision on such interim accommodation.[357]

9.211 The review function may be contracted out.[358]

Local connection reviews

9.212 The particular considerations relevant to a local connection have been considered in chapter 7.[359]

Impact of the Human Rights Act 1998

9.213 The review procedure is not the determination of a civil right for the purposes of Article 6[360] of the ECHR.[361] Even if it was, it was considered in *Runa Begum*[362] that an internal review coupled with the right to an appeal to the county court under HA 1996 s204 comprised compliance with Article 6, an approach followed in *Ali v Birmingham City Council*.[363]

354 *Feld v Barnet LBC; Pour v Westminster City Council*, above.

355 See Welsh Code para 20.29.

356 See paras 10.49–10.57.

357 *R (Abdi) v Lambeth LBC* [2007] EWHC 1565 (Admin), [2008] HLR 5.

358 See para 9.5; and English Code of Guidance para 19.9. See Housing (Wales) Act 2014 (Consequential Amendments) Regulations 2015 SI No 752, amending the Local Authorities (Contracting Out of Allocation of Housing and Homelessness Functions) Order 1996 SI No 3205 so as to apply to H(W)A 2014 Part 2.

359 Paras 7.104–7.107.

360 'In the determination of his civil rights and obligations . . . everyone is entitled to a fair and public hearing within a reasonable time by an independent and impartial tribunal established by law . . .'

361 See paras 12.117–12.122.

362 *Runa Begum v Tower Hamlets LBC* [2003] UKHL 5, [2003] 2 AC 430, [2003] HLR 32.

363 [2010] UKSC 8.

9.214 In *Ali v UK*,[364] which was the latter case at the European Court of Human Rights, *Runa Begum* was qualified to the extent that it was held that Article 6(1) is engaged once an authority has decided that a duty is owed under HA 1996 s193 because there is a sufficiently certain right to amount to a 'civil right'; in agreement with *Runa Begum* and *Ali* at the Supreme Court, however, it was also held that there was no violation of Article 6 as the rights to a reasoned decision, review and appeal were adequate safeguards.

9.215 In *Poshteh v Kensington and Chelsea RLBC*,[365] the Supreme Court declined to depart from its decision in *Ali v Birmingham City Council*, notwithstanding *Ali v UK*: the decision in *Ali v UK* did not engage in any detail with the decision in *Ali v Birmingham City Council*; the scope and limit of the concept of a 'civil right' was suitable for consideration by the Grand Chamber of the European Court of Human Rights; without such a decision, it was not appropriate to depart from the fully reasoned decision in *Ali v Birmingham City Council*.

Procedure on review

9.216 Once the applicant has requested a review, the authority must notify the applicant that he or she – or someone acting on the applicant's behalf – may make representations in writing.[366] If the applicant has not already been informed of the procedure to be followed,[367] then the notification must also set out what it is.[368]

9.217 The purpose of this requirement is to invite the applicant to state his or her grounds for requesting a review (if the applicant has not

364 App No 40378/10, [2015] HLR 46.

365 [2017] UKSC 36; [2017 HLR 28.

366 English Review Procedure Regs 2018 reg 5(3)(a). Where the review is under HA 1996 s202(1)(ba)(i), (bc), the representations must be received within two weeks beginning with the day on which the review was requested (or such longer period as may be agreed); the same two week period also applies to a review under s202(1)(bb) where the effect of the decision is to bring the s195(2) duty to an end. Where the case concerns a local connection referral that has been referred to a referee (see paras 7.82–7.89), it is the referee who must make the notification: reg 5(4)(a). Welsh Review Procedure Regs 2015 reg 2, gives a right to make representations in writing, orally, or both.

367 English Review Procedure Regs 2018 reg 5(3)(c); Welsh Review Procedure Regs 2015 reg 2(2)(b).

368 The suggestion in the 1996 edition of the Code of Guidance that authorities should have an approved document setting out their procedure available to the public is not included in the present Code.

already done so) and to elicit any new information that the applicant may have in relation to it.[369]

9.218 Where the applicant's legal representatives requested information from the authority prior to making representations, and the authority failed to provide the information or await the representations prior to making a review decision, the decision was unlawful.[370]

9.219 The original regulations[371] required the reviewer to consider any representations made by the applicant and to carry out the review on the basis of the facts known to him or her at its date. The latter requirement is not explicit in the current English Review Procedure Regs 2018.[372] This change notwithstanding, the reviewing officer:

> . . . is not simply considering whether the initial decision was right on the material before it at the date it was made. He may have regard to information relevant to the period before the decision but only obtained thereafter and to matters occurring after the initial decision.[373]

9.220 There is nothing in the regulations which prevents a reviewing officer from making a decision which is less favourable to the applicant than the original decision.[374]

9.221 If there is a deficiency or irregularity in the original decision, or in the way it was made, but the reviewer is nonetheless minded to make a decision which is against the interests of the applicant, the reviewer must notify the applicant that he or she is so minded and of the reasons why, and that the applicant or someone on the applicant's

369 English Code of Guidance para 19.13; Welsh Code para 20.11.

370 *Aw-Aden v Birmingham City Council* [2005] EWCA Civ 1834 at [21], although as the authority subsequently reconsidered the decision it was in fact upheld by the Court of Appeal.

371 Allocation of Housing and Homelessness (Review Procedures and Amendment) Regulations 1996 SI No 3122 reg 8(1).

372 The former is included: English Review Procedure Regs 2018 reg 7(1). Where the review is being conducted by a referee (see paras 7.82–7.89, above) the referee must send any representations to both authorities involved and seek their comments: reg 5(5). The position is the same in Wales: reg 4.

373 *Mohamed v Hammersmith and Fulham LBC* [2001] UKHL 57, [2002] HLR 7 at [26]. As to reviews of suitability, see paras 9.194–9.199.

374 *Temur v Hackney LBC* [2014] EWCA Civ 877, [2014] HLR 39.

behalf may make representations to him or her, orally or in writing or both, which representations the reviewer must consider.[375]

9.222 If the applicant is represented, notification to his or her solicitor suffices for the purposes of this requirement.[376] This procedure is capable of remedying any defect in the original decision letter and is suitable as a means for challenging the original decision of a local authority, rather than judicial review.[377]

9.223 The duty is two-fold:

a) first, to consider whether there was a deficiency or irregularity in the original decision or in the manner in which it was made; and
b) second, if there was – and if the review officer is nonetheless minded to make a decision adverse to the applicant on one or more issues – to serve a 'minded to find' notice on the applicant explaining the reasons for the reviewer's provisional views.[378]

9.224 The review officer is only under a duty to 'consider' the representations, on the face of it not necessarily to give any notification or indication of that consideration.[379] Where consideration of deficiency and/or irregularity has taken place, but no reasons have been given for an adverse conclusion in relation to it,[380] the review procedure could still be susceptible on public law grounds.[381] Accordingly, in practice a local authority is now effectively obliged to state in every review decision letter why there is no deficiency or irregularity in the original

375 English Review Procedure Regs 2018 reg 7(2). The Court of Appeal has assumed – without argument – that the wording of the previous regulations (Allocation of Housing and Homelessness (Review Procedures) Regulations 1999 reg 8(2)(b)) gave the applicant the right to choose how representations are made – orally, in writing, or orally and in writing: see *Lambeth LBC v Johnston* [2008] EWCA Civ 690, [2009] HLR 10 at [53]; and *Hall v Wandsworth LBC; Carter v Wandsworth LBC* [2004] EWCA Civ 1740, [2005] HLR 23 at [25]–[26]. In Wales, see Welsh Review Procedure Regs 2015 reg 5(2).

376 *Maswaku v Westminster City Council* [2012] EWCA Civ 669; *El Goure v Kensington and Chelsea RLBC* [2012] EWCA Civ 670.

377 *R (Lynch) v Lambeth LBC* [2007] HLR 15.

378 *Lambeth LBC v Johnston*, above.

379 *Johnston*, above, per Rimer LJ at [51].

380 A poorly worded letter which, however, had addressed all the important aspects of the case and which meant that a reasonable reader would have had no doubt about the basis of the decision sufficed in one (*Nagi*) of the three cases heard together in *Makisi v Birmingham City Council; Yosief v Birmingham City Council; Nagi v Birmingham City Council* [2011] EWCA Civ 355, [2011] HLR 27.

381 *Johnston*, per Rimer LJ at [54].

decision, and consequently why no 'minded to find' letter has been sent.

9.225 Neither 'deficiency' nor 'irregularity' is defined in either the English or Welsh Review Procedure Regs.[382] 'Deficiency' is not confined to an error of law in the original decision; there is a deficiency if there is 'something lacking' in it which is of sufficient importance to the fairness of the procedure to justify the additional procedural safeguard: *Hall* and *Carter*.[383]

9.226 A reviewing officer should therefore apply English Review Procedure Regs 2018 reg 7(2)[384] whenever the officer considers that an important aspect of the case was either not addressed or was not addressed adequately by the original decision-maker.

9.227 In *Mitu*,[385] the original decision held both that the applicant was not in priority need and that he had become homeless intentionally; the review concluded that he was not homeless intentionally but upheld the finding on priority need; there was nonetheless a deficiency in the original decision, and what is now reg 7(2) therefore applied.

9.228 This may be contrasted with *Mohamoud v Birmingham City Council*,[386] in which the applicant had rejected a flat and the authority decided that its duty towards her had been discharged; on review, she claimed for the first time that she had misunderstood what she had originally been told by the authority and that she had thought that she would receive up to three offers of accommodation, a confusion that could have arisen as English was not her first language. The review officer rejected these contentions and upheld the original decision. The court held that this should have triggered a 'minded to' letter under what is now reg 7(2).

9.229 If circumstances have changed between the original decision and decision on review,[387] reviewers will need to undertake further

382 See English Code of Guidance para 19.21 which suggests matters which might be included (eg failure to take into account relevant considerations; failure to base decision on the facts; bad faith or dishonesty; error of law; decisions which are contrary to the purpose of the HA 1996; irrational or unreasonable decisions; procedurally unfair decisions); see also Welsh Code para 20.13, which contains the same list of examples as in the English Code.

383 *Hall v Wandsworth LBC; Carter v Wandsworth LBC*, above. See now English Code of Guidance para 19.22, Welsh Code para 21.9 reflecting this decision.

384 Or Welsh Review Procedure Regs 2015 reg 5(2).

385 *Mitu v Camden LBC* [2011] EWCA Civ 1249, [2012] HLR 10.

386 [2014] EWCA Civ 227, [2014] HLR 22.

387 As in *Mohamed v Hammersmith and Fulham LBC* [2001] UKHL 57, [2002] HLR 7, HL.

enquiries before reaching a decision and may need to serve a 'minded to find' letter,[388] even though strictly there was no deficiency in the original decision at the time it was taken.

9.230 Applicants should be aware that it is not only new circumstances which count in the applicant's favour which are to be taken into account, but also any developments which adversely affect the applicant's entitlement.[389] A change of circumstances may yet lead to the loss of a qualifying element in the previous decision, for example, priority need.[390] The requirement to allow further representations, including an oral hearing,[391] will apply.

9.231 An adverse change will not, however, cause the loss of an element of the first decision if that decision was itself unlawful. In *Robinson*,[392] the authority unlawfully decided that the applicant was not in priority need, notwithstanding that she was only 17 years old at the time.[393] By the time of the review, she was 18 and no longer in priority need. The authority unsuccessfully sought to uphold its original decision on that basis: it was held that the proper decision on the review should be that an unlawful decision had been made such as to have denied the applicant her rights; she should therefore have been given the rights to which she was entitled had a lawful decision been made, and the reviewer should accordingly have found her to be in priority need.[394]

9.232 The court applied the dictum of Chadwick LJ in *Crawley BC v B*[395] that:

388 *Banks v Kingston upon Thames RLBC* [2008] EWCA Civ 1443, [2009] HLR 29. In the original decision, the applicant was found to be not homeless. Between the original decision and the review decision, the applicant was served with notice to quit by his landlord. The reviewer found that the applicant was homeless, and went on to consider the question of priority need without giving the applicant the opportunity to make representations on that issue, before deciding it against the applicant. The applicant successfully appealed to the Court of Appeal that the change in question under consideration invoked his right to receive a 'minded to find' letter in accordance with what is now English Review Procedure Regs 2018 reg 7(2).

389 See further para 9.171.

390 For example, a dependent child leaving home, death of a vulnerable co-resident.

391 See para 2.238.

392 *Robinson v Hammersmith and Fulham LBC* [2006] EWCA Civ 1122, [2006] 1 WLR 3295, [2007] HLR 7.

393 See paras 5.73–5.80.

394 *Robinson v Hammersmith and Fulham LBC*, above, at [32].

395 (2000) 32 HLR 636, CA, at 651.

> . . . an applicant ought not to be deprived, by events which had occurred between the date of the original decision and the date of the appeal, of some benefit or advantage to which he would have been entitled if the original decision had been taken in accordance with the law.

9.233 Points made earlier about enquiries before the first decision are equally relevant here.[396] For example, if the reviewer fails to make sufficient enquiries into a matter, or fails to make those enquiries that a reasonable authority would make, the decision is susceptible to challenge. Subject to this, the point of the review is to cure any defects in the original decision and therefore a failure to conduct sufficient enquiries at the first stage can be resolved at this stage by the person conducting the review.

9.234 It is incumbent on the applicant to put forward the matters and evidence which the applicant wishes to be taken into account: see *Cramp*.[397] This is particularly important where a 'minded to find' letter has been sent because a failure to challenge anything in it is likely to bar any argument on appeal that the authority had failed to carry out further enquiries in respect of the matters raised in the letter.[398]

9.235 In *Pieretti v Enfield LBC*,[399] however, it was said that the approach in *Cramp* requires qualification where the applicant is a disabled[400] person: where a decision-maker (whether under HA 1996 s184 or s202) is not expressly invited to consider a putative[401] disability, he or she must still have due regard to the need to take steps to take account of it.

9.236 In *Bellouti*, 'it was for Mr Bellouti to put forward the material on which he relied in support of his assertion of priority need'.[402] Bearing in mind that a decision can only be based on the information available to the authority, there may therefore be difficulty complaining to

396 See paras 9.57–9.162.

397 See para 9.90.

398 *R (Lynch) v Lambeth LBC* [2007] HLR 15.

399 [2010] EWCA Civ 1104, [2011] HLR 3.

400 *Pieretti* concerned Disability Discrimination Act 1995 s49A; this has been replaced with the broader 'public sector equality duty' in EqA 2010 s149 and, as such, the full range of 'protected characteristics' should be considered, ie age, disability, gender reassignment, pregnancy or maternity, race, sex, sexual orientation, religion or belief.

401 The decision-maker is, however, entitled to ask for evidence of an alleged disability and, if none is provided, may conclude that there is no disability: *Birmingham City Council v Wilson* [2016] EWCA Civ 1137, [2017] HLR 4.

402 *Bellouti v Wandsworth LBC* [2005] EWCA Civ 602, [2005] HLR 46, at [59].

the county court (on appeal) of a failure to make enquiries if a matter has not been raised before the review, at least sufficiently to put the reviewer on notice, or to call for him or her to make such further enquiries as are necessary.

9.237 The review must be carried out fairly. Applicants should be given the opportunity to refute matters on which the authority wishes to rely: *Robinson*.[403]

9.238 The right to make representations 'orally or in writing or both orally and in writing' is not satisfied by a telephone interview: the right includes a right exercisable at a face-to-face meeting, though amounts to no more than a 'simple and relatively brief opportunity' for the applicant (with or without someone acting on his or her behalf) to make oral representations to the review officer; it does not authorise the calling of third party witnesses or cross-examination.[404]

9.239 What comprises fairness in carrying out a review has to be determined having regard to the basis of the decision under review. In *Goodger*,[405] the authority's decision-making file was not disclosed to the applicant's advisers until a few days before the review. There was no procedural unfairness, however, as the applicant had known the case against him and the decision of intentional homelessness had been the only one possible in the circumstances.

9.240 Where an applicant deliberately withholds information so as to hinder the authority's enquiries, the authority may be entitled to decide matters against the applicant.[406]

403 *Robinson v Brent LBC* (1999) 31 HLR 1015, CA. See further, para 9.140, on the fairness of conducting enquiries by authorities.

404 *Makisi v Birmingham City Council; Yosief v Birmingham City Council; Nagi v Birmingham City Council* [2011] EWCA Civ 355, [2011] HLR 27. The court does not appear to have been assisted by *Bury MBC v Gibbons* [2010] EWCA Civ 327, [2010] HLR 33, in which it had been said that, while there were some cases (such as that) in which the requirements of what is now English Review Procedure Regs 2018 reg 7(2) could not be satisfied without a face-to-face meeting with the applicant, in other cases it would be sufficient for representations to be made over the telephone. There is no reference in the judgment to *Lomotey v Enfield LBC* [2004] EWCA Civ 627, [2004] HLR 45 in which it had been said that a refusal to hold a face-to-face hearing had not been unfair, but in that case it was not argued that what is now reg 7(2) gave a right to an oral hearing (to the contrary, it was conceded that it did not apply).

405 *Goodger v Ealing LBC* [2002] EWCA Civ 751, [2003] HLR 6.

406 *R (Abdi) v Lambeth LBC* [2007] EWHC 1565 (Admin), [2008] HLR 5, although a case about accommodation pending review. This issue commonly arises in the context of assessments under the Children Act (CA) 1989, ie where a parent appears to the authority to be withholding information for the purposes of trying to secure accommodation with a child under CA 1989 s17(6): see eg *R (MN and KN) v Hackney LBC* [2013] EWHC 1205 (Admin), para 13.46.

9.241 As at the initial enquiry stage,[407] authorities may obtain expert medical opinion. If this raises new issues or contentious points on which the applicant has not been able to comment, the applicant should normally be given a chance to do so in the interests of fairness.

9.242 If, however, the advice is merely directed to assisting the authority to assess the weight to be given to evidence on matters which are already fully in play, there is no automatic obligation to disclose it to the applicant before the authority reaches its decision.[408]

Time

9.243 The English and Welsh Review Procedure Regs[409] normally require authorities to notify applicants of their decision within eight weeks of the request for the review being made.[410] There are exceptions for certain local connection reviews: these have been considered in chapter 7 (see paras 7.82, 7.100–7.103).

9.244 The parties may, however, agree a longer period.[411]

Notification of review decision

9.245 The authority must notify the applicant of the outcome of the decision.[412] Where the decision is against the interests of the applicant,[413] reasons for the decision must be included.[414]

9.246 The notification of the decision on the review must also inform the applicant of his or her right of appeal to the county court on a point of law.[415] There is no obligation to give reasons for deciding the

407 See para 9.57.

408 *Hall v Wandsworth LBC; Carter v Wandsworth LBC* [2004] EWCA Civ 1740, [2005] HLR 23. See also *Shala v Birmingham City Council* [2007] EWCA Civ 624, [2008] HLR 8, in particular [19]–[23].

409 See para 9.204.

410 English Review Procedure Regs 2018 reg 9(1)(b). Where the review is under HA 1996 s202(1)(ba)(i), (bb) or (bc) (footnote 365 above), it must be notified within three weeks; in Wales, reg 6(1)(a).

411 English Code para 19.23; Welsh Code para 20.15.

412 HA 1996 s203(4); H(W)A 2014 s86(3).

413 Identifying decisions to refer to another authority separately out of an abundance of caution, as the applicant may be presumed so to have considered it when he or she elected to seek a review under HA 1996 s203.

414 See para 9.179.

415 See chapter 12.

review in the applicant's favour nor, therefore, any appeal from such a decision (or its reasoning).[416]

Housing pending review

9.247 This is considered in chapter 10.[417]

Reasons

9.248 Both a) the original decision and b) a decision reached on a review the outcome of which is adverse to the applicant, must contain sufficient reasons.[418]

9.249 In cases where there has been an internal review,[419] it is likely to be the reasons in the review decision which will be the focus of any challenge, although these may well rely on, reflect or be elaborated by, the first decision, which may therefore remain relevant.

9.250 What is imported by the requirement to give reasons is considered in chapter 12.[420]

416 *Akhtar v Birmingham City Council* [2011] EWCA Civ 383, [2011] HLR 28, in which the applicant rejected a second offer on an erroneous assumption as to why an earlier review had been successful; nor had it been unfair to explain the basis of the first review decision. See also *Solihull MBC v Khan* [2014] EWCA Civ 41, [2014] HLR 33.

417 See paras 10.49–10.57.

418 HA 1996 ss184(3), 203(4); H(W)A 2014 s86(4).

419 See para 9.186.

420 See paras 12.78–12.109.

CHAPTER 10

Discharge of homelessness duties

continued

Introduction

Overview

10.1 The Housing Act (HA) 1996 Part 7 and the Housing (Wales) Act (H(W)A) 2014 Part 2 impose duties on local authorities:

a) to make enquiries and carry out assessments;
b) to provide help to those threatened with homelessness and to the homeless;
c) to make and notify decisions;
d) to protect property; and
e) to secure that accommodation is made available.

10.2 Duties on a local connection referral (see chapter 7) and relating to property (see chapter 8) have already been considered; so also have the duties to entertain applications, make enquiries and reach decisions (see chapter 9). Other statutory duties (eg under children and social care legislation) are considered in chapter 13.

10.3 This chapter is accordingly concerned with the remaining duties under HA 1996 Part 7 and H(W)A 2014 Part 2. These will be considered under the following headings:

a) interim accommodation;
b) accommodation pending review;
c) assessment and plan;
d) duties to those threatened with homelessness;
e) initial help duty towards the homeless;
f) other duties to the intentionally homeless; and,
g) other duties to the unintentionally homeless in priority need.

Contracting out of functions

10.4 The power of an authority to contract out functions under HA 1996 Part 7 and H(W)A 2014 Part 2 has been discussed at the start of chapter 9.

Co-operation

England

10.5 An English authority is entitled to ask another local housing or social services authority (in England, Wales or Scotland) to exercise its own functions in relation to a case with which the authority is dealing or,

may ask such an authority, a private registered provider of social housing, a registered social landlord or a housing action trust, or a development corporation, registered housing association or Scottish Homes to co-operate in rendering assistance to the authority in the discharge its functions.[1] The other authority (or body) must co-operate with the housing authority by rendering such assistance as is reasonable in the circumstances.[2]

Wales

10.6 In Wales, where all authorities are unitary and therefore have both housing and social services functions, the corresponding provisions require each authority to make arrangements to promote co-operation between those of its officers who exercise its social services functions and those who exercise its functions as the local housing authority, with a view to achieving the following objectives in its area:

a) the prevention of homelessness;
b) that suitable accommodation is or will be available for people who are or may become homeless;
c) that satisfactory support is available for people who are or may become homeless; and
d) the effective discharge of its functions under H(W)A 2014 Part 2.[3]

10.7 In addition, the authority may request the co-operation in the exercise of its functions of the following persons (whether in Wales or England): a local housing authority; a social services authority; a registered social landlord; a private registered provider of social housing; or a housing action trust.[4] The body is bound to comply with the request unless it considers that doing so would be incompatible with its own duties, or would otherwise have an adverse effect on the exercise of its functions.[5]

10.8 The authority may seek information it requires in order to exercise its functions under H(W)A 2014 Part 2 from the same bodies, in

1 HA 1996 s213(1), (2). A Scottish authority may also ask for co-operation under this provision: HA 1996 s213(3).
2 HA 1996 s213(1). As to the effect of this, see *R v Northavon DC ex p Smith* [1994] 2 AC 402, (1994) 26 HLR 659, HL; see paras 13.84–13.96.
3 H(W)A 2014 s95(1).
4 H(W)A 2014 s95(5). The Welsh Ministers may add or omit persons from this list, other than a Minister of the Crown: H(W)A 2014 s95(6), (7).
5 H(W)A 2014 s95(2).

which case that body must comply with the request unless it considers that doing so would be incompatible with its own duties or would otherwise have an adverse effect on the exercise of the body's functions.[6]

10.9 In the case of both a co-operation and an information request, a body which decides not to comply with the request must give the local housing authority which made the request written reasons for its decision.[7]

Notifications

10.10 In a number of cases, the legislation requires notification to be made to an applicant, of a decision or other matter, eg a written record. In all cases, the notice or other matter must be in writing and, if not received by the applicant, is treated as having been given if made available at the authority's office for a reasonable period for collection by the applicant or on his or her behalf; where there is a right to review, the notice will invariably need to say so and specify the time (21 days or such longer period as may be allowed) with which the review must be sought.[8] In some cases, the secretary of state or Welsh Ministers may make provision by regulations as to the procedure to be followed in connection with notices.[9]

Interim accommodation

Overview

Generally

10.11 If an authority has reason to believe that an applicant may be eligible for assistance and homeless, it has to secure that accommodation is

6 H(W)A 2014 s95(3).
7 H(W)A 2014 s95(4).
8 HA 1996, ss184(5), (6), 189A(12), 193B(3), (7), (8), 195(7), (9), 199A(3), (7), 200(6), 202(1), (3), 203(8); H(W)A 2014 ss84(1), (3), (4), 85(5), 86.
9 HA 1996 s193B(7).

made available for the applicant's occupation pending any decision that it may make as a result of its enquiries.[10]

10.12 This duty exists irrespective of questions of local connection.[11] The test is exhaustive: the authority cannot qualify it by adding any further criteria, for example, that an applicant must be at risk of harm in his or her current accommodation if not provided with other accommodation pending the decision.[12]

10.13 The threshold test for the provision of accommodation pending decision is very low:[13] it only requires authority to have 'reason to believe' that an applicant may be homeless, eligible for assistance and have a priority need for the duty to secure accommodation to be activated[14] – although the authority itself may take action that obviates the homelessness before a decision is taken.[15]

10.14 A local housing authority may be able to leave an applicant in current accommodation (where it remains available) in satisfaction of the duty under HA 1996 s188(1).[16]

10 HA 1996 s188(1); H(W)A 2014 s68. This duty is met by an offer of suitable accommodation. If the applicant does not take up the offer then – absent a material change in circumstances which affects the suitability of the accommodation – he or she cannot require the authority to make a further offer of interim accommodation: *R (Brooks) v Islington LBC* [2015] EWHC 2657 (Admin), [2016] HLR 2.

11 HA 1996 s188(2); H(W)A 2014 s68(4); see paras 7.108–7.111.

12 *R (Kelly and Mehari) v Birmingham City Council* [2009] EWHC 3240 (Admin), [2009] JHL D24.

13 *R (M) v Hammersmith and Fulham LBC* [2006] EWCA Civ 917. The case was appealed to the House of Lords (*R (M) v Hammersmith and Fulham LBC* [2008] UKHL 14, [2008] 1 WLR 535, [2008] 4 All ER 271; see also paras 5.74–5.75) but the point on the threshold for HA 1996 s188(1) was not in issue. A similar point on the threshold was made in the High Court in *R (Aweys) v Birmingham City Council* [2007] EWHC 52 (Admin), [2007] HLR 27, not pursued on appeal, see above; see also para 9.55.

14 HA 1996 s188(1), H(W)A 2014 s68.

15 *Hanton-Rhouila v Westminster City Council* [2010] EWCA Civ 1334, [2011] HLR 12.

16 *Birmingham City Council v Ali; Moran v Manchester City Council (Secretary of State for Communities and Local Government and another intervening)* [2009] UKHL 36, [2009] HLR 41. See also *R (Edwards and others) v Birmingham CC* [2016] EWHC 173 (Admin), [2016] HLR 11 in which the authority were entitled to rely on an applicant's 'self-certification' as to the suitability of property he or she was occupying on a 'homeless at home' application; this was not objectionable so long as the applicant was aware of his or her right to interim accommodation and knew he or she could return to request it at a later date.

England

Re-application following private sector offer

10.15 From 9 November 2012, when Localism Act (LA) 2011 s149(2) came into force in England,[17] the duty also arises if the authority has reason to believe that the new duty in HA 1996 s195A may apply to the applicant.[18] Consequent on the extended powers of an authority to discharge the full duty in HA 1996 s193[19] by using private sector accommodation,[20] section 195A provides for the full duty to recur even if there is no priority need,[21] if the applicant becomes homeless[22] again within two years of acceptance of the offer, provided that he or she is still eligible for assistance, and did not become homeless intentionally.[23] When assessing whether this duty has arisen, the authority must disregard any restricted person.[24]

Ending the duty – without priority need

10.16 Since commencement of the Homelessness Reduction Act (HRA) 2017,[25] in England, the duty to secure interim accommodation ends on different dates depending on what the authority decides. If the authority concludes that the applicant is not in priority need, and the authority also decides that it does not owe him or her an initial

17 Localism Act 2011 (Commencement No 2 and Transitional Provisions) (England) Order 2012 SI No 2599 art 2.

18 HA 1996 s188(1A). This is only applicable where the duty to secure accommodation had arisen but had not ceased before 9 November 2012: Localism Act 2011 (Commencement No 2 and Transitional Provisions) (England) Order 2012 SI No 2599 art 3.

19 Paras 10.118–10.263.

20 LA 2011 s148, amending HA 1996 s193.

21 Ie, it has been lost since the original application, eg if a child leaves home.

22 Defined to mean when valid notice under HA 1988 s21, expires (see Arden & Dymond, *Manual of housing law*, 10th edn, LAG, 2017, para 2.203: there is no need for the applicant to await proceedings for possession or an order: HA 1996 s195A(2).

23 This duty applies only to the first re-application: HA 1996 s195A(6).

24 HA 1996 s195(1), (5). As to restricted person, see paras 10.241–10.250.

25 3 April 2018: see Homelessness Reduction Act 2017 (Commencement and Transitional and Savings Provisions) Regulations 2018 SI No 167 reg 3, only applicable to applications made and reviews sought on or after that date – see reg 4.

help duty under HA 1996 s189B(2) (paras 10.76–10.96),[26] the duty ends when the authority notifies the applicant of that decision.[27]

10.17 If the authority decides that there is no priority need but the that it does owe the initial help duty, the interim accommodation duty ends when the authority notifies the applicant of its decision that, on the coming to an end of its initial help duty, it does not owe the applicant any duty under either HA 1996 s190 (duties to the intentionally homeless: paras 10.97–10.117) or s193 (principal duty: paras 10.118–10.263).[28]

Ending the duty – with priority need

10.18 In any other case,[29] the duty comes to an end on the later of either when the HA 1996 s189B(2) duty comes to an end or the authority notifies the applicant that it does not owe him or her a duty under that section, or when the authority notifies the applicant of its decision as to what other duty (if any) it owes to the applicant under HA 1996 Part 7 following the initial help duty.[30] These alternatives will also apply to the duty under HA 1996 s188(1A) (re-application following private sector offer: para 10.15).[31]

Wales

10.19 In Wales, the duty ends if the authority notifies the applicant that it has no initial help duty because it is not satisfied that the applicant is homeless and eligible.[32] If such a duty is owed, the accommodation duty ends when the authority notifies the applicant that the initial help duty has come to an end and that a duty is or is not owed to the applicant under H(W)A 2014 s75 (paras 10.118–10.263).[33]

10.20 If the reason for the decision that there is no such principal duty is either on the ground that the applicant became homeless intentionally (in the circumstances which gave rise to the application) or on the ground that it had previously secured accommodation to the applicant following a previous application for help, at any time within

26 Ie is either not eligible for assistance and/or not homeless: HA 1996 s189B(1).
27 HA 1996 s188(1ZA).
28 HA 1996 s188(1ZA).
29 Ie when it is decided that there is a priority need.
30 HA 1996 s188(1ZB).
31 HA 1996 s188(1A).
32 H(W)A 2014 s69(2).
33 H(W)A 2014 s69(3).

the period of five years before the day on which the applicant was notified that a duty was owed to him or her, the duty does not come to end.[34]

10.21 In either of these cases, the accommodation duty continues until the authority is satisfied that the period of accommodation has been sufficient to allow the applicant a reasonable opportunity of securing his or her own accommodation,[35] not being less than 56 days that the initial help duty was applicable.[36]

10.22 The duty also ends if the applicant, having been notified of the possible consequences, refused an offer of suitable interim accommodation, or became homeless intentionally from that accommodation, or voluntarily ceased to occupy such accommodation as his or her only or principal home.[37]

10.23 The duty also comes to an end if: the authority is no longer satisfied that the applicant is eligible; or the authority is satisfied that a mistake of fact led to the decision that the duty was owed at all; or the authority is satisfied that the applicant has withdrawn his or her application; or the authority is satisfied that the applicant is unreasonably failing to co-operate with the it in connection with the exercise of its homelessness functions which relate to the applicant.[38]

10.24 The duty comes to an end even if a review is sought, although the authority has a discretion to continue to secure suitable accommodation pending a decision on the review.[39]

General considerations

Reason to believe

10.25 The threshold – 'reason to believe'[40] – is designedly low; the authority should provide the accommodation when it is needed and then make

34 H(W)A 2014 s69(4), (5).
35 H(W)A 2014 s69(5).
36 H(W)A 2014 s69(6).
37 H(W)A 2014 s69(7)–(9).
38 H(W)A 2014 ss69(12), 79.
39 H(W)A 2014 s69(10), (11).
40 Whether this threshold is met is primarily a matter for the authority; any review is on conventional *Wednesbury* grounds: *R (Edwards) v Birmingham City Council* [2016] EWHC 173 (Admin), [2016] HLR 11.

further enquiries.[41] Even this threshold was not reached in *Burns*,[42] however, where the authority had no reason to believe that the applicant was eligible. The applicant, who had married a European Union (EU) national, had been refused a residence permit by the Home Office, which refusal the authority was entitled to take at face value so that it was reasonable for it to have refused interim accommodation without making any further enquiries.

10.26 In *R (Edwards) v Birmingham City Council*,[43] it was held that, although the threshold is a low one, the authority is nonetheless entitled to question a person who claims to be homeless at home to clarify whether in fact there is reason to believe that the accommodation occupied by that person is such that it may not be reasonable for him or her to continue to occupy it; the applicant's assertion to this effect – or one on the applicant's behalf – does not have to be accepted on its face.

Available for occupation

10.27 The requirement to make accommodation available for the applicant's occupation is, by definition, a requirement to make it available for the applicant and for any person who might reasonably be expected to reside with him or her.[44] The meaning of this has been considered in chapter 4, above.[45]

Securing accommodation

10.28 An authority may discharge its interim accommodation duties by providing its own accommodation; by arranging for it to be provided by someone else; or by giving advice such as will secure that it is provided by someone else.[46] These provisions are considered below, in relation to the principal housing duty.[47]

41 *R (M) v Hammersmith and Fulham LBC* [2008] UKHL 14, [2008] 1 WLR 535 at [36].

42 *R (Burns) v Southwark LBC* [2004] EWHC 1901 (Admin), [2004] JHL D105; see also, by way of example *R (Omar) v Wandsworth LBC* [2015] EWHC 4110 (Admin).

43 [2016] EWHC 173 (Admin), [2016] HLR 11.

44 HA 1996 s176; H(W)A 2014 s68.

45 Paras 4.16–4.38; and see, in particular, *Sharif v Camden LBC* [2013] UKSC 10, [2013] HLR 16 in which it was held that two flats yards apart in the same building can comprise accommodation in which a household can live together.

46 HA 1996 s206(1); H(W)A 2014 ss95, 96; see further para 10.135.

47 Paras 10.118–10.263.

10.29 The requirement calls for some action on the part of the authority. In *Sidhu*,[48] a women's refuge, not even in the same area, provided accommodation, but as the authority had not been involved in procuring it, it could not rely on it as a discharge of its duty.

10.30 The fact that the accommodation was in another area was not itself fundamental to the result, but it may not be without relevance. Many such refuges are funded by local authorities. In such circumstances, there are two reasons why accommodation in a refuge in the same area, which is provided voluntarily and other than at the arrangement of the authority may be less susceptible to challenge:

a) as a matter of practice, the refuge is not entirely independent of the authority; and
b) the provision of funds for the refuge may be held to denote a sufficient degree of participation or assistance by the authority,[49] although probably only if the accommodation is provided at the express request of the authority, or it is agreed – or at the lowest 'understood' – that the organisation will accommodate those referred to it by the authority; anything more vague should not qualify.

10.31 The authority may require a person housed under this provision to pay such reasonable charges[50] as it may determine, or to pay an amount towards the payment made by the authority to a third party for accommodation – for example, a contribution towards the cost of private sector accommodation.[51] If the authority provides its own accommodation, it can in any event make a reasonable charge under HA 1985 s24.

10.32 The provision of assistance under HA 1996 Part 7 or H(W)A 2014 Part 2 is not, however, contingent on ability to pay,[52] although there is no reason why – even if the applicant is unable to make a payment – an authority should not reserve the right to payment, eg against a future change of fortunes on the part of an applicant.

48 *R v Ealing LBC ex p Sidhu* (1982) 2 HLR 45, QBD.

49 It may depend on the circumstances, including the powers under which assistance was provided and the terms of assistance.

50 Which can be 'nil': *R (Yekini) v Southwark LBC* [2014] EWHC 2096 (Admin).

51 HA 1996 s206(2); H(W)A 2014 s90. If accommodation is provided or secured by the authority but is subsequently found not to be suitable on grounds of costs (para 10.192), it is difficult to see how it can have been a 'reasonable charge'; if that is correct, it would provide a basis for the applicant to seek to resist a claim for arrears.

52 *R v Secretary of State for Social Security ex p B and Joint Council for the Welfare of Immigrants* (1996) 29 HLR 129, CA.

Security

10.33 In *Miah*,[53] *Buscombe*[54] and *Hayden*,[55] some doubt was cast on whether accommodation provided under the Housing (Homeless Persons) Act (H(HP)A) 1977 amounted to a tenancy or licence within the security provisions of what is now HA 1985 Part 4. In *Walsh*,[56] however, the authority's argument that any temporary accommodation so provided would necessarily be by way of licence was rejected by the House of Lords and the letting was held to amount to a tenancy.[57]

10.34 The importance of this issue is diminished[58] by the exclusion of security of tenure under the HAs 1985[59] and 1988[60] for homeless applicants, although it may still bear on determination of the right of occupation at common law, disrepair claims and whether or not court proceedings are required to evict an occupier.[61]

10.35 The exclusion from assured protection under the HA 1988 lasts for a period of 12 months beginning on the date on which the applicant is notified of the decision on his or her application,[62] unless the landlord notifies him or her to the contrary, either that it is to be a fully assured tenancy or an assured shorthold tenancy.[63]

10.36 For these purposes, a 'private sector landlord' is any landlord who is not within HA 1985 s80(1);[64] the term therefore includes registered

53 *Family Housing Association v Miah* (1982) 5 HLR 94, CA.

54 *Restormel DC v Buscombe* (1982) 14 HLR 91, CA.

55 *Kensington and Chelsea RLBC v Hayden* (1984) 17 HLR 114, CA.

56 *Eastleigh DC v Walsh* [1985] 1 WLR 525, (1985) 17 HLR 392, HL.

57 See also *Street v Mountford* [1985] AC 809, (1985) 17 HLR 402, HL.

58 If not eliminated: see next paragraph.

59 HA 1985 Sch 1 para 4 as amended by H(W)A 2014 Sch 3 para 1; such a tenancy will become secure if the authority notifies the tenant that the tenancy is to be regarded as a secure tenancy. In *Tompkins v Wandsworth LBC* [2015] EWCA Civ 846, [2015] HLR 44, use of an incorrect form of tenancy agreement was held not to amount to 'notification' for these purposes.

60 HA 1996 s209; H(W)A 2014 s92.

61 A homeless person who has been granted a daily licence to occupy a room with a lock in a local authority hostel is entitled to exclude trespassers: *Thomas v Director of Public Prosecutions* [2009] EWHC 3906 (Admin).

62 Or, in the case of a review or appeal to the county court, of the date on which he or she is notified of the outcome of the review or of when the appeal is finally determined.

63 HA 1996 s209(2); H(W)A 2014 s92(2).

64 Ie, local authorities, new town corporations, housing action trusts, urban development corporations, or housing co-operatives within the meaning of HA 1985 s27B.

providers of social housing and registered social landlords.[65] It follows that someone initially provided with interim accommodation but left in it for long enough afterwards could become assured through the passage of time; secure protection under the HA 1985 is not, however, likewise limited by time, only by whether or not it is provided under HA 1996 Part 7 or H(W)A 2014 Part 2.

Quality

10.37 Under H(HP)A 1977 and HA 1985, as unamended, there was no statutory standard governing the quality of accommodation provided.[66] Under HA 1985, as amended by Housing and Planning Act 1986,[67] statutory requirements for suitability were introduced, but were not applicable to accommodation pending enquiries. The suitability requirements[68] of HA 1996 and H(W)A 2014 are, however, applicable to every requirement to secure that accommodation is available, including the interim duties. An authority does not have to give reasons why it considers that a property offered under these provisions is suitable.[69] Suitability is considered below in relation to the principal housing duty.[70]

10.38 In *Ali* and *Moran*,[71] it was observed that 'what is regarded as suitable for discharging the interim duty may be rather different from what is regarded as suitable for discharging the more open-ended duty in [HA 1996] section 193(2)'. This accords with two earlier decisions on the quality of temporary accommodation under the H(HP)A 1977, even though there was then no statutory suitability requirement,[72] although both related to temporary accommodation for the intentionally homeless.[73]

65 HA 1996 s217; H(W)A 2014 s99.

66 *R v Hillingdon LBC ex p Puhlhofer* [1986] AC 484, (1986) 18 HLR 158, HL.

67 Section 14(3).

68 See HA 1996 ss206(1) and 210(1) and H(W)A 2014 s59, (paras 10.162–10.204). See, eg *R (Lindsay) v (1) Watford BC (2) Hertfordshire CC* High Court (QBD), 13 October 2017, in which it was considered doubtful that bed and breakfast accommodation was suitable for an applicant whose complex medical and mental health issues made it impossible for her to live independently.

69 *Akhtar v Birmingham City Council* [2011] EWCA Civ 383, [2011] HLR 28; *Solihull MBC v Khan* [2014] EWCA Civ 41, [2014] HLR 33.

70 See paras 10.162–10.204.

71 *Birmingham City Council v Ali; Moran v Manchester City Council (Secretary of State for Communities and Local Government and another intervening)* [2009] UKHL 36, [2009] 1 WLR 1506 at [18].

72 See para 10.37.

73 See para 10.97.

10.39 In *Glidden*,[74] the authority was alleged to have been in breach of its temporary duty because the accommodation provided was in substantial disrepair, requiring works to prevent it becoming statutorily unfit for human habitation. It was held that the authority could have regard to the time for which accommodation was likely to be occupied: while some quality of accommodation would fall below the line of acceptable discharge of even a temporary duty, accommodation needing works to pre-empt statutory unfitness did not necessarily do so; accommodation so unfit that it is not even repairable, however, might well have been inadequate even for a temporary purpose.

10.40 In *Ward*,[75] accommodation on a caravan site described by a social worker as being in appalling condition was nonetheless an adequate discharge of the temporary duty, having regard to the family's wish to live on a site, rather than in a permanent structure.

Area

10.41 There are constraints on out-of-area placements which apply to discharge under this section: these are considered below in relation to the full duty.[76]

Termination of accommodation

10.42 On occasion, in particular when enquiries have taken some time (for example, into accommodation abroad), a local authority will wish to terminate a right of occupation, either because it wants to move the applicant elsewhere or because of some fault on the part of the applicant[77] or it will have to deal with the position which arises if another landlord providing accommodation on its behalf has taken or wants to evict the applicant.

10.43 It is clear that the authority may move the occupier, for example, for reasons of cost, provided the new accommodation is also suitable, and it is otherwise acting reasonably. Where the accommodation is lost because of the applicant's default, it is not open to an authority to conclude that the applicant has thereby become homeless intentionally, as this would not have been the accommodation the loss of

74 *R v Exeter City Council ex p Gliddon* (1984) 14 HLR 103, QBD.
75 *R v Southampton City Council ex p Ward* (1984) 14 HLR 114, QBD.
76 See paras 10.147–10.161.
77 Eg non-payment of charges, nuisance and annoyance, damage to property.

which gives rise to the homelessness application requiring a decision: see *Din*.[78] It may, however, be that no further interim duty is owed.[79]

10.44 Where the applicant refuses the accommodation offered (under HA 1996 s188), the authority may nonetheless be able to conclude that it has discharged its duty under this section, and decline to provide further accommodation pursuant to it,[80] albeit that it will still be bound to consider and discharge the appropriate HA 1996 s193 duty following its decision under s184, based on the accommodation lost which led to the homelessness which gave rise to the application.

10.45 In reaching its decision on whether or not that loss amounted to intentionality, the loss of the intervening accommodation will therefore not be relevant,[81] save if and so far as the conduct involved can properly be considered to have some evidential value in reaching a view on the earlier loss of accommodation, for example, analogous conduct.

10.46 Since commencement of the HRA 2017,[82] if the authority has continued accommodation while discharging the initial help duty,[83] there are statutory provisions governing refusal of offers and non co-operation, which are likely to apply[84] which may render it unnecessary to resort to previous case-law.

78 *Din v Wandsworth LBC* [1983] 1 AC 657, (1983) 1 HLR 73, HL. Consider, too, that HA 1996 s193(6)(b) makes explicit provision for an authority to determine that its duty towards a homeless applicant – following a decision that the applicant is homeless, in priority need and not intentionally homeless – has been discharged in the event of becoming intentionally homeless from *that* accommodation; it would be anomalous to reach the same conclusion in relation to temporary accommodation *pending* a decision.

79 In *R v Kensington and Chelsea RLBC ex p Kujtim* (2000) 32 HLR 579, (1999) 2 CCLR 460, CA, the duty to provide accommodation under National Assistance Act 1948 s21 (see now chapter 13 for the provisions replacing that section) was held not to be absolute. Where the applicant manifests a persistent and unequivocal refusal to observe the authority's reasonable requirements in relation to occupation of the accommodation, the authority is entitled to treat its duty as discharged and to refuse to provide further accommodation.

80 Consider *R (Brooks) v Islington LBC* [2015] EWHC 2657 (Admin), [2016] HLR 2 where the applicant refused an offer of interim accommodation and the authority did not have to make a further offer. The same point may be made by parity of reasoning with *R v Westminster City Council ex p Chambers* (1982) 6 HLR 15, QBD on refusal of a final offer (before statutory provision was made to govern such refusals): see para 10.211.

81 *R v Islington LBC ex p Hassan* (1995) 27 HLR 485, QBD.

82 3 April 2018: see Homelessness Reduction Act 2017 (Commencement and Transitional and Savings Provisions) Regulations 2018 SI No 167 reg 3, only applicable to applications made and reviews sought on or after that date – see reg 4.

83 Paras 10.76–10.96.

84 Paras 10.86–10.91.

Eviction

10.47 Accommodation provided under HA 1996 Part 7 or H(W)A 2014 Part 2 is not protected by Protection from Eviction Act (PEA) 1977 s3, and the applicant may be evicted without a court order; any challenge based on Article 8 of the European Convention on Human Rights (ECHR) can, however, be raised on an appeal to the county court against any decision which means that a full duty is not to be accepted.[85]

10.48 If court proceedings are used, it seems likely that they can be resisted both on the basis that the authority's decision to seek possession is ultra vires in domestic public law,[86] or on the basis of Article 8[87] and/or (where appropriate) that it would amount to unlawful discrimination under the Equality Act (EqA) 2010.[88]

Accommodation pending review

10.49 The duty to provide interim accommodation under HA 1996 s188 comes to an end even if a review is sought.[89] The duty is, however, replaced with a power to provide accommodation pending the review.[90] The authority is not obliged of its own motion to consider whether to exercise this power, but may await a request from the applicant before deciding whether to do so.[91] As a refusal to house pending a review is not a decision that is itself susceptible to the statutory review process, any challenge has to be by way of judicial review.[92]

85 *R (ZH and CN) v Newham LBC and Lewisham LBC* [2014] UKSC 62, [2015] HLR 6.

86 *Barber v Croydon LBC* [2010] EWCA Civ 51, [2010] HLR 26.

87 *Powell v Hounslow LBC; Frisby v Birmingham CC; Hall v Leeds CC* [2011] UKSC 8, [2011] HLR 23.

88 *Akerman-Livingstone v Aster Communities Ltd* [2015] UKSC 15, [2015] HLR 20.

89 HA 1996 s188(3); H(W)A 2014 s69. See also *R (Faizi) v Brent LBC* [2015] EWHC 2449 (Admin).

90 HA 1996 s188(3); H(W)A 2014 s69(11).

91 *R (Ahmed) v Waltham Forest LBC* [2001] EWHC (Admin) 540, [2001] JHL D89.

92 *R v Camden LBC ex p Mohammed* (1998) 30 HLR 315, QBD. This sets a high bar: consider *R (Abdusemed) v Lambeth LBC*, High Court (Administrative Court), 19 February 2016; *HousingView*, 29 February 2016, where interim relief on judicial review was refused to a woman whom the authority had declined to house pending review even though she was walking the streets during the day and spending the night at a local mosque. See para 12.140.

10.50 As an applicant has an unfettered right to a review,[93] it is not envisaged that the discretion to house pending review will be exercised as a matter of course. An authority may therefore decide to exercise the discretion only in exceptional circumstances: *Mohammed*.[94]

10.51 In exercising its discretion, the authority must balance the objective of maintaining fairness between other homeless persons – in circumstances where it has decided that no duty is owed to the applicant – and proper consideration of the possibility that the applicant may be right.[95] In carrying out this balancing exercise, certain matters will always require consideration, although other matters may also be relevant:

a) the merits of the case and the extent to which it can properly be said that the decision was one which was either contrary to the apparent merits or was one which involved a very fine balance of judgment;
b) whether consideration is required of new material, information or argument which could have a real effect on the decision under review;
c) the personal circumstances of the applicant and the consequences to him or her of a decision not to exercise the discretion.[96]

10.52 In *Lumley*,[97] Brooke LJ explained that the merits of the case meant 'the merits of the applicant's case that the council's original decision was flawed'. In that case, the decision was quashed because the initial decision that the applicant was not in priority need was seriously flawed and the authority had failed to take the flaws into account when considering the exercise of its discretion to house pending review.

10.53 In every case, the principles must be applied to the relevant facts and a properly reasoned decision provided.[98] In *Mohammed*,[99] the judge found that the council had considered the matters set out properly, but he nonetheless quashed its decision not to house the applicant pending review because it had failed to give her an opportunity

93 Paras 9.186–9.199.

94 *R v Camden LBC ex p Mohammed*. See also *R v Hammersmith and Fulham LBC ex p Fleck* (1997) 30 HLR 679, QBD and *R v Newham LBC ex p Bautista* April 2001 *Legal Action* 22. See also, English Code of Guidance paras 15.25–15.27.

95 *R v Camden LBC ex p Mohammed* (1998) 30 HLR 315, QBD.

96 *R v Camden LBC ex p Mohammed* (1998) 30 HLR 315, QBD.

97 *R v Newham LBC ex p Lumley* (2001) 33 HLR 11, QBD.

98 See *R (Paul-Coker) v Southwark LBC* [2006] EWHC 497 (Admin), [2006] HLR 32.

99 *R v Camden LBC ex p Mohammed* (1997) 30 HLR 315, QBD.

to explain inconsistencies in her statements and had therefore failed to take into account a relevant and material consideration in exercising its discretion.

10.54 In *Nacion*,[100] the Court of Appeal applied *Mohammed* to a decision under the discretion to house pending an appeal.[101] Housing pending appeal is considered in chapter 12, below, as part of the machinery for enforcement of duties.[102]

10.55 There is, however, a difference between housing pending review and housing pending appeal, as recognised by Brooke LJ in *Lumley*:[103] in *Nacion* there had already been a review, so that 'most of the errors, if any, made on the first consideration of the case should have been put right by the senior officer who conducted the review', while pending review, there will only have been the one decision and consideration. Accordingly, the bar may be a little lower when considering housing pending review than when considering housing pending appeal.

10.56 In deciding when to terminate accommodation provided pending a decision following an unsuccessful review, an authority must give the person reasonable notice so that he or she can have an opportunity to make alternative arrangements.[104]

10.57 It was previously held that there is no requirement for a local housing authority to take into consideration possible duties owed to the children of an applicant under Children Act (CA) 1989, or the potential break-up of the family, when deciding whether to continue to provide accommodation under HA 1996 s188(3),[105] although the correctness of this must now be in doubt given the impact of ECHR Article 8, CA 2004 s11[106] and the trend of homelessness legislation under HRA 2017.

100 *R v Brighton and Hove Council ex p Nacion* (1999) 31 HLR 1095, CA.

101 HA 1996 s204(4). But see now section 204A, allowing an appeal from such a refusal to be made to the county court itself – paras 12.238–12.247.

102 Paras 12.238–12.247.

103 (2001) 33 HLR 11, QBD.

104 *R v Newham LBC ex p Ojuri (No 5)* (1998) 31 HLR 631, QBD.

105 *R (Hassan) v Croydon LBC* [2009] JHL D56, Administrative Court.

106 Local authorities must have regard 'to the need to safeguard and promote the welfare of children' when discharging their functions: CA 2004 s11 (England) s28 (Wales). This includes functions under HA 1996 Part 7: *Huzrat v Hounslow LBC* [2013] EWCA Civ 1865, [2014] HLR 17. See also *Nzolameso v Westminster City Council* [2015] UKSC 22, [2015] HLR 22: when considering whether accommodation is suitable for a family, the authority must identify the principal needs of the children both individually and collectively when making the decision.

Assessment and plan

England

10.58 Since the HRA 2017 came into force,[107] there has been a new duty of 'assessment' applicable to all applicants whom an English authority is satisfied are homeless or threatened with homelessness[108] and eligible[109] for assistance.[110] Priority need is therefore not needed. The duty is to 'make an assessment of the applicant's case',[111] which must include an assessment of the circumstances which resulted in the applicant's homelessness or being threatened with homelessness, the applicant's housing needs,[112] and the applicant's needs for support[113] in order to be able to have and retain suitable accommodation.[114] The authority has to notify the applicant in writing of the assessment it makes.[115]

10.59 The next stage is for the authority to try to agree with the applicant what steps he or she is to be required to take in order to secure that he or she[116] has and is able to retain suitable accommodation, and what steps the authority is to take under HA 1996 Part 7 for those purposes.[117]

107 3 April 2018: see Homelessness Reduction Act 2017 (Commencement and Transitional and Savings Provisions) Regulations 2018 SI No 167 reg 3, only applicable to applications made and reviews sought on or after that date – see reg 4.

108 Chapter 4.

109 Chapter 3.

110 HA 1996 s189A.

111 HA 1996 s189A(1).

112 In particular, what accommodation would be suitable for him or her and anyone with whom he or she resides or might reasonably be expected to reside.

113 Together with anyone with whom he or she resides or might reasonably be expected to reside.

114 HA 1996 s189A(2).

115 HA 1996 s189A(3).

116 Together with anyone with whom he or she resides or might reasonably be expected to reside.

117 HA 1996 s189A(4). This could include the applicant and the authority working together to ensure that the applicant is receiving all welfare benefits to which he or she might be entitled, whether as of right or pursuant to any discretionary scheme. For example, if the applicant is entitled to housing benefit or universal credit and requires further financial assistance in order to meet his or her housing costs, then the authority has power to make a discretionary housing payment (DHP): Discretionary Financial Assistance Regulations 2001 SI No 1167 and Discretionary Housing Payments (Grants) Order 2001 SI No 2340. Such payments can be made in any amount and for any period of time and are a

10.60 If the authority and the applicant reach an agreement, the authority has to record it in writing.[118] If they cannot reach agreement, the authority has to record in writing why it could not agree; what steps it considers it would be reasonable to require the applicant to take; and what steps the authority is to take under HA 1996 Part 7 for those purposes.[119] Either class of record can include any advice the authority considers appropriate, including the steps the authority thinks it would be 'a good idea for the applicant to take', albeit that the applicant is not to be required to take.[120] The authority has to give the applicant a copy of the written record.[121]

10.61 Until the authority decides that it owes the applicant no duty under any of the remaining provisions of Part 7, the authority has to keep the assessment under review, together with the appropriateness of any agreement reached or steps recorded.[122] If the assessment of the mandatory considerations (circumstances resulting in homelessness or being threatened with homelessness, housing needs and needs for support)[123] changes, the authority must notify the applicant, in writing, of how its assessment has changed (whether by providing a revised written assessment or otherwise); the same is true if the authority's assessment otherwise changes in a way that it considers it appropriate to notify the applicant.[124]

10.62 If the authority considers that any agreement reached or any step recorded under it is no longer appropriate, it must notify the applicant in writing to this effect and that any subsequent failure to take a step that was agreed or recorded is to be disregarded; the provisions governing attempt to reach agreement, or to record a failure to do so, described above (paras 10.59–10.60) re-apply.[125]

legitimate tool for preventing homelessness: *R (Halvai) v Hammersmith and Fulham LBC* [2017] EWHC 802 (Admin). A refusal to provide such – or other financial – assistance can, however, only be challenged on conventional public law grounds: cf *R (Conville) v Richmond upon Thames LBC* [2005] EWHC 1430 (Admin), [2006] HLR 1, not appealed on this point, see [2006] EWCA Civ 718, [2006] HLR 45.

118 HA 1996 s189A(5).
119 HA 1996 s189A(6).
120 HA 1996 s189A(7).
121 HA 1996 s189A(8).
122 HA 1996 s189A(9).
123 See para 10.25.
124 HA 1996 s189A(10).
125 HA 1996 s189A(11).

Wales

10.63 In Wales, the H(W)A 2014 contains similar – but not identical – duties.[126] If it appears to the authority that an applicant may be homeless or threatened with homelessness, it must carry out an assessment of the person's case.[127] The assessment must consider whether the applicant is eligible.[128] If the applicant is eligible, the assessment must then address:

a) how the applicant has become homeless or threatened with homelessness;
b) the applicant's housing needs and those of anyone with whom he or she lives or might reasonably be expected to live;
c) the support required to meet those needs; and
d) whether or not the authority has any duty under H(W)A 2014 Part 2 to the applicant.[129]

10.64 The assessment must seek to identify what the applicant wishes to achieve with the authority's help; the authority must consider whether the exercise of any of its powers under Part 2 can contribute to that outcome.[130] The assessment must be kept under review.[131]

10.65 The authority must notify the applicant of the outcome of the assessment (and of any review) and, insofar as any issue is decided against his or her interests, give reasons for the decision.[132] It must also inform the applicant or his or her right to request a review.[133]

10.66 Additional notification duties[134] apply where a duty under H(W)A 2014 s75[135] is owed only because of a restricted person[136] or where the authority has already notified or intends to notify another authority under the local connection provisions.[137]

126 H(W)A 2014 applies from 27 April 2015: see Housing (Wales) Act 2014 (Commencement No 3 and Transitory, Transitional and Saving Provisions) Order 2015 SI No 1272.

127 H(W)A 2014 s62(1), (4), (5).

128 H(W)A 2014 s62(3).

129 H(W)A 2014 s62(5).

130 H(W)A 2014 s62(6). See also above, footnote 117.

131 H(W)A 2014 s62(8), (9).

132 H(W)A 2014 s63(1).

133 H(W)A 2014 s63(4).

134 H(W)A 2014 s63(2), (3).

135 Ie the full duty.

136 As to which, see para 3.149.

137 As to which, see paras 7.100–7.103.

Duties to those threatened with homelessness

England

10.67 Since commencement of the HRA 2017,[138] a new duty has been imposed on English authorities – replacing previous provisions to be found in HA 1996 s195 as enacted – in all cases where the authority is satisfied that an applicant is threatened with homelessness[139] and eligible[140] for assistance.[141] Priority need is again[142] not relevant to whether or not there is a duty.[143]

10.68 The authority is obliged to take reasonable steps to help the applicant to secure that accommodation does not cease to be available for his or her occupation.[144] The term 'reasonable steps' is not defined; plainly, however, it cannot mean 'no steps'. Authorities cannot refuse as a matter of policy to take any action until physical eviction: each case must be considered on its merits, and where it is obvious that homelessness will ensue steps must be taken to prepare for it.[145]

10.69 In deciding what steps to take, the authority has to have regard to its assessment (paras 10.58–10.66) of the applicant's case.[146] The obligation is without prejudice to the authority's right to recover possession of any accommodation.[147]

138 3 April 2018: see Homelessness Reduction Act 2017 (Commencement and Transitional and Savings Provisions) Regulations 2018 SI No 167 reg 3, only applicable to applications made and reviews sought on or after that date – see reg 4.

139 See paras 4.141–4.148.

140 Chapter 3.

141 HA 1996 s195(1).

142 Para 10.58.

143 It is highly relevant, however, to the rights that the applicant will enjoy: see further below, paras 10.118–10.263.

144 HA 1996 s195(2). The duties apply even although an issue of local connection may apply: see *Williams v Exeter City Council*, September 1981 *LAG Bulletin* 211, CC, under the Housing (Homeless Persons) Act 1977.

145 *R v Newham LBC ex p Khan* (2001) 33 HLR 29, QBD, under the predecessor provisions of HA 1996 s195 (as enacted).

146 HA 1996 s195(3).

147 HA 1996 s195(4). The provision does not make an authority's refusal to withdraw 'stop notices', under planning legislation perverse, even though it would render the applicants, a group of travelling showmen, homeless: *R v Chiltern DC ex p Dyason* (1990) 23 HLR 387, QBD.

10.70 The authority can give notice bringing this duty to an end when it is satisfied that any one of the following circumstances is applicable:[148]

a) the applicant both has suitable accommodation which is available for his or her occupation[149] and there is a reasonable prospect of the applicant having suitable accommodation[150] available for at least six months[151] from the date of the notice;
b) the authority has complied with the duty to take reasonable steps and the period of 56 days beginning with the day that the authority was first satisfied that the applicant is threatened with homeless and eligible has ended (whether or not he or she is still threatened with homelessness);[152]
c) the applicant has become homeless;[153]
d) the applicant has refused an offer of suitable accommodation and, on the date of refusal, there was a reasonable prospect that suitable accommodation would be available for occupation by the applicant for at least six months or such longer period[154] as may be prescribed;
e) the applicant has become homeless intentionally[155] from any accommodation that has been made available to him or her as a result of the authority's exercise of its functions under this duty;
f) the applicant is no longer eligible for assistance; or
g) the applicant has withdrawn the application for accommodation or assistance in obtaining it.

10.71 The duty may also be brought to an end under HA 1996 s193B (deliberate and unreasonable refusal to co-operate: paras 10.88–10.91),[156]

148 HA 1996 s195(5), (8). The notice must specify which of the circumstances applies and inform the applicant that he or she has a right to request a review of the decision to bring the duty to an end and of the time within which such a request must be made: HA 1996 s195(7).

149 See paras 4.16–4.38.

150 It need not be the same accommodation.

151 Or such longer period not exceeding 12 months as may be prescribed.

152 The authority cannot give notice to the applicant in this circumstances if a valid notice has been given to the applicant under HA 1988 s21 (see *Manual of housing law*, para 2.203) which will expire within 56 days or has expired and is in respect of the only accommodation that is available for his or her occupation (see para 4.120): HA 1996 s195(6).

153 So that the initial help duty will apply: see paras 10.76–10.96.

154 Not exceeding 12 months.

155 Chapter 6.

156 HA 1996 s195(10).

although this does not end a right to accommodation for an applicant who is homeless, eligible, in priority need and not homeless intentionally (para 10.91).[157] This additional circumstance is considered further below (paras 10.85–10.91).

Wales

10.72 In Wales, if an authority is satisfied that an applicant is eligible and threatened with homelessness, it must 'help to secure' that accommodation does not cease to be available to the applicant.[158] This duty cannot be used to prevent the authority itself obtaining vacant possession of any accommodation; accordingly, it cannot be raised as a defence by a tenant in possession proceedings by the authority.[159]

10.73 The duty to help to secure that accommodation does not cease to be available requires the authority to take reasonable steps to help, having regard to (among other things) the need to make the best use of its resources.[160] It does not require the authority to offer accommodation, whether under H(W)A 2014 Part 6 or otherwise.[161]

10.74 An authority can help to secure that suitable accommodation does not cease to be available either by providing some form of assistance itself or arranging for someone else to provide it.[162] Examples in the H(W)A 2014 of what may be provided or arranged are:

a) mediation;
b) grants or loans;
c) guarantees;
d) support in management of debt, mortgage or rent arrears;
e) security measures for applicants at risk of abuse;
f) advocacy or other representation;
g) accommodation;
h) information and advice; and
i) other services, goods or facilities.[163]

157 HA 1996 s193C(3), (4).
158 H(W)A 2014 s66(1).
159 H(W)A 2014 s66(2).
160 H(W)A 2014 s65(a).
161 H(W)A 2014 ss65(b)–(c).
162 H(W)A 2014 s64(1).
163 H(W)A 2014 s64(2).

10.75 The authority can give notice[164] bringing this duty to and end if the authority is satisfied that:[165]

a) the applicant has become homeless;[166]
b) the applicant is no longer threatened with homelessness and suitable accommodation is likely to remain available for his or her occupation for at least another six months;[167]
c) the applicant refuses an offer of accommodation – which the authority is satisfied was suitable and was likely to be available for at least the next six months – from any person, having been notified in writing of the possible consequences of refusal or acceptance of the offer;[168]
d) the applicant ceases to be eligible;[169]
e) a mistake of fact led to authority to notify the applicant that it owed him or her a duty to help to secure accommodation for the applicant;[170]
f) the applicant has withdrawn the application;[171] or
g) the applicant is unreasonably failing to co-operate with the authority.[172]

Initial help duty

England

Overview

10.76 Since the HRA 2017 came into force,[173] there has been a new duty[174] applicable where the authority is satisfied that an applicant is

164 H(W)A 2014 s84: the authority has to provide reasons why it considers the duty has come to an end, and inform the applicant of the right to a review and of the time within which it must be sought. See also para 10.10.
165 H(W)A 2014 s67.
166 H(W)A 2014 s67(2).
167 H(W)A 2014 s67(3).
168 H(W)A 2014 s67(4).
169 H(W)A 2014 s79(2).
170 H(W)A 2014 s79(3).
171 H(W)A 2014 s79(4).
172 H(W)A 2014 s79(5).
173 3 April 2018: see Homelessness Reduction Act 2017 (Commencement and Transitional and Savings Provisions) Regulations 2018, SI No 167 reg 3, only applicable to applications made and reviews sought on or after that date – see reg 4.
174 Also based on provisions already in force in Wales: see paras 10.63–10.66.

homeless[175] and eligible[176] for assistance;[177] the duty does not, however, arise where the authority refers the application to another local housing authority in England under the local connection provisions (see paras 7.63–7.69).[178] The duty also[179] arises regardless of priority need.

10.77 The duty is to take reasonable steps[180] to help the applicant to secure that suitable accommodation becomes available for his or her occupation[181] for at least six months or such longer period[182] as may be prescribed.[183] In deciding what steps to take, the authority must have regard to its assessment of the applicant's case (paras 10.58–10.66).[184]

10.78 It may be stressed that, while the authority can fulfil the duty by providing accommodation,[185] it is only a duty to take reasonable steps to help to secure accommodation. It seems highly likely that the courts will take the view that what is reasonable for the authority to do is a matter for the authority, rather than the court: compare the duty in HA 1996 s213,[186] to render 'such assistance . . . as is reasonable in the circumstances' in which the authority's decision to refuse to assist was upheld on the basis that it was for it to decide whether or not to do so would unduly prejudice the discharge of its functions.[187]

10.79 It is also currently considered that the duty does not give rise to a duty of care on the part of the authority to ensure that any accommodation towards which the applicant is directed is safe. In *Ephraim v Newham LBC*,[188] the plaintiff had been directed by the authority – by way of advice and assistance[189] – to a guesthouse, a house in multiple

175 Chapter 4.
176 Chapter 3.
177 HA 1996 s189B(1).
178 HA 1996 s189B(2).
179 Paras 10.58, 10.67.
180 See the observation at para 10.68: reasonable steps cannot mean no steps.
181 See paras 4.16–4.38.
182 Not exceeding 12 months.
183 HA 1996 s189B(2).
184 HA 1996 s189B(3).
185 Although this is not explicitly stated, it is not merely implied but supported by other provisions of the HRA 2017, amending HA 1996: see, in particular, HRA 2017 s6, amending HA 1996 s205, and s7(1) adding s193A.
186 See paras 13.84–13.96.
187 *R v Northavon DC ex p Smith* [1994] 2 AC 402, (1994) 26 HLR 659, HL.
188 *Ephraim v Newham LBC* (1992) 25 HLR 208, CA.
189 Under the predecessor provision to HA 1996 s192 prior to repeal by HRA 2017 s5(1), (6).

occupation (HMO). She took up occupation in a bedsitting room in it. The HMO lacked proper fire precautions. Subsequently, there was a fire in the property and she suffered severe injuries. She sued, unsuccessfully alleging that Newham LBC was under a duty of care to satisfy itself that the premises to which it had referred her were reasonably safe, particularly in relation to fire.

10.80 It was held that the imposition of such a duty would put the authority in the dilemma of having either to inspect a particular property, or else not advise people to seek available accommodation; it was more desirable that the authority should give advice which enables homeless people to obtain accommodation, even though some of the properties where they obtain accommodation might prove not to be properly equipped, than it was to restrict the range of advice and make it more difficult for homeless people to find housing.[190]

When the duty comes to an end

Generally

No priority need

10.81 Where the applicant is eligible for assistance and homeless, but not in priority need, the authority may give notice that it has complied with its duty under HA 1996 s189B(2) (para 10.10) and that 56 days have elapsed since it did so.[191] The period begins with the day when the authority is first satisfied that the applicant was owed the initial help duty under section 189B (paras 10.76–10.96); the notice must specify that this is the ground on which it relies for concluding that it has complied with its duty, and must inform the applicant that he or she has a right to request a review of the decision to bring the duty to an end and of the time within which such a request must be made.[192]

10.82 The authority is not obliged to cease to help simply because an applicant is not in priority need. There is no explicit power to afford

190 It is, however, arguable that the initial help duty is intended to impose a more active obligation on authorities than the former 'advice and assistance' duty which might be considered to suggest a higher duty of care, reliance being also placed on an authority's HMO duties: see Arden, Brown and Madge-Wyld, *Quiet enjoyment, protection from rogue landlords*, LAG, 2017, chapter 5. The decision is one which seems ripe for consideration by the Supreme Court, in light of a range of developments as to duty of care by public authorities in other areas of the law.

191 HA 1996 s189B(5), (7)(b).

192 HA 1996 s189B(6). See also para 10.10.

initial help to those not in priority need. The section is case in terms of allowing the authority to serve notice stating that it has complied with its initial help duty on a number of grounds, of which this is one.[193] The authority could, accordingly, decide it will continue to comply with the duty until other grounds for termination – those applicable to applicants in priority need (paras 10.83–10.91) – exist.[194] Financial pressures do, however, mean that this is likely to be the exception rather than the norm.

With priority need

10.83 Where the authority is satisfied that the applicant does have a priority need[195] and is not satisfied that the applicant became homeless intentionally,[196] the duty comes to an end 56 days following the day the authority was first satisfied that the applicant was homeless and eligible.[197] The duty is normally followed by the principal housing duty under HA 1996 s193.[198]

10.84 The authority may also give notice bringing the duty to an end when it is satisfied that any one of certain circumstances is applicable.[199] The circumstances are as follows:[200]

a) the applicant both has suitable accommodation which is available for the applicant's occupation and there is a reasonable prospect of him or her having suitable accommodation[201] available for at least six months[202] from the date of the notice;

193 HA 1996 s189B(5)–(7).

194 Cf HA 1996 s189B(4), applicable where there is a priority need: para 10.83. While it may at first blush seem odd that the duty is brought to an end where there *is* a priority need (and no intentionality), and *not* where there is no priority need, it is explained by the fact that in such circumstances, other, more substantial, duties of course come into play.

195 Chapter 5.

196 Chapter 6.

197 HA 1996 s189B(4), unless disapplied by s193A (refusal of final accommodation offer or final Part 6 offer): s193(1A).

198 HA 1996 s193(1) unless disapplied by s193A (refusal of final accommodation offer or final Part 6 offer): s193(1A) (para 10.119).

199 HA 1996 s189B(5). The notice must specify which of the circumstances applies and inform the applicant of his or her right to a review and of the time within which a review must be sought: HA 1996 s189B(6).

200 HA 1996 s189B(7).

201 It need not be the same accommodation.

202 Or such longer period not exceeding 12 months as may be prescribed.

b) the authority has complied with the duty to take reasonable steps and the period of 56 days beginning with the day that the authority is first satisfied that the applicant was homeless and eligible has ended (whether or not he or she has secured accommodation);
c) the applicant has refused an offer of suitable accommodation and, on the date of refusal, there was a reasonable prospect that suitable accommodation would be available for occupation by the applicant for at least six months or such longer period[203] as may be prescribed;
d) the applicant has become homeless intentionally from any accommodation that has been made available to him or her as a result of the authority's exercise of its functions under this duty;
e) the applicant is no longer eligible for assistance; or
f) the applicant has withdrawn the application for accommodation or assistance in obtaining it.

Additional circumstances

10.85 Additionally, the duty can be brought to an end under:

a) HA 1996 s193A – refusal of final offer (see para 10.264); or
b) HA 1996 s193B – deliberate and unreasonable refusal to co-operate (see paras 10.88–10.91),[204]

although – by HA 1996 s193C – the latter will not end a right to accommodation for an applicant who is homeless, eligible, in priority need and not homeless intentionally (para 10.91)[205] who will continue to enjoy the benefit of the principal housing duty in section 193(1).[206]

Refusal of final offer

10.86 The first of these additional circumstances in which the initial help duty can be brought to an end is if the applicant, having been informed of the consequences of refusal and of his or her right to request a review of the suitability of the accommodation,[207] refuses

203 Not exceeding 12 months.

204 HA 1996 s189B(9). This is also applicable to termination of the duty to those who are threatened with homelessness intentionally (paras 10.67–10.71): HA 1996 s195(1).

205 HA 1996 s193C(3), (4).

206 HA 1996 s193(1).

207 Paras 9.194–9.199.

either a final accommodation offer,[208] or a final Part 6[209] offer.[210] If it is brought to an end on this basis, the principal housing duty in HA 1996 s193 (paras 10.118–10.263) does not apply.[211]

10.87 The authority cannot approve a final accommodation offer or make a final Part 6 offer unless it is satisfied that it is suitable for the applicant;[212] nor can it approve or make such an offer if the applicant is under contractual or other obligations in respect of his or her existing accommodation, which he or she is not able to bring to an end before he or she would have to take up the offer.[213] The provisions are modelled on, and similar to, those which may determine that a section 193 duty has ceased.[214]

Deliberate and unreasonable refusal to co-operate

10.88 The second of the additional circumstances in which the initial help duty can be brought to an end – which can also bring to an end the new duty to those threatened with homelessness (paras 10.67–10.75) – arises where the authority gives notice to an applicant that it considers that the applicant has deliberately and unreasonably refused to take any step that he or she agreed to take or that was recorded by the authority under the assessment and plan provisions considered above (paras 10.58–10.66).[215]

10.89 The refusal must be both deliberate and unreasonable. When deciding whether a refusal is unreasonable, the authority must have regard to the particular circumstances and needs of the applicant (whether identified in its assessment of his or her case or not).[216]

208 This is an offer of an assured shorthold tenancy made by a private landlord – including a private registered provider of social housing (England) or a registered social landlord (Wales) – in relation to any accommodation which is, or may become, available for the applicant's occupation, made, with the approval of the authority, in pursuance of arrangements made by the authority in discharge of the initial help duty, which is a fixed term tenancy for a period of at least six months: HA 1996 s193A(4).

209 This is an offer of accommodation under Part 6 made in writing in discharge of the authority's initial help duty, which states that it is a final offer for that purpose: HA 1996 s193A(5).

210 HA 1996 s193A(1), (2).

211 HA 1996 s193A(3).

212 HA 1996 s193A(6).

213 HA 1996 s193A(7).

214 See paras 10.118–10.263.

215 HA 1996 s193B(1), (2).

216 HA 1996 s193B(6).

10.90 The notice must explain why the authority is giving it and its effect, and inform the applicant that he or she has a right to request a review[217] of the decision to give the notice and of the time within which such a request must be made.[218] No notice may be given without a prior 'relevant warning' notice[219] and a reasonable period[220] has elapsed since it was given.[221] The decision to give the notice must be made by an officer of the authority and authorised by a second officer who was not involved in the decision to give the notice and who is at least as senior as the person who made the decision to serve the notice.[222]

10.91 If either duty[223] is brought to an end on this basis,[224] then while the principal housing duty in HA 1996 s193 (paras 10.118–10.263) will not apply,[225] the homeless who are eligible and in priority need but not homeless intentionally will be entitled to accommodation under section 193C (para 10.267).[226] This is considered below, alongside other duties to the unintentionally homeless in priority need.[227] Otherwise, the duty under s193 is still owed.[228]

Wales

Overview

10.92 If an authority is satisfied that an applicant is homeless and eligible for assistance, whether or not he or she has a priority need or may be homeless intentionally, it must help to secure that accommodation is

217 See paras 9.186–9.199.

218 HA 1996 s193B(3).

219 This is a notice given by the authority after the refusal to take the agreed or recorded step, which warns the applicant that, if he or she continues deliberately and unreasonably to refuse to take the step after receiving the notice, the authority intends to give the notice which will bring the duty to an end, and which explains the consequences of that notice: HA 1996 s193B(5).

220 This is not defined.

221 HA 1996 s193B(4).

222 Homelessness (Review Procedure etc) Regulations 2018 SI No 223 reg 3. The process adopted in connection with notices under HA 1996 s193B(2) must be in writing, kept under review and comply with the requirements of reg 3: reg 2.

223 HA 1996 ss189B(2), 195(2).

224 Which will be the effect of a notice which fulfils all its requirements: HA 1996 s193C(1), (2).

225 HA 1996 s193C(3).

226 HA 1996 s193C(4).

227 See para 10.118.

228 HA 1996 s193(1).

available for him or her.[229] The duty does not apply if the authority refers the application to another local housing authority[230] in England or Wales.[231]

10.93 The duty requires the authority to take reasonable steps to help, having regard to (among other things) the need to make the best use of its resources.[232] It does not require the authority to offer accommodation, whether under Part 6 or otherwise.[233]

When the duty comes to an end

10.94 This duty lasts for 56 days,[234] although the authority can decide on a shorter period if reasonable steps to secure accommodation for the applicant have been taken.[235]

10.95 The duty will come to an end before the end of that period if one of the following occurs:

a) the authority is satisfied that the applicant has suitable accommodation available for occupation, which accommodation is likely to be available for occupation by the applicant for a period of at least six months;[236]
b) the applicant refuses an offer of accommodation from any person, having been notified in writing of the possible consequences of refusal or acceptance of the offer, provided that the authority is satisfied that the accommodation was suitable for the applicant and was likely to be available for at least the next six months;[237]
c) the applicant ceases to be eligible;[238]
d) a mistake of fact led the authority to notify the applicant that it owed him or her a duty to help to secure accommodation for the applicant;[239]
e) the applicant has withdrawn the application;[240]

229 H(W)A 2014 s73(1).
230 H(W)A 2014 s73(2).
231 H(W)A 2014 s18(1).
232 H(W)A 2014 s65(a).
233 H(W)A 2014 s65(b)–(c).
234 H(W)A 2014 s74(2).
235 H(W)A 2014 s74(3).
236 H(W)A 2014 s74(4).
237 H(W)A 2014 s74(5).
238 H(W)A 2014 s79(2).
239 H(W)A 2014 s79(3).
240 H(W)A 2014 s79(4).

f) the applicant is unreasonably failing to co-operate with the authority.[241]

Unreasonable failure to co-operate

10.96 While HA 1996 as amended by HRA 2017 contains detailed provisions governing the refusal of an applicant in England to co-operate (paras 10.88–10.91), H(W)A 2014 has no equivalent. The Welsh Code of Guidance suggests that authorities should satisfy themselves that the applicant is not failing to co-operate because he or she is vulnerable, has an unmet support need or has difficulty communicating and recommends a 'minded to' letter be sent before discharging any duty.[242]

Other duties to the intentionally homeless

England

Advice and assistance

10.97 Since the HRA 2017 came into force,[243] the long-standing duty to provide advice and assistance formerly applicable where an applicant was either not in priority need, or else in priority need but was homeless intentionally,[244] now *only* applies to the intentionally homeless in priority need, and then only once the duty under HA 1996 s189B(2) (initial help duty: paras 10.76–10.96) has come to an end (on whatever ground). When discharging it, an authority must have regard to its assessment under HA 1996 s189A (paras 10.58–10.66).[245]

Accommodation

10.98 This class of applicant benefits from the additional duty imposed on an authority to secure that suitable[246] accommodation is made

241 H(W)A 2014 s79(5).

242 Paras 15.86–15.89. The English Code suggests that an authority 'should take into account any particular difficulties that the applicant may have in managing communications when considering if failure to cooperate is deliberate and unreasonable': para 14.52.

243 3 April 2018: Homelessness Reduction Act 2017 (Commencement and Transitional and Savings Provisions) Regulations 2018 SI No 167 reg 3, only applicable to applications made on or after that date – see reg 4.

244 HA 1996 ss190(2), 192(2).

245 HA 1996 s190(4).

246 See HA 1996 ss205, 206.

available for the applicant's occupation[247] – which means for the occupation of the applicant and of any person who might reasonably be expected to reside with him or her – 'for such period as' the authority considers 'will give him a reasonable opportunity of himself securing accommodation for his occupation'.[248]

10.99 The observations on quality[249] and termination made in relation to interim accommodation (paras 10.37–10.40) also apply to accommodation provided under this power, as do those on availability (para 10.27), payment (para 10.31), security (paras 10.33–10.36), exclusion from PEA 1977 (para 10.47) and defences on eviction (para 10.47). How accommodation may be provided,[250] suitability[251] and the constraints on out-of-area placements[252] (which are all considered below in relation to the principal duty) also apply to discharge under this section.

10.100 This duty has given rise to a number of problems. The first question is from when does time run when determining what comprises a reasonable opportunity. Whether or not an applicant seeks internal review does not affect this issue: time runs from the date of the decision regardless of whether an internal review is sought: *Conville*.[253]

10.101 In *Dyson*,[254] the applicant was told on 21 May that she would be provided with one month's accommodation from 25 May (the date when her homelessness would actually occur). This decision appears to have been taken by an official, but appears to have required ratification by a committee. The time was subsequently extended to 6 July, but it was not until 3 July that committee ratification was communicated to the applicant. Time was nonetheless held to run from the notification by the official, of which the letter of 3 July was mere confirmation.

10.102 In *de Falco*,[255] only four days had been allowed between notification of decision and the expiry of what is now HA 1996 s188 accommodation. The Master of the Rolls thought that this period was probably adequate, having regard to several weeks in accommoda-

247 HA 1996 s176.
248 HA 1996 s190(2)(a).
249 See also paras 10.37–10.40.
250 See para 10.135.
251 See paras 10.162–10.204.
252 See paras 10.147–10.162.
253 *R (Conville) v Richmond upon Thames LBC* [2005] EWHC 1430 (Admin), [2006] HLR 1, not appealed on this point see [2006] EWCA Civ 718, [2006] HLR 45.
254 *Dyson v Kerrier DC* [1980] 1 WLR 120, CA.
255 *de Falco, Silvestri v Crawley BC* [1980] QB 460, CA.

tion provided by the authority prior to its decision. He was, however, also influenced by the time during which the applicants had been accommodated between the issue of proceedings and the hearing before the Court of Appeal. As *de Falco* was the hearing of an interlocutory appeal for an interlocutory injunction to house until trial, he treated that matter as conclusive as a matter of the court's discretion.

10.103 The same point influenced Bridge LJ, although he was otherwise of the view that time prior to communication of the local authority's decision was irrelevant so that only time since that decision was communicated could count. As the purpose of the provisions is to give the applicant time to find somewhere else to live once it has been decided that the authority need not provide full assistance, this view seems preferable.[256]

10.104 The courts may be less generous towards an applicant who lives with another person who has previously been found homeless intentionally, and who has already enjoyed a period of HA 1996 s190(2)(a) accommodation, although such a person may indeed reapply and it seems to be an irresistible inference from *Lewis*[257] and the other cases on this point[258] that such a person will then be entitled to a new period of section 190(2)(a) accommodation; it is strongly arguable that he or she can and should benefit from the reasoning of Bridge LJ in *de Falco*.

10.105 Some reconciliation of merits and principle may be found in the extent of acquiescence or participation in the act which results in the finding of intentionality and therefore the extent to which an adverse finding should have been anticipated.

10.106 In *Smith v Bristol City Council*,[259] a county court judge held that, even where a substantial period of warning had been given to the applicant, the authority was still obliged to give more time:

> I cannot accept that 'no time' can in any circumstances be a reasonable period . . . [A] reasonable time must be given to the applicant after she actually becomes homeless . . .

256 Sir David Cairns thought that the decision was unreviewable, although this proposition does not find any support elsewhere and is wholly out of line with a more modern approach in public law.

257 *R v North Devon DC ex p Lewis* [1981] 1 WLR 328, QBD.

258 See paras 6.11–6.27. See also *R (Savage) v Hillingdon LBC* [2010] EWHC 88 (Admin), [2010] JHL D44, where it was held that it was for the authority to determine what period of time afforded a reasonable opportunity of securing accommodation.

259 December 1981 *LAG Bulletin* 287, CC.

10.107 When an authority decides for how long it should secure that accommodation is available so as to give an applicant a reasonable opportunity of securing accommodation for himself or herself, pursuant to its duty under HA 1996 s190(2)(a), it may not have regard to considerations peculiar to itself, ie the extent of its resources and other demands.[260] While it is for the authority to decide what is a reasonable opportunity, subject to the usual principles of intervention,[261] what is reasonable for these purposes is to be assessed by reference to the particular needs and circumstances of the applicant, including the availability of other accommodation; if the applicant is not making reasonable efforts to pursue other possibilities, however, that will be a strong indication that he or she should not be given more time; and, even if the applicant makes reasonable efforts, a moment will normally be reached when time will expire if those possibilities have not come to fruition; the opportunity is no more than that – it cannot be converted into a duty to provide long-term accommodation.[262]

10.108 The English Code no longer suggests any particular time frame:[263]

> A few weeks may provide the applicant with a reasonable opportunity to secure accommodation for him or herself. However, some applicants might require longer, and others, particularly where the housing authority provides pro-active and effective advice and assistance, might require less time.[264]

10.109 It continues that:

> . . . authorities will need to take into account (a) the particular needs and circumstances of the applicant and the resources available to them to secure accommodation . . . (b) the housing circumstances in the local area and the length of time it might reasonably take to secure accommodation . . . (c) arrangements that have already been made by the applicant which are likely to be successful within a reasonable timescale.[265]

10.110 This much is clear: an applicant's circumstances must be individually considered, and if it can be shown that the time allowed has been reached without regard to them or was such a short period that no

260 *R (Conville) v Richmond upon Thames LBC* [2006] EWCA Civ 718, [2006] HLR 45.

261 See chapter 12.

262 *R (Conville) v Richmond upon Thames LBC*, above.

263 Previous editions of the Code referred to 28 days being adequate in most cases.

264 English Code of Guidance para 15.14; Welsh Code paras 9.27, 17.45–17.46.

265 English Code of Guidance para 15.15; Welsh Code paras 9.27, 17.45–17.46.

authority could have considered that it gave the applicant a reasonable opportunity to find somewhere for himself or herself, the courts will order sufficient time.[266]

10.111 It would seem from *Monaf*[267] that – at least where the housing authority is also a social services authority – the authority ought to have regard to its duties under the CA 1989 s20(1)[268] when determining this period.[269] Prior to this stage, the housing authority should in any event have sought the applicant's consent to refer the case to the social services authority,[270] so that the latter authority can consider exercise of its powers under the CA 1989.[271]

10.112 A further issue is raised by 'policies'. In particular, the frequency with which all kinds of applicants receive identical offers of 28 days' accommodation suggests that many authorities operate a policy under this provision.[272] If an inflexible policy can be proven, it can be set aside.[273] If, however, the 28-day rule is merely a guideline, genuinely reconsidered in each case, it will be valid.

Wales

10.113 In Wales, the position is somewhat different. Where the authority decides that a person is eligible for assistance, homeless and in priority need, it has a duty to secure that accommodation is made available for his or her occupation (unless it refers the applicant to another authority under the local connection provisions of the legislation).[274]

266 *Lally v Kensington and Chelsea RLBC* (1980) *Times* 27 March, ChD.

267 *R v Tower Hamlets LBC ex p Monaf* (1988) 20 HLR 529, CA.

268 See paras 13.67–13.83.

269 Moreover, local authorities must now have regard 'to the need to safeguard and promote the welfare of children' when discharging their functions: CA 2004 s11 (England); s28 (Wales). This includes functions under HA 1996 Part 7: *Huzrat v Hounslow LBC* [2013] EWCA Civ 1865, [2014] HLR 17. See also *Nzolameso v Westminster City Council* [2015] UKSC 22, [2015] HLR 22: when considering whether accommodation is suitable for a family, the authority must identify the principal needs of the children both individually and collectively when making the decision.

270 See further HA 1996 s213A; and para 13.84.

271 See further paras 13.58–13.107.

272 In *Birmingham City Council v Ali; Moran v Manchester City Council (Secretary of State for Communities and Local Government and another intervening)* [2009] UKHL 36, [2009] 1 WLR 1506 at [17], Baroness Hale commented: 'We are told that up to six weeks is usually thought enough for this although there is no statutory limit.'

273 See paras 12.54–12.55.

274 H(W)A 2014 s75(1), (2); see chapter 7.

10.114 When discharging this duty, however, the authority has power to consider whether or not the applicant became homeless intentionally.[275]

10.115 If the authority decides to exercise that power, the principal duty to accommodate under H(W)A 2014 s75[276] will arise either if the authority is not satisfied that the applicant is homeless intentionally or if the applicant is:

a) a pregnant woman or a person with whom she resides or might reasonably be expected to reside;
b) a person with whom a dependent child resides or might reasonably be expected to reside;
c) a person who had not attained the age of 21 when the application was made or a person with whom such a person resides or might reasonably be expected to reside; or
d) a person who had attained the age of 21, but not the age of 25, when the application was made and who was looked after, accommodated or fostered at any time while under the age of 18, or a person with whom such a person resides or might reasonably be expected to reside.[277]

10.116 In these circumstances, the full duty will arise if:

a) the applicant has no suitable accommodation available for occupation, or suitable accommodation which it is not likely will be available for occupation for at least six months starting on the day on which the applicant is notified[278] that the full duty will not apply;
b) the applicant is eligible for help and has a priority need for accommodation; and
c) the authority has not previously secured an offer of accommodation to the applicant under these provisions following a previous application for help, at any time within the period of five years before the day on which the applicant was notified[279] that a duty was owed to him or her under them.[280]

275 H(W)A 2014 s78; see para 6.3.

276 Paras 10.118–10.263.

277 H(W)A 2014 s75(3).

278 Under H(W)A 2014 s84.

279 The applicant is to be treated as notified on the day the notice is sent or first made available for collection: H(W)A 2014 s75(4).

280 H(W)A 2014 s75(3).

10.117 If the full duty does not arise for any of these reasons, or because the applicant is not within the H(W)A 2014 s75(3) class,[281] then the initial duty to help[282] is limited to 56 days.[283]

Other duties towards the unintentionally homeless in priority need

Introduction

10.118 Duties towards those whom the authority is satisfied are eligible, homeless, in priority need and not intentionally homeless, are governed by HA 1996 s193 and H(W)A 2014 s75. Since the HRA 2017 came into force in England,[284] the HA 1996 s193 duty does not arise until the authority's duty under HA 1996 s189B(2) (initial help duty: paras 10.76–10.96) has come to an end.[285] Likewise, in Wales, the H(W)A 2014 s75 duty does not arise until the initial help duty in H(W)A 2014 s73 duty has come to an end.[286]

10.119 In England, the HA 1996 s193 duty does not arise at all, however, if it has been disapplied by HA 1996 s193A(3) (refusal of final offer: para 10.86) or if the authority has given notice to the applicant under section 193B(2) (deliberate and unreasonable refusal to co-operate: paras 10.88–10.91),[287] although in the latter case it is replaced by duties under s193C (paras 10.267–10.272).

10.120 In Wales, the H(W)A 2014 s75 duty can only arise where the section 73 duty has come to an end and the applicant is eligible, in priority need, not intentionally homeless[288] and does not have suitable accommodation available for his or her occupation or, if he or she does have such accommodation, it is not likely that it will be available for at least six months: accordingly, if the section 73 duty has come to an end because the applicant accepted other accommodation or

281 See paras 10.113–10.117.

282 See paras 10.92–10.95.

283 H(W)A 2014 s74(2).

284 3 April 2018: Homelessness Reduction Act 2017 (Commencement and Transitional and Savings Provisions) Regulations 2018 SI No 167 reg 3, only applicable to applications made and reviews sought on or after that date – see reg 4.

285 HA 1996 s193(1).

286 H(W)A 2014 s75(1).

287 HA 1996 s193(1A).

288 Assuming the authority is applying the intentionality provisions: H(W)A 2014 ss77, 78. See also H(W)A 2014 s75(3).

refused an offer or unreasonably refused to co-operate with the authority, the section 75 duty will not be owed.[289]

Housing Act 1996 s193 and Housing (Wales) Act 2014 s75

Overview

10.121 Under HA 1996 s193, the duty towards the unintentionally homeless is to secure that accommodation is available for occupation by the applicant until the duty ceases in accordance with the sections;[290] it is the principal – or 'highest' – duty under the Acts, sometimes referred to as permanent or indefinite, although it will be seen that neither description is wholly accurate; in particular, housing may be provided under HA 1996 s193(2) pending a final arrangement, which may continue for years.

10.122 The observations on availability (para 10.27), payment (paras 10.31–10.32) and security (paras 10.33–10.36) made in relation to interim accommodation (paras 10.11–10.48) in principle also apply to accommodation provided under this power, save that there is no exclusion from assured security under HA 1996 s209 for accommodation so provided, although as it is likely to be provided on a shorthold basis[291] it is not required.

10.123 Whether exclusion from PEA 1977 (para 10.47) applies once the principal duty is owed, has been held to be a question of fact in each case.[292] In *Bucknall*, the applicant was provided with temporary accommodation under HA 1996 s188; when the authority subsequently decided that it owed her the section 193(2) duty, it said that she should continue to occupy the sane accommodation pending identification of a suitable property. The authority subsequently offered her a property which she rejected; it served notice to quit which did not comply with the requirements of the PEA 1977.[293] As she had been told that she should occupy the accommodation for an

289 H(W)A 2014 s75(1).

290 HA 1996 s193(2) and (3); s193(3) was amended by the Homelessness Act 2002 to remove the restriction on the duty to a period of two years. In Wales, see H(W)A 2014 ss75 and 76; as in England, there is no 'two-year' restriction.

291 See *Manual of housing law*, para 1.246.

292 *Bucknall v Dacorum BC* [2017] EWHC 2094 (QB), [2017] HLR 40.

293 Section 5, and the Notices to Quit etc (Prescribed Information) Regulations 1988 SI No 2201: see *Manual of housing law*, para 2.58.

indefinite period, it was held that the PEA 1977 applied and that, as the notice was invalid, her tenancy had not been terminated.

10.124 This conclusion is somewhat narrower than might be thought. In *R (ZH and CN) v Lewisham LBC*,[294] Lady Hale referred to the 'generally accepted view that the protection of section 3 of the 1977 Act will apply once the local authority have accepted that they owe the family the "full housing duty"',[295] presumably picking up the local authorities' submission that the 'licences were expressly limited to the period to be taken to provide a decision'[296] and the secretary of state's submission that the premises were 'temporary accommodation while the council made inquiries'.[297]

10.125 Other observations on defences on eviction (para 10.47) will apply should an authority seek to evict an applicant while he or she is still being housed under HA 1996 Part 7 or H(W)A 2014 Part 2.

10.126 A number of issues fall to be considered:

a) postponement of the duty;
b) means of discharge;
c) out-of-area placements;
d) suitability of accommodation;
e) cessation of duty.

Postponement of the duty

10.127 Discharge of the duty may not be postponed for any extraneous reason: see *Khalique*,[298] where the authority sought to postpone making an offer of accommodation pending a reduction in arrears of rent owed by the applicant.[299] This does not mean that the applicant's arrears may not be taken into account when deciding whether or not to make an HA 1996 Part 6 allocation,[300] which is governed by its own provisions.[301]

10.128 There are, however, apparently conflicting decisions as to whether the duty under HA 1996 s193 to secure suitable accommodation may be postponed at all, although these have tended to conflate the

294 [2014] UKSC 62, [2015] AC 1259, [2015] HLR 6.
295 At [165].
296 At 1287F.
297 At 1288D. See also Lord Hodge at [16] and [45].
298 *R v Tower Hamlets LBC ex p Khalique* (1994) 26 HLR 517, QBD.
299 See also *R v Newham LBC ex p Miah* (1995) 28 HLR 279, QBD.
300 Both *Khalique* and *Miah* preceded HA 1996: accordingly, discharge and offer of permanent accommodation were commonly synonymous. The proposition in the text applies the principle in *Khalique* to the provisions post-1996.
301 See paras 11.12–11.74.

provision of suitable accommodation on a temporary basis with an allocation or other final offer of suitable accommodation.

10.129 In *Anderson*,[302] the authority had failed to make any suitable offers to the applicant in 16 months after accepting that she was homeless because of overcrowding in her current accommodation. A number of offers of accommodation had been made, but it was accepted by the authority that these had been reasonably refused. One offer remained outstanding and subject to review. Moses J said:[303]

> The statutory scheme under the Housing Act shows that there is no time limit within which a housing authority is obliged under the statute to comply with a duty to secure available accommodation for those who fall within section 193 . . . The provisions within the Housing Act, which require housing authorities to put in place an allocations policy and to comply with that policy, are contained in Part 6 of the Housing Act. They demonstrate that there will be those to whom a duty is owed under section 193 of the Act who will not be housed immediately or within any particular time-limit. There may be those in respect of whom, the housing authority will be under an obligation, in accordance with their allocations policy, to give a greater priority.

10.130 In *Sembi*,[304] the applicant, a woman of 52 who was confined to a wheelchair, was accepted as homeless and offered accommodation in a nursing home occupied mainly by the elderly and terminally ill. The authority accepted that the nursing home was not suitable in the long term, but considered it suitable as temporary accommodation. The judge held that there had been no failure by the authority to discharge its duty under HA 1996 s193. Jowitt J cited the passage from *Anderson* with approval.

10.131 In *Begum*,[305] however, Collins J held that duties under the HA 1996 – whether under section 193 or otherwise[306] – could not

302 *R v Southwark LBC ex p Anderson* (1998) 32 HLR 96, QBD.

303 *R v Southwark LBC ex p Anderson* (1998) 32 HLR 96 at 98, QBD.

304 *R v Merton LBC ex p Sembi* (1999) 32 HLR 439, QBD.

305 *R v Newham LBC ex p Begum* (1999) 32 HLR 808, QBD. See also *R (Khan) v Newham LBC* [2001] EWHC (Admin) 589, [2001] JHL D90, where Newham LBC conceded that it was in breach of the duty (through the provision of inadequate bed and breakfast-type accommodation), and a mandatory order requiring the authority to provide suitable accommodation within two months was made. Cf *Begum v Tower Hamlets LBC* [2002] EWHC 633 (Admin), [2002] JHL D58, where, again, the authority acknowledged that the accommodation was unsuitable but the court refused to make a mandatory order in the absence of any evidence of the time within which suitable accommodation could be provided.

306 Ie, also under HA 1996 ss188, 190, 200.

be deferred. Accordingly, the authority could not defer providing accommodation which was suitable for the applicant and his family, including for the applicant's mother who used a wheelchair. He accepted that where there were great difficulties in finding suitable accommodation, a court would not enforce the duty unreasonably, for example within a few days, but only if the authority was doing all that it could to comply with it.[307]

10.132 This conflict has in practice now been overtaken by *Ali* and *Moran*,[308] where a clear distinction was drawn between the duty to secure that suitable accommodation is available for a homeless family under HA 1996 s193(2) and allocation under Part 6. Thus, suitability for the purpose of section 193(2) does not imply permanence or security of tenure; there are degrees of suitability and what is suitable in the short term may not be suitable for a longer period; when the time comes that the applicant cannot continue to occupy his or her current accommodation for another night, the authority must act immediately.[309] Accordingly, Birmingham County Council could decide that applicants were homeless even though they could remain in their current accommodation for a while.[310]

10.133 When considering the question whether a local housing authority has left an applicant in accommodation which it would not be reasonable for him or her to continue to occupy for too long a period, the question is primarily one for the authority; a court should normally be slow to accept that the authority has left an applicant in unsatisfactory accommodation for too long; in resolving this issue it is necessary to take account of the severe constraints on budgets and personnel, and the limited housing stock.[311]

10.134 The decision allows an authority to conclude that an applicant is already homeless without necessarily providing fresh accommodation at once, on the basis that current accommodation is suitable in the short term: hence, no question of postponement of duty arises.

307 The authority had not, however, done all that it could, because it had adopted a policy not to consider its own stock to discharge its duty under HA 1996 s193.

308 *Birmingham City Council v Ali; Moran v Manchester City Council (Secretary of State for Communities and Local Government and another intervening)* [2009] UKHL 36, [2009] 1 WLR 1506.

309 At [47].

310 At [48].

311 At [50].

Means of discharge

10.135 By HA 1996 s206 or H(W)A 2014 s76, a local authority may discharge its duty under section 193 in one of three ways:[312]

a) by securing that suitable accommodation provided by it is available for the applicant;
b) by securing that the applicant obtains suitable accommodation from some other person; or
c) by giving the applicant such advice and assistance as will secure that suitable accommodation is available from some other person.

10.136 As a matter of language, and construction, HA 1996 s206 is exhaustive of the means of providing accommodation, and so it cannot be used – even in conjunction with Local Government Act 1972 s111 – to guarantee the provision of accommodation by another.[313]

10.137 Since the HRA 2017 came into force in England,[314] bringing with it the new initial help duty (paras 10.76–10.96) and new duties to those in priority need (para 10.58), HA 1996 s206 only applies where the authority decides to discharge those duties by securing that accommodation is available for an applicant's accommodation.[315]

Resources

10.138 The issue of resources is not irrelevant to how an authority decides to discharge its duty. Thus, if an applicant has a particular and perhaps unusual need, the authority can – in deciding whether to meet it by purchasing a property on the open market – take into account the cost of doing so.[316]

312 HA 1996 s206(1); H(W)A 2014 ss64, 76.

313 *Crédit Suisse v Waltham Forest LBC* (1996) 29 HLR 115, CA. It may, however, be that the general power of competence in LA 2011 s1, could be used, although this depends on construction of the limits on that power in LA 2011 s2. See paras 13.116–13.120.

314 3 April 2018: Homelessness Reduction Act 2017 (Commencement and Transitional and Savings Provisions) Regulations 2018 SI No 167 reg 3, only applicable to applications made and reviews sought on or after that date – see reg 4.

315 HA 1996 s205(3).

316 *R v Lambeth LBC ex p Ekpo-Wedderman* (1999) 31 HLR 498, QBD. See also *R v Lambeth LBC ex p A1* (1997) 30 HLR 933, CA, where the homeless applicant's challenge to a decision of the authority not to exercise its powers under HA 1985 ss9 and 17 to add to its stock failed.

10.139 In *Calgin*,[317] the cost of providing accommodation was likewise held to be a factor that the authority could take into account in deciding how to discharge its duty.

10.140 In *Sheridan v Basildon BC*,[318] the applicants were travellers living at unauthorised sites in Basildon's area; they applied under HA 1996 Part 7; the authority accepted that they were owed the full housing duty under HA 1996 s193(2). Having decided that there were no suitable traveller sites in their area, Basildon offered them tenancies of conventional properties, which were refused, relying, inter alia, on a regional planning strategy which had recommended that the authority provide further pitches, so that Basildon ought to be required to purchase land to be used as a traveller site, an argument that failed: while it might be said that, as a matter of planning policy, Basildon should have provided suitable sites, it was unrealistic to expect a HA 1996 s202 review to consider such matters; planning policy was outside the expertise of housing officers and Parliament could not have intended such matters to fall within the scope of a section 202 review; nor was there any basis for requiring Basildon to purchase land; the section 193 duty was to be discharged within the existing resources of the authority.

Advice and assistance

10.141 Advice and assistance such that the applicant secures accommodation from another under HA 1996 s206(1)(c) or H(W)A 2014 s64 seems wide enough to cover advice and assistance leading to house purchase by an applicant who is financially able to undertake it.[319] It may also cover the provision of mediation designed to ensure that a 16- or 17-year-old applicant returns to live in his or her family home.[320]

Discharge through another

10.142 The authority may discharge the duty by securing an assured shorthold tenancy from a private sector landlord.[321]

317 *R (Calgin) v Enfield LBC* [2005] EWHC 1716 (Admin), [2006] HLR 4.

318 [2012] EWCA Civ 335, [2012] HLR 29. See also *Slattery v Basildon BC* [2014] EWCA Civ 30, [2014] HLR 16, following *Sheridan*.

319 See English Code of Guidance para 3.7(k), including through shared equity or similar schemes for low cost home ownership.. There is no equivalent in the Welsh Code.

320 See *Robinson v Hammersmith and Fulham LBC* [2006] EWCA Civ 1122, [2007] HLR 7 at [39].

321 HA 1996 s193(7AC); H(W)A 2014 s76(2)(b).

10.143 The provision of successful mediation which enables a 16- or 17-year-old applicant to return to live in the family home may be considered to secure 'accommodation from some other person'.[322]

10.144 Some other person may be a person or body – or an authority – abroad. In *Browne,*[323] a woman with no local connection with Bristol, and no local connection with the area of any other housing authority in England, Wales or Scotland, was offered assistance to return to her home town of Tralee, Ireland, where the authorities were prepared to ensure that she was housed. In order to sustain its decision, Bristol CC did not need to know the exact details of the accommodation to be made available to her.[324]

10.145 The arrangement was, however, only appropriate once it was established by Bristol CC that, in its opinion, the woman ran no risk of domestic violence in Tralee. It would seem from the report that had there been a risk of domestic violence, the arrangement would not have been acceptable, for otherwise Bristol CC would have managed to circumvent the spirit of the local connection provisions,[325] even though, not being a referral to another authority in the UK, its letter did not apply.

Discharge by authority

10.146 Although an authority may now use its own stock without limit of time to house an applicant under HA 1996 Part 7 or H(W)A 2014 Part 2,[326] applicants do not become secure tenants, unless and until so notified.[327]

Out-of-area placements

10.147 Authorities have not uncommonly sought to discharge duties by placing applicants in the area of another authority. In the early case of *Wyness v Poole BC,*[328] a county court rejected an attempt to house

322 See *Robinson v Hammersmith and Fulham LBC* [2006] EWCA Civ 1122 at [39].

323 *R v Bristol City Council ex p Browne* [1979] 1 WLR 1437, DC.

324 The decision preceded the introduction of the requirement of suitability. Today, an authority would be bound to take steps to satisfy itself about suitability, even if only by appropriate enquiries – this accords with the approach taken in *Browne* to domestic violence: see text.

325 See para 7.51.

326 Cf HA 1996 s207, which was repealed by the Homelessness Act 2002.

327 HA 1985 Sch 1 para 4, as amended by H(W)A 2014 Sch 3 para 1. Notification that the tenancy is to be secure is an allocation under Part 6 (see para 11.15).

328 July 1979 *LAG Bulletin* 166, CC.

an applicant in the area of another authority, when the local connection provisions were inapplicable because of an employment connection, because living in the area of that other authority would have meant that the employment would have to be given up. The court held that no reasonable authority could so discharge the duty.[329]

10.148 In *Parr v Wyre BC*,[330] an authority sought to discharge its duty by securing an offer of accommodation in Birmingham, an area with which the applicants had no connection at all. There were no details available of the accommodation to be provided, and the applicants had a limited time in which to accept. While it was common ground that discharge could be in another area, the Court of Appeal, distinguishing *Browne*,[331] did not uphold the offer: the offer had to be of 'appropriate accommodation', in terms both of size of family and of area. In *Puhlhofer*,[332] however, the House of Lords rejected introduction of the qualification 'appropriate'.[333]

10.149 HA 1996 s208 introduced a new requirement that 'So far as reasonably practicable', the authority must secure accommodation in its own area:[334] this is as applicable to temporary accommodation as it is to permanent, and is particularly pertinent where the authority provide accommodation under HA 1996 s193(2) pending a final offer.

10.150 In *Sacupima*,[335] Latham LJ stated[336] that 'the clear and sensible purpose' of HA 1996 s208 is 'to ensure that so far as possible that authorities do not simply decant homeless persons into areas for which other authorities are responsible'.[337] A failure to consider section 208 was a significant factor in rendering the decision in *Cafun*[338] unlawful.

329 See also paras 10.147–10.161, on out-of-area placements.

330 (1982) 2 HLR 71, CA.

331 Paras 10.144–10.145.

332 *R v Hillingdon LBC ex p Puhlhofer* [1986] AC 484, (1986) 18 HLR 158, HL.

333 See paras 4.7–4.9.

334 HA 1996 s208(1). Note that this requirement is disapplied in England in relation to eligible asylum-seekers, if there is written agreement with another authority that it may place asylum-seekers in its area: HA 1996 s208(1A).

335 *R v Newham LBC ex p Sacupima* (2001) 33 HLR 2, CA.

336 *R v Newham LBC ex p Sacupima*, above, at [31].

337 A failure by one authority to notify another under s208 made a significant contribution to the problems that arose in conducting a needs assessment under CA 1989 s17: see *R (AM) v Havering LBC and Tower Hamlets LBC* [2015] EWHC 1004 (Admin). See para 13.58.

338 See para 10.151.

10.151 In *Cafun*,[339] the authority purported to discharge its duty by referring the applicant to another (neighbouring) authority with which it had a reciprocal agreement. It failed to consider either whether accommodation in the neighbouring area would be suitable for the particular applicant, or the limits on out-of-area placements.[340] The decision was quashed.

10.152 In *Yumsak*,[341] a decision by Enfield LBC, in whose area the applicant had lived for the previous eight years since arriving as an asylum-seeker[342] and where her children were in school, to secure accommodation for an applicant in bed and breakfast accommodation in Birmingham, with which city the applicant had no connection, was held to be irrational and an infringement of the applicant's rights under ECHR Article 8(1).[343]

10.153 In *Calgin*,[344] the authority, a London borough, had a policy of providing accommodation to some homeless households outside its district because of an acute shortage of affordable housing locally. The applicant was offered accommodation in Birmingham and challenged its suitability. On review, the authority decided that the accommodation was suitable and that its policy was not incompatible with HA 1996 s208 because it was not reasonably practical to provide accommodation locally.

10.154 The decision was upheld: it was for the authority to decide whether or not it was reasonably practical to obtain accommodation within its district, an assessment with which the court would only interfere on *Wednesbury* grounds.[345] The decision to use out-of-district accommodation for a small proportion of those seeking accommodation was not *Wednesbury* unreasonable.

10.155 Subsequent to these cases, the Homelessness (Suitability of Accommodation) (England) Order 2012[346] made distance from the authority's area a mandatory consideration. The law was then considered and developed by the Supreme Court in *Nzolameso v*

339 *R (Cafun) v Bromley LBC* 17 October 2000, CO/1481/2000, QBD (unreported).

340 See paras 10.147–10.161.

341 *R (Yumsak) v Enfield LBC* [2002] EWHC 280 (Admin), [2002] JHL D38.

342 Acceptance of her refugee status, bringing an end to her assistance from the social services department of the council, prompted her homelessness application.

343 Paras 12.123–12.125.

344 *R (Calgin) v Enfield LBC* [2005] EWHC 1716 (Admin), [2006] HLR 4.

345 See paras 12.23–12.35, 12.62.

346 SI No 2601.

Westminster City Council,[347] in which it was held that if it is not reasonably practicable to accommodate in its own district, an authority must try to place the household as close as possible to where it had previously been living.

10.156 It was held that authorities should adopt policies relating to the procurement of temporary accommodation, which should be approved by elected members and made available to the public; the policy should explain how accommodation will be allocated and what factors will be taken into account in allocating out-of-borough units.[348]

10.157 *Nzolameso* has, in turn, been incorporated in part into statutory form by the Homelessness (Suitability of Accommodation) (England) Order 2012,[349] and into the English Code.[350] This is considered below,[351] as it is applicable not merely to out-of-area placements but to all placements, ie it also goes to where accommodation is located within an authority's district.

Notification of other authority

10.158 Under HA 1996 s208(2), if the authority accommodates someone in another area, it must – within 14 days of the accommodation being made available to the applicant[352] – give notice to the local housing authority for the area in which that accommodation is situated.

10.159 The notice must state:

a) the name of the applicant;
b) the number and description of the persons residing with the applicant;
c) the address of the accommodation;
d) the date on which it became available; and
e) the function under which it was made available.[353]

10.160 The notification function is designed to allow the notified authority to refer the applicant back under the local connection provisions,[354]

347 *Nzolameso v Westminster City Council* [2015] UKSC 22, [2015] HLR 22.
348 *Nzolameso v Westminster City Council*, above.
349 SI No 2601.
350 English Code paras 17.46–17.61.
351 Paras 10.191–10.198.
352 HA 1996 s208(4); in Wales, see H(W)A 2014 s91(2)–(3).
353 HA 1996 s208(3). For example, under HA 1996 s193, s200 or s190. In Wales, see H(W)A 2014 s91(3).
354 See HA 1996 s198(4); H(W)A 2014 s75.

should a later application be made to it for assistance: as such, it is considered in chapter 7.[355]

10.161 Since the HRA 2017 came into force in England,[356] bringing with it the new initial help duty (paras 10.76–10.96) and new duties to those in priority need, HA 1996 s208 only applies where the authority decides to discharge those duties by securing that accommodation is available for an applicant's accommodation,[357] ie it does not apply where the help proffered suggests that the applicant move to another area to find his or her own accommodation.

Suitability of accommodation

10.162 The duty to provide suitable accommodation is a continuing one; authorities must consider any changes in circumstances which occur while they are discharging their duty: *Zaher*.[358]

10.163 Suitability is statutorily governed by HA 1996 s210 and H(W)A 2014 s59,[359] which identify considerations which must be taken into account – the law governing housing conditions, overcrowding and HMOs.[360] The obligation is to 'have regard to' these provisions of HA 1985 and HA 2004.

10.164 Even now, and save so far as overtaken by the specific grounds of unsuitability in the secondary legislation,[361] the statutory wording is

355 See para 7.66.

356 3 April 2018: Homelessness Reduction Act 2017 (Commencement and Transitional and Savings Provisions) Regulations 2018 SI No 167 reg 3, only applicable to applications made and reviews sought on or after that date – see reg 4.

357 HA 1996 s205(3).

358 *R (Zaher) v Westminster City Council* [2003] EWHC 101 (Admin), [2003] JHL D41.

359 See also para 10.189 where asylum-seekers are concerned.

360 Additionally, in Wales, regard must be had to H(W)A 2014 Part 1 (landlord licencing).

361 In England, there are three such orders: Homelessness (Suitability of Accommodation) (England) Order 2012 SI No 2601; Homelessness (Suitability of Accommodation) (England) Order 2003 SI No 3326; Homelessness (Suitability of Accommodation) Order 1996 SI No 3204. There is also a specific order for accommodation provided for asylum-seekers: Homelessness (Asylum-seekers) (Interim Period) (England) Order 1999 SI No 3126. In Wales, there is only one order: Homelessness (Suitability of Accommodation) (Wales) Order 2015 SI No 1268.

not strong enough to prevent an authority using overcrowded[362] or hazardous property[363] or an HMO which falls below standard, although it will vitiate a decision in relation to which the authority had ignored these considerations; the wording is sufficient, however, to require the authority to justify a decision to use such substandard accommodation,[364] and the secondary legislation will be definitive in some circumstances.[365]

10.165 Older cases accordingly fall to be reconsidered in the light of any statutory (primary and secondary) considerations which may have followed them, but will still be relevant where the statutory considerations are not mandatory[366] and the authority otherwise disclaims compliance on the ground of insufficient accommodation which meets the standard to which they refer. They may even be of some relevance where the considerations are mandatory, so far as they are illustrative of the matters which Parliament has subsequently addressed (and in some cases, which it may be contended which Parliament has sought to redress). They are accordingly considered first, with statutory considerations addressed below, under the heading 'Added considerations' (paras 10.190–10.195).

Physical condition

10.166 In *Campbell*,[367] a cockroach-infested property was not suitable for the applicant, a decision which, on its facts, could still stand. On the other hand, in *Jibril*,[368] an offer of a five-bedroom house with only one toilet – situated in the bathroom – for a family of 12 was held to be within the 'margin of appreciation' of that which an authority could consider suitable.

362 See *Harouki v Kensington and Chelsea RLBC* [2007] EWCA Civ 1000, [2008] HLR 16 in which it was said that the wording of HA 1996 s210 recognises that accommodation is not necessarily unsuitable because it is statutorily overcrowded.

363 The English Code of Guidance para 17.24 recommends that, when determining the suitability of accommodation, authorities should, as a minimum, ensure that all accommodation is free of category 1 hazards under HA 2004 Part 1. See now the Homelessness (Suitability of Accommodation) (England) Order 2012 SI No 2601 art 3 – private sector accommodation which the authority is of the view is not in a reasonable physical condition is not suitable.

364 Consider *Padfield v Minister of Agriculture, Fisheries and Food* [1968] AC 997, HL; see para 12.50.

365 Homelessness (Suitability of Accommodation) (England) Order 2012 SI No 2601 art 3; see paras 10.191–10.198.

366 As last footnote.

367 *R v Lambeth LBC ex p Campbell* (1994) 26 HLR 618, QBD.

368 *R v Camden LBC ex p Jibril* (1997) 29 HLR 785, QBD.

10.167 In *Khan*,[369] the authority conceded that a bed and breakfast property with communal kitchen and bathroom facilities – in which the applicant, his wife and their four children occupied two bedrooms on different floors – was unsuitable. Ordering the authority to find alternative accommodation, the judge stressed that bed and breakfast accommodation should only be used in the short term and that authorities should look for alternative ways to discharge their HA 1996 s193 duty. This has now been embodied in statutory constraints on use of bed and breakfast: see paras10.196–10.203.

10.168 In *Flash*,[370] a one-bedroom flat provided to the applicant and her grandson was suitable: the grandson could sleep in the living room. In *El-Dinnaoui*,[371] the complaint was about an offer on the ninth floor of a block of flats; the applicant's wife had a fear of heights; the reviewing officer concluded that the appellant's wife would have settled into the flat over time. That conclusion failed to give proper weight to the medical evidence; she had collapsed during her visit to the flat and had been taken to hospital; the collapse had been caused by a panic attack; the discharging doctor had recorded that she had a lifelong fear of high buildings; her GP had advised that, owing to the severity of her symptoms, she should be offered a flat on a lower floor to avoid further panic attacks; it had not been open to the reviewing officer to conclude that the wife merely had a general dislike of heights rather than a fear which made it impractical for her to live above a certain floor level.

Other considerations

10.169 In *Awua*,[372] it was said that suitability is primarily a matter of space and arrangement, but that other matters, such as whether the applicant can afford the rent, may also be material.[373]

10.170 In *Maloba*,[374] on the related issue of whether accommodation was reasonable to continue to occupy, it was held that the question was not limited to consideration of the size, structural quality and amenities of accommodation.

369 *R (Khan) v Newham LBC* [2001] EWHC (Admin) 589, [2001] JHL D90.
370 *R (Flash) v Southwark LBC* [2004] EWHC 717 (Admin), [2004] JHL D60.
371 *El-Dinnaoui v Westminster City Council* [2013] EWCA Civ 231, [2013] HLR 23.
372 *R v Brent LBC ex p Awua* [1996] AC 55, (1995) 27 HLR 453, HL.
373 This decision preceded the statutory instrument (see para 10.191) requiring authorities to take affordability into account.
374 *Waltham Forest LBC v Maloba* [2007] EWCA Civ 1281, [2008] HLR 26 at [59]–[61].

10.171 The statutory considerations (primary and secondary)[375] are accordingly not exhaustive.

10.172 Thus, in *Kaur*,[376] (decided before the Homelessness (Suitability of Accommodation) (England) Order 1996 required consideration of affordability – see para 10.191), it had been held that accommodation secured for the applicant in the private sector was not suitable because the contractual rent exceeded the amount which would be met in housing benefit and the shortfall could not be afforded from the applicant's own resources.

Personal circumstances

10.173 In deciding the question of suitability, the authority must consider the individual needs of the applicant and his or her family, including needs as to work, education and health.[377]

10.174 In *Omar*,[378] a political refugee was offered accommodation in a basement flat in an estate. The condition of the premises and the layout of the estate strongly reminded the applicant of the prisons in which she had been held and abused, to such an extent that she maintained that she would rather commit suicide than live there. The court held that the accommodation must be suitable for the person to whom the duty was owed, in determining which the authority should have regard to the relevant circumstances of the applicant as well as to the matters set out in HA 1996 s210.

10.175 *Omar* was considered in *Dolan*,[379] where the authority's decision to offer accommodation was flawed because it had separated out medical and social considerations and had not taken an overall view of the applicant's needs: 'the ultimate decision as to suitability must be the result of a composite assessment'.

10.176 *Omar* was also considered in *Karaman*,[380] where the applicant's terror of her husband's domestic violence was such that the authority's decision to house her within two miles of where her husband was believed to be living was *Wednesbury* unreasonable.

375 Paras 10.162–10.204.

376 *R v Tower Hamlets LBC ex p Kaur* (1994) 26 HLR 597, QBD.

377 *R v Newham LBC ex p Sacupima* (2001) 33 HLR 1, QBD and (2001) 33 HLR 2, CA. See also *R v Newham LBC ex p Ojuri (No 3)* (1998) 31 HLR 452, QBD.

378 *R v Brent LBC ex p Omar* (1991) 23 HLR 446, QBD.

379 *R v Lewisham LBC ex p Dolan* (1992) 25 HLR 68, QBD.

380 *R v Haringey LBC ex p Karaman* (1996) 29 HLR 366, QBD. Cf *R v Lambeth LBC ex p Woodburne* (1997) 29 HLR 836, QBD.

10.177 In *Slater,*[381] Ward LJ said of a young single mother who was fleeing domestic violence 'that the particular needs of the applicant, for example, to be protected from domestic violence and to be located near to support networks, are relevant when considering suitability'.

10.178 In *Haque,*[382] it was held that where a person has a disability (or other protected characteristic under the Equality Act (EqA) 2010), the 'public sector equality duty' in EqA 2010 s149 requires the authority:

a) to recognise that the appellant has a disability;
b) to focus on specific aspects of his or her impairments to the extent that they are relevant to the suitability of the accommodation;
c) to focus on the disadvantages he or she might suffer when compared to a person without those impairments;
d) to focus on his or her accommodation needs arising from those impairments and the extent to which the accommodation meets those needs;
e) to recognise that the appellant's particular needs might require him or her to be treated more favourably than a person without a disability; and
f) to review the suitability of the accommodation, paying due regard to those matters.[383]

Family

10.179 An authority has a wide discretion to determine who is within an applicant's household.[384] In *Ariemuguvbe,*[385] the claimant was living in a three-bedroom property with her husband, five adult children who had come to the UK from Nigeria in 1998 who had overstayed their visitor's visas, and three grandchildren. The claimant argued that the points allocated to her under the authority's allocation

381 *Slater v Lewisham LBC* [2006] EWCA Civ 394, [2006] HLR 37 at [30].

382 *Hackney LBC v Haque* [2017] EWCA Civ 4, [2017] HLR 14.

383 There is no need to refer in terms to EqA 2010 s149; what matters is whether the substance has been complied with: *Haque*; *Poshteh v Kensington and Chelsea RLBC* [2015] EWCA Civ 711, [2015] HLR 36. *Poshteh* went on appeal to the Supreme Court ([2017] UKSC 36, [2017] HLR 28) where there was no substantive discussion of the nature of the duty under EqA 2010 s149 and the argument that it had not been considered by the review officer was dismissed as an example of the 'over-zealous linguistic analysis' deprecated in *Holmes-Moorhouse v Richmond upon Thames LBC* [2009] UKHL 7, [2009] HLR 34.

384 *R (Ariemuguvbe) v Islington LBC* [2009] EWCA Civ 1308.

385 *R (Ariemuguvbe) v Islington LBC*, above.

scheme should be increased to take account of the five adult children.[386]

10.180 It was held that the authority was entitled to conclude that it was not appropriate to allocate a larger property to the claimant, because her five children were all independent adults, some having their own families, who should have been able to make their own housing arrangements; also, they were subject to immigration control[387] in circumstances where providing accommodation for them would amount to them having recourse to public funds in breach of their conditions of entry to the UK.[388]

Racial harassment

10.181 Issues of racial harassment and violence are also relevant. In *Abdul Subhan*,[389] Tower Hamlets LBC offered a Bangladeshi applicant accommodation in a block of flats in which there was active racial harassment. The authority had itself set up a Racial Incidents Panel, had been provided with details of incidents of racial harassment by the local law centre, and had received reports from a research project set up by the Home Office Crime Prevention Unit. The decision to make the offer was quashed because the authority had failed to take into account the material on harassment which was before it.

Separation

10.182 Accommodation which split a family between two hostels was held not to be suitable in *Surdonja*.[390] In *Camden LBC v Sharif*,[391] however, the accommodation was split between two flats, yards apart in the same building. The decision that the flats were suitable was not challenged. The challenge was confined to whether it was accommodation which was available: see paras 4.16–4.38.

Location

10.183 Independently of the requirement, applicable in England, to consider locality under the Homelessness (Suitability of Accommodation) (England) Order 2012,[392] location will in any event impact on

386 *R (Ariemuguvbe) v Islington LBC*, above.

387 See paras 3.154–3.176.

388 *R (Ariemuguvbe) v Islington LBC*, above, at [19].

389 *R v Tower Hamlets LBC ex p Abdul Subhan* (1992) 24 HLR 541, QBD; see also *R v Southwark LBC ex p Solomon* (1994) 26 HLR 693, QBD.

390 *R v Ealing LBC ex p Surdonja* (1998) 31 HLR 686, QBD.

391 [2013] UKSC 10, [2013] HLR 16.

392 SI No 2601 art 2.

suitability,[393] and an authority must consider how location will affect employment, education and healthcare for the applicant and his or her family.[394]

10.184 In *Abdullah*,[395] the review officer had taken into account the appellant's submissions and the medical evidence provided and was entitled to conclude that the medical evidence meant no more than that it would be advantageous for the appellant to live near to her family and friends, rather than meaning that was being necessary for her to do so; it was also open to the reviewer to assume that social services would provide assistance where necessary, regardless of where the appellant lived.[396]

Adaptations

10.185 The suitability of accommodation offered by an authority pursuant to HA 1996 s193(2) is not to be judged exclusively by reference to the condition of the accommodation at the time of the offer: regard may be had to proposed adaptations or alterations provided that the proposals can fairly be regarded as certain, binding and enforceable; adaptations that are proposed after the date of the offer are, however, irrelevant to the question of suitability.[397]

Security

10.186 In *Wingrove* and *Mansoor*,[398] Evans LJ thought that the tenure, or time element, of suitability had to be proportionate to the circumstances of the case, including the needs of the applicant – for example,

393 See also the discussion at paras 10.147–10.161, on discharging the duty by securing accommodation outside the authority's area.

394 *R v Newham LBC ex p Sacupima* (2001) 33 HLR 1, QBD and (2001) 33 HLR 2, CA; *R v Newham LBC ex p Ojuri (No 3)* (1998) 31 HLR 452, QBD; *R (Yumsak) v Enfield LBC* [2002] EWHC 280 (Admin), [2002] JHL D38. See above paras 10.150–10.152, 10.173. The English Code of Guidance is somewhat less generous, referring to 'the needs of the applicant and their household' and how any health problems will be met (para 17.58), but the Welsh Code adds 'Authorities should also consider factors such as access to schools and other services and facilities (eg, GPs and informal support networks) with a view to maintaining stability for the household, particularly in respect of children's schooling, wherever possible' (para 19.11).

395 *Abdullah v Westminster City Council* [2007] EWCA Civ 1566, [2007] JHL D89.

396 The decision in *Shala v Birmingham City Council* [2007] EWCA Civ 624, [2008] HLR 8 was not considered: see para 5.49. While this may not have led to a different result, the same principles must surely apply to how the authority approaches the medical evidence.

397 *Boreh v Ealing LBC* [2008] EWCA Civ 1176, [2009] HLR 22 at [31].

398 *R v Wandsworth LBC ex p Wingrove; R v Wandsworth LBC ex p Mansoor* [1997] QB 953, CA.

the need for the applicant's children to remain in an area to attend the same school for a number of years. Suitability for the purpose of HA 1996 s193(2) does not imply permanence or security of tenure;[399] thus, even pre-LA 2011,[400] an assured shorthold tenancy could be suitable: see *Wingrove* and *Mansoor*[401] and *Griffiths*.[402]

Gypsies

10.187 Where the applicant is a gypsy, authorities must give special consideration to securing accommodation that will facilitate his or her traditional way of life: *Codona*.[403] Nonetheless, in *Codona*, the authority was unable to find any suitable accommodation other than bed and breakfast accommodation in the short term, and a decision that it was suitable was not unlawful and did not violate the applicant's rights under ECHR Articles 8 and 14.[404]

10.188 A person who has adopted a lifestyle similar to that of a gypsy, but is not a gypsy, is not entitled to the special protection afforded to gypsies under human rights jurisprudence.[405]

Asylum-seekers

10.189 In relation to eligible asylum-seekers in England,[406] HA 1996 s210 is modified[407] so that in considering whether accommodation is suitable for the applicant or any person who might reasonably be expected to reside with him or her, the authority must have regard to the fact that the accommodation is to be temporary, pending the applicant's claim for asylum; the authority may not have regard to any preference the applicant, or any person who might reasonably be expected to reside with him or her, may have as to the locality of the accommodation; the authority must, however, have regard to the desirability, in general, of securing accommodation in areas in which

399 *Birmingham City Council v Ali; Moran v Manchester City Council (Secretary of State for Communities and Local Government and another intervening)* [2009] UKHL 36, [2009] 1 WLR 1506 at [47].

400 See paras 10.231–10.236.

401 *R v Wandsworth LBC ex p Wingrove; R v Wandsworth LBC ex p Mansoor* [1997] QB 953, CA, per Sir Thomas Bingham MR at 923G.

402 *Griffiths v St Helens MBC* [2006] EWCA Civ 160, [2006] 1 WLR 2233, [2006] HLR 29.

403 *Codona v Mid-Bedfordshire DC* [2005] EWCA Civ 925, [2005] HLR 1. See also *R (Price) v Carmarthenshire CC* [2003] EWHC 42 (Admin), [2003] JHL D43.

404 See also paras 12.123–12.128.

405 *Steward v Kingston Upon Thames LBC* [2007] EWCA Civ 565, [2007] HLR 42.

406 See para 3.174.

407 HA 1996 s210(1A).

there is a ready supply of accommodation: see Homelessness (Asylum-seekers) (Interim Period) (England) Order 1999.[408]

Added considerations

10.190 The secretary of state and Welsh Ministers have power to specify circumstances in which accommodation is (or is not) to be regarded as suitable and to specify other matters to be taken into account or disregarded.[409]

England

10.191 This power has been used in England to require authorities to take affordability into account when determining suitability: see Homelessness (Suitability of Accommodation) Order 1996.[410]

10.192 This requires the authority to consider:

a) the financial resources available to the person;
b) the costs of the accommodation;
c) payments being made under a court order to a spouse, or former spouse;
d) any payments made to support children, whether under a court order or under the Child Support Act 1991; and
e) the applicant's other reasonable living expenses.[411]

408 SI No 3126. HA 1996 s206(1A). This is intended to encourage authorities in areas of high demand for social housing to seek accommodation outside the district: see 2002 edition of the Code of Guidance annex 12 para 7.

409 HA 1996 s210(2); H(W)A 2014 s59(3).

410 SI No 3204 (appendix B). The English Code does not directly address the impact of the 'benefit cap' (Welfare Reform Act 2012 s96), although government policy is for discretionary housing payments to be used to cover any shortfall between the contractual rent and the housing benefit/housing element of universal credit: see Department for Work and Pensions (DWP) Circular HB/CTB G6/12 – Annex A, June 2012.

411 See further paras 4.121–4.129. See also English Code of Guidance paras 17.44–17.45. The authority can take into account all forms of income (including social security benefits of all kinds, not just housing benefit/ housing element of universal credit): *Samuels v Birmingham City Council* [2015] EWCA Civ 1051, [2015] HLR 47 (permission to appeal to the Supreme Court has been granted).

10.193 The power has also been used in England[412] to require the authority to consider the location of accommodation,[413] including:

a) where it is outside the authority's own area, its distance from that area;[414]
b) the significance of any disruption to employment, caring responsibilities or education;[415]
c) proximity and accessibility to medical facilities and other support which is currently used by or provided to the applicant or a member of his or her household and which is essentially to that person's wellbeing;[416] and,

412 Homelessness (Suitability of Accommodation) (England) Order 2012 SI No 2601 art 2, in force from 9 November 2012: it was brought into force contemporaneously with the new provisions governing private sector discharge: paras 10.237–10.240.

413 From the point of view of all members of the household – English Code para 17.2. Authorities are urged to seek accommodation as close as possible to previous accommodation as 'accommodation for an applicant in a different location can cause difficulties for some applicants . . . Where possible the authority should seek to retain established links with schools, doctors, social workers and other key services and support': para 17.48.

414 Where otherwise suitable and affordable accommodation is available nearer to the authority's own district 'the accommodation which it has secured is not likely to be suitable unless the authority has a justifiable reason or the applicant has specified a preference' – English Code para 17.47.

415 '[A]ccount should be taken of the type and importance of the care household members provide and the likely impact the withdrawal would cause': English Code para 17.49. 'When securing accommodation for families with children housing authorities should be mindful of their duties under section 11 of the Children Act 2004 to discharge their functions with regard to the need to safeguard and promote the welfare of children. This would include minimising the disruption to the education of children and young people, particularly (but not solely) at critical points in time such as leading up to taking GCSE (or their equivalent) examinations': English Code para 17.50. 'Before a family that includes a school age child is placed out of district, the housing authority should liaise with the receiving authority and make every reasonable effort to ensure arrangements are or will be put in place to meet the child's educational needs': English Code para 17.51 – see also *R (E) v Islington LBC* [2017] EWHC 1440 (Admin) where no such arrangements were made for a child placed in the area of another authority so that there was a breach of ECHR Protocol 1 Article 2 (right to education).

416 'Housing authorities should consider the potential impact on the health and well being of an applicant or any person reasonably expected to reside with them, were such support removed or medical facilities were no longer accessible. They should also consider whether similar facilities are accessible and available near the accommodation being offered and whether there would be any specific difficulties in the applicant or person residing with them using those essential facilities, compared to the support they are currently receiving': English Code para 17.52.

d) proximity and accessibility to local services, amenities and transport.[417]

10.194 Additionally, the authority may not consider private rented sector accommodation[418] as suitable if any of the following applies.[419]

a) the authority considers that the accommodation is not in a reasonable physical condition;[420]
b) the authority considers that any electrical equipment supplied with the accommodation does not meet Electrical Equipment (Safety) Regulations 1994 regs 5 and 7;[421]
c) the authority considers that the landlord has not taken reasonable fire safety precautions in respect of the accommodation and furnishings;[422]

417 'Housing authorities should avoid placing applicants in isolated accommodation away from public transport, shops and other facilities where possible': English Code para 17.53.

418 Since the HRA 2017 came into force on 3 April 2018 (see Homelessness Reduction Act 2017 (Commencement and Transitional and Savings Provisions) Regulations 2018 SI No 167 reg 3, only applicable to applications made and reviews sought on or after that date – see reg 4), reg 3 spells out that the requirements apply not only to private sector offers under HA 1996 s193(7F) (paras 10.231–10.240) but also to the suitability of final offers under HA 1996 ss193A (para 10.162) and 193C (para 10.267) and of accommodation for applicants in priority need by way of arrangements with private landlords under the initial help duty in HA 1996 s189B (paras 10.76–10.96) and the replacement provisions governing threatened with homelessness in HA 1996 s195 (paras 10.67–10.75): HRA 2017 s12. The amendments are without prejudice to any power by order to amend or revoke reg 3: HRA 2017 s12(5).

419 Homelessness (Suitability of Accommodation) (England) Order 2012 SI No 2601 art 3, in force from 9 November 2012: see above, footnote 361.

420 'Housing authorities are advised to ensure it is visited by a local authority officer or someone acting on their behalf able to carry out an inspection. Attention should be paid to signs of damp or mould and indications that the property would be cold as well as to a visual check made of electrical installations and equipment (for example; looking for loose wiring, cracked or broken electrical sockets, light switches that do not work and appliances which do not appear to have been safety tested)': English Code para 17.16.

421 SI No 3260.

422 Eg, consideration of Regulatory Reform (Fire Safety) Order 2005 SI No 1541, which applies to the common or shared parts of multi-occupied residential buildings, and Furniture and Furnishings (Fire) (Safety) Regulations 1988 SI No 1324, as amended: 'Housing authorities and fire and rescue authorities should work together to ensure the safety of domestic premises including the provision of fire safety advice to households. Housing authorities will need to satisfy themselves that these regulations have been adhered to': English Code para 17.18.

d) the authority considers that the landlord has not taken reasonable precautions to prevent carbon monoxide poisoning in the accommodation;[423]
e) the authority considers that the landlord is not a fit and proper person to act as landlord, after considering if he or she has committed any one of a number of specified categories of offence,[424] or has practiced unlawful discrimination in or in connection with carrying on any business,[425] contravened any provision of housing law,[426] or acted otherwise than in accordance with any approved[427] and applicable code of practice for the management of an HMO;
f) the accommodation is an unlicensed HMO which ought to be licensed;[428]
g) the accommodation is or forms part of residential property which does not have a valid energy performance certificate[429] or a current gas safety record;[430]
h) the landlord has not provided the authority with a written tenancy agreement which he or she proposes to use for the purposes of

423 English Code para 17.19: 'Housing authorities are asked to satisfy themselves that there are reasonable precautions to prevent the possibility of carbon monoxide poisoning in the accommodation, where such a risk exists. Since 2015, private sector landlords have been required to have at least one smoke alarm installed on every storey of their properties and a carbon monoxide alarm in any room containing a solid fuel burning appliance (for example a coal fire or wood burning stove). After that, the landlord must make sure the alarms are in working order at the start of each new tenancy.'

424 Offences involving fraud or other dishonest, violence or illegal drugs, or offences attracting notification requirements in Sexual Offences Act 2003 Sch 3. When placing households outside of their own district, authorities should check with the authority for the receiving district to see whether it has taken enforcement activity against the landlord and may consult the Rogue Landlord database (Housing and Planning Act 2016): English Code para 17.21.

425 On the grounds of sex, race, age, disability, marriage or civil partnership, pregnancy or maternity, religion or belief, sexual orientation, gender identity or reassignment.

426 Including landlord and tenant law.

427 Under HA 2004 s133.

428 Under HA 2004 s54 or s55.

429 As required by the Energy Performance of Buildings (England and Wales) Regulations 2012 SI No 3118.

430 In accordance with Gas Safety (Installation and Use) Regulations 1998 SI No 2451 reg 36.

the private rented sector offer and which the authority considers adequate.[431]

10.195 While the decision in *Ephraim v Newham LBC*,[432] considered in relation to advice and assistance which helped the applicant to find accommodation where there was no obligation to secure it for her, remains correct in law on its face (paras 10.79–10.80), its reasoning relied on the absence of any duty to inspect; while the 2012 Order does not explicitly require an authority to inspect, it is almost impossible for it to comply without doing so, and the English Code does envisage inspection.[433] In these cases, therefore, it may well be that *Ephraim* would not apply and that an authority may be held liable for injury, loss or damage if it places an applicant in non-compliant accommodation.

10.196 Bed and breakfast accommodation is not in itself necessarily unsuitable,[434] but the Homelessness (Suitability of Accommodation) (England) Order 2003[435] limits its use: where it is provided to families (including pregnant women), it is not to be regarded as suitable, save where there is no other accommodation available and then only for a period not exceeding six weeks (or periods not exceeding six weeks in total).[436]

10.197 Bed and breakfast accommodation is defined[437] as accommodation (whether or not breakfast is provided) which is not separate and self-contained and in which more than one household share one or more of the following:

a) a toilet;
b) personal washing facilities; or
c) cooking facilities.

431 'It is expected that the local authority should review the tenancy agreement to ensure that it sets out, ideally in a clear and comprehensible way, the tenant's obligations, for example a clear statement of the rent and other charges, and the responsibilities of the landlord, but does not contain unfair or unreasonable terms, such as call-out charges for repairs or professional cleaning at the end of the tenancy': English Code para 17.14. 'Whilst a local authority will not be able to check that a tenant's deposit has been placed in a tenancy deposit protection scheme prior to them taking the tenancy housing authorities should remind prospective landlords and tenants of their responsibilities in this area': English Code para 17.22..

432 *Ephraim v Newham LBC* (1992) 25 HLR 208, CA.

433 See above, footnote 420.

434 See English Code of Guidance para 17.40 suggesting its use in emergencies or as a last resort, but also stating that authorities should avoid using it wherever possible (para 17.30).

435 SI No 3326 (appendix B).

436 See further para 10.167.

437 Suitability Order 2003 art 2.

10.198 Accommodation owned or managed by an authority, a registered provider of social housing or a voluntary organisation[438] is, however, exempt from the prohibition.

Wales

10.199 There is no need for an affordability statutory instrument in Wales because H(W)A 2014 s59(2) requires authorities to have regard to whether or not accommodation is affordable.[439]

10.200 The Homelessness (Suitability of Accommodation) (Wales) Order 2015[440] requires Welsh authorities to take into account the following additional matters when considering suitability of accommodation for a person in priority need:

a) the specific health needs of the person;
b) the proximity and accessibility of the support of the family or other support services;
c) any disability of the person;
d) the proximity and accessibility of medical facilities, and other support services which:
    i) are currently used by or provided to the person; and
    ii) are essential to the wellbeing of the person;
e) where the accommodation is situated outside the area of the authority, the distance of the accommodation from the area of the authority;
f) the significance of any disruption which would be caused to the employment, caring responsibilities or education of the person by the location of the accommodation; and
g) the proximity of alleged perpetrators and victims of domestic abuse.

10.201 Additionally, the authority may not consider private rented sector accommodation as suitable if any of the following applies.[441]

a) the authority is of the view that the accommodation is not in a reasonable physical condition;
b) the authority is of the view that the accommodation does not comply with all statutory requirements (such as, where applicable, requirements relating to fire, gas, electrical, carbon monoxide and other safety; planning; and licences for HMOs);

438 See para 14.29 as to the definition of voluntary organisation.

439 See also see Welsh Code para 19.26 on factors to be taken into account when assessing affordability under H(W)A 2014 s59(2).

440 SI No 1268 (Welsh Suitability Order).

441 Welsh Suitability Order Part 3.

c) the authority is of the view that the landlord is not a fit and proper person within the meaning of H(W)A 2014 s20, to act in the capacity of landlord.

10.202 As in England,[442] bed and breakfast accommodation is not in itself necessarily unsuitable,[443] but, since 27 April 2015, there have been restrictions on its use and that of other shared accommodation, both as regards quality and duration.[444] Bed and breakfast or shared accommodation will be unsuitable for a person who is, or who may be, in priority need unless:

a) offered in response to an emergency (eg fire, flood) and no other accommodation is reasonably available;
b) the applicant has been offered other suitable accommodation but has chosen bed and breakfast; or
c) it is used for less than a fixed period (two weeks, or six weeks if the accommodation meets a 'higher standard', as defined in the Schedule to the Order, taking into account, among other things, room size, heating facilities, storage facilities, toilet and washing facilities).

10.203 'Bed and breakfast accommodation' is defined in substantially the same way as under the 2003 English Suitability Order; 'shared accommodation' is likewise defined as accommodation which is not separate and self-contained premises; or in which a toilet, personal washing facilities or cooking facilities are not available to the applicant or are shared by more than one household.[445]

Enquiries into suitability

10.204 Although there is no explicit statutory duty to enquire into questions of suitability, it is implicit: authorities cannot otherwise reach a decision that accommodation is suitable for the particular applicant.[446] The principles developed in relation to HA 1996 s184

442 See paras 10.196–10.198.

443 See Welsh Code paras 5.40, 19.56–19.62.

444 Homelessness (Suitability of Accommodation) (Wales) Order 2015 SI No 1268. See also the previous restrictions in the Homelessness (Suitability of Accommodation) (Wales) Order 2006 SI No 650.

445 Welsh Suitability Order 2015 reg 2. The only differences from the English order are that the accommodation must be 'commercially provided' and must not be registered under the Care Standards Act 2000.

446 Likewise, if a complaint is made, the authority must decide whether an inspection is required: *Firoozmand v Lambeth LBC* [2015] EWCA Civ 952, [2015] HLR 45.

enquiries[447] therefore also apply to enquiries as to suitability: *Thomas*.[448]

Viewing property

10.205 There is no requirement[449] that authorities provide applicants with an opportunity to view and comment on the suitability of any accommodation before moving into it or before a decision is made on its suitability: *Khatun*.[450] It is not oppressive, perverse or disproportionate to the fair and efficient administration of HA 1996 Part 7 for an authority to require an applicant who has not viewed a property to decide whether or not to accept it on pain of immediate cancellation of his or her current accommodation if he or she does not do so, as applicants can challenge suitability by internal review after moving in.[451]

Challenges to suitability

10.206 Challenge to the suitability of an offer is by review under HA 1996 s202 (H(W)A 2014 s85)[452] and appeal under s204 (H(W)A 2014 s88).[453] Save in exceptional circumstances, a decision on suitability of offer may not be challenged in a defence to eviction from temporary accommodation.[454]

Cessation of the duty

10.207 The duty under HA 1996 s193 or H(W)A 2014 s75 will terminate in the following circumstances.[455]

447 See paras 9.57–9.160.

448 *R v Islington LBC ex p Thomas* (1997) 30 HLR 111, QBD. See also *R v South Holland DC ex p Baxter* (1998) 30 HLR 1069, QBD.

449 The current edition of the English Code (para 15.46) however, 'recommends that applicants are given the chance to view accommodation that is offered on anything other than an interim basis, before being required to decide whether they accept or refuse an offer, and before being required to sign any written agreement relating to the accommodation (eg a tenancy agreement)'; see also Welsh Code para 3.65.

450 *Khatun v Newham LBC* [2004] EWCA Civ 55, [2004] HLR 29.

451 See paras 9.186–9.199.

452 See paras 9.186–9.199.

453 See para 12.194.

454 *Tower Hamlets LBC v Rahnara Begum* [2005] EWCA Civ 116, [2006] HLR 9.

455 But see also para 10.48, on the possibility of a public law defence (whether on domestic grounds or under the ECHR).

Eligibility

10.208 The duty will cease if the applicant ceases to be eligible for assistance,[456] for example, if his or her immigration status changes.[457]

Loss of accommodation

10.209 If the applicant becomes homeless intentionally from the accommodation made available, or otherwise voluntarily ceases to occupy it as his or her only or principal home,[458] the duty will cease.[459]

Offers

10.210 A number of instances terminate the duty through offers of accommodation. Although the LA 2011, which made a number of changes to the provisions governing subsequent applications, came into force on 9 November 2012,[460] the length of time during which applicants may remain in Part 7/Part 2 accommodation before the duty towards them is discharged means that it continues to be necessary to consider the position both before and since the LA 2011, as well as before and since the H(W)A 2014 and, somewhat more obviously, since the HRA 2017 came into force.[461]

Refusal of suitable offers

10.211 ***England pre-LA 2011 and Wales pre-H(W)A 2014.*** By HA 1996 s193(5), in relation to applications made before commencement of the LA 2011 s148(3)[462] in respect of which the duty to secure accommodation had arisen but had not ceased by that date,[463] and continuing in Wales for applications made prior to 27 April 2015,[464] the duty ceases

456 See chapter 3.

457 HA 1996 s193(6)(a); H(W)A 2014 s79(2).

458 See *Crawley BC v Sawyer* (1998) 20 HLR 98, CA.

459 HA 1996 s193(6)(b) and (d); H(W)A 2014 s76(6).

460 9 November 2012: Localism Act 2011 (Commencement No 2 and Transitional Provisions) (England) Order 2012 SI No 2599 art 2.

461 3 April 2018: Homelessness Reduction Act 2017 (Commencement and Transitional and Savings Provisions) Regulations 2018 SI No 167 reg 3, only applicable to applications made and reviews sought on or after that date – see reg.4.

462 9 November 2012: Localism Act 2011 (Commencement No 2 and Transitional Provisions) (England) Order 2012 SI No 2599 art 2.

463 Localism Act 2011 (Commencement No 2 and Transitional Provisions) (England) Order 2012 SI No 2599 art 3.

464 For applications made on or after that date, H(W)A 2014 applies: see Housing (Wales) Act 2014 (Commencement No 3 and Transitory, Transitional and Saving Provisions) Order 2015 SI No 1272 art 7.

if the applicant is made an offer of suitable accommodation which he or she refuses, having been warned that the authority will regard itself as having discharged its duty if he or she does so[465] and having been informed of the right to an internal review.[466]

10.212 This provision operates to bring to an end the full housing duty regardless of whether the accommodation offered to the applicant is temporary or permanent.[467]

10.213 Thus, where an authority had placed an applicant in accommodation pursuant to its duty under HA 1996 s193(2), pending a final offer, which accommodation became unsuitable because of the applicant's change of circumstances so that the applicant had to move, the authority's duty ceased under subsection (5) when the applicant refused a new offer of suitable alternative section 193(2) accommodation.[468] Nor had the authority acted unfairly as it had followed the procedural safeguards set out in the subsection and had not led the applicant to believe that she was entitled to any additional procedural protection.

10.214 The authority must notify the applicant that it considers the duty to have been discharged.[469] As such notification comprises a decision as to what duty is owed to the applicant, ie that there is no duty because it has ceased,[470] it must comply with HA 1996 s184, which means that it must give reasons and inform the applicant of his or her right to a review and be in writing.[471]

465 In *Maswaku v Westminster City Council* [2012] EWCA Civ 669, [2012] HLR 37 an offer letter which informed the applicant that, should she refuse it, she would have to find her own accommodation, was a sufficient warning for this purpose.

466 HA 1996 s193(5). This condition even applied to an offer of an assured shorthold tenancy at the point in time when applicants were not obliged to accept shorthold tenancies (paras 10.231–10.236), where it had not been held out as an offer of a 'qualifying' offer under section 193(7B): see *Griffiths v St Helens BC* [2006] EWCA Civ 160, [2006] 1 WLR 2233, [2006] HLR 29 although – at that time – it was on the basis that the offer is only a stage in the final rehousing exercise.

467 *Griffiths v St Helens MBC*, above.

468 *Muse v Brent LBC* [2008] EWCA Civ 1447.

469 HA 1996 s193(5). Given the applicant's right to challenge the suitability of the offer, the reasons should encompass why the authority considers the accommodation to be suitable for the applicant. Surprisingly there is no express requirement that the notification has to be in writing. In Wales, see H(W)A 2014 s84.

470 HA 1996 s184(1); H(W)A 2014 s84.

471 See para 10.10.

10.215 ***England post-LA 2011 and Wales post-H(W)A 2014.*** Since LA 2011 s148(3) came into force in England,[472] the duty does not cease by reason of HA 1996 s193(5), in the case either of an offer of accommodation under Part 6[473] or of private sector accommodation,[474] but is governed instead by discrete provisions which determine when the duties come to an end: these are considered below.[475]

10.216 In substance, HA 1996 s193(5) is now limited to a refusal of a suitable offer of further interim accommodation. In Wales, the position is the same: the refusal of an offer of suitable interim accommodation brings the duty to an end.[476]

Part 6 offer

10.217 ***England pre-LA 2011 and Wales pre-H(W)A 2014.*** In relation to applications made before commencement of LA 2011 s148(3),[477] in respect of which the duty to secure accommodation had arisen but had not ceased by that date,[478] and continuing in Wales for applications made prior to 27 April 2015,[479] the duty will cease if the applicant accepts an offer of accommodation under Part 6.[480]

10.218 The duty will also cease if the applicant, having been informed of the possible consequences of refusal[481] and of his or her right to request a review of the suitability of the accommodation, refuses a final offer of accommodation under Part 6.[482] A final offer of accommodation cannot be made unless the authority is satisfied that the

472 9 November 2012: Localism Act 2011 (Commencement No 2 and Transitional Provisions) (England) Order 2012 SI No 2599 art 2.

473 Paras 10.217–10.230.

474 Paras 10.231–10.240.

475 Paras 10.217–10.230, 10.231–10.240.

476 H(W)A 2014 s76(3)(a).

477 9 November 2012: Localism Act 2011 (Commencement No 2 and Transitional Provisions) (England) Order 2012 SI No 2599 art 2.

478 Localism Act 2011 (Commencement No 2 and Transitional Provisions) (England) Order 2012 SI No 2599 art 3.

479 For applications made on or after that date, the H(W)A 2014 applies: see Housing (Wales) Act 2014 (Commencement No 3 and Transitory, Transitional and Saving Provisions) Order 2015 SI No 1272 art 7.

480 HA 1996 s193(6)(c); see chapter 11. Such an offer could have been made by way of nomination to become the assured tenant of a private registered provider of social housing (England) or a registered social landlord (Wales): HA 1996 s159(1)(c).

481 HA 1996 s193(7).

482 HA 1996 s193(7); in Wales, see H(W)A 2014 s76(3).

accommodation is suitable for the applicant and that it is reasonable for him or her to accept it.[483]

10.219 The questions of suitability and whether it is reasonable for the applicant to accept the offer have to be considered separately.[484]

10.220 In judging whether it is unreasonable to refuse an offer:

> ... the decision-maker must have regard to all the personal characteristics of the applicant, her needs, her hopes and her fears and then taking account of those individual aspects, the subjective factors, ask whether it is reasonable, an objective test, for the applicant to accept. The test is whether a right-thinking local housing authority would conclude that it was reasonable that *this applicant* should have accepted the offer of *this* accommodation.[485]

10.221 An offer is a final offer for this purpose if it is in writing and states that it is a final offer for the purposes of HA 1996 s193(7).

10.222 The exact wording of section 193(7) does not need to be followed, provided that the notification contains every matter of substance which the subsection requires; the authority should, however, convey to the applicant that it is satisfied both that the accommodation is suitable for him or her and that it is reasonable for him or her to accept it.[486]

10.223 In *Begum*,[487] the notification was inadequate because it merely stated that the accommodation offered was a reasonable and suitable offer of permanent accommodation. The requirements may, however, be fulfilled by information in more than one document, provided that they can properly be read together.[488]

10.224 An applicant's genuine belief that it was not reasonable to accept an offer of accommodation is not conclusive of whether it was reasonable to do so; if the authority has evidence which entitles it to consider that the belief was not objectively reasonable, even if that evidence was not available to the applicant at the time of the refusal,

483 HA 1996 s193(7F)(a).

484 *Slater v Lewisham LBC* [2006] EWCA Civ 394, [2006] HLR 37, where the authority had failed to apply its mind to the element of reasonableness.

485 Ward LJ in *Slater v Lewisham LBC* (emphasis in original).

486 *Tower Hamlets LBC v Rahanara Begum* [2005] EWCA Civ 116, [2006] HLR 9 at [27], though that case concerned HA 1996 s193(7)(b) prior to its amendment by the Homelessness Act 2002.

487 *Tower Hamlets LBC v Rahanara Begum* [2005] EWCA Civ 116, [2006] HLR 9.

488 *Vilvarasa v Harrow LBC* [2010] EWCA Civ 1278, [2010] HLR 11 – the information was spread across two letters, one in July (which did not specify the property in question) and one in August (which did so); the two documents could be read together.

the authority may nonetheless decide that it was reasonable for the applicant to accept the offer: *Ahmed*.[489]

10.225 It had been held that an offer under Part 6 which does not satisfy the requirements of subsection (7) may nonetheless serve to discharge the authority's duty if it satisfied the requirements of section 193(5) (para 10.211): *Omar*.[490] In *Ravichandran*,[491] however, it was said that *Omar* should be confined to its own facts. It is submitted that this is correct: it is difficult to see how compliance with the less stringent requirements of section 193(5) could properly be considered compliance with the detailed requirements of section 193(7).[492]

10.226 The courts will not easily interfere with an authority's allocation scheme,[493] nor, therefore, with its policy in relation to Part 6 offers to homeless persons: thus, once a homeless person housed in temporary accommodation achieved the requisite number of points to qualify to bid on an appropriate property, he was given only two months in which to make a voluntary bid before a successful 'auto-bid' was generated on his behalf,[494] which auto-bid could be treated as a final offer, refusal of which meant that the authority's duty could lawfully be treated as discharged.[495]

10.227 It would seem, however, to have been central to the court's decision that, before the two months began, a housing officer would visit, which would allow any particular personal considerations or difficulties to be taken into account before the bid was placed on his behalf.

10.228 ***England post-LA 2011 and Wales post-H(W)A 2014.*** The law considered in relation to pre-LA 2011/H(W)A 2014 applicants is

489 *Ahmed v Leicester City Council* [2007] EWCA Civ 843, [2008] HLR 6.

490 *Omar v Birmingham City Council* [2007] EWCA Civ 610, [2007] HLR 43 at [29] and [36]; see also *Tower Hamlets LBC v Rahanara Begum* [2005] EWCA Civ 116, [2006] HLR 9 at [27].

491 *Ravichandran v Lewisham LBC* [2010] EWCA Civ 755, [2010] HLR 42.

492 The issue does not arise in relation to the post-LA 2011/H(W)A 2014 applications considered under the next heading, in respect of which HA 1996 s193(5) is expressed only to apply to an offer which is neither a Part 6 offer nor an offer of private sector accommodation.

493 See *R (Ahmad) v Newham LBC* [2009] UKHL 14, [2009] HLR 31; paras 11.106–11.115.

494 Ie a bid by an officer of the authority on his behalf.

495 *R (Tout a Tout) v Haringey LBC; R (Heff) v Haringey LBC* [2012] EWHC 873 (Admin), [2012] JHL D77.

largely the same for applications in relation to which the duty had not arisen before commencement of LA 2011 s148(3)[496] and those in Wales made prior to 27 April 2015.

10.229 The duty will cease if the applicant accepts an offer of accommodation under Part 6.[497] The duty will also cease if the applicant, having been informed of the possible consequences of refusal and acceptance[498] and of his or her right to request a review of the suitability of the accommodation, refuses a final offer of accommodation under Part 6.[499] An offer is a final offer for this purpose if it is in writing and states that it is a final offer for the purposes of HA 1996 s193(7).[500] Accordingly, the earlier cases considered at paras 10.217–10.227 will remain relevant.

10.230 Apart from the requirement in England to inform the applicant about the possible consequences of acceptance as well as of refusal (para 10.229), the other difference is that the issue considered at para 10.225[501] is not relevant to these post-LA 2011/H(W)A 2014 applications, as HA 1996 s193(5) is now expressed to apply only to an offer which is neither a Part 6 offer nor an offer of private sector accommodation.[502]

Private sector accommodation offers

10.231 ***England pre-LA 2011 and Wales pre-H(W)A 2014.*** The following provisions applied until LA 2011 s148 came into force in England,[503] and continue to apply to applications made before that date, in relation to which the duty to secure accommodation had arisen but had

496 9 November 2012: Localism Act 2011 (Commencement No 2 and Transitional Provisions) (England) Order 2012 SI No 2599 art 2.

497 HA 1996 s193(6)(c); H(W)A 2014 s76(2). See chapter 11.

498 HA 1996 s193(7) as amended from 9 November 2012. In Wales, see H(W)A 2014 s76(3).

499 HA 1996 s193(7); in Wales, see H(W)A 2014 s76(3). Such an offer may include a nomination to become the assured tenant of a private registered provider of social housing (England) or a registered social landlord (Wales): HA 1996 s159(1)(c).

500 HA 1996 s193(7A). There is no such requirement in Wales.

501 Ie whether an offer under HA 1996 Part 6 which does not satisfy the requirements of HA 1996 s193(7) may nonetheless serve to discharge the authority's duty if it satisfied the requirements of s193(5).

502 See also Supplementary Suitability Guidance 2012 para 19.

503 9 November 2012: Localism Act 2011 (Commencement No 2 and Transitional Provisions) (England) Order 2012 SI No 2599 art 2.

not ceased by it;[504] in Wales they apply to applications made prior to 27 April 2015.[505]

10.232 The duty will cease if the applicant accepts an offer of an assured (but not an assured shorthold) tenancy from a private landlord.[506] The duty will also cease if the applicant accepts a 'qualifying offer' of an assured shorthold.[507]

10.233 An offer qualifies if:

a) it is made with the approval of the authority,[508] pursuant to arrangements made between it and the private landlord in order to bring the HA 1996 s193 duty to an end;
b) the tenancy is a fixed-term tenancy;[509] and
c) it is accompanied by a statement in writing, which states the term of the tenancy being offered and explains in ordinary language that there is no obligation to accept the offer, but that if it is accepted the duty under HA 1996 s193 will cease.[510]

10.234 An applicant is free to reject a qualifying offer; the duty under HA 1996 s193 is not discharged,[511] and acceptance is only effective if the applicant signs a statement acknowledging that he or she has read and understood the statement made with the offer.[512]

10.235 An offer of accommodation let on an assured shorthold tenancy which does not comply with the requirements of HA 1996 s193(7D)

504 Localism Act 2011 (Commencement No 2 and Transitional Provisions) (England) Order 2012 SI No 2599 art 3.

505 For applications made on or after that date, the H(W)A 2014 applies: see Housing (Wales) Act 2014 (Commencement No 3 and Transitory, Transitional and Saving Provisions) Order 2015 SI No 1272 art 7.

506 HA 1996 s193(6)(cc); as defined by HA 1996 s217(1). A private landlord is any landlord other than one within HA 1985 s80 and therefore includes a private registered provider of social housing (England) or a registered social landlord (Wales): HA 1996 s217 and H(W)A 2014 s99.

507 HA 1996 s193(7B).

508 The offer may not be approved unless the authority is satisfied that the accommodation is suitable for the applicant and that it is reasonable for him or her to accept the offer: HA 1996 s193(7F)(b). For this purpose, however, an applicant may reasonably be expected to accept an offer even though he or she is under contractual or other obligations in respect of his or her existing accommodation, those obligations can be brought to an end before he or she is required to take up the offer: HA 1996 s193(8).

509 As defined by HA 1988 s45(1), ie, any tenancy other than a periodic tenancy.

510 HA 1996 s193(7D).

511 HA 1996 s193(7C).

512 HA 1996 s193(7E).

(para 10.233) cannot be a qualifying offer but, if refused, section 193(5) can nevertheless operate to bring the authority's duty under section 193(2) to an end, provided that the requirements of the latter subsection have been fulfilled, as qualified in the case of an assured shorthold.[513]

10.236 If an applicant accepts an offer of an assured shorthold tenancy that is not a qualifying offer, which accommodation subsequently ceases to be available, the authority will continue to owe him or her a duty under section 193(2) (provided that the applicant's circumstances have not otherwise materially changed).[514]

10.237 ***England post-LA 2011 and Wales post-H(W)A 2014.*** An offer of private rented sector accommodation by an authority leads to cessation of the duty even if the tenancy is an assured shorthold.[515] A private rented sector accommodation offer is of an assured shorthold tenancy, from a private landlord[516] to the applicant in respect of any accommodation which is, or may become, available for the applicant's occupation, which is made with the approval of the authority in pursuance of arrangements made between it and the landlord, with a view to bringing its duty to an end; the tenancy must be for a fixed term of at least 12 months[517] or – otherwise than in a restricted case – such longer period as the secretary of state may by regulations prescribe.[518]

10.238 In England, the offer must comply with specified qualifying conditions: the applicant must be informed in writing of the consequences of refusal or acceptance, that he or she has the right to a review of the suitability of the accommodation and – otherwise than in a restricted case – that he or she will be entitled to further assistance from the authority if a new application is made within two years of acceptance,[519] even if he or she is no longer in priority need,

513 *Griffiths v St Helens MBC* [2006] EWCA Civ 160, [2006] 1 WLR 2233.

514 *Griffiths v St Helens MBC*, above.

515 HA 1996 s193(7AA); H(W)A 2014 s76(2)–(4).

516 Ie any landlord other than one within HA 1985 s80 and thus including a private registered provider of social housing (England) or a registered social landlord (Wales): HA 1996 s217.

517 In Wales, six months: see H(W)A 2014 s76(4)(c).

518 HA 1996 s193(7AC). There is no equivalent in Wales.

519 Homelessness in this case arises when a valid notice under HA 1988 s21, expires (HA 1996 s195A(2)); see *Manual of housing law*, para 2.203.

provided that he or she is not ineligible when that application is made nor had become homeless intentionally.[520]

10.239 In Wales, he or she need only be informed in writing of the consequences of refusal and acceptance and of his or her right to seek a review.[521]

10.240 While there is (in these cases) still a requirement that the authority considers the accommodation suitable[522] for the applicant, there is no longer a requirement that the authority additionally considers it reasonable[523] for the applicant to accept the offer. The latter is replaced by a prohibition on the offer if the applicant is under contractual or other obligations in respect of his or her existing accommodation which he or she cannot bring to an end before being required to take up the offer.[524]

Restricted cases

10.241 ***England pre-LA 2011 and Wales pre-H(W)A 2014.*** The following provisions governing restricted cases applied until the LA 2011 s148 came into force in England,[525] and continue to apply to applications made before that date, in relation to which the duty to secure accommodation had arisen but had not ceased by it,[526] and in Wales they apply to applications made prior to 27 April 2015.[527]

10.242 A restricted case[528] is one where the authority is only satisfied that the applicant is homeless, threatened with homelessness or in priority need because of a restricted person.[529]

520 HA 1996 ss193(7AA)–(7AD), 195A(1), (5), (6). Similar provision is made for those threatened with homelessness, which is defined as arising arises once a valid notice under HA 1988 s21 is served (see *Manual of housing law*, para 2.203): HA 1996 s195A(3)–(5). Subsection (3) concerns those threatened with homelessness and, once HRA 2017 came into force, it was repealed and new duties apply (paras 10.67–10.71): HRA 2017 s4(4).

521 H(W)A 2014 ss76(3), 84.

522 HA 1996 s193(7F); H(W)A 2014 s76(2).

523 HA 1996 193(7F) as it read prior to amendment by LA 2011.

524 HA 1996 s193(7F), (8): see 'Reasonable refusals', paras 10.251–10.253 below.

525 9 November 2012: Localism Act 2011 (Commencement No 2 and Transitional Provisions) (England) Order 2012 SI No 2599 art 2.

526 Localism Act 2011 (Commencement No 2 and Transitional Provisions) (England) Order 2012 SI No 2599 art 3.

527 For applications made on or after that date, the H(W)A 2014 applies: see Housing (Wales) Act 2014 (Commencement No 3 and Transitory, Transitional and Saving Provisions) Order 2015 SI No 1272 art 7. As to applications under H(W)A 2014, see paras 10.246–10.250.

528 HA 1996 s193(3B). See para 3.148.

529 HA 1996 s184(7). See para 3.149.

10.243 If the authority only owes a full housing duty[530] to the applicant because of the restricted person, then, so far as reasonably practicable, it must bring the duty to an end by making a private accommodation offer.[531] Where it is not reasonably practicable to do so, the authority may discharge its duty under the other provisions of HA 1996 s193, but should continue to try to bring the duty to an end with a private accommodation offer.[532]

10.244 A private accommodation offer is of an assured shorthold tenancy made by a private landlord[533] to the applicant in relation to any accommodation which is, or may become, available for the applicant's occupation, which is made with the approval of the authority in pursuance of arrangements made between it and the landlord with a view to bringing the authority's duty to an end; the tenancy must be for a fixed term of at least 12 months.[534]

10.245 When making a private accommodation offer, the authority must inform the applicant of the possible consequences of refusal and of the right to request a review of the suitability of the accommodation.[535] The duty ceases if the applicant either accepts or refuses the private accommodation offer.[536]

10.246 ***England post-LA 2011 and in Wales post-H(W)A 2014.*** In a restricted case,[537] the authority must, so far as is reasonably practicable, bring the full housing duty to an end by arranging for a private accommodation offer to be made.[538]

10.247 This means an offer of an assured shorthold tenancy made by a private landlord to the applicant, made with the approval of the authority in pursuance of arrangements made by between it and the landlord with a view to bringing the authority's duty to an end; the tenancy must be a fixed tenancy for a period of at least 12 months.[539]

530 Under HA 1996 s193(2).

531 HA 1996 s193(7AD).

532 Department of Communities and Local Government (DCLG) Guidance Note, 16 February 2009, para 14.

533 Ie any landlord other than one within HA 1985 s80 and thus including a private registered provider of social housing (England) or a registered social landlord (Wales): HA 1996 s217 and H(W)A 2014 s99.

534 HA 1996 s193(7AC).

535 HA 1996 s193(7AB).

536 HA 1996 s193(7AA).

537 See para 3.148.

538 HA 1996 s193(7AD).

539 HA 1996 s193(7AC).

10.248 The full housing duty ends if the applicant, having been informed of the possible consequences of refusal of the offer and the right to request a review of the suitability of the accommodation,[540] either accepts or refuses a private accommodation offer.[541]

10.249 The authority must inform the applicant that the basis for the decision was that the duty was only owed because of a restricted person,[542] identify the restricted person by name, and explain both why the person is a restricted person and that it is necessary to bring the duty to an end with a private accommodation offer.[543]

10.250 In Wales, as in England, a duty owed to a restricted person must, so far as is reasonably practicable, be brought to an end by securing an offer of accommodation from a private sector landlord.[544]

Reasonable refusals

10.251 Until LA 2011 s148 came into force in England,[545] an authority was not to make a final offer of accommodation under Part 6,[546] approve a private accommodation offer[547] or approve an offer of an assured shorthold tenancy,[548] unless satisfied that the accommodation was suitable for the applicant and that it was reasonable for him or her to accept the offer:[549] this is of continuing application to an application made before that date in respect of which the accommodation duty had arisen but had not ceased by that date.[550] It is also of continuing

540 HA 1996 s193(7AB).

541 HA 1996 s193(7AA).

542 HA 1996 s184(3A). Since HRA 2017 came into force in England on 3 April 2018 (Homelessness Reduction Act 2017 (Commencement and Transitional and Savings Provisions) Regulations 2018 SI No 167 reg 3, only applicable to applications made and reviews sought on or after that date – see reg 4), the duty also arises if the authority decides that a duty would be owed after its duty under HA 1996 s189B(2) comes to an end: HA 1996 s184(3A).

543 HA 1996 s184(3).

544 H(W)A 2014 s76.

545 9 November 2012: Localism Act 2011 (Commencement No 2 and Transitional Provisions) (England) Order 2012 SI No 2599 art 2.

546 HA 1996 s193(7F)(a).

547 HA 1996 s193(7F)(ab), inserted by the Housing and Regeneration Act 2008 s314 with effect from 2 March 2009 except in relation to applications for an allocation of social housing or housing assistance or for accommodation made before that date, see the Housing and Regeneration Act 2008 (Commencement No 1 and Saving Provisions) Order 2009 SI No 415 art 2.

548 HA 1996 s193(7F)(b).

549 HA 1996 s193(7F).

550 Localism Act 2011 (Commencement No 2 and Transitional Provisions) (England) Order 2012 SI No 2599 art 3.

application for applications made to Welsh authorities prior to 27 April 2015.[551]

10.252 From LA 2011, the requirement that it is reasonable to accept the offer was replaced by a prohibition on making the offer if the applicant is under contractual or other obligations in respect of his or her existing accommodation which he or she cannot bring to an end before being required to take up the offer.[552]

10.253 In Wales, there is no analogous restriction on the offer.

Keeping offers open

10.254 In *Khatun*,[553] the Court of Appeal reviewed earlier cases in which it had been held that an offer (under HA 1985 Part 3) should remain open for consideration by the applicant for a reasonable time.[554]

10.255 It was held that – while an authority may have regard to the applicant's subjective view on suitability – the cases did not support the proposition that the authority is bound to do so.

10.256 It was also held that an applicant does not have a right to view and comment on a property offered by a local authority in discharge of a duty to him or her before being required to decide whether or not to accept it, although a policy denying an applicant an opportunity to view and comment on the suitability of accommodation offered in discharge of a duty under the HA 1996 would be struck down if no reasonable authority could fail to give him or her such an opportunity.

10.257 It was said that it was not oppressive, perverse or disproportionate to the fair and efficient administration of the authority's scheme for housing the homeless for the authority to require an applicant who had not viewed accommodation offered in discharge of a duty to decide whether or not to accept it on pain of cancellation of his bed and breakfast accommodation if he did not accept; moreover, while the authority's policy of not allowing applicants a reasonable period to consider whether to accept offers of accommodation represented a departure from the recommendations in the Code of Guidance,

551 For applications made on or after that date, H(W)A 2014 applies: see Housing (Wales) Act 2014 (Commencement No 3 and Transitory, Transitional and Saving Provisions) Order 2015 SI No 1272 art 7.

552 HA 1996 s193(7F), (8): para 10.240.

553 *Khatun v Newham LBC* [2004] EWCA Civ 55, [2004] HLR 29.

554 *R v Wandsworth LBC ex p Lindsay* (1986) 18 HLR 502, QBD. The same had been held in *Parr v Wyre BC* (1982) 2 HLR 71, CA, which was disapproved in *R v Hillingdon LBC ex p Puhlhofer* [1986] AC 484, (1986) 18 HLR 158, HL, so far as it was based on the introduction of the word 'appropriate'. See also *R v Ealing LBC ex p Denny* (1995) 27 HLR 424, CA.

it could not be criticised as it pursued the lawful aim of moving families out of bed and breakfast accommodation as quickly as possible.

10.258 Given the right to seek a review of suitability after moving in, authorities may therefore insist that an applicant makes a decision whether or not to accept an offer at the time that it is made, without holding it open to afford him or her an opportunity to view it.

10.259 The position is different where the authority knows that admittedly relevant material, for example, medical evidence, is yet to be produced. In *Hazeltine,*[555] the applicant challenged suitability on medical grounds; the authority agreed to keep the offer open, but only for a limited period, before the end of which it would not have received or evaluated the medical reports that it had requested from her. The authority's proposal was that, if she accepted the offer, she should abandon her challenge to it, but that, if she did not do so, the authority would determine the issue of suitability retrospectively, ie, if considered unsuitable she would get another offer, but if suitable she would not and the authority would take the position that it had discharged its duty to her. The court held that this procedure was not fair.

10.260 Where an authority notifies an applicant that it has ceased to be subject to the duty under HA 1996 s193(2), because the applicant has refused an offer of suitable accommodation under section 193(5), the authority is not obliged to keep the accommodation available during the period when the applicant has the right to request a review or until the authority has reached its review decision.[556]

Review

10.261 There is a right to seek an internal review of the suitability of accommodation offered under HA 1996 s193(5) or (7),[557] which may be exercised whether or not the applicant has accepted the offer of accommodation.[558]

555 *R v Wycombe DC ex p Hazeltine* (1993) 25 HLR 313, CA. See *Khatun v Newham LBC*, above, at [37] where *Hazeltine* was held to be consistent with the decision in that case.

556 *Osseily v Westminster City Council* [2007] EWCA Civ 1108, [2008] HLR 18 at [11].

557 HA 1996 s202(1A); H(W)A 2014 s85.

558 HA 1996 s202(1A); reversing the effect of *Alghile v Westminster City Council* (2001) 33 HLR 57, CA, so as to afford the applicant the option of moving into the property while still contesting its suitability. In Wales, see H(W)A 2014 s85.

Re-application

10.262 A person towards whom the authority has been under a duty under HA 1996 s193 which has ceased, may re-apply.[559] This prevents an authority from simply relying on the previous discharge.[560] Rather, the authority must reconsider the case, so that a new duty will arise unless the authority can properly conclude that the applicant no longer fulfils the preconditions, for example, is not eligible or became intentionally homeless.[561]

10.263 This is, however, subject to the discussion in *Fahia*[562] and *Rikha Begum*[563] of when a further application may be made and when it may be said to be identical with a previous application, such that there is no application before the authority at all.[564]

Alternative provisions under the Homelessness Reduction Act 2017 – England

Housing Act 1996 s193A

10.264 As noted,[565] since the HRA 2017 came into force,[566] the initial help duty can be brought to an end if the applicant, having been informed of the consequences of refusal and of his or her right to request a

559 HA 1996 s193(9); H(W)A 2014 s62(2).

560 Cf paras 9.26–9.44. The case-law discussed there would suggest that, notwithstanding HA 1996 s193(9), an authority may refuse to accept a new application from an applicant who has refused a suitable offer of accommodation if the application is based on exactly the same facts.

561 See also para 10.15, for the right to re-apply with two years even if not in priority need.

562 *R v Harrow LBC ex p Fahia* [1998] 1 WLR 1396, (1998) 30 HLR 1124, HL.

563 *Rikha Begum v Tower Hamlets LBC* [2005] EWCA Civ 340, [2005] HLR 34: HA 1996 s193(9) is expressly considered at [53]. See also *R (Kensington and Chelsea RLBC) v Ealing LBC* [2017] EWHC 24 (Admin), [2017] HLR 13 at [18].

564 See the full discussion of repeat applications at paras 9.26–9.44 and, in particular, the conclusion in para 9.37 that the distinction is rarely one on which an authority can rely, ie a new application will normally need to be accepted. The corollary is that HA 1996 ss193(9) and 85 add little.

565 See paras 10.81–10.91.

566 3 April 2018: see Homelessness Reduction Act 2017 (Commencement and Transitional and Savings Provisions) Regulations 2018 SI No 167 reg 3, only applicable to applications made and reviews sought on or after that date – see reg 4.

review of the suitability of the accommodation,[567] refuses either a final accommodation offer,[568] or a final Part 6[569] offer.[570]

10.265 The authority cannot, however, approve a final accommodation offer or make a final Part 6 offer unless it is satisfied that it is suitable for the applicant;[571] nor can it approve or make such an offer if the applicant is under contractual or other obligations in respect of his or her existing accommodation, which he or she is not able to bring to an end before he or she would have to take up the offer.[572]

10.266 If it is brought to an end on this basis, the principal housing duty in section 193 does not apply.[573]

HA 1996 s193C

10.267 Also since HRA 2017 came into force,[574] HA 1996 s193 does not apply when either the duty towards those threatened with homelessness (para10.67) or the initial help duty (paras 10.67–10.75) is brought to an end by reason of the applicant's deliberate and unreasonable refusal to co-operate (paras 10.88–10.91).[575] In either case, however, an applicant who is homeless, eligible, in priority need and not homeless intentionally will be entitled to accommodation under HA 1996 s193C instead.[576]

567 See paras 9.192–9.199.

568 This is an offer of an assured shorthold tenancy made by a private landlord – including a private registered provider of social housing (England) or a registered social landlord (Wales) – in relation to any accommodation which is, or may become, available for the applicant's occupation, made, with the approval of the authority, in pursuance of arrangements made by the authority in discharge of the initial help duty, which is a fixed term tenancy for a period of at least six months: HA 1996 s193A(4) added by HRA 2017 s7(1).

569 This is an offer of accommodation under Part 6 made in writing in discharge of the authority's initial help duty, which states that it is a final offer for that purpose: HA 1996 s193A(5).

570 HA 1996 s193A(1), (2).

571 HA 1996 s193A(6).

572 HA 1996 s193A(7).

573 HA 1996 s193A(3).

574 3 April 2018: Homelessness Reduction Act 2017 (Commencement and Transitional and Savings Provisions) Regulations 2018 SI No 167 reg 3, only applicable to applications made and reviews sought on or after that date – see reg 4.

575 HA 1996 ss195(10), 189B(9).

576 HA 1996 s193C(3), (4).

10.268 The authority's duty under HA 1996 s193C is to secure that accommodation is available for occupation by the applicant.[577] Much of the law considered in relation to section 193 will apply: the general provisions referred to at para 10.118 (observations on availability: para 10.27; payment: paras 10.31–10.32; and security: paras 10.33–10.36), subject to the same qualification applicable to assured security as in paras 10.33–10.36, and it remains to be seen whether the exclusion from PEA 1977 (para 10.47) applies to this duty:[578] it is submitted that the close relationship between sections 193 and 193C suggests that it should also not do so.

10.269 Observations on defences on eviction (para 10.47) will likewise apply should an authority seek to evict an applicant while he or she is still being housed under this provision. In addition, the following headings in relation to section 193 should also apply save so far as qualified specific statutory qualification: postponement of the duty (paras 10.127–10.134); means of discharge (paras 10.135–10.136); out-of-area placements (paras 10.147–10.161); suitability of accommodation (paras 10.162–10.204); keeping offers open (paras 10.254–10.260).

10.270 The duty will cease if the applicant:

a) ceases to be eligible for assistance;
b) becomes homeless intentionally from accommodation made available for his or her occupation;
c) accepts an offer of an assured tenancy from a private landlord; or
d) otherwise voluntarily ceases to occupy, as his or her only or principal home,[579] the accommodation made available for his or her occupation.[580]

10.271 The duty will also cease if the applicant, having been informed of the possible consequences of refusal or acceptance and of his or her right to request a review[581] of the suitability of the accommodation,

577 HA 1996 s193C(3), (4).
578 See the discussion at para 10.123.
579 See *Manual of housing law*, paras 1.62–1.73.
580 HA 1996 s193C(5).
581 See paras 9.186–9.199.

refuses or accepts a final accommodation offer,[582] or a final Part 6[583] offer.[584]

10.272 The authority cannot approve a final accommodation offer or make a final Part 6 offer unless it is satisfied that it is suitable for the applicant;[585] nor can it approve or make such an offer if the applicant is under contractual or other obligations in respect of his or her existing accommodation, which he or she is not able to bring to an end before he or she would have to take up the offer.[586]

582 This is an offer of an assured shorthold tenancy made by a private landlord – including a private registered provider of social housing (England) or a registered social landlord (Wales) – in relation to any accommodation which is, or may become, available for the applicant's occupation, made, with the approval of the authority, in pursuance of arrangements made by the authority in discharge of the HA 1996 s193C duty, which is a fixed term tenancy for a period of at least six months: HA 1996 s193C(7).

583 This is an offer of accommodation under HA 1996 Part 6 made in writing in discharge of the authority's HA 1996 s193C duty, which states that it is a final offer for that purpose: HA 1996 s193C(8).

584 HA 1996 s193C(6).

585 HA 1996 s193C(9).

586 HA 1996 s193C(10).

CHAPTER 11

Allocations

continued

Introduction

11.1 Local authorities hold the bulk of their housing stock under Housing Act (HA) 1985 Part 2.

11.2 Until 1996, the statutory constraints on the allocation of that stock were to be found in HA 1985 s22, which required that in the selection of tenants, certain groups were to be given a reasonable preference, including (by amendment in 1977) homeless people, a formulation so loose that there was negligible case-law under it.

11.3 Under HA 1985 Part 3, duties towards the homeless could be discharged by allocating housing held by the authority under HA 1985 Part 2 or any other power.[1] The Housing Act (HA) 1996 was intended to reduce the proportion of permanent housing which went directly to homeless people, whether from an authority's own stock or by way of nomination to the stock of registered providers of social housing; accordingly, it repealed and replaced HA 1985 s22,[2] with, among other provisions regulating allocation, its own categories of reasonable preference.

11.4 Under the 1996 Act, homelessness was not in itself one of the grounds of preference – although the homeless could qualify, along with others, on the grounds of, for example, unsatisfactory housing conditions, temporary or insecure housing, a particular need for settled accommodation, or social or economic circumstances which made it difficult for them to secure settled accommodation.[3]

11.5 HA 1996 also introduced a statutory requirement to maintain a housing register, which the authority could keep in such form as it thought fit and which it could, if it wished, maintain in common with other landlords, eg other social housing landlords.[4]

11.6 In 1997, following the general election of that year, a degree of direct priority for homeless people was restored in the allocation of permanent stock by regulations.[5]

1 HA 1985 s69(1)(a).

2 See para 11.83 onwards.

3 HA 1996 s167 as enacted.

4 See generally, HA 1996 ss162–166 as enacted; as to common registers, see HA 1996 s162(3).

5 Allocation of Housing (Reasonable and Additional Preference) Regulations 1997 SI No 1902.

11.7 Subsequently, the Homelessness Act 2002 extensively amended HA 1996 Part 6,[6] primarily:

a) to remove the detailed requirements governing the housing register;
b) to remove the power of local authorities to impose blanket restrictions on groups of people;[7]
c) to introduce arrangements to exclude or give a lower priority to those guilty of 'serious unacceptable behaviour'; and
d) to advance the policy of more applicant choice in the allocation of housing.

11.8 In England, the provisions were changed again by the Localism Act (LA) 2011, primarily by re-introducing a right for local authorities to determine for themselves who qualifies for an allocation, subject to any regulations which require them to include or exclude specified classes of person.

11.9 This chapter addresses allocations under the following headings:

a) meaning of 'allocation';
b) qualifying persons;
c) applications for housing;
d) the allocation scheme;
e) procedure;
f) internal reviews and challenges; and
g) allocation of housing by registered providers of social housing/registered social landlords.

11.10 Criminal offences which may be committed in relation to housing applications under HA 1996 Part 6 – as under Part 7 – are considered in chapter 15. The secretary of state and Welsh Ministers have power – which has been exercised – to issue guidance to local authorities on the exercise of their functions under Part 6.[8]

6 The amendments came into force in Wales on 27 January 2003 (Homelessness Act 2002 (Commencement) (Wales) Order 2002 SI No 1736) and 31 January 2003 in England (Homelessness Act 2002 (Commencement No 3) (England) Order 2002 SI No 3114).

7 A practice facilitated by the wording of the former HA 1996 s161(4), which provided that authorities could decide what classes of persons were or were not 'qualifying persons' for the purposes of an allocation of housing.

8 *Allocation of accommodation: guidance for local housing authorities in England*, Department for Communities and Local Government (DCLG), 2012, replacing all previous guidance (see para 1.2 of the guidance), although note that earlier codes will be relevant to applications which precede it (ie before commencement of the changes effected by the LA 2011, which came into force on 18 June 2012 – see para 11.72), as to which see previous editions of this book. See also the 2018 English Code of Guidance which, although issued under HA 1996 s182 in

11.11 The interaction of allocation schemes with other statutory duties, in particular the Care Act (CA) 2014 and Children Act (CA) 1989 ss17 and 20, is considered in chapter 13.

Meaning of 'allocation'

11.12 The provisions of HA 1996 Part 6 apply only to the allocation of housing accommodation, as defined by HA 1996 s159(2).[9]

Selecting a person to be a secure or introductory tenant

11.13 Any selection of a person to be a secure[10] or introductory tenant,[11] whether or not of property held under HA 1985 Part 2, is an allocation.[12] Selection is not synonymous with the grant of a tenancy:[13] the provisions accordingly govern how people are selected to become tenants, but the grant itself is a separate process under HA 1985 Part 2; it follows that a grant that is not in accordance with the HA 1996 Part 6 allocations policy of the authority is not invalid[14] for that reason.[15]

Part 7, touches on allocations at paras 2.44–2.50, remarking at para 2.45 that: 'Housing authorities may need to review their allocations schemes in response to the 2017 Act, to ensure that they deliver the requirements of the legislation and are sufficiently geared towards preventing homelessness.' In October 2017, the then DCLG issued a consultation paper on how to improve access to social housing for victims of domestic abuse (*Improving access to social housing for victims of domestic abuse: consultation*) but, at the time of writing, no response to the consultation paper had been published. In Wales, see the *Code of guidance for local authorities: allocation of accommodation and homelessness*, Welsh Government, March 2016 ('Welsh Code of Guidance'). See also the Housing Association Circular RSL 004/15 (replacing circular RSL 003/12, which itself replaced RLS 023/09) which requires all housing associations registered in Wales to take account of the Welsh Code.

9 An authority will not normally owe a duty of care to anyone seeking an allocation under HA 1996 Part 6; the remedy for a person dissatisfied with a decision is to seek internal review or use the ombudsman service: *R (Darby, as administratix of the estate of Lee Rabbetts) v Richmond upon Thames LBC* [2015] EWHC 909 (QB). As to internal review, see paras 11.149–11.152; and see paras 11.162–11.167 on the ombudsman. Ultimately, judicial review may be available.

10 HA 1985 Part 4.

11 Introductory tenancies were brought in by HA 1996 Part 5 Chapter 1.

12 HA 1996 s159(2)(a).

13 Ie, the disposal of stock by way of the grant of a tenancy, under HA 1985 s32.

14 Cf para 11.82.

15 *Birmingham City Council v Qasim* [2009] EWCA Civ 1080, [2010] HLR 19.

11.14 For this purpose, 'tenancy' includes 'licence'.[16]

11.15 'Selection' includes notifying a tenant or licensee who is not currently secure that he or she is to become so.[17] The transition from introductory to secure tenant, effected by the passage of time,[18] is not, however, a selection in itself: the allocation process was at the introductory tenancy stage.[19]

Nominations

11.16 Nomination of a person to be the secure or introductory tenant (or licensee) of another, for example, of a housing action trust, is an allocation.[20]

11.17 Likewise, the nomination of a person to become an assured tenant of a private registered provider of social housing or registered social landlord is an allocation: accordingly, this does not include a nomination to a tenancy that will not be assured under HA 1988 Sch 1, but it does include nomination to an assured shorthold.[21]

11.18 Nominations include those made in pursuance of an arrangement (whether or not legally enforceable) to require that accommodation is made available to a person or a number of persons nominated by the authority.[22]

11.19 These provisions reflect long-standing arrangements with housing associations and trusts to which funding has been provided,[23] linked to a right on the part of an authority to nominate a proportion (or even all) of the tenants to a particular property, group of properties (for example, block of flats), or to an association's stock as a whole.

11.20 The wording of HA 1996 s159(4) is oxymoronic: if the entitlement is to 'require' that accommodation is made available to a person or number of persons, it is 'legally enforceable'. It may be that what

16 HA 1996 s159(3); see HA 1985 s79(3).

17 HA 1996 s159(3). For example, under HA 1985 Sch 1 paras 4 (homeless persons), 5 (temporary accommodation for persons taking up employment) and 10 (student lettings), as amended by HA 1996 Schs 16 and 17.

18 HA 1996 s125.

19 See last paragraph.

20 HA 1996 s159(2)(b).

21 HA 1996 s159(2)(c).

22 HA 1996 s159(4).

23 Whether under Local Government Act 1988 Part 3 or HA 1996 s22. (Since 1 April 2010, the latter provision has only been applicable in Wales as a result of amendments by Housing and Regeneration Act 2008.)

was in mind is that a particular nomination is not legally enforceable, because such arrangements commonly work by way of proportions of voids, but the wording does not lend itself to this, because it is the arrangement that must 'require' – even if putatively not 'legally enforceable'. To give the wording some meaning (within the apparent intention of the provision), it would seem that a voluntary nomination arrangement not made by deed and for which there is no consideration will still qualify.

Exemptions

11.21 In England, HA 1996 s159(4A) and (4B)[24] provide that the allocation provisions do not apply to anyone who is already a secure or introductory tenant, or an assured tenant of a private registered provider of social housing or a registered social landlord, unless the person has applied to the authority for a transfer and the authority decide that the applicant is entitled to a reasonable preference[25] in the allocation.[26]

11.22 The position is different in Wales:[27] HA 1996 s159(5) exempts from these allocation provisions an allocation to anyone who is already a secure or introductory tenant (whether or not of the same landlord), unless the allocation involves a transfer of housing accommodation for that person which has been made on his or her application.[28] Those moved at the behest of the landlord – for example, for redevelopment – are exempt from both sets of provisions.

11.23 Also exempt from HA 1996 Part 6 are the categories specified in HA 1996 s160:

24 As amended by the Homelessness Act 2002 s13 and the LA 2011 s145.

25 See paras 11.98–11.105.

26 HA 1996 s159(4A), (4B), as amended by LA 2011 s145(2). So far as concerns assured tenants, the wording is difficult: HA 1996 s159(4B) refers to someone within section 159(4A)(a) or (b), the former referring to local authority tenants, the latter to private registered providers and registered social landlords; it is, however, an unusual use of the word 'transfer' and if section 159(4B) had only referred to section 159(4A), it may have been assumed that it applied only to local authority tenants.

27 HA 1996 s159(5), as amended by the Homelessness Act 2002 s13.

28 Before amendment, transfers were also exempt. The re-inclusion within the provisions of transfer applications accords with the practice of many local authorities to deal with transfer applications on the same basis as those of new applicants (see, eg *R v Islington LBC ex p Reilly and Mannix* (1998) 31 HLR 651, QBD).

a) succession to secure tenancy on death, or devolution of a fixed term in such circumstances that the tenancy remains secure;[29]
b) assignment by way of exchange of secure tenancy or to a person who could have succeeded to it;[30]
c) transfers by way of surrender and re-grant where one of the tenancies is a flexible tenancy[31] or an assured shorthold tenancy;[32]
d) transfers of secure or introductory tenancies under the provisions of matrimonial and related domestic legislation;[33]
e) becoming a secure tenant following an introductory tenancy;[34]
f) succession to an introductory tenancy;[35]
g) assignment of an introductory tenancy to a person who could have succeeded to it.[36]

11.24 The secretary of state and the Welsh Ministers may prescribe other categories of allocation which are to fall outside HA 1996 Part 6, subject to restrictions or conditions, including by reference to a specific category or proportion of housing.[37]

11.25 This power has been exercised to exempt allocation of housing to:[38]

a) those entitled to rehousing under Land Compensation Act 1973 s39;[39]
b) those whose homes are repurchased under HA 1985 s554 or s555;[40] and
c) in England, those to whom accommodation is let on a family intervention tenancy.[41]

29 HA 1985 ss87–90.
30 HA 1985 s92.
31 See HA 1985 s107A.
32 LA 2011 s158.
33 Matrimonial Causes Act 1973 s24; Matrimonial and Family Proceedings Act 1984 s17; CA 1989 Sch 1 para 1; and Civil Partnership Act 2004 Sch 5 Part 2 or Sch 7 para 9(2) or (3).
34 HA 1996 s125.
35 HA 1996 s133.
36 HA 1996 s134.
37 HA 1996 s160(4) and (5).
38 Allocation of Housing (England) Regulations 2002 SI No 3264 reg 3 and Allocation of Housing (Wales) Regulations 2003 SI No 239 reg 3.
39 Following compulsory purchase or a number of specified actions leading to loss of the home, eg a demolition order under HA 1985 or a prohibition order under HA 2004.
40 Repurchase of a designated defective dwelling.
41 As to family intervention tenancies, see HA 1985 s79 and Sch 1 para 4ZA.

Eligibility and qualification

11.26 The principal class of person to whom a property cannot be allocated is someone who is ineligible because of immigration status.[42] This has been considered in chapter 3. The English Code of Guidance suggests that eligibility be considered both when an initial application is made and when considering making an allocation, especially where a substantial period of time has elapsed since the application.[43]

11.27 If a person is ineligible, then the authority may not allocate a tenancy to the person, even jointly with someone else who is qualified.[44]

11.28 This does not mean that an allocation may not be made to someone who is eligible simply because a member of his or her household is not, although the fact that a member is ineligible may in some circumstances need to be taken into account when determining an applicant's housing needs under an allocation scheme.[45]

11.29 This is, in any event, unlikely to arise because, under HA 1996 Part 7 or Housing (Wales) Act (H(W)A) 2014 Part 2, such cases (known as 'restricted cases') are, so far as is reasonably practicable, to be dealt with by way of an offer of private sector accommodation (see paras 5.8–5.11).

11.30 Unless a person is ineligible, he or she may therefore – subject to the following paragraphs – be allocated housing accommodation by an authority.[46]

Transfer applicants

11.31 Where an applicant[47] is an existing secure or introductory tenant, or an assured tenant of housing accommodation allocated[48] to him or her by a local housing authority, the applicant is not disqualified on the basis of his or her immigration status.[49]

42 HA 1996 s160ZA(1) in England; HA 1996 s160A(1) in Wales.

43 *Allocation of accommodation: guidance for local housing authorities in England*, para 3.2. There is no similar advice in the Welsh Code.

44 HA 1996 s160ZA(1)(b); HA 1996 s160A(1)(c) in Wales.

45 See paras 3.198–3.206.

46 HA 1996 s160A(2).

47 In England only, an applicant whom the authority considers is entitled to a reasonable preference, HA 1996 s160ZA(5), referring to s159(4B). See para 11.21.

48 See para 11.21.

49 HA 1996 s160ZA(5) (England) and s160A(6) (Wales).

Ineligibility for unacceptable behaviour in Wales

11.32 Local authorities in Wales may disqualify those who – or whose household members[50] – have been guilty of unacceptable behaviour serious enough to make them unsuitable to be tenants of the authority and who – in the circumstances at the time their application is considered – are unsuitable to be tenants of the authority because of the unacceptable behaviour.[51]

11.33 'Unacceptable behaviour' is defined as behaviour which would, if the person was either a secure tenant or a member of a secure tenant's household, entitle a landlord to a possession order under any of grounds 1–7 of HA 1985 Sch 2[52] or the 'absolute' ground for possession in HA 1985 s84A.[53]

11.34 Accordingly, a former assured or protected tenant evicted on analogous grounds could be treated as disqualified.

11.35 The 'discretionary' grounds[54] are:

- *Ground 1*[55] – Rent arrears or breach of tenancy.
- *Ground 2*[56] – Behaviour which caused or is likely to cause a nuisance or annoyance to those persons residing, visiting or otherwise engaging in a lawful activity in the locality of the dwelling, or to any person employed (whether or not by the landlord) in connection with the exercise of the landlord's housing management functions, which behaviour is directly or indirectly related to or affects those functions; or, conviction for using the dwelling for immoral or illegal purposes or committing an indictable offence in or in the locality of the dwelling house.[57]

50 'Household' is not defined, but is presumably wider than 'family'.

51 HA 1996 s160A(7). It has been held that this does not entitle an authority to take into account criminal convictions which are 'spent' under the Rehabilitation of Offenders Act 1974: see R *(YA) v Hammersmith and Fulham LBC* [2016] EWHC 1850 (Admin), [2016] HLR 39. Even if – contrary to the apparent effect of the Rehabilitation of Offenders Act 1974 – an argument could be mounted to the contrary, it is very difficult indeed to see how it could be reasonable in public law terms to take it into account.

52 HA 1996 s160A(8)(a).

53 HA 1996 s160A(8)(aa).

54 Ie those where reasonableness must also be proven: HA 1985 s84(2).

55 HA 1988 Sch 2 grounds 8, 10, 11 and 12; Rent Act (RA) 1977 Sch 15 case 1.

56 HA 1988 Sch 2 ground 14; RA 1977 Sch 15 case 2.

57 A number of cases have relied on this ground, and the Court of Appeal has either upheld possession orders or substituted possession where it has originally been refused: see *Kensington and Chelsea RLBC v Simmonds* (1996) 29 HLR 507; *Bristol City Council v Mousah* (1997) 30 HLR 32; *Darlington LBC v Sterling* (1997) 29 HLR 309; *West Kent HA v Davies* (1998) 31 HLR 415; *Camden*

- *Ground 2A*[58] – Domestic violence causing a partner or other family member to leave the property.[59]
- *Ground 3*[60] – Deterioration of the dwelling-house due to waste, neglect or default.
- *Ground 4*[61] – Deterioration of furniture provided by the landlord due to ill-treatment.
- *Ground 5*[62] – Tenancy induced by a false statement.[63]
- *Ground 6*[64] – Premium received or paid in connection with a mutual exchange.
- *Ground 7*[65] – Eviction from a dwelling within the curtilage of a building held for non-housing purposes due to conduct such that given the nature of the building it would not be right for occupation to continue.

11.36 The 'absolute ground'[66] is the new ground introduced by Anti-social Behaviour, Crime and Policing Act (ASBCPA) 2014 s94, where a

LBC v Gilsenan (1998) 31 HLR 81; *Portsmouth City Council v Bryant* (2000) 32 HLR 906; *Newcastle City Council v Morrison* (2000) 32 HLR 891; *Lambeth LBC v Howard* (2001) 33 HLR 58; *New Charter HA v Ashcroft* [2004] EWCA Civ 310, [2004] HLR 36; *London and Quadrant Housing Trust v Root* [2005] EWCA Civ 43, [2005] HLR 28; *Manchester City Council v Higgins* [2006] HLR 14; *Sandwell MBC v Hensley* [2008] HLR 22. These cases reflect a hardening of attitudes towards those guilty of anti-social behaviour and, in turn, make it easier for authorities to conclude that an applicant is disqualified on this ground, although authorities will need to be careful to consider each case and, in particular, the issue of reasonableness on its own merits not on the basis of policy. For the equivalent provision under HA 1988 Sch 2 ground 14, see eg, *Knowsley Housing Trust v Prescott* [2009] EWHC 924 (QB), [2009] L&TR 24. See also *Brent LBC v Corcoran* [2010] EWCA Civ 774, [2010] HLR 43 concerning breach of licence conditions for caravan pitches by reason of anti-social behaviour.

58 HA 1988 Sch 2 ground 14A; there is no equivalent under the RA 1977.

59 See *Camden LBC v Mallett* (2001) 33 HLR 20, CA.

60 HA 1988 Sch 2 ground 13; RA 1977 Sch 15 case 3.

61 HA 1988 Sch 2 ground 15; RA 1977 Sch 15 case 4.

62 HA 1988 Sch 2 ground 17; there is no equivalent under the RA 1977.

63 Including those made as part of a homelessness application. Cf *Rushcliffe BC v Watson* (1991) 24 HLR 124, CA; *Shrewsbury and Atcham BC v Evans* (1997) 30 HLR 123, CA; and *Lewisham LBC v Akinsola* (1999) 32 HLR 414, CA; *Waltham Forest LBC v Roberts* [2004] EWCA Civ 940, [2005] HLR 2.

64 There is no equivalent under HA 1988 or RA 1977, although in each case, if the tenancy agreement prohibits assignment (whether absolutely or only with the consent of the landlord), an assignment in breach of such a term may give rise to a basis for possession under HA 1988 Sch 2 ground 12 or RA 1977 Sch 15 case 1.

65 There is no equivalent under either the HA 1988 or RA 1977.

66 HA 1988 Sch 2 ground 7A. There is no requirement also to prove that it is reasonable to make the order sought.

secure tenant (or a person residing in or visiting the property) has engaged in specified anti-social behaviour (eg breached an injunction under ASBCPA 2014 s1, convicted of a breach of a criminal behaviour order under ASBCPA 2014 s30).

11.37 HA 1985 Sch 2 grounds 1–7 are discretionary grounds for possession, and as such the court has to be satisfied that it is reasonable to grant possession before an order can be made.[67] Authorities will therefore need to address this issue of reasonableness for themselves,[68] ie they will need to reach a public law decision (that in itself is not so unreasonable as to be irrational or perverse)[69] on whether or not a county court would have found it reasonable to make the order.

11.38 There need not have been an eviction on the particular ground relied on, only behaviour which would entitle the landlord to a possession order under one of them.[70]

11.39 Sight must not be lost of the overriding test, whether the authority is satisfied that the applicant or member of the applicant's household has been guilty of behaviour 'serious enough to make [the applicant] unsuitable to be' its tenant, and that – in the circumstances at the time of his or her application – the applicant is thus unsuitable.[71]

11.40 The latter qualification means that the fact that an order for possession has been made on a relevant ground will not be sufficient on its own,[72] nor will a fixed rule or practice to treat all those evicted on one of the relevant grounds as qualifying under the first limb of the test (ie past unsuitability) be lawful.[73] The separation in HA 1996 s160A(7) between past conduct and suitability at time of application is likely to be strictly applied.

11.41 Criminal convictions for drug-related offences can be sufficient.[74] Convictions for sexual offences, including offences against children, were sufficient to render an applicant for a transfer ineligible, even though he had been assessed as having a critical need for ground-floor accommodation and, due to his disabilities, was unable to climb stairs; if he had been allocated the ground-floor flat that he had

67 HA 1985 s84(2).
68 See Welsh Code para 2.34.
69 Cf para 12.62.
70 See Welsh Code para 2.33.
71 Still or, eg if there has been a period of good behaviour, again.
72 See Welsh Code para 2.35.
73 See paras 12.54–12.55.
74 *R (Dixon) v Wandsworth LBC* [2007] EWHC 3075 (Admin), [2008] JHL D21.

identified, then he would have had easy access to a playground, which posed an obvious risk to children in the area.[75]

11.42 Conduct leading to an outright, a suspended or a postponed order can suffice, because postponement and suspension are under HA 1985 s85, which does not come into play unless an order under section 84 is available. There is a difficult relationship here. In *Portsmouth City Council v Bryant*,[76] it was said that: 'In deciding whether it is reasonable to make an order under section 84(2) the judge can properly take into account his power under section 85(2) to suspend that order.' The burden of the decision was that a court could decide to make an order because it had power to suspend or postpone knowing that it intended to do so, where if there were no such power it might not make an order at all.

11.43 It follows that there is a material difference between an outright order made under HA 1996 s84 and one made in contemplation of the exercise of the section 85 power to suspend or postpone. On the face of it, any such order could suffice; on the other hand, if the conduct was such that a court would have been likely to suspend or postpone, it is tantamount to recognising that a court would have been operating from the premise that the conduct had not yet reached the point at which the occupier was – in terms of the overriding issue for the authority – unsuitable to be a tenant.

11.44 In turn, this should impact on the overriding issue (whether or not the conduct was sufficient to make the applicant unsuitable to be a tenant). Accordingly, it is submitted that the authority should ask itself whether it was likely that an outright, suspended or postponed order would have been made: if one of the latter two, while it still has the right to treat the applicant as unsuitable, it should nonetheless be able to justify why.

11.45 The Welsh Code of Guidance suggests that the authority needs 'to satisfy itself that if a possession order were granted it would have been an outright order'.[77] It may be thought that this is an overstatement of the law; the essential issue is selection of tenants, to which conduct is, on the face of it, not irrelevant;[78] on the other hand, there is much practical merit in this reconciliation.

11.46 Relevant too would seem to be the distinction drawn in some of the anti-social behaviour cases between conduct by the tenant himself

75 *R (M) v Hackney LBC* [2009] EWHC 2255 (Admin), [2010] JHL D1.

76 (2000) 32 HLR 906, CA, per Simon Brown LJ at 916.

77 At para 2.35.

78 See also para 12.41.

or herself and conduct by a member of the tenant's household which the tenant had failed to control, such that an outright order might be made in the first case but a suspended order in the second, depending on the degree of acquiescence.[79]

11.47 Thus, a transfer applicant against whom a suspended order has been made (which has not subsequently led to eviction) would prima facie still be suitable. Likewise, a person against whom a suspended order was made on the ground of, for example, nuisance and annoyance, but put into effect because of arrears,[80] would be in a different class from an applicant whose order was put into effect because of continued nuisance or annoyance.

11.48 The position of a former tenant who has abandoned a property owing several hundred pounds of arrears may also usefully be considered. On an application for housing from the local authority, the authority may consider that the arrears are such that an order would have been made, so that the applicant can be considered to have committed unacceptable behaviour. The authority should, however, also consider whether – if the tenant had decided not to abandon, but had instead waited and defended a possession action based on the arrears – an outright or a suspended order would have been made.[81]

Disqualification in England

Overview

11.49 The previous class of ineligibility based on anti-social behaviour was replaced in England by a power entitling the local authority to decide for itself who does – or does not – qualify for an allocation.[82] Accommodation can only be allocated to someone who qualifies according to those local criteria (or to joint tenants, one of whom so qualifies).[83] The power is, however, subject to the overriding immig-

79 See, eg, *Gallagher v Castle Vale HAT* [2001] EWCA Civ 944, (2001) 33 HLR 72; see also *Kensington and Chelsea RLBC v Simmonds* (1996) 29 HLR 507, CA, per Simon Brown LJ at 512; *Newcastle City Council v Morrison* (2000) 32 HLR 891, CA; *Manchester City Council v Higgins* [2005] EWCA Civ 1423, [2006] HLR 14; and *Knowsley Housing Trust v McMullen (by her litigation friend)* [2006] EWCA Civ 539, [2006] HLR 43. Cf *London and Quadrant Housing Trust v Root* [2005] EWCA Civ 43, [2005] HLR 28.

80 See *Sheffield City Council v Hopkins* [2001] EWCA Civ 1023, [2002] HLR 12.

81 See, eg *Lambeth LBC v Henry* (2000) 32 HLR 874, CA.

82 HA 1996 s160ZA(7), added by LA 2011 s146 with effect from 18 June 2012, see fn 8.

83 HA 1996 s160ZA(6), added by LA 2011 s146 with effect from 18 June 2012, see fn 8.

ration criteria considered in chapter 3, ie there can be no allocation in contravention of them.[84]

11.50 Although there is power to decide what persons are or are not qualifying persons,[85] it has been held that it may not be used to disqualify a person entitled to a reasonable preference.[86] It follows that an English authority which wants to adopt a restriction similar to that applicable in Wales[87] would need to frame it carefully.

11.51 Authorities are under a duty to seek to eliminate discrimination:[88] they must be careful not to offend anti-discrimination legislation in relation to those with protected characteristics,[89]

11.52 Discrimination may be:

a) direct, ie treating a person less favourably because of a protected characteristic[90] – although treating the disabled more favourably is not discrimination;[91] or

84 HA 1996 s160ZA(7), added by LA 2011 s146; see paras 11.26–11.30.

85 HA 1996 s160ZA(7).

86 Under HA 1996 s166A(3), see *R (Jakimaviciute) v Hammersmith and Fulham LBC* [2014] EWCA Civ 1438, [2015] HLR 5 – exclusion of those in suitable long-term private rented accommodation; *R (Alemi) v Westminster City Council* [2014] EWHC 3858 (Admin) – not able to bid for local authority accommodation for first 12 months; *R (HA) v Ealing LBC* [2015] EWHC 2375 (Admin) – five-year residential qualification. Given the statutory and policy background, this is a surprising conclusion, leaving Wales in a position to exclude the anti-social with a reasonable preference, where English authorities cannot do so: the first of these judgments rejected an approach based on examination of the previous statutory position in England and analysis of what the subsequent legislation had intended to change; it may be that this conclusion would not withstand Supreme Court consideration. That court also rejected guidance advising against such policies, which, however, implied that the secretary of state thought that legally they were possible: see para 11.60.

87 Paras 11.32–11.48.

88 Equality Act (EqA) 2010 s149.

89 EqA 2010 s4: age, disability, gender reassignment, marriage and civil partnership, pregnancy and maternity, race, religion and belief, sex and sexual orientation. Some of these (age, marriage and civil partnership) are not protected in relation to the disposal and management of premises, but it may be doubted whether disposal here goes as far as formulating an allocation scheme: see EqA 2010 s38: '(3) A reference to disposing of premises includes, in the case of premises subject to a tenancy, a reference to– (a) assigning the premises, (b) sub-letting them, or (c) parting with possession of them. (4) A reference to disposing of premises also includes a reference to granting a right to occupy them.'

90 EqA 2010 s13.

91 EqA 2010 s13(3).

b) indirect, as defined:[92] this occurs if the authority applies to an applicant a provision, criterion or practice which is discriminatory in relation to a relevant protected characteristic,[93] meaning a provision, criterion or practice which, while applied to others, puts, or would put, persons with that characteristic at a particular disadvantage when compared to persons without it, which provision, criterion or practice cannot be shown to be a proportionate means of achieving a legitimate aim.[94]

11.53 Nor can authorities otherwise discriminate under Article 14 of the European Convention on Human Rights (ECHR).[95] Thus, in *R (HA) v Ealing LBC*,[96] a requirement that applicants had lived in the borough for five years was held to violate Article 14[97] in respect of female victims of domestic violence; on the other hand, in *R (H) v Ealing LBC*,[98] a majority of the Court of Appeal expressed the provisional view that the provision and allocation of social housing was a social welfare benefit which did not, without more, fall within the ambit of Article 8, so that no issue under Article 14 would arise.

11.54 An allocation scheme which gave priority to people who were working or volunteered in the local community was held to be indirectly discriminatory against disabled persons,[99] but the discrimination was justified: it was legitimate for the authority to seek to

92 EqA 2010 s19.

93 EqA 2010 s19(1). Indirect discrimination does not apply to the protected characteristic of pregnancy and maternity: EqA 2010 s19(3).

94 EqA 2010 s19(2).

95 Article 14 provides that the rights protected by the ECHR must be enjoyed by all persons without discrimination on 'any ground such as sex, race, colour, language, religion, political or other opinion, national or social origin, association with a national minority, property, birth or other status'. Although disability discrimination is not expressly mentioned in Article 14, it has been held that it is also prohibited under Article 14: *AM (Somalia) v Entry Clearance Officer* [2009] EWCA Civ 634, [2009] UKHRR 1073.

96 [2015] EWHC 2375 (Admin).

97 It also offended the prohibition on the exclusion of those with a reasonable preference: para 11.50, footnote 86. In October 2017, the (then) DCLG issued a consultation paper (*Improving access to social housing for victims of domestic abuse: consultation*) proposing that where an authority operates a residence requirement for those who wish to apply for an allocation of social housing, it should be disapplied for victims of domestic abuse who are housed in refuges or other forms of temporary accommodation.

98 [2017] EWCA Civ 1127, [2018] HLR 2.

99 Who would be less likely to be able to work or to volunteer.

ensure that their tenants included a reasonable proportion of working people and to encourage volunteering.[100]

11.55 The scheme accorded with para 4.27 of the *Allocation of accommodation: guidance for local housing authorities in England* (which encourages authorities to 'consider how they can use their allocation policies to support those households who want to work as well as those who . . . are contributing . . . through voluntary work'). There was no alternative measure which could have been applied to achieve these legitimate aims.

11.56 Likewise, an allocation scheme which reserved a proportion of lettings for working households was indirectly discriminatory against women (as persons likely to be caring for children), the elderly and the disabled because they were less likely to be able to secure paid employment but the discrimination was justified as the authority was entitled to reward those who were in work and encourage others to seek work; the policy was a rational means of achieving those legitimate aims.[101]

11.57 See also *R (C) v Islington LBC*,[102] in which it was held that provisions of an allocation scheme which prioritised existing social housing tenants who wanted to move were potentially discriminatory against homeless people, victims of domestic violence and women; but that any discrimination was justified as it served the legitimate purpose of encouraging existing tenants to move to smaller homes and free up larger units.[103]

11.58 An authority cannot rely on 'spent' criminal convictions to exclude an otherwise qualified applicant.[104]

Regulations

11.59 The power to decide who qualifies to apply is subject to the power of the secretary of state by regulations to prescribe classes of persons who are, or are not, to be treated as qualifying persons and to prescribe criteria that may not be used in deciding what classes of persons are not qualifying persons.[105]

100 *R (XC) v Southwark LBC* [2017] EWHC 736 (Admin), [2017] HLR 24.
101 *R (H) v Ealing LBC* [2017] EWCA Civ 1127, [2018] HLR 2.
102 [2017] EWHC 1288 (Admin), [2017] HLR 32.
103 The claim was, however, allowed in part on a different point, see footnote 252.
104 *R (YA) v Hammersmith and Fulham LBC* [2016] EWHC 1850 (Admin), [2016] HLR 39.
105 HA 1996 s160ZA(8), added by LA 2011 s146.

11.60 Authorities may not disqualify – on the basis that they have no local connection with their areas – the following applicants:

a) someone who is serving in the regular forces,[106] or who has served in the regular forces within five years of the date of application;
b) someone who has recently ceased, or will cease, to be entitled to reside in accommodation provided by the Ministry of Defence following the death of that person's spouse or civil partner, which spouse or civil partner had served in the regular forces and whose death was attributable (wholly or partly) to that service;
c) someone who is serving or has served in the reserve forces[107] and who is suffering from a serious injury, illness or disability which is attributable (wholly or partly) to that service; or[108]
d) a person with the 'right to move'.[109]

Guidance

11.61 Pre-*Jakimaviciute*[110] guidance[111] suggested that authorities should avoid setting qualifying criteria which disqualify groups of people whose members are likely to qualify for a reasonable preference,

106 The Royal Navy, the Royal Marines, the regular army or the Royal Air Force: see Armed Forces Act 2006 s374 (applied by Allocation of Housing (Qualification Criteria for Armed Forces) (England) Regulations 2012 SI No 1869 reg 2).

107 The Royal Fleet Reserve, the Royal Naval Reserve, the Royal Marines Reserve, the Regular Reserve, the Army Reserve, the Royal Air Force Reserve or the Royal Auxiliary Air Force: see Armed Forces Act 2006 s374 (applied by Allocation of Housing (Qualification Criteria for Armed Forces) (England) Regulations 2012 SI No 1869 reg 2).

108 Allocation of Housing (Qualification Criteria for Armed Forces) (England) Regulations 2012 SI No 1869 reg 3. It is intended that such persons will be given additional preference (see para 11.85) – see *Allocation of accommodation: guidance for local housing authorities in England*, para 4.14.

109 Allocation of Housing (Qualification Criteria for Right to Move) (England) Regulations 2015 SI No 967. This is a three-stage test. First, the person must be a secure or introductory tenant or an assured tenant of a social landlord (reg 4(a)); second, the person must be entitled to a reasonable preference because he or she needs to move to a particular locality in the authority's district, where failure to meet that need would cause hardship (reg 4(b)); third, the person must have a 'need to move', either because he or she works in the authority's district or he or she has been offered work in its district and has a genuine intention of taking up the offer (regs 4(c) and 5). See also *Right to move: statutory guidance on social housing allocations for local housing authorities in England*, DCLG, March 2015.

110 *R (Jakimaviciute) v Hammersmith and Fulham LBC* [2014] EWCA Civ 1438, [2015] HLR 5, at [40]: see para 11.50.

111 *Allocation of accommodation: guidance for local housing authorities in England.*

which pursuant to *Jakimaviciute* would be unlawful. Guidance also suggests that authorities should avoid allocating to people who already own their own homes, save in exceptional circumstances, eg, elderly owner occupiers who cannot stay in their own home and need to move into sheltered accommodation.[112] It also notes that there may be reasons for applying different qualification criteria in relation to existing tenants from those which apply to new applicants, eg, to ensure that residency requirements do not restrict existing social tenants moving to take up work or downsizing to a smaller home; and, authorities could apply different qualification criteria in relation to different stock, eg, properties which are hard to let.[113]

11.62 The guidance reminds authorities that there may always be exceptional circumstances when it will be necessary not to apply criteria in the case of an individual applicant, eg, an intimidated witness who needs to move quickly to another area; authorities are encouraged to include provision for dealing with exceptional cases within their qualification rules.[114] As with eligibility,[115] authorities are advised to consider whether an applicant qualifies for an allocation at the time of the initial application and when considering making an allocation, 'particularly where a long time has elapsed since the original application'.[116]

Notification

11.63 An authority which decides that an applicant is ineligible must notify[117] him or her of the decision and of the grounds for it in writing.[118]

Re-applications

11.64 In Wales, an applicant who is treated as ineligible due to serious unacceptable behaviour may make a fresh application if he or she

112 *Allocation of accommodation: guidance for local housing authorities in England*, para 3.23.

113 *Allocation of accommodation: guidance for local housing authorities in England*, para 3.24.

114 *Allocation of accommodation: guidance for local housing authorities in England*, para 3.25.

115 See para 11.26.

116 *Allocation of accommodation: guidance for local housing authorities in England*, para 3.26.

117 If the notification is not received by the applicant, it is to be treated as having been received if it is made available at the authority's office for a reasonable period for collection: HA 1996 s160ZA(10) (England) and s160(10) (Wales).

118 HA 1996 s160ZA(9), (10) (England); s160A(9), (10) (Wales).

considers that he or she should no longer be treated as ineligible[119] – for example, because rent arrears have been cleared, or because someone who had been guilty of anti-social behaviour is no longer part of his or her household.[120]

11.65 Likewise, in England, an applicant who is not being treated as a qualifying person by an English authority may (if he or she considers that he or she should now be treated as a qualifying person) make a fresh application to the authority for an allocation.[121]

11.66 Superficially, the entitlement to re-apply might seem to suggest an analogy with the law on re-applications for assistance under HA 1996 Part 7.[122] This would, however, be wrong because, while the test – whether the application is made on exactly the same facts – in relation to a homelessness re-application is in principle a question for the authority to determine,[123] the obligation to reconsider qualification for an allocation arises when *the applicant* considers that he or she should no longer be treated as ineligible or that he or she should be treated as a qualifying person.

11.67 That said, it is unlikely that an authority can be required to reconsider application after application, week in week out, each to be followed by a review,[124] without some basis for suggesting a relevant change.

11.68 There would seem to be two broad approaches – either:

a) the courts will oblige authorities to engage in consideration (and review), but they will be entitled to do no more than ask whether there has been a change 'in the [applicant's] circumstances'[125] and what that change is, so that if the applicant fails to put forward anything which could justify reconsideration, the authority may reach the same decision on that basis alone; or
b) the courts will impose a somewhat more rigorous test along the lines of whether 'a reasonable applicant' could himself or herself consider that there had been any material change such as to lead him or her to consider that he or she should no longer be treated as ineligible or should not be treated as qualifying.

119 HA 1996 s160A(11).

120 Cf the distinction drawn at para 11.46: see *Gallagher v Castle Vale HAT* [2001] EWCA Civ 944, (2001) 33 HLR 72; *Kensington and Chelsea RLBC v Simmonds* (1996) 29 HLR 507, CA.

121 HA 1996 s160ZA(11), added by LA 2011 s146.

122 See paras 9.26–9.53.

123 See *Rikha Begum v Tower Hamlets LBC* [2005] EWCA Civ 340, [2005] HLR 34; see paras 9.36–9.37.

124 See para 11.149.

125 Cf the wording of HA 1996 s160(7)(b).

The latter seems less likely.

11.69 In practice, the issue is only likely to reach court where there has been something that could lead the applicant to re-apply, both because a challenge will have to be by way of judicial review for which permission will be required and in order to procure public funding to make a claim.

11.70 Nonetheless, authorities need to determine a proper response to such applications. The safest course is for authorities to ask the applicant to identify the putative change and ensure that that they consider it along with any other material changes of which they are aware, including, for example, to their own policies and/or in the overall demographics of an area.[126] The Welsh Code of Guidance suggests that unless there has been a considerable lapse of time, it will be for the applicant to show that his or her circumstances or behaviour have changed,[127] ie, the first approach in para 11.68.

Existing applicants

11.71 The eligibility provisions of HA 1996 s160A came into force on 27 January 2003 in Wales and 31 January 2003 in England. All applicants who were on a local authority housing register immediately before that date, or who had made an application which had not yet been determined, were to be treated as persons who had applied for an allocation of housing, which had the effect of applying the provisions of section 160A to them.

11.72 From 18 June 2012, local authorities in England may only allocate accommodation in accordance with the provisions of HA 1996 s160ZA and their own allocation scheme.

11.73 Any entitlement to an allocation of housing will largely depend on the allocation scheme of the local housing authority to which the applicant has applied.[128] An authority must take steps to bring to the attention of those likely to be affected by it any alteration to its allocation scheme which reflects a major change of policy.[129] Some applicants may therefore find that, following a change in allocation scheme by the local housing authority, they are no longer be entitled to an allocation of housing either because they are ineligible or because they do not satisfy the authority's qualification criteria.

126 See, in particular, HA 1996 s166(3).

127 Welsh Code para 2.40.

128 See paras 11.80–11.124.

129 HA 1996 s168(3).

11.74 If an authority decides that an applicant is ineligible or is not a qualifying person, it must serve the applicant with a written notice of that decision together with the reasons for it.[130] An applicant has the right to a statutory review of that decision.[131]

Applications for housing

Housing register

11.75 Prior to amendment by the Homelessness Act 2002, HA 1996 Part 6 required all local authorities to establish and maintain a housing register. That requirement has now been repealed.

Consideration of applications

11.76 All applications must, if made in accordance with the procedures laid down in an authority's allocation scheme,[132] be considered by that authority.[133] It is a matter for the authority how it records that application and the information contained in it.

Advice and information

11.77 All authorities must make available, free of charge, advice and information about the right to make an application for an allocation of housing.[134] They must also provide the necessary assistance in making an application to those who are likely otherwise to have difficulty in doing so.[135]

11.78 All applicants must be informed of the right to request information about their applications,[136] and about any decisions made in relation to them,[137] and to seek an internal review.[138]

130 HA 1996 s160ZA(9).
131 HA 1996 s166A(9)(c).
132 See para 11.80.
133 HA 1996 s166(3). Provided proper consideration has been given, a court will not interfere with the authority's findings or how it decides to treat the application: see, eg *R (Heaney) v Lambeth LBC* [2006] EWHC 3332 (Admin), [2007] JHL D25.
134 HA 1996 s166(1)(a).
135 HA 1996 s166(1)(b).
136 Under HA 1996 s166A(9)(a) (England) or s167(4A)(a) (Wales): see paras 11.145–11.148.
137 Under HA 1996 s166A(9)(b) (England) or s167(4A)(b) (Wales): see para 11.148.
138 Under HA 1996 s167(4A)(c); see para 11.149.

Disclosure of information

11.79 The fact that a person is an applicant for housing must not be disclosed – without the consent of the applicant – to any other member of the public.[139]

The allocation scheme

Introduction

11.80 Each local housing authority must establish an allocation scheme for determining priorities between qualifying persons[140] and for the procedure to be followed in allocating housing accommodation.[141] Authorities in England must – when preparing or modifying their schemes – have regard to their homelessness strategy,[142] as well as to their 'current tenant strategy';[143] London boroughs will also have to have regard to the London housing strategy,[144] prepared by the Mayor.[145]

Choice-based housing

11.81 The scheme must include a statement of the authority's policy on offering applicants a 'choice of housing accommodation' or 'the opportunity to express preferences' about the accommodation to be allocated to them.[146]

Unlawful allocations

11.82 Allocation from the waiting list must be in accordance with the scheme.[147] An allocation which is not in accordance with the scheme

139 HA 1996 s166(4).

140 See paras 11.26–11.74.

141 HA 1996 s167(1) (from commencement of LA 2011 s147, in England, s166A(1)).

142 Under Homelessness Act 2002 s1: see paras 14.3–14.19.

143 The strategy under LA 2011 s150, pursuant to which authorities decide, among other matters, whether and when to grant flexible tenancies, ie outside of full security.

144 Under LA 2011 s151.

145 HA 1996 s166A(12).

146 HA 1996 s166A(2) (England); s167(1A) (Wales).

147 HA 1996 s166A(14) (England). See *Sahardid v Camden LBC* [2004] EWCA Civ 1485, [2005] HLR 11; *R (Bibi) v Camden LBC* [2004] EWHC 2527 (Admin),

will be ultra vires.[148] Notwithstanding what might be thought the obvious purpose of this provision, to constrain lettings that are not in accordance with the scheme, it has been held that a non-compliant tenancy is nonetheless valid.[149]

Categories of reasonable preference

Generally

11.83 When establishing priorities, a reasonable preference must be given to:[150]

a) those who are homeless (within the meaning of HA 1996 Part 7 or in Wales H(W)A 2014 Part 2);[151]
b) those who are owed a duty by any local housing authority under HA 1996 s190(2),[152] s193(2)[153] or s195(2)[154] (or under HA 1985 s65(2) or s68(2))[155] or who are occupying accommodation secured under HA 1996 s192(3),[156] or, in Wales, those who are owed any duty under H(W)A 2014 s66, s73 or s75;[157]

[2005] HLR 18, where failures by the local authority to apply the scheme led to the quashing of its decisions. Cf *R (Osei) v Newham LBC* [2010] EWHC 368 (Admin), [2010] JHL D37.

148 See *R v Macclesfield BC ex p Duddy* [2001] JHL D16, QBD (allocation to a former employee outside the provisions of the scheme).

149 *Birmingham City Council v Qasim* [2009] EWCA Civ 1080, [2010] HLR 19.

150 HA 1996 s166A(3) (England); s167(2) (Wales)).

151 See chapter 4. The class is not qualified in any way (cf HA 1996 ss167(2)(b) and 166A(3)(b)), and therefore encompasses those who are homeless but not in priority need. There is no requirement that an applicant should have applied as homeless before an authority must consider whether or not he or she qualifies under this ground (again, cf HA 1996 s167(2)(b)/s166A(3)(b)): *R (Alam) v Tower Hamlets LBC* [2009] EWHC 44 (Admin), [2009] JHL D47.

152 See para 10.98. This is the duty to those who are in priority need but intentionally homeless. Any exclusion or reduction of preference for this group must be in accordance with HA 1996 s160ZA(7) or s166A(5) (England) or s160A(7) (see para 11.28) or s167(2A) or (2B) (Wales) (see paras 11.69–11.72).

153 The duty to those who are eligible, in priority need and not intentionally homeless: see para 10.118.

154 The duty to those threatened with homelessness unintentionally: see para 10.89.

155 The equivalent duties under the HA 1985 to the unintentionally homeless.

156 Those unintentionally homeless who are not in priority need but who are offered housing under the discretionary power: see para 10.82.

157 H(W)A 2014 s66 – duty to help to secure accommodation for those threatened with homelessness; s73 – initial duty owed to those who are eligible and homeless; s75 – full duty equivalent to HA 1996 s193(2).

c) those in insanitary or overcrowded housing or otherwise in unsatisfactory housing conditions;
d) those who need to move on medical or welfare grounds (including grounds relating to a disability);[158] and
e) those who need to move to a particular locality in the district of the authority, where failure to meet that need would cause hardship (to themselves or others).[159]

11.84 Reasonable preference must not be given to an applicant who only falls within any of the reasonable preference categories because of a restricted person.[160] A 'restricted person' is someone who is ineligible,[161] subject to immigration control,[162] and who either does not have leave to enter or remain in the UK, or whose leave is subject to a condition to maintain and accommodate him or herself, and any dependants, without recourse to public funds.[163] An authority should take care that its published allocation scheme reflects restricted cases.[164]

11.85 Additional preference may be given to sub-groups within those specified, being persons with urgent housing needs.[165] This means

158 The express reference to disability was added by HA 2004 s223 because of concerns that local authorities were interpreting the need for a move on 'medical' grounds too narrowly. *Allocation of accommodation: guidance for local housing authorities in England*, para 4.10, envisages that this could include care leavers, a person moving on from a drug or alcohol recovery programme, young adults with learning disabilities and those who provide care or support, eg foster carers, those approved to adopt, or those being assessed to foster or adopt, special guardians, and family and friend carers who – without fostering or adopting – have taken care of a child because the parents are unable to do so. The extension to disability is not found in H(W)A 2014, but see also Welsh Code paras 3.31–3.33.

159 'This would include, for example, a person who needs to move to a different locality in order to give or receive care, to access specialised medical treatment, or to take up a particular employment or training opportunity': *Allocation of accommodation: guidance for local housing authorities in England*, para 4.11; Welsh Code para 4.23.

160 HA 1996 s166A(4) (England); s167(2ZA) (Wales).

161 See para 3.149.

162 See paras 3.154–3.176.

163 HA 1996 s184(7); and see para 3.164.

164 DCLG Guidance Note, 16 February 2009, para 17.

165 HA 1996 s166A(3) (England); s167(2) (Wales). See also *R (Heaney) v Lambeth LBC* [2006] EWHC 3332 (Admin), [2007] JHL D25, where the applicant asserted that she had an urgent housing need arising out of the distress caused by continuing to live in a property in which one of her daughters had died and, as such, that she qualified within the authority's category for transfer on an urgent basis, a claim which the authority rejected. Recognising that the authority had set a high threshold for inclusion in the relevant category, and that it had considered all the evidence, the court held that the authority was entitled to reach the conclusion that the applicant did not meet the criteria.

giving those applicants 'additional weight' or 'an extra head start, but does not require an allocation to be made to applicants entitled to it ahead of all others'.[166]

11.86 The English guidance reminds authorities to 'consider, in the light of local circumstances, the need to give effect to this provision', offering, by way of illustration, those who need to move suddenly because of a life-threatening illness or sudden disability, families in such severe overcrowding that it poses a serious health hazard, and those who require urgent rehousing as a result of violence or threats of violence, whether intimidated witnesses or as a result of serious anti-social behaviour or domestic violence.[167]

11.87 There is no requirement for an authority to frame an allocation scheme to provide for cumulative preference, ie affording greater priority to applicant who falls within more than category of one reasonable preference.[168]

11.88 The English guidance encourages authorities to take advantage of the flexibility available to them to meet local needs and local priorities.[169]

Regulations

11.89 The secretary of state and the Welsh Ministers have power to specify further categories of reasonable preference or to amend or repeal any part of HA 1996 s166A(3) (England) or s167(2) (Wales).[170] This power has not been exercised in relation to the amended section 167(2) in Wales.

11.90 In England, this has been used to provide that additional preference should be given to:

166 *R (L and D) v Lambeth LBC* [2001] EWHC (Admin) 900, (2002) JHL D1 (upheld on appeal, *Lambeth LBC v A; Lambeth LBC v Lindsay* [2002] EWCA Civ 1084, [2002] HLR 57). There is nothing objectionable in an authority adopting a 'points threshold', below which an applicant cannot bid under the authority's choice procedures (as to which, see para 11.81): *R (Woolfe) v Islington LBC* [2016] EWHC 1907 (Admin), [2016] HLR 42.

167 *Allocation of accommodation: guidance for local housing authorities in England*, para 4.13.

168 *R (Ahmad) v Newham LBC* [2009] UKHL 14, [2009] HLR 31. See also *Allocation of accommodation: guidance for local housing authorities in England*, para 4.5. See further paras 11.106–11.116.

169 *Allocation of accommodation: guidance for local housing authorities in England*, para 4.19.

170 HA 1996 s166A(7) (England); s167(3) (Wales).

- former members of the armed forces;
- serving members who need to move because of a serious injury, medical condition or disability sustained as a result of service;
- bereaved spouses and civil partners of members of the armed forces leaving services accommodation following the death; and
- serving or former members of the reserve forces who need to move because of a serious injury, medical condition or disability sustained as a result of service

who have urgent housing needs.[171]

Considerations

11.91 For the purpose of defining how preference is to be awarded to those within these categories, an authority's allocation scheme may take into account:[172]

a) the financial resources open to an applicant to meet his or her housing costs;
b) any behaviour of an applicant (or a member of the applicant's household) which affects his or her suitability to be a tenant;[173]
c) any local connection[174] which exists between an applicant and the authority's area.[175]

11.92 Here, therefore, authorities in England as in Wales may have regard to anti-social behaviour.

11.93 The secretary of state and Welsh Ministers may specify factors which the local authority may not take into account when allocating housing accommodation.[176] This power has not been exercised.

11.94 Insofar as authorities can and do adopt their own policies to allocation decisions, they cannot adopt policies so rigid as to fetter

171 Housing Act 1996 (Additional Preference for Armed Forces) (England) Regulations 2012 SI No 2989. See also *Allocation of accommodation: guidance for local housing authorities in England*, para 4.14.

172 HA 1996 s166A(5) (England), s167(2A) (Wales).

173 See further paras 11.95–11.97.

174 As defined by HA 1996 s199; see paras 7.8–7.9.

175 Accordingly, a scheme is not unlawful because it includes reference to whether an applicant has a local connection when determining priority as between two applicants otherwise in the same band of priority: *R (Boolen) v Barking and Dagenham LBC* [2009] EWHC 2196 (Admin), [2009] JHL D113.

176 HA 1996 s166A(8) (England); s167(4) (Wales).

their consideration of the individual circumstances of particular applicants for housing.[177]

Anti-social behaviour – Wales

11.95 HA 1996 s167, applies only in Wales. It is a discrete provision allowing an authority to afford no preference at all for an applicant who – in the circumstances at the time his or her case is considered – does not deserve to be treated as a member of a group who are to be given preference, because the applicant, or a member of the applicant's household, has been guilty of such serious unacceptable behaviour that he or she is unsuitable to be a tenant of the authority.[178] Such behaviour is defined in the same way as for ineligibility.[179]

11.96 Thus, in Wales, there are three ways of dealing with the anti-social:[180]

a) ineligibility;[181]
b) taking the behaviour into account for the purpose of defining how preference is to be awarded within the statutory categories;[182] and
c) excluding them from any preference.[183]

Only the second of these is available in England.[184]

11.97 An applicant must be notified in writing of a decision that he or she is a person to whom HA 1996 s167(2C) applies,[185] and of the grounds for it.[186] There is provision for review of such a decision.[187]

177 See *R v Canterbury City Council ex p Gillespie* (1987) 19 HLR 7, QBD; *R v Bristol City Council ex p Johns* (1992) 25 HLR 249, QBD; *R v Newham LBC ex p Campbell* (1993) 26 HLR 183, QBD; *R v Newham LBC ex p Watkins* (1993) 26 HLR 434, QBD; *R v Newham LBC ex p Dawson* (1994) 26 HLR 747, QBD; *R v Islington LBC ex p Aldabbagh* (1994) 27 HLR 271, QBD; *R v Lambeth LBC ex p Njomo* (1996) 28 HLR 737, QBD; *R v Southwark LBC ex p Melak* (1996) 29 HLR 223, QBD; *R v Gateshead MBC ex p Lauder* (1997) 29 HLR 360, QBD; and *R v Lambeth LBC ex p Ashley* (1996) 29 HLR 385, QBD. See also paras 12.54–12.55.
178 HA 1996 s167(2B) and (2C).
179 See paras 11.32–11.48.
180 Whose conduct rises to the prescribed level.
181 Paras 11.32–11.48.
182 Para 11.83.
183 Para 11.93.
184 See paras 11.91–11.92.
185 HA 1996 s167(4A)(b).
186 HA 1996 s167(4A)(c).
187 See paras 11.149–11.152.

Meaning of 'reasonable preference'

Generally

11.98 The requirement to give a 'reasonable preference' to certain groups was also to be found in HA 1985 s22. In relation to that section, reasonable preference meant that the criteria must be an 'important factor in making a decision about the allocation of housing',[188] and that 'positive favour should be shown to applications which satisfy any of the relevant criteria'.[189]

11.99 More recently, HA 1996 s167(2)[190] was said to provide those within it with a 'reasonable head start', although still not guaranteed an allocation.[191]

11.100 The test is whether they are given a reasonable preference relative to persons who are not so entitled; whether a preference is reasonable is a decision for the authority; a scheme may still give reasonable preference to applicants who do not fall within HA 1996 s166A(3) (England) or s167(2) (Wales) provided that such non-statutory preferences do not dominate the scheme at the expense of the statutory preference categories.[192]

11.101 Reasonable preference does, however, imply a power to choose between different applicants on 'reasonable grounds . . . it is not unreasonable to prefer good tenants to bad tenants'.[193] Other grounds could include refusal of a previous, suitable offer; the refusal was a matter the authority was entitled to take into account.[194]

11.102 There is therefore no reason why an authority's own principles of allocation should not include reference to arrears of rent[195] (but not,

188 Per Tucker J in *R v Lambeth LBC ex p Ashley* (1996) 29 HLR 385, QBD at 387.

189 Per Judge LJ in *R v Wolverhampton MBC ex p Watters* (1997) 29 HLR 931, CA at 938.

190 Which in England, is now found in HA 1996 s166A(3).

191 See per Collins J in *R (A) v Lambeth LBC; R (Lindsay) v Lambeth LBC* [2002] EWCA Civ 1084, [2002] HLR 57 at [15].

192 *R (Lin) v Barnet LBC* [2007] EWCA Civ 132, [2007] HLR 30.

193 Per Carnwath J in *R v Newham LBC ex p Miah* (1995) 28 HLR 279, at 288.

194 *R (Cranfield-Adams) v Richmond upon Thames LBC* [2012] EWHC 3334 (Admin), [2012] All ER(D) 114 (Jun), JHL D10.

195 *R v Newham LBC ex p Miah*, above; *R v Lambeth LBC ex p Njomo* (1996) 28 HLR 737, QBD; *R v Islington LBC ex p Aldabbagh* (1994) 27 HLR 271, QBD. See now HA 1996 ss166A(5)(b) and 167(2A)(b), and in Wales (2B) and (2C) allowing behaviour to be taken into account; see paras 11.83, 11.95–11.97. They may also go to discretionary disqualification under section 160A(7) in Wales.

it is suggested, other categories of debt, such as arrears of local taxation).[196]

11.103 It has been held that there was no impropriety in requiring a victim of domestic violence, whom the authority agreed ought to be rehoused, to clear her arrears from a previous tenancy before being made an offer – the authority was entitled to have regard to the fact that the claimant was one of a number of persons in need of emergency re-housing; as other such persons did not have such debts, it was not irrational to conclude that she should be given a lower priority than them.[197]

11.104 On the other hand, an authority – whose allocation scheme provided for overpayments of housing benefit to be taken into account when determining priority – could not take them into account when the overpayment was statute-barred under the Limitation Act 1980: it was unlawful and irrational to reduce the applicant's preference on account of debts which were not recoverable.[198]

11.105 The requirement to give a reasonable preference to the specified groups does not prevent an authority allocating a quota of all vacancies to one particular group (for example, homeless persons).[199]

R (Ahmad) v Newham LBC

11.106 A line of cases on reasonable preference within local authority allocation schemes was reversed by the House of Lords in *Ahmad*.[200] Those cases had held that a reasonable authority is bound to include within its scheme a mechanism for identifying, and giving added

196 *R v Forest Heath DC ex p West and Lucas* (1991) 24 HLR 85, CA: all local taxpayers are to be treated the same way, regardless of their need for housing.

197 *R (Osei) v Newham LBC Lettings Agency* [2010] EWHC 368 (Admin), [2010] JHL D37. A policy of not allocating to those in arrears also prevented an allocation on the basis of overcrowding in *R (Babakandi) v Westminster City Council* [2011] EWHC 1756 (Admin), [2011] JHL D105, although the Director of Housing had a discretion not to apply the policy in 'exceptional circumstances'; the fact that those circumstances were not spelled out did not make the scheme unlawful.

198 *R (Joseph) v Newham LBC* [2009] EWHC 2983 (Admin), [2010] JHL D37.

199 *R v Islington LBC ex p Reilley and Mannix* (1998) 31 HLR 651, QBD; *R v Westminster LBC ex p Al-Khorshan* (2000) 33 HLR 6, QBD; *R (Babakandi) v Westminster City Council* [2011] EWHC 1756 (Admin), [2011] JHL D105.

200 [2009] UKHL 14, [2009] HLR 31.

preference, to those with 'cumulative need', ie, who qualified within more than one category of reasonable preference.[201]

11.107 In *Ahmad*, Newham LBC's allocations policy was challenged on two principal grounds: first, that it failed to determine priority between people in the reasonable preference groups in accordance with the gravity of their individual needs, ie, cumulative needs; and second, that the policy of allocating up to five per cent of properties advertised under the authority's choice-based lettings scheme to existing tenants (without a reasonable preference) who wished to transfer to another similar property failed to give reasonable preference to those within HA 1996 s167(2).[202]

11.108 In both the High Court and the Court of Appeal, the scheme was held to be unlawful, principally because the mechanism for determining priority between those with a reasonable preference was by length of time since registration, not by relative need.[203] The scheme was also found to be unlawful because of the allocation of five per cent of properties to tenants seeking a transfer.

11.109 The House of Lords held that an authority cannot be required to afford preference by reference to cumulative need,[204] as HA 1996 s167(2) provides only that a local authority may afford additional preference to those within the priority groups who have an urgent need,[205] and section 167(2A) provides only that it may determine priorities between those within priority groups by reference to other considerations.[206]

11.110 In relation to the challenge to its choice-based scheme, the authority was entitled to allocate properties to people who did not fall within a category of reasonable preference; HA 1996 s167(2)[207] only requires that the categories set out in that subsection are given a 'reasonable preference' – it does not require that they should be given absolute priority over everyone else.[208] Moreover, allocating a proportion of the

201 *R v Islington LBC ex p Reilly and Mannix* (1998) 31 HLR 651, QBD; *R v Westminster City Council ex p Al-Khorsan* (1999) 33 HLR 77; *R (A) v Lambeth LBC* [2002] EWCA Civ 1084, [2002] HLR 57. See also *R (Cali and others) v Waltham Forest LBC* [2006] EWHC 2950 (Admin), [2007] HLR 1. See, generally, the 7th edition of this book, at paras 11.70–11.83.

202 In England, see now HA 1996 s166A(3).

203 Per Richards LJ [2008] EWCA Civ 140 at [69].

204 See Baroness Hale at [14] and Lord Neuberger at [39]–[43].

205 See para 11.85. In England, see now HA 1996 s166A(5).

206 See para 11.91.

207 In England, see now HA 1996 s166A(3).

208 See Baroness Hale at [18]–[19].

available housing stock to transfer applicants who were already tenants of the local authority neither increased nor decreased the available housing stock – the property left by the transferring tenant becomes available to others.[209]

11.111 The importance of the case is not merely the dismissal of the judicially created requirement of provision for cumulative need, but its statement about judicial intervention generally:

> . . . as a general proposition, it is undesirable for the courts to get involved in questions of how priorities are accorded in housing allocation policies. Of course, there will be cases where the court has a duty to interfere, for instance if a policy does not comply with statutory requirements, or if it is plainly irrational. However, it seems unlikely that the legislature can have intended that Judges should embark on the exercise of telling authorities how to decide on priorities as between applicants in need of rehousing, save in relatively rare and extreme circumstances. Housing allocation policy is a difficult exercise which requires not only social and political sensitivity and judgment, but also local expertise and knowledge.[210]
>
> In relation to the provision of accommodation under the National Assistance Act 1948, my noble and learned friend, Baroness Hale of Richmond, then Hale LJ, said in *R (Wahid) v Tower Hamlets London Borough Council* [2002] EWCA Civ 287, [2003] HLR 13, para 33, '[n]eed is a relative concept, which trained and experienced social workers are much better equipped to assess than are lawyers and courts, provided that they act rationally'. Precisely the same is true of relative housing needs under Part 6 of the 1996 Act, and trained and experienced local authority housing officers.
>
> If section 167[211] carries with it the sort of requirements which can be said to be implied by the decisions of the Court of Appeal and the Deputy Judge in this case, then Judges would become involved in considering details of housing allocation schemes in a way which would be both unrealistic and undesirable. Because of the multifarious factors involved, the large number of applicants, and the relatively small number of available properties at any one time, any scheme would be open to attack, and it would be a difficult and very time-consuming exercise for a Judge to decide whether the scheme

209 At [17]–[21].

210 This judicial restraint was applied in the planning case of *R (McDonagh) v Hackney LBC* [2012] EWHC 373, [2012] JHL D60, upholding a policy whereby Gypsies and Travellers who wanted a pitch on a caravan site had to provide documentary evidence of an address in the authority's area at which correspondence could be sent to them and to re-register every year; there was nothing irrational about the policy as it ensured that applicants had connections to the local area and that the waiting list was up-to-date.

211 In England, see now HA 1996 s166A.

before him was acceptable. If it was not, then the consequences would also often be unsatisfactory: either the authority would be in a state of some uncertainty as to how to reformulate the scheme, or the Judge would have to carry out the even more difficult and time-consuming (and indeed inappropriate) exercise of deciding how the scheme should be reformulated to render it acceptable. As Baroness Hale said, that point is well made by looking at the Deputy Judge's order in this case, which requires the Scheme to be reconsidered 'in accordance with the law set out in this judgment'.[212]

11.112 In contrast, however, in *Birmingham City Council v Ali*,[213] the same committee of the House of Lords as in *Ahmad* – cognisant that in that case it had 'made it clear that the courts should be very slow indeed to interfere with a local housing authority's allocation policy, unless it breached the requirements of Part 6'[214] – nonetheless held that Birmingham City Council's allocations policy was unlawful by reason of irrationality.

11.113 Under that policy, if it was accepted that a family was homeless because of overcrowding in, or the condition of, its current accommodation, so that a 'full' duty was owed,[215] the authority would discharge its duty under HA 1996 s193(2) by leaving the family in the existing accommodation until suitable permanent accommodation could be found; such applicants were, however, awarded a lower priority than where the authority placed a homeless family in temporary accommodation.

11.114 Some caution is needed before applying this to similar policies. There was little argument on this part of the case.[216] While the conclusion of the Court of Appeal that those who were homeless in their current accommodation could not lawfully be left in it under HA 1996 Part 7[217] was not supported by the House of Lords,[218] it was only irrational on a 'relatively narrow aspect': the authority had not justified the difference in treatment – its 'bald statement' that 'those in greatest need are dealt with first' was insufficient; on the face of it, those in (their current) unsuitable accommodation were in greater need than those in other temporary accommodation which had not

212 Lord Neuberger, with whom the other members of the Committee agreed, at [46]–[48].

213 [2009] UKHL 36, [2009] HLR 41.

214 At [62].

215 See paras 10.118–10.263.

216 See Baroness Hale at [57].

217 See paras 10.38 and 10.132–10.134.

218 At [61].

been subject to an unsuitability finding; if there was evidence to that effect, it had not been put forward.[219]

11.115 In the post-*Ahmad* decision of *Kabashi*,[220] the authority's allocation scheme took waiting time into account, but re-set the date whenever a change of circumstances led to re-assessment of an applicant's rehousing needs (with no residual discretion to disapply the provision). The applicant's need for a three-bedroom property changed to a need for two bedrooms, with the result that her waiting time was re-set to a later date. This was not unlawful: the authority had explained that, in its experience, those adversely affected by applicants moving from the waiting list for three-bed properties to two-bed properties perceived such interloping as unfair queue jumping; it was not for the court to second-guess that policy.

Children

11.116 Where an authority – as it will invariably do – takes children into account for the purposes of determining priority and nature of accommodation under its scheme, a child arrangement order under CA 1989 s8 will be relevant in deciding whether or not a child is to be taken into account, but it is not determinative of the authority's allocation decision.[221]

Carers, adopters and fosterers

11.117 Carers who need to stay overnight should, where possible, merit a spare room;[222] likewise, applications from prospective fosterers or adopters 'who would require an extra bedroom to accommodate a foster or adoptive child', should lead authorities 'to weigh up the risk that the application to foster or adopt may be unsuccessful (leading to the property being under-occupied), against the wider benefits which would be realised if the placement was successful'.[223] Authorities are encouraged to work with children's services to meet

219 At [62]–[63].

220 *R (Kabashi) v Redbridge LBC* [2009] EWHC 2984 (Admin), [2011] JHL D1.

221 *R (Bibi) v Camden LBC* [2004] EWHC 2527 (Admin), [2005] HLR 18. See also *Holmes-Moorhouse v Richmond upon Thames LBC* [2009] UKHL 7, [2009] HLR 34.

222 *Allocation of accommodation: guidance for local housing authorities in England*, para 4.29.

223 *Allocation of accommodation: guidance for local housing authorities in England*, para 4.30.

the needs of prospective and approved foster carers and adopters, so that children's services can fulfil their duties under CA 1989 s22G, to ensure sufficient accommodation in the area to meet the needs of 'looked after children',[224] eg by setting aside a quota of properties for people who need to move to larger accommodation in order to foster or adopt.[225]

Armed forces

11.118 Authorities are 'strongly encouraged' to take into account the needs of current and former members of the armed forces when determining their allocation policies, 'and to give sympathetic consideration to the housing needs of family members of serving or former service personnel who may have been disadvantaged by the requirements of military service and, in particular, the need to move from base to base'[226] – eg by affording preference to those who have recently left or who are close to leaving the service, or to determine priorities between those with a reasonable preference, or, if using financial resources to determine priorities, disregarding any lump sum received as compensation for injury or disability sustained on active service, or by setting aside a proportion of properties for them under a local lettings policy.[227]

Households in or seeking work

11.119 Authorities are also 'urged' to consider using policies to support households in or seeking work, 'as well as those who – while unable to engage in paid employment – are contributing to their community in other ways, for example, through voluntary work'[228] – eg, by giving preference to those in low paid work, or employment-related training, or greater priority to those with a reasonable preference who are working or actively seeking work, or using local lettings policies to allocate to households 'in particular types of employment where, for

224 See para 13.79.

225 *Allocation of accommodation: guidance for local housing authorities in England*, para 4.31.

226 *Allocation of accommodation: guidance for local housing authorities in England*, para 4.24. See also paras 11.60, 11.90.

227 *Allocation of accommodation: guidance for local housing authorities in England*, para 4.25. As to local lettings, see paras 11.121–11.122.

228 *Allocation of accommodation: guidance for local housing authorities in England*, para 4.27. See paras 11.54–11.56 .

example, skills are in short supply',[229] or by using 'flexible tenancies'[230] either to support households in low paid work or to incentivise people 'to take up employment opportunities'.[231]

Under-occupation

11.120 When determining criteria for property sizes, authorities should take account of the provisions in the Welfare Reform Act 2012 which reduce housing benefit to under-occupiers.[232]

Choice-based and local lettings

11.121 Subject to the 'reasonable preference' categories, the allocation scheme may contain provisions about the allocation of particular housing accommodation either to a person who makes a specific application for it[233] or to persons of a particular description, whether or not within the reasonable preference groups.[234]

11.122 Allocation to persons 'of a particular description' comprises the statutory basis for local lettings policies outside the general priorities of HA 1996 s166A(3) or s167(2).[235]

Consultation

11.123 By HA 1996 s166A(13) (England) and s167(7) (Wales), the authority must afford all registered providers of social housing and registered social landlords with whom it has nomination arrangements the opportunity to comment on an allocation scheme before it is adopted or before it is altered in any way that reflects 'a major change of policy'. The expression 'major change of policy' is not statutorily defined.[236]

229 *Allocation of accommodation: guidance for local housing authorities in England*, para 4.27. As to local lettings, see paras 11.121–11.122.
230 See para 14.10.
231 *Allocation of accommodation: guidance for local housing authorities in England*, para 4.28.
232 *Allocation of accommodation: guidance for local housing authorities in England*, para 4.22; see Housing Benefit Regulations 2006 SI No 213 reg B13; and Universal Credit Regulations 2013 SI No 376 Sch 4.
233 Eg through advertisement and 'bidding'.
234 HA 1996 s166A(6) (England); s167(2E) (Wales).
235 *Allocation of accommodation: guidance for local housing authorities in England*, para 4.21. See further, Welsh Code, para 3.71–3.74 on local lettings policies.
236 *Allocation of accommodation: guidance for local housing authorities in England*, para 5.2 suggests any amendment affecting the relative priority of a large

11.124 In an appropriate case, it may be that a person awaiting an allocation will have a legitimate expectation that he or she will enjoy the same priority under the new scheme as the old, in which case he or she will in principle be entitled to continue to enjoy it;[237] in considering whether a statement is sufficiently clear and unambiguous to found the basis of a legitimate expectation, the court should ascertain the meaning which the defendant's statements would reasonably convey to a particular claimant in the light of all the background knowledge available to him or her at the time the statement was made.

Procedure

Introduction

11.125 Allocations are a matter for an authority's executive.[238]

11.126 The secretary of state and, in Wales, the Welsh Ministers, may prescribe the principles of procedure to be followed when framing allocation schemes.[239]

11.127 In Wales, local housing authority officers must be included among the persons by whom allocation decisions can be taken, except where an express decision has been made not to delegate the decision, ie, to retain it as an executive decision.[240]

11.128 In both England and Wales, elected members may not be involved in allocation decisions where the accommodation to be allocated, or the applicant's sole or main residence, is in the member's ward.[241]

number of applicants or a significant alteration to procedures. See also Welsh Code para 4.26.

237 See, eg *R (Alansi) v Newham LBC* [2013] EWHC 3722 (Admin), [2014] HLR 25, in which the claim was, however, unsuccessful.

238 See para 12.59.

239 HA 1996 s166A(10) (England); s167(5) (Wales).

240 Local Housing Authorities (Prescribed Principles for Allocation Schemes) (Wales) Regulations 1997 SI No 45 reg 3 and Sch para 2.

241 1997 SI No 45 reg 3 and Sch para 1; and Allocation of Housing (Procedure) Regulations 1997 SI No 483 reg 3. *Allocation of accommodation: guidance for local housing authorities in England*, para 5.8, reminds authorities of this, but at para 5.9 also notes that: 'The regulations do not prevent an elected Member from representing their [sic] constituents in front of the decision making body, or from participating in the decision making body's deliberations prior to its decision. The regulations also do not prevent elected Members' involvement in policy decisions that affect the generality of housing accommodation in their division or electoral ward rather than individual allocations; for example, a decision that certain types of property should be prioritised for older people.' See also Welsh Code paras 4.35–4.37.

Enquiries

11.129 Unlike under HA 1996 Part 7 or H(W)A 2014 Part 2,[242] there is no express provision requiring an authority to make enquiries before determining an application. Nevertheless, a body charged with a statutory function must make or cause to be made such enquiries as will allow it to be satisfied that it can properly discharge its role.[243]

11.130 In *Crowder*,[244] a decision that the applicant's daughter was no longer living with her – and that she should accordingly only be considered for single person accommodation – was quashed because of the authority's failure to make adequate enquiries.

11.131 In *Maali*,[245] the authority's decision was quashed because of flaws in the medical assessment. The claimant, an asthmatic, occupied a third-floor maisonette under a secure tenancy granted by the authority, together with her three children, the eldest of whom also suffered from asthma. She applied to be transferred to another property, contending that she and her eldest daughter were having difficulty climbing the stairs and that she therefore fell within the emergency medical category (group B) of the authority's allocation scheme.

11.132 In August 2003, the authority's housing medical adviser concluded that the medical conditions were not severe enough to justify the need for an emergency transfer because: i) the fact that the claimant and her child had to climb stairs was positive as exercise helped alleviate the symptoms of asthma; and ii) when the claimant's asthma worsened, she went to stay with friends in order to obtain help with childcare and would continue to do so even if transferred to another property.

11.133 The authority accordingly assessed her as being within a mainstream category (group D) of its allocation scheme. The court concluded that the assessment was *Wednesbury* unreasonable: the medical adviser had wrongly attributed the stays with friends to a need for assistance with childcare rather than to the difficulties that she was experiencing in reaching the third floor. Nor was there any basis for the adviser's conclusion that, because exercise was beneficial to asthmatics, the climbing of stairs was positive.

242 See paras 9.57–9.70.

243 See *R v Islington LBC ex p Thomas* (1997) 30 HLR 111, QBD, per Roger Henderson QC at 120 (in relation to whether accommodation provided under HA 1985 s65(2) was suitable). See also *Secretary of State for Education and Science v Tameside BC* [1977] AC 1014, per Lord Diplock at 1065.

244 *R v Oxford City Council ex p Crowder* (1998) 31 HLR 485, QBD.

245 *R (Maali) v Lambeth LBC* [2003] EWHC 2231 (Admin), [2003] JHL D83.

11.134 In *Bauer-Czarnomski*,[246] the applicant lived in a four-bedroom house with his parents, both of whom suffered from mental health problems and required 24-hour assistance which he provided. In 2004, he applied to the authority for his own accommodation and was placed in the lowest band. In 2006, he submitted a report from his doctor which explained that, because he was required to be permanently available to assist his parents, his sleep was frequently disturbed and he was not able to rest, with the result that his own health was being harmed.

11.135 The authority obtained a report from a different doctor which accepted that the living arrangements had adverse implications for the applicant's health, but went on to advise that there was no need to place him in a higher band as the physical condition of the house did not affect his well-being. In particular, it noted that he had his own bedroom and was able to maintain a degree of independence and separation from other family members.

11.136 In reliance on that report, the authority refused to put the applicant into a higher band, a decision which was quashed because the authority's medical report had gone beyond an assessment of the applicant's medical need; it had not been for a doctor to advise on the priority to be afforded to him and in taking account of it, and the authority therefore had regard to an immaterial and irrelevant consideration; in any event, having regard to the medical evidence, the decision to leave the applicant in band D was perverse.

11.137 In *Adow*,[247] the authority's allocation scheme provided that every application which claimed a medical need would be 'assessed on its merits by the medical assessment officer in the quality and review team'. The applicant was the respondent's tenant in a one-bedroom flat in which she lived with her partner and her four children; she adduced evidence from a paediatrician and her family GP to show that the cramped conditions in which she was living were having an adverse impact on her health and that of her family.

11.138 The authority – contrary to its policy – did not refer the case to a medical assessment officer, but instead engaged an external doctor to evaluate the medical evidence and make a decision as to her housing needs: the authority accepted that this was unlawful.

246 *R (Bauer-Czarnomski) v Ealing LBC* [2010] EWHC 130 (Admin), [2010] JHL D38.

247 *R (Adow) v Newham LBC* [2010] EWHC 951 (Admin), [2010] JHL D101.

Information

Scheme

11.139 Since the HA 1980, authorities have been obliged to publish details of their allocation provisions: see HA 1985 s106. The details must be sufficient both to enable applicants to ascertain how the practices of a local authority will affect them, and so that the legality of the practice may be determined.[248]

11.140 Lack of publication does not, however, make a policy ultra vires.[249] Thus, it was sufficient for a social services procedure for making housing nominations to be provided in a short and comprehensible form; nor did the social services department have to give reasons for refusing to make a nomination to housing unless asked to do so.[250]

11.141 Likewise, where it was held that the local authority was entitled to adopt its local connection policy so long as it was rational and like cases were treated alike, the policy did not have to be set out in the allocations scheme itself because it was not a central feature of the scheme.[251]

11.142 On the other hand, where the scheme wrongly suggested that the applicant could not bid for a property, but there was in fact a separate policy which would have allowed her to do so, the claim for judicial review was allowed.[252] See also para 11.57.

11.143 There is a similar and overlapping duty to HA 1985 s106 in HA 1996 Part 6, that an authority must publish a summary of its scheme and provide a copy of the summary free of charge to any member of the public who asks for one.[253] The authority must keep the full scheme available for inspection at its principal office, although a reasonable fee may be charged to any member of the public who asks for a copy.[254]

11.144 Where an authority makes an alteration to its scheme reflecting a major change in policy,[255] it must, within a reasonable period, take

248 *R (Faarah) v Southwark LBC* [2008] EWCA Civ 807, [2009] HLR 12 (how registration dates were determined).

249 *R v Newham LBC ex p Miah* (1995) 28 HLR 279, QBD.

250 *R (Yazar) v Southwark LBC* [2008] EWHC 515 (Admin), [2008] JHL D55.

251 *R (Boolen) v Barking and Dagenham LBC* [2009] EWHC 2196 (Admin), [2009] JHL D113.

252 *R (C) v Islington LBC* [2017] EWHC 1288 (Admin), [2017] HLR 32; cf para 11.57.

253 HA 1996 s168(1). This is not confined to a member of the public in the authority's area.

254 HA 1996 s168(2).

255 Cf para 11.123.

such steps as it considers reasonable to bring the effect of the alteration to the attention of those likely to be affected by it.[256]

Applications

11.145 The scheme must include a right for an applicant to request such general information as enables him or her to assess how his or her application is likely to be treated; this must, in particular, include whether the applicant is likely to be a member of a group to which a preference will be given.[257]

11.146 A person is also entitled to be given general information that will enable him or her to assess whether accommodation appropriate to his or her needs is likely to be made available and, if so, how long it is likely to be before housing accommodation actually becomes available.[258]

11.147 English guidance encourages authorities to consider how accurate and anonymised information on waiting list applicants and lettings outcomes could be published.[259] The Welsh Code of Guidance suggests[260] that it is important for authorities to provide 'regular, accurate and generalised information on how housing is allocated and how waiting lists are managed, working actively to dispel any myths and misconceptions which may arise'.

11.148 The scheme must also afford an applicant the opportunity to request information about any decision about the facts of his or her case.[261]

Internal review and challenge

11.149 An applicant in England has the right to request an internal review of any decision taken under HA 1996 s166A(9)(b) (decision about the facts of his or her case) or under s160ZA(9) (eligibility) and to be notified of the outcome and the grounds for it.[262] Likewise, an applicant in Wales has the same rights in respect of a decision under HA

256 HA 1996 s168(3).

257 HA 1996 s166A(9)(a)(i) (England); s167(4A)(a)(i) (Wales).

258 HA 1996 s166A(9)(a)(ii) (England); s167(4A)(a)(ii) (Wales).

259 *Providing social housing for local people: statutory guidance on social housing allocations for local authorities in England*, DCLG, December 2013.

260 Welsh Code para 3.58.

261 HA 1996 s166A(9)(b) (England); s167A(4A)(c) (Wales).

262 HA 1996 s166A(9)(c) (England).

1996 s167(4A)(b) (unacceptable conduct) or under s160A(9) (eligibility, whether on the grounds of immigration status or conduct).[263]

11.150 Prior to its repeal, HA 1996 s165 permitted regulations to be made governing the conduct of internal reviews under Part 6.[264] There is no such provision in connection with section 166A(9) or section 167(4A). Authorities nonetheless must ensure that any review is fair to the applicant.[265] A decision on an application under Part 6 is not, however, a determination of a civil right or obligation for the purposes of Article 6 of the ECHR (right to a fair trial).[266]

11.151 There is no appeal to the county court against the review decision;[267] any challenge has to be by way of judicial review.[268]

11.152 There is nothing to prevent authorities establishing a voluntary review or appeal process that goes beyond the statutory right to review.[269] If the authority does add such a voluntary review process, it is likely to be considered necessary for anyone who is dissatisfied with the priority which he or she has been given to use this before seeking judicial review.[270]

Allocations by private registered providers of social housing (England) and registered social landlords (Wales)

Generally

11.153 Private registered providers (PRPs) of social housing (England) and registered social landlords (RSLs) (Wales) are obliged to co-operate with local housing authorities in offering accommodation to people

263 HA 1996 s167(4A)(d) (Wales).

264 Allocation of Housing and Homelessness (Review Procedures) Regulations 1999 SI No 71.

265 Cf paras 12.66–12.70.

266 See paras 12.117–12.122.

267 Cf paras 12.194–12.266.

268 See chapter 12.

269 See, eg *R v Southwark LBC ex p Mason* (1999) 32 HLR 88, QBD (panel reviewing the suitability of offers).

270 See chapter 12. The person could, of course, also complain to the local government ombudsman – see paras 12.268–12.287.

with priority under the authority's allocation scheme, to such extent as is reasonable in the circumstances.[271]

11.154 In practice, many local authorities now maintain no housing stock of their own, but have transferred it either to PRPs or RSLs specially formed for the purpose, or to other providers, by way of large-scale voluntary stock transfers, in connection with which they will necessarily have reserved rights to ensure that they can discharge their homelessness duties, ie, by way of nomination.

11.155 Even where the authority has retained some or all of its housing stock, it is likely to have nomination arrangements with PRPs and RSLs in its area. Such providers are among the partners with which local authorities will normally develop their homelessness strategies.[272]

11.156 Guidance in England says:[273]

> Nomination agreements should set out the proportion of lettings that will be made available; any criteria which the Private Registered Provider has adopted for accepting or rejecting nominees; and how any disputes will be resolved. Housing authorities will want to put in place arrangements to monitor effective delivery of the nomination agreement so they can demonstrate they are meeting their obligations under Part 6.

11.157 PRPs in England are regulated under Part 2 of the Housing and Regeneration Act (H&RA) 2008;[274] RSLs in Wales[275] are regulated under HA 1996 Part 1.[276]

11.158 PRPs in England were formerly regulated by the Housing Corporation – which had been the regulator of housing associations and trusts since the HA 1974 – until it was abolished and replaced[277]

271 HA 1996 s170. See also *Allocation of accommodation: guidance for local housing authorities in England*, para 6.1. See also the Housing Association Circular RSL 004/15, issued by the Welsh Government in April 2015 (replacing circular RSL 003/12, which itself replaced RLS 023/09) which requires all housing associations registered in Wales to take account of the Welsh Code.

272 See paras 14.9–14.17.

273 *Allocation of accommodation: guidance for local housing authorities in England*, para 6.3. In Wales, see paras 1.7 and 4.18 of the Welsh Code, reminding associations to have regard to the *Regulatory Framework for Housing Associations Registered in Wales.*

274 As amended by LA 2011 Part 7 Chapter 5 and Schs 16 and 17.

275 Still called 'registered social landlords' under HA 1996 Part 1.

276 Albeit amended in parts by H&RA 2008.

277 H&RA 2008 s64; its functions were transferred to the TSA: Transfer of Housing Corporation Functions (Modifications and Transitional Provisions) Order 2008 SI No 2839.

by what was statutorily called the Office for Tenants and Social Landlords,[278] known as the Tenant Services Authority (TSA).[279] From 1 April 2012, the TSA was itself abolished and its functions transferred to the Regulation Committee of the Homes and Communities Agency (HCA): those functions are due to transfer to a new body corporate, the Regulator of Social Housing, in early April 2018.[280]

11.159 In Wales, regulation of RSLs was the responsibility of the National Assembly for Wales ('the Assembly') from 1 July 1999.[281] The regulatory function was transferred to the Welsh Ministers on 1 April 2012.[282] The Welsh Ministers remain responsible for regulation in Wales.

11.160 It is not possible to describe either system of regulation here in any detail,[283] although a small number of matters affecting allocation are considered below.[284] It suffices to say that PRPs and RSLs are subject to regulatory regimes under one or other Act – HA 1996 or H&RA 2008. This means that, while not subject to direct statutory

278 H&RA 2008 s81.

279 Unlike the former Housing Corporation, the TSA did not have power to provide financial assistance to registered providers; that role is now undertaken by the Homes and Communities Agency (HCA).

280 From 15 January 2012, the HCA was required to set up a Regulation Committee pursuant to H&RA 2008 s94B, brought into force by Localism Act 2011 (Commencement No 2 and Transitional and Saving Provision) Order 2012 SI No 57. The Regulation Committee took over the functions previously undertaken by the TSA on 1 April 2012 – the same date on which the TSA was abolished: see Localism Act 2011 (Commencement No 4 and Transitional, Transitory and Saving Provisions) Order 2012 SI No 628. In November 2016, the (then) DCLG proposed that the regulatory functions of the HCA should be transferred to a new non-departmental public body (see *Proposal on using a Legislative Reform Order to establish the social housing regulator as an independent body*). In February 2018, a draft Legislative Reform Order (the Legislative Reform (Regulator of Social Housing) (England) Order 2018) was laid before Parliament; it establishes the Regulator of Social Housing as a new body corporate.

281 National Assembly for Wales (Transfer of Functions) Order 1999 SI No 672.

282 Housing and Regeneration Act 2008 (Commencement No 7 and Transitional and Saving Provisions) Order 2010 SI No 862 art 2. The Welsh Ministers remain the 'relevant authority' for the purposes of HA 1996 Part 1. The regulatory framework is that published in 2011.

283 See, generally, Arden and Partington's *Housing law*, Sweet & Maxwell, paras 1–203 onwards; and Arden & Dymond, *Manual of housing law*, 10th edn, LAG, 2017, chapter 8. In general terms, the HCA may set managements standards requiring local authorities and PRPs to comply with rules about, inter alia, allocating accommodation (H&RA 2008 s193, as amended by LA 2011); the standards are presently contained in Tenancy Involvement and Empowerment Standard (July 2017).

284 See paras 11.168–11.178.

rules on allocation in the same way that local authorities are, their actions, including in relation to allocations, are nonetheless susceptible to review by their regulators and, in turn, susceptible to complaints to those regulators by those adversely affected by their actions and/or inaction.

11.161 Regulators have a range of sanctions available, including powers of inspection of performance by and/or enquiry into PRPs or RSLs, extending ultimately to the de-registration or winding up of providers whose performance is inadequate.[285]

11.162 In England, complaints can also be made to an independent scheme approved by the secretary of state.[286] HA 1996 Sch 2 sets out the general provisions governing the membership, approval and registration of such a scheme in England. The Housing Ombudsman Service (HOS) is the approved scheme of which every PRP must be a member.[287] Failure to comply with the requirement to be a member of the scheme may result in an application to the High Court by the secretary of state for an order directing the provider to comply.[288] In Wales, there is no requirement for an RSL to be a member of any scheme as the Public Services Ombudsman for Wales (PSOW) already has jurisdiction over every registered social landlord.[289]

11.163 Where a complaint is made to the HOS,[290] the ombudsman has the power to investigate and determine that complaint by reference to what is, in the opinion of the ombudsman, 'fair in all the circumstances of the case'.[291] In Wales, the investigation must be carried out in such manner as he or she thinks 'appropriate in the circumstances of the case'.[292]

285 See H&RA 2008 Part 1 Chapters 4, 6 and 7; HA 1996 Part 1 and Sch 1.

286 HA 1996 Sch 2 para 3. In Wales, the function was transferred to the Public Services Ombudsman in 2006, see Public Services Ombudsman (Wales) Act 2005 (PSO(W)A 2005).

287 HA 1996 Sch 2 para 1(1). If the relevant provisions of the LA 2011 are brought into force, local authorities will also fall within the jurisdiction of the housing ombudsman, see para 12.268. In February 2018, the Ministry of Housing, Communities and Local Government (MHCLG) issued a consultation paper (*Strengthening consumer redress in the housing market: consultation*) seeking views on, among other things, the creation of a single ombudsman to cover all housing complaints, regardless of the nature of the landlord or tenure of the occupier.

288 HA 1996 Sch 2 para 1(2).

289 PSO(W)A 2005 ss7, 41, Sch 3.

290 As to which, in England, see para 12.228 as to the procedure for making a complaint through a 'designated person' rather than directly.

291 HA 1996 Sch 2 para 7.

292 PSO(W)A 2005 s13.

11.164 If the complaint is upheld, the ombudsman has power to order the PRP to pay compensation to the complainant or even to order that the member or the complainant is not to exercise or require the performance of contractual or other obligations or rights existing between them.[293] In Wales, the ombudsman does not have a directly corresponding power; a body which is subject to a complaint referred to the ombudsman may, however, make a payment to, or provide any other benefit for, the person aggrieved in respect of the matter which is the subject of the complaint.[294]

11.165 If the PRP fails to comply with the ombudsman's determination, the ombudsman has the power to order it to publish that failure in such manner as he or she sees fit.[295] If the PRP fails to comply with the order to publish, the ombudsman has the power to take such steps as he or she thinks appropriate to publish what the PRP ought to have published and to recover the costs of doing so from the PRP.[296] In Wales, the authority must publicise the report.[297]

11.166 It has been held that PRPs[298] may qualify as public authorities within the Human Rights Act 1998, in respect of some aspects of their management of their social housing stock (including service of notice to quit or of seeking possession) and, in addition to the requirement to conform to the ECHR rights, that in such circumstances they are also susceptible to the principles of domestic public law in respect of such activities, even if they would not otherwise be.[299]

11.167 At first instance, those aspects explicitly included the allocation of social housing; while this was not overruled per se, it was not the basis on which the decision that such providers may be public authorities for the purposes of the Human Rights Act 1998 was upheld: rather, it was held that service of notice to quit or to seek possession is a public function for the purposes of that Act, which means that such providers are public authorities in respect of such service; while allocation was not directly in issue, however, it seems also to qualify

293 HA 1996 Sch 2 para 7(2). There is no power to enforce against the complainant in Wales.
294 PSO(W)A 2015 s34.
295 HA 1996 Sch 2 para 7(3).
296 HA 1996 Sch 2 para 7(5).
297 PSO(W)A 2005 s17, although the ombudsman has power to waive this requirement: ss17, 21.
298 And, therefore, RSLs in Wales.
299 *R (Weaver) v London & Quadrant Housing Trust* [2008] EWHC 1377 (Admin), [2008] JHL D94 and on appeal [2009] EWCA Civ 587, [2010] 1 WLR 363, [2009] HLR 40. See para 12.7. The proposition as to susceptibility was conceded on appeal.

and in *R (McIntyre) v Gentoo Group Ltd*,[300] the principle was held to include allocation. Whether or not other acts of management qualify may well depend on a detailed investigation into and assessment of the functions of allocating and managing housing of the particular registered provider.[301]

England

11.168 The Regulator of Social Housing[302] enjoys a range of powers in relation to the provision of social housing, including that of setting standards, which may include requiring PRPs to comply with rules about, inter alia, allocation criteria,[303] in relation to which it may issue codes of practice amplifying the standard.[304] The statutory objectives of the Regulation Committee include economic and consumer objectives, the latter of which include ensuring that actual or potential tenants of social housing have an appropriate degree of choice and protection.[305]

11.169 The secretary of state may direct the HCA to issue a standard, or make directions about its content or to require regard to be had to specified objectives when setting a standard.[306] The Regulation Committee must comply with any such direction.[307] Standards issued by the HCA may require PRPs to comply with specified rules about a wide range of matters including criteria for allocating accommodation.[308]

300 [2010] EWHC 5 (Admin), [2010] JHL D22 and D40, in particular at [25].

301 *Weaver* at [68]–[72]. See also *Aston Cantlow and Wilmcote with Billisley Parochial Church Council v Wallbank* [2003] UKHL 37, [2004] 1 AC 546. In *R (Macleod) v Peabody Trust Governors* [2016] EWHC 737 (Admin), [2016] HLR 27, it was held that the association was not amenable to judicial review in connection with the refusal to allow an assignment of a tenancy which, however, did not fall to be treated as social housing because it had been acquired by the association without the use of any public funds.

302 Assuming the draft Legislative Reform Order (the Legislative Reform (Regulator of Social Housing) (England) Order 2018) comes into effect; otherwise, it would remain the Regulation Committee of the Homes and Communities Agency – see para 11.158.

303 H&RA 2008 s193(2)(a).

304 H&RA 2008 s195.

305 H&RA 2008 s92K.

306 H&RA 2008 s197.

307 H&RA 2008 s197(7).

308 H&RA 2008 s193(2)(a).

11.170 Failure to meet a standard is a ground for action by the Regulation Committee,[309] including the use of enforcement powers ranging from notices, fines and compensation, to orders to require the appointment of a manager over the whole of a PRP's functions or specified functions, or the transfer of functions to another PRP, and to the removal or suspension of officers or employees or their disqualification.[310]

11.171 Specific provision is made for the Regulation Committee to exercise any of the powers of regulation where there is a failure (or an anticipated failure) to meet any of the consumer standards where the Regulation Committee has reason to believe that there has been or may be a serious detriment caused to a tenant or potential tenant.[311]

11.172 In March 2015, the Regulation Committee issued *The regulatory framework for social housing in England from April 2015*[312] which took effect from 1 April 2015. The framework covers key areas of regulation including the regulation of consumer standards. The framework specifies outcomes and expectations of standards relating to economic and consumer standards that reflect the statutory objectives of the HCA.[313]

Wales

11.173 The statutory framework governing RSLs in Wales under HA 1996 Part 1 has been the responsibility of the Welsh Ministers since 1 April 2010.[314] The Welsh Ministers have responsibility for maintaining a register of providers, financial regulation, setting of performance standards and the power to issue guidance.

11.174 The Welsh Ministers also have some enforcement powers, although not as extensive as the powers granted to the HCA. From October 2011, the Welsh Ministers have had the power to set standards to be met by RSLs in Wales.[315] Welsh Ministers have the power to issue guidance that relates to a matter addressed by a standard and which amplifies the standard.[316]

309 H&RA 2008 s198.
310 H&RA 2008 Part 1 Chapter 7.
311 H&RA 2008 ss198A, 198B.
312 The Social Housing Regulator, March 2015. Replacing the 2012 Guidance.
313 H&RA 2008 s92K. See para 11.168.
314 Prior to that, it was the responsibility of the Welsh Assembly. See para 11.159.
315 HA 1996 s33A.
316 HA 1996 s33B.

11.175 In December 2011, the Welsh Ministers issued *The regulatory framework for housing associations registered in Wales*[317] ('Welsh Framework'). The purpose of the Welsh Framework is to 'ensure that housing associations provide good quality homes and services to tenants and others who use their services'.[318] The framework does not set out any expectations that relate specifically to allocations, but its principles include close working relationships between the Welsh Ministers, housing associations, their tenants and service users and their key partners.[319]

11.176 Enforcement powers include service of an enforcement notice in specified cases,[320] prosecution in relation to matters relied on in enforcement notices,[321] imposition of penalties,[322] and a power to require a landlord to pay compensation to an affected person for failure to meet a standard or comply with an undertaking given by a landlord to the Welsh Ministers.[323]

11.177 The Welsh Ministers also have powers of inspection[324] and inquiry[325] into the affairs of landlords. There is power for Welsh Ministers to remove[326] and appoint[327] officers in certain circumstances, to petition for the winding up of an RSL[328] and to take control of assets following dissolution or winding up of a landlord.[329]

11.178 Housing Association Circular RSL 004/15 requires all housing associations registered in Wales to take account of the Welsh Code (ie the Code under Part 6) governing allocations[330] when 'addressing key delivery outcomes' for the Welsh Framework.

317 Pursuant to HA 1996 s36.
318 Welsh Framework para 1.9.
319 Welsh Framework para 2.1.
320 HA 1996 s50C.
321 HA 1996 s50G.
322 HA 1996 s50H.
323 HA 1996 s50O.
324 HA 1996 Sch 1 Part 3A.
325 HA 1996 Sch 1 Part 4.
326 HA 1996 Sch 1 Part 2 para 4.
327 HA 1996 Sch 1 Part 2 paras 6–8.
328 HA 1996 Sch 1 Part 2 para 14.
329 HA 1996 Sch 1 Part 2 paras 15–15A.
330 See para 11.10.

CHAPTER 12

Enforcement

Introduction

12.1 Housing Act (HA) 1996 Parts 6 and 7 and Housing (Wales) Act (H(W)A) 2014 Part 2 all contain provision for the *internal* review of decisions, which are considered elsewhere in this book.[1] This chapter is concerned with the *external* enforcement of an applicant's rights, ie, what an applicant, who remains dissatisfied with the decision of the authority *after* internal review (if any), can do to challenge or change it by way of recourse to the courts or the ombudsman.

12.2 The only route available to a dissatisfied applicant for an allocation of housing under HA 1996 Part 6 is by way of a claim for judicial review in the High Court, which means that permission must be obtained from the court to bring the claim; HA 1996 Part 7 and H(W)A 2014 Part 2, however, provide for a statutory appeal to the county court[2] on a 'point of law' as of right, and this is the procedure that will normally be used in homelessness cases, although there remain a few circumstances in which judicial review either remains available or may be the only recourse.[3]

12.3 The divergence is practical rather than substantive because an appeal on a point of law confers on the county court the same jurisdiction as that available on a claim for judicial review, engaging the same legal basis for challenge.

12.4 This chapter is divided into two parts: The first part contains the substantive law, applicable either on judicial review or on statutory appeal. The second part deals with the procedure governing how to bring a claim in either court and when to do so. It also deals with complaints to the Local Government Ombudsman. In an annex, a number of specimen documents have been produced, both to illustrate the principles under consideration here, and to assist when applying them.

Substantive law

Introduction

12.5 The general principles which underlie a challenge on a point of law are those of administrative – or public – law, which have been largely,

1 Discussed in chapter 11 (HA 1996 Part 6) and chapter 10 (HA 1996 Part 7 and H(W)A 2014 Part 2).

2 HA 1996 s204; H(W)A 2014 s88.

3 Para 12.140.

but far from exclusively,[4] developed in the course of proceedings for judicial review, and comprise a significant area of law in its own right.[5] The overwhelming bulk of homelessness and allocations case-law is of this order, ie an illustration of the operation of the principles of administrative law, in relation to the statutes governing homelessness and allocations. The jurisprudence that the courts develop in the context of homelessness has itself added to the general body of administrative law, as well as contributing to the growth of housing law.

12.6 The issue in such cases is not what decision the court would reach, but whether a decision can be said to be ultra vires, ie outwith the powers of the body making the decision. This is so whether the challenge is brought by way of judicial review or as a statutory appeal.[6]

12.7 Domestic administrative law includes the obligations imposed on public bodies by the Human Rights Act (HRA) 1998 and the rights from the European Convention on Human Rights ('the Convention'/ ECHR) that the HRA 1998 imports. This has three consequences: first, it adds to the categories of illegality – if an administrative law decision is unlawful under the provisions of HRA 1998, it is ultra vires; second, it reinforces and develops existing administrative law; third, public authorities within its purview include private registered providers of social housing and registered social landlords in respect of some aspects of their management of social housing stock (including service of notice to quit or of seeking possession), which means that, in addition to the requirement to conform to the Convention rights, they are (in these respects) also susceptible to the principles of domestic public law, even if they would not otherwise be.[7]

4 The important Court of Appeal decision in *Crédit Suisse v Allerdale MBC* [1997] QB 306, CA, was an appeal from a decision of the Commercial Court; *Boddington v British Transport Police* [1999] 2 AC 143, HL, which is also of considerable importance, was a criminal prosecution.

5 See the two leading textbooks in the area: Wade and Forsyth, *Administrative law*, 11th edn, OUP, 2014; and Woolf, Jowell, Donnelly and Hare, *De Smith's Judicial review*, 8th edn, Sweet & Maxwell, 2018.

6 *Nipa Begum v Tower Hamlets LBC* [2000] 1 WLR 306, (2000) 32 HLR 445, CA, approved by the House of Lords in *Runa Begum v Tower Hamlets LBC* [2003] UKHL 5, [2003] 2 AC 430, [2003] HLR 32, see particularly Lord Bingham at [7]. *Runa Begum* was followed in *Ali v Birmingham City Council* [2010] UKSC 8, [2010] HLR 22. This did not, however, allow a firm of solicitors with a Legal Aid Agency contract for public law work (but not housing) to conduct HA 1996 s204 appeals: *Bhatia Best Ltd v Lord Chancellor* [2014] EWHC 746 (QB), [2014] 1 WLR 3487.

7 *R (Weaver) v London & Quadrant Housing Trust* [2008] EWHC 1377, [2008] JHL D94 and on appeal [2009] EWCA Civ 587, [2010] 1 WLR 363, [2009] HLR 40. The proposition as to susceptibility was conceded. See paras 11.166–11.167.

12.8 The developing – and expanding – body of 'administrative law' is that with which this part of this chapter is concerned. It is addressed as follows.

a) the nature of a challenge;
b) the general principles of administrative law;
c) substantive grounds for challenge;
d) procedural grounds for challenge.

12.9 This important caveat needs to be entered at the start. Public law is not about absolutes: many aspects of it engage degrees of right and wrong, which will depend on the facts of the individual challenge, rather than 'rules' – as it has been said, 'in law, context is everything'.[8]

12.10 Thus, a general duty to make enquiries will differ depending on the context: a duty to make enquiries under the homelessness provisions will import different practical obligations than will a duty to make enquiries into another, entirely different area – for example, a police enquiry into the commission of a crime (hence, the proposition that local authority enquiries do not have to amount to 'CID-type enquiries').[9] Likewise, and plainly, what is factually relevant to one area of activity will not necessarily be relevant to another.

12.11 Because administrative law derives from a variety of sources and is applied to (and therefore continues to be developed in relation to) a wide range of activities, many of which are very far from the specific issues raised by HA 1996 Parts 6 and 7 and H(W)A 2014 Part 2, cases which have been developed in other areas therefore need to be treated with some caution: there may be more room for manoeuvre (either way) over how they function under Parts 6, 7 or 2 than may at first appear; or, they may simply not be relevant. Decisions on the specific statutory provisions are one thing; decisions on principles of decision-making quite another.

The nature of a challenge

12.12 At the heart of administrative law is the proposition that Parliament intends public bodies always to act properly, in the sense of reasonably and lawfully.

8 *R (Daly) v Secretary of State for the Home Department* [2001] UKHL 26, [2001] 2 AC 532.

9 *Lally v Kensington and Chelsea RLBC* (1980) *Times* 26 March, QBD.

12.13 The role of the courts is, however, supervisory rather than appellate: the court[10] must review the decision-making processes of the body in question, rather than determine for itself what decision the authority should make.[11] Provided that the authority does not err in how it reaches the decision,[12] the substance of the decision is for the authority, not for the court, and it is the authority's view or decision which must prevail.[13]

12.14 There is rarely only one decision which an authority may reach: one individual's view of what is reasonable will often quite properly differ from that of another, and Parliament has entrusted decision-making under HA 1996 Parts 6 and 7 and H(W)A 2014 Part 2 to authorities, not to the courts.

10 Whether Administrative Court on judicial review or county court on appeal. The Court of Appeal has expressed its disapproval of county court judges who have overstepped their role (*Kruja v Enfield LBC* [2004] EWCA Civ 1769, [2005] HLR 13 – see para 12.195) and emphasised that decision-making on matters such as the vulnerability of applicants is for the local authority: *Osmani v Camden LBC* [2004] EWCA Civ 1706, [2005] HLR 22.

11 See, eg *R v Northumberland Compensation Appeal Tribunal ex p Shaw* [1952] 1 KB 338, CA, per Denning LJ at 346–347: 'The Court of King's Bench has an inherent jurisdiction to control all inferior tribunals, not in an appellate capacity but in a supervisory capacity. This control extends not only to seeing that the inferior tribunals keep within their jurisdiction, but also to seeing that they observe the law . . . The King's Bench does not substitute its own views for those of the tribunal, as a Court of Appeal would do. It leaves it to the tribunal to hear the case again, and in a proper case may command it to do so.' See also *R v Secretary of State for Trade and Industry ex p Lonrho plc* [1989] 1 WLR 525, HL per Lord Keith of Kinkel at 535: 'The question is not whether the Secretary of State came to . . . a conclusion which meets with the approval of the . . . Court but whether the discretion was properly exercised.' This is the same approach as the appellate court adopts when considering an appeal against a discretionary decision of a judge: eg, *Woodspring DC v Taylor* (1982) 4 HLR 95, CA.

12 In any of the acknowledged senses – see paras 12.19–12.128.

13 See, eg *R v Secretary of State for the Home Department ex p Khawaja* [1984] AC 74, HL per Lord Scarman at 100, referring to the *Wednesbury* principle: 'The principle excluded the court from substituting its own view of the facts for that of the authority'; *R v Secretary of State for the Home Department ex p Brind* [1991] 1 AC 696, HL per Lord Lowry at 767: 'The judges are not, generally speaking, equipped by training or experience or furnished with the necessary knowledge and advice, to decide the answer to an administrative problem where the scales are evenly balanced, but they have a much better chance of reaching the right answer where the question is put in a *Wednesbury* form'; see also *Wednesbury* itself, below, footnote 25 and para 12.23, where Lord Greene MR, at 234, refers to the court as 'a judicial authority which is concerned, and concerned only, to see whether the local authority have contravened the law by acting in excess of the powers which Parliament has confided in them'.

12.15 In *Puhlhofer*,[14] Lord Brightman said:[15]

> I am troubled at the prolific use of judicial review for the purpose of challenging the performance by local authorities of their functions under the Act of 1977. Parliament intended the local authority to be the judge of fact. The Act abounds with the formula when, or if, the housing authority are satisfied as to this, or that, or have reason to believe this, or that. Although the action or inaction of a local authority is clearly susceptible to judicial review where they have misconstrued the Act, or abused their powers or otherwise acted perversely, I think that great restraint should be exercised in giving leave to proceed by judicial review. The plight of the homeless is a desperate one, and the plight of the applicants in the present case commands the deepest sympathy. But it is not, in my opinion, appropriate that the remedy of judicial review, which is a discretionary remedy, should be made use of to monitor the actions of local authorities under the Act save in the exceptional case. The ground upon which the courts will review the exercise of an administrative discretion is abuse of power, for example, bad faith, a mistake in construing the limits of the power, a procedural irregularity, or unreasonableness in the *Wednesbury*[16] sense – unreasonableness verging on an absurdity: see the speech of Lord Scarman in *R v Secretary of State for the Environment ex p Nottinghamshire CC*.[17] Where the existence or non-existence of a fact is left to the judgment and discretion of a public body and that fact involves a broad spectrum ranging from the obvious to the debatable to the just conceivable, it is the duty of the court to leave the decision of that fact to the public body to whom Parliament has entrusted the decision-making power save in a case where it is obvious that the public body, consciously or unconsciously, are acting perversely.
>
> . . . I express the hope that there will be a lessening in the number of challenges which are mounted against local authorities who are endeavouring, in extremely difficult circumstances, to perform their duties under the Homeless Persons Act with due regard for all their other housing problems.[18]

12.16 There are echoes of this in the HA 1996 Part 6 decision of the House of Lords in *R (Ahmad) v Newham LBC*.[19]

14 *R v Hillingdon LBC ex p Puhlhofer* [1986] AC 484, (1986) 18 HLR 158, HL.

15 At 518.

16 *Associated Provincial Picture Houses Ltd v Wednesbury Corporation* [1948] 1 KB 223, CA.

17 *Nottinghamshire CC v Secretary of State for the Environment* [1986] AC 240, HL.

18 The same principles apply on a statutory appeal – the county court must at all times bear in mind the public law exercise in which it is engaged: *Crawley BC v B* (2000) 32 HLR 636, CA.

19 [2009] UKHL 14, [2009] HLR 31.

> 46. . . . [A]s a general proposition, it is undesirable for the courts to get involved in questions of how priorities are accorded in housing allocation policies. Of course, there will be cases where the court has a duty to interfere, for instance if a policy does not comply with statutory requirements, or if it is plainly irrational. However, it seems unlikely that the legislature can have intended that Judges should embark on the exercise of telling authorities how to decide on priorities as between applicants in need of rehousing, save in relatively rare and extreme circumstances. Housing allocation policy is a difficult exercise which requires not only social and political sensitivity and judgment, but also local expertise and knowledge.
>
> 47. In relation to the provision of accommodation under the National Assistance Act 1948, my noble and learned friend, Baroness Hale of Richmond, then Hale LJ, said in *R (Wahid) v Tower Hamlets LBC*[20] '[n]eed is a relative concept, which trained and experienced social workers are much better equipped to assess than are lawyers and courts, provided that they act rationally'. Precisely the same is true of relative housing needs under Part 6 of the 1996 Act, and trained and experienced local authority housing officers.
>
> 48. If section 167 carries with it the sort of requirements which can be said to be implied by the decisions of the Court of Appeal and the Deputy Judge in this case, then Judges would become involved in considering details of housing allocation schemes in a way which would be both unrealistic and undesirable . . .
>
> . . .
>
> 55. This is not to say that there could never be circumstances in which a scheme, which complies with the statutory requirements, could be susceptible to judicial review on grounds of irrationality. Such a suggestion would be unmaintainable not least because it would represent an abdication of judicial responsibility. However, what is important is to emphasise that once a housing allocation scheme complies with the requirements of section 167 and any other statutory requirements, the courts should be very slow to interfere on the ground of alleged irrationality.

12.17 The discretion conferred by Parliament, embodied in this more limited,[21] supervisory approach, does not lead to the conclusion that an authority's decision under HA 1996 Part 6 or Part 7 or H(W)A

20 [2002] EWCA Civ 287, [2003] HLR 2 at [33].

21 Than when an appeal approach allows a court to substitute its own view of the facts.

2014 Part 2 is above reproach.[22] It is the purpose of public law to ensure that public authorities, entrusted with an apparently blanket power to reach 'subjective' decisions, nonetheless do so in accordance with the law.

12.18 A discretionary decision may still be ultra vires and without effect in law: it may be unreasonable in the *Wednesbury* sense – ie a decision which no reasonable authority, properly directing itself, could have reached; it may be a decision that is contrary to the law as properly understood; it may be a decision which has been reached without affording the applicant his or her due procedural safeguards; or it may be a decision which is not based on all the relevant information.

Ultra vires

12.19 Local authorities may only act within their powers. If they do not do so, they are acting unlawfully, and their actions and decisions will be so treated[23] – this is the ultra vires doctrine and a decision so made will be unlawful because:

a) on the face of the statute there was no authority to engage in the action at all; or
b) the statute has been misconstrued; or
c) the authority has misapplied the statute, for example, by failing to use the powers to implement the purpose of the statute; or
d) a decision has been reached under the statute by reference to something which is irrelevant, or in ignorance of something which is relevant, to the way the power under the statute is intended to be operated, or which is so unreasonable – or irrational or perverse – that no reasonable authority could have reached it.

12.20 If it can be shown that a public body such as a local authority has approached its decision unlawfully then, regardless of the reason, the decision will be void and the courts will not give effect to it.

12.21 In so saying, the propositions in the last two paragraphs assume:

a) that there are no differences between the legal consequences of decisions which there was no power at all to take (ie, those which

22 See per Lord Wilberforce in *Secretary of State for Education and Science v Tameside MBC* [1977] AC 1014, HL, at 1047: 'The section is framed in a "subjective" form . . . This form of section is quite well-known and *at first sight* might seem to exclude judicial review . . .' (emphasis added).

23 Subject to issues of forum: cf *Wandsworth LBC v Winder* [1985] AC 461, HL; *Avon CC v Buscott* [1988] QB 656, CA; and *Hackney LBC v Lambourne* (1992) 25 HLR 172, CA; *Manchester City Council v Cochrane* [1999] 1 WLR 809, CA.

are said to be outside the four corners of a statute) and those which there was power to take but which have been taken in some way improperly;[24] and

b) that once it is decided that a decision is ultra vires, it must be treated as if it had at all times been void for all purposes.

12.22 There has been a number of cases which have considered these two (overlapping) issues, and they are issues which will doubtless continue to be discussed.[25] For the purposes of this book, however, those propositions normally suffice in practice.[26]

The general principles of administrative law

Wednesbury

12.23 The classic statement of the court's role and function when addressing public law issues is that of Lord Greene MR in *Wednesbury*:[27]

> What, then, is the power of the courts? They can only interfere with an act of executive authority if it be shown that the authority has

24 See, in particular, *Crédit Suisse plc v Allerdale MBC* [1997] QB 306, CA, per Neill LJ at 343: 'I know of no authority for the proposition that the *ultra vires* decisions of local authority can be classified into categories of invalidity . . .' But cf *Charles Terence Estates Ltd v Cornwall CC* [2012] EWCA Civ 1439, [2013] 1 WLR 466, [2013] HLR 12, at [27]–[37], [44]–[53].

25 *Anisminic Ltd v Foreign Compensation Commission* [1969] 2 AC 147, HL, would nonetheless seem to be definitive: a decision wrongly reached, for whatever reason, was considered to be void and a nullity, because decision-makers have no jurisdiction to make unlawful decisions (see, in particular, per Lord Reid, at 171, using similar terms to describe unlawfulness as the classic definition by Lord Greene MR in *Wednesbury*, see para 12.53). In *Boddington v British Transport Police* [1999] 2 AC 143, HL, however, the majority of the Committee was not willing simply to assume invalidity for all purposes and at all times, because people would in the meantime have regulated their lives on the basis of a decision's validity.

26 It today appears to be accepted in homelessness law that a decision improperly taken may be retaken: see *Crawley BC v B*, above (see further para 12.252); *Porteous v West Dorset DC* [2004] EWCA Civ 244, (2004) HLR 30 at [7]–[9] (fundamental mistake of fact); and *Islington LBC v Uckac* [2006] EWCA Civ 340, [2006] HLR 35 (on mistake of fact, but by counsel's concession). Although the discussion in *Porteous* is in terms of revisiting and changing or rescinding an earlier decision, the basis of the argument in both cases was that the earlier decision was void and it is hard to see any other basis: unless void, the authority is what is known as functus officio, ie, it has no further function – it has had an application and it has reached its decision; accordingly, to uphold the later decision, the earlier one had to be void.

27 *Associated Provincial Picture Houses Ltd v Wednesbury Corporation* [1948] 1 KB 223, CA.

contravened the law. It is for those who assert that the local authority has contravened the law to establish that proposition ... It is not to be assumed prima facie that responsible bodies like the local authority in this case will exceed their powers; but the court, whenever it is alleged that the local authority have contravened the law, must not substitute itself for that authority ... When an executive discretion is entrusted by Parliament to a body such as the local authority in this case, what appears to be an exercise of that discretion can only be challenged in the courts in a strictly limited class of case ... When discretion of this kind is granted the law recognises certain principles upon which that discretion must be exercised, but within the four corners of those principles the discretion ... is an absolute one and cannot be questioned in any court of law. What then are those principles? They are well understood. They are principles which the court looks to in considering any question of discretion of this kind. The exercise of such a discretion must be a real exercise of the discretion. If, in the statute conferring the discretion, there is to be found expressly or by implication matters which the authority exercising the discretion ought to have regard to, then in exercising the discretion it must have regard to those matters. Conversely, if the nature of the subject-matter and the general interpretation of the Act make it clear that certain matters would not be germane to the matter in question, the authority must disregard those irrelevant collateral matters.[28]

There have been in the cases expressions used relating to the sort of things that authorities must not do ... I am not sure myself whether the permissible grounds of attack cannot be defined under a single head ... Bad faith, dishonesty – those of course, stand by themselves – unreasonableness, attention given to extraneous circumstances, disregard of public policy and things like that have all been referred to, according to the facts of individual cases, as being matters which are relevant to the question. If they cannot all be confined under one head, they at any rate ... overlap to a very great extent. For instance, we have heard in this case a great deal about the meaning of the word 'unreasonable'.

It is true the discretion must be exercised reasonably. Now what does that mean? ... It has frequently been used and is frequently used as a general description of the things that must not be done ... A person entrusted with a discretion must ... direct himself properly in law. He must call his own attention to the matters which he is bound to consider. He must exclude from his consideration matters which are irrelevant to what he has to consider. If he does not obey those rules, he may truly be said, and often is said, to be acting 'unreasonably'. Similarly, there may be something so absurd that no sensible person

28 At 228.

could ever dream that it lay within the powers of the authority. Warrington LJ in *Short v Poole Corporation*[29] gave the example of the red-haired teacher, dismissed because she had red hair. That is unreasonable in one sense. In another sense it is taking into consideration extraneous matters. It is so unreasonable that it might almost be described as being done in bad faith; and, in fact, all these things run into one another . . .[30]

It is true to say that, if a decision on a competent matter is so unreasonable that no reasonable authority could ever have come to it, then the courts can interfere . . . But to prove a case of that kind would require something overwhelming . . . [The] proposition that the decision of the local authority can be upset if it is proved to be unreasonable, really meant that it must be proved to be unreasonable in the sense that the court considers it to be a decision that no reasonable body could have come to. It is not what the court considers unreasonable, a different thing altogether . . . The effect of the legislation is not to set up the court as an arbiter of the correctness of one view over another. It is the local authority that are set in that position and, provided they act, as they have acted, within the four corners of their jurisdiction, this court . . . cannot interfere . . .[31]

The court is entitled to investigate the action of the local authority with a view to seeing whether they have taken into account matters which they ought not to take into account, or, conversely, have refused to take into account or neglected to take into account matters which they ought to take into account. Once that question is answered in favour of the local authority, it may still be possible to say that, although the local authority have kept within the four corners of the matters which they ought to consider, they have nevertheless come to a conclusion so unreasonable that no reasonable authority could ever have come to it. In such a case, again, I think the court can interfere. The power of the court to interfere in each case is not as an appellate authority to override a decision of the local authority, but as a judicial authority which is concerned, and concerned only, to see whether the local authority have contravened the law by acting in excess of the powers which Parliament has confided in them.[32]

12.24 This statement, in particular the last passage, remains the cornerstone of domestic administrative law, even if there are cases in which it has been questioned.[33]

29 [1926] Ch 66, CA.
30 At 229.
31 At 230–231.
32 At 233–234.
33 See further below, paras 12.28–12.35.

CCSU

12.25 The central principles of public law derived from Lord Greene's comments in *Wednesbury* were subsequently re-classified by Lord Diplock under the headings of 'illegality', 'irrationality' and 'procedural impropriety' in *CCSU*:[34]

> By 'illegality' as a ground of judicial review I mean that the decision-maker must understand correctly the law that regulates his decision-making power and must give effect to it. Whether he has or not is par excellence a justiciable question to be decided, in the event of dispute, by those persons, the judges, by whom the judicial power of the state is exercisable.
>
> By 'irrationality' I mean what can by now be succinctly referred to as '*Wednesbury* unreasonableness' . . . It applies to a decision which is so outrageous in its defiance of logic or of accepted moral standards that no sensible person who had applied his mind to the question to be decided could have arrived at it. Whether a decision falls within this category is a question that judges by their training and experience should be well-equipped to answer, or else there would be something badly wrong with our judicial system . . . 'Irrationality' by now can stand upon its own feet as an accepted ground on which a decision may be attacked by judicial review.
>
> I have described the third head as 'procedural impropriety' rather than failure to observe basic rules of natural justice or failure to act with procedural fairness towards the person who will be affected by the decision. This is because susceptibility to judicial review under this head covers also failure by an administrative tribunal to observe procedural rules that are expressly laid down in the legislative instrument by which its jurisdiction is conferred, even where such failure does not involve any denial of natural justice . . .

Human Rights Act 1998 and proportionality

12.26 As noted above,[35] the HRA 1998 is relevant in a number of ways, including, first, that it imports specific articles of the ECHR; and, second, because of its influence on the development of the principles

34 *Council of Civil Service Unions v Minister for the Civil Service* [1985] AC 374, HL ('*CCSU*'). The statement was described by Lord Scarman as 'a valuable and already "classical"' statement of the law, albeit 'certainly not exhaustive': *R v Secretary of State for the Environment ex p Nottinghamshire CC* [1986] AC 240, HL at 249.

35 See para 12.7.

of domestic administrative law. It is the second of these aspects which is relevant under this heading. The first is considered below.[36]

12.27 In *CCSU*,[37] Lord Diplock had raised – but did not answer – the question whether or not the principle of 'proportionality'[38] might be imported into domestic law from Europe.[39]

12.28 From the early 1990s, doubt began to be cast on whether the *Wednesbury* test – affording a decision-maker a wide ambit of discretion – was suitable to deal with cases that involved what were recognisable as fundamental rights, and it began to be suggested that the *Wednesbury* test required adaptation so as to subject such cases to what has been called 'anxious scrutiny',[40] meaning a closer degree of factual scrutiny than the conventional *Wednesbury* approach.[41]

12.29 Comparing the differences, it has been observed that there are three potential approaches to the standard of review that may be applied when there is challenge on public law grounds:[42]

a) the conventional *Wednesbury* approach;
b) an approach based on fundamental rights which requires the court to 'insist that that fact be respected by the decision-maker, who is accordingly required to demonstrate either that his proposed action does not in truth interfere with the right, or, if it does, that there exist considerations which may reasonably be accepted as amounting to a substantial objective justification for the interference'; and

36 See paras 12.114–12.128.

37 See para 12.25.

38 'Proportionality' is the doctrine that there has to be a reasonable relationship between the governmental (including local) action under review and its purpose in a given context.

39 At 410. What Lord Diplock had in mind was not the ECHR but European Union (EU) law, in which proportionality also plays a substantial part. Some have considered that proportionality was in any event already inherent in *Wednesbury* unreasonableness: see *R v Secretary of State Home Department ex p Leech* [1994] QB 198, CA; *R v Chief Constable of Sussex ex p International Trader's Ferry* [1999] 2 AC 418, HL.

40 *R v Ministry of Defence ex p Smith* [1996] QB 517, CA; *Bugdaycay v Secretary of State for the Home Department* [1987] AC 514, HL; sometimes referred to as 'Super-*Wednesbury*' – *Vilvarajah v UK* (1991) 14 EHRR 248, ECtHR.

41 See *R v Ministry of Agriculture, Fisheries and Food ex p First City Trading Limited* [1997] 1 CMLR 250, QBD; see also *R v Secretary of State for Health ex p Eastside Cheese Co* [1999] 3 CMLR 123, CA.

42 *R (Mahmood) v Secretary of State for the Home Department* [2001] 1 WLR 840, CA.

c) an approach based on claims which directly engage rights guaranteed by the ECHR, which requires the court to decide whether there has in fact been a violation of a convention right.[43]

12.30 This trend towards different standards of review depending on the rights in issue appears to imply a weakening of the dominance of the *Wednesbury* test for determining public law challenges. In *Daly*,[44] Lord Steyn (although suggesting that in most cases the courts would reach the same conclusion regardless of the basis on which the decision was scrutinised) said that:

> . . . the day will come when it will be more widely recognised that [*Wednesbury*] was an unfortunately retrogressive decision in English administrative law, insofar as it suggested that there are degrees of unreasonableness and that only a very extreme degree can bring an administrative decision within the legitimate scope of judicial invalidation. The depth of judicial review and the deference due to administrative discretion vary with the subject matter. It may well be, however, that the law can never be satisfied in any administrative field merely by a finding that the decision under review is not capricious or absurd.[45]

12.31 The reference to subject-matter is the key element for present purposes: see also Lord Steyn's comment in the same case that 'in

43 Those categories were not 'hermitically sealed': 'There is, rather, what may be called a sliding scale of review; the graver the impact of the decision in question upon the individual affected by it, the more substantial the justification that will be required . . . [C]ases where, objectively, the individual is most gravely affected will be those where what we have come to call his fundamental rights are or are said to be put in jeopardy' (at [19]).

44 *R (Daly) v Secretary of State for the Home Department* [2001] UKHL 26, [2001] 2 AC 532. In *R (Pro-Life Alliance) v British Broadcasting Corporation* [2003] UKHL 23, [2004] 1 AC 185, Lord Walker extensively cited with approval the passages under consideration here: see [134]–[135]. See also per Lord Bingham in *A and others v Secretary of State for the Home Department; X and another v Secretary of State for the Home Department* [2004] UKHL 56, [2005] 2 AC 68, at [40].

45 Per Lord Cooke at [32]. The Court of Appeal has observed that 'the *Wednesbury* test is moving closer to proportionality' but also said that 'it is not for this court to perform the burial rights' – *R (Association of British Civilian Internees (Far East Region)) v Secretary of State for Defence* [2003] EWCA Civ 473, [2003] 3 WLR 80.

law, context is everything'.[46] In *Runa Begum*,[47] it could accordingly still be held that it was appropriate for the decision-maker to make findings of fact without any scrutiny other than the usual grounds for judicial review, because homelessness decisions are administrative in nature and do not engage substantive Convention rights:[48] there was therefore no need for any intensification of the traditional approach to review, or for anxious scrutiny[49] of, the decision.

12.32 In *R (Association of British Civilian Internees (Far East Region)) v Secretary of State for Defence*,[50] the Court of Appeal suggested that the time had come for the *Wednesbury* approach to be dispensed with, noting that its strictness had been relaxed in recent years so that it was, in any event, moving closer to proportionality, so much so that in some cases it was not possible to see daylight between the two tests.

12.33 In *R (Keyu) v Secretary of State for Foreign and Commonwealth Affairs*,[51] however, Lord Neuberger said that reconsideration of the basis on which courts review decisions of the executive, specifically whether *Wednesbury* rationality should be replaced by a structured proportionality assessment, would require a panel of nine Supreme Court justices because the move from rationality to proportionality could have far-reaching consequences and implications which were profound in constitutional terms.[52]

46 *Daly*, at [28].

47 *Runa Begum v Tower Hamlets LBC* [2003] UKHL 5, [2003] 2 AC 430, [2003] HLR 32. *Runa Begum* was followed in *Ali v Birmingham City Council* [2010] UKSC 8, [2010] HLR 22. In *Ali v UK* App No 40378/10, [2015] HLR 46, the same case at ECtHR, it was held that Article 6(1) was engaged once the authority decided that a duty was owed under HA 1996 s193 as that was a sufficiently certain right to amount to a 'civil right'; but it was also held that there was no violation of Article 6 as the right to a reasoned decision, review and appeal were adequate safeguards. In *Poshteh v Kensington and Chelsea RLBC* [2017] UKSC 36, [2017] AC 624, [2017] HLR 28, however, it was held that *Ali v UK* did not provide a sufficient reason to depart from the fully considered decision in *Ali v Birmingham City Council* and the Supreme Court should await full consideration of the Issue by a Grand Chamber of the European Court before deciding whether (and if so how) to modify its position.

48 See further paras 12.114–12.128.

49 See *R v Ministry of Agriculture, Fisheries and Food ex p First City Trading Limited* [1997] 1 CMLR 250, QBD; see also *R v Secretary of State for Health ex p Eastside Cheese Co* [1999] 3 CMLR 123, CA.

50 [2003] EWCA Civ 473, [2003] QB 1397, per Lord Phillips at [34]–[35].

51 [2015] UKSC 69.

52 At [132]–[133]. Lord Kerr, at [271] agreed with the need for a panel of nine but also said that the question would have to be addressed by the Supreme Court sooner rather than later.

12.34 What then is the current position? *Runa Begum* concludes that what may be called the highest standard of judicial scrutiny of the three identified[53] is not applicable to challenges under Part 7. It implies that nothing more than conventional *Wednesbury* is applicable. Nonetheless, it remains open to argument that housing is a fundamental right, within the 'middle' standard of review.

12.35 Even if forced back to *Wednesbury*, that may not be the end of it: the *Wednesbury* approach is clearly under pressure or, as it has been put, the law is engaged in a 'long trek away from *Wednesbury* irrationality'.[54] Perhaps the simplest approach is to view the *Wednesbury* approach as an absolute minimum, while acknowledging that, sometimes, it will not be enough.[55]

Grounds for challenge – practical classification

12.36 Having considered the general principles on which public law decisions may be challenged, we turn to consider the practical classification of grounds for challenge, utilising *CCSU*,[56] supplemented by the specific (relevant) provisions of the HRA 1998.[57]

12.37 As effectively recognised in *Wednesbury*,[58] when applied in a practical context, grounds tend to overlap one another: thus a failure to have regard to a relevant fact may also be an error of law; a failure to give reasons for a decision may not only be unlawful for failure to comply with the duty to do so but may also found a challenge based on the fairness of the procedure.[59]

12.38 Moreover, the distinction between a point of law (challengeable on administrative law principles) and a question of fact (which is not) is not a straightforward distinction and there will be cases where matters of pure fact arise:

53 See para 12.31.

54 Per Lord Walker in *R (ProLife Alliance) v British Broadcasting Corporation* [2003] UKHL 23, [2004] 1 AC 185, at [131].

55 In reality, the *Wednesbury* test is sufficiently flexible – open-textured – in any event to allow courts to apply it to the same effect as if another test were permissible. Certainly, they have no difficulty catching the more egregious errors and in justices when they wish to do so.

56 See para 12.25.

57 Cf paras 12.114–12.128.

58 See para 12.23.

59 The overlapping nature of grounds is illustrated by the specimen documents annexed to this chapter.

> The cases do not support the proposition that *any* conclusion that a legal or statutory concept applies to a particular set of facts is a question of law, although in practice they permit considerable elasticity in their application.[60]

Illegality

Misdirection of law

12.39 A decision-maker must 'understand correctly the law that regulates his or her decision-making power and must give effect to it',[61] ie, the decision-maker must understand and apply the law correctly. Thus in *Islam*,[62] the authority's misunderstanding of the test to be applied when determining whether a person was homeless intentionally under the Housing (Homeless Persons) Act 1977 was a misdirection of law sufficient to vitiate the decision.[63] When a court reconsiders an issue, eg the meaning of vulnerable,[64] it is reconsidering the correct legal interpretation of an issue and – if finding against the authority – holding that previous usage was a misdirection.

Decisions must be based on the facts

12.40 While it is of the essence of *Puhlhofer*[65] that matters of fact are for the decision-maker, this does not mean that factual errors are irrelevant. In *Adan*,[66] Brooke LJ commented:[67]

> In very many cases, although it could be said that an administrative body had made a material mistake of fact the decision is vulnerable on other more conventional grounds: for procedural impropriety . . . or because a factor had been taken into account which should not have been taken into account . . . or because there was no evidence on which the decision could have been safely based . . . What is quite clear is that a court of supervisory jurisdiction does not, without more,

60 *Adan v Newham LBC* [2001] EWCA Civ 1916, [2002] HLR 28, per Hale LJ at [66] (emphasis in original).

61 *CCSU* at 410F, per Lord Diplock.

62 *R v Hillingdon LBC ex p Islam* [1983] 1 AC 688, HL. See also *Anisminic Ltd v Foreign Compensation Commission* [1969] 2 AC 147, HL and *R (Q) v Secretary of State for the Home Department* [2003] EWCA Civ 364, [2004] QB 36.

63 If the decision-maker incorrectly thinks that it does not have a power, that is also a misdirection of law: *National Aids Trust v National Health Service Commissioning Board (NHS England)* [2016] EWHC 2005 (Admin).

64 *Hotak v Southwark LBC; Kanu v Southwark LBC; Johnson v Solihull MBC* [2015] UKSC 30, [2015] HLR 23.

65 See para 12.15.

66 *Adan v Newham LBC*, above.

67 At [41].

have the power to substitute its own view of the primary facts for the view reasonably adopted by the body to whom the fact-finding power has been entrusted.

12.41 If it can be shown that a decision proceeded on the basis of an incorrect understanding of the facts, that there was no evidence to support the finding of fact made, or that there was no account taken of the facts, there may be scope for a challenge on the basis that the decision was at odds with the factual matrix,[68] in particular where there are fundamental rights at stake.[69]

12.42 It has also for some time been recognised that the court is entitled to decide what the facts are if they comprise 'precedent facts' or as they are sometimes called, 'jurisdictional facts',[70] ie, if the facts establish the right to exercise a power or the obligation to perform a duty,[71] the court is entitled to reach a decision for itself as to what the facts are.[72]

12.43 Where there has been a review,[73] however, the issue will be whether the reviewer could, as a matter of public law, have reached the relevant decision on the facts, rather than whether those facts exist,[74] as the scheme of the HA 1996 means that 'there is no jurisdiction ... for the County Court to set itself up as a finder of the

68 *Secretary of State for Education and Science v Tameside MBC* [1977] AC 1014, HL, at 1047.

69 In *R (Wilkinson) v Broadmoor Special Hospital Authority* [2001] EWCA Civ 1545, [2002] 1 WLR 419, it was suggested that, where fundamental rights were at issue, the court 'must now inevitably reach its own view' on the facts. See also *R (Murphy) v Secretary of State for the Home Department* [2005] EWHC 140 (Admin), [2005] 1 WLR 3516. But cf the discussion above, paras 12.13–12.17.

70 Eg, *R v Secretary of State for the Environment ex p Powis* [1981] 1 WLR 584, CA per Dunn LJ at 595H.

71 *R v Secretary of State for Home Department ex p Khawaja* [1984] AC 74, HL. See also per Baroness Hale in *R (A) (FC) v Croydon LBC; R (M) (FC) v Lambeth LBC* [2009] UKSC 8, at [29]–[30].

72 See *Khawaja*, above, per Lord Wilberforce at 105; *R v Oldham BC ex p Garlick* [1993] AC 509, HL, per Lord Griffiths at 520E.

73 See para 9.184 and following.

74 *Bubb v Wandsworth LBC* [2011] EWCA Civ 1285, [2012] HLR 13, where the issue was whether the applicant had received the authority's letter warning her of the possible consequences of refusal of an offer, and of her right to request a review of the suitability of the accommodation, under HA 1996 s193(7), (7F); the reviewing officer had been entitled to conclude that she had done so. Cf *R (A) v Croydon LBC* [2009] UKSC 8, [2009] 1 WLR 2557, where the age of a child for the purposes of Children Act 1989 s20 was held to be one for the court, distinguishing (at [28]) between 'a number of different value judgments' contained in the CA 1989 and 'a different kind of question [to which there] is a right or a wrong answer' (of which age was an example).

relevant primary facts for itself'.[75] See also the discussion of the judgment of the Supreme Court in *Ali v Birmingham City Council*[76] below.[77]

12.44 In *Tameside* at the Court of Appeal,[78] Scarman LJ suggested that an error of fact – not merely precedent fact – might be sufficient of itself to vitiate an authority's decision where that error could be said to be a 'misunderstanding or ignorance of an established and relevant fact': this approach has found significant subsequent support.[79] There are now several examples of administrative decisions quashed because they were reached on a material error[80] of fact,[81] although opinions differ as to whether they are examples of failing to take into

75 *Bubb* at [20]. See also *Richmond upon Thames v Kubicek* [2012] EWHC 3292 (QB) where it was held that the county court judge had been wrong to list a trial of a preliminary issue (and hear factual evidence) to resolve a dispute between the authority and the applicant as to what had been said during HA 1996 s184 enquiries.

76 [2010] UKSC 8.

77 See paras 12.117–12.122.

78 *Secretary of State for Education and Science v Tameside MBC* (1976) 120 SJ 539, CA.

79 Lord Slynn, in *R v Criminal Injuries Compensation Board ex p A* [1999] 2 AC 330, HL accepted the existence of such a doctrine, a view he re-affirmed in *R (Alconbury Developments Ltd) v Secretary of State for the Environment, Transport and the Regions* [2001] UKHL 23, [2003] 2 AC 295 at [53], but in neither case was this reasoning adopted by the Committee and, in the first, Lord Slynn himself 'preferred' to decide the case on the alternative ground of breach of natural justice amounting to unfairness (at 345). In *E v Secretary of State for the Home Department* [2004] EWCA Civ 49, [2004] QB 1044, Carnwath LJ considered the history in some detail. How far the House of Lords can be said to have endorsed Scarman LJ's approach may be in some doubt: see *E* at [55].

80 Or 'fundamental mistake of fact': see *Porteous v West Dorset DC* [2004] EWCA Civ 244, per Mantell LJ at [9].

81 See also *Mason v Secretary of State for the Environment and Bromsgrove DC* [1984] JPL 332; *Jagendorf & Trott v Secretary of State for the Environment and Krasucki* [1986] JPL 771; *R v Hillingdon LBC ex p Thomas* (1987) 19 HLR 196; *R v Legal Aid Committee No 10 (East Midlands) ex p McKenna* [1990] COD 358, (1989) *Times* 20 December, DC; *Simplex GE (Holdings) Ltd v Secretary of State for the Environment* [1988] 3 PLR 25, CA; *R v London Residuary Body ex p ILEA* (1987) *Times* 3 July, CA. See also *R (Meredith) v Merthyr Tydfil CBC* [2002] EWHC 634 (Admin); *R (Kathro) v Rhondda Cynon Taff CBC* [2001] EWHC (Admin) 527, [2002] Env LR 196; *R (McLellan) v Bracknell Forest BC* [2001] EWCA Civ 1510, [2002] QB 1129; *Martin Hill v Bedfordshire CC* [2007] EWHC 2435 (Admin), [2008] ELR 191; *R (March) v Secretary of State for Health* [2010] EWHC 765 (Admin); *Manydown Ltd v Basingstoke and Deane BC* [2012] EWHC 977 (Admin); *R (Watt) v Hackney LBC* [2016] EWHC 1978 (Admin).

account a relevant consideration,[82] a stand-alone ground[83] or are as an aspect of fairness.[84] It must nonetheless be said that mistake of fact is still some way from a generally accepted ground of judicial review.[85]

Taking into account irrelevant considerations

12.45 It is sufficient to void a decision on the basis that an irrelevant factor has been taken into account if the factor is significant, or potentially of influence, meaning that, if it had not been taken into account, the decision might have been different. The authority must take such steps as are reasonable to find out the relevant facts.[86] When housing is in issue, 'consideration of common humanity' is a

82 *Secretary of State for Education and Science v Tameside MBC*, above, per Lord Diplock at 1066F–1067A. See also *Crake v Supplementary Benefits Commission* [1982] 1 All ER 498, QBD at 508, cited in *Aslam v South Bedfordshire DC* [2001] EWCA Civ 514, [2001] RVR 65, itself cited in *E v Secretary of State for the Home Department*, above, at [38].

83 *R (Alconbury Developments and others) v Secretary of State for the Environment, Transport and the Regions*, above at [53], [169]; *R v Criminal Injuries Compensation Board ex p A*, above, at [344]; *Runa Begum v Tower Hamlets LBC* [2003] UKHL 5, [2003] 2 AC 430, at [7]–[11].

84 *E v Secretary of State for the Home Department*, above, and see further, paras 12.66–12.70. 'What mattered was that, because of their failure, and through no fault of her own, the claimant had not had "a fair crack of the whip" (see *Fairmount Investments v Secretary of State for the Environment* [1976] 1 WLR 1255, HL per Lord Russell at 1266/A). If it is said that this is taking "fairness" beyond its traditional role as an aspect of procedural irregularity it is no further than its use in cases such as *HTV Ltd v Price Commission* [1976] ICR 170, CA approved by the House of Lords in *R v IRC ex p Preston* [1985] AC 825, at 865–866). In our view, the time has now come to accept that a mistake of fact giving rise to unfairness is a separate head of challenge in an appeal on a point of law, at least in those statutory contexts where the parties share an interest in co-operating to achieve the correct result. Asylum law is undoubtedly such an area.' Per Carnwath LJ in *E* at [65]–[66].

85 See *Wandsworth LBC v A* [2000] 1 WLR 1246, CA, at 1255/H-1256/C: 'While there may, possibly, be special considerations that apply in the more formalised area of planning inquiries . . . and while the duty of "anxious scrutiny" imposed in asylum cases by *R v Secretary of State for the Home Department ex p Bugdaycay* [[1987] AC 514, HL] renders those cases an uncertain guide for other areas of public law; none the less . . . there is still no general right to challenge the decision of a public body on an issue of fact alone. The law in this connection continues, in our respectful view, to be as stated for a unanimous House of Lords by Lord Brightman in *R v Hillingdon LBC ex p Puhlhofer* . . .'

86 Per Lord Diplock in *Secretary of State for Education and Science v Tameside MBC* [1977] AC 1014, HL, at p1065; see also *R v Lincolnshire CC and Wealden DC ex p Atkinson* [1995] 8 Admin LR 529, DC and *R v Hillingon LBC ex p McDonagh* (1998) 31 HLR 531, QBD.

relevant consideration in its own right.[87] While the resources available to an authority will be relevant to how it discharges its duty,[88] they are not relevant[89] to the question whether there is a duty at all.[90]

12.46 There is no general proposition which governs what is a relevant consideration: the question is what the Act requires to be taken into account, not what the court thinks may be relevant.[91]

Disproportionate weight for relevant considerations

12.47 It is not just taking something irrelevant into account that may vitiate the decision, but also giving disproportionate weight to a

87 *Ex p Atkinson, ex p McDonagh*, above; *R v Kerrier ex p Uzell* (1995) 71 P&CR 566, QBD; *R v Brighton and Hove Council ex p Marmont* (1998) 30 HLR 1046, QBD.

88 *R v Lambeth LBC ex p A and G* (1998) 30 HLR 933, CA. Consider, however, *Conville v Richmond upon Thames LBC* [2006] EWCA Civ 718, [2006] HLR 45, where financial considerations were not relevant when determining the period for which an authority must provide an applicant with accommodation under section 190(2)(a) to afford her or him a 'reasonable opportunity to secure accommodation'. Nonetheless, homelessness and allocations must be considered in their context: 'But the social norm must be applied in the context of a scheme for allocating scarce resources. It is impossible to consider only what would be desirable in the interests of the family if resources were unlimited . . .'; 'There seems to me no reason in logic why the fact that Parliament has made the question of priority need turn upon whether a dependent child might reasonably be expected to reside with the applicant should require that question to be answered without regard to the purpose for which it is being asked, namely, to determine priority in the allocation of a scarce resource. To ignore that purpose would not be a rational social policy. It does not mean that a housing authority can say that it does not have the resources to comply with its obligations under the Act. Parliament has placed upon it the duty to house the homeless and has specified the priorities it should apply. But so far as the criteria for those priorities involve questions of judgment, it must surely take into account the overall purpose of the scheme': per Lord Hoffmann in *Holmes-Moorhouse v Richmond upon Thames LBC* [2009] UKHL 7, [2009] HLR 34, at [12] and [16].

89 Save so far as it may be said that consideration of the general housing circumstances of an area as an element in a decision on homelessness, and on intentionality, might be said to import 'resources' by the back-door (see para 4.93).

90 Cf *R v Birmingham City Council ex p Mohammed* [1999] 1 WLR 33, (1999) 31 HLR 392, QBD where it was said that to treat resources as relevant when deciding whether or not to approve a disabled facilities grant would be to downgrade a duty to a discretion. See, generally, *R v East Sussex CC ex p Tandy* [1998] AC 714, HL; see also *R v Bristol City Council ex p Penfold* (1997–98) 1 CCLR 315, QBD. Compare also *R(Conville) v Richmond upon Thames LBC* [2006] EWCA Civ 718, [2006] HLR 1, and *Holmes-Moorhouse v Richmond upon Thames LBC* [2009] UKHL 7, [2009] HLR 34.

91 *Re Findlay* [1985] AC 318, HL, at 333; see also *R v Hillingdon LBC ex p McDonagh* (1999) 31 HLR 531, QBD.

relevant consideration. In *Ashton*,[92] excessive reliance had been placed on the prevailing housing circumstances of the area when considering intentional homelessness;[93] the decision-maker had not appreciated that 'it is something that must be weighed carefully in the balance with the other factors upon which the decision . . . is reached'.[94]

Failure to take into account relevant considerations

12.48 Just as taking into account the irrelevant may vitiate a decision, so may a failure to take into account the relevant, such as the effect of a medical condition on the need for a transfer from accommodation.[95] The authority must take reasonable steps to acquaint itself with what is relevant.[96]

12.49 Some considerations derive from statute and therefore must be taken into account: consider the requirements under HA 1996 ss169(1) and 182(1) and H(W)A 2014 s98(1) to have regard to Codes of Guidance when determining applications under HA 1996 Parts 6 and 7 and H(W)A 2014 Part 2.[97] The requirement to 'have regard' to the Code of Guidance does not mean that the authority is bound by it, or bound to apply it: it simply means that the Code is a relevant consideration to which regard must be had.[98]

12.50 An authority may depart from a Code eg because it considers the Code to be incorrect[99] or in conflict with the requirements of statute,[100] but the reasons for any departure should be explained.[101] If the decision-maker wrongly takes the view that a consideration is not

92 *R v Winchester City Council ex p Ashton* (1991) 24 HLR 520, CA.

93 See para 6.38.

94 At p526.

95 *R v Islington LBC ex p Aldabbagh* (1995) 27 HLR 271, QBD.

96 Per Lord Diplock in *Secretary of State for Education and Science v Tameside MBC* [1977] AC 1014, HL, at 1065.

97 As to which, see *R v Wandsworth LBC ex p Hawthorne* [1994] 1 WLR 1442, CA.

98 An authority need not, however, spell out every paragraph of the Code to which it has had regard, see eg *Birmingham City Council v Balog* [2013] EWCA Civ 1582, [2014] HLR 14 and footnote 187, below.

99 See, eg, *R v Brent LBC ex p Awua* [1996] AC 55, (1995) 27 HLR 453, HL.

100 In which case, it is always the statute which prevails: see, eg, *R v Waveney DC ex p Bowers* [1983] QB 238, (1982) 4 HLR 118, CA; *Griffin v Westminster City Council* [2004] EWCA Civ 108, [2004] HLR 32.

101 See *Padfield v Minister of Agriculture, Fisheries and Food* [1968] AC 997, HL; see also, eg, *de Falco, Silvestri v Crawley BC* [1980] QB 460, CA; *Khatun v Newham LBC* [2004] EWCA Civ 55, [2005] QB 37.

relevant, and therefore has no regard to it, his or her decision cannot stand and he or she will be required to think again.[102]

12.51 A failure to take into account a relevant consideration will be sufficient to found a claim only if consideration of the relevant fact would have made a difference to the decision.[103] In *R v Newham LBC ex p Bones*,[104] it was held that regard to the wrong (earlier) Code would invalidate a decision, if there was a substantive point of difference, including a change of emphasis.

Promoting the object of legislation[105]

12.52 Powers conferred for public purposes must be used in a way that Parliament can be presumed to have intended.[106] In *Khalique*,[107] the authority was entitled to provide temporary accommodation (in discharge of the HA 1996 Part 7 duty) provided the entitlement to permanent accommodation was not deferred so as 'to frustrate the purpose of the legislation and the rights which it gives to individuals, nor deferred or withheld for some improper or illicit reason'.[108]

12.53 Likewise, in *Robinson v Hammersmith and Fulham LBC*,[109] the authority could not defer a decision until the applicant, a child, reached an age at which she would not be in priority need so that she would no longer be entitled to assistance.[110]

Fettering discretion

12.54 An authority must reach its own decision on each individual case; it may not fetter its discretion by approaching a decision with a pre-determined policy on how it will deal with cases that fall within a particular class.[111] That is not to say that – if good administration requires it – an authority cannot adopt a policy in order to *guide* the

102 *Tesco Stores Ltd v Secretary of State for the Environment* [1995] 1 WLR 759, HL, at 764G–H.

103 *R v Wandsworth LBC ex p Onwudiwe; R v Secretary of State for Health ex p Eastside Cheese Co* [1999] EuLR 968, CA.

104 (1992) 25 HLR 357, QBD.

105 See, generally, *Padfield v Minister of Agriculture, Fisheries and Food* [1968] AC 997, HL; see also *Meade v Haringey LBC* [1979] 1 WLR 637, CA, and *R v Braintree DC ex p Halls* (2000) 32 HLR 770, CA.

106 *R v Tower Hamlets LBC ex p Chetnik Developments Ltd* [1988] AC 858, HL.

107 *R v Tower Hamlets LBC ex p Khalique* (1994) 26 HLR 517, QBD.

108 *Khalique*, at 522.

109 [2006] EWCA Civ 1122, at [31].

110 See paras 5.76–5.79.

111 *British Oxygen Co Ltd v Minister of Technology* [1971] AC 610, HL. See also *R v Secretary of State for the Environment ex p Brent LBC* [1982] QB 593, DC.

future exercise of its discretion. Where it does so, however, it must consider the application of that policy individually in every case where it is sought to make an exception.[112] This approach was adopted and applied by the House of Lords in *Re Betts*.[113]

12.55 A policy of requiring all applicants who were joint tenants of an authority to serve notice to quit (thereby terminating the tenancy) before they could be accepted as homeless owing to domestic violence under HA 1996 Part 7 was held to be unlawful in *Hammia*.[114] In *Savage*,[115] the applicant was refused assistance by way of a rent deposit in order to secure private rented accommodation because she had been found to be homeless intentionally; although the authority's policy was not unlawful, because it required officers to consider its application in every case, it had been misunderstood and misapplied in the present case.

Unlawful delegation or dictation

12.56 The authority cannot avoid its duties by simply adopting the decision of another body.[116] A distinction must be drawn, however, between adoption of the decision of another body and the proper use of others to assist in reaching a decision.[117] The authority may employ staff,[118] and has implied power to employ contractors or agents and to enter into contracts with them.[119] These resources can all be used when reaching a decision. What cannot be abdicated – save so far as statutorily permitted – is responsibility for the essential elements of a decision, which are to determine *what* is to be done or *what* is to happen (in contrast to – even if overlapping with – *how* something is to be done), ie, the underlying decision rather than its day-to-day management.[120]

112 *British Oxygen Co Ltd v Minister of Technology*, above, at 625E.

113 [1983] 2 AC 613, (1983) 10 HLR 97, HL; see chapter 8.

114 *R (Hammia) v Wandsworth LBC* [2005] EWHC 1127 (Admin), [2005] HLR 46.

115 *R (Savage) v Hillingdon LBC* [2010] EWHC 88 (Admin), [2010] JHL D44.

116 *Lavender & Sons v Minister of Housing and Local Government* [1970] 1 WLR 1231, QBD.

117 In *R v West Dorset DC ex p Gerrard* (1994) 27 HLR 150, QBD, under HA 1985 Part 3, the authority could enlist the assistance of a third party but had to take the 'active and dominant' part in the investigative process. But cf the approach in *R v Hertsmere BC ex p Woolgar* (1995) 27 HLR 703, QBD, likewise under HA 1985 Part 3: see paras 9.177–9.178. The actual results are now overtaken by statutory provision: see para 12.57.

118 Local Government Act (LGA) 1972 s112.

119 *Crédit Suisse v Allerdale BC* [1997] QB 306, CA, at 346. There is now express power to contract, in Local Government (Contracts) Act 1997 s1.

120 *Crédit Suisse v Allerdale BC* [1995] 1 Lloyd's Rep 315, Comm Ct; [1997] QB 306, CA.

12.57 Statute permits many functions to be designated by order as capable of being exercised by others who are not members or employees of the authority.[121] Under this provision, the Local Authorities (Contracting Out of Allocation of Housing and Homelessness Functions) Order 1996[122] permits a wide range of functions under both HA 1996 Parts 6 and 7 and H(W)A 2014 Part 2 to be contracted out,[123] including enquiry and even decision-making on homelessness.[124]

The authority's decision must be reached properly

12.58 Under the LGA 1972, it is the full authority[125] which is prima facie entrusted with functions, including the function of reaching decisions, and only the authority can perform its functions[126] save so far as it is permitted to delegate it: the general power of delegation in local government (LGA 1972 s101) permits delegation to a committee, subcommittee or officer. That power does not permit delegation to a single member, because there cannot be a committee or subcommittee of one.[127] It does, however, permit delegation to an officer, to be exercised in consultation with a member, so long as the member does not play the dominant role to the extent that the officer cannot be said to have reached the decision himself or herself.[128]

12.59 Under Local Government Act (LGA) 2000, however, local authorities now function in what may be described as two parts: an

121 Deregulation and Contracting Out Act 1994 s70. See para 9.5.

122 SI No 3205; as amended by Housing (Wales) Act 2014 (Consequential Amendments) Regulations 2015 SI No 752 so as to extend to H(W)A 2014 Part 2. See generally *Tachie v Welwyn Hatfield BC* [2013] EWHC 3972 (QB).

123 The 'public sector equality duty' imposed on authorities by Equality Act 2010 s149, does not prevent contracting out: see above, para 9.5 – *Panayiotou v Waltham Forest LBC; Smith v Haringey LBC* [2017] EWCA Civ 1624, [2017] HLR 48.

124 See chapter 9.

125 Subject to exceptions.

126 *Gardner v London Chatham and Dover Railway Co (No 1)* (1867) LR 2 Ch App 201, CA; *Marshall v South Staffordshire Tramways Co* [1895] 2 Ch 36, CA; *Parker v Camden LBC* [1986] Ch 162, CA; *Crédit Suisse plc v Waltham Forest LBC* [1997] QB 362, CA.

127 *R v Secretary of State for the Environment ex p Hillingdon LBC* [1986] 1 WLR 807, CA. There is statutory power to delegate to a single member in circumstances which do not apply here: see Local Government and Public Involvement in Health Act 2007 s236.

128 *R v Port Talbot BC ex p Jones* [1988] 2 All ER 208, QBD. See also *R v Tower Hamlets LBC ex p Khalique* (1994) 26 HLR 517, QBD.

executive and the full authority. Decisions not conferred on the authority by statute, statutory instrument or (where the matter is left to the authority to decide) under what is known as 'local choice',[129] *must* be taken by the executive.[130] Decisions on allocations and homelessness are – by this route – matters for the executive.[131] Decisions to be taken by the executive may be dealt with in any way that the LGA 2000 permits, which includes delegation to an individual member of the executive, or to a committee or sub-committee of the executive, or to an officer (or, in some circumstances, an area committee not of the executive but of the authority itself).[132]

12.60 A decision of an executive is treated as that of, and is binding on, the authority;[133] it is not a delegation to the executive but a decision taken on behalf of the authority:[134] the authority cannot 'overrule' it in the way that, for example, it can 'overrule' one of its own committees or officers (and could formerly overrule all committees and officers), although it does have power to consider an executive decision and to require the executive to reconsider it.[135] Nor, conversely, can the executive overrule a decision of the authority.[136]

12.61 A general category of 'appeals' is within the 'local choice' class.[137] It does not seem that this includes reviews under HA 1996 Parts 6 and 7 because a review can take into account facts arising subsequent to the original decision[138] which means that it is not exclusively an

129 LGA 2000 s9D(3) (England); s13(3)(b) (Wales).

130 LGA 2000 s9D(2) (England); s13(2), (10) (Wales).

131 LGA 2000 ss9D, 13; Local Authorities (Functions and Responsibilities) (England) Regulations 2000 SI No 2853; and Local Authorities (Executive Arrangements) (Functions and Responsibilities) (Wales) Regulations 2007 SI No 399.

132 LGA 2000 ss9E–9EB (England); ss14–16, 18 (Wales).

133 LGA 2000 s9D (England); s13(9), (10)(a) (Wales).

134 LGA 2000 s9D (England); s13(9) (Wales).

135 LGA 2000 s9F (England); s21 (Wales). All authorities must maintain at least one 'overview and scrutiny' committee to exercise such powers, on which the executive cannot be represented; they may, however, maintain more than one, referable to different functions.

136 This is implicit in the allocation of functions to the different parts of the authority.

137 Local Authorities (Functions and Responsibilities) (England) Regulations 2000 SI No 2853 reg 3(1) and Sch 2 para 2; and Local Authorities (Executive Arrangements) (Functions and Responsibilities) (Wales) Regulations 2007 SI No 399, Sch 2 para 2.

138 *Mohamed v Hammersmith and Fulham LBC* [2001] UKHL 57, [2002] 1 AC 547, see para 9.217.

'appeal' and there remain issues of judgment that fall within the 'execution' of functions that should fall on the executive.

Irrationality

Wednesbury

12.62 As noted,[139] the authority may not reach a decision which no reasonable authority could have reached – such a decision, sometimes referred to as a perverse decision, is conclusive evidence that the decision is irrational and therefore void. There is a high threshold to cross.[140]

Bad faith/improper purposes or motives

12.63 A decision will be unlawful if it can be shown that the decision-maker acted in bad faith or was motivated by some aim or purpose that is not considered legitimate. This is part of the (obvious) principle that the decision-maker may not use the powers entrusted to him or her for purposes which fall outwith his or her authority.[141] Acting in bad faith stands alone as a ground and will automatically vitiate a decision.[142]

12.64 Although frequently alleged by dissatisfied applicants, both grounds are difficult to establish[143] and must be fully particularised and proven.[144]

12.65 A power conferred on a local authority may not lawfully be exercised to promote the electoral advantage of a political party.[145] If several purposes are being pursued and the dominant purpose is legitimate, however, the decision will not be unlawful.[146]

139 See para 12.23.

140 See, eg, *R v Westminster City Council ex p Moozary-Oraky* (1993) 26 HLR 214, QBD at para 6.60; *R v Southwark LBC ex p Hughes* (1998) 30 HLR 1082, QBD. at para 7.35; *R (IA) v Westminster City Council* [2013] EWHC 1273 (QB) at para 9.75; *R (Bauer-Czarnomski) v Ealing LBC* [2010] EWHC 130 (Admin), [2010] JHL D38 at paras 11.134–11.136.

141 *R v Tower Hamlets LBC ex p Chetnik Developments Ltd* [1988] AC 858, HL.

142 *Wednesbury*, see para 12.20; *Smith v East Elloe Rural DC* [1956] AC 736, HL.

143 In *Cannock Chase DC v Kelly* [1978] 1 WLR 1, CA, it was suggested that the term should be used only in respect of a dishonest misuse of power.

144 *Cannock Chase DC v Kelly* [1978] 1 WLR 1, CA.

145 *Magill v Porter* [2001] UKHL 67, [2002] 2 AC 357.

146 *Magill v Porter* [2001] UKHL 67, [2002] 2 AC 357.

Procedural impropriety

Fairness and Article 6

12.66 A decision-maker must act fairly and in accordance with the principles of natural justice, as supplemented and developed by Article 6 of the ECHR (right to a fair trial) in appropriate cases.[147]

12.67 What constitutes fairness has been described as 'essentially an intuitive judgment'[148] and what it demands will depend on the context of the decision, the statute which confers the decision-making power on the decision-maker, and the legal and administrative system within which the decision is taken. Fairness will commonly require that a person adversely affected by the decision should have an opportunity to make representations on his or her own behalf either before the decision is taken or with a view to procuring its modification; that requirement necessarily carries with it a need on the part of the applicant to be informed of the gist of the case which he or she has to answer.[149]

12.68 The influence of Article 6 in this area generally has been considerable, but has not yet had a significant impact in relation to claims under HA 1996 Part 6 or Part 7 or H(W)A 2014 Part 2.[150] Any defects which may exist in the statutory procedure for internal review can be rectified by the right of an applicant to appeal to the county court or by judicial review.[151]

12.69 That is not to say that the existence of a statutory scheme will always be deemed sufficient. The courts may, if they consider the circumstances of the case justify it, impose more stringent requirements to ensure that a matter has been decided fairly.[152] Thus, while review of a homelessness decision has to be carried out by a senior

147 As to which, see paras 12.117–12.123.

148 *R v Secretary of State for the Home Department ex p Doody* [1994] 1 AC 531, HL, at 560/D.

149 *R v Secretary of State for the Home Department ex p Doody*, above.

150 See further paras 12.117–12.123.

151 See also *R (Alconbury Developments Ltd) v Secretary of State for the Environment, Transport and the Regions* [2001] UKHL 23, [2003] 2 AC 295.

152 *Wiseman v Borneman* [1971] AC 297, HL; *R v Hull Prison Visitors ex p St Germain (No 2)* [1979] 1 WLR 1401, QBD; *Lloyd v McMahon* [1987] AC 625, HL; *R v Civil Service Appeal Board ex p Cunningham* [1991] 4 All ER 310, CA; *R v Secretary of State for the Home Department ex p Doody* [1994] 1 AC 531, HL; *R v Higher Education Funding Council ex p Institute of Dental Surgery* [1994] 1 WLR 242, DC; *R v Kensington and Chelsea RLBC ex p Grillo* (1995) 28 HLR 94, CA; and *R v Ministry of Defence ex p Murray* [1998] COD 134, QBD.

officer not involved in the original decision,[153] mere compliance with this would per se not prevent a challenge to the review[154] if the reviewer – though senior and not involved – could, for other reasons,[155] be said to be biased against the applicant.

12.70 Leaving aside Article 6, the principles of natural justice require both that no one should be a judge in his or her own cause (bias); and that an applicant has the right to be heard.[156]

Bias

12.71 For a decision to be quashed on the ground of bias, it is not necessary to show that the decision-maker was in fact biased; it is sufficient for there to be an apparent bias.[157]

12.72 In *R v Gough*[158] it had been held that, in the absence of actual bias, the court should decide for itself whether, in all of the circumstances relevant to the issue of bias, there was a real danger that the decision-maker/decision-making body had been biased. In *Re Medicaments and Related Classes of Goods (No 2)*,[159] however, it was said that the court should ask whether a fair-minded and informed observer would conclude that there was a real possibility or danger of bias.

12.73 The House of Lords has approved this 'modest adjustment of the test in *Gough*',[160] subject to omission of the phrase 'real danger'; accordingly, the appropriate test for bias is now 'whether the fair-minded and informed observer, having considered the facts, would conclude that there was a real possibility that the tribunal was biased'.[161]

153 See HA 1996 s202 and Homelessness (Review Procedure etc) Regulations 2018 SI No 223 reg 8. The Welsh regulations only require that the review officer be someone who was not involved in the original decision (Homelessness (Review Procedure) (Wales) Regulations 2015 SI No 1266 reg 3; see also Welsh Code para 20.9).

154 Cf *Feld v Barnet LBC* [2005] EWCA Civ 1307, [2005] HLR 9.

155 Eg, past contact/dealings suggesting something other than full disinterestedness, or even some private or personal reason.

156 *Ridge v Baldwin* [1964] AC 40, HL.

157 By Localism Act (LA) 2011 s25, there is no apparent bias in relation to a decision taken after 12 January 2012 (but capable of referring to things done beforehand) simply because the decision-maker has previously done something that directly or indirectly indicates what view he or she took, or would or might take, in relation to a matter relevant to the decision. This only applies, however, to members (elected or co-opted) of an authority and will rarely apply in homelessness or allocation cases, although it could do so.

158 [1993] AC 646, HL.

159 [2001] 1 WLR 700, CA.

160 See *Magill v Porter* [2001] UKHL 67, [2002] 2 AC 357, at [103].

161 *Magill v Porter*, at [103].

12.74 In *Feld*,[162] the authority only had one reviewing officer, who conducted both an initial review and a subsequent re-review following a successful complaint to the ombudsman (of which she was not the subject, and in the report on which she was not criticised). The applicant asserted that this gave rise to the appearance of bias.

12.75 The Court of Appeal dismissed the claim. The fair-minded and informed observer would take into account that a decision under HA 1996 s202 is an administrative decision which Parliament has entrusted to senior local authority officers, who have received training; the observer would also consider the practical constraints (financial and administrative) imposed on local housing authorities. Taking those factors into account, there would not be said to have been any bias in the decision-making process, based either on the officer's conduct of the previous review or on the successful complaint to the ombudsman.[163]

12.76 In *De-Winter Heald v Brent LBC*,[164] the Court of Appeal held that an objective and well-informed observer would not think that there was a real danger of bias on the part of a contracted-out reviewer, and therefore rejected the contention that the review decisions in the appeals were marred by apparent bias; there was no reason why a person contracted to carry out a review on an authority's behalf should necessarily be less impartial than an authority employee; whether he may be regarded as less independent depends on the facts, in particular the terms of the contract between the authority and the reviewer; eg a long contractual term terminable only for serious breach would suggest that there was a high degree of independence on the part of the reviewer.[165]

162 *Feld v Barnet LBC*, above.

163 'Adopting a balanced approach such an observer will accept that investigation by and even adverse comment from the Ombudsman is one of the slings and arrows of local government misfortune with which broad shouldered officials have to cope. [The officer] was not herself involved nor the subject of criticism. She could be expected to bear criticism of the department not only with fortitude but with indifference . . .': per Ward LJ at [49].

164 [2009] EWCA Civ 930, [2010] HLR 8.

165 At [52]. If there is any doubt about the validity of the contract, an applicant will need to consider its terms; if the authority will not willingly disclose it, the applicant can seek a copy under the Freedom of Information Act 2000 or make an application for pre-action disclosure under CPR 31.16, but a challenge to it cannot be made in pleadings without a clear basis and, unless pleaded, it will not later be possible to obtain the agreement by disclosure in the course of a section 204 appeal as it will not relate to any pleaded issue: *Servis v Newham LBC*, High Court, 1 May 2018 (*HousingView* 8 May 2018).

Right to be heard

12.77 This has two elements: first, to inform the party affected about what is being said; and second, to afford him or her the opportunity to answer it.[166] This does not amount to a requirement for an oral hearing – so as to require any internal review to be a full hearing[167] – but does require, where a decision is reached without a hearing, that the applicant is given an opportunity to put his or her case in response to adverse findings.[168]

Reasons

12.78 While there is no universal obligation to give reasons in all circumstances, in general they should be given unless there is a proper justification for not doing so.[169] The internal review requirements in both HA 1996 Parts 6 and 7 and H(W)A 2014 Part 2 contain express provision for reasons to be given for decisions.[170]

12.79 A failure to provide reasons would give rise to a ground of challenge and would suffice to quash the decision.[171] The requirement is a manifestation of the need for the applicant to be aware of the decision against him or her and to be able to challenge that decision if necessary,[172] so that it is the substance rather than the form that is of importance.

12.80 The authority must apply the facts to the legal background and reach a 'properly or adequately reasoned decision'.[173] In *Paul-Coker*,

166 *Board of Education v Rice* [1911] AC 179, HL; *Kanda v Government of the Federation of Malaya* [1962] AC 362, PC.

167 Consider *Runa Begum* and *Ali v Birmingham City Council*, paras 12.117–12.122.

168 This is not a limitless right and there is no absolute right to the last word: *Bellouti v Wandsworth LBC* [2005] EWCA Civ 602, [2005] HLR 46.

169 Reasons will be required where fairness requires it, or a particular decision is aberrant, where the failure to give reasons may frustrate a right of appeal (because without reasons a party will not know whether there is an appealable ground or not) and where a party has a legitimate expectation that reasons will be given: *Oakley v South Cambridgeshire DC* [2017] EWCA Civ 71 at [30]–[31]. See also *R (Sambotin) v Brent LBC* [2017] EWHC 1190 (Admin), para 9.159, n258, in which the authority sought to revisit and change its own earlier decision without a lawful basis for doing so (no fraud, deception or fundamental mistake of fact): the court additionally held that the authority had been under a duty to give reasons for reaching a second decision, with which duty it had failed to comply (permission to appeal has been granted).

170 HA 1996 ss167(4A), 203(4); H(W)A 2014 s86(4).

171 *R v Westminster City Council ex p Ermakov* [1996] 2 All ER 302, CA. Reasons should be 'proper, adequate and intelligible': *Westminster City Council v Great Portland Estates plc* [1985] 1 AC 661, HL.

172 *R v Islington LBC ex p Hinds* (1995) 27 HLR 65, QBD.

173 *R (Paul-Coker) v Southwark LBC* [2006] EWHC 497 (Admin), [2006] HLR 32.

the applicant successfully claimed judicial review of the authority's decision to refuse her accommodation pending review on the grounds that the authority had not applied the correct legal criteria to her circumstances and that there was a 'complete absence of any explanation or reasoning' in the authority's decision letter. This success, based on inadequacy of reasons, was considered 'an exceptional case'.[174]

12.81 The nature and extent of reasons must relate to the substantive issues raised by an applicant (or by an applicant's adviser): see *Re Poyser & Mills Arbitration*,[175] approved by the House of Lords in *Westminster City Council v Great Portland Estates plc*,[176] and again in *Save Britain's Heritage v Secretary of State for the Environment*.[177]

12.82 'The reasons that are set out must be reasons which will not only be intelligible, but which deal with the substantive points that have been raised', per Megaw J in *Posyer*. 'The three criteria suggested in the dictum of Megaw J are that the reasons should be proper, intelligible and adequate', per Lord Bridge in *Save Britain's Heritage*. In *Edwin H Bradley & Sons Ltd v Secretary of State for the Environment*,[178] Glidewell J added to the dictum of Megaw J that reasons can be briefly stated (also approved in *Great Portland Estates*).

12.83 In *Baruwa*[179] it was said to be:

> . . . trite law that where, as here, an authority is required to give reasons for its decision it is required to give reasons which are proper, adequate, and intelligible and enable the person affected to know why they have won or lost. That said, the law gives decision-makers a certain latitude in how they express themselves and will recognise that not all those taking decisions find it easy in the time available to express themselves with judicial exactitude.

12.84 The purpose of the obligation to give reasons is to enable the recipient to see whether they might be challengeable in law: see *Thornton v Kirklees MBC*.[180] In *Mohammed*,[181] Latham J considered the role of

174 *R (Paul-Coker) v Southwark LBC*, at [52].
175 [1964] 2 QB 467, QBD.
176 [1985] AC 661, HL.
177 [1991] 1 WLR 153. See also *Givaudan v Minister of Housing and Local Government* [1967] 1 WLR 250, QBD; *Mountview Court Properties Ltd v Devlin* (1970) 21 P&CR 689, QBD.
178 (1982) 264 EG 926, QBD.
179 *R v Brent LBC ex p Baruwa* (1997) 29 HLR 915, CA.
180 [1979] QB 626, CA, which appears to have been a judicial summary of counsel's submission, rather than a judicial observation in its own right. See further *R v Tynedale DC ex p Shield* (1987) 22 HLR 144, QBD.
181 *R v Camden LBC ex p Mohammed* (1998) 30 HLR 315, QBD at p323.

reasons in the light of the right to seek an internal review of the decision:

> ... the purpose to be served by the giving of such reasons ... is to enable the applicant to put before the local housing authority a proper case based upon a full understanding of the council's previous[182] decision to refuse accommodation.

12.85 Reasons should accordingly be sufficient to enable the applicant to form a view as to whether to challenge the decision on a point of law.[183] Merely stating the words of the Act 'parrot-fashion', with no substantive explanation for the decision, is insufficient.[184] Reasons should be in sufficient detail to show the principles on which the decision-maker has acted and that have led to his or her decision; they need not be elaborate nor need they deal with every argument presented in support of the case.[185]

12.86 Not every factor which weighed with the decision-maker in the appraisal of the evidence has to be identified and explained, but the issues which were vital to the conclusion should be identified, and the manner in which they were resolved, explained.[186] The question is whether it is possible to understand the decision-maker's thought processes when he or she was making material findings.[187]

12.87 Authorities are entitled to give their reasons quite simply:

> ... their decision and their reasons are not to be analysed in minute detail. They are not to be gone through as it were with a fine-tooth comb. They are not to be criticised by saying: 'They have not mentioned this or that'.[188]

12.88 In the context of a decision on review, it has been said that reasons contained in the decision letter are not to be treated as if they are statutes or judgments and that it is important to read a decision

182 Ie, initial.

183 *Osmani v Camden LBC* [2004] EWCA Civ 1706, [2005] HLR 22. See also *R v Croydon LBC ex p Graham* (1993) 26 HLR 286, at 291–292.

184 *R v Newham LBC ex p Lumley* (2001) 33 HLR 124: this was a concession by counsel, but is again obviously correct. The decision in *Kelly v Monklands DC* (1985) 12 July, Ct of Session (OH), that a mere recital of the words of the Act was sufficient, is unlikely to be followed unless the relevant factual issues for determination by the authority are both clear and confined to something which the wording of HA 1996 serves to address.

185 *Eagil Trust Co Ltd v Pigott Brown* [1985] 3 All ER 119, CA.

186 *English v Emery Reimbold & Strick Ltd* [2002] EWCA Civ 605, [2002] 1 WLR 2409.

187 *R (Iran) and others v Secretary of State for the Home Department* [2005] EWCA Civ 982.

188 *Tickner v Mole Valley DC* [1980] 2 April, CA transcript.

letter as a whole to get its full sense: *Osmani*.[189] Nevertheless, if a decision-maker fails to address in his or her decision letter an issue 'so startling that one would not expect it to pass without individual comment', the court may be justified in inferring that it has not received any or any sufficient consideration: *Bariise*.[190]

12.89 In *Graham*,[191] Sir Thomas Bingham MR said:

> I readily accept that these difficult decisions are decisions for the housing authority and certainly a pedantic exegesis of letters of this kind would be inappropriate. There is, nonetheless, an obligation under the Act to give reasons and that must impose on the council a duty to give reasons which are intelligible and which convey to the applicant the reasons why the application has been rejected in such a way that if they disclose an error of reasoning the applicant may take such steps as may be indicated.

12.90 This passage was cited with approval in *Hinds*,[192] in which the duty had been complied with because the reasons were intelligible and conveyed clearly to the applicant why his application had been rejected. In *Carpenter*,[193] in contrast, the decision letter was considered 'manifestly defective' because it failed to address the reasons why the applicant had left his previous accommodation and, accordingly, defeated the purpose of the section, 'to enable someone who is entitled to a decision to see what the reasons are for that decision and to challenge those reasons if they are apparently inadequate'.

12.91 A court should not approve incomprehensible or misguided reasoning, but a judge should not adopt an unfair or unrealistic approach when considering or interpreting review decisions;[194] a decision can often survive despite the existence of an error in the reasoning advanced to support it – for example, the error may be irrelevant to the outcome; it may be too trivial to affect the outcome; it may be obvious from the rest of the reasoning, read as a whole, that the decision would have been the same notwithstanding the error; there may be more than one reason for the conclusion, while the error only undermines one of the reasons;

189 *Osmani v Camden LBC* [2004] EWCA Civ 1706, [2004] HLR 22. See also *William v Wandsworth LBC; Bellamy v Hounslow LBC* [2006] EWCA Civ 535, [2006] HLR 42.

190 *R v Brent LBC ex p Bariise* (1998) 31 HLR 50, CA, per Millett LJ at 58.

191 *R v Croydon LBC ex p Graham* (1993) 26 HLR 286, CA at 291–292.

192 *R v Islington LBC ex p Hinds* (1996) 28 HLR 302, CA. See also *R v Camden LBC ex p Adair* (1996) 29 HLR 236, QBD; and *R v Wandsworth LBC ex p Dodia* (1997) 30 HLR 562, QBD.

193 *R v Northampton BC ex p Carpenter* (1992) 25 HLR 349, QBD.

194 *Holmes-Moorhouse v Richmond upon Thames LBC* [2009] UKHL 7, [2009] HLR 34, at [47].

or, the decision may be the only one which could rationally have been reached: in all such cases, the error should not, save perhaps in wholly exceptional circumstances, justify the decision being quashed.[195]

12.92 Although they may be checked by people with legal experience or qualifications before they are sent out, review decisions are prepared by housing officers, who occupy a post of considerable responsibility and who have substantial experience in the housing field, but they are not lawyers; it is not therefore appropriate to subject their decisions to the same sort of analysis as may be applied to a contract drafted by solicitors, to an Act of Parliament, or to a court's judgment; rather, a benevolent approach should be adopted. Nor should the court take too technical view of the language used, or search for inconsistencies, or adopt a nit-picking approach when confronted with an appeal against a review decision.[196]

12.93 This approach does, however, need to be read subject to the requirements of the public sector equality duty[197] where it is engaged,[198] not only when the issue is vulnerability[199] but by parity of reasoning in all cases where it falls for consideration, ie it must be possible to see how the authority has addressed that duty.

12.94 In *City of Gloucester v Miles*,[200] the Court of Appeal held that – to comply with the requirement to state reasons – a notification of intentional homelessness[201] ought to have stated:

a) that the authority was satisfied that the applicant for accommodation became homeless intentionally;
b) when the applicant was considered to have become homeless;
c) why the applicant was said to have become homeless at that time, ie, what is the deliberate act or omission in consequence of which it is concluded that at that time the applicant ceased to occupy accommodation which was available for his or her occupation; and
d) that it would have been reasonable for the applicant to continue to occupy that accommodation.

195 *Holmes-Moorhouse* at [51].

196 *Holmes-Moorhouse* at [50]; a review officer need not refer to every relevant passage of the Code of Guidance, see. *Birmingham City Council v Balog* [2013] EWCA Civ 1582, [2014] HLR 14 and *Samuels v Birmingham City Council* [2015] EWCA Civ 1051, [2015] HLR 47.

197 See para 9.91.

198 *Hotak v Southwark LBC and other appeals* [2015] UKSC 30, [2015] 2 WLR 1341, [2015] HLR 23, at [79].

199 See also para 5.35.

200 (1985) 17 HLR 292, CA.

201 See chapter 6.

12.95 In *ex p H*,[202] it was held that, while the authority was entitled to express itself quite simply and could not be criticised for not having gone into great detail, it was nonetheless incumbent on it to say what was the deliberate act or omission in consequence of which it had been concluded that the applicant had ceased to occupy accommodation available for his occupation and which it would have been reasonable for him to continue to occupy. In the context of the case, that required more than a statement that he could have continued to occupy under his council tenancy in Northern Ireland.

12.96 Likewise, in *Baruwa*,[203] the decision letter should have clarified why the applicant was regarded as having spent money on non-essential items and why the authority regarded this as having caused the applicant's homelessness. It is not necessary, however, that the decision letter set out arithmetical calculations or itemised what an applicant could or could not afford.[204]

12.97 In *Monaf*,[205] the court quashed the decision of the authority on the basis that its letters did not disclose that it had carried out the proper balancing act called for, to determine whether or not it would have been reasonable for applicants to remain in accommodation in Bangladesh or to come back to the UK.

12.98 In *Adair*,[206] the court described a decision letter which merely recited that the authority had taken into account all the evidence and that the applicant did not fall within any of the categories of priority need as being completely devoid of reasoning and inadequate.[207] The decision letter should have set out why the applicant was considered not to be a vulnerable person in the light of the medical evidence which he had put forward.

12.99 In *Khan*,[208] a decision letter which addressed only one of a number of grounds on which local connection was being claimed was held to be defective. In *McCarthy*,[209] however, the decision letter was upheld, even though it had not dealt with the suitability of the applicant's

202 *R v Hillingdon LBC ex p H* (1988) 20 HLR 554, QBD. See also *R v Southwark LBC ex p Davies* (1993) 26 HLR 677, QBD.

203 *R v Brent LBC ex p Baruwa* (1997) 29 HLR 915, CA. See also *Robinson v Brent LBC* (1999) 31 HLR 1015, CA.

204 *Bernard v Enfield LBC* [2001] EWCA Civ 1831.

205 *R v Tower Hamlets LBC ex p Monaf* (1988) 20 HLR 529, CA.

206 *R v Camden LBC ex p Adair* (1996) 29 HLR 236, QBD.

207 See also *R v Brent LBC ex p Bariise* (1998) 31 HLR 50, CA, at 58.

208 *R v Slough BC ex p Khan* (1995) 27 HLR 492, QBD.

209 *R v Sedgemoor DC ex p McCarthy* (1996) 28 HLR 608, QBD.

current accommodation, because the applicant had not raised that issue with the authority.

12.100 In *O'Connor,*[210] the authority concluded that the applicants were intentionally homeless. Both initial and review decision letters, however, failed to identify the date at which the authority considered that the homelessness had commenced and therefore had not considered whether the omission at that time had been in good faith. Although the letter was 'thoughtful and factually sound', the decision was quashed because it failed to address the questions raised by HA 1996 s191(2).

12.101 In *Augustin,*[211] it was held that a later letter from the authority could rectify the shortcomings of an earlier notification (which, however, was not itself considered defective, albeit that it was 'sparse' – per Auld J in the court below – or 'cryptic' and brief – per Glidewell LJ in the Court of Appeal; the notification had given the applicant the information she needed).

12.102 The courts may be slow to intervene on the basis of want of adequate reasons unless the applicant, or the applicant's adviser, offers the authority an opportunity to remedy a defective decision letter, by way of a 'prompt request for details', to which the authority has failed to respond.[212] In judicial review cases, the pre-action protocol[213] requires a letter before action[214] and the same is expected before a county court appeal is launched.[215]

12.103 The issue of additional evidence to amplify reasons arises in the context of appeals, where the person undertaking the review sometimes submits a witness statement containing further reasoning for his or her decision. Such evidence cannot be admitted as of right. Statements which are aimed at clarification and do not alter or contradict anything in the decision letter are, however, properly admitted.[216]

210 *O'Connor v Kensington and Chelsea RLBC* [2004] EWCA Civ 394, [2004] HLR 37.

211 *R v Westminster City Council ex p Augustin* (1993) 25 HLR 281, CA.

212 *R v Camden LBC ex p Mohammed* (1997) 30 HLR 315, at 323, cited with approval in *R v Newham LBC ex p Lumley* (2000) 33 HLR 124, at 136–137.

213 See para 12.140.

214 See para 12.141.

215 See para 12.208.

216 *Hijazi v Kensington and Chelsea RLBC* [2003] EWCA Civ 692, [2003] HLR 73. See also *Hall v Wandsworth LBC; Carter v Wandsworth LBC* [2004] EWCA Civ 1740, [2005] HLR 23.

12.104 In *Graham*[217] and *Ermakov*,[218] the Court of Appeal held that – save in exceptional circumstances – the courts will not permit the reasons given in the notification to be supplemented.[219] In *John*,[220] however, non-disclosure of the proper reasons for the decision in the decision letter did not prevent the authority from relying on proper reasons and justifying its decision accordingly. In *Hobbs*,[221] the Court of Appeal upheld the High Court decision to admit affidavit evidence amplifying and explaining earlier evidence as to reasons.

12.105 In *Baruwa*,[222] it was also recognised that there are cases:

> . . . where . . . one could look at the affidavit[223] . . . by way of amplification of the reasons for the decision. Looking at such an affidavit is often a sensible course and saves the bother and expense of going back to the decision-maker to make a new decision which will incorporate the material which appears in the affidavit.

12.106 In practice, the courts have not invariably held authorities to the reasons given. The decision in *de Falco*[224] was, so far as relevant, that:

> . . . the council is of the opinion that you became homeless intentionally because you came to this country without having ensured that you had permanent accommodation to come to.

12.107 This was clearly, and has since expressly been held to be, wrong.[225] The court upheld it by finding that the applicants were homeless intentionally because they had left accommodation (in Italy) before coming to this country.

12.108 In *Islam*,[226] at the Court of Appeal, the court was similarly willing to disregard the express words used by the authority, and consider

217 *R v Croydon LBC ex p Graham* (1993) 26 HLR 286, CA.

218 *R v Westminster City Council ex p Ermakov* (1995) 28 HLR 819, CA; see also *R v Southwark LBC ex p Dagou* (1995) 28 HLR 72, QBD.

219 These were pre-county court appeal, judicial review cases, but the same principles apply: *Samuels v Birmingham City Council* [2015] EWCA Civ 1051, [2015] HLR 47.

220 *R v Swansea City Council ex p John* (1982) 9 HLR 56, QBD. Another judicial review, pre-county court appeal case.

221 *Hobbs v Sutton LBC* (1993) 26 HLR 132, CA. See also *R v Bradford City Council ex p Parveen* (1996) 28 HLR 681, QBD.

222 *R v Brent LBC ex p Baruwa* (1997) 29 HLR 915, QBD at 929. See also *Samuels v Birmingham City Council* [2015] EWCA Civ 1051, [2015] HLR 47 where the authority was entitled to lead evidence to rebut an allegation of factual error made for the first time the afternoon before the HA 1996 s204 appeal hearing.

223 Or witness statement or evidence on an appeal to the county court.

224 *De Falco, Silvestri v Crawley BC* [1980] QB 460, CA.

225 See para 6.147.

226 *R v Hillingdon LBC ex p Islam* [1983] 1 AC 688, (1981) 1 HLR 107, HL.

whether there had been what in substance could be considered intentional homelessness. In *Chambers*,[227] the decision that applicants had become homeless intentionally was not sustainable, but relief was refused on the alternative approach that the authority had discharged its duties to the applicants by an earlier offer.

12.109 These earlier cases should be treated with some caution. *De Falco* could as easily be described as a decision (at an interlocutory hearing) on discretion. The result in *Islam* was overturned on appeal.[228] *Chambers* was explicitly a decision on relief (discretion).

Legitimate expectation

12.110 The requirement of fairness means that an authority must respect any legitimate expectation which an applicant may enjoy,[229] provided that to conform to the expectation would not interfere or conflict with the authority's statutory duty.[230] Conventionally, legitimate expectation refers to a legitimate *procedural* expectation, as to how a matter is to be handled, such as an assurance that no decision will be taken, at all or on an aspect of a matter, until there has been a further opportunity to comment or until the authority has managed to contact someone, or that it will only be taken by an officer of a particular level of seniority or by a panel (member or officer).[231]

12.111 At its most narrow, it may refer only to the procedure to be adopted before an existing right or privilege is removed,[232] although as the concept is a part of the overall duty of fairness, it may equally be used to infer the loss of an opportunity to acquire a benefit or advantage. This does not easily translate into a legitimate substantive expectation of a particular outcome of a decision-making process as opposed to its procedure. For legitimate expectation to give rise to a substantive entitlement requires a clear and unambiguous representation, devoid of qualification, on which it was reasonable to rely.[233]

12.112 There is, however, no requirement that an applicant should detrimentally have changed his or her position in reliance on the

227 *R v Westminster City Council ex p Chambers* (1982) 6 HLR 24, QBD.

228 *R v Hillingdon LBC ex p Islam*, above, see para 6.151.

229 *R v North and East Devon Health Authority ex p Coughlan* [2001] QB 213, CA.

230 *R v Attorney General of Hong Kong ex p Ng Yuen Shiu* [1983] 2 AC 629, PC, at 638/f.

231 *Schmidt v Secretary of State for Home Affairs* [1969] 2 Ch 149, CA; *R v Devon CC ex p Baker* [1995] 1 All ER 73, CA.

232 *Council of Civil Service Unions v Minister for the Civil Service* [1985] 1 AC 374, HL, per Lord Diplock at 413.

233 *R v IRC ex p MFK Underwriting* [1990] 1 WLR 1545, QBD at 1569/G.

promise.[234] The question is whether it would be an abuse of power to frustrate the legitimate expectation. It is for the court to determine whether there is a sufficient overriding interest to justify a departure from what has previously been promised.[235] In one case, the substantive right to take over a tenancy was upheld.[236]

12.113 No appeal to legitimate expectation can, however, widen an authority's duties under either HA 1996 Part 6 or Part 7 or H(W)A 2014 Part 2.[237] Nonetheless, where a promise of a 'permanent' home had been made to homeless applicants, a legitimate expectation had arisen which was sufficient to justify derogation from the authority's housing allocation scheme, and which required the authority to provide reasons if the expectation was not to be fulfilled.[238]

Human Rights Act 1998

12.114 The scheme of the HRA 1998 is to require all domestic legislation to be read and given effect (as far as is possible) in a manner that is compatible with the Convention rights contained in the Act[239] and to render it unlawful for a 'public authority'[240] – including local authorities and registered providers of social housing in respect of some aspects of their management of their social housing stock, including service of notice to quit or of seeking possession[241] – to act in a way which is incompatible with one or more of the Convention rights.[242]

234 *R v Newham LBC ex p Bibi and Al-Nashed* [2001] EWCA Civ 607, (2001) 33 HLR 84.

235 *R v North and East Devon Health Authority ex p Coughlan*, above.

236 *R v Lambeth LBC ex p Trabi* (1997) 30 HLR 975, QBD.

237 *R v Lambeth LBC ex p Ekpo-Wedderman* (1998) 31 HLR 498, QBD; *Obiorah v Lewisham LBC* [2013] EWCA Civ 325, [2013] HLR 35. The same must be true of H(W)A 2014 Part 2.

238 *R v Newham LBC ex p Bibi and Al-Nashed* [2001] EWCA Civ 607, (2001) 33 HLR 84; cf. *Obiorah v Lewisham LBC* [2013] EWCA Civ 325 where a similar claim was not upheld on the facts. See also *R (Alansi) v Newham LBC* [2013] EWHC 3722 (Admin), [2014] HLR 25: authority entitled to resile from a clear promise as a result of changes made to its allocation scheme.

239 HRA 1998 s3(1). *R (Morris) v Westminster City Council (No 3)* [2005] EWCA Civ 1184, [2006] 1 WLR 505, [2006] HLR 8.

240 As defined in HRA 1998 s6(3).

241 *R (Weaver) v London & Quadrant Housing Trust* [2008] EWHC 1377 (Admin), [2008] JHL D94 and on appeal [2009] EWCA Civ 587, [2009] HLR 40; see paras 11.166–11.167 on other acts of management and allocation.

242 HRA 1998 s6(1).

12.115 A person who claims that a public authority has acted unlawfully on this basis may bring proceedings against the authority or rely on the Convention right in any legal proceedings.[243]

12.116 The Convention rights which are relevant to a claim brought against HA 1996 Part 6 or Part 7 or H(W)A 2014 Part 2 decisions are:

- *Article 6* – Everyone, in the determination of his or her civil rights and obligations, is entitled to a fair and public hearing within a reasonable time by an independent and impartial tribunal established by law.
- *Article 8 – Rights to respect for private and family life and home*, interference with which is permitted to the extent that it is in accordance with law and necessary in a democratic society in the interests of national security, public safety, economic well-being of the country, the prevention of disorder or crime, the protection of health or morals or the rights and freedoms of others.
- *Article 14 – Prohibition on discrimination* on grounds of sex, race, colour, language, religion, political or other opinion, national or social origin, association with a national minority, property, birth or other status.

Article 6

12.117 Internal reviews do not need to be compliant with Article 6, as homelessness rights are not civil rights within it.[244] Even if they were, it was held in *Runa Begum*[245] that an internal review coupled with the right to an appeal to the county court under HA 1996 s204 comprised compliance with Article 6. This approach was followed in *Ali v Birmingham City Council*.[246]

12.118 In *Ali v UK*,[247] the same case at the European Court of Human Rights, it was held that Article 6(1) was engaged once the authority decided that a duty was owed under HA 1996 s193 because there was a sufficiently certain right to amount to a 'civil right'; nonetheless, in agreement with *Runa Begum* and *Ali* at the Supreme Court, it was also held that there was no violation of Article 6 as the rights to a reasoned decision, review and appeal were adequate safeguards.

243 HRA 1998 s7(1).

244 *Ali v Birmingham City Council* [2010] UKSC 8, [2010] HLR 22.

245 *Runa Begum v Tower Hamlets LBC* [2003] UKHL 5, [2003] 2 AC 430, [2003] HLR 32.

246 [2010] UKSC 8.

247 App No 40378/10, [2015] HLR 46.

12.119 In *Poshteh v Kensington and Chelsea RLBC*,[248] however, the Supreme Court refused to depart from its decision in *Ali v Birmingham City Council*, notwithstanding *Ali v UK*, for the reasons referred to at para 9.211.

12.120 For the purpose of illustrating the principle, the position may be contrasted with *Tsfayo*,[249] a challenge at the European Court of Human Rights to a decision of a housing benefit review board to refuse to find good reason for backdating a claim, in which it was held that judicial review had not provided the claimant with access to a court of full jurisdiction for the purpose of Article 6(1), because the question in issue for the board – which lacked independence[250] – was a simple one of fact, not involving professional knowledge or specialist experience; judicial review was an inappropriate jurisdiction for the resolution of factual issues.

12.121 This was distinguished in *Ali v Birmingham City Council*, where the issue was whether the homeless person had received a letter warning her – in accordance with HA 1996 s193(5) – that if she did not accept the accommodation offered, the authority would consider that its duty had been discharged.[251] This was held not to be a matter of simple fact required by *Tsfayo* to be considered by a court of full jurisdiction: see also the discussion of *Bubb v Wandsworth LBC*,[252] above.[253]

12.122 Article 6 was also relied on in a challenge to the legality of contracting out review decisions.[254] The Court of Appeal rejected the argument that a third party would be any less impartial than an employee of the authority; in any event, the authority accepted the contracted out review as its own decision and the availability of an appeal to the county court under HA 1996 s204 ensured compliance with Article 6, following *Runa Begum*.[255]

248 [2017] UKSC 36.

249 *Tsfayo v UK* App no 60860/00, [2007] HLR 19, ECtHR.

250 And perhaps impartiality: it was relevant to the decision that – had the claim been allowed – the authority (of some of whose members the board was comprised) would have received only 50 per cent rather than 95 per cent subsidy: at [19]. Review is now by way of appeal to the First Tier Tribunal (Social Entitlement Chamber).

251 See para 10.210.

252 [2011] EWCA Civ 1285, [2011] HLR 13.

253 See para 12.43 and footnote 74, above.

254 *De-Winter Heald and others v Brent LBC* [2009] EWCA Civ 930 at [4].

255 *Runa Begum v Tower Hamlets LBC*, above.

Article 8

12.123 Article 8 does not comprise a right to housing to be provided by the state.[256] Given this, it does not currently seem likely that a claim for breach of the right to respect for the home under Article 8 will succeed[257] where an authority has properly applied the provisions of HA 1996 Part 7 or H(W)A 2014 Part 2 and reached the conclusion that there is no substantive duty to house an applicant, because the provisions of HA 1996 Part 7 and H(W)A 2014 Part 2 are themselves compliant with the ECHR (and, indeed, go further than any duties under Article 8).

12.124 Thus, in *Hackney LBC v Ekinci*,[258] the Court of Appeal rejected the applicant's argument that he was in priority need through his 17-year-old wife.[259] Pill LJ said:[260]

> There is no breach of article 8(1) in Parliament enacting a scheme of priorities whereby applications for accommodation by homeless persons are to be determined by local housing authorities whose resources will inevitably be limited . . .

12.125 Claims may also be made under Article 8 in relation to the right to respect for family life. Generally, social welfare measures provided by the state do not fall within the ambit of Article 8, as they are not specifically designed to promote or protect family life.[261] Although this principle was applied to HA 1996 Part 7 generally in *Morris* and

256 *X v Federal Republic of Germany* (1965) 8 Yearbook of the ECHR 158; *Chapman v UK* (2001) 33 EHRR 18, (2001) 10 BHRC 48; *O'Rourke v UK* App No 39022/97, ECtHR. See also *Lambeth LBC v Kay; Leeds City Council v Price* [2006] UKHL 10, [2006] 2 AC 465, [2006] HLR 22. Cf *Mazari v Italy* App No 36448/97, (2000) 30 EHRR CD 218, suggesting that a right may arise in some limited, extreme circumstances, where there is a positive obligation towards the applicant under Article 8.

257 See *R (Morris) v Newham LBC* [2002] EWHC 1262 (Admin), [2002] JHL D77, where a claim that the failure to comply with the authority's duty under HA 1996 s193 was a breach of ECHR Article 8 and gave rise to a right to damages was rejected.

258 [2001] EWCA Civ 776, [2002] HLR 2.

259 See, further, chapter 5.

260 At [16].

261 See *R (Carson) v Secretary of State for Work and Pensions* [2003] EWCA Civ 797, [2003] 3 All ER 577 at [28], upheld [2005] UKHL 37, [2006] 1 AC 173. See also *R (Couronne and others) v (1) Crawley BC (2) Secretary of State for Work and Pensions (3) First Secretary of State; R (Bontemps and others) v Secretary of State for Work and Pensions* [2006] EWHC 1514 (Admin), [2006] JHL D106, in which the application of the 'habitual residence' test in deciding whether a homeless applicant is eligible (see chapter 3) was held to have nothing to do with promoting respect for private and/or family life; accordingly, the claimants' case was not within the ambit of Article 8.

Badu,[262] the Court of Appeal considered that the particular section under consideration, HA 1996 s185(4),[263] nonetheless fell within the ambit of Article 8 'because it sets out to give effect to a legislative policy of preserving family life for the homeless'.[264]

Article 14

12.126 Article 14 will be breached if it applies directly to another Convention right or if it can be said to fall within the ambit of another Convention right, even if no specific right under that article is said to have been breached.[265] Courts should approach Article 14 in a structured way, considering:

- whether the facts fall within the ambit of one or more Convention rights;[266]
- whether there is a difference in treatment of the claimant and persons put forward for comparison;
- whether chosen comparators are in an analogous situation to the complainant; and
- whether the difference in treatment has an objective and reasonable justification.[267]

12.127 In *Morris (No 2)*,[268] it was held that – in addition – the courts should ask whether any difference in treatment between the complainant

262 *R (Morris) v Westminster City Council; R (Badu) v Lambeth LBC and First Secretary of State* [2005] EWCA Civ 1184, [2006] 1 WLR 505, [2006] HLR 8. See paras 3.151, 5.8.

263 HA 1996 s185(4) provides that a person from abroad who is ineligible is to be disregarded in determining whether another person is homeless or in priority need.

264 *R (Morris) v Westminster City Council; R (Badu) v Lambeth LBC and First Secretary of State*, above, at 25.

265 *M v Secretary of State for Work and Pensions* [2006] UKHL 11, [2006] 2 AC 91, at [11]–[14].

266 The right does not, however, have to be engaged – thus, even if there is no claim under Article 8, there may be a claim under Article 14 because the subject-matter is family, private life or home: *M v Secretary of State for Work and Pensions* [2006] UKHL 11, [2006] 2 AC 91, at [11]–[14].

267 *Wandsworth LBC v Michalak* [2002] EWCA Civ 271, [2003] 1 WLR 617 (see also *Ghaidan v Godin-Mendoza* [2004] UKHL 30, [2004] HLR 46). In *R (Carson) v Secretary of State for Work and Pensions* [2005] UKHL 37, [2006] 1 AC 173, Lord Nicholls said that the criteria derived from *Michalak* may not be appropriate in every case and that it may be appropriate simply to consider whether the alleged discrimination can withstand scrutiny.

268 *R (Morris) v Westminster City Council (No 3)* [2004] EWHC 2191 (Admin), [2005] HLR 7. The decision was upheld on appeal: [2005] EWCA Civ 1184, [2006] 1 WLR 505, [2006] HLR 8.

and his or her comparator is based on one or more of the grounds set out in Article 14.[269] Having found that HA 1996 s185(4)[270] fell within the ambit of Article 8, the court went on to consider whether the section was in breach of Articles 8 and 14. As the distinction in section 185(4) in effect discriminated on the ground of nationality, and could not be justified,[271] the section was declared incompatible with ECHR under HRA 1998 s4.[272]

12.128 In *R (RJM) v Secretary of State for Work and Pensions*,[273] the House of Lords accepted that being a homeless person was a 'personal characteristic', and accordingly that being a homeless person fell within the category of 'other status' within the meaning of Article 14. In view of the reach of Article 14,[274] the decision might yet, therefore, have wider implications in future homelessness cases than has yet been appreciated.

Procedural law

Introduction

12.129 There are two courts to which a dissatisfied applicant will be able to turn: a) the Administrative Court, by way of proceedings for judicial review; and b) the county court, by way of a statutory appeal against a decision made under HA 1996 Part 7 or H(W)A 2014 Part 2. In this section, we consider the procedure to be followed in relation to each.

Which court?

12.130 Decisions made by local authorities under HA 1996 Parts 6 and 7 and H(W)A 2014 Part 2 are administrative law decisions and

269 See also *R (S) v Chief Constable of South Yorkshire Police* [2004] UKHL 39, [2004] 1 WLR 2196.

270 See paras 3.143–3.152.

271 The government sought to justify the section on the basis that it was a necessary element of immigration control in order to prevent benefit tourism. This was rejected on the basis that the parent applicants in the cases (both of whom had children who were ineligible and were thus held not in priority need because of the application of section 185(4)) were both lawfully and habitually resident here. In *Bah v UK* App No 56328/07, [2012] HLR 2, however, the ECtHR held that there was no contravention.

272 Some changes were made as a result of the declaration – see paras 3.143–3.145.

273 [2008] UKHL 63, [2009] 1 AC 311.

274 See paras 12.126–12.128.

therefore, without more, would prima facie only be justiciable by way of judicial review in the Administrative Court. Judicial review is, however, a remedy of 'last resort'[275] and the provision of a statutory appeal (or any form of alternative remedy) generally precludes recourse to it unless the case can in some way be distinguished from the category for which the appeal – or alternative – procedure is provided.[276]

12.131 The existence of a scheme of internal review under Parts 6 and 7 and Part 2 accordingly requires the applicant – save in exceptional cases – to pursue that review before going to court. More significantly for current purposes, the existence of a statutory appeal against a decision under HA 1996 Part 7 and H(W)A 2014 Part 2 will generally preclude a dissatisfied applicant from seeking to challenge that decision by proceedings for judicial review.

12.132 Examples of decisions outside HA 1996 Parts 6 and 7 and H(W)A 2014 Part 2, where judicial review has proceeded notwithstanding the existence of an alternative – or internal – procedure, include cases where it is not the individual decision that is in issue but the underlying legality of a decision – for example, a policy – of which the individual case is a mere application,[277] and where the decision was made without jurisdiction or contained an error of law.[278]

12.133 In *R v East Yorkshire Borough of Beverley Housing Benefits Review Board ex p Hare*,[279] the court allowed judicial review proceedings to continue – and granted relief – even though the applicant had an alternative remedy by way of appeal (under the then provisions) to a housing benefit review board, because the point raised was in part a point of statutory interpretation of general importance on which it was therefore appropriate for the court to rule.

12.134 Even these circumstances are, however, unlikely to lead to the grant of permission to seek judicial review under HA 1996 Part 7 or H(W)A 2014 Part 2 to a homeless person aggrieved by a decision on

275 Ie, any proper alternative remedy should be exhausted before the Administrative Court will permit a case to be heard: *R v Hammersmith and Fulham LBC ex p Burkett* [2002] UKHL 23, [2002] 1 WLR 1593; *R (Bancoult) v Secretary of State for the Foreign and Commonwealth Office* [2001] QB 1067, CA.

276 *R v Secretary of State for the Home Department ex p Swati* [1986] 1 WLR 477, CA.

277 *R v Paddington Valuation Officer ex p Peachey Property Corporation Ltd* [1966] 1 QB 380, CA.

278 *R v Hillingdon LBC ex p Royco Homes Ltd* [1974] QB 720, QBD.

279 (1995) 27 HLR 637, QBD.

his or her application which could otherwise be appealed to the county court,[280] because the appeal procedure itself – being on a 'point of law'[281] – embraces the same grounds as those on which judicial review would be available.[282]

12.135 The intention of the HA 1996 s204 appeal procedure was to transfer the bulk of the work from the High Court to the county court.[283] Accordingly, permission to bring a challenge by way of judicial review was refused where the reason the applicant could not appeal to the county court was simply because the applicant was out of time[284] to do so: while the court did not rule out *ever* granting permission where an applicant was out of time, the applicant would have to show 'really exceptional circumstances'.[285]

12.136 It would nonetheless be wrong to think that the High Court – through the Administrative Court – has nothing to do with homelessness. A number of HA 1996 Part 7 cases have come before it and the use of judicial review has been approved where:

a) an authority refused to house pending an internal review;[286]
b) an authority refused to consider a request for accommodation pending review;[287]
c) the decision letter from the authority was so unsatisfactory that any internal review would be unfair to the applicant, and the authority refused to rectify the deficiency in the letter;[288]

280 The issue does not arise if the issue raised *cannot* be brought by way of appeal to the county court, as there is no 'alternative remedy'.

281 HA 1996 s204(1); H(W)A 2014 s88(1).

282 See paras 12.36–12.128.

283 'Prior to 1997, many of these unhappy cases fell to be considered by nominated judges dealing with the Crown Office list. Such was the pressure that a particular deputy High Court judge sat almost continuously dealing with homelessness cases and other such cases frequently had to be referred to other deputy High Court judges. Therefore, Parliament incorporated into the Housing Act 1996 another route whereby complaints could be dealt with': per Tucker J in *R v Brent LBC ex p O'Connor* (1998) 31 HLR 923, QBD, at 924.

284 See para 12.203.

285 *R v Brent LBC ex p O'Connor*, above, at 925.

286 *R v Camden LBC ex p Mohammed* (1998) 30 HLR 315, QBD (see further para 12.102). Prior to the county court acquiring power to make an interim order to house (see para 12.138), this would also have been true of a refusal to house pending appeal to the county court.

287 *R (Casey) v Restormel BC* [2007] EWHC 2554 (Admin), [2008] JHL D27.

288 *R v Camden LBC ex p Mohammed*, above.

d) the challenge was to the legality of a policy of the authority: see *Byfield*,[289] a challenge to a policy that applicants could not seek an internal review of the suitability of an offer of accommodation unless the offer was rejected; this was an unlawful fetter on the right to an internal review and was accordingly properly brought by way of judicial review;[290]
e) the case raised an important matter of law: *Sadiq*;[291]
f) an authority had not made a decision in response to a request for accommodation: *Lusamba*;[292]
g) the decision was to refuse to make a local connection referral to another authority, which decision is not reviewable under HA 1996 s202:[293] *Sareen*;[294]
h) the authority refused to extend time to apply for an internal review under HA 1996 s202(3):[295] *Lewisham*,[296] *Slaiman*;[297]

289 (1997) 31 HLR 913, QBD. It is conceivable that such a challenge might be brought by an interested pressure group; see, eg, *R v Inland Revenue Commissioners ex p National Federation of Self-employed and Small Businesses Ltd* [1982] AC 617, HL; *R v Secretary of State for Social Services ex p Child Poverty Action Group* [1990] 2 QB 540, CA; *R v Her Majesty's Inspectorate of Pollution ex p Greenpeace Ltd* [1994] 4 All ER 329, QBD; *R v Secretary of State for Foreign and Commonwealth Affairs ex p World Development Movement Ltd* [1995] 1 WLR 386, QBD.

290 The substance of this decision was overruled in *Alghile v Westminster City Council* [2001] EWCA Civ 363, 33 HLR 57; in turn, *Alghile* was overturned by the statutory amendment that permits an applicant to seek a review of accommodation while accepting it: HA 1996 s202(1A). These do not, however, affect the underlying point being made here, that a challenge to an unlawful policy may yet be brought by judicial review.

291 *R v Brent LBC ex p Sadiq* (2000) 33 HLR 47, QBD. Moses J, while acknowledging that the applicant should have sought a review and county court appeal, referred to the residual jurisdiction of the High Court and said that the case raised an important point, which might well have had to be considered by the Court of Appeal in any event.

292 *R (Lusamba) v Islington LBC* [2008] EWHC 1149 (Admin), [2008] JHL D89. If, however, a decision is subsequently made by the authority, then there is no point in pursuing the substantive hearing.

293 In Wales, H(W)A 2014 s85. See also see also *R (Savage) v Hillingdon LBC* [2010] EWHC 88 (Admin) where it was said that it was doubtful that the manner in which an authority chose to discharge their duties under HA 1996 s190(2) and (4) (duties to persons who are eligible, homeless, in priority need but became homeless intentionally) could be dealt with by way of review under HA 1996 s202.

294 *Hackney LBC v Sareen* [2003] EWCA Civ 351, [2003] HLR 54. See further chapter 7.

295 In Wales, H(W)A 2014 s85(5); see further chapter 10.

296 *R (C) v Lewisham LBC* [2003] EWCA Civ 927, [2004] HLR 4.

297 *R (Slaiman) v Richmond upon Thames LBC* [2006] EWHC 329 (Admin), [2006] HLR 20.

i) an appeal under HA 1996 s204 would not provide an effective remedy: in *Aguiar*,[298] the applicant received his costs on a compromised judicial review application, in part because the remedy sought[299] would not have been available in appeal proceedings under HA 1996 s204;

j) the person seeking judicial review was a third party, not the applicant: in *Hammia*,[300] the authority applied a policy that victims of domestic violence, if a joint tenant of the authority, must first serve a notice to quit their existing home as a condition of acceptance as homeless; the applicant's husband, who lost his security of tenure because of the notice, successfully challenged this policy by proceedings for judicial review;

k) following a local connection referral, the authority to which the applicant had been referred wished to challenge a substantive finding, for example, that the applicant is unintentionally homeless: *Bantamagbari*;[301]

l) there were exceptional circumstances: *Van der Stolk*.[302]

12.137 In addition, there remain a number of circumstances, not yet considered by the courts, in which it is likely that judicial review will continue to be available, for example:

a) where, otherwise than so far as governed by the local connection provisions of HA 1996 ss200–201,[303] two authorities are at odds, eg under the co-operation provisions of HA 1996 s213;[304]

298 *R (Aguiar) v Newham LBC* [2002] EWHC 1325 (Admin), [2002] JHL D92.

299 An order that the authority were required to carry out a HA 1996 s202 review.

300 *R (Hammia) v Wandsworth LBC* [2005] EWHC 1127 (Admin), [2005] HLR 46.

301 *R (Bantamagbari) v Westminster City Council* [2003] EWHC 1350 (Admin), [2003] JHL D70.

302 *R (Van der Stolk) v Camden LBC* [2002] EWHC 1261 (Admin), [2002] JHL D77, where the authority had failed properly to consider medical evidence provided after the time limit to appeal had passed and the applicant's mental health was deteriorating. See also *RW v Sheffield City Council* [2005] EWHC 720 (Admin), where two local authorities were disputing responsibility for the applicant under the local connection provisions, and neither would house in the interim. '[T]he claimant having been caught between two stools and faced with an exceptional situation, I consider that it is appropriate, notwithstanding the existence of alternative remedies, to entertain judicial review proceedings': per Gibb J at [34].

303 In Wales, H(W)A 2014 ss80–83. See para 7.51 onwards. Cf *Sheffield*, last footnote, where the dispute was not covered by the statutory arbitration provisions.

304 See chapter 13.

b) where what is in issue is discharge of the property duties, which are not subject to internal review or, therefore, to appeal (see HA 1996 ss211 and 212[305]);

c) where an applicant seeks an internal review on the facts alone, ie, without reference to a point of law, but the authority does not conduct the internal review (or notify the applicant of the outcome) within the prescribed time: there may need to be an application for judicial review to compel the authority to conduct the internal review or to notify the applicant of the outcome.[306]

12.138 Accordingly, judicial review is some way from obsolete in cases under HA 1996 Parts 6 and 7 and H(W)A 2014 Part 2. Permission to pursue a judicial review for a 'pre-emptive' declaration in advance of any homelessness or threatened homelessness, that the applicant should not be considered intentionally homeless, while not within the review or appeal provisions (for want of any decision), would, however, seem likely to be refused.[307]

12.139 In the following paragraphs, the procedural steps to be followed when challenging a decision either in the Administrative Court – by way of judicial review against a decision under HA 1996 Part 6 or in those circumstances where decisions under HA 1996 Part 7 or H(W)A 2014 Part 2 may still be challenged by way of proceedings for judicial review – or the county court, by way of statutory appeal, are considered. See also the annex to this chapter for specimen documents.

Judicial review

Procedure

12.140 The procedure for claiming judicial review is to be found in Civil Procedure Rules[308] (CPR) Part 54.[309] Cases are now commonly – but not invariably – heard by a single High Court judge. All parties should comply with the pre-action protocol for judicial review.

305 In Wales, H(W)A 2014 ss93, 94. See chapter 8.

306 See further para 12.199.

307 See *R v Hillingdon LBC ex p Tinn* (1988) 20 HLR 305, QBD. Like every 'absolute' proposition, there may yet be exceptions, for example, where the court apprehends – with a degree of reason – *such* unlawful conduct by an authority that it feels impelled to intervene, even if the conditions for a prohibiting order are not fulfilled.

308 1998 SI No 3132.

309 See also the accompanying PD and Senior Courts Act 1981 s31.

Compliance or non-compliance will be taken into account when giving directions for the case management of proceedings or when making an order for costs.[310] The protocol will not, however, be appropriate where there is an urgent need for an interim order, for example, to secure interim accommodation under HA 1996 s188(3), although informal (or 'short') notice should nonetheless be given.[311]

Letter before claim

12.141 The pre-action protocol requires the claimant to send a letter to the defendant before making the claim, to identify the issues in dispute and to establish whether litigation can be avoided.[312] The letter should contain the date and details of the decision, act or omission being challenged and a clear summary of the facts on which the claim is based. It should also contain the details of any relevant information that the claimant is seeking to obtain and an explanation of why this is considered relevant.[313] The letter should set out a date for reply, which in most circumstances will be 14 days.[314] A claim should not usually be made until the proposed reply date has passed.[315]

Letter of response

12.142 The authority should respond within 14 days.[316] If this is not possible, an interim reply should be sent and a reasonable extension proposed.[317] The reply must indicate clearly whether or not the claim is being conceded.[318] Failure to comply with the requirement to respond may lead to a costs order. In *R v Kensington and Chelsea RLBC ex p Ghebregiogis*,[319] a comprehensive letter before action had been sent to the authority by the applicant's solicitors explaining the applicant's position and dealing with the authority's adverse

310 See Judicial Review Pre-action Protocol para 7 and CPR Costs PDs.

311 Judicial Review Pre-action Protocol para 6. See further para 12.157 onwards on challenges to refusals to house pending internal review.

312 Judicial Review Pre-action Protocol para 14. A suggested standard format is provided at annex A to the Protocol.

313 Judicial Review Pre-action Protocol para 16.

314 See standard letter, annex A, para 13.

315 Judicial Review Pre-action Protocol para 18.

316 Judicial Review Pre-action Protocol para 20. A standard format letter is provided at annex B to the Protocol.

317 Judicial Review Pre-action Protocol para 21.

318 Judicial Review Pre-action Protocol para 22.

319 (1994) 27 HLR 602, QBD.

contentions, following which the applicant commenced judicial review proceedings. Just before the application for permission came on for hearing, the authority changed its mind. The applicant successfully sought his costs: the authority should have considered the case properly when it received the letter.

Permission

12.143 Permission must be sought to bring an application for judicial review.[320] Where a claim has become academic, even if as a result of a change of circumstances between issue of proceedings and hearing,[321] it is only in exceptional circumstances, and where there is good reason to do so in the public interest, that permission to claim judicial review will be granted.

12.144 Such exceptional circumstances include where a large number of similar cases either exist or are anticipated or where there is a discrete point of statutory construction which does not involve detailed consideration of the facts.[322]

12.145 In very different circumstances,[323] an applicant had obtained alternative accommodation before the hearing. The authority failed to file an acknowledgement of service and only produced a witness statement the day before the hearing. It contended that no remedy should be granted because it was in the process of revising the relevant policy. A declaration was nonetheless granted: the conduct of the authority in failing to file an acknowledgement of service and producing a witness statement shortly before the substantive hearing

320 The requirement for permission represents the most significant difference between the procedure to be followed on a claim for judicial review and an appeal under HA 1996 s204 or H(W)A 2014 s88, which is as of right.

321 See *R v Secretary of State for the Home Department, ex p Salem* [1999] 1 AC 450; *R (Rushbridger) v Attorney-General* [2004] 1 AC 357, HL.

322 *R (McKenzie) v Waltham Forest LBC* [2009] EWHC 1097 (Admin), [2009] JHL D94. See *R (Raw) v Lambeth LBC* [2010] EWHC 507 (Admin), [2010] JHL D40, D104 where the authority conceded the applicant's entitlement to assistance under its rent deposit scheme after the issue of his claim, which it invited him to withdraw, which he refused to do. The Administrative Court dismissed the claim as it was not in the public interest to hear academic claims and the court's resources were better spent on cases directly affecting the rights and obligations of the parties; nor was there evidence of other cases in which the authority had applied its policy or that the issue raised would need to be resolved by the courts in the near future. If a claim is fact-sensitive, it will not be permitted to proceed: *R (Zoolife International Ltd) v Secretary of State for the Environment* [2007] EWHC 2995 (Admin), [2008] ACD 44.

323 *R (Adow) v Newham LBC* [2010] EWHC 951 (Admin), [2010] JHL D101; for the facts, see para 11.137.

was unacceptable; the court had the distinct impression that the authority was anxious to hide its position as far as possible. It was right that the court should mark its disapproval of such conduct.

Time

12.146 Application for permission must be made 'promptly and in any event within three months from the date when grounds for the application first arose'.[324] The three-month period runs from the time when application for permission can first be made.[325]

12.147 The former explicit power (to be found in RSC Order 53 r4) to extend time for 'good reason' has not been retained, although the general jurisdiction of the court to extend time under CPR 3.1 is available. Any application to extend time must be set out in the claim form with grounds.[326] The parties may not agree to extend time,[327] nor will the court be enthusiastic about granting permission when an application has grown stale.[328] Delay in obtaining legal aid may constitute an acceptable reason for granting permission belatedly.[329] Where the challenge is to the lawfulness of a policy and the relief sought is to restrain its further implementation, the need to ensure that a prima facie unlawful policy is discontinued is likely to comprise a good reason for extending time.[330]

12.148 When permission to pursue judicial review out of time is granted, it is not a final decision on time: it may still be raised at the full hearing of the application for judicial review itself.[331]

Form of application

12.149 An application must be made on form N461, in accordance with CPR Part 54. The claim form must include or be accompanied by

324 CPR 54.5.

325 PD 54A para 4.1. When what is under challenge is a policy, time only begins to run when it affects the individual applicant: *R v Tower Hamlets LBC ex p Mohib Ali* (1993) 25 HLR 218, DC; *R v Newham LBC ex p Ajayi* (1994) 28 HLR 25, QBD.

326 PD 54A para 54.6.

327 CPR 54.5(2).

328 See *R v Rochester City Council ex p Trotman* (1983) *Times* 13 May.

329 *R v Stratford on Avon DC ex p Jackson* [1985] 1 WLR 1319, CA; see also *R v Dacorum BC ex p Brown* (1989) 21 HLR 405, QBD.

330 *R (Lin) v Barnet LBC* [2006] EWHC 1041 (Admin), [2006] HLR 44.

331 *R v Dairy Produce Quota Tribunal ex p Caswell* [1990] 2 AC 738, HL; caution should, however, be exercised when re-opening the issue of delay at the substantive hearing: *R (Lichfield Securities Ltd) v Lichfield DC* [2001] EWCA Civ 304, [2001] 3 PLR 33.

a detailed statement of the grounds and a statement of the facts relied on.[332]

Supporting documents

12.150 In addition, the following must also be supplied: any written evidence in support of the claim; a copy of the decision that the applicant[333] seeks to have quashed; any documents which will be relied on; copies of relevant statutory material; and a list of essential documents for advance reading. Two copies of the relevant documents in a paginated and indexed bundle must be filed.[334] Where it is not possible to file all of the documents immediately, the applicant must say which are to follow and explain why they are not currently available.

12.151 In the usual case, the applicant's full case must be made out in the initial application, without anticipating additional oral evidence or later elaboration. This makes the initial papers very important indeed. This means that the case must be made out from the outset.

Duty of care

12.152 There is a high duty of care on the part of all applicants to make full and frank disclosure in an application for permission, even if it is unhelpful to the case.[335] Non-disclosure is not necessarily fatal if it causes no advantage to the applicant and no prejudice to the respondent but, even if it does not lead to the refusal of permission, it could still affect relief at the end of the day.[336] The obligation is to make full and candid disclosure of the material facts known to the applicant and to make proper enquiries before making the application; there is a breach of the disclosure duty if the applicant has not disclosed any additional material facts which he or she would have known if he or she had made proper enquiries before making the application.[337]

332 A form of N461, including the statement of grounds and statement of facts, is annexed to this chapter.

333 Under the CPR, a person claiming judicial review is now (as in other cases) a claimant (see CPR 2.3(1): 'a claimant is a person who makes a claim' and CPR 54.1 referring to a 'claim for judicial review'); the term 'applicant' is, however, used in this book to denote applicant under either HA 1996 Part 6 or Part 7 or H(W)A 2014 Part 2.

334 PD 54A paras 5.6–5.9.

335 See also paras 12.177–12.180, on an application for interim relief, where there is an analogous duty of disclosure.

336 See *R v Wirral MBC ex p Bell* (1994) 27 HLR 234, QBD.

337 *R (Lawer) v Restormel BC* [2007] EWHC 2299 (Admin), [2008] HLR 20.

12.153 Proper disclosure for this purpose means specifically identifying all relevant documents for the judge, drawing his or her attention to the particular passages in the documents which are material and taking appropriate steps to ensure that the judge correctly appreciates the significance of what he or she is being asked to read; that burden of full and frank disclosure is more onerous where a telephone application is being made to a judge who has none of the papers before him or her, nor is it obviated by giving informal notice to the other party.[338]

Service

12.154 The claim form (and accompanying documents) must be served on the defendant(s) within seven days of the date of issue,[339] together with an acknowledgment of service form, which must be filed by the respondent authority not more than 21 days after service of the claim form.[340]

Pre-permission response

12.155 In the acknowledgement of service, the defendant must set out a summary of the grounds for contesting the claim, any directions which will be sought and other applications which will be made at the permission stage. A respondent who does not return the acknowledgment of service form within 14 days of service will lose the right to take part in the permission hearing (although not the right to take part in the substantive application) without the court's express permission to do so.[341] A respondent authority may not apply to set aside permission where it has been served with the claim form,[342] but may do so where there has been a failure to serve by the applicant.[343]

Paper applications

12.156 Applications for permission to proceed will, unless the court directs otherwise, be decided by a judge without hearing oral submissions.

338 See para 12.140.

339 CPR 54.7. Where the relief sought in the claim form includes a declaration of incompatibility under HRA 1998 s4, the Crown must be given 21 days' notice and/or joined as an interested party or second defendant to the claim: CPR 19.4A(1), and see *R (Morris) v Westminster City Council* [2003] EWHC 2266 (Admin), [2004] HLR 18.

340 CPR 54.8.

341 CPR 54.9.

342 CPR 54.13.

343 *R (Webb) v Bristol City Council* [2001] EWHC (Admin) 696, [2001] JHL D90.

Interim applications

12.157 Any applications for interim relief should be made in accordance with CPR Parts 23 and 25 and may be considered with the application for permission.[344] Even where an interim application – for example, to house pending the substantive hearing – is made at the same time as permission is sought, there does not have to be an oral hearing if the court does not consider it appropriate.[345]

12.158 Failure to comply with any order of the court – or an undertaking given in lieu of an order – may amount to contempt of court.[346]

Attendance of respondent

12.159 Unless the court directs otherwise, the respondent authority does not need to attend any permission hearing. Where it does so, the court will not generally make an order for costs against the applicant.[347]

Post-permission response

12.160 If permission is granted, the respondent must, within 35 days of service of the order granting permission, file and serve detailed grounds for contesting the claim and any written evidence on which reliance is to be placed.[348]

Further stages

12.161 If permission is granted, then a full hearing will be listed. At least 21 days prior to that hearing, the applicant must file a full skeleton argument. The respondent must file a skeleton at least 14 days in advance.[349] Where permission is, on the papers, refused (or granted only subject to conditions or on certain grounds), the applicant may, within seven days, request that the decision be reconsidered

344 There is a duty of full disclosure – see para 12.151.

345 CPR 23.8.

346 See *R (Bempoa) v Southwark LBC* [2002] EWHC 153 (Admin), [2002] JHL D44, where, in proceedings under the National Assistance Act 1948 s21, the authority through its social services department undertook not to evict the applicant, pending an assessment of his needs. Notwithstanding this, the authority's housing department evicted him from his accommodation and refused to reinstate him. The undertaking bound all departments in the authority, which was held to be in contempt.

347 PD 54A paras 8.5–8.6.

348 CPR 54.14.

349 PD 54A para 15.

at an oral hearing.[350] If the oral hearing does not lead to a successful reconsideration, then the applicant may appeal. An appeal against a refusal of permission – generally or on specific grounds, or against conditions – lies to the Court of Appeal, but only with its permission.[351]

Disclosure

12.162 Application for disclosure of documents may be made (by either party) at the same time as permission is sought or after it has been granted.[352] Unless the court makes an order for disclosure, it is not required.[353] On discovery, only material that is privileged – because it has been produced in the course of, or in anticipation of, the proceedings – may be withheld.

12.163 Through disclosure, the applicant will be able to inspect the authority's minutes, emails and other memoranda dealing with his or her application. An examination of the authority's standing orders should also be undertaken in every case, as these may reveal a want of authorised delegation or sub-delegation:[354] these should be available on the authority's website but otherwise may be sought as part of the disclosure exercise. It may be said that few authorities can withstand such close legal scrutiny without revealing *some* flaws in their procedure, although these flaws may do no more than cause minor embarrassment without invalidating the whole process.[355]

Further appeal

12.164 If permission is refused, the refusal may be appealed to the Court of Appeal; this must be pursued within seven days.[356] If successful, the Court of Appeal may i) grant permission to appeal; or (more commonly) ii) grant permission to apply for judicial review and direct

350 CPR 54.12. No such application may be made, however, if the refusal of permission records that the application is totally without merit: CPR 54.12(7). As to the meaning of 'totally without merit' in this context see *R (Wasif) v Secretary of State for the Home Department* [2016] EWCA Civ 82, [2016] 1 WLR 2793. Such a litigant can still seek permission to appeal from the Court of Appeal: *Wasif.*

351 CPR 52.8.

352 CPR 54.16.

353 PD 54A.12(1).

354 See chapter 9.

355 Applicants should be wary of pinning too many hopes on an administrative error.

356 CPR 52.8(3).

that the case be heard by the High Court; or iii) grant permission to apply for judicial review but order that the Court of Appeal will hear the case itself.[357]

Hearing

12.165 In the usual course, evidence will be that which was served (in writing) with the application for permission,[358] supplemented by any evidence in reply and any further evidence in response; not uncommonly there will be two or three exchanges of evidence. Oral evidence is possible, but only at the discretion of the court.[359] Permission to cross-examine witnesses is rarely granted.[360]

Burden of proof

12.166 As noted,[361] the burden of proof lies on a person seeking to show that a decision is void; the allegations must be both substantiated and particularised: *Wednesbury*[362] and *Cannock Chase DC v Kelly*.[363]

12.167 It is never enough to say simply that the applicant is a homeless person and in priority need, because this would not be enough to raise the inference of a duty. The duty arises only when the authority is satisfied, or has reason to believe, or considers that the fact or state of affairs is as it is claimed to be. It must be alleged that it has refused or failed to reach a decision, or that such decision as has been reached must be treated by the courts as void, for want of compliance with such of the foregoing principles as are identified; the factual basis for this allegation must be set out.

Costs

12.168 The costs of and incidental to all proceedings in the High Court are in the discretion of the court.[364] The general provisions concerning costs (ie, those contained in CPR Part 44) are applicable to judicial

357 CPR 52.8.

358 See para 12.209.

359 The court has an inherent power to give directions requiring oral evidence and cross-examination in a claim for judicial review: *R (G) v Ealing LBC (No 2)* [2002] EWHC 250 (Admin), [2002] MHLR 140. See further CPR 54.16 (referring to CPR 8.6(1)).

360 *Bubb v Wandsworth LBC* [2011] EWCA Civ 1285, [2012] HLR 13 at [24]–[25].

361 See para 12.209.

362 *Associated Provincial Picture Houses Ltd v Wednesbury Corporation* [1948] 1 KB 223, CA.

363 [1978] 1 WLR 1, CA.

364 *R (Burkett) v Hammersmith and Fulham LBC* [2004] EWCA Civ 1342.

review proceedings.[365] Accordingly, the usual order is for costs to follow the event so that the successful party will be able to recover costs.[366] The court has, however, a broad discretion to take into account all factors, including the conduct of the parties; where either party's conduct has prolonged litigation unnecessarily or has had the effect of increasing the costs burden on the other without proper cause, the court may deprive the successful party of all or a proportion of the costs.[367]

12.169 The courts may depart from the general rule on an issue-by-issue basis: where a party unsuccessfully raises an issue that takes up a significant part of the hearing, the party may be denied costs in relation to that issue, even if successful in the claim overall.[368]

12.170 Publicly funded litigants should not be treated differently from those who are not; nonetheless, the consequences for solicitors who do such work is a factor which must be taken into account: it is one thing for solicitors who do a substantial amount of publicly funded work, and who have to fund the substantial overheads that sustaining a legal practice involves, to take the risk of being paid at lower rates if a publicly funded case turns out to be unsuccessful, but quite another for them to be unable to recover remuneration at inter partes rates in the event that it is successful.[369]

365 This includes the wasted costs jurisdiction under Senior Courts Act 1981 s51 and CPR 48.7, where a legal representative has acted improperly, unreasonably or negligently, causing another party to incur unnecessary costs and it is just to make such an order: see generally *Ridehalgh v Horsefield* [1994] Ch 205, CA: see *R (Grimshaw) v Southwark LBC* [2013] EWHC 4504 (Admin) (proceedings challenging decision to terminate provision of temporary accommodation followed by accepted offer of accommodation about which claimant's solicitors failed to inform the court).

366 CPR 44.2(2)(a). See, eg *Mendes and another v Southwark LBC* [2009] EWCA Civ 594, [2010] HLR 3, at [23] and [24].

367 CPR 44.2(1)–(5).

368 *AEI Rediffusion Music Ltd v Phonographic Performance Ltd (Costs)* [1999] 1 WLR 1507, CA; *R (Bateman) v Legal Services Commission (Costs)* [2001] EWHC 797 (Admin), [2002] ACD 29.

369 *R (E) v Governing Body of JFS and the Admissions Appeal Panel of JFS and others; R (E) v Governing Body of JFS and the Admissions Appeal Panel of JFS (United Synagogue) and others* [2009] UKSC 1 at [25]. The dicta of Scott Baker J in *R (Boxall) v Waltham Forest LBC* (2001) 4 CCLR 258, QBD that the fact that the claimants were legally aided was immaterial when deciding what, if any, costs order to make between the parties in a case where they were successful, was approved. See also *Bunning v King's Lynn and West Norfolk Council* [2016] EWCA Civ 1037, [2017] HLR 9, accepting the general principle, but, on the facts, making no order as to costs (claimant had prima facie been in breach of an injunction but her subsequent compliance rendered the committal proceedings academic).

12.171 Where a claim for judicial review is settled (most commonly, in the present context, where an authority agrees to withdraw its decision and reconsider it) but the costs remain in dispute, the principles are as set out in *R (Boxall) v Waltham Forest LBC*:[370]

a) the court has power to make a costs order even where parties have settled the substantive claim;
b) it will ordinarily be irrelevant that the claimant is in receipt of public funding for his or her claim;
c) the overriding objective is to do justice between the parties without incurring unnecessary court time and costs;
d) how far the court will be prepared to look into the substantive issues will depend on the circumstances of the particular case, including the amount of costs at stake and the conduct of the parties;
e) in the absence of a good reason to make any other order, the fall-back position is to make no order as to costs; and
f) the court should take care not to discourage parties from settling judicial review proceedings.

12.172 *Boxall* has been approved and applied in a number of other cases, drawing out the proposition that where the claimant has secured the substantive relief sought, it would normally comprise a good reason to award him or her the costs;[371] a judge should not be tempted too readily to adopt the fall-back position of making no order.[372]

12.173 The *Boxall* approach was applied by the Court of Appeal in *Harripaul v Lewisham LBC*:[373] The applicant was dissatisfied with both the original section 184 decision and the subsequent section 202 review and unsuccessfully appealed to the county court under section 204, from which the Court of Appeal granted permission to

370 (2001) 4 CCLR 258, QBD.

371 *Brawley v Marczynski & Business Lines Ltd* [2002] EWCA Civ 756, [2002] 4 All ER 1060; *R (Scott) v Hackney LBC* [2009] EWCA Civ 217; *Mendes v Southwark LBC* [2009] EWCA Civ 594, [2010] HLR 3; *R (Bhata) v Secretary of State for the Home Department* [2011] EWCA Civ 895. In *R (J) v Hackney LBC* [2010] EWHC 3021 (Admin), [2010] JHL D20, under Children Act 1989, the good reason was not only the rejection of the authority's argument that its concession followed a recent decision resulting from a development in the law (rejected on the basis that the law had not radically altered the legal landscape) but also flowed from the conduct of the authority which was sufficiently poor to justify an award of costs: it had taken 12 months to file an acknowledgement of service and five months after the new case to settle the matter; it had also been unreasonable for the authority to require an oral hearing to determine costs.

372 *R (Scott) v Hackney* LBC, above, at [51].

373 [2012] EWCA Civ 266, [2012] HLR 24.

appeal, in response to which the authority offered to carry out a fresh review. The appeal was dismissed by consent, but the parties were unable to agree who should bear the costs of the appeal. The Court of Appeal held that the authority should do so: the case was akin to a judicial review and the *Boxall* principles applied; the applicant had obtained the substantive relief that she sought and it was for the authority to show why it should not pay the costs; no such reasons existed on the facts.

12.174 In *R (M)*,[374] the Court of Appeal went somewhat further, holding that where a claimant obtains all the relief which he or she seeks (whether by consent or after a contested hearing),[375] he or she is ordinarily[376] entitled to all his or her costs, unless there is a good reason to the contrary; where, however, the claimant obtains only some of the relief which he or she is seeking, the issue is more complex: it may be appropriate to make an order for costs based on individual issues in proceedings; in many cases, the correct order will be 'no order as to costs'; each case will turn on its own facts.[377]

12.175 The court has power to order that costs be set off.[378] This may permit a set off against damages or costs to which a legally aided person has become or becomes entitled in the action; the set-off is no different from and no more extensive than the set-off available to or against parties who are not legally aided; the broad criterion is that the claims of both claimant and defendant claim are so closely

374 *R (M) v Croydon LBC* [2012] EWCA Civ 595; see further *R (Dempsey) v Sutton LBC* [2013] EWCA Civ 863.

375 But not where the relief is obtained as the result of the actions of a third party, see *R (Naureen) v Salford City Council* [2012] EWCA Civ 1795 – the claimant became entitled to housing benefit because the secretary of state granted her leave to remain, rather than because of any act or concession on the part of the authority. See also *RL v Croydon LBC* [2018] EWCA Civ 726: permission for judicial review in respect of an alleged failure to carry out a Children Act s17 assessment was refused because the authority had, albeit belatedly, carried out the assessment that it was the purpose of the proceedings to secure; while this led to the provision of accommodation and support, the appropriate costs order was 'no order' because the relief was not obtained as a result of proceedings, but as a result of the completion of the assessment.

376 See also *R (Hunt) v North Somerset Council* [2015] UKSC 51, [2015] 1 WLR 3575 in which it was held that a person who establishes that a public authority has acted unlawfully should ordinarily recover costs, even if no relief is obtained.

377 As to the procedure to be adopted where the parties have settled a judicial review claim but cannot agree costs, see guidance as to how the parties should assist the court when applications for costs are made following settlement of claims for judicial review, Administrative Court Office, December 2013.

378 CPR 44.12.

connected that it would be inequitable to allow the claimant's claim without taking into account the defendant's claim.[379]

12.176 While an assisted person is protected against the making of enforceable orders for payment of costs, that protection is not available to prevent an order for costs being set off.[380] While there will rarely be claim and counterclaim in HA 1996 Parts 6 and 7 (or H(W)A 2014 Part 2) cases,[381] the implication is that it may be possible to set off costs orders made in different judicial reviews, or even county court appeals, and perhaps even costs orders made in the county court against orders made in the High Court, if the proceedings are closely connected.

Remedies and relief

Interim relief

12.177 Where a challenge is by judicial review, the normal principle on an application for an interim injunction is that an order will be granted if it can be shown that the balance of convenience is in its favour.[382] In *de Falco, Silvestri v Crawley BC*,[383] however, Lord Denning MR said that in a homeless person's action, it is necessary to show that there was a strong prima facie case of breach by the authority as, almost invariably, the applicant would be unable to give a worthwhile undertaking in damages should the applicant eventually lose.[384]

12.178 The *de Falco* approach would also seem to conflict with Lord Denning MR's own approach in *Allen v Jambo Holdings Ltd*,[385] a case in which the owners of an aircraft sought discharge of a *Mareva* injunction on the ground that the plaintiff, who was legally aided, could not give a valuable cross-undertaking in damages.

> It is said that whenever a *Mareva* injunction is granted the plaintiff has to give the cross-undertaking in damages. Suppose the widow should lose this case altogether. She is legally-aided. Her undertaking is worth nothing. I would not assent to that argument . . . A legally-aided plaintiff is by our statutes not to be in any worse position by

379 *Lockley v National Blood Transfusion Service* [1992] 1 WLR 492, CA.
380 *Hill v Bailey* [2003] EWHC 2835 (Ch).
381 Whether formally so or in practice.
382 *American Cyanamid v Ethicon* [1975] AC 396, HL; *Fellowes v Fisher* [1976] QB 122, CA.
383 *De Falco, Silvestri v Crawley BC* [1980] QB 460, CA.
384 In *Cyanamid*, ability to give a meaningful undertaking in damages was already a factor to be weighed up in determining the balance of convenience.
385 [1980] 1 WLR 1252, CA.

reason of being legally-aided than any other plaintiff would be. I do not see why a poor plaintiff should be denied a *Mareva* injunction just because he is poor, whereas a rich plaintiff would get it . . .

12.179 In *R v Kensington and Chelsea RLBC ex p Hammell,*[386] it was contended by the authority that, following *Puhlhofer,*[387] it would be necessary to show something akin to 'exceptional circumstances' before an interim injunction could be granted. The court rejected this argument: interim relief is discretionary, although the discretion is one that must be exercised in accordance with principles of law; in a clear case of breach, there is therefore likely to be no issue of whether or not such relief should be granted.

12.180 In *R v Cardiff City Council ex p Barry,*[388] it was held that, as a strong prima facie case had to be made out for a court to grant permission for judicial review of an authority's decision, interim relief would be the usual concomitant of the grant of permission. In relation to a challenge to a refusal to house pending review,[389] however, this approach was rejected in *R v Camden LBC ex p Mohammed*[390] (itself approved in *R v Brighton and Hove Council ex p Nacion*[391]) because a review is as of right, available to everyone who is the subject of an adverse decision, so that – unlike on an application for permission to apply for judicial review – no prima facie case has to be made out.[392]

12.181 The principles on which the discretion to house pending review is to be exercised by the authority have been considered in chapter 10;[393] their application to housing pending appeal[394] is considered below.[395] Whether the development of those principles will have an impact in other cases in which permission is sought to claim judicial review – on other grounds – is unclear, but there is no apparent reason why they should do so, or why *Hammell*[396] should not continue to apply.

12.182 Orders granted without notice should be for a defined and short period, though sometimes it may be appropriate to decline to make

386 [1989] QB 518, (1988) 20 HLR 666, CA.
387 *R v Hillingdon LBC ex p Puhlhofer* [1986] AC 484, (1986) 18 HLR 158.
388 (1989) 22 HLR 261, CA.
389 Under the power in HA 1996 s188(3); or H(W)A 2014 s69(10), (11).
390 (1998) 30 HLR 315, QBD.
391 (1999) 31 HLR 1095, CA.
392 (1998) 30 HLR 315, at 320.
393 See paras 10.49–10.57.
394 Under HA 1996 s204A or H(W)A 2014 s88(1), (5).
395 See paras 12.238–12.247.
396 See para 12.179.

an immediate order and direct instead an oral hearing within one or two days. This gives the defendant the opportunity to mount an opposition to the application.[397] There is a duty of full and frank disclosure of all relevant facts and law on an application for interim relief:[398] thus, in *Konodyba*,[399] an interim order for interim accommodation was set aside because the applicant had failed to disclose that she was the tenant of a property in Bishop's Stortford in which she could live pending determination of her application under HA 1996 Part 7.

Substantive hearing

12.183 The Administrative Court may:

a) quash a decision (a quashing order);
b) compel an authority to make a decision or a particular decision, or re-take a decision that has been quashed (a mandatory order);[400]
c) prohibit an authority from taking some action (a prohibiting order); or
d) make a declaration,[401] for example, to declare a decision ultra vires or void.

12.184 Although the Administrative Court cannot substitute its own decision for that of the authority, the findings of fact or law it makes may on occasion be such that there is only one decision that the authority can lawfully make, ie, with which it is left. In such cases, either directly or indirectly, the court will (in substance) order the authority to come to that decision.[402]

12.185 It may also be that the Administrative Court would order the authority to come to a particular decision where it is necessary in

397 *R (Casey) v Restormel BC* [2007] EWHC 2554 (Admin), [2008] JHL D27.

398 *R (Lawer) v Restormel BC* [2007] EWHC 2299 (Admin), [2008] HLR 20.

399 *Konodyba v Kensington and Chelsea RLBC* [2011] EWHC 2653 (Admin), [2011] JHL D10. Upheld on appeal [2012] EWCA Civ 982.

400 Where the court does so, the authority is bound by its conclusions and cannot go behind the findings of the High Court; if it disagrees with that decision, its recourse is to appeal: *Kuteh v Secretary of State for Education* [2014] EWCA Civ 1586.

401 CPR 54.3(1).

402 See *Barty-King v Ministry of Defence* [1979] 2 All ER 80, QBD. See also, eg *R v Ealing LBC ex p Parkinson* (1997) 29 HLR 179, QBD per Laws J at 185–186; *R (Cunningham) v Exeter Crown Court* [2003] EWHC 184 (Admin), [2003] 2 Cr App R (S) 64, per Clarke LJ at [22]; *R (S) v Secretary of State for the Home Department* [2007] EWCA Civ 546, [2007] Imm AR, 781, per Carnwath LJ at [46].

order to restore a right of which the claimant has been unlawfully deprived.[403]

12.186 In an appropriate case, the Administrative Court may award damages as compensation for wrongful action or wrongful refusal to act.[404] This is not available where damages are the sole remedy claimed; the court must be satisfied that, if the claim had been made in a private law action, the claimant would have been awarded damages.

Refusal of relief

12.187 A court may refuse relief, notwithstanding a finding of procedural error on the part of the authority, if the error would plainly have made no difference to the authority's decision.[405] This is not the case if reconsideration *could* lead to a different decision: it is not enough for the authority to assert that it could reach the same decision on reconsideration; the error must be such that it *would* have made no difference.

Appeals

12.188 Appeals from a full judicial review application require permission from either the High Court, or – if refused – from the Court of Appeal.[406]

Confidentiality

12.189 Both the High Court and the county court[407] have inherent jurisdiction to make an order granting anonymity to an applicant, and to support it with an order under Contempt of Court Act 1981 s11

403 Consider *Crawley LBC v B* (2000) 32 HLR 636, CA, at 651–652, see para 12.253; and *Robinson v Hammersmith and Fulham LBC* [2006] EWCA Civ 1122, [2006] 1 WLR 3295, [2007] HLR 7, at [31], see paras 9.231, 12.261.

404 CPR 54.3(2).

405 *R (Bibi) v Newham LBC* [2001] EWCA Civ 607, [2002] 1 WLR 237, at [40]: 'The court has two functions – assessing the legality of actions by administrators and, if it finds unlawfulness on the administrators' part, deciding what relief it should give.' See also *R v Secretary of State for the Environment ex p Walters; R v Brent LBC ex p O'Malley* (1997) 30 HLR 328, CA; *R v Islington LBC ex p B* (1997) 30 HLR 706, QBD. See also Senior Courts Act 1981 s31(2A), providing that the court must refuse relief if it is 'highly likely that the outcome for the applicant would not have been substantially different' notwithstanding the conduct complained of.

406 CPR 52.3(1). Permission may only be granted where there is a real prospect of success or some other compelling reason: CPR 52.6.

407 *Norman v Mathews* (1916) 85 LJKB 857, *affirmed* (1916) 23 TLR 369, CA.

preventing publication of an applicant's name, address and photograph.[408] Such an order should be made, however, only where it can be shown that a failure to do so would render the attainment of justice doubtful or, in effect, impracticable.[409]

12.190 If no order is sought and obtained before proceeding, then:

a) no subsequent order can relate back; with the result that
b) it might become inappropriate to make an order in relation to the substantive proceedings themselves simply by reason of any publicity derived from preliminary proceedings.

12.191 The proper course, therefore, is to apply to the court without notice under Contempt of Court Act 1981 s11 at the same time as proceedings are to be issued, if appropriate asking for a hearing to be in camera. If there is power to make an order because the preconditions are satisfied, the court can grant it for a short time, for notice to be given to the press.[410] In some cases, it may be necessary for papers not to be lodged until the application can be dealt with immediately, so as to prevent disclosure by way of inspection of office documents.[411]

12.192 Additionally, the court has power under CPR 39.2(4) to order that the identity of any party or witness should not be disclosed if it considers non-disclosure necessary in order to protect the interests of that party or witness.

Minors

12.193 A court may also require reports not to identify parties for the purpose of protecting the interests of children indirectly involved in a case.[412]

Appeal to county court

Procedure

Point of law

12.194 An appeal to the county court lies on a point of law.[413] 'Point of law' includes:

408 *R v Westminster City Council ex p Castelli; R v Same ex p Tristran-Garcia* (1995) 27 HLR 125.
409 *In the matter of D* (1997–98) 1 CCLR 190, at 196K.
410 *In the matter of D*, above.
411 *In the matter of D*, above.
412 See *Crawley BC v B* (2000) 32 HLR 636, CA, at 638. See CPR 39.2(3)(d).
413 HA 1996 s204(1); H(W)A 2014 s88(1).

> . . . not only matters of legal interpretation but also the full range of issues[414] which would otherwise be the subject of an application to the High Court for judicial review, such as procedural error and questions of *vires*, to which I add, also of irrationality and (in)adequacy of reasons.[415]

12.195 The jurisdiction does not permit judges to reach their own decisions of fact; to do so is in excess of the statutory jurisdiction.[416] Where an authority considered that an applicant was not vulnerable[417] because of mental illness, it was not for the judge to conclude that he was mentally ill (and accordingly vulnerable): 'Some decision-makers might have arrived at a different conclusion. It is elementary that matters of that kind were not for the judge . . .'[418]

12.196 There are, however, exceptions. First, the discussion of when error of fact may comprise a public law failure sufficient to vitiate a decision is as applicable in the county court as otherwise: this may involve the court considering the facts from the perspective of whether there has been such an error.[419]

12.197 Second, an applicant who will face eviction from temporary accommodation if his or her HA 1996 s204 appeal is unsuccessful is entitled to raise his or her Article 8 rights[420] during that appeal,[421]

414 Cf the first part of this chapter: 'Substantive law', paras 12.5–12.128.

415 *Nipa Begum v Tower Hamlets LBC* [2000] 1 WLR 306, (1999) 32 HLR 445, CA per Auld LJ at 452. *Nipa Begum* was approved by the House of Lords in *Runa Begum v Tower Hamlets LBC* [2003] UKHL 5, [2003] 2 AC 430, [2003] HLR 32, see particularly Lord Bingham at [7].

416 *Kruja v Enfield LBC* [2004] EWCA Civ 1769, [2005] HLR 13. See also *Aw-Aden v Birmingham City Council* [2005] EWCA Civ 1834, in which it was held that the judge had made inappropriate findings of fact. See also *Bubb v Wandsworth LBC* [2011] EWCA Civ 1285, [2012] HLR 13 and *Richmond upon Thames LBC v Kubickek* [2012] EWHC 3292 (QB), again reiterating that the county court should not set itself up as a finder of fact.

417 And accordingly not in priority need – see chapter 5.

418 *Kruja v Enfield LBC* [2004] EWCA Civ 1769, [2005] HLR 13 at [23]. See also *Wandsworth LBC v Watson* [2010] EWCA Civ 1558, [2011] HLR 9, where the authority's appeal was allowed because the recorder had effectively substituted her own decision as to risk of violence in relation to an offer of accommodation for that of the authority.

419 Para 12.44.

420 Para 12.123.

421 *R (ZH and CN) v Newham LBC and Lewisham LBC* [2014] UKSC 62, [2015] AC 1259, [2015] HLR 6 at [64].

provided occupation can be said to be as a home,[422] which, on the basis of how Article 8 is understood and applied domestically,[423] means that the court may be required independently to determine the facts for itself, eg if what is asserted is that the authority has come to the wrong decision[424] in concluding that the applicant is not in priority need or is intentionally homeless because it has erred in relation to the facts.[425]

From what decision?

12.198 The point of law under challenge will usually be one made in relation to the internal review rather than the original decision, as any error on the original decision will either have been remedied on or replaced by the review (with or without the same or another error of law).

12.199 There is an exception to this where no notification of a decision on an internal review is given within the time prescribed for it[426] (or, if notification has been given, if it does not comply with the minimum statutory requirements, ie, to give reasons and advise of the right to appeal and the time for appeal – see HA 1996 s203(4), (5) and H(W)A 2014 s86(4), (5) – so that it is treated as not having

422 This is an autonomous test which requires 'the existence of sufficient and continued links with a specific place': see, eg, *Hounslow LBC v Powell* [2011] UKSC 8, [2011] 2 AC 186, [2011] HLR 23, per Lord Hope at [33] but is not a high bar and will commonly be fulfilled by homeless people (who, after all, of definition have nowhere else to call home) who have been in the accommodation for a relatively short time, perhaps as little as a month.

423 *Manchester City Council v Pinnock* [2010] UKSC 45, [2011] 2 AC 104, [2011] HLR 7; *Hounslow LBC v Powell* (above).

424 Because it is strongly arguable that it would not be disproportionate to evict someone on a materially erroneous assessment of his or her circumstances.

425 'A fair procedure requires the occupant to have a right to raise the issue of the proportionality of the interference and to have that issue determined by an independent tribunal': *Pinnock*, above, at [45] cited in *R (ZH and CN) v Newham LBC and Lewisham LBC* at [63]. 'It is only in very exceptional cases that the applicant will succeed in raising an arguable case of a lack of proportionality where an applicant has no right under domestic law to remain in possession of a property' which 'is so particularly where an authority seeks to recover possession of interim accommodation provided under s.188 of the 1996 Act'; and, it is for the occupier to raise the question: nevertheless, 'In an appropriate case the court, if satisfied that eviction was disproportionate, could prohibit the eviction for as long as that was the case, for example if the local authority did not provide alternative accommodation': *R (ZH and CN) v Newham LBC and Lewisham LBC* at [65]–[66].

426 HA 1996 s203(7); H(W)A 2014 s85; see para 9.243 for the prescribed times.

been given: see HA 1996 s203(6) and H(W)A 2014 s88(2)).[427] In such a case, an appeal lies against the original decision: in effect, the authority's delay in notifying the outcome of the review means that it loses the opportunity to remedy any error in the original decision.

12.200 The original decision may nonetheless continue to be relevant if the review simply ignores an error in it which continues to have an effect, whether because it has been adopted or because – even if expressed differently – it influences how the court should construe the decision on review. In either event, however, the appeal must be on a point of law, whether it is in relation to the internal review or – for want of a review decision within time – in relation to the original decision.[428]

Review and reconsideration

12.201 There is no right to a review of a decision on an earlier review.[429] Not uncommonly, however, even where there has been a review, a local authority will be willing to reconsider its decision, for example, following receipt of a letter before action.[430] A complaint about the decision on such a reconsideration may still lie to the county court[431] if, but only if, the complaint can be described as still comprising an appeal from the original review decision[432] (which in turn will raise the issue of whether it is still in time).[433]

12.202 In the alternative, it is possible that the decision to reconsider can in context be construed as a withdrawal of the original review decision.[434]

Time for appeal

12.203 The appeal must be brought within 21 days of the applicant being notified of the decision on the internal review, or when the applicant should have been so notified.[435] Where the court office is closed on the final day for lodging the appeal, time is extended until the next

427 HA 1996 s204(1)(b); H(W)A 2014 s88(1)(b).
428 HA 1996 s204(1); H(W)A 2014 s88(1).
429 HA 1996 s202(2); H(W)A 2014 s85(4).
430 See para 12.207.
431 *R v Westminster City Council ex p Ellioua* (1998) 31 HLR 440, CA.
432 *Demetri v Westminster City Council* [2000] 1 WLR 772, CA, at 780/A–B.
433 See para 12.203.
434 See para 12.207.
435 HA 1996 s204(2); H(W)A 2014 s88(2).

day that the office is open.[436] Delivery of the notice of appeal is sufficient to constitute filing; there is no requirement that a court officer receive or authenticate the notice.[437]

Extension of time

12.204 The 21-day limit has been acknowledged as short, indeed 'draconian, as some might think'.[438] Prior to amendment by the Homelessness Act 2002 there was no power for the court to extend time.[439] By HA 1996 s204(2A) and H(W)A 2014 s88(3), the county court now has power to extend time – before or after the 21-day period has expired – for 'good reason'.

12.205 Delay in obtaining public funding to bring an appeal may well constitute an acceptable reason for extension of time[440] as may incompetent legal advice, although there has to be evidence of the latter.[441] Where the applicant was profoundly deaf and had been seeking legal assistance that she could understand and follow, there was a good reason for her appeal not to have been brought within the 21-day time limit.[442]

12.206 The merits of the appeal are irrelevant to deciding whether there is good reason to extend time; the merits come in at the next stage, when – having decided that there is a good reason –

436 *Calverton Parish Council v Nottingham City Council* [2015] EWHC 503 (Admin); *Aadan v Brent LBC* (2000) 32 HLR 848, CA; *Pritam Kaur v S Russell & Sons Ltd* [1973] QB 336. See also *Croke v Secretary of State for Communities and Local Government* [2016] EWHC 248 (Admin) in which the claimant's agent arrived at the court office at 4.25pm on the last day for lodging an appeal. A security guard refused him entry to the court building. The documents were filed a few days later. The High Court held that the principle in *Calverton, Aadan* and *Kaur* did not apply: the court office had been open and available to accept the papers; litigants had to appreciate that there would be security procedures to be completed before being allowed access to the court and had to allow sufficient time to deal with them.

437 *Van Aken v Camden LBC* [2002] EWCA Civ 1724, [2003] 1 WLR 684, [2003] HLR 33.

438 *R v Brent LBC ex p O'Connor* (1998) 31 HLR 923, QBD, per Tucker J at 925.

439 *Honig v Lewisham LBC* (1958) 122 JPJ 302; and *Gwynedd CC v Grunshaw* (1999) 32 HLR 610, CA. See also *O'Connor*, above.

440 *R v Stratford on Avon DC ex p Jackson* [1985] 1 WLR 1319, CA; see also *R v Dacorum BC ex p Brown* (1989) 21 HLR 405, QBD. Cf *Peake v Hackney LBC* [2013] EWHC 2528 (QB) (that time for appeal expired on Christmas Day did not necessarily comprise good reason: nor did the imposition of a time limit give rise to any arguable issue under Article 6).

441 *Poorsalehy v Wandsworth LBC* [2013] EWHC 3687 (QB); it does not automatically follow from the failure to issue in time.

442 *Barrett v Southwark LBC* [2008] EWHC 1568 (QB), [2008] JHL D107.

the court has to decide whether it should exercise its discretion to extend time.[443]

Agreement to further review

12.207 Where an authority agrees to reconsider the review decision, it is possible that the agreement will in substance comprise an agreement on the part of the authority to revoke or withdraw its original decision. Alternatively, it may comprise an agreement to waive, extend or suspend the time limit for appeal from it, or to take no time point.[444] Such an agreement does, however, need to be clearly spelled out.[445] Where an applicant seeking reconsideration is not represented, the authority should take it on itself to make clear the basis on which it is agreeing to reconsider and, in particular, should point out if time to appeal is not being extended.[446]

Letter before action

12.208 The provisions of CPR Part 52 do not require the applicant (or the applicant's legal advisers) to write a letter before action setting out the applicant's case on appeal. Prior to the introduction of the statutory appeal,[447] however – when challenges against adverse decisions were made by way of judicial review – a letter before claim should nonetheless have been written.[448] Given the introduction of a requirement for a pre-action letter in judicial review proceedings,[449] and the fact that the question of costs is a matter for the discretion of the court,[450] the same principles should now be applied (in the absence of special circumstances rendering such a letter impossible, impracticable or pointless).

443 *Short v Birmingham City Council* [2004] EWHC 2112 (QB), [2005] HLR 6. If a judge is minded to strike out an appeal as being outside the 21-day time limit, the applicant is entitled to proper notice so as to enable him or her to meet the point: *Dawkins v Central Bedfordshire Council* [2013] EWHC 4757 (QB).

444 *Demetri v Westminster City Council* [2000] 1 WLR 772, CA, at 780/C–D and 781/E–G. An agreement to conduct a further review could constitute a good reason for the applicant being unable to bring the appeal in time, and would be likely to do so if public funding was not available until after its outcome.

445 *Demetri.*

446 *Demetri,* at 781/H-782/A.

447 And prior to the introduction of the requirement for a pre-action protocol letter in judicial review cases.

448 *R v Horsham DC ex p Wenman* [1995] 1 WLR 680, QBD; *R v Secretary of State for the Home Department ex p Begum* [1995] COD 177.

449 See para 12.141.

450 See Senior Courts Act 1981 s51 and CPR 44.2.

Supporting documents

12.209 The appeal will need to be brought in accordance with CPR Part 52 and the associated Practice Directions (PDs).[451] Three copies of the appellant's notice (plus a further copy for each respondent) must be filed, together with grounds of appeal[452] and a copy of the decision under appeal. Any amendment to the appellant's notice or grounds of appeal normally requires the permission of the court.[453]

12.210 When issuing an appeal, the appellant must file and serve proposed case management directions, with which – within 14 days – the authority must either agree or to which it must propose alternatives.[454] Within the same period, the authority must also disclose any relevant documents which have not previously been disclosed; within 14 days of their receipt, the grounds of appeal may be amended as of right to deal with any new material.[455]

12.211 Notwithstanding the discretion to amend the notice of appeal (other than as of right to deal with new material),[456] the Court of Appeal has emphasised the importance of the grounds in setting the agenda for the appeal hearing and in enabling the respondent (and the court) to understand that agenda from the outset. In one case, Brooke LJ commented that:

> It is thoroughly bad practice to state the barest possible grounds in the original notice of appeal . . ., and then to delay formulating and serving very substantial amended grounds of appeal for five months so that they surfaced for the first time less than a week before the appeal hearing.[457]

Response

12.212 While a respondent's notice may be filed where a respondent seeks to uphold a decision for reasons different from, or additional to, those previously given,[458] this is unlikely to be appropriate in a home-

451 See in particular, PD 52D para 28.1.
452 PD 52B para 4.1; see form N161.
453 CPR 52.17. Note, however, that – unless the court has ordered otherwise – there is a right to amend 'as of right' within 14 days of the authority disclosing relevant material: see para 12.209; CPR PD52D para 28(1)(5)(d).
454 CPR Part 52, PD 52D para 28.1(5)(a), (b).
455 CPR Part 52, PD 52D para 28.1(5)(c), (d).
456 See para 12.209 and footnote 443.
457 *Cramp v Hastings BC; Phillips v Camden LBC* [2005] EWCA Civ 1005 at [72].
458 CPR 52.13.

lessness appeal. If the review (or, on occasion, the original) decision is wrong, then the authority should consent to it being quashed, and proceed to make a fresh decision on the correct basis. The only obvious circumstance when the authority could ask the court to substitute one (wrong) decision with a fresh decision is if the fresh decision is the only decision open to the authority as a matter of law.[459]

12.213 While an authority may well need to concede one or more elements of a challenge before the appeal comes to a hearing, the authority may not withdraw its decision so as to pre-empt the appeal if continuing the appeal could lead to an enduring benefit to the applicant. In *Deugi*,[460] the applicant not only sought to quash the original decision but also sought a variation of it; its withdrawal would have deprived the applicant of the opportunity to seek the variation.

District judges

12.214 As soon as it was appreciated that the CPR permitted district judges to hear Part 52 appeals,[461] a new PD was introduced to prevent them doing so.[462]

12.215 As with judicial review,[463] it is only exceptionally that the court will hear oral evidence,[464] eg where relevant evidence has come to light since the review was concluded.[465]

Costs

12.216 The general rule that costs should follow the event applies even where the matter is remitted to the authority for a fresh decision. It is not appropriate for the county court judge to refuse costs on the basis that it is considered inevitable that the authority will reach the same adverse decision (and that it will be upheld on review and appeal); it is inappropriate for the judge to reach any conclusion on that issue.[466]

459 See paras 12.248–12.261.

460 *Tower Hamlets LBC v Deugi* [2006] EWCA Civ 159, [2006] HLR 28.

461 See the comments of Sir Richard Scott V-C in *Crawley BC v B* (2000) 32 HLR 636, CA.

462 CPR Part 2, PD 2B.9.

463 See para 12.150.

464 *Bubb v Wandsworth LBC* [2011] EWCA Civ 1285, [2012] HLR 13 at [24]–[25].

465 *Bubb* at [26].

466 *Rikha Begum v Tower Hamlets LBC* [2005] EWCA Civ 340, [2005] HLR 34.

12.217 The principles applicable to costs where a claim for judicial review is settled[467] – that a claimant who has secured the substantive relief sought should normally be awarded his or her costs[468] – are also applicable to appeals under HA 1996 s204.[469]

12.218 The court has power to order that costs be set off.[470] The implication of this – discussed above – is that it may be possible to set off costs orders made in the county court against orders made in the High Court, if the proceedings are closely connected,[471] as well as costs in other county court proceedings.

12.219 In *Maloba*,[472] the county court ordered the authority to pay two-thirds of the appellant's costs in relation to a section 204 appeal and refused the authority's application for a stay pending the outcome of any future appeal against its fresh review decision, in which it hoped to be successful and therefore to secure a costs award in its favour, which it would then seek to be set off against those awarded against it in the present case.[473]

12.220 The Court of Appeal accepted that the court's discretion was wide enough in principle to enable it to grant such a stay if it considers it just to do so, but refused to overturn the judge's decision.[474] It was cautious about introducing a general practice which would have the effect of depriving solicitors who acted for successful legally aided clients of payment at normal commercial rates without being able to assess properly the potential wider consequences that this would have.[475]

12.221 It may be observed that it is hard to see that such an anticipatory order could ever be successful unless there was a history of unsuccessful challenges, in which the instant success was a rare or only

467 See paras 12.171–12.176.

468 *R (M) v Croydon LBC* [2012] EWCA Civ 595, [2012] 1 WLR 2607.

469 *Harripaul v Lewisham LBC* [2012] EWCA Civ 266, [2012] HLR 24. See also *Unichi v Southwark LBC* [2013] EWHC 3681 (QB) (authority refused to await conclusion of review pending receipt of psychologist's report which was provided after review issued and on receipt of which authority agreed to carry out a fresh review: the applicant had obtained the substantive relief she had sought; the authority had been alerted to the importance of the report but had decided to conclude the review before it was available; the costs were payable immediately rather than held against any further proceedings).

470 CPR 44.12.

471 See para 12.175.

472 *Waltham Forest LBC v Maloba* [2007] EWCA Civ 1281, [2008] HLR 26.

473 *Maloba* at [65].

474 *Maloba* at [71].

475 *Maloba* at [73].

occurrence. Even so, it would necessarily assume that the same solicitors would be acting, for those who had been successful should surely not properly be deprived of their success-based costs in the event that other solicitors pursued an unsuccessful case.

Wasted costs

12.222 In *Wilson*,[476] a first-instance decision that non-legal officers of an authority could be ordered personally to pay costs, in substance for causing unnecessary legal expenditure by failing to respond to litigation, was overturned and held to have been wrongly made. Lawyers, however, are susceptible to such orders ('wasted costs orders') under Senior Courts Act 1981 s51[477] and CPR 46.8.

12.223 It is appropriate to make a wasted costs order against a legal representative only if:

a) the legal representative acted improperly, unreasonably or negligently;[478]
b) the legal representative's conduct caused a party to incur unnecessary costs; and
c) it is just in all the circumstances to order the legal representative to compensate that party for the whole or part of the costs.[479]

12.224 The test is a moderately high one:

i) improper conduct is that which would attract a sanction from a professional body or which would fairly be stigmatised as being improper;
ii) unreasonable conduct is that which is vexatious or is designed to harass the other side rather than to advance a resolution of the case, or which does not have a reasonable explanation;[480]
iii) negligent conduct is not that which would found a common law action for damages,[481] but a question as to whether the legal

476 *R v Lambeth LBC ex p Wilson* (1997) 30 HLR 64, CA.

477 Inserted by Courts and Legal Services Act 1990 s4.

478 *KOO Golden East Mongolia v Bank of Nova Scotia* [2008] EWHC 1120 (QB), per Silber J; *Hallam Peel & Co v Southwark LBC* [2008] EWCA Civ 1120.

479 The test derives from *Re A Barrister (wasted costs order) (No 1 of 1991)* [1992] 3 All ER 429, CA, and is now incorporated into the PD accompanying CPR Part 48 (at para 53.5).

480 '[The] courts can be trusted to differentiate between errors of judgment and true negligence': *Arthur JS Hall & Co (a firm) v Simons* [2002] 1 AC 615, HL.

481 This is not negligence in any technical sense, see *Re Sternberg, Reed, Taylor and Gill* (1999) *Times* 26 July, CA and *Dempsey v Johnstone* [2003] EWCA Civ 1134, [2003] All ER (D) 515.

> representative conducted himself or herself with the competence to be expected of a professional person.[482]

It must be something akin to abuse of process; a breach of the lawyer's duty to the court.[483]

12.225 A rising tendency to seek an order for wasted costs was curtailed by the Court of Appeal in *Ridehalgh v Horsefield*,[484] where it was said that the courts should be anxious to avoid satellite litigation. Reinforcing the point, the House of Lords has held[485] that wasted costs orders should be confined to questions which are apt for summary disposal by the courts:[486]

> Save in the clearest case, applications against the lawyers acting for an opposing party are unlikely to be apt for summary determination, since any hearing to investigate the conduct of a complex action is itself likely to be expensive and time-consuming. The desirability of compensating litigating parties who have been put to unnecessary expense by the unjustified conduct of their opponents' lawyers is, without doubt, an important public interest, but it is, as the Court of Appeal pointed out in *Ridehalgh v Horsefield* . . . only one of the public interests which have to be considered.[487]

12.226 As a guide, matters such as the following are apt for wasted costs:

- failure to appear;
- conduct which leads to an otherwise avoidable step in the proceedings or the prolongation of a hearing by gross repetition or extreme slowness in the presentation of evidence or argument;
- wasting court time; and
- abuse of process which results in excessive cost.[488]

12.227 Costs that arise as a consequence of difficulties with public funding are unlikely to lead to an order for wasted costs. Where a

482 See *Ridehalgh v Horsefield* [1994] Ch 205, CA.

483 *Persaud (Luke) v Persaud (Mohan)* [2003] EWCA Civ 394, [2003] PNLR 26, CA at [27].

484 [1994] Ch 205, CA; see also *Re A Barrister (wasted costs order)* [1993] QB 293, CA. See *Arthur JS Hall & Co v Simons* [2002] 1 AC 615 and *R v Camden LBC ex p Martin* [1997] 1 WLR 359, QBD, where it was held that there was no power to make a wasted costs order in favour of a person who elects to oppose an ex parte application for permission to seek judicial review.

485 *Medcalf v Mardell* [2002] UKHL 27, [2003] 1 AC 120.

486 See *Wall v Lefever* [1998] 1 FCR 605, CA, where wasted costs orders were said to provide a 'salutary and summary remedy' in clear cases. See also *R v Luton Family Proceedings Court Justices ex p R* [1998] 1 FCR 605, CA.

487 *Medcalf v Mardell* [2002] UKHL 27, [2003] 1 AC 120, per Lord Bingham at [24].

488 *Medcalf*, approving *Harley v McDonald* [2001] 2 AC 678, PC.

solicitor sought an adjournment on the day before the hearing because of difficulties with his client's funding, his failure was an error of judgment, not an act which attracted liability for wasted costs.[489]

12.228 Where a court refuses to make a wasted costs order, it will only be in very rare circumstances that an appeal court will intervene.[490]

Further appeal

12.229 Under the Access to Justice Act 1999 (Destination of Appeals) Order 2016,[491] the appropriate forum for appeal from a county court section 204 or section 88 appeal is to the Court of Appeal as the section 204 or section 88 appeal is itself an 'appeal' (from the decision of the authority), so that an appeal against the county court judge is a second appeal, to be determined by the Court of Appeal.[492]

12.230 A consequence of the 'second appeal' status is that permission cannot be granted by the county court; it must be obtained from the Court of Appeal.[493] An application for permission to appeal must be made in accordance with CPR Part 52. Permission must be requested in an appellant's notice, which must be served within such period as directed by the lower court,[494] or – if no such direction is made – within 21 days of the decision being appealed.[495]

12.231 Witness statements in support of an application for permission to appeal are only appropriate for relevant and admissible evidence (if any) going to the issue before the court and nothing else: submissions in support of the appeal are for advocates to make in skeleton arguments.[496]

12.232 Where a county court has ordered a further review and the authority seeks permission to appeal, the parties should agree that the

489 *Re A Solicitor (wasted costs order)* [1993] 2 FLR 959, CA.

490 *Persaud v Persaud*, above.

491 SI No 917.

492 An appeal against a decision on costs is, however, treated as a first appeal and is therefore to the High Court: see *Handley v Lake Jackson Solicitors* [2016] EWCA Civ 465, [2016] HLR 23; and Access to Justice Act 1999 (Destination of Appeals) Order 2016 reg 5. The county court judge can therefore grant permission to appeal; indeed, it is good practice to ask for permission: *P v P* [2015] EWCA Civ 447.

493 CPR 52.7.

494 Which may be longer or shorter than the period of 21 days required under the CPR: CPR 52.12.

495 CPR 52.12.

496 *William v Wandsworth LBC; Bellamy v Hounslow LBC* [2006] EWCA Civ 535, [2006] HLR 42.

obligation to undertake a fresh review is suspended pending outcome of the appeal. If agreement is not reached, an authority may apply to the Court of Appeal to stay the effect of the order made by the county court. In the event that an authority does undertake a fresh review pending the appeal, however, it is verging on an abuse for the authority not to inform the Court of Appeal that it has done so.[497]

12.233 Permission to bring a second appeal will be granted only if the court is satisfied that:

a) the appeal has a real prospect of success and raises an important point of principle or practice;[498] or
b) there is some other compelling reason for the appeal to be heard.[499]

12.234 Where an appeal raises an important point of principle which has not previously been determined, permission will normally be granted under CPR 52.7(2)(a).[500] When determining whether there is some other compelling reason to grant permission under CPR 52.7(2)(b), the court should apply the following principles:
a) the prospects of success on appeal must be very high;
b) even where the prospects of success are very high, the court may nonetheless conclude that justice does not require the appellant to have the opportunity of a second appeal; but, conversely,
c) if the prospects of success are not very high, there may nevertheless be a compelling reason for a second appeal if the court is satisfied that the first appeal was tainted by procedural irregularity such as to render it unfair.[501]

12.235 In the context of a homelessness appeal, permission was refused in *Azimi*,[502] where the decision of the county court was reached primarily on the facts. By contrast, in *Cramp*,[503] the Court of Appeal gave

497 *William*, above.

498 CPR 52.7(2)(a).

499 CPR 52.7(2)(b).

500 *Uphill v BRB (Residuary) Ltd* [2005] EWCA Civ 60, [2005] 1 WLR 2070. *Uphill* does not comment on the 'real prospect of success' limb as that was only introduced for appeals issued after 3 October 2016: see Civil Procedure (Amendment No 3) Rules 2016 SI No 788.

501 *Upill*, above.

502 *Azimi v Newham LBC* (2000) 33 HLR 51, CA. See also *Ryde v Enfield LBC* [2005] EWCA Civ 1281 (no important point of principle or practice) and *Gentle v Wandsworth LBC* [2005] EWCA Civ 1377 (no obvious injustice).

503 *Cramp v Hastings BC; Phillips v Camden LBC* [2005] EWCA Civ 1005, [2005] HLR 48.

permission to appeal against a decision that an authority's enquiries had been inadequate because the appeal raised an important point of practice. Brooke LJ said:[504]

> In view of the amount of public money that is in issue in cases like this, it would in my judgment be quite wrong for this court to feel that the judgment in *Uphill*[505] represented a fetter on its power to put things right if it has occasion to believe that things are going wrong in an important way in the practical operation of the statutory scheme in Part 7 of the 1996 Act (up to and including the appeal on a point of law to the county court).

12.236 In *Elrify*,[506] it was pointed out that the second appeal is really only the first appeal from a judicial decision, because the appeal to the county court is not in respect of a judicial decision but from the authority's own review decision. This does not mean that CPR 52.7 is inapplicable, but it does mean that the court can take a somewhat more relaxed approach to a second appeal in a homelessness case that has clear merits.[507]

12.237 On an appeal to the Court of Appeal, the primary question is normally not whether the county court judge deciding the first appeal was right, but whether the decision being appealed is right, or at least one that the decision-maker was entitled to reach.[508]

Remedies and relief

Interim relief

12.238 Authorities have power under HA 1996 s204(4) and H(W)A 2014 s88(5) to house pending any appeal (and any subsequent appeal). Interim relief will not be needed on a county court appeal if the authority agrees to use this power.

12.239 Prior to amendment by the Homelessness Act 2002, if an authority refused to exercise this power, the county court could not grant an interim injunction because the applicant had no substantive rights to which an interim injunction could properly be said to be ancillary;[509] accordingly, the only recourse was by way of judicial review.

504 At [66].

505 See para 12.234.

506 *Elrify v Westminster City Council* [2007] EWCA Civ 332, [2007] HLR 36.

507 *Elrify*, at [24].

508 *Danesh v Kensington and Chelsea RLBC* [2006] EWCA Civ 1404, [2007] HLR 17 at [30].

509 *Ali v Westminster City Council* (1998) 31 HLR 349, CA.

12.240 Under HA 1996 s204A or H(W)A 2014 s89, an applicant with a right to appeal to the county court against a local authority's decision on review[510] may now also appeal to the county court if the authority refuses to exercise its power to secure interim accommodation under section 204(4) or section 88, or is only willing to do so for a limited period ending before the final determination of the main appeal.[511]

12.241 Once the county court has dismissed an appeal under section 204, however, it has no remaining function under section 204A so cannot consider an appeal against an authority's decision not to secure interim accommodation for the appellant pending a further appeal to the Court of Appeal.[512]

12.242 This right to appeal under HA 1996 s204A or H(W)A 2014 s89 may be exercised even before the applicant has appealed under section 204 or section 88, provided the latter appeal is against the authority's decision on review: this excludes the possibility of a section 204A or section 89 appeal where the applicant only has a right to appeal against the section 184 or section 86 decision because the authority has not notified the review decision in time.[513] In these circumstances, judicial review remains the only remedy.[514]

12.243 As a matter of good practice, an applicant should include appeals under section 204 and section 204A in one appellant's notice[515] although, if this is not possible, the appeals may be included in separate notices.[516] An appeal under section 204A or section 89 may[517] include an application for an order under section 204A(4)(a) or section 89(4)(a) requiring the authority to secure that accommodation is available for the applicant's occupation.[518]

12.244 If the court makes such an order without notice, the appellant's notice must be served on the authority together with the order.

510 HA 1996 s204A(1); H(W)A 2014 s89(1).

511 HA 1996 s204A(2); H(W)A 2014 s89(2).

512 *Johnson v Westminster City Council* [2013] EWCA Civ 773, [2013] HLR 45. The appropriate course of action is to seek judicial review.

513 HA 1996 s204(1)(b); H(W)A 2014 s88(1)(b).

514 *Davies v Watford BC* [2018] EWCA Civ 529.

515 CPR Part 52D PD para 24.2(1). The PD has not been amended to reflect the position in Wales, but it seems unlikely that a different approach would be thought to apply.

516 CPR Part 52D PD para 24.2(2).

517 And usually will.

518 PD 52D para 28.1(4).

Such an order will normally require the authority to secure that accommodation is available until a hearing date when the authority can make representations as to whether the order should be continued.[519]

12.245 The primary power given to the county court[520] is to order the authority to secure accommodation for the applicant pending determination of the appeal or such earlier time that the court may specify. The court is bound either to quash the authority's section 204(4) decision on accommodation pending appeal, or to confirm it.[521] If the county court decides to quash, it may order the authority to exercise the power for such period as may be specified in the order, up to but not beyond the determination of the main appeal.[522] The power may be exercised only if the court is satisfied that failure to exercise the section 204(4) power would substantially prejudice the applicant's ability to pursue the main appeal.

12.246 Contempt of Court Act 1981 s2(2) uses a similar, although not identical, phrase of 'substantial risk that the course of justice will be seriously prejudiced'. In that context, it has been held that:

> . . . 'substantial' as a qualification of 'risk' does not have the meaning 'weighty' but rather means 'not insubstantial' or 'not minimal'.[523]

12.247 In deciding whether to confirm or quash, the court must apply judicial review principles.[524] In effect, this means applying the approach to decisions to provide interim accommodation in *R v Camden LBC ex p Mohammed*,[525] described above,[526] so that the court can only order the provision of accommodation only if the authority has failed to direct itself properly in accordance with it: *Francis*.[527]

519 PD 52D para 28.1(4).

520 HA 1996 s204A(4)(a); H(W)A 2014 s89(4)(a).

521 HA 1996 s204A(4)(b); H(W)A 2014 s89(4)(b).

522 HA 1996 s204A(5), (6)(b); H(W)A 2014 s89(6), (7).

523 Per Donaldson MR in *Attorney-General v News Group Newspapers Ltd* [1987] QB 1, CA.

524 HA 1996 s204A(4); H(W)A 2014 s89(5).

525 (1998) 30 HLR 315, QBD, as approved in *R v Brighton and Hove Council ex p Nacion* (1999) 31 HLR 1095, CA in relation to challenges under HA 1996 s204 prior to the addition of s204A (see para 12.179).

526 See paras 10.49–10.59. When considering an application for interim accommodation pending an appeal against an authority's review decision, an authority must take into account the grounds of appeal: *Lewis v Havering LBC* [2006] EWCA Civ 1793, [2007] HLR 20.

527 *Francis v Kensington and Chelsea RLBC* [2003] EWCA Civ 443, [2003] HLR 50.

Powers on appeal

12.248 Under its appeal powers, the county court can confirm a decision, or quash it or vary the decision as it thinks fit.[528]

12.249 The power to vary gives the county court a somewhat wider range of powers than a court on judicial review.[529] This does not, however, empower the court to extend its scope beyond 'point of law' (within the meaning given to that phrase that has already been considered).[530] It follows that the power can usually only be used to quash a decision, remitting the matter back to the authority for re-determination, unless – the point of law having been determined – there is only one decision which the authority could lawfully take.[531]

12.250 It may, however, be argued that even though the appeal is confined to a point of law, the power to vary – if the applicant has been successful – allows the court to substitute its own decision for that of the authority (even where matters of judgment or evaluation of facts are inherent).

12.251 It is not a complete answer to say that, since the appeal itself has been on a point of law, there will not be the evidential material before the court on which to do so, because:

a) that will not be true in all cases (and would therefore merely limit the occasions when the power could be used); and
b) it is, in any event, a chicken-and-egg point, for if the court has the wider powers, then material can still be put before it even if only directed or relevant to the exercise of its powers.

12.252 Although this argument is consistent with Parliament having conferred wider powers on the county court than are available on judicial review,[532] it would nonetheless not seem to be available in

528 HA 1996 s204(3); H(W)A 2014 s88(4). Whether the court can refuse to grant relief when the appeal has been overtaken by events and is accordingly pointless is still open. Compare the difference of views in *O'Connor v Kensington and Chelsea RLBC* [2004] EWCA Civ 394, [2004] HLR 37 between the proposition that the court can only refuse to grant relief where the appeal is an abuse of process and the proposition that the court ought to be able to make no order if the appeal is pointless.

529 As noted in *Nipa Begum v Tower Hamlets LBC* [2000] 1 WLR 306, (1999) 32 HLR 445, CA at 313F: see further para 12.193.

530 See para 12.194.

531 See para 12.184.

532 Sedley LJ in *Begum* agreed with Auld LJ as to the ambit of the powers (see para 12.248): 'The jurisdiction of the county court is *at least* as wide as that of a court of judicial review': at 327/B–C, emphasis added.

most cases.[533] The 'decision' which the court has jurisdiction to vary, is a decision for the authority under HA 1996 s202(1) or H(W)A 2014 s85(1), as to eligibility, suitability or local connection or – most relevantly here – 'as to what duty (if any) is owed' to the applicant, under the principal sections.

12.253 Thus, in *Crawley BC v B*,[534] it was held that, once the existing decision had been quashed because of an error of law (admitted by the authority), the authority had to reconsider, which required it to make enquiries and reach a further decision. This will, of course, require the authority to establish (properly) whether or not it has reason to believe, or is of the opinion, or is satisfied as to a particular state of affairs. It is only once the relevant precondition (state of mind of the authority) exists, that the decision about duty can be taken:[535]

> The question, therefore, is whether the judge was entitled, or required, on the material before him, to do more than simply quash the decision ... I would accept that, if that material had shown that the *only* decision as to its duty to provide accommodation or assistance that the Council, acting rationally, could reach was that the duty was that imposed by section 193(2) of the Act, the judge could properly have pre-empted further consideration by making an order to that effect ...[536]

12.254 There is, however, an exception where the power to vary may be used to substitute a decision in the applicant's favour, without remission back to the authority, in order to reinstate a benefit of which the applicant should not have been deprived:

> I would accept, also, that there could be circumstances in which a judge might properly take the view that an applicant ought not to be deprived, by events which had occurred between the date of the original decision and the date of the appeal, of some benefit or advantage to which he would have been entitled if the original decision had been taken in accordance with the law ...[537]

533 See further para 12.256.

534 *Crawley BC v B* (2000) 32 HLR 636, CA.

535 'The decision that the authority has to make is ... as to the category into which its duty falls under the 1996 Act. Although subject to the discipline of sections 202 and 204, that remains a decision based on the satisfaction of the authority as to the issues (which are issues of fact and judgment) of priority need and intentionality. As is well-established, a conclusion as to a public body's satisfaction can only be challenged on public law grounds.' *Crawley BC v B*, above, per Buxton LJ at 645.

536 *Crawley BC v B*, above, per Chadwick LJ at 651; emphasis added.

537 *Crawley BC v B*, above, at 651–652.

12.255 This passage was adopted in *Robinson v Hammersmith and Fulham LBC*[538] in support of the proposition – in relation to a decision on a review – that:

> If the original decision was unlawful . . . the review decision maker should have so held and made a decision that would have restored to the appellant the rights she would have had if the decision had been lawful.

12.256 It would therefore seem that the power to vary does import an alternative to quashing a decision – and its remission to the authority – *either*:

a) where the variation relates to, reflects or rectifies the error of law itself, for example, where the decision can be identified in light of the authority's factual findings and/or evaluation, so that remission to the authority is unnecessary;[539] or
b) where it restores rights of which the applicant has been deprived.

12.257 Thus, in *Ekwuru*,[540] the authority could not, on the material before it, lawfully conclude that the applicant was intentionally homeless. The applicant had twice successfully appealed against the decision of the local authority, upheld on review, that he was intentionally homeless and on each occasion the decision had been quashed and remitted to the authority. Following the second appeal, the authority again found him intentionally homeless and for a third time upheld this decision on review. On appeal, the county court judge again quashed the decision and remitted it. The applicant appealed against the failure of the judge to vary the decision.

12.258 The Court of Appeal concluded that, on the material before it at the date of the third review decision, the authority could not lawfully have concluded that the applicant was intentionally homeless. Accordingly, nothing could be gained by remitting the application for further investigation because there was no real prospect that the authority would discover further material which permitted it properly to conclude that the applicant was intentionally homeless. The circumstances of the case were, however, described as 'exceptional'.[541]

12.259 In *Deugi*,[542] the authority's decision on eligibility and priority need was at issue on appeal, but the judge, having quashed the authority's

538 [2006] EWCA Civ 1122, at [31].
539 Ie, where the only rational conclusion that the authority can reach is that proposed by the applicant: *Slater v Lewisham LBC* [2006] EWCA Civ 394.
540 *Ekwuru v Westminster City Council* [2003] EWCA Civ 1293, [2004] HLR 14.
541 Per Schiemann LJ at [31].
542 *Tower Hamlets LBC v Deugi* [2006] EWCA Civ 159, [2006] HLR 28.

decision, varied it to include a finding that the applicant was not intentionally homeless:

> The question for the judge was whether there was any real prospect that Tower Hamlets, acting rationally and with the benefit of further enquiry, might have been satisfied that Mrs Deugi was intentionally homeless.[543]

12.260 Only if there had been no such prospect could the judge properly have varied the decision. On the facts of the case, there remained a possibility that further enquiries could yet lead to a finding of intentional homelessness, for which reason the decision could only be quashed. [544]

12.261 In *Robinson*,[545] the initial decision ought to have been that the applicant was in priority need (because she was 17),[546] but she had turned 18 by the time of the review. On a strict application of *Mohamed*,[547] the review decision would therefore have concluded that the applicant was – regardless of the correctness of the first decision – not in priority need. The Court of Appeal rejected this:

> I am not persuaded that the above passages[548] have any application to a situation such as the present. It was not in issue in *Mohamed* whether an unlawful decision by the original decision maker had denied rights to the person affected by the decision to which he would otherwise have been entitled.[549]

Damages

12.262 Damages can only be awarded in the county court in respect of a claim within its jurisdiction arising in contract or tort. An award of

543 Per May LJ at [36]. This formulation was said (at [37]) 'to be seen as an amalgam of Chadwick LJ [in *Crawley BC v B*] and Schiemann LJ [in *Ekwuru*], [and] is intended to reflect the fact that the appeal process is in the nature of judicial review'.

544 See also *R (P) v Ealing LBC* [2013] EWCA Civ 1579, [2014] HLR 5 (county court judge wrong to vary a decision to find that an applicant was homeless as it was 'quite impossible' to say that there was no real prospect of any other conclusion) and *R (Woolfe) v Islington LBC* [2016] EWHC 1907 (Admin) (authority had wrongly applied their allocation policy so that the refusal to award the applicant points based on her residence in the borough was quashed and remitted for further investigation and consideration).

545 [2006] EWCA Civ 1122.

546 See para 5.76.

547 *Mohamed v Hammersmith and Fulham LBC* [2001] UKHL 57, [2002] 1 AC 547 – see paras 9.219–9.224.

548 From *Mohamed*.

549 At [31].

compensation is not one of the powers conferred on the county court in relation to a section 204 or section 88 appeal.

12.263 Notwithstanding some differences of opinion over the years,[550] no action will lie for breach of statutory duty for failure properly to perform duties under HA 1996 Part 7,[551] absent some separate cause of action, for example, negligence,[552] or indeed contract.[553] Nor will action for misfeasance in public office[554] be easy to maintain.[555]

Confidentiality

12.264 As noted above,[556] the court has inherent jurisdiction to make an order granting anonymity to an applicant. The same principles are applicable here.[557]

Ancillary relief

12.265 Ancillary relief in the county court is available only where final relief is available.[558] It follows that if the authority has failed to carry out the review but the only basis for complaining about the original decision is on the facts, ie, if there is still no appeal to

550 *Thornton v Kirklees MBC* [1979] QB 626, CA; *Cocks v Thanet DC* [1983] 2 AC 286, (1983) 6 HLR 15, HL; *Mohram Ali v Tower Hamlets LBC* [1993] QB 407, (1992) 24 HLR 474, CA; *Tower Hamlets LBC v Abdi* (1992) 25 HLR 80, CA; *R v Lambeth LBC ex p Barnes* (1992) 25 HLR 140, QBD; *Hackney LBC v Lambourne* (1992) 25 HLR 172, CA; *R v Northavon DC ex p Palmer* (1995) 27 HLR 576, CA.

551 *O'Rourke v Camden LBC* [1998] AC 188, HL; *R (Morris) v Newham LBC* [2002] EWHC 1262 (Admin), [2002] JHL D77; *R (Darby) v Richmond Upon Thames LBC* [2015] EWHC 909 (QB). The same must be true of H(W)A 2014 Part 2.

552 See further *Ephraim v Newham LBC* (1993) 25 HLR 207, CA.

553 For example, in respect of the conditions in accommodation occupied under contract (tenancy or licence), under which the authority is the landlord.

554 Where an officer of a public authority either: i) maliciously exercises a power with the intent to injure a person or persons; or ii) acts knowing that he or she has no power to act where to do so will probably injure a third party: *Three Rivers DC v Bank of England (No 3)* [2003] 2 AC 1, HL. Authorities can themselves be liable for the misfeasance of an officer on the basis of vicarious liability, cf *AA v Southwark LBC* [2014] EWHC 500 (QB) where the authority were liable for the behaviour of housing officers who had engaged in a tortious conspiracy to evict Mr AA.

555 Consider *R (Khazai and others) v Birmingham City Council* [2010] EWHC 2576 (Admin), [2011] JHL D9, where it was held that an email containing unlawful instructions was the product of 'oversight and ill-considered drafting' rather than 'anything more sinister' and as being the work of one person rather than an institutional decision.

556 See para 12.189.

557 See paras 12.189–12.192.

558 County Courts Act 1984 s38.

the county court on a point of law, then – notwithstanding the provisions of HA 1996 s204(1) or H(W)A 2014 s88(1)[559] – the county court cannot make a mandatory order to require the authority to carry out the review.[560]

12.266 As in the Administrative Court on a claim for judicial review, a county court judge on a homelessness appeal may refuse relief on the basis that, notwithstanding a procedural error on the part of the authority, the error would have made no difference to the authority's decision. Where a court identifies procedural flaws in an authority's decision-making process, that decision may, however, only be upheld where the court is satisfied that a properly directed authority would *inevitably* have reached the same decision.

12.267 The test of inevitability is a strict test; regardless of how slight, if the possibility exists that a proper assessment of the circumstances might produce a different decision, the authority must conduct and consider such an assessment.[561]

Ombudsman

12.268 One further forum for challenge[562] is the Local Government Ombudsman,[563] who may investigate claims of maladministration against local authorities, where the claimant can show that he or she has sustained injustice in consequence of the maladministration.[564] If the provisions of LA 2011 ss180–182 are brought fully into force,[565] jurisdiction over maladministration in England in actions taken in relation to the provision or management of social housing will transfer to the housing ombudsman.[566]

559 See para 12.194.

560 See para 12.228–12.249.

561 *Ali v Newham LBC* [2002] HLR 20, CA.

562 For reasons of space, it is not practicable to describe the procedure here in any detail.

563 LGA 1974 Part 3. In England this is called the Commission for Local Administration in England or the 'ombudsman'.

564 LGA 1974 s26.

565 Localism Act 2011 (Commencement No 2 and Transitional Provisions) Order 2013 SI No 722 brought the relevant provisions into force for limited purposes only and no further commencement order has been made: jurisdiction therefore remains with the local government ombudsman.

566 Jurisdiction for all other complaints relating to maladministration generally (such as matters relating to health or education) will remain with the local government ombudsman. See para 12.269.

12.269 'Maladministration' is not defined. In *Eastleigh BC*,[567] Lord Donaldson stated that:[568]

> . . . administration and maladministration in the context of the work of a local authority is concerned with the *manner* in which decisions by the authority are reached and the *manner* in which they are or are not implemented. Administration has nothing to do with the nature, quality or reasonableness of the decision itself.

12.270 The powers of the ombudsman in England were extended by the Local Government and Housing Act 1989[569] and by the Local Government and Public Involvement in Health Act 2007.[570] The latter extends jurisdiction in England from maladministration to include alleged or apparent maladministration in connection with the authority's administrative functions, alleged or apparent failure in a service which the authority has the function to provide, and alleged or apparent failure to provide such a service.[571]

12.271 The ombudsman can recommend that compensation be paid to a complainant. Where maladministration is found, this will usually be ordered, and compensation has commonly been recommended in homelessness cases.

12.272 Complaint to the ombudsman may be particularly appropriate where there are delays in making decisions and inadequacies in decision letters. Even where the applicant is eventually adequately housed, it may be worthwhile proceeding with the complaint in order to obtain compensation.

12.273 Complaints must generally be made within 12 months of the maladministration complained of – although there is discretion to take complaints outside that period, if the ombudsman considers it reasonable so to do.[572]

567 *R v Local Commissioner for the South etc ex p Eastleigh BC* [1988] 1 QB 855, CA.

568 *Eastleigh BC* at 863E/F, as a summary of the decision in *R v Local Commissioner for Administration for the North etc ex p Bradford MBC* [1979] QB 287, CA. Emphasis in original.

569 LGA 1972 Part 2, substituted by the Local Government and Housing Act 1989.

570 Part 9.

571 LGA 1972 s26(1), substituted by Local Government and Public Involvement in Health Act 2007 s173(2) with effect from 1 April 2008, by virtue of Local Government and Public Involvement in Health Act 2007 (Commencement No 5 and Transitional, Saving and Transitory Provision) Order 2008 SI No 917 reg 2(1)(i).

572 LGA 1974 s26B.

12.274 Currently, any person (or his or her representative) can make a direct complaint to the ombudsman.[573] The complaint must generally be made in writing.[574]

12.275 A complaint may also be made by way of referral from a member of a local authority,[575] and a matter may even be considered if it comes to the attention of the ombudsman during the course of an investigation and it appears to the ombudsman that a member of the public has, or may have, suffered injustice in consequence of the matter.[576] The ombudsman has a wide discretion to conduct any investigation in any manner he or she deems appropriate, and to make such inquiries as he or she thinks fit.[577]

12.276 At the conclusion of the investigation, the ombudsman will usually produce a report.[578] If the ombudsman concludes that there has been maladministration, a failure in a service or a failure to provide a service, then the report is laid before the local authority concerned,[579] which must consider the report and, within three months beginning with the date on which they received the report, notify the ombudsman of what action the authority has taken or proposes to take.[580]

12.277 If the ombudsman is not satisfied by the steps taken or proposed to be taken, he or she will produce a further report including his or her own recommendations as to the action the authority should take.[581] The ombudsman has power to publish a copy of the further report, and a separate power to require the authority to publish a statement in a local newspaper about the complaint, including details of the ombudsman's recommendations.[582]

12.278 Authorities have power to make payments to those who have suffered injustice as a result of maladministration, whether or not recommended to do so by the ombudsman.[583]

573 LGA 1974 s26A.

574 The LGO also accepts complaints through an online form or via telephone, see: www.lgo.org.uk/make-a-complaint/how-to-complain.

575 LGA 1974 s26C.

576 LGA 1974 s26D.

577 LGA 1974 s28.

578 LGA 1974 s30(1).

579 LGA 1974 s31.

580 LGA 1974 s31(2).

581 LGA 1974 s31(2A).

582 LGA 1974 s31(2D).

583 LGA 2000 s92.

12.279 If LA 2011 ss180–182 come fully into force,[584] the complaints procedure in England[585] will change considerably.[586] The primary change is in the way complaints are commenced. Under the new procedure, complaints to the housing ombudsman will usually have to be made by a member of the public writing to a 'designated person' and for the designated person to refer the complaint to the ombudsman.[587] Designated persons will include an MP, a member of the local housing authority for the district in which the property concerned is located, or a designated tenant panel.

12.280 The 'designated tenant panel' is a new entity: it is defined as a group of tenants recognised by a social landlord[588] for the purpose of referring complaints against it.[589]

12.281 Exceptionally, there will be no requirement that the complaint be made by such a referral:

a) where the social landlord has its own complaints procedure and more than eight weeks have elapsed since that procedure was exhausted;[590]
b) where a designated person refused in writing to refer the complaint to the ombudsman;[591]
c) where a designated person has agreed in writing to the complaint being made otherwise than by referral.[592]

12.282 Enforcement of decisions by the housing ombudsman will be strengthened. Under the new scheme, the secretary of state will have the power to make provision (by statutory instrument) for the housing ombudsman to be able to apply to a court or tribunal for an order that his or her determination is to be enforced as if it were an order of the court.[593]

584 See para 12.268.
585 The complaints procedure in Wales will remain the same: see para 12.232. There are currently no plans to change this.
586 By inserting new paras 7A–7D into HA 1996 Sch 2, as well as making amendments to the LGA 1974.
587 LA 2011 s180, new HA 1996 Sch 2 para 7A.
588 Including a local authority: LA 2011 s181, new HA 1996 s51(2)(za).
589 LA 2011 s180, new HA 1996 Sch 2 para 7C(1).
590 LA 2011 s180, new HA 1996 Sch 2 para 7B(1).
591 LA 2011 s180, new HA 1996 Sch 2 para 7B(2)(a)(i).
592 LA 2011 s180, new HA 1996 Sch 2 para 7B(2)(a)(ii).
593 LA 2011 s180, new HA 1996 Sch 2 para 7D(1).

12.283 The local government ombudsman regularly publishes details of complaints that have been received.[594] A report in 2011 made the following recommendations, based on an analysis of complaints.

a) authorities should decide on the same day an application is received whether to offer interim accommodation;
b) appropriate arrangements should be put in place to ensure that vulnerable applicants are referred to social services;
c) there should be a proactive approach to identifying actual or potential homelessness when applicants join the housing register and/or provide new information;
d) clear records should be kept of all interviews with applicants, advice given to applicants and decisions made on applications.

12.284 The 2011 report also indicates that maladministration is likely to be found where authorities:

a) use homelessness prevention techniques to block or delay consideration of an application;
b) insist that applicants complete a specific form or be interviewed by a specialist homelessness assessment officer;
c) place a burden of proof on the applicant to demonstrate that he or she is homeless; or
d) defer taking an application merely because it does not appear that the applicant would be in priority need.

12.285 In Wales, the Public Services Ombudsman for Wales has responsibility not only for local administration but also for the health service in Wales, social housing in Wales and for the functions of the former Welsh Administration Ombudsman.

12.286 He or she therefore has power to investigate maladministration and service failure by the Welsh Assembly, Welsh health service, health service providers in Wales, local authorities in Wales and Welsh registered providers of social housing.[595] He or she has power to investigate[596] complaints by or on behalf of a person who claims to

594 There were 169 such reports published for England for 2016/17; thematic reports are published intermittently, eg *Still no place like home*, December 2017 (use of bed and breakfast and other unsuitable accommodation) and *Homelessness: how councils can ensure justice for homeless people*, July 2011 (analysis of complaints received arising out of HA 1996 Part 7).

595 Public Services Ombudsman (Wales) Act (PSO(W)A) 2005 Sch 3.

596 PSO(W)A 2005 ss8, 10.

have suffered injustice or hardship[597] arising from maladministration by an authority in connection with a relevant action,[598] failure in a relevant service[599] provided by an authority and failure by an authority to provide a relevant service.[600]

12.287 The Public Services Ombudsman for Wales also has power, subject to consultation, to issue guidance to local authorities about good administrative practice.[601]

Annex: Specimen documents

12.288 The following are examples of the forms[602] and pleadings both those used in judicial review proceedings, based on an allocation decision and a failure to carry out an assessment, and two appeals against homelessness decisions in the county court:

Allocation decision

a) judicial review pre-action protocol letter before claim;
b) judicial review claim form;
c) judicial review statement of grounds and facts relied on;
d) judicial review acknowledgement of service;
e) judicial review summary grounds for contesting the claim;

Assessment decision

f) judicial review pre-action protocol letter before claim;
g) judicial review statement of grounds and facts relied on;
h) judicial review summary grounds for contesting the claim;

Intentional homelessness decision

i) county court appellant's notice and draft directions;
j) county court grounds of appeal;

Initial help duty

k) county court grounds of appeal.

597 PSO(W)A 2005 s4.
598 PSO(W)A 2005 s7(3).
599 PSO(W)A 2005 s7(4).
600 PSO(W)A 2005 s7.
601 PSO(W)A 2005 s31.
602 The forms in this section are all © Crown Copyright. For reasons of space and simplicity, only one copy of the prescribed forms, eg the prescribed form for a county court appeal, is included, despite there being two sample pleadings included.

Leo & Nevil Solicitors
2404 Nashville Road
Warden
WAR7 8QB

Warden Drane District Council
Legal Services Department
Civic Centre
Warden High Road
Warden
WAR1 9SX

20 June 2017

Your ref: LE/HSG/FIELDS/86915
Our ref: LH/H/FIELDS/01533

Dear Sir/Madam

The following is a letter before claim written in accordance with the pre action protocol for judicial review claims and follows the structure of the model letter in Annex A of the pre-action protocol.

1. Proposed claim for judicial review
To: Warden Drane District Council, Housing Department, Civic Centre, Warden High Road, Warden, WAR1 9SX
Copied to: Warden Drane District Council, Legal Services Department, Civic Centre, Warden High Road, Warden, WAR1 9SX

2. The claimant
The proposed claimant is Ms Jane Fields, 16A Maxwell Square, Warden WAR16 1AB.

3. Reference details
Your ref: LE/HSG/FIELDS/86915.

4. The Claimant's Legal Advisors
Leo & Nevil Solicitors, 2404 Nashville Road, Warden WAR7 8QB. Our ref: LH/H/FIELDS/01533

5. The details of the matter being challenged
The assessment of the claimant by the defendant under its allocation scheme, and the defendant's refusal to increase her points.

6. Interested Parties
None

7. The issue(s)
There are five. First, whether the claimant has been awarded a reasonable preference in accordance with section 166A(3) of the Housing Act 1996 ('the Act'). Secondly, whether the defendant's allocation scheme is in breach

of section 166A(3) of the Act. Thirdly, whether the defendant's discretion to award additional preference complies with section 166A(3) of the Act. Fourthly, whether the defendant has properly applied its allocation scheme to the claimant and, in particular, whether it has acted lawfully by refusing to exercise its residual discretion in her favour, and whether it has properly assessed the issue of overcrowding. Fifthly, whether the defendant's allocation scheme and the application of it to the claimant's case are perverse.

8. The details of the action that the defendant is expected to take
The defendant is required to reassess the claimant and award her more than 250 points under its allocation scheme, and redraft its scheme so that reasonable and additional preference is properly awarded.

9. ADR Proposals
The claimant is prepared to have a without prejudice meeting and/or negotiations to try to resolve this matter without litigation, as suggested by para 9 of the pre-action protocol for judicial review claims. If the defendant has other suggestions for alternative dispute resolution, the claimant is willing to consider them.

10. The details of information sought
An explanation by the defendant of how its allocation scheme purports to operate lawfully in relation to the award of reasonable and additional preference.

11. The details of any documents that are considered relevant and necessary
A full copy of the defendant's allocation scheme so that the claimant can satisfy herself that the copy that she has seen is the one being applied by the defendant.

12. The address for reply and service of court documents
This is set out at 4 above.

13. Proposed reply date
The claimant expects a reply within 14 days of receipt of this letter.

Yours sincerely,

Judicial Review
Claim Form

Notes for guidance are available which explain how to complete the judicial review claim form. Please read them carefully before you complete the form.

In the High Court of Justice Administrative Court	
Help with Fees - Ref no. (if applicable)	HWF- -

For Court use only	
Administrative Court Reference No.	
Date filed	

Seal

Is your claim in respect of refusal of an application for fee remission? ☐ Yes ☐ No

SECTION 1 Details of the claimant(s) and defendant(s)

Claimant(s) name and address(es)

name
Jane Fields

address
16A Maxwell Square
Warden
WAR16 1AB

Telephone no. 012557 932831
Fax no. n/a
E-mail address jane.fields@googliemail.com

Claimant's or claimant's legal representatives' address to which documents should be sent.

name
Leo & Nevil Solicitors

address
2404 Nashville Road
Warden
WAR7 8QB

Telephone no. 012557 168932
Fax no. n/a
E-mail address housing@leoandnevil.co.uk

Claimant's Counsel's details

name
Julia Clunes

address
Justice Chambers
Warden Drane
Warden, WAR 1AA

Telephone no. 012557 204204
Fax no. n/a
E-mail address julia.clunes@justicechambers.com

1st Defendant

name
Warden Drane District Council

Defendant's or (where known) Defendant's legal representatives' address to which documents should be sent.

name
Warden Drane District Council – Legal Services

address
Civic Centre
Warden High Road
Warden, WAR1 9SX

Telephone no. 012557 132000
Fax no. n/a
E-mail address legal@warden.gov.uk

2nd Defendant

name

Defendant's or (where known) Defendant's legal representatives' address to which documents should be sent.

name

address

Telephone no.
Fax no.
E-mail address

SECTION 2 Details of other interested parties

Include name and address and, if appropriate, details of DX, telephone or fax numbers and e-mail

name	name
address	**address**
Telephone no. / **Fax no.**	**Telephone no.** / **Fax no.**
E-mail address	**E-mail address**

SECTION 3 Details of the decision to be judicially reviewed

Decision:
Failure by the defendant authority to operate a lawful allocation scheme and properly to afford the claimant the appropriate preference within the terms of the scheme

Date of decision:
30 May 2016 and continuing

Name and address of the court, tribunal, person or body who made the decision to be reviewed.

name	address
Housing Department, Warden Drane DC	Civic Centre Warden High Road Warden, WAR1 9SX

SECTION 4 Permission to proceed with a claim for judicial review

I am seeking permission to proceed with my claim for Judicial Review.

Is this application being made under the terms of Section 18 Practice Direction 54 (Challenging removal)? ☐ Yes ☑ No

Are you making any other applications? If Yes, complete Section 8. ☐ Yes ☑ No

Is the claimant in receipt of a Civil Legal Aid Certificate? ☑ Yes ☐ No

Are you claiming exceptional urgency, or do you need this application determined within a certain time scale? If Yes, complete Form N463 and file this with your application. ☐ Yes ☑ No

Have you complied with the pre-action protocol? If No, give reasons for non-compliance in the box below. ☑ Yes ☐ No

Have you issued this claim in the region with which you have the closest connection? (Give any additional reasons for wanting it to be dealt with in this region in the box below). If No, give reasons in the box below. ☑ Yes ☐ No

Does the claim include any issues arising from the Human Rights Act 1998?
If Yes, state the articles which you contend have been breached in the box below. ☐ Yes ☑ No

SECTION 5 Detailed statement of grounds

☐ set out below ☑ attached

Please see attached statement of facts and grounds

SECTION 6 Aarhus Convention claim

I contend that this claim is an Aarhus Convention claim ☐ Yes ☑ No

If Yes, indicate in the following box if you do not wish the costs limits under CPR 45.43 to apply.

If you have indicated that the claim is an Aarhus claim set out the grounds below, including (if relevant) reasons why you want to vary the limit on costs recoverable from a party.

SECTION 7 Details of remedy (including any interim remedy) being sought

1) Quashing order to quash the defendant's allocation scheme.

2) Further or alternatively, a declaration that the scheme is unlawful in that it failed to afford the statutory preferences required by s.166A(3), Housing Act 1996

3) Further or other relief

4) Costs

SECTION 8 Other applications

I wish to make an application for:-

SECTION 9 Statement of facts relied on

Please see attached

Statement of Truth

I believe (The claimant believes) that the facts stated in this claim form are true.

Full name____________________

Name of claimant's solicitor's firm ____________________

Signed____________________ Position or office held____________________

Claimant ('s solicitor) (if signing on behalf of firm or company)

SECTION 10 Supporting documents

If you do not have a document that you intend to use to support your claim, identify it, give the date when you expect it to be available and give reasons why it is not currently available in the box below.

Please tick the papers you are filing with this claim form and any you will be filing later.

- [x] Statement of grounds — [ ] included [x] attached
- [x] Statement of the facts relied on — [ ] included [x] attached
- [ ] Application to extend the time limit for filing the claim form — [ ] included [ ] attached
- [ ] Application for directions — [ ] included [ ] attached
- [ ] Any written evidence in support of the claim or application to extend time
- [ ] Where the claim for judicial review relates to a decision of a court or tribunal, an approved copy of the reasons for reaching that decision
- [x] Copies of any documents on which the claimant proposes to rely
- [x] A copy of the legal aid or Civil Legal Aid Certificate *(if legally represented)*
- [x] Copies of any relevant statutory material
- [x] A list of essential documents for advance reading by the court *(with page references to the passages relied upon)*
- [ ] Where a claim relates to an Aarhus Convention claim, a schedule of the claimant's financial resources. — [ ] included [ ] attached

If Section 18 Practice Direction 54 applies, please tick the relevant box(es) below to indicate which papers you are filing with this claim form:

- [ ] a copy of the removal directions and the decision to which the application relates — [ ] included [ ] attached
- [ ] a copy of the documents served with the removal directions including any documents which contains the Immigration and Nationality Directorate's factual summary of the case — [ ] included [ ] attached
- [ ] a detailed statement of the grounds — [ ] included [ ] attached

Reasons why you have not supplied a document and date when you expect it to be available:-

Signed ______________________________ Claimant ('s Solicitor)________________________

IN THE HIGH COURT OF JUSTICE **Claim No.**
QUEEN'S BENCH DIVISION
ADMINISTRATIVE COURT

BETWEEN

THE QUEEN
(on the application of
JANE FIELDS) **Claimant**

–and–

WARDEN DRANE
DISTRICT COUNCIL **Defendant**

STATEMENT OF FACTS AND GROUNDS

STATEMENT OF FACTS

Introductory

1. The claimant is a 33 year old woman with 3 children – Sally (aged 12), Margaret (aged 11) and Peter (aged 10). Peter is quadriplegic and is confined to a wheel-chair. Sally suffers from severe attention-deficit and hyper-activity disorder. The claimant is unable to work as she is the sole carer of Peter.
2. On 14 July 2016, she applied to the defendant authority for accommodation under Part 6 of the Housing Act 1996, and was duly registered on the authority's housing register.

Background

3. In January 2016, the claimant, her partner and her children moved to private rented accommodation in the authority's area in order to be closer to family members who were able to provide support to Sally and Peter.
4. In March 2016, the claimant left the accommodation that she shared with her former partner, due to domestic violence. The claimant secured her current accommodation, which is a one-bedroom flat, occupied under a private tenancy. The flat is located on the second-floor. There is no lift.
5. She applied to the authority as homeless under Part 7 of the Housing 1996. The authority found that – although she was eligible for assistance and in priority need – the claimant was not homeless as she had

accommodation that was available for her occupation and that is was reasonable for her to continue to occupy it. That decision was upheld on review and the claimant did not appeal.

6. The claimant applied to be registered on the authority's housing register. She provided medical evidence as to her children's medical needs and information on the overcrowded nature of her current accommodation, in particular that:
   (a) there are two girls, a disabled boy and the claimant living in a one-bedroom flat, the girls share the only bedroom and the claimant and her son sleep in the living room;
   (b) the bedroom is 8 foot x 8 foot – there is room for two single beds but no other furniture;
   (c) Sally's severe ADHD causes her to act impulsively and without regard to the consequences of her actions, this can have dangerous consequences in a confined space and places the other members of the household at risk; and,
   (d) the claimant has severe difficulties taking Peter out of the flat as she has to carry him down two flights of stairs and return for his wheelchair – although she is currently able to carry Peter, it is unlikely that she will be able to do so as he grows.
7. In September 2016, the authority assessed the medical needs of Peter and Sally and visited the flat to assess its size and determine whether it was overcrowded. As a result of those assessments (and expert evidence obtained by the claimant), the authority found that it was statutorily overcrowded, that both children had medical needs and that the family had a need for accommodation with an additional bedroom.
8. The current position is that the claimant is registered on the authority's housing register, awaiting an allocation of two-bedroom accommodation, in accordance with Part 6 of the Housing 1996.

The authority's allocation scheme

9. The authority's allocation scheme operates principally – but not exclusively – by means of 'choice-based lettings'. In broad terms, this means that applicants are given points to reflect their priority according to criteria set out in the scheme, and are informed of the types of property for which they are eligible. They may then bid for any properties of the appropriate type which are advertised as available to let. The bidding applicant with the highest number of points is offered the property. It is estimated by the authority that an applicant requires a minimum of 250 points before there is any realistic possibility that he will be able successfully to bid for accommodation.
10. In summary, the principal material provisions of the scheme are as follows.
11. Part 1 of the Scheme governs applications under Part 6 of the Housing Act 1996. The scheme provides that all applications are to be assessed using a points system.

12. Paragraphs 1.3 and 1.4 of the scheme make provision for various categories of applicant (those owed a duty as homeless under Part 7, Housing Act 1996; young people leaving care; people moving to larger accommodation to foster or adopt a child; people with learning disabilities; applicants who have successfully completed rehabilitation from drug or alcohol dependency) to be afforded 300 points, thereby essentially obtaining an overriding priority for accommodation.

Points for overcrowding

13. Where an applicant claims to reside in overcrowded accommodation, the application is referred to a panel which assesses the accommodation. The panel has power to award a maximum of 12 points. Those points are awarded on the basis of a space assessment; the scheme assumes that a room which is 60 square feet can accommodate two persons of any age and no account is taken of the sex of the occupants or their relationship to one another.
14. On the basis of the space assessment, the panel calculates the number of bedrooms required and may award an applicant three points for each extra bedroom required.

Medical and Welfare points

15. The scheme allows 10 points to be awarded on medical or welfare grounds. Paragraph. 2.4 provides:

> 'The panel may award a set 10 points on medical or welfare grounds. In calculating the amount of points (if any) to award, the panel shall have regard to any medical reports supplied but ultimately shall use their absolute discretion to award a household points on this basis.'

General points

16. All applicants are entitled to 'time points' awarded at the rate of 10 points for every year spent on the waiting list for accommodation.
17. Additionally, all applicants may receive 100 income points if they are 'unable (on financial grounds) to meet their own housing needs'.
18. Local connection points, at the rate of 50, are awarded to those applicants who live in the Borough and have done so by choice for five years.
19. The authority retains an absolute discretion to award up to 75 additional points, if it considers the circumstances justify doing so. Provision is also made for the award of other points, including for existing tenants of the authority who apply for a transfer to smaller accommodation.

The claimant's points

20. The claimant has been awarded the following points:

100 income points
10 time points

10 medical and welfare points
3 overcrowding points

21. The overcrowding panel calculated the claimant's entitlement to points on the basis that the household requires only one additional bedroom as the house comprises only four persons.
22. In assessing the need for medical and welfare points, the panel had regard to medical reports submitted in relation to both Peter and Sally. The panel accepted that both children had medical and welfare needs that were not being met in their current accommodation. On the basis of that conclusion they awarded the set 10 points.
23. The claimant has bid for a number of properties under the choice-based scheme, but 173 points has been insufficient for any bid to be successful.

Pre-claim correspondence

24. The claimant has been in correspondence with the authority since September 2016, seeking the award of additional points. The claimant has sought three additional overcrowding points, on the basis that her household requires a three bedroom property. She has also sought to obtain additional medical and welfare points on the basis that two of her children have (accepted) medical and welfare needs, such that she should be entitled to a further 10 points on that basis.
25. The claimant has also asked the authority to exercise its residual discretion to award 50 further points on the grounds that her household's need for alternative accommodation is severe.
26. The authority has refused those requests. In letters dated 12 December 2016, 14 February 2017, and 16 May 2017, the authority has consistently stated that the claimant is not entitled to further points and has refused to exercise the residual discretion.
27. The only suggestions offered by the letters were that the claimant take up a council scheme to obtain a private sector tenancy or else move to another area where accommodation is in greater supply.
28. On 20 June 2017, the claimant's legal representatives sent the authority a pre-action protocol letter before action, which asserted (a) that the authority's allocation scheme was unlawful, alternatively (b) that the way in which the allocation scheme had been applied to the claimant was unlawful. The authority was invited to withdraw its scheme or to award the claimant sufficient points

STATEMENT OF GROUNDS

Allocations Law

29. The claimant and her children remain in the flat, awaiting an allocation of accommodation under Part 6. By section 166A(14) of the Housing Act 1996, the authority may only lawfully allocate such accommodation in accordance with the provisions of its allocation scheme.

30. This section provides that every local housing authority shall have an allocation scheme for determining priorities, and as to the procedure to be followed in allocating housing accommodation (s166A(1)).
31. As a person who resides in overcrowded and unsatisfactory housing conditions and as a person who needs to move on medical or welfare grounds, the claimant is entitled to a reasonable preference in the allocation of Part 6 accommodation. Section 166A(3) provides that such preference must be afforded to certain priority groups, in the following terms.

> '(2) As regards priorities, the scheme shall be framed so as to secure that reasonable preference is given to –
>
> . . .
>
> (c) people occupying insanitary or overcrowded housing or otherwise living in unsatisfactory housing conditions;
> (d) people who need to move on medical or welfare grounds (including any grounds relating to a disability); and
>
> . . .'.

The scheme may also be framed so as to give additional preference to particular descriptions of people within this subsection (being descriptions of people with urgent housing needs).'

32. Although the courts should be slow to interfere with the allocation policy of a local authority (*R (Ahmad) v Newham LBC* [2009] UKHL 14, [2009] HLR 31), where an allocation scheme is clearly irrational, even on a relatively narrow aspect, it should be struck down. The purpose of an allocation scheme should be justified properly and authorities should not rely on 'bald statements': *Birmingham City Council v Ali; Moran v Manchester City Council (Secretary of State for Communities and Local Government and another intervening)* [2009] UKHL 36, [2009] HLR 41.
33. Overcrowded housing (para 31, above), is defined in Part 10, Housing Act 1985. A property is overcrowded if either the room standard (s325) or space standard is contravened.
34. The room standard is contravened when the number of people sleeping in a dwelling and the number of rooms available as sleeping accommodation is such that two persons of opposite sexes who are not living together as man and wife are forced to sleep in the same room:
    (a) children under the age are left out of the account; and,
    (b) a room is available as sleeping accommodation if it is of a type normally used in the locality either as a bedroom, living room or other habitable room.
35. The Space Standard provides that the permitted number of persons per room is the smaller of the number of persons obtained from the following two calculation methods:

    Where a house consists of:
    1 room – 2 persons

2 rooms – 3 persons
3 rooms – 5 persons
4 rooms – 7½ persons
5 rooms or more – 2 for each room
Or

110 sq. ft. or more	2
90 sq. ft. or more but less than 110 sq. ft.	1½
70 sq. ft. or more but less than 90 sq. ft.	1
50 sq. ft. or more but less than 70 sq. ft.	½

No account shall be taken of a child under the age of one.
A child of one to ten counts as a ½ unit.

GROUND ONE Error of law – no reasonable preference

36. The effect of the scheme is not to confer any reasonable preference at all on the claimant; unless and until the claimant has resided in the authority's area for five years, she has and will have no preference at all in practical terms.

37. The claimant has been awarded 10 points on medical grounds and a further 3 on the grounds of overcrowding. Those additional points give her no increased priority in practice; although the claimant and her family could remain in their current accommodation, when she is evicted or has to leave because she can no longer physically manage with her disabled son on the second floor, she will be entitled to apply as homeless and receive an additional 300 points.

38. The claimant and her family have no chance whatsoever of bidding successfully for a property unless or until they become homeless. Thus the claimant is in an even worse position than if she were to be evicted from her accommodation, as she would then receive 300 points as a homeless person.

39. In the context of the scheme, the award of a maximum 12 overcrowding points and 10 medical points is *de minimis* and has no effect on priority whatsoever, unless the applicant has a preference in another category.

40. The absence of any real preference can be seen by analysis of the points awarded to the claimant. Aside from the 10 medical points and the 3 overcrowding points, she has received 100 income points, 10 time points.

41. The only points which are related to the claimant's statutory right to a reasonable preference are the 13 points received for overcrowding and medical need. She will not be able to increase her points total at all, unless her circumstances change and she falls within another category of need.

42. The claimant's points total is significantly below that needed to have any possibility of successfully bidding for a property under Part 6. The only option that the authority has been able to suggest is that, with three children, one of whom is disabled, she could move out of the area where she has lived since childhood.

43. To describe a scheme which operates in this way as securing a reasonable preference to persons who have a medical need or a need based on overcrowding (section 166A(3)(c) and (d)), is a misuse of language.

GROUND TWO Error of law – frustrating the purpose of the 1996 Act

44. The provision of a maximum of 23 points to families with medical needs in overcrowded accommodation does not amount to securing a reasonable or any preference, and is contrary to – and frustrates – the scheme of Part 6 of the Housing 1996.

45. It is plain from the scheme itself, from the correspondence referred to above, and from the manner in which the scheme is operated, that the scheme is designed to keep families in overcrowded accommodation or with medical needs from being eligible for accommodation for as long as possible before permitting them sufficient points to have any prospect at all of bidding successfully for a tenancy under Part 6.

46. This is demonstrated by the following matters:
    (a) the availability of only 10 points on medical grounds;
    (b) the availability of only 12 points on the grounds of overcrowding, regardless of how overcrowded the property is;
    (c) the availability of 300 points where an alternative statutory preference category (homelessness) exists.

47. This is unlawful and conflicts with and frustrates the purposes of the 1996 Act, in particular the statutory intention concerning the statutory preference to be afforded to those with medical need or those in overcrowded accommodation.

GROUND THREE Irrationality – discretion

48. The scheme purports to confer 'additional preference' on persons who, in the absolute discretion of the defendant, have circumstances that give them 'urgent housing needs'. The only provision under the scheme for the award of additional points (other than waiting time) is the defendant's residual discretion to award up to 75 points. This is not a rational means by which to assess need, nor is it a rational means by which a person in the position of the claimant could ever achieve an additional preference, having regard to the maximum points available under the 'additional preference discretion'.

GROUND FOUR Policy applied unlawfully

49. In the alternative, if the policy is not unlawful, the application of the policy to the claimant's circumstances has been unlawful.

Failure to exercise the residual discretion

50. It is unlawful to fail to give any proper priority to the claimant's claim, not least because to do so requires her to remain in statutorily overcrowded accommodation that is fundamentally unsuitable to the medical needs of her household.

51. In the claimant's case, there were compelling factors which ought to have led to an exercise of discretion in her favour: namely the matters set out at paragraph 6, above.

Failure properly to assess the issue of overcrowding

52. The claimant has been awarded 3 points on the grounds of overcrowding, on the basis that her household only requires one additional bedroom (ie two bedrooms in total). If that conclusion is correct, the claimant would be required to share a bedroom with her disabled son, while her two daughters – one of whom has a medical need – would also be required to share a room.
53. In concluding that two-bedroom accommodation would suffice for the claimant's household, the authority has acted irrationally and contrary to the medical evidence that was before it when making its decision on overcrowding.

GROUND FIVE Perversity

54. Further, or alternatively, the defendant's policy, and the treatment which the defendant has given to the claimant's application are both unreasonable in the *Wednesbury* sense.

Julia Clunes
Justice Chambers, Warden

N462

Judicial Review
Acknowledgment of Service

In the High Court of Justice Administrative Court	
Claim No.	
Claimant(s) (including ref.)	Jane Fields (LH/H/fields/01533)
Defendant(s)	Warden Drane DC (LE/HSG/Fields/86915)
Interested Parties	

Name and address of person to be served

name
Warden Drane DC

address
Civic Centre
Warden High Rd
Warden
WAR 1 96X

SECTION A

Tick the appropriate box

1. I intend to contest all of the claim	☑	complete sections B, C, D and F
2. I intend to contest part of the claim	☐	
3. I do not intend to contest the claim	☐	complete section F
4. The defendant (interested party) is a court or tribunal and **intends** to make a submission.	☐	complete sections B, C and F
5. The defendant (interested party) is a court or tribunal and **does not intend** to make a submission.	☐	complete sections B and F
6. The applicant has indicated that this is a claim to which the Aarhus Convention applies.	☐	complete sections E and F
7. The **Defendant** asks the Court to consider whether the outcome for the claimant would have been **substantially different** if the conduct complained of had not occurred [see s.31(3C) of the Senior Courts Act 1981]	☐	A summary of the grounds for that request must be set out in/accompany this Acknowledgment of Service

Note: If the application seeks to judicially review the decision of a court or tribunal, the court or tribunal need only provide the Administrative Court with as much evidence as it can about the decision to help the Administrative Court perform its judicial function.

SECTION B

Insert the name and address of any person you consider should be added as an interested party.

name

address

Telephone no. | Fax no.

E-mail address

name

address

Telephone no. | Fax no.

E-mail address

SECTION C

Summary of grounds for contesting the claim. If you are contesting only part of the claim, set out which part before you give your grounds for contesting it. If you are a court or tribunal filing a submission, please indicate that this is the case.

Please see attached summary grounds of resistance

SECTION D

Give details of any directions you will be asking the court to make, or tick the box to indicate that a separate application notice is attached.

None

If you are seeking a direction that this matter be heard at an Administrative Court venue other than that at which this claim was issued, you should complete, lodge and serve on all other parties Form N464 with this acknowledgment of service.

SECTION E

Response to the claimant's contention that the claim is an Aarhus claim

Do you deny that the claim is an Aarhus Convention claim? ☐ Yes ☑ No

If Yes, please set out your grounds for denial in the box below.

SECTION F

*delete as appropriate

*(I believe)(The defendant believes) that the facts stated in this form are true.

*I am duly authorised by the defendant to sign this statement.

(If signing on behalf of firm or company, court or tribunal)

Position or office held

(To be signed by you or by your solicitor or litigation friend)

Signed

Date

Give an address to which notices about this case can be sent to you	If you have instructed counsel, please give their name address and contact details below.
name Legal Services	**name** Clare Ronethun
address Warden Drane DC Civic Centre Warden High Rd Warden WAR1 96X	**address** Smith Chambers 96 Smith Lane London ECR1 9SS
Telephone no. 012557 123000 — **Fax no.** n/a	**Telephone no.** 0207 999 8118 — **Fax no.** n/a
E-mail address Legal@warden.gov.uk	**E-mail address** clairer@smithchambers.law.co.uk

Completed forms, together with a copy, should be lodged with the Administrative Court Office (court address, over the page), at which this claim was issued within 21 days of service of the claim upon you, and further copies should be served on the Claimant(s), any other Defendant(s) and any interested parties within 7 days of lodgement with the Court.

Administrative Court addresses

- Administrative Court in **London**

  Administrative Court Office, Room C315, Royal Courts of Justice, Strand, London, WC2A 2LL.

- Administrative Court in **Birmingham**

  Administrative Court Office, Birmingham Civil Justice Centre, Priory Courts, 33 Bull Street, Birmingham B4 6DS.

- Administrative Court in **Wales**

  Administrative Court Office, Cardiff Civil Justice Centre, 2 Park Street, Cardiff, CF10 1ET.

- Administrative Court in **Leeds**

  Administrative Court Office, Leeds Combined Court Centre, 1 Oxford Row, Leeds, LS1 3BG.

- Administrative Court in **Manchester**

  Administrative Court Office, Manchester Civil Justice Centre, 1 Bridge Street West, Manchester, M3 3FX.

IN THE HIGH COURT OF JUSTICE **Claim No.**
QUEEN'S BENCH DIVISION
ADMINISTRATIVE COURT

BETWEEN

THE QUEEN
(on the application of
JANE FIELDS) **Claimant**

-and-

WARDEN DRANE
DISTRICT COUNCIL **Defendant**

SUMMARY GROUNDS FOR
CONTESTING THE CLAIM

Lawfulness of the allocations policy

1. The defendant's allocation policy is lawful and cannot successfully be challenged for the following reasons.

Error of law – reasonable preference

2. The scheme complies with the requirements of Part 6 of the Housing Act 1996. A reasonable preference is afforded in accordance with section 166A(3) as all of the priority groups are afforded points that would not be available to persons who did not qualify under those categories.
3. It cannot be said that the preference awarded on overcrowding or medical grounds is not a reasonable preference. When affording a reasonable preference the requirement is that persons entitled to such a preference must be given a 'head start' over other applicants (*R (A) v Lambeth LBC* [2002] EWCA Civ 1084, [2002] HLR 57). The scheme achieves this by providing additional points for need arising on medical or overcrowding grounds.
4. In designing the allocations scheme the authority has determined – as it is entitled to do – that priority on those grounds should be given less (but still reasonable) preference when compared with other categories of need such as the homeless. The extent of the reasonable preference is a matter for the authority to determine and can be challenged only on *Wednesbury* grounds.

Error of law – frustration of the purpose of the 1996 Act

5. An additional preference is given to, *inter alia*, the homeless. That is permissible under the terms of the statute (s166A) and accords with the

purpose of the interrelationship between Parts 6 and 7 of the Act. The authority cannot be criticised for deciding to award additional preference to the homeless over those in other priority groups.

6. It is absurd to suggest that the scheme is designed to keep families in overcrowded accommodation or with medical needs from being eligible for accommodation for as long as possible. Families falling within those groups are awarded additional points, thereby enhancing their possibility of successfully bidding for accommodation under the choice-based lettings scheme.

Irrationality – discretion

7. It is not irrational to have a residual discretion (*R v Islington LBC, ex p Reilly and Mannix* (1998) 31 HLR 651, QBD see also *R (Ahmad) v Newham LBC* [2009] UKHL 14, [2009] HLR 31), such a discretion is necessary to ensure that the scheme operates efficiently and can be adapted to unforeseen or individual circumstances.

Unlawful application of the policy

8. The authority's failure to exercise the residual discretion can only be challenged on *Wednesbury* grounds. It is for local authorities to determine the allocation of accommodation and they are afforded a wide margin of appreciation when doing so and when applying the scheme. It is not possible for the claimant to demonstrate that the decision not to exercise the residual discretion is so unreasonable as to be perverse.

9. Further, the issue of overcrowding has been considered in accordance with the scheme and the authority's policy for assessing overcrowding. There is no challenge to that policy and the claim under this head must fail. On the claimant's own case, the authority had regard to the medical evidence submitted and it is a matter for the authority – applying its policies – to determine the weight to be given to that medical evidence.

Challenge futile

10. In any event, the defendant is currently in the process of updating its scheme in accordance with its modernisation agenda and its commitment to continuous improvements in its services. It is envisaged that the new allocations scheme will be in place some time during 2017/18. The defendant cannot move any more quickly to replace its existing policy than this, whatever rulings the court may make on this application.

11. The claimant should await adoption of the new policy and challenge that within three months of its adoption if she believes that she has grounds for so doing.

12. For those reasons, it is submitted that the claimant is not entitled to the relief claimed, or to any relief.

Claire Ronethun
Smith Chambers, London

Leo & Nevil Solicitors
2404 Nashville Road
Warden
WAR7 8QB

Warden Drane District Council
Legal Services Department
Civic Centre
Warden High Road
Warden
WAR1 9SX

20 April 2018

Your ref: LE/HSG/PEAK/1955
Our ref: LH/H/PEAK/1678

Dear Sir/Madam

This is a letter before claim written in accordance with the pre-action protocol for judicial review claims. It follows the structure of the model letter in Annex A of the pre-action protocol.

1. Proposed claim for judicial review
To: Warden Drane District Council, Housing Department, Civic Centre, Warden High Road, Warden, WAR1 9SX

And copied to: Warden Drane District Council, Legal Services Department, Civic Centre, Warden High Road, Warden, WAR1 9SX

2. The claimant
Mr Anthony Peak, 15 Golden Square, Warden, WAR14 1AB

3. Your reference details]
Your ref: LE/HSG/PEAK/1955

4. The claimant's legal advisers
Leo & Nevil Solicitors, 2404 Nashville Road, Warden, WAR7 8QB

5. The details of the matter being challenged
Failure to carry out an assessment under s.189A, Housing Act 1996

6. Interested Parties
There are no interested parties

7. The issue
Mr Peak is the assured shorthold tenant of 15 Golden Square, Warden, WAR14 1AB. His landlord recently served him with notice under s.21, Housing Act 1988. That notice expires on 1 May 2018. Accordingly, he is threatened with homelessness for the purposes of s.175(4), Housing Act 1996.

Following a telephone conversation with an officer of the authority, he attended a meeting at your offices on 19 April 2018. At that meeting he provided a copy of the s.21 notice and explained that, once the notice expired, he would have no other accommodation available to him. He also provided a copy of his UK passport.

At that stage, the authority should have been satisfied that he was threatened with homelessness and eligible for assistance so that, by s.189A, Housing Act 1996, they were required to carry out an assessment of his case. Such an assessment should have included an assessment of

(a) the circumstances that caused him to become threatened with homelessness;
(b) his housing needs including, in particular, what accommodation would be suitable for him; and,
(c) what support would be necessary for him to be able to have and retain suitable accommodation.

In fact, he was given a cursory interview by a housing caseworker, who took a copy of his documents, asked him a number of questions and then provided him with an annotated map of the local area, showing the location of estate agents and letting agents. He was told to go and talk to those agents and to return only if they were unable to find any accommodation for him. He was given no notification in writing of an assessment nor was he provided with any written statement of steps to be taken or failure to agree steps, as required by s189A(3)–(8).

8. The details of the action that the defendant is expected to take
The authority is expected to carry out an assessment under s.189A with immediate effect.

9. ADR proposals
It is not clear what form of alternative dispute resolution might be appropriate here, but the claimant confirms that he is willing to have a without prejudice meeting to try and resolve this matter without litigation.

10. The details of any information sought
Details of what, if any, training the authority provided to its officers prior to s.189A coming into force.

11. Details of what documents are considered relevant and necessary
A copy of any document that the authority considers amounts to a s.189A assessment so that Mr Peak can see what assessment was produced.
A copy of the notes of the meeting made by the housing caseworker so that Mr Peak can check them for accuracy.
Copies of any policies (including internal policies) which are relevant to s.189A assessments so that Mr Peak can see what the authority expects of its employees and how they are to interact with the public.

12. The address for reply and service of court documents
This is the address set out at 4, above.

13. Proposed reply date
The claimant expects a reply within 14 days of the date of this letter. If a longer period is required, please contact us immediately to explain why and make proposals.

IN THE HIGH COURT OF JUSTICE **Claim No.**
QUEEN'S BENCH DIVISION
ADMINISTRATIVE COURT

BETWEEN

THE QUEEN
(on the application of
ANTHONY PEAK)

Claimant

–and–

WARDEN DRANE
DISTRICT COUNCIL

Defendant

STATEMENT OF FACTS AND GROUNDS

Introduction

1. Mr Peak seeks a mandatory order requiring the defendant to carry out an assessment under s.189A, Housing Act 1996.

Factual background

2. Mr Peak is the assured shorthold tenant of 15 Golden Square, Warden, WAR14 1AB. His landlord recently served him with notice under s.21, Housing Act 1988. That notice expires on 1 May 2018.
3. Following a telephone conversation with an officer of the authority, he attended a meeting at the housing department on 19 April 2018. At that meeting he provided a copy of the s.21 notice and explained that, once the notice expired, he would have no other accommodation available to him. He also explained that he was a UK citizen and provided his UK passport.
4. He was asked to complete a short *pro-forma* document and then met with a housing officer for a short interview. The face-to-face interview lasted around 10 minutes. The officer told him that, as a healthy man, he was unlikely ever to obtain any significant support from the defendant and would be most unlikely to be provided with accommodation (whether permanent social housing or temporary accommodation).
5. He was told that there were ample private rental opportunities in the local area and was given an annotated map of the local area, showing the location and contact details of local letting agents. He was told to speak

to those agents and only to return if none were able to offer him a new private sector tenancy, He was given no written notification or any other information in writing.

Legal framework

6. Part 7, Housing Act 1996 governs the duties of local housing authorities towards homeless persons or persons threatened with homelessness.

Threatened with homelessness

7. A person is threatened with homelessness if either:
   (a) it is likely that he will become homeless within 56 days; or,
   (b) he has been given a valid notice under s21, Housing Act 1988 (notice only ground for possession) in respect of the only accommodation that is available for his occupation and that notice will expire within 56 days

   (s.175(4), (5), Housing Act 1996).

Assessment duty

8. Where an applicant approaches a local housing authority and the authority are satisfied that he is:
   (a) homeless or threatened with homelessness; and,
   (b) eligible for assistance

   then the authority must make an assessment of his case (s.189A(1), inserted by s.3, Homelessness Reduction Act 2017 and came in force since 3 April 2018).
9. The assessment must include an assessment of, *inter alia*:
   (a) the circumstances that caused the applicant to become homeless or threatened with homelessness,
   (b) the housing needs of the applicant including, in particular, what accommodation would be suitable for the applicant; and,
   (c) what support would be necessary for the applicant to be able to have and retain suitable accommodation (s.189A(2)).
10. The authority must notify the applicant, in writing, of the assessment that is made (s.189A(3)). Thereafter, the authority must try to agree with the applicant, *inter alia*, steps that the applicant and the authority will take for the purposes of securing that the applicant has and is able to retain suitable accommodation (s.189A(4)).
11. If an agreement is reached, the authority must record it in writing (s.189A(5)) and provide the applicant with a copy of it (s189A(7)). If no agreement is reached, the authority must record the reasons why no agreement was reached, what steps the authority consider that it would be reasonable for the applicant and the authority to take so as to secure that he has and is able to retain suitable accommodation (s.189A(6)) and provide the applicant with a copy of it (s189A(7)).

12. This assessment and any agreement must be kept under review until such time as the authority consider that no duty is owed under Part 7, 1996 Act (s.189A(9)).

Code of Guidance

13. When discharging functions under Part 7, an authority must have regard to any guidance issued by the Secretary of State (s.182). That guidance is presently found in the Homelessness Code of Guidance 2018. It provides, *inter alia*, that when discharging the s.189A duty authorities 'should adopt a positive and collaborative approach toward applicants, taking account of their particular needs and making all reasonable efforts to engage their cooperation' (para.11.2).

Ground 1: breach of statutory duty

14. The claimant is threatened with homelessness. The s.21 notice relates to his only accommodation and requires him to vacate the property in a few weeks (much less than 56 days: see s.175(5)). As a British Citizen he is also eligible for assistance (s.185). Accordingly, the authority were obliged to carry out an assessment of his case, which they have not done.
15. The pro-forma document and short face-to-face interview cannot be considered an 'assessment'. In order to be a meaningful assessment, the authority must make proper enquiries of the circumstances and needs of the applicant: see, by analogy, *R (MM) v Lewisham LBC* [2009] EWHC 416 (Admin) (an assessment of need under the Children Act 1989).
16. Moreover, it must include consideration of the circumstances that caused the applicant to become homeless or threatened with homelessness, his housing and support needs. There has been no such consideration of these matters.
17. Finally, no written copy of the assessment has been provided.

Conclusion

18. The defendant has failed to comply with the assessment duty in s.189A, Housing Act 1996 and must be compelled to do so.

Julia Clunes
Justice Chambers, Warden

IN THE HIGH COURT OF JUSTICE **Claim No.**
QUEEN'S BENCH DIVISION
ADMINISTRATIVE COURT

BETWEEN

THE QUEEN
(on the application of
ANTHONY PEAK)

Claimant

–and–

WARDEN DRANE
DISTRICT COUNCIL

Defendant

SUMMARY GROUNDS FOR
CONTESTING THE CLAIM

The defendant resists the claim in its entirety.

Claim premature

1. The defendant agrees that:
   (a) the claimant telephoned the authority to seek assistance with his housing situation;
   (b) he was given an initial appointment on 19 April 2018;
   (c) at that appointment, he provided a copy of a notice under s.21, Housing Act 1988 and of his UK passport, completed a *pro-forma* questionnaire about his circumstances and had a short meeting with a housing officer; and,
   (d) he was given details of local estate agents.
2. As to (a)–(c), these factors are not sufficient for the defendant to have been 'satisfied' that the claimant is threatened with homelessness, *i.e.* as at 19 April 2018, the defendant was not satisfied that the claimant was likely to become homeless within 56 days. Nor was the defendant satisfied that the claimant had been given a valid notice under s.21, Housing Act 1988.
3. The purpose of the meeting on 19 April 2018 was to gather information so as to enable the defendant to decide whether it was satisfied that the claimant was threatened with homelessness. In particular, it was to see whether the claimant had any defence to the s.21 notice, *e.g.*:

(a) was the notice in the prescribed form, as required by the Assured Tenancies and Agricultural Occupancies (Forms) (England) Regulations 2015?
(b) had the landlord served a gas safety certificate, energy performance certificate and the 'How to Rent' booklet, as required by the Assured Shorthold Tenancy Notices and Prescribed Requirements Regulations 2015?
(c) had a tenancy deposit been paid and had the deposit been duly protected as required by s.213, Housing Act 2004?

4. There is nothing objectionable in an authority having a process to obtain this information which would affect the landlord's right to recover possession. To the contrary, the 2018 Code of Guidance expressly envisages that there should be an 'initial interview' (para.11.3) and that, save in the most obvious of cases, the authority should then carry out further inquiries (para.11.4)
5. Likewise, there is nothing objectionable in an authority providing assistance to prevent homelessness even before being satisfied that the s.189A duty is owed. Prevention and relief work may take place alongside the s.189A process (para.11.26).

No practical benefit

6. Even if it is assumed that the claimant is owed the s.189A duty, the outcome will – in substance – simply be that he is given details of private letting agents in the local area:
   (a) there is nothing about his personal circumstances that caused him to become threatened with homelessness, his landlord has simply decided to recover possession;
   (b) his only housing need is for an equivalent property to the one that he is about to lose;
   (c) he is a healthy man with no identified support needs.
7. In those circumstances, it is inevitable that a s.189A assessment will simply result in the authority providing him with details of how to obtain a new private tenancy and him contacting the relevant letting agents.

Conclusion

8. For those reasons, it is submitted that the claimant is not entitled to the relief claimed, or to any relief.

Claire Ronethun
Smith Chambers, London

Appellant's notice

(All appeals except small claims track appeals and appeals to the Family Division of the High Court)

For Court use only	
Appeal Court Ref. No.	
Date filed	

Notes for guidance are available which will help you complete this form. Please read them carefully before you complete each section.

SEAL

Section 1 Details of the claim or case you are appealing against

Claim or Case no.

Fee Account no. (if applicable)

Help with Fees - Ref no. (if applicable) HWF- -

Name(s) of the ☐ Claimant(s) ☑ Applicant(s) ☐ Petitioner(s)

JANE FIELDS

Name(s) of the ☐ Defendant(s) ☑ Respondent(s)

WARDEN DRANE DC

Details of the party appealing ('The Appellant')

Name

Elizabeth Leahy

Address (including postcode)

16A Maxwell Square
Warden
WAR 16 6AB

Tel No.	012557 932831
Fax	n/a
E-mail	elizabeth.leahy@googliemail.com

Details of the Respondent to the appeal

Name

Warden Drane District Council

Address (including postcode)

Housing Department
Civic Centre
Warden High Rd
Warden
WAR1 96X

Tel No.	012557 132000
Fax	n/a
E-mail	housing@warden.gov.uk

Details of additional parties (if any) are attached ☐ Yes ☑ No

Section 2 Details of the appeal

From which court is the appeal being brought?

- ☐ The County Court at
- ☐ The Family Court at
- ☐ High Court
  - ☐ Queen's Bench Division
  - ☐ Chancery Division
  - ☐ Family Division
- ☑ Other (please specify)
  A decision of Warden Drane DC under s.202 Housing Act 1996

What is the name of the Judge whose decision you want to appeal?

n/a

What is the status of the Judge whose decision you want to appeal?

- ☐ District Judge or Deputy
- ☐ Circuit Judge or Recorder
- ☐ Tribunal Judge
- ☐ Master or Deputy
- ☐ High Court Judge or Deputy
- ☐ Justice(s) of the Peace

What is the date of the decision you wish to appeal against?

28 July 2017

Is the decision you wish to appeal a previous appeal decision? ☐ Yes ☑ No

Section 3 Legal representation

Are you legally represented? ☑ Yes ☐ No

If Yes, is your legal representative (please tick as appropriate)

☑ a solicitor

☐ direct access counsel instructed to conduct litigation on your behalf

☐ direct access counsel instructed to represent you at hearings only

Name of your legal representative

Leo & Nevil Solicitors

The address (including postcode) of your legal representative

Address		
23204 Nashville Road Warden WAR7 8QB	Tel No.	012557 168932
	Fax	n/a
	E-mail	housing@leoandnevil.co.uk
	DX	896432 Warden 2
	Ref.	LN/h/fields/01532

Are you, the Appellant, in receipt of a Civil Legal Aid Certificate? ☑ Yes ☐ No

Is the respondent legally represented? ☑ Yes ☐ No

If 'Yes', please give details of the respondent's legal representative below

Name and address (including postcode) of the respondent's legal representative

Address		
Legal Services Warden Drane DC Civic Centre Warden High Road Warden WAR1 96X	Tel No.	012557 132000
	Fax	n/a
	E-mail	legal@warden.gov.uk
	DX	162 Warden 1
	Ref.	LE/HSG/Fields/86914

Section 4 Permission to appeal

Do you need permission to appeal? ☐ Yes ☑ No

Has permission to appeal been granted?

☐ **Yes** (Complete Box A) ☐ **No** (Complete Box B)

Box A

Date of order granting permission

Name of Judge granting permission

Box B

I

the Appellant('s legal representative) seek permission to appeal.

If permission to appeal has been granted **in part** by the lower court, do you seek permission to appeal in respect of the grounds refused by the lower court? ☐ Yes ☐ No

Section 5 Other information required for the appeal

Please set out the order (or part of the order) you wish to appeal against

Decision of the local authority that the appellant is intentionally homeless.

Have you lodged this notice with the court in time? (There are different types of appeal - see Guidance Notes N161A) ☑ Yes ☐ No

If **'No'** you must also complete **Part B of Section 10 and Section 11**

Section 6 Grounds of appeal

Please state, in numbered paragraphs, **on a separate sheet** attached to this notice and entitled 'Grounds of Appeal' (also in the top right hand corner add your claim or case number and full name), why you are saying that the Judge who made the order you are appealing was wrong.

☑ I confirm that the grounds of appeal are attached to this notice.

Section 7 Arguments in support of grounds for appeal

☐ I confirm that the arguments (known as a 'Skeleton Argument') in support of the 'Grounds of Appeal' are set out **on a separate sheet** and attached to this notice.

OR (in the case of appeals other than to the Court of Appeal)

☑ I confirm that the arguments (known as a 'Skeleton Argument') in support of the 'Grounds of Appeal' will follow within 14 days of filing this Appellant's Notice. A skeleton argument should only be filed if appropriate, in accordance with CPR Practice Direction 52B, paragraph 8.3.

Section 8 Aarhus Convention Claim

For applications made under the Town and Country Planning Act 1990 or Planning (Listed Buildings and Conservation Areas) Act 1990

I contend that this claim is an Aarhus Convention Claim ☐Yes ☑No

If Yes, and you are appealing to the Court of Appeal, any application for an order to limit the recoverable costs of an appeal, pursuant to CPR 52.19, should be made in section 10.

If Yes, indicate in the following box if you do not wish the costs limits under CPR 45 to apply. If you have indicated that the claim is an Aarthus claim set out the grounds below

Section 9 What are you asking the Appeal Court to do?

I am asking the appeal court to:-
(please tick the appropriate box)

☐ set aside the order which I am appealing

☑ vary the order which I am appealing and substitute the following order. Set out in the following space the order you are asking for:-

The court is asked to allow the appeal and substitute a decision that the appellant is not intentionally homeless. Alternatively, the court is asked to quash the decision and remit the matter back to the defendant for further consideration and redetermination

☐ order a new trial

Section 10 Other applications

Complete this section **only** if you are making any additional applications.

Part A

☐ I apply for a stay of execution. (You must set out in Section 11 your reasons for seeking a stay of execution and evidence in support of your application.)

Part B

☐ I apply for an extension of time for filing my appeal notice. (You must set out in Section 11 the reasons for the delay and what steps you have taken since the decision you are appealing.)

Part C

☑ I apply for an order that:

The court make case management directions in the form attached

(You must set out in Section 11 your reasons and your evidence in support of your application.)

Section 11 Evidence in support

In support of my application(s) in Section 10, I wish to rely upon the following reasons and evidence:

By CPR PD 52D para 28, the appellant is required to serve proposed case management directions with this appeal. The appellant proposes:

1) The defendant shall, by [insert date 14/21 days hence], disclose a full copy of the housing file (and any other document relevant to this appeal if not otherwise contained in the housing file) to the appellant.

2) Any application by the appellant to amend the grounds of appeal must be made within 14 days of receipt of the documents referred to in (1), above.

3) Any witness statements of fact must be exchanged by 4pm on [insert date 21 days after the date in (1), above]

4) The appellant must liaise with the respondent and seek to agree paginated and indexed bundle for use at the appeal. Such bundle must be filed and served not less than 14 days before the hearing of this appeal.

5) Each party must file and serve a skeleton argument not less than 7 days before the hearing of this appeal. The advocates who will argue the appeal must lodge an agreed bundle of authorities not less than 3 days before the hearing of this appeal.

Statement of Truth – This must be completed in support of the evidence in Section 11

I believe (The appellant believes) that the facts stated in this section are true.

Full name

Name of appellant's legal representative firm

signed
Appellant ('s legal representative)

position or office held
(if signing on behalf of firm or company)

Section 12 Supporting documents

To support your appeal you should file with this notice all relevant documents listed below. To show which documents you are filing, please tick the appropriate boxes.

If you do not have a document that you intend to use to support your appeal complete the box over the page.

In the County Court or High Court:

- ☑ three copies of the appellant's notice for the appeal court and three copies of the grounds of appeal;
- ☑ one additional copy of the appellant's notice and grounds of appeal for each of the respondents;
- ☐ one copy of the sealed (stamped by the court) order being appealed;
- ☐ a copy of any order giving or refusing permission to appeal; together with a copy of the judge's reasons for allowing or refusing permission to appeal; and
- ☑ a copy of the Civil Legal Aid Agency Certificate (if legally represented).

In the Court of Appeal:

- ☐ three copies of the appellant's notice and three copies of the grounds of appeal on a separate sheet attached to each appellant's notice;
- ☐ one additional copy of the appellant's notice and one copy of the grounds of appeal for each of the respondents;
- ☐ one copy of the sealed (stamped by the court) order or tribunal determination being appealed;
- ☐ a copy of any order giving or refusing permission to appeal together with a copy of the judge's reasons for allowing or refusing permission to appeal;
- ☐ one copy of any witness statement or affidavit in support of any application included in the appellant's notice;
- ☐ where the decision of the lower court was itself made on appeal, a copy of the first order, the reasons given by the judge who made it and the appellant's notice of appeal against that order;
- ☐ in a claim for judicial review or a statutory appeal a copy of the original decision which was the subject of the application to the lower court;
- ☐ one copy of the skeleton arguments in support of the appeal or application for permission to appeal;
- ☐ a copy of the approved transcript of judgment; and
- ☐ a copy of the Civil Legal Aid Certificate (if applicable)
- ☐ where a claim relates to an Aarhus Convention claim, a schedule of the claimant's financial resources

Reasons why you have not supplied a document and date when you expect it to be available:-

Title of document and reason not supplied	Date when it will be supplied
Skeleton argument - it is proposed to file and serve this once the full housing file has been disclosed	14 days after the disclosure of the housing file

Section 13 The notice of appeal must be signed here

Signed [ ] Appellant('s legal representative)

IN THE COUNTY COURT AT WARDEN **Claim No. WXN1234**

BETWEEN

ELIZABETH LEAHY **Appellant**

–and–

WARDEN DRANE DISTRICT COUNCIL **Respondent**

GROUNDS OF APPEAL

This is an appeal under the Housing Act 1996 s204, against the decision of the authority's reviewing officer (under HA 1996 s202) to uphold the decision that the appellant had made herself homeless intentionally homeless from 1 Warden Lane, Warden, WD9 9ZX.

A person is intentionally homeless if he deliberately does or fails to do anything in consequence of which he ceases to occupy settled accommodation which is available for his occupation and which it would have been reasonable for him to continue to occupy: Housing Act 1996 s191(1). In each case, the ground of appeal raises a point of law.

GROUND ONE: The authority misdirected itself in law in finding that it would be reasonable for the appellant to continue to occupy the matrimonial home because she could exclude her husband

1.1 A person is homeless if he has no accommodation which he has a legal entitlement to occupy (s175(1)), but shall not be treated as having accommodation unless it is accommodation which it would be reasonable for him to continue to occupy: s175(3). Section 177(1) provides that it is not reasonable for a person to continue to occupy accommodation if it is probable that such occupation will lead to domestic or other violence or threats of violence against him or against a person who might reasonably be expected to reside with him.

1.2 The only question that an authority should ask when determining whether accommodation is suitable on the grounds of violence or threats of violence is whether it is probable that continued occupation of the accommodation will lead to violence or threats of violence against the applicant; it is irrelevant whether the applicant has or could have availed him/herself of any alternative remedies to address the domestic violence: *Bond v Leicester City Council* [2001] EWCA Civ 1544, [2002] HLR 6.

1.3 In its review decision letter, the authority states that it would be reasonable for the Appellant to continue to occupy the matrimonial home because:

> *'There are steps which Ms Leahy may take to ask the court to oust her husband, John Jones, from their jointly owned property. It does not make sense to consider the first option in such cases to be rehousing by a local authority when a home-owner has suitable accommodation which they may use the process of law to secure and to protect them in residence there yet chooses not to do so.'*

1.4 In so finding, the authority misdirected itself in law by concluding that it was reasonable for the Appellant to continue to occupy the matrimonial home because the Appellant should have considered obtaining and/or obtained an injunction excluding her husband from the matrimonial home.

GROUND TWO: The authority gave inadequate reasons for finding that it was not probable that occupation of the marital home by the Appellant would lead to violence or threats of violence from her husband

2.1 Where on review under section 202 of the Housing Act 1996, a local authority confirms an earlier decision, it is required to give reasons for doing so: s203(4), and see *R v Croydon LBC, ex p Graham* (1993) 26 HLR 286, CA, and *R v Brent LBC ex p Bariise* (1998) 31 HLR 50, CA.

2.2 In its decision letter, the authority disputes whether the Appellant would be at risk of violence from her husband were she to return to live at the matrimonial home:

> *'That she says she is in fear – and for the sake of argument I am willing to accept that she is – does not mean that it is likely or probable that violence or threats of violence will be carried out. Just because Ms Leahy fears it does not make it so . . . Whilst I do not dispute Ms Leahy version of past events, ie that violence occurred in the past, it does not mean that it is probable that domestic violence, other violence or threats of violence are likely to be carried out against her, or those who normally reside with her.'*

2.3 No reasons are given for not accepting the Appellant's belief that she would be subjected to violence or for disregarding the evidence submitted on her behalf and, accordingly, the authority has failed to provide any or any adequate reasoning for its decision.

GROUND THREE: the authority failed to make sufficient enquiries

3.1 The obligation on a reviewing officer is to have regard to all matters as they appear to him at the date of the review: *Sahardid v Camden LBC* [2004] EWCA Civ 1485, [2005] HLR 11. The officer is also under an obligation to make sufficient enquiries into all matters relevant to an application, including the risk of domestic violence (*Patterson v Greenwich LBC* (1993) 26 HLR 159, CA).

3.2 On 9 September 2016, representations were made on behalf of the Appellant. Those representations detailed the history of violence from the Appellant's husband and her concerns about the likely repetition of that violence since her husband was released from prison. The Appellant – and her then advisers – provided the authority with details of persons who could support her application and her account, including details of a next-door neighbour, Becky Dodgson, who was aware of the domestic violence suffered by the Appellant.

3.3 Once the husband's release from prison had been drawn to the authority's attention, it was obliged to make reasonable inquiries into the Appellant's concern that there was a probability of threats of violence towards her. In failing to do so, the authority acted in breach of its duties under Part 7.

3.4 In circumstances where the authority was minded not to believe that the Appellant was at risk of domestic violence, it was incumbent on it to make enquiries of the neighbour in order to determine whether the Appellant's assertions could be corroborated. In failing to do so, the authority erred in law by failing to make sufficient enquiries into the Appellant's application.

GROUND FOUR: The authority failed to put adverse findings to the Appellant

4.1 In conducting its inquiries, the authority must put basic issues to the applicant that may be decided against him to enable him to comment on them (*R v Tower Hamlets LBC ex p Rouf* (1989) 21 HLR 294, QBD); the applicant must have an opportunity to deal with the generality of material which will adversely affect him: *R v Gravesham BC ex p Winchester* (1986) 18 HLR 208, QBD.

4.2 The authority found that it was not probable that the Appellant and her daughter were at risk of violence or threats of violence if they returned to the property; in so finding they dismissed the evidence put forward by the Appellant as to her belief and the evidence put forward in support of the Appellant. That finding was a finding that was central to the authority's decision. The authority failed, however, to put that finding to the Appellant and in so doing breached the principles of natural justice and/or acted unfairly towards the Appellant by failing to put adverse findings to her and allow her an opportunity to comment on them.

GROUND FIVE: Failure to have regard to relevant considerations

5.1 In the representations put to the authority on behalf of the Appellant, the authority was informed that the Appellant's husband had been released from prison and had been seen in the vicinity of 1 Warden Lane and had been associating with the Appellant's neighbours.

5.2 The authority's decision letter is silent on this point or its effect. In failing to consider the effect which this would have on the Appellant's application, the authority failed to have regard to a relevant consideration.

GROUND SIX: Error of fact

6.1 The authority made a number of findings when reaching its decision that the Appellant did a deliberate act that rendered her intentionally homeless which are based on errors of fact.

6.2 In reaching its conclusions, the authority makes a number of key findings: '*You took no steps to oust your husband from the property*'; '*you did not report the alleged incidents to anyone*', and '*Your daughter has not expressed any symptoms of being scared of your husband*'.

6.3 These findings are factually incorrect:

(a) the Appellant did take steps to exclude her husband from the marital home, by contacting a solicitor and discussing her options regarding an exclusion order;

(b) the Appellant did report incidents of domestic violence to the police and to her doctor; copies of the crime incident numbers and a letter from her doctor were supplied to the authority;

(c) the authority did receive evidence that the Appellant's daughter was receiving counselling for stress consequent upon her experiences of violence from her husband.

6.4 Accordingly, the decision is based on errors of fact, which are so fundamental to the authority's conclusions that the decision that there was an intentional act cannot be said to be sustainable.

GROUND SEVEN: Reasonableness

7.1 When authorities make decisions, they must have regard to all relevant matters, ignore irrelevant matters and not come to a decision that no reasonable authority could make ('*Wednesbury* unreasonableness'): *Associated Provincial Picture House v Wednesbury Corporation* [1948] 1 KB 223, CA, *per* Lord Greene MR at 229, 234.

7.2 The decision that the accommodation at 1 Warden Lane Road was suitable as permanent accommodation was a decision which no reasonable authority, properly directing itself, could have reached, because, *inter alia*:

- the authority did not consider that accommodation which may be suitable on a temporary basis may not be suitable on a permanent basis;
- the authority did not have any or any adequate regard to the fact that the Appellant's husband had been released from prison; and,
- the authority failed to have regard to the Appellant's concerns for her own safety and that of her family.

7.3 Further or alternatively, the decision to dismiss the Appellant's belief that she would be subject to domestic violence were she to return was – on the basis of the facts and the evidence before the authority – a decision that no reasonable authority could have reached. Having regard to all the circumstances, the decision was so unreasonable as to be perverse.

Julia Clunes
Justice Chambers

IN THE COUNTY COURT AT WARDEN **Claim No. WXN1234**

BETWEEN

ANTHONY PEAK **Appellant**

–and–

WARDEN DRANE DISTRICT COUNCIL **Respondent**

GROUNDS OF APPEAL

Introduction

1. This is an appeal under s.204, Housing Act 1996 against a decision of the respondent that its duty under s.189B(2) had been discharged. These Grounds of Appeal raise a point of law.

Background

2. Mr Peak was the assured shorthold tenant of 15 Golden Square, Warden, WAR14 1AB. In February 2018, his landlord served him with notice under s.21, Housing Act 1988. That notice expired on 1 May 2018. Mr Peak did not vacate the property and the landlord issued possession proceedings. On 1 August 2018, a possession order was made and, on 1 September 2018, bailiffs enforced the order and evicted Mr Peak.
3. On 2 September 2018, Mr Peak applied to the defendant for homelessness assistance under Part 7. Housing Act 1996. The authority carried out an assessment under s.189A, 1996 act and concluded that:
   (a) his homelessness was caused by the decision of the landlord to recover possession in order to re-let the property at a higher rent;
   (b) suitable accommodation for Mr Peak would be either a bedsit or a one bed flat; and,
   (c) Mr Peak did not need any support in order to have and retain such accommodation.
4. The s.189A assessment concluded that the authority should assist Mr Peak by providing details of local letting agents and that Mr Peak should contact those agents. Details were provided and Mr Peak contacted over 30 different agents. Despite this, he has been unable to secure private sector accommodation because he does not have sufficient savings to be able to pay a deposit.
5. The authority also decided that Mr Peak was homeless and eligible for assistance, so that the duty in s.189B arose. That duty is to '. . . take reasonable steps to help the applicant to secure that suitable accom-

modation becomes available for the applicant's occupation for at least (a) 6 months, or (b) such longer period not exceeding 12 months as may be prescribed' (s.189B(2)).

6. The authority considered that this duty was satisfied by the provision of details of local letting agents. Accordingly, 56 days after deciding that the s.189B duty had arisen, the authority gave notice under ss.189B(6), (7) that the s.189B(2) duty had ceased. That decision was upheld on review (s.202).

Ground 1: duty not discharged

7. The duty under s.189B(2) is to '. . . take reasonable steps to help the applicant to secure that suitable accommodation becomes available for the applicant's occupation for at least (a) 6 months, or (b) such longer period not exceeding 12 months as may be prescribed'.
8. Mere provision of the details of estate agents is not sufficient for these purposes.
   (a) providing information which is already in the public domain is not a 'reasonable step to help' the applicant;
   (b) the 'reasonable step' would be to provide financial support (whether by way of a guarantee or providing funds for a deposit) so as to enable him to obtain private sector accommodation
   (c) the Code of Guidance envisages such support being provided (para.11.23(c)).
9. Given that all 30 of the agents identified by the authority have refused to let a property to the appellant unless he provides a deposit, the only rational conclusion that can be reached is that the 'reasonable step' for the authority to take is to provide that deposit.

Ground 2: misdirection in law

10. The s.202 review decision concluded that:

> 's 56 days have now passed, even though you have not yet secured accommodation, I am required to bring the s.189B(2) duty to an end . . .'

11. That is a misdirection of law. The authority have a discretion to bring the s.189B(2) duty to an end after 56 days (see s.189B(5) – the authority 'may' give notice if the conditions in s.189B(7) are met).

Ground 3: Failure to exercise discretion / failure to consider relevant factors

12. As a consequence of the misdirection identified in Ground 2, the authority has failed even to consider exercising its discretion to continue to perform the s.189B(2) duty. It has failed to appreciate that it has a power to do so and has failed to take into account all relevant matters, including the personal circumstances of the appellant. He has not yet secured accommodation and there is a significant risk of him sleeping rough.

These are factors to which the authority should have had regard, as the 2018 Code of Guidance makes clear:

> 'During the relief stage, where an applicant does not have a priority need . . . the authority may want to consider continuing the relief duty for longer. Considerations may include the needs of the applicant; the risk of the applicant sleeping rough; the prospects of securing accommodation within a reasonable period; the resources available to the housing authority, and any wider implications of bringing the duty to an end (for example, in the case of an applicant who has dependent children and who became homeless intentionally where Children Act duties may apply if accommodation could not be secured).' (para.14.19)

Julia Clunes
Justice Chambers

CHAPTER 13

Other statutory provisions

continued

Introduction

Overview

13.1 The National Assistance Act (NAA) 1948 was the direct precursor of homeless persons legislation.[1] That Act was also a precursor of the Children Act (CA) 1989.[2] Two factors placed a much greater housing emphasis on those Acts in recent years:[3]

a) the exclusion from housing assistance of categories of immigrants;[4] and
b) the stricter controls on housing under Housing Act (HA) 1996 Parts 6 and 7.[5]

13.2 The NAA 1948 has now been replaced, in England by the Care Act (CA) 2014 and in Wales by the Social Services and Well-being (Wales) Act (SSWB(W)A) 2014; the CA 1989 now only applies in England, with the equivalent provisions in Wales to be found in SSWB(W)A 2014.[6]

13.3 This book does not comprise a comprehensive study of the broader welfare provisions of any of this legislation. There is, however, an overlap: the facts of many of the cases often suggest circumstances that would, but for legislative changes, formerly have been dealt with under homelessness legislation; indeed, many of those cases refer directly to that legislation.

13.4 Also overlapping with homelessness is the asylum support scheme under the Immigration and Asylum Act (IAA) 1999.

1 See paras 1.8–1.22.

2 See NAA 1948 ss21 and 29, as enacted, amended to apply only to persons aged 18 and over by CA 1989 s108(5) and Sch 13 para 11; see the observations of Laws LJ in *R (A) v Lambeth LBC* [2001] EWCA Civ 1624, [2002] HLR 13 at [1].

3 Benefit caps and other recent measures will also enhance dependence on social welfare duties.

4 See paras 1.61–1.62, 1.84.

5 See paras 1.69–1.82.

6 Cases decided under NAA 1948 are, however, likely to have some bearing on the application of the new legislative schemes under CA 2014 and SSWB(W)A 2014. In *R (GS) v Camden LBC* [2016] EWHC 1762 (Admin), [2016] HLR 43 it was held that the case law on the meaning of 'care and attention' in NAA 1948 s21, applies to 'care and support' in CA 2014 s9; thus a need for accommodation is not itself a need for care and support; to be eligible for accommodation under Part 1 of the SSWB(W)A 2014, an applicant must have other needs which mean that he or she is not capable of living independently. For case-law on the NAA 1948, see the 9th edition of this work, LAG, 2012, paras 13.7–13.35.

13.5 In addition, because it has been held to be an available source of power with which to assist in appropriate circumstances, reference may also be made to the power of general competence under the Localism Act (LA) 2011 in England, replacing the well-being powers of the Local Government Act (LGA) 2000, which remain available in Wales.

13.6 In this chapter, we therefore consider the relevant provisions of the following:

a) CA 2014 / SSWB(W)A 2014;
b) IAA 1999;
c) CA 1989 / SSWB(W)A 2014;
d) LGA 2000 / LA 2011;
e) other statutory provisions.

Social services authorities

13.7 Much of this chapter concerns relationships between housing authorities and social services authorities and the powers of the latter. All Welsh authorities – counties and county boroughs – are social services authorities; all London borough councils and the Common Council of the City of London, and all other unitary authorities in England, whether termed district, county or otherwise, are social services authorities.

13.8 Where there remains two-tier local government, the position depends on whether the area is a metropolitan area or not – in the former, a district council will be the social services authority; in the latter, it will be the county council.[7]

Care Act 2014/Social Services and Well-being (Wales) Act 2014

Generally

13.9 Adults with needs for care and support may be provided with residential care by local authorities under the CA 2014 in England or the SSWB(W)A 2014 in Wales.

7 See London Government Act 1963, Local Authority Social Services Act 1970, LGA 1972 and LGA 1985.

13.10 In England, CA 2014 Part 1 came into force on 1 April 2015.[8] In Wales, the SSWB(W)A 2014 came fully into force on 6 April 2016.[9] Under both Acts, local authorities[10] have a wide range of duties and powers, not all of them duties towards individuals.

13.11 English authorities have to provide or arrange for the provision of services, facilities or resources, or take other steps, to achieve the Acts' objectives.[11] Regulations may permit an authority to charge, or prohibit an authority from charging, for the provision of services, facilities or resources, or for taking other steps.[12]

13.12 Welsh authorities have to seek to promote the well-being of people who need care and support and of carers who need support.[13] They must provide or arrange for the provision of a range and level of services which they consider will achieve specified purposes in

8 Where a person was being provided with assistance under NAA 1948 Part 3, on 1 April 2015, the authority had one year in which to assess his needs under the CA 2014 by carrying out a review of his case: Care Act 2014 (Transitional Provision) Order 2015 SI No 995 art 2. Until such a review was completed, the NAA 1948 continued to apply to that person. If the authority failed to complete a review under the 2014 Act before 1 April 2016, the person was automatically treated as having needs which he or she is entitled to have met under the CA 2014. That automatic entitlement continues until the authority complete a review.

9 Social Services and Well-being (Wales) Act 2014 (Commencement No 3, Savings and Transitional Provisions) Order 2016 SI No 412 Sch 1 para 2 provides that SSWB(W)A 2014 does not apply where a person was receiving support or services prior to 6 April 2016 but that the authority must carry out a review of that person's case by 1 April 2017. Once the review has been carried out, the SSWB(W)A 2014 will apply. If the authority failed to complete a review by 1 April 2017, the person was automatically treated as having needs which he is entitled to have met under the SSWB(W)A 2014. That automatic entitlement continues until the authority completes a review.

10 A county council in England, a district council for an area in England for which there is no county council, a London borough council, or the Common Council of the City of London: CA 2014 s1(4); the council of a county or county borough in Wales: SSWB(W)A 2014 s197(1).

11 CA 2014 s2(1). The objectives are to contribute towards preventing or delaying the development by adults in its area of needs for care and support; to contribute towards preventing or delaying the development by carers in its area of needs for support: reduce the needs for care and support of adults in its area; to reduce the needs for support of carers in its area: CA 2014 s2(1); in Wales, see para 13.12.

12 CA 2014 s2(3). A charge may cover only the cost that the local authority incurs in providing or arranging for the provision of the service, facility or resource or for taking the other step: CA 2014 s2(5).

13 SSWB(W)A 2014 s5.

their areas.[14] Regulations govern what authorities may or may not charge.[15]

13.13 In order to meet needs, authorities may provide, among other things, accommodation in a care home or in premises of some other type.[16]

Duty and power to meet needs for care and support

Duty

13.14 In respect of both CA 2014 and SSWB(W)A 2014, the duty to meet needs arises where an adult is ordinarily resident[17] in the local authority's area (or present in its area and of no settled residence)[18] and that adult has needs which meet the eligibility criteria.[19]

14 SSWB(W)A 2014 s5(1). The purposes are to contribute towards preventing or delaying the development of people's needs for care and support; to reduce the needs for care and support of people who have such needs; to promote the upbringing of children by their families, where that is consistent with the well-being of children; to minimise the effect on disabled people of their disabilities; to contribute towards preventing people from suffering abuse or neglect; to reduce the need for proceedings for care or supervision orders under the Children Act 1989, criminal proceedings against children, any family or other proceedings in relation to children which might lead to them being placed in local authority care, or proceedings under the inherent jurisdiction of the High Court in relation to children; to encouraging children not to commit criminal offences; to avoid the need for children to be placed in secure accommodation; and, to enable people to live their lives as independently as possible: s5(2).

15 SSWB(W)A 2014 ss59–62.

16 CA 2014 s8(1)(a); SSWB(W)A 2014 s34(2)(a).

17 A person's ordinary residence is determined in accordance with CA 2014 s39 or SSWB(W)A 2014 s194. In particular, both Acts provide for a person provided with accommodation under certain statutory provisions to be treated as ordinarily resident in the area in which he or she was ordinarily resident before being provided with that accommodation. The statutory provisions include the National Health Service Act 2006 and National Health Service (Wales) Act 2006 thereby addressing *R (Kent CC) v Secretary of State for Health* [2015] EWCA Civ 81, [2015] 1 WLR 1221 (person ordinarily resident for purposes of NAA 1948 in Kent, despite not having lived there prior to having been placed in NHS accommodation). In determining where someone is resident, any period and place of detention in hospital is to be disregarded: *R (Hertfordshire CC) v Hammersmith and Fulham LBC* [2011] EWCA Civ 77; *R (Wiltshire CC) v Hertfordshire CC* [2014] EWCA Civ 712, [2014] HLR 41.

18 CA 2014 s18(1)(a); SSWB(W)A 2014 s35(2).

19 CA 2014 s18(1); SSWB(W)A 2014 s35(3)(a). In Wales, the duty may arise even if the adult's needs do not meet the eligibility criteria, provided that the authority considers it necessary to meet those needs in order to protect the adult from abuse or neglect or a risk of abuse or neglect: SSWB(W)A 2014 s35(3)(b).

13.15 The duty is not, however, triggered where there would be a charge for meeting the needs,[20] unless one of three conditions is met:[21]

a) The first condition is that the adult's financial resources are at or below the financial limit.
b) The second condition is that, if the adult's financial resources are above the financial limit, the adult nonetheless asks the authority to make the arrangements to meet his or her needs.[22]
c) The third condition is that the adult lacks capacity to arrange for the provision of care and support and there is no person authorised under the Mental Capacity Act 2005 to make such provision for him or her or otherwise in a position to do so on his or her behalf.[23]

13.16 The phrase 'ordinarily resident' was considered in *Shah*,[24] under the Education Act 1962: it was held that a person's long-term future intentions or expectations are not relevant; the test is not what a person's real home is, but whether a person can show a regular, habitual mode of life in a particular place, the continuity of which has persisted despite temporary absences; a person's attitude is only relevant in two respects – residence must be voluntarily adopted; and there must be a settled purpose in living in the particular place or country.[25]

13.17 In *R (Cornwall CC) v Secretary of State for Health*,[26] *Shah* was said to be 'the leading modern authority on the meaning' of ordinary residence[27] although 'the meaning of the term . . . may be strongly influenced by the particular statutory context'.[28]

13.18 In England, an adult's needs meet the eligibility criteria if:

20 Under CA 2014 s14 or SSWB(W)A 2014 s59.

21 CA 2014 s18(1)(c); SSWB(W)A 2014 s35(4)(a). There is also a cap on care costs in England but this has not yet been brought into force: CA 2014 ss15 and 18(1)(b).

22 The costs both of meeting the care needs and of making the arrangements to do so being met by the adult, see CA 2014 s14 and SSWB(W)A 2014 s59.

23 CA 2014 s18(2)–(4); SSWB(W)A 2014 s35(4)(b). The financial limit is set by regulations: Care and Support (Charging and Assessment of Resources) Regulations 2014 SI No 2672 (England); Care and Support (Charging) (Wales) Regulations 2015 SI No 1843 (Wales).

24 *R v Barnet LBC ex p Shah* [1983] 2 AC 309, HL.

25 *Shah* at 349C.

26 [2015] UKSC 46, [2015] HLR 32.

27 *Cornwall* at [41].

28 *Cornwall* at [43].

a) they arise from or are related to a physical or mental impairment or illness;
b) as a result of those needs the adult is unable to achieve two or more specified personal outcomes;[29] and
c) as a consequence there is (or is likely to be) a significant impact on the adult's well-being.[30]

13.19 In Wales, an adult's needs meet the eligibility criteria if:

a) they arise from the adult's physical or mental ill-health, age, disability, dependence on alcohol or drugs, or other similar circumstances;
b) they relate to one or more of a list of specified matters;[31] and
c) the adult is not able to meet the need or needs.[32]

Power

13.20 In England, the power to meet needs is engaged where the adult is ordinarily resident in the authority's area[33] or is present in its area but of no settled residence, and the authority is satisfied that it is not under a duty to meet the adult's needs,[34] ie not under the duty considered at para 13.14, above.[35] The power may also be exercised to

29 The specified outcomes are: managing and maintaining nutrition; maintaining personal hygiene; managing toilet needs; being appropriately clothed; being able to make use of the adult's home safely; maintaining a habitable home environment; developing and maintaining family or other personal relationships; accessing and engaging in work, training, education or volunteering; making use of necessary facilities or services in the local community including public transport, and recreational facilities or services; and, carrying out any caring responsibilities the adult has for a child: Care and Support (Eligibility Criteria) Regulations 2015 SI No 313 reg 2(2).

30 Care and Support (Eligibility Criteria) Regulations 2015 SI No 313 reg 2(1).

31 The ability to carry out self-care or domestic routines; the ability to communicate; protection from abuse or neglect; involvement in work, education, learning or in leisure activities; maintenance or development of family or other significant personal relationships; development and maintenance of social relationships and involvement in the community; and fulfilment of caring responsibilities for a child: Care and Support (Eligibility) (Wales) Regulations 2015 SI No 1578 reg 3(b).

32 Care and Support (Eligibility) (Wales) Regulations 2015 SI No 1578 reg 3.

33 See para 13.14.

34 Ie not under a duty pursuant to CA 2014 s18: CA 2014 s19(1).

35 The only restrictions on this power are those found in CA 2014 ss21–23 (exclusions for certain illegal immigrants, NHS services and housing services) discussed below (see paras 13.23–13.30). In Wales, see SSWB(W)A 2014 ss46–48, to the same effect.

support an adult who is ordinarily resident in another authority's area.[36] The power may also be exercised where the adult has needs which appear to the authority to be urgent even though an assessment has not yet been carried out.[37]

13.21 In Wales, the power is expressed rather more broadly. An authority may meet an adult's needs for care and support if he or she is either within or ordinarily resident in its area but presently outside of it.[38] The power to meet needs may be used whether or not an assessment (para 13.22) has been completed.[39]

Assessment of need

13.22 Where it appears[40] to a local authority that an adult may have needs for care and support, the authority must assess whether he or she does so and, if so, what those needs are.[41] If a person refuses an assessment, the authority need not carry one out.[42] Where the authority is satisfied, on the basis of the needs assessment, that a person has needs for care and support, it must determine whether his or her needs meet the eligibility criteria and, if satisfied that they do so, it must, among other things, consider what could be done to meet those needs.[43]

36 This power cannot be used unless the authority which is exercising the power has notified the authority for the area where the adult is ordinarily resident that they intend to provide support (CA 2014 s14(2)(c)) and, in any event, is subject to limitations as to what charges the authority may impose (CA 2014 s14(2)(b)).

37 CA 2014 s19.

38 SSWB(W)A 2014 s36(1).

39 SSWB(W)A 2014 s36(3).

40 Under the pre-CA 2014 law, there was no need to request an assessment so long as the person had come to the attention of the local authority: *R v Gloucester CC ex p RADAR* (1997–98) 1 CCLR 476. It must, however, 'appear' to the authority that a person has a need: *R (NM) v Islington LBC* [2012] EWHC 414 (Admin).

41 CA 2014 s9(1); SSWB(W)A 2014 s19(1). Statutory guidance on assessments under CA 2014 has been issued, see CA 2014 s78 and *Care and support statutory guidance* (last updated 27 February 2017), chapter 6. In Wales, see SSWB(W)A 2014 s145 and the Code of Practice on the exercise of social services functions in relation to SSWB(W)A 2014 Part 3 (Assessing the needs of individuals).

42 CA 2014 s11(1); SSWB(W)A 2014 s20(1). A lack of capacity does not, in itself, amount to a refusal (CA 2014 s11(2)(a); SSWB(W)A 2014 s20(2)). A person who refuses an assessment is entitled to change his or her mind and require one at a later date, see CA 2014 s11(3) and SSWB(W)A 2014 s20(3).

43 CA 2014 s13; SSWB(W)A 2014 s32.

Immigrants and asylum-seekers

13.23 A local authority may not meet the needs for care and support of an adult to whom IAA 1999 s115, applies if his or her needs for care and support have arisen solely because he or she is destitute or because of the physical effects (or anticipated physical effects) of being destitute.[44]

13.24 The effect of this is to exclude those who are subject to immigration control (unless re-included by regulations) from making an application for assistance under CA 2014 or SSWB(W)A 2014, where the need for care and attention arises solely from destitution. Their needs are, instead, intended to be met under the IAA 1999.

13.25 Local authorities accordingly have no power to provide any accommodation for non-asylum-seeking immigrants who are merely destitute and who do not have children. In the case of asylum-seekers whose need for care and attention does not arise because of destitution, however, but because of, eg, disability, responsibility for meeting their care needs remains with the local authority.[45]

13.26 These exclusions are subject to what is commonly known as the 'human rights'[46] exception:[47] they do not prevent the exercise of a power or the performance of a duty if, and to the extent that, its exercise or performance is necessary for the purpose of avoiding a breach of a person's rights under the European Convention on Human Rights (ECHR).

13.27 A similar exclusion was found in (now repealed) NAA 1948 s21(1A). Under that Act, it was held that the starting-point was to ask whether support should be provided in order to avoid a violation of a right under the ECHR, before applying any eligibility criteria or assessing the applicant's need for care and attention.[48]

44 CA 2014 s21(1); SSWB(W)A 2014 s46(1). These provisions follow a similar exclusion contained in NAA 1948 s21(1A). See also Nationality, Immigration and Asylum Act (NIAA) 2002 Sch 3 para 1.

45 *Westminster City Council v National Asylum Support Service* [2002] UKHL 38, [2002] 1 WLR 2958; *O v Wandsworth LBC* (2001) 33 HLR 39, CA. See also *R (M) v Slough BC* [2008] UKHL 52, [2008] 1 WLR 1808, where *O* was applied and *R (Murua) v Croydon LBC* [2001] EWHC Admin 830, QBD; *R (Mani) v Lambeth LBC* [2003] EWCA Civ 836, (2003) 6 CCLR 376; and *R (SL) v Westminster City Council* [2013] UKSC 27, [2013] 1 WLR 1445.

46 It is not limited to human rights but also extends to rights under the EU treaties: see NIAA 2002, Sch 3 para 3(b).

47 NIAA 2002 Sch 3 para 3(a).

48 *R (N) v Lambeth LBC* [2006] EWHC 3427 (Admin).

13.28 In *PB*,[49] the claimant was a homeless Jamaican woman and an illegal overstayer. She had contact with her oldest child who lived with his father in the UK, but the other four children, all born in the UK, were the subject of care proceedings and not living with her at the time. The authority refused to assist her under NAA 1948 s21, on the basis that she could return to Jamaica. This was unlawful because the authority had not considered whether her right to respect for family life under ECHR Article 8[50] would be breached if she were forced to leave the UK while care proceedings were pending.

13.29 In *Binomugisha*,[51] the authority withdrew CA 1989[52] support from a 19-year-old failed asylum-seeker with mental health problems who had made a further application for leave to remain in the UK on the basis that it would be a breach of Article 8 to remove him to Uganda. The Home Office had not yet made a decision on that application. The claimant asserted that the authority owed him a duty under the leaving care provisions of the CA 1989[53] and under NAA 1948 s21. It was held that where there is an outstanding Article 8 claim, the question for the authority is whether that application was manifestly unfounded; while responsibility for making decisions on such applications lay with the Home Office, pending that decision the authority would have to consider whether it was necessary to provide a service in order to prevent a breach of ECHR Article 3 (prohibition of torture and inhuman or degrading treatment or punishment).

13.30 In *AW*[54] it was held that a purported fresh claim, either for asylum or under Article 3, by an asylum-seeker whose original claim had been rejected, did not always necessitate the provision of support in order to avoid a breach of the ECHR; in considering the issue, regard must be had to all the relevant circumstances, including – where appropriate – the matters which were alleged to give rise to the fresh claim.[55] Accordingly, the human rights exception does not bite simply because a human rights claim has been made to the UK Visas and

49 *R (PB) v Haringey LBC and (1) Secretary of State for Health (2) Secretary of State for Communities and Local Government (interested parties)* [2006] EWHC 225 (Admin), [2007] HLR 13.

50 See paras 12.123–12.125.

51 *R (Gordon Binomugisha) v Southwark LBC* [2006] EWHC 2254 (Admin), [2007] ACD 35.

52 See paras 13.58–13.107.

53 See paras 13.97–13.107.

54 *R (AW) v Croydon LBC* [2005] EWHC 2950 (QB), (2006) 9 CCLR 252.

55 *R (AW) v Croydon LBC*. The decision on appeal did not affect this part of the judgment below – see *Croydon LBC and Hackney LBC v R (AW, A and Y)* [2007] EWCA Civ 266, [2007] 1 WLR 3168.

Immigration (UKVI): it only applies where the provision of community care service is necessary for the purpose of avoiding a breach of a person's human rights.[56] A leading example is where an applicant had limited life expectancy and could die at any time.[57]

Provision of housing accommodation

13.31 A local authority may not meet needs for care and support by doing anything which it, or another local authority, is required to do under HA 1996,[58] or Housing (Wales) Act (H(W)A) 2014.[59] In relation to NAA 1948 s21, it was held that once the local authority had assessed an applicant's needs as satisfying the relevant criteria, it had to provide accommodation on a continuing basis so long as the need of the applicant remains as originally assessed: *R v Kensington and Chelsea RLBC ex p Kujtim*.[60] It was also held that residential accommodation could include 'ordinary' housing accommodation.[61]

13.32 A duty to supply such accommodation arose where a person needed care and attention, including housing accommodation, that was not otherwise available. The need for care and attention was, however, a precondition of such a duty.[62] Although both CA 2014 and SSWB(W)A 2014 use the phrase 'care and support' instead of NAA 1948's 'care and attention', the case-law on the NAA 1948 still applies.[63]

13.33 Under NAA 1948, the courts adopted a relatively generous approach.[64] In the context of psychiatric care, it was held[65] that the

56 NIAA 2002 Sch 3 para 3.

57 *R (De Almeida) v Kensington and Chelsea RLBC* [2012] EWHC 1082 (Admin).

58 CA 2014 s21(1)(a).

59 SSWB(W)A 2014 s48(a).

60 [1999] 4 All ER 161, (1999) 32 HLR 579, CA.

61 See *R v Bristol City Council ex p Penfold* (1998) 1 CCLR 315, QBD; *R v Wigan MBC ex p Tammadge* (1998) 1 CCLR 581, QBD; *R (Batantu) v Islington LBC* (2001) 33 HLR 76, QBD; and *Khana v Southwark LBC* [2001] EWCA Civ 999, CA; cf *R (Wahid) v Tower Hamlets LBC* [2001] EWHC Admin 641, QBD, where Stanley Burnton J doubted the correctness of the proposition, but felt constrained by the existing case-law.

62 *Khana*, above. It should not be used to circumvent the controls in HA 1996 Part 6.

63 See *R (SG) v Haringey LBC* [2015] EWHC 2579 (Admin), (2015) CCLR 444 (the appeal did not deal with this issue: [2017] EWCA Civ 322); *R (GS) Camden LBC* [2016] EWHC 1762 (Admin), [2016] HLR 43.

64 *R v Hammersmith LBC ex p M; R v Lambeth LBC ex p P and X; R v Westminster City Council ex p A* (1998) 30 HLR 10.

65 *R (Pajaziti and Pajaziti) v Lewisham LBC and Secretary of State for the Home Department (interested party)* [2007] EWCA Civ 1351.

question is whether the individual's need for care and attention by way of the provision of residential accommodation is made materially more acute by reason of his or her psychiatric disorder. A claimant may, however, have mental health needs that do not necessitate the provision of accommodation, for example where the claimant is able to manage the practicalities of day-to-day life and does not need looking after.[66]

13.34 *R (M)*[67] comprises a comprehensive review of the meaning of 'care and attention' in NAA 1948: the natural and ordinary meaning of the words 'care and attention' in that context is 'looking after', which means doing something for the person being cared for which the person cannot or should not be expected to do for himself or herself, such as household tasks, protection from risks, or personal care – eg feeding, washing or toileting.

13.35 In *R (SL) v Westminster City Council*,[68] the Supreme Court stressed that it was not enough that the authority was doing something that the applicant could not do for himself as that could lead to absurd conclusions (eg if the authority had to buy a refrigerator for him if he had no money); the need in question had to be linked to the provision of accommodation.

13.36 In *R (Nassery) v Brent LBC*,[69] the claimant suffered from mental health problems, had previously self-harmed and had made a number of suicide attempts. He sought accommodation under NAA 1948 s21 on the basis that he needed the assistance of a social worker to access medical help and that he had difficulty cooking as he suffered lapses in concentration. The authority carried out an assessment of his needs and concluded that he did not need such assistance and was not in need of care and attention. The claimant unsuccessfully sought judicial review of this conclusion:[70] the authority had considered all relevant evidence and had been entitled to reach its conclusion that he was not in need of care and attention; he had previously been able to access medical services via his general practitioner (GP) and his mental health had been stable for some time; his contention that he was unable to cook was contrary to earlier statements made by him; the authority was entitled to conclude that the risk of self-harm did not amount to a need for care and attention.

66 *R (Okil) v Southwark LBC* [2012] EWHC 1202 (Admin).
67 *R (M) v Slough BC* [2008] UKHL 52, [2008] 1 WLR 1808.
68 [2013] UKSC 27, [2013] HLR 30.
69 [2011] EWCA Civ 539, [2011] PTSR 1639.
70 [2010] EWHC 2326 (Admin).

13.37 In the Court of Appeal, the claimant unsuccessfully sought to raise a new issue (that he had become obsessive and anxious about the most basic of decisions in life that he was essentially unable to function): new matters that had arisen since the initial assessment should be the subject of a request for a new assessment.

Discharge of the duty

13.38 The duty to meet needs is not absolute. Where an applicant manifests a persistent and unequivocal refusal to observe the authority's reasonable requirements in relation to occupation of accommodation, the authority is entitled to treat its duty as discharged and to refuse to provide further accommodation.[71]

13.39 The duty may also be discharged by the unreasonable refusal of an offer of accommodation. In *Khana v Southwark LBC*,[72] the applicant was a severely disabled elderly Kurdish woman. She lived with her husband and daughter in the latter's one-bedroom flat. Following assessment, the authority offered her and her husband a placement in a residential home on the basis that it was the only form of residential accommodation which would meet her needs for care and attention. The offer was refused by the applicant and her husband, who asserted they would only accept a two-bedroom, ground-floor flat, where the family could continue to live together. Given its conclusion as to needs, the authority was held to have discharged its duty and, in any event, the refusal was unreasonable and as such discharged the authority from any further duty for so long as the refusal was maintained.

Immigration and Asylum Act 1999

13.40 IAA 1999 Part 6 came into force on 3 April 2000. It excludes persons subject to immigration control[73] from social security benefits and most other welfare provisions.[74] At the same time, however, it also set up a scheme for asylum support. The National Asylum Support Service (NASS) was established within the Immigration and Nationality Directorate (IND) of the Home Office, to administer the

71 *R v Kensington and Chelsea RLBC ex p Kujtim* (2000) 32 HLR 579.

72 *Khana v Southwark LBC* [2001] EWCA Civ 999, (2001) 4 CCLR 267. See also *R (Patrick) v Newham LBC* (2001) 4 CCLR 48, QBD.

73 See paras 3.154–3.176.

74 IAA 1999 s115.

scheme. In July 2006 the Home Office announced that NASS no longer existed as a separate department.

13.41 Asylum support is now administered in two separate ways:

a) those who made their first asylum claim on or after 5 March 2007 have their support processed by the New Asylum Model (NAM) 'case owner' who is processing his or her asylum claim; and
b) those who claimed before that date are known as 'legacy cases' and have their asylum and support claims dealt with by the Casework Resolution Directorate (CRD), subsequently renamed the Case Assurance and Audit Unit (CAAU).

13.42 In April 2007, the Border and Immigration Agency (BIA) replaced the IND. The BIA was replaced by the United Kingdom Border Agency which, in turn, has been replaced by the Home Office's UKVI centre.

13.43 The EU has attempted to implement a common policy for the treatment of asylum-seekers across Europe by enacting Council Directive 2003/9/EC[75] which lays down minimum standards for their reception. The directive has been implemented into domestic law by amending the Immigration Rules[76] and enacting new regulations[77] which apply to a person whose claim for asylum is recorded on or after 5 February 2005.[78]

13.44 Under the IAA 1999 s95(1) the secretary of state may provide, or arrange for the provision of support for asylum-seekers or the dependants of asylum-seekers who appear to him or her to be destitute or to be likely to become destitute within the prescribed period. That period is 14 days, or 56 days if they are already receiving asylum support.[79] The power to provide support has, by regulation, become a duty.[80] An asylum-seeker is a person who is not under 18 and who has made a claim for asylum which has been recorded by the secretary of state but which has not been determined.[81] A claim for asylum means a claim that it would be contrary to the UK's obligations under the Refugee Convention,[82] or under ECHR Article 3, for the

75 The directive came into force on 6 February 2003.
76 HC 395.
77 Asylum Seekers (Reception Conditions) Regulations 2005 SI No 7 and Asylum Support (Amendment) Regulations 2005 SI No 11.
78 Asylum Seekers (Reception Conditions) Regulations 2005 SI No 7 reg 1(2).
79 Asylum Support Regulations (AS Regs) 2000 SI No 704 reg 7.
80 Asylum Seekers (Reception Conditions) Regulations 2005 SI No 7 reg 5.
81 IAA 1999 s94(1).
82 Convention Relating to the Status of Refugees 1951.

claimant to be removed from, or required to leave, the UK.[83] Dependants include a spouse, a child of the claimant or the claimant's spouse, who is under 18 and dependent on the claimant,[84] and other prescribed persons.[85]

13.45 Assistance under these provisions is in theory excluded in the case of some classes of immigrant, being those classes (subject to exceptions, including the over-arching exception for British citizens and persons under the age of 18,[86] and the human rights/ European Community (EC) Treaty exceptions)[87] considered in chapter 3.[88] In practice, the government does not usually apply these eligibility criteria when making asylum support decisions, but applies the principles set out in these paragraphs.[89]

13.46 A person is destitute if he or she does not have adequate accommodation or any means of obtaining it; or has adequate accommodation or the means of obtaining it but cannot meet his or her other essential living needs.[90] This test involves consideration of the claimant and the claimant's dependants.[91]

13.47 The secretary of state may not arrange or provide asylum support unless satisfied that the claim for asylum was made as soon as reasonably practicable after the person's arrival in the UK.[92] This does not apply if support is necessary to avoid a breach of the ECHR or if the household includes a dependent child who is under 18 years old.[93] The House of Lords has held that there would be a breach of ECHR Article 3 when an individual faces an imminent prospect of serious suffering caused or materially aggravated by denial of shelter, food or the most basic necessities of life: *R (Limbuela) v Secretary of State of the Home Department*.[94]

13.48 The government has interpreted the judgment as meaning that support 'should be provided under [NIAA 2002] section 55(5)(a) when an applicant (or his adult dependant(s)) faces an imminent

83 IAA 1999 s94(1).
84 IAA 1999 s94(1).
85 The list is set out in the AS Regs 2000 reg 2(4).
86 See para 3.102.
87 See paras 3.189–3.197.
88 See paras 3.17–3.139.
89 See paras 13.53–13.56.
90 IAA 1999 s95(3).
91 IAA 1999 s95(4).
92 NIAA 2002 s55(1).
93 NIAA 2002 s55(5).
94 [2005] UKHL 66, [2006] 1 AC 396.

prospect of serious suffering caused or materially aggravated by denial of support'.[95] The judgment that this calls for, however, also requires the decision-maker to be satisfied that the asylum-seeker has some means of meeting his or her need for food and washing facilities.

13.49 The secretary of state may provide, or arrange for the provision of, temporary support to destitute asylum-seekers and their dependants until a decision is reached on eligibility for support under IAA 1999 s95.[96] This is usually in a hotel or hostel, arranged by one of the voluntary organisations funded by the Home Office, which are known as the Asylum Support Partnership (ASP) and which provide reception assistance.

13.50 The secretary of state should arrange for the asylum-seeker to be offered support under IAA 1999 s95, as soon as it has been decided that he or she is eligible. This support can include providing accommodation that appears to be adequate for the needs of the supported person and his or her dependants, and providing for their essential living needs.[97] Before deciding what form of support to provide or continue to provide, the secretary of state must take certain matters into account and ignore others.[98] The asylum-seeker's resources must be taken into account when deciding the kind and level of support.[99]

13.51 An asylum-seeker stops being an asylum-seeker for support purposes 28 days after the secretary of state notifies him or her of a favourable asylum decision, or 21 days after notification of a refusal. If there is an appeal, the period ends 28 days after any final appeal is disposed of.[100]

13.52 This does not apply if the asylum-seeker has a dependent child under 18 in the household: in those circumstances, the person continues to be treated as an asylum-seeker for support purposes so long as the child is under 18 and within the household.[101] An asylum-seeker will not benefit from this provision if the secretary of state has certified that he or she is a refused asylum-seeker with a dependent child under 18 who is refusing to leave the UK.[102]

95 UKVI, *Section 55 guidance*, Version 12, 1 June 2015.
96 IAA 1999 s98.
97 IAA 1999 s96(1).
98 IAA 1999 s97(1), (2) and (4).
99 AS Regs 2000 reg 12.
100 IAA 1999 s94(3) and AS Regs 2000 reg 2(2).
101 IAA 1999 s94(5).
102 NIAA 2002 Sch 3 para 7A, substituted by the Asylum and Immigration (Treatment of Claimants, etc) Act 2004, with effect from 1 December 2004.

13.53 Under IAA 1999 s4(2),[103] the secretary of state may provide, or arrange for the provision of, facilities for the accommodation of a person (and any dependant) if the person was, but is no longer, an asylum-seeker, and the person's claim for asylum was rejected, if the person can satisfy one of the five conditions set out in the applicable regulations.[104]

13.54 Those conditions are that:

a) the person is taking all reasonable steps to leave the UK or place himself or herself in a position in which he or she is able to leave, which may include complying with attempts to obtain a travel document to facilitate his or her departure;
b) the person is unable to leave the UK because he or she cannot travel for physical reasons or for some other medical reason;
c) the person is unable to leave the UK because in the opinion of the secretary of state there is currently no viable route of return available;
d) the person has made an application for judicial review of a decision in relation to his or her asylum claim,[105] and has been granted permission to proceed pursuant to Civil Procedure Rules (CPR) Part 54; or
e) the provision of accommodation is necessary for the purpose of avoiding a breach of rights under the ECHR.[106]

103 The former power to provide, or arrange for the provision of, support to a person who has arrived in the UK and been granted temporary admission or who has been detained, whether or not he or she is also a former asylum-seeker under IAA 1999 s4(1) was repealed from 15 January 2018 by Immigration Act 2016 Sch 11, para 1: Immigration Act 2016 (Commencement No 7 and Transitional Provisions) Regulations 2017 SI No 1241, reg 2; see also guidance on transitional provisions *Support provided under section 4(1) of the Immigration and Asylum Act 1999: handling transitional cases*, Home Office, February 2018. The IAA 1999 s4(1) power was replaced by Immigration Act 2016 Sch 10 which provides that the secretary of state has power to provide or arrange for the provision of facilities for the accommodation of a person on 'immigration bail'. See the Home Office January 2018 guidance *Immigration Bail.*

104 Immigration and Asylum (Provision of Accommodation to Failed Asylum-Seekers) Regulations (IA(PAFAS) Regs) 2005 SI No 930. As to support under s4(2), see *Asylum Support, section 4(2): policy and process*, Home Office, February 2018.

105 *R (NS (Somalia)) v First Tier Tribunal (Social Security Entitlement Chamber) and Secretary of State for the Home Department* [2009] EWHC 3819 (Admin), Staden J, on 6 November 2009.

106 IA(PAFAS) Regs 2005 reg 3(2).

13.55 The power to provide support under IAA 1999 s4 is expressed in terms of 'facilities for accommodation', so it may be provided in the form of accommodation with living expenses attached. Unlike support under IAA 1999 s95 (see para 13.44), it is not possible for an applicant to stay with a friend and only claim a subsistence allowance. The support usually comprises vouchers for living expenses, with a room in a communal private rented house arranged by an accommodation provider. Sometimes the package is full board in hostel accommodation. The accommodation provider will issue weekly supermarket vouchers, which may be delivered to the applicant, or the applicant may need to collect them from an office. Unlike accommodation under IAA 1999 s95, there is no requirement for IAA 1999 s4 accommodation to be adequate – section 4 is a more limited and less advantageous duty for the applicant than the duty imposed by section 95: *R (Kiana) v Secretary of State for the Home Department*.[107]

13.56 In *R (VC) v Newcastle City Council*,[108] the High Court described IAA 1999 s4(2) as a 'residuary power', but added that the mere fact that support is or may be available under section 4 does not, of itself, exonerate a local authority from what would otherwise be a power or duty under other statutory provisions:[109] thus, where a local authority had assessed a child as being in need within CA 1989 s17 or was already providing services under that power, it would not be able to justify the non-provision or discontinuance of assessed services on the ground that support under IAA 1999 s4 is available unless it can be shown that the secretary of state is actually able and willing (or if not willing could be compelled) to provide support, which support would meet the assessed needs of the child.

Children Act 1989/Social Services and Well-being (Wales) Act 2014

Generally

13.57 CA 1989 Part 3 confers general powers and imposes general duties on local authorities in England exercising social service functions in

107 [2010] EWHC 1002 (Admin).
108 [2011] EWHC 2673 (Admin), [2012] PTSR 546. The other statutory powers and duties in *VC* referred in particular to CA 1989 s17. See para 13.66.
109 At [86].

respect of children and families in their area.[110] From 6 April 2016, SSWB(W)A 2014 applies in Wales in its place.[111]

Children Act 1989

Children Act 1989 s17

13.58 Under CA 1989 s17(1), authorities are required to safeguard and promote the welfare of children within their areas[112] whom they assess as being in need and, insofar as is consistent with that duty, to promote the upbringing of such children by their families.[113] The section sets out duties of a general character intended for the benefit of children in need in the area of the social services authority.[114] Other duties – and specific duties in subsequent provisions of the CA 1989 – must be performed in individual cases by reference to

110 A local authority exercising a social services function in respect of children and families in their area is a 'children's services authority' as defined by CA 2004 s65(1). This mirrors the definition of a 'social services authority' save for the addition of the Council of the Isles of Scilly. See para 13.7.

111 Social Services and Well-being (Wales) Act 2014 (Commencement No 3, Savings and Transitional Provisions) Order 2016 SI No 412.

112 A child will be within an authority's area if physically present: it is not necessary that the child be 'ordinarily resident' in the area; it is possible for a child to be 'within' more than one authority's area for the purposes of CA 1989 s17, eg where the child is living in one area but attends school in another – see *R (Sandra Stewart) v Wandsworth LBC and others* [2001] EWHC 709 (Admin), [2002] 1 FLR 469; *R (N) v (1) Newham LBC (2) Essex CC* [2013] EWHC 2475 (Admin). Although an authority needs only to assess those children within its area, it can provide services outside of the area in order to meet those assessed needs: *R (J) v Worcestershire CC* [2014] EWCA Civ 1518 (services provided to Romany Gypsy child).

113 CA 1989 s17(1)(b).

114 In *R (AM) v Havering LBC and Tower Hamlets LBC* [2015] EWHC 1004 (Admin), [2015] PTSR 1242, an application under Part 7 was made to Tower Hamlets who provided temporary accommodation in Havering without notifying the latter under HA 1996 s208 (see para 10.150), which accommodation was withdrawn following a decision that the applicant was intentionally homeless; Tower Hamlets started but did not complete an assessment under CA 1989 s17, but referred the applicant to Havering, who refused to conduct an assessment under section 17 on the basis that Tower Hamlets should do it; claims for judicial review against both authorities were allowed – having started the assessment, Tower Hamlets should have completed it; and, Havering had a duty since the family had moved to its area. The problems which had arisen were 'significantly aggravated' by the failure of Tower Hamlets to give notice to Havering under HA 1996 s208. Had it done so, the two authorities would have been able to co-operate by, for example, one conducting the Children Act assessment on behalf of both.

the general duty under section 17(1), but section 17(1) does not itself impose an individual duty.[115]

13.59 The provision is excluded in the case of some classes of immigrant, being those classes (subject to exceptions, including the overarching exception for British citizens and persons under the age of 18,[116] and the human rights/EC Treaty exceptions)[117] considered in chapter 3.[118] In view of the exception for persons under the age of 18, the exclusion has no effect on them, but it may prevent the use of CA 1989 s17 for adult members of the family.

13.60 Although CA 1989 s17(1) is a general duty, when discharging it authorities have available the specific powers and duties set out in Schedule 2 Part 1, including assessment of the child's needs.[119] By section 17(6), such services may include assistance in kind or cash, and may include the provision of accommodation, possibly together with family.[120] Local Authority Circular 2003/13 (*Guidance on accommodating children in need and their families*) provides that 'social services departments might find it helpful to refer . . . to Chapter 12 of the [Homelessness Code of Guidance]' when considering what accommodation to provide for families under section 17(6). The English Code confirms[121] that bed and breakfast accommodation is not suitable for families and should only be used as a last resort and, even then, for no more than six weeks (para 12.14). This is, however, only guidance and does not render a decision to provide accommodation under section 17[122] in bed and breakfast accommodation unlawful under section 17.[123] A child in need within

115 *R (G) v Barnet LBC; R (W) v Lambeth LBC; R (A) v Lambeth LBC* [2003] UKHL 57, [2004] AC 208, [2004] HLR 10. See also *R (Bates) v Barking and Dagenham LBC* [2012] EWHC 4218 (Admin).

116 See para 3.102.

117 See paras 3.189–3.197.

118 See paras 3.17–3.139.

119 Section 17(2).

120 The Act was amended by Adoption and Children Act 2002 s116(1) to include references to accommodation following the decision of the Court of Appeal in *R (A) v Lambeth LBC* [2001] EWCA Civ 1624, [2002] HLR 13, which suggested that there was no power to provide accommodation (although this was subsequently held to have been decided per incuriam: *R (W) v Lambeth LBC* [2002] EWCA Civ 613, [2002] HLR 41, (2002) 5 CCLR 203). See para 13.74.

121 See paras 14–252 to 14–254.

122 But see paras 10.196–10.203 where the accommodation is provided under HA 1996 Part 7.

123 *R (C, T, M, U) v Southwark LBC* [2014] EWHC 3983 (Admin); on appeal, this issue was not pursued: [2016] EWCA Civ 707, [2016] HLR 36.

section 17(10) is eligible for the provision of assistance, but has no absolute right to it.[124]

13.61 In *R (G) v Barnet LBC*,[125] the House of Lords held that it was unlawful for a local authority to adopt a general policy of only accommodating homeless children pursuant to their duty under CA 1989 s20[126] while refusing to exercise its power under section 17 to accommodate other members of the family. The provisions of CA 1989 s17(6), and in particular the inclusion of the power to provide accommodation,[127] should now be read in the light of Local Authority Circular, *Guidance on accommodating children in need and their families*[128] and the observations of Baroness Hale in *R (G) v Southwark LBC*,[129] suggesting that children in need of accommodation will almost always involve children needing to be accommodated with their families.

13.62 The assessment of need carried out under CA 1989 s17 should not be dealt with summarily and requires proper enquiry and consideration:[130] *R (MM) v Lewisham LBC*.[131] In that case, the claimant, a 17-year-old girl, had been living in a women's refuge for four months when she was referred to the social services department of Lewisham

124 *R(G) v Barnet LBC; R(W) v Lambeth LBC; R(A) v Lambeth LBC* [2003] UKHL 57, [2004] AC 208, [2004] HLR 10.

125 [2003] UKHL 57, [2004] AC 208, [2004] HLR 10. See also paras 13.58, 13.74.

126 See paras 13.67–13.83. In *R (Bates) v Barking and Dagenham LBC* [2012] EWHC 4218 (Admin), a refusal to use CA 1989 s17 instead of making an offer to accommodate the claimant's children (without her) under section 20 was upheld where the authority was trying to prompt the claimant to organise herself better and seek appropriate assistance, which was a legitimate aim and a lawful decision on the facts.

127 Adoption and Children Act 2002 s116(1).

128 Para 13.60.

129 [2009] UKHL 26, [2009] 1 WLR 1299 at [30].

130 Where the child or the child's family are foreign nationals, this is likely to include whether they have a 'right to rent' as defined in Immigration Act (IA) 2014 Part 3 Ch 1. In *R (U, U, by their mother and litigation friend BU) v Milton Keynes Council* [2017] EWHC 3050 (Admin), the authority had concluded that the children were not 'in need' because their mother had sufficient resources to enable her to obtain privately rented accommodation; the family were Nigerian nationals with no right to remain in the UK and they contended that they had no 'right to rent'. The failure to consider whether the IA 2014 applied was a material omission and the decision that the children were not 'in need' was quashed. Where an authority is faced with an applicant who has the financial means to rent privately but who is disqualified by virtue of the IA 2014, one solution might be to apply to the secretary of state (IA 2014 s21(3)) for a limited right to rent to be granted to the applicant. See also *R (Michael Stewart) v Birmingham City Council* [2018] EWHC 61 (Admin).

131 *R (MM) v Lewisham LBC* [2009] EWHC 416 (Admin).

LBC by a support worker at the refuge. The support worker informed the social services department that the reasons for the referral were that the claimant was fleeing domestic violence, vulnerable, lacking life-skills and that she was shortly to be placed in hostel accommodation. The social services department made no enquiries of its own and determined that the referral was 'vague'. It also decided that, as the claimant was in receipt of benefits and had accommodation provided for her, she was not a child in need under CA 1989 s17 and was not therefore entitled to assistance from social services. The claimant applied for judicial review of that decision on the basis that the authority had failed to carry out a proper assessment. The High Court agreed that the decision could not stand. The consideration given to the referral was no more than 'cursory' and 'fell far below' the standard required by law.[132]

13.63 An authority is, however, entitled to draw adverse inferences from a failure by parents to co-operate with the assessment: *R (MN and KN) v Hackney LBC*[133] in which the parents failed to provide information about their income and other sources of assistance from friends or relatives, entitling the authority to conclude that there was no immediate risk of homelessness and that the children were not 'in need'.

13.64 A local authority must consider the policy of the secretary of state when deciding whether to withdraw accommodation provided under CA 1989 s17(6): *R (Clue) v Birmingham City Council*.[134] The claimant and her eldest son were Jamaican citizens who had come to the UK as visitors and overstayed. The claimant was refused leave to remain. No action was taken to remove her and her son to Jamaica. She subsequently had three more children in the UK. Accommodation for the entire family was being funded by the local authority under CA 1989 s17(6). After the birth of her youngest child, the claimant made a further application for leave to remain, by which time her eldest child had been continuously in the UK for seven years. The policy of the secretary of state for the Home Department

132 *R (MM)* at [14]. The assessment must also be revisited if circumstances change, see eg *R (CO) v Lewisham LBC* [2017] EWHC 1676 (Admin), where an initial conclusion that children were not 'in need' because they were receiving financial and other support from wider family members could not be relied on once it had been withdrawn; there should have been a proper reconsideration of the position.

133 [2013] EWHC 1205 (Admin).

134 *R (Clue) v Birmingham City Council* [2010] EWCA Civ 460, [2011] 1 WLR 99, [2010] 2 FLR 1011, (2010) 13 CCLR 276.

was that it would normally be inappropriate forcibly to remove a family with a child who had been continuously in the country for seven years because such a child would, in most cases, have established ties which rendered it right and fair that the family should be allowed to remain.[135] The authority nonetheless decided to withdraw funding for the accommodation and pay the cost of returning the family to Jamaica, even though no action had been taken by immigration authorities to remove the claimant and her family from the country.

13.65 It was held that the authority was required by NIAA 2002 Sch 3 para 1 to determine whether its proposed course of action would breach the ECHR rights of the claimant or any of her family members. Although the policy of the secretary of state was not binding, the authority had failed to give sufficient weight to it, in the light of which it was likely that the claimant and her eldest daughter would be permitted to remain in the UK. If the claimant and her family were to return to Jamaica, that would render the application for indefinite leave to remain academic and defeat the purpose of the policy; the authority was not intended to be allowed to pre-empt the decision of the secretary of state on applications for leave to remain. In *R (KA) v Essex CC*[136] it was held that the effect of *Clue* was that, save where the case was obviously hopeless or abusive, an authority could not deny support under the CA 1989 if the effect would be to negate an ECHR right.

13.66 A local authority cannot automatically withdraw, or decline to offer, support under CA 1989 s17(6) to a child whom it had assessed to be 'in need' simply on the basis that support is available under the IAA 1999 s4.[137] It can only do so in the unlikely event that it can be shown that the secretary of state is able and willing, or could be compelled, to provide IAA 1999 s4 support, which support would suffice to meet the child's assessed needs.

CA 1989 s20

13.67 CA 1989 s20 provides that:

> (1) Every local authority shall provide accommodation for any child in need within their area who appears to them to require accommodation as a result of:

135 DP 56/96.

136 [2013] EWHC 43 (Admin), [2013] 1 WLR 1163.

137 *R (VC) v Newcastle City Council* [2011] EWHC 2673 (Admin), [2012] JHL D3, QBD.

a) there being no person who has parental responsibility for him;
b) his being lost or having been abandoned; or
c) the person who has been caring for him being prevented (whether or not permanently, and for whatever reason) from providing him with suitable accommodation or care.

. . .

(3) Every local authority shall provide accommodation for any child in need within their area who has reached the age of sixteen and whose welfare the authority consider is likely to be seriously prejudiced if they do not provide him with accommodation.

(4) A local authority may provide accommodation for any child within their area (even though a person who has parental responsibility for him is able to provide him with accommodation) if they consider that to do so would safeguard or promote the child's welfare.

13.68 CA 1989 s20 therefore contains both a power and a duty to provide accommodation for the child.[138] The duty is imposed on social services authorities to house children in the circumstances set out in section 20(1) and to house young people in the circumstances set out in section 20(3); the power arises under section 20(4). An authority may enter into arrangements with another local authority for assistance in the discharge of the duty under CA 1989 s20, but that does not permit it to pass the child 'from pillar to post' between authorities: *R (G) v Southwark LBC*.[139]

13.69 Following this decision,[140] the Department for Communities and Local Government[141] issued new guidance in April 2010, subsequently updated and re-issued jointly with the Department for Education in April 2018 as *Prevention of homelessness and provision of accommodation for 16 and 17 year old young people who may be homeless and/or require accommodation.*[142] The guidance says that if the young person

138 When deciding how to discharge the duty, and, in particular, whether or not to house parents with the child or children, the authority must consider the family rights of the child/children under ECHR Article 8: *R (PK and another) v Harrow LBC* [2014] EWHC 584 (Admin).

139 [2009] UKHL 26, [2009] 1 WLR 1299, per Baroness Hale at [28].

140 *R (G) v Southwark LBC*, above.

141 As it then was: it is now the Ministry of Housing, Communities and Local Government.

142 Available at www.gov.uk/government/publications/provision-of-accommodation-for-16-and-17-year-olds-who-may-be-homeless-and-or-require-accommodation.

makes an initial approach to housing services, the authority should commence inquiries under HA 1996 Part 7 and, if appropriate, secure interim accommodation, which should not normally be in bed and breakfast accommodation and should not be in an 'all-ages night shelter', even in an emergency (paras. 5.9–5.15). The accommodation should be provided until the children's services authority has assessed whether a duty is owed under CA 1989 s20. If no duty is owed under CA 1989 s20, then the housing authority should consider whether any duty is owed under HA 1996 Part 7 although that does not obviate the need for the children's services authority to consider the provision of services under CA 1989 s17.

13.70 The guidance stresses the importance of preventative work, including mediation, in seeking to resolve family problems which may have led the young person to become homeless. It recognises that such steps should be undertaken alongside the statutory assessment procedures and that it is unlawful to delay the statutory assessment in order to attempt mediation.[143] The guidance supersedes those parts of circular 2003/13 (guidance on accommodating children in need and their families) that related to homeless 16- and 17-year-olds.

13.71 Whether a person is a child is a question of jurisdictional fact which the court determines for itself, so that the court is not confined to the judicial review approach of asking whether or not the authority could have reached its decision on that point: *R (A) v Croydon LBC and (1) Secretary of State for the Home Department (2) Children's Commissioner; R (M) v Lambeth LBC and (1) Secretary of State for the Home Department (2) Children's Commissioner.*[144] Whether a child is 'in need', however, is an evaluative question to be determined by the authority, subject to judicial review on conventional public law grounds: *R (A); R (M)*.

13.72 Where the age of a person is in dispute, the approach to be taken is that set out in *R (CJ) v Cardiff City Council:*[145] in determining a person's age for the purposes of the CA 1989, the court's role is inquisitorial and it must decide, on the balance of probabilities, if the person in question was a child at the material time; there is no burden of proof for either party to overcome.[146]

143 See 2018 guidance, chapter 2. See also *Robinson v Hammersmith and Fulham LBC* [2006] EWCA Civ 1122, [2006] 1 WLR 3295, [2007] HLR 7; see paras 9.164, 12.53.

144 [2009] UKSC 8, [2009] 1 WLR 2557, [2010] 1 All ER 469. See, in particular, the opinions of Lady Hale at [14]–[33] and Lord Hope at [51]–[54].

145 [2011] EWCA Civ 1590, [2012] HLR 20.

146 [2011] EWCA Civ 1590, [2012] HLR 20, per Lord Justice Pitchford at [21]–[24].

13.73 In *R (FZ) v Croydon LBC*,[147] the Court of Appeal issued procedural guidance to local authorities to be applied in age assessment cases:

a) Where an authority is minded to reach a decision that is adverse to the applicant, it must give the applicant a fair and proper opportunity to deal with important points prior to reaching any final conclusion.
b) Applicants are entitled to have an adult present at any interview.
c) The correct test for the court to apply is not whether the authority had reached a reasonable decision, but what determination the court makes of the claimant's age for itself.
d) The court is not required to come to the same conclusions as the local authority on all matters, eg credibility.
e) Considering the balance of probabilities at the permission stage is unhelpful.
f) The burden on the Administrative Court in deciding disputes of fact in age assessment cases is a significant use of resources. In the majority of cases, it would be appropriate to transfer age assessment disputes to the Upper Tribunal, which has sufficient judicial review jurisdiction for this purpose.[148]

13.74 Where an authority provides a child with accommodation pursuant to its duty under CA 1989 s20, it is not obliged by section 23(6)[149] to

147 [2011] EWCA Civ 59, [2011] HLR 22. See also *R (AK) v Secretary of State for the Home Department* [2011] EWHC 3188 (Admin) and *R (K) v Birmingham City Council* [2011] EWHC 1559 (Admin). The guidance given in *FZ* has not yet been incorporated into any government guidance. The UK Border Agency (UKBA) guidance *Assessing age* still refers to *R (B) v Merton LBC* [2003] EWHC 1689 (Admin), [2003] 4 All ER 280. The UKBC guidance is available at: www.ukba.homeoffice.gov.uk/sitecontent/documents/policyand-law/asylumprocessguidance/specialcases/guidance/assessing-age?view=Binary. See also *Age assessment: joint working guidance* (June 2015), which also still refers to the *Merton* case, while recognising that there have been subsequent decisions. It is available at www.gov.uk/government/uploads/system/uploads/attachment_data/file/432724/Age_Assessment_Joint_Working_Guidance__April_2015__Final_agreed_v2_EXT.pdf.

148 A local authority undertaking age assessments for the purposes of the CA 1989 is not bound by any previous age assessment carried out by the secretary of state or the First-tier Tribunal (Immigration and Asylum Chamber) on appeal: *R (Kadri) v Birmingham City Council* [2012] EWCA Civ 1432, [2013] HLR 4.

149 CA 1989 s23(6) provided that an authority may provide accommodation with a child's family, relatives or any other suitable person and, so far as is reasonably practicable and consistent with the child's welfare, the authority must make the placement with a parent, person with parental responsibility, relative, friend or other person connected with him or her; see now CA 1989 s22C.

make arrangements to enable the child to live with a parent, relative, friend or other person connected with him or her.[150]

13.75 A duty is only owed under CA 1989 s20 to a 'child in need'. Once a social services department has determined that it owes a duty to a child to provide accommodation under section 20, it cannot sidestep it by securing accommodation pursuant to a different statutory provision, eg, CA 1989 s17, HA 1996 Part 7[151] or Children and Families Act (CFA) 2014 Part 3.[152] If, however, a child approaches a local housing authority directly and asks for accommodation which is then provided under HA 1996 Part 7, such accommodation can be taken into consideration at the point that the authority carries out its assessment of the child's needs in order to determine if a duty under CA 1989 s20 exists; accordingly, a determination that adequate housing is already being provided under an alternative legislative provision – so that no duty is owed – is not in these circumstances an unlawful or irrational conclusion.[153] Likewise, where a child leaves home in order to live on his or her own, there is no duty on the authority to house the child under CA 1989 s20.[154] A duty may, however, be owed under HA 1996 Part 7.[155]

13.76 To activate the duty to provide accommodation under CA 1989 s20, notice must be given or a referral made to the social services

150 *R (G) v Barnet LBC; R (W) v Lambeth LBC; R (A) v Lambeth LBC* [2003] UKHL 57, [2004] AC 208, [2004] HLR 10. But see the obiter comments of Lord Nichols at [52] and [55]–[56] on the best interests of the child(ren) and the importance of maintaining the relationship between parent(s) and child(ren). In *R (Bates) v Barking and Dagenham LBC* [2012] EWHC 4128 (Admin), a refusal to house the claimant with her children under CA 1989 s20 was upheld: the authority was trying to prompt the claimant to organise herself better and seek appropriate assistance, which was a legitimate aim and a lawful decision on the facts.

151 *R (S) v Sutton LBC* [2007] EWCA Civ 790, (2007) 10 CCLR 615 considered and applied in *R (G) v Southwark LBC* [2009] UKHL 26, [2009] 1 WLR 1299.

152 *R (O) v East Riding of Yorkshire CC* [2011] EWCA Civ 196, [2011] 3 All ER 137. CFA 2014 Part 3 replaced the Education Act 1996 Part 4 in England. CFA 2014 makes provision for the assessment of a child with special educational needs (as defined in CFA 2014 s20): CFA 2014 s36. Following a positive assessment an Education, Health and Care Plan must be produced by a local authority (CFA 2014 s37). The plan must deal with any social care needs of the child, which includes any services provided by the Local Authority Social Services Act 1970 (CFA 2014 ss21, 70).

153 *R (B) v Nottingham City Council* [2011] EWHC 2933 (Admin), [2012] JHL D2, QDB.

154 *R (AH) v Cornwall Council* [2010] EWHC 3192 (Admin), [2011] PTSR, D23.

155 *R (AH) v Cornwall Council*, above.

authority;[156] a social services authority cannot be criticised for not doing something that it had not been given notice it should be doing.[157] Nonetheless, where a child assessed as being in need is erroneously referred to the housing department rather than the social services department of a unitary authority, the accommodation provided by the authority should be treated as having been provided under CA 1989 s20.[158]

13.77 It is a question of fact what statutory power has been used to secure accommodation; it is not open to a court to deem a child to have been accommodated under CA 1989 s20 where some other power was, in fact, used to provide accommodation.[159] Where a local authority is found to have wrongly failed to provide accommodation to someone under section 20 (eg, due to an erroneous assessment of age), it can exercise discretionary powers (such as under LGA 2000 or LA 2011)[160] in order to provide him or her with some or all of the support services to which he or she would otherwise have been entitled as a formerly looked after child.[161]

13.78 In considering discharge of the duty under CA 1989 s20, CA 1989 s1[162] does not apply to judicial review proceedings involving a challenge to a local authority decision on where to accommodate a child: the role of the court is to review the decision of the local authority. As such, it is not determining a question with respect to the upbringing of the child; there is a number of ways in which the authority could meet the needs of the child and it is for the authority to choose between them.[163]

13.79 A child in need provided with accommodation pursuant to the duty or power in CA 1989 s20 is a 'looked after child' for the purposes

156 Para 13.7.

157 *R (M) v Hammersmith and Fulham LBC* [2008] UKHL 14, [2008] 1 WLR 535.

158 *R (TG) v Lambeth LBC* [2011] EWCA Civ 526, [2011] HLR 33.

159 *R (M) v Hammersmith and Fulham LBC*, above; *R (GE (Eritrea)) v Secretary of State for the Home Department* [2014] EWCA Civ 1490, [2015] 1 WLR 4123.

160 Paras 13.114–13.120.

161 *R (GE (Eritrea)) v Secretary of State for the Home Department*, [2014] EWCA Civ 1490, [2015] 1 WLR 4123; *R (A) v Enfield LBC* [2016] EWHC 567 (Admin), [2016] HLR 33. As to looked after – and formerly looked after – children, see paras 13.79, 13.97–13.107.

162 This provides that when a court determines any question with respect to the upbringing of a child or the administration of a child's property or the application of any income arising from it, the child's welfare is the court's paramount consideration.

163 *R (O) v Hammersmith and Fulham LBC* [2011] EWCA Civ 925, [2012] 1 WLR 1057.

of the general duty in CA 1989 s22. A 'looked after child' may be either a child in the care of the local authority,[164] or a child provided with accommodation by the authority in the exercise of a social services function within the meaning of the Local Authority Social Services Act 1970, other than a function exercised pursuant to CA 1989 ss17, 23B and 23C.[165]

13.80 The duty under CA 1989 s22 towards a 'looked after' child is to safeguard and promote the child's welfare and to make such use of services available for children cared for by his or her own parents as appears reasonable to the authority for a particular child.[166] The duty was extended by section 52 of the Children Act 2004[167] to include a particular duty to promote the child's educational achievement.

13.81 An authority may discharge the duty under CA 1989 s22 by the provision of accommodation for children in care,[168] or by the maintenance of looked after children (other than by provision of accommodation);[169] the provisions also deal with the class of persons with whom a local authority is permitted to make arrangements for a looked after child to be accommodated and the matters to which an authority should have regard when placing a looked after child in accommodation,[170] the circumstances in which an authority must carry out a review before placing a looked after child in accommodation,[171] and the terms under which a child may be placed in a children's home.[172]

13.82 Whether a child has been a 'looked after child' for the purposes of CA 1989 Part 3 is germane to the nature and extent of the duty owed to any child by a local authority once he or she reaches the age of 16 or 17 and becomes a 'relevant child' entitled to advice and assistance under different statutory provisions relating to duties owed by authorities to children leaving care[173] which may include the provision of accommodation.[174]

164 CA 1989 s22(1)(a).
165 CA 1989 s22(1)(b).
166 CA 1989 s22(3).
167 Inserting section 22(3A) into CA 1989.
168 CA 1989 s22A.
169 CA 1989 s22B.
170 CA 1989 s22C.
171 CA 1989 s22D.
172 CA 1989 s22E.
173 See paras 13.82–13.87.
174 CA 1989 s24A.

13.83 Since commencement of the Homelessness Reduction Act (HRA) 2017 on 3 April 2018,[175] where accommodation for a child in care has been provided under CA 1989 s22A,[176] in circumstances which mean that the child has been normally resident in the district of a local housing authority for a continuous period of at least two years, some or all of which falls before he or she turns 16, he or she is deemed to have a local connection with that district, although ceases to do so once he or she turns 21, unless a local connection can be established on any of the other grounds for it:[177] see paras 7.8–7.50. As this operates by way of amendment of the principal Act, there is no reason to think that time before the commencement date is to be disregarded.

Co-operation and notification

England

13.84 Just as housing authorities can seek the co-operation of social services authorities under HA 1996 s213,[178] social services authorities can ask housing authorities to assist them, in which event the housing authority must comply with the request if it is compatible with its own statutory or other duties and obligations and does not unduly prejudice the discharge of any of its own functions.[179] Such joint working is encouraged by MHCLG[180] and Department for Education in the joint guidance *Prevention of homelessness and provision of accommodation for 16 and 17 year old young people who may be homeless and/or require accommodation.*[181] The duty to co-operate does not apply where one department of a local authority seeks help from another department of the same authority.[182]

175 Homelessness Reduction Act 2017 (Commencement and Transitional and Savings Provisions) Regulations 2018 SI No 167 reg 3, only applicable to applications made and reviews sought on or after that date – see reg 4.

176 See para 13.81.

177 HA 1996 s199(10), added by HRA 2017 s8.

178 See para 9.58.

179 CA 1989 s27. See also CA 2004 s10 which places a duty on 'children's services authorities' (see footnote 109) to make arrangements to promote co-operation between the authority, relevant partners (including district authorities) and other persons or bodies engaged in activities in relation to children, to improve the well-being of children and young people in the authority's area.

180 Joint guidance, April 2018.

181 Available at www.gov.uk/government/publications/provision-of-accommodation-for-16-and-17-year-olds-who-may-be-homeless-and-or-require-accommodation.

182 *R v Tower Hamlets LBC ex p Byas* (1992) 25 HLR 105, CA; *R (C1) v Hackney LBC* [2014] EWHC 3670 (Admin), [2015] PTSR 1011; and, *R (M and A) v Islington LBC* [2016] EWHC 332 (Admin), [2016] HLR 19.

13.85 In *Smith*,[183] the housing authority refused a request from the social services authority for assistance in housing a family with children whom the housing authority had previously found to be intentionally homeless. In the Court of Appeal, it was held that the housing authority could not simply refuse to help by reference to the finding of intentionality. The House of Lords allowed an appeal: although housing and social services authorities were expected to co-operate, if the housing authority could not assist – because no solution was forthcoming which did not unduly prejudice the discharge of its functions – then in the final analysis the children remained the responsibility of the social services authority.

13.86 A further referral and co-operation duty is imposed on English local housing authorities by amendment of HA 1996 Part 7 by the Homelessness Act 2002,[184] which arises[185] where the local housing authority has reason to believe that a homeless applicant with children may be:

a) ineligible for assistance;[186]
b) homeless intentionally;[187] or
c) threatened with homelessness intentionally.[188]

13.87 Given the low standard of satisfaction needed ('have reason to believe'),[189] the housing authority may reach this conclusion prior to a final decision on the homelessness application, and the procedures for referral put into place by CA 1989 s27 should commence before the applicant is notified of the decision under HA 1996 s184.[190] In anticipation of this duty, the housing authority must have in place

183 *R v Northavon DC ex p Smith* [1994] 2 AC 402, (1994) 26 HLR 659, HL.

184 This followed the decision of the Court of Appeal in *R (A) v Lambeth LBC* [2001] EWCA Civ 1624, [2002] HLR 13, subsequently upheld in the House of Lords at [2003] UKHL 57, [2004] AC 208, [2004] HLR 10.

185 HA 1996 s213A(1).

186 See chapter 3.

187 See chapter 6. Formerly, this also applied where the applicant was threatened with homelessness; that reference was repealed from 3 April 2018, when HRA 2017 came into force (see Homelessness Reduction Act 2017 (Commencement and Transitional and Savings Provisions) Regulations 2018 reg 3, only applicable to applications made and reviews sought on or after that date – see reg 4), as it was replaced with new provisions (paras 10.58–10.61): HA 1996, s213A(1) as amended by HRA 2017 s4(7)(a)).

188 See para 6.6.

189 The same standard as triggers the homelessness enquiry duty: see para 9.60.

190 See para 9.179.

arrangements to invite the applicant to give his or her consent to a referral either to the social services authority for the area (where a separate authority) or to the social services department (in the case of a unitary authority).[191] Where consent is obtained, the social services authority or department, as may be, must be made aware of the case and notified of any subsequent decision by the authority.[192] These provisions do not affect any other power to disclose information to social services, with or without the consent of the applicant – for example, where the housing authority receives information which might indicate that a child in the family is at risk of significant harm.[193]

13.88 Once a social services authority is made aware that an applicant is ineligible for assistance and homeless intentionally, it may request the local housing authority to provide it with advice and assistance in the exercise of its functions under CA 1989 Part 3;[194] the housing authority must provide 'such advice and assistance as is reasonable in the circumstances'.[195]

13.89 A unitary authority must likewise make arrangement for ensuring that its housing department provides its social services department with such advice and assistance as is reasonably requested.[196] These duties are additional to those in CA 1989 s27.[197] They do not, however, reverse the position in *Smith*,[198] that where the housing authority/department is unable to provide any assistance, the ultimate responsibility for ensuring that the needs of the children are met remains with the social services authority/department.

191 HA 1996 s213(2)(a), (3)(a).

192 HA 1996 s213A(2)(b), (3)(b).

193 HA 1996 s213A(4). See also English Code of Guidance para 13.7.

194 HA 1996 s213A(5). This provision formerly referred also to being threatened with homelessness: it was repealed from 3 April 2018, on the commencement of HRA 2017 (3 April 2018: see Homelessness Reduction Act 2017 (Commencement and Transitional and Savings Provisions) Regulations 2018 reg 3, only applicable to applications made and reviews sought on or after that date – see reg 4), as it was replaced by new provisions (paras 10.58–10.62): HRA 2017 s4(7)(b).

195 HA 1996 s213A(5).

196 HA 1996 s213A(6). This overturns the decision in *R v Tower Hamlets LBC ex p Byas* (1992) 25 HLR 105, CA, where it was held that the previous duty requiring authority to co-operate (HA 1996 s213) did not apply where one department of a local authority sought help from another department of the same authority.

197 See para 13.84.

198 See para 13.85. See also English Code of Guidance para 13.9.

13.90 Since HRA 2017 came into force,[199] in England the secretary of state has had power to specify by regulations a public authority, or public authorities of a particular description, who will be under notification duties under HA 1996 s213B;[200] public authority means anyone – other than a local housing authority – with functions of a public nature.[201] While most of the HRA 2017 came into force on 3 April 2018 (subject to transitional provisions), the referral duty only applies from 1 October 2018.[202]

13.91 The regulations specify the following:[203]

a) the governor of a prison[204] or the director of a contracted out prison;[205]
b) the governor of a young offender institution;[206]
c) the governor of a secure training centre[207] or the director of a contracted out secure training centre;[208]
d) the principal of a secure college;[209]
e) a youth offending team;[210]
f) a provider of probation services;
g) an officer, designated by the Secretary of State for Work and Pensions for the purposes of HA 1996 s213B, employed by the secretary of state at an office known as a Jobcentre Plus office;
h) a social services authority;
i) a person who performs a function of a local authority pursuant to a direction under Education Act 1996 s497A(4) or (4A);[211]

199 3 April 2018: see Homelessness Reduction Act 2017 (Commencement and Transitional and Savings Provisions) Regulations 2018 reg 3, only applicable to applications made and reviews sought on or after that date – see reg 4.

200 HA 1996 s213B(4), (5) added by HRA 2017 s10.

201 This is likely to rely on the same phrase in the definition of public authority under Human Rights Act 1998 s6(3); see para 12.95.

202 Homelessness (Review Procedure etc) Regulations 2018 SI No 223 reg 1(3).

203 Homelessness (Review Procedure etc) Regulations 2018 Part 4, Schedule. See also English Code of Guidance Chapter 4.

204 Prison Act 1952 s53(1).

205 Criminal Justice Act 1991 s84(4).

206 Prison Act 1952 s43(1)(a).

207 Prison Act 1952 s43(1)(b).

208 Criminal Justice and Public Order Act 1994 s15.

209 Prison Act 1952 s43(1)(c).

210 Crime and Disorder Act 1998 s39(1).

211 Those provisions confer power on the secretary of state to secure the proper performance of local authority education functions; see Children Act 2004 s50 and Childcare Act 2006 s15.

j) an NHS trust and an NHS foundation trust, but only in connection with the provision of emergency department and urgent treatment centres and in-patient treatment; and,
k) the Secretary of State for Defence, but only in relation to members of the regular armed forces.

13.92 The duty arises if the specified public authority considers that a person in England in relation to whom the authority exercises any functions is or may be homeless or threatened with homelessness, and asks the person to agree to it notifying a local housing authority in England of its opinion and of how he or she may be contacted by the local housing authority.[212] The duty does not arise unless the person identifies a local housing authority in England to which he or she would like the notification to be made.[213] If these conditions are fulfilled, the public authority must notify that local housing authority of its opinion and of the contact information.[214]

13.93 Note, however, that unless the notification also asserts, in whatever terms, that the individual is applying to the housing authority for accommodation or assistance in obtaining it, the duty to make enquiries under HA 1996 s184[215] does not on the face of it appear to arise,[216] although it is strongly arguable that this is the intention of HA 1996 s213B and that section 184 should be construed commensurately with it; it is difficult to see what other purpose section 213B could have sought to achieve.

Wales

13.94 In Wales, a notification duty arises where an authority has reason to believe that an applicant with whom a person under the age of 18 normally resides, or might reasonably be expected to reside, may be

212 HA 1996 s213B(2), added by HRA 2017 s10.
213 HA 1996 s213B(3), added by HRA 2017 s10.
214 HA 1996 s213B(3), added by HRA 2017 s10.
215 See para 9.60.
216 The English Code of Guidance puts it this way: 'A referral made by a public authority to the housing authority under section 213B will not in itself constitute an application for assistance under Part 7, but housing authorities should always respond to any referral received . . . If the housing authority's subsequent contact with the individual following receipt of the referral reveals details that provide the housing authority with reason to believe that they might be homeless or threatened with homelessness and the individual indicates they would like assistance it will trigger an application for assistance under Part 7' (paras 4.19–4.20).

ineligible for help, may be homeless, but that a duty under H(W)A 2014 s68,[217] s73[218] or s75[219] is not likely to apply, or that the authority has reason to believe that an applicant may be threatened with homelessness and that a duty under section 66[220] is not likely to apply.[221]

13.95 In such cases, the authority must make arrangements for ensuring that the applicant is invited to consent to the referral to the social services department of the essential facts of his or her case, and, if he or she has given that consent, that the social services department is made aware of those facts and of the subsequent decision in respect of his or her case.[222]

13.96 The authority must also make arrangements to ensure that where it makes a decision that an applicant is ineligible for help, became homeless intentionally or became threatened with homelessness intentionally, its housing department provides the social services department with such advice and assistance as the social services department reasonably requests.[223]

Children leaving care

13.97 In certain circumstances, local social services authorities are under a duty to provide services[224] to children who are about to leave the care of the local authority and to children who were previously in its care. The statutory scheme governing these duties was introduced by the Children (Leaving Care) Act 2000. There are three categories towards whom a local authority might owe a duty:

a) an eligible child;
b) a relevant child;
c) a former relevant child.

217 Paras 10.11–10.18.
218 Paras 10.92–10.95.
219 Paras 10.118–10.263.
220 Para 10.62.
221 H(W)A 2014 s96(1).
222 H(W)A 2014 s96(2).
223 H(W)A 2014 s96(4).
224 From 1 April 2018, the Children and Social Work Act 2017 has placed authorities under a duty to publish information about what support is available to eligible, relevant and former relevant children, including information about what accommodation is available from the authority (Children and Social Work Act 2017 s2): Children and Social Work Act 2017 (Commencement No 3) Regulations 2018 SI No 346.

13.98 An 'eligible child' is a child aged 16 or 17 who has been 'looked after'[225] by a local authority[226] for a prescribed period,[227] which is 13 weeks.[228] The duty owed to an eligible child is not the provision of accommodation per se, but to arrange for the child to have a personal advisor[229] and to carry out an assessment of the child's needs to determine what advice, assistance and support it would be appropriate for the authority to provide both while it is still looking after the eligible child and after it ceases to do so.[230] Such assistance and support can include the provision of accommodation. The authority must complete a pathway plan following the assessment which the authority must keep under regular review.[231]

13.99 A 'relevant child' is a child aged 16 or 17 who would otherwise be an eligible child because he or she was looked after by a local authority for a prescribed period, but whom the authority has ceased to look after and who is not now being looked after by any authority.[232] The duty owed to a relevant child is the same as that owed to an eligible child, but includes a requirement for the authority to 'stay in touch'[233] with the relevant child; the duty requires the authority to provide the relevant child with suitable accommodation unless the authority is satisfied that the relevant child's welfare does not require it.[234]

13.100 Under CA 1989 s23B(10), regulations may be made to govern the meaning of 'suitable accommodation'. Schedule 2 to the Care

225 See para 13.79.

226 It must be by the authority, not (for example) pursuant to an informal agreement by a family member during care proceedings (*Re B (a child) (looked-after child)* [2013] EWCA Civ 964, [2014] FLR 277; *R (O) v Doncaster MBC* [2014] EWHC 2309 (Admin); *R (T) v Hertfordshire CC* [2016] EWCA Civ 1108, [2017] HLR 10. The position would be different if the child had been placed with a relative by the authority pursuant to its power under CA 1989 s22C.

227 CA 1989 Sch 2 Part 2 para 19B.

228 Care Planning, Placement and Case Review (England) Regulations 2010 SI No 959 from 1 April 2011. For a child who was an eligible child prior to 1 April 2011, see the Children (Leaving Care) (England) Regulations 2001 SI No 2874. The prescribed period is the same under both sets of regulations. The period need not be continuous, see CA 1989 Sch 2 para 19B(2)(b).

229 CA 1989 Sch 2 Part 2 para 19C.

230 CA 1989 Sch 2 Part 2 para 19B.

231 CA 1989 Sch 2 Part 2 para 19B.

232 CA 1989 s23A.

233 CA 1989 s23B(1).

234 CA 1989 s23B.

Leavers (England) Regulations 2010[235] provides that matters to be taken into consideration when determining the suitability of accommodation include the facilities and services provided, the state of repair of the accommodation, safety, location, support, tenancy status and the financial commitments involved for the relevant child and their affordability.[236] The authority should also take into consideration the child's views about the accommodation, his or her understanding of rights and responsibilities in relation to the accommodation, and his or her understanding of funding arrangements.[237]

13.101 A 'former relevant child' is a person aged 18 years or over who was previously a relevant child[238] or who was an eligible child[239] immediately before he ceased to be looked after by the local authority.[240] The duty owed to a former relevant child is for the local authority to take reasonable steps to stay in touch, or if it loses touch to re-establish contact, and to appoint a personal advisor, carry out an assessment and create a care plan which it must keep under review.[241]

13.102 While there is no duty to provide accommodation, there is power for the authority to provide other assistance,[242] which is wide enough to include a contribution towards accommodation expenses in connection with education expenses.[243] When considering whether to exercise that power, the authority cannot take into account the possibility of support that might be provided under IAA 1999 s95.[244] Nor can the authority withdraw support in circumstances where to do so would be tantamount to pre-empting a decision on an asylum application.[245]

235 SI No 2571.
236 Care Leavers (England) Regulations 2010 SI No 2571 Sch 2 para 1.
237 Care Leavers (England) Regulations 2010 SI No 2571 Sch 2 para 2.
238 See para 13.99.
239 See para 13.98.
240 CA 1989 s23C.
241 CA 1989 s23C.
242 Under CA 1989 s23C(4).
243 *R (Sabiri) v Croydon LBC* [2012] EWHC 1236 (Admin).
244 *R (O) v Barking and Dagenham LBC* [2010] EWCA Civ 1101, [2011] 1 WLR 1283, [2011] 1 FLR 734, [2011] HLR 4, (2010) 13 CCLR 591.
245 *R (Birara) v Hounslow LBC* [2010] EWHC 2113 (Admin), [2010] 3 FCR 21, (2010) 13 CCLR 685.

13.103 In *R (TG) v Lambeth LBC,*[246] a social worker employed by the authority's Youth Offending Team[247] correctly identified the applicant as a child in need for the purposes of CA 1989 Part 3,[248] but failed to make the necessary referral to the social services department. Accommodation was instead provided by the housing department. The authority accordingly denied that the claimant was a former relevant child as it had not provided the accommodation pursuant to CA 1989 s20 and refused to provide services to the claimant as if he or she was a relevant child or former relevant child.

13.104 The Court of Appeal held that the social worker was to be regarded as the 'eyes and ears' of the social services department and that, as she had assisted the applicant to find accommodation, it should be 'treated or deemed'[249] to have been provided under CA 1989 s20; the claimant was therefore, and was to be treated as, a former relevant child for the purposes of CA 1989 with all the rights and benefits that flowed from that.

13.105 See also *R (R) v Croydon LBC,*[250] where the court held that, where the local authority undoubtedly knew that the claimant was a child and entitled to accommodation under CA 1989 s20, accommodation provided by (what is now) UKVI should be deemed to have been provided by the local authority.[251]

13.106 The courts will, however, only intervene where litigation is necessary. Thus, judicial review was not available where the authority, while denying that claimants were 'former relevant children' for the purposes of CA 1989 s23C, had nevertheless agreed voluntarily to

246 [2011] EWCA Civ 526, [2011] HLR 33.

247 Local authorities – as defined in Crime and Disorder Act 1998 s42(1) – must establish Youth Offending Teams, who are responsible for, among other things, the supervision and rehabilitation of young offenders: Crime and Disorder Act 1998 ss38(4) and 39(7). A youth offending team must include at least one person who is a social worker in the local authority's social services department: Crime and Disorder Act 1998 s39(5)(a).

248 See para 13.75.

249 At [43]. In *R (GE (Eritrea)) v Secretary of State for the Home Department* [2014] EWCA Civ 1490, [2015] 1 WLR 4123, it was said that *TG* was not a case of (impermissible – see para 13.77) deeming, but, rather, a case where the 'provision of accommodation by the local authority could be attributed to its social services function' (at [33]).

250 [2013] EWHC 4243 (Admin), [2012] JHL D58.

251 Although this decision was doubted in *R (GE (Eritrea)) v Secretary of State for the Home Department* [2014] EWCA Civ 1490, [2015] 1 WLR 4123, which reiterated that 'deeming' is impermissible, cf para 13.77.

offer them all the services equivalent to those to which they would have been entitled if they had been.[252]

13.107 Note that[253] so long as an authority in England has a duty under CA 1989 s23C towards a former relevant child, then, if the authority is a local housing authority as well as a social services authority,[254] the former relevant child is deemed to have a local connection with its area; and if the authority is not a local housing authority,[255] a local connection with every district in its area:[256] paras 7.26–7.27.

Social Services and Well-being (Wales) Act 2014

13.108 From 6 April 2016, the position in respect of children in Wales has been governed by the SSWB(W)A 2014. Welsh local authorities[257] have both a duty and a power to meet the care and support needs of a child.[258] In order to meet needs, authorities may provide, inter alia, 'accommodation in a care home, children's home or premises of some other type'.[259]

13.109 Where it appears to a local authority that a child may need care and support in addition to, or instead of, the care and support provided by his or her family, the authority must assess whether he or she does have such needs and, if so, what those needs are.[260] As part of that assessment, the authority must seek to identify outcomes that the child wishes to achieve, that persons with parental responsibility wish to achieve for the child, and that persons specified in regulations[261] wish to achieve for the child.[262] Where the authority is

252 *R (C) v Nottingham City Council* [2010] EWCA Civ 790, [2011] 1 FCR 127.

253 Since 3 April 2018, commencement of HRA 2017: 3 April 2018: see Homelessness Reduction Act 2017 (Commencement and Transitional and Savings Provisions) Regulations 2018 reg 3, only applicable to applications made and reviews sought on or after that date – see reg.4.

254 Para 13.7.

255 Ie county council in non-metropolitan areas.

256 HA 1996 s199(8), added by HRA 2017 s8, with effect from 3 April 2018: see Homelessness Reduction Act 2017 (Commencement and Transitional and Savings Provisions) Regulations 2018 reg 3, only applicable to applications made and reviews sought on or after that date – see reg.4.

257 The council of a county or county borough in Wales: SSWB(W)A 2014 s197(1).

258 SSWB(W)A 2014 ss37 and 38. There is also a duty and a power to meet the needs for care and support of a child carer: SSWB(W)A 2014 ss42 and 45.

259 SSWB(W)A 2014 s34(2)(a).

260 SSWB(W)A 2014 s21(1).

261 No such regulations have yet been made.

262 SSWB(W)A 2014 s21(4)(b).

satisfied, on the basis of the needs assessment, that a person has needs for care and support, it must determine whether his or her needs meet the eligibility criteria and, if satisfied that they do so, it must, among other things, consider what could be done to meet those needs.[263]

13.110 Subject to exceptions,[264] the duty to meet a child's needs arises where:

a) the child is in the authority's area;[265] and
b) either the child's needs meet the eligibility criteria (see next paragraph); or the local authority considers it necessary to meet the child's needs in order to protect the child from abuse or neglect (or a risk of abuse or neglect), or other harm (or a risk of such harm).[266]

13.111 The child's needs meet the eligibility criteria if:

a) the need arises from the child's physical or mental ill-health, age, disability, dependence on alcohol or drugs, or other similar circumstances, or if the need is one that if unmet is likely to have an adverse effect on the child's development;[267]
b) the need relates to one or more of a list of specified matters;[268]
c) the need is one that neither the child, the child's parents nor other persons in a parental role is able to meet;[269] and
d) the child is unlikely to meet one or more of his or her personal outcomes unless, among other things, care and support is provided.[270]

13.112 The power to meet a child's needs for care and support is expressed in very broad terms. An authority may meet any child's needs for care

263 SSWB(W)A 2014 s32.
264 The duty does not apply if the authority is satisfied that the child's needs are being met by the child's family or a carer, or if the child is being looked after by a local authority or a Health and Social Care Trust: SSWB(W)A 2014 s37(5), (6).
265 SSWB(W)A 2014 s37(2).
266 SSWB(W)A 2014 s37(3).
267 Care and Support (Eligibility) (Wales) Regulations 2015 SI No 1578 reg 4(1)(a). References to a child's development include the physical, intellectual, emotional, social and behavioural development of that child: reg 4(2)(i).
268 The ability to carry out self-care or domestic routines; the ability to communicate; protection from abuse or neglect; involvement in work, education, learning or in leisure activities; maintenance or development of family or other significant personal relationships; development and maintenance of social relationships and involvement in the community; and, achieving developmental goals: Care and Support (Eligibility) (Wales) Regulations 2015 SI No 1578 reg 4(1)(b).
269 Care and Support (Eligibility) (Wales) Regulations 2015 SI No 1578 reg 4(1)(c).
270 Care and Support (Eligibility) (Wales) Regulations 2015 SI No 1578 reg 4(1)(d). The personal outcomes are those identified under SSWB(W)A 2014 s21(4)(b): reg 1(3).

and support if he or she is either within its area, or ordinarily resident in its area but presently outside of it.[271] The power to meet needs may be used whether or not an assessment has been completed.[272]

13.113 Further duties to provide accommodation for children are contained in SSWB(W)A 2014 s76. These are, so far as material, in the same terms as CA 1989 s20.[273]

Local Government Act 2000/Localism Act 2011

13.114 The LGA 2000 provided a new power of 'well-being' applicable in both England and Wales. Section 2 provides, so far as relevant:

> (1) Every local authority are to have power to do anything which they consider is likely to achieve any one or more of the following objects –
>
> . . .
>
> (b) the promotion or improvement of the social well being of their area.

13.115 The power continues to apply in Wales. It can be exercised for the benefit of the whole or any part of the local authority's area,[274] or of all or any persons resident or present in it.[275] Well-being powers cannot, however, be used where there is a prohibition, restriction or limitation on the authority's power to act 'contained in' any enactment, whenever passed or made.[276] The courts have inclined against finding implied restrictions and have tended to interpret the limitation as referring only to cases where these is an express provision.[277] Use of

271 SSWB(W)A 2014 s38(1).

272 SSWB(W)A 2014 s38(3).

273 Likewise, similar duties exist for those leaving care, see SSWB(W)A 2014 Part 6; and the Care Leavers (Wales) Regulations 2015 SI No 1820.

274 LGA 2000 s2(2)(a).

275 LGA 2000 s2(2)(b).

276 LGA 2000 s3(1).

277 *R (J) v Enfield LBC* [2002] EWHC 432 (Admin), [2002] HLR 38; *R (Theophilus) v Lewisham LBC* [2002] EWHC 1371 (Admin), [2002] 3 All ER 851; *R (W) v Lambeth LBC* [2002] EWCA Civ 613, [2002] HLR 41, (2002) 5 CCLR 203, per Brooke LJ at [75]; *R (Khan) v Oxfordshire CC* [2004] EWCA Civ 309, [2004] HLR 41; *R (Grant) v Lambeth LBC* [2004] EWCA Civ 1711, [2005] HLR 27; *R (Richards) West Somerset Council* [2008] EWHC 3215 (Admin). The power under LGA 2000 s2 does not, however, enable an authority to promote its own economic well-being: *Brent LBC v Risk Management Partners Ltd* [2009] EWCA Civ 490 (the point did not arise on the subsequent Supreme Court appeal: [2011] UKSC 7, [2011] 2 AC 34).

the provision is, however, excluded in the case of some classes of immigrant, being those classes (subject to exceptions, including the overarching exception for British citizens and persons under the age of 18,[278] and the human rights/EC Treaty exceptions)[279] considered in chapter 3.[280]

13.116 From 18 February 2012, LA 2011 s1 introduced a further new power, to replace well-being in England (but not Wales), being a 'power of general competence'.[281] The repeal of well-being powers in England, and the amendment of the LGA 2000 to confine its operation to Wales, however, did not take effect until 4 April 2012.[282]

13.117 The power of general competence is a power to do anything that individuals – with full capacity – generally may do, even though they are in nature, extent or otherwise unlike anything the authority may do without the power, or unlike anything that other public bodies may do.[283] The power may be exercised anywhere in the UK or elsewhere, and is not limited by the existence of any other power of the authority which overlaps the general power, just as any such other power is not limited by the existence of the general power.[284]

13.118 If, however, exercise of the power 'overlaps with' a pre-commencement power which is subject to restrictions, those restrictions apply to exercise of the power 'so far as it is overlapped' by the pre-commencement power;[285] nor can the authority do anything which they are unable to do by reason of a pre-commencement limitation; nor can the general power be used to do anything which they are unable to do by virtue of a post-commencement limitation[286] which is expressed to apply to it or to all of the authority's powers (or to all of the authority's powers subject to exceptions which do not include the general power).[287]

278 See para 3.102.

279 See paras 3.189–3.197.

280 See paras 3.17–3.139.

281 Localism Act 2011 (Commencement No 3) Order 2012 SI No 411.

282 Localism Act 2011 (Commencement No 5 and Transitional, Savings and Transitory Provisions) Order 2012 SI No 1008.

283 LA 2011 s1(2).

284 LA 2011 s1(5), (6).

285 LA 2011 s2(1).

286 On the difference in treatment between a pre- and post-commencement limitation, see *R (GS) Camden LBC* [2016] EWHC 1762 (Admin), [2016] HLR 43 at [61]: only an express limitation can comprise a post-commencement limitation.

287 LA 2011 s2(2).

13.119 While LGA 2000 s2 was primarily intended for strategic use,[288] cases under it nonetheless affirmed its availability for use as a 'safety-net', including the provision of accommodation.[289] These cases will be applicable under LA 2011, which has been held to encompass the provision of accommodation.[290]

13.120 The power in LGA 2000 s2 was likewise held to be wide enough to permit an authority to fund travel arrangements for a person unlawfully in the UK, where exercising that power was necessary to avoid breaching the person's rights under the ECHR.[291] There is no reason to believe that LA 2011 s1 will be interpreted differently. The power will not, however, become a duty even if use of the power is the only way to avoid a breach of human rights: *Morris*,[292] applying the decision of the House of Lords in *Hooper*,[293] and overruling the decision in *J*.[294]

Other statutory provisions

Child Abduction and Custody Act 1985

13.121 Child Abduction and Custody Act (CACA) 1985 s5 provides:

> Where an application has been made to a court in the United Kingdom under the Convention, the court may, at any time before the application is determined, give such interim directions as it thinks fit for the purpose of securing the welfare of the child concerned or of preventing changes in the circumstances relevant to the determination of the application.

13.122 The convention referred to in section 5 is the Hague Convention.[295] The word 'directions' refers to orders of the court directing the

288 See the requirement in LGA 2000 s2(3) to have regard to the authority's community strategy (made under LGA 2000 s4) in determining whether and how to use the power.

289 See, eg, *R (J) v Enfield LBC* [2002] EWHC 432 (Admin), [2002] HLR 38.

290 *R (GS) Camden LBC* [2016] EWHC 1762 (Admin), [2016] HLR 43.

291 *R (Grant) v Lambeth LBC*, above; see also *R (Theophilus) v Lewisham LBC*, above, authorising a student loan to someone not otherwise entitled to assistance.

292 *R (Morris) v Westminster City Council (No 3)* [2005] EWCA Civ 1184, [2006] 1 WLR 505, [2006] HLR 8.

293 *R (Hooper) v Secretary of State for Work and Pensions* [2005] UKHL 29, [2005] 1 WLR 1681.

294 *R (J) v Enfield LBC*, above.

295 CACA 1985 s1.

provision of accommodation.[296] In *Re A (children) (abduction: interim powers)*,[297] the Court of Appeal held that the provisions of CACA 1985 s5 should be construed widely and that the court has the power to direct a local authority to provide accommodation for an alleged abductor and an allegedly abducted child, pending determination of an application for the return of the child. Moreover, it held that an order for the provision of accommodation is an order made for the purpose of securing the welfare of the child; accordingly, interim directions can include an order that a child, or a child's family, are provided with accommodation.[298]

296 *Re A (children) (abduction: interim powers), sub nom EA v GA* [2010] EWCA Civ 586, [2011] 2 WLR 1269.
297 [2010] EWCA Civ 586, [2011] Fam 179, [2011] 2 WLR 1269.
298 [2010] EWCA Civ 586, [2011] Fam 179, [2011] 2 WLR 1269.

CHAPTER 14

Strategy, advice, aid and practice

Introduction

14.1 In this chapter, we consider what might be called the 'general' functions related to homelessness, imposed on local housing authorities for the benefit of their areas. There are three such functions:

a) to maintain a homelessness strategy;
b) to provide advisory services; and
c) to provide assistance to the voluntary sector.

14.2 In addition, in England the secretary of state has power to issue codes of practice relating to homelessness or the prevention of homelessness about the exercise by a local housing authority of functions under Part 7 of the Housing Act (HA) 1996, staff training and monitoring, which power is also considered in this chapter.

Homelessness strategies

14.3 By Homelessness Act 2002 s1, all local housing authorities are required to carry out a homelessness review and formulate and publish a strategy based on that review:[1] by Homelessness Act 2002 s1(3) and (4), the first such strategy had to be drawn up within a year of the section coming into force,[2] and thereafter at least every five years.[3]

14.4 This exercise is to be carried out with the assistance of the local social services authority.[4] Both the housing and social services

1 Homelessness Act 2002 s1(1). Para 20 of *Fair and flexible: statutory guidance on social housing allocations for local authorities in England* (Department for Communities and Local Government (DCLG), December 2009) spells out the importance the government places on the prevention of homelessness and encourages local authorities to use their allocations policies to assist with homeless strategies. In Wales, see the Welsh Code of Guidance chapter 5.

2 That was by 31 July 2003 in England, 30 September 2003 in Wales.

3 An English authority which was categorised as an 'excellent authority' or a three- or four-star authority under an order made under Local Government Act 2003 s99(4) was exempt from the requirement to publish further strategies: Local Authorities' Plans and Strategies (Disapplication) (England) Order 2005 SI No 157. Section 99 was repealed with effect from 1 April 2015 by the Local Audit and Accountability Act 2014 Sch 12 para 53. All English authorities are now required to publish a homelessness strategy 'as of 01 April 2017': English Code of Guidance para 2.3.

4 Homelessness Act 2002 s1(2). Within the meaning of the Local Authority Social Services Act 1970 or Part 8, Social Services and Well-Being (Wales) Act 2014) (see Homelessness Act 2002 s4, for both definitions) (see para 2.19).

authorities have to take the strategy into account in exercising their functions.[5]

14.5 Initially, these provisions applied to both England and Wales: since 1 December 2014, the position in Wales has been governed by Housing (Wales) Act (H(W)A) 2014 s50. A Welsh authority must carry out a homelessness review for its area, and formulate and adopt a homelessness strategy based on the results of that review.[6] There is no requirement that the exercise be carried out with the assistance of the local social services authority as all Welsh authorities are unitary, ie have both housing and social service functions. The strategy must be taken into account by the authority when exercising any of its functions.[7] The strategy must be adopted in 2018, with a new strategy every fourth year thereafter.[8]

Reviews

14.6 'Homelessness review' is defined in Homelessness Act 2002 s2 and H(W)A 2014 s51 as a review of:

a) the current and likely future levels of homelessness in an authority's district;[9]
b) the activities carried out in the authority's area for:[10]
   i) preventing homelessness;[11]
   ii) securing that accommodation[12] is or will be available in the area for people who are or may become homeless;[13] and

5 Homelessness Act 2002 s1(5), (6).
6 H(W)A 2014 s50(1). The strategy can form part of the Well-Being Plan under the Well-being of Future Generations (Wales) Act 2015; Welsh Code para.5.4.
7 H(W)A 2014 s50(4).
8 H(W)A 2014 s50(2). The Welsh Code of Guidance notes that the strategy should reflect the Welsh Government's Ten Year Homeless Plan (July 2009), para 5.7.
9 See English Code of Guidance paras 2.17–2.18; Welsh Code paras 5.17–5.37.
10 See English Code of Guidance paras 2.14–2.29.
11 The English Code draws particular attention to the needs of Gypsies and Travellers, see para 2.16.
12 H(W)A 2014 s51(1)(b)(ii) refers to suitable accommodation.
13 The English Code stresses the need to ensure a sufficient supply of accommodation and to increase the supply of new housing (paras 2.31–2.33 and 2.37–2.42); as regards the latter, it encourages authorities to have regard to the National Planning Policy Framework and to ensure that their Local Plan (see Planning and Compulsory Purchase Act 2004) 'meets the full, objectively assessed need for market and affordable housing in the housing market area, as far as is consistent with the policies set out in the Framework' (para 2.39).

iii) providing support[14] for such people or for those who have been homeless and need support to prevent it recurring;[15] and

c) the resources available to the authority, the social services authority,[16] other public authorities, voluntary organisations[17] and other persons for such activities.[18]

Guidance

14.7 Guidance on carrying out a review is available in *Homelessness strategies: a good practice handbook*,[19] chapter 2 of the English Code of Guidance and, in Wales, in the *Code of guidance for local authorities on the allocation of accommodation and homelessness*.[20] The review should include an assessment of the needs of all homeless people, including those who have become homeless intentionally and those who are not in priority need. The review of needs and an audit of services should identify both where needs are not being met and where there is unnecessary duplication in the supply of services. The review of resources should cover staff, property and funding and include existing provision as well as plans for the future.

Publication

14.8 On completion of the review, an authority must arrange for the results to be available for inspection by members of the public, at

14 Support means 'advice, information or assistance': Homelessness Act 2002 s4. There is no definition in H(W)A 2014.

15 In Wales, the requirement is for 'satisfactory support': H(W)A 2014 s51(1)(b)(iii).

16 This is omitted from H(W)A 2014 s51(1)(c) as all Welsh authorities are unitary and, as such, also social services authorities; instead, a Welsh authority is required to have regard to any resources available to it in the exercise of other statutory functions, ie it is required to have regard to social service as well as housing resources.

17 By Homelessness Act 2002 s4, this has the same definition as HA 1996 s180(3), ie 'a body (other than a public or local authority) whose activities are not carried on for profit'.

18 See English Code of Guidance paras 2.27–2.29 and 2.43 (the latter encouraging close partnership working with the private sector); Welsh Code paras 5.38–5.40.

19 Department of Transport, Local Government and Regions (DTLR), February 2002. See, in particular, chapter 4. See also *Local authorities' homelessness strategies: evaluation and good practice*, Office of the Deputy Prime Minister (ODPM), 2004.

20 March 2016, see chapter 5.

reasonable hours, without charge, and provide a copy on payment of a reasonable charge.[21]

Strategies

Overview

14.9 'Homelessness strategy' is defined in Homelessness Act 2002 s3(1) and H(W)A 2014 s52(1) as one formulated in order to:

a) prevent homelessness in an authority's area;[22]
b) secure that sufficient accommodation is and will be available in that area for people who are or may become homeless;[23] and
c) provide satisfactory support[24] for such people or those who have been homeless and need support to prevent it recurring.[25]

14.10 In England, there is no requirement that specific objectives or plans, such as housing a proportion of homeless applicants outside an authority's district, should be included in the strategy: it is therefore a matter of discretion for the authority whether or not to include such matters.[26] Since 7 June 2012,[27] however, an authority in England must – when formulating or modifying a homelessness strategy – have regard to its current allocation scheme under

21 Homelessness Act 2002 s2(3); H(W)A 2014 s51(2). In Wales, the results must also be published on the authority's website, if it has one.

22 On prevention, see further English Code of Guidance paras 2.25–2.26 and para 2.30; Welsh Code paras 5.44–5.48.

23 English Code paras 2.31–2.56; Welsh Code paras 5.49–5.53.

24 In England, 'support' means 'advice, information or assistance': Homelessness Act 2002 s4; see also English Code paras 2.57–2.75, stressing the need to consider single people, rough sleepers, families, victims of domestic abuse and those in temporary accommodation. It is undefined in Wales.

25 H(W)A 2014 s52 does not refer to the need to prevent homelessness recurring. See also Welsh Code paras 5.54–5.59.

26 *R (Calgin) v Enfield LBC* [2005] EWHC 1716 (Admin), [2006] HLR 4. In *Nzolameso v Westminster City Council* [2015] UKSC 22, [2015] HLR 22, however, the Supreme Court held that an authority should have a policy for procuring sufficient units of temporary accommodation to meet the anticipated demand for the coming year; that policy should reflect the authority's duties under the HA 1996 and the Children Act (CA) 2004; it should be approved by the democratically accountable members of the authority; the authority should also have a policy for allocating those units; where there is an anticipated shortfall of accommodation in its district, the policy should explain the factors which will be taken into account in offering accommodation further away; and, both policies should be publicly available. It would clearly be possible to include this policy in the Homelessness Strategy.

27 Ie the commencement of LA 2011 s153.

HA 1996 s166A,[28] and its current tenancy strategy under Localism Act (LA) 2011 s150,[29] and (in the case of a London borough council) the current London Housing Strategy.[30] It should also ensure that the strategy 'is co-ordinated with the Health and Wellbeing Strategy' under the Health and Social Care Act 2012.

14.11 In Wales, the strategy must include details of both general and specific actions planned by the authority, including actions expected to be taken by other public authorities and voluntary organisations, in relation to those who may be in particular need of support if they are or may become homeless, in particular:

a) people leaving prison or youth detention accommodation;
b) young people leaving care;
c) people leaving the regular armed forces of the Crown;
d) people leaving hospital after medical treatment for mental disorder as an inpatient; and
e) people receiving mental health services in the community.[31]

Functions

14.12 The strategy may encompass specific objectives or action falling within both housing and social service functions.[32]

Partnership

14.13 The strategy may also include provision for action to be taken by other public authorities, voluntary organisations[33] or persons who might be capable of contributing to the achievement of any of the strategic objectives, but only if given approval to include such provision by that contributing authority, organisation or person,[34] ie, an authority cannot rely on what others might do, otherwise than with their consent.

14.14 In order to encourage partnership working, an authority is under a duty positively to consider the extent to which any of the objectives

28 See para 11.80.
29 Ie flexible tenancies.
30 Homelessness Act 2002 s3(7A).
31 H(W)A 2014 s52(6); see also Welsh Code para 5.65.
32 Homelessness Act 2002 s3(2); H(W)A 2014 s52(2). See also the guidance on developing action plans in *Local authorities' homelessness strategies: evaluation and good practice* (ODPM, 2004). See Welsh Code chapter 5.
33 By Homelessness Act 2002 s4. In Wales, see H(W)A 2014 ss52(3). The definition of 'voluntary organisation' is the same as in HA 1996 s180(3): see para 14.29 footnote 70 and H(W)A 2014 s99.
34 Homelessness Act 2002 s3(3), (4); H(W)A 2014 s52(3), (4).

of the strategy can be achieved through action involving two or more of the local authority, social services authority, another public authority, any voluntary organisation or any person.[35]

Guidance

14.15 In England, in addition to the needs assessment and audit of services emerging from the homelessness review, the strategy should include action on planning and implementing the strategy, including:[36]

a) the involvement of partner agencies – public, voluntary and private – in formulating and implementing the strategy;
b) consultation with other agencies in contact with homeless people, even if not involved in service provision;
c) consultation with service-users and other homeless people;
d) defining key aims and objectives of the strategy;
e) agreeing priorities for action;
f) a timetabled and costed programme;
g) identification of which agencies will do what and when;
h) mechanisms for joint and partnership work;
i) mechanisms of monitoring and evaluation of the strategy and individual elements of the programme, including targets and performance indicators; and
j) mechanisms for regular review and amendment of the strategy in the light of the monitoring and evaluation.

On strategies to prevent homelessness, further guidance is also available in *Homelessness prevention: a guide to good practice*.[37]

14.16 As the allocation of accommodation under HA 1996 Part 6 is one of the ways in which the main homelessness duty can be discharged, allocation policies and procedures should be consistent with the local authority's homelessness strategy.[38] In addition, since 7 June 2012, see also the obligation for an authority to have regard to its allocation scheme, and its current tenancy strategy, and – in the case of a London borough council – the current London housing strategy.[39]

14.17 In Wales, the strategy should 'prioritise the need for prevention' and adequate consideration and resources should be devoted to

35 Homelessness Act 2002 s3(5); H(W)A 2014 s52(5).

36 *Homelessness strategies: a good practice handbook*, DTLR, 2002, para 2.1.5.

37 DCLG, June 2006.

38 *Allocation of accommodation: guidance for local housing authorities in England*, DCLG, 2012, para 4.2; English Code of Guidance paras 2.44–2.49.

39 See para 14.10.

preventative services, eg information, advice, short-term support and mediation.[40] Related areas, such as money advice and debt counselling, should also be included.[41] Discretionary Housing Payments are particularly important and ought to be prioritised where they can be used most effectively to prevent homelessness.[42] The private rented sector plays a 'critical role' and strategic planning 'must reflect' that, both as regards prevention and sustaining tenancies and helping the homeless to move into accommodation.[43]

Review of strategy

14.18 The strategy must be kept under review by the authority,[44] and may be modified.[45] Any modifications must be published.[46] Any public or local authorities, voluntary organisations or other persons as the authority considers appropriate must be consulted prior to both adopting or modifying the strategy.[47]

Publication

14.19 The published strategy, and any modifications, must be available for inspection, at reasonable hours, without charge, by members of the public and available for purchase on payment of a reasonable charge.[48]

Provision of advice and assistance

England

14.20 From 3 April 2018,[49] English housing authorities have been under a duty to provide, or secure the provision of, a service, to be available

40 Welsh Code para 5.44.
41 Welsh Code para 5.45.
42 Welsh Code para 5.47.
43 Welsh Code para 5.53.
44 See *Preventing homelessness: a strategy health check*, non-statutory guidance published in September 2006 by the DCLG.
45 Homelessness Act 2002 s3(6); H(W)A 2014 s52(7).
46 Homelessness Act 2002 s3(7); H(W)A 2014 s52(9), (10), (11).
47 Homelessness Act 2002 s3(8); H(W)A 2014 s52(8).
48 Homelessness Act 2002 s3(9); H(W)A 2014 s52(9).
49 Commencement of HRA 2017: see Homelessness Reduction Act 2017 (Commencement and Transitional and Savings Provisions) Regulations 2018 SI No 167 reg 3. See English Code of Guidance Chapter 3.

free of charge to any person in its district, providing information and advice on:

a) preventing homelessness;
b) securing accommodation when homeless;
c) the rights of persons who are homeless or threatened with homelessness;
d) the duties of the authority, under Part 7;
e) any help that is available from the authority or anyone else, whether under Part 7 or otherwise, for persons in the district who are homeless or may become homeless (whether or not they are threatened with homelessness); and
f) how to access that help.[50]

14.21 The service has to be designed to meet the needs of persons in the authority's district including, in particular, the needs of:

a) people released from prison or youth detention accommodation;[51]
b) care leavers;[52]
c) former members of the regular armed forces;[53]
d) victims of domestic abuse;[54]
e) people leaving hospital;[55]
f) people suffering from a mental illness or impairment; and
g) any other group which the authority identifies as being at particular risk of homelessness in its district.[56]

50 HA 1996 s179(1).
51 'Youth detention accommodation' means a secure children's home, a secure training centre, a secure college, a young offender institution, accommodation provided by or on behalf of a local authority for the purpose of restricting the liberty of children, accommodation provided for that purpose under CA 1989 s82(5), or accommodation, or accommodation of a description, for the time being specified by order under Powers of Criminal Courts (Sentencing) Act 2000 s107(1)(e): HA 1996 s179(5).
52 People who are former relevant children within CA 1989 s23C(1) – see para 13.101.
53 The regular forces as defined by Armed Forces Act 2006 s374 – see para 7.37.
54 For this purpose, domestic abuse means physical violence, threatening, intimidating, coercive or controlling behaviour, emotional, financial, sexual or any other form of abuse, where the victim is associated with the abuser. Financial abuse includes having money or other property stolen, being defrauded, being put under pressure in relation to money or other property, and having money or other property misused.
55 Hospital has the same meaning as in the National Health Service Act 2006 s275(1).
56 HA 1996 s179(2).

14.22 As under the pre- Homelessness Reduction Act (HRA) 2017 provision,[57] the authority may provide grants or loans to a person providing the service on its behalf.[58] Assistance may also be given by way of the use of premises, furniture or other goods and even the services of staff.[59]

14.23 Where advice is provided by the authority, it is trite – but should be borne in mind – that appropriate advice in the interests of the applicant must be given.[60]

Wales

14.24 In Wales, H(W)A 2014 s60 requires authorities to ensure that provision of advice and information about homelessness and the prevention of homelessness is available free of charge in their areas both to people who are in the area and to anyone who has a local connection with the area.

14.25 The advice and information must include details about how the homelessness service operates in the authority's area, other help which might be available for people who are homeless or may become homeless (whether or not threatened with homelessness) and how to access it.[61] Where someone may become homeless (not necessarily threatened with homelessness in the statutory sense), assistance must be provided to access help which is available to prevent the person becoming homeless.[62]

14.26 The authority must work with other public authorities, voluntary organisations and others to ensure that the service is designed to meet the needs of groups at particular risk of homelessness, including in particular:[63]

57 HA 1996, s179 (see below, paras 14.29–14.34).

58 HA 1996 s179(3).

59 HA 1996 s179(4).

60 *Robinson v Hammersmith and Fulham LBC* [2006] EWCA Civ 1122, [2006] 1 WLR 3295, [2007] HLR 7, per Jacob LJ at [45], considering – with reference to HA 1996 s179 – advice to mediate offered to a 17-year-old: 'A near 18 [year] old who came to the authority could obviously not be properly advised to mediate if the effect of mediation would be to delay the actual s.184 decision past the 18th birthday' (thus causing the loss of automatic priority need – see para 5.67).

61 H(W)A 2014 s60(2).

62 H(W)A 2014 s60(3).

63 H(W)A 2014 s60(4).

a) people leaving prison[64] or youth detention accommodation;[65]
b) young people leaving care;
c) people leaving the regular armed forces of the Crown;[66]
d) people leaving hospital after medical treatment for mental disorder as an inpatient; and
e) people receiving mental health services in the community.

14.27 The authority does not have to provide this service itself but may secure that it is provided on its behalf by or in partnership with some other organisation.[67] Where it does provide advice, see para 14.20.

14.28 The duty to provide advice and information to persons in the area is applicable even to those who are ineligible for assistance.[68]

Aid to voluntary organisations – England[69]

14.29 Voluntary organisations have long played an important role in assisting homeless people. Bodies such as housing associations have provided significant assistance to local authorities in the discharge of their obligations towards the homeless, especially those in special categories of need. The definition of voluntary organisation[70] is wide enough to include housing associations and other non-profit-making social landlords.[71]

64 This has the same meaning as in the Prison Act 1952 s53(1).

65 'Youth detention accommodation' means a secure children's home, a secure training centre, a young offender institution, accommodation provided, equipped and maintained by the Welsh Ministers under section 82(5) of the Children Act 1989 for the purpose of restricting the liberty of children or accommodation, or accommodation of a description, for the time being specified by order under Powers of Criminal Courts (Sentencing) Act 2000 s107(1)(e): H(W)A 2014 s99.

66 As defined by the Armed Forces Act 2006 s374.

67 Two or more authorities may provide a combined service: H(W)A 2014 s60(5); see further: Welsh Code paras 9.9–9.12.

68 H(W)A 2014 s60.

69 There is no equivalent to these provisions in Wales, although the Welsh Code does discuss the circumstances in which an authority might provide assistance to a voluntary body, at paras 9.13–9.16.

70 Ie 'a body (other than a public or local authority) whose activities are not carried on for profit': HA 1996 s180(3).

71 *Goodman v Dolphin Square Trust Ltd* (1979) 38 P&CR 257, CA.

14.30 The powers permit the secretary of state, or local housing authorities, to give voluntary organisations money by way of grant or loan.[72]

14.31 A local housing authority may also assist by letting a voluntary organisation use premises belonging to it, on such terms and conditions as may be agreed, and by making available furniture or other goods – by way of gift, loan or otherwise – or the services of staff employed by it.[73] Assistance under HA 1996 s179 or s180 may be given on such terms and conditions as the secretary of state or authority may determine.[74]

14.32 No assistance of any kind is to be given, however, unless the voluntary organisation first gives an undertaking:

a) to use the money, furniture or other goods or premises made available to it for a purpose specified in the undertaking; and
b) that – if required to do so by the body providing the assistance – it will, within 21 days of notice served upon it, certify such information as may reasonably be required by the notice as to the manner in which assistance given to it is being used.[75]

14.33 In every case in which assistance is provided, the conditions must include a requirement that the voluntary organisation: keeps proper books of account and has them audited in a specified manner; keeps records indicating how the assistance has been used; and submits accounts and records for inspection by the body providing the assistance.[76]

14.34 If it appears to the body providing the assistance that the voluntary organisation is not using the assistance for the purposes specified in the undertaking, it is obliged to take all reasonable steps to recover an amount of money equal to the amount of the assistance from the organisation. No such amount is recoverable, however, unless the voluntary organisation has first been served with a notice specifying the amount alleged to be recoverable and the basis on which it has been calculated.[77]

72 HA 1996 s180(1).
73 HA 1996 s180(2).
74 HA 1996 s181(2).
75 HA 1996 s181(3).
76 HA 1996 s181(4).
77 HA 1996 s181(5), (6).

Code of Practice – England

14.35 Since 3 April 2018,[78] in England the secretary of state has had power to issue codes of practice relating to homelessness or homelessness prevention to local housing authorities,[79] in particular concerning the exercise by a local housing authority of functions under HA 1996 Part 7, staff training relating to the exercise of those functions and monitoring by the authority of the exercise of those functions.[80] A code may apply to all local housing authorities or to a local housing authority specified or described in the code, and may contain different provision for different kinds of local housing authority.[81]

14.36 The secretary of state must lay a draft of the code before parliament, which is subject to negative resolution by either House of Parliament not to approve it; if there is no such resolution within 40 days[82] of the date the code is laid,[83] then the code may be issued.[84] A code may be revised from time to time revise and reissued or revoked: the procedural requirements do not apply to the reissue of a code;[85] accordingly, they do apply to revision or revocation. The secretary of state must publish the current version of each code of practice in whatever manner he or she thinks fit.[86]

14.37 A local housing authority must have regard to a code of practice[87] in exercising its functions.[88]

78 Commencement of HRA 2017: see Homelessness Reduction Act 2017 (Commencement and Transitional and Savings Provisions) Regulations 2018 SI No 167 reg 3.

79 HA 1996 s214A(1).

80 HA 1996 s214A(2).

81 HA 1996 s214A(3).

82 No account is taken of any period during which parliament is dissolved or prorogued, or both Houses are adjourned for more than four days. HA 1996 s214A(8).

83 If laid before the two Houses on different dates, the later such date, HA 1996 s214A(7)(b).

84 HA 1996 s214A(4)–(8).

85 HA 1996 s214A(9)–(10).

86 HA 1996 s214A(11).

87 See para 12.49.

88 HA 1996 s214A(12).

CHAPTER 15

Criminal offences

Introduction

15.1 To prevent abuse of Housing Act (HA) 1996 Parts 6 and 7 and Housing (Wales) Act (H(W)A) 2014 Part 2, some attempts to obtain accommodation are classified as criminal offences. There are three such offences:[1]

a) making a false statement;
b) withholding information; and
c) failing to notify changes.

15.2 Offences under these provisions are prosecuted in the magistrates' court, and are punishable by a fine.[2]

Making a false statement

15.3 In all cases, the offence is sufficiently widely drafted to catch not merely the applicant but someone who makes representations on behalf of an applicant, which could therefore include an adviser. As the homelessness offences require proof of intent to induce the authority to believe something which is not true, however, the prosecutor must include proof of such intent as part of the prosecution, so this would be a rare event. Advisers should, however, bear the possibility in mind when deciding in what terms to relay information to an authority.[3]

15.4 The elements of the offences differ depending on whether made in connection with an allocation (HA 1996 Part 6) or homelessness application (HA 1996 Part 7, H(W)A 2014 Part 2).

Homelessness

15.5 An offence is committed by anyone who knowingly or recklessly makes a statement which is false in a material particular with intent to induce an authority, in connection with the exercise of its functions under HA 1996 Part 7 or H(W)A Part 2, to believe that the

1 HA 1996 ss171, 214; H(W)A 2014 s97.

2 For HA 1996 Parts 6 and 7, the fine may not exceed level 5 on the standard scale, but level 5 is presently unlimited (see Criminal Justice Act 1982 s37 and Legal Aid, Sentencing and Punishment of Offenders Act 2012 s85). For H(W)A 2014 Part 2, the fine may not exceed level 4 on the standard scale, currently £2,500: Criminal Justice Act 1982 s37.

3 As a criminal offence, the standard of proof is beyond reasonable doubt but the element of intent may be proved by natural inference from acts.

person making the statement or any other person is entitled to accommodation or assistance[4] in accordance with the provisions of HA 1996 Part 7 or H(W)A 2014 Part 2.[5]

Allocations

15.6 An offence is committed by anyone who knowingly or recklessly makes a statement which is false in any material particular in connection with the exercise by an authority of its functions under HA 1996 Part 6: there is no requirement that there be an intent to induce an authority to believe anything.[6]

Withholding information

15.7 An offence is committed by anyone who knowingly withholds information which the authority has reasonably required the person to give in connection with the exercise of its functions under HA 1996 Parts 6 and 7 or H(W)A 2014 Part 2.[7] This is a widely drafted provision, allowing an authority to require information from, for example, a relative or a former landlord.

15.8 As with the 'false statement' offence (above), the offence is different as between 'allocations' and 'homelessness' cases.

Homelessness

15.9 Under HA 1996 s214(1) and H(W)A 2014 s97(1), an intent must be shown to induce the authority, in connection with the exercise of its HA 1996 Part 7 or H(W)A 2014 Part 2 functions, to believe that the person withholding the information, or any other person, is entitled to accommodation or assistance.[8] Accordingly, it is directed at

4 Defined for the purposes of HA 1996 s214 as 'the benefit of any duty under HA 1996 Part 7, which relates to accommodation or to assistance in obtaining accommodation' (s183). There is no equivalent definitional provision in HA 1996 Part 6 or H(W)A 2014 Part 2.

5 HA 1996 s214(1); H(W)A 2014 s97(1).

6 HA 1996 s171(1).

7 HA 1996 ss171(1), 214(1); H(W)A 2014 s97(1).

8 Defined for the purposes of HA 1996 s214 as 'the benefit of any duty under HA 1996 Part 7, which relates to accommodation or to assistance in obtaining accommodation' (s183). There is no equivalent definition in HA 1996 Part 6 or H(W)A 2014 Part 2.

the person withholding information that would be harmful to an applicant, rather than at someone who refuses to provide helpful information.

Allocations

15.10 There is no equivalent 'intent' provision in HA 1996 s171(1): an offence is committed where a person knowingly withholds information which the authority have reasonably required him to give in connection with the exercise of its functions under HA 1996 Part 6.

Failure to notify changes

15.11 An offence of failure to notify changes arises only in relation to HA 1996 Part 7 and H(W)A 2014. It may only be committed by an applicant.

15.12 An applicant is under a positive duty to inform the authority as soon as possible of any change of facts material to his or her application, which occurs before receipt of notification of the authority's decision on his or her application, under HA 1996 s184 or H(W)A 2014 s63.[9] The offence is failure to notify the authority of the change as soon as possible.

15.13 The obligation only arises before the authority's notification, even though the circumstances to be taken into account on an internal review include any that have changed between that decision and the decision on the review.[10] It follows that a failure to notify the authority of a change adverse to the applicant's interests after the decision would seem to be exempt from this obligation, even though the authority is entitled to take a change into account,[11] but the point has never been explicitly tested and it may yet be that the courts would find a way to apply the requirement in this circumstances.

9 HA 1996 s214(2). The statutory language would not seem to be capable of being extended to the decision on the review, especially bearing in mind that as a criminal offence is involved, it is to be interpreted narrowly.

10 See paras 9.171–9.176.

11 Although there is no reference to HA 1996 s214 in *Mohamed v Hammersmith and Fulham LBC* [2001] UKHL 57, [2002] HLR 7, it formed a substantive part of the argument and it would therefore seem that Lord Slynn's conclusion at [25] confirms this analysis: 'I find nothing in the statutory language which requires the review to be confined to the date of the initial application or determination.'

15.14 The extent of the obligation is less straightforward than the two offences previously considered. Of particular difficulty is the issue of what constitutes a 'material change of facts'. In accordance with the usual principles of criminal law, the courts should interpret the provisions narrowly, ie in favour of the accused.

15.15 A related duty is imposed on authorities: to explain to an applicant, in ordinary language, the nature of the applicant's duty to notify them of material changes and that failure to do so is a criminal offence.[12] The English Code of Guidance[13] suggests that this obligation is 'explained in ordinary language, and conveyed sensitively to avoid intimidating applicants'.

15.16 It is a defence for the applicant to show that he or she was not given such an explanation. It is also a defence to show that the applicant had a reasonable excuse for non-compliance.[14]

12 HA 1996 s214(2); H(W)A 2014 s97(3), (4).

13 English Code of Guidance para 18.10. There is no equivalent In the Welsh Code.

14 HA 1996 s214(3); H(W)A 2014 s97(4)–(5).

APPENDICES

continued

APPENDIX A

Statutes[1]

In addition to the Housing Act 1996 Parts 6 and 7, Housing (Wales) Act 2014 Part 2, Schs 2 and 3 Pt 1 are reproduced in the ebook version of *Homelessness and Allocations*

1 © Crown Copyright. Legislation reproduced, as amended, up to date to 3 April 2018.

HOUSING ACT 1996

PART 6: ALLOCATION OF HOUSING ACCOMMODATION

159 Allocation of housing accommodation

(1) A local housing authority shall comply with the provisions of this Part in allocating housing accommodation.

(2) For the purposes of this Part a local housing authority allocate housing accommodation when they–

(a) select a person to be a secure or introductory tenant of housing accommodation held by them,

(b) nominate a person to be a secure or introductory tenant of housing accommodation held by another person, or

(c) nominate a person to be an assured tenant of housing accommodation held by [a private registered provider of social housing or][2] a registered social landlord.

(3) The reference in subsection (2)(a) to selecting a person to be a secure tenant includes deciding to exercise any power to notify an existing tenant or licensee that his tenancy or licence is to be a secure tenancy.

(4) The references in subsection (2)(b) and (c) to nominating a person include nominating a person in pursuance of any arrangements (whether legally enforceable or not) to require that housing accommodation, or a specified amount of housing accommodation, is made available to a person or one of a number of persons nominated by the authority.

[(4A) Subject to subsection (4B), the provisions of this Part do not apply to an allocation of housing accommodation by a local housing authority in England to a person who is already–

(a) a secure or introductory tenant, or

(b) an assured tenant of housing accommodation held by a private registered provider of social housing or a registered social landlord.

(4B) The provisions of this Part apply to an allocation of housing accommodation by a local housing authority in England to a person who falls within subsection (4A)(a) or (b) if–

(a) the allocation involves a transfer of housing accommodation for that person,

(b) the application for the transfer is made by that person, and

(c) the authority is satisfied that the person is to be given reasonable preference under section 166A(3).][3]

[(5) The provisions of this Part do not apply to an allocation of housing accommodation [by a local housing authority in Wales][4] to a person who is already

2 Words inserted by Housing and Regeneration Act 2008 (Consequential Provisions) Order 2010 SI No 866 Sch 2 para 100 (1 April 2010, subject to savings and transitional provisions specified in SI No 866 Sch 3 para 4).

3 Added by Localism Act (LA) 2011 s145(2) (15 January 2012 for the purpose specified in SI 2012 No 57 art 4(1)(j) subject to transitional and savings provisions specified in SI 2012 No 57 arts 6, 7, 9, 10 and 11; 18 June 2012 otherwise).

4 Words inserted by LA 2011 s145(3) (15 January 2012 for the purpose specified in SI 2012 No 57 art 4(1)(j) subject to transitional and savings provisions specified in SI 2012 No 57 arts 6, 7, 9, 10 and 11; 18 June 2012 otherwise).

a secure or introductory tenant unless the allocation involves a transfer of housing accommodation for that person and is made on his application.][5]

(7) Subject to the provisions of this Part, a local housing authority may allocate housing accommodation in such manner as they consider appropriate.

160 Cases where provisions about allocation do not apply

(1) The provisions of this Part about the allocation of housing accommodation do not apply in the following cases.

(2) They do not apply where a secure tenancy–

(a) vests under section 89 of the Housing Act 1985 (succession to periodic secure tenancy on death of tenant),

(b) remains a secure tenancy by virtue of section 90 of that Act (devolution of term certain of secure tenancy on death of tenant),

(c) is assigned under section 92 of that Act (assignment of secure tenancy by way of exchange),

(d) is assigned to a person who would be qualified to succeed the secure tenant if the secure tenant died immediately before the assignment, [. . .][6]

[(da) is granted in response to a request under section 158 of the Localism Act 2011 (transfer of tenancy), or][7]

(e) vests or is otherwise disposed of in pursuance of an order made under–

(i) section 24 of the Matrimonial Causes Act 1973 (property adjustment orders in connection with matrimonial proceedings),

(ii) section 17(1) of the Matrimonial and Family Proceedings Act 1984 (property adjustment orders after overseas divorce, &c.), [. . .][8]

(iii) paragraph 1 of Schedule 1 to the Children Act 1989 (orders for financial relief against parents) [, or][9]

[(iv) Part 2 of Schedule 5, or paragraph 9(2) or (3) of Schedule 7, to the Civil Partnership Act 2004 (property adjustment orders in connection with civil partnership proceedings or after overseas dissolution of civil partnership, etc.).][10]

(3) They do not apply where an introductory tenancy–

(a) becomes a secure tenancy on ceasing to be an introductory tenancy,

(b) vests under section 133(2) (succession to introductory tenancy on death of tenant),

(c) is assigned to a person who would be qualified to succeed the introductory tenant if the introductory tenant died immediately before the assignment, or

5 Section 159(5) substituted for s159(5)–(6) by Homelessness Act 2002 s13 (31 January 2003 as SI 2002 No 3114).

6 Possible drafting error: s160(1)(da) is purportedly inserted but s160(1)(d) does not exist so (da) is inserted after s160(2)(da) by LA 2011 Pt 7 s159(7) (1 April 2012 subject to SI 2012 No 628 arts 9, 11, 14, 15 and 17).

7 Possible drafting error, s160(1)(da) is purportedly inserted but s160(1)(d) does not exist so (da) is inserted after s160(2)(da) by LA 2011 s159(7), which is where it appears to belong (1 April 2012 subject to SI 2012 No 628 arts 9, 11, 14, 15 and 17).

8 Word repealed by Civil Partnership Act (CPA) 2004 Sch 30 para 1 (5 December 2005 as SI 2005 No 3175).

9 Added by CPA 2004 Sch 8 para 60 (5 December 2005).

10 Added by CPA 2004 Sch 8 para 60 (5 December 2005).

(d) vests or is otherwise disposed of in pursuance of an order made under–
  (i) section 24 of the Matrimonial Causes Act 1973 (property adjustment orders in connection with matrimonial proceedings),
  (ii) section 17(1) of the Matrimonial and Family Proceedings Act 1984 (property adjustment orders after overseas divorce, &c.), [. . .][11]
  (iii) paragraph 1 of Schedule 1 to the Children Act 1989 (orders for financial relief against parents) [, or][12]
  [(iv) Part 2 of Schedule 5, or paragraph 9(2) or (3) of Schedule 7, to the Civil Partnership Act 2004 (property adjustment orders in connection with civil partnership proceedings or after overseas dissolution of civil partnership, etc.).][13]

(4) They do not apply in such other cases as the Secretary of State may prescribe by regulations.

(5) The regulations may be framed so as to make the exclusion of the provisions of this Part about the allocation of housing accommodation subject to such restrictions or conditions as may be specified.
In particular, those provisions may be excluded–
(a) in relation to specified descriptions of persons, or
(b) in relation to housing accommodation of a specified description or a specified proportion of housing accommodation of any specified description.

[160ZA Allocation only to eligible and qualifying persons: England

(1) A local housing authority in England shall not allocate housing accommodation–
(a) to a person from abroad who is ineligible for an allocation of housing accommodation by virtue of subsection (2) or (4), or
(b) to two or more persons jointly if any of them is a person mentioned in paragraph (a).

(2) A person subject to immigration control within the meaning of the Asylum and Immigration Act 1996 is ineligible for an allocation of housing accommodation by a local housing authority in England unless he is of a class prescribed by regulations made by the Secretary of State.

(3) No person who is excluded from entitlement to [universal credit or][14] housing benefit by section 115 of the Immigration and Asylum Act 1999 (exclusion from benefits) shall be included in any class prescribed under subsection (2).

(4) The Secretary of State may by regulations prescribe other classes of persons from abroad who are ineligible to be allocated housing accommodation by local housing authorities in England.

(5) Nothing in subsection (2) or (4) affects the eligibility of a person who falls within section 159(4B).

(6) Except as provided by subsection (1), a person may be allocated housing accommodation by a local housing authority in England (whether on his application or otherwise) if that person–

11 Word repealed by CPA 2004 Sch 30 para 1 (5 December 2005 as SI 2005 No 3175).

12 Added by CPA 2004 Sch 8 para 60 (5 December 2005).

13 Added by CPA 2004 Sch 8 para 60 (5 December 2005).

14 Words inserted by Universal Credit (Consequential, Supplementary, Incidental and Miscellaneous Provisions) Regulations 2013 SI No 630 reg 12(3) (29 April 2013).

(a) is a qualifying person within the meaning of subsection (7), or
(b) is one of two or more persons who apply for accommodation jointly, and one or more of the other persons is a qualifying person within the meaning of subsection (7).

(7) Subject to subsections (2) and (4) and any regulations under subsection (8), a local housing authority may decide what classes of persons are, or are not, qualifying persons.

(8) The Secretary of State may by regulations–
(a) prescribe classes of persons who are, or are not, to be treated as qualifying persons by local housing authorities in England, and
(b) prescribe criteria that may not be used by local housing authorities in England in deciding what classes of persons are not qualifying persons.

(9) If a local housing authority in England decide that an applicant for housing accommodation–
(a) is ineligible for an allocation by them by virtue of subsection (2) or (4), or
(b) is not a qualifying person,
they shall notify the applicant of their decision and the grounds for it.

(10) That notice shall be given in writing and, if not received by the applicant, shall be treated as having been given if it is made available at the authority's office for a reasonable period for collection by him or on his behalf.

(11) A person who is not being treated as a qualifying person may (if he considers that he should be treated as a qualifying person) make a fresh application to the authority for an allocation of housing accommodation by them.][15]

[160A Allocation only to eligible persons [: Wales][16]

(1) A local housing authority [in Wales][17] shall not allocate housing accommodation–
(a) to a person from abroad who is ineligible for an allocation of housing accommodation by virtue of subsection (3) or (5);
(b) to a person who the authority have decided is to be treated as ineligible for such an allocation by virtue of subsection (7); or
(c) to two or more persons jointly if any of them is a person mentioned in paragraph (a) or (b).

(2) Except as provided by subsection (1), any person may be allocated housing accommodation by a local housing authority [in Wales][18] (whether on his application or otherwise).

(3) A person subject to immigration control within the meaning of the Asylum and Immigration Act 1996 (c. 49) is (subject to subsection (6)) ineligible for an

15 Added by LA 2011 s146(1) (15 January 2012 for purposes specified in SI 2012 No 57 art 4(1)(k) subject to transitional and savings provisions specified in SI 2012 No 57 arts 6, 7, 9, 10 and 11; 18 June 2012 otherwise).

16 Word inserted by LA 2011 s146(2)(a) (15 January 2012 for purposes specified in SI 2012 No 57 art 4(1)(k) subject to transitional and savings provisions specified in SI 2012 No 57 arts 6, 7, 9, 10 and 11; 18 June 2012 otherwise).

17 Words inserted by LA 2011 s146(2)(b) (15 January 2012 for purposes specified in SI 2012 No 57 art 4(1)(k) subject to transitional and savings provisions specified in SI 2012 No 57 arts 6, 7, 9, 10 and 11; 18 June 2012 otherwise).

18 Words inserted by LA 2011 s146(2)(c) (15 January 2012 for purposes specified in SI 2012 No 57 art 4(1)(k) subject to transitional and savings provisions specified in SI 2012 No 57 arts 6, 7, 9, 10 and 11; 18 June 2012 otherwise).

allocation of housing accommodation by a local housing authority [in Wales][19] unless he is of a class prescribed by regulations made by the Secretary of State.

(4) No person who is excluded from entitlement to [universal credit or][20] housing benefit by section 115 of the Immigration and Asylum Act 1999 (c. 33) (exclusion from benefits) shall be included in any class prescribed under subsection (3).

(5) The Secretary of State may by regulations prescribe other classes of persons from abroad who are (subject to subsection (6)) ineligible for an allocation of housing accommodation, either in relation to local housing authorities [in Wales][21] generally or any particular local housing authority [in Wales][22].

(6) Nothing in subsection (3) or (5) affects the eligibility of a person who is already–
   (a) a secure or introductory tenant;
   (b) an assured tenant of housing accommodation allocated to him by a local housing authority [in Wales][23].

(7) A local housing authority [in Wales][24] may decide that an applicant is to be treated as ineligible for an allocation of housing accommodation by them if they are satisfied that–
   (a) he, or a member of his household, has been guilty of unacceptable behaviour serious enough to make him unsuitable to be a tenant of the authority; and
   (b) in the circumstances at the time his application is considered, he is unsuitable to be a tenant of the authority by reason of that behaviour.

(8) The only behaviour which may be regarded by the authority as unacceptable for the purposes of subsection (7)(a) is–
   (a) behaviour of the person concerned which would (if he were a secure tenant of the authority) entitle the authority to a possession order under section 84 of the Housing Act 1985 (c. 68) on any ground mentioned in Part 1 of Schedule 2 to that Act (other than ground 8); or

19 Words inserted by LA 2011 s146(2)(d) (15 January 2012 for purposes specified in SI 2012 No 57 art 4(1)(k) subject to transitional and savings provisions specified in SI 2012 No 57 arts 6, 7, 9, 10 and 11; 18 June 2012 otherwise).

20 Words inserted by Universal Credit (Consequential, Supplementary, Incidental and Miscellaneous Provisions) Regulations 2013 SI No 630 Pt 2 reg 12(4) (29 April 2013).

21 Words inserted by LA 2011 s146(2)(e)(i) (15 January 2012 for purposes specified in SI 2012 No 57 art 4(1)(k) subject to transitional and savings provisions specified in SI 2012 No 57 arts 6, 7, 9, 10 and 11; 18 June 2012 otherwise).

22 Words inserted by LA 2011 s146(2)(e)(ii) (15 January 2012 for purposes specified in SI 2012 No 57 art 4(1)(k) subject to transitional and savings provisions specified in SI 2012 No 57 arts 6, 7, 9, 10 and 11; 18 June 2012 otherwise).

23 Words inserted by LA 2011 s146(2)(f) (15 January 2012 for purposes specified in SI 2012 No 57 art 4(1)(k) subject to transitional and savings provisions specified in SI 2012 No 57 arts 6, 7, 9, 10 and 11; 18 June 2012 otherwise).

24 Words inserted by LA 2011 s146(2)(g) (15 January 2012 for purposes specified in SI 2012 No 57 art 4(1)(k) subject to transitional and savings provisions specified in SI 2012 No 57 arts 6, 7, 9, 10 and 11; 18 June 2012 otherwise).

[(aa) behaviour of the person concerned which would (if he were a secure tenant of the authority) entitle the authority to a possession order under section 84A of the Housing Act 1985; or][25]
(b) behaviour of a member of his household which would (if he were a person residing with a secure tenant of the authority) entitle the authority to [a possession order of the type referred to in paragraph (a) or (aa)][26].

(9) If a local housing authority [in Wales][27] decide that an applicant for housing accommodation–
(a) is ineligible for an allocation by them by virtue of subsection (3) or (5); or
(b) is to be treated as ineligible for such an allocation by virtue of subsection (7),

they shall notify the applicant of their decision and the grounds for it.

(10) That notice shall be given in writing and, if not received by the applicant, shall be treated as having been given if it is made available at the authority's office for a reasonable period for collection by him or on his behalf.

(11) A person who is being treated by a local housing authority [in Wales][28] as ineligible by virtue of subsection (7) may (if he considers that he should no longer be treated as ineligible by the authority) make a fresh application to the authority for an allocation of housing accommodation by them.][29]

161–165

[. . .][30]

[166 Applications for housing accommodation

(1) A local housing authority shall secure that–
(a) advice and information is available free of charge to persons in their district about the right to make an application for an allocation of housing accommodation; and
(b) any necessary assistance in making such an application is available free of charge to persons in their district who are likely to have difficulty in doing so without assistance.

[(1A) A local housing authority in England shall secure that an applicant for an allocation of housing accommodation is informed that he has the rights mentioned in section 166A(9).][31]

25 Added by Anti-social Behaviour, Crime and Policing Act 2014 (Consequential Amendments) (Wales) Order 2015 SI No 1321 art 2(2)(a) (19 May 2015).

26 Words substituted by Anti-social Behaviour, Crime and Policing Act 2014 (Consequential Amendments) (Wales) Order 2015 SI No 1321 art 2(2)(b) (19 May 2015).

27 Words inserted by LA 2011 s146(2)(h) (15 January 2012 for purposes specified in SI 2012 No 57 art 4(1)(k) subject to transitional and savings provisions specified in SI 2012 No 57 arts 6, 7, 9, 10 and 11; 18 June 2012 otherwise).

28 Words inserted by LA 2011 s146(2)(i) (15 January 2012 for purposes specified in SI 2012 No 57 art 4(1)(k) subject to transitional and savings provisions specified in SI 2012 No 57 arts 6, 7, 9, 10 and 11; 18 June 2012 otherwise).

29 Added by Homelessness Act 2002 s14(2) (27 January 2003 as SI 2002 No 1736).

30 Repealed by Homelessness Act 2002 s14(1) (31 January 2003 as SI 2002 No 3144).

31 Added by LA 2011 s147(2)(a) (15 January 2012 for purposes specified in SI 2012 No 57 art 4(1)(k) subject to transitional and savings provisions specified in SI 2012 No 57 arts 6, 7, 9, 10 and 11; 18 June 2012 otherwise).

(2) A local housing authority [in Wales][32] shall secure that an applicant for an allocation of housing accommodation is informed that he has the rights mentioned in section 167(4A).

(3) Every application made to a local housing authority for an allocation of housing accommodation shall (if made in accordance with the procedural requirements of the authority's allocation scheme) be considered by the authority.

(4) The fact that a person is an applicant for an allocation of housing accommodation shall not be divulged (without his consent) to any other member of the public.

(5) In this Part *'district'* in relation to a local housing authority has the same meaning as in the Housing Act 1985 (c. 68).][33]

[166A Allocation in accordance with allocation scheme: England[34]

(1) Every local housing authority in England must have a scheme (their 'allocation scheme') for determining priorities, and as to the procedure to be followed, in allocating housing accommodation.
For this purpose 'procedure' includes all aspects of the allocation process, including the persons or descriptions of persons by whom decisions are taken.

(2) The scheme must include a statement of the authority's policy on offering people who are to be allocated housing accommodation–
(a) a choice of housing accommodation; or
(b) the opportunity to express preferences about the housing accommodation to be allocated to them.

(3) As regards priorities, the scheme shall, subject to subsection (4), be framed so as to secure that reasonable preference is given to–
(a) people who are homeless (within the meaning of Part 7);
(b) people who are owed a duty by any local housing authority under section 190(2), 193(2) or 195(2) (or under section 65(2) or 68(2) of the Housing Act 1985) or who are occupying accommodation secured by any such authority under section 192(3);
(c) people occupying insanitary or overcrowded housing or otherwise living in unsatisfactory housing conditions;
(d) people who need to move on medical or welfare grounds (including any grounds relating to a disability); and
(e) people who need to move to a particular locality in the district of the authority, where failure to meet that need would cause hardship (to themselves or to others).
The scheme may also be framed so as to give additional preference to particular descriptions of [people within one or more of paragraphs (a) to (e)] (being descriptions of people with urgent housing needs).

32 Words inserted by LA 2011 s147(2)(b) (15 January 2012 for purposes specified in SI 2012 No 57 art 4(1)(k) subject to transitional and savings provisions specified in SI 2012 No 57 arts 6, 7, 9, 10 and 11; 18 June 2012 otherwise).

33 Existing s166 is substituted and moved under a new heading entitled Applications for housing accommodation by Homelessness Act 2002 s15 (27 January 2003 as SI 2002 No 1736).

34 Section 166A was added by LA 2011 s147(4) (15 January 2012 for purposes specified in SI 2012 No 57 art 4(1)(k) subject to transitional and savings provisions specified in SI 2012 No 57 arts 6, 7, 9, 10 and 11; 18 June 2012 otherwise).

[The scheme must be framed so as to give additional preference to a person with urgent housing needs who falls within one or more of paragraphs (a) to (e) and who–

(i) is serving in the regular forces and is suffering from a serious injury, illness or disability which is attributable (wholly or partly) to the person's service,

(ii) formerly served in the regular forces,

(iii) has recently ceased, or will cease to be entitled, to reside in accommodation provided by the Ministry of Defence following the death of that person's spouse or civil partner who has served in the regular forces and whose death was attributable (wholly or partly) to that service, or

(iv) is serving or has served in the reserve forces and is suffering from a serious injury, illness or disability which is attributable (wholly or partly) to the person's service.

For this purpose 'the regular forces' and 'the reserve forces' have the meanings given by section 374 of the Armed Forces Act 2006.][35]

(4) People are to be disregarded for the purposes of subsection (3) if they would not have fallen within paragraph (a) or (b) of that subsection without the local housing authority having had regard to a restricted person (within the meaning of Part 7).

(5) The scheme may contain provision for determining priorities in allocating housing accommodation to people within subsection (3); and the factors which the scheme may allow to be taken into account include–

(a) the financial resources available to a person to meet his housing costs;

(b) any behaviour of a person (or of a member of his household) which affects his suitability to be a tenant;

(c) any local connection (within the meaning of section 199) which exists between a person and the authority's district.

(6) Subject to subsection (3), the scheme may contain provision about the allocation of particular housing accommodation–

(a) to a person who makes a specific application for that accommodation;

(b) to persons of a particular description (whether or not they are within subsection (3)).

(7) The Secretary of State may by regulations–

(a) specify further descriptions of people to whom preference is to be given as mentioned in subsection (3), or

(b) amend or repeal any part of subsection (3).

(8) The Secretary of State may by regulations specify factors which a local housing authority in England must not take into account in allocating housing accommodation.

(9) The scheme must be framed so as to secure that an applicant for an allocation of housing accommodation–

(a) has the right to request such general information as will enable him to assess–

(i) how his application is likely to be treated under the scheme (including in particular whether he is likely to be regarded as a member of a group of people who are to be given preference by virtue of subsection (3)); and

35 subs(3)(e) was inserted by the Housing Act 1996 (Additional Preference for Armed Forces) (England) Regulations 2012 SI No 2989 reg 2(b) (30 November 2012).

(ii) whether housing accommodation appropriate to his needs is likely to be made available to him and, if so, how long it is likely to be before such accommodation becomes available for allocation to him;

(b) has the right to request the authority to inform him of any decision about the facts of his case which is likely to be, or has been, taken into account in considering whether to allocate housing accommodation to him; and

(c) has the right to request a review of a decision mentioned in paragraph (b), or in section 160ZA(9), and to be informed of the decision on the review and the grounds for it.

(10) As regards the procedure to be followed, the scheme must be framed in accordance with such principles as the Secretary of State may prescribe by regulations.

(11) Subject to the above provisions, and to any regulations made under them, the authority may decide on what principles the scheme is to be framed.

(12) A local housing authority in England must, in preparing or modifying their allocation scheme, have regard to–

(a) their current homelessness strategy under section 1 of the Homelessness Act 2002,

(b) their current tenancy strategy under section 150 of the Localism Act 2011, and

(c) in the case of an authority that is a London borough council, the London housing strategy.

(13) Before adopting an allocation scheme, or making an alteration to their scheme reflecting a major change of policy, a local housing authority in England must–

(a) send a copy of the draft scheme, or proposed alteration, to every private registered provider of social housing and registered social landlord with which they have nomination arrangements (see section 159(4)), and

(b) afford those persons a reasonable opportunity to comment on the proposals.

(14) A local housing authority in England shall not allocate housing accommodation except in accordance with their allocation scheme.]

167 Allocation in accordance with allocation scheme [: Wales][36]

(1) Every local housing authority [in Wales][37] shall have a scheme (their 'allocation scheme') for determining priorities, and as to the procedure to be followed, in allocating housing accommodation.

For this purpose *'procedure'* includes all aspects of the allocation process, including the persons or descriptions of persons by whom decisions are to be taken.

[(1A) The scheme shall include a statement of the authority's policy on offering people who are to be allocated housing accommodation–

(a) a choice of housing accommodation; or

(b) the opportunity to express preferences about the housing accommodation to be allocated to them.][38]

36 Word inserted by LA 2011 s147(5)(a) (15 January 2012 for purposes specified in SI 2012 No 57 art 4(1)(k) subject to transitional and savings provisions specified in SI 2012 No 57 arts 6, 7, 9, 10 and 11; 18 June 2012 otherwise).

37 Words inserted by Localism Act 2011s.147(5)(b) (15 January 2012 for purposes specified in SI 2012 No 57 art 4(1)(k) subject to transitional and savings provisions specified in SI 2012 No 57 arts 6, 7, 9, 10 and 11; 18 June 2012 otherwise).

38 Amended by Homelessness Act 2002 s16 (31 January 2003 as SI 2002 No 3114).

[(2) As regards priorities, the scheme shall [, subject to subsection (2ZA),][39] be framed so as to secure that reasonable preference is given to–

(a) people who are homeless [(within the meaning of Part 2 of the Housing (Wales) Act 2014)][40];

[(b) people who are owed any duty by a local housing authority under section 66, 73 or 75 of the Housing (Wales) Act 2014;][41]

(c) people occupying insanitary or overcrowded housing or otherwise living in unsatisfactory housing conditions;

(d) people who need to move on medical or welfare grounds; and

(e) people who need to move to a particular locality in the district of the authority, where failure to meet that need would cause hardship (to themselves or to others).

The scheme may also be framed so as to give additional preference to particular descriptions of people within this subsection (being descriptions of people with urgent housing needs).

[(2ZA) People are to be disregarded for the purposes of subsection (2) if they would not have fallen within paragraph (a) or (b) of that subsection without the local housing authority having had regard to a restricted person (within the meaning of [Part 2 of the Housing (Wales) Act 2014][42]).][43]

(2A) The scheme may contain provision for determining priorities in allocating housing accommodation to people within subsection (2); and the factors which the scheme may allow to be taken into account include–

(a) the financial resources available to a person to meet his housing costs;

(b) any behaviour of a person (or of a member of his household) which affects his suitability to be a tenant;

(c) any local connection (within the meaning of [section 81 of the Housing (Wales) Act 2014][44]) which exists between a person and the authority's district.

(2B) Nothing in subsection (2) requires the scheme to provide for any preference to be given to people the authority have decided are people to whom subsection (2C) applies.

(2C) This subsection applies to a person if the authority are satisfied that–

(a) he, or a member of his household, has been guilty of unacceptable behaviour serious enough to make him unsuitable to be a tenant of the authority; and

(b) in the circumstances at the time his case is considered, he deserves by reason of that behaviour not to be treated as a member of a group of people who are to be given preference by virtue of subsection (2).

(2D) Subsection (8) of section 160A applies for the purposes of subsection (2C)(a) above as it applies for the purposes of subsection (7)(a) of that section.

39 Words inserted by Housing and Regeneration Act (HRA) 2008 Sch 15(1) para 2(2) (2 March 2009 for purposes specified in SI 2009 No 415 art 2).

40 Words substituted by Housing (Wales) Act 2014 (H(W)A) 2014 anaw 7 Sch 3(1) para 3(a)(i) (27 April 2015).

41 Substituted by H(W)A 2014 anaw 7 Sch 3(1) para 3(a)(ii) (27 April 2015).

42 Words substituted by H(W)A 2014 Sch 3(1) para 3(b) (27 April 2015)

43 Added by H&RA 2008 Sch 15(1) para 2(3) (March 2, 2009 for purposes specified in SI 2009 No 415 art 2).

44 Words substituted by H(W)A 2014 Sch 3(1) para 3(c) (27 April 2015).

(2E) Subject to subsection (2), the scheme may contain provision about the allocation of particular housing accommodation–
(a) to a person who makes a specific application for that accommodation;
(b) to persons of a particular description (whether or not they are within subsection (2)).][45]

(3) The Secretary of State may by regulations–
(a) specify further descriptions of people to whom preference is to be given as mentioned in subsection (2), or
(b) amend or repeal any part of subsection (2).

(4) The Secretary of State may by regulations specify factors which a local housing authority [in Wales][46] shall not take into account in allocating housing accommodation.

[(4A) The scheme shall be framed so as to secure that an applicant for an allocation of housing accommodation–
(a) has the right to request such general information as will enable him to assess–
(i) how his application is likely to be treated under the scheme (including in particular whether he is likely to be regarded as a member of a group of people who are to be given preference by virtue of subsection (2)); and
(ii) whether housing accommodation appropriate to his needs is likely to be made available to him and, if so, how long it is likely to be before such accommodation becomes available for allocation to him;
(b) is notified in writing of any decision that he is a person to whom subsection (2C) applies and the grounds for it;
(c) has the right to request the authority to inform him of any decision about the facts of his case which is likely to be, or has been, taken into account in considering whether to allocate housing accommodation to him; and
(d) has the right to request a review of a decision mentioned in paragraph (b) or (c), or in section 160A(9), and to be informed of the decision on the review and the grounds for it.][47]

(5) As regards the procedure to be followed, the scheme shall be framed in accordance with such principles as the Secretary of State may prescribe by regulations.

(6) Subject to the above provisions, and to any regulations made under them, the authority may decide on what principles the scheme is to be framed.

(7) Before adopting an allocation scheme, or making an alteration to their scheme reflecting a major change of policy, a local housing authority [in Wales][48] shall–
(a) send a copy of the draft scheme, or proposed alteration, to every [private registered provider of social housing and][49] registered social landlord with which they have nomination arrangements (see section 159(4)), and

45 Amended by Homelessness Act 2002 s16 (31 January 2003 as SI 2002 No 3114).

46 Words inserted by LA 2011 s147(5)(c) (15 January 2012 for purposes specified in SI 2012 No 57 art 4(1)(k) subject to transitional and savings provisions specified in SI 2012 No 57 arts 6, 7, 9, 10 and 11; 18 June 2012 otherwise).

47 Amended by Homelessness Act 2002 s16 (31 January 2003 as SI 2002 No 3114).

48 Words inserted by LA 2011 s147(5)(d) (15 January 2012 for purposes specified in SI 2012 No 57 art 4(1)(k) subject to transitional and savings provisions specified in SI 2012 No 57 arts 6, 7, 9, 10 and 11; 18 June 2012 otherwise).

49 Words inserted by Housing and Regeneration Act 2008 (Consequential Provisions) Order 2010 No 866 Sch 2 para 101 (1 April 2010: insertion has effect subject to savings and transitional provisions specified in SI 2010 No 866 Sch 3 para 4).

(b) afford those persons a reasonable opportunity to comment on the proposals.

(8) A local housing authority [in Wales][50] shall not allocate housing accommodation except in accordance with their allocation scheme.

168 Information about allocation scheme

(1) A local housing authority shall publish a summary of their allocation scheme and provide a copy of the summary free of charge to any member of the public who asks for one.

(2) The authority shall make the scheme available for inspection at their principal office and shall provide a copy of the scheme, on payment of a reasonable fee, to any member of the public who asks for one.

(3) When the authority make an alteration to their scheme reflecting a major change of policy, they shall within a reasonable period of time [take such steps as they consider reasonable to bring the effect of the alteration to the attention of those likely to be affected by it][51].

169 Guidance to authorities by the Secretary of State

(1) In the exercise of their functions under this Part, local housing authorities shall have regard to such guidance as may from time to time be given by the Secretary of State.

(2) The Secretary of State may give guidance generally or to specified descriptions of authorities.

170 Co-operation between [certain][52] social landlords and local housing authorities

Where a local housing authority so request, a [private registered provider of social housing or][53] registered social landlord shall co-operate to such extent as is reasonable in the circumstances in offering accommodation to [people with priority under the authority's allocation scheme].[54]

171 False statements and withholding information

(1) A person commits an offence if, in connection with the exercise by a local housing authority of their functions under this Part–

(a) he knowingly or recklessly makes a statement which is false in a material particular, or

(b) he knowingly withholds information which the authority have reasonably required him to give in connection with the exercise of those functions.

50 Words inserted by LA 2011 s147(5)(e) (15 January 2012 for purposes specified in SI 2012 No 57 art 4(1)(k) subject to transitional and savings provisions specified in SI 2012 No 57 arts 6, 7, 9, 10 and 11; 18 June 2012 otherwise).

51 Words substituted by Homelessness Act 2002 Sch 1 para 4 (31 January 2003 as SI 2002 No 3114).

52 Word substituted by Housing and Regeneration Act 2008 (Consequential Provisions) Order 2010 SI No 866 Sch 2 para 102(b) (1 April 2010: substitution has effect subject to savings and transitional provisions specified in SI 2010 No 866 Sch 3 para 4).

53 Words inserted by Housing and Regeneration Act 2008 (Consequential Provisions) Order 2010 SI No 866 Sch 2 para 102(a) (1 April 2010: insertion has effect subject to savings and transitional provisions specified in SI 2010 No 866 Sch 3 para 4).

54 Words substituted by Homelessness Act 2002 Sch 1 para 5 (31 January 2003 as SI 2002 No 3114).

(2) A person guilty of an offence under this section is liable on summary conviction to a fine not exceeding level 5 on the standard scale.

172 Regulations

(1) Regulations under this Part shall be made by statutory instrument.

(2) No regulations shall be made under [section 166A(7) or 167(3)][55] (regulations amending provisions about priorities in allocating housing accommodation) unless a draft of the regulations has been laid before and approved by a resolution of each House of Parliament.

(3) Any other regulations under this Part shall be subject to annulment in pursuance of a resolution of either House of Parliament.

(4) Regulations under this Part may contain such incidental, supplementary and transitional provisions as appear to the Secretary of State appropriate, and may make different provision for different cases including different provision for different areas.

173 Consequential amendments: Part VI

The enactments mentioned in Schedule 16 have effect with the amendments specified there which are consequential on the provisions of this Part.

174 Index of defined expressions: Part VI

The following Table shows provisions defining or otherwise explaining expressions used in this Part (other than provisions defining or explaining an expression used in the same section–

allocation (of housing)	section 159(2)
allocation scheme	[section 166A and 167][56]
assured tenancy	section 230
[district (of local housing authority)	section 165(5)][57]
[repealed][58]	
[repealed][59]	
introductory tenancy and introductory tenant	sections 230 and 124
local housing authority	section 230
[repealed][60]	
registered social landlord	sections 230 and 2
secure tenancy and secure tenant	section 230

55 Words inserted by LA 2011 s147(6) (15 January 2012 subject to transitional and savings provisions specified in SI 2012 No 57 arts 6, 7, 9, 10 and 11).

56 Words inserted by LA 2011 s147(7) (June 7, 2012).

57 Entry inserted by Homelessness Act 2002 Sch 1 para 6 (31 January 2003 as SI 2003 No 3114).

58 Entry repealed by Homelessness Act 2002 Sch 2 para 1 (31 January 2003 as SI 2003 No 3114).

59 Entry repealed by Homelessness Act 2002 Sch 2 para 1 (31 January 2003 as SI 2003 No 3114).

60 Entry repealed by Homelessness Act 2002 Sch 2 para 1 (31 January 2003 as SI 2003 No 3114).

PART 7: HOMELESSNESS

175 Homelessness and threatened homelessness

(1) A person is homeless if he has no accommodation available for his occupation, in the United Kingdom or elsewhere, which he–
- (a) is entitled to occupy by virtue of an interest in it or by virtue of an order of a court,
- (b) has an express or implied licence to occupy, or
- (c) occupies as a residence by virtue of any enactment or rule of law giving him the right to remain in occupation or restricting the right of another person to recover possession.

(2) A person is also homeless if he has accommodation but–
- (a) he cannot secure entry to it, or
- (b) it consists of a moveable structure, vehicle or vessel designed or adapted for human habitation and there is no place where he is entitled or permitted both to place it and to reside in it.

(3) A person shall not be treated as having accommodation unless it is accommodation which it would be reasonable for him to continue to occupy.

(4) A person is threatened with homelessness if it is likely that he will become homeless within [56][61] days.

[(5) A person is also threatened with homelessness if–
- (a) a valid notice has been given to the person under section 21 of the Housing Act 1988 (orders for possession on expiry or termination of assured shorthold tenancy) in respect of the only accommodation the person has that is available for the person's occupation, and
- (b) that notice will expire within 56 days.][62]

176 Meaning of accommodation available for occupation

Accommodation shall be regarded as available for a person's occupation only if it is available for occupation by him together with–
- (a) any other person who normally resides with him as a member of his family, or
- (b) any other person who might reasonably be expected to reside with him.

References in this Part to securing that accommodation is available for a person's occupation shall be construed accordingly.

177 Whether it is reasonable to continue to occupy accommodation

(1) It is not reasonable for a person to continue to occupy accommodation if it is probable that this will lead to domestic violence [or other violence][63] against him, or against–
- (a) a person who normally resides with him as a member of his family, or
- (b) any other person who might reasonably be expected to reside with him.

[. . .][64]

61 Word substituted by Homelessness Reduction Act (HRA) 2017 s1(2) (3 April 2018: substitution has effect subject to transitional and savings provisions specified in SI 2018 No 167 reg 4(1)).

62 Added by HRA 2017 s1(3) (3 April 2018: insertion has effect subject to transitional and savings provisions specified in SI 2018 No 167 reg 4(1)).

63 Amended by Homelessness Act 2002 s10 (31 July 2002 as SI 2002 No 1799).

64 Amended by Homelessness Act 2002 s10 (31 July 2002 as SI 2002 No 1799).

[(1A) For this purpose *'violence'* means–
(a) violence from another person; or
(b) threats of violence from another person which are likely to be carried out;
and violence is 'domestic violence' if it is from a person who is associated with the victim.][65]
(2) In determining whether it would be, or would have been, reasonable for a person to continue to occupy accommodation, regard may be had to the general circumstances prevailing in relation to housing in the district of the local housing authority to whom he has applied for accommodation or for assistance in obtaining accommodation.
(3) The Secretary of State may by order specify–
(a) other circumstances in which it is to be regarded as reasonable or not reasonable for a person to continue to occupy accommodation, and
(b) other matters to be taken into account or disregarded in determining whether it would be, or would have been, reasonable for a person to continue to occupy accommodation.

178 Meaning of associated person

(1) For the purposes of this Part, a person is associated with another person if–
(a) they are or have been married to each other;
[(aa) they are or have been civil partners of each other;][66]
(b) they are cohabitants or former cohabitants;
(c) they live or have lived in the same household;
(d) they are relatives;
(e) they have agreed to marry one another (whether or not that agreement has been terminated);
[(ea) they have entered into a civil partnership agreement between them (whether or not that agreement has been terminated);][67]
(f) in relation to a child, each of them is a parent of the child or has, or has had, parental responsibility for the child.
(2) If a child has been adopted or [falls within subsection (2A)][68], two persons are also associated with each other for the purposes of this Part if–
(a) one is a natural parent of the child or a parent of such a natural parent, and
(b) the other is the child or a person–
(i) who has become a parent of the child by virtue of an adoption order or who has applied for an adoption order, or
(ii) with whom the child has at any time been placed for adoption.
[(2A) A child falls within this subsection if–
(a) an adoption agency, within the meaning of section 2 of the Adoption and Children Act 2002, is authorised to place him for adoption under section 19 of that Act (placing children with parental consent) or he has become the subject of an order under section 21 of that Act (placement orders), or

65 Amended by Homelessness Act 2002 s10 (31 July 2002 as SI 2002 No 1799).
66 Added by CPA 2004 Sch 8 para 61(2) (5 December 2005).
67 Added by CPA 2004 Sch 8 para 61(3) (5 December 2005).
68 Words substituted by Adoption and Children Act 2002 Sch 3 para 90 (30 December 2005).

(b) he is freed for adoption by virtue of an order made–
(i) in England and Wales, under section 18 of the Adoption Act 1976,
(ii) in Scotland, under section 18 of the Adoption (Scotland) Act 1978, or
(iii) in Northern Ireland, under Article 17(1) or 18(1) of the Adoption (Northern Ireland) Order 1987.][69]

(3) In this section–

['*adoption order*' means an adoption order within the meaning of section 72(1) of the Adoption Act 1976 or section 46(1) of the Adoption and Children Act 2002;][70]

'*child*' means a person under the age of 18 years;

['*civil partnership agreement*' has the meaning given by section 73 of the Civil Partnership Act 2004;][71]

['*cohabitants*' means–
(a) a man and a woman who, although not married to each other, are living together as husband and wife, or
(b) two people of the same sex who, although not civil partners of each other, are living together as if they were civil partners;

and '*former cohabitants*' shall be construed accordingly;][72]

'*parental responsibility*' has the same meaning as in the Children Act 1989; and

'*relative*', in relation to a person, means –
(a) the father, mother, stepfather, stepmother, son, daughter, stepson, stepdaughter, grandmother, grandfather, grandson or granddaughter of that person or of that person's [spouse, civil partner, former spouse or former civil partner][73], or
(b) the brother, sister, uncle, aunt, niece or nephew (whether of the full blood or of the half blood or by [marriage or civil partnership][74]) of that person or of that person's [spouse, civil partner, former spouse or former civil partner][75],

and includes, in relation to a person who is living or has lived with another person as husband and wife, a person who would fall within paragraph (a) or (b) if the parties were married to each other.

[179 Duty of local housing authority in England to provide advisory services

(1) Each local housing authority in England must provide or secure the provision of a service, available free of charge to any person in the authority's district, providing information and advice on–
(a) preventing homelessness,
(b) securing accommodation when homeless,
(c) the rights of persons who are homeless or threatened with homelessness, and the duties of the authority, under this Part,

69 Added by Adoption and Children Act 2002 Sch 3 para 91 (30 December 2005).
70 Definition substituted by Adoption and Children Act 2002 Sch 3 para 92 (30 December 2005).
71 Definition inserted by CPA 2004 Sch 8 para 61(4) (5 December 2005).
72 Definition substituted by CPA 2004 Sch 8 para 61(5) (5 December 2005).
73 Words substituted by CPA 2004 Sch 8 para 61(6) (5 December 2005).
74 Word substituted by CPA 2004 Sch 8 para 61(7) (5 December 2005).
75 Words substituted by CPA 2004 Sch 8 para 61(6) (5 December 2005).

(d) any help that is available from the authority or anyone else, whether under this Part or otherwise, for persons in the authority's district who are homeless or may become homeless (whether or not they are threatened with homelessness), and
(e) how to access that help.

(2) The service must be designed to meet the needs of persons in the authority's district including, in particular, the needs of–
(a) persons released from prison or youth detention accommodation,
(b) care leavers,
(c) former members of the regular armed forces,
(d) victims of domestic abuse,
(e) persons leaving hospital,
(f) persons suffering from a mental illness or impairment, and
(g) any other group that the authority identify as being at particular risk of homelessness in the authority's district.

(3) The authority may give to any person by whom the service is provided on behalf of the authority assistance by way of grant or loan.

(4) The authority may also assist any such person–
(a) by permitting the person to use premises belonging to the authority,
(b) by making available furniture or other goods, whether by way of gift, loan or otherwise, and
(c) by making available the services of staff employed by the authority.

(5) In this section–
'care leavers' means persons who are former relevant children (within the meaning given by section 23C(1) of the Children Act 1989);
'domestic abuse' means–
(a) physical violence,
(b) threatening, intimidating, coercive or controlling behaviour, or
(c) emotional, financial, sexual or any other form of abuse, where the victim is associated with the abuser;
'financial abuse' includes–
(a) having money or other property stolen,
(b) being defrauded,
(c) being put under pressure in relation to money or other property, and
(d) having money or other property misused;
'hospital' has the same meaning as in the National Health Service Act 2006 (see section 275(1) of that Act);
'regular armed forces' means the regular forces as defined by section 374 of the Armed Forces Act 2006;
'youth detention accommodation' means–
(a) a secure children's home,
(b) a secure training centre,
(c) a secure college,
(d) a young offender institution,
(e) accommodation provided by or on behalf of a local authority for the purpose of restricting the liberty of children;
(f) accommodation provided for that purpose under section 82(5) of the Children Act 1989, or

(g) accommodation, or accommodation of a description, for the time being specified by order under section 107(1)(e) of the Powers of Criminal Courts (Sentencing) Act 2000 (youth detention accommodation for the purposes of detention and training orders).][76]

180 Assistance for voluntary organisations

(1) The Secretary of State or a local housing authority [in England][77] may give assistance by way of grant or loan to voluntary organisations concerned with homelessness or matters relating to homelessness.

(2) A local housing authority may also assist any such organisation–

(a) by permitting them to use premises belonging to the authority,

(b) by making available furniture or other goods, whether by way of gift, loan or otherwise, and

(c) by making available the services of staff employed by the authority.

(3) A *'voluntary organisation'* means a body (other than a public or local authority) whose activities are not carried on for profit.

181 Terms and conditions of assistance

(1) This section has effect as to the terms and conditions on which assistance is given under section 179 or 180.

(2) Assistance shall be on such terms, and subject to such conditions, as the person giving the assistance may determine.

(3) No assistance shall be given unless the person to whom it is given undertakes–

(a) to use the money, furniture or other goods or premises for a specified purpose, and

(b) to provide such information as may reasonably be required as to the manner in which the assistance is being used.

The person giving the assistance may require such information by notice in writing, which shall be complied with within 21 days beginning with the date on which the notice is served.

(4) The conditions subject to which assistance is given shall in all cases include conditions requiring the person to whom the assistance is given–

(a) to keep proper books of account and have them audited in such manner as may be specified,

(b) to keep records indicating how he has used the money, furniture or other goods or premises, and

(c) to submit the books of account and records for inspection by the person giving the assistance.

(5) If it appears to the person giving the assistance that the person to whom it was given has failed to carry out his undertaking as to the purpose for which the assistance was to be used, he shall take all reasonable steps to recover from that person an amount equal to the amount of the assistance.

(6) He must first serve on the person to whom the assistance was given a notice specifying the amount which in his opinion is recoverable and the basis on which that amount has been calculated.

76 Substituted by HRA 2017 s2 (3 April 2018).

77 Words inserted by H(W)A 2014 Sch 3(1) para 6 (27 April 2015: insertion has effect subject to transitional provisions as specified in SI 2015 No 1272 art 7).

182 Guidance by the Secretary of State

(1) In the exercise of their functions relating to homelessness and the prevention of homelessness, a local housing authority or social services authority [in England][78] shall have regard to such guidance as may from time to time be given by the Secretary of State.

(2) The Secretary of State may give guidance either generally or to specified descriptions of authorities.

183 Application for assistance

(1) The following provisions of this Part apply where a person applies to a local housing authority [in England][79] for accommodation, or for assistance in obtaining accommodation, and the authority have reason to believe that he is or may be homeless or threatened with homelessness.

(2) In this Part–

'applicant' means a person making such an application,

'assistance under this Part' means the benefit of any function under the following provisions of this Part relating to accommodation or assistance in obtaining accommodation, and

'eligible for assistance' means not excluded from such assistance by section 185 (persons from abroad not eligible for housing assistance) or section 186 (asylum seekers and their dependants).

(3) Nothing in this section or the following provisions of this Part affects a person's entitlement to advice and information under section 179 (duty to provide advisory services).

184 Inquiry into cases of homelessness or threatened homelessness

(1) If the local housing authority have reason to believe that an applicant may be homeless or threatened with homelessness, they shall make such inquiries as are necessary to satisfy themselves–

(a) whether he is eligible for assistance, and

(b) if so, whether any duty, and if so what duty, is owed to him under the following provisions of this Part.

(2) They may also make inquiries whether he has a local connection with the district of another local housing authority in England, Wales or Scotland.

(3) On completing their inquiries the authority shall notify the applicant of their decision and, so far as any issue is decided against his interests, inform him of the reasons for their decision.

[(3A) If the authority decide that a duty is [, or after the authority's duty to the applicant under section 189B(2) comes to an end would be,][80] owed to the applicant under [section 193(2)][81] but would not have done so without having had regard to a restricted person, the notice under subsection (3) must also–

78 Words inserted by H(W)A 2014 Sch 3(1) para 7 (27 April 2015: insertion has effect subject to transitional provisions as specified in SI 2015 No 1272 art 7).

79 Words inserted by H(W)A 2014 Sch 3(1) para 8 (27 April 2015: insertion has effect subject to transitional provisions as specified in SI 2015 No 1272 art 7).

80 Words inserted by HRA 2017 s5(3)(a) (3 April 2018: insertion has effect subject to transitional and savings provisions specified in SI 2018 No 167 reg 4(1)).

81 Words repealed by HRA 2017 s4(3)(a) (3 April 2018: repeal has effect subject to transitional and savings provisions specified in SI 2018 No 167 reg 4(1)).

(a) inform the applicant that their decision was reached on that basis,
(b) include the name of the restricted person,
(c) explain why the person is a restricted person, and
(d) explain the effect of section 193(7AD)[. . .][82].][83]

(4) If the authority have notified or intend to notify another local housing authority [in England under section 198(A1) (referral of cases where section 189B applies)][84], they shall at the same time notify the applicant of that decision and inform him of the reasons for it.

(5) A notice under subsection (3) or (4) shall also inform the applicant of his right to request a review of the decision and of the time within which such a request must be made (see section 202).

(6) Notice required to be given to a person under this section shall be given in writing and, if not received by him, shall be treated as having been given to him if it is made available at the authority's office for a reasonable period for collection by him or on his behalf.

[(7) In this Part *'a restricted person'* means a person–
(a) who is not eligible for assistance under this Part,
(b) who is subject to immigration control within the meaning of the Asylum and Immigration Act 1996, and
(c) either–
(i) who does not have leave to enter or remain in the United Kingdom, or
(ii) whose leave to enter or remain in the United Kingdom is subject to a condition to maintain and accommodate himself, and any dependants, without recourse to public funds.][85]

185 Persons from abroad not eligible for housing assistance

(1) A person is not eligible for assistance under this Part if he is a person from abroad who is ineligible for housing assistance.

(2) A person who is subject to immigration control within the meaning of the Asylum and Immigration Act 1996 is not eligible for housing assistance unless he is of a class prescribed by regulations made by the Secretary of State.

[(2A) No person who is excluded from entitlement to [universal credit or][86] housing benefit by section 115 of the Immigration and Asylum Act 1999 (exclusion from benefits) shall be included in any class prescribed under subsection (2).][87]

(3) The Secretary of State may make provision by regulations as to other descriptions of persons who are to be treated for the purposes of this Part as persons from abroad who are ineligible for housing assistance.

82 Words repealed by HRA 2017 s4(3)(b) (3 April 2018: repeal has effect subject to transitional and savings provisions specified in SI 2018 No 167 reg 4(1)).

83 Added by H&RA 2008 Sch 15(1) para 3(2) (2 March 2009 for purposes specified in SI 2009 No 415 art 2).

84 Words substituted by HRA 2017 s5(3)(b) (3 April 2018: substitution has effect subject to transitional and savings provisions specified in SI 2018 No 167 reg 4(1)).

85 Added by H&RA 2008 Sch 15(1) para 3(3) (2 March 2009 for purposes specified in SI 2009 No 415 art 2).

86 Words inserted by Universal Credit (Consequential, Supplementary, Incidental and Miscellaneous Provisions) Regulations 2013 No 630 Pt 2 reg 12(5) (29 April 2013).

87 Substituted by Homelessness Act 2002 Sch 1 para 7(1) (26 February 2002).

(4) A person from abroad who is not eligible for housing assistance shall be disregarded in determining for the purposes of this Part whether [a person falling within subsection (5)][88] –
(a) is homeless or threatened with homelessness, or
(b) has a priority need for accommodation.

[(5) A person falls within this subsection if the person–
(a) falls within a class prescribed by regulations made under subsection (2); but
(b) is not a national of an EEA State or Switzerland.][89]

186 Asylum-seekers and their dependants

(1) An asylum-seeker, or a dependant of an asylum-seeker who is not by virtue of section 185 a person from abroad who is ineligible for housing assistance, is not eligible for assistance under this Part if he has any accommodation in the United Kingdom, however temporary, available for his occupation.

(2) For the purposes of this section a person who makes a claim for asylum–
(a) becomes an asylum-seeker at the time when his claim is recorded by the Secretary of State as having been made, and
(b) ceases to be an asylum-seeker at the time when his claim is recorded by the Secretary of State as having been finally determined or abandoned.

(3) For the purposes of this section a person–
(a) becomes a dependant of an asylum-seeker at the time when he is recorded by the Secretary of State as being a dependant of the asylum-seeker, and
(b) ceases to be a dependant of an asylum-seeker at the time when the person whose dependant he is ceases to be an asylum-seeker or, if it is earlier, at the time when he is recorded by the Secretary of State as ceasing to be a dependant of the asylum-seeker.

(4) In relation to an asylum-seeker, *'dependant'* means a person–
(a) who is his spouse or a child of his under the age of eighteen, and
(b) who has neither a right of abode in the United Kingdom nor indefinite leave under the Immigration Act 1971 to enter or remain in the United Kingdom.

(5) In this section a *'claim for asylum'* means a claim made by a person that it would be contrary to the United Kingdom's obligations under the Convention relating to the Status of Refugees done at Geneva on 28th July 1951 and the Protocol to that Convention for him to be removed from, or required to leave, the United Kingdom.

187 Provision of information by Secretary of State

(1) The Secretary of State shall, at the request of a local housing authority [in England][90], provide the authority with such information as they may require–
(a) as to whether a person is [a person to whom section 115 of the Immigration and Asylum Act 1999 (exclusion from benefits) applies][91], and

88 Words substituted by H&RA 2008 Sch 15(1) para 4(2) (2 March 2009 for purposes specified in SI 2009 No 415 art 2).

89 Added by H&RA 2008 Sch 15(1) para 4(3) (2 March 2009 for purposes specified in SI 2009 No 415 art 2).

90 Words inserted by H(W)A 2014 Sch 3(1) para 9 (27 April 2015: insertion has effect subject to transitional provisions as specified in SI 2015 No 1272 art 7).

91 Words substituted by Immigration and Asylum Act (IAA) 1999 s117(6) (2 April 2000).

(b) to enable them to determine whether such a person is eligible for assistance under this Part under section 185 (persons from abroad not eligible for housing assistance).

(2) Where that information is given otherwise than in writing, the Secretary of State shall confirm it in writing if a written request is made to him by the authority.

(3) If it appears to the Secretary of State that any application, decision or other change of circumstances has affected the status of a person about whom information was previously provided by him to a local housing authority under this section, he shall inform the authority in writing of that fact, the reason for it and the date on which the previous information became inaccurate.

[188 Interim duty to accommodate in case of apparent priority need

[(1) If the local housing authority have reason to believe that an applicant may be homeless, eligible for assistance and have a priority need, they must secure that accommodation is available for the applicant's occupation.

(1ZA) In a case in which the local housing authority conclude their inquiries under section 184 and decide that the applicant does not have a priority need–

(a) where the authority decide that they do not owe the applicant a duty under section 189B(2), the duty under subsection (1) comes to an end when the authority notify the applicant of that decision, or

(b) otherwise, the duty under subsection (1) comes to an end upon the authority notifying the applicant of their decision that, upon the duty under section 189B(2) coming to an end, they do not owe the applicant any duty under section 190 or 193.

(1ZB) In any other case, the duty under subsection (1) comes to an end upon the later of–

(a) the duty owed to the applicant under section 189B(2) coming to an end or the authority notifying the applicant that they have decided that they do not owe the applicant a duty under that section, and

(b) the authority notifying the applicant of their decision as to what other duty (if any) they owe to the applicant under the following provisions of this Part upon the duty under section 189B(2) coming to an end.][92]

[(1A) But if the local housing authority have reason to believe that the duty under section 193(2) may apply in relation to an applicant in the circumstances referred to in section 195A(1), they shall secure that accommodation is available for the applicant's occupation [until the later of paragraph (a) or (b) of subsection (1ZB)][93] regardless of whether the applicant has a priority need.

(2) The duty under this section arises irrespective of any possibility of the referral of the applicant's case to another local housing authority (see sections 198 to 200).

[(2A) For the purposes of this section, where the applicant requests a review under section 202(1)(h) of the authority's decision as to the suitability of accommodation offered to the applicant by way of a final accommodation offer or a final Part 6 offer (within the meaning of section 193A), the authority's duty to the applicant

92 Section 188(1)–(1ZB) substituted for s188(1) by HRA 2017 s5(4)(a) (3 April 2018: substitution has effect subject to transitional and savings provisions specified in SI 2018 No 167 reg 4(1)).

93 Words substituted by HRA 2017 s5(4)(b) (3 April 2018: substitution has effect subject to transitional and savings provisions specified in SI 2018 No 167 reg 4(1)).

under section 189B(2) is not to be taken to have come to an end under section 193A(2) until the decision on the review has been notified to the applicant.

(3) Otherwise, the duty under this section comes to an end in accordance with subsections (1ZA) to (1A), regardless of any review requested by the applicant under section 202.
But the authority may secure that accommodation is available for the applicant's occupation pending a decision on review.][94]][95]

189 Priority need for accommodation

(1) The following have a priority need for accommodation–
   (a) a pregnant woman or a person with whom she resides or might reasonably be expected to reside;
   (b) a person with whom dependent children reside or might reasonably be expected to reside;
   (c) a person who is vulnerable as a result of old age, mental illness or handicap or physical disability or other special reason, or with whom such a person resides or might reasonably be expected to reside;
   (d) a person who is homeless or threatened with homelessness as a result of an emergency such as flood, fire or other disaster.
(2) The Secretary of State may by order–
   (a) specify further descriptions of persons as having a priority need for accommodation, and
   (b) amend or repeal any part of subsection (1).
(3) Before making such an order the Secretary of State shall consult such associations representing relevant authorities, and such other persons, as he considers appropriate.
(4) No such order shall be made unless a draft of it has been approved by resolution of each House of Parliament.

[189A Assessments and personalised plan

(1) If the local housing authority are satisfied that an applicant is–
   (a) homeless or threatened with homelessness, and
   (b) eligible for assistance,
   the authority must make an assessment of the applicant's case.
(2) The authority's assessment of the applicant's case must include an assessment of–
   (a) the circumstances that caused the applicant to become homeless or threatened with homelessness,
   (b) the housing needs of the applicant including, in particular, what accommodation would be suitable for the applicant and any persons with whom the applicant resides or might reasonably be expected to reside ('other relevant persons'), and
   (c) what support would be necessary for the applicant and any other relevant persons to be able to have and retain suitable accommodation.

94 Section 188(2A) and (3) substituted for s188(3) by HRA 2017 s5(4)(c) (3 April 2018: substitution has effect subject to transitional and savings provisions specified in SI 2018 No 167 reg 4(1)).

95 Added by LA 2011 s149(2) (9 November 2012: insertion has effect as SI 2012 No 2599 subject to transitional provisions specified in SI 2012 No 2599 art 2).

(3) The authority must notify the applicant, in writing, of the assessment that the authority make.

(4) After the assessment has been made, the authority must try to agree with the applicant–

(a) any steps the applicant is to be required to take for the purposes of securing that the applicant and any other relevant persons have and are able to retain suitable accommodation, and

(b) the steps the authority are to take under this Part for those purposes.

(5) If the authority and the applicant reach an agreement, the authority must record it in writing.

(6) If the authority and the applicant cannot reach an agreement, the authority must record in writing–

(a) why they could not agree,

(b) any steps the authority consider it would be reasonable to require the applicant to take for the purposes mentioned in subsection (4)(a), and

(c) the steps the authority are to take under this Part for those purposes.

(7) The authority may include in a written record produced under subsection (5) or (6) any advice for the applicant that the authority consider appropriate (including any steps the authority consider it would be a good idea for the applicant to take but which the applicant should not be required to take).

(8) The authority must give to the applicant a copy of any written record produced under subsection (5) or (6).

(9) Until such time as the authority consider that they owe the applicant no duty under any of the following sections of this Part, the authority must keep under review–

(a) their assessment of the applicant's case, and

(b) the appropriateness of any agreement reached under subsection (4) or steps recorded under subsection (6)(b) or (c).

(10) If–

(a) the authority's assessment of any of the matters mentioned in subsection (2) changes, or

(b) the authority's assessment of the applicant's case otherwise changes such that the authority consider it appropriate to do so,

the authority must notify the applicant, in writing, of how their assessment of the applicant's case has changed (whether by providing the applicant with a revised written assessment or otherwise).

(11) If the authority consider that any agreement reached under subsection (4) or any step recorded under subsection (6)(b) or (c) is no longer appropriate–

(a) the authority must notify the applicant, in writing, that they consider the agreement or step is no longer appropriate,

(b) any failure, after the notification is given, to take a step that was agreed to in the agreement or recorded under subsection (6)(b) or (c) is to be disregarded for the purposes of this Part, and

(c) subsections (4) to (8) apply as they applied after the assessment was made.

(12) A notification under this section or a copy of any written record produced under subsection (5) or (6), if not received by the applicant, is to be treated as having been given to the applicant if it is made available at the authority's office for a reasonable period for collection by or on behalf of the applicant.][96]

96 Added by HRA 2017 s3(1) (3 April 2018).

[189B Initial duty owed to all eligible persons who are homeless

(1) This section applies where the local housing authority are satisfied that an applicant is–
  (a) homeless, and
  (b) eligible for assistance.

(2) Unless the authority refer the application to another local housing authority in England (see section 198(A1)), the authority must take reasonable steps to help the applicant to secure that suitable accommodation becomes available for the applicant's occupation for at least–
  (a) 6 months, or
  (b) such longer period not exceeding 12 months as may be prescribed.

(3) In deciding what steps they are to take, the authority must have regard to their assessment of the applicant's case under section 189A.

(4) Where the authority–
  (a) are satisfied that the applicant has a priority need, and
  (b) are not satisfied that the applicant became homeless intentionally,
  the duty under subsection (2) comes to an end at the end of the period of 56 days beginning with the day the authority are first satisfied as mentioned in subsection (1).

(5) If any of the circumstances mentioned in subsection (7) apply, the authority may give notice to the applicant bringing the duty under subsection (2) to an end.

(6) The notice must–
  (a) specify which of the circumstances apply, and
  (b) inform the applicant that the applicant has a right to request a review of the authority's decision to bring the duty under subsection (2) to an end and of the time within which such a request must be made.

(7) The circumstances are that the authority are satisfied that–
  (a) the applicant has–
    (i) suitable accommodation available for occupation, and
    (ii) a reasonable prospect of having suitable accommodation available for occupation for at least 6 months, or such longer period not exceeding 12 months as may be prescribed, from the date of the notice,
  (b) the authority have complied with the duty under subsection (2) and the period of 56 days beginning with the day that the authority are first satisfied as mentioned in subsection (1) has ended (whether or not the applicant has secured accommodation),
  (c) the applicant has refused an offer of suitable accommodation and, on the date of refusal, there was a reasonable prospect that suitable accommodation would be available for occupation by the applicant for at least 6 months or such longer period not exceeding 12 months as may be prescribed,
  (d) the applicant has become homeless intentionally from any accommodation that has been made available to the applicant as a result of the authority's exercise of their functions under subsection (2),
  (e) the applicant is no longer eligible for assistance, or
  (f) the applicant has withdrawn the application mentioned in section 183(1).

(8) A notice under this section must be given in writing and, if not received by the applicant, is to be treated as having been given to the applicant if it is made available at the authority's office for a reasonable period for collection by or on behalf of the applicant.

(9) The duty under subsection (2) can also be brought to an end under–
   (a) section 193A (consequences of refusal of final accommodation offer or final Part 6 offer at the initial relief stage), or
   (b) sections 193B and 193C (notices in cases of applicant's deliberate and unreasonable refusal to co-operate).][97]

190 Duties to persons becoming homeless intentionally

[(1) This section applies where–
   (a) the local housing authority are satisfied that an applicant–
      (i) is homeless and eligible for assistance, but
      (ii) became homeless intentionally,
   (b) the authority are also satisfied that the applicant has a priority need, and
   (c) the authority's duty to the applicant under section 189B(2) has come to an end.][98]

(2) [The authority must–][99]
   (a) secure that accommodation is available for his occupation for such period as they consider will give him a reasonable opportunity of securing accommodation for his occupation, and
   (b) provide him with [(or secure that he is provided with) advice and assistance][100] in any attempts he may make to secure that accommodation becomes available for his occupation.

[. . .][101]

[[(4) In deciding what advice and assistance is to be provided under this section, the authority must have regard to their assessment of the applicant's case under section 189A.][102]

(5) The advice and assistance provided under subsection (2)(b) [. . .][103] must include information about the likely availability in the authority's district of types of accommodation appropriate to the applicant's housing needs (including, in particular, the location and sources of such types of accommodation).][104]

191 Becoming homeless intentionally

(1) A person becomes homeless intentionally if he deliberately does or fails to do anything in consequence of which he ceases to occupy accommodation which is available for his occupation and which it would have been reasonable for him to continue to occupy.

97 Added by HRA 2017 s5(2) (3 April 2018: insertion has effect subject to transitional and savings provisions specified in SI 2018 No 167 reg 4(1)).

98 Substituted by HRA 2017 s5(5)(a) (3 April 2018: substitution has effect subject to transitional and savings provisions specified in SI 2018 No 167 reg 4(1)).

99 Words substituted by HRA 2017 s5(5)(b) (3 April 2018: substitution has effect subject to transitional and savings provisions specified in SI 2018 No 167 reg 4(1)).

100 Words substituted by Homelessness Act 2002 Sch 1 para 9 (31 July 2002 as SI 2002 No 1799).

101 Repealed by HRA 2017 s5(5)(c) (3 April 2018: repeal has effect subject to transitional and savings provisions specified in SI 2018 No 167 reg 4(1)).

102 Substituted by HRA 2017 s3(2) (3 April 2018).

103 Words repealed by HRA 2017 s5(5)(d) (3 April 2018: repeal has effect subject to transitional and savings provisions specified in SI 2018 No 167 reg 4(1)).

104 Added by Homelessness Act 2002 Sch 1 para 10 (31 July 2002 as SI 2002 No 1799).

(2) For the purposes of subsection (1) an act or omission in good faith on the part of a person who was unaware of any relevant fact shall not be treated as deliberate.

(3) A person shall be treated as becoming homeless intentionally if–

(a) he enters into an arrangement under which he is required to cease to occupy accommodation which it would have been reasonable for him to continue to occupy, and

(b) the purpose of the arrangement is to enable him to become entitled to assistance under this Part,

and there is no other good reason why he is homeless.

[. . .][105]

192 Duties to persons found to be homeless or threatened with homelessness

[. . .][106]

[193 Duty to persons with priority need who are not homeless intentionally

[(1) This section applies where–

(a) the local housing authority–

(i) are satisfied that an applicant is homeless and eligible for assistance, and

(ii) are not satisfied that the applicant became homeless intentionally,

(b) the authority are also satisfied that the applicant has a priority need, and

(c) the authority's duty to the applicant under section 189B(2) has come to an end.][107]

[(1A) But this section does not apply if–

(a) section 193A(3) disapplies this section, or

(b) the authority have given notice to the applicant under section 193B(2).][108]

(2) Unless the authority refer the application to another local housing authority (see section 198), they shall secure that accommodation is available for occupation by the applicant.

(3) The authority are subject to the duty under this section until it ceases by virtue of any of the following provisions of this section.

(3A) [. . .][109]

(3B) In this section *'a restricted case'* means a case where the local housing authority would not be satisfied as mentioned in subsection (1) without having had regard to a restricted person.

[(5) The local housing authority shall cease to be subject to the duty under this section if–

(a) the applicant, having been informed by the authority of the possible consequence of refusal or acceptance and of the right to request a review of

105 Repealed by Homelessness Act 2002 Sch 2 para 1 (31 July 2002 as SI 2002 No 1799).

106 Repealed by HRA 2017 s5(6) (3 April 2018: repeal has effect subject to transitional and savings provisions specified in SI 2018 No 167 reg 4(1)).

107 Substituted by HRA 2017 s5(7) (3 April 2018: substitution has effect subject to transitional and savings provisions specified in SI 2018 No 167 reg 4(1)).

108 Added by HRA 2017 s7(2) (3 April 2018).

109 Repealed by LA 2011 s148(2) (9 November 2012: substitution has effect as SI 2012 No 2599 art 2 subject to transitional provisions specified in SI 2012 No 2599 art 3).

the suitability of the accommodation, refuses an offer of accommodation which the authority are satisfied is suitable for the applicant,
(b) that offer of accommodation is not an offer of accommodation under Part 6 or a private rented sector offer, and
(c) the authority notify the applicant that they regard themselves as ceasing to be subject to the duty under this section.][110]

(6) The local housing authority shall cease to be subject to the duty under this section if the applicant–
(a) ceases to be eligible for assistance,
(b) becomes homeless intentionally from the accommodation made available for his occupation,
(c) accepts an offer of accommodation under Part VI (allocation of housing), or
(cc) accepts an offer of an assured tenancy (other than an assured shorthold tenancy) from a private landlord,
(d) otherwise voluntarily ceases to occupy as his only or principal home the accommodation made available for his occupation.

(7) The local housing authority shall also cease to be subject to the duty under this section if the applicant, having been informed of the possible consequence of refusal [or acceptance][111] and of his right to request a review of the suitability of the accommodation, refuses a final offer of accommodation under Part 6.

(7A) An offer of accommodation under Part 6 is a final offer for the purposes of subsection (7) if it is made in writing and states that it is a final offer for the purposes of subsection (7).

(7AA) [The][112] authority shall also cease to be subject to the duty under this section if the applicant, having been informed [in writing][113] of the matters mentioned in subsection (7AB)–
(a) accepts a [private rented sector offer][114], or
(b) refuses such an offer.

(7AB) The matters are–
(a) the possible consequence of refusal [or acceptance][115] of the offer, and
(b) that the applicant has the right to request a review of the suitability of the accommodation [, and

110 Substituted by LA 2011 s148(3) (9 November 2012: substitution has effect as SI 2012 No 2599 art 2 subject to transitional provisions specified in SI 2012 No 2599 art 3).

111 Words inserted by LA 2011 s148(4) (9 November 2012: insertion has effect as SI 2012 No 2599 art 2 subject to transitional provisions specified in SI 2012 No 2599 art 3).

112 Words repealed by LA 2011 s148(5)(a) (9 November 2012: repeal has effect as SI 2012 No 2599 art 2 subject to transitional provisions specified in SI 2012 No 2599 art 3).

113 Words inserted by LA 2011 s148(5)(b) (9 November 2012: insertion has effect as SI 2012 No 2599 art 2 subject to transitional provisions specified in SI 2012 No 2599 art 3).

114 Words substituted by LA 2011 s148(5)(c) (9 November 2012: substitution has effect as SI 2012 No 2599 art 2 subject to transitional provisions specified in SI 2012 No 2599 art 3).

115 Words inserted by LA 2011 s148(6)(a) (9 November 2012: insertion has effect as SI 2012 No 2599 art 2 subject to transitional provisions specified in SI 2012 No 2599 art 3).

(c) in a case which is not a restricted case, the effect under section 195A of a further application to a local housing authority within two years of acceptance of the offer.][116]

(7AC) For the purposes of this section an offer is a [private rented sector offer][117] if–

(a) it is an offer of an assured shorthold tenancy made by a private landlord to the applicant in relation to any accommodation which is, or may become, available for the applicant's occupation,

(b) it is made, with the approval of the authority, in pursuance of arrangements made by the authority with the landlord with a view to bringing the authority's duty under this section to an end, and

(c) the tenancy being offered is a fixed term tenancy (within the meaning of Part 1 of the Housing Act 1988) for a period of at least 12 months.

(7AD) In a restricted case the authority shall, so far as reasonably practicable, bring their duty under this section to an end as mentioned in subsection (7AA).

[. . .][118]

(7F) The local housing authority shall not–

(a) make a final offer of accommodation under Part 6 for the purposes of subsection (7); [or][119]

(ab) approve a [private rented sector offer][120] [,][121]

[. . .][122]

unless they are satisfied that the accommodation is suitable for the applicant and that [subsection (8) does not apply to the applicant][123].

[(8) This subsection applies to an applicant if–

(a) the applicant is under contractual or other obligations in respect of the applicant's existing accommodation, and

(b) the applicant is not able to bring those obligations to an end before being required to take up the offer.][124]

116 Added by LA 2011 s148(6)(b) (9 November 2012: insertion has effect as SI 2012 No 2599 art 2 subject to transitional provisions specified in SI 2012 No 2599 art 3).

117 Words substituted by LA 2011 s148(7) (9 November 2012: substitution has effect as SI 2012 No 2599 art 2 subject to transitional provisions specified in SI 2012 No 2599 art 3).

118 Repealed by LA 2011 Pt 7 s148(8) (9 November 2012: repeal has effect as SI 2012 No 2599 art 2 subject to transitional provisions specified in SI 2012 No 2599 art 3).

119 Word inserted by LA 2011 s148(9)(a) (9 November 2012: insertion has effect as SI 2012 No 2599 art 2 subject to transitional provisions specified in SI 2012 No 2599 art 3).

120 Words substituted by LA 2011 s148(9)(b) (9 November 2012: substitution has effect as SI 2012 No 2599 art 2 subject to transitional provisions specified in SI 2012 No 2599 art 3).

121 Repealed by LA 2011 s148(9)(c) (9 November 2012: repeal has effect as SI 2012 No 2599 art 2 subject to transitional provisions specified in SI 2012 No 2599 art 3).

122 Repealed by LA 2011 s148(9)(c) (9 November 2012: repeal has effect as SI 2012 No 2599 art 2 subject to transitional provisions specified in SI 2012 No 2599 art 3).

123 Words substituted by LA 2011 Pt 7 c1 s148(9)(d) (9 November 2012: substitution has effect as SI 2012 No 2599 art 2 subject to transitional provisions specified in SI 2012 No 2599 art 3).

124 Substituted by LA 2011 Pt 7 c1 s148(10) (9 November 2012: substitution has effect as SI 2012 No 2599 art 2 subject to transitional provisions specified in SI 2012 No 2599 art 3).

(9) A person who ceases to be owed the duty under this section may make a fresh application to the authority for accommodation or assistance in obtaining accommodation.

[(10) The appropriate authority may provide by regulations that subsection (7AC)(c) is to have effect as if it referred to a period of the length specified in the regulations.

(11) Regulations under subsection (10)–
(a) may not specify a period of less than 12 months, and
(b) may not apply to restricted cases.

(12) In subsection (10) *'the appropriate authority'* –
(a) in relation to local housing authorities in England, means the Secretary of State;
(b) in relation to local housing authorities in Wales, means the Welsh Ministers.][125]

[193A Consequences of refusal of final accommodation offer or final Part 6 offer at the initial relief stage

(1) Subsections (2) and (3) apply where–
(a) a local housing authority owe a duty to an applicant under section 189B(2), and
(b) the applicant, having been informed of the consequences of refusal and of the applicant's right to request a review of the suitability of the accommodation, refuses–
(i) a final accommodation offer, or
(ii) a final Part 6 offer.

(2) The authority's duty to the applicant under section 189B(2) comes to an end.

(3) Section 193 (the main housing duty) does not apply.

(4) An offer is a 'final accommodation offer' if–
(a) it is an offer of an assured shorthold tenancy made by a private landlord to the applicant in relation to any accommodation which is, or may become, available for the applicant's occupation,
(b) it is made, with the approval of the authority, in pursuance of arrangements made by the authority in the discharge of their duty under section 189B(2), and
(c) the tenancy being offered is a fixed term tenancy (within the meaning of Part 1 of the Housing Act 1988) for a period of at least 6 months.

(5) A *'final Part 6 offer'* is an offer of accommodation under Part 6 (allocation of housing) that–
(a) is made in writing by the authority in the discharge of their duty under section 189B(2), and
(b) states that it is a final offer for the purposes of this section.

(6) The authority may not approve a final accommodation offer, or make a final Part 6 offer, unless they are satisfied that the accommodation is suitable for the applicant and that subsection (7) does not apply.

(7) This subsection applies to an applicant if–
(a) the applicant is under contractual or other obligations in respect of the applicant's existing accommodation, and

125 Added by LA 2011 Pt 7 c1 s148(11) (9 November 2012: insertion has effect as SI 2012 No 2599 art 2 subject to transitional provisions specified in SI 2012 No 2599 art 3).

(b) the applicant is not able to bring those obligations to an end before being required to take up the offer.][126]

[193B Notices in cases of an applicant's deliberate and unreasonable refusal to co-operate

(1) Section 193C applies where–
(a) a local housing authority owe a duty to an applicant under section 189B(2) or 195(2), and
(b) the authority give notice to the applicant under subsection (2).
(2) A local housing authority may give a notice to an applicant under this subsection if the authority consider that the applicant has deliberately and unreasonably refused to take any step–
(a) that the applicant agreed to take under subsection (4) of section 189A, or
(b) that was recorded by the authority under subsection (6)(b) of that section.
(3) A notice under subsection (2) must–
(a) explain why the authority are giving the notice and its effect, and
(b) inform the applicant that the applicant has a right to request a review of the authority's decision to give the notice and of the time within which such a request must be made.
(4) The authority may not give notice to the applicant under subsection (2) unless–
(a) the authority have given a relevant warning to the applicant, and
(b) a reasonable period has elapsed since the warning was given.
(5) A *'relevant warning'* means a notice–
(a) given by the authority to the applicant after the applicant has deliberately and unreasonably refused to take any step–
(i) that the applicant agreed to take under subsection (4) of section 189A, or
(ii) that was recorded by the authority under subsection (6)(b) of that section,
(b) that warns the applicant that, if the applicant should deliberately and unreasonably refuse to take any such step after receiving the notice, the authority intend to give notice to the applicant under subsection (2), and
(c) that explains the consequences of such a notice being given to the applicant.
(6) For the purposes of subsections (2) and (5), in deciding whether a refusal by the applicant is unreasonable, the authority must have regard to the particular circumstances and needs of the applicant (whether identified in the authority's assessment of the applicant's case under section 189A or not).
(7) The Secretary of State may make provision by regulations as to the procedure to be followed by a local housing authority in connection with notices under this section.
(8) A notice under this section must be given in writing and, if not received by the applicant, is to be treated as having been given to the applicant if it is made

126 Added by HRA 2017 s7(1) (3 April 2018: s7(1) came into force on 12 February 2018 as specified in SI 2018 No 167 reg 2(a) for the limited purpose of enabling the exercise of the power to make regulations conferred by 1996 s193B(7); 3 April 2018 as SI 2018 No 167 reg 3(g) otherwise).

available at the authority's office for a reasonable period for collection by or on behalf of the applicant.][127]

[193C Notice under section 193B: consequences

(1) In the circumstances mentioned in section 193B(1), this section applies in relation to a local housing authority and an applicant.

(2) The authority's duty to the applicant under section 189B(2) or 195(2) comes to an end.

(3) Subsection (4) applies if the authority–

(a) are satisfied that the applicant is homeless, eligible for assistance and has a priority need, and

(b) are not satisfied that the applicant became homeless intentionally.

(4) Section 193 (the main housing duty) does not apply, but the authority must secure that accommodation is available for occupation by the applicant.

(5) The authority cease to be subject to the duty under subsection (4) if the applicant–

(a) ceases to be eligible for assistance,

(b) becomes homeless intentionally from accommodation made available for the applicant's occupation,

(c) accepts an offer of an assured tenancy from a private landlord, or

(d) otherwise voluntarily ceases to occupy, as the applicant's only or principal home, the accommodation made available for the applicant's occupation.

(6) The authority also cease to be subject to the duty under subsection (4) if the applicant, having been informed of the possible consequences of refusal or acceptance and of the applicant's right to request a review of the suitability of the accommodation, refuses or accepts–

(a) a final accommodation offer, or

(b) a final Part 6 offer.

(7) An offer is 'a final accommodation offer' if–

(a) it is an offer of an assured shorthold tenancy made by a private landlord to the applicant in relation to any accommodation which is, or may become, available for the applicant's occupation,

(b) it is made, with the approval of the authority, in pursuance of arrangements made by the authority with a view to bringing the authority's duty under subsection (4) to an end, and

(c) the tenancy being offered is a fixed term tenancy (within the meaning of Part 1 of the Housing Act 1988) for a period of at least 6 months.

(8) A *'final Part 6 offer'* is an offer of accommodation under Part 6 (allocation of housing) that is made in writing and states that it is a final offer for the purposes of this section.

(9) The authority may not approve a final accommodation offer, or make a final Part 6 offer, unless they are satisfied that the accommodation is suitable for the applicant and that subsection (10) does not apply.

(10) This subsection applies to an applicant if–

127 Added by HRA 2017 s7(1) (3 April 2018: s7(1) came into force on 12 February 2018 as specified in SI 2018 No 167 reg 2(a) for the limited purpose of enabling the exercise of the power to make regulations conferred by 1996 s193B(7); 3 April 2018 as SI 2018 No 167 reg 3(g) otherwise).

(a) the applicant is under contractual or other obligations in respect of the applicant's existing accommodation, and
(b) the applicant is not able to bring those obligations to an end before being required to take up the offer.][128]

194 Duties to persons found to be homeless or threatened with homelessness

[. . .][129]

[195 Duties in cases of threatened homelessness

(1) This section applies where the local housing authority are satisfied that an applicant is–
(a) threatened with homelessness, and
(b) eligible for assistance.

(2) The authority must take reasonable steps to help the applicant to secure that accommodation does not cease to be available for the applicant's occupation.

(3) In deciding what steps they are to take, the authority must have regard to their assessment of the applicant's case under section 189A.

(4) Subsection (2) does not affect any right of the authority, whether by virtue of contract, enactment or rule of law, to secure vacant possession of any accommodation.

(5) If any of the circumstances mentioned in subsection (8) apply, the authority may give notice to the applicant bringing the duty under subsection (2) to an end.

(6) But the authority may not give notice to the applicant under subsection (5) on the basis that the circumstances in subsection (8)(b) apply if a valid notice has been given to the applicant under section 21 of the Housing Act 1988 (orders for possession on expiry or termination of assured shorthold tenancy) that–
(a) will expire within 56 days or has expired, and
(b) is in respect of the only accommodation that is available for the applicant's occupation.

(7) The notice must–
(a) specify which of the circumstances apply, and
(b) inform the applicant that the applicant has a right to request a review of the authority's decision to bring the duty under subsection (2) to an end and of the time within which such a request must be made.

(8) The circumstances are that the authority are satisfied that–
(a) the applicant has–
(i) suitable accommodation available for occupation, and
(ii) a reasonable prospect of having suitable accommodation available for occupation for at least 6 months, or such longer period not exceeding 12 months as may be prescribed, from the date of the notice,
(b) the authority have complied with the duty under subsection (2) and the period of 56 days beginning with the day that the authority are first satisfied as mentioned in subsection (1) has ended (whether or not the applicant is still threatened with homelessness),

128 Added by HRA 2017 s7(1) (3 April 2018: s7(1) came into force on 12 February 2018 as specified in SI 2018 No 167 reg 2(a) for the limited purpose of enabling the exercise of the power to make regulations conferred by 1996 s193B(7); 3 April 2018 as SI 2018 No 167 reg 3(g) otherwise.

129 Repealed by Homelessness Act 2002 Sch 2 para 1 (31 July 2002 as SI 2002 No 1799).

(c) the applicant has become homeless,
(d) the applicant has refused an offer of suitable accommodation and, on the date of refusal, there was a reasonable prospect that suitable accommodation would be available for occupation by the applicant for at least 6 months or such longer period not exceeding 12 months as may be prescribed,
(e) the applicant has become homeless intentionally from any accommodation that has been made available to the applicant as a result of the authority's exercise of their functions under subsection (2),
(f) the applicant is no longer eligible for assistance, or
(g) the applicant has withdrawn the application mentioned in section 183(1).

(9) A notice under this section must be given in writing and, if not received by the applicant, is to be treated as having been given to the applicant if it is made available at the authority's office for a reasonable period for collection by or on behalf of the applicant.

(10) The duty under subsection (2) can also be brought to an end under sections 193B and 193C (notices in cases of applicant's deliberate and unreasonable refusal to co-operate).][130]

[195A Re-application after private rented sector offer

(1) If within two years beginning with the date on which an applicant accepts an offer under section 193(7AA) (private rented sector offer), the applicant re-applies for accommodation, or for assistance in obtaining accommodation, and the local housing authority–
(a) is satisfied that the applicant is homeless and eligible for assistance, and
(b) is not satisfied that the applicant became homeless intentionally,
the duty under section 193(2) applies regardless of whether the applicant has a priority need.

(2) For the purpose of subsection (1), an applicant in respect of whom a valid notice under section 21 of the Housing Act 1988(orders for possession on expiry or termination of assured shorthold tenancy) has been given is to be treated as homeless from the date on which that notice expires.
[. . .][131]

(5) Subsection (1) [. . .][132] does not apply to a case where the local housing authority would not be satisfied as mentioned in that subsection without having regard to a restricted person.

(6) Subsection (1) [. . .][133] does not apply to a re-application by an applicant for accommodation, or for assistance in obtaining accommodation, if the immediately preceding application made by that applicant was one to which subsection (1) [. . .][134] applied.][135]

130 Substituted by HRA 2017 s4(2) (3 April 2018: substitution has effect subject to transitional and savings provisions specified in SI 2018 No 167 reg 4(1)).

131 Repealed by HRA 2017 s4(4)(a) (3 April 2018: repeal has effect subject to transitional and savings provisions specified in SI 2018 No 167 reg 4(1)).

132 Words repealed by HRA 2017 s4(4)(b) (3 April 2018: repeal has effect subject to transitional and savings provisions specified in SI 2018 No 167 reg 4(1)).

133 Words repealed by HRA 2017 s4(4)(c) (3 April 2018: repeal has effect subject to transitional and savings provisions specified in SI 2018 No 167 reg 4(1)).

134 Words repealed by HRA 2017 s4(4)(c) (3 April 2018: repeal has effect subject to transitional and savings provisions specified in SI 2018 No 167 reg 4(1)).

135 Added by LA 2011 Pt 7 c1 s149(4) (9 November 2012: insertion has effect as SI 2012 No 2599 subject to transitional provisions specified in SI 2012 No 2599 art 3).

196 Duties to persons found to be homeless or threatened with homelessness

[. . .][136]

197 Duty where other suitable accommodation available

[. . .][137]

198 Referral of case to another local housing authority

[(A1) If the local housing authority would be subject to the duty under section 189B (initial duty owed to all eligible persons who are homeless) but consider that the conditions are met for referral of the case to another local housing authority in England, they may notify that other authority of their opinion.][138]

(1) If the local housing authority would be subject to the duty under section 193 (accommodation for those with priority need who are not homeless intentionally) but consider that the conditions are met for referral of the case to another local housing authority, they may notify that other authority of their opinion.

(2) The conditions for referral of the case to another authority are met if–

(a) neither the applicant nor any person who might reasonably be expected to reside with him has a local connection with the district of the authority to whom his application was made,

(b) the applicant or a person who might reasonably be expected to reside with him has a local connection with the district of that other authority, and

(c) neither the applicant nor any person who might reasonably be expected to reside with him will run the risk of domestic violence in that other district.

[(2ZA) The conditions for referral of the case to another authority are also met if–

(a) the application is made within the period of two years beginning with the date on which the applicant accepted an offer from the other authority under section 193(7AA) (private rented sector offer), and

(b) neither the applicant nor any person who might reasonably be expected to reside with the applicant will run the risk of domestic violence in the district of the other authority.][139]

[(2A) But the conditions for referral mentioned in subsection (2) [or (2ZA)][140] are not met if–

(a) the applicant or any person who might reasonably be expected to reside with him has suffered violence (other than domestic violence) in the district of the other authority; and

(b) it is probable that the return to that district of the victim will lead to further violence of a similar kind against him.

136 Repealed by HRA 2017 s4(5) (3 April 2018: repeal has effect subject to transitional and savings provisions specified in SI 2018 No 167 reg 4(1)).

137 Repealed by Homelessness Act 2002 Sch 2 para 1 (31 July 2002 as SI 2002 No 1799).

138 Added by HRA 2017 s5(8) (3 April 2018).

139 Added by LA 2011 Pt 7 s149(6) (9 November 2012: insertion has effect as SI 2012 No 2599 art 2 subject to transitional provisions specified in SI 2012 No 2599 art 3).

140 Added by LA 2011 Pt 7 s149(7) (9 November 2012: insertion has effect as SI 2012 No 2599 art 2 subject to transitional provisions specified in SI 2012 No 2599 art 3).

(3) For the purposes of subsections (2), [(2ZA)][141] and (2A) *'violence'* means–
(a) violence from another person; or
(b) threats of violence from another person which are likely to be carried out;
and violence is 'domestic violence' if it is from a person who is associated with the victim.][142]

(4) The conditions for referral of the case to another authority are also met if–
(a) the applicant was on a previous application made to that other authority placed (in pursuance of their functions under this Part) in accommodation in the district of the authority to whom his application is now made, and
(b) the previous application was within such period as may be prescribed of the present application.

[(4A) Subsection (4) is to be construed, in a case where the other authority is an authority in Wales, as if the reference to 'this Part' were a reference to Part 2 of the Housing (Wales) Act 2014.][143]

(5) The question whether the conditions for referral of a case which does not involve a referral to a local housing authority in Wales are satisfied shall be decided by agreement between the notifying authority and the notified authority or, in default of agreement, in accordance with such arrangements as the Secretary of State may direct by order.

[(5A) The question whether the conditions for referral of a case involving a referral to a local housing authority in Wales shall be decided by agreement between the notifying authority and the notified authority or, in default of agreement, in accordance with such arrangements as the Secretary of State and the Welsh Ministers may jointly direct by order.][144]

(6) An order may direct that the arrangements shall be–
(a) those agreed by any relevant authorities or associations of relevant authorities, or
(b) in default of such agreement, such arrangements as appear to the Secretary of State [or, in the case of an order under subsection (5A), to the Secretary of State and the Welsh Ministers][145] to be suitable, after consultation with such associations representing relevant authorities, and such other persons, as he thinks appropriate.

(7) [An order under this section shall not][146] be made unless a draft of the order has been approved by a resolution of each House of Parliament [and, in the case of a joint order, a resolution of the National Assembly for Wales.][147]

141 Added by LA 2011 Pt 7 s149(8) (9 November 2012: insertion has effect as SI 2012 No 2599 art 2 subject to transitional provisions specified in SI 2012 No 2599 art 3).
142 Substituted by Homelessness Act 2002 s10 (31 July 2002 as SI 2002 No 1799 art 2).
143 Added by H(W)A 2014 Sch 3(1) para 11(a) (27 April 2015: insertion has effect subject to transitional provisions as specified in SI 2015 No 1272 art 7).
144 Added by H(W)A 2014 Sch 3(1) para 11(c) (27 April 2015: insertion has effect subject to transitional provisions as specified in SI 2015 No 1272 art 7).
145 Added by H(W)A 2014 Sch 3(1) para 11(d) (27 April 2015: insertion has effect subject to transitional provisions as specified in SI 2015 No 1272 art 7).
146 Words substituted by H(W)A 2014 Sch 3(1) para 11(e)(i) (27 April 2015: insertion has effect subject to transitional provisions as specified in SI 2015 No 1272 art 7).
147 Words substituted by H(W)A 2014 Sch 3(1) para 11(e)(ii) (27 April 2015: insertion has effect subject to transitional provisions as specified in SI 2015 No 1272 art 7).

199 Local connection

(1) A person has a local connection with the district of a local housing authority if he has a connection with it–

(a) because he is, or in the past was, normally resident there, and that residence is or was of his own choice,

(b) because he is employed there,

(c) because of family associations, or

(d) because of special circumstances.

[. . .][148]

(3) Residence in a district is not of a person's own choice if–

[. . .][149]

(b) he, or a person who might reasonably be expected to reside with him, becomes resident there because he is detained under the authority of an Act of Parliament.

[. . .][150]

(5) The Secretary of State may by order specify [. . .][151] circumstances in which–

(a) a person is not to be treated as employed in a district, or

(b) residence in a district is not to be treated as of a person's own choice.

[(6) A person has a local connection with the district of a local housing authority if he was (at any time) provided with accommodation in that district under section 95 of the Immigration and Asylum Act 1999 (support for asylum seekers).

(7) But subsection (6) does not apply–

(a) to the provision of accommodation for a person in a district of a local housing authority if he was subsequently provided with accommodation in the district of another local housing authority under section 95 of that Act, or

(b) to the provision of accommodation in an accommodation centre by virtue of section 22 of the Nationality, Immigration and Asylum Act 2002 (c. 41) (use of accommodation centres for section 95 support).][152]

[(8) While a local authority in England have a duty towards a person under section 23C of the Children Act 1989 (continuing functions in respect of former relevant children)–

(a) if the local authority is a local housing authority, the person has a local connection with their district, and

(b) otherwise, the person has a local connection with every district of a local housing authority that falls within the area of the local authority.

(9) In subsection (8), 'local authority' has the same meaning as in the Children Act 1989 (see section 105 of that Act).

(10) Where, by virtue of being provided with accommodation under section 22A of the Children Act 1989 (provision of accommodation for children in care), a

148 Repealed by H&RA 2008 Sch 16 para 1 (1 December 2008 as SI 2008 No 3068).

149 Repealed by H&RA 2008 Sch 16 para 1 (1 December 2008 as SI 2008 No 3068).

150 Repealed by H&RA 2008 Sch 16 para 1 (1 December 2008 as SI 2008 No 3068).

151 Word repealed by H&RA 2008 Sch 16 para 1 (1 December 2008 as SI 2008 No 3068).

152 Added by Asylum and Immigration (Treatment of Claimants, etc) Act 2004 s11(1) (4 January 2005).

person is normally resident in the district of a local housing authority in England for a continuous period of at least two years, some or all of which falls before the person attains the age of 16, the person has a local connection with that district.

(11) A person ceases to have a local connection with a district under subsection (10) upon attaining the age of 21 (but this does not affect whether the person has a local connection with that district under any other provision of this section).][153]

[199A Duties to the applicant whose case is considered for referral or referred under section 198(A1)

(1) Where a local housing authority ('the notifying authority') notify an applicant that they intend to notify or have notified another local housing authority in England ('the notified authority') under section 198(A1) of their opinion that the conditions are met for referral of the applicant's case to the notified authority, the notifying authority–

(a) cease to be subject to any duty under section 188 (interim duty to accommodate in case of apparent priority need), and

(b) are not subject to the duty under section 189B (initial duty owed to all eligible persons who are homeless).

(2) But, if the notifying authority have reason to believe that the applicant may have a priority need, they must secure that accommodation is available for occupation by the applicant until the applicant is notified of the decision as to whether the conditions for referral of the applicant's case are met.

(3) When it has been decided whether the conditions for referral are met, the notifying authority must give notice of the decision and the reasons for it to the applicant.

The notice must also inform the applicant of the applicant's right to request a review of the decision and of the time within which such a request must be made.

(4) If it is decided that the conditions for referral are not met–

(a) the notifying authority are subject to the duty under section 189B,

(b) the references in subsections (4) and (7)(b) of that section to the day that the notifying authority are first satisfied as mentioned in subsection (1) of that section are to be read as references to the day on which notice is given under subsection (3) of this section, and

(c) if the notifying authority have reason to believe that the applicant may have a priority need, they must secure that accommodation is available for occupation by the applicant until the later of–

(i) the duty owed to the applicant under section 189B coming to an end, and

(ii) the authority deciding what other duty (if any) they owe to the applicant under this Part after the duty under section 189B comes to an end.

(5) If it is decided that the conditions for referral are met–

(a) for the purposes of this Part, the applicant is to be treated as having made an application of the kind mentioned in section 183(1) to the notified authority on the date on which notice is given under subsection (3),

(b) from that date, the notifying authority owes no duties to the applicant under this Part,

153 Added by HRA 2017 s8 (3 April 2018).

(c) where the notifying authority have made a decision as to whether the applicant is eligible for assistance, is homeless or became homeless intentionally, the notified authority may only come to a different decision if they are satisfied that–
  (i) the applicant's circumstances have changed, or further information has come to light, since the notifying authority made their decision, and
  (ii) that change in circumstances, or further information, justifies the notified authority coming to a different decision to the notifying authority, and

(d) the notifying authority must give to the notified authority copies of any notifications that the notifying authority have given to the applicant under section 189A(3) or (10) (notifications of the notifying authority's assessments of the applicant's case).

(6) A duty under subsection (2) or paragraph (c) of subsection (4) ceases as provided in the subsection or paragraph concerned even if the applicant requests a review of the authority's decision upon which the duty ceases. The authority may secure that accommodation is available for the applicant's occupation pending the decision on review.

(7) A notice under this section must be given in writing and, if not received by the applicant, is to be treated as having been given to the applicant if it is made available at the authority's office for a reasonable period for collection by or on behalf of the applicant.][154]

200 Duties to applicant whose case is considered for referral or referred [under section 198(1)][155]

(1) Where a local housing authority notify an applicant that they intend to notify or have notified another local housing authority [under section 198(1)][156] of their opinion that the conditions are met for the referral of his case to that other authority–
  (a) they cease to be subject to any duty under section 188 (interim duty to accommodate in case of apparent priority need), and
  (b) they are not subject to any duty under section 193 (the main housing duty),

but they shall secure that accommodation is available for occupation by the applicant until he is notified of the decision whether the conditions for referral of his case are met.

[(1A) A local housing authority in England may not notify an applicant as mentioned in subsection (1) until the authority's duty to the applicant under section 189B(2) (initial duty owed to all eligible persons who are homeless) has come to an end.][157]

(2) When it has been decided whether the conditions for referral are met, the

154 Added by HRA 2017 s5(9) (3 April 2018: insertion has effect subject to transitional and savings provisions specified in SI 2018 No 167 reg 4(1)).

155 Words inserted by HRA 2017 s5(10)(a) (3 April 2018: insertion has effect subject to transitional and savings provisions specified in SI 2018 No 167 reg 4(1)).

156 Words inserted by HRA 2017 s5(10)(b) (3 April 2018: insertion has effect subject to transitional and savings provisions specified in SI 2018 No 167 reg 4(1)).

157 Added by HRA 2017 s5(10)(c) (3 April 2018: insertion has effect subject to transitional and savings provisions specified in SI 2018 No 167 reg 4(1)).

notifying authority shall notify the applicant of the decision and inform him of the reasons for it.

The notice shall also inform the applicant of his right to request a review of the decision and of the time within which such a request must be made.

[(3) If it is decided that the conditions for referral are not met, the notifying authority are subject to the duty under section 193 (the main housing duty).

(4) If it is decided that those conditions are met [and the notified authority is not an authority in Wales][158], the notified authority are subject to the duty under section 193 (the main housing duty) [; for provision about cases where it is decided that those conditions are met and the notified authority is an authority in Wales, see section 83 of the Housing (Wales) Act 2014 (cases referred from a local housing authority in England)][159].][160]

(5) The duty under subsection (1), [. . .][161] ceases as provided in that subsection even if the applicant requests a review of the authority's decision (see section 202).

The authority may [secure][162] that accommodation is available for the applicant's occupation pending the decision on a review.

(6) Notice [. . .][163] given to an applicant under this section shall be given in writing and, if not received by him, shall be treated as having been given to him if it is made available at the authority's office for a reasonable period for collection by him or on his behalf.

201 Application of referral provisions to cases arising in Scotland

Sections 198 and 200 (referral of application to another local housing authority and duties to applicant whose case is considered for referral or referred) apply–

(a) to applications referred by a local authority in Scotland in pursuance of sections 33 and 34 of the Housing (Scotland) Act 1987, and

(b) to persons whose applications are so transferred,

as they apply to cases arising under this Part (the reference in section 198 to this Part being construed as a reference to Part II of that Act).

[201A Cases referred from a local housing authority in Wales

(1) This section applies where an application has been referred by a local housing authority in Wales to a local housing authority in England under section 80 of the Housing (Wales) Act 2014 (referral of case to another local housing authority).

(2) If it is decided that the conditions in that section for referral of the case are met, the notified authority are subject to the duty under section 193 of this Act

158 Words inserted by H(W)A 2014 Sch 3(1) para 12(a) (27 April 2015: insertion has effect subject to transitional provisions as specified in SI 2015 No 1272 art 7).

159 Words inserted by H(W)A 2014 Sch 3(1) para 12(b) (27 April 2015: insertion has effect subject to transitional provisions as specified in SI 2015 No 1272 art 7).

160 Substituted by Homelessness Act 2002 Sch 1 para 15 (31 July 2002 as SI 2002 No 1799).

161 Words repealed by Homelessness Act 2002 Sch 2 para 1 (31 July 2002 as SI 2002 No 1799).

162 Substituted by Homelessness Act 2002 Sch 1 para 15(b) (31 July 2002 as SI 2002 No 1799).

163 Words repealed by HRA 2017 s5(10)(d) (3 April 2018: repeal has effect subject to transitional and savings provisions specified in SI 2018 No 167 reg 4(1)).

in respect of the person whose case is referred (the main housing duty); for provision about cases where it is decided that the conditions for referral are not met, see section 82 of the Housing (Wales) Act 2014 (duties to applicant whose case is considered for referral or referred).

(3) References in this Part to an applicant include a reference to a person to whom a duty is owed by virtue of subsection (2).][164]

[202 Right to request review of decision

(1) An applicant has the right to request a review of–

(a) any decision of a local housing authority as to his eligibility for assistance,

(b) any decision of a local housing authority as to what duty (if any) is owed to him under [sections 189B to 193C and 195][165] (duties to persons found to be homeless or threatened with homelessness),

[(ba) any decision of a local housing authority–

(i) as to the steps they are to take under subsection (2) of section 189B, or

(ii) to give notice under subsection (5) of that section bringing to an end their duty to the applicant under subsection (2) of that section,

(bb) any decision of a local housing authority to give notice to the applicant under section 193B(2) (notice given to those who deliberately and unreasonably refuse to cooperate),

(bc) any decision of a local housing authority–

(i) as to the steps they are to take under subsection (2) of section 195, or

(ii) to give notice under subsection (5) of that section bringing to an end their duty to the applicant under subsection (2) of that section,][166]

(c) any decision of a local housing authority to notify another authority under section 198(1) (referral of cases),

(d) any decision under section 198(5) whether the conditions are met for the referral of his case,

(e) any decision under section 200(3) or (4) (decision as to duty owed to applicant whose case is considered for referral or referred),

(f) any decision of a local housing authority as to the suitability of accommodation offered to him in discharge of their duty under any of the provisions mentioned in paragraph (b) or (e) or as to the suitability of accommodation offered to him as mentioned in section 193(7), [. . .][167]

164 Added by H(W)A 2014 Sch 3(1) para 13 (27 April 2015: insertion has effect subject to transitional provisions as specified in SI 2015 No 1272 art 7).

165 Words repealed by HRA 2017 s9(2)(a)(i) and (ii) (3 April 2018: repeal has effect as SI 2018 No 167 reg 3(i) subject to transitional and savings provisions specified in SI 2018 No 167 reg 4(2)).

166 Added by HRA 2017 s9(2)(b) (3 April 2018: s9(2)(b) came into force on 12 February 2018 as specified in SI 2018 No 167 reg 2(b) for the limited purpose of enabling the exercise of the power to make regulations conferred by HA 1996 s203(1) as to the procedure to be followed in relation to reviews under 1996 s202(1)(ba)-(bc) and (h); 3 April 2018 as specified in SI 2018 No 167 reg 3(i) subject to transitional and savings provisions specified in SI 2018 No 167 reg 4(2) otherwise).

167 Word repealed by HRA 2017 s9(2)(c) (3 April 2018: repeal has effect as SI 2018 No 167 reg 3(i) subject to transitional and savings provisions specified in SI 2018 No 167 reg 4(2)).

(g) any decision of a local housing authority as to the suitability of accommodation offered to him by way of a [private rented sector offer][168] (within the meaning of section 193) [, or

(h) any decision of a local housing authority as to the suitability of accommodation offered to the applicant by way of a final accommodation offer or a final Part 6 offer (within the meaning of section 193A or 193C).][169]

[(1A) An applicant who is offered accommodation as mentioned in section 193(5), (7) or (7AA) may under subsection (1)(f) or (as the case may be) (g) request a review of the suitability of the accommodation offered to him whether or not he has accepted the offer.][170]

[(1B) An applicant may, under subsection (1)(h), request a review of the suitability of the accommodation offered whether or not the applicant has accepted the offer.][171]

(2) There is no right to request a review of the decision reached on an earlier review.

(3) A request for review must be made before the end of the period of 21 days beginning with the day on which he is notified of the authority's decision or such longer period as the authority may in writing allow.

(4) On a request being duly made to them, the authority or authorities concerned shall review their decision.

203 Procedure on a review

(1) The Secretary of State may make provision by regulations as to the procedure to be followed in connection with a review under section 202.
Nothing in the following provisions affects the generality of this power.

(2) Provision may be made by regulations–

(a) requiring the decision on review to be made by a person of appropriate seniority who was not involved in the original decision, and

(b) as to the circumstances in which the applicant is entitled to an oral hearing, and whether and by whom he may be represented at such a hearing.

(3) The authority, or as the case may be either of the authorities, concerned shall notify the applicant of the decision on the review.

(4) If the decision is–

(a) to confirm the original decision on any issue against the interests of the applicant, or

(b) to confirm a previous decision–

(i) to notify another authority under section 198 (referral of cases), or

(ii) that the conditions are met for the referral of his case,

they shall also notify him of the reasons for the decision.

168 Words substituted by LA 2011 Pt 7 c1 s149(9) (9 November 2012: substitution has effect as SI 2012 No 2599 subject to transitional provisions specified in SI 2012 No 2599 art 3).

169 Added by HRA 2017 s9(2)(d) (3 April 2018: s9(2)(d) came into force on February 12, 2018 as specified in SI 2018 No 167 reg 2(b) for the limited purpose of enabling the exercise of the power to make regulations conferred by 1996 s203(1) as to the procedure to be followed in relation to reviews under 1996 s202(1)(ba)-(bc) and (h); 3 April 2018 as specified in SI 2018 No 167 reg 3(i) subject to transitional and savings provisions specified in SI 2018 No 167 reg 4(2) otherwise).

170 Added by Homelessness Act 2002 s8(2)(b) (February 26, 2002).

171 Added by HRA 2017 s9(3) (3 April 2018: insertion has effect as SI 2018 No 167 reg 3(i) subject to transitional and savings provisions specified in SI 2018 No 167 reg 4(2)).

(5) In any case they shall inform the applicant of his right to appeal to [the county court][172] on a point of law, and of the period within which such an appeal must be made (see section 204).

(6) Notice of the decision shall not be treated as given unless and until subsection (5), and where applicable subsection (4), is complied with.

(7) Provision may be made by regulations as to the period within which the review must be carried out and notice given of the decision.

(8) Notice required to be given to a person under this section shall be given in writing and, if not received by him, shall be treated as having been given if it is made available at the authority's office for a reasonable period for collection by him or on his behalf.

204 Right of appeal to county court on point of law

(1) If an applicant who has requested a review under section 202–

(a) is dissatisfied with the decision on the review, or

(b) is not notified of the decision on the review within the time prescribed under section 203,

he may appeal to the county court on any point of law arising from the decision or, as the case may be, the original decision.

(2) An appeal must be brought within 21 days of his being notified of the decision or, as the case may be, of the date on which he should have been notified of a decision on review.

[(2A) The court may give permission for an appeal to be brought after the end of the period allowed by subsection (2), but only if it is satisfied–

(a) where permission is sought before the end of that period, that there is a good reason for the applicant to be unable to bring the appeal in time; or

(b) where permission is sought after that time, that there was a good reason for the applicant's failure to bring the appeal in time and for any delay in applying for permission.][173]

(3) On appeal the court may make such order confirming, quashing or varying the decision as it thinks fit.

(4) Where the authority were under a duty under section 188, 190, [199A][174] or 200 to secure that accommodation is available for the applicant's occupation [, [. . .][175] they may][176] secure that accommodation is so available–

(a) during the period for appealing under this section against the authority's decision, and

172 Words substituted by Crime and Courts Act 2013 Sch 9(3) para 52(1)(b) (22 April 2014: substitution has effect as SI 2014 No 954 subject to savings and transitional provisions specified in 2013 c22 s15 and Sch 8 and transitional provision specified in SI 2014 No 954 arts 2(c) and 3).

173 Amended by Homelessness Act 2002 Sch 1 para 17(a) (30 September 2002 as SI 2002 No 2324).

174 Word inserted by HRA 2017 s5(11) (3 April 2018: insertion has effect subject to transitional and savings provisions specified in SI 2018 No 167 reg 4(1)).

175 Words repealed by HRA 2017 s4(6) (3 April 2018: repeal has effect subject to transitional and savings provisions specified in SI 2018 No 167 reg 4(1)).

176 Amended by Homelessness Act 2002 Sch 1 para 17 (31 July 2002 as SI 2002 No 1799).

(b) if an appeal is brought, until the appeal (and any further appeal) is finally determined.

[204A Section 204(4): appeals

(1) This section applies where an applicant has the right to appeal to the county court against a local housing authority's decision on a review.

(2) If the applicant is dissatisfied with a decision by the authority–

(a) not to exercise their power under section 204(4) ('the section 204(4) power') in his case;

(b) to exercise that power for a limited period ending before the final determination by the county court of his appeal under section 204(1) ('the main appeal'); or

(c) to cease exercising that power before that time,

he may appeal to the county court against the decision.

(3) An appeal under this section may not be brought after the final determination by the county court of the main appeal.

(4) On an appeal under this section the court–

(a) may order the authority to secure that accommodation is available for the applicant's occupation until the determination of the appeal (or such earlier time as the court may specify); and

(b) shall confirm or quash the decision appealed against,

and in considering whether to confirm or quash the decision the court shall apply the principles applied by the High Court on an application for judicial review.

(5) If the court quashes the decision it may order the authority to exercise the section 204(4) power in the applicant's case for such period as may be specified in the order.

(6) An order under subsection (5)–

(a) may only be made if the court is satisfied that failure to exercise the section 204(4) power in accordance with the order would substantially prejudice the applicant's ability to pursue the main appeal;

(b) may not specify any period ending after the final determination by the county court of the main appeal.][177]

205 Discharge of functions: introductory

(1) The following sections have effect in relation to the discharge by a local housing authority of their functions under this Part to secure that accommodation is available for the occupation of a person–

section 206 (general provisions),

[. . .][178]

section 208 (out-of-area placements),

section 209 (arrangements with private landlord).

(2) In [sections 206 and 208][179] those functions are referred to as the authority's 'housing functions under this Part'.

177 Added by Homelessness Act 2002 s11 (30 September 2002 as SI 2002 No 1736)

178 Entry repealed by Homelessness Act 2002 Sch 2 para 1 (31 July 2002 as SI 2002 No 1799).

179 Words substituted by Homelessness Act 2002 Sch 1 para 18 (31 July 2002 as SI 2002 No 1799).

[(3) For the purposes of this section, a local housing authority's duty under section 189B(2) or 195(2) is a function of the authority to secure that accommodation is available for the occupation of a person only if the authority decide to discharge the duty by securing that accommodation is so available.][180]

206 Discharge of functions by local housing authorities

(1) A local housing authority may discharge their housing functions under this Part only in the following ways–
(a) by securing that suitable accommodation provided by them is available,
(b) by securing that he obtains suitable accommodation from some other person, or
(c) by giving him such advice and assistance as will secure that suitable accommodation is available from some other person.

(2) A local housing authority may require a person in relation to whom they are discharging such functions–
(a) to pay such reasonable charges as they may determine in respect of accommodation which they secure for his occupation (either by making it available themselves or otherwise), or
(b) to pay such reasonable amount as they may determine in respect of sums payable by them for accommodation made available by another person.

207 Discharge of functions: provision of accommodation by the authority

[. . .][181]

208 Discharge of functions: out-of-area placements

(1) So far as reasonably practicable a local housing authority shall in discharging their housing functions under this Part secure that accommodation is available for the occupation of the applicant in their district.

(2) If they secure that accommodation is available for the occupation of the applicant outside their district, they shall give notice to the local housing authority in whose district the accommodation is situated.

(3) The notice shall state–
(a) the name of the applicant,
(b) the number and description of other persons who normally reside with him as a member of his family or might reasonably be expected to reside with him,
(c) the address of the accommodation,
(d) the date on which the accommodation was made available to him, and
(e) which function under this Part the authority was discharging in securing that the accommodation is available for his occupation.

(4) The notice must be in writing, and must be given before the end of the period of 14 days beginning with the day on which the accommodation was made available to the applicant.

[209 Discharge of interim duties: arrangements with private landlord

(1) This section applies where in pursuance of any of their housing functions under section 188, 190, 200 or 204(4) (interim duties) a local housing authority make arrangements with a private landlord to provide accommodation.

180 Added by HRA 2017 s6 (3 April 2018).
181 Repealed by Homelessness Act 2002 Sch 2 para 1 (31 July 2002 as SI 2002 No 1799).

(2) A tenancy granted to the applicant in pursuance of the arrangements cannot be an assured tenancy before the end of the period of twelve months beginning with–
  (a) the date on which the applicant was notified of the authority's decision under section 184(3) or 198(5); or
  (b) if there is a review of that decision under section 202 or an appeal to the court under section 204, the date on which he is notified of the decision on review or the appeal is finally determined,

unless, before or during that period, the tenant is notified by the landlord (or in the case of joint landlords, at least one of them) that the tenancy is to be regarded as an assured shorthold tenancy or an assured tenancy other than an assured shorthold tenancy.][182]

210 Suitability of accommodation

(1) In determining for the purposes of this Part whether accommodation is suitable for a person, the local housing authority shall have regard to [Parts 9 and 10 of the Housing Act 1985][183] (slum clearance [and overcrowding) and Parts 1 to 4 of the Housing Act 2004][184].

(2) The Secretary of State may by order specify–
  (a) circumstances in which accommodation is or is not to be regarded as suitable for a person, and
  (b) matters to be taken into account or disregarded in determining whether accommodation is suitable for a person.

211 Protection of property of homeless persons and persons threatened with homelessness

(1) This section applies where a local housing authority have reason to believe that–
  (a) there is danger of loss of, or damage to, any personal property of an applicant by reason of his inability to protect it or deal with it, and
  (b) no other suitable arrangements have been or are being made.

(2) If the authority have become subject to a duty towards the applicant under–

section 188 (interim duty to accommodate),

[section 189B (initial duty owed to all eligible persons who are homeless),][185]

section 190, 193 or 195 (duties to persons found to be homeless or threatened with homelessness), or

section 200 (duties to applicant whose case is considered for referral or referred),

then, whether or not they are still subject to such a duty, they shall take reasonable steps to prevent the loss of the property or prevent or mitigate damage to it.

(3) If they have not become subject to such a duty, they may take any steps they consider reasonable for that purpose.

182 Substituted by Homelessness Act 2002 Sch 1 para 19 (31 July 2002 as SI 2002 No 1799).

183 Amended by HA 2004 Sch 15 para 43 (6 April 2006 as SI 2006 No 1060).

184 Amended by HA 2004 Sch 15 para 43 (6 April 2006 as SI 2006 No 1060).

185 Words inserted by HRA 2017 s5(12) (3 April 2018: insertion has effect subject to transitional and savings provisions specified in SI 2018 No 167 reg 4(1)).

(4) The authority may decline to take action under this section except upon such conditions as they consider appropriate in the particular case, which may include conditions as to–
(a) the making and recovery by the authority of reasonable charges for the action taken, or
(b) the disposal by the authority, in such circumstances as may be specified, of property in relation to which they have taken action.
(5) References in this section to personal property of the applicant include personal property of any person who might reasonably be expected to reside with him.
(6) Section 212 contains provisions supplementing this section.

212 Protection of property: supplementary provisions

(1) The authority may for the purposes of section 211 (protection of property of homeless persons or persons threatened with homelessness)–
(a) enter, at all reasonable times, any premises which are the usual place of residence of the applicant or which were his last usual place of residence, and
(b) deal with any personal property of his in any way which is reasonably necessary, in particular by storing it or arranging for its storage.
(2) Where the applicant asks the authority to move his property to a particular location nominated by him, the authority–
(a) may, if it appears to them that his request is reasonable, discharge their responsibilities under section 211 by doing as he asks, and
(b) having done so, have no further duty or power to take action under that section in relation to that property.
If such a request is made, the authority shall before complying with it inform the applicant of the consequence of their doing so.
(3) If no such request is made (or, if made, is not acted upon) the authority cease to have any duty or power to take action under section 211 when, in their opinion, there is no longer any reason to believe that there is a danger of loss of or damage to a person's personal property by reason of his inability to protect it or deal with it.
But property stored by virtue of their having taken such action may be kept in store and any conditions upon which it was taken into store continue to have effect, with any necessary modifications.
(4) Where the authority–
(a) cease to be subject to a duty to take action under section 211 in respect of an applicant's property, or
(b) cease to have power to take such action, having previously taken such action,
they shall notify the applicant of that fact and of the reason for it.
(5) The notification shall be given to the applicant–
(a) by delivering it to him, or
(b) by leaving it, or sending it to him, at his last known address.
(6) References in this section to personal property of the applicant include personal property of any person who might reasonably be expected to reside with him.

213 Co-operation between relevant housing authorities and bodies

(1) Where a local housing authority [in England][186]–

(a) request another relevant housing authority or body, in England, Wales or Scotland, to assist them in the discharge of their functions under this Part, or

(b) request a social services authority, in England, Wales or Scotland, to exercise any of their functions in relation to a case which the local housing authority are dealing with under this Part,

the authority or body to whom the request is made shall co-operate in rendering such assistance in the discharge of the functions to which the request relates as is reasonable in the circumstances.

(2) In subsection (1)(a) *'relevant housing authority or body'* means –

(a) in relation to England and Wales, a local housing authority, a new town corporation, [a private registered provider of social housing][187] a registered social landlord or a housing action trust;

(b) in relation to Scotland, a local authority, a development corporation, a registered housing association or Scottish Homes.

Expressions used in paragraph (a) have the same meaning as in the Housing Act 1985; and expressions used in paragraph (b) have the same meaning as in the Housing (Scotland) Act 1987.

(3) Subsection (1) above applies to a request by a local authority in Scotland under section 38 of the Housing (Scotland) Act 1987 as it applies to a request by a local housing authority in England and Wales (the references to this Part being construed, in relation to such a request, as references to Part II of that Act).

[213A Co-operation in certain cases involving children

(1) This section applies where a local housing authority have reason to believe that an applicant with whom a person under the age of 18 normally resides, or might reasonably be expected to reside–

(a) may be ineligible for assistance; [or][188]

(b) may be homeless and may have become so intentionally [.][189]

[. . .][190]

(2) A local housing authority shall make arrangements for ensuring that, where this section applies–

(a) the applicant is invited to consent to the referral of the essential facts of his case to the social services authority for the district of the housing authority (where that is a different authority); and

186 Words inserted by H(W)A 2014 Sch 3(1) para 14 (27 April 2015: insertion has effect subject to transitional provisions as specified in SI 2015 No 1272 art 7).

187 Words inserted by Housing and Regeneration Act 2008 (Consequential Provisions) Order 2010 No 866 Sch 2 para 103 (1 April 2010: insertion has effect subject to savings and transitional provisions specified in SI 2010 No 866 Sch 3 para 4).

188 Word inserted by HRA 2017 s4(7)(a)(i) (3 April 2018: insertion has effect subject to transitional and savings provisions specified in SI 2018 No 167 reg 4(1)).

189 Repealed by HRA 2017 s4(7)(a)(ii) (3 April 2018: repeal has effect subject to transitional and savings provisions specified in SI 2018 No 167 reg 4(1)).

190 Repealed by HRA 2017 s4(7)(a)(ii) (3 April 2018: repeal has effect subject to transitional and savings provisions specified in SI 2018 No 167 reg 4(1)).

(b) if the applicant has given that consent, the social services authority are made aware of those facts and of the subsequent decision of the housing authority in respect of his case.

(3) Where the local housing authority and the social services authority for a district are the same authority (a 'unitary authority'), that authority shall make arrangements for ensuring that, where this section applies–

(a) the applicant is invited to consent to the referral to the social services department of the essential facts of his case; and

(b) if the applicant has given that consent, the social services department is made aware of those facts and of the subsequent decision of the authority in respect of his case.

(4) Nothing in subsection (2) or (3) affects any power apart from this section to disclose information relating to the applicant's case to the social services authority or to the social services department (as the case may be) without the consent of the applicant.

(5) Where a social services authority–

(a) are aware of a decision of a local housing authority that the applicant is ineligible for [assistance or became homeless intentionally],[191] and

(b) request the local housing authority to provide them with advice and assistance in the exercise of their social services functions under Part 3 of the Children Act 1989 [or Part 6 of the Social Services and Well-being (Wales) Act 2014],[192]

the local housing authority shall provide them with such advice and assistance as is reasonable in the circumstances.

(6) A unitary authority shall make arrangements for ensuring that, where they make a decision of a kind mentioned in subsection (5)(a), the housing department provide the social services department with such advice and assistance as the social services department may reasonably request.

(7) In this section, in relation to a unitary authority–

'the housing department' means those persons responsible for the exercise of their housing functions; and

'the social services department' means those persons responsible for the exercise of their social services functions under Part 3 of the Children Act 1989 [or Part 6 of the Social Services and Well-being (Wales) Act 2014][193].][194]

191 Words substituted by HRA 2017 s4(7)(b) (3 April 2018: substitution has effect subject to transitional and savings provisions specified in SI 2018 No 167 reg 4(1)).

192 Words inserted by Social Services and Well-being (Wales) Act 2014 (Consequential Amendments) Regulations 2016 No 413 reg 150(a) (6 April 2016: insertion has effect subject to savings and transitional provisions as specified in SI 2016 No 413 Sch 1 para 3).

193 Words inserted by Social Services and Well-being (Wales) Act 2014 (Consequential Amendments) Regulations 2016 No 413 reg 150(b) (6 April 2016: insertion has effect subject to savings and transitional provisions as specified in SI 2016 No 413 Sch 1 para 3).

194 Added by Homelessness Act 2002 s12 (30 September 2002 as SI 2002 No 1736).

[213B Duty of public authority to refer cases in England to local housing authority

(1) This section applies if a specified public authority considers that a person in England in relation to whom the authority exercises functions is or may be homeless or threatened with homelessness.

(2) The specified public authority must ask the person to agree to the authority notifying a local housing authority in England of–
(a) the opinion mentioned in subsection (1), and
(b) how the person may be contacted by the local housing authority.

(3) If the person–
(a) agrees to the specified public authority making the notification, and
(b) identifies a local housing authority in England to which the person would like the notification to be made,
the specified public authority must notify that local housing authority of the matters mentioned in subsection (2)(a) and (b).

(4) In this section *'specified public authority'* means a public authority specified, or of a description specified, in regulations made by the Secretary of State.

(5) In subsection (4) *'public authority'* means a person (other than a local housing authority) who has functions of a public nature.][195]

214 False statements, withholding information and failure to disclose change of circumstances

(1) It is an offence for a person, with intent to induce a local housing authority to believe in connection with the exercise of their functions under this Part that he or another person is entitled to accommodation or assistance in accordance with the provisions of this Part, or is entitled to accommodation or assistance of a particular description–
(a) knowingly or recklessly to make a statement which is false in a material particular, or
(b) knowingly to withhold information which the authority have reasonably required him to give in connection with the exercise of those functions.

(2) If before an applicant receives notification of the local housing authority's decision on his application there is any change of facts material to his case, he shall notify the authority as soon as possible.
The authority shall explain to every applicant, in ordinary language, the duty imposed on him by this subsection and the effect of subsection (3).

(3) A person who fails to comply with subsection (2) commits an offence unless he shows that he was not given the explanation required by that subsection or that he had some other reasonable excuse for non-compliance.

(4) A person guilty of an offence under this section is liable on summary conviction to a fine not exceeding level 5 on the standard scale.

[214A Codes of practice

(1) The Secretary of State may from time to time issue one or more codes of practice dealing with the functions of a local housing authority in England relating to homelessness or the prevention of homelessness.

195 Added by HRA 2017 s10 (3 April 2018: s10 came into force on 12 February 2018 as specified in SI 2018 No 167 reg 2(c) for the limited purpose of making regulations conferred by HA 1996 s213B(4). Fully in force from 1 October 2018).

(2) The provision that may be made by a code of practice under this section includes, in particular, provision about–
  (a) the exercise by a local housing authority of functions under this Part;
  (b) the training of an authority's staff in relation to the exercise of those functions;
  (c) the monitoring by an authority of the exercise of those functions.
(3) A code of practice may–
  (a) apply to all local housing authorities or to the local housing authorities specified or described in the code;
  (b) contain different provision for different kinds of local housing authority.
(4) The Secretary of State may issue a code of practice under this section only in accordance with subsections (5) and (6).
(5) Before issuing the code of practice, the Secretary of State must lay a draft of the code before Parliament.
(6) If–
  (a) the Secretary of State lays a draft of the code before Parliament, and
  (b) no negative resolution is made within the 40-day period,
  the Secretary of State may issue the code in the form of the draft.
(7) For the purposes of subsection (6)–
  (a) a *'negative resolution'* means a resolution of either House of Parliament not to approve the draft of the code, and
  (b) *'the 40-day period'* means the period of 40 days beginning with the day on which the draft of the code is laid before Parliament (or, if it is not laid before each House of Parliament on the same day, the later of the two days on which it is laid).
(8) In calculating the 40-day period, no account is to be taken of any period during which–
  (a) Parliament is dissolved or prorogued, or
  (b) both Houses are adjourned for more than four days.
(9) The Secretary of State may–
  (a) from time to time revise and reissue a code of practice under this section;
  (b) revoke a code of practice under this section.
(10) Subsections (4) to (6) do not apply to the reissue of a code of practice under this section.
(11) The Secretary of State must publish the current version of each code of practice under this section in whatever manner the Secretary of State thinks fit.
(12) A local housing authority must have regard to a code of practice under this section in exercising their functions.][196]

215 Regulations and orders

(1) In this Part *'prescribed'* means prescribed by regulations of the Secretary of State.
(2) Regulations or an order under this Part may make different provision for different purposes, including different provision for different areas.
(3) Regulations or an order under this Part shall be made by statutory instrument.
(4) Unless required to be approved in draft, regulations or an order under this

196 Added by HRA 2017 s11 (3 April 2018).

Part shall be subject to annulment in pursuance of a resolution of either House of Parliament.

216 Transitional and consequential matters

(1) The provisions of this Part have effect in place of the provisions of Part III of the Housing Act 1985 (housing the homeless) and shall be construed as one with that Act.

(2) Subject to any transitional provision contained in an order under section 232(4) (power to include transitional provision in commencement order), the provisions of this Part do not apply in relation to an applicant whose application for accommodation or assistance in obtaining accommodation was made before the commencement of this Part.

(3) The enactments mentioned in Schedule 17 have effect with the amendments specified there which are consequential on the provisions of this Part.

217 Minor definitions: Part VII

(1) In this Part, subject to subsection (2)–

['*private landlord*' means a landlord who is not within section 80(1) of the Housing Act 1985 (c. 68) (the landlord condition for secure tenancies);][197]

'*relevant authority*' means a local housing authority or a social services authority; and

'*social services authority*' means [–

(a) in relation to England a local authority for the purposes of the Local Authority Social Services Act 1970, as defined in section 1 of that Act;

[(b) in relation to Wales, a local authority exercising social services functions for the purposes of the Social Services and Well-being (Wales) Act 2014.][198]][199].

(2) In this Part, in relation to Scotland–

(a) '*local housing authority*' means a local authority within the meaning of the Housing (Scotland) Act 1988, and

(b) '*social services authority*' means a local authority for the purposes of the Social Work (Scotland) Act 1968.

(3) References in this Part to the district of a local housing authority–

(a) have the same meaning in relation to an authority in England or Wales as in the Housing Act 1985, and

(b) in relation to an authority in Scotland, mean the area of the local authority concerned.

197 Definition inserted by Homelessness Act 2002 Sch 1 para 20 (31 July 2002 as SI 2002 No 1799).

198 Added by Social Services and Well-being (Wales) Act 2014 (Consequential Amendments) Regulations 2016 No 413 reg 151(b) (6 April 2016: insertion has effect subject to savings and transitional provisions as specified in SI 2016 No 413 Sch 1 para 3).

199 Added by Social Services and Well-being (Wales) Act 2014 (Consequential Amendments) Regulations 2016 No 413 reg 151(a) (6 April 2016: insertion has effect subject to savings and transitional provisions as specified in SI 2016 No 413 Sch 1 para 3).

218 Index of defined expressions: Part VII

The following Table shows provisions defining or otherwise explaining expressions used in this Part (other than provisions defining or explaining an expression used in the same section)–

accommodation available for occupation	section 176
applicant	section 183(2)
assistance under this Part	section 183(2)
associated (in relation to a person)	section 178
assured tenancy and assured shorthold tenancy	section 230
district (of local housing authority)	section 217(3)
eligible for assistance	section 183(2)
homeless	section 175(1)
housing functions under this Part (in [sections 206 and 208][200])	section 205(2)
intentionally homeless	section 191
[. . .][201]	
local connection	section 199
local housing authority–	
-in England and Wales	section 230
-in Scotland	section 217(2)(a)
[. . .][202]	
prescribed	section 215(1)
priority need	section 189
[private landlord	section 217(1)][203]
reasonable to continue to occupy accommodation	section 177
registered social landlord	section 230
relevant authority	section 217(1)
[restricted person	section 184(7)][204]
social services authority	section 217(1) and (2)(b)
threatened with homelessness	section 175(4)

200 Amended by Homelessness Act 2002 Sch 1 para 21 (31 July 2002 as SI 2002 No 1799).

201 Entry repealed by HRA 2017 s4(8) (3 April 2018: repeal has effect subject to transitional and savings provisions specified in SI 2018 No 167 reg 4(1)).

202 Entry repealed by Homelessness Act 2002 Sch 2 para 1 (31 July 2002 as SI 2002 No 1799).

203 Amended by Homelessness Act 2002 Sch 1 para 21 (31 July 2002 as SI 2002 No 1799).

204 Entry inserted by H&A 2008 Sch 15(1) para 8 (2 March 2009 for purposes specified in SI 2009 No 415 art 2).

APPENDIX B

Statutory instruments[1]

In addition to these statutory instruments, the following Welsh SIs are reproduced in the ebook version of *Homelessness and Allocations:*

- Homelessness (Intentionality) (Specified Categories) (Wales) Regulations 2015
- Homelessness (Review Procedure) (Wales) Regulations 2015
- Homelessness (Suitability of Accommodation) (Wales) Order 2015
- Allocation of Housing and Homelessness (Eligibility) (Wales) Regulations 2014

Homelessness (Review Procedure etc) Regulations 2018 SI No 223

PART 1: GENERAL

1 Citation, commencement and interpretation

(1) These Regulations may be cited as the Homelessness (Review Procedure etc) Regulations 2018.
(2) This Part, and Parts 2, 3 and 5, come into force on 3rd April 2018.
(3) Part 4 comes into force on 1st October 2018.
(4) In these Regulations any reference to a section, save where the context otherwise appears, is to that section in the Housing Act 1996.

PART 2: NOTICES IN CASES OF APPLICANT'S DELIBERATE AND UNREASONABLE REFUSAL TO CO-OPERATE

2 Notice procedure

A local housing authority must ensure that its procedure in connection with notices under section 193B(2) (Notices in cases of applicant's deliberate and unreasonable refusal to co-operate)–
(a) is in writing,
(b) is kept under review, and
(c) makes provision which complies with regulation 3.

3 Decision to give notice

(1) A local housing authority may not give a notice under section 193B(2) unless the decision to give the notice–
(a) is made by an officer of that local housing authority, and
(b) is authorised by an appropriate person.
(2) For the purposes of paragraph (1)(b)–
(a) 'appropriate person' means a person who–
(i) is at least as senior as the person mentioned in paragraph (1)(a),
(ii) works for that local housing authority or the local authority, and
(iii) was not involved in the decision to give the notice, and
(b) a person works for a local housing authority or a local authority if the person–
(i) works under a contract of employment with that authority,
(ii) works under any other contract with that authority,
(iii) is supplied to that authority as an agency worker (within the meaning of regulation 3 of the Agency Workers Regulations 2010), or
(iv) is seconded to work for that authority.

PART 3: REVIEW OF LOCAL HOUSING AUTHORITY DECISIONS UNDER SECTION 202

4 Interpretation of this Part

In this Part–
'A' means the applicant;
'the authority' means the local housing authority who made the original decision;

'notified authority' means a local housing authority who receive a notification under section 198(A1) or (1);
'notifying authority' means a local housing authority who give a notification under section 198(A1) or (1);
'original decision' means a decision of a local housing authority in relation to which a request for a review has been made;
'request for a review' means a request for a review made under section 202;
'the reviewer' means–
(a) where the original decision falls within section 202(1)(d)–
(i) the notifying authority and the notified authority, where the review is carried out by those authorities,
(ii) the person appointed to carry out the review in accordance with regulation 6, where the case falls within that regulation,
(b) where the original decision falls within any other sub-paragraph of section 202(1), the authority.

5 Request for a review and notification of review procedure

(1) A request for a review must be made to the authority where the original decision falls within–
(a) section 202(1)(a) (decision as to A's eligibility for assistance),
(b) section 202(1)(b) (decision as to what duty, if any, is owed to A under sections 189B to 193C and 195: duties to persons found to be homeless or threatened with homelessness),
(c) section 202(1)(ba) (decision as to the steps they are to take under section 189B(2) or to give notice under section 189B(5) to bring to an end their duty to A under section 189B(2)),
(d) section 202(1)(bb) (decision to give notice to A under section 193B(2): notice given to those who deliberately and unreasonably refuse to cooperate),
(e) section 202(1)(bc) (decision as to the steps they are to take under section 195(2) or to give notice under section 195(5) bringing to an end their duty to A under section 195(2)),
(f) section 202(1)(c) (decision to notify another authority under section 198(1): referral of cases),
(g) section 202(1)(e) (decision under section 200(3) or (4): decision as to the duty owed to A whose case is considered for referral or referred),
(h) section 202(1)(f) (decision as to the suitability of accommodation offered to A in discharge of their duty under any of the provisions mentioned in section 202(1)(b) or (e) or as to the suitability of accommodation offered to A as mentioned in section 193(7)),
(i) section 202(1)(g) (decision as to the suitability of accommodation offered to A by way of a private rented sector offer within the meaning of section 193), or
(j) section 202(1)(h) (decision as to the suitability of accommodation offered to A by way of a final accommodation offer or a final Part 6 offer within the meaning of section 193A or 193C).

(2) A request for a review must be made to the notifying authority where the original decision falls within section 202(1)(d) (decision under section 198(5) whether conditions are met for the referral of A's case).

(3) Except in the case of a request for a review falling within regulation 6, the authority must–

(a) notify A that A, or someone acting on A's behalf, may make representations in writing to the authority in connection with the review,

(b) in the case of a request for a review falling–

(i) within section 202(1)(ba)(i) or (bc), or

(ii) within section 202(1)(bb) where the effect of the notice given under section 193B(2) is to bring the authority's duty to A under section 195(2) to an end,

notify A that any such representations must be made within two weeks beginning with the day on which A requested the review, or such longer period as A and the reviewer may agree in writing,

(c) if they have not already done so, notify A of the procedure to be followed in connection with the review.

(4) In the case of a request for a review falling within regulation 6, the person appointed in accordance with that regulation must–

(a) notify A that A, or someone acting on A's behalf, may make representations in writing to that person in connection with the review, and

(b) notify A of the procedure to be followed in connection with the review.

6 Initial procedure where the original decision was made under the Decisions on Referrals Order

(1) Where the original decision under section 198(5) (whether the conditions are met for the referral of the case) was made under the Homelessness (Decisions on Referrals) Order 1998 (the Decisions on Referrals Order), a review of that decision must, subject to paragraph (2), be carried out by a person appointed by the notifying authority and the notified authority.

(2) If a person is not appointed in accordance with paragraph (1) within five working days beginning with the day on which the request for a review is made, the review must be carried out by a person–

(a) from the panel constituted in accordance with paragraph 3 of the Schedule to the Decisions on Referrals Order (the panel), and

(b) appointed in accordance with paragraph (3) below.

(3) The notifying authority must within five working days beginning with the end of the period specified in paragraph (2) request the chairman of the Local Government Association or their nominee (the proper officer) to appoint a person from the panel and the proper officer must do so within seven days of the request.

(4) The notifying authority and the notified authority must within five working days of the appointment of the person from the panel (the appointed person) provide the appointed person with the reasons for the original decision and the information and evidence on which that decision was based.

(5) The appointed person must–

(a) send to the notifying authority and the notified authority any representations made under regulation 5, and

(b) invite those authorities to respond to those representations.

(6) The appointed person must not be the same person as the person who made the original decision.

(7) For the purposes of this regulation 'working day' means any day other than a Saturday, a Sunday, Christmas Day, Good Friday, or a day which is a bank

holiday under the Banking and Financial Dealings Act 1971 in England and Wales.

7 Procedure on a review

(1) The reviewer must, subject to compliance with the provisions of regulation 9, consider–
(a) any representations made under regulation 5 and, in a case falling within regulation 6, any responses to them, and
(b) any representations made under paragraph (2).

(2) If the reviewer considers that there is a deficiency or irregularity in the original decision, or in the manner in which it was made, but is minded nonetheless to make a decision which is against the interests of A on one or more issues, the reviewer must notify A–
(a) that the reviewer is so minded and the reasons why, and
(b) that A, or someone acting on A's behalf, may make representations to the reviewer orally or in writing, or both orally and in writing.

8 Decision on the review

(1) Paragraph (2) applies where–
(a) the reviewer is, or includes, the authority,
(b) the original decision was made by an officer of the authority, and
(c) the decision on the review is to be made by an officer of the authority.

(2) Where this paragraph applies, the officer making the decision on the review must be someone who–
(a) was not involved in the original decision, and
(b) is more senior than the officer who made the original decision.

9 Notification of the decision on a review

(1) Notice of the decision on a review under section 203(3) must be given to A–
(a) where the original decision falls within–
(i) section 202(1)(ba)(i) or (bc), or
(ii) section 202(1)(bb) and the effect of the notice given under section 193B(2) is to bring the authority's duty to A under section 195(2) to an end,
three weeks beginning with the day on which the request for the review is made or, where A makes representations under regulation 7, beginning with the day on which those representations are received,
(b) where the original decision falls within–
(i) section 202(1)(a), (b), (ba)(ii), (c), (d), (e), (f), (g), or (h), or
(ii) section 202(1)(bb) and the effect of the notice given under section 193B(2) is to bring the authority's duty to A under section 189B(2) to an end,
eight weeks beginning with the day on which the request for the review is made,
(c) where the original decision falls within section 202(1)(d) and the review is carried out by the notifying authority and the notified authority, ten weeks beginning with the day on which the request for the review is made,
(d) in a case falling within regulation 6, twelve weeks beginning with the day on which the request for the review is made,
or within such longer period as A and the reviewer may agree in writing.

(2) In a case falling within regulation 6, the appointed person must notify their decision on the review and the reasons for it, in writing, to the notifying authority and the notified authority–
  (a) within a period of eleven weeks beginning with the day on which the request for the review is made, or
  (b) where a longer period has been agreed in accordance with paragraph (1), by no later than one week before the expiry of that longer period.

PART 4: DUTY TO REFER

10 Specified public authorities

The public authorities set out in the Schedule are specified for the purposes of section 213B (Duty of public authority to refer cases in England to local housing authority).

PART 5: REVOCATION

11 Revocation and transitional provision

(1) Subject to paragraph (2), the Allocation of Housing and Homelessness (Review Procedures) Regulations 1999 are revoked.

(2) The Allocation of Housing and Homelessness (Review Procedures) Regulations 1999 continue in force in relation to any request for a review under section 202 made prior to the coming into force of this Part.

SCHEDULE: SPECIFIED PUBLIC AUTHORITIES

Regulation 10

1 The governor of a prison within the meaning given in section 53(1) of the Prison Act 1952.

2 The director of a contracted out prison within the meaning given in section 84(4) of the Criminal Justice Act 1991.

3 The governor of a young offender institution provided under section 43(1)(a) of the Prison Act 1952.

4 The governor of a secure training centre provided under section 43(1)(b) of the Prison Act 1952.

5 The director of a contracted out secure training centre within the meaning given in section 15 of the Criminal Justice and Public Order Act 1994.

6 The principal of a secure college provided under section 43(1)(c) of the Prison Act 1952.

7 A youth offending team established under section 39(1) of the Crime and Disorder Act 1998.

8 A provider of probation services.

9 An officer, designated by the Secretary of State for Work and Pensions for the purposes of section 213B, employed by the Secretary of State at an office known as a Jobcentre Plus office.

10 A social services authority.

11 A person who performs a function of a local authority pursuant to a direction under section 497A(4) or (4A) of the Education Act 1996 (which confers power on the Secretary of State to secure the proper performance of local authority education functions, and is applied to social services functions relating to

children by section 50 of the Children Act 2004 and to functions relating to childcare by section 15 of the Childcare Act 2006).

12 (1) An NHS trust and an NHS foundation trust, but only in connection with the provision of the following NHS health services–

(a) emergency department and urgent treatment centres,

(b) in-patient treatment.

(2) For the purposes of paragraph (1)–

'emergency department and urgent treatment centres' includes–

(a) accident and emergency services provided in a hospital,

(b) services known as urgent treatment centres,

(c) any other providers of community and primary urgent care services,

'NHS foundation trust' has the meaning given in section 30 of the National Health Service Act 2006,

'NHS health services' means any kind of health services provided as part of the health service continued under, and for the purposes of, section 1(1) of the National Health Service Act 2006, and

'NHS trust' means an NHS trust established under section 25 of the National Health Service Act 2006.

13 The Secretary of State for Defence, but only in relation to members of the regular armed forces.

Allocation of Housing (Qualification Criteria for Right to Move) (England) Regulations 2015 SI No 967

1 Citation, commencement and application

(1) These Regulations may be cited as the Allocation of Housing (Qualification Criteria for Right to Move) (England) Regulations 2015.

(2) These Regulations come into force on 20th April 2015.

(3) These Regulations apply in relation to England only.

2 Interpretation

Any reference in these Regulations to a section is a reference to a section of the Housing Act 1996.

3 Criterion that may not be used in deciding what classes of persons are not qualifying persons

(1) In deciding whether a person is a qualifying person under section 160ZA(7), a local housing authority may not use the criterion set out in paragraph (2) if the allocation involves a transfer of housing accommodation for that person from the district of another local housing authority in England.

(2) The criterion is that a relevant person must have a local connection with the district of the local housing authority.

(3) In this regulation 'local connection' has the meaning given by section 199.

4 Relevant person

For the purposes of regulation 3, a relevant person is a person who–

(a) falls within section 159(4A)(a) or (b),

(b) is to be given reasonable preference under section 166A(3)(e), and

(c) has a need to move falling within regulation 5(1).

5 Need to move

(1) Subject to paragraph (2), for the purposes of regulation 4, a relevant person has a need to move because the relevant person–

(a) works in the district of the local housing authority, or

(b)

(i) has been offered work in the district of the local housing authority, and

(ii) the authority is satisfied that the relevant person has a genuine intention of taking up the offer of work.

(2) This regulation does not apply if the need to move is associated with work or the offer of work which is–

(a) short-term or marginal in nature,

(b) ancillary to work in another district, or

(c) voluntary work.

(3) In this regulation 'voluntary work' means work where no payment is received by the relevant person or the only payment due to be made to the relevant person by virtue of being so engaged is a payment in respect of any expenses reasonably incurred by the relevant person in the course of being so engaged.

Allocation of Housing (Qualification Criteria for Armed Forces) (England) Regulations 2012 SI No 1869

1 Citation and commencement

(1) These Regulations may be cited as the Allocation of Housing (Qualification Criteria for Armed Forces) (England) Regulations 2012.

(2) These Regulations come into force on 24th August 2012.

2 Interpretation

In these Regulations–

'the 1996 Act' means the Housing Act 1996;

'local connection' has the meaning given by section 199 of the 1996 Act; and

'regular forces' and 'reserve forces' have the meanings given by section 374 of the Armed Forces Act 2006.

3 Criterion that may not be used in deciding what classes of persons are not qualifying persons

(1) In deciding what classes of persons are not qualifying persons under section 160ZA(7) of the 1996 Act, a local housing authority in England may not use the criterion set out in paragraph (2).

(2) The criterion is that a relevant person must have a local connection to the district of a local housing authority.

(3) A relevant person is a person who–

(a) is serving in the regular forces or who has served in the regular forces within five years of the date of their application for an allocation of housing under Part 6 of the 1996 Act;

(b) has recently ceased, or will cease to be entitled, to reside in accommodation provided by the Ministry of Defence following the death of that person's spouse or civil partner where–

(i) the spouse or civil partner has served in the regular forces; and

(ii) their death was attributable (wholly or partly) to that service; or

(c) is serving or has served in the reserve forces and who is suffering from a serious injury, illness or disability which is attributable (wholly or partly) to that service.

Homelessness (Suitability of Accommodation) (England) Order 2012 SI No 2601

1 Citation, commencement and application

(1) This Order may be cited as the Homelessness (Suitability of Accommodation) (England) Order 2012 and comes into force on 9th November 2012.

(2) This Order applies in relation to England only.

2 Matters to be taken into account in determining whether accommodation is suitable for a person

In determining whether accommodation is suitable for a person, the local housing authority must take into account the location of the accommodation, including–

(a) where the accommodation is situated outside the district of the local housing authority, the distance of the accommodation from the district of the authority;

(b) the significance of any disruption which would be caused by the location of the accommodation to the employment, caring responsibilities or education of the person or members of the person's household;

(c) the proximity and accessibility of the accommodation to medical facilities and other support which–

(i) are currently used by or provided to the person or members of the person's household; and

(ii) are essential to the well-being of the person or members of the person's household; and

(d) the proximity and accessibility of the accommodation to local services, amenities and transport.

3 Circumstances in which accommodation is not to be regarded as suitable for a person

(1)[2] For the purposes [of a private rented sector offer under section 193(7F) of the Housing Act 1996] *mentioned in paragraph (2)*,[3] accommodation shall not be regarded as suitable where one or more of the following apply–

(a) the local housing authority are of the view that the accommodation is not in a reasonable physical condition;

(b) the local housing authority are of the view that any electrical equipment supplied with the accommodation does not meet the requirements of Schedule 1 to the Electrical Equipment (Safety) Regulations 2016;

(c) the local housing authority are of the view that the landlord has not taken reasonable fire safety precautions with the accommodation and any furnishings supplied with it;

(d) the local housing authority are of the view that the landlord has not taken reasonable precautions to prevent the possibility of carbon monoxide poisoning in the accommodation;

2 Numbered as para (1) by Homelessness Reduction Act 2017 s12(1), (2). Not yet in force: see Homelessness Reduction Act 2017 s13(3).

3 Words in square brackets revoked and subsequent words in italics substituted by Homelessness Reduction Act 2017 s12(1), (3). Not yet in force: see Homelessness Reduction Act 2017 s13(3).

(e) the local housing authority are of the view that the landlord is not a fit and proper person to act in the capacity of landlord, having considered if the person has:
   (i) committed any offence involving fraud or other dishonesty, or violence or illegal drugs, or any offence listed in Schedule 3 to the Sexual Offences Act 2003 (offences attracting notification requirements);
   (ii) practised unlawful discrimination on grounds of sex, race, age, disability, marriage or civil partnership, pregnancy or maternity, religion or belief, sexual orientation, gender identity or gender reassignment in, or in connection with, the carrying on of any business;
   (iii) contravened any provision of the law relating to housing (including landlord or tenant law); or
   (iv) acted otherwise than in accordance with any applicable code of practice for the management of a house in multiple occupation, approved under section 233 of the Housing Act 2004;
(f) the accommodation is a house in multiple occupation subject to licensing under section 55 of the Housing Act 2004 and is not licensed;
(g) the accommodation is a house in multiple occupation subject to additional licensing under section 56 of the Housing Act 2004 and is not licensed;
(h) the accommodation is or forms part of residential property which does not have a valid energy performance certificate as required by the Energy Performance of Buildings (Certificates and Inspections) (England and Wales) Regulations 2007;
(i) the accommodation is or forms part of relevant premises which do not have a current gas safety record in accordance with regulation 36 of the Gas Safety (Installation and Use) Regulations 1998; or
(j) the landlord has not provided to the local housing authority a written tenancy agreement, which the landlord proposes to use for the purposes of a private rented sector offer, and which the local housing authority considers to be adequate.

(2) The purposes are–
   (a) determining, in accordance with section 193(7F) of the Housing Act 1996, whether a local housing authority may approve a private rented sector offer;
   (b) determining, in accordance with section 193A(6) or 193C(9) of that Act, whether a local housing authority may approve a final accommodation offer made by a private landlord;
   (c) determining whether any accommodation–
      (i) secured for a person who has a priority need by a local housing authority in discharge of their functions under section 189B(2) or 195(2) of that Act, and
      (ii) made available for occupation under a tenancy with a private landlord,
   is suitable for the purposes of the section concerned.[4]

4 Inserted by Homelessness Reduction Act 2017 s12(1), (4). Not yet in force: see Homelessness Reduction Act 2017 s13(3).

Allocation of Housing and Homelessness (Miscellaneous Provisions) (England) Regulations 2006 SI No 2527

1 Citation, commencement, interpretation and application

(1) These Regulations may be cited as the Allocation of Housing and Homelessness (Miscellaneous Provisions) (England) Regulations 2006 and shall come into force on 9th October 2006.

(2) In these Regulations, 'the 1996 Act' means the Housing Act 1996.

(3) These Regulations apply to England only.

2 Amendment of the classes of person from abroad who are eligible for an allocation of accommodation and for housing assistance

(1) The Allocation of Housing and Homelessness (Eligibility) (England) Regulations 2006 are amended as follows.

(2) For regulation 3(d), substitute–

'(d) Class D–a person who has humanitarian protection granted under the Immigration Rules.'.

(3) For regulation 5(1)(d), substitute–

'(d) Class D–a person who has humanitarian protection granted under the Immigration Rules; and'.

3 Prescribed period for referral of case to another local housing authority

For the purposes of section 198(4)(b) of the 1996 Act (referral of case to another local housing authority), the prescribed period is the aggregate of–

(a) five years; and

(b) the period beginning on the date of the previous application and ending on the date on which the applicant was first placed in pursuance of that application in accommodation in the district of the authority to whom the application is now made.

4 Transitional provisions

The amendments made by these Regulations shall not have effect in relation to an applicant whose application for–

(a) an allocation of housing accommodation under Part 6 of the 1996 Act; or

(b) housing assistance under Part 7 of the 1996 Act,

was made before 9th October 2006.

Allocation of Housing and Homelessness (Eligibility) (England) Regulations 2006 SI No 1294

1 Citation, commencement and application

(1) These Regulations may be cited as the Allocation of Housing and Homelessness (Eligibility) (England) Regulations 2006 and shall come into force on 1st June 2006.

(2) These Regulations apply to England only.

2 Interpretation

(1) In these Regulations–

'the 1996 Act' means the Housing Act 1996;

'the Accession Regulations 2013' means the Accession of Croatia (Immigration and Worker Authorisation) Regulations 2013;

'the EEA Regulations' means the Immigration (European Economic Area) Regulations 2006;

'the Human Rights Convention' means the Convention for the Protection of Human Rights and Fundamental Freedoms, agreed by the Council of Europe at Rome on 4thNovember 1950 as it has effect for the time being in relation to the United Kingdom;

'the Immigration Rules' means the rules laid down as mentioned in section 3(2) of the Immigration Act 1971 (general provisions for regulation and control);

'the Refugee Convention' means the Convention relating to the Status of Refugees done at Geneva on 28th July 1951, as extended by Article 1(2) of the Protocol relating to the Status of Refugees done at New York on 31st January 1967; and

'sponsor' means a person who has given an undertaking in writing for the purposes of the Immigration Rules to be responsible for the maintenance and accommodation of another person.

(2) For the purposes of these Regulations–

(a) 'jobseeker', 'self-employed person', and 'worker' have the same meaning as for the purposes of the definition of a 'qualified person' in regulation 6(1) of the EEA Regulations; and

(b) subject to paragraph (3), references to the family member of a jobseeker, self-employed person or worker shall be construed in accordance with regulation 7 of those Regulations.

(3) For the purposes of regulations 4(2)(d) and 6(2)(d) 'family member' does not include a person who is treated as a family member by virtue of regulation 7(3) of the EEA Regulations.

(4) [Revoked].

3 Persons subject to immigration control who are eligible for an allocation of housing accommodation

The following classes of persons subject to immigration control are persons who are eligible for an allocation of housing accommodation under Part 6 of the 1996 Act–

(a) Class A – a person who is recorded by the Secretary of State as a refugee within the definition in Article 1 of the Refugee Convention and who has leave to enter or remain in the United Kingdom;

(b) Class B – a person–
   (i) who has exceptional leave to enter or remain in the United Kingdom granted outside the provisions of the Immigration Rules; and
   (ii) who is not subject to a condition requiring him to maintain and accommodate himself, and any person who is dependent on him, without recourse to public funds;

(c) Class C – a person who is habitually resident in the United Kingdom, the Channel Islands, the Isle of Man or the Republic of Ireland and whose leave to enter or remain in the United Kingdom is not subject to any limitation or condition, other than a person–
   (i) who has been given leave to enter or remain in the United Kingdom upon an undertaking given by his sponsor;
   (ii) who has been resident in the United Kingdom, the Channel Islands, the Isle of Man or the Republic of Ireland for less than five years beginning on the date of entry or the date on which his sponsor gave the undertaking in respect of him, whichever date is the later; and
   (iii) whose sponsor or, where there is more than one sponsor, at least one of whose sponsors, is still alive;

(d) Class D – a person who has humanitarian protection granted under the Immigration Rules;

(e) Class E – a person who is habitually resident in the United Kingdom, the Channel Islands, the Isle of Man or the Republic of Ireland and who has limited leave to enter the United Kingdom as a relevant Afghan citizen under paragraph 276BA1 of the Immigration Rules; and

(f) Class F – a person who has limited leave to enter or remain in the United Kingdom on family or private life grounds under Article 8 of the Human Rights Convention, such leave granted–
   (i) under paragraph 276BE(1), paragraph 276DG or Appendix FM of the Immigration Rules, and
   (ii) who is not subject to a condition requiring that person to maintain and accommodate himself, and any person dependent upon him, without recourse to public funds.

4 Other persons from abroad who are ineligible for an allocation of housing accommodation

(1) A person who is not subject to immigration control is to be treated as a person from abroad who is ineligible for an allocation of housing accommodation under Part 6 of the 1996 Act if–

(a) subject to paragraph (2), he is not habitually resident in the United Kingdom, the Channel Islands, the Isle of Man, or the Republic of Ireland;

(b) his only right to reside in the United Kingdom–
   (i) is derived from his status as a jobseeker or the family member of a jobseeker; or
   (ii) is an initial right to reside for a period not exceeding three months under regulation 13 of the EEA Regulations; or
   (iii) is a derivative right to reside to which he is entitled under regulation 15A(1) of the EEA Regulations, but only in a case where the right exists under that regulation because the applicant satisfies the criteria in regulation 15A(4A) of those Regulations; or

(iv) is derived from Article 20 of the Treaty on the Functioning of the European Union, in a case where the right to reside arises because a British citizen would otherwise be deprived of the genuine enjoyment of the substance of their rights as a European Union citizen; or

(c) his only right to reside in the Channel Islands, the Isle of Man or the Republic of Ireland–

(i) is a right equivalent to one of those mentioned in sub-paragraphs (b)(i), (ii) or (iii) which is derived from the Treaty on the Functioning of the European Union; or

(ii) is derived from Article 20 of the Treaty on the Functioning of the European Union, in a case where the right to reside–

(a) in the Republic of Ireland arises because an Irish citizen, or

(b) in the Channel Islands or the Isle of Man arises because a British citizen also entitled to reside there

would otherwise be deprived of the genuine enjoyment of the substance of their rights as a European Union citizen.

(2) The following are not to be treated as persons from abroad who are ineligible for an allocation of housing accommodation pursuant to paragraph (1)(a)–

(a) a worker;

(b) a self-employed person;

(c) a person who is treated as a worker for the purpose of the definition of 'qualified person' in regulation 6(1) of the EEA Regulations pursuant to–

(i) [Revoked].

(ii) regulation 5 of the Accession Regulations 2013 (right of residence of an accession State national subject to worker authorisation);

(d) a person who is the family member of a person specified in sub-paragraphs (a)–(c);

(e) a person with a right to reside permanently in the United Kingdom by virtue of regulation 15(c), (d) or (e) of the EEA Regulations; and

(f) [Revoked].

(g) a person who is in the United Kingdom as a result of his deportation, expulsion or other removal by compulsion of law from another country to the United Kingdom;

(h) [Revoked].

(i) [Revoked].

5 Persons subject to immigration control who are eligible for housing assistance

(1) The following classes of persons subject to immigration control are persons who are eligible for housing assistance under Part 7 of the 1996 Act–

(a) Class A – a person who is recorded by the Secretary of State as a refugee within the definition in Article 1 of the Refugee Convention and who has leave to enter or remain in the United Kingdom;

(b) Class B – a person–

(i) who has exceptional leave to enter or remain in the United Kingdom granted outside the provisions of the Immigration Rules; and

(ii) whose leave to enter or remain is not subject to a condition requiring him to maintain and accommodate himself, and any person who is dependent on him, without recourse to public funds;

(c) Class C – a person who is habitually resident in the United Kingdom, the Channel Islands, the Isle of Man or the Republic of Ireland and whose leave to enter or remain in the United Kingdom is not subject to any limitation or condition, other than a person–
  (i) who has been given leave to enter or remain in the United Kingdom upon an undertaking given by his sponsor;
  (ii) who has been resident in the United Kingdom, the Channel Islands, the Isle of Man or the Republic of Ireland for less than five years beginning on the date of entry or the date on which his sponsor gave the undertaking in respect of him, whichever date is the later; and
  (iii) whose sponsor or, where there is more than one sponsor, at least one of whose sponsors, is still alive;
(d) Class D – a person who has humanitarian protection granted under the Immigration Rules;
(e) [Revoked].
(f) Class F – a person who is habitually resident in the United Kingdom, the Channel Islands, the Isle of Man or the Republic of Ireland and who has limited leave to enter the United Kingdom as a relevant Afghan citizen under paragraph 276BA1 of the Immigration Rules; and
(g) Class G – a person who has limited leave to enter or remain in the United Kingdom on family or private life grounds under Article 8 of the Human Rights Convention, such leave granted–
  (i) under paragraph 276BE(1), paragraph 276DG or Appendix FM of the Immigration Rules, and
  (ii) who is not subject to a condition requiring that person to maintain and accommodate himself, and any person dependent upon him, without recourse to public funds.

(2) [Revoked].
(3) [Revoked].

6 Other persons from abroad who are ineligible for housing assistance

(1) A person who is not subject to immigration control is to be treated as a person from abroad who is ineligible for housing assistance under Part 7 of the 1996 Act if–
(a) subject to paragraph (2), he is not habitually resident in the United Kingdom, the Channel Islands, the Isle of Man, or the Republic of Ireland;
(b) his only right to reside in the United Kingdom–
  (i) is derived from his status as a jobseeker or the family member of a jobseeker; or
  (ii) is an initial right to reside for a period not exceeding three months under regulation 13 of the EEA Regulations; or
  (iii) is a derivative right to reside to which he is entitled under regulation 15A(1) of the EEA Regulations, but only in a case where the right exists under that regulation because the applicant satisfies the criteria in regulation 15A(4A) of those Regulations; or
  (iv) is derived from Article 20 of the Treaty on the Functioning of the European Union in a case where the right to reside arises because a British citizen would otherwise be deprived of the genuine enjoyment of the substance of the rights attaching to the status of European Union citizen; or

(c) his only right to reside in the Channel Islands, the Isle of Man or the Republic of Ireland–
   (i) is a right equivalent to one of those mentioned in sub-paragraph (b)(i), (ii) or (iii) which is derived from the Treaty on the Functioning of the European Union; or
   (ii) is derived from Article 20 of the Treaty on the Functioning of the European Union, in a case where the right to reside–
      (a) in the Republic of Ireland arises because an Irish citizen, or
      (b) in the Channel Islands or the Isle of Man arises because a British citizen also entitled to reside there

   would otherwise be deprived of the genuine enjoyment of the substance of their rights as a European Union citizen.

(2) The following are not to be treated as persons from abroad who are ineligible for housing assistance pursuant to paragraph (1)(a)–
(a) a worker;
(b) a self-employed person;
(c) a person who is treated as a worker for the purpose of the definition of 'qualified person' in regulation 6(1) of the EEA Regulations pursuant to–
   (i) [Revoked].
   (ii) regulation 5 of the Accession Regulations 2013 (right of residence of an accession State national subject to worker authorisation);
(d) a person who is the family member of a person specified in sub-paragraphs (a)–(c);
(e) a person with a right to reside permanently in the United Kingdom by virtue of regulation 15(c), (d) or (e) of the EEA Regulations; and
(f) [Revoked].
(g) a person who is in the United Kingdom as a result of his deportation, expulsion or other removal by compulsion of law from another country to the United Kingdom;
(h) [Revoked].
(i) [Revoked].

7 Revocation

Subject to regulation 8, the Regulations specified in column (1) of the Schedule are revoked to the extent mentioned in column (3) of the Schedule.

8 Transitional provisions

The revocations made by these Regulations shall not have effect in relation to an applicant whose application for–
(a) an allocation of housing accommodation under Part 6 of the 1996 Act; or
(b) housing assistance under Part 7 of the 1996 Act,

was made before 1st June 2006.

Homelessness (Suitability of Accommodation) (England) Order 2003 SI No 3326

1 Citation, commencement and application

(1) This Order may be cited as the Homelessness (Suitability of Accommodation) (England) Order 2003 and shall come into force on 1st April 2004.

(2) This Order applies in relation to the duties of local housing authorities in England to make accommodation available for occupation by applicants under Part 7 of the Housing Act 1996.

2 Interpretation

In this Order–

'applicant with family commitments' means an applicant–

(a) who is pregnant;
(b) with whom a pregnant woman resides or might reasonably be expected to reside; or
(c) with whom dependent children reside or might reasonably be expected to reside;

'B&B accommodation' means accommodation (whether or not breakfast is included)–

(a) which is not separate and self-contained premises; and
(b) in which any one of the following amenities is shared by more than one household–
(i) a toilet;
(ii) personal washing facilities;
(iii) cooking facilities,

but does not include accommodation which is owned or managed by a local housing authority, a non-profit registered provider of social housing or a voluntary organisation as defined in section 180(3) of the Housing Act 1996; and

any reference to a numbered section is a reference to a section of the Housing Act 1996.

3 Accommodation unsuitable where there is a family commitment

Subject to the exceptions contained in article 4, B&B accommodation is not to be regarded as suitable for an applicant with family commitments where accommodation is made available for occupation–

(a) under section 188(1), 190(2), 193(2) or 200(1); or
(b) under section 195(2), where the accommodation is other than that occupied by the applicant at the time of making his application.

4 Exceptions

(1) Article 3 does not apply–

(a) where no accommodation other than B&B accommodation is available for occupation by an applicant with family commitments; and
(b) the applicant occupies B&B accommodation for a period, or a total of periods, which does not exceed 6 weeks.

(2) In calculating the period, or total period, of an applicant's occupation of B&B accommodation for the purposes of paragraph (1)(b), there shall be disregarded–

(a) any period before 1st April 2004; and
(b) where a local housing authority is subject to the duty under section 193 by virtue of section 200(4), any period before that authority became subject to that duty.

Homelessness (Priority Need for Accommodation) (England) Order 2002 SI No 2051

1 Citation, commencement and interpretation

(1) This Order may be cited as the Homelessness (Priority Need for Accommodation) (England) Order 2002 and shall come into force on the day after the day on which it is made.

(2) This Order extends to England only.

(3) In this Order–

'looked after, accommodated or fostered' has the meaning given by section 24(2) of the Children Act 1989 or, as the case may be, section 104(3) of the Social Services and Well-being (Wales) Act 2014; and

'relevant student' means a person to whom section 24B(3) of the Children Act 1989 or, as the case may be, section 114(5) or 115(6) of the Social Services and Well-being (Wales) Act 2014 applies–

(a) who is in full-time further or higher education; and

(b) whose term-time accommodation is not available to him during a vacation.

2 Priority need for accommodation

The descriptions of person specified in the following articles have a priority need for accommodation for the purposes of Part 7 of the Housing Act 1996.

3 Children aged 16 or 17

(1) A person (other than a person to whom paragraph (2) below applies) aged sixteen or seventeen who is not a relevant child for the purposes of section 23A of the Children Act 1989 or, as the case may be, is not a category 2 young person within the meaning of section 104(2) of the Social Services and Well-being (Wales) Act 2014.

(2) This paragraph applies to a person to whom a local authority owe a duty to provide accommodation under section 20 of that Act (provision of accommodation for children in need) or, as the case may be, section 76 of the Social Services and Well-being (Wales) Act 2014 (accommodation for children without parents or who are lost or abandoned etc).

4 Young people under 21

(1) A person (other than a relevant student) who–

(a) is under twenty-one; and

(b) at any time after reaching the age of sixteen, but while still under eighteen, was, but is no longer, looked after, accommodated or fostered.

5 Vulnerability: institutional backgrounds

(1) A person (other than a relevant student) who has reached the age of twenty-one and who is vulnerable as a result of having been looked after, accommodated or fostered.

(2) A person who is vulnerable as a result of having been a member of Her Majesty's regular naval, military or air forces.

(3) A person who is vulnerable as a result of–

(a) having served a custodial sentence (within the meaning of section 76 of the Powers of Criminal Courts (Sentencing) Act 2000);

(b) having been committed for contempt of court or any other kindred offence;
(c) having been remanded in custody (within the meaning of paragraph (b), (c) or (d) of section 88(1) of that Act).

6 Vulnerability: fleeing violence or threats of violence
A person who is vulnerable as a result of ceasing to occupy accommodation by reason of violence from another person or threats of violence from another person which are likely to be carried out.

Homelessness (Decisions on Referrals) Order 1998 SI No 1578

1 Citation and commencement

This Order may be cited as the Homelessness (Decisions on Referrals) Order 1998 and shall come into force on the twenty eighth day after the day on which it is approved by resolution of each House of Parliament.

2 Arrangements for deciding whether conditions for referral are satisfied

The arrangements set out in the Schedule to this Order are those agreed by the Local Government Association, the Welsh Local Government Association, the Association of London Government and the Convention of Scottish Local Authorities, and shall be the arrangements for the purposes of section 198(5) and (6)(a) of the Housing Act 1996.

3 Revocation of order

(1) Subject to paragraph (2), the Housing (Homeless Persons) (Appropriate Arrangements) Order 1978 ('the 1978 Order') is hereby revoked.

(2) The 1978 Order shall remain in force for any case where a notified authority has received a notification under section 67(1) of the Housing Act 1985 or section 198(1) of the Housing Act 1996 (referral to another local housing authority) prior to the date on which this Order comes into force.

SCHEDULE: THE ARRANGEMENTS

Article 2

Appointment of person by agreement between notifying authority and notified authority

1 Where the question whether the conditions for referral of a case are satisfied has not been decided by agreement between the notifying authority and the notified authority, the question shall be decided by a person appointed by those authorities.

Appointment of person other than by agreement between notifying authority and notified authority

2 If within a period of 21 days commencing on the day on which the notified authority receives a notification under section 198(1) of the Housing Act 1996 a person has not been appointed in accordance with paragraph 1, the question shall be decided by a person–

(a) from the panel constituted in accordance with paragraph 3, and
(b) appointed in accordance with paragraph 4.

3 (1) Subject to sub-paragraph (2), the Local Government Association shall establish and maintain a panel of persons from which a person may be appointed to decide the question whether the conditions for referral of a case are satisfied.

(2) The Local Government Association shall consult such other associations of relevant authorities as they think appropriate before–

(a) establishing the panel,
(b) inviting a person to join the panel after it has been established, and
(c) removing a person from the panel.

4 (1) The notifying authority and the notified authority shall jointly request the Chairman of the Local Government Association or his nominee ('the proper officer') to appoint a person from the panel.

(2) If within a period of six weeks commencing on the day on which the notified authority receives a notification under section 198(1) of the Housing Act 1996 a person has not been appointed, the notifying authority shall request the proper officer to appoint a person from the panel.

Procedural requirements

5 (1) Subject to the following provisions of this paragraph, the procedure for deciding whether the conditions for referral of a case are satisfied shall be determined by the appointed person.

(2) The appointed person shall invite written representations from the notifying authority and the notified authority.

(3) The appointed person may also invite–

(a) further written representations from the notifying authority and the notified authority,

(b) written representations from any other person, and

(c) oral representations from any person.

(4) If the appointed person invites representations from any person, those representations may be made by a person acting on his behalf, whether or not legally qualified.

Notification of decision

6 The appointed person shall notify his decision, and his reasons for it, in writing to the notifying authority and the notified authority.

Costs

7 (1) The notifying authority and the notified authority shall pay their own costs incurred in connection with the arrangements set out in this Schedule.

(2) Where a person has made oral representations, the appointed person may give directions as to the payment by the notifying authority or the notified authority or both authorities of any travelling expenses reasonably incurred by that person.

Meaning of 'appointed person'

8 In this Schedule "appointed person" means a person appointed in accordance with paragraph 1 or 4.

Homelessness (Suitability of Accommodation) Order 1996 SI No 3204[5]

1 Citation and commencement

This Order may be cited as the Homelessness (Suitability of Accommodation) Order 1996 and shall come into force on 20th January 1997.

2 Matters to be taken into account

In determining whether it would be, or would have been, reasonable for a person to continue to occupy accommodation and in determining whether accommodation is suitable for a person there shall be taken into account whether or not the accommodation is affordable for that person and, in particular, the following matters–

(a) the financial resources available to that person, including, but not limited to–
- (i) salary, fees and other remuneration;
- (ii) social security benefits;
- (iii) payments due under a court order for the making of periodical payments to a spouse or a former spouse, or to, or for the benefit of, a child;
- (iv) payments of child support maintenance due under the Child Support Act 1991;
- (v) contributions to the costs in respect of the accommodation which are or were made or which might reasonably be expected to be, or have been, made by other members of his household;
- (vi) pensions
- (vii) financial assistance towards the costs in respect of the accommodation, including loans, provided by a local authority, voluntary organisation or other body;
- (viii) benefits derived from a policy of insurance;
- (ix) savings and other capital sums;

(b) the costs in respect of the accommodation, including, but not limited to–
- (i) payments of, or by way of, rent;
- (ii) payments in respect of a licence or permission to occupy the accommodation;
- (iii) mortgage costs;
- (iv) payments of, or by way of, service charges;
- (v) mooring charges payable for a houseboat;
- (vi) where the accommodation is a caravan or a mobile home, payments in respect of the site on which it stands;
- (vii) the amount of council tax payable in respect of the accommodation;
- (viii) payments by way of deposit or security in respect of the accommodation;
- (ix) payments required by an accommodation agency;

5 Revoked in relation to Wales.

(c) payments which that person is required to make under a court order for the making of periodical payments to a spouse or a former spouse, or to, or for the benefit of, a child and payments of child support maintenance required to be made under the Child Support Act 1991;
(d) that person's other reasonable living expenses.

Local Authorities (Contracting Out of Allocation of Housing and Homelessness Functions) Order 1996 SI No 3205

1 Citation, commencement and interpretation

(1) This Order may be cited as the Local Authorities (Contracting Out of Allocation of Housing and Homelessness Functions) Order 1996.

(2) This article and article 3 of this Order shall come into force on 20th January 1997 and article 2 of this Order shall come into force on 1st April 1997.

(3) In this Order–

'the Act' means the Housing Act 1996;

'an authority' means a local housing authority as defined in the Housing Act 1985.

(4) Any expressions used in this Order which are also used in the Act have the same meaning as they have in the Act

2 Contracting out of allocation of housing functions

Any function of an authority which is conferred by or under Part VI of the Act (allocation of housing accommodation), except one which is listed in Schedule 1 to this Order, may be exercised by, or by employees of, such person (if any) as may be authorised in that behalf by the authority whose function it is.

3 Contracting out of homelessness functions

Any function of an authority which is conferred by or under Part VII of the Act (homelessness) [or Chapter 2 of Part 2 of the Housing (Wales) Act 2014 (help for people who are homeless or threatened with homelessness)], except one which is listed in Schedule 2 to this Order, may be exercised by, or by employees of, such person (if any) as may be authorised in that behalf by the authority whose function it is.

SCHEDULE 1: ALLOCATION OF HOUSING FUNCTIONS OF A LOCAL HOUSING AUTHORITY EXCLUDED FROM CONTRACTING OUT

Article 2

Functions conferred by or under any of the following provisions of the Act:

(a) section 161(4) (classes of persons qualifying for allocations);

(b) section 162 (the housing register) so far as they relate to any decision about the form of the register;

(c) section 167 (allocation in accordance with allocation scheme) so far as they relate to adopting or altering an allocation scheme (including decisions on what principles the scheme is to be framed) and to the functions in subsection (7) of that section;

(d) section 168(2) (information about allocation scheme) so far as they relate to making the allocation scheme available for inspection at the authority's principal office.

SCHEDULE 2: HOMELESSNESS FUNCTIONS OF A LOCAL HOUSING AUTHORITY EXCLUDED FROM CONTRACTING OUT

Article 3

Functions conferred by or under any of the following provisions of the Act:

(a) section 179(2) and (3) (duty of local housing authority to provide advisory services);

(b) section 180 (assistance for voluntary organisations);

(c) section 213 (co-operation between relevant housing authorities and bodies).

Functions conferred by or under section 95 of the Housing (Wales) Act 2014.

APPENDIX C

Guidance[1]

In addition to this Guidance, the following are reproduced in the ebook version of *Homelessness and Allocations:*

- Code of Guidance to Local Authorities on the Allocation of Accommodation and Homelessness 2016 (Wales)

1 © Crown copyright.

Homelessness code of guidance for local authorities: Guidance on how local authorities should exercise their homelessness functions in accordance with the Homelessness Reduction Act 2017 from 3 April 2018 (February 2018)

DEFINITIONS

Definitions used in the code of guidance
Throughout this code of guidance:

- 'the 1996 Act' means the Housing Act 1996
- 'the 2002 Act' means the Homelessness Act 2002
- 'the 2017 Act' means the Homelessness Reduction Act 2017
- 'the housing authority' means the local housing authority
- 'the Code' means the Homelessness code of guidance for local authorities (2018)
- 'the Convention' means the European Convention on Human Rights
- 'the Eligibility Regulations' means the Allocation of Housing and Homelessness (Eligibility) (England) Regulations 2006
- 'personalised housing plans' means personalised plans
- 'the 2002 Order' means the Homelessness (Priority Need for Accommodation) (England) Order 2002
- 'the 2003 Order' means the Homelessness (Suitability of Accommodation) (England) Order 2003

OVERVIEW OF THE HOMELESSNESS LEGISLATION

A summary of the homelessness legislation and the duties, powers and obligations on housing authorities and others towards people who are homeless or threatened with homelessness.

1. This overview provides a summary of the homelessness legislation and the duties, powers and obligations on housing authorities and others towards people who are homeless or at risk of homelessness. **It does not form part of the statutory code of guidance.**

The homelessness legislation

2. The primary homelessness legislation – that is, Part 7 of the Housing Act 1996 – provides the statutory under-pinning for action to prevent homelessness and provide assistance to people threatened with or actually homeless.
3. In 2002, the government amended the homelessness legislation through the Homelessness Act 2002 and the Homelessness (Priority Need for Accommodation) (England) Order 2002 to:
   (a) ensure a more strategic approach to tackling and preventing homelessness, in particular by requiring a homelessness strategy for every housing authority district; and
   (b) strengthen the assistance available to people who are homeless or threatened with homelessness by extending the priority need categories to homeless 16 and 17 year olds; care leavers aged 18, 19 and 20; people who are vulnerable as a result of time spent in care, the armed forces, prison or

custody, and people who are vulnerable because they have fled their home because of violence.

4. The Homelessness Reduction Act 2017 significantly reformed England's homelessness legislation by placing duties on local authorities to intervene at earlier stages to prevent homelessness in their areas. It also requires housing authorities to provide homelessness services to all those affected, not just those who have 'priority need'. These include:
   (a) an enhanced prevention duty extending the period a household is threatened with homelessness from 28 days to 56 days, meaning that housing authorities are required to work with people to prevent homelessness at an earlier stage; and
   (b) a new duty for those who are already homeless so that housing authorities will support households for 56 days to relieve their homelessness by helping them to secure accommodation.

Homelessness review and strategy

5. Under the Homelessness Act 2002, all housing authorities must have in place a homelessness strategy based on a review of all forms of homelessness in their district. The strategy must be renewed at least every 5 years. The social services authority must provide reasonable assistance.
6. The strategy must set out the authority's plans for the prevention of homelessness and for securing that sufficient accommodation and support are or will be available for people who become homeless or who are at risk of becoming so.

Duty to refer

7. The Homelessness Reduction Act 2017 introduced a duty on certain public authorities to refer service users who they think may be homeless or threatened with homelessness to a housing authority. The service user must give consent, and can choose which authority to be referred to. The housing authority should incorporate the duty to refer into their homelessness strategy and establish effective partnerships and working arrangements with agencies to facilitate appropriate referrals.

Duty to provide advisory services

8. The housing authority has a duty to provide advice and information about homelessness and the prevention of homelessness and the rights of homeless people or those at risk of homelessness, as well as the help that is available from the housing authority or others and how to access that help. The service should be designed with certain listed vulnerable groups in mind and authorities can provide it themselves or arrange for other agencies to do it on their behalf.

Applications and inquiries

9. Housing authorities must give proper consideration to all applications for housing assistance, and if they have reason to believe that an applicant may be homeless or threatened with homelessness, they must make inquiries to see whether they owe them any duty under Part 7 of the 1996 Act. This assessment process is important in enabling housing authorities to identify the assistance which an applicant may need, either to prevent them from becoming homeless,

or to help them to find another home. In each case, the authority will need to first decide whether the applicant is eligible for assistance and threatened with or actually homeless. Certain applicants who are 'persons from abroad' are not eligible for any assistance under Part 7 except free advice and information about homelessness and the prevention of homelessness.

10. Broadly speaking, a person is threatened with homelessness if they are likely to become homeless within 56 days. An applicant who has been served with valid notice under section 21 of the Housing Act 1988 to end their assured shorthold tenancy is also threatened with homelessness, if the notice has expired or will expire within 56 days and is served in respect of the only accommodation that is available for them to occupy.

11. An applicant is to be considered homeless if they do not have accommodation that they have a legal right to occupy, which is accessible and physically available to them (and their household) and which it would be reasonable for them to continue to live in.

Assessments and personalised housing plans

12. Housing authorities have a duty to carry out an assessment in all cases where an eligible applicant is homeless or threatened with homelessness. This will identify what has caused the homelessness or threat of homelessness, the housing needs of the applicant and any support they need in order to be able to secure and retain accommodation. Following this assessment, the housing authority must work with the person to develop a personalised housing plan which will include actions (or 'reasonable steps') to be taken by the authority and the applicant to try and prevent or relieve homelessness.

Prevention duty

13. Housing authorities have a duty to take reasonable steps to help prevent any eligible person (regardless of priority need status, intentionality and whether they have a local connection) who is threatened with homelessness from becoming homeless. This means either helping them to stay in their current accommodation or helping them to find a new place to live before they become actually homeless. The prevention duty continues for 56 days unless it is brought to an end by an event such as accommodation being secured for the person, or by their becoming homeless.

Relief duty

14. If the applicant is already homeless, or becomes homeless despite activity during the prevention stage, the reasonable steps will be focused on helping the applicant to secure accommodation. This relief duty lasts for 56 days unless ended in another way. If the housing authority has reason to believe a homeless applicant may be eligible for assistance and have a priority need they must be provided with interim accommodation.

Main housing duty

15. If homelessness is not successfully prevented or relieved, a housing authority will owe the main housing duty to applicants who are eligible, have a priority need for accommodation and are not homeless intentionally. Certain categories of household, such as pregnant women, families with children, and households

that are homeless due to an emergency such as a fire or flood, have priority need if homeless. Other groups may be assessed as having priority need because they are vulnerable as a result of old age, mental ill health, physical disability, having been in prison or care or as a result of becoming homeless due to domestic abuse.

16. Under the main housing duty, housing authorities must ensure that suitable accommodation is available for the applicant and their household until the duty is brought to an end, usually through the offer of a settled home. The duty can also be brought to an end for other reasons, such as the applicant turning down a suitable offer of temporary accommodation or because they are no longer eligible for assistance. A suitable offer of a settled home (whether accepted or refused by the applicant) which would bring the main housing duty to an end includes an offer of a suitable secure or introductory tenancy with a local authority, an offer of accommodation through a private registered provider (also known as a housing association) or the offer of a suitable tenancy for at least 12 months from a private landlord made by arrangement with the local authority.

Suitable accommodation

17. Housing authorities have various powers and duties to secure accommodation for homeless applicants, either on an interim basis, to prevent or relieve homelessness, to meet the main housing duty or as a settled home. Accommodation must always be 'suitable' and there are particular standards set when private rented accommodation is secured for households which have priority need.
18. Under the Homelessness (Suitability of Accommodation) (England) Order 2003, bed and breakfast accommodation is not considered suitable for families with children and households that include a pregnant woman, except where there is no other accommodation available, and then only for a maximum of 6 weeks. The Secretary of State considers that bed and breakfast accommodation is unsuitable for 16 and 17 year olds.

Intentional homelessness

19. A person would be homeless intentionally where homelessness was the consequence of a deliberate action or omission by that person. A deliberate act might be a decision to leave the previous accommodation even though it would have been reasonable for the person (and everyone in the person's household) to continue to live there. A deliberate omission might be non-payment of rent that led to rent arrears and eviction despite the rent being affordable.
20. Where people have a priority need but are intentionally homeless the housing authority must provide advice and assistance to help them find accommodation for themselves and secure suitable accommodation for them for a period that will give them a reasonable chance of doing so.
21. If, despite this assistance, homelessness persists, any children in the household could be in need under the Children Act 1989, and the family should be referred (with consent) to the children's social services authority.

Local connection and referrals to another authority

22. Broadly speaking, for the purpose of the homelessness legislation, people may have a local connection with a district because of residence, employment

or family associations in the district, or because of special circumstances. (There are exceptions, for example, residence in a district while serving a prison sentence there does not establish a local connection.) Where applicants meet the criteria for the relief duty or for the main housing duty, and the authority considers that the applicant does not have a local connection with the district but does have one somewhere else, the housing authority dealing with the application can ask the housing authority in that other district to take responsibility for the case. However, applicants cannot be referred to another housing authority if they, or any member of their household, would be at risk of violence in the district of the other authority.

23. The definition of a 'local connection' for young people leaving care was amended by the Homelessness Reduction Act 2017 so that a young homeless care leaver has a local connection to the area of the local authority that looked after them. Additional provision is made for care leavers who have been placed in accommodation, under section 22A of the Children Act 1989, in a different district to that of the children's services authority that owes them leaving care duties. If they have lived in the other district for at least 2 years, including some time before they turned 16, they will also have a local connection with that district until they are 21.

Reviews and appeals

24. Housing authorities must provide written notifications to applicants when they reach certain decisions about their case, and the reasons behind any decisions that are against the applicant's interests. Applicants can ask the housing authority to review most aspects of their decisions, and, if still dissatisfied, can appeal to the county court on a point of law.
25. Housing authorities have the power to accommodate applicants pending a review or appeal to the county court. When an applicant who is being provided with interim accommodation requests a review of the suitability of accommodation offered to end the relief duty, the authority has a duty to continue to accommodate them pending a review.

CHAPTER 1
Introduction

The purpose of the code and the relevant equality duties that housing authorities need to consider in carrying out their duties.

Purpose of the code

1.1 The Secretary of State for the Ministry of Housing, Communities and Local Government is issuing this code of guidance to local housing authorities (referred to as housing authorities) in England under section 182 of the Housing Act 1996 (the 1996 Act). In accordance with section 182(1) of the 1996 Act, housing authorities are required to have due regard to this statutory guidance in exercising their functions relating to homelessness and prevention of homelessness, including their functions under Part 7 of the 1996 Act (as amended) and under the Homelessness Act 2002 (the 2002 Act). This code replaces and consolidates the previous version published in 2006 and the supplementary guidance issued in August 2009, November 2012 and November 2014.

1.2 Under section 182(1), social services authorities in England are also required to have regard to guidance given by the Secretary of State (such as this code) when exercising their functions relating to homelessness and the prevention of homelessness. Further guidance applicable to social services authorities is also issued jointly with the Secretary of State for Health and Social Care and the Secretary of State for Education.

1.3 The code provides guidance on how housing authorities should exercise their functions relating to homelessness and threatened homelessness and apply the statutory duties in practice. This is not a substitute for legislation and therefore any policy context on the law documented in the code should be considered only as the department's understanding at the time of issue. While it is intended that the code will be updated periodically, housing authorities are expected to keep up to date with developments in legislation and case law.

1.4 The Secretary of State has the power to issue statutory codes of practice, providing further guidance on how housing authorities should deliver and monitor their homelessness and homelessness prevention functions. Any codes of practice will focus on specific functions of housing authorities in order to drive up standards.

Who is the code for?

1.5 The code is issued specifically for local authority members and staff. It is also of direct relevance to private registered providers of social housing. Private registered providers have a duty under the 1996 Act to co-operate with housing authorities in exercising their homelessness functions. Private registered providers are subject to the Regulator of Social Housing's[2] Regulatory Standards, in particular the expectation that they will co-operate with local authority strategic housing functions, as set out in the Tenancy and Home and Community Standards.

1.6 Many of the activities discussed in the code require joint planning and operational co-operation between housing authorities and social services authorities, health authorities, criminal justice agencies, voluntary sector organisations and the diverse range of bodies working in the private rented sectors – so the code is also relevant to these agencies.

Homelessness legislation

1.7 Part 7 of the 1996 Act sets out the powers and duties of housing authorities where people apply to them for accommodation or assistance in obtaining accommodation in cases of homelessness or threatened homelessness.

1.8 The Homelessness Act 2002 (the 2002 Act) places a requirement on housing authorities in England to formulate and publish a homelessness strategy based on the results of a review of homelessness in their district. The 2002 Act

2 The regulation of social housing is the responsibility of the Regulation Committee, a statutory committee of the Homes and Communities Agency (HCA). The organisation refers to itself as the Regulator of Social Housing in undertaking the functions of the Regulation Committee. References in any enactment or instrument to the Regulator of Social Housing are references to the HCA acting through the Regulation Committee. Homes England is the trading name of the HCA's non-regulation functions.

also amended a number of provisions in Part 7 of the 1996 Act to strengthen the safety net for vulnerable people.

1.9 The Homelessness Reduction Act 2017 (the 2017 Act) places a set of duties on housing authorities to intervene at earlier stages to prevent homelessness in their areas and to take reasonable steps to prevent and relieve homelessness for all eligible applicants, not just those that have priority need under the Act.

Equality

1.10 Housing authorities need to ensure that policies and decisions relating to homelessness and threatened homelessness do not amount to unlawful conduct under the Equality Act 2010 and also comply with the public sector equality duty.

1.11 The Equality Act 2010 provides protection from unlawful discrimination in the provision of goods, services and public functions, housing, transport and education in relation to the protected characteristics set out in the legislation, which are:

(a) age;
(b) disability;
(c) gender reassignment;
(d) pregnancy and maternity (which includes breastfeeding);
(e) marriage and civil partnership;
(f) race;
(g) religion or belief;
(h) sex; and,
(i) sexual orientation.

1.12 The public sector equality duty in section 149(1) of the Equality Act 2010 requires public authorities, including housing authorities, to integrate equality considerations into the decision-making process from the outset, including in the development, implementation and review of their policies and services. This includes policies and services relating to homelessness and threatened homelessness. Other agencies and bodies who carry out public functions on behalf of local authorities also have a duty to comply with the public sector equality duty in the delivery of those public functions.

1.13 Specifically, under section 149(1) Equality Act 2010, public authorities in exercising their functions (or a person exercising public functions that is not a public authority (section 149(2)) must have due regard to the need to:

(a) eliminate discrimination, harassment, victimisation and any other conduct that is prohibited by or under the Equality Act 2010;
(b) advance equality of opportunity between persons who share a relevant protected characteristic and persons who do not share it; and,
(c) foster good relations between persons who share a relevant protected characteristic and persons who do not share it.

1.14 The 3 limbs of the duty, listed above, apply to all protected characteristics apart from marriage and civil partnership, which is only relevant to the first limb (eliminating discrimination and so on).

1.15 In order to comply with the public sector equality duty housing authorities need to do the following:

(a) plan how to factor in equality considerations;
(b) collect sufficient information to develop a reasonable understanding of what the equality impacts might be;

(c) identify any equality impact the policy or service might have;
(d) justify any decision that it takes;
(e) re-evaluation to consider whether any alternative approaches might be possible;
(f) record how many equality impacts are taken;
(g) inform decision-makers; and,
(h) continue to review equality impacts as the policy or service is implemented or developed.

1.16 The duty to have due regard to these equality issues will also apply when decisions are taken in respect of individual applications for homelessness assistance. Applicants should receive fully considered decisions which, in accordance with the public sector equality duty, show due regard to any equality impacts of the decision.

1.17 Housing authorities are also subject to the Equality Act 2010 (Specific Duties and Public Authorities) Regulations 2017 if they are covered under Schedule 2 to those regulations, which would include most housing authorities. These regulations require public authorities to publish information to demonstrate their compliance with the public sector equality duty and set and publish equality objectives.

1.18 Further information about the Equality Act 2010 and the public sector equality duty is available from the Equality and Human Rights Commission and the Government Equalities Office.

Human Rights Act 1998

1.19 In addition, when someone is receiving services from (or is on the receiving end of public functions carried out by) a public sector organisation or others who deliver services or carry out public functions on their behalf, they will also have rights under the Human Rights Act 1998.

1.20 Section 3 of the Human Rights Act 1998 specifies that when interpreting the law, so far as it is possible to do so, primary and secondary legislation must be read and given effect in a way which is compatible with the European Convention on Human Rights (the Convention). Section 6 of the Human Rights Act 1998 provides that it is unlawful for a public authority to act in a way which is incompatible with a Convention right. Therefore, housing authorities and other agencies that carry out public functions on behalf of housing authorities must do so in a way that is compatible with Convention rights.

1.21 Housing authorities should pay particular attention to the promotion and protection of rights of vulnerable and disadvantaged groups such as people with disabilities, ethnic minorities, victims of sexual discrimination, children and elderly people.

1.22 Schedule 1 to the Human Rights Act 1998 gives further effect to a number of Convention rights and freedoms in domestic UK law. There are 3 Articles which are particularly important for the purposes of this code, as follows:
(a) Article 3 – is the prohibition of torture whereby every person has the absolute right not to be tortured or subjected to treatment or punishment that is inhuman or degrading;
(b) Article 4 – is the prohibition of slavery and forced labour whereby every person has the right not to be held in slavery or required to perform forced labour; and,

(c) Article 8 – is the right to respect for private and family life whereby every person has the right to respect for their private and family life, their home and their correspondence. This right can be interfered with only in specified circumstances: where it is necessary in the interests of national security, public safety or the economic well-being of the country, for the prevention of disorder or crime, for the protection of health or morals, or for the protection of the rights and freedoms of others.

1.23 Under Article 3, housing authorities have an obligation to prevent a person being subjected to treatment or punishment that is inhuman or degrading, to investigate any allegations of such treatment, and to protect vulnerable individuals who they know or should know are at risk of such treatment.

1.24 Under Article 4, housing authorities should try to ensure that their policies or decisions take measures to protect victims of modern slavery or trafficking and to protect individuals who they are aware are at risk of such treatment.

1.25 Under Article 8, housing authorities should try to ensure that their policies or decisions do not interfere with a person's right to respect for private and family life, their home and their correspondence.

1.26 If a housing authority does decide that it will be difficult to avoid interfering with someone's Article 8 rights, it will need to make sure that the policy or action is necessary, pursues one of the recognised legitimate aims and is proportionate to that aim. A housing authority may be asked to produce reasons for its decisions.

1.27 Housing authorities may also need to consider whether there are situations putting them under obligation to take active steps to promote and protect individuals' Article 8 rights from systematic interference by third parties, for example, private businesses.

1.28 Housing authorities are expected to consider the human rights implications of their actions in the exercise of their powers, or risk having their decisions overturned as a result and the planning and delivery of their services affected.

1.29 Further information about the Human Rights Act 1998 is available from the Equality and Human Rights Commission.

Safeguarding

1.30 Housing authorities have a duty to safeguard and promote the welfare of children and to co-operate to promote the well-being of all children, including 16–17 year olds, in the area as set out in the Children Act 2004.

1.31 Housing authorities also have a duty to co-operate with children's services in relation to children in need when requested to do so, as long as this is compatible with their own statutory or other duties and obligations and does not unduly prejudice the discharge of any of their functions.

1.32 Children's needs are paramount, and the welfare, needs and wishes of each child should be put first, so that every child receives the support they need.

1.33 All professionals who come into contact with children and their families must be alert to their needs and any risks of harm that individual abusers or potential abusers may pose, and respond proactively to them when dealing with their housing situation.

1.34 All professionals must share appropriate information in a timely way and can discuss any concerns about an individual child with colleagues, and with children's services. This will include identifying where current or changing housing arrangements might affect risk to children.

1.35 All professionals contribute to whatever actions are needed to safeguard and promote a child's welfare and take part in regularly reviewing the outcomes for the child against specific plans and outcomes.

1.36 The duties placed on housing authorities are set out in the government's inter-agency statutory guidance: Working together to safeguard children: A guide to inter-agency working to safeguard and promote the welfare of children. The specific duties towards 16- and 17-year-olds who are at risk of homelessness or who are homeless, and the legal duties children's services authorities and housing authorities have towards them are set out in the government's statutory guidance: Provision of accommodation for 16- and 17-year-old young people who may be homeless and/or require accommodation.

CHAPTER 2
Homelessness strategies and reviews

Guidance on housing authority duties to carry out a homelessness review and publish a homelessness strategy.

2.1 This chapter provides guidance on housing authorities' duties to carry out a homelessness review and to formulate and publish a strategy based on the results of that review.

Duty to formulate a homelessness strategy

2.2 Section 1(1) of the 2002 Act gives housing authorities the power to carry out a homelessness review for their district and formulate and publish a homelessness strategy based on the results of the review. Section 1(4) requires housing authorities to publish a new homelessness strategy, based on the results of a further homelessness review, within the period of 5 years beginning with the day on which their last homelessness strategy was published. However, housing authorities can conduct homelessness reviews and publish homelessness strategies more frequently if circumstances in the district change.

2.3 There was an exemption from this requirement for 'excellent authorities' as classified by the Secretary of State by virtue of the Local Authorities' Plans and Strategies (Disapplication) (England) Order 2005. This regulation was revoked by the Local Audit and Accountability Act 2014 and all housing authorities are required to publish homelessness strategies as of 1 April 2017.

2.4 In conducting a review of homelessness and to formulate a new strategy, housing authorities will need to take into account the additional duties introduced through the 2017 Act. Authorities are encouraged to take the opportunity to involve all relevant partners in developing a strategy that involves them in earlier identification and intervention to prevent homelessness.

2.5 For a homelessness strategy to be effective, housing authorities should ensure that it is consistent with other local plans and is developed with, and has the support of, all relevant local authority departments and partners. Corporate and partnership involvement in identifying strategic objectives will help to ensure all relevant departments and agencies are committed to supporting their delivery.

2.6 The homelessness strategy should link with other strategies and programmes that aim to address the wide range of factors that could contribute to homelessness in the local area. It will be important to consider how these strategies and programmes, which could encompass aspects of local health, justice or economic policy for example, can help achieve the objectives of the homelessness strategy and vice-versa.

2.7 Housing authorities should consider the benefits of cross-boundary co-operation. A county-wide approach will be particularly important in non-unitary authorities, where housing and homelessness services are provided by the district authority whilst other key services, such as social services, are delivered at the county level. Housing authorities should ensure that the homelessness strategy for their district forms part of a coherent approach to tackling homelessness with neighbouring authorities. Housing authorities may wish to collaborate to produce a joint homelessness strategy covering a sub-regional area. London boroughs should have regard to the London Housing Strategy when formulating their homelessness strategies.

2.8 Each local authority has a legal duty under the Health and Social Care Act 2012 to take such steps as it considers appropriate for improving the health of the people in its area. This includes people experiencing homelessness or at risk of homelessness. Housing authorities should ensure that their homelessness strategy is co-ordinated with the Health and Wellbeing Strategy, and that their review of homelessness informs and is informed by the Joint Strategic Needs Assessment.

2.9 To be effective the homelessness strategy will need to be based on realistic assumptions and be developed and owned jointly with partners who will be responsible for its delivery. Sections 1(5) and (6) of the 2002 Act require housing and social services authorities to take the homelessness strategy into account when exercising their functions. Authorities can combine housing and homelessness strategies in a single document where it is coherent to do so.

2.10 Housing authorities must consult public or local authorities, voluntary organisations or other persons as they consider appropriate before adopting or modifying a homelessness strategy. Housing authorities will also wish to consult with service users and specialist agencies that provide support to homeless people in the district. Section 3(4) provides that a housing authority cannot include in a homelessness strategy any specific action expected to be taken by another body or organisation without their approval.

2.11 As part of the homelessness strategy housing authorities should develop effective action plans, to help ensure that the objectives set out in the homelessness strategy are achieved. Action plans could include, for example, targets, milestones and arrangements for monitoring and evaluation.

2.12 Housing authorities must make copies of their homelessness review and the homelessness strategy available for inspection at their principal office at all reasonable hours and without charge, and the strategy must be available to any member of the public, on request (for which a reasonable charge can be made). Housing authorities are advised to publish the strategy and review documents on their website.

2.13 Housing authorities must keep their homelessness strategy under review and may modify it accordingly. Before modifying the strategy, they must consult on the same basis as required before adopting a strategy. Circumstances that might prompt modification of a homelessness strategy include but not be limited to: anything that may affect the composition of homelessness and/or the risk of homelessness in the district; anything that may change the delivery of the strategy; changes to the relationships between the partners involved in the strategy; or changes to the organisational structure of the housing authority.

Reviewing homelessness and formulating a strategy

2.14 Under section 2(1) of the 2002 Act, a homelessness review means a review by a housing authority of:

(a) the levels, and likely future levels, of homelessness in their district;

(b) the activities which are carried out for any the following purposes (or which contribute to achieving any of them):

  (i) preventing homelessness in the housing authority's district;

  (ii) securing that accommodation is or will be available for people in the district who are or may become homeless; and

  (iii) providing support for people in the district who are homeless or who may become at risk of homelessness; or who have been homeless and need support to prevent them becoming homeless again; and,

(c) the resources available to the housing authority, the social services authority for the district, other public authorities, voluntary organisations and other persons for the activities outlined in (b) above.

2.15 The purpose of the review is to determine the extent to which the population in the district is homeless or at risk of becoming homeless, assess the likely extent in the future, identify what is currently being done and by whom, and identify what resources are available, to prevent and tackle homelessness.

2.16 Housing authorities are reminded that when drawing up their homelessness strategies for preventing and reducing homelessness, they must consider the needs of all groups of people in their district who are homeless or likely to become homeless, including Gypsies and Travellers. The periodical review of housing needs under section 8 of the Housing Act 1985 is a statutory requirement on housing authorities. This requires housing authorities to assess and understand the accommodation needs of people residing or resorting to their district. Under section 124 of the Housing and Planning Act 2016, which amends section 8 of the Housing Act 1985, housing authorities have a statutory duty to consider the needs of people residing in or resorting to their district with respect to sites for caravans and the mooring of houseboats.

Identifying current and future levels of homelessness

2.17 Homelessness is defined by sections 175 to 178 of the 1996 Act. For further guidance on homelessness and threatened with homelessness see Chapter 6. The review must take account of all forms of homelessness within the meaning of the 1996 Act and should therefore consider a wide population of households who are homeless or at risk of becoming homeless. This will include people sleeping rough, and those whose accommodation and circumstances make them more likely than others to become homeless including sleeping rough.

2.18 When carrying out the review housing authorities should consider including the following as a basis for assessing current and future levels of homelessness in their district:

(a) homelessness casework records and other local sources of data;
(b) trends in homelessness approaches and in underlying causes;
(c) which cohorts may be more likely to become homeless or be threatened with homelessness;
(d) the profile of households who have experienced homelessness in their district;
(e) equality monitoring data, including that relating to homelessness applications and outcomes;
(f) the range of factors that may affect future levels of homelessness;
(g) the personal and structural factors that may contribute to people becoming homeless; and,
(h) any planned legislation or local policy changes that are likely to impact on levels of homelessness for particular groups in the district.

Reviewing activities carried out and resources required

2.19 The public, private and voluntary sectors can all contribute, directly or indirectly, to the prevention of homelessness and the provision of accommodation and support for homeless people. The housing authority should therefore consider the activities of all relevant agencies and organisations, as well as the resources available to them, which may contribute to the delivery of services.

2.20 Having mapped all the current activities, the housing authority should consider whether these are appropriate and adequate to meet the aims of the strategy, and whether any realignment of resources or additional provision is needed.

Assistance from social services

2.21 In non-unitary districts, where the social services authority and the housing authority are different authorities, section 1(2) of the 2002 Act requires the social services authority to give the housing authority such assistance as may be reasonably required in carrying out a homelessness review and formulating and publishing a homelessness strategy. **Since a large proportion of people who are homeless or at risk of homelessness will be vulnerable adults or have children in their care, it will always be necessary to seek assistance from the social services authority to formulate an effective homelessness strategy.** In unitary authorities, the authority must ensure that the social services department assists the housing department in carrying out a homelessness review and formulating and publishing a homelessness strategy.

2.22 The social services authority must comply with all reasonable requests for assistance from housing authorities within their district. For the purposes of formulating a strategy, this might include providing information about the current and projected numbers of vulnerable adults within the district that might be at higher risk of homelessness, and the care, support and accommodation available to them. Children's social care services could provide, for example, future projections of young people leaving care who are likely to require accommodation and support, families provided with accommodation who are ineligible for assistance (some of which might become eligible), and the numbers of safeguarding alerts involving domestic abuse, poor housing conditions or other factors that might indicate a need for homelessness assistance.

Formulating the strategy

2.23 Having carried out a homelessness review the housing authority will be in a position to formulate its homelessness strategy based on the results of that review as required by section 1(1)(b) of the 2002 Act. In formulating its strategy, a housing authority will need to consider the necessary levels of activity required to achieve the aims set out in the paragraph below and the sufficiency of the resources available to them as revealed by the review.

2.24 Under section 3(1) of the 2002 Act a homelessness strategy means a strategy for:

(a) preventing homelessness in the district (see paragraphs 2.25–2.29 below);
(b) securing that sufficient accommodation is and will be available for people in the district who are or may become homeless (see paragraphs 2.30–2.56 below); and,
(c) securing the satisfactory provision of support for people in the district who are or may become homeless or who have been homeless and need support to prevent them becoming homeless again (see paragraphs 2.57–2.75 below).

Preventing homelessness

2.25 Under section 3(1)(a) of the 2002 Act, a homelessness strategy must include a strategy for **preventing** homelessness in the district. Furthermore, the 2017 Act strengthens statutory duties to prevent homelessness for all eligible applicants, including those who do not have priority need or may be considered intentionally homelessness and regardless of local connection. The 2017 Act also creates a new duty on certain public authorities to refer users of their services who are threatened with homelessness to a housing authority of their choice, which enables earlier identification of people at risk of becoming homeless through their interactions with other services.

2.26 When developing their homelessness strategy, local authorities will wish to look beyond the statutory requirements to consider the economic and social reasons for investing in activities that prevent homelessness, and may wish to learn from other local authorities and service providers who have adopted a more preventative approach.

Reviewing homelessness prevention activities and resources

2.27 Housing authorities will need to gain a good understanding of the causes of homelessness in their district, both to inform the development of successful interventions, and to assist in securing the commitment of stakeholders who can contribute toward preventing homelessness.

2.28 Housing authorities should establish good links with service providers who have early contact with people who are at risk of becoming homeless, review and learn from their activities and consider how they might be improved. Housing authorities should also consider how they might identify and interact with those households that are not receiving services, in order to prevent homelessness.

2.29 As part of their homelessness review, housing authorities should identify resources that are allocated to activities that prevent homelessness as well as those that respond to households becoming homeless, and consider how these might be realigned. This will be particularly important for delivering the duties contained in the 2017 Act. Upstream prevention activities are likely to produce direct savings in temporary accommodation and other costs for the authority, and will also help to reduce pressures on wider services, such as health, housing and employment, in the longer term.

Formulating a strategy to prevent homelessness

2.30 Elements of a prevention strategy should include:

(a) **advice and information:** available to residents in the district, or who may return to the district, which assists them in having appropriate information or access to services that will help to prevent them becoming homeless. Maintaining a high level of awareness about housing options and homelessness amongst partner agencies will also contribute to preventing homelessness. For further guidance on advice and information on homelessness and threatened with homelessness see Chapter 3;

(b) **early identification:** authorities should consider how they might identify people at risk of homelessness at an earlier stage, and the interventions that could be put in place to prevent them from being threatened with or becoming homeless. The 'duty to refer' (section 213B of the 1996 Act) should engage public bodies to assist with earlier identification, and housing authorities should develop local protocols or referral arrangements with appropriate agencies, whether or not they are included within that duty. For further advice on duty to refer see Chapter 4;

(c) **pre-crisis intervention:** authorities should consider whether sufficient activity is in place to intervene proactively where a household may be at risk of homelessness in the future. This might include, for example, having joint working arrangements with environmental health services to ensure tenants are not displaced through enforcement action other than in a planned way, involving children's early help services to support families at risk of losing their social housing tenancy, or funding a court duty advice service that identifies households at risk of mortgage repossession or loss of private rented accommodation;

(d) **preventing recurring homelessness:** an analysis of local data should identify applicants most at risk of repeat homelessness which will inform decisions about allocation of resources, particularly for housing related support to help sustain settled accommodation; and,

(e) **Partnership arrangements:** the homelessness strategy should set out how partners will be involved in all of the above activities, and what practical arrangements are needed (for example, joint protocols and procedures) to ensure the continued commitment to joint working to prevent homelessness and improve outcomes.

Ensuring a sufficient supply of accommodation

2.31 Section 3(1)(b) of the 2002 Act provides that one of the purposes of the homelessness strategy is to secure that sufficient accommodation is and will be available for people who are or may become homeless.

2.32 A shortage of affordable housing can lead to increasing numbers of people being accommodated in temporary accommodation whilst waiting for settled housing to bring the main homelessness duty to an end. 'Settled housing' in this context will primarily be social housing and good quality private sector accommodation. For further guidance on securing accommodation see Chapter 16.

2.33 Through the homelessness review, housing authorities should estimate the likely demand for assistance to prevent or relieve homelessness, and to meet the needs of those who are owed the main housing duty. They should include within the strategy what actions are required to ensure sufficient supply of accommodation to meet the estimated need.

Reviewing accommodation needs and resources

2.34 Housing authorities need to consider the range of accommodation that is available and is likely to be required for people who are, or may become, homeless. Landlords, accommodation providers and housing developers across all sectors may contribute to the review, and to the development of a strategy for provision of accommodation in the district.

2.35 Housing authorities should review the existing supply of accommodation available to people who are homeless or at risk of homelessness and identify where there are gaps, or where existing resources do not match the most pressing needs.

2.36 This might include reviewing supply and demand for:

(a) social and affordable housing held by the housing authority and private registered providers;

(b) temporary accommodation provided on an interim basis, or under the section 193(2) main housing duty;

(c) private rented accommodation, including shared housing options for young single people;

(d) supported accommodation available for particular cohorts of people in need of accommodation with support; and,

(e) low cost home ownership schemes.

Increasing the supply of new housing

2.37 National guidance on planning and affordable housing is contained in the National Planning Policy Framework and supporting planning guidance. The Framework acts as guidance for local planning authorities both in drawing up Local Plans and making decisions about planning applications.

2.38 The Framework sets out that local planning authorities should have a clear understanding of housing needs in their area. They should prepare a Strategic Housing Market Assessment to assess their full housing needs, working with neighbouring authorities where housing market areas cross administrative boundaries.

2.39 The Framework asks local authorities to use their evidence base to ensure that their Local Plan meets the full, objectively assessed needs for market and affordable housing in the housing market area, as far as is consistent with the policies set out in the Framework.

2.40 To deliver a wide choice of high quality homes, widen opportunities for home ownership and create sustainable, inclusive and mixed communities, the Framework asks local planning authorities to:

(a) plan for a mix of housing based on current and future demographic trends, market trends and the needs of different groups in the community (such as, but not limited to, families with children, young single people, older people, people with disabilities, service families and people wishing to build their own homes);

(b) identify the size, type, tenure and range of housing that is required in particular locations, reflecting local demand;

(c) where they have identified that affordable housing is needed, set policies that meet this need within development sites, unless off-site provision or a financial contribution of broadly equivalent value can be robustly justified and the agreed approach contributes to the objective of creating mixed and balanced communities. Such policies should be sufficiently flexible to take account of changing market conditions over time.

2.41 Local planning authorities are expected to review their Plans regularly and ensure that they are kept up-to-date.

2.42 Another important means of providing affordable housing is through planning obligations, which might be sought in the context of granting planning permission for new housing development. Section 106 of the Town and Country Planning Act 1990 enables a local planning authority to seek agreement from developers to enter into planning obligations to mitigate the impact of otherwise unacceptable development. More detailed guidance on the use of planning obligations is contained within the Planning Practice Guidance.

Accessing the private rented sector

2.43 Housing authorities are encouraged to work in close partnership with local landlords and to develop opportunities to expand the provision of private rented accommodation that is available to people threatened with or actually homeless. Housing authorities should engage private landlords in developing the homelessness strategy, and in identifying how they might support its delivery. There may be opportunities to provide grant funding to landlords to improve poor quality accommodation or to bring empty properties back in to use for homeless households. Housing authorities should also review their private rented access schemes to ensure they meet a broad range of needs, including for single people at risk of homelessness.

Access to social housing

2.44 In developing their homelessness strategy, housing authorities should review how allocation arrangements for their own stock, and nominations, to private registered providers contribute to preventing or relieving homelessness.

2.45 Allocations schemes will be designed to reflect local priorities and needs, but must also provide reasonable preference to people who are homeless or are owed specific homelessness duties as set out in section 166A(3) of the 1996 Act. This will include providing reasonable preference to people who are owed the prevention (section 195(2)) or relief (section 189B) duty. Housing authorities may need to review their allocations schemes in response to the 2017 Act, to ensure that they deliver the requirements of the legislation and are sufficiently geared towards preventing homelessness.

2.46 Housing authorities are encouraged to develop an annual lettings plan to match anticipated supply against applicant demand, taking into account the need to prevent homelessness and to provide settled accommodation to people owed the main housing duty. As well as considering the proportion of lettings that should be made available to applicants who are owed the main housing duty (section 193(2)), housing authorities will want to consider whether the lettings plan facilitates or reduces access to housing for groups they know to be at risk of becoming homeless in their area. Housing authorities may also wish to review what part social housing allocations should play in facilitating move-on from any supported accommodation that forms part of the authority's wider homelessness response.

2.47 The Localism Act 2011 amended Part 6 of the 1996 Act to enable housing authorities to set their own qualification criteria for applicants wishing to join their housing register, to address local priorities and needs. Authorities can also provide reduced preference to applicants because of their previous conduct, which might include anti-social behaviour or rent arrears. However, housing authorities should not apply qualification criteria which would exclude from their allocation schemes homeless households who would be entitled to reasonable preference in the allocation of housing.

2.48 Housing authorities are encouraged to keep under review the impact of their allocations policies upon people at risk of homelessness, including single people who may be less able to establish their residency or may have a history of offending or other behaviour that impacts on their ability to access social housing. It is for the authority to decide its allocation scheme based on local priorities, but in doing so it should be aware of and take into consideration the impact of policies and procedures (which may be unintentional and/or indirect) on applicants who may be at risk of homelessness in the district.

2.49 It is important that housing authorities work effectively with private registered providers to help them prevent and tackle homelessness in the district. Private registered providers have a key role to play in sustaining tenancies, reducing evictions and abandonment, and preventing homelessness through their housing management functions. All parties will wish to ensure that there are effective procedures to identify early those tenants at risk of becoming homeless and that referral processes are in place.

2.50 The Secretary of State considers that, where local authority or private registered providers stock is provided as temporary accommodation (under section 193(2)); the housing authority should give consideration to the scope for allocating the accommodation as a secure or assured tenancy, as appropriate. This is especially the case where a household has been living in a particular property for anything other than a short-term emergency stay.

Temporary accommodation

2.51 Housing authorities should review their need for and use of temporary accommodation and, where necessary, identify what improvements will be made to procurement plans within their homelessness strategy. The aim will be to maximise the supply of good quality accommodation to meet the needs of homeless households, and reduce the financial burden of temporary accommodation on the applicant, authority and public purse. Housing authorities who use bed and breakfast to accommodate families in emergencies should consider including a plan to reduce or eliminate its use. For further guidance on securing accommodation see Chapter 16.

Supported housing and refuges

2.52 Housing authorities will need to work with partners to assess the need, and plan strategically, for supported housing provision to help prevent and resolve homelessness for people with support needs, and to consider whether existing local needs are met or to commission provision (either new units or additional support) to address these needs. Supported housing should be of good quality and suitable for the needs of the client group it is intended for. For example, supported accommodation with shared facilities will not normally be suitable for longer-term placements for families with pregnant women and/or children.

2.53 Refuge provision is very important for victims of domestic abuse at high risk who need to flee from highly dangerous perpetrators, and victims will very often need to be placed in a refuge in another area in order to be safe from the perpetrator. Housing authorities will need to work together to assess and meet the need for refuge provision across local authority boundaries, for example, across a region or sub-region, to help ensure provision for people fleeing both from and to individual housing authority areas.

Empty homes

2.54 Local authorities are encouraged to make use of their powers and the incentives available to tackle empty homes. Through the new homes bonus, local authorities can earn the same financial reward for bringing an empty home back into use as building a new one. They can also charge up to 150% council tax for a home left empty for over 2 years. Housing authorities may wish to consider introducing local schemes that incentivise landlords to bring empty properties back into use, for example by providing grant funding subject to the refurbished accommodation being made available for homeless households.

Disabled facilities grant

2.55 Uptake of the disabled facilities grant – a mandatory entitlement administered by housing authorities for eligible disabled people in all housing tenures – can enable homeowners to remain living an independent life at home. Authorities are required to give a decision within 6 months of receiving an application. The grant is subject to a maximum limit and is means tested to ensure that funding goes to those most in need.

2.56 For guidance on securing accommodation for homeless applicants see Chapter 16.

Securing the provision of support

2.57 Section 3(1)(c) of the 2002 Act provides that the homelessness strategy should secure the satisfactory provision of support for people in the district who are or may be homeless, or who have been homeless and need support to prevent them becoming homeless again.

Reviewing resources and activities to provide support

2.58 Housing authorities should consider all the current activities which contribute to the provision of support for people who are, or may be at risk of becoming, homeless and those who have been homeless and need support to prevent them becoming homeless again. The range of providers whose activities will be making a contribution to this area are likely to embrace the public, private, voluntary and charitable sectors.

2.59 The 2017 Act introduced duties for housing authorities to assess the support needs of all applicants who are homeless or threatened with homelessness, and agree a personalised housing plan which should include reasonable steps required to meet any support needs identified. This more systematic assessment arrangement for all applicants will enable the generation of much improved data on the support needs of homeless people, which can be used as part of the homelessness review and to inform the homelessness strategy as well as commissioning plans. For further guidance on assessments and personalised housing plans see Chapter 11.

2.60 Housing authorities should consider mapping support services and activities in the district to assist in developing the homelessness strategy and to identify areas, both geographic and thematic, in which services are duplicated and/or where gaps in service provision can be identified.

2.61 Housing authorities should explore how budgets and resources from a wide range of sources can be used to provide support for people in their district. Due to the cross-cutting nature of homelessness there will be opportunities, for example, for the housing authority to work with organisations specialising in primary care, substance dependency, mental health or employment and training.

2.62 In two-tier authority areas it will be necessary to engage the upper tier authority, which holds responsibility for commissioning housing related support, in identifying resources available to meet support needs across all cohorts that are at high risk of homelessness.

Formulating a strategy to provide support

2.63 In formulating their homelessness strategies, housing authorities need to recognise that for some households homelessness cannot be tackled, or prevented, solely through the provision of accommodation. Some households will require a range of support services, which may include housing related support to help them sustain their accommodation, as well as personal support relating to factors such as relationship breakdown, domestic abuse, mental health problems, drug and alcohol addiction, poverty, debt and unemployment.

2.64 Housing-related support services have a key role in preventing homelessness occurring or recurring. The types of housing-related support that households who have experienced homelessness may need include:

(a) support in establishing a suitable home – help, advice and support in finding and maintaining suitable accommodation for independent living in the community;

(b) support with daily living skills – help, advice and training in the day-to-day skills needed for living independently, such as budgeting and cooking;

(c) support in accessing benefits, health and community care services – information, advice and help in claiming benefits or accessing community care or health services;

(d) help in establishing and maintaining social support – help in rebuilding or establishing social networks that can help counter isolation and help support independent living.

Support for single people

2.65 Housing authorities will be aware that some individuals may be at particular risk of homelessness, for example young people leaving care, ex-offenders, veterans, people with mental health problems or individuals leaving hospital, and may require a broader package of resettlement support. When developing their homelessness strategies, housing authorities should consider carefully how to work effectively to prevent homelessness amongst these groups and ensure that appropriate support is available.

2.66 Housing authorities should work with key partners to assess and meet the support needs of people at risk of homelessness. Where appropriate, accommodation and support services might be jointly commissioned, with children's social care, health, criminal justice agencies and other partners, in order to share and maximise resources and ensure a more holistic service response.

2.67 Many young people who have experienced homelessness will be in particular need of support to develop skills to manage their affairs and prepare to take on and sustain a tenancy and operate a household budget. Those estranged from their family, particularly care leavers, may lack the advice and support normally available to young people.

Support for rough sleepers

2.68 In districts where there is evidence that people are sleeping rough, the homelessness strategy should include objectives to work toward eliminating rough sleeping. This would include reviewing existing support arrangements, identifying which do or do not work, and where appropriate looking for alternative ways to provide accommodation and support that might improve outcomes for people who have slept rough. Accommodation and support solutions will vary according to the profile and particular needs of rough sleepers in the district, but authorities will wish to consider whether existing arrangements are working, or whether 'Housing First' or other service models might be more effective.

2.69 Housing authorities should consider what actions will assist in preventing rough sleeping, particularly for those groups that are over represented amongst those identified as sleeping rough, which includes people who have been in care or in prison, people who have mental health problems and those with a history of drug or alcohol misuse. Housing authorities cannot tackle rough sleeping alone and should involve partners in health, social care and criminal justice, as well as third sector and charitable service providers to develop and deliver the strategy.

2.70 Housing authorities should also consider joint working with agencies to tackle issues such as street drinking, begging, drug misuse and anti-social behaviour. Such collaborative working can help reduce the numbers of people sleeping rough and provide effective services targeted at those who are homeless or at risk of becoming homeless.

Support for families

2.71 Housing authorities should consider what support is available, or could be made available to support families who are at risk of homelessness, including preventing them from becoming homeless. Early Help services commissioned or delivered by children's social care authorities can contribute to the identification of families that are struggling to maintain accommodation, and require help and support before problems escalate and they are placed at imminent risk of homelessness. Involving providers of services to children and families in developing the strategy will contribute to improving early intervention, as well as drawing in resources available to support families who become homeless or require support to access and sustain settled accommodation.

2.72 Housing authorities will also wish to involve teams responsible for delivering the 'troubled families' programme in developing and delivering a strategy that helps to prevent the most vulnerable families from becoming homeless.

Support for victims of domestic abuse

2.73 In formulating their homelessness strategies, housing authorities should consider the particular needs that victims of domestic abuse have for safe accommodation, which will include having accommodation placements available outside the district. Housing authorities should also work cooperatively with other local authorities and commissioners to provide services to tackle domestic abuse; and should involve any local Violence Against Women and Girls Forum and service provider(s) in developing the homelessness strategy.

2.74 Housing authorities should also work closely with local refuge providers to develop fair and efficient move on arrangements, and should be mindful that policies and practices do not disadvantage people who have lost settled accommodation because of domestic abuse.

Households in temporary accommodation

2.75 The provision of support to households placed in temporary accommodation is essential to ensure that they are able to continue to enjoy a reasonable quality of life and access the range of services they need. In formulating their homelessness strategies, housing authorities should consider what arrangements need to be in place to ensure that households placed in temporary accommodation, within their district or outside, are able to access relevant support services. In particular households will need to be able to access:

(a) primary care services such as health visitors and GPs;
(b) appropriate education services;
(c) relevant social services; and,
(d) employment and training services.

CHAPTER 3
Advice and information about homelessness and the prevention of homelessness

Guidance on housing authority duties to provide free advice and information about homelessness and the prevention of homelessness, and to ensure they design advice to meet the needs of particular vulnerable groups.

3.1 Housing authorities have a duty to provide or secure the provision of advice and information about homelessness and the prevention of homelessness, free of charge. These services will form part of the offer to applicants who are also owed other duties under Part 7, for example the prevention and relief duties. **They must also be available to any other person in their district**, including people who are not eligible for further homelessness services as a result of their immigration status. The provision of up to date, comprehensive, tailored advice and information will play an important part in delivering the housing authority's strategy for preventing homelessness.

3.2 Housing authorities may wish to consider providing information for those who are ineligible for further homelessness services on how to access any other assistance available in the area, for example through charitable or faith groups.

3.3 Under section 179(1) of the 1996 Act, authorities must provide information and advice on:

(a) preventing homelessness;
(b) securing accommodation when homeless;
(c) the rights of people who are homeless or threatened with homelessness, and the duties of the authority;
(d) any help that is available from the authority or anyone else for people in the authority's district who are homeless or may become homeless (whether or not they are threatened with homelessness); and,
(e) how to access that help.

3.4 Early applications for homelessness assistance maximise the time and opportunities available to prevent homelessness. Information provided through authorities' websites and other channels should therefore:

(a) help enable people to take action themselves where possible; and,
(b) actively encourage them to seek assistance from the authority in good time if they need it.

3.5 Section 179(2) states that housing authorities must design advice and information services to meet the needs of people within their district including, in particular, the needs of the following groups:

(a) people released from prison or youth detention accommodation;
(b) care leavers;
(c) former members of the regular armed forces;
(d) victims of domestic abuse;
(e) people leaving hospital;
(f) people suffering from a mental illness or impairment; and,
(g) any other group that the authority identify as being at particular risk of homelessness in their district.

3.6 Housing authorities will need to work with other relevant statutory and non-statutory service providers to identify groups who are at particular risk and to develop appropriate provision that is accessible to those who are likely to need it. In some circumstances tailored advice and information will be best delivered in a targeted and planned way when it is most likely to be needed – for example, in preparation for leaving care, being discharged from hospital or being released from custody, but it should also be widely accessible as a universal service. Appropriate provision will need to be made to ensure accessibility for people with particular needs, including those with mobility difficulties, sight or hearing loss and learning difficulties, as well as those for whom English is not their first language.

3.7 Many people concerned about a risk of homelessness will be seeking practical advice and assistance to help them remain in their accommodation or secure alternative accommodation. Advice on the following issues may help to prevent people from becoming threatened with homelessness:

(a) tenants' rights and rights of occupation;

(b) what to do about harassment and threats of illegal eviction;
(c) rights to benefits including assistance with making claims as required;
(d) how to protect and retrieve rent deposits;
(e) rent and mortgage arrears;
(f) how to manage debt;
(g) help available to people at risk of violence and abuse;
(h) grants available for housing repair and/or adaptation;
(i) how to obtain accommodation in the private rented sector – e.g. details of landlords and letting agents within the district, any accreditation schemes, and information on rent guarantee and deposit schemes;
(j) how to apply for social housing; and,
(k) how to access shared-ownership or other low cost home ownership schemes.

3.8 The legislation does not specify how housing authorities should ensure that advice and information on homelessness and the prevention of homelessness are made available. They could do this in a number of ways, for example:
(a) provide the service themselves;
(b) ensure that it is provided by another organisation; or,
(c) ensure that it is provided in partnership with another organisation.
For further guidance on contracting out homelessness functions see Chapter 5.

3.9 Under section 179(3), housing authorities may give grants or loans to other persons who are providing advice and information about homelessness and the prevention of homelessness on behalf of the housing authority. Under section 179(4), housing authorities may also assist such persons (e.g. voluntary organisations) by:
(a) allowing them to use premises belonging to the housing authority;
(b) making available furniture or other goods, by way of gift, loan or some other arrangement; and,
(c) making available the services of staff employed by the housing authority.

3.10 Housing authorities should monitor the provision of advisory services to ensure they continue to meet the needs of all sections of the community and help deliver the aims of their homelessness strategy.

CHAPTER 4
The duty to refer cases in England to housing authorities

Guidance on the duty on specified public bodies to refer service users that may be homeless or threatened with homelessness to a local housing authority.

4.1 Under section 213B the public authorities specified in regulations are required to notify a housing authority of service users they consider may be homeless or threatened with homelessness (i.e. it is likely they will become homeless within 56 days). Before making a referral a public authority must:
(a) have consent to the referral from the individual;
(b) allow the individual to identify the housing authority in England which they would like the notification to be made to; and,
(c) have consent from the individual that their contact details can be supplied so the housing authority can contact them regarding the referral.

4.2 The duty to refer only applies to public authorities in England and individuals can only be referred to housing authorities in England.

4.3 The public authorities which are subject to the duty to refer are specified in the Homelessness (Review Procedure etc.) Regulations 2018. The public services included in the duty are as follows:

(a) prisons;
(b) youth offender institutions;
(c) secure training centres;
(d) secure colleges;
(e) youth offending teams;
(f) probation services (including community rehabilitation companies);
(g) Jobcentre Plus;
(h) social service authorities;
(i) emergency departments;
(j) urgent treatment centres; and,
(k) hospitals in their function of providing inpatient care.

The Secretary of State for Defence is also subject to the duty to refer in relation to members of the regular forces. The regular forces are the Royal Navy, the Royal Marines, the regular army and the Royal Air Force.

4.4 The most appropriate approach to discharging the duty will vary between public authorities and it is their responsibility to decide how to do so. The expected response following a disclosure from a service user that they are homeless or at risk of homelessness is for the public authority to refer the case (with consent) to a housing authority identified by the service user. Public authorities are not expected to conduct housing needs assessments as part of the section 213B duty to refer.

The procedure for referrals

4.5 The procedure for referrals should be decided by service partners in each local area. The housing authority should incorporate the duty to refer into their wider homelessness strategy and joint working arrangements and establish local arrangements with agencies in regard to referrals. These arrangements should focus on identifying people at risk of homelessness as early as possible to maximise the opportunities to prevent homelessness.

4.6 Housing authorities are responsible for setting up local procedures for managing referrals, and should ensure that all referral information is stored securely so that it can be linked to case files for use in data returns and be included in an applicant's assessment and/or personalised housing plan as appropriate.

4.7 It is recommended that housing authorities set up a single point of contact which public authorities can use for submitting referrals. This should be shared with all relevant local agencies and be clearly accessible on the housing authority website for referrals made by public authorities in different districts.

4.8 Local procedures should be tailored to each public authority. For example, arrangements with prisons should ensure that the referral is made well in advance of the release date and that, with the individual's consent, appropriate information is supplied with the referral. When designing procedures, it may be helpful to include consideration of information to be given to people being referred to help inform their decision on which housing authority they wish to be referred to. This might include information on how local connection arrangements might affect a person who is homeless and wishes to be referred to a district where they have no local connection.

4.9 Housing authorities should include information about how they will respond where the referral indicates that an individual is at risk of sleeping rough, or is already sleeping rough in their procedures for responding to referrals.

4.10 Some public authorities that are subject to the duty to refer will be required to provide accommodation for certain individuals as part of their own legal duties, for example as an element of care or supervision. Examples include social services authorities with a duty to accommodate a lone 16- or 17-year-old under the Children Act 1989 or a vulnerable adult under the Care Act 2014. Housing authorities will wish to agree arrangements with relevant authorities to ensure that when they receive referrals from these authorities appropriate alternative joint working approaches are in place and the primary responsibility to provide accommodation which would prevent or address homelessness lies with the other service.

4.11 Authorities are encouraged to establish arrangements with partners that go beyond referral procedures, aiming to maximize the impact of shared efforts on positive outcomes for service users who may have multiple needs. Such arrangements can advance the objectives of partner agencies and deliver efficiencies for the public purse.

4.12 Referring authorities should be mindful that for certain individuals, rather than making a referral, it may be more appropriate to assist them to approach a housing authority directly for assistance. This might apply, for example for clients with particular support needs.

What constitutes a referral

4.13 Under section 213B the referral to a housing authority must include the individual's name and contact details and the agreed reason for referral (e.g. that the individual is homeless or at risk of homelessness).

4.14 Housing authorities may want to develop standard referral mechanisms or forms. For example, it may be helpful for public authorities to expand on the minimum legal requirement in section 213B(3) for information to be captured in a referral (that is, of the public authority's opinion that the service user is or may be homeless or threatened with homelessness and their contact details), although housing authorities should be mindful of the service context of each referring agency when considering this.

4.15 Further referral information may include:

(a) whether an individual is already homeless, and if not when they are likely to become homeless;

(b) whether the individual is at risk of rough sleeping on the date the referral is made and if so whether this is imminent;

(c) risk assessment information, considering risks to the individual and to others; and,

(d) key medical information where relevant.

Consent

4.16 Housing authorities are advised to request that referring agencies confirm that the referee has given their consent to the referral as part of referral procedures.

Multiple/repeat referrals

4.17 When establishing local arrangements, housing authorities should consider the issues of multiple and repeat referrals and agree protocols with service partners to mitigate these.

4.18 There may be circumstances in which an individual's application has been closed by the housing authority and a new referral is received shortly after. The housing authority should respond to the referral and make contact with the individual to evaluate if there has been any change in relevant facts since the last application, which would warrant inquiries being made into any new application for assistance under Part 7.

Action upon the receipt of a referral

4.19 A referral made by a public authority to the housing authority under section 213B will not in itself constitute an application for assistance under Part 7, but housing authorities should always respond to any referral received. The housing authority may wish to contact the individual via a phone-call, email or letter using the contact details provided in the referral. If a response is not received from the direct contact with the individual, the authority should provide information on accessing advice and assistance including the housing authority's website, opening hours, address and 24-hour contact details via a phone-call, email or letter.

4.20 If the housing authority's subsequent contact with the individual following receipt of the referral reveals details that provide the housing authority with reason to believe that they might be homeless or threatened with homelessness and the individual indicates they would like assistance it will trigger an application for assistance under Part 7.

CHAPTER 5
Contracting out homelessness functions

Guidance on contracting out homelessness functions.

5.1 This chapter provides guidance on contracting out homelessness functions and housing authorities' statutory obligations with regard to the discharge of those functions.

5.2 The Local Authorities (Contracting Out of Allocation of Housing and Homelessness Functions) Order 1996 (1996 Order) enables housing authorities to contract out certain functions under Parts 6 and 7 of the 1996 Act. The 1996 Order is made under section 70 of the Deregulation and Contracting Out Act 1994 (1994 Act). In essence, the 1996 Order allows the contracting out of executive functions while leaving the responsibility for making strategic decisions with the housing authority.

5.3 The 1996 Order provides that the majority of functions under Part 7 of the 1996 Act can be contracted out. These include:

(a) making arrangements to secure that advice and information about homelessness, and the prevention of homelessness, is available free of charge within the housing authority's district;

(b) making inquiries about and deciding a person's eligibility for assistance;

(c) making inquiries about and deciding whether any duty and, if so, what duty is owed to a person under Part 7;

(d) assessing eligible applicants' cases and agreeing a personalised housing plan;
(e) undertaking prevention and relief duties owed to an applicant;
(f) making referrals to another housing authority;
(g) carrying out reviews of decisions; and,
(h) securing and helping to secure accommodation to discharge homelessness duties.

5.4 Where decision-making in homelessness cases is contracted out, housing authorities may wish to consider retaining the review function under section 202 of the 1996 Act. This may provide an additional degree of independence between the initial decision and the decision on review.

5.5 The 1994 Act provides that a contract made:
(a) may authorise a contractor to carry out only part of the function concerned;
(b) may specify that the contractor is authorised to carry out functions only in certain cases or areas specified in the contract;
(c) may include conditions relating to the carrying out of the functions, e.g. prescribing standards of performance;
(d) shall be for a period not exceeding 10 years and may be revoked at any time by the Minister or the housing authority. Any subsisting contract is to be treated as having been repudiated in these circumstances; and,
(e) shall not prevent the housing authority from exercising themselves the functions to which the contract relates.

5.6 Schedule 2 to the 1996 Order lists the homelessness functions in Part 7 of the 1996 Act that may not be contracted out, for example the provision of assistance by way of grant or loan to voluntary organisations concerned with homelessness or related matters under section 180 of the 1996 Act.

5.7 Housing authorities also cannot contract out their functions under the Homelessness Act 2002 which relate to homelessness reviews and strategies. These include:
(a) section 1(1): carry out a homelessness review for the district, and formulate and publish a homelessness strategy based on the results of that review;
(b) section 1(4): publish a new homelessness strategy within 5 years from the day on which their last homelessness strategy was published; and,
(c) section 3(6): keep their homelessness strategy under review and modify it from time to time.

For further advice on homelessness reviews and strategies see Chapter 2.

5.8 Homelessness reviews and the formulation of strategies can, however, be informed by research commissioned from external organisations.

5.9 The 1994 Act also provides that the housing authority is responsible for any act or omission of the contractor in exercising functions under the contract, except:
(a) where the contractor fails to fulfil conditions specified in the contract relating to the exercise of the function; or,
(b) where criminal proceedings are brought in respect of the contractor's act or omission.

5.10 Where there is an arrangement in force under section 101 of the Local Government Act 1972 whereby one housing authority exercises the functions of another, the 1994 Act provides that the authority exercising the function is not allowed to contract it out without the principal authority's consent.

5.11 Where a housing authority has contracted out the operation of any homelessness functions, the housing authority remains statutorily responsible and accountable for the discharge of those functions. This includes any public sector equality duty obligations under section 149 of the Equality Act 2010. The housing authority will therefore need to ensure that the contract provides for delivery of the homelessness functions in accordance with both the statutory obligations and the authority's own policies on tackling and preventing homelessness.

5.12 Housing authorities should ensure they have adequate contractual, monitoring and quality assurance mechanisms in place to ensure their statutory duties are being fully discharged.

CHAPTER 6
Homeless or threatened with homelessness

Guidance on how to determine whether a person is homeless or threatened with homelessness according to legislation.

6.1 This chapter provides guidance on how to determine whether a person is 'homeless' or 'threatened with homelessness' for the purposes of the 1996 Act.

6.2 Under section 184, if a housing authority has reason to believe that a person applying to the housing authority for accommodation, or assistance in obtaining accommodation, may be homeless or threatened with homelessness, it must make inquiries to satisfy itself whether the applicant is eligible for assistance and if so, what duties – if any – are owed to that person. For further guidance on applications for assistance see Chapter 18.

Threatened with homelessness

6.3 Under section 175(4), a person is 'threatened with homelessness' if they are likely to become homeless within 56 days. Under section 175(5), a person is also threatened with homelessness if a valid notice under section 21 of the Housing Act 1988 has been issued in respect of the only accommodation available for their occupation, and the notice will expire within 56 days. Section 195 provides that where applicants are threatened with homelessness and eligible for assistance, housing authorities must take reasonable steps to help prevent their homelessness. For further guidance on the duty to help prevent homelessness see Chapter 12.

Homeless

6.4 There are a number of different factors that determine whether a person is homeless. Under section 175, a person is homeless if they have no accommodation in the UK or elsewhere which is available for their occupation and which that person has a legal right to occupy. A person is also homeless if they have accommodation but cannot secure entry to it, or the accommodation is a moveable structure, vehicle or vessel designed or adapted for human habitation and there is nowhere it can lawfully be placed in order to provide accommodation. A person who has accommodation is to be treated as homeless where it would not be reasonable for them to continue to occupy that accommodation. Housing authorities should ask themselves whether the person is homeless at the date of making the decision on their application.

Available for occupation

6.5 Section 176 provides that accommodation shall be treated as available for a person's occupation only if it is available for occupation by them together with:

(a) any other person who normally resides with them as a member of the family; or,

(b) any other person who might reasonably be expected to reside with them.

6.6 Both of these groups of people constitute members of the applicant's household, and accommodation will only be considered to be available if it is available for occupation by both the applicant and all members of their household.

6.7 The first group covers those members of the family who normally reside with the applicant. It is a question of fact as to who is living with the applicant, and housing authorities are not required to satisfy themselves that it is reasonable for this member of the family to normally reside with them. The phrase 'as a member of the family', although not defined for these purposes in legislation, will include those with close blood or marital relationships and cohabiting partners, and, where such a person is an established member of the household, the accommodation must provide for them as well.

6.8 The second group relates to any other person, and includes those who may not have been living as part of the household at the time of the application but whom it would be reasonable to expect to live with the applicant as part of their household. People in this group might include a companion for an elderly or disabled person, or children who are being fostered by the applicant or a member of their family. This group will also include those members of the family who were not living as part of the household at the time of the application but who nonetheless might reasonably be expected to form part of it.

6.9 In relation to the second group, it is for the housing authority to assess whether any other person might reasonably be expected to live with the applicant and there will be a range of situations that the authority will need to consider. Persons who would normally live with the applicant but who are unable to do so because there is no accommodation in which they can all live together should be included in the assessment. When dealing with a family which has split up, housing authorities will need to take a decision as to which members of the family normally reside, or might be expected to reside, with the applicant. A court may have made a residence order indicating with whom the children are to live, but in many cases it will be a matter of agreement between the parents and a court will not have been involved.

Legal right to occupy accommodation

6.10 Under section 175(1), a person is homeless if they have no accommodation available for occupation in the UK or somewhere else which they have a legal right to occupy by virtue of:

(a) an interest in it (e.g. as an owner, lessee or tenant) or by virtue of a court order;

(b) an express or implied licence to occupy it (e.g. as a lodger, as an employee with a service occupancy, or when living with a relative); or,

(c) any enactment or rule of law giving them the right to remain in occupation or restricting the right of another person to recover possession (e.g. a person with a right to retain occupation as a statutory tenant under the Rent Act 1977 where that person's contractual rights to occupy have expired or been terminated).

6.11 A person who has been occupying accommodation as a licensee whose licence has been terminated (and who does not have any other accommodation available for their occupation) is homeless because they no longer have a legal right to continue to occupy, despite the fact that the person may continue to occupy but as an unauthorised occupier. This may include, for example:

(a) those required to leave hostels or hospitals; or,

(b) former employees occupying premises under a service occupancy which is dependent upon contracts of employment which have ended.

People asked to leave accommodation by family or friends

6.12 Some applicants may have been asked to leave their current accommodation by family or friends with whom they have been living. In such cases, the housing authority will need to consider carefully whether the applicant's licence to occupy the accommodation has in fact been revoked, rendering the applicant homeless. Authorities are encouraged to be sensitive to situations where parents or carers have been providing a home for a family member with care or support needs (for example, a person with learning difficulties) for a number of years and who are genuinely finding it difficult to continue with that arrangement, but are reluctant to revoke their licence to occupy formally until alternative accommodation can be secured.

6.13 In some cases the applicant may be unable to stay in their accommodation and in others there may be scope for preventing or postponing homelessness, and providing them with an opportunity to plan their future accommodation with assistance from the housing authority. However, housing authorities will need to be sensitive to the possibility that for some applicants it may not be safe for them to remain in, or return to, their home because of a risk of violence or abuse.

6.14 People living with family and friends may have genuine difficulties in finding alternative accommodation that can lead to friction and disputes within their current home, culminating in a threat of homelessness. In some cases external support, or the offer of assistance with securing alternative housing, may help to reduce tension and prevent homelessness. The use of mediation services may assist here.

6.15 In cases involving 16- and 17-year-olds threatened with exclusion from the family home children's services authorities will be the lead agency, but should work closely with housing authorities to prevent homelessness and support young people to remain within the family network, wherever it is safe and appropriate for them to do so.

6.16 Housing authorities will also need to be alert to the possibility of collusion where family or friends agree to revoke a licence to occupy accommodation that would have been reasonable for the person to continue to occupy, as part of an arrangement whose purpose is to enable the applicant to be entitled to assistance under Part 7. For further guidance on intentional homelessness see Chapter 9.

Tenant given notice

6.17 With certain exceptions, a person who has been occupying accommodation as a tenant and who has received a valid notice to quit, or notice that the landlord requires possession of the accommodation, would have the right to remain in occupation until a warrant for possession was executed (following the granting of an order for possession by the court). The exceptions are tenants with resident landlords and certain other tenants who do not benefit from the Protection from Eviction Act 1977.

6.18 Housing authorities should note that the fact that a tenant has a right to remain in occupation does not necessarily mean that they are not homeless. In assessing whether an applicant is homeless in cases where they are a tenant who has a right to remain in occupation pending execution of a warrant for possession, the housing authority will also need to consider whether it would be reasonable for them to continue to occupy the accommodation in the circumstances (section 175(3) of the 1996 Act). For guidance on cases involving service of a section 21 notice see paragraphs 6.35–6.38.

6.19 Some tenants may face having to leave their accommodation because their landlord has defaulted on the mortgage of the property they rent. Where a mortgage lender starts possession proceedings, the lender is obliged to give written notice of the proceedings to the occupiers of the property before an order for possession is granted. The notice must be given after issue of the possession summons and at least 14 days before the court hearing. Housing authorities will need to consider whether it would be reasonable for an applicant to continue to occupy the accommodation after receiving notice of possession proceedings from the lender. Housing authorities should not consider it reasonable for an applicant to remain in occupation until eviction by a bailiff.

Inability to secure entry to accommodation

6.20 Under section 175(2)(a), a person is also homeless if they have a legal entitlement to accommodation, but is unable to secure entry to it, for example:

(a) those who have been evicted illegally; or,

(b) those whose accommodation is being occupied illegally by squatters.

6.21 Housing authorities will want to support applicants to pursue the legal remedies available to them to regain possession of their accommodation. However, an authority cannot refuse to assist an applicant who is homeless and eligible for assistance under Part 7 simply because such remedies are available.

Accommodation consisting of a moveable structure

6.22 Section 175(2)(b) provides that a person is homeless if they have accommodation available for their occupation which is a moveable structure, vehicle or vessel designed or adapted for human habitation (e.g. a caravan or houseboat), and there is nowhere that they are entitled or permitted to place it and reside in it. The site or mooring for the moveable structure need not be permanent in order to avoid homelessness.

Reasonable to continue to occupy

6.23 Section 175(3) provides that a person shall not be treated as having accommodation unless it is accommodation which it would be reasonable for them to continue to occupy. There are a number of provisions relating to whether or not it is reasonable for someone to continue to occupy accommodation and these are discussed below. There is no simple test of reasonableness. It is for the housing authority to make a judgement on the facts of each case, taking into account the circumstances of the applicant.

Domestic abuse or other violence

6.24 Section 177(1) provides that it is not reasonable for a person to continue to occupy accommodation if it is probable that this will lead to domestic abuse or other violence against:
(a) the applicant;
(b) a person who normally resides with the applicant as a member of the applicant's family; or,
(c) any other person who might reasonably be expected to reside with the applicant.
For further guidance on domestic abuse or other violence in determining whether a person is homeless see Chapter 21.

General housing circumstances in the district

6.25 Section 177(2) provides that, in determining whether it is reasonable for a person to continue to occupy accommodation, housing authorities may have regard to the general housing circumstances prevailing in the housing authority's district.

6.26 This comparison might be appropriate, for example, where it was suggested that an applicant was homeless because of poor physical conditions in their current home. In such cases it would be open to the authority to consider whether the condition of the property was so bad in comparison with other accommodation in the district that it would not be reasonable to expect someone to continue to live there.

6.27 Consideration of the general circumstances prevailing in the housing authority's district might also be appropriate in cases of homelessness due to overcrowding.

Affordability

6.28 Affordability must be considered in all cases. The *Homelessness (Suitability of Accommodation) Order 1996* requires the housing authority to consider the affordability of the accommodation for the applicant. The Order specifies, among other things, that in determining both whether it would be (or would have been) reasonable for a person to continue to occupy accommodation and whether the accommodation is suitable, a housing authority must take into account whether the accommodation is affordable for them and must, in particular, take account of:
(a) the financial resources available to them;
(b) the costs of the accommodation;
(c) maintenance payments (to a spouse, former spouse or in respect of a child); and,
(d) their reasonable living expenses
For further guidance on affordability and suitability of accommodation see Chapter 17.

Tenant given notice of intention to recover possession

6.29 In cases where the applicant has been occupying accommodation as a tenant and has received a valid notice to quit, or a notice that the landlord intends to recover possession, housing authorities should make contact with the landlord at an early stage. This will be necessary both to understand the circumstances in which the applicant has become threatened with homelessness, and to establish what reasonable steps may be taken by the housing authority and by the applicant to prevent their homelessness.

6.30 A housing authority can give notice to end the section 195(2) prevention duty where 56 days has passed since the prevention duty was accepted, whether or not the applicant is still threatened with homelessness (section 195(8)(b)). However, section 195(6) of the 1996 Act prevents an authority from doing this if the applicant has been given a valid section 21 notice which will expire within 56 days, or has already expired, in respect of the only accommodation available for the applicant's occupation. This means an applicant in these circumstances cannot be 'timed out' of the prevention duty if they remain threatened with homelessness, and the authority must continue to help the applicant to retain or secure accommodation until the prevention duty ends in another way.

6.31 However, an authority should give notice to end the section 195 prevention duty when an applicant has become homeless, triggering a section 189B relief duty. It follows that housing authorities will be required to assess at what point a tenant who has been served a valid section 21 becomes homeless and is owed a relief duty; and that expiry of a valid section 21 notice does not automatically render the person homeless for the purposes of the 1996 Act. Under section 175 of the 1996 Act, an applicant must be considered homeless if they have no accommodation to which they have a legal right to occupy that is available to them and reasonable for them to continue to occupy.

6.32 In determining whether it would be reasonable for an applicant to continue to occupy accommodation following expiry of a valid section 21 notice the authority will need to consider all the factors relevant to the case and decide the weight that each should attract. If the landlord confirms a willingness to consider delaying or halting action to recover possession if certain steps are taken, it will usually be reasonable for the tenant to remain in occupation to allow time for action to be taken which may prevent homelessness. This might include, for example, resolving problems with a benefit claim or establishing a manageable repayment schedule for rent arrears.

6.33 Authorities should not adopt a blanket policy or practice on the point at which it will no longer be reasonable for an applicant to occupy following the expiry of a section 21 notice. As well as the factors set out elsewhere in this chapter, factors which may be relevant include the preference of the applicant (who may, for example, want to remain in the property until they can move into alternative settled accommodation if there is the prospect of a timely move, or alternatively to leave the property to avoid incurring court costs); the position of the landlord; the financial impact of court action and any build up of rent arrears on both landlord and tenant; the burden on the courts of unnecessary proceedings where there is no defence to a possession claim; and the general cost to the housing authority. Housing authorities will be mindful of the need to maintain good relations with landlords providing accommodation in the district.

6.34 Throughout any period that an applicant remains in occupation whilst the landlord pursues possession action, the housing authority should keep the reasonable steps in the applicant's personalised housing plan under regular review, and maintain contact with the tenant and landlord to ascertain if there is any change in circumstances which affects whether or not it continues to be reasonable for the applicant to occupy.

6.35 The Secretary of State considers that where an applicant is:

(a) an assured shorthold tenant who has received a valid notice in accordance with section 21 of the Housing Act 1988;

(b) the housing authority is satisfied that the landlord intends to seek **possession and further efforts from the housing authority to resolve the situation and persuade the landlord to allow the tenant to remain in the property are unlikely to be successful**; and,

(c) there would be no defence to an application for a possession order;

then it is unlikely to be reasonable for the applicant to continue to occupy beyond the expiry of a valid section 21 notice, unless the housing authority is taking steps to persuade the landlord to allow the tenant to continue to occupy the accommodation for a reasonable period to provide an opportunity for alternative accommodation to be found.

6.36 The Secretary of State considers that it is highly unlikely to be reasonable for the applicant to continue to occupy beyond the date on which the court has ordered them to leave the property and give possession to the landlord.

6.37 Housing authorities should not consider it reasonable for an applicant to remain in occupation up until the point at which a court issues a warrant or writ to enforce an order for possession.

6.38 **Housing authorities should ensure that homeless families and vulnerable individuals who are owed a section 188 interim accommodation duty or section 193(2) main housing duty are not evicted through the enforcement of an order for possession as a result of a failure by the authority to make suitable accommodation available to them.**

Other relevant factors

6.39 Other factors which may be relevant in determining whether it would be reasonable for an applicant to continue to occupy accommodation include:

(a) **physical characteristics:** it would not be reasonable for an applicant to continue to occupy accommodation if the physical characteristics of the accommodation were unsuitable for the applicant because, for example, they are a wheelchair user and access was limited;

(b) **type of accommodation:** some types of accommodation, for example women's refuges, direct access hostels and night shelters are intended to provide very short-term, temporary accommodation in a crisis and should not be regarded as being reasonable to continue to occupy in the medium and longer-term;

(c) **people fleeing harassment:** in some cases severe harassment may fall short of actual violence or threats of violence likely to be carried out. Housing authorities should consider carefully whether it would be, or would have been, reasonable for an applicant to continue to occupy accommodation in circumstances where they have fled, or are seeking to leave, their home because of non-violent forms of harassment, for example verbal abuse or damage to property. Careful consideration should be given to applicants who may be at risk of witness intimidation. In some criminal cases the police may provide alternative accommodation for witnesses, but usually this will apply for the duration of the trial only. Witnesses may have had to give up their home or may feel unable to return to it when the trial has finished.

6.40 This is not an exhaustive list and authorities will need to take account of all relevant factors when considering whether it is reasonable for an applicant to continue to occupy accommodation.

CHAPTER 7
Eligibility for assistance

Guidance on the provisions relating to an applicant's eligibility for homelessness services.

7.1 This chapter provides guidance on the provisions relating to an applicant's eligibility for homelessness services.

7.2 Housing authorities have a duty to provide or secure the provision of advice and information about homelessness and the prevention of homelessness, free of charge which must be available to any person in their district. All applicants, including those who are ineligible as a result of their immigration status, will be able to access this form of assistance from the housing authority. Housing authorities should refer applicants to appropriate support which they may be entitled to where relevant.
For further guidance on the provision of advice and information on homelessness and the prevention of homelessness see Chapter 3.

7.3 Part 7 of the 1996 Act includes provisions that make certain people from abroad ineligible for housing assistance. Housing authorities will therefore need to satisfy themselves that applicants are eligible before providing housing assistance. The provisions on eligibility are complex and housing authorities will need to ensure that they have procedures in place to carry out appropriate checks on housing applicants.

7.4 Housing authorities should ensure that staff who are required to screen applicants about eligibility for assistance are given training in the complexities of the housing provisions, the housing authority's duties and responsibilities under the Equality Act 2010 and are able to deal with applicants in a sensitive manner.

7.5 Local authorities are reminded that Schedule 3 to the Nationality, Immigration and Asylum Act 2002 provides that certain persons shall not be eligible for support or assistance provided through the exercise of housing authorities' powers to secure accommodation pending a review (section 188(3)) or pending an appeal to the county court (section 204(4)). For further guidance see 7.21–7.22.

Persons from abroad

7.6 A person will not be eligible for assistance under Part 7 if they are a person from abroad who is ineligible for housing assistance under section 185 of the 1996 Act. In particular:

(a) a 'person subject to immigration control' is not eligible for housing assistance unless they come within a class prescribed in regulations made by the Secretary of State; and,

(b) the Secretary of State can make regulations to provide for other descriptions of person from abroad who, although they are not subject to immigration control, are to be treated as ineligible for housing assistance.

7.7 The regulations that set out which classes of persons from abroad are eligible or ineligible for housing assistance are the Allocation of Housing and Homelessness (Eligibility) (England) Regulations 2006 (the Eligibility Regulations). Persons subject to immigration control are not eligible for housing assistance unless they fall within a class of persons prescribed in regulation 5 of the Eligibility Regulations. Persons who are not subject to immigration control will be eligible for housing assistance unless they fall within a description of persons who are to be treated as persons from abroad who are ineligible for assistance by virtue of regulation 6 of the Eligibility Regulations.

Persons subject to immigration control

7.8 The term 'person subject to immigration control' is defined in section 13(2) of the Asylum and Immigration Act 1996 as a person who requires leave to enter or remain in the United Kingdom (whether or not such leave has been given).

7.9 Only the following categories of person do not require leave to enter or remain in the UK:

(a) British citizens;
(b) certain Commonwealth citizens with a right of abode in the UK;
(c) citizens of an EEA country (EEA nationals) and their family members, who have a right to reside in the UK that is derived from European Union law or any provision made under section 2(2) of the European Communities Act 1972. The question of whether an EEA national (or family member) has a right to reside in the UK (or in another Member State e.g. the Republic of Ireland) will depend on their circumstances at that particular time, e.g. whether the EEA national is, for the purposes of the Immigration (European Economic Area) Regulations 2016, a jobseeker, a worker, a self-employed person, and so on;
(d) persons who are exempt from immigration control under the Immigration Acts, including diplomats and their family members based in the United Kingdom, and some military personnel.

For the purposes of this guidance, 'EEA nationals' means nationals of any of the EU member states (excluding the UK), and nationals of Iceland, Norway, Liechtenstein and Switzerland.

7.10 Any person who does not fall within one of the 4 categories in paragraph 7.9 above will be a person subject to immigration control and will be ineligible for housing assistance unless they fall within a class of persons prescribed by regulation 5 of the Eligibility Regulations (see paragraph 7.12 below).

7.11 If there is any uncertainty about an applicant's immigration status, it is recommended that authorities contact the Home Office. In some circumstances, local authorities may be under a duty to contact the Home Office (see paragraph 7.23).

Persons subject to immigration control who are eligible for housing assistance

7.12 Generally, persons subject to immigration control are not eligible for housing assistance. However, by virtue of regulation 5 of the Eligibility Regulations, the following classes of person subject to immigration control are eligible for housing assistance:

(a) a person whose refugee status has been recognised by the Secretary of State and who has leave to enter and remain in the UK. Persons granted refugee status are usually granted 5 years' limited leave to remain in the UK. (Prior to 30 August 2005, it was the policy to provide immediate settlement (indefinite leave to remain) for persons granted refugee status);

(b) a person who has discretionary leave to enter or remain in the United Kingdom granted outside the provisions of the Immigration Rules; and whose leave to enter or remain is not subject to a condition requiring them to maintain and accommodate themselves, and any person who is dependent on them, without recourse to public funds;

(c) a person with current leave to enter or remain in the UK with no condition or limitation, and who is habitually resident in the UK, the Channel Islands, the Isle of Man or the Republic of Ireland: such a person will have indefinite leave to enter or indefinite leave to remain and will be regarded as having settled status. However, where indefinite leave to enter or indefinite leave to remain status was granted as a result of an undertaking that a sponsor would be responsible for the applicant's maintenance and accommodation, the person must have been resident in the UK, the Channel Islands, the Isle of Man or the Republic of Ireland for 5 years since the date of entry – or the date of the sponsorship undertaking, whichever is later – for the applicant to be eligible. Where a sponsor has (or, if there was more than one sponsor, all of the sponsors have) died within the first 5 years, the applicant will be eligible for housing assistance;

(d) a person who has humanitarian protection granted under the Immigration Rules;

(e) a person who is habitually resident in the United Kingdom, the Channel Islands, the Isle of Man or the Republic of Ireland and who has limited leave to enter the United Kingdom as a relevant Afghan citizen under paragraph 276BA1 of the Immigration Rules;

(f) a person who has limited leave to enter or remain in the United Kingdom on family or private life grounds under Article 8 of the Human Rights Act, such leave granted under paragraph 276BE (1), paragraph 276DG or Appendix FM of the Immigration Rules, and who is not subject to a condition requiring that person to maintain and accommodate themselves, and any person dependent upon them, without recourse to public funds.

Asylum seekers

7.13 Under section 186 of the 1996 Act, an asylum seeker who would otherwise be eligible for housing assistance will be ineligible if they have any accommodation available in the UK for their occupation, however temporary. This exclusion is only relevant to pre-April 2000 asylum seekers who are eligible for homelessness assistance.

Other persons from abroad who are ineligible for assistance

7.14 By virtue of regulation 6 of the Eligibility Regulations, a person who is not subject to immigration control and who falls within one of the following descriptions of persons is to be treated as a person from abroad who is ineligible for housing assistance:

(a) a person who is not habitually resident in the UK, the Channel Islands, the Isle of Man or the Republic of Ireland (subject to certain exceptions – see paragraph 7.15 below);
(b) a person whose only right to reside in the UK is derived from their status as a jobseeker (or their status as the family member of a jobseeker). For this purpose, 'jobseeker' has the same meaning as for the purpose of regulation 6(1)(a) of the Immigration (European Economic Area) Regulations 2016 (the EEA Regulations);
(c) a person whose only right to reside in the UK is an initial right to reside for a period not exceeding 3 months under regulation 13 of the EEA Regulations;
(d) a person whose only right to reside in the UK is a derivative right to reside to which they are entitled under regulation 16(1) of the EEA Regulations, but only in a case where the right exists under that regulation because the applicant satisfies the criteria in regulation 16(5) of those Regulations;
(e) a person whose only right to reside in the UK is derived from Article 20 of the Treaty on the Functioning of the European Union in a case where the right to reside arises because a British citizen would otherwise be deprived of the genuine enjoyment of the substance of the rights attaching to the status of European Union citizen (also know as '*Zambrano* carers');
(f) a person whose only right to reside in the Channel Islands, the Isle of Man or the Republic of Ireland –
    (i) is a right equivalent to one of those mentioned in sub-paragraph (b–d) above which is derived from the Treaty on the Functioning of the European Union; or
    (ii) is derived from Article 20 of the Treaty on the Functioning of the European Union, in a case where the right to reside in the Republic of Ireland arises because an Irish citizen, or in the Channel Islands or the Isle of Man arises because a British citizen also entitled to reside there and would otherwise be deprived of the genuine enjoyment of the substance of their rights as a European Union citizen.

Persons exempted from the requirement to be habitually resident

7.15 Certain persons from abroad are not subject to the requirement to be habitually resident in the UK, the Channel Islands, the Isle of Man or the Republic of Ireland. Such a person will be eligible for assistance even if not habitually resident, if they are:

(a) an EEA national who is in the UK as a worker (which has the same meaning as it does for the purposes of regulation 6(1) of the EEA Regulations);
(b) an EEA national who is in the UK as a self-employed person (which has the same meaning as it does for the purposes of regulation 6(1) of the EEA Regulations);
(c) a person who is treated as a worker for the purpose of the definition of 'qualified person' in regulation 6(1) of the EEA Regulations pursuant to regulation 5 of the Accession of Croatia (Immigration and Worker Authorisation) Regulations 2013 (as amended), (right of residence of an accession State national subject to worker authorisation);

(d) a person who is a family member of a person referred to in (a) to (c) above;
(e) a person with a right to reside permanently in the UK by virtue of regulation 15(c), (d) or (e) of the EEA Regulations;
(f) a person who is in the UK as a result of their deportation, expulsion or other removal by compulsion of law from another country to the UK.

7.16 On (a) and (b), authorities should note that a person who is not currently working or self-employed will retain their status as a worker or self-employed person in certain circumstances. On (c), authorities should note that an accession state worker will generally only be treated as a worker if they hold an accession worker authorisation document and are working in accordance with the conditions set out in that document. On (d), authorities should note that 'family member' does not include a person who is an extended family member who is treated as a family member by virtue of regulation 7(3) of the EEA Regulations.

7.17 For further guidance on EEA right to reside see pages 6–8 of Home Office guidance on administrative removal of EEA nationals.

The habitual residence test

7.18 The term 'habitual residence' is intended to convey a degree of permanence in the person's residence in the UK, the Channel Islands, the Isle of Man or the Republic of Ireland; it implies an association between the individual and the place of residence and relies substantially on fact.

7.19 The Secretary of State considers that it is likely that applicants who have been resident in the UK, Channel Islands, the Isle of Man or the Republic of Ireland continuously during the 2-year period prior to their housing application will be habitually resident. In such cases, therefore, housing authorities may consider it unnecessary to make further enquiries to determine whether the person is habitually resident, unless there are other circumstances that need to be taken into account. A period of continuous residence in the UK, Channel Islands, the Isle of Man or the Republic of Ireland might include periods of temporary absence. Where 2 years' continuous residency has not been established, housing authorities will need to conduct further enquiries to determine whether the applicant is habitually resident.

7.20 A person will not generally be habitually resident anywhere unless they have taken up residence and lived there for a period. There will be cases where the person concerned is not coming to the UK for the first time, and is resuming a previous period of habitual residence.
For further guidance on habitual residence see Annex 1.

Persons ineligible under certain provisions by virtue of Schedule 3 to the Nationality, Immigration and Asylum Act 2002

7.21 Section 54 of, and Schedule 3 to, the Nationality, Immigration and Asylum Act 2002 have the effect of making certain applicants for housing assistance ineligible for accommodation under section 188(3) (power to accommodate pending a review) or section 204(4) (power to accommodate pending an appeal to the county court) of the 1996 Act. The following classes of person will be ineligible for assistance under those powers:
(a) a person who has refugee status abroad, i.e. a person:
(i) who does not have the nationality of an EEA State, and

(ii) who the government of an EEA State other than the UK has determined is entitled to protection as a refugee under the Refugee Convention;

(b) a person who has the nationality of an EEA State other than the UK (but see paragraph 7.22 below);

(c) a person who was (but is no longer) an asylum seeker and who fails to co-operate with removal directions issued in respect of them;

(d) a person who is in the UK in breach of the immigration laws (within the meaning of section 50A of the British Nationality Act 1981) and is not an asylum seeker;

(e) certain persons who are failed asylum seekers with dependent children, where the Secretary of State has certified that, in their opinion, such a person has failed without reasonable excuse to take reasonable steps to leave the UK voluntarily or place themselves in a position where they are able to leave the UK voluntarily, and that person has received the Secretary of State's certificate more than 14 days previously;

(f) a person who is the dependant of a person who falls within class (a), (b) or (c) above.

7.22 **However, section 54 and Schedule 3 do not prevent the exercise of an authority's powers under section 188(3) and section 204(4) of the 1996 Act to the extent that such exercise is necessary for the purpose of avoiding a breach of a person's rights under the European Convention of Human Rights or rights under EU Treaties.** Among other things, this means that a local authority can exercise these powers to accommodate an EEA national who has a right to reside in the UK under EU law.

7.23 Paragraph 14 of Schedule 3 provides, among other things, that authorities must inform the Secretary of State where the powers under section 188(3) or section 204(4) apply, or may apply, to a person who is, or may come, within classes (c) or (d) in paragraph 7.21 by contacting the Home Office.

7.24 For further guidance, local authorities should refer to Guidance to Local Authorities and Housing Authorities about the Nationality, Immigration and Asylum Act, section 54 and Schedule 3, and the Withholding and Withdrawal of Support (Travel Assistance and Temporary Accommodation) Regulations 2002, issued by the Home Office.

Restricted cases

7.25 A restricted case is a case where the housing authority would not be satisfied that the applicant had a priority need for accommodation without having had regard to a 'restricted person' within the household. This would be the case, for example, where an applicant who is an eligible British citizen who would not have priority need if they applied alone, does have priority need because of their dependent children who are 'restricted persons'.

7.26 A restricted person means a person who is not eligible for assistance under Part 7 of the 1996 Act and is subject to immigration control and either:

(a) does not have leave to enter or remain in the UK; or,

(b) does have leave but it is subject to a condition of no recourse to public funds.

7.27 In a restricted case, the housing authority must, so far as reasonably practical, bring the section 193(2) duty to an end by arranging for an offer of an assured shorthold tenancy to be made to the applicant by a private landlord (a private rented sector offer of at least 12 months in length).

7.28 Where a housing authority considers a household member of an applicant may be a restricted person who does not have leave to enter or remain in the UK, or if there is uncertainty about the immigration status of any household member, it is recommended that the authority contact the Home Office.

CHAPTER 8
Priority need

Guidance on the categories of applicant who have a priority need for accommodation if they become homeless.

8.1 This chapter provides guidance on the categories of applicant who have a priority need for accommodation under the homelessness legislation.

8.2 Housing authorities have duties to try and prevent or relieve homelessness for all applicants who are eligible for assistance and are homeless or threatened with homelessness, irrespective of whether or not they may have a priority need for accommodation. If a housing authority is unable to prevent an applicant from becoming homeless, or to help them to secure accommodation within the 'relief' stage, they are required to reach a decision as to whether the applicant has a priority need for accommodation.

8.3 Section 188(1) of the 1996 Act requires housing authorities to secure that accommodation is available for an applicant if they have reason to believe that the applicant **may** be homeless, eligible for assistance and have a priority need. The housing authority may bring this 'interim' accommodation duty to an end during the relief stage if they subsequently find that the applicant does not have priority need (or are not eligible or not homeless) and issues a decision that the applicant will not be owed further duties at the end of the relief duty. For further guidance on accommodation duties see Chapter 15. Section 193(2) of the 1996 Act requires housing authorities to secure accommodation for applicants who have a priority need for accommodation section 189(1) and the Homelessness (Priority Need for Accommodation) (England) Order 2002 (the '2002 Order') provide that the following categories of applicant have a priority need for accommodation:

(a) a pregnant woman or a person with whom she resides or might reasonably be expected to reside (see paragraph 8.5);

(b) a person with whom dependent children reside or might reasonably be expected to reside (see paragraphs 8.6–8.12);

(c) a person who is vulnerable as a result of old age, mental illness, learning disability or physical disability or other special reason, or with whom such a person resides or might reasonably be expected to reside (see paragraphs 8.13–8.18);

(d) a person aged 16 or 17 who is not a 'relevant child' or a child in need to whom a local authority owes a duty under section 20 of the Children Act 1989 (see paragraphs 8.19–8.23);

(e) a person under 21 who was (but is no longer) looked after, accommodated or fostered between the ages of 16 and 18 (except a person who is a 'relevant student');

(f) a person aged 21 or more who is vulnerable as a result of having been looked after, accommodated or fostered (except a person who is a 'relevant student') (see paragraphs 8.28–8.31);

(g) a person who is vulnerable as a result of having been a member of Her Majesty's regular naval, military or air forces (see paragraphs 8.32–8.33);
(h) a person who is vulnerable as a result of:
  (i) having served a custodial sentence;
  (ii) having been committed for contempt of court or any other kindred offence; or,
  (iii) having been remanded in custody;(see paragraphs 8.34–8.35);
(i) a person who is vulnerable as a result of ceasing to occupy accommodation because of violence from another person or threats of violence from another person which are likely to be carried out (see paragraphs 8.36–8.37);
(j) a person who is homeless, or threatened with homelessness, as a result of an emergency such as flood, fire or other disaster.

8.4 Once a housing authority has notified an applicant that they have a priority need and have been accepted as owed the section 193(2) duty it cannot subsequently change that decision if the applicant subsequently ceases to have a priority need (e.g. because a dependent child leaves home), except where a review has been requested and the change takes place before the review decision. Any change of circumstance prior to the decision on the homelessness application should be taken into account. However, once all the relevant inquiries are completed, the housing authority should not defer their decision on the case in anticipation of a possible change of circumstance.

Pregnant women

8.5 A pregnant woman, and anyone with whom she lives or might reasonably be expected to live, has a priority need for accommodation. This is regardless of the length of time that the woman has been pregnant. Normal confirmation of pregnancy, e.g. a letter from a medical professional, such as a midwife, should be adequate evidence of pregnancy. If a pregnant woman suffers a miscarriage or terminates her pregnancy before a decision is reached as to whether she is owed section 193(2) main housing duty the housing authority should consider whether she continues to have a priority need as a result of some other factor (e.g. she may be vulnerable as a result of another special reason – see paragraph 8.38).

Dependent children

8.6 Applicants have a priority need if one or more dependent children is living with them or might reasonably be expected to live with them. There must be actual dependence on the applicant, although the child need not be wholly and exclusively dependent on them. There must also be actual residence (or a reasonable expectation of residence) with some degree of permanence or regularity, rather than a temporary arrangement whereby the children are merely staying with the applicant for a limited period (see paragraphs 8.10 and 8.11). Similarly, the child need not be wholly and exclusively resident (or expected to reside wholly and exclusively) with the applicant.

8.7 The 1996 Act does not define dependent children, but housing authorities may wish to treat as dependent all children under 16, and all children aged 16–18 who are in, or are about to begin, full-time education or training or who for other reasons are unable to support themselves and who live at home. The meaning of dependency is not however, limited to financial dependency. Thus, while children aged 16 and over who are in full-time employment and are financially independent of their parents would not normally be considered to be dependents, housing authorities should remember that such children may not be sufficiently mature to live independently of their parents, and there may be sound reasons for considering them to be dependent. The Secretary of State considers that it will be very rare that a 16- or 17-year-old child who is living at home will not be considered to be dependent.

8.8 Dependent children need not necessarily be the applicant's own children, but could, for example, be related to the applicant or their partner, or be adopted or fostered by the applicant. There must, however, be some form of parent/child relationship.

8.9 Housing authorities may receive applications from a parent who is separated from their former spouse or partner. In some cases where parents separate, the court may make a residence order indicating with which parent the child normally resides. In such cases the child may be considered to reside with the parent named in the order, and would not normally be expected to reside with the other parent. However, in many cases the parents come to an agreement themselves as to how the child is cared for, and a court order will not be required.

8.10 Residence does not have to be full-time and a child can be considered to reside with either parent or with both parents. However, there must be some regularity to the arrangement for it to establish residence. Housing authorities should be mindful that where parents separate, there will generally be a presumption towards shared residence though this will not always be on the basis of an equal amount of time being spent living with both parents.

8.11 If the child is not currently residing with the applicant, the housing authority will need to decide whether, in the circumstances in which the applicant is homeless it would be reasonable for the child to do so. An agreement for joint residency between a child's parents, or a joint residence order by a court, will not automatically lead to a conclusion that it would be reasonable for the child to reside with the parent making the application, and housing authorities will need to consider each case individually. In doing so, housing authorities should take into account the specific needs and circumstances of the child, including whether suitable accommodation is available to them with their other parent.

8.12 Where the applicant's children are being looked after by a children's social services authority, whether subject to a care order or being accommodated under a voluntary agreement, and they are not currently living with the applicant, liaison with the social services authority will be essential. Joint consideration with social services will ensure that the best interests of the applicant and the children are served. This may, for example, enable a family to be reunited subject to suitable accommodation being available.

Vulnerability

8.13 A person has a priority need for accommodation if they are vulnerable as a result of:

(a) old age;
(b) mental illness or learning disability or physical disability;
(c) having been looked after, accommodated or fostered and is aged 21 or more;

(d) having been a member of Her Majesty's regular naval, military or air forces;
(e) having been in custody;
(f) ceasing to occupy accommodation because of violence from another person or threats of violence from another person which are likely to be carried out; or,
(g) any other special reason.

8.14 In the case of (a), (b) and (g) only, a person with whom a vulnerable person lives or might reasonably be expected to live also has a priority need for accommodation and can therefore make an application on behalf of themselves and that vulnerable person.

8.15 It is a matter of evaluative judgement whether the applicant's circumstances make them vulnerable. When determining whether an applicant in any of the categories set out in paragraph 8.13 is vulnerable, the housing authority should determine whether, if homeless, the applicant would be significantly more vulnerable than an ordinary person would be if they became homeless. The assessment must be a qualitative composite one taking into account all of the relevant facts and circumstances, and involves a consideration of the impact of homelessness on the applicant when compared to an ordinary person if made homeless. The housing authority should consider whether the applicant would suffer or be at risk of suffering harm or detriment which the ordinary person would not suffer or be at risk of suffering, such that the harm or detriment would make a noticeable difference to their ability to deal with the consequences of homelessness.

8.16 When assessing an applicant's vulnerability, a housing authority may take into account the services and support available to them from a third party, including their family. This would involve considering the needs of the applicant, the level of support being provided to them, and whether with such support they would or would not be significantly more vulnerable than an ordinary person if made homeless. In order to reach a decision that a person is not vulnerable because of the support they receive the housing authority must be satisfied that the third party will provide the support on a consistent and predictable basis. In each case a housing authority should consider whether the applicant, even with support, would be vulnerable.

8.17 Housing authorities must be mindful of the Equality Act 2010 and their public sector equality duties towards people who have a protected characteristic. For further guidance on the Equality Act 2010 see Chapter 1. If the applicant has a disability (or another relevant protected characteristic) the authority should assess the extent of such disability and the likely effect of the disability, when taken together with any other features, on the applicant if and when homeless. They will then need to decide whether the impact of this makes the applicant significantly more vulnerable as a result.

8.18 Some of the factors which may be relevant to determining whether an applicant is vulnerable are set out below.

16 and 17 year olds

8.19 The specific duties towards 16 and 17 year olds who are at risk of homelessness or who are homeless, and the legal duties children's services authorities and housing authorities have towards them are set out in the government's statutory guidance: Provision of accommodation for 16 and 17 year old young people who may be homeless and/or require accommodation.

8.20 16 and 17 year old homeless applicants have a priority need for accommodation except those who are:
(a) a relevant child; or,
(b) a child in need who is owed a duty under section 20 of the Children Act 1989.

8.21 A relevant child is a child aged 16 or 17 who has been looked after by a local authority for at least 13 weeks since the age of 14 and has been looked after at some time while 16 or 17 and who is not currently being looked after (i.e. an 'eligible child' for the purposes of paragraph 19B of Schedule 2 to the Children Act 1989). In addition, a child is also a relevant child if they would have been looked after by the local authority as an eligible child but for the fact that on their 16th birthday they were detained through the criminal justice system, or in hospital, or if they returned home on family placement and that has broken down (see section 23A of the Children Act 1989 and regulation 3 of the Care Leavers (England) Regulations 2010).

8.22 The primary responsibility for a child in need who requires accommodation, including a 16 and 17 year old who is homeless lies with the relevant children's services authority. The Children Act 1989 (section 20) places a duty on children's services authorities to accommodate a child in need, and in almost all circumstances a homeless 16–17 year old would be a child in need.

8.23 However, there remain circumstances when the housing authority will have duties towards a homeless 16 and 17 year olds, including when the young person, having been fully informed of the implications, and being judged to have capacity to make that decision, declines to become looked after under the Children Act and instead applies for assistance under homelessness legislation. By definition these young people are nearing adulthood where a smooth and supported transition will be necessary to protect against the risk of homelessness re-occurring. As both children's services and housing authorities have duties towards this group it is essential that services are underpinned by written joint protocols which set out clear, practical arrangements for providing services that are centered on young people and their families and prevent young people from being passed over and back between housing and children's services authorities.

Old age

8.24 Old age alone is not sufficient for the applicant to be considered vulnerable. However, it may be that as a result of old age the applicant would be significantly more vulnerable than an ordinary person would be if homeless. Housing authorities should not use a fixed age beyond which vulnerability occurs automatically (or below which it can be ruled out); each case will need to be considered in the light of the individual circumstances.

Mental illness or learning disability or physical disability

8.25 Housing authorities should have regard to any advice from medical professionals, social services or current providers of care and support. In cases where there is doubt as to the extent of any vulnerability authorities may also consider seeking a clinical opinion. However, the final decision on the question of vulnerability will rest with the housing authority. In considering whether such applicants are vulnerable, authorities will need to take account of all relevant factors including:

(a) the nature and extent of the illness and/or disability;
(b) the relationship between the illness and/or disability and the individual's housing difficulties; and,
(c) the relationship between the illness and/or disability and other factors such as drug/alcohol misuse, offending behaviour, challenging behaviour, age and personality disorder.

8.26 Assessment of vulnerability due to mental health problems will require co-operation between housing authorities, social services authorities and mental health agencies. Housing authorities should consider carrying out joint assessments or using a trained mental health practitioner as part of an assessment team. NHS mental health services provide help under the Care Programme Approach (CPA) for eligible patients, including people with severe mental illness (including personality disorder), who also have problems with housing. People who are homeless on discharge from hospital following a period of treatment for mental illness are likely to be vulnerable. Effective arrangements for liaison between housing, social services and mental health services will be essential in such cases but authorities will also need to be sensitive to direct approaches from former patients who have been discharged and may be homeless.

8.27 Learning or physical disabilities or long-term or acute illnesses which give rise to vulnerability may be readily discernible, but advice from health or social services should be sought wherever necessary.

Having been looked after, accommodated or fostered and aged 21 or over

8.28 A person aged 21 or over who is vulnerable as a result of having been looked after, accommodated or fostered has a priority need (other than a person who is a 'relevant student'). The terms 'looked after, accommodated or fostered' are set out in section 24(2) of the Children Act 1989) and this includes any person who has been:

(a) looked after by a local authority (i.e. has been subject to a care order or accommodated under a voluntary agreement);
(b) accommodated by or on behalf of a voluntary organisation;
(c) accommodated in a private children's home;
(d) accommodated for a consecutive period of at least 3 months:
  (i) by any Local Health Board, Special Health Authority or by a local authority in the exercise of education functions; or,
  (ii) in any care home or independent hospital or in any accommodation provided pursuant to arrangements made by the Secretary of State, the National Health Service Commissioning Board or a clinical commissioning group under the National Health Service Act 2006 or by a National Health Service trust or an NHS foundation trust, or by a local authority in Wales in the exercise of education functions; or,
(e) privately fostered.

8.29 A 'relevant student' means a care leaver under 25 to whom section 24B(3) of the Children Act 1989 applies, and who is in full-time further or higher education and whose term-time accommodation is not available during a vacation.

Under section 24B(5), where a social services authority is satisfied that a person is someone to whom section 24B(3) applies and needs accommodation during a vacation they must provide accommodation or the means to enable it to be secured.

8.30 Housing authorities will need to make inquiries into an applicant's childhood history to establish whether they have been looked after, accommodated or fostered in any of these ways. If so, they will need to consider whether they are vulnerable as a result.

8.31 For further guidance on assessing vulnerability, and on providing assistance to applicants who are care leavers see Chapter 22.

Having been a member of the armed forces

8.32 A person who is vulnerable as a result of having been a member of Her Majesty's regular armed forces has a priority need for accommodation. Former members of the armed forces will include a person who was previously a member of the regular naval, military or air forces.

8.33 For further guidance on assessing vulnerability, and on providing assistance to applicants who are veterans see Chapter 24.

Having been in custody

8.34 A person who is vulnerable as a result of having served a custodial sentence, been committed for contempt of court or remanded in custody has a priority need for accommodation.

8.35 For further guidance on assessing vulnerability, and on providing assistance to applicants who have been in custody or detention see Chapter 23.

Having left accommodation because of violence

8.36 A person has a priority need if they are vulnerable as a result of having to leave accommodation because of violence from another person, or threats of violence from another person that are likely to be carried out. It will usually be apparent from the assessment of the reason for homelessness whether the applicant has had to leave accommodation because of violence or threats of violence. In cases involving violence, the safety of the applicant and ensuring confidentiality must be of paramount concern.

8.37 For further guidance on dealing with cases involving domestic violence see Chapter 21.

Other special reason

8.38 Section 189(1)(c) provides that a person has a priority need for accommodation if they are vulnerable for any 'other special reason.' The legislation envisages that vulnerability can arise because of factors that are not expressly provided for in statute. Each application must be considered in the light of the facts and circumstances of the case. Moreover, other special reasons giving rise to vulnerability are not restricted to the physical or mental characteristics of a person. Where applicants have a need for support but have no family or friends on whom they can depend they may be vulnerable as a result of another special reason.

8.39 Housing authorities must keep an open mind and should avoid blanket policies that assume that particular groups of applicants will, or will not, be vulnerable for any other special reason. Where a housing authority considers that an applicant may be vulnerable, it will be important to make an in-depth assessment of the circumstances of the case. Guidance on certain categories of applicants who may be vulnerable as a result of any other special reason is given below. The list below is not exhaustive and housing authorities must ensure that they give proper consideration to every application on the basis of the individual circumstances. In addition, housing authorities will need to be aware that an applicant may be considered vulnerable for any other special reason because of a combination of factors which taken alone may not necessarily lead to a decision that they are vulnerable (e.g. drug and alcohol problems, common mental health problems, a history of sleeping rough, no previous experience of managing a tenancy).

8.40 **Young people:** the 2002 Order makes specific provision for certain categories of young homeless people. However, there are many other young people who fall outside these categories who could be vulnerable if homeless. Most young people can expect a degree of support from families, friends or an institution (e.g. a college or university) with the practicalities and costs of finding, establishing, and managing a home for the first time. But some young people, particularly those who are forced to leave the parental home or who cannot remain there because they are being subjected to violence or sexual abuse, may lack this back-up network and be less able than others to establish and maintain a home for themselves. Moreover, a young person who is homeless without adequate financial resources to live independently may be at risk of abuse or exploitation.

8.41 **People fleeing harassment:** housing authorities should consider whether harassment falls under the general definition of domestic abuse. For further guidance see Chapter 21 and paragraphs 8.36–8.37 above. In some cases, however, severe harassment may fall short of actual violence or threats of violence likely to be carried out. Housing authorities should consider carefully whether applicants who have fled their home because of non-violent forms of harassment, for example, psychological or emotional or damage to property, are vulnerable as a result.

8.42 **Victims of trafficking and of modern slavery:** housing authorities should ensure that staff have an awareness of the possibility that applicants may be victims of trafficking or of modern slavery, and are able to assess whether or not they are vulnerable as a result. For guidance on assessing vulnerability, and on providing assistance to applicants who are victims of trafficking or modern slavery see Chapter 25.

CHAPTER 9
Intentional homelessness

Guidance on determining whether an applicant has become homeless intentionally under homelessness legislation.

9.1 This chapter provides guidance on determining whether an applicant became homeless intentionally under section 191 of the 1996 Act.

9.2 The prevention and relief duties owed to applicants who are eligible for assistance and homeless, or threatened with homelessness, apply irrespective of whether or not they may be considered to be homeless intentionally.

9.3 Applicants who have a priority need, and whose homelessness has not been successfully relieved, are owed a lesser duty if they have become homeless intentionally than would be owed to them if they were homeless unintentionally. This reflects the general expectation that, wherever possible, people should take responsibility for their own accommodation needs and not behave in a way which might lead to the loss of their accommodation.

9.4 Where a housing authority finds an eligible applicant has a priority need but is homeless intentionally and the relief duty has come to an end, they have a duty to secure accommodation which is available to the applicant to provide reasonable opportunity for them to find their own accommodation. The authority must also provide advice and assistance in any attempts the applicant might make to secure accommodation. For further guidance on the accommodation duty owed to intentionally homeless applicants see Chapter 15.

9.5 It is for housing authorities to satisfy themselves in each individual case whether an applicant is homeless intentionally. Generally, it is not for applicants to 'prove their case.' The exception is where an applicant seeks to establish that, as a member of a household where another member has been found or is likely to be found to have caused intentional homelessness of the household, they did not acquiesce in the behaviour that led to homelessness. In such cases, acquiescence may be assumed by the housing authority in the absence of material which indicates to the contrary.

9.6 Housing authorities must not adopt general policies which seek to pre-define circumstances that do or do not amount to intentional homelessness. In each case, housing authorities must form a view in the light of all their inquiries about that particular case. Where the original loss of settled accommodation occurred some years earlier and the facts are unclear, it may not be possible for the housing authority to satisfy themselves that the applicant became homeless intentionally.

Definition of intentional homelessness

9.7 Section 191(1) provides that a person becomes homeless intentionally if **ALL** of the following apply:

(a) they deliberately do or fail to do anything in consequence of which they cease to occupy accommodation; and,
(b) the accommodation is available for their occupation; and,
(c) it would have been reasonable for them to continue to occupy the accommodation.

However, for this purpose, an act or omission made in good faith by someone who was unaware of any relevant fact must not be treated as deliberate (see paragraph 9.23).

9.8 Section 191(3) provides that a person must be treated as homeless intentionally if:

(a) the person enters into an arrangement under which they are required to cease to occupy accommodation which it would have been reasonable for the person to continue to occupy; and,
(b) the purpose of the arrangement is to enable the person to become entitled to assistance under Part 7; and,
(c) there is no other good reason why the person is homeless.

Whose conduct results in intentional homelessness?

9.9 Every applicant is entitled to individual consideration of their application. This includes applicants where another member of their family or household has made, or is making, a separate application. It is the applicant who must deliberately have done or failed to do something which resulted in homelessness.

9.10 Where a housing authority has found an applicant to be homeless intentionally, nothing in the 1996 Act prevents another member of their household from making a separate application. Situations may arise where one or more members of a household found to be intentionally homeless were not responsible for the actions or omissions that led to the homelessness. For example, a person may have deliberately failed to pay the rent or defaulted on the mortgage payments, which resulted in homelessness against the wishes or without the knowledge of their partner.

9.11 However, where applicants were not directly responsible for the act or omission which led to their family or household becoming homeless, but they acquiesced in that behaviour, then they may be treated as having become homeless intentionally themselves. In considering whether an applicant has acquiesced in certain behaviour, the housing authority should take into account whether the applicant could reasonably be expected to have taken that position through a fear of actual or probable violence.

Cessation of occupation

9.12 For intentional homelessness to be established there must have been actual occupation of accommodation which has ceased. However, occupation need not necessarily involve continuous occupation at all times, provided the accommodation was at the disposal of the applicant and available for their occupation. The accommodation which has been lost can be outside the UK. Housing authorities are reminded that applicants cannot be considered to have become homeless intentionally because of failing to take up an offer of accommodation. However, an applicant whose refusal of a suitable offer of accommodation brought to an end the section 193(2) duty under which they were at the time accommodated, resulting in the loss of that accommodation, may be considered to be intentionally homeless.

Consequence of a deliberate act or omission

9.13 For homelessness to be intentional, the ending of occupation of the accommodation must be a consequence of a deliberate act or omission by the applicant. Having established that there was a deliberate act or omission, the housing authority will need to decide whether the loss of the applicant's home is the reasonably likely result of that act or omission. This is a matter of cause and effect. An example would be where a person voluntarily gave up settled accommodation that it would have been reasonable for them to continue to occupy, moved into alternative accommodation of a temporary or unsettled nature and subsequently became homeless when required to leave the alternative accommodation. Housing authorities will, therefore, need to look back to the last period of settled accommodation and the reasons why the applicant left that accommodation, to determine whether the current incidence of homelessness is the reasonably likely result of a deliberate act or omission.

Ceasing to be intentionally homeless

9.14 Where a person becomes homeless intentionally, that condition may continue until the link between the causal act or omission and the intentional homelessness has been broken. It could be broken by an intervening event which, irrespective of any act or omission on the part of the applicant, would have itself led to their being homeless at the point at which the housing authority was carrying out inquiries into their application for assistance. This might be the case where, for example, an applicant gave up accommodation without sufficient good reason but at the later point at which they applied for assistance due to homelessness this accommodation would no longer have been available to them, or reasonable for them to occupy.

9.15 The causal link between a deliberate act or omission and intentional homelessness is more typically broken by a period in settled accommodation which follows the intentional homelessness. Whether accommodation is settled will depend on the circumstances of the case, with factors such as security of tenure and length of residence being relevant. Occupation of accommodation that was merely temporary rather than settled, for example, staying with friends on an insecure basis, may not be sufficient to break the link with the earlier intentional homelessness. However, a period in settled accommodation is not the only way in which a link with the earlier intentional homelessness may be broken: some other event, such as the break-up of a marriage resulting in homelessness, may be sufficient.

Deliberate act or omission

9.16 For homelessness to be intentional, the act or omission that led to the loss of accommodation must have been deliberate, and applicants must always be given the opportunity to explain such behaviour. An act or omission should not generally be treated as deliberate, even where deliberately carried out, if it is forced upon the applicant through no fault of their own. Moreover, an act or omission made in good faith where someone is genuinely ignorant of a relevant fact must not be treated as deliberate (see paragraph 9.23).

9.17 Generally, an act or omission should not be considered deliberate where, for example:

(a) the act or omission was non-payment of rent or mortgage costs which arose from financial difficulties which were beyond the applicant's control, or were the result of Housing Benefit or Universal Credit delays;

(b) the housing authority has reason to believe the applicant is incapable of managing their affairs, for example, by reason of age, mental illness or disability;

(c) the act or omission was the result of limited mental capacity; or a temporary aberration or aberrations caused by mental illness, frailty, or an assessed substance misuse problem;

(d) the act or omission was made when the applicant was under duress;

(e) imprudence or lack of foresight on the part of an applicant led to homelessness but the act or omission was in good faith.

9.18 An applicant's actions would not amount to intentional homelessness where they have lost their home, or were obliged to sell it, because of rent or mortgage arrears resulting from significant financial difficulties, and the applicant was genuinely unable to keep up the rent or mortgage payments even after claiming benefits, and no further financial help was available.

9.19 Where an applicant has lost a former home due to rent arrears, the reasons why the arrears accrued should be fully explored, including examining the applicant's ability to pay the housing costs at the time the commitment was taken on. Similarly, in cases which involve mortgagors, housing authorities will need to look at the reasons for mortgage arrears together with the applicant's ability to pay the mortgage commitment when it was taken on, given the applicant's financial circumstances at the time.

9.20 Examples of acts or omissions which may be regarded as deliberate (unless any of the circumstances set out in paragraph 9.17 apply) include the following, where someone:

(a) chooses to sell their home in circumstances where they are under no risk of losing it;
(b) has lost their home because of willful and persistent refusal to pay rent or mortgage payments;
(c) could be said to have significantly neglected their affairs having disregarded sound advice from qualified people;
(d) voluntarily surrenders adequate accommodation in this country or abroad which it would have been reasonable for them to continue to occupy;
(e) is evicted because of their anti-social behaviour, nuisance to neighbours or harassment;
(f) is evicted because of violence or threats of violence or abuse by them towards another person;
(g) leaves a job with tied accommodation and the circumstances indicate that it would have been reasonable for them to continue in the employment and reasonable to continue to occupy the accommodation.

Available for occupation

9.21 For homelessness to be intentional the accommodation must have been available for the applicant, their household and any other person reasonably expected to live with them. For further guidance on availability for occupation see Chapter 6.

Reasonable to continue to occupy the accommodation

9.22 An applicant cannot be treated as intentionally homeless unless it would have been reasonable for them to have continued to occupy the accommodation. For further guidance on reasonable to continue to occupy see Chapter 6. It will be necessary for the housing authority to give careful consideration to the circumstances of the applicant and the household, in each case, and with particular care in cases where violence and abuse has been alleged. For further guidance on domestic violence and abuse see Chapter 21.

Act or omissions in good faith

9.23 Acts or omissions made by the applicant in good faith where they were genuinely unaware of a relevant fact must not be regarded as deliberate. Provided that the applicant has acted in good faith, there is no requirement that ignorance of the relevant fact be reasonable.

9.24 A general example of an act made in good faith would be a situation where someone gave up possession of accommodation in the belief that they had no legal right to continue to occupy the accommodation and, therefore, it would not be reasonable for them to continue to occupy it. This could apply where someone leaves rented accommodation in the private sector having received a valid notice to quit or notice that the assured shorthold tenancy has come to an end and the landlord requires possession of the property, and the former tenant was genuinely unaware that they had a right to remain until the court granted an order for possession and a warrant or writ for possession to enforce it.

9.25 Where there was dishonesty there could be no question of an act or omission having been made in good faith.

9.26 Other examples of acts or omissions that could be made in good faith might include situations where:

(a) a person gets into rent arrears, being unaware that they may be entitled to Housing Benefit, Universal Credit or other social security benefits;

(b) an owner-occupier faced with foreclosure or possession proceedings to which there is no defence, sells before the mortgagee recovers possession through the courts or surrenders the property to the lender; or,

(c) a tenant, faced with possession proceedings to which there would be no defence, and where the granting of a possession order would be mandatory, surrenders the property to the landlord.

9.27 In (c) although the housing authority may consider that it would have been reasonable for the tenant to continue to occupy the accommodation, the act should not be regarded as deliberate if the tenant made the decision to leave the accommodation in ignorance of relevant facts.

Applicant enters into an arrangement

9.28 Housing authorities will need to be alert to the possibility of collusion by which a person may claim that they are obliged to leave available accommodation that would have been reasonable for them to continue to occupy in order to take advantage of the homelessness legislation. Collusion is not confined to arrangements with friends or relatives but can also occur between landlords and tenants. Housing authorities, while relying on experience, nonetheless need to be satisfied that collusion exists, and must not rely on hearsay or unfounded suspicions in finding that an applicant became intentionally homeless under section 191(3).

9.29 For collusion to amount to intentional homelessness, section 191(3) specifies that there should be no other good reason for the applicant's homelessness. Examples of other good reasons include overcrowding or an obvious breakdown in relations between the applicant and their host or landlord. In some cases involving collusion the applicant may not actually be homeless, if there is no genuine need for the applicant to leave the accommodation. For further guidance on applicants asked to leave by family or friends see Chapter 6.

9.30 Specific guidance relating to intentional homelessness can also be found in the following chapters:

- Chapter 21: domestic abuse
- Chapter 22: care leavers
- Chapter 23: people with an offending history
- Chapter 24: former members of the armed forces

CHAPTER 10
Local connection and referrals to another housing authority

Guidance on the provisions relating to an applicant's local connection with an area and explains the procedures for referring an applicant to another housing authority.

10.1 This chapter provides guidance on the provisions relating to an applicant's 'local connection' with an area and explains the conditions and procedures for referring an applicant to another housing authority. The chapter includes how local connection is assessed, particular arrangements that apply for certain groups such as care leavers and former asylum seekers, the process and conditions for referrals between authorities, cross-border referrals and dealing with disputes.

Local Authorities Agreement

10.2 Local authority bodies have together agreed guidelines for local authorities on procedures for referral between them, and for resolving disputes that arise when housing authorities are unable to agree whether conditions for a referral from one authority to another are met. Although these procedures have been adopted by local authority organisations in England, Scotland and Wales, and are now widely used, housing authorities are reminded that they should consider each case individually on its own particular facts.

Assessing local connection

10.3 When a housing authority makes inquiries to determine whether an applicant is eligible for assistance and owed a duty under Part 7, it may also make inquiries under section 184(2) to establish an applicant's local connection.

10.4 Section 199(1) provides that a person has a local connection with the district of a housing authority if they have a connection with it because:

(a) they are, or were in the past, normally resident there, and that residence was of their own choice; or,
(b) they are employed there; or,
(c) they have family associations living there; or,
(d) of any special circumstances.

10.5 For the purposes of (a), above, 'normal residence' is to be understood as meaning 'the place where at the relevant time the person in fact resides.' Residence in temporary accommodation provided by a housing authority can constitute normal residence of choice and can contribute towards a local connection.

10.6 In the case of a person who is street homeless or insecurely accommodated (sofa surfing) the housing authority will need to carry out a different type of inquiry to be satisfied as to their 'normal residence' than would be required for an applicant who has become homeless from more settled accommodation. If an applicant has no settled accommodation elsewhere, and from inquiries the authority is satisfied that they do in fact reside in the district, then there will be normal residence for the purposes of the 1996 Act.

10.7 The Local Authorities Agreement suggests that a working definition of normal residence sufficient to establish a local connection should be residence for at least 6 months in an area during the previous 12 months, or for 3 years during the previous 5 year period.

10.8 With regard to (b) the applicant should actually work in the district: it would not be sufficient that their employers' head office was located there.

10.9 For the purposes of (c), where the applicant raises family associations, this may extend beyond partners, parents, adult children or siblings. They may include associations with other family members such as step-parents, grandparents, grandchildren, aunts or uncles provided there are sufficiently close links in the form of frequent contact, commitment or dependency. Family associations should be determined with regard to the fact-specific circumstances of the individual case. For example, the actual closeness of the family association may count for more than the degree of blood relation. A housing authority should not identify a local connection through family associations with an area other than the one where the applicant positively wants to live.

10.10 The Local Authorities Agreement recommends that in order to give rise to a local connection, the family members relied upon as family associations should have been resident in the district for a period of at least 5 years at the date of application from homelessness assistance. Housing authorities should remain cautious in applying this guideline to every case. For example, in cases of refugees or other recent arrivals to the UK, a housing authority should bear in mind that the relatives may not have had 5 years in which to build up a residence period in any district in the UK.

10.11 With regard to (d), special circumstances might include the need to be near special medical or support services which are available only in a particular district.

10.12 Decisions about the application of (a) to (d) must be based on the facts at the date of the decision (or review of the decision), not the date of the application.

10.13 The test regarding local connection, as set out in section 199(1) should be applied, and the additional provisions for care leavers (see paragraph 10.17) and asylum seekers (see paragraph 10.23) where relevant, in order to establish whether the applicant has the required local connection. The fact that an applicant may satisfy one of these grounds will not necessarily mean that they have been able to establish a local connection.

10.14 The overriding consideration should always be whether the applicant has a connection 'in real terms' with an area and the housing authority must consider the applicant's individual circumstances, particularly any exceptional circumstances, before reaching a decision.

10.15 **Housing authorities are not generally required to make any inquiries as to whether an applicant has a local connection with an area.** However, by virtue of section 11 of the Asylum and Immigration (Treatment of Claimants, etc.) Act 2004, housing authorities will need to consider local connection in cases where the applicant is a former asylum seeker:

(a) who was provided with accommodation in Scotland under section 95 of the Immigration and Asylum Act 1999; and,

(b) whose accommodation was not provided in an accommodation centre by virtue of section 22 of the Nationality, Immigration and Asylum Act 2002.

10.16 In such cases, by virtue of section 11(2)(d) and (3) of the Asylum and Immigration (Treatment of Claimants, etc.) Act 2004, local connection to a district in England, Wales or Scotland will be relevant to what duty is owed under section 193. (See paragraphs 10.23 – 10.29 below).

Care leavers

10.17 Section 199(8) to (11) makes specific provisions relating to local connection for care leavers.

10.18 A young person owed leaving care duties under section 23C of the Children Act 1989 will have a local connection to the area of the children services authority that owes them the duties. If the children services authority is a county council and not a housing authority, the young person will have a local connection with every housing authority district falling within the area of the children services authority.

10.19 Where a care leaver is aged under 21 and normally lives in a different area to that of a local authority that owes them leaving care duties, and has done for at least 2 years including some time before they turned 16, the young person will also have a local connection in that area.

10.20 For further guidance on assessments and provision of services for care leavers see Chapter 22.

Ex-service personnel

10.21 Section 315 of the Housing and Regeneration Act 2008 amended the local connection test to enable armed forces personnel to establish a local connection in an area through residing there by choice, or being employed there, in the same way as a civilian. For further guidance on former members of the armed forces see Chapter 24.

Ex-prisoners and detainees under the Mental Health Act 1983

10.22 Detention in prison (whether convicted or not) does not establish residency of choice in the district the prison is in, and so will not create a local connection with that district. The same is true of those detained under the Mental Health Act 1983. For further guidance on people with an offending history see Chapter 23.

Former asylum seekers

10.23 Section 199(6) provides that a person has a local connection with the district of a housing authority if they were (at any time) provided with accommodation there under section 95 of the Immigration and Asylum Act 1999 (section 95 accommodation).

10.24 Under section 199(7), however, a person does not have a local connection by virtue of section 199(6):

(a) if they have been subsequently provided with section 95 accommodation in a different area. Where a former asylum seeker has been provided with section 95 accommodation in more than one area, the local connection is with the area where accommodation was last provided; or,

(b) if they have been provided with section 95 accommodation in an accommodation centre in the district by virtue of section 22 of the Nationality, Immigration and Asylum Act 2002.

10.25 A local connection with a district by virtue of section 199(6) does not override a local connection by virtue of section 199(1). Thus, a former asylum seeker who has a local connection with a district because they were provided with accommodation there under section 95 may also have a local connection elsewhere for some other reason, for example, because of employment or family associations.

Former asylum seekers provided with section 95 accommodation in Scotland

10.26 Under Scottish legislation, a person does not establish a local connection with a district in Scotland if they are resident there in section 95 accommodation. Consequently, if such a person made a homelessness application to a housing authority in England, and did not have a local connection with the district of that authority, the fact that they had been provided with section 95 accommodation in Scotland would not establish conditions for referral to the relevant local authority in Scotland.

10.27 Sections 11(2) and (3) of the Asylum and Immigration (Treatment of Claimants, etc.) Act 2004 provides that where a housing authority in England or Wales is satisfied that an applicant is eligible for assistance, unintentionally homeless and in priority need and:

(a) applicant has been provided with section 95 accommodation in Scotland at any time;
(b) the section 95 accommodation was not provided in an accommodation centre by virtue of section 22 of the Nationality, Immigration and Asylum Act 2002;
(c) the applicant does not have a local connection anywhere in England and Wales (within the meaning of section 199 of the 1996 Act); and,
(d) the applicant does not have a local connection anywhere in Scotland (within the meaning of section 27 of the Housing (Scotland) Act 1987);

then the duty to the applicant under section 193 (the main housing duty) shall not apply.

10.28 However, the authority:

(a) may secure that accommodation is available for occupation by the applicant for a period giving them a reasonable opportunity of securing accommodation for their occupation; and,
(b) may provide the applicant (or secure that they are provided with) advice and assistance in any attempts they may make to secure accommodation for their occupation.

10.29 When dealing with an applicant in these circumstances, housing authorities will need to take into account the wishes of the applicant but should consider providing such advice and assistance as would enable the applicant to make an application for housing to the Scottish authority in the district where the section 95 accommodation was last provided, or to another Scottish authority of the applicant's choice. If they were unintentionally homeless and in priority need, it would be open to them to apply to any Scottish housing authority and they would be owed a main housing duty.

Referrals to another housing authority

10.30 If a housing authority's inquires under section 184(2) determine that an applicant has a local connection with the district of another housing authority in England, Wales or Scotland, section 198 allows a housing authority (the notifying authority) to refer a case to another housing authority (the notified authority) at the point of the relief duty or main housing duty. Before making a referral the notifying authority must decide if the conditions for referral are met (see 10.32). Referrals cannot be made to Welsh or Scottish authorities where the section 189B relief duty is owed.

10.31 The Secretary of State recommends that the notified authority should respond to a referral within 10 working days.

10.32 **Referrals are discretionary only: housing authorities are not required to refer applicants to other authorities.** Housing authorities may have a policy about how they exercise their discretion to refer a case. This must not, however, extend to deciding in advance that in all cases where there is a local connection to another district the case should be referred.

10.33 There may be instances where an applicant has a local connection to the district where they applied but the housing authority considers that there is a stronger local connection elsewhere. In such cases, a housing authority can not decide to transfer responsibility to another housing authority; however, they will still be able to seek assistance from the other housing authority in securing accommodation, under section 213. For further guidance on securing accommodation see Chapter 16.

10.34 Where a person has a local connection with the districts of more than one other housing authority, the notifying housing authority should take account of the applicant's preference in deciding which housing authority to notify.

10.35 If neither an applicant, nor any person who might reasonably be expected to live with them, has a local connection with any district in Great Britain, the duty to secure accommodation or help to secure accommodation will rest with the housing authority that has received the application.

Referrals to another housing authority in England at the relief stage

10.36 Referrals cannot be made to Welsh or Scottish authorities at the relief stage – the English authority the applicant has applied to will be subject to the relief duty, if one is owed.

10.37 Section 198(A1) enables a housing authority to refer applicants who do not have a local connection to their district to another housing authority in England where they do have such a connection. Before making a referral, the notifying authority must be satisfied that the applicant is homeless and eligible for assistance and therefore owed the (section 189B) relief duty and that the conditions for referral are met (see paragraph 10.51).

10.38 Section 189B sets out the initial duties owed to all eligible people who are homeless, that is the relief duty, **unless** the authority refers the application to another housing authority. Section 199A(b) states that the housing authority is not subject to the relief duty at the point that they have notified the applicant that they intend to refer or have referred their case to another housing authority. It follows that a housing authority will owe the relief duty until such time as the applicant has been issued with this notification. If the authority believes that the applicant has no local connection and **may** have a connection elsewhere, they should take reasonable steps to try and relieve the applicant's homelessness until they issue the first notification as outlined in 10.39 below.

10.39 When the notifying authority intends to refer or have referred a case to another housing authority, there are 2 points at which applicants must be notified:

(c) when the notifying authority has decided that the conditions for referral are met and intend to notify, or have notified, another local authority of that opinion;
(d) when, following referral, it has been decided that the conditions for referral are or are not met. The notification must provide notice of the decision and the reasons for it.

10.40 From the date that the first notice is issued the authority will not be subject to the relief duty and will cease to be subject to the section 188 (interim accommodation) duty. However if they have reason to believe the applicant may be in priority need they will have a section 199A(2) duty to provide interim accommodation to the applicant whilst a decision is made on whether the conditions for referral are met.

10.41 From the date the second notice (b) is issued to the applicant, if it is decided that the conditions for referral are met, the applicant is to be treated as having made an application to the notified authority. At this point, the notifying authority's duties under Part 7 of the 1996 Act come to an end. The 56 day period of the relief duty will start from the date of the second notification.

10.42 If the notifying authority has made a decision as to whether the applicant is eligible for assistance, is homeless or became homeless intentionally, the notified authority may only come to a different decision if they are satisfied that the applicants circumstances have changed; or further information has come to light since the notifying authority made their decision, and that the changes or information warrant a different decision.

10.43 The notifying authority must give the notified authority a copy of the applicant's section 189A(3) assessment and any revisions made to it, and should also (with the applicant's consent) provide any personalised housing plan that has been agreed with the applicant which remains relevant. The notifying authority should provide this documentation as quickly as possible.

10.44 If it is decided that the conditions for referral are not met the applicant's case will remain with the notifying authority and they will be subject to the relief duty under section 189(B)(2). The 56-day period of the relief duty will start from the date of the second notification.

Referrals to another housing authority in England, Wales or Scotland at the end of the relief duty

10.45 Section 198(1) enables a housing authority to refer an applicant who is owed the main housing duty but does not have a local connection to their district, to another housing authority in England, Wales or Scotland if it considers that the conditions for referral are met. Before making a referral, it is the responsibility of the notifying authority to determine that the applicant is unintentionally homeless, eligible for assistance and has a priority need; and is owed the main housing duty.

10.46 The notifying authority cannot issue a notice of referral under section 198(1) until their duties to the applicant under section 189B(2), the relief duty, have come to an end.

10.47 As set out in paragraph 10.38 above when the notifying authority intends to refer a case to another housing authority, there are 2 notification points. At the point that the housing authority issues the first notice which notifies the applicant that they have or will be referring their case to another housing authority the notifying authority will cease to be subject the section 188 duty to provide interim accommodation from the date of the notice and will not be subject to any duty under section 193. However, they will be subject to a section 200(1) duty to provide interim accommodation until a decision is reached on whether the conditions for referral are met.

10.48 From the date the second notice (b) is issued to the applicant, (which sets out the decision on whether the conditions for referral have been met), if it is decided that the conditions for referral are met, the notifying authority's duty to provide accommodation under section 200(1) comes to an end and the notified authority will be subject to the main housing duty.

10.49 If it is decided that the conditions for referral are not met the applicant's case will remain with the notifying authority and they will be subject to the main housing duty under section 193.

10.50 A notified authority which disagrees on a finding as to the application of the main housing duty (section 193) to the applicant must challenge the notifying authority's finding (for example as to intentionality) by way of judicial review.

Conditions for referral

10.51 Sections 198(2)(2ZA) and (4) describe the conditions which must be satisfied before a referral may be made. A notifying authority may only refer an applicant to whom the relief duty or main housing duty applies to another housing authority if all of the following are met:

(a) neither the applicant nor any person who might reasonably be expected to live with them has a local connection with its district; and,

(b) the applicant or a person who might reasonably be expected to live with them has a local connection with the district of the authority to be notified; and,

(c) none of them will be at risk of domestic or other violence, or threat of domestic or other violence which is likely to be carried out, in the district of the authority to be notified.

Or:

(a) the application is made within 2 years of the applicants acceptance of a private rented sector offer from the other authority under section 193(7AA); and,

(b) neither the applicant or any person who might reasonably be expected to live with them will be at risk of domestic or other violence, or threat of domestic or other violence which is likely to be carried out, in the district of the authority to be notified.

For further guidance on referrals to another housing authority in this circumstance see Chapter 18 on re-applications.

Or:

(a) the applicant was placed in the authority's district by another authority as a result of a previous homelessness application to the other authority; and,

(b) the fresh application for assistance has been made within a prescribed period of the first application.

The Allocation of Housing and Homelessness (Miscellaneous Provisions) (England) Regulations 2006 set out that the 'prescribed period' is the total of 5 years plus the period between the date of the previous application and the date the applicant was first placed in accommodation in the district of the authority to whom the application is now made.

Risk of violence

10.52 A housing authority cannot refer an applicant to another housing authority if they or anyone who might reasonably be expected to reside with them would be at risk of violence. The housing authority is under a positive duty to enquire whether the applicant would be at such a risk and, if they would, should not assume that the applicant will take steps to deal with the threat.

10.53 Section 198(3) defines violence as violence from another person or threats of violence from another person which are likely to be carried out. This is the same definition as appears in section 177 in relation to whether it is reasonable to continue to occupy accommodation and the circumstances to be considered as to whether a person runs a risk of violence are the same.

10.54 Housing authorities should be alert to the deliberate distinction which is made in section 198(3) between actual violence and threatened violence. A high standard of proof of actual violence in the past should not be imposed. The threshold is that there must be:

(a) no risk of domestic violence (actual or threatened) in the other district; and,
(b) no risk of other violence (actual or threatened) in the other district.

For further guidance on cases involving domestic abuse see Chapter 21.

Cross-border referrals

10.55 Paragraph 10.30 above sets out the circumstances under which a local housing authority can refer a case to another housing authority in Wales or Scotland, and the conditions for referral apply to all referrals. Following a referral, the Local Authorities Agreement sets out that the legislation relevant to the location of the notified authority should be applied when reaching an agreement on whether the conditions for referral are met. There are no arrangements in place to enable referrals to be made between England and Northern Ireland or the Republic of Ireland.

Applicants' rights to request a review

10.56 Applicants have the right to request a review of various decisions relating to local connection and referrals. Under section 202(1)(c), an applicant is able to request a review of a housing authority's decision to notify another housing authority that the conditions for referral are met where the main housing duty is owed (notice a – see 10.39). Applicants cannot request a review of the equivalent section 198(A1) decision at the relief stage. Applicants have a right to request a review of the decision on whether the conditions for referral are met at both the stage of the relief duty or main housing duty under section 202(1)(e) (notice b – see 10.39). For further guidance on reviews see Chapter 19.

10.57 The notifying authority's interim duty to accommodate under section 188, 199A(2) or 200(1) ends regardless of whether the applicant requests a review of a decision that the conditions for referral are met. However, where the applicant does request a review the notifying authority has powers under section 199A(6) and section 200(5) to secure that accommodation is available pending the review decision. For further guidance on powers to secure accommodation see Chapter 15.

10.58 There is no right to request a review of a decision not to refer a case, although a failure by a housing authority to consider whether it has the discretion to refer an applicant may be amenable to challenge though judicial review. The same is true of an unreasonable use of the discretion. For further guidance on reviews see Chapter 19.

Disputes

10.59 The question of whether the conditions for referral are met in a particular case at the point of the relief duty or the main housing duty should be decided by agreement between the housing authorities concerned (section 198(5)).

10.60 If they cannot agree, the decision should be made in accordance with such arrangements as may be directed by order of the Secretary of State (section 198(5)). The Homelessness (Decisions on Referrals) Order 1998 sets out that where a decision cannot be reached by agreement between the notifying authority and the notified authority, the question shall be decided by a person appointed by those authorities.

10.61 The Order directs that the arrangements to be followed in such a dispute are the arrangements agreed between the local authority associations (i.e. the Local Government Association (LGA), the Convention of Scottish Local Authorities, the Welsh Local Government Association and London Councils). The LGA has issued guidelines for housing authorities on invoking the disputes procedure.

10.62 If the authorities are unable to appoint a person to make this decision within 21 days from the date on which the notified authorities receives a notification, sections (2) to (4) of the Schedule to the Order set out the arrangements for appointing a person. These sections **only apply** where a housing authority in England, Wales or Scotland seek to refer a homelessness case under section 198(1) to another housing authority in England or Wales, at the point of the main housing duty and they are unable to agree to appoint a person to decide whether the conditions for referral are met. They **do not apply** where a housing authority in England seek to refer a homelessness case to another authority in England under section 198(A1) at the point of the relief duty.

10.63 The Secretary of State has issued the below guidance to set out the arrangements housing authorities should take in the event of them being unable to agree on a person to be appointed to make the decision on whether the conditions for referral of a case are met under section 198(A1) at the point of the relief duty. Housing authorities are strongly recommended to follow this guidance:

(a) if the notified and notifying authority are unable to appoint a person to make a decision on their behalf on the referral of a case within 21 days from the day on which the notified authority received a notification under section 198(A1), They should jointly request the Chair of the LGA or their nominee (the proper officer) to appoint a person to make this decision;

(b) the Secretary of State recommends that the authorities request that the LGA appoint a person from the panel of persons they have established to decide the question of whether the conditions for a referral of a case are satisfied. The LGA are required to establish this panel under the Homelessness (Decisions on Referrals) Order 1998 to appoint persons to make decisions on referrals of cases under section 198(1). Housing authorities are recommended to utilise this existing procedure;

(c) if within a period of 6 weeks from the day on which the notified authority received a notification under section 198(A1), a person still has not been appointed, the notifying authority is recommended to request the proper officer to appoint a person from the panel specified above.

10.64 Broadly speaking, both section (2) to (4) of the Schedule to the order and the guidance above provide that in the event of 2 housing authorities being unable to agree on a person to be appointed to make the decision for them they should agree to make a joint request to the LGA to appoint someone. If unable to agree on that the notifying housing authority must make such a request of the LGA. In all cases relating to notifications under section 198(1) the appointed person must be drawn from a panel established by the LGA for this purpose. It is recommended that for cases relating to notification under section 198(A1) the housing authorities request that the appointed person is drawn from this panel.

10.65 Section 5, 6 and 7 of the Homelessness (Decisions on Referrals) Order 1998 sets out the procedure to be followed by the appointed person when making their decision and the arrangements for meeting associated costs. These provisions apply regardless of the means by which a person has been appointed. The appointed person must invite written representations from the notifying and notified authority and shall notify their decision and their reasons for it, in writing to the notifying authority and the notified authority. The notifying and notified authority must pay their own costs incurred in connection with these arrangements.

10.66 The Homelessness (Decisions on Referrals) (Scotland) Order 1998 applies under the Scottish homelessness legislation. The arrangements in the latter apply in cases where a housing authority in England, Wales or Scotland refers a homelessness case to a housing authority in Scotland, and they are unable to agree whether the conditions for referral are met.

10.67 Where an English or Welsh housing authority seek to refer a case to a Scottish housing authority, a request to the local authority association to appoint an arbitrator should be made to the Convention of Scottish Local Authorities.

CHAPTER 11
Assessments and personalised plans

Guidance on the initial assessments required to determine the duties owed to a person applying for homelessness assistance; personalised housing plans and the reasonable steps to be taken to prevent or relieve homelessness.

11.1 This chapter provides guidance on the (section 189A of the 1996 Act) assessments that housing authorities must carry out to determine the duties owed to a person applying for assistance, and the needs and circumstances of those applicants who are eligible for assistance and homeless or threatened with homelessness. It includes guidance on personalised plans and the reasonable steps applicants and housing authorities may take to prevent or relieve homelessness.

Overview: assessments and personalised plans

11.2 The section 189A duties to assess an applicant's case and develop a personalised plan provide a framework for housing authorities and applicants to work together to identify appropriate actions to prevent or relieve the applicant's homelessness. In performing these duties, the Secretary of State considers that housing authorities should adopt a positive and collaborative approach toward applicants, taking account of their particular needs and making all reasonable efforts to engage their cooperation. Personalised plans are more frequently referred to as 'personalised housing plans', and so this term is adopted throughout this guidance.

Initial assessments

11.3 Every person applying for assistance from a housing authority stating that they are or are going to be homeless will require an initial interview. If there is reason to believe that they may be homeless or threatened with homelessness within 56 days the housing authority must carry out an assessment to determine if this is the case, and whether they are eligible for assistance. If the applicant is not eligible for assistance or if the authority is satisfied that they are not homeless or threatened with homelessness within 56 days, they must be given a written section 184 notification of the decision reached. For further guidance on eligibility see Chapter 7 and for further guidance on notifications see Chapter 18.

11.4 In some circumstances it will be possible to determine that an applicant is not threatened with homelessness at first approach, but in most cases further enquires will need to be carried out to find out more about their housing circumstances before being satisfied that they are not threatened with homelessness within 56 days. If the applicant believes they are threatened with homelessness and there is reason to believe that this is the case then further investigations will be required.

11.5 Guidance on whether a person is homeless or threatened with homelessness is provided in Chapter 6. It should be noted that applicants who have been served a valid section 21 notice to end an assured shorthold tenancy of their only available home, which expires within 56 days, are threatened with homelessness.

11.6 Housing authorities are encouraged to take a flexible approach toward applications for assistance where there is an evidenced risk of homelessness, which might not necessarily result in homelessness within 56 days. Rather than advise the applicant to return when homelessness is more imminent, the housing authority may wish to accept a prevention duty and begin to take reasonable steps to prevent homelessness. However, where there is no risk of homelessness in the foreseeable future the housing authority should offer advice and assistance to the applicant as appropriate.

Assessment of circumstances and needs (section 189A(2))

11.7 Applicants who are eligible and homeless or threatened with homelessness must have an assessment of their case, which includes assessing:

(a) the circumstances that have caused them to be homeless or threatened with homelessness;

(b) their housing needs, and what accommodation would be suitable for them, their household and anybody who might reasonably be expected to live with them; and,

(c) the support that would be necessary for them, and anybody who will be living with them, to have and sustain suitable accommodation.

11.8 When assessing the **circumstances** leading to a threat of homelessness housing authorities will need applicants to provide all relevant information to inform their assessment. This will usually include enquiring into their accommodation history at least as far back as their last settled address, and the events that led to them being threatened with or becoming homeless.

11.9 Applicants should be encouraged to share information without fear that this will reduce their chances of receiving support, and questions should be asked in a sensitive way and with an awareness that the applicant may be reluctant to disclose personal details if they lack confidence that their circumstances will be understood and considered sympathetically. Housing authorities should ensure staff have sufficient skills and training to conduct assessments of applicants who may find it difficult to disclose their circumstances, including people at risk of domestic abuse, violence or hate crime.

11.10 When assessing the **housing needs** of an applicant housing authorities will need to consider the individual members of the household, and all relevant needs. This should include an assessment of the size and type of accommodation required, any requirements to meet the needs of a person who is disabled or has specific medical needs, and the location of housing that is required. The applicant's wishes and preferences should also be considered and recorded within the assessment; whether or not the housing authority believes there is a reasonable prospect of accommodation being available that will meet those wishes and preferences.

11.11 An assessment of the applicant's and household member's **support needs** should be holistic and comprehensive, and not limited to those needs which are most apparent or have been notified to the housing authority by a referral agency. Housing authorities will wish to adopt assessment tools that enable staff to tease out particular aspects of need, without appearing to take a 'checklist' approach using a list of possible needs. Some applicants may be reluctant to disclose their needs and will need sensitive encouragement to do so, with an assurance that the purpose of the assessment is to identify how the housing authority can best assist them to prevent or relieve homelessness.

11.12 Some applicants will identify care and support needs that cannot be met by the housing authority; or which require health or social care services to be provided alongside help to secure accommodation. Housing authorities should be mindful of duties under the Care Act 2014 including those relating to assessment and adult safeguarding; and the use of Care Act powers to meet urgent care and support needs where an assessment has not been completed.

Arrangements for carrying out assessments

11.13 Housing authorities should provide assessment services that are flexible to the needs of applicants. The Secretary of State considers an individual and interactive process will be required to fully and effectively assess circumstances and needs. Whilst advice and information services could be provided via an online process, housing authorities could not rely solely on such means to complete assessments into individual circumstances and needs for people who are homeless or threatened with homelessness within 56 days.

11.14 In most circumstances assessments will require at least one face to face interview. However, where that is not possible or does not meet the applicant's needs, assessments could be completed on the telephone or internet or with the assistance of a partner agency. For example, an applicant who is in prison, hospital or in other circumstances where they cannot attend an interview, could have an assessment completed through a video link or with the help of a partner agency able to complete an assessment form, provide information and assist with communication where needed.

11.15 Some applicants may find it more convenient to complete an assessment through telephone or internet interviews, but there should be an opportunity for the assessment to be completed through a face to face meeting where the applicant's needs indicate this is necessary, or if the applicant requests it.

11.16 Assessments should be specific to the applicant and the results of the assessment must be notified in writing to them.

Responding to referrals for assistance

11.17 Housing authorities will receive referrals of customers from other service providers, both statutory and non-statutory, including public authorities with a statutory duty to refer people who are homeless or threatened with homelessness. Some referring agencies will be better equipped than others to establish the threat of homelessness, or to conduct assessments of needs, and housing authorities will need to supplement the information provided within a referral with their own assessment and enquiries. For further guidance on duty to refer see Chapter 4.

Reasonable steps

11.18 Housing authorities should work alongside applicants to identify practical and reasonable steps for the housing authority and the applicant to take to help the applicant retain or secure suitable accommodation. These steps should be tailored to the household, and follow from the findings of the assessment, and must be provided to the applicant in writing as their personalised housing plan.

11.19 Housing authorities will wish to develop resources and tools that can be used regularly to address common issues, whilst also ensuring genuine personalisation in response to the wide range of circumstances and needs experienced by applicants. The Secretary of State expects this to result in significant variation in the staff time and other resources invested with each applicant in accordance with the nature and complexity of the issues they face.

11.20 Personalised housing plans should be realistic, taking account of local housing markets and the availability of relevant support services, as well as the applicant's individual needs and wishes. For example, a plan which limited the search for accommodation to a small geographic area where the applicant would like to live would be unlikely to be reasonable if there was little prospect of finding housing there that they could afford. The plan might instead enable the applicant to review accommodation prices in their preferred areas as well as extending their home search to more affordable areas and property types. In their interactions with applicants, housing authorities are encouraged to provide sufficient information and advice to encourage informed and realistic choices to be identified and agreed for inclusion in the plan.

11.21 Through their assessments, housing authorities might identify support needs that cannot be easily met from existing service provision. Improvements in assessments and data capture will enable authorities to build up better information to assess needs and inform commissioning arrangements for the future. The Secretary of State recognises that 'reasonable steps' will vary between housing authority areas, and will be affected by housing markets and availability of services to support vulnerable people. However, every authority should engage in efforts to identify and measure needs and prioritise funding for the provision of services, as well as the development of partnerships, appropriately.

11.22 It would not be reasonable to agree steps for an applicant that were reliant on them engaging with a service provision that is not currently available in the district or which is unlikely to be offered to them. If the applicant is already receiving services from an agency that might contribute to preventing or relieving homelessness, the housing authority may wish to seek the applicant's consent to involving them in developing and agreeing reasonable steps, and in delivering the personalised housing plan.

11.23 The Secretary of State expects the type of reasonable steps a housing authority might take to prevent or relieve homeless to include but not be limited to the following, irrespective of whether the applicant may have a priority need or be homeless intentionally:

(a) attempting mediation/conciliation where an applicant is threatened with parent/family exclusion;
(b) assessing whether applicants with rent arrears might be entitled to Discretionary Housing Payment;
(c) providing support to applicants, whether financial or otherwise, to access private rented accommodation;
(d) assisting people at risk of violence and abuse wishing to stay safely in their home through provision of 'sanctuary' or other measures;
(e) helping to secure or securing an immediate safe place to stay for people who are sleeping rough or at high risk of sleeping rough.

Process and timing

11.24 Housing authorities are required to notify applicants of the assessments they have made, and also provide written personalised housing plans. In practice, these 2 notifications might be combined to provide a clearer response to applicants.

11.25 The duty to issue written notifications should not prevent a housing authority from taking immediate action to assist an applicant where necessary. An officer may, for example, contact a young applicant's parents or carers, perhaps through a same day home visit, if they have been asked to leave, or make immediate contact with a landlord where there is an imminent threat of eviction. In these cases prevention work would begin in parallel with the assessment and planning process, having regard to initial assessment findings and with the agreement of the applicant.

11.26 Where initial prevention or relief work is undertaken in parallel with the assessment and planning process it follows that in some cases successful prevention or relief will have been largely achieved before the assessment and personalised housing plan have been completed and the applicant has been informed in writing. Where this is the case, the record of actions taken might be included in the section 189A assessment, whilst any further steps needed to sustain the accommodation arrangements are included in the personalised housing plan.

11.27 Wherever possible and appropriate, housing authorities should prioritise efforts to prevent homelessness so that households can remain in their accommodation or, helped to secure a new home rather than becoming homeless.

This might include, for example, achieving agreement for a young family to remain in the parental home pending an offer of Part 6 accommodation; or agreeing steps through which the housing authority and applicant might resolve outstanding benefit difficulties to clear or reduce rent arrears.

11.28 Housing authorities must take reasonable steps to prevent homelessness whether or not the applicant has a local connection with their area. If the applicant is actually homeless the authority may refer them to another authority where they have a local connection, and must provide copies of the assessment, and any revisions to it that have been notified to the applicant, as part of the referral arrangement. If the housing authority has agreed a personalised housing plan with the applicant they should also forward the plan to the notified authority if it has relevance, and with the applicant's consent. For further guidance on local connection see Chapter 10.

Reaching agreement and reviewing the plan (section 189A(4) to (11))

11.29 Housing authorities should make every effort to secure the agreement of applicants to their personalised housing plans. Identifying and attempting to address personal wishes and preferences will help achieve that agreement, and improve the likelihood that the plan will be successful in preventing or relieving homelessness.

11.30 If the housing authority is unable to reach an agreement with the applicant about the reasonable steps to be included in their personalised housing plan, they must record why they could not agree; and provide the written plan to the applicant indicating what steps they consider it reasonable for the applicant and the housing authority to take.

11.31 The personalised housing plan may include steps that the housing authority considers advisable for the applicant to take (recommended steps), but which the applicant is not required to take if they choose not to do so (section 189A(7)), as well as steps which they are required to take (mandatory steps). The relevant duty (prevention or relief) cannot be ended for failure to co-operate with recommended steps. The use of recommended steps might enable the authority to provide or refer the applicant to a broader range of advice and support, for example to address wider needs or to help increase their housing options in the future through employment support. Mandatory steps should be limited to those which the housing authority considers are required in order to prevent or relieve homelessness. The plan must set out clearly which steps are mandatory and which are recommended.

11.32 Assessments and personalised housing plans must be kept under review throughout the prevention and relief stages, and any amendments notified to the applicant. Housing authorities will wish to establish timescales for reviewing plans, and these are likely to vary according to individual needs and circumstances. Some applicants will need more intensive housing authority involvement to achieve a successful outcome than others, and the timescales for regular contact and reviews should reflect this. Personalised housing plans agreed during the prevention stage will need to be reviewed if an applicant subsequently becomes homelessness, enabling housing authorities and applicants to focus on steps required to help secure accommodation.

11.33 If the housing authority become aware that the information the applicant has provided for their assessment is inaccurate or if there is new information or a relevant change in the applicant's circumstances and needs there will be a need to initiate a review of the assessment and plan. The housing authority should also arrange a review if they believe the applicant is not cooperating with the personalised housing plan for whatever reason.

11.34 If the housing authority considers that their assessment of the applicant's circumstances and needs have changed, or that the agreement reached as to reasonable steps is no longer appropriate they must notify the applicant in writing. The housing authority must notify the applicant if it considers any of the agreed steps are no longer appropriate, and there will be no consequence of failure to take any of the 'removed' steps after written notification is given.

11.35 For practical purposes a review of the plan might be conducted by telephone, email or video-link, especially if the applicant is unable to or declining to attend office based appointments.

11.36 Applicants have a right under section 202 to request a review of the reasonable steps the housing authority has included within their personalised housing plan within the prevention and relief stages. Housing authorities should encourage applicants to raise any concerns they have about their plan and work to resolve disagreements to minimise the occasions on which the applicant will feel the need to request a review.

CHAPTER 12
Duty in cases of threatened homelessness (the prevention duty)

Guidance on duties owed to applicants who are threatened with becoming homeless, to try and prevent their homelessness.

12.1 Section 195 of the 1996 Act – the 'prevention duty' – places a duty on housing authorities to work with people who are threatened with homelessness within 56 days to help prevent them from becoming homelessness. This chapter provides guidance on how to fulfil the prevention duty and the ways in which it can be ended.

12.2 Housing authorities may become aware of residents who are threatened with becoming homeless but not within 56 days, and possibly not within any specified time period; and are encouraged to offer assistance where possible rather than delay providing support which may be effective in preventing homelessness.

12.3 The section 195 duty applies when the housing authority is satisfied that the applicant is both threatened with homelessness and eligible for assistance. For further guidance on eligibility see Chapter 7 and for further guidance on threatened with homelessness see Chapter 6. The housing authority is obliged to take reasonable steps to help the applicant either remains in their existing accommodation or secure alternative accommodation. For further guidance on reasonable steps see Chapter 11.

12.4 The first option to be explored with the applicant should be enabling them to remain in their current home, where suitable. Where this is not possible, the focus should be on helping to secure alternative accommodation that the applicant can move into in a planned way. This will often involve taking steps to extend an applicant's stay in their existing accommodation until they can move.

12.5 The housing authority cannot refer an applicant to another district during the prevention duty, even if the conditions for referral that would apply during the relief and main housing duties are met. For further guidance on local connection see Chapter 10. This means the housing authority is obliged to take reasonable steps to help the applicant retain their existing accommodation or secure alternative accommodation wherever that may be. If the applicant is living at distance from the housing authority to which they have applied, one reasonable step to be agreed with the applicant might be for the receiving authority to make contact with the housing authority where the applicant is living to request their assistance in efforts to prevent homelessness.

12.6 Housing authorities may find it helpful to establish protocols for collaboration with relevant neighbouring authorities to improve outcomes and efficiency in localities where applicants frequently seek help in a different district to the one where they live.

12.7 The reasonable steps taken by both the authority and the applicant to help prevent homelessness should be those set out in the personalised housing plan drawn up and reviewed as set out in section 189A of the 1996 Act. For further guidance on personalised housing plans see Chapter 11. The housing authority will need to have arrangements in place for accessible and timely communication with applicants to maximise the effectiveness of their joint efforts to prevent homelessness.

12.8 Housing authorities must take into account the needs and circumstances of the applicant as they work to fulfil the prevention duty, recognising that there are a range of factors that will affect an applicants' ability to take action to help prevent their homelessness. For some more vulnerable applicants, the factors that have contributed to their being threatened with homelessness may also affect their ability to work with the housing authority to resolve that threat. The housing authority will want to seek to understand these factors and tailor the support it provides, both directly and through engaging relevant specialist services, accordingly.

12.9 Where homelessness is prevented, but an applicant's needs may put them at risk of a further threat of homelessness, the housing authority will want to work with relevant support and specialist services to help promote sustainability.

12.10 Where an applicant has to leave their accommodation without any reasonable prospect of an imminent return, or if it otherwise ceases to be reasonable for them to occupy before a suitable alternative is available, further duties should be considered under section 189B (the relief duty).

CHAPTER 13
Relief duty

Guidance on duties owed to applicants who are homeless, to try and relieve their homelessness.

13.1 Section 189B of the 1996 Act – the 'relief duty' – requires housing authorities to help people who are homeless to secure accommodation. This chapter of the code provides guidance on how to fulfil the relief duty.

13.2 The duty applies when the housing authority is satisfied that the applicant is both homeless and eligible for assistance. The housing authority is obliged to take reasonable steps to help the applicant secure suitable accommodation with a reasonable prospect that it will be available for their occupation for at least 6 months.

13.3 Where the housing authority have reason to believe that an applicant may be homeless, eligible and have a priority need they must provide interim accommodation under section 188(1) whilst fulfilling the relief duty. For further guidance on interim duties to accommodate see Chapter 15.

13.4 If the housing authority would be subject to the relief duty but consider that the conditions are met for referral to another housing authority in England (not Scotland or Wales) they have the discretion to notify that housing authority of their opinion (section 198(A1)). For further guidance on local connection see Chapter 10.

13.5 The reasonable steps to be taken by both the housing authority and the applicant to help secure accommodation must include those set out in the personalised housing plan drawn up and reviewed as set out in section 189A. For further guidance on assessments and personalised housing plans see Chapter 11. The housing authority will need to have arrangements in place for accessible and timely communication with applicants to maximise the effectiveness of their joint efforts.

13.6 Housing authorities must take into account their assessment of the applicant's case under section 189A (which includes consideration of an applicant's housing needs, circumstances leading to homelessness, and support required) as they work to fulfil the relief duty, recognising that there are a range of factors that will affect an applicant's ability to take action to secure accommodation. For some applicants, the circumstances, needs or issues that have contributed to their being homeless may also affect their ability to work with the housing authority. The housing authority's duty to have regard to the applicant's section 189A assessment will assist the authority with understanding the applicant's particular situation and tailoring the support it provides under the relief duty, both directly and through engaging relevant specialist services, accordingly.

13.7 Housing authorities will want to ensure that people who are sleeping rough and eligible for assistance are supported to apply to them for housing assistance, and should seek to prevent applicants from starting to sleep rough during the course of the relief duty. For further guidance on joint working to address rough sleeping see the homelessness strategy see Chapter 2 and for further guidance on personalised plans see Chapter 11. Specific considerations in relation to applicants who are (or are at imminent risk of) sleeping rough and are or may be owed the relief duty include:

(a) working with other agencies and/or commissioned services to ensure rough sleepers are aware of, and have support to seek, housing assistance from the authority and in the provision of appropriate accommodation and/or support;

(b) if the authority does not have reason to believe that the applicant may have a priority need and has not therefore provided interim accommodation under section 188(1), the use of discretionary powers to secure emergency accommodation to prevent nights on the streets, taking into account the risk of harm applicants may face. For further guidance on discretionary powers to secure emergency accommodation see Chapter 15;

(c) if using discretion to enquire into whether an applicant has a local connection, remembering that normal residence does not require a settled address and may include periods sleeping rough. For further guidance on local connection see Chapter 10.

13.8 Where homelessness is relieved, but an applicant's needs, as set out in the personalised housing plan, may put them at risk of a further threat of homelessness, the housing authority should work with relevant support and specialist services to help promote sustainability.

13.9 Housing authorities may conduct and complete their inquiries into the duties that will be owed to an applicant under section 193(2), the main housing duty during the period in which they are attempting to relieve homelessness under the section 189B duty. However, this activity must not detract from the housing authority's work to relieve the applicant's homelessness. **Where the housing authority considers an applicant is unlikely to be owed a section 193(2) main housing duty they must not limit or reduce the assistance they provide during the relief duty for this reason.**

13.10 Housing authorities are advised against issuing a section 184 notification accepting the section 193 (main housing duty) during the relief stage. The section 193 duty cannot commence until the relief duty has come to an end and issuing notification during the relief stage might detract from activities to relieve their homelessness.

13.11 Housing authorities may issue a section 184 decision to the applicant, that when the relief duty ends they will owe them a duty under section 190 because they have a priority need but are intentionally homeless. Although the section 190 duty cannot commence until the relief duty has come to an end, the authority may wish to alert an applicant that the main housing duty will not be owed. It may be beneficial to review the personalised housing plan at this point to help maximise joint efforts to relieve homelessness.

13.12 If the authority has provided interim accommodation under section 188 and subsequently finds that the applicant does not have a priority need during the relief duty stage, a section 184 notification that neither the main housing duty nor the section 190 duty will be owed once the relief duty ends will bring the section 188 duty to an end (section 188(1ZA)(b)). The relief duty will continue to be owed until it ends in one of the circumstances in subsections (7) or (9) of section 189B. For further guidance on interim duties to accommodate see Chapter 15, and for guidance on ending the prevention and relief duty see Chapter 14.

CHAPTER 14
Ending the prevention and relief duties

Guidance on how the prevention and relief duties come to an end.

14.1 This chapter provides guidance on how the (section 195) prevention and (section 189B) relief duties come to an end.

14.2 There are 7 circumstances under which both the prevention and relief duties can be brought to an end. In addition to these common circumstances the prevention duty will end where the applicant has become homeless, and the relief duty will end when 56 days has passed and the housing authority is satisfied that the applicant has a priority need and is homeless unintentionally, or on refusal of a final accommodation offer or Part 6 offer.

14.3 The housing authority must give the applicant notice in order to end the duties except under section 189B (4) where 56 days have passed since the start of the relief duty and the housing authority is satisfied the applicant has a priority need and is homeless unintentionally. For further guidance on notifications see Chapter 18 and for further guidance on reviews see Chapter 19. Guidance on bringing the duties to an end under each circumstance is set out below.

14.4 Chapter 15 provides guidance on the ending of interim accommodation duties following the end of relief duties.

Circumstances in which both prevention and relief duties may end

A – the housing authority is satisfied that the applicant has suitable accommodation available for occupation and a reasonable prospect of suitable accommodation being available for at least 6 months from the date of the notice. Note that the Secretary of State has a power to increase this minimum period up to a maximum of 12 months (sections 195(8)(a) and 189B(7)(a)).

14.5 Housing authorities must allow applicants a reasonable period for considering offers of accommodation that will bring the prevention and relief duties to an end. There is no set reasonable period – housing authorities must take into account the applicant's circumstances in each case.

14.6 Applicants should be given the opportunity to view accommodation before being required to decide whether to accept or refuse an offer, and before being required to sign any written agreement relating to the accommodation (for example, a tenancy agreement). If the accommodation is in another area and it is not practical to travel to view, sufficient information about the property and the locality should be made available to them. This may, for example, include photographs and the opportunity to ask questions of the landlord or agent.

14.7 Where new tenancies are secured housing authorities are encouraged to adopt policies favouring longer tenancies than the legal minimum where market conditions in their area allow. It is recommended that, wherever possible, minimum tenancy lengths of 12 months are secured to provide more stability to individuals and particularly to families with children.

14.8 In some circumstances, determining reasonable prospect will be less clear cut. For example, a landlord may agree to allow the applicant to stay in their accommodation having previously issued a section 21 notice. Ideally in this case they would issue a new tenancy, but they may instead choose to leave the existing tenancy running, with the section 21 notice in place until it expires.

14.9 Where this is the case it is the responsibility of the housing authority to satisfy itself that there is a reasonable prospect of the accommodation being available for at least 6 months. This may, for example, involve securing written confirmation from the landlord that the applicant can remain in the accommodation on condition that they comply with documented conditions, and the housing authority having a reasonable expectation that the applicant is in a position to comply.

14.10 Where an applicant has remained at or returned home or gone to stay with friends or extended family, for example, through the use of mediation or negotiation, it is the responsibility of the housing authority to satisfy itself that accommodation will be available for at least 6 months. There may, for example, be an open ended agreement (perhaps with reasonable conditions), or an agreement that the applicant can stay until they have secured alternative accommodation (whether that happens before or after 6 months).

14.11 There may be other circumstances where there is a reasonable prospect of suitable accommodation being available for at least 6 months, but this not necessarily being the same accommodation throughout. For example, an applicant with support needs may be placed in short term supported accommodation which forms part of a planned accommodation and support pathway overseen by the housing authority. This may meet the conditions for ending the duty under this subsection if there is a clear, documented expectation that the applicant will be supported to make a planned move directly to more settled supported or independent accommodation through the pathway service.

14.12 The housing authority should take into account the support needs and vulnerabilities of an applicant, which will have been identified during assessment, in determining whether they can reasonably expect the applicant to sustain the accommodation for at least 6 months.

B – the housing authority has complied with the prevention or relief duty and 56 days have passed (regardless of whether the applicant is still threatened with homelessness in the case of the prevention duty or whether they have secured accommodation in the case of the relief duty) (sections 195 (8)(b) and 189B (7)(b)).

14.13 Under the prevention duty (section 195(6)), the 56 day period does not apply where the applicant has been given a valid section 21 notice that will expire within 56 days or has expired and is in respect of the only accommodation that is available for the applicant's accommodation. This is to ensure continuity of prevention services where an applicant remains in the property after the expiry of their section 21 notice or longer than 56 days from the duty starting and also remains threatened with homelessness.

14.14 Where a housing authority is satisfied that, despite the section 21 notice, the landlord has agreed not to pursue possession and there is a reasonable prospect of the accommodation being available for at least 6 months the prevention duty may be ended (section 195(8)(a)) (see paragraphs 14.7 and 14.8 above).

14.15 The housing authority can continue to deliver the prevention or relief duty with any applicant for longer than 56 days and issue a notice to end it under this subsection at any point after this date; as long as no other duties take precedence (for example, the relief duty takes precedence where an applicant previously owed the prevention duty becomes homeless).

14.16 Where the housing authority is satisfied that the applicant has a priority need and has become homeless unintentionally, the relief duty comes to an end after 56 days (section 189B(4)). Housing authorities should not delay completing their inquiries as to what further duties will be owed after the relief duty. Where the housing authority has the information it requires to make a decision as to whether the applicant is in priority need and became homeless unintentionally, it should be possible to notify the applicant on or around day 57. In cases where significant further investigations are required it is recommended that housing authorities aim to complete their inquiries and notify the applicant of their decision within a maximum of 15 working days after 56 days have passed.

14.17 Housing authorities should not have a blanket policy of ending the prevention and relief duties after 56 days where they have the discretion to continue it; instead they should in each case take the applicant's circumstances into account.

14.18 Where the applicant remains at risk of homelessness and the housing authority considers there is still the chance that homelessness can be prevented, it will be in the interests of both the applicant and the housing authority for work to continue to help the applicant avoid homelessness, whereupon they may make a new application to the housing authority for help under the relief duty.

14.19 During the relief stage, where an applicant does not have a priority need or they have a priority need and have become homeless intentionally, the authority may want to consider continuing the relief duty for longer. Considerations may include the needs of the applicant; the risk of the applicant sleeping rough; the prospects of securing accommodation within a reasonable period; the resources available to the housing authority, and any wider implications of bringing the duty to an end (for example, in the case of an applicant who has dependent children and who became homeless intentionally where Children Act duties may apply if accommodation could not be secured).

C – an applicant who was owed the prevention duty has become homeless (section 195(8)(c)).

14.20 Where an applicant in these circumstances is owed the relief duty the housing authority will want to provide a seamless transition between the prevention and relief duties, including notifying the applicant of any further duties owed to them at the same time as issuing the notice advising that the prevention duty has ended. These notifications may be combined.

14.21 Where interim accommodation is to be provided, this should be arranged as a priority. Authorities should take the opportunity to plan interim accommodation in advance whenever it is possible to do so, in order to minimise distress and disruption for the applicant and provide maximum opportunity for planning for, for example, children's journeys to school.

14.22 The housing authority and the applicant will then need to review the assessment and personalised plan undertaken under section 189A, devising new reasonable steps to help secure that accommodation becomes available for the applicant under the relief duty. For further guidance on assessments and personalised housing plans see Chapter 11.

D – the applicant has refused an offer of suitable accommodation and, on the date of refusal, there was a reasonable prospect that suitable accommodation would be available for the minimum prescribed period (sections 195(8)(d) and 189B(7)(c)).

14.23 There is an important distinction between the consequences of refusal of an offer of suitable accommodation at the prevention and relief stages.

14.24 During the prevention stage the housing authority can bring the prevention duty to an end but refusal does not affect any further duties that may be owed to the applicant if they become homeless.

14.25 During the relief stage the housing authority can bring the relief duty to an end through a suitable offer of accommodation (section 189B(7)(c)) and there will be no consequences affecting any main housing duty owed to the applicant if they refuse it.

14.26 However, the housing authority can also bring the relief duty to an end through a final accommodation offer (section 189B(9)(a)) or a final Part 6 offer. Refusal of either of these types of offer will preclude the applicant from subsequently being owed the main housing duty (section 193A(3)). A final accommodation offer must be of an assured shorthold tenancy of at least 6 months duration, and the applicant must have been informed of the consequences of refusal as well as the right to request a review of the suitability of the offer. For guidance on the suitability of offers see Chapter 17.

14.27 It will be up to the housing authority to decide whether or not to end the prevention or relief duty when a suitable offer, other than a final offer or Part 6 offer, is refused. In reaching their decision a housing authority should consider the applicant's circumstances, the reason for their refusal, the reasonable steps they are taking to secure accommodation that better suits their needs and preferences and, in the case of the prevention duty, the likelihood of the applicant subsequently becoming homeless and applying for help under the relief duty.

14.28 For many applicants, working with the housing authority to prevent or relieve their homelessness will provide an opportunity to explore what realistic options are available to them and consider what compromises they may wish to make in order to achieve the best option for them. The opportunity to consider more than one property can play an important part in this process.

E – the applicant has become homeless intentionally from any accommodation that has been made available to them as a result of reasonable steps taken by the housing authority during the prevention or relief duty, whichever is relevant (sections 195(8)(e) and 189B(7)(d)).

14.29 Where the prevention duty ends under this circumstance, the applicant's entitlement to the relief duty will not be affected as the relief duty applies irrespective of whether or not an applicant is considered to be intentionally homeless.

14.30 Where the applicant has a priority need and the relief duty has ended under this circumstance, the main housing duty will not apply. An applicant should only be considered intentionally homeless under this provision if they have ceased to occupy accommodation which it would have been reasonable for them to continue to occupy, and which has been provided to them within the 'reasonable steps' provisions of the Act (sections 195(2) and 189B(2)). In most cases where such accommodation has been secured the housing authority will already have notified the applicant that the prevention or relief duty has come to an end, and so there will be very limited circumstances in which the duty is brought to an end through the provision of section 195(8)(e) and 189B(7)(d).

14.31 Under section 190, duties to persons becoming homeless intentionally, the housing authority will need to secure that accommodation is available for the applicant's occupation for long enough to give them a reasonable opportunity of securing accommodation and provide advice and assistance in any attempts the applicant makes to secure accommodation. This advice must have regard to the assessment the housing authority made under section 189A, assessment and personalised plans. For further guidance on intentional homelessness see Chapter 9.

F – the applicant is no longer eligible for assistance (sections 195(8)(f) and 189B(7)(e)).

14.32 In circumstances where an applicant is found not to be eligible for assistance, the housing authority must provide, or secure the provision, of information and advice as set out in section 179. For further guidance on eligibility see Chapter 7. If (section 188) interim accommodation has been provided, notice periods should take account of the needs of the applicant and the time required for them to access assistance. For households including children or particularly vulnerable adults who are owed duties under the Children Act 1989 or Care Act 2014, local authorities should consider having arrangements in place to manage a transition in responsibilities, so that there is no break in the provision of accommodation for applicants who cease to be eligible for 1996 Act support.

G – the applicant has withdrawn their application for homelessness assistance (sections 195(8)(g) and 189B(7)(f)).

14.33 Some applicants will cease contact with the authority rather than explicitly withdraw their application. It is recommended that local authorities have procedures in place to attempt to maintain or regain contact with applicants who have ceased contact prior to deciding to end the prevention or relief duty under this subsection. These efforts should take into account the circumstances and needs of the applicant, and use varied communication channels to help prevent, for example, losing contact with someone because they have lost their mobile phone. For further guidance on losing contact with applicants see Chapter 18.

14.34 It is recommended that where the housing authority considers that the applicant has withdrawn their application because they have failed to maintain contact, the duty is ended under this subsection rather than because 56 days has passed. This will help to ensure accurate data relating to the reasons why duties end.

H – deliberate and unreasonable refusal to co-operate (sections 195(10) and 189B(9)(b)).

14.35 The prevention and relief duties can also be brought to and end as a result of the applicant's deliberate and unreasonable refusal to co-operate. For further guidance on non-cooperation see Chapter 14. Where the **prevention duty** is brought to an end due to deliberate and unreasonable refusal to co-operate, the applicant's entitlements under any other section of Part 7, including the relief and main housing duties, are not affected.

14.36 Where the **relief duty** is brought to an end as a result of the applicant's deliberate and unreasonable refusal to co-operate the **main housing duty will not apply**. However, under section 193C(4) the housing authority will, be required to secure that accommodation is available for an applicant who has priority need and is unintentionally homeless, until such time as they make a final accommodation offer or a final Part 6 offer of suitable accommodation, or the duty comes to an end for another of the reasons set out in section 193C(5).

Notification to end the prevention duty

14.37 Section 195(8) provides the circumstances in which the housing authority can give notice under section 195(5) to the applicant to bring the prevention duty to an end. For further guidance on the prevention duty see Chapter 12.

14.38 The notice must specify which of the circumstances in section 195(8) apply and inform the applicant that they have a right to request a review of the housing authority's decision to bring the duty to an end, and of the time frame within which such a request must be made.

14.39 Section 195(6) prevents a housing authority from bringing the prevention duty to an end after 56 days if the applicant has been given a valid section 21 notice which will expire in 56 days or has expired, and is in respect of their only available accommodation. This means that the housing authority will continue to owe a prevention duty beyond the initial 56 days, until the applicant is served with a section 195(5) notice on the basis that another of the circumstance set out in section 195(8) applies.

Notification to end the relief duty (section 189B(7))

14.40 Section 189B(7) provides the circumstances in which the housing authority can give notice under section 189B(5) to the applicant bringing the relief duty under section 189B(2) to an end. For further guidance on the relief duty see Chapter 13.

14.41 The notice must specify which of the circumstances in section 189B(7) apply and inform the applicant that they have right to request a review of the authority's decision to bring the relief duty under section 189B(2) to an end, and of the time frame within which such a request must be made.

14.42 Housing authorities may refer an applicant's case to another housing authority in England during the relief duty if the applicant does not have a local connection with the authority to which they have applied, and does have a local connection to another district where they would not be at risk of violence. For guidance on local connection referrals see Chapter 10.

Deliberate and unreasonable refusal to co-operate (sections 193B and 193C)

14.43 Both the prevention and relief duties can be brought to an end under section 193B and section 193C if an applicant deliberately and unreasonably refuses to take any of the steps that they agreed to take, or the housing authority set out for them to take where agreement could not be reached, in their personalised housing plan (subsections (4) and (6)(b) of section 189A).

14.44 Before bringing either duty to an end by issuing a section 193B(2) notice, the housing authority must first issue a warning letting the applicant know that if they deliberately and unreasonably refuse to take any of the steps in their personalised housing plan after receiving the warning the authority intends to issue a notice bringing the prevention or relief duty, whichever is relevant, to an end. The warning must explain the consequences of a notice being given and the housing authority must allow a reasonable period after the warning is given before issuing a notice (section 193B(4) and (5)). There is no set reasonable period, but housing authorities should ensure sufficient time is given to allow the applicant to rectify the non-co-operation and prevent a notice being issued to end the prevention or relief duty. This will vary according to the particular needs and circumstances of the applicant.

14.45 Notices issued under section 193B(2) must explain why the housing authority are giving notice and its effect, and inform the applicant of their right to request a review of the decision to issue the notice (section 202(1)) and that a request for a review must be made within 21 days of being notified of that decision, or such longer period as the housing authority may allow in writing (section 202(3)).

14.46 Regulations relating to the procedure to be followed by housing authorities in connection with notices under section 193B (section 193B(7)) are set out in the Homelessness (Review Procedure etc.) Regulations 2018 – these relate to decisions to issue a notice.

14.47 The ending of the **prevention duty** under sections 193B and 193C will not affect the housing authority's assessment of what duties are owed if the applicant subsequently seeks help having become homeless.

14.48 For applicants who are eligible for assistance, unintentionally homeless and have a priority need, the ending of the relief duty under sections 193B and 193C will mean that section 193 (the main housing duty) will not apply. However, the housing authority must secure that accommodation is available for occupation by the applicant by making a final accommodation offer or final Part 6 offer (sections 193C(4) to (10). For further guidance on accommodation duties and powers see Chapter 15.

Meaning of deliberate and unreasonable refusal

14.49 Section 193B(6) provides that the housing authority must have regard to the particular circumstances and needs of the applicant, whether or not identified in the assessment under section 189A, in deciding whether refusal by the applicant is unreasonable.

14.50 Housing authorities should make reasonable efforts to obtain the co-operation of the applicant, including seeking to understand the reasons for their lack of co-operation, before invoking and during the use of section 193B. Where an applicant appears not to be co-operating the housing authority should review their assessment of the applicant's case and the appropriateness of the steps in the personalised housing plan (section 189A(9)) and explain the consequences of not co-operating before issuing a warning under section 193B(4). For further guidance on personalised housing plans see Chapter 11.

14.51 Where the applicant is receiving support from other services, for example the leaving care team, an offender management service, or a family support service, the housing authority should alert relevant service(s) to the problem as soon as possible and seek to involve them in supporting the applicant to resolve the situation. Having local information sharing arrangements in place will facilitate this.

14.52 The housing authority should take into account any particular difficulties that the applicant may have in managing communications when considering if failure to cooperate is deliberate and unreasonable, particularly if they are street homeless or moving between temporary places to stay such as the homes of different family and friends.

14.53 The housing authority should be satisfied of the following before ending the prevention or relief duty under sections 193B and 193C:

(a) the steps recorded in the applicant's personalised housing plan are reasonable in the context of the applicant's particular circumstances and needs;

(b) the applicant understands what is required of them in order to fulfil the reasonable steps, and is therefore in a position to make a deliberate refusal;

(c) the applicant is not refusing to co-operate as a result of a mental illness or other health need, for which they are not being provided with support, or because of a difficulty in communicating;
(d) the applicant's refusal to co-operate with any step was deliberate and unreasonable in the context of their particular circumstances and needs. For example, if they prioritised attending a Jobcentre or medical appointment, or fulfilling a caring responsibility, above viewing a property, this is unlikely to constitute a deliberate and unreasonable refusal to cooperate. However, if the applicant persistently failed to attend property viewings or appointments without good reason; or they actively refused to engage with activity required to help them secure accommodation, then this might be considered deliberate and unreasonable refusal to cooperate.

Please see Chapters 21–24 for client group specific considerations sections.

Notices in cases of an applicant's deliberate and unreasonable refusal to co-operate (section 193B(2))

14.54 Under section 193B(2), the housing authority may give a notice to an applicant if they consider that the applicant has deliberately and unreasonably refused to take one or more of the steps in their personalised housing plan.

14.55 Before serving this notice, the housing authority must have given a relevant warning to the applicant and a reasonable period of time has elapsed since the warning. The relevant warning must be a written notice to warn the applicant that if they deliberately and unreasonably refuse to take any step in their personalised housing plan the housing authority will issue a notice under section 193B(2), and explain the consequences of a section 193B(2) notice being served.

14.56 A housing authority must develop a procedure to be followed when issuing notices bringing their prevention or relief duties to an end under section 193B(2). The procedure must:
(a) be in writing;
(b) be kept under review; and,
(c) make provision for the decision to give a notice under section 193B(2) to be made by an officer of that housing authority and authorised by an appropriate person.

14.57 The original decision to issue the notice must be made by an officer of the housing authority and then receive authorisation by an appropriate person. An 'appropriate person' is someone of at least an equivalent seniority to the officer who made the original decision to issue a notice, and they must:
(a) work for the housing authority or local authority; and,
(b) not have been involved in the original decision to issue the notice.

14.58 The housing authority's procedures may provide that second sign off of the decision to issue a notice can be given by an appropriate person from another service within the local authority (or upper tier local authority). For example, in the case of a care leaver, second sign off by an officer of at least an equivalent seniority within Children's Services may be appropriate.

14.59 The appropriate person conducting the second sign off should give particular consideration as to whether the original decision to issue the notice had due regard to the circumstances and needs of the applicant, whether or not these were properly identified in the authority's assessment of the applicant's case under section 189A.

CHAPTER 15
Accommodation duties and powers

Guidance on housing authority duties and powers to secure accommodation for applicants; how they arise and are brought to an end, including under the main housing duty.

15.1 This chapter provides guidance on the housing authority's duties to secure accommodation for applicants, how they arise and are brought to an end; and the powers within the 1996 Act to secure accommodation for homeless households.

15.2 The chapter includes:
(a) duties to provide interim accommodation;
(b) powers to provide accommodation pending review or appeal;
(c) duties to prevent and relieve homelessness, including a power to provide accommodation;
(d) the section 193C(4) duty to secure accommodation for applicants who are homeless, eligible for assistance, have priority need and are not intentionally homeless but have deliberately and unreasonably refused to cooperate;
(e) the section 193(2) duty to secure accommodation for applicants who are homeless, eligible for assistance, have priority need and are not intentionally homeless (the main housing duty).

Duties to provide interim accommodation

15.3 The 1996 Act provides 4 circumstances in which a housing authority must secure accommodation on an interim basis until a decision or other event occurs. These are set out below.

Section 188 interim duty to accommodate

15.4 Section 188(1) requires housing authorities to secure that accommodation is available for an applicant (and their household) if they have reason to believe that the applicant may:
(a) be homeless;
(b) be eligible for assistance; and,
(c) have a priority need.

15.5 The threshold for triggering the section 188(1) duty is low as the housing authority only has to have a **reason to believe** (rather than being satisfied) that the applicant **may** be homeless, eligible for assistance and have a priority need.

15.6 The section 188(1) interim accommodation duty applies even where the housing authority considers the applicant may not have a local connection with their district and may have one with the district of another housing authority giving rise to the possibility of referral (section 188(2)). For further guidance on local connection see Chapter 10.

Ending the section 188 interim duty

15.7 The section 188(1) interim duty comes to an end when applicants are notified of certain decisions in relation to their application.

15.8 Following inquiries, where the housing authority concludes that an **applicant does not have a priority need**, the section 188(1) duty ends when **either**:

(a) the housing authority notifies the applicant of the decision that they do not owe a section 189B(2) relief duty; **or,**
(b) the housing authority notifies them of a decision that, once the section 189B(2) relief duty comes to an end, they do not owe a duty under section 190 (duties to persons becoming homeless intentionally) or section 193(2) (the main housing duty owed to applicants with priority need who are not homeless intentionally).

15.9 So, an applicant who the housing authority has found to be not in priority need within the 56 day 'relief stage' will no longer be owed a section 188(1) interim duty to accommodate, but will continue to be owed a section 189B(2) relief duty until that duty ends or is found not to be owed.

15.10 For any other case (including for **applicants who have a priority need,** and for applicants who the housing authority have reason to believe will be owed a duty because they have **reapplied within 2 years of accepting a private rented sector offer** (for further guidance on reapplication after a private rented sector offer see Chapter 18), the section 188(1) interim duty will end at **whichever is the later of:**
(a) the housing authority notifies them of what duty (if any) they are owed under Part 7 of the 1996 Act once the section 189B(2) relief duty comes to an end;
(b) the housing authority notifies them that they are not owed the section 189B(2) relief duty, or that this duty has come to an end;
(c) the housing authority notifies them of a decision following their request for a review as to the suitability of a final accommodation offer or Part 6 offer made within the section 189B relief stage.

15.11 In summary, a housing authority may bring the section 188(1) interim accommodation duty to an end within the 56 day period (the relief stage) by issuing a section 184 decision that the applicant does not have priority need; or by issuing a notification that the relief duty is not owed or has been brought to an end. If neither of these notifications is issued within the 56 day period, the section 188(1) interim accommodation duty will be brought to an end by notification of what further duties are owed, if any, under section 193 or section 190. However, in the event that the relief duty is brought to an end following refusal of a final accommodation or Part 6 offer, and the applicant requests a review as to the suitability of the accommodation offered, the section 188(1) duty will continue until a decision on the review has been notified to the applicant.

15.12 In circumstances where an applicant is found not to be eligible for assistance, the housing authority must provide, or secure the provision of, information and advice as set out in section 179. If (section 188) interim accommodation has been provided, notice periods should take account of the needs of the applicant and the time required for them to access assistance. For households including children or particularly vulnerable adults who are owed duties under the Children Act 1989 or Care Act 2014, local authorities should consider having arrangements in place to manage a transition in responsibilities, so that there is no break in the provision of accommodation for applicants who cease to be eligible for support under the 1996 Act.

Section 190(2): duty to provide accommodation to applicants who are intentionally homeless

15.13 On reaching a decision that an applicant has priority need and is intentionally homeless, the housing authority must secure accommodation for a period of time that will provide a reasonable opportunity for them to find their own accommodation.

15.14 In determining the period of time for which accommodation will be secured under section 190(2) housing authorities must consider each case on its merits. A few weeks may provide the applicant with a reasonable opportunity to secure accommodation for themselves. However, some applicants might require longer and others, particularly where the housing authority provides pro-active and effective assistance, might require less time.

15.15 Housing authorities will need to take into account:

(a) the particular needs and circumstances of the applicant and the resources available to them to secure accommodation. This might include any health or support needs that make it more difficult for the applicant to find and secure accommodation, as well as the support available from their family or social network;

(b) the housing circumstances in the local area, and the length of time it might reasonably take to secure accommodation. In assessing this the housing authority might reflect on the efforts previously made by both the housing authority and the applicant to relieve their homelessness, and why these had not proved successful;

(c) arrangements that have already been made by the applicant which are likely to be successful within a reasonable timescale. For example, if the applicant has secured accommodation that is not yet available to occupy or can demonstrate that accommodation will be so secured, the housing authority should consider providing section 190(2) accommodation until the applicant is able to take up the accommodation.

Section 199A(2) and section 200(1): duties to accommodate applicants with no local connection pending outcome of referral

15.16 If the housing authority has notified an applicant that it proposes to refer the case to another housing authority, the notifying authority has a duty under section 199A(2) (if referral is in the relief stage of an applicant who the authority has reason to believe may have a priority need) or section 200(1) (if referral is in the section 193 main housing duty stage of an applicant who has a priority need and is unintentionally homeless) to secure that accommodation is available for the applicant until they are notified of the decision whether the conditions for referral are met. At this point the duty under section 199A(2) or 200(1) will come to an end and a duty under section 189B or section 193(2) will be owed by either the notified housing authority or the notifying housing authority. For further guidance on referrals to another housing authority see Chapter 10.

Suitability of accommodation

15.17 Section 206(1) provides that all accommodation provided under Part 7 of the 1996 Act must be suitable for the applicant and their household, and the suitability requirements under section 210 apply. For further guidance on the suitability of accommodation see Chapter 17. Housing authorities may take into account the interim nature of a placement when assessing whether or not it is suitable; as accommodation may be suitable for a few days or weeks that would not be suitable for a longer term placement.

15.18 The applicant does not have the right to ask for a statutory review under section 202 of the housing authority's decision as to the suitability of interim accommodation, but housing authorities are reminded that such decisions could be subject to judicial review.

Ending interim accommodation arrangements

15.19 When a housing authority is satisfied that they are under no further duty to secure interim accommodation or where this duty has ended, the housing authority will need to terminate the applicant's right of occupation. In the first instance, a housing authority should look to the terms of the licence or tenancy under which interim accommodation has been provided to establish the length of the notice period required.

15.20 Interim accommodation is usually provided under licences excluded from the requirement to issue 4 weeks written notice provided by the Protection from Eviction Act 1977. The courts have applied this principle in cases where the accommodation provided was B&B accommodation in a hotel, and where it was a self-contained flat. Consequently, housing authorities are required only to provide an applicant with reasonable notice to vacate the accommodation, and do not need to apply for a possession order from the court. However, housing authorities are public bodies and so must act reasonably by giving the applicant at least some opportunity to find alternative accommodation before the interim accommodation is terminated. What is considered 'reasonable notice' would depend on the facts of the case, taking into account the circumstances of the applicant and allowing time for them to consider whether to request a review of the decision.

15.21 In cases involving applicants who have children under 18 where the housing authority have reason to believe that the applicant may be ineligible for assistance or may be homeless intentionally, the housing authority must, subject to the applicant's consent, alert the children's services authority to the case. A referral to the children's services authority may also be made without the applicant's consent where there are safeguarding concerns, in accordance with local procedures.

Refusal or loss of interim accommodation

15.22 Where an applicant rejects an offer of interim accommodation (or accepts and moves into the interim accommodation and then later rejects it), this will bring the housing authority's interim accommodation duty to an end – unless it is reactivated by any change of circumstances. Note, however, that an applicant's rejection of interim accommodation does not end other duties that the housing authority may owe under Part 7.

Discretionary powers to secure accommodation

15.23 Housing authorities have powers to secure accommodation for certain applicants who request a review of certain decisions on their case, and to certain applicants requesting accommodation pending determination of a county court appeal.

15.24 The fact that a housing authority has decided that an applicant is **not eligible** for housing assistance under Part 7 does not preclude it from exercising its powers to secure accommodation pending a review or appeal. However, housing authorities should note that section 54 of, and schedule 3 to, the Nationality, Immigration and Asylum Act 2002 prevent them from exercising their powers to accommodate an applicant pending a review or appeal to the county court, where the applicant is a person who falls within one of a number of classes of person specified in schedule 3 unless there would otherwise be a breach of the person's rights under the European Court of Human Rights or rights under EU Treaties (see paragraph 7.22). For further guidance on eligibility see Chapter 7.

Powers to accommodate pending a review

15.25 Under section 202, applicants have the right to ask for a review of a housing authority's decision on a number of issues relating to their case, and may also request that accommodation is secured for them pending a decision on the review. For further guidance on reviews see Chapter 19. Housing authorities have powers to accommodate applicants pending a decision on reviews under section 188(3), section 199A(6) and section 200(5) of the 1996 Act.

15.26 In considering whether to secure accommodation pending review housing authorities will need to balance the objective of maintaining fairness between homeless persons in circumstances where they have decided that no duty is owed to them, against proper consideration of the possibility that the applicant might be right. Housing authorities should consider the following, along with any other relevant factors:

(a) the merits of the applicant's case that the original decision was flawed and the extent to which it can properly be said that the decision was one which was either contrary to the apparent merits or was one which involved a very fine balance of judgment;

(b) whether any new material, information or argument has been put to them which could alter the original decision; and,

(c) the personal circumstances of the applicant and the consequences to them of a decision not to exercise the discretion to accommodate.

15.27 Where an applicant is refused accommodation pending a review, they may seek to challenge the decision through judicial review.

Power to accommodate pending an appeal to the county court

15.28 Where an applicant is dissatisfied with a housing authority's section 202 review decision or are not notified of the review decision within the proper time limits, an applicant has the right to appeal to the county court on a point of law arising from the review decision or original homelessness decision. For further guidance on reviews see Chapter 19. Under section 204(4), housing authorities have the power to accommodate certain applicants:

(a) during the period for making an appeal against their decision; and,

(b) if an appeal is brought, until it and any subsequent appeals are finally determined.

15.29 This power may be exercised where the housing authority was previously under a duty to secure accommodation for the applicant's occupation under section 188, section 190, section 199A or section 200; and may be exercised whether or not the housing authority has exercised its powers to accommodate the applicant pending review.

15.30 In deciding whether to exercise this power, housing authorities will need to adopt the same approach, and consider the same factors, as for a decision whether to exercise their power to accommodate pending a review (see paragraph 15.26).

15.31 Under section 204A, applicants have a right to appeal to the county court against decisions on the use of the section 204(4) power to accommodate. This enables an appeal against decisions not to secure accommodation for them pending their main appeal, or to stop securing accommodation, or to secure accommodation for only a limited period before final determination of the main appeal by the county court).

15.32 In deciding a section 204A appeal, if the court quashes the decision of the housing authority, it may order the authority to accommodate the applicant, but only where it is satisfied that failure to do so would substantially prejudice the applicant's ability to pursue the main appeal on the homelessness decision. For further guidance on reviews see Chapter 19.

Powers to secure accommodation to prevent or relieve homelessness

15.33 Housing authorities have duties to help prevent and relieve homelessness for eligible applicants who are threatened with becoming homelessness within 56 days, or are homeless. The section 195(2) prevention duty requires authorities to take reasonable steps to help the applicant to secure that accommodation does not cease to be available to them, and the relief duty requires housing authorities to take reasonable steps to help the applicant to secure that suitable accommodation becomes available to them for at least 6 months. For further guidance on the prevention duty see Chapter 12 and for further guidance on the relief duty see Chapter 13.

15.34 Section 205(3) of the 1996 Act enables housing authorities to discharge the section 189B(2) relief and/or section 195(2) prevention duties by securing accommodation for an applicant, where it decides to do so. The power to secure accommodation to applicants to prevent or relieve homelessness, regardless of priority need status, provides more flexibility to pursue appropriate housing options for applicants.

15.35 Housing authorities might use the section 205(3) power to deliver accommodation services for groups that are at higher risk of homelessness, for example young people with low incomes. The power might also be used to provide additional help to those least able to secure accommodation directly from a private landlord, such as people with an offending history or people with a mental health problem. Housing authorities will wish to consider local priorities, needs and resources when considering how the power might best be utilised in their district.

Section 193C(4): duty to accommodate applicants who have deliberately and unreasonably refused to co-operate pending final offer

15.36 Applicants who have priority need but are no longer owed a section 189B relief duty following service of a section 193B notice due to their deliberate and unreasonable refusal to co-operate will not be owed the section 193 main housing duty but will be owed an accommodation duty under section 193C(4).

15.37 This section 193C(4) duty ends if the applicant accepts or refuses a final accommodation offer or a final Part 6 offer. A 'final accommodation offer' is an offer of an assured shorthold tenancy made by a private landlord with the approval of the housing authority, with a view to bringing the section 193C(4) duty to an end. The offer must be of a fixed term tenancy (within the meaning of Part 1 of the Housing Act 1988) of at least 6 months duration, and the accommodation must be suitable for the applicant. A 'final Part 6 offer' is a suitable housing allocation (under Part 6 of the 1996 Act) made in writing, and which states that it is a final offer for the purposes of this section. A housing authority must not approve a final accommodation offer or make a final Part 6 offer if the applicant has a contractual obligation in respect of their existing accommodation which they are unable to bring to an end before being required to take up the offer. For further guidance on suitability see Chapter 17.

15.38 The section 193C(4) duty will also end if the applicant:

(a) ceases to be eligible for assistance;

(b) becomes homeless intentionally from the accommodation provided under section 193C(4);

(c) accepts an offer of an assured tenancy from a private landlord; or,

(d) voluntarily ceases to occupy as their only or principal home, the accommodation provided.

Duty to secure accommodation under the section 193(2) 'main housing duty'

15.39 Where an applicant is unintentionally homeless, eligible for assistance and has a priority need for accommodation, the housing authority has a duty under section 193(2) to secure that accommodation is available for their occupation (unless it refers the application to another housing authority under section 198). This is commonly known as 'the main housing duty'. **However, the main housing duty will not be owed to an applicant who has turned down a suitable final accommodation offer or Part 6 offer made during the section 189B(2) relief stage, or has been given notice under section 193B(2) due to their deliberate and unreasonable refusal to co-operate.** For further guidance on deliberate and unreasonable refusal to co-operate see Chapter 14.

15.40 The accommodation secured must be available for occupation by the applicant together with any other person who normally resides with them as a member of their family, or any other person who might reasonably be expected to reside with them. It must be suitable for their occupation. For further guidance on suitability see Chapter 17.

15.41 The housing authority will cease to be subject to the duty under section 193(2) (the main housing duty) in the following circumstances:

(a) the applicant **accepts a suitable offer of accommodation under Part 6** (an allocation of social housing) (section 193(6)(c)). This would include an offer of an assured tenancy of a private registered provider property via the housing authority's allocation scheme;

(b) the applicant **accepts an offer of an assured tenancy** (other than an assured shorthold tenancy) from a private landlord (section 193(6)(cc)). This could include an offer of an assured tenancy made by a private registered provider;

(c) the applicant **accepts or refuses a private rented sector offer – an offer of an assured shorthold tenancy of at least 12 months made by a private landlord (section 193(7AA))**. For this to be the case the applicant must have been informed in writing of the possible consequences of refusing or accepting the offer, their right to request a review of the suitability of the accommodation, and the duties that would be owed to them on re-application if they became unintentionally homeless from the accommodation within 2 years of accepting the offer;

(d) the applicant **refuses a final offer of accommodation under Part 6** (an allocation of social housing). The main housing duty does not end unless the applicant is informed of the possible consequences of refusal and of their right to ask for a review of the suitability of the accommodation (section 193(7)), the offer is made in writing and states that it is a final offer (section 193(7A)), and the housing authority is satisfied that the accommodation is suitable and that it would be reasonable for the applicant to accept it (section 193(7F));

(e) the applicant **refuses an offer of temporary accommodation** which the housing authority is satisfied is suitable for the applicant (section 193(5)). For this to be the case the applicant must have been informed of the possible consequences of refusal and of their right to ask for a review of the suitability of the accommodation, and have been notified by the housing authority that it regards itself as having discharged its duty.

15.42 The main housing duty will also end if the applicant:

(a) **ceases to be eligible** for assistance as defined in section 185 of the 1996 Act;

(b) **becomes homeless intentionally** from accommodation made available to them under section 193. For further guidance on intentional homelessness see Chapter 9;

(c) voluntarily **ceases to occupy** as their principal home the accommodation made available under section 193.

15.43 In restricted cases housing authorities should, as far as is reasonably practicable, bring the section 193(2) duty to an end through the offer of a assured shorthold tenancy of at least 12 months duration with a private landlord (section 193(7AD)). The applicant will not be owed a section 195A duty if they re-apply as unintentionally homeless within 2 years of accepting the offer. For further guidance on restricted cases see Chapter 7.

Pre-Localism Act 2011 cases

15.44 In circumstances where the housing authority accepted a section 193(2) duty on an application made before 9 November 2012, that duty cannot be brought to an end through an offer of private rented accommodation unless that offer meets the requirements of 'a qualifying offer'.

15.45 A qualifying offer must be of a fixed-term tenancy of at least 12 months duration and be accompanied by a written statement that states the term of the tenancy being offered and explains in ordinary language that there is no obligation on the applicant to accept the offer, but if the offer is accepted the housing authority will cease to be subject to the section 193 duty. The applicant must have signed a statement acknowledging that he or she has understood the written statement accompanying the offer.

Making suitable offers

15.46 The Secretary of State recommends that applicants are given the chance to view accommodation that is offered on anything other than an interim basis, before being required to decide whether they accept or refuse an offer, and before being required to sign any written agreement relating to the accommodation (e.g. a tenancy agreement). Where housing authorities are making offers of accommodation outside their district they should take particular care to ensure that applicants have sufficient information about the location of the accommodation and the services that would be available to them there and that applicants are given a reasonable amount of time to consider the offer made before reaching a decision. Under section 202(1A), an applicant who is offered accommodation can request a review of its suitability whether or not they have accepted the offer. For further guidance on suitability see Chapter 17 and for further guidance on reviews see Chapter 19.

15.47 Where an applicant has contractual or other obligations in respect of their existing accommodation (e.g. a tenancy agreement or lease), the housing authority can only reasonably expect an offer to be taken up if the applicant is able to bring those obligations to an end before being required to take up the offer (section 193(8)).

15.48 Housing authorities should allow applicants a reasonable period for considering offers of accommodation that will bring the main housing duty to an end whether accepted or refused. There is no set reasonable period; some applicants may require longer than others depending on their circumstances, whether they wish to seek advice in making their decision and whether they are already familiar with the property or locality in question. Longer periods may be required where the applicant is in hospital or temporarily absent from the district. In deciding what a reasonable period is, housing authorities must take into account the applicant's circumstances.

15.49 For further guidance on accommodation arrangements see:

- Chapter 16: Securing accommodation
- Chapter 17: Suitability of accommodation

CHAPTER 16
Securing accommodation

Guidance on the various ways in which housing authorities can secure suitable accommodation for applicants.

16.1 This chapter provides guidance on the ways in which housing authorities can ensure that suitable accommodation is available for applicants.

Securing and helping to secure accommodation

16.2 Housing authorities have various duties and powers to secure accommodation for an applicant, which require them to directly let or ensure a property owned by another landlord is made available to the applicant. The Homelessness Reduction Act 2017 introduced the duty to 'help to secure' accommodation for all applicants who are eligible for assistance and threatened with homelessness or homeless.

16.3 'Helping to secure' does not mean that the housing authority has a duty to directly find and secure the accommodation, but involves them working with applicants to agree (where possible) reasonable steps that the applicant and the housing authority can take to identify and secure suitable accommodation.

16.4 In providing 'help to secure', the housing authority is able to provide support and advice to households who are taking some responsibility for securing their own accommodation. This approach is intended to increase choice and control for applicants and allow the housing authority to help to resolve particular problems rather than direct resources at securing accommodation for households regardless of what assistance they need. It remains open to the housing authority to secure accommodation for eligible applicants where appropriate.

General considerations

16.5 Section 206(1) provides that a housing authority may discharge its housing functions under Part 7 in the following ways:

(a) by securing that suitable accommodation provided by them is available for the applicant;
(b) by securing that the applicant obtains suitable accommodation from some other person; or,
(c) by giving the applicant such advice and assistance as will secure that suitable accommodation is available from some other person.

16.6 Accommodation secured must be available and suitable for occupation by the applicant and any other person who normally resides with them as a member of their family, or any other person who might reasonably be expected to reside with them. Section 208(1) requires housing authorities to secure accommodation within their district, in so far as is reasonably practicable. For further guidance on suitability of accommodation see Chapter 17.

16.7 In deciding what accommodation is to be secured, housing authorities will need to consider whether the applicant has any support needs, as identified in their (section 189A) personalised housing plan, and taking in to account any additional information available from health or social care services, or from other agencies providing services to them.

16.8 Where a housing authority has a duty under section 193(2) to secure accommodation for an applicant it should consider, where availability of suitable housing allows, securing settled (rather than temporary) accommodation that will bring the duty to an end in the immediate or short term.

16.9 Housing authorities may secure accommodation by giving advice and assistance to an applicant that will secure that accommodation becomes available for them from another person (section 206(1)(c)). However, where an authority has a duty to secure accommodation, they will need to ensure that the advice and assistance provided results in suitable accommodation actually being secured. Merely assisting the applicant in any efforts that they might make to find accommodation would not be sufficient if suitable accommodation did not actually become available.

Local authority owned accommodation

16.10 Housing authorities may secure temporary accommodation through its own stock (i.e. held under Part 2 of the Housing Act 1985). In considering whether to do so authorities will need to balance the requirements of applicants owed a duty under Part 7 against the need to provide accommodation for others who have reasonable preference for an allocation under Part 6 of the 1996 Act.

16.11 Paragraph 4 of Schedule 1 to the Housing Act 1985 provides that a tenancy granted by a housing authority in pursuance of any function under Part 7 is not a secure tenancy unless the housing authority notifies the tenant that it is such. Housing authorities are reminded that the allocation of secure and introductory tenancies must be made in accordance with their allocation scheme framed under the provisions of Part 6.

Private registered provider owned accommodation

16.12 Under section 213 of the 1996 Act, where requested by a housing authority, a private registered provider must assist the housing authority in carrying out their duties under the homelessness legislation by co-operating with them as far as is reasonable in the circumstances. Private registered providers have a duty under the 1996 Act to co-operate with housing authorities in exercising their homelessness functions. Private registered providers are subject to the Regulator of Social Housing's[3] Regulatory Standards, in particular the expectation that they will co-operate with local authorities' strategic housing function, set out in the Tenancy and Home and Community Standards.

Co-operation between social housing providers

16.13 Under section 213 other social landlords have a duty to co-operate, as far as is reasonable in the circumstances, with a housing authority in carrying out their housing functions under Part 7 of the 1996 Act, if asked to do so.

16.14 Housing authorities may be able to assist one another by providing temporary or settled accommodation for homeless applicants. Under section 213(1), where one housing authority requests another to help them discharge a function under Part 7, the other housing authority must co-operate in providing such assistance as far as is reasonable in the circumstances.

16.15 This could be particularly appropriate in the case of applicants who would be at risk of violence or serious harassment in the district of the housing authority to whom they have applied for assistance. Other housing authorities may also be able to provide accommodation in cases where the applicant has special housing needs and the other housing authority has accommodation available which is appropriate to those needs. Housing authorities are encouraged to consider entering into reciprocal and co-operative arrangements where these might prove beneficial to authorities and to applicants.

Privately owned accommodation

16.16 Housing authorities may seek the assistance of private landlords in providing suitable accommodation direct to applicants, as well as engaging

3 The regulation of social housing is the responsibility of the Regulation Committee, a statutory committee of the Homes and Communities Agency (HCA). The organisation refers to itself as the Regulator of Social Housing in undertaking the functions of the Regulation Committee. References in any enactment or instrument to the Regulator of Social Housing are references to the HCA acting through the Regulation Committee. Homes England is the trading name of the HCA's non-regulation functions.

them in schemes that enable applicants to find their own private rented accommodation.

16.17 A general consent under section 25 of the Local Government Act 1988 (The general consent under section 25 of the Local Government Act 1988 for financial assistance to any person 2010) allows housing authorities to provide financial assistance to private landlords in order to secure accommodation for people who are homeless or at risk of homelessness. This could involve, for example, making small one-off grants (finders' fees) to landlords to encourage them to let dwellings to households owed a homelessness duty; paying rent deposits or indemnities to ensure accommodation is secured for such households; and making one-off grant payments which would prevent an eviction. There is no limit set on the amount of financial assistance that can be provided, however housing authorities are obliged to act reasonably and in accordance with their fiduciary duty to local tax and rent payers.

Private rented sector offers

16.18 Private rented accommodation can be used to prevent or relieve homelessness, or to bring the main housing duty (section 193) to an end, but in all cases enabling the applicant to exercise some choice over the accommodation offered to them is likely to increase the acceptance rate, and engage the cooperation of both applicants and landlords.

16.19 Housing authorities are encouraged to develop a private rented sector access scheme which provides opportunities for all applicants, including those who do not have a priority need, to access private rented accommodation. The level of help and support the authority is able to provide through such a scheme will vary to reflect local housing markets and available resources, but might include offers of bonds and guarantees, as well as payments towards deposits and incentives. Housing authorities will need to be mindful of the need to identify shared housing options for younger people, and will wish to work with landlords willing to provide suitable Houses in Multiple Occupation (HMOs).

16.20 Whilst housing authorities must ensure any accommodation offered to homeless applicants is suitable, there are additional suitability requirements that apply to private rented accommodation offered under section 193(7)(F) to end the main housing duty, or secured for applicants in priority need to prevent or relieve their homelessness. Private rented sector accommodation must meet the requirements of Article 3 if it is to be considered suitable when offered:

(a) to bring to an end the section 193(2) main housing duty (section 193(7F));

(b) as a final accommodation offer made in the 189B relief stage (sections 193A(6) and 193C(9)); or,

(c) to an applicant who has priority need, in order to prevent or relieve their homelessness.

For further guidance on the suitability of private rented sector offers see Chapter 17.

16.21 Housing authorities may make Discretionary Housing Payments (DHP) to help an applicant secure accommodation and to meet a shortfall between the rent and the amount of Housing Benefit or Universal Credit payable to them. However, where they do this housing authorities should take into account how sustainable any arrangement will be in the longer term when considering suitability of accommodation. Payments of DHP are governed by the Discretionary Financial Assistance Regulations 2001.

16.22 Housing authorities are encouraged to secure assured shorthold tenancies of at least 12 months wherever possible, and if a private rented sector offer is being made to end the section 193 duty it must always be for a tenancy of at least 12 months and comply with other requirements of section 193(7AA).

Temporary accommodation provided by a private landlord

16.23 Section 209 governs security of tenure where a private landlord provides accommodation to assist a housing authority to discharge an interim duty. Any such accommodation is exempt from statutory security of tenure until 12 months from the date on which the applicant is notified of the authority's decision under section 184(3) or section 198(5) or from the date on which the applicant is notified of the decision on any review under section 202 or an appeal under section 204, unless the landlord notifies the applicant that the tenancy is an assured or assured shorthold tenancy.

16.24 Where a private landlord or private registered provider lets accommodation directly to an applicant to assist a housing authority to discharge any other homelessness duty, the tenancy granted will be an assured shorthold tenancy unless the tenant is notified that it is to be regarded as an assured tenancy.

Accommodation leased from a private landlord

16.25 Accommodation leased from a private landlord can provide housing authorities with a source of good quality, self-contained accommodation which can be let to applicants. When entering into leases, as when borrowing, local authority capital finance rules require authorities to be satisfied that the associated liabilities are affordable.

16.26 Housing authorities may wish to consider contracting with private registered providers for assistance in discharging their housing functions under arrangements whereby the private registered provider leases and/or manages accommodation owned by private landlords, which can be let to households to prevent or relieve homelessness or as temporary accommodation. A general consent under section 25 of the Local Government Act 1988 (The general consent under section 25 of the Local Government Act 1988 for financial assistance to registered social landlords or to private landlords to relieve or prevent homelessness 2010) allows housing authorities to provide private registered providers with financial assistance in connection with such arrangements. Housing authorities must reserve the right to terminate such agreements, without penalty, after 3 years.

16.27 Housing authorities are encouraged to test approaches that would enable temporary accommodation to become settled accommodation and so reduce the uncertainty and lack of security that households in temporary accommodation can face. This could include converting private sector leased accommodation used as temporary accommodation into settled housing when the lease comes to an end. If the accommodation is suitable for the households needs, and the landlord would be prepared to let directly to them, the housing authority may wish to arrange for a section 193(7AA) private rented sector offer to end the section 193(2) duty. For further guidance on accommodation duties see Chapter 15. Similarly, where a private registered provider holds the lease of accommodation owned by a private sector landlord, the accommodation might also be offered to the applicant (if suitable) as a section 193(7AA) offer to end the main housing duty (section 193(2)).

16.28 When considering conversion of temporary into settled accommodation, the interests and needs of the household, and the affordability of the new letting arrangement for the applicant, should be taken into account before any offer is made.

Bed and breakfast accommodation

16.29 Bed and breakfast (B&B) is defined in the Homelessness Suitability Order 2003 as a form of privately owned accommodation in which residents share facilities such as kitchens, bathrooms and/or toilets, and is usually paid for on a nightly basis.

16.30 Housing authorities must not use B&B to accommodate families with children or pregnant women except where there is no alternative available, and then for a maximum period not exceeding 6 weeks. Guidance states that B&B type accommodation is never suitable for 16–17 year olds.

Privately owned 'annexe' accommodation

16.31 Some housing authorities access the private market to secure self-contained accommodation (sometimes referred to as 'annexe' accommodation) for households, which is typically paid for on a nightly basis and typically involves family members sharing a large room with one another. This type of accommodation is unlikely to be suitable for families on anything but a short-term basis.

Lodgings

16.32 Lodgings provided by householders may be suitable for some applicants. Housing authorities may wish to establish a network of such landlords in their district, and might consider operating supported lodgings schemes for people with support needs, for example young people needing to gain skills for living independently.

Hostels and supported housing

16.33 Hostels and supported housing schemes may be owned and managed by local authorities, private registered providers, charities or private landlords and may be available through direct access, local referral arrangements or as direct temporary accommodation placements. The quality of accommodation provided within hostels varies considerably, and authorities should be particularly careful when securing or helping to secure accommodation with non-commissioned providers of hostel places that are not monitored or quality assessed.

16.34 Hostel accommodation typically involves some sharing of facilities, and in some hostels this includes sharing bedrooms as well as kitchens and bathing facilities.

16.35 Where hostel accommodation is used to accommodate vulnerable young people or families with children, the Secretary of State considers that it would be inappropriate to accommodate these groups alongside vulnerable adults. Housing authorities should be alert to the risks that may be associated with placing families with children, and young people, in mixed hostel settings, and should avoid doing so in circumstances where the housing authority does not have control over all of the placements.

16.36 Hostels can offer short-term accommodation to people who are experiencing homelessness, and housing authorities will wish to ensure they make the most effective use of services available, and that accommodation is suitable for the applicants placed there. Hostel accommodation that involves families or pregnant women sharing facilities with other households will not be suitable for longer-term placements.

16.37 Supported housing is usually, although not exclusively, commissioned by a local authority or other public body in order to meet the accommodation and support needs of particular groups who require such assistance. It can provide a highly valuable source of accommodation particularly for young people and for adults who need a period of stability and individual support to help them to prepare to live independently.

16.38 Housing authorities that have commissioned supported housing services will wish to keep the uptake, utilisation and move-on arrangements for these services under regular review to ensure that they meet local needs and that resources are maximised. In two-tier local authority areas, housing authorities should ensure that evidence of homelessness and support needs is available and informs commissioning priorities at upper tier level, and that there is collaboration across the districts to ensure efficient referral and move on from supported housing services. For further guidance on homelessness strategies and reviews see Chapter 2.

16.39 A placement in a short-stay hostel or supported housing scheme will be only be sufficient to meet a housing authority's duties to prevent or relieve homelessness where there is a planned pathway to ensure that accommodation will continue to be available to them for at least 6 months.

Refuges for victims of domestic abuse

16.40 Housing authorities should develop close links with refuges within their district, and neighbouring districts, to ensure they have access to emergency accommodation for applicants who are fleeing domestic or other violence or who are at risk of such violence. Refuge placements will usually require the applicant to speak directly to the service provider, and to indicate that they want and need refuge accommodation.

16.41 Housing authorities should recognise that placing an applicant in a refuge will generally be on a short-term basis, except where a longer period of support is required to enable applicants to prepare to manage independently. Housing authorities should work together with refuge providers to ensure efficient and planned move on from refuge provision, to maximise the use of refuge spaces. For further guidance on domestic abuse see Chapter 21.

Housing First accommodation

16.42 Housing First is an approach to ending long term homelessness for people with complex needs. It has been developed specifically to meet the needs of the most challenging client groups who have previously been unable to sustain housing. Although there are some variations in approach between different providers of Housing First, the central principles include providing a home without any requirement to engage with services, flexible support available for as long as needed, enabling individuals to have choice and control, and to reduce harm.

Caravans, houseboats and other moveable accommodation

16.43 Under section 175(2) applicants are homeless if the accommodation available for their occupation is a caravan, houseboat, or other movable structure and they do not have a place where they are entitled, or permitted, to put it and live in it. If a duty to secure accommodation arises in such cases, the housing authority is not required to make equivalent accommodation available (or provide a site or berth for the applicant's own accommodation). However, the housing authority must consider whether such options are reasonably available, particularly where this would provide the most suitable solution to the applicant's accommodation needs.

16.44 The circumstances described in paragraph 16.43 will be particularly relevant in the case of Gypsies and Travellers. Where a duty to secure accommodation arises but an appropriate site is not immediately available, the housing authority may need to provide an alternative temporary solution until a suitable site, or some other suitable option, becomes available. Some Gypsies and Travellers may have a cultural aversion to the prospect of 'bricks and mortar' accommodation. In such cases, the housing authority should seek to provide an alternative solution. However, where the housing authority is satisfied that there is no prospect of a suitable site for the time being, there may be no alternative solution. Housing authorities must give consideration to the needs and lifestyle of applicants who are Gypsies and Travellers when considering their application and how best to discharge a duty to secure suitable accommodation, in line with their obligations to act consistently with the Human Rights Act 1998, and in particular the right to respect for private life, family and the home; as well as their duties under section 149 of the Equality Act 2010.

16.45 Although mobile homes may sometimes provide emergency or short-term accommodation for applicants who do not usually occupy movable accommodation, housing authorities will need to be satisfied that the accommodation is suitable for the applicant and their household, paying particular regard to their needs, requirements and circumstances and the conditions and facilities on the site. Caravans designed primarily for short-term holiday use should not be regarded as suitable as temporary accommodation for applicants.

Tenancies for minors

16.46 There are legal complications associated with the grant of a tenancy to a minor because a minor cannot hold a legal estate in land. In most cases a 16–17 year old who has become homeless will be accommodated under section 20 of the Children Act 1989 and/or through provision of supported housing or supported lodgings, and will not be ready to manage their own tenancy until they reach adulthood. If housing authorities are securing accommodation for 16–17 year olds within social housing or private rented stock there will need to be sufficient support in place, and a license agreement may be more appropriate depending on the arrangements in place. Where a minor is considered able to manage a tenancy independently this could be granted to a minor and held on trust. Authorities will need to take into account how the terms of any tenancy will be enforced in the event that there is a breach in tenancy conditions.

CHAPTER 17
Suitability of accommodation

Guidance on housing authority duties to ensure that accommodation secured for homeless applicants is suitable.

17.1 This chapter provides guidance on the factors to be taken into account when determining the suitability of accommodation secured and helped to secure under the 1996 Act. This includes (temporary) accommodation secured under interim accommodation duties or the main housing duty as well as settled accommodation which would bring the prevention, relief or main housing duty to an end.

17.2 Section 206 provides that where a housing authority discharges its functions to secure that accommodation is available for an applicant the accommodation must be suitable. This applies in respect of all powers and duties to secure accommodation under Part 7, including interim duties. The accommodation must be suitable in relation to the applicant and to all members of their household who normally reside with them, or who might reasonably be expected to reside with them.

17.3 Section 210 of the 1996 Act sets out matters a housing authority must have regard to when determining suitability. Section 210(2) provides for the Secretary of State to specify by order the circumstances in which accommodation is or is not to be regarded as suitable for someone, and matters to be taken into account or disregarded in determining whether accommodation is suitable.

17.4 Space and arrangement will be key factors in determining the suitability of accommodation. However, consideration of whether accommodation is suitable will require an assessment of all aspects of the accommodation in the light of the relevant needs, requirements and circumstances of the homeless person and their household. The location of the accommodation will always be a relevant factor.

17.5 Housing authorities will need to consider carefully the suitability of accommodation for households with particular medical and/or physical needs. Physical access to and around the home, space, bathroom and kitchen facilities, access to a garden and modifications to assist people with sensory loss as well as mobility needs are all factors which might need to be taken into account.

17.6 Account will need to be taken of any social considerations relating to the applicant and their household that might affect the suitability of accommodation, including any risk of violence, racial or other harassment in a particular locality. Where domestic violence or abuse is involved and the applicant is not able to stay in the current home, housing authorities may need to consider the need for alternative accommodation whose location can be kept a secret and which has security measures and staffing to protect the occupants.

17.7 Accommodation that is suitable for a short period, for example accommodation used to discharge an interim duty pending inquiries under section 188, may not necessarily be suitable for a longer period, for example to discharge a duty under section 193(2).

17.8 Housing authorities have a continuing obligation to keep the suitability of accommodation under review, and to respond to any relevant change in circumstances which may affect suitability, until such time as the accommodation duty is brought to an end.

17.9 Housing authorities are required to assess whether accommodation is suitable for each household individually, and case records should demonstrate that they have taken the statutory requirements into account in securing the accommodation.

Standards of accommodation

17.10 Section 210(1) requires a housing authority to have regard to the following provisions when assessing the suitability of accommodation for an applicant:

(a) Parts 9 and 10 of the Housing Act 1985 (the '1985 Act') (slum clearance and overcrowding); and,

(b) Parts 1 to 4 of the Housing Act 2004 (the '2004 Act') (housing conditions, licensing of houses in multiple occupation, selective licensing of other residential accommodation, additional control provisions in relation to residential accommodation).

Suitability of private rented accommodation

17.11 Article 3 of the Homelessness (Suitability of Accommodation) (England) Order 2012 concerns the suitability of privately rented accommodation offered to certain applicants who are homeless or threatened with homelessness.

17.12 Private rented sector accommodation must meet the requirements of Article 3 if it is to be considered suitable when offered:

(a) to bring to an end the section 193(2) main housing duty (section 193(7F));

(b) as a final accommodation offer made in the 189B relief stage (sections 193A(6) and 193C(9)); or,

(c) to an applicant who has priority need, in order to prevent or relieve their homelessness.

17.13 A private rented property must not be regarded as suitable if the housing authority are of the view any of the following apply:

(a) it is not in a reasonable physical condition;

(b) electrical equipment supplied with the accommodation does not meet the requirements of Schedule 1 to the Electrical Equipment (Safety) Regulations 2016;

(c) the landlord has not taken reasonable fire safety precautions with the accommodation and any furnishings supplied with it;

(d) the landlord has not taken reasonable precautions to prevent the possibility of carbon monoxide poisoning in the accommodation (see 17.20 below);

(e) the landlord is not a fit and proper person to act in the capacity of landlord (see 17.21 below).

17.14 A private rented property must not be regarded as suitable if any of the following apply:

(a) it is a house in multiple occupation subject to licensing under section 55 of the Housing Act 2004 and is not licensed;

(b) it is subject to additional licensing under section 56 of the Housing Act 2004 and is not licensed;

(c) it forms part of residential property which does not have a valid Energy Performance Certificate as required by the Energy Performance of Buildings (England and Wales) Regulations 2012;

(d) it is or forms part of relevant premises which do not have a current gas safety record in accordance with regulation 36 of the Gas Safety (Installation and Use) Regulations 1998;

(e) the landlord has not provided a written tenancy agreement to the housing authority which the landlord proposes to use for the purposes of a private rented sector offer, and which the housing authority considers to be adequate. It is expected that the housing authority should review the tenancy agreement to ensure that it sets out, ideally in a clear and comprehensible way, the tenant's obligations, for example a clear statement of the rent and other charges, and the responsibilities of the landlord, but does not contain unfair or unreasonable terms, such as call-out charges for repairs or professional cleaning at the end of the tenancy.

17.15 The particular requirements of Article 3 do not apply to accommodation secured for households that do not have priority need, or to accommodation that the authority helped the applicant to secure (for example through a bond guarantee or financial assistance) but which the applicant identified themselves. However, the Secretary of State expects housing authorities to make reasonable efforts to ensure private rented accommodation secured for applicants who do not have priority need is safe, and in reasonable condition; and that all applicants looking for their own accommodation have sufficient guidance to enable them to consider standards.

17.16 To determine whether or not accommodation meets the requirements set out in Article 3 housing authorities are advised to ensure it is visited by a local authority officer or someone acting on their behalf able to carry out an inspection. Attention should be paid to signs of damp or mould and indications that the property would be cold as well as to a visual check made of electrical installations and equipment (for example; looking for loose wiring, cracked or broken electrical sockets, light switches that do not work and appliances which do not appear to have been safety tested).

Additional health and safety requirements

17.17 The Regulatory Reform (Fire Safety) Order 2005 applies to the common or shared parts of multi occupied residential buildings. It places a duty on landlords, owners or managing agents to carry out a fire risk assessment of the common parts and implement and maintain appropriate and adequate fire safety measures to manage the risk that lives could be lost in a fire. As part of their responsibilities, landlords should put in place appropriate management and maintenance systems to ensure any fire safety equipment or equipment which may represent a fire hazard, is maintained in good working order, and in accordance with the manufacturers' instructions. Landlords are also required to ensure that furniture and furnishings supplied must comply with the Furniture and Furnishings (Fire) (Safety) Regulations 1988 (as amended).

17.18 Housing authorities and fire and rescue authorities should work together to ensure the safety of domestic premises including the provision of fire safety advice to households. Housing authorities will need to satisfy themselves that these regulations have been adhered to.

17.19 Housing authorities are asked to satisfy themselves that there are reasonable precautions to prevent the possibility of carbon monoxide poisoning in the accommodation, where such a risk exists. Since 2015, private sector landlords have been required to have at least one smoke alarm installed on every storey of their properties and a carbon monoxide alarm in any room containing a solid fuel burning appliance (for example a coal fire or wood burning stove). After that, the landlord must make sure the alarms are in working order at the start of each new tenancy.

Fit and proper landlords

17.20 Housing authorities must satisfy themselves that landlords are fit and proper people to act in the capacity of a landlord. This assessment involves consideration if the landlord has:

(a) committed any offences involving fraud or other dishonesty, violence or illegal drugs, or that are listed in Schedule 3 to the Sexual Offences Act 2003 (offences attracting notification requirements);

(b) practised unlawful discrimination on grounds of sex, race, age, disability, marriage or civil partnership, pregnancy or maternity, religion or belief, sexual orientation, gender identity or gender reassignment in, or in connection with, the carrying on of any business;

(c) contravened any provision of the law relating to housing (including landlord or tenant law); or,

(d) acted otherwise than in accordance with any applicable code of practice for the management of a house in multiple occupation, approved under section 233 of the Housing Act 2004.

17.21 The Secretary of State recommends that when placing households outside of their district that the authority liaise with the receiving district to check whether that authority has taken any enforcement activity against the landlord. The Housing and Planning Act 2016 introduced a range of measures to tackle rogue landlords including a database of rogue landlords or letting agents who have been banned; convicted of certain offences; or received multiple civil penalties for housing offences. Housing authorities could check this database as part of their inquiries.

Tenancy deposit scheme

17.22 Whilst a local authority will not be able to check that a tenant's deposit has been placed in a tenancy deposit protection scheme prior to them taking the tenancy housing authorities should remind prospective landlords and tenants of their responsibilities in this area.

Housing Health and Safety Rating System (HHSRS)

17.23 Housing authorities are obliged under section 3 of the Housing Act 2004 to keep the housing conditions in their area under review with a view to identifying any action that may need to be taken by them under the Household Health and Safety Ratings System legislation (HHSRS).

17.24 When determining the suitability of accommodation secured under the homelessness legislation, housing authorities should, as a minimum, ensure that all accommodation is free of Category 1 hazards. In the case of an out of district placement it is the responsibility of the placing authority to ensure that accommodation is free of Category 1 hazards.

Overcrowding

17.25 Part 10 of the 1985 Act is intended to tackle the problems of overcrowding in dwellings. Section 324 provides a definition of overcrowding which in turn relies on the room standard specified in section 325 and the space standard in section 326. Housing authorities must be mindful of these provisions when securing or helping to secure accommodation for homeless applicants.

17.26 A room provided within an HMO may be defined as a 'dwelling' under Part 10 of the 1985 Act and the room and space standards will therefore apply. Housing authorities should also note that 'crowding and space' is one of the hazards assessed by the HHSRS. Any breach of the room and space standards under Part 10 is likely to constitute a Category 1 hazard.

Houses in Multiple Occupation (HMOs)

17.27 Housing authorities must have regard to regulations governing the required standards for any Houses in Multiple Occupation (HMO) that may be secured or helped to secure for an applicant.

17.28 A property is an HMO if it satisfies the conditions set out in sections 254(2) to (4), has been declared an HMO under section 255 or is a converted block of flats to which section 257 applies. Privately owned bed and breakfast or hostel accommodation that is used to accommodate a household pursuant to a homelessness function, and which is the household's main residence, will fall within this definition of an HMO.

17.29 A housing authority will have to be satisfied that an HMO is suitable for the number of households or occupants it is licensed for and meets statutory standards relating to shared amenities and facilities. These standards are set out in Schedule 3 to the Licensing and Management of Houses in Multiple Occupation and Other Houses (Miscellaneous Provisions) (England) Regulations 2006. These 'amenity standards' will run alongside the consideration of health and safety issues under HHSRS.

Bed and breakfast accommodation

17.30 Bed and breakfast (B&B) accommodation caters for very short-term stays only and affords residents only limited privacy, and may lack or require sharing of important amenities, such as cooking and laundry facilities. Wherever possible, housing authorities should avoid using B&B accommodation as accommodation for homeless applicants, unless, in the very limited circumstances where it is likely to be the case, it is the most appropriate option for the applicant.

17.31 Living in B&B accommodation can be particularly detrimental to the health and development of children. Under section 210(2), the Secretary of State has made the Homelessness (Suitability of Accommodation) (England) Order 2003 (the 2003 Order). The 2003 Order specifies that B&B accommodation is not to be regarded as suitable for applicants with family commitments provided with accommodation under Part 7.

17.32 Housing authorities should, therefore, use B&B accommodation to discharge a duty to secure accommodation for applicants with family commitments only as a last resort and then only for a maximum of 6 weeks. Applicants with family commitments means an applicant:

(a) who is pregnant;
(b) with whom a pregnant woman resides or might reasonably be expected to reside; or,
(c) with whom dependent children reside or might reasonably be expected to reside.

17.33 For the purpose of the 2003 Order, B&B accommodation means accommodation (whether or not breakfast is included):
(a) which is not separate and self-contained premises; and,
(b) in which any of the following amenities is shared by more than one household:
(i) a toilet;
(ii) personal washing facilities; or,
(iii) cooking facilities.

17.34 B&B accommodation does not include accommodation which is owned or managed by a housing authority, a private registered provider or a voluntary organisation as defined in section 180(3) of the 1996 Act.

17.35 The 2003 Order provides that if no alternative accommodation is available for the applicant the housing authority may accommodate the family in B&B for a period, or periods, not exceeding 6 weeks in result of a single homelessness application. Where B&B accommodation is secured for an applicant with family commitments, the Secretary of State considers that the authority should notify the applicant of the effect of the 2003 Order, and, in particular, that the authority will be unable to continue to secure B&B accommodation for such applicants any longer than 6 weeks, after which the authority must secure alternative, suitable accommodation.

17.36 When determining whether accommodation other than B&B accommodation is available for use, housing authorities will need to take into account, among other things, the cost to the authority of securing the accommodation, the affordability of the accommodation for the applicant and the location of the accommodation. A housing authority is under no obligation to include in its considerations accommodation which is to be allocated in accordance with its allocation scheme, published under section 167 of the 1996 Act.

17.37 If there is a significant change in an applicant's circumstances that would bring the applicant within the scope of the 2003 Order, the 6 week period should start from the date the authority was informed of the change of circumstances not the date the applicant was originally placed in B&B accommodation.

17.38 If the conditions for referring a case are met and another housing authority accepts responsibility for an applicant under section 200(4), any time spent in B&B accommodation before this acceptance should be disregarded in calculating the 6 week period.

17.39 B&B accommodation is not suitable for 16 and 17 year old applicants even on an emergency basis.

17.40 The Secretary of State considers that the limited circumstances in which B&B accommodation may provide suitable accommodation could include those where:
(a) emergency accommodation is required at very short notice (for example to discharge an interim duty to accommodate); or,
(b) there is simply no better alternative accommodation available and the use of B&B accommodation is necessary as a last resort.

17.41 The Secretary of State considers that where housing authorities are unable to avoid using B&B accommodation to accommodate applicants, they should ensure that such accommodation is of a good standard and is used for the shortest period possible.

Standards of B&B accommodation

17.42 Where B&B accommodation is used to accommodate an applicant and is their main residence, it falls within the definition of an HMO. Local authorities have a power under the 2004 Act to issue an HMO Declaration confirming HMO status where there is uncertainty about the status of a property.

17.43 The government recognises that living conditions in HMOs should not only be healthy and safe but should also provide acceptable, decent standards for people who may be unrelated to each other and who are sharing basic facilities. The government has set out in regulation the minimum 'amenity standards' required for a property to be granted an HMO licence. These standards will only apply to HMOs covered by mandatory licensing or those HMOs that will be subject to additional licensing, and will not apply to the majority of HMOs. However, housing authorities (or groups of authorities) can adopt their own local classification, amenity specification or minimum standards for B&B and other shared accommodation provided as temporary accommodation under Part 7.

Affordability

17.44 Under section 210(2), the Secretary of State has made the Homelessness (Suitability of Accommodation) Order 1996. The 1996 Order specifies that in determining whether it would be, or would have been, reasonable for a person to occupy accommodation and in determining whether accommodation is suitable a housing authority must take into account whether the accommodation is affordable by them, and in particular must take account of:

(a) the financial resources available to them (i.e. all forms of income), including, but not limited to:
   - (i) salary, fees and other remuneration (from such sources as investments, grants, pensions, tax credits etc.);
   - (ii) social security benefits
   - (iii) payments due under a court order for the making of periodical payments to a spouse or a former spouse, or to, or for the benefit of, a child;
   - (iv) payments of child support maintenance due under the Child Support Act 1991;
   - (v) pensions;
   - (vi) contributions to the costs in respect of the accommodation which are or were made or which might reasonably be expected to be, or have been, made by other members of their household (most members can be assumed to contribute, but the amount depends on various factors including their age and income);
   - (vii) financial assistance towards the costs in respect of the accommodation, including loans, provided by a local authority, voluntary organisation or other body;

(viii) benefits derived from a policy of insurance (such as cover against unemployment or sickness);

(b) savings and other capital sums which may be a source of income or might be available to meet accommodation expenses;

(c) the costs in respect of the accommodation, including, but not limited to:

(i) payments of, or by way of, rent (including rent default/property damage deposits);

(ii) payments in respect of a licence or permission to occupy the accommodation;

(iii) mortgage costs (including an assessment of entitlement to support for mortgage interest (SMI) in income support/income-based jobseeker's allowance/income-related employment and support allowance/universal credit);

(iv) payments of, or by way of, service charges (e.g. maintenance or other costs required as a condition of occupation of the accommodation);

(v) mooring charges payable for a houseboat;

(vi) where the accommodation is a caravan or a mobile home, payments in respect of the site on which it stands;

(vii) the amount of council tax payable in respect of the accommodation;

(viii) payments by way of deposit or security in respect of the accommodation;

(ix) payments required by an accommodation agency;

(d) payments which that person is required to make under a court order for the making of periodical payments to a spouse or former spouse, or to, or for the benefit of, a child and payments of child support maintenance required to be made under the Child Support Act 1991; and,

(e) other reasonable living expenses

17.45 Housing authorities will need to consider whether the applicant can afford the housing costs without being deprived of basic essentials such as food, clothing, heating, transport and other essentials specific to their circumstances. Housing costs should not be regarded as affordable if the applicant would be left with a residual income that is insufficient to meet these essential needs. Housing authorities may be guided by Universal Credit standard allowances when assessing the income that an applicant will require to meet essential needs aside from housing costs, but should ensure that the wishes, needs and circumstances of the applicant and their household are taken into account. The wider context of the applicant's particular circumstances should be considered when considering their household expenditure especially when these are higher than might be expected. For example, an applicant with a disabled child may have higher travel costs to ensure that the child is able to access additional support or education that they require and so this should be taken into account when assessing their essential needs, and the income that they have available for accommodation costs.

Location of accommodation

17.46 The suitability of the location for all the members of the household must be considered by the authority. Section 208(1) of the 1996 Act requires that authorities shall, in discharging their housing functions under Part 7 of the 1996 Act, in so far as is reasonably practicable, secure accommodation within the authority's own district.

17.47 Where it is not reasonably practicable to secure accommodation within district and an authority has secured accommodation outside their district, the housing authority is required to take into account the distance of that accommodation from the district of the authority. Where accommodation which is otherwise suitable and affordable is available nearer to the authority's district than the accommodation which it has secured, the accommodation which it has secured is not likely to be suitable unless the applicant has specified a preference.

17.48 Generally, where possible, housing authorities should try to secure accommodation that is as close as possible to where an applicant was previously living. Securing accommodation for an applicant in a different location can cause difficulties for some applicants. Where possible the authority should seek to retain established links with schools, doctors, social workers and other key services and support.

17.49 In assessing the significance of disruption to employment, account will need to be taken of their need to reach their normal workplace from the accommodation secured. In assessing the significance of disruption to caring responsibilities, account should be taken of the type and importance of the care household members provide and the likely impact the withdrawal would cause.

17.50 When securing accommodation for families with children housing authorities should be mindful of their duties under section 11 of the Children Act 2004 to discharge their functions with regard to the need to safeguard and promote the welfare of children. This would include minimising the disruption to the education of children and young people, particularly (but not solely) at critical points in time such as leading up to taking GCSE (or their equivalent) examinations.

17.51 Before a family that includes a school age child is placed out of district, the housing authority should liaise with the receiving authority and make every reasonable effort to ensure arrangements are or will be put in place to meet the child's educational needs. Local authorities have a duty to ensure that school places are available for children who have moved in to their area, but particular care should be taken by housing authorities when placing families that may require more support to access school places, to ensure educational needs will be met.

17.52 Account should also be taken of medical facilities and other support currently provided for the applicant and their household. Housing authorities should consider the potential impact on the health and wellbeing of an applicant or any person reasonably expected to reside with them, were such support to be removed or medical facilities were no longer accessible. They should also consider whether similar facilities are accessible and available near the accommodation being offered and whether there would be any specific difficulties in the applicant or person residing with them using those essential facilities, compared to the support they are currently receiving.

17.53 Housing authorities should avoid placing applicants in isolated accommodation away from public transport, shops and other facilities, where possible.

17.54 In some circumstances there will be clear benefits for the applicant of being accommodated outside of the district. This could occur, for example, where the applicant, and/or a member of their household, would be at risk of domestic abuse or other violence in the district and need to be accommodated elsewhere to reduce the risk of further contact with the perpetrator(s). Another example might be where, upon the advice of the relevant provider of offender management services (Probation Service, Community Rehabilitation Company or Youth Offending Team), ex-offenders or drug/alcohol users would benefit from being accommodated outside the district to help break links with previous contacts which could exert a negative influence.

17.55 There may also be advantages in enabling some applicants to access employment opportunities outside of their current district. The availability, or otherwise, of employment opportunities in the new area may help to determine if that area is suitable for the applicant.

17.56 The Secretary of State considers that applicants whose household has a need for social services support or a need to maintain links with other essential services within the borough, for example families with children who are subject to safeguarding arrangements, should be given particular attention when temporary accommodation is allocated, to try and ensure it is located in or close to the housing authorities own district. Careful consideration should be given to applicants with a mental illness or learning disability who may have a particular need to remain in a specific area, for example to maintain links with health service professionals and/or a reliance on existing informal support networks and community links. Such applicants may be less able than others to adapt to any disruption caused by being placed in accommodation in another district.

17.57 Housing authorities, particularly those that find it necessary to make out of district placements, are advised to develop policies for the procurement and allocation of temporary accommodation which will help to ensure suitability requirements are met. This would provide helpful guidance for staff responsible for identifying and making offers of accommodation, and would make local arrangements, and the challenges involved with sourcing accommodation, clearer to applicants.

17.58 When making offers of accommodation to an applicant a housing authority should make clear in the offer letter why they consider the property to be suitable, taking into account the needs of the applicant and their household. If any members of the household have health problems the authority should state how their medical needs may be met in the district where the accommodation is located. For families with school age children, the authority should set out how the impact on their education has been assessed and what arrangements have been made for their education in the area of placement.

17.59 Where a housing authority places an applicant in accommodation outside the district under any part of the Act, section 208(2) requires them to notify the authority in whose district the accommodation is situated of the placement. The notification requirement applies to all out of district placements and not just those arranged under interim accommodation duties or the section 193(2) main housing duty. The notification must include:

(a) the name of the applicant;
(b) the number and description of other persons who normally reside with the applicant as a member of his or her family or might reasonably be expected to do so;
(c) the address of the accommodation;
(d) the date on which the accommodation was made available;
(e) which function the housing authority is discharging in securing the accommodation; and,

(f) the notice must be given in writing within 14 days of the accommodation being made available to the applicant.

17.60 Applicants should be given a reasonable amount of time to consider offers of accommodation outside their district (for further guidance see 15.46). In considering what amount of time is to be considered reasonable, housing authorities should take into account how familiar the applicant might be with the district offered, and the length of time that the household are likely to be living there.

17.61 Housing authorities should record how decisions to place an applicant out of district have been reached, taking into account the household's collective and individual needs.

Households with pets

17.62 Housing authorities will need to be sensitive to the importance of pets to some applicants, particularly elderly people and rough sleepers who may rely on pets for companionship. Although it will not always be possible to make provision for pets, the Secretary of State recommends that housing authorities give careful consideration to this aspect when making provision for applicants who wish to retain their pet.

Right to request a review of suitability

17.63 Applicants may ask for a review on request of the housing authority's decision that the accommodation offered to them is suitable under section 202(1)(f), although this right does not apply in the case of interim accommodation secured under sections 188, 190, 200(1), 204(4). For further guidance on accommodation duties see Chapter 15. Under section 202(1A) an applicant may request a review as to suitability regardless of whether or not they accept the accommodation. This applies equally to offers of accommodation made under section 193(5) to discharge the section 193(2) main housing duty and to offers of an allocation of accommodation made under section 193(7) that would bring that duty to an end. This means that the applicant is able to ask for a review of suitability without inadvertently bringing the main housing duty to an end. Housing authorities should note that although there is no right of review of a decision on the suitability of accommodation secured under interim accommodation duties such decisions could nevertheless be subject to judicial review in the High Court. For further guidance see Chapter 19.

CHAPTER 18
Applications, decisions and notifications

Guidance on procedural requirements related to homelessness applications and the notification of decisions.

18.1 This chapter provides guidance on dealing with applications for accommodation or assistance in obtaining accommodation, reapplications to a housing authority within 2 years of acceptance of a private rented sector offer and the circumstances in which an authority has a duty to notify an applicant of its decision.

Service provision

18.2 A need for accommodation, or assistance in obtaining accommodation, can arise at anytime. Housing authorities will therefore need to provide access to advice and assistance at all times during normal office hours, and have arrangements in place for 24 hour emergency cover, e.g. by enabling telephone access to an appropriate duty officer. The police and other relevant services should be provided with details of how to access the service outside normal office hours.

18.3 It is recommended that housing authorities should give proper consideration to the location of, and accessibility to, advice and information about homelessness and the prevention of homelessness, including the need to ensure privacy during interviews.

18.4 Housing authorities should publicise their opening hours, address, and the 24 hour contact details. For example, this information could be accessible on the housing authority's website. Translated information and interpreting services should be made available to applicants for who English is not a first language, and the availability of these services publicised to residents and community organisations. For more guidance on arrangements for carrying out assessments see 11.13 to 11.16.

Form of an application

18.5 Applications can be made to any department of the local authority and expressed in any particular form; they need not be expressed as explicitly seeking assistance under Part 7. As long as the communication seeks accommodation or assistance in obtaining accommodation and includes details that give the housing authority reason to believe that they might be homeless or threatened with homelessness, this will constitute an application.

18.6 Housing authorities should take particular attention to identify instances where information on an inquiry about a social housing allocation scheme, or an application for an allocation of housing under Part 6, provides reason to believe that the applicant might be homeless or threatened with homelessness. This should be regarded as an application for homelessness assistance.

18.7 A referral of a case made by a public authority to the housing authority under section 213B of the 1996 Act, the duty to refer, will not in itself constitute an application. However, housing authorities should make contact with the person referred and determine whether they have reason to believe that the applicant may be homeless or threatened with homelessness. For further guidance on the duty to refer see Chapter 4.

Persons making an application

18.8 An application can be made by any individual who has the mental capacity to do so. There is no statutory minimum age, but applications from dependent children should not be considered. A child aged 16–17 may make an application in their own right, and will require a Children Act 1989 assessment to be completed if they are homeless.

Applications to more than one housing authority

18.9 In some cases applicants may apply to more than one housing authority simultaneously and housing authorities should be alert to cases where an applicant is doing this. In such cases, where a housing authority has reason to believe that the applicant may be homeless or threatened with homelessness, it may wish to contact the other housing authorities involved, to agree which housing authority will take responsibility for conducting inquiries. Where another housing authority has previously made decisions about an applicant's circumstances, a housing authority considering a fresh application may wish to have regard to those decisions. However, housing authorities should not rely solely on decisions made by another housing authority and will need to make their own inquiries in order to reach an independent decision on whether any duty, and if so which duty, is owed under Part 7. Any arrangements for the discharge of any of their functions by another housing authority must comply with section 101 of the Local Government Act 1972.

Withholding or falsifying information

18.10 Under section 214, it is an offence for a person, knowingly or recklessly to make a false statement, or knowingly to withhold information, with intent to induce the housing authority to believe that they, or another person, are entitled to accommodation or assistance under Part 7. If, before the applicant receives notification of a decision, there is any change of facts material to their case, they must inform the housing authority of this as soon as possible. Housing authorities must ensure that all applicants are made aware of these obligations and that they are explained in ordinary language. Housing authorities are advised to ensure that the obligations are conveyed sensitively to avoid intimidating applicants.

Further applications

18.11 There is no period of disqualification if someone wants to make a fresh application. Where a person whose application has been previously considered and determined under Part 7 makes a fresh application, the housing authority will need to decide whether there are any new facts which render it different from the earlier application. If no new facts are revealed, or any new facts are of a trivial nature, the housing authority would not be required to consider the new application and can instead rely on its previous decision. However, where the fresh application does reveal a change in relevant facts, the housing authority must treat the fresh application in the same way as it would any other application for accommodation or assistance in obtaining accommodation under Part 7.

18.12 In the majority of re-application cases where the applicant has previously refused an offer of suitable accommodation, the housing authority will be entitled to rely on the ending of its duties following the refusal of accommodation. However, if, after the refusal of accommodation, the applicant's factual circumstances change, the housing authority can no longer rely on the completion of the earlier duty and must consider the fresh application.

18.13 For example, if an applicant makes a further application following a relationship breakdown which has changed the membership of the household, this should be treated as a new application following a factual change of circumstances.

Withdrawn applications

18.14 It is recommended that housing authorities have procedures in place for dealing with applications that are withdrawn or where someone fails to maintain contact with the housing authority after making an application. The

Secretary of State considers that it would be reasonable to consider an application closed where the applicant has not responded to any form of contact for 56 days or longer. Any further approach from the applicant after this time may need to be considered as a fresh application. Where an applicant renews contact within 56 days the housing authority will need to consider any change of circumstances that may affect the application.

18.15 If an applicant dies before a decision is reached on their application, the housing authority can substitute another member of the late applicant's household as applicant upon the consent of that household member.

Reapplication to a housing authority within 2 years of acceptance of a private rented sector offer

18.16 Under section 195A(1) (re-application after private rented sector offer), the section 193(2) duty will apply regardless of whether the applicant has a priority need where:

(a) a person makes a re-application for assistance within 2 years of accepting a private rented sector offer under section 193(7AA); and,

(b) the applicant is eligible for assistance and has become homeless unintentionally.

18.17 The date from which the 2 years begins is the date of acceptance of the private rented sector offer, not the date when the tenancy was granted or when the applicant moved in.

18.18 Housing authorities should be aware that if, following the expiry of the initial 12 month assured shorthold tenancy, an applicant secures their own accommodation and then subsequently becomes homeless within 2 years of the original private rented sector offer then the re-application duty will still apply.

18.19 Given the 2 year re-application duty, housing authorities are advised to keep the household circumstances under review as they approach the expiry of the 12 month tenancy so they can help actively prevent homelessness wherever possible.

18.20 If the applicant is found to have become homeless intentionally but does have a priority need, the housing authority must secure short-term accommodation for the applicant under section 190(2)(a) for such period as they consider will give them a reasonable opportunity of securing accommodation.

Referrals to another housing authority

18.21 Housing authorities should note that the section 193(2) duty on re-application will apply regardless of whether or not the housing authority receiving the re-application is the same housing authority that arranged the private rented sector offer. This means that the housing authority receiving the re-application cannot simply refer the applicant to the housing authority which made the private rented sector offer but must first carry out investigations to determine whether the applicant is eligible and homeless through no fault of their own, under section 195A. It is for the receiving housing authority to establish whether the applicant has become homeless unintentionally. Once established, this matter cannot be reopened.

18.22 Once the receiving housing authority has established that the applicant is unintentionally homeless and eligible for assistance, they may refer the applicant to the housing authority that made the private rented sector offer.

The conditions for referral of the case to the other housing authority are met once it has been established that the re-application has been made within 2 years and neither the applicant nor any person who might reasonably be expected to reside with the applicant will be at risk of violence, in the district of the other housing authority. The term 'violence' should not be given a restrictive meaning, and 'domestic violence' should be understood to include physical violence, threatening or intimidating behaviour, and any other form of abuse which directly or indirectly may give rise to harm; between persons who are, or have been, intimate partners, family members or members of the same household, regardless of gender identity or sexual orientation.

18.23 The housing authority which made the private rented sector offer will owe the reapplication duty and it will be their responsibility to secure accommodation is available for occupation by the applicant. Housing authorities are expected to respond quickly to referrals and requests for information.

18.24 Housing authorities are reminded to consider the conditions for referral of a case to another housing authority as set out under section 198(2ZA). For further guidance on referrals to another housing authority see Chapter 10 and risk of domestic abuse see Chapter 21.

18.25 Referrals regarding re-applications are not subject to any consideration of local connection.

When re-application does not apply

18.26 The provisions under section 195A do not apply in a restricted case. Additionally, these provisions do not apply in a case where the applicant has previously made a re-application which resulted in their being owed the duty under section 193(2) by virtue of section 195A(1) This effectively means that an applicant can only be owed the re-application duty once following each private rented sector offer. For further guidance on restricted cases see Chapter 7.

Interim duty to accommodate

18.27 Under section 188(1A), if the housing authority have reason to believe that the re-application duty may apply, they must secure interim accommodation for the applicant regardless of whether or not they have a priority need.

18.28 Housing authorities should note that the duty under section 188(1A) will apply regardless of whether the housing authority receiving the re-application is the same authority that arranged the private rented sector offer.

Notifications to applicants

18.29 Housing authorities are required to provide written notifications to applicants of certain decisions reached in relation to their applications under Part 7. In all cases notifications should be clearly written in plain language, and include information about the right to request a review and the timescales that apply. Housing authorities might also include information about independent advice services available to the applicant. In cases where the applicant may have difficulty understanding the implications of the decision, it is recommended that housing authorities consider arranging for a member of staff to provide and explain the notification in person.

18.30 Written notification not received by the applicant can be treated as having been given to them, if it is made available at the housing authority's office for a reasonable period that would allow it to be collected by the applicant or by someone acting on their behalf.

Combining notifications

18.31 There will be circumstances in which more than one notification will be required at the same time and it will be more practicable to combine the necessary information within one notification letter. Housing authorities will need to take particular care to ensure the information provided to the applicant is clear and comprehensive, and that they are made aware of review rights in respect of each of the decisions about which they are being notified.

Notification on decisions about duties owed section 184(3)

18.32 If a housing authority has reason to believe that a person applying for assistance may be homeless or threatened with homelessness, the housing authority must make such inquiries as are necessary to satisfy itself whether the applicant is eligible for assistance and if so, whether any duty, and if so what duty, is owed to that person under Part 7 of the 1996 Act. When a housing authority has completed its inquiries it must notify the applicant in writing of its decisions.

18.33 Where a decision is against the applicant's interests the notification must explain clearly and fully the reasons for the decision. In cases where contradictory factual accounts are put before the housing authority, and it prefers one account to another, the decisions letter should explain why a particular account was preferred.

Notification bringing duties to an end

18.34 Housing authorities can give notice to the applicant bringing their duties to an end at each stage. The conditions and requirements for these notifications are set out separately under each provision.

18.35 A notice bringing duties to an end must explain why the housing authority are giving the notice and its effect, and inform the applicant that they have a right to request a review of the authority's decision to give the notice and of the time within which such a request must be made. For further guidance on how and when the prevention and relief duties can be ended and on issuing notices in cases of an applicant's deliberate and unreasonable refusal to co-operate see Chapter 14.

CHAPTER 19
Review of decisions and appeals to the county court

Guidance on the procedures to be followed when an applicant requests a review of decisions reached on their homelessness application.

19.1 This chapter provides guidance on the procedures to be followed when an applicant requests the housing authority to review any decision on their case.

Right to request a review

19.2 Applicants have the right to request the housing authority review their decisions on homelessness cases in some circumstances. If the request is made in accordance with section 202 the housing authority, or housing authorities, concerned must review the relevant decision.

19.3 Under section 202(1) an applicant has the right to request a review of a housing authority's decision:

(a) of their eligibility for assistance (section 202(1)(a));
(b) what duty (if any) is owed to them in relation to the duties owed to persons found to be homeless or threatened with homelessness (section 202(1)(b));
(c) of the steps they are to take in their personalised housing plan at the prevention duty (section 202(1)(bc)(i));
(d) to give notice to bring the prevention duty to an end (section 202(1)(bc)(ii));
(e) of the steps they are to take in their personalised housing plan at the relief duty (section 202(1)(ba)(i));
(f) to give notice to bring the relief duty to an end (section 202(1)(ba)(ii));
(g) to give notice under section 193B(2) in cases of deliberate and unreasonable refusal to co-operate (section 202(1)(bb));
(h) to notify their case to another authority under section 198(1) (i.e. a decision to refer the applicant at the main housing duty, to another housing authority because they consider that the conditions for referral are met) (section 202(1)(c));
(i) under section 198(5) as to whether the conditions are met for the referral of their case to another housing authority at the relief duty or main housing duty (including a decision reached either by agreement between the notifying and notified authority, or taken by a person appointed under the Homelessness (Decisions on Referrals) Order 1998 where agreement cannot be reached) (section 202(1)(d));
(j) under section 200(3) (i.e. where a decision is made that the conditions for referral are not met and so the notifying housing authority owe the section 193 main housing duty) or a decision under section 200(4) (i.e. a decision that the conditions for referral to a notified authority in Wales are met and the notified authority owe the section 193 main housing duty) (section 202(1)(e));
(k) as to the suitability of accommodation offered to the applicant under any of the provisions in paragraph (b) or (j) above or the suitability of accommodation offered under section 193(7) in relation to allocations under Part 6 (section 202(1)(f)). Applicants can request a review of the suitability of accommodation whether or not they have accepted the offer (section 202(1B));
(l) as to the suitability of accommodation offered to the applicant by way of a private rented sector offer under section 193 (section 202(1)(g)); or,
(m) as to the suitability of accommodation offered to the applicant by way of a final accommodation offer or a final Part 6 offer under section 193A or 193C (section 202(1)(h)). Applicants can request a review of the suitability of accommodation whether or not they have accepted the offer.

19.4 An applicant must request a review before the end of the period of 21 days beginning with the day on which they are notified of the housing authority's decision. The housing authority may specify, in writing, a longer period during which a review may be requested.

19.5 In reviewing a decision, housing authorities will need to have regard to any information relevant to the period before the decision was made (even if only obtained afterwards) as well as any new relevant information obtained since the decision.

19.6 In the case of (i) above (a decision on whether the conditions are met for the referral of the applicant's case to another housing authority) the request for a review must be made to the notifying authority.

19.7 There is no right to request a review of a decision reached on an earlier review.

The Review Procedures Regulations

19.8 **The Allocation of Housing and Homelessness (Review Procedures) Regulations 1999 have been revoked and replaced by the Homelessness (Review Procedure etc.) Regulations 2018.** These regulations set out the procedures to be followed by housing authorities in carrying out reviews under Part 7.

Who may carry out the review

19.9 A review may be carried out by the housing authority itself which made the original decision or by someone acting as an agent of the housing authority. For further guidance on contracting out homelessness functions see Chapter 5. Where the review is to be carried out by an officer of the housing authority, the officer must not have been involved in the original decision, and they must be senior to the officer (or officers) who took that decision. Seniority for these purposes means seniority in rank or grade within the housing authority's organisational structure. The seniority provision does not apply where a committee or sub-committee of elected members took the original decision.

19.10 The same officer is able to carry out multiple reviews relating to a single case as long as they were not involved in the original decisions.

19.11 Where the decision under review is a joint decision by a notifying housing authority and the notified housing authority as to whether the conditions of referral of a case are satisfied, section 202(4) requires that the review should be carried out jointly by the 2 housing authorities.

19.12 Where the decision under review was taken by a person appointed by the notifying and notified authority, the review of that decision must also be carried out by a person appointed by the 2 authorities (see paragraph 19.25).

Written representations

19.13 An applicant is not required to provide grounds or reasons for challenging the housing authority's decision in their request for review, but should be invited to do so. The purpose of this is to invite the applicant to state their grounds for requesting a review (if they have not already done so) and to elicit any new information and particular issues that the applicant may have in relation to their request for a review.

19.14 Regulation 5 requires the housing authority to notify the applicant that they, or someone acting on their behalf, may make written representations in connection with the request for a review.

19.15 Regulation 5 also provides that the housing authority must notify the applicant that if they chose to make written representations where the request for review relates to:

(a) the reasonable steps in an applicant's personalised housing plan (during the prevention or relief duty) (section 202(1)(ba)(i) or (bc)(i)); or,

(b) a notice bringing the prevention duty to an end (including where the reason for this is deliberate and unreasonable refusal to co-operate) (section 202(1)(bc)(ii) and (bb)).

The representations must be made to the housing authority within 2 weeks from the day on which the applicant requested the review. The regulations provide that this 2 week period is open to be extended to a longer period if the applicant and reviewing authority agree in writing.

19.16 Applicants should already have been provided with copies of their assessments and personalised housing plan which they will be able to share with any legal representatives. Housing authorities should provide further copies or any further information requested as quickly as possible to minimise delays.

19.17 Where the request for a review falls outside of the decisions listed under 19.15, written representations should be made within a reasonable period to allow sufficient time for the housing authority to respond to the review within the prescribed timeframe (see paragraph 19.23).

19.18 The housing authority must also notify the applicant of the procedure to be followed in connection with the review (if this information has not been provided earlier).

19.19 Regulation 5 also provides that:

(a) where the original decision was made jointly by the notifying and notified housing authorities under section 198(5), the notification should be made by the notifying housing authority; and,

(b) where the original decision was made by a person appointed in accordance to the Homelessness (Decisions on Referrals) Order 1998, the notification should be made by the person appointed to carry out the review.

Oral hearings

19.20 Regulation 7 provides that in cases where a review has been requested, if the housing authority, authorities or person carrying out the review consider that there is a deficiency or irregularity in the original decision, or in the manner in which it was made, but they are minded nonetheless to make a decision that is against the applicant's interests on one or more issues, they should notify the applicant:

(a) that they are so minded and the reasons why; and,

(b) that the applicant, or someone acting on their behalf, may, within a reasonable period, make oral representations, further written representations, or both oral and written representations.

19.21 Such deficiencies or irregularities would include:

(a) failure to take into account relevant considerations and to ignore irrelevant ones;

(b) failure to base the decision on the facts;

(c) bad faith or dishonesty;

(d) mistake of law;

(e) decisions that run contrary to the policy of Part 7 of the 1996 Act;

(f) irrationality or unreasonableness; or,

(g) procedural unfairness, e.g. where an applicant has not been given a chance to comment on matters relevant to a decision.

19.22 The reviewer must consider whether there is 'something lacking' in the decision, i.e. were any significant issues not addressed or addressed inadequately, which could have led to unfairness. An original decision could subsequently be rendered deficient because of intervening events which occurred between the date of the original decision and the review decision.

Period during which review must be completed

19.23 Regulation 9 provides that the period within which the applicant (or the applicant's authorised agent) must be notified of the decision on a review is:

(a) 3 weeks from the day of the request for a review, or 3 weeks from the day on which representations are received, where the original decision falls within section 202(1)(ba)(i), (bc), or section 202(1) (bb) and the effect of the notice is to bring the prevention duty to an end;

(b) 8 weeks from the day of the request for a review, where the original decision falls within section 202(1)(a), (b), (ba)(ii), (c), (d), (e), (f), (g), or section 202(1) (bb) and the effect of the notice is to bring the relief duty to an end;

(c) 10 weeks, where the original decision falls within section 202(1)(d) and was made jointly by 2 housing authorities under section 198(5) (a decision on whether the conditions for referral are met);

(d) 12 weeks, where the original decision falls within section 202(1)(d) and it was taken by a person appointed by the notifying authority and the notified authority in accordance with the Schedule to the Homelessness (Decisions on Referrals) Order 1998.

The regulations provide that in all of these cases it is open to the reviewing authority to seek the applicant's agreement to an extension of the prescribed period. Any such agreement must be given in writing.

Late representations

19.24 The regulations require the reviewer(s) to consider any written representations received subject to compliance with the requirement to notify the applicant of the decision on review within the period of the review, i.e. the period prescribed in the regulations or any extended period agreed in writing between the applicant and housing authority. It may in some circumstances be necessary to make further enquiries of the applicant about information they have provided. The reviewer(s) should be flexible about allowing such further exchanges, having regard to the time limits for reviews prescribed in the regulations. If this leads to significant delays, the applicant may be approached to agree an extension in the period for the review. Similarly, if an applicant has been invited to make oral representations and this requires additional time to arrange, the applicant should be asked to agree an appropriate extension.

Procedures for reviews of section 198(5) decisions made by an appointed person

19.25 Where the original decision under section 198(5) was made by a person appointed in accordance with the Schedule to the Homelessness (Decisions on Referrals) Order 1998, regulation 6 requires that a review must be carried out by a person appointed by the notifying authority and the notified authority. If the authorities are unable to reach agreement on an appointed person, and where the review is of the original decision on whether the conditions for referral of a case under section 198(1) are met, the review must be carried out by a person appointed from the panel by the chair of the Local Government Association (LGA), or their nominee.

19.26 The appointed person must not be the same person as the person who made the original decision and they must comply with the relevant procedures set out in the regulations. Specifically, they must invite written representations from the applicant and send copies of these to the 2 housing authorities, inviting them to respond. The reviewer is also required to notify in writing the 2 housing authorities of their decision on review and the reasons for it at least a week before the end of the prescribed period of 12 weeks (or of any extended period agreed with the applicant). This allows the housing authorities adequate time to notify the applicant of the decision before expiry of the period.

19.27 Paragraphs (2)–(4) of regulation 6 set out the procedure to be followed when the notifying and notified authority are unable to appoint a person to carry out a review by agreement. These provisions currently apply to decisions on notifications under section 198(1) at the point of the main housing duty. However local authorities are encouraged to also follow these arrangements in relation to the review of decisions on notifications under section 198(A1).

19.28 Paragraphs (2)–(4) of regulation 6 set out that if the 2 housing authorities fail to appoint a person to carry out the review within 5 working days of the date of the request for a review, the notifying housing authority must request the chair of the LGA or their nominee to appoint a person from the panel. The chair, in turn, must within 7 days of that request appoint a person from the panel to undertake the review. The housing authorities are required to provide the reviewer with the reasons for the original decision, and the information on which that decision is based, within 5 working days of their appointment.

Notification of decision on review

19.29 Section 203 requires a housing authority to notify the applicant in writing of their decision on the review. The authority must also notify the applicant of the reasons for their decision where it:

(a) confirms the original decision on any issue against the interests of the applicant;

(b) confirms a previous decision to notify another housing authority under section 198(1) (referral of case under the main housing duty); or,

(c) confirms a previous decision that the conditions for referral in section 198 (referral of case under the relief duty or main housing duty) are met in the applicant's case.

19.30 Where the review is carried out jointly by 2 housing authorities under section 198(5), or by a person appointed in accordance to the Homelessness (Decisions on Referrals) Order 1998, the notification may be made by either of the 2 housing authorities concerned.

19.31 At this stage, the housing authority making the notification must advise the applicant of their right to appeal to the county court under section 204 against a review decision on a point of law, and of the period in which to appeal.

Powers to accommodate pending a review

19.32 Under section 188(2A), where an applicant refuses a final accommodation offer or a final Part 6 offer in the relief stage and requests a review under section 202(1)(h) of the housing authority's decision as to the suitability of the accommodation offered, the relief duty to the applicant continues to apply despite section 193A(2), and the housing authority must continue to provide interim accommodation for applicants in priority need until the decision on the review has been notified to the applicant.

19.33 Sections 188(3), 199A(6) and 200(5) give housing authorities powers to secure accommodation for certain applicants pending the decision on a review. For further guidance on powers to secure accommodation see Chapter 15.

Prevention and relief activity following a review decision

19.34 In circumstances where the outcome of one of the following decisions are in the applicants favour, review officers are recommended to use their discretion to assess the impact of the failure across the whole period of the relevant duty and make recommendations which seek to remedy this:

(a) the decision on reasonable steps in the personalised housing plan; or,
(b) the decision to issue a notice bringing the prevention or relief duties to an end.

19.35 For example, if an applicant's personalised housing plan was completed 3 days after the start of the prevention or relief duty and a review found that steps were unreasonable, the review officer may recommend that the authority work with the applicant to agree new steps and resume prevention or relief activity for a further 53 days.

19.36 Where an applicant requests a review of the authority's decision as to whether the conditions are met for the referral of their case to another housing authority at the relief stage the relief duty will rest with the notified authority whilst the review is conducted. If the review officer decides that the conditions for referral were not met and that the applicant should not have been referred to another housing authority, they are encouraged to make recommendations based on the following considerations:

(a) the reasonable wishes of the applicant;
(b) the relief activity that has taken place to date by both or either authorities;
(c) how relevant this activity is in the geographical context of the notifying authority given the successful review decision; and,
(d) whether the applicant is in priority need and therefore if they should directly proceed to the main duty after the 56 day period.

Appeals to the county court

19.37 Section 204 provides an applicant who has requested a section 202 review with the right of appeal on a point of law to the county court if:

(a) they are dissatisfied with the decision on a review; or,
(b) they are not notified of the decision on the review within the time prescribed in regulations made under section 203.

19.38 An appeal must be brought by an applicant within 21 days of:

(a) the date on which they are notified of the decision on review; or,
(b) the date on which they should have been notified (i.e. the date marking the end of the period for the review prescribed in the regulations, or any extended period agreed in writing by the applicant).

19.39 The court may give permission for an appeal to be brought after 21 days, but only where it is satisfied that:

(a) (where permission is sought within the 21 day period), there is good reason for the applicant to be unable to bring the appeal in time; or,
(b) (where permission is sought after the 21 day period has expired), there was a good reason for the applicant's failure to bring the appeal in time and for any delay in applying for permission.

19.40 On an appeal, the county court is empowered to make an order confirming, quashing or varying the housing authority's decision as it thinks fit. It is important, therefore, that housing authorities have in place review procedures that are robust, fair, and transparent.

Power to accommodate pending an appeal to the county court

19.41 Section 204(4) gives housing authorities the power to accommodate certain applicants during the period for making an appeal, and pending determination of the appeal and any subsequent appeal. For further guidance on powers to secure accommodation see Chapter 15.

Local Government and Social Care Ombudsman

19.42 Applicants may complain to the Local Government and Social Care Ombudsman if they consider that they have been caused injustice as a result of maladministration in relation to their application for assistance under Part 7 by a housing authority. The Ombudsman may investigate the way a decision has been made, but may not question the merits of a decision properly reached. For example, maladministration would occur where a housing authority:
(a) took too long to do something;
(b) did not follow their own rules or the law;
(c) broke their promises;
(d) treated the applicant unfairly; or,
(e) gave the applicant the wrong information.

19.43 There are some matters an Ombudsman cannot investigate. These include:
(a) matters the applicant knew about more than 12 months before they wrote to the Ombudsman or to a councillor, unless the Ombudsman considers it reasonable to investigate despite the delay;
(b) matters about which the applicant has already taken court action against the housing authority, for example, an appeal to the county court under section 204; and,
(c) matters about which the applicant could go to court, unless the Ombudsman considers there are good reasons why the applicant could not reasonably be expected to do so.

19.44 Where there is a right of review, and/or a complaints procedure within the housing authority, the Ombudsman would expect an applicant to pursue their rights through these arrangements before making a complaint. If there is any doubt about whether the Ombudsman can look into a complaint, the applicant should seek advice from the Ombudsman's office.

CHAPTER 20
Protection of personal property

Guidance on the duties and powers housing authorities have to protect the personal property of an applicant who is homeless.

20.1 This chapter provides guidance on the duty and powers housing authorities have to protect the personal property of an applicant.

20.2 Under section 211(1) and (2), where a housing authority has become subject to a duty to an applicant under specified provisions of Part 7 and it has reason to believe that:

(a) there is a danger of loss of, or damage to, the applicant's personal property;
(b) because the applicant is unable to protect it or deal with it; and,
(c) no other suitable arrangements have been, or are being, made,

then, whether or not the housing authority is still subject to such a duty, it must take reasonable steps to prevent the loss of, or to prevent or mitigate damage to, any personal property of the applicant.

20.3 The specified provisions are:

(a) section 188 (interim duty to accommodate);
(b) section 189B (initial duty owed to all eligible persons who are homeless); and,
(c) section 190, section 193 or section 195 (duties to persons found to be homeless or threatened with homelessness); or section 200 (duties to an applicant whose case is considered for referral or is referred).

20.4 In all other circumstances, housing authorities have a power to take any steps they consider reasonable to protect in the same way, an applicant's personal property (section 211(3)).

20.5 Section 212 makes provisions supplementing section 211. For the purposes of both section 211 and section 212, the personal property of an applicant includes the personal property of any person who might reasonably be expected to reside with them (section 211(5)) and section 212(6)).

20.6 A danger of loss or damage to personal property means that there is a likelihood of harm, not just that harm is a possibility. Applicants may be unable to protect their property if, for example, they are ill or are unable to afford to have it stored themselves.

20.7 Under section 212(1), in order to protect an applicant's personal property, a housing authority can enter, at all reasonable times, the applicant's current or former home, and deal with the property in any way which seems reasonably necessary.

20.8 Where a housing authority does take steps to protect personal property it must take reasonable care of it and deliver it to the owner when reasonably requested to do so. Housing authorities may find it helpful to take a log of the applicant's personal property as part of this process.

20.9 The applicant can request the housing authority to move their property to a particular location. If the housing authority considers that the request is reasonable, they may discharge their responsibilities under section 211 by doing as the applicant asks. Where such a request is met, the housing authority will have no further duty or power to protect the applicant's property, and it must inform the applicant of this consequence before complying with the request (section 212(2)).

20.10 Housing authorities may impose conditions on the assistance they provide (section 211(4)). Conditions may include making a reasonable charge for storage of property and reserving the right to dispose of property in certain circumstances specified by the housing authority – e.g. if the applicant loses touch with them and cannot be traced after a certain period (section 211(4)).

20.11 Where a request to move personal property to another location is either not made or not carried out, the duty or power to take any action under section 211 ends when the housing authority believes there is no longer any danger of loss or damage to the property because of the applicant's inability to deal with or protect it (section 212(3)). This may be the case, for example, where an applicant recovers from illness or finds accommodation where they are able to place their possessions, or becomes able to afford the storage costs themselves. However, where the housing authority has discharged the duty under section 211 by placing property in storage, it has a discretionary power to continue to keep the property in storage. Where it does so, any conditions imposed by the housing authority continue to apply and may be modified as necessary.

20.12 Where the housing authority ceases to be under a duty, or ceases to have a power, to protect an applicant's personal property under section 211, it must notify the applicant of this and give the reasons for it. The notification must be delivered to the applicant or sent to the applicant's last known address (section 212(5)). For further guidance on notifications see Chapter 18.

CHAPTER 21
Domestic abuse

Guidance on providing homelessness services to people who have experienced or are at risk of domestic violence or abuse.

21.1 This chapter provides guidance on providing homelessness services to people who have experienced domestic violence or abuse, or are at risk of domestic violence or abuse.

Understanding domestic violence and abuse

21.2 Domestic violence or abuse is 'domestic' in nature if the perpetrator is a person who is associated with the victim. It is not limited to physical violence or confined to instances within the home.

21.3 Housing authorities must take account of the cross-government definition of domestic violence and abuse when designing and delivering services. This defines domestic violence and abuse as:

21.4 Any incident or pattern of incidents of controlling, coercive, threatening behaviour, violence or abuse between those aged 16 or over who are, or have been, intimate partners or family members regardless of gender. The abuse can encompass, but is not limited to:

(a) **psychological** – including: intimidation, insults, isolating the person from friends and family, criticising, denying the abuse, treating the person as inferior, threatening to harm children or take them away, forced marriage;

(b) **physical** – this can include: shaking, smacking, punching, kicking, presence of finger or bite marks, bruising, starving, tying up, stabbing, suffocation, throwing things, using objects as weapons, female genital mutilation.

Physical effects are often in areas of the body that are covered and hidden (i.e. breasts, legs and stomach);

(c) **sexual** – including rape (including the threat of rape), sexual assault, forced prostitution, ignoring religious prohibitions about sex, refusal to practise safe sex, sexual insults, passing on sexually transmitted diseases, preventing breastfeeding;

(d) **financial** – not letting the person work, undermining efforts to find work or study, refusing to give money, asking for an explanation of how every penny is spent, making the person beg for money, gambling, not paying bills, building up debt in the other person's name;

(e) **emotional** – including: swearing, undermining confidence, making racist, sexist or other derogatory remarks, making the person feel unattractive, calling the person stupid or useless, eroding the person's independence, keeping them isolated from family or friends.

21.5 **Controlling behaviour** is a range of acts designed to make a person subordinate and/or dependent by isolating them from sources of support, exploiting their resources and capacities for personal gain, depriving them of the means needed for independence, resistance and escape and regulating their everyday behaviour.

21.6 **Coercive behaviour** is an act or a pattern of acts of assault, threats, humiliation and intimidation or other abuse that is used to harm, punish, or frighten their victim.

21.7 **So-called honour-based abuse** is also a form of domestic abuse, explained by the perpetrator of the abuse on the grounds that it was committed as a consequence of the need to protect or defend the honour of the family; it can include all the types of abuse listed above and specific crimes such as forced marriage and female genital mutilation.

21.8 Domestic violence and abuse can affect anyone regardless of their age, gender identity or reassignment, race, religion, class, sexual orientation and marital status. Housing authorities should bear in mind that the provisions of the Equality Act 2010 for public authorities apply to policies, practice and procedures relating to homelessness and domestic violence and abuse.

21.9 An important factor in ensuring that an authority develops a strong and appropriate response to domestic abuse is understanding what domestic abuse is, the context in which it takes place in and the impacts are on victims; as well as how the impacts may be different on different groups of people. Specialist training for staff and managers will help them to provide a more sensitive response and to identify, with applicants, housing options which are safe and appropriate to their needs.

Identifying abuse and preventing homelessness

21.10 Housing authorities should have policies in place to identify and respond to domestic abuse. Alongside their role in tackling homelessness authorities should take an active role in identifying victims and referring them for help and support. They are key partners in local domestic violence partnerships and should be represented at their local multi-agency risk assessment conference (MARAC).

21.11 The MARAC leads multi-agency safety planning for high-risk victims of domestic abuse. It brings together the police, independent domestic violence advisers, children's social services, health, social landlords and other relevant agencies. They share information and write a safety plan for each victim and family, which may include actions by any agency present. The housing authority should be consistently represented at the MARAC and encourage relevant social landlords to also be represented.

21.12 Victims can experience many incidents of abuse before calling the police or reporting it to another agency. Housing providers may be able to identify abuse at earlier stages and should consider how they can best provide support to their residents. By understanding the indicators of domestic abuse through training and professional development, housing officers can increase their confidence to speak to people experiencing abuse, risk assess and safety plan alongside them.

21.13 Housing authorities should also be alert to the wider role they play in ensuring victim safety. Procedures should be in place to keep all information on victims safe and secure. In many cases, particularly where extended family members or multiple perpetrators may be involved, for example in female genital mutilation, forced marriage and so called honour based violence cases, perpetrators go to great lengths to seek information on victims.

21.14 The housing authority must be alert to the possibility of employees being, or having links to, perpetrators. Housing authorities should not disclose information about an applicant to anybody outside the organisation without consent, and should be particularly alert to the need to maintain confidentiality wherever domestic abuse is involved. In some circumstances, it may be necessary to restrict access to cases where abuse is disclosed to only named members of staff. Housing authorities should also consider how they flag case files so they can identify those victims who have been referred to the MARAC and may present as homeless.

21.15 Households at risk of domestic abuse often have to leave their homes and the area where they have lived. There is a clear need for victims of abuse and their children to be able to travel to different areas in order for them to be safe from the perpetrator, and housing authorities should extend the same level of support to those from other areas as they do to their own residents.

Duties to those homeless or threatened with homelessness

21.16 Section 177(1) of the 1996 Act provides that it is not reasonable for a person to continue to occupy accommodation if it is probable that this will lead to domestic violence or other violence against:

(a) the applicant;
(b) a person who normally resides as a member of the applicant's family; or,
(c) any other person who might reasonably be expected to reside with the applicant.

21.17 Section 177(1A) provides that 'violence' means violence from another person or threats of violence from another person which are likely to be carried out. 'Domestic violence' is violence or threats of violence which are likely to be carried out by a person who is associated with the victim. Domestic violence is not confined to instances within the home.

21.18 In the context of defining domestic violence, section 178 provides that, for the purposes of Part 7 of the 1996 Act, a person is associated with another if:

(a) they are, or have been, married to each other;
(b) they are or have been civil partners of each other;

(c) they are, or have been, cohabitants;
(d) they live, or have lived, in the same household;
(e) they are relatives, i.e. father, mother, stepfather, stepmother, son, daughter, stepson, stepdaughter, grandmother, grandfather, grandson, granddaughter, brother, sister, uncle, aunt, niece or nephew (whether of full blood, or of half blood or by marriage or civil partnership) of that person or of that person's spouse or former spouse. A person is also included if they would fall into any of these categories in relation to cohabitees or former cohabitees if they were married to each other;
(f) they have agreed to marry each other, whether or not that agreement has been terminated;
(g) they have entered into a civil partnership agreement between them, whether or not that agreement has been terminated;
(h) in relation to a child, each of them is a parent of the child or has, or has had, parental responsibility for the child (within the meaning of the Children Act 1989). A child is a person under 18 years of age;
(i) if a child has been adopted or 'freed for adoption' (section 18 of the Adoption Act 1976), 2 persons are also associated if one is the natural parent or grandparent of the child and the other is the child or a person who has become the parent by virtue of an 'adoption order' (section 72(1), Adoption Act 1976) or has applied for an adoption order or someone with whom the child has at any time been placed for adoption.

21.19 The term 'violence' should not be given a restrictive meaning, and 'domestic violence' should be understood to include physical violence, threatening or intimidating behaviour, and any other form of abuse which directly or indirectly may give rise to harm; between persons who are, or have been, intimate partners, family members or members of the same household, regardless of gender identity or sexual orientation.

21.20 An assessment of the likelihood of a threat of violence or abuse being carried out should not be based on whether there has been actual violence or abuse in the past. Assessments must be based on the facts of the case and should be devoid of any value judgements about what an applicant should or should not do, or should or should not have done, to mitigate the risk of any violence and abuse.

21.21 It is essential that inquiries do not provoke further violence and abuse. Housing authorities **should not approach the alleged perpetrator,** since this could generate further violence and abuse. Housing authorities may, however, wish to seek information from friends and relatives of the applicant, social services, health professionals, MARACs, a domestic abuse support service or the police, as appropriate. This is not an exhaustive list and there may be other sources of evidence that would be appropriate. In some cases, corroborative evidence of actual or threatened violence may not be available, for example, because there were no adult witnesses and/or the applicant was too frightened or ashamed to report incidents to family, friend or the police. Housing authorities should not have a blanket approach toward domestic abuse which requires corroborative or police evidence to be provided.

21.22 There may be occasions where victims of abuse seek emergency assistance having left behind ID and other documentation that may be required to support their application. Housing authorities should work with police;

domestic abuse agencies (as appropriate) and the applicant to ensure that essential documentation can be recovered or replaced without putting the applicant at further risk of abuse.

21.23 In many cases involving violence and abuse, the applicant may be in considerable distress and an officer trained in dealing with the particular circumstances should conduct the interview. Applicants should be given the option of being interviewed by an officer of the same sex if they so wish. Housing authorities should be aware that this may be the first time a victim has disclosed their abuse and that the period during which a victim is planning or making their exit, is often the **most dangerous time** for them and any children they have.

21.24 The following services are among those subject to the duty to refer, meaning they are required to refer service users in England they consider may be homeless or threatened with homelessness within 56 days to a housing authority, with the service user's consent:

(a) emergency departments;
(b) urgent treatment centres;
(c) hospitals in their function of providing in patient care; and,
(d) adults and children's social care services.

For further guidance on the duty to refer see Chapter 4.

Prevention and relief duties

21.25 Following an application for assistance under Part 7 of the 1996 Act, whether an applicant is threatened with homelessness or is actually homeless will be a matter for the housing authority to assess taking into account all of the relevant circumstances. For example, a person at risk of domestic violence or abuse may be threatened with homelessness because a perpetrator is soon to be released from custody (and so the person is likely to become homeless within 56 days); but would be actually homeless if the perpetrator was in the community and presented a risk to them at their home (and so it is not reasonable for the person to continue to occupy the accommodation).

21.26 When developing a personalised housing plan the housing authority should be particularly sensitive to an applicant's wishes and respectful of their judgement about the risk of abuse, unless there is evidence to the contrary. For further guidance on assessments and personalised housing plans see Chapter 11. Victims should be allowed sufficient time and space to absorb and understand the options available to them.

21.27 The reasonable steps that a housing authority might take to help an applicant to retain or secure safe accommodation might include provision of sanctuary scheme or other security measures, assistance to find alternative accommodation, or help to access legal remedies such as injunctions where these might be effective. Single people might also be assisted to access supported housing, or helped to gain more support from family and friends through the intervention of the housing authority.

21.28 Sanctuary schemes can prevent homelessness by enabling victims to remain safely in their home where it is their choice, and it is safe to do so. A sanctuary comprises enhanced security measures in the home which delay or prevent a perpetrator from gaining entry into and within a property, and allow time for the police to arrive. Use of sanctuary is not appropriate if the perpetrator lives at, or retains a legal right to enter the home, or if the victim continues to be at risk in the vicinity around the home.

21.29 Housing authorities may wish to inform applicants of the option of seeking an injunction against the perpetrator. Where applicants wish to pursue this option, authorities should inform them that they should seek legal advice and that they may be eligible for legal aid.

21.30 Housing authorities should recognise that injunctions ordering a person not to molest (non-molestation orders), or not to live in the home or enter the surrounding area (occupation orders) may not be effective in deterring some perpetrators from carrying out further violence, abuse or incursions, and applicants may not have confidence in their effectiveness. Consequently, applicants should not be expected to return home on the strength of an injunction. To ensure applicants who have experienced actual or threatened violence get the support they need, authorities should inform them of appropriate specialist organisations in the area as well as agencies offering counselling and support.

21.31 When dealing with domestic violence and abuse within the home, where the authority is the landlord, housing authorities should consider the scope for evicting the perpetrator and allowing the victim to remain in their home. However, where there would be a probability of violence if the applicant continued to occupy their present accommodation, the housing authority must treat the applicant as homeless and should not expect them to remain in, or return to, the accommodation. **In all cases involving violence the safety of the applicant and their household should be the primary consideration at all stages of decision making as to whether or not the applicant remains in their own home.**

Assessing priority need

21.32 A person has a priority need if they are vulnerable as a result of having to leave accommodation because of violence from another person, or threats of violence from another person that are likely to be carried out. (Article 6, Homelessness (Priority Need for Accommodation) (England) Order 2002).

21.33 It is not only domestic violence and abuse that is relevant, but all forms of violence, including racially motivated violence or threats of violence likely to be carried out. In assessing whether it is likely that threats of violence are likely to be carried out, a housing authority should only take into account the probability of violence, and not actions which the applicant could take (such as injunctions against the perpetrators).

21.34 In considering whether applicants are vulnerable as a result of leaving accommodation because of violence or threats of violence likely to be carried out, a housing authority may wish to take into account the following factors:

(a) the nature of the violence or threats of violence (there may have been a single but significant incident or a number of incidents over an extended period of time which have had a cumulative effect);

(b) the impact and likely effects of the violence or threats of violence on the applicant's current and future wellbeing;

(i) whether the applicant has any existing support networks, particularly by way of family or friends; and,

(ii) the continuing threat from the perpetrator.

For further guidance on priority need see Chapter 8.

Providing suitable accommodation

21.35 There are a number of accommodation options for victims of domestic abuse, and housing authorities will need to consider which are most appropriate for each person on a case by case basis taking into account their circumstances and needs. This may include safe temporary accommodation and/or a managed transfer. Housing authorities may, for example, provide temporary accommodation whilst action is taken to exclude or to arrest and detain a perpetrator. Opportunities to plan for victims to remain or return to their homes are much improved by housing authorities working with partners in the MARAC to reduce risk.

21.36 For victims at risk from highly dangerous perpetrators, refuges will usually be the most appropriate choice. Refuges provide key short term, intensive support for those who flee from abuse. Given the intensity of the support and the vulnerability of the victims, attention should be paid to the length of time they spend in a refuge. Refuges are not simply a substitute for other forms of temporary accommodation. The housing authority should work with the refuge provider to consider how long a person needs to stay before the provision of other accommodation (which may be temporary in the absence of settled accommodation) may be more appropriate, potentially with floating support if needed.

21.37 Account will need to be taken of any social considerations relating to the applicant and their household that might affect the suitability of accommodation offered to them to prevent or relieve homelessness, or under the main housing duty. Any risk of violence or racial harassment in a particular locality should be taken into account. Where domestic violence is involved and the applicant is not able to stay in the current home, housing authorities may need to consider the need for accommodation that would not be found by the perpetrator (which may involve an out of district placement) and which has security measures and appropriately trained staff to protect the occupants. Housing authorities may consider implementing a reciprocal agreement with other housing authorities and providers to facilitate out of area moves for victims of domestic violence and abuse.

Local connection referrals

21.38 A housing authority cannot refer an applicant to another housing authority where they have a local connection if that person or any person who might reasonably be expected to reside with them would be at risk of violence and abuse in that other district. The housing authority is under a positive duty to enquire whether the applicant would be at such a risk and, if they would, it should not be assumed that the applicant will take steps to deal with the threat. For further guidance on local connection see Chapter 10.

21.39 Section 198(3) defines violence as violence from another person or threats of violence from another person which are likely to be carried out. Housing authorities should be alert to the deliberate distinction which is made in section 198(3) between actual violence and threatened violence. A high standard of proof of actual violence in the past should not be imposed. The threshold is that there must be:

(a) no risk of domestic violence (actual or threatened) in the other district; and,
(b) no risk of non-domestic violence (actual or threatened) in the other district. Nor should 'domestic violence' be interpreted restrictively.

Eligibility

21.40 People who have no recourse to public funds are not generally eligible for homelessness assistance. However, the Destitute Domestic Violence Concession supports those who have entered or stayed in the UK as a spouse, unmarried partner, same-sex or civil partner of a British Citizen, or settled citizen and this relationship has permanently broken down due to domestic violence and abuse. A victim may be eligible if:
(a) they came to the UK or were granted leave to stay in the UK as the spouse or partner of a British Citizen or someone settled in the UK;
(b) their relationship has permanently broken down due to domestic violence and abuse.

21.41 They can then apply to the Home Office for limited leave to remain (3 months) under the Destitute Domestic Violence Concession to enable them to access public funds and advice, whilst they prepare and submit an application for indefinite leave to remain (or to make alternative arrangements).

CHAPTER 22
Care leavers

Guidance on providing homelessness services to care leavers.

22.1 This chapter provides guidance on specific duties towards care leavers who are homeless or threatened with homelessness. It covers:
(a) corporate parenting duties placed on housing authorities;
(b) joint working arrangements between housing authorities and children's services authorities;
(c) prevention and relief of homelessness;
(d) assessing whether or not a care leaver has a priority need for accommodation; and,
(e) the provision of suitable accommodation.

Corporate parenting duties

22.2 Local authorities have duties and powers to assist young people who are leaving and have left local authority care. As a corporate parent to all children in care and care leavers all parts of a local authority, including a housing authority, must have regard to the need:
(a) to act in the best interests, and promote the physical and mental health and well-being, of those children and young people;
(b) to encourage those children and young people to express their views, wishes and feelings;
(c) to take into account the views, wishes and feelings of those children and young people;
(d) to help those children and young people gain access to, and make the best use of, services provided by the local authority and its relevant partners;

(e) to promote high aspirations, and seek to secure the best outcomes, for those children and young people;
(f) for those children and young people to be safe, and for stability in their home lives, relationships and education or work; and,
(g) to prepare those children and young people for adulthood and independent living.

Children and Social Work Act 2017 (Part 1, (1(a–g))

22.3 There is a duty on children's services authorities to appoint a Personal Adviser to provide support to care leavers until they reach their 25th birthday (except where the young person no longer wants a Personal Adviser) (Part 1(3), Children and Social Work Act 2017). The support provided by Personal Advisers should be based on the needs of the young person as set out in their statutory Pathway Plan. This may include support from a housing authority.

22.4 Any joint working arrangements between a children's services authority and a housing authority for care leavers' transition to independent living should include ensuring the delivery of effective preparation for independence with planned, sustainable moves into supported or independent accommodation. Local processes and/or practices should not involve care leavers routinely being treated as homeless when care placements come to an end in order to place the housing authority under an obligation to secure accommodation under Part 7 of the 1996 Act.

Joint working arrangements

22.5 The Secretary of State for the Ministry of Housing, Communities and Local Government and the Secretary of State for Education consider that all young people leaving care should have safe and appropriate accommodation to meet their needs. By working together, housing authorities and children's services authorities can better ensure that as a corporate parent, the appropriate accommodation and support is available to care leavers.

22.6 Housing authorities, children's services authorities and other relevant departments within local authorities, are advised to develop joint protocols or procedures to ensure that each department plays a full role in providing corporate parenting support to young people leaving care. In two-tier areas all housing authorities in the county should be party to these arrangements.

22.7 A joint protocol should cover arrangements for achieving planned, supportive transitions to independent living; identifying homelessness risk early and acting to prevent it, and providing a quick, safe, joined up response for care leavers who do become homeless.

Advice and information

22.8 Advisory services provided by housing authorities' under section 179 must be designed to meet the needs of care leavers in their district (section 179(2)(b)). For further guidance on the provision of advice and information on homelessness see Chapter 3. Housing authorities should work with children's services authorities and consult with care leavers themselves to ensure the advice and information is:
(a) designed and delivered in an appropriate format for the age of the client group;

(b) available through communication channels which care leavers are most likely to access;
(c) understood by children's services authority staff.

22.9 It is recommended that housing options advice be made available to young people preparing to leave care to help them to make informed choices and avoid becoming homeless. Housing authorities may wish to provide training and information to social workers, Personal Advisers and others who have responsibility to support looked after young people, to ensure that the most up to date and accurate information on housing options is available to them.

Prevention and relief of homelessness

22.10 There is a duty on specified public bodies to refer to a housing authority (with consent) any household which is threatened with homelessness or is homeless within 56 days to a housing authority with the service user's consent (section 213B). The following services are among those subject to the duty to refer:
(a) social service authorities; and,
(b) custodial institutions, youth offending teams and probation services.

22.11 For further guidance on duty to refer see Chapter 4. Specific referral arrangements should be made for care leavers and set out in the joint protocol or procedures.

22.12 When a young person aged between 18 and 24 approaches directly or is referred to a housing authority, if it is known that they are a care leaver or the young person says they are a care leaver, then the children's services authority which has responsibility for them should be informed as soon as possible, with consent from the young person.

22.13 Where there is a duty to assess a care leaver's housing and other support needs and develop a personalised housing plan, arrangements should be in place to enable the Personal Adviser to be involved in the assessment process with the young person's consent. For further guidance on assessments and personalised housing plans see Chapter 11. Where there is no agreed local working arrangement, or where the young person has been looked after by a children's services authority which is not part of local joint protocol arrangements, the housing authority must continue without delay with the duties owed to the young person under Part 7 of the 1996 Act.

22.14 Where a care leaver has a personalised housing plan this should be informed, by their Pathway Plan (section 23C(3)(b) of the Children Act 1989). The Secretary of State for the Ministry of Housing, Communities and Local Government considers it appropriate for housing authorities to involve a young person's Personal Adviser in assessing their needs and circumstances and developing a personalised housing plan that is appropriate to them. The young person's consent must be obtained, and it would be advisable to seek their consent for the Personal Adviser to continue to be informed and involved in efforts to prevent or relieve homelessness. The Personal Adviser may also be requested to take actions to deliver the personalised housing plan.

22.15 There are specific legal requirements in relation to local connection for care leavers (section 199(8) to (11). For further guidance on local connection see Chapter 10.

22.16 Subject to arrangements for consent, where a housing authority is concerned that a care leaver may not be co-operating with the required steps set out in the personalised housing plan this should be shared as soon as possible with the Personal Adviser to enable joint early action to remind the young person of the actions to be taken and the consequences of not doing so. For further guidance on deliberate and unreasonable refusal to co-operate see Chapter 14. Joint working to understand mitigating factors and resolve issues should continue throughout any action related to deliberate and unreasonable refusal to co-operate.

22.17 The Secretary of State for the Ministry of Housing, Communities and Local Government considers that all attempts should be made by housing authorities to avoid the impact of intentionally homeless decisions in relation to care leavers aged 18–25. For further guidance on intentional homelessness see Chapter 9. It will be a matter for the housing authority to determine whether or not a care leaver has become homeless intentionally, taking into account all relevant facts. To inform this assessment, housing authorities should consult with the relevant children's services authority and obtain advice and information as to the young person's emotional and mental well-being, maturity and general ability to understand the impact of their actions.

22.18 The personalised housing plan should be reviewed and, the housing authority and Personal Adviser or other officer should work together with the young person to try and resolve the issues.

22.19 Children's services authorities have a duty to 'former relevant' care leavers in terms of accommodation if there are no other options available and the welfare of the care leaver requires it (section 23C(4c) of the Children Act 1989).

Assessing priority need

22.20 Section 193 of the 1996 Act requires housing authorities to secure accommodation for applicants who have a priority need, and whose homelessness has not been prevented or relieved.

22.21 Categories and definitions of people who have priority need are set out in Chapter 8, and include young people under 21 who were looked after between the ages of 16 and 18; and people aged 21 or more who are vulnerable as a result of having been looked after, accommodated or fostered. Both of these categories exclude 'relevant students', who are owed particular accommodation and support duties under the Children (Leaving Care) Act. It should be noted that a young person who was looked after when aged 16 or 17 will be in priority need when they are 18, 19 or 20 years old, whether or not they qualify for care leaving services from a children's services authority.

22.22 Guidance on priority need and vulnerability is contained in Chapter 8, and should be taken into account when assessing whether a person aged 21 or over is vulnerable as a result of having been looked after, accommodated or fostered. Factors that a housing authority may wish to consider include:

(a) the length of time that the applicant was looked after, accommodated or fostered;

(b) the reasons why they were looked after, accommodated or fostered;

(c) the length of time since the applicant left care, and whether they have been able to obtain and maintain accommodation during any of that period;

(d) whether the applicant has any existing support networks, particularly including family, friends or a mentor.

22.23 Housing authorities should take particular care in assessing whether a care leaver aged 21 or over is vulnerable, and should take into account whether, if homeless, they would be at particular risk of exploitation, abuse or involvement in offending behaviour as a result of having been looked after, accommodated or fostered.

Suitable accommodation for care leavers

22.24 Housing authorities and children's services authorities should adopt a shared strategic approach to the provision of suitable accommodation for care leavers.

22.25 In considering suitability, all authorities should bear in mind that care leavers who are homeless will be particularly vulnerable and in need of support. They may lack skills in managing their affairs and require help with managing their own accommodation and operating a household budget. Many care leavers are likely to lack the advice and support normally available to other young people from family, friends and a mentor.

22.26 There should be no blanket presumption that at 18 a young person who has left care will be ready for their own tenancy; this should be a matter of individual assessment. Options will be based on their individual preferences, needs, circumstances and the local provision available and might include, for example, supported lodgings, supported accommodation or independent accommodation with visiting support.

22.27 Bed and breakfast accommodation, including hotels and nightly let accommodation with shared facilities, is not considered suitable for care leavers aged under 25 and should only be used in exceptional circumstances and for short periods.

22.28 The specific needs and circumstances of care leavers should be taken into account in determining suitability of accommodation in relation to its location. For example, in the absence of strong family support networks they may wish to live as near as possible to another significant adult such as a friend or ex-foster carer; or need to avoid certain locations due to childhood experiences or associations.

22.29 Housing authorities may want to involve Personal Advisers in decisions about the suitability of accommodation and inform them prior to making an offer of accommodation, with the young person's consent. For further guidance on suitability of accommodation see Chapter 17.

CHAPTER 23
People with an offending history

Guidance on providing homelessness services to people with an offending history.

23.1 This chapter provides guidance on providing homelessness services to people with an offending history.

23.2 People with an offending history are over represented amongst single people who are homeless and sleep rough, and a lack of accommodation is likely to have a negative impact on prospects for successful resettlement and rehabilitation. Female offenders often have complex needs which affect their access to suitable and sustainable accommodation on release from custody.

23.3 Housing authorities will need to work in collaboration with HM Prisons providers of probation services (National Probation Service (NPS) and Community Rehabilitation Companies (CRCs)), Youth Offending Services, as well as other relevant partners to prevent people leaving custody, or living in the community, from becoming homeless. The duty to refer introduced through the 2017 Act provides an impetus to develop effective referral arrangements and accommodation pathways that involve all relevant agencies to provide appropriate jointly planned help and support to prevent home-lessness.

23.4 Housing authorities should work closely with Youth Offending Services and children's social care services to ensure joint and advanced planning around the needs of young people leaving custody. Particular care should be taken to ensure that young people aged 16–17 and care leavers aged 18–24 do not leave custody without an accommodation plan in place. This will also require cooperation between housing authorities and children's social care services in advance of release.

23.5 Housing authorities and offender management services (i.e. prisons, youth offending services and probation providers) should work together to ensure the accommodation needs of people leaving custody and those serving their sentence in the community are met. Probation providers have a responsibility to support people under their supervision to reduce reoffending. CRCs and the NPS must provide direct support to help people find accommodation. Housing authorities should continue to work with these agencies, as well as prisons and voluntary sector organisations, to ensure their clients access suitable accommodation

23.6 The following criminal justice services are subject to the duty to refer, meaning they are required to refer service users in England they consider may be homeless or threatened with homelessness within 56 days to a local housing authority, with the service user's consent:

(a) prisons (public and private);
(b) young offender institutions;
(c) secure training centres;
(d) secure colleges;
(e) youth offending teams; and,
(f) probation providers (CRCs and NPS).

For further guidance on duty to refer see Chapter 4.

Advice and information

23.7 People with an offending history generally face additional barriers in accessing housing, and therefore will need targeted advice and information to help them to secure accommodation.

23.8 Section 179(2)(a) of the 1996 Act requires authorities to provide information and advice which is designed to meet the needs of people released from prison or youth detention. Advice and information to people with an offending history may be delivered via the housing authority's website, social media, through leaflets or through dedicated advice services, and will be most effective if developed in consultation or jointly with offender management services in the district (i.e. prisons, youth offending services and probation providers).

Housing authorities may also wish to consult with prisoners or people with an offending history before developing resources tailored to their particular needs.

23.9 Advice and information should reflect local circumstances and arrangements but might include:

(a) the support available to people going in to custody which will enable them to retain a tenancy or license, or to surrender it so that rent arrears do not accrue;

(b) housing benefit or universal credit entitlement for people in custody;

(c) tenancy rights and how to protect a tenancy where it is appropriate to do so;

(d) housing options for people leaving custody, including access to the social housing register, supported housing and help available to secure private rented accommodation; and,

(e) support services for people with an offending history that might help them to secure and/or to sustain accommodation on release.

23.10 It is recommended that housing advice be made available to people whilst in custody, and that housing authorities collaborate with prisons from which offenders are released to their districts, together with probation providers, to provide accessible advice on housing options available to them. For further guidance on providing advice and information see Chapter 3.

Prevention

23.11 Housing authorities should put in place arrangements that will help to prevent people with an offending history from becoming homeless. Policies and partnerships designed to reduce homelessness might include, but not be limited to, the areas set out in 23.12 to 23.15 below.

Preventing loss of accommodation due to offending behaviour:

23.12 Tenants may be at risk of becoming homeless because of their own or others' anti-social or offending behaviour. Housing authorities should ensure that their housing management procedures include early contact with a tenant who they believe may be responsible for behaviour that could result in their becoming homeless, and that private landlords and private registered providers are encouraged to alert them where tenants are threatened with eviction. Where offender management services continue to be involved with the person they should be alerted of any risk of homelessness, so that joint plans may be put in place to try and prevent homelessness and provide additional support where appropriate.

23.13 Sometimes people with an offending history, and their families, become homeless because it is no longer safe for them to remain in their tenancy. Young people, who become involved in gang related activity, whether as victims or perpetrators, sometimes face particular risks. Housing authorities should work with police, offender managers and specialist services to coordinate activity to minimise risk and prevent homelessness. This will also help reduce re-offending and promote community safety.

Preventing loss of accommodation whilst a person is in custody:

23.14 Prison services and probation providers carry out assessments to identify resettlement needs, including the need for accommodation, at the start of a prisoner's period in custody. Sentence planning arrangements require plans for resettlement to be reviewed throughout the sentence and appropriate support arranged to meet a person's needs on leaving custody.

23.15 Assessing an offender's housing needs at the start of a period in custody will help to identify if assistance is required to end, sustain or transfer an existing tenancy, access welfare support to meet rent costs while in prison, or close down an existing tenancy appropriately. Housing authorities are advised to assist the Prison service and probation providers in providing advice to prisoners and taking action to ensure they can sustain or surrender their accommodation while in custody.

Preventing homelessness on leaving custody:

23.16 If a prisoner is assessed as requiring assistance with accommodation on release, there will usually be sufficient time to consider their options and take action to try and prevent their homelessness. In most cases, but particularly with young people, contact should be made with family to try and support a return home (where safe to do so) if only on a temporary basis. Where a person preparing to leave custody cannot return to family or another safe address, housing authorities should work with the applicant and liaise with offender manager and support services to agree and to deliver reasonable steps to prevent them from becoming homeless on release.

Assessing priority need

23.17 Housing authorities have a duty to help secure accommodation for any applicant threatened with homelessness on leaving custody, irrespective of priority need. For further guidance on prevention duty see Chapter 12, for further guidance on the relief duty see Chapter 13 and for further guidance on assessments and plans see Chapter 11.

23.18 Where activity to prevent or relieve homelessness is unsuccessful the authority will need to assess whether the person has a priority need for accommodation and is owed the main housing duty. For further guidance on priority need see Chapter 8 and for further guidance on accommodation duties see Chapter 15. **A person who is vulnerable as a result of having served a custodial sentence, been committed for contempt of court or remanded in custody has a priority need for accommodation.**

23.19 Assessments of vulnerability should be composite, taking into account all relevant factors that might contribute to a person being significantly more vulnerable if homeless than an ordinary person would be if homeless. In determining whether applicants who fall within this category are vulnerable as a result of their period in custody a housing authority will need to take into account all of the relevant factors including:

(a) the length of time the applicant served in custody or detention (although authorities should not assume that vulnerability could not occur as a result of a short period in custody or detention);

(b) whether the applicant is receiving supervision from a criminal justice agency e.g. the providers of probation services (NPS and CRCs) or youth offending team. Housing authorities should have regard to any advice from criminal justice agency staff regarding their view of the applicant's general vulnerability, but the final decision on the question of vulnerability for the purposes of the homelessness legislation will rest with the housing authority;

(c) the length of time since the applicant was released from custody or detention, and the extent to which the applicant has been able to obtain and/or maintain accommodation during that time;

(d) whether the applicant has any existing support networks and how much of a positive influence these networks are likely to be in the applicant's life.

23.20 Housing authorities should take into account the assessments of housing and support needs completed by offender management services, or voluntary organisations acting on behalf of these agencies.

Intentional homelessness

23.21 People with an offending history may apply for homelessness assistance after losing their accommodation due to a period in custody. In considering whether such an applicant is homeless intentionally the housing authority will have to decide whether:

(a) there was a likelihood that ceasing to occupy the accommodation could reasonably have been regarded at the time as a likely consequence of committing the offence; and,

(b) the accommodation would have otherwise continued to be available to the person at the point in time when they applied for homelessness assistance.

23.22 Housing authorities must consider each application on a case by case basis, in the light of all the facts and circumstances, including the age and maturity of the applicant, and should discuss the matter with the relevant provider of probation services. Authorities should not adopt a blanket policy which assumes that people who have lost accommodation whilst in custody will or will not be assessed as intentionally homeless.

Local connection

23.23 Housing authorities may receive applications from people leaving custody who do not have a local connection to their district but do have a connection to another local authority area. For further guidance on local connection see Chapter 10. If the applicant is eligible for assistance and threatened with homelessness the housing authority taking the application will have a section 195 prevention duty, whether or not the applicant has a local connection. Detention in prison (whether convicted or not) does not establish residency of choice in the district the prison is in, and so will not create a local connection with that district.

23.24 However, if the applicant is homeless the receiving authority may, if it is satisfied that the conditions are met, make a referral to another district where the applicant has a local connection. If the notified authority accepts that the conditions for referral are met they will take on the section 189B relief duty, as well as a duty to provide accommodation if there is reason to believe the applicant may be in priority need.

23.25 In considering whether or not a referral should be made, the authority that has taken the application should consider the particular circumstances of the applicant, and any risks involved in referring them to another local authority area. An applicant cannot be referred to another area where they would be at risk of violence. The authority will also want to take into account the considerations identified in paragraphs 23.26 and 23.27 below where relevant, before making a final decision.

Suitability of accommodation

23.26 Section 208(1) requires housing authorities to secure accommodation within their district, in so far as is reasonably practicable. There may be circumstances in which there are clear benefits for the applicant of being accommodated outside of the district. This could occur where upon the advice of the relevant provider of probation service (NPS or CRC) or through Multi Agency Public Protection Arrangements (MAPPA) it is decided that a person with an offending history should be placed outside the district to reduce risk of reoffending, or to help break links with previous contacts who could exert a negative influence.

23.27 There may also be instances where a criminal justice agency or MAPPA advise that in order to ensure appropriate distance between the applicant and their victims, the applicant should reside in a particular area, where they do not have a local connection.

23.28 When assessing the accommodation needs of a person with an offending history an authority will need to take into account their support needs, which in some cases might be complex. Young people leaving custody are likely to require accommodation with some level of support if they are to maintain their tenancy or license and avoid reoffending.

Accessing accommodation

23.29 People with an offending history face barriers to accessing accommodation across tenures. Housing authorities providing help to secure or securing accommodation should be aware of the provisions of the Rehabilitation of Offenders Act 1974 (as amended by the Legal Aid, Sentencing and Punishment of Offenders Act 2012). The Rehabilitation of Offenders Act 1974 sets out timescales for when convictions become spent, after which it is unlawful for social and private landlords to take spent convictions into account when determining whether the person is suitable for housing.

CHAPTER 24
Former members of the armed forces

Guidance on providing homelessness services to former members of the armed forces.

24.1 This chapter provides guidance on providing homelessness services to former members of the armed forces, who are referred to throughout as veterans.

24.2 Members of Her Majesty's regular naval, military and air forces are generally provided with accommodation by the Ministry of Defence (MOD), but are required to leave this when they are discharged from the service.

24.3 Housing authorities that have a significant number of service personnel stationed in their area will need to work closely with relevant partners, such as the Joint Service Housing Advice Office and MOD's resettlement services, to ascertain likely levels of need for housing assistance amongst people leaving the forces and plan their services accordingly.

24.4 The Secretary of State for Defence is subject to the duty to refer in relation to members of the regular forces. The Secretary of State is required to refer members of the regular forces in England he considers may be homeless or threatened with homelessness within 56 days to a local housing authority, with the individual's consent. For further guidance on the duty to refer see Chapter 4. The regular forces are the Royal Navy, the Royal Marines, the regular army and the Royal Air Force.

Advice and information

24.5 The principal responsibility for providing housing information and advice to Service personnel lies with the armed forces up to the point of discharge and these services are delivered through the Joint Service Housing Advice Officeand through Veterans UK. Some people, who have served in the armed forces for a long period, and those who are medically discharged, may be offered assistance with resettlement by the MOD's resettlement staff.

24.6 Housing authorities have a duty (section 179) to provide advisory services free of charge to people in their district. The service must be designed to meet the needs of certain groups, which include former members of the regular armed forces. This duty will be particularly relevant for housing authorities who have armed forces stationed within their districts, and in these circumstances authorities are encouraged to consult with the services concerned about how best to deliver local housing advice to prevent veterans from becoming homeless. For further guidance on providing advice and information on homelessness and threatened with homelessness see Chapter 3.

Veterans required to leave service accommodation

24.7 The MOD recognises that housing authorities will need to be satisfied that entitlement to occupy service accommodation will end on a certain date in order to determine whether applicants who are service personnel and approaching their date of discharge may be homeless or threatened with homelessness.

24.8 For this purpose, the MOD issues a Certificate of Cessation of Entitlement to Occupy Service Accommodation 6 months before discharge. These certificates indicate the date on which entitlement to occupy service accommodation ends, and the Secretary of State considers that housing authorities should not insist upon a court order for possession to establish that entitlement to occupy has ended.

Priority need

24.9 A person who is vulnerable as a result of having been a member of Her Majesty's regular armed forces (a veteran) has a priority need for accommodation. Veterans will include a person who was previously a member of the regular naval, military or air forces.

24.10 In considering whether veterans are vulnerable (as set out in paragraph 6.9 above) as a result of their time spent in the forces, a housing authority may wish to take into account the following factors:

(a) the length of time the applicant spent in the armed forces (although authorities should not assume that vulnerability could not occur as a result of a short period of service);

(b) the type of service the applicant was engaged in (those on active service may find it more difficult to cope with civilian life);
(c) whether the applicant spent any time in a military hospital (this could be an indicator of a serious health problem or of post-traumatic stress);
(d) whether HM Forces' medical and welfare advisers have judged an individual to be particularly vulnerable in their view and have issued a Medical History Release Form giving a summary of the circumstances causing that vulnerability;
(e) the length of time since the applicant left the armed forces, and whether they have been able to obtain and/or maintain accommodation during that time; and,
(f) whether the applicant has any existing support networks, particularly by way of family or friends.

Intentional homelessness

24.11 Where service personnel are required to vacate service quarters as a result of taking up an option to give notice to leave the service, and in so doing are acting in compliance with their contractual engagement, they should not be considered to have become homeless intentionally. For further guidance on intentional homelessness see Chapter 9.

Local connection

24.12 Section 315 of the Housing and Regeneration Act 2008 amended section 199 of the 1996 Act to enable members of the armed forces to establish a local connection through residence or employment in the same way as a civilian. For further guidance on local connection see Chapter 10.

CHAPTER 25
Modern slavery and trafficking

Guidance on providing homelessness services to victims of modern slavery.

25.1 This chapter provides guidance on modern slavery in relation to applicants who are threatened with homelessness or homeless.

What is modern slavery and trafficking

25.2 Modern slavery is a serious and often hidden crime in which people are exploited for criminal gain. The impact can be devastating for victims. Modern slavery comprises slavery, servitude, and forced or compulsory labour and human trafficking. The common factors are that a victim is, or is intended to be, used or exploited for someone else's (usually financial) gain, without respect for their human rights.

25.3 Modern slavery can take many different forms. The following are types of exploitation which commonly occur in the UK and individuals may experience more than one form of abuse:

(a) **sexual exploitation:** victims are coerced into sex work or sexually abusive situations. This includes child sexual exploitation. Victims may be brought to the UK on the promise of legitimate employment, or moved around the UK to be sexually exploited. In some cases they may know they will be involved in sex work, but are forced into a type or frequency they did not agree to. Victims are more commonly female but can also be male;

(b) **domestic servitude:** domestic servitude typically involves victims working in a private family home where they are ill treated, humiliated, subjected to unbearable conditions or working hours or made to work for little or no pay. The victim could be used in this way by their own family members or partner. Again, it is very difficult for them to leave, for example because of threats, the perpetrator holding their passport, or using a position of power over the victim;

(c) **labour exploitation:** labour exploitation usually involves unacceptably low pay, poor working conditions or excessive wage deductions, but is not solely about this. In order to constitute modern slavery there will also be some form of coercion meaning that victims cannot freely leave for other employment or exercise choice over their own situation. Where the perpetrator is taking advantage of a child or vulnerable person, an offence can be committed without the element of coercion;

(d) **criminal exploitation:** criminal exploitation is the exploitation of a person to commit a crime for someone else's gain. For example victims could be coerced into shoplifting, pick-pocketing, entering into a sham marriage, benefit fraud, begging or drug cultivation such as cannabis farming;

(e) other forms of exploitation include organ or tissue removal; forced begging and illegal adoption. For further information, see Modern slavery awareness and victim identification guidance.

Identification

25.4 Modern slavery is a highly complex crime. There is no typical victim of slavery – victims can be men, women and children of all ages, ethnicities and nationalities (including British) and cut across the population. But it is normally more prevalent amongst the most vulnerable groups, and within minority or socially excluded groups. Child victims are victims of child abuse and should therefore be treated as such using existing child protection procedures and statutory protocols.

25.5 Victims of modern slavery can be found anywhere. There are certain industries where they are currently more prevalent, such as nail bars, car washes, agriculture and fishing, building sites and the sex industry. Other high risk situations include when there is a need for a sudden injection of workers into the work force, such as seasonal staff or construction for a major event. However victims may also pass through transport hubs, health services and other public places or be found in private homes.

25.6 In all cases decision makers should be alive to the possibility that applicants for assistance under Part 7 are victims of modern slavery, or are otherwise vulnerable. Particular care should be paid to children, especially where there are doubts about the relationship with any purported guardian. **Children's social services should be alerted to any safeguarding concerns immediately.**

The National Referral Mechanism

25.7 The National Referral Mechanism (NRM) is the process by which people who may be victims of modern slavery are identified and supported by the UK Government.

25.8 **Local authorities, as designated first responder organisations, should refer any individual they suspect to be a victim of modern slavery to the NRM.** Adults have to provide informed consent to be referred to the NRM, but children do not need to consent and must be referred to the NRM if there are suspicions that the child has been a victim of modern slavery.

25.9 Following the referral of an adult or child into the NRM, an initial 'reasonable grounds' decision will be made within 5 days. If this decision is positive, the individual will be entitled to access safe accommodation provided through a central-government funded Victim Care Contract. If the person would otherwise be destitute during that 5 day period they can access emergency accommodation by contacting the Salvation Army. However, the person may be referred to the housing authority to provide accommodation if the individual is a British citizen who is homeless, eligible and has or may have a priority need.

25.10 In some instances, the adult involved may not give consent to a referral to the NRM. In this case, instead of referring the case, the local authority has a duty to notify the Home Office under section 52 of the Modern Slavery Act 2015. For further information, see Guidance for public authorities on duty to notify.

What support is provided by the National Referral Mechanism

25.11 The provision of support through the NRM is a devolved matter in the United Kingdom and differs depending on whether the victim is an adult or child. The below information covers the support offer to adult and child victims in England and Wales.

Adult support and assistance

25.12 If an adult receives a positive 'reasonable grounds' decision through the NRM, they are entitled to support for a minimum period of 45 days. This is provided through a central-government funded Victim Care Contract and includes accommodation, subsistence, counselling, access to mental, physical and dental health services, and signposting to legal services.

25.13 Whilst in support, a 'conclusive grounds' decision will be made on their case through the NRM and they will be provided with a letter setting out whether there was enough evidence to conclude that they are indeed a victim of modern slavery. The individual will then receive a short period of move-on support focused on their transition out of central government-funded support, which may include liaising with housing authorities or local homelessness services.

Children support and assistance

25.14 Children are supported locally and are not provided with support and assistance through Victim Care Contract, unless with a parent who is a potential victim. Housing authorities should refer unaccompanied children to children's services in line with local safeguarding procedures.

Applications and inquiries under Part 7

25.15 In many cases involving modern slavery or trafficking, the applicant may be in considerable distress and officers would benefit from appropriate training to enable them to conduct such interviews. Applicants should be given the option of being interviewed by an officer of the same sex if they wish.

25.16 Housing authorities should refer any individual they suspect to be a victim of modern slavery to the NRM (see paragraphs 25.7 to 25.10).

25.17 A person who has been a victim of trafficking or modern slavery may have a priority need for accommodation if they are assessed as being vulnerable according to section 189(1)(c) of the 1996 Act. In assessing whether they are vulnerable a housing authority should take into account advice from specialist agencies providing services to the applicant, such as their assigned support provider under the NRM. Many victims of modern slavery suffer from poor mental health and often lack support structures in the area they are residing. If a victim of modern slavery is threatened with homelessness or is homeless this significantly increases their risk to being re-trafficked or exposed to further exploitation. For further guidance on priority need see Chapter 8.

25.18 Section 188(1) of the 1996 Act requires housing authorities to secure that accommodation is available for an applicant if they have reason to believe that the applicant may be homeless, eligible for assistance and have a priority need. If housing authorities believe an individual may be vulnerable as a result of being a victim of modern slavery following a referral to the NRM housing authorities should ensure that accommodation is available while they are waiting for an initial 'reasonable grounds' decision.

25.19 Housing authorities may find it helpful to establish local, joint working arrangements with NRM support providers where appropriate to help identify people at risk of homelessness as early as possible and maximise the opportunities to prevent homelessness.

Suitability of accommodation

25.20 There will be a number of accommodation options for victims of modern slavery. Housing authorities should consider which are most appropriate for each person on a case by case basis taking into account their specific circumstances and needs.

25.21 Account will need to be taken of any special considerations relating to the applicant and their household or their experiences that might affect the suitability of accommodation. Where there is no other option for applicants who have suffered modern slavery but to be accommodated in an emergency hostel or bed and breakfast accommodation, the accommodation may need to be gender-specific as well as have appropriate security measures depending on their needs and circumstances. Any risk of violence or racial harassment in a particular locality should also be taken into account, and housing authorities should be mindful that individuals who have left their traffickers remain at risk of being re-trafficked.

25.22 Whilst authorities should, as far as is practicable, aim to secure accommodation within their own district, they should also recognise that there can be benefits for some applicants to be accommodated outside of the district. This could occur in cases of modern slavery or trafficking where the applicant, and/or a member of their household, would be vulnerable to further exploitation and needs to be accommodated outside the district to reduce the risk of further contact with the perpetrator(s) and to help break links which could exert a negative influence.

ANNEX 1
The habitual residence test

Guidance on considering housing applications from persons who are subject to the habitual residence test.

1. In practice, when considering housing applications from persons who are subject to the habitual residence test, it is only necessary to investigate habitual residence if the applicant has arrived or returned to live in the UK during the 2 year period prior to making the application.

Definition of habitually resident

2. The term 'habitually resident' is not defined in legislation. Local authorities should always consider the overall circumstances of a case to determine whether someone is habitually resident in the UK, the Channel Islands, the Isle of Man or the Republic of Ireland.

General principles

3. When deciding whether a person is habitually resident in a place, consideration must be given to all the facts of each case in a common sense way. It should be remembered that:
   (a) the test focuses on the fact and nature of residence;
   (b) a person who is not resident somewhere cannot be habitually resident there. Residence is a more settled state than mere physical presence in a country. To be resident a person must be seen to be making a home. It need not be the only home or a permanent home but it must be a genuine home for the time being. For example, a short stay visitor or a person receiving short term medical treatment is not resident;
   (c) the most important factors for habitual residence are the length, continuity and general nature of actual residence rather than intention;
   (d) the practicality of a person's arrangements for residence is a necessary part of determining whether it can be described as settled and habitual;
   (e) established habitual residents who have periods of temporary or occasional absence of long or short duration may still be habitually resident during such absences.

Action on receipt of an application

Applicant came to live in the UK during the previous 2 years

4. If it appears that the applicant came to live in the UK during the previous 2 years, authorities should make further enquiries to decide if the applicant is habitually resident, or can be treated as such.

Factors to consider

5. The applicant's stated reasons and intentions for coming to the UK will be relevant to the question of whether they are habitually resident. If the applicant's stated intention is to live in the UK, and not return to the country from which they came, that intention must be consistent with their actions.
6. To decide whether an applicant is habitually resident in the UK, authorities should consider the factors set out below. However, these do not provide an

exhaustive check list of the questions or factors that need to be considered. Further enquiries may be needed. The circumstances of each case will dictate what information is needed, and all relevant factors should be taken into account.

Why has the applicant come to the UK?

7. If the applicant is returning to the UK after a period spent abroad, and it can be established that the applicant was previously habitually resident in the UK and is returning to resume their former period of habitual residence, they will be immediately habitually resident.
8. In determining whether an applicant is returning to resume a former period of habitual residence authorities should consider:
   (a) when did the applicant leave the UK?
   (b) how long did the applicant live in the UK before leaving?
   (c) why did the applicant leave the UK?
   (d) how long did the applicant intend to remain abroad?
   (e) why did the applicant return?
   (f) did the applicant's partner and children, if any, also leave the UK?
   (g) did the applicant keep accommodation in the UK?
   (h) if the applicant owned property, was it let, and was the lease timed to coincide with the applicant's return to the UK?
   (i) what links did the applicant keep with the UK?
   (j) have there been other brief absences? If yes, obtain details
   (k) why has the applicant come to the UK?
9. If the applicant has arrived in the UK within the previous 2 years and is not resuming a period of habitual residence, consideration should be given to their reasons for coming to the UK, and in particular to the factors set out below.

Applicant is joining family or friends

10. If the applicant has come to the UK to join or rejoin family or friends, authorities should consider:
    (a) has the applicant sold or given up any property abroad?
    (b) has the applicant bought or rented accommodation or are they staying with friends?
    (c) is the move to the UK intended to be permanent?

Applicant's plans

11. Authorities should consider the applicant's plans, e.g.:
    (a) if the applicant plans to remain in the UK, is the applicant's stated plan consistent with their actions?
    (b) were any arrangements made for employment and accommodation (even if unsuccessful) before the applicant arrived in the UK?
    (c) did the applicant buy a one-way ticket?
    (d) did the applicant bring all their belongings?
    (e) is there any evidence of links with the UK, e.g. membership of clubs?
12. The fact that a person may intend to live in the UK for the foreseeable future does not, of itself, mean that habitual residence has been established. However, the applicant's intentions along with other factors, for example the disposal of property abroad, may indicate that the applicant is habitually resident in the UK.

13. An applicant who intends to reside in the UK for only a short period, for example for a holiday or to visit friends is unlikely to be habitually resident in the UK.

Length of residence in the UK

14. To be habitually resident in a country an applicant must have actually taken up residence and lived there for a period. It is not sufficient that the applicant came to the UK voluntarily and for settled purposes. They must be resident in fact for an appropriate period of time which demonstrates that their residence has become, and is likely to remain, habitual in nature. The appropriate period of time need not be lengthy if the facts indicate that a person's residence has become habitual in nature at an early stage. In some circumstances the period can be as little as a month, but it must be a period which is more than momentary in a claimant's life history. A period of between 1 and 3 months is likely to be appropriate to demonstrate that a person's residence is habitual in nature.

Length of residence in another country

15. Authorities should consider the length and continuity of an applicant's residence in another country:
    (a) how long did the applicant live in the previous country?
    (b) does the applicant have any remaining ties with their former country of residence?
    (c) has the applicant stayed in different countries outside the UK?
16. It is possible that a person may own a property abroad but still be habitually resident in the UK. A person who has a home or close family in another country would normally retain habitual residence in that country. A person who has previously lived in several different countries but has now moved permanently to the UK may be habitually resident here.

Centre of interest

17. An applicant is likely to be habitually resident in the UK, the Channel Islands, the Isle of Man or the Republic of Ireland, despite spending time abroad, if their centre of interest is located in one of these places.
18. People who maintain their centre of interest in the UK, the Channel Islands, the Isle of Man or the Republic of Ireland, for example a home, a job, friends, membership of clubs, are likely to be habitually resident there. People who have retained their centre of interest in another country and have no particular ties with the UK, the Channel Islands, the Isle of Man or the Republic of Ireland, are unlikely to be habitually resident in the UK, the Channel Islands, the Isle of Man or the Republic of Ireland.
19. Authorities should take the following into account when deciding the centre of interest:
    (a) home;
    (b) family ties;
    (c) club memberships;
    (d) finance accounts.
20. If the centre of interest appears to be in the UK, the Channel Islands, the Isle of Man or the Republic of Ireland but the applicant has a home somewhere else, authorities should consider the applicant's intentions regarding the property.

21. In certain cultures, e.g. the Asian culture, it is quite common for a person to live in one country but have property abroad that they do not intend to sell. Where such a person has lived in the UK, the Channel Islands, the Isle of Man or the Republic of Ireland for many years, the fact that they have property elsewhere does not necessarily mean that they intend to leave, or that the applicant's centre of interest is elsewhere.

ANNEX 2

Note: In its response to consultation on the draft Code of Guidance, the government indicated that it intended to attach the Local Government Association's Procedures for Referrals of Homeless Applicants to Another Local Authority 2018, at that time itself also being consulted on, once finalised, as Annex 2 to the 2018 Code of Guidance, in the same way that the previous version of the Procedures was attached as Annex 18 to the previous Code of Guidance. At time of printing, the Procedures had been agreed by the local authority associations which are party to it but the government had not yet formally added it to the published Code. What follows is the final version of the Procedures, provided by the LGA and reproduced with its permission. While, therefore, it is not formally part of the 2018 Code of Guidance, it does represent the agreement between the associations.

PROCEDURES FOR REFERRALS OF HOMELESS APPLICANTS TO ANOTHER LOCAL AUTHORITY[4]

AGREED BY:

LOCAL GOVERNMENT ASSOCIATION (LGA)
CONVENTION OF SCOTTISH LOCAL AUTHORITIES (CoSLA)
WELSH LOCAL GOVERNMENT ASSOCIATION (WLGA)
(*'the local authority associations'*)

Guidelines for Local Authorities on Procedures for Referral

These procedures and guidelines concern the situation where, under Part 7 of the Housing Act 1996, a local housing authority consider that the conditions for referral of the case to another local housing authority are met and notifies the other authority of its opinion. Referrals are discretionary only. Housing authorities are not required to make inquiries as to whether, for example, an applicant has a local connection with another district and, where they decide to do so, there is no requirement to refer applicants to another authority if the conditions for referral are met. Authorities may have a policy about how they may exercise their discretion. However, they cannot decide in advance that a referral will be made in all cases where an applicant may, for example, have a local connection with another district.

1 SCOPE AND PURPOSE

1.1 These procedures and guidelines mainly concern local housing authorities in England and the legal framework which applies to them, but they also cover cross-border issues in relation to Scotland and Wales. They apply following the changes made to Part 7 of the Housing Act 1996 by the Homelessness Reduction Act 2017. Authorities in England may notify another authority of their opinion that the conditions for referral are met if the notifying authority would be subject to a duty under either s189B (the 'initial' or 'relief' duty) or s193 (the 'main' housing duty) of the Housing Act 1996; but referrals cannot be made to Scottish or Welsh authorities at the relief stage. Authorities should follow the relevant statutory provisions and have regard to governmental guidance when considering referrals; the information given below in relation to those provisions and guidance is by way of an overview only.

1.2 Section 198 of the Housing Act 1996 provides that:

(5) The question whether the conditions for referral of a case which does not involve a referral to a local housing authority in Wales are satisfied shall be determined by agreement between the notifying authority and the notified authority or, in default of agreement, in accordance with such arrangements as the Secretary of State may direct by order.

(5A) The question whether the conditions for referral of a case involving a referral to a local housing authority in Wales shall be decided by agreement between the notifying authority and the notified authority or, in default of agreement, in accordance with such arrangements as the Secretary of State and the Welsh Ministers may jointly direct by order.

(6) An order may direct that the arrangements shall be:

(a) those agreed by any relevant authorities or associations of relevant authorities, or

(b) in default of such agreement, such arrangements as appear to the Secretary of State or, in the case of an order under subsection (5A), to the Secretary of State and the Welsh Ministers to be suitable, after consultation with such associations representing relevant authorities, and such other persons, as he thinks appropriate.

1.3 Similar provision is made in s80(5) and (6) of the Housing (Wales) Act 2014 in relation to Wales and in s33(4) and (5) of the Housing (Scotland) Act 1987 in relation to Scotland. However, s8 of the Homelessness (Scotland) Act 2003 (not yet in force) gives Scottish ministers the power to suspend or vary the circumstances under which a homeless applicant may be referred by a Scottish local authority to another authority in Scotland. Please note any future orders made will need to be taken into account.

1.4 The LGA, CoSLA and the WLGA, the local authority associations in England, Scotland and Wales, have agreed guidelines for referrals which they recommend to local housing authorities. The relevant statutory framework contains detailed provisions in relation to referrals, including where it appears that the applicant does not have a local connection with the area of the authority receiving the housing application but does have one with another area in England, Scotland or Wales. There are, however, considerable areas of possible disagreement and dispute in determining whether the conditions of referral are met in any particular case. Although, in the last resort, disagreements can only be resolved by the courts, the associations are anxious to avoid, as far as possible, legal disputes between local authorities. The associations therefore issue these agreed guidelines on the procedures and criteria to be followed, and recommend them for general adoption by all their members. **These Guidelines are without prejudice to the duty of local authorities to treat each case on its merits and to take into account existing and future case law.** Furthermore, these Guidelines only apply to the issues of local connection and whether the conditions for referral are met.

1.5 In *R v Eastleigh BC ex p Betts* [1983] 2 AC 613, the House of Lords considered the application of the referral arrangements agreed between the local authority associations. Their Lordships decided that a rigid application of the arrangements would constitute a fetter on an authority's discretion. **The agreement could be taken into account, and applied as a guideline, provided its application to each case is given individual consideration.**

1.6 A previous version of this agreement was considered by the Court of Appeal in *Ozbek v Ipswich BC* [2006] EWCA Civ 534, [2006] HLR 41, the following being said at [37]–[38]:

> one purpose – indeed, perhaps, the principal purpose – of the Referral Guidelines and their predecessor, the Agreement on Procedures, is to facilitate agreement between authorities on the question whether the conditions for referral are met; or to provide a basis for speedy and inexpensive resolution of disputes between authorities on that question. . . . [T]hat purpose is unlikely to be achieved unless authorities do follow the guidance which those guidelines provide by applying that guidance 'generally to all applications which come before them'. [A]n authority is not to be criticised for following that guidance in the individual case, provided that they have not closed their mind to the possibility that the particular facts of that case may require a departure from the guidance which they would apply more generally.
>
> . . . The conditions for referral – set out in s198(2) of the 1996 Act – include (a) that the applicant does not have a local connection with the notifying authority and (b) that the applicant does have a local connection with the notified authority. It is desirable (if the statutory scheme is to work smoothly) that both notifying authority and notified authority should be able to agree on both conditions. Or, to put the point another way, it is desirable that the notified authority – who is being asked to assume the burden of providing accommodation for the applicant in the place of the notifying authority – should be able to accept the view of the notifying authority both that the applicant has no local connection with the district of the notifying authority and that the applicant does have a local connection with their own district. Ready agreement is unlikely to be achieved on those two points unless both the notifying authority and the notified authority are able to approach the question from a common basis. It is the need for that common basis which, as it seems to me, provides the imperative for all authorities to apply the guidelines 'generally to all applications which come before them'.

2 DEFINITIONS

2.1 For the purposes of this agreement, the relevant statutory definitions apply. All references in this agreement to an '*applicant*' are to be taken as references to a housing applicant to whom the relevant duty would be owed but for the decision to refer the case to another authority.

2.2 The authority to whom the applicant applies for accommodation or assistance and which decides to refer the case to another authority is the *'notifying authority'*.

2.3 Where the notifying authority consider that the conditions for referral are met, including where neither the applicant nor any person who might reasonably reside with the applicant has a local connection with its district but does have one with another local authority district and notifies the other local authority of its opinion, the authority which they notify is known as the *'notified authority'*.

2.4 The principal context in which the question of referral may arise concerns *'local connection'*, defined as explained below, but the conditions for referral may also be met in certain other cases. These guidelines provide a framework within which the referral procedures may be applied.

3 CRITERIA FOR NOTIFICATION

3.1 The criteria for notification are set out in the statutory framework and are addressed in governmental guidance. The following is designed to provide merely an overview.

3.2 Before a local authority can consider referring an applicant to another local authority under s198(A1) it must first be satisfied that the applicant is
(i) eligible for assistance and
(ii) homeless.

3.3 Before a local authority can consider referring an applicant to another local authority under s198(1) it must be satisfied that, in addition to meeting the two criteria noted above, the applicant also:
(i) is in priority need and
(ii) did not become homeless intentionally.

3.4 Before making a referral the notifying authority must be satisfied that the conditions of referral are met. Broadly, the conditions for referral will be met if:
(a) neither the applicant nor any person who might reasonably be expected to reside with the applicant has a local connection with the district of the authority to which the application was originally made,
(b) either the applicant or any person who might reasonably be expected to reside with the applicant has a local connection with the district of the other authority,
(c) neither the applicant nor any person who might reasonably be expected to reside with the applicant would run the risk of domestic violence in that other district and
(d) neither the applicant nor any person who might reasonably be expected to reside with the applicant has suffered any other violence in that other district and it is not probable that returning to that district would lead to further violence of a similar kind.

3.5 The conditions for referral will also be met if the application is made within a period of two years beginning with the date on which the applicant accepted a 'private rented sector' offer from the other authority under s193(7AA), provided that (c) and (d), above, are met.

3.6 The conditions for referral will also be met if the applicant was placed in the authority's district by another authority as a result of a previous application to that authority and the second application is made within the prescribed period (5 years) of the first.

3.7 In deciding whether or not to make a referral, authorities should also consider the Court of Appeal decision in the case of *R v Newham LBC ex p Tower Hamlets LBC* [1991] 1 WLR 1032. The notifying authority should have regard to any decisions made by the notified authority that may have a bearing on the case in question (eg a previous decision that the applicant was intentionally homeless) as well as any other material considerations, which should include the general housing circumstances prevailing in the district of the notifying authority and in the district of the notified authority. The notifying authority should also consider whether it is in the public interest to accept a duty to secure accommodation.

3.8 Should a local authority wish to accept a duty to secure accommodation for an applicant who does not have a local connection with its district, nothing in this agreement shall prevent the authority from providing such assistance. The decision to make a referral is discretionary and could be challenged if the discretion was considered to have been exercised unreasonably.

3.9 Under s202 of the Housing Act 1996, applicants have the right to request a review of certain decisions made by the local authority about their application, including a decision to notify another authority under s198(1) and a decision that the conditions are met for referral of the case to another authority.

4 LOCAL CONNECTION

4.1 The test for establishing a local connection is set out in s199 of the Housing Act 1996 and addressed in detail in governmental guidance. The following is designed to provide merely an overview.

4.2 The relevant date for deciding whether or not a local connection has been established is not the date when the application for housing assistance was made but the date of the decision or, if there is a review, the date of the review decision (see the House of Lords' judgment in *Mohamed v Hammersmith and Fulham LBC* [2001] 1 AC 547). Moreover, if inquiries prior to a decision have been prolonged, the notifying authority should also consider whether there may have been any material change in circumstances that might affect the question of whether a local connection has been established.

4.3 A local connection may be established where the following grounds apply, subject to the exceptions below:

(i) the applicant or a person who might reasonably be expected to reside with the applicant is, or in the past was, normally resident in the district. It is suggested that a working definition of 'normal residence' should be residence for at least 6 months in the area during the previous 12 months, or for not less than 3 years during the previous 5-year period. The period taken into account should be up to the date of the authority's decision. This should include any periods living in temporary accommodation secured by the authority under s188 (interim duty pending inquiries);

(ii) the applicant or a person who might reasonably be expected to reside with the applicant is at present employed in the district. The local authority should obtain confirmation from the employer that the person is in employment and that the employment is not of a casual nature;

(iii) the applicant or a person who might reasonably be expected to reside with the applicant has family associations in the district. Family associations normally arise where an applicant or a person who might reasonably be expected to reside with the applicant has parents, adult children or brothers or sisters who have been resident in the district for a period of at least 5 years at the date of the decision, and the applicant indicates a wish to be near them. Only in exceptional circumstances would the residence of relatives other than those listed above be taken to establish a local connection, but the circumstances may be sufficient and all cases will be fact-specific. The residence of dependent children in a different district from their parents would not be residence of their own choice and therefore would not establish a local connection with that district. However, a referral should not be made to another local authority on the grounds of a local connection because of family associations if the applicant objects to those grounds;

(iv) there are special circumstances which the authority considers establish a local connection with the district. This may be particularly relevant where the applicant has been in prison or hospital and his or her circumstances do not conform to the criteria in (i)–(iii) above. Where, for example, an applicant seeks to return to a district where he or she was brought up or lived for a considerable length of time in the past, there may be grounds for considering that the applicant has a local connection with that district because of special circumstances. An authority must exercise its discretion when considering whether special circumstances apply.

4.4 A notifying authority should not refer an applicant to another authority on grounds of a local connection because of special circumstances without the prior consent of the notified authority. Alternatively, authorities may come to an informal arrangement in such cases on a reciprocal basis, subject to the agreement of the applicants.

4.5 There are certain circumstances where the local connection provisions set out above may be modified. More detail is contained in governmental guidance. See:

(i) care leavers;
(ii) ex-service personnel;
(iii) ex-prisoners and detainees under the Mental Health Act 1983;
(iv) former asylum seekers.

5 PROCEDURES IN MAKING A REFERRAL

5.1 If an authority considers that the conditions for referral in s198 Housing Act 1996 are likely to be met in a particular case it should make any necessary enquiries in the area/s where there may be a local connection. These should be undertaken as soon as possible. An authority that is considering making a referral must investigate all the circumstances of the case with the same thoroughness as if it were not considering a referral.

5.2 Under s184(4) Housing Act 1996, if a housing authority notifies or intends to notify another authority in England under s198(A1) (ie at the relief duty stage) that it considers that the conditions for referral of a case are met, the authority must at the same time notify the applicant of this decision and the reasons for it. Under s184(5) of the 1996 Act, the notice must also inform the applicant of his right, under s202, to request a review of the decision and that any request must be made within 21 days, or such longer period as the authority allows in writing.

5.3 See further below as to the duty to ensure that suitable accommodation is available for occupation by the applicant, where an authority notifies an applicant, either as above under s198(A1) or for the purposes of s200(1) (ie at the s193 main duty stage).

5.4 In general, the notified authority is bound by any decision made by the notifying authority as to whether the applicant is eligible, homeless, unintentionally homeless, and in priority need; there is no provision for the notified authority to challenge the decision other than judicial review in the High Court. For notifications made under s198(A1), however, where the notifying authority has made a decision as to whether the applicant is eligible, homeless or became homeless intentionally, the notified authority may come to a different decision but only if it is satisfied the applicant's circumstances have changed or further information has come to light since the notifying authority made its decision, and that the change in circumstances or further information justifies coming to a different decision (s199A(5)(c)).

5.5 When it has been decided whether the conditions for referral are met, the notifying authority must notify the applicant of the decision and the reason for it (s199A(3) and s200(2)). The applicant must also be informed of his right to ask for a review of the decision and that any request must be made within 21 days or such longer period as the authority may allow in writing.

5.6 The local authority associations' disputes procedure should be used only where there is a disagreement over the question of whether the conditions for referral are met and not for resolving disagreement on any other matter.

6 MAKING THE NOTIFICATION TO THE OTHER AUTHORITY

6.1 All notifications and arrangements concerning an applicant should be made by telephone and then confirmed in writing. A specimen standard notification form is attached, which authorities are advised to use. If telephone contact cannot be made, an email or fax should be sent. Where the notified authority accepts that the conditions for referral are met, it should not wait for the receipt of written confirmation of notification before making appropriate arrangements to secure accommodation for the applicant and his or her household.

6.2 Each authority should nominate an officer responsible for making decisions about applications notified by another authority. Appropriate arrangements should also be put in place to ensure cover during any absences of the designated officer.

6.3 The notified authority should normally accept the facts of the case relating to residence, employment, family associations etc., as stated by the notifying authority, unless they have clear evidence to the contrary. It is the notifying authority's duty to make inquiries into the circumstances of homelessness with the same degree of care and thoroughness before referring a case to another authority as it would for any other case.

6.4 Local authorities should try to avoid causing undue disruption to the applicant which could arise from the operation of the criteria and procedures set out above. For instance, where it is agreed that the conditions for referral are met, the two authorities involved could agree, subject to the applicants' consent, to enter into a reciprocal arrangement so as to avoid having to move a household which may already have made arrangements within the notifying authority's area for schooling, medical treatment etc. Such arrangements could involve provision via nominations to other social housing providers such as registered social landlords. Authorities are reminded that there is no requirement to refer applicants to another authority even where it is agreed that the conditions for referral are met.

6.5 Once written confirmation of notification has been received the notified authority should, within 10 days, reply to the notifying authority. If, despite reminders, there is an unreasonable delay by the notified authority in formally responding to the notification, the notifying authority may ask its local authority association to intercede on its behalf.

7 ARRANGEMENTS FOR SECURING ACCOMMODATION

7.1 Where an authority notifies an applicant that it intends to notify or has notified another authority of their opinion that the conditions for referral are met at the s193 main duty stage, it has a duty under s200(1) to ensure that suitable accommodation is available for occupation by the applicant until s/he is notified of the decision whether the conditions for referral are met. A similar duty arises under s199A(2) where the notifying authority similarly notifies an applicant in relation to a s198(A1) referral at the s189B relief duty stage, but only if it has reason to believe that the applicant may have a priority need. The notifying authority may also have a duty (under s211) to take reasonable steps for the protection of property belonging to the applicant or anyone who might reasonably be expected to reside with the applicant.

7.2 If it is decided that the conditions for referral are not met, the notifying authority will be subject to either the s189B relief duty (see s199A(4)(a)) or the s193 main duty (see s200(3)), depending on whether the referral arose under s198(A1) or s198(1).

7.3 If it is decided that the conditions for referral are met, then either

(i) under s199A(5)(a), the applicant is treated as having made an application to the notified authority on the date on which the applicant is given notice that the referral conditions are met, or

(ii) under s200(4), the notified authority will be subject to the s193 main duty and must ensure that suitable accommodation is available for the applicant,

as the case may be.

7.4 The local authority associations recommend that once a notified authority has accepted that the conditions of referral are met it shall reimburse the notifying authority for any expenses which may reasonably have been incurred in providing temporary accommodation, including protection of property. If the notifying authority delays unduly before advising an authority of its intention to refer an applicant then the notified authority shall only be responsible for expenses incurred after the receipt of notification. In normal circumstances a period of more than 30 working days, commencing from the date when the notifying authority had reason to believe that the applicant may be homeless or threatened with homelessness and commenced inquiries under s184, should be considered as constituting undue delay.

8 RIGHT OF REVIEW OF REFERRAL DECISIONS

8.1 Under s202(1)(c) Housing Act 1996, applicants have the right to request a review of a decision by the authority under s198(1) to notify another authority of its opinion that the conditions for referral are met.

8.2 Further, under s202(1)(d), applicants have the right to request a review of any decision whether the conditions for referral are met (whether the notification was made under s198(A1) or s198(1)).

9 STATUTORY PROCEDURE ON REVIEW

9.1 The procedural requirements for a review are set out in the Homelessness (Review Procedure etc) Regulations 2018 SI No 223. There is some overlap between the requirements for reviews in general, considered here so far as they are relevant to referrals, and the requirements for reviews of a referee's decision under the Disputes Procedure, considered below.

9.2 The notifying authority must notify the applicant:
(i) that the applicant, or someone acting on the applicant's behalf, may make written representations; and
(ii) of the review procedures.

9.3 If the reviewer acting for the notifying authority considers that there is an irregularity in the original decision, or in the manner in which it was made, but is minded nonetheless to make a decision which is against the interests of the applicant, the reviewer must notify the applicant:
(i) that the reviewer is so minded, and the reasons why; and
(ii) that the applicant, or someone acting on the applicant's behalf, may make further written and/or oral representations.

9.4 In carrying out a review the reviewer must:
(i) consider any representations made by, or on behalf of, the applicant;
(ii) consider any further written and/or oral representations made by, or on behalf of, the applicant in response to a notification referred to in paragraph 9.3(ii) above; and
(iii) make a decision on the basis of the facts known at the date of the review.

9.5 In general, the applicant must be notified of the decision on a review within:
(i) eight weeks from the date on which a request for review was made, or
(ii) such longer period as the applicant may agree in writing.

9.6 Where the decision under review is a joint decision by the notifying housing authority and the notified housing authority, s202(4) requires that the review be carried out jointly by the two housing authorities. In that situation, the applicant must be notified of the decision on a review within:
(i) ten weeks from the date on which a request for review was made, or
(ii) such longer period as the applicant may agree in writing.

9.7 Where the decision under s198(5) was taken by a referee, the procedure is described in the *Guidelines for Invoking the Disputes Procedure*, below.

9.8 Section 204 gives applicants the right to appeal to the county court on a point of law if dissatisfied with the decision on the review (or the initial decision, if a review decision is not made within the relevant prescribed time limit).

10 DISPUTES BETWEEN AUTHORITIES

10.1 Where a notified authority considers the conditions for referral are not met it should write to the notifying authority giving its reasons in full, within 10 days. The letter should contain all the reasons for its opinion, to avoid delay and minimise any inconvenience for the applicant.

10.2 The Homelessness (Decisions on Referrals) Order 1998 SI No 1578 sets out the arrangements for determining whether the conditions for referral are met, should the notifying and the notified authority fail to agree.

10.3 Where two authorities cannot reach agreement on whether the conditions for referral are met they must seek to agree on a referee who will make the decision. The LGA has established an independent panel of referees for this purpose. A referee should be appointed within 21 days of the notified authority receiving the notification.

10.4 Authorities invoking the disputes procedure should, having first agreed on the proposed referee, establish that he or she is available and willing to accept the case. Each authority is then responsible for providing the referee with such information as he or she requires to reach a decision, making copies of the submission available to the applicant and ensuring prompt payment of fees and expenses. The *Guidelines for Invoking the Disputes Procedure* set out in greater detail the requirements and timescale for the disputes procedure.

10.5 If the authorities are unable to agree on the choice of a referee, they must jointly request that the LGA appoint a referee on their behalf from the independent panel.

10.6 If a referee has still not been appointed within six weeks of the notified authority receiving the referral, the notifying authority must request the LGA to appoint a referee.

10.7 The local authority associations should only be involved in the direct appointment of referees as a last resort. Under normal circumstances authorities should jointly agree the arrangements between themselves in accordance with the *Guidelines for Invoking the Disputes Procedure*.

10.8 Authorities invoking the disputes procedure should be bound by the decision of the referee, including the apportionment of fees and expenses, subject to a further decision by a referee where the applicant asks for a review of the initial decision.

11 CROSS-BORDER DISPUTES

11.1 In Scotland, the main homelessness law is the Housing (Scotland) Act 1987, while in Wales it is the Housing (Wales) Act 2014. Both make similar provision to s198 of the Housing Act 1996: s33 of the Housing (Scotland) Act 1987 and s80 of the Housing (Wales) Act 2014. Where relevant, regard should be had to the appropriate national governmental guidance. Note that the position of former asylum seekers with regard to local connection may be quite different in Scotland from England and Wales.

11.2 Where there is a cross-border dispute, it is the legislation relevant to the location of the *notified* authority which should be applied in determining whether the conditions for referral are met.

11.3 The review procedure in Scotland and Wales respectively is governed by ss35A and 35B of the Housing (Scotland) Act 1987 and the Homelessness (Review Procedure) (Wales) Regulations 2015 SI No 1266.

11.4 The Homelessness (Decisions on Referrals (Scotland) Order 1998 SI No 1603 sets out the arrangements for determining whether the conditions for referral are met, should the notifying and the notified authority fail to agree, where the notifying authority is in Scotland. These are in the same terms as for England, but the referee is appointed through CoSLA.

Guidelines for Invoking the Disputes Procedure

12 DETERMINING DISPUTES

12.1 The local authority associations have been concerned to establish an inexpensive, simple, speedy, fair and consistent way of resolving disputes between authorities arising from the referral of homeless applicants.

12.2 For the purpose of this Disputes Procedure, arbitrators are referred to as 'referees'. Referees will not normally be entitled to apply the criteria set out in this agreed procedure without the consent of the local authorities involved in the dispute. Where the issues in the case are evenly balanced, referees may have regard to the wishes of the applicant.

12.3 In determining disputes referees will need to apply the relevant statutory framework and have regard to the appropriate national governmental guidance.

13 ARRANGEMENTS FOR APPOINTING REFEREES

13.1 Referees will be approached by the authorities in dispute, both of which must agree that the referee should be invited to accept the appointment, to establish whether they are willing and able to act in a particular dispute. The referee should be appointed within 21 days of the notified authority receiving the referral. If the local authorities are unable to agree on the choice of referee they should contact the LGA in accordance with section 10 of the *Guidelines for Local Authorities on Procedures for Referral.*

13.2 A referee will be given an initial indication of the reason for the dispute by the relevant authorities or the local authority association. The referee's jurisdiction is limited to the issue of whether the conditions for referral are met.

13.3 A referee must not have any personal interest in the outcome of the dispute and should not accept the appointment if he or she is, or was, employed by, or is a council tax payer in, one of the disputing local authorities, or if he or she has any connection with the applicant.

14 PROCEDURES FOR DETERMINING THE DISPUTE

14.1 The general procedures to be followed by a referee in determining a dispute are outlined in the Schedule to the Homelessness (Decisions on Referrals) Order 1998 SI No 1578. It is recommended that the following, more detailed, procedures are applied to *all* cases.

14.2 Following appointment, the referee shall invite the notifying and notified authorities to submit written representations within a period of ***fourteen*** working days, specifying the closing date, and requiring them to send copies of their submission to the applicant and to the other authority involved in the dispute. Authorities must have the opportunity to see each other's written statements, and should be allowed a further period of ***ten*** working days to comment thereon before the referee proceeds to determine the issue. The referee may also invite further written representations from the authorities, if considered necessary.

14.3 The homeless applicant to whom the dispute relates is not a direct party to the dispute but the referee may invite written or oral representations from the applicant, or any other person, which is proper and relevant to the issue. Where the referee invites representations from a person they may be made by another person acting on the person's behalf, whether or not the other person is legally qualified.

14.4 The disputing authorities should make copies of their submissions available to the applicant. The authorities should have the opportunity to comment on any information from the applicant (or any other source) upon which the referee intends to rely in reaching his/her decision.

14.5 Since the applicant's place of abode is in question, and temporary accommodation and property storage charges may be involved, it is important that a decision should be reached as quickly as possible – normally within ***a month*** of the receipt of the written representations and comments from the notifying and notified authority. This period will commence at the end of the process described in paragraph 14.2. In the last resort, a referee may determine a dispute on the facts before him/her if one authority has, after reminders, failed to present its case without reasonable cause.

15 ORAL HEARINGS

15.1 Where an oral hearing is necessary or more convenient (eg where the applicant is illiterate, English is not his/her first language or further information is necessary to resolve issues in dispute), it is suggested that the notifying authority should be invited to present its case first, followed by the notified authority and any other persons whom the referee wishes to hear. The applicant may be invited to provide information on relevant matters. The authorities should then be given a right to reply to earlier submissions.

15.2 The referee will have to arrange the venue for the hearing and it is suggested that the offices of the notifying authority would often be the most convenient location.

15.3 Where a person has made oral representations the referee may direct either or both authorities to pay reasonable travelling expenses. The notifying and notified authorities will pay their own costs.

15.4 The referee's determination must be in writing even when there is an oral hearing.

16 NOTIFICATION OF DETERMINATION

16.1 The written decision of the referee should set out:

(a) the issue(s) which s/he has been asked to determine
(b) the findings of fact which are relevant to the question(s) in issue
(c) the decision
(d) the reasons for the decision.

The referee's determination is binding upon the participating local authorities, subject to the applicant's right to ask for a review of the decision under s202 of the Housing Act 1996 (and possible right of appeal to the county court on a point of law under s204).

17 COSTS OF DETERMINATION

17.1 Referees will be expected to provide their own secretarial services and to obtain their own advice on points of law. The cost of so doing, however, will be costs of the determination and recoverable as such.

18 CIRCULATION OF DETERMINATION

18.1 Referees should send copies of the determination to both disputing authorities and to the LGA. The LGA will circulate copies to other members of the Panel of Referees as an aid to settling future disputes and promoting consistency in decisions.

18.2 The notifying authority should inform the applicant of the outcome promptly.

19 PAYMENT OF FEES AND COSTS

19.1 The local authority associations recommend a flat rate fee of £500 per determination (including determinations made on a review) which should be paid in full and as speedily as possible after the determination has been received. However, in exceptional cases where a dispute takes a disproportionate time to resolve, a referee may negotiate a higher fee. In addition, the referee may claim the actual cost of any travelling, secretarial or other incidental expenses which s/he has incurred, including any additional costs arising from the right of review or the right of appeal to a county court on a point of law.

19.2 The LGA will determine such additional fees as may be appropriate for any additional work which may subsequently arise should there be a further dispute or appeal after the initial determination has been made or should a referee be party to an appeal, under s204 Housing Act 1996, to the county court on a point of law.

19.3 The referee's fees and expenses, and any third party costs, would normally be recovered from the unsuccessful party to the dispute, although a referee may choose to apportion expenses between the disputing authorities if s/he considers it warranted. Referees are advised, when issuing invoices to local authorities, to stipulate that payment must be made within **28 days**.

20 REOPENING A DISPUTE

20.1 Once a determination on a dispute is made, a referee is not permitted to reopen the case, even though new facts may be presented to him or her, unless a fresh determination is required to rectify an error arising from a mistake or omission.

21 REVIEW OF REFEREE'S DECISION

21.1 Section 202(1)(d) Housing Act 1996 gives an applicant the right to request a review of any decision made under this Dispute Procedure. The procedural requirements for a review are set out in the Homelessness (Review Procedure etc) Regulations 2018 SI No 223. There is some overlap between the requirements for reviews of a referee's decision under the Disputes Procedure, considered here, and the requirements for reviews in general, considered above so far as they are relevant to referrals.

21.2 If an applicant asks for a review of a referee's decision the notifying and notified authority must, within five working days, appoint another referee ('the reviewer') from the panel. This applies even if the original referee was appointed by the LGA. The reviewer must be a different referee from the referee who made the initial decision. If the two authorities fail to appoint a reviewer within this period then the notifying authority must, within five working days, request the LGA to appoint a reviewer and the LGA must do so within seven days of the request.

21.3 The authorities are required to provide the reviewer with the reasons for the initial decision, and the information on which the decision is based, within five working days of his or her appointment. The two authorities should decide between them who will be responsible for notifying the applicant of the reviewer's decision, once received.

21.4 The reviewer is required to:
(i) notify the applicant that he or she, or someone acting on his or her behalf, may make written representations,
(ii) notify the applicant of the review procedures, and
(iii) send copies of the applicant's representations to the two authorities and invite them to respond.

21.5 If the reviewer considers that there is an irregularity in the original decision, or in the manner in which it was made, but is minded nonetheless to make a decision which is against the interests of the applicant on one or more issues, the reviewer must notify the applicant:
(a) that the reviewer is so minded and the reasons why, and
(b) that the applicant, or someone acting on his behalf, may make further written and/or oral representations.

21.6 In carrying out a review, the reviewer is required to:
(i) consider any representations made by, or on behalf of, the applicant,
(ii) consider any responses to (i) above,
(iii) consider any further written and/or oral representations made by, or on behalf of, the applicant in response to a notification referred to in paragraph 21.5(b), and
(iv) make a decision on the basis of the facts known at the date of the review.

21.7 The applicant must be notified of the decision on a review within twelve weeks from the date on which the request for the review was made, or such longer period as the applicant may agree in writing. The two authorities must be advised in writing of the decision on the review, and the reasons for it, **at least a week before the end of the period** in order to allow them adequate time to notify the applicant. Copies of the decision should also be sent to the LGA.

22 CROSS-BORDER DISPUTES

22.1 For cross-border cases, see Section 11 of the Guidelines, above.

Procedures for Referrals of Homeless Applicants on the Grounds of Local Connecton with Another Local Authority Standard Notification Form

A – NOTIFYING AUTHORITY DETAILS

Contact Name ______________________________

Authority ______________________________

Telephone Number ______________ Fax Number ______________

E-mail ______________________________

Address for Correspondence ______________________________

____

B – APPLICANT DETAILS

Name of Main Applicant ______________ Date of Birth ______________

Current Address ______________________________

____

____

____

____

C – FAMILY MEMBERS

Name	Relationship	Date of Birth

D – ADDRESSES IN LAST 5 YEARS (include dates and types of tenure)

____

____

____

____

____

____

____

____

E – PRESENT/PREVIOUS EMPLOYMENT DETAILS

Employer Telephone No ____________

Address______________________________________

Contact Name and Job Title__________________________

Previous Employer_____________________________

Date from Date to ________

Address______________________________________

F – REASONS FOR HOMELESSNESS

____

____

____

____

____

____

H – PROIRITY NEED CATEGORY

____

____

____

____

____

I – LOCAL CONNECTION DETAILS

____

____

____

____

____

J – WISHES OF THE APPLICANT(S) (in the context of the referral)

____

____

____

____

____

K – THE NOTIFYING AUTHORITY CONSIDER THE CONDITIONS FOR REFERRAL ARE MET BECAUSE:

____

____

____

____

____

L – ANY SUPPLEMENTARY INFORMATION
(attach supporting documentation if relevant)

I confirm that, in accordable with the s198 Housing Act 1996, this authority considers that neither the applicant nor any person who might reasonably be expected to reside with the applicant would run the risk of domestic violence or face a probability of other violence in the district of your authority, if this referral is made.

Signed ______________________ Date ______________

Right to move: statutory guidance on social housing allocations for local housing authorities in England (March 2015)

Introduction

1. This is guidance by the Secretary of State for Communities and Local Government under section 169 of the Housing Act 1996 ('the 1996 Act'). Local housing authorities housing authorities) are required to have regard to it in exercising their functions under Part 6 of the 1996 Act.
2. It is in addition to the Guidance for Local Housing Authorities in England on the Allocation of Accommodation issued in June 2012 ('the 2012 guidance').
3. References to sections in this guidance are references to sections in the 1996 Act.
4. Housing authorities are encouraged to review their existing allocation policies and revise them, where appropriate, in the light of this guidance as soon as possible.

PURPOSE OF THE GUIDANCE

5. The Government is committed to increasing mobility for social tenants to enable tenants to meet their aspirations, and to support them into work. We want to ensure that tenants are not prevented from taking up an employment opportunity because they cannot find a suitable place to live, recognising that long term unemployment is damaging for individuals and communities. That is why in the Autumn Statement 2013 we set out our intention to introduce a Right to Move for social tenants who need to move to take up a job or live closer to employment or training.
6. We've already taken some important steps in the right direction. *HomeSwap* Direct is helping social tenants search for a new home across the country. Through the Localism Act, we have given local authorities the freedom to make better use of the social housing stock by taking transferring tenants who are not in housing need out of the allocation legislation, allowing authorities to develop appropriate policies for transferring tenants, without the risk of challenge from those in greater need on the waiting list.
7. The Government has also taken decisive steps to increase the supply of affordable housing. The current Affordable Homes Programme is on track to deliver 170,000 homes between 2011 and 2015 with £19.5 billion of public and private investment. A further £38 billion of public and private investment will help deliver another 275,000 new affordable homes between 2015 and 2020.
8. To give effect to the Right to Move we have introduced regulations to prevent local authorities applying a local connection test that could disadvantage tenants who need to move across local authority boundaries for work related reasons. This guidance is intended to assist local authorities to implement these regulations.
9. The Government has made clear that we expect social homes to go to people who genuinely need and deserve them. That is why the Localism Act has maintained the protection provided by the statutory reasonable preference

criteria which ensure that priority for social housing continues to be given to those in the greatest housing need.

10. Another important aim of this guidance, therefore, is to assist local authorities to apply the allocation legislation to ensure that tenants who need to move within or across local authority boundaries are given appropriate priority under local authorities' allocation schemes.

QUALIFICATION

11. Section 160ZA(7) provides that local authorities may decide who does or does not qualify for an allocation of social housing, subject to any regulations made under subsection 8 which provides that the Secretary of State may prescribe that certain classes of persons are or are not qualifying persons, or that certain criteria cannot be taken into account in deciding who qualifies.
12. Subject to parliamentary scrutiny, the Allocation of Housing (Qualification Criteria for Right to Move) (England) Regulations 2015 SI No 967 ('the qualification regulations 2015') will come into force on 20 April. These provide that local authorities must not disqualify certain persons on the grounds that they do not have a local connection with the authority's district. Specifically, a local connection may not be applied to existing social tenants seeking to transfer from another local authority district in England who:
    - have reasonable preference under s166(3)(e) because of a need to move to the local authority's district to avoid hardship, and
    - need to move because the tenant works in the district, or
    - need to move to take up an offer of work
13. This will ensure that existing tenants who are seeking to move between local authority areas in England in order to be closer to their work, or to take up an offer of work (hereafter referred to together as 'work related reasons'), will not be disadvantaged.
14. We have made a similar provision for certain members of the Armed Forces community, by regulating to prevent local authorities from applying a local connection requirement to disqualify them,[1] in order to give effect to the Government's commitment that those who serve in the Armed Forces are not disadvantaged in their access to social housing by the need to move from base to base. Aside from members of the Armed Forces and transferring tenants who will benefit from the Right to Move, the Government has made clear that we expect local authorities to ensure that only long standing local residents, or those with a well established local association should qualify for social housing, and has issued statutory guidance to ensure that local authorities apply a residency test to social housing of at least two years.[2]

Local connection

15. Local connection is defined by s199. A person has a local connection because of normal residence (current or previous) of their own choice, employment, family associations, or special circumstances.

1 Allocation of Housing (Qualification Criteria for Armed Forces) (England) Regulations 2012 SI No 1869.

2 Providing Social Housing for Local People: Statutory guidance on social housing allocations for local authorities in England.

Need to move

16. The qualification regulations 2015 apply to transferring tenants who have reasonable preference under s166A(3)(e), that is to say the local authority is satisfied that they need to move to a particular locality in the district of the housing authority, where failure to meet that need would cause hardship (to themselves or others).
17. The local authority must ensure, therefore, not simply that the tenant needs to move for work, but that, if they were unable to do so, it would cause them hardship.
18. Local authorities must be satisfied that the tenant needs, rather than wishes, to move for work related reasons. In the Secretary of State's view the factors that local authorities should take into account in determining whether a tenant needs to move to be closer to work or to take up a job offer include:
    - the distance and/or time taken to travel between work and home
    - the availability and affordability of transport, taking into account level of earnings
    - the nature of the work and whether similar opportunities are available closer to home
    - other personal factors, such as medical conditions and child care, which would be affected if the tenant could not move
    - the length of the work contract
    - whether failure to move would result in the loss of an opportunity to improve their employment circumstances or prospects, for example, by taking up a better job, a promotion, or an apprenticeship
19. This is not an exhaustive list and local authorities may wish to consider providing for other appropriate factors to take into account in the light of local circumstances.

Work

20. The qualification regulations 2015 only apply if work is not short-term or marginal in nature, nor ancillary to work in another district. Voluntary work is also excluded.

Short-term

21. In determining whether work is short-term, the Secretary of State considers that the following are relevant considerations:
    - *whether work is regular or intermittent*

    This is likely to be particularly relevant in the case of the self-employed.
    - *the period of employment and whether or not work was intended to be short-term or long-term at the outset*

    In the Secretary of State's view a contract of employment that was intended to last for less than 12 months could be considered to be short-term.

Marginal

22. The following considerations would be relevant in determining whether work is marginal:
    - *the number of hours worked*

    In the Secretary of State's view employment of less than 16 hours a week could be considered to be marginal in nature. This is the threshold below which a person may be able to claim Income Support and the threshold for a single person's entitlement to Working Tax Credit.

- *the level of earnings*

23. Local authorities should take into account all the relevant factors when reaching a decision. The fact that a tenant only works 15 hours a week, for example, may not be determinative if they are able to demonstrate that the work is regular and the remuneration is substantial.

Ancillary

24. Work must not be ancillary to work in another local authority's district. This means that, if the person works occasionally in the local authority's district, even if the pattern of work is regular, but their main place of work is in a different local authority's district, the work is excluded from the ambit of these regulations.
25. A further relevant consideration would be whether the tenant is expected eventually to return to work in the original local authority district. If a local authority has reason to believe this is the case, they should seek verification from the tenant's employer.
26. A person who seeks to move into a local authority to be closer to work in a neighbouring authority – for example, where the transport links are better in the first local authority's area – is also excluded from these regulations. However, there is nothing to prevent local authorities looking sympathetically on tenants seeking to move into their authority's district for this reason, if they choose to do so.

Voluntary work

27. The regulations exclude voluntary work. Voluntary work means work where no payment is received or the only payment is in respect of any expenses reasonably incurred.

Apprenticeship

28. The term 'work' includes an apprenticeship. This is because an apprenticeship normally takes place under an apprenticeship agreement which is an employment contract (specifically a contract of service).

Genuine intention to take up an offer of work

29. Where the tenant has been offered a job and needs to move to take it up, they must be able to demonstrate to the local authority's satisfaction that they have a genuine intention to take up the offer.
30. Local authorities may wish to ask to see a letter of acceptance and may wish to contact the employer to verify the position. Authorities may also wish to seek clarification from the tenant by interviewing them over the telephone or in person.

Verification and evidence

31. Local authorities will want to satisfy themselves that the work or job-offer is genuine and should seek appropriate documentary evidence.
32. Appropriate evidence could include:
    - a contract of employment
    - wage/salary slips covering a certain period of time, or bank statements (this is likely to be particularly relevant in the case of zero-hours contracts)

- tax and benefits information – eg proof that the applicant is in receipt of working tax credit (if eligible)
- a formal offer letter

33. Additionally, local authorities may wish to contact the employer to verify the position.
34. Authorities are strongly advised to consider whether an applicant qualifies for an allocation under the qualification regulations 2015 both at the time of the initial application and when considering making an allocation.

PRIORITISATION

35. The qualification regulations will ensure that tenants who need to move between local authority districts for work related reasons are not disadvantaged by a local connection test. However, to deliver the Right to Move, it is also important that tenants who need to move for work, within or across local authority boundaries, are given appropriate priority under local authorities' allocation schemes.

Hardship reasonable preference

36. Section 166A(3) provides that housing authorities must frame their allocation scheme to ensure that reasonable preference is given to people who need to move to a particular locality in the authority's district, where failure to meet that need would cause hardship (to themselves or others).
37. Paragraph 4.11 of the 2012 guidance sets out the Secretary of State's view that 'hardship' would include, for example, a person who needs to move to a different locality to take up a particular employment, education or training opportunity.
38. This guidance goes further and strongly encourages all local authorities to apply the hardship reasonable preference category to tenants who are seeking to transfer and who need to move within the local authority district or from another local authority district to be closer to work, or to take up an offer of work.
39. In considering whether a transferring tenant needs to move for work related reasons to avoid hardship to themselves (or others), they may wish to take account of the guidance set out in paragraphs 16 to 34 above.
40. Where a tenant is seeking to move within the same local authority district, local authorities are encouraged to take a more flexible approach. This is because the tenant is already accommodated in the district and any move to another social home will therefore be broadly stock neutral (that is to say the transfer creates another void which can be used to meet other housing needs). In particular, local authorities should consider whether or not the issue of whether work is short-term, marginal, ancillary or voluntary carries the same weight in relation to a within district move.

Setting aside a proportion of lets for cross-boundary moves

41. In framing their allocation scheme to determine their allocation priorities, local authorities will wish to strike a balance between the interests of transferring tenants who need to move into their district for work related reasons and the demand from other applicants in identified housing need.
42. The Secretary of State considers that an appropriate way to do so would be for a local authority to set a quota for the proportion of properties that it expects

to allocate each year to transferring tenants who need to move into their district for work related reasons ('the Right to Move quota'). The Secretary of State strongly encourages all local authorities to adopt such an approach and considers that an appropriate quota would be at least 1%.

43. Local authorities should publish the quota as part of their allocation scheme, together with their rationale for adopting the specific percentage. They should review and revise the proportion as appropriate, in the light of changing circumstances.
44. Local authorities may wish to set aside a higher proportion than 1%. Authorities that decide to set a quota that is lower than 1%, should be ready to explain publicly why they have chosen to do so.
45. It is important that local authorities are open and accountable, to their own tenants and the wider community as well as to tenants seeking to move into the area for work related reasons. Accordingly, local authorities are encouraged to report locally on demand for and lettings outcomes in relation to the Right to Move quota.

Area based choice based lettings schemes

46. We are aware that in some parts of the country, local authorities participate in area-based choice based lettings schemes that bring together a number of authorities and Private Registered Providers of social housing, often with a common allocation policy that applies to all the partner local authorities.
47. We consider that such schemes provide an excellent basis for cross-boundary mobility, particularly as housing and employment markets are likely to be similar across the partner authorities. Accordingly, we strongly encourage all local authorities that participate in area-based choice based lettings schemes to consider how they can provide for tenants to move between partner authorities for work related reasons, for example, by providing for a quota of lettings to be made available for this group.

Providing social housing for local people: statutory guidance on social housing allocations for local authorities in England (December 2013)

Introduction

1. This is guidance by the Secretary of State for Communities and Local Government under section 169 of the Housing Act 1996 (the 1996 Act). Local housing authorities (housing authorities) are required to have regard to it in exercising their functions under Part 6 of the 1996 Act.
2. It is in addition to the Guidance for Local Housing Authorities in England on the Allocation of Accommodation issued in June 2012 (the 2012 guidance).
3. References to sections in this guidance are references to sections in the 1996 Act.
4. Housing authorities are encouraged to review their existing allocation policies and revise them, where appropriate, in the light of this guidance as soon as possible.

Purpose of the guidance

5. Social housing – stable and affordable – is of enormous importance for the millions who live in it now and for those who look to it to provide the support they need in future. The way it is allocated is key to creating communities where people choose to live and are able to prosper.
6. The Government has made clear that we expect social homes to go to people who genuinely need and deserve them. That is why the Localism Act has maintained the protection provided by the statutory reasonable preference criteria which ensure that priority for social housing continues to be given to those in the greatest housing need.
7. The Localism Act has also given back to local authorities the freedom to better manage their social housing waiting list, as well as providing authorities with greater flexibility to enable them to tackle homelessness by providing homeless households with suitable private sector accommodation. Local authorities can now decide who qualifies for social housing in their area, and can develop solutions which make best use of the social housing stock. This guidance is intended to assist housing authorities to make full use of the flexibilities within the allocation legislation to better meet the needs of their local residents and their local communities.
8. The Government has also taken decisive steps to increase the supply of affordable housing, with £19.5 billion of public and private investment in the current Spending Review, and up to £23.3 billion more money invested from 2015 to 2018 alongside receipts from Right to Buy sales.
9. This investment in new affordable housing will help to meet housing need. We now want to see local authorities take an approach to social housing allocations which gives greater priority to those in need who have invested in and demonstrated a commitment to their local community.
10. The Prime Minister has made clear the Government's determination to tackle the widespread perception that the way social housing is allocated is unfair, and to address concerns that the system favours households who have little

connection to the local area over local people and members of the Armed Forces. Another important aim of this guidance, therefore, is to encourage authorities to be open and transparent about who is applying for and being allocated social housing in their area.

Qualification for social housing

11. Section 160ZA(6) provides that housing authorities may only allocate accommodation to people who are defined as 'qualifying persons' and section 160ZA(7) gives them the power to decide the classes of people who are, or are not, qualifying persons.
12. The Government is of the view that, in deciding who qualifies or does not qualify for social housing, local authorities should ensure that they prioritise applicants who can demonstrate a close association with their local area. Social housing is a scarce resource, and the Government believes that it is appropriate, proportionate and in the public interest to restrict access in this way, to ensure that, as far as possible, sufficient affordable housing is available for those amongst the local population who are on low incomes or otherwise disadvantaged and who would find it particularly difficult to find a home on the open market.
13. Some housing authorities have decided to include a residency requirement as part of their qualification criteria, requiring the applicant (or member of the applicant's household) to have lived within the authority's district for a specified period of time in order to qualify for an allocation of social housing. The Secretary of State believes that including a residency requirement is appropriate and strongly encourages all housing authorities to adopt such an approach. The Secretary of State believes that a reasonable period of residency would be at least two years.
14. We are aware that in some parts of the country, housing authorities share a common allocation policy with their neighbours and may wish to adopt a broader residency test which would be met if an applicant lives in any of the partners' districts. Such an approach might be particularly appropriate where an established housing market area spans a number of local authority districts, and could help promote labour mobility within a wider geographical area.
15. Housing authorities may wish to consider whether there is a need to adopt other qualification criteria alongside a residency requirement to enable and ensure that applicants who are not currently resident in the district who can still demonstrate a strong association to the local area are able to qualify. Examples of such criteria might include:
    - family association – for example, where the applicant has close family who live in the district and who have done so for a minimum period of time
    - employment in the district – for example, where the applicant or member of their household is currently employed in the district and has worked there for a certain number of years
16. Whatever qualification criteria for social housing authorities adopt, they will need to have regard to their duties under the Equality Act 2010, as well as their duties under other relevant legislation such as section 225 of the Housing Act 2004.
17. Housing authorities are reminded of the desirability of operating a housing options approach (see paragraph 3.19 of the 2012 guidance) as part of a move to a managed waiting list. In this way, people who have not lived in the area

long enough to qualify for social housing can be provided with advice and any necessary support to help them find appropriate alternative solutions.

Providing for exceptions

18. Housing authorities should consider the need to provide for exceptions from their residency requirement; and must make an exception for certain members of the regular and reserve Armed Forces – see further at paragraph 23 below. Providing for appropriate exceptions when framing residency requirements would be in line with paragraphs 3.22 and 3.24 of the 2012 guidance.
19. It is important that housing authorities retain the flexibility to take proper account of special circumstances. This can include providing protection to people who need to move away from another area, to escape violence or harm; as well as enabling those who need to return, such as homeless families and care leavers whom the authority have housed outside their district, and those who need support to rehabilitate and integrate back into the community.
20. There may also be sound policy reasons not to apply a residency test to existing social tenants seeking to move between local authorities. Housing authorities should assist in tackling under-occupation, for example allowing tenants to move if they wish to downsize to a smaller social home. There may also be sound housing management reasons to disapply a residency test for hard to let stock.
21. These examples are not intended to be exhaustive and housing authorities may wish to consider providing for other appropriate exceptions in the light of local circumstances. In addition, authorities retain a discretion to deal with individual cases where there are exceptional circumstances.
22. The Government wants to increase opportunities for hardworking households. That is why we have announced an intention to introduce a Right to Move for social tenants seeking to move to take up a job or be closer to their work, whether within the local authority district or across local authority boundaries. We will consult on options for implementing this policy in Spring 2014. In the meantime, we expect housing authorities to make appropriate exceptions to their residency test for social tenants so as not to impede labour market mobility.

Members of the Armed Forces

23. The Government is committed to ensuring that Service personnel and their families have access to appropriate accommodation when they leave the Armed Forces. The Allocation of Housing (Qualification Criteria for Armed Forces) (England) Regulations 2012 SI No 1869 ensure that, where housing authorities decide to use a local connection[1] requirement as a qualification criterion, they must not apply that criterion to the following persons so as to disqualify them from an allocation of social housing:

1 As defined by HA 1996 s199. A person has a local connection with the district of a housing authority if he has a connection because of normal residence there (either current or previous) of his own choice, employment there, family connections or special circumstances.

a) those who are currently serving in the regular forces or who were serving in the regular forces at any time in the five years preceding their application for an allocation of social housing
b) bereaved spouses or civil partners of those serving in the regular forces where (i) the bereaved spouse or civil partner has recently ceased, or will cease to be entitled, to reside in Ministry of Defence accommodation following the death of their service spouse or civil partner, and (ii) the death was wholly or partly attributable to their service
c) existing or former members of the reserve forces who are suffering from a serious injury, illness, or disability which is wholly or partly attributable to their service

24. The Regulations give effect to the Government's commitment that those who serve in the regular and reserve Armed Forces are not disadvantaged in their access to social housing by the requirements of their service.
25. When adopting a residency test, we expect housing authorities to also consider the wider needs of the Armed Forces community, and to be sympathetic to changing family circumstances, recognising, for example, that the spouses and partners of Service personnel can also be disadvantaged by the need to move from base to base.

Prioritising local connection

26. Housing authorities have the ability to take account of any local connection between the applicant and their district when determining relative priorities between households who are on the waiting list (s166A(5)). For these purposes, local connection is defined by reference to s199 of the 1996 Act.
27. Housing authorities should consider whether, in the light of local circumstances, there is a need to take advantage of this flexibility, in addition to applying a residency requirement as part of their qualification criteria. Examples of circumstances in which the power might be useful would include:
    - dealing sensitively with lettings in rural villages by giving priority to those with a local connection to the parish, as part of a local lettings policy (section 166A(6)(b) – see paragraph 4.21 of the 2012 guidance)
    - where a group of housing authorities apply a wider residency qualification test, to give greater priority to people who live or work (or have close family) in any of the partner authorities' own district

Information about allocations

28. It is important that applicants and the wider community understand how social housing is allocated in their area, and that they know who is getting that social housing, so that they can see that the allocation system is fair and the authority is complying with its allocation scheme. We would encourage housing authorities to consider how accurate and anonymised information on waiting list applicants and lettings outcomes could be routinely published, to strengthen public confidence in the fairness of their allocation scheme.

Allocation of accommodation: guidance for local housing authorities in England (June 2012)

CHAPTER 1
Scope of guidance and definition of an allocation

1.1 This guidance is issued to local housing authorities ('housing authorities') in England under s169 of the Housing Act 1996 ('the 1996 Act'). Housing authorities are required to have regard to it in exercising their functions under Part 6 of the 1996 Act ('Part 6'). In so far as this guidance comments on the law, it can only reflect the Department's understanding at the time of issue.

1.2 This guidance replaces all previous guidance on social housing allocations.

Definition of an 'allocation'

1.3 For the purposes of Part 6, a housing authority allocates accommodation when it:
- selects a person to be a secure or introductory tenant of accommodation held by that authority
- nominates a person to be a secure or introductory tenant of accommodation held by another housing authority
- nominates a person to be an assured tenant of accommodation held by a Private Registered Provider (or Registered Social Landlord in Wales) (s159(2))

1.4 The term 'assured tenant' includes a person with an assured shorthold tenancy, including of an Affordable Rent property.[1] 'Secure tenant' includes a person with a flexible tenancy granted under s107A of the Housing Act 1985.[2]

Allocations to existing tenants

1.5 Provisions in relation to existing tenants are contained in s159(4A) and (4B). These provide that Part 6 does not apply to an allocation of accommodation by a housing authority to a tenant of a local authority or Private Registered Provider unless:
- the allocation involves a transfer made at the tenant's request, and
- the authority is satisfied that the tenant has reasonable preference.

Accordingly, social tenants applying to the housing authority for a transfer who are considered to have reasonable preference for an allocation must be treated on the same basis as new applicants in accordance with the requirements of s166A(3).

1.6 Transfers at the tenant's request, where the authority is satisfied the tenant does not have reasonable preference, do not fall within Part 6 and housing authorities may set their own transfer policies in relation to these tenants. Authorities should consider how to make the best use of this flexibility. Providing tenants with greater opportunities to move within the social sector

1 Affordable Rent is not subject to the national rent regime but is subject to other rent controls that require a rent (including service charges, where applicable) of no more than 80% of the local market rent.

2 Inserted by s154 of the Localism Act 2011.

can help promote social and economic mobility and make the best use of social housing stock.

1.7 Authorities should consider the importance of giving social tenants who under-occupy their accommodation appropriate priority for a transfer. This will be important in light of the measure in the Welfare Reform Act 2012 which will reduce Housing Benefit entitlement for working age social sector tenants who under-occupy their property (measured in accordance with the Local Housing Allowance size criteria) from April 2013.[3] Authorities should also consider whether there are other provisions that might make it more difficult for under-occupiers to move, such as a prohibition against tenants with minor rent arrears transferring, and the scope for removing or revising these in relation to under-occupiers.

1.8 Housing authorities may decide to operate a separate allocation system for transferring tenants who are not in the reasonable preference categories (with a separate waiting list and lettings policy) or to continue with a single allocation system which covers all applicants but which, for example, rewards transferring tenants with a good tenancy record, or gives a degree of priority to those who want to move for work.

1.9 Transfers that the housing authority initiates for management purposes do not fall within Part 6. These would include a temporary decant to allow repairs to a property to be carried out. The renewal of a flexible tenancy in the same property also does not fall within Part 6; neither do mutual exchanges between existing tenants, including exchanges between secure and assured tenants and those with flexible tenancies (under s107A of the Housing Act 1985). Other specific exemptions from the provisions of Part 6 are set out in s160 of the 1996 Act and the Allocation of Housing (England) Regulations 2002 (SI No 3264).

CHAPTER 2
Overview of the amendments to Part 6 made by the Localism Act 2011

2.1 The Localism Act 2011 introduces significant amendments to Part 6. The main policy objectives behind these amendments are to:

- enable housing authorities to better manage their housing waiting list by giving them the power to determine which applicants do or do not qualify for an allocation of social housing. Authorities will be able to operate a more focused list which better reflects local circumstances and can be understood more readily by local people. It will also be easier for authorities to manage unrealistic expectations by excluding people who have little or no prospect of being allocated accommodation
- make it easier for existing social tenants to move by removing the constraints of Part 6 from those social tenants who apply to the housing authority for a transfer, unless they have reasonable preference. Housing

3 The LHA size criteria allow one bedroom for each: adult couple; any other adult (aged 16 or over); two children of the same sex aged 10 or over; two children under 10 regardless of sex; any other child.

authorities will be able to strike a balance between meeting the needs of existing tenants and new applicants for social housing, while making best use of their stock. Part 6 continues to apply to transferring tenants with reasonable preference, ensuring they continue to receive priority under the authority's allocation scheme

- maintain the protection provided by the statutory reasonable preference criteria – ensuring that priority for social housing goes to those in the greatest need

2.2 The detailed changes to Part 6 contained in the Localism Act 2011 are set out in the following paragraphs.

2.3 By virtue of new s159(4B) the term 'allocation' continues to apply to a transfer at the request of an existing secure, introductory or assured tenant where the authority is satisfied that he or she has 'reasonable preference' for an allocation. Existing secure, introductory and assured tenants seeking a transfer who are not considered to have reasonable preference are now outside the scope of Part 6 (s159(4A).

2.4 New s160ZA replaces s160A in relation to allocations by housing authorities in England. Social housing may only be allocated to 'qualifying persons' and housing authorities are given the power to determine what classes of persons are or are not qualified to be allocated housing (s160ZA(6) and (7)). These requirements are in addition to the provisions on eligibility in respect of persons from abroad (s160ZA(2) and (4)) which continue to be set centrally. The power for a housing authority to decide that an applicant is to be treated as ineligible by reason of unacceptable behaviour serious enough to make him unsuitable to be a tenant is redundant and has therefore been repealed.

2.5 New s166A requires housing authorities in England to allocate accommodation in accordance with a scheme which must be framed to ensure that certain categories of applicants are given reasonable preference. With certain exceptions, s166A replicates the provisions in s167 which continues to apply to allocations by housing authorities in Wales. Section 166A(9) includes a new requirement for an allocation scheme to give a right to review a decision on qualification in s160AZ(9), and to be informed of the decision on the review and the grounds for it. This is in addition to the existing right to review a decision on eligibility. Section 166A(12) is new and provides that authorities must have regard to their homelessness and tenancy strategies when framing their allocation scheme.

2.6 The provisions in s167 which allow for no preference to be given to a person guilty of serious unacceptable behaviour (s167(2B)–(2D)) are not reproduced in s166A. However, the power to take behaviour – whether good or poor – into account in determining priorities between people in the reasonable preference categories remains (new s166A(5)(b)).

2.7 The requirement for an allocation scheme to contain a statement of the authority's policy on offering a choice of accommodation or the opportunity to express preferences about their accommodation is retained (s166A(2)). However, the requirement to provide a copy of this statement to people to whom they owe a homelessness duty (under s193(3A) or s195(3A) of the 1996 Act) is repealed.[4]

4 Localism Act 2011 ss148(2) and 149(3).

CHAPTER 3
Eligibility and qualification

3.1 Housing authorities must consider all applications made in accordance with the procedural requirements of the authority's allocation scheme (s166(3)). In considering applications, authorities must ascertain:

- if an applicant is eligible for an allocation of accommodation, and
- if he or she qualifies for an allocation of accommodation

Eligibility

3.2 An applicant may be ineligible for an allocation of accommodation under s160ZA(2) or (4). Authorities are advised to consider applicants' eligibility at the time of the initial application and again when considering making an allocation to them, particularly where a substantial amount of time has elapsed since the original application.

Joint tenancies

3.3 Under s160ZA(1)(b), a housing authority must not grant a joint tenancy to two or more people if any one of them is a person from abroad who is ineligible. However, where two or more people apply and one of them is eligible, the authority may grant a tenancy to the person who is eligible. In addition, while ineligible family members must not be granted a tenancy, they may be taken into account in determining the size of accommodation which is to be allocated.

Existing tenants

3.4 The eligibility provisions do not apply to applicants who are already secure or introductory tenants or assured tenants of a Private Registered Provider. Most transferring tenants fall outside the scope of the allocation legislation (s159(4A)); while those who are considered to have reasonable preference for an allocation are specifically exempted from the eligibility provisions by virtue of s160ZA(5).

Persons from abroad

3.5 A person may not be allocated accommodation under Part 6 if he or she is a person from abroad who is ineligible for an allocation under s160ZA of the 1996 Act. There are two categories for the purposes of s160ZA:

(i) *a person subject to immigration control* – such a person is not eligible for an allocation of accommodation unless he or she comes within a class prescribed in regulations made by the Secretary of State (s160ZA(2)), and

(ii) *a person from abroad other than a person subject to immigration control* – regulations may provide for other descriptions of persons from abroad who, although not subject to immigration control, are to be treated as ineligible for an allocation of accommodation (s160ZA(4)).

3.6 The regulations setting out which classes of persons from abroad are eligible or ineligible for an allocation are the Allocation of Housing and Homelessness (Eligibility) (England) Regulations 2006 (SI No 1294) ('the Eligibility Regulations').

Persons subject to immigration control

3.7 The term 'person subject to immigration control' is defined in s13(2) of the Asylum and Immigration Act 1996 as a person who under the Immigration

Act 1971 requires leave to enter or remain in the United Kingdom (whether or not such leave has been given).

3.8 The following categories of persons do not require leave to enter or remain in the UK:

(i) British citizens

(ii) certain Commonwealth citizens with a right of abode in the UK

(iii) Irish citizens, who are not subject to immigration control in the UK because the Republic of Ireland forms part of the Common Travel Area (see paragraph 3.11 (iii) below) with the UK which allows free movement

(iv) EEA nationals,[5] and their family members, who have a right to reside in the UK that derives from EU law. Whether an EEA national (or family member) has a particular right to reside in the UK (or another Member State) will depend on the circumstances, particularly their economic status (eg whether he or she is a worker, self-employed, a student, or economically inactive)

(v) persons who are exempt from immigration control under the Immigration Acts, including diplomats and their family members based in the UK, and some military personnel.

3.9 Any person who does not fall within one of the four categories in paragraph 3.11 will be a person subject to immigration control and will be ineligible for an allocation of accommodation unless they fall within a class of persons prescribed by regulation 3 of the Eligibility Regulations (see further below).

3.10 If there is any uncertainty about an applicant's immigration status, housing authorities are recommended to contact the UK Border Agency (UKBA). UKBA provides a service to housing authorities to confirm the immigration status of an applicant from abroad (non-asylum-seekers) by email at LA@UKBA.gsi.gov.uk. Where UKBA indicates the applicant may be an asylum seeker, enquiries of their status can be made to the Immigration Enquiry Bureau helpline on 0870 606 7766.

3.11 Regulation 3 of the Eligibility Regulations provides that the following classes of persons subject to immigration control are eligible for an allocation of accommodation:

(i) *a person granted refugee status*: granted 5 years' limited leave to remain in the UK

(ii) *a person granted exceptional leave to enter or remain in the UK without condition that they and any dependants should make no recourse to public funds*: granted for a limited period where there are compelling humanitarian or compassionate circumstances for allowing them to stay. However, if leave is granted on condition that the applicant and any dependants are not a charge on public funds, the applicant will not be eligible for an allocation of accommodation. Exceptional leave to remain (granted at the Secretary of State's discretion outside the Immigration Rules) now takes the form of 'discretionary leave'.

5 European Economic Area nationals are nationals of any EU member state (except the UK), and nationals of Iceland, Norway, Liechtenstein and Switzerland.

(iii) *a person with current leave to enter or remain in the UK with no condition or limitation, and who is habitually resident in the UK, the Channel Islands, the Isle of Man or the Republic of Ireland* (the Common Travel Area): such a person will have indefinite leave to enter (ILE) or remain (ILR) and is regarded as having settled status. However, where ILE or ILR status is granted as a result of an undertaking that a sponsor will be responsible for the applicant's maintenance and accommodation, the person must have been resident in the Common Travel Area for five years since the date of entry – or the date of the sponsorship undertaking, whichever is later – to be eligible. Where all sponsors have died within the first five years, the applicant will be eligible for an allocation of accommodation.

(iv) *a person who has humanitarian protection granted under the Immigration Rules:*[6] a form of leave granted to persons who do not qualify for refugee status but would face a real risk of suffering serious harm if returned to their state of origin (see paragraphs 339C–344C of the Immigration Rules (HC 395))

Other persons from abroad who may be ineligible for an allocation

3.12 By virtue of regulation 4 of the Eligibility Regulations, a person who is not subject to immigration control and who falls within one of the following descriptions is to be treated as a person from abroad who is ineligible for an allocation of accommodation:

(i) a person who is not habitually resident in the Common Travel Area (subject to certain exceptions – see paragraph 3.14 below)

(ii) a person whose only right to reside in the UK is derived from his status as a jobseeker (or his status as the family member of a jobseeker). 'Jobseeker' has the same meaning as in regulation 6(1) of the Immigration (European Economic Area) Regulations 2006 (SI 2006/1003) ('the EEA Regulations').

(iii) a person whose only right to reside in the UK is an initial right to reside for a period not exceeding three months under regulation 13 of the EEA Regulations

(iv) a person whose only right to reside in the Common Travel Area is a right equivalent to one of the rights mentioned in (ii) or (iii) above and which is derived from EU Treaty rights

3.13 See annex 2 for guidance on rights to reside in the UK derived from EU law.

3.14 The following persons from abroad are eligible for an allocation of accommodation even if they are not habitually resident in the Common Travel Area:

(a) an EEA national who is in the UK as a worker (which has the same meaning as in regulation 6(1) of the EEA Regulations)

(b) an EEA national who is in the UK as a self-employed person (which has the same meaning as in regulation 6(1) of the EEA Regulations)

(c) a person who is treated as a worker for the purposes of regulation 6(1) of the EEA Regulations, pursuant to the Accession (Immigration and Worker Authorisation) Regulations 2006 (ie nationals of Bulgaria and

6 Inserted by the Allocation of Housing and Homelessness (Miscellaneous Provisions) (England) Regulations 2006.

Romania required to be authorised by the Home Office to work until they have accrued 12 months uninterrupted authorised work)[7]

(d) a person who is a family member of a person referred to in (a) to (c) above

(e) a person with a right to reside permanently in the UK by virtue of regulation 15(c), (d) or (e) of the EEA Regulations

(f) a person who left Montserrat after 1 November 1995 because of the effect of volcanic activity there

(g) a person who is in the UK as a result of his deportation, expulsion or other removal by compulsion of law from another country to the UK. This could include EEA nationals, if the person was settled in the UK and exercising EU Treaty rights prior to deportation from the third country. Where deportation occurs, most countries will signal this in the person's passport.

3.15 A person who is no longer working or no longer in self-employment will retain his or her status as a worker or self-employed person in certain circumstances. However, accession state workers requiring authorisation will generally only be treated as a worker when they are actually working as authorised and will not retain 'worker' status between jobs until they have accrued 12 months continuous authorised employment. 'Family member' does not include a person who is an extended family member who is treated as a family member by virtue of regulation 7(3) of the EEA Regulations (see annexes 2 and 3 for further guidance).

3.16 The term 'habitual residence' is intended to convey a degree of permanence in the person's residence in the Common Travel Area; it implies an association between the individual and the place of residence and relies substantially on fact.

3.17 Applicants who have been resident in the Common Travel Area continuously during the two-year period prior to their housing application are likely to be habitually resident (periods of temporary absence, e.g. visits abroad for holidays or to visit relatives may be disregarded). Where two years' continuous residency has not been established, housing authorities will need to conduct further enquiries to determine whether the applicant is habitually resident (see annex 4 for further guidance).

Qualification

3.18 Housing authorities may only allocate accommodation to people who are defined as 'qualifying persons' (s160ZA(6)(a)). Subject to the requirement not to allocate to persons from abroad who are ineligible and the exception for members of the Armed and Reserve Forces in paragraph 3.27 below, a housing authority may decide the classes of people who are, or are not, qualifying persons.

3.19 Housing authorities are encouraged to adopt a housing options approach as part of a move to a managed waiting list. A strong and pro-active housing options approach brings several benefits: people are offered support to access the housing solution which best meets their needs (which might be private rented housing, low cost home ownership or help to stay put); expectations

7 As of 1 May 2011, nationals of the 8 Eastern European countries (A8 nationals) which acceded to the EU in 2004 are no longer required to register with the Workers Registration Scheme in order to work in the UK. Regulation 4(2)(c) of the Eligibility Regulations no longer applies to applications from A8 workers as of that date. Rather applications from A8 workers should be considered on the same basis as those from other EU workers under regulation 4(2)(a).

about accessing social housing are properly managed; and social housing is focused on those who need it most. A lower waiting list can also be a by-product.

3.20 In framing their qualification criteria, authorities will need to have regard to their duties under the equalities legislation, as well as the requirement in s166A(3) to give overall priority for an allocation to people in the reasonable preference categories.

3.21 Housing authorities should avoid setting criteria which disqualify groups of people whose members are likely to be accorded reasonable preference for social housing, for example on medical or welfare grounds. However, authorities may wish to adopt criteria which would disqualify individuals who satisfy the reasonable preference requirements. This could be the case, for example, if applicants are disqualified on a ground of anti-social behaviour.

3.22 When deciding what classes of people do not qualify for an allocation, authorities should consider the implications of excluding all members of such groups. For instance, when framing residency criteria, authorities may wish to consider the position of people who are moving into the district to take up work or to escape violence, or homeless applicants or children in care who are placed out of borough.

3.23 The Government believes that authorities should avoid allocating social housing to people who already own their own homes. Where they do so, this should only be in exceptional circumstances; for example, for elderly owner occupiers who cannot stay in their own home and need to move into sheltered accommodation.

3.24 There may be sound policy reasons for applying different qualification criteria in relation to existing tenants from those which apply to new applicants. For example, where residency requirements are imposed, authorities may wish to ensure they do not restrict the ability of existing social tenants to move to take up work or to downsize to a smaller home. Authorities may decide to apply different qualification criteria in relation to particular types of stock, for example properties which might otherwise be hard to let.

3.25 Whatever general criteria housing authorities use to define the classes of persons who do not qualify for social housing, there may be exceptional circumstances where it is necessary to disapply these criteria in the case of individual applicants. An example might be an intimidated witness[8] who needs to move quickly to another local authority district. Authorities are encouraged to make explicit provision for dealing with exceptional cases within their qualification rules.

3.26 As with eligibility, authorities are advised to consider whether an applicant qualifies for an allocation at the time of the initial application and when considering making an allocation, particularly where a long time has elapsed since the original application.

Members of the Armed Forces and the Reserve Forces

3.27 Subject to Parliamentary scrutiny, we will regulate to provide that authorities must not disqualify the following applicants on the grounds that they do not have a local connection[9] with the authority's district:

8 'Intimidated witnesses include Protected Persons as specified in Section 82 and schedule 5 of the Serious Organised Crime and Police Act 2005.'

9 As defined by s199 of the 1996 Act.

(a) members of the Armed Forces and former Service personnel, where the application is made within five[10] years of discharge
(b) bereaved spouses and civil partners of members of the Armed Forces leaving Services Family Accommodation following the death of their spouse or partner
(c) serving or former members of the Reserve Forces who need to move because of a serious injury, medical condition or disability sustained as a result of their service

3.28 These provisions recognise the special position of members of the Armed Forces (and their families) whose employment requires them to be mobile and who are likely therefore to be particularly disadvantaged by local connection requirements; as well as those injured reservists who may need to move to another local authority district to access treatment, care or support.

Joint tenants

3.29 In the case of an allocation to two or more persons jointly, at least one of the persons must be a qualifying person (s160ZA(6)(b)) and all of them must be eligible.

Fresh applications

3.30 Applicants who have previously been deemed not to qualify may make a fresh application if they consider they should now be treated as qualifying, but it will be for the applicant to show that his or her circumstances have changed (s160ZA(11)).

Reviews of decisions on eligibility and qualification

3.31 For guidance on decisions and reviews see chapter 5.17

CHAPTER 4
Framing an allocation scheme

4.1 Housing authorities are required by s166A(1) to have an allocation scheme for determining priorities, and for defining the procedures to be followed in allocating housing accommodation; and they must allocate in accordance with that scheme (s166A(14)). All aspects of the allocation process must be covered in the scheme, including the people by whom decisions are taken. In the Secretary of State's view, qualification criteria form part of an allocation scheme.

4.2 All housing authorities must have an allocation scheme, regardless of whether they own housing stock and whether they contract out the delivery of any of their allocation functions (see further chapter 6). When framing or modifying their scheme, authorities must have regard to their current tenancy and homelessness strategies (s166A(12)).

10 Five years reflects guidelines issued by the local authorities associations which propose a working definition of normal residence for the purposes of establishing a local connection (see paragraph 4.1(i) to Annex 18 of the Homelessness Code of Guidance 2006).

Choice and preference options

4.3 An allocation scheme must include a statement as to the housing authority's policy on offering people a choice of accommodation or the opportunity to express preferences about the accommodation to be allocated to them (s166A). It is for housing authorities to determine their policy on providing choice or the ability to express preferences.

Reasonable preference

4.4 In framing their allocation scheme to determine allocation priorities, housing authorities must ensure that reasonable preference is given to the following categories of people (s166A(3):

(a) people who are homeless within the meaning of Part 7 of the 1996 Act (including those who are intentionally homeless and those not in priority need)

(b) people who are owed a duty by any housing authority under section 190(2), 193(2) or 195(2) of the 1996 Act (or under section 65(2) or 68(2) of the Housing Act 1985) or who are occupying accommodation secured by any housing authority under s192(3)

(c) people occupying insanitary or overcrowded housing or otherwise living in unsatisfactory housing conditions

(d) people who need to move on medical or welfare grounds, including grounds relating to a disability,[11] and

(e) people who need to move to a particular locality in the district of the housing authority, where failure to meet that need would cause hardship (to themselves or others)

4.5 In framing their allocation scheme to give effect to s166A(3), housing authorities should have regard to the following considerations:

- the scheme must be framed so as to give reasonable preference to applicants who fall within the categories set out in s166A(3), over those who do not
- although there is no requirement to give equal weight to each of the reasonable preference categories, authorities will need to demonstrate that, overall, reasonable preference has been given to all of them
- there is no requirement for housing authorities to frame their scheme to afford greater priority to applicants who fall within more than one reasonable preference category (cumulative preference) over those who have reasonable preference on a single, non-urgent basis.[12]

Otherwise, it is for housing authorities to decide how to give effect to the provisions of s166A(3) in their allocation scheme.

Restricted persons

4.6 Applicants should not be given reasonable preference under paragraph (a) or (b) of s166A(3) if they would only qualify for reasonable preference by taking into account a 'restricted person' within the meaning of Part 7 (s166A(4)). A restricted person is a person subject to immigration control who is not eligible

11 The words 'including grounds relating to a disability were added by the Housing Act 2004.

12 (*R (Ahmad) v London Borough of Newham* [2009] UKHL 14, [2009] HLR 31.

for homelessness assistance because he or she does not have leave to enter or remain in the UK or has leave which is subject to a 'no recourse to public funds' condition (s184(7) of the 1996 Act).

Homeless or owed a homelessness duty

4.7 The requirement for housing authorities to frame their allocation scheme to give reasonable preference to people who are owed certain homeless duties remains the case, notwithstanding the amendments to Part 7 made by the Localism Act which give authorities the power to end the main homelessness duty with an offer of private rented accommodation, without requiring the applicant's consent.

Overcrowding

4.8 The Secretary of State takes the view that the bedroom standard is an appropriate measure of overcrowding for allocation purposes, and recommends that all housing authorities should adopt this as a minimum. The bedroom standard allocates a separate bedroom to each:

- married or cohabiting couple
- adult aged 21 years or more
- pair of adolescents aged 10–20 years of the same sex
- pair of children aged under 10 years regardless of sex

Medical and welfare grounds

4.9 The medical and welfare reasonable preference category includes people who need to move because of their disability or access needs, and this includes people with a learning disability as well as those with a physical disability.

4.10 'Welfare grounds' would encompass a wide range of needs, including, but not limited to, the need to:

- provide a secure base from which a care leaver, or a person who is moving on from a drug or alcohol recovery programme, can build a stable life
- provide accommodation, with appropriate care and support, for those who could not be expected to find their own accommodation, such as young adults with learning disabilities who wish to live independently in the community
- provide or receive care or support. This would include foster carers, those approved to adopt, or those being assessed for approval to foster or adopt, who need to move to a larger home in order to accommodate a looked after child or a child who was previously looked after by a local authority. It would also include special guardians, holders of a residence order and family and friends carers who are not foster carers but who have taken on the care of a child because the parents are unable to provide care

Hardship grounds

4.11 This would include, for example, a person who needs to move to a different locality in order to give or receive care, to access specialised medical treatment, or to take up a particular employment, education or training opportunity.

4.12 Possible indicators of the criteria which apply to reasonable preference categories (c) and (d) are given in annex1.

Additional preference

4.13 Section 166A(3) gives housing authorities the power to frame their allocation scheme to give additional preference to particular descriptions of people who fall within the statutory reasonable preference categories and have urgent housing needs. All housing authorities must consider, in the light of local circumstances, the need to give effect to this provision. Examples of people with urgent housing needs to whom housing authorities should consider giving additional preference within their allocation scheme include:

- those who need to move urgently because of a life threatening illness or sudden
- disability
- families in severe overcrowding which poses a serious health hazard
- those who are homeless and require urgent re-housing as a result of violence or threats of violence, including intimidated witnesses, and those escaping serious anti-social behaviour or domestic violence

Members of the Armed and Reserve Forces

4.14 Subject to parliamentary approval, we will regulate to require authorities to frame their allocation scheme to give additional preference to the following categories of people who fall within one or more of the reasonable preference categories and who have urgent housing needs:

(a) former members of the Armed Forces
(b) serving members of the Armed Forces who need to move because of a serious injury, medical condition or disability sustained as a result of their service
(c) bereaved spouses and civil partners of members of the Armed Forces leaving Services Family Accommodation following the death of their spouse or partner
(d) serving or former members of the Reserve Forces who need to move because of a serious injury, medical condition or disability sustained as a result of their service

Determining priorities between households with a similar level of need

4.15 Authorities may frame their allocation scheme to take into account factors in determining relative priorities between applicants in the reasonable (or additional) preference categories (s166A(5)). Examples of such factors are given in the legislation: financial resources, behaviour and local connection. However, these examples are not exclusive and authorities may take into account other factors instead or as well as these.

Financial resources available to a person to meet his housing costs

4.16 This would enable a housing authority, for example, to give less priority to owner occupiers (wherever the property is situated).

Behaviour

4.17 This would allow for greater priority to be given to applicants who have been model tenants or have benefited the community, for example.

Local connection

4.18 Local connection is defined by s199 of the 1996 Act. A person has a local connection because of normal residence (current or previous) of their own choice, employment, family associations, or special circumstances. Residence is not of a person's choice if it is the consequence of being detained in prison or in hospital under the Mental Health Act. As a result of changes to s199 introduced in 2008[13] a person serving in the Armed Forces can establish a local connection with a local authority district through residence or employment there, in the same way as a civilian.

Including local priorities alongside the statutory reasonable preference categories

4.19 As the House of Lords made clear in the case of *R (Ahmad) v Newham LBC*,[14] s166A(3)[15] only requires that the people encompassed within that section are given 'reasonable preference'. It 'does not require that they should be given absolute priority over everyone else'.[16] This means that an allocation scheme may provide for other factors than those set out in s166A(3) to be taken into account in determining which applicants are to be given preference under a scheme, provided that:

- they do not dominate the scheme, and
- overall, the scheme operates to give reasonable preference to those in the statutory reasonable preference categories over those who are not

The Secretary of State would encourage authorities to consider the scope to take advantage of this flexibility to meet local needs and local priorities.

4.20 The House of Lords also made clear that, where an allocation scheme complies with the reasonable preference requirements and any other statutory requirements, the courts should be very slow to interfere on the ground of alleged irrationality.[17]

Local lettings policies

4.21 Section 166A(6)(b) of the 1996 Act enables housing authorities to allocate particular accommodation to people of a particular description, whether or not they fall within the reasonable preference categories, provided that overall the authority is able to demonstrate compliance with the requirements of s166A(3). This is the statutory basis for so-called 'local lettings policies' which may be used to achieve a wide variety of housing management and policy objectives.

Households affected by the under-occupation measure

4.22 When framing the rules which determine the size of property to allocate to different households and in different circumstances, housing authorities are free to set their own criteria, provided they do not result in a household being statutorily overcrowded. However, in setting these criteria, authorities will want to take account of the provision in the Welfare Reform Act 2012 which will reduce Housing Benefit to under-occupiers.

13 Amendment to s199 of the 1996 Act made by s315 of the Housing and Regeneration Act 2008.

14 [2009] UKHL 14.

15 Previously s167(2), which continues to apply to allocations by housing authorities in Wales.

16 Baroness Hale at para [18].

17 Lord Neuberger at para [55].

4.23 Social tenants affected by the under-occupation measure may choose to move to more suitably sized accommodation in the private rented sector. One way to encourage tenants to consider this option might be to ensure they are given some degree of preference for an allocation if they apply for a new social tenancy at a later date.

Members of the Armed Forces

4.24 Authorities are also strongly encouraged to take into account the needs of all serving or former Service personnel when framing their allocation schemes, and to give sympathetic consideration to the housing needs of family members of serving or former Service personnel who may themselves have been disadvantaged by the requirements of military service and, in particular, the need to move from base to base. This would be in line with terms of the Government's Armed Forces Covenant published in May 2011.

4.25 Examples of ways in which authorities can ensure that Service personnel and their families are given appropriate priority, include:

- using the flexibility within the allocation legislation to set local priorities alongside the statutory reasonable preference categories so as to give preference, for example, to those who have recently left, or are close to leaving, the Armed Forces[18] (see paragraph 4.19 above)
- using the power to determine priorities between applicants in the reasonable preference categories, so that applicants in housing need who have served in the Armed Forces are given greater priority for social housing over those who have not (see paragraph 4.15 above)
- If taking into account an applicant's financial resources in determining priorities between households with a similar level of need (see paragraph 4.16 above), disregarding any lump sum received by a member of the Armed Forces as compensation for an injury or disability sustained on active service
- setting aside a proportion of properties for former members of the Armed Forces under a local lettings policy (see paragraph 4.21 above)

4.26 A number of organisations provide specialist housing and support for veterans, such as the Royal British Legion, Stoll, Haig Homes, Alabare and Norcare, and housing authorities are encouraged to liaise with them to ensure that former Service personnel are able to access the housing option which best suits their needs.

Households in work or seeking work

4.27 Local authorities are urged to consider how they can use their allocation policies to support those households who want to work, as well as those who – while unable to engage in paid employment – are contributing to their community in other ways, for example, through voluntary work. The flexibilities which authorities are encouraged to make use of to meet the needs of Service personnel would apply equally here. This might involve, for example, framing an allocation scheme to give some preference to

18 MoD issues a Certificate of Cessation of Entitlement to Occupy Service Living Accommodation 6 months before discharge.

households who are in low paid work or employment-related training, even where they are not in the reasonable preference categories; or to give greater priority to those households in the reasonable preference categories who are also in work or who can demonstrate that they are actively seeking work. Alternatively, it might involve using local lettings policies to ensure that specific properties, or a specified proportion of properties, are allocated to households in particular types of employment where, for example, skills are in short supply.

4.28 Authorities should also consider how best they can make use of the new power to offer flexible tenancies to support households who are in low paid work, and incentivise others to take up employment opportunities.

Carers

4.29 In making accommodation offers to applicants who receive support from carers who do not reside with them but may need to stay overnight, housing authorities should, wherever possible, take account of the applicant's need for a spare bedroom.

Prospective adopters and foster carers

4.30 When considering housing applications from prospective foster carers or adopters who would require an extra bedroom to accommodate a foster or adoptive child, authorities will wish to weigh up the risk that the application to foster or adopt may be unsuccessful (leading to the property being under-occupied), against the wider benefits which would be realised if the placement was successful.

4.31 Children's services have a duty under s22G of the Children Act 1989 to ensure sufficient accommodation to meet the needs of the looked after children in their area. Authorities should work together with children's services to best meet the needs of prospective and approved foster carers and adopters, so that children's services can meet their s22G duty. One way to strike an appropriate balance would be to set aside a quota of properties each year for people who need to move to larger accommodation in order to foster or adopt a child on the recommendation of children's services.

4.32 The advice in paragraph 4.22 is particularly relevant in relation to prospective foster carers, as foster children are not taken into account in determining the household size for the purposes of the under-occupation measure in the Welfare Reform Act. However, current and prospective foster carers affected by the measure may be eligible to apply for a Discretionary Housing Payment.

General information about particular applications

4.33 Under s166A(9), allocation schemes must be framed so as to give applicants the right to request from housing authorities general information that will enable them to assess:

(a) how their application is likely to be treated under the scheme and, in particular, whether they are likely to have reasonable preference

(b) whether accommodation appropriate to their needs is likely to be made available and, if so, how long it is likely to be before such accommodation becomes available

Notification about decisions and the right to a review of a decision

4.34 An allocation scheme must be framed so as to give applicants the right to be informed of certain decisions and the right to review certain decisions (s166A(9)). For further advice on decisions and reviews, see chapter 5.

CHAPTER 5
Allocation scheme management

Publishing and consulting on allocation schemes

5.1 Housing authorities must publish a summary of their allocation scheme and, if requested, provide a free copy of it (s168(1)). They must also make the full scheme available for inspection at their principal office and, if requested, provide a copy of it on payment of a reasonable fee (s168(2)).

5.2 When an alteration is made to a scheme reflecting a major change of policy, an authority must ensure within a reasonable time that those likely to be affected by the change have the effect brought to their attention, taking such steps as the housing authority considers reasonable (s168(3)). A major policy change would include, for example, any amendment affecting the relative priority of a large number of applicants or a significant alteration to procedures. Housing authorities should be aware that they still have certain duties under s106 of the Housing Act 1985.

5.3 Section 166A(13) requires authorities, before adopting an allocation scheme, or altering a scheme to reflect a major change of policy, to:

- send a copy of the draft scheme, or proposed alteration, to every Private Registered Provider[19] with which they have nomination arrangements, and
- ensure they have a reasonable opportunity to comment on the proposals

Advice and information

5.4 Housing authorities must ensure that advice and information is available free of charge to everyone in their district about the right to apply for an allocation of accommodation (s166(1)(a)). This would include general information about application procedures; as well as information about qualification and prioritisation criteria.

5.5 If a person is likely to have difficulty making an application without assistance, the authority must secure that any necessary assistance is available free of charge (s166(1)(b)).

5.6 Housing authorities must inform applicants that they have the right to the following general information (s166(1A)):

- information that will enable them to assess how their application is likely to be treated under the authority's allocation scheme, and, in particular, whether they are likely to fall within the reasonable preference categories, and
- information about whether accommodation appropriate to their needs is likely to be made available to them and, if so, how long it is likely to be before such accommodation becomes available. Maintaining a database of housing suitable for applicants with access needs would assist with this.

19 And, where relevant, every Registered Social Landlord in Wales with which they have nomination arrangements.

5.7 Section 166(4) prohibits housing authorities from divulging to other members of the public that a person is an applicant for social housing, unless they have the applicant's consent. Furthermore, authorities should process any personal data they hold about applicants consistently with the Data Protection Act 1998. If authorities are unclear about their obligations and responsibilities under the Data Protection Act they should contact the Information Commissioner.

Elected Members' Involvement in Allocation Decisions

5.8 The Allocation of Housing (Procedure) Regulations 1997 (SI 1997/483) prevent an elected Member from being part of a decision-making body at the time an allocation decision is made, when either:
- the accommodation concerned is situated in their division or electoral ward, or
- the person subject to the decision has their sole or main residence there

5.9 The regulations do not prevent an elected Member from representing their constituents in front of the decision making body, or from participating in the decision making body's deliberations prior to its decision. The regulations also do not prevent elected Members' involvement in policy decisions that affect the generality of housing accommodation in their division or electoral ward rather than individual allocations; for example, a decision that certain types of property should be prioritised for older people.

Offences related to information given or withheld by applicants

5.10 Section 171 makes it an offence for anyone, in connection with the exercise by a housing authority of its functions under Part 6, to:
- knowingly or recklessly give false information
- knowingly withhold information which the housing authority has reasonably required the applicant to give in connection with the exercise of those functions

5.11 The circumstances in which an offence is committed could include providing false information:
- on an application form for social housing
- in response to a request for further information in support of the application
- during review proceedings

5.12 Ground 5 in Schedule 2 to the Housing Act 1985 (as amended by s146 of the 1996 Act) enables a housing authority to seek possession of a tenancy granted as a result of a false statement by the tenant or a person acting at the tenant's instigation.

Fraudulent or incorrect allocations

5.13 Authorities may also wish to take action to minimise the risk of staff allocating incorrectly or even fraudulently, for example to applicants who do not have sufficient priority under the allocation scheme or do not meet the authority's qualification criteria. Appropriate steps might include vetting staff who take allocation decisions or providing for decisions to be validated by employing senior staff to undertake random checks.

Decisions and reviews

Information about decisions and reviews

5.14 Housing authorities must inform applicants that they have the right to information about certain decisions which are taken in respect of their application and the right to review those decisions (s166(1A)).

5.15 By virtue of s160ZA (9) and (10) housing authorities must notify an applicant in writing of any decision that he or she:

- is ineligible for an allocation of accommodation under s160ZA(2) or (4), or
- is not a qualifying person under s160ZA(7).

5.16 The notification must give clear grounds for the decision based on the relevant facts of the case. Section 160ZA(10) provides that, where a notification is not received by an applicant, it can be treated as having been given to him or her, if it is made available at the housing authority's office for a reasonable period. Where an authority considers that an applicant may have difficulty in understanding the implications of a decision on ineligibility or disqualification, it would be good practice to make arrangements for the information to be explained verbally in addition to providing a written notice.

5.17 Applicants also have the right, on request, to be informed of any decision about the facts of their case which has been, or is likely to be, taken into account in considering whether to make an allocation to them (s166A(9)(b)).

5.18 Under s166A(9)(c) applicants have the right to request a review of any of the decisions mentioned in paragraphs 5.15 and 5.17 above and to be informed of the decision on the review and the grounds for it.

Procedures on review

5.19 Review procedures should be clearly set out, including timescales for each stage of the process, and must accord with the principles of transparency and fairness. Failure to put in place a fair procedure for reviews, which allows for all relevant factors to be considered, could result in a judicial review of any decision reached. The following are general principles of good administrative practice:

(i) Applicants should be notified of the timescale within which they must request a review. 21 days from the date the applicant is notified of the decision is well-established as a reasonable timescale. A housing authority should retain the discretion to extend this time limit in exceptional circumstances.

(ii) Applicants should be notified that the request for review should be made in writing, and that it would also be acceptable for the request to be submitted by a representative on their behalf. Applicants should also be advised of the information which should accompany the request.

(iii) Authorities should consider whether to advise that provision can be made for verbal representations, as well as written submissions, to be made.

(iv) The review should be carried out by an officer who is senior to the person who made the original decision. Alternatively, authorities may wish to appoint a panel to consider the review. If so, it should not include any person involved in the original decision.

(v) The review should be considered on the basis of the authority's allocation scheme, any legal requirements and all relevant information. This should include information provided by the applicant on any relevant developments since the original decision was made – for instance, the settlement of arrears or establishment of a repayment plan, or departure of a member of the household responsible for anti-social behaviour

(vi) Reviews should be completed wherever practicable within a set deadline. Eight weeks is suggested as a reasonable timescale. The applicant should be notified of any extension to this deadline and the reasons for this

(vii) Applicants must be notified in writing of the outcome of the review. The notification must set out the reasons for the decision. This will assist the applicant and the authority if, for example, the applicant is not satisfied with the outcome and decides to seek a judicial review or to take their case to the Local Government Ombudsman.

CHAPTER 6
Private Registered Providers and contracting out

Working with Private Registered Providers

6.1 Private Registered Providers have a duty under s170 to cooperate with housing authorities – where the authority requests it – to such extent as is reasonable in the circumstances in offering accommodation to people with priority under the authority's allocation scheme. Similarly, s213 provides that, where a Private Registered Provider has been requested by a housing authority to assist them in the discharge of their homelessness functions under Part 7, it must cooperate to the same extent.

6.2 Housing authorities must comply with the requirements of Part 6 when they nominate an applicant to be the tenant of a Private Registered Provider. A housing authority nominates for these purposes when it does so 'in pursuance of any arrangements (whether legally enforceable or not) to require that housing accommodation, or a specified amount of housing accommodation, is made available to a person or one of a number of persons nominated by the authority' (s159(4)).

6.3 Nomination agreements should set out the proportion of lettings that will be made available; any criteria which the Private Registered Provider has adopted for accepting or rejecting nominees; and how any disputes will be resolved. Housing authorities will want to put in place arrangements to monitor effective delivery of the nomination agreement so they can demonstrate they are meeting their obligations under Part 6.

6.4 The Secretary of State expects that Affordable Rent homes will be allocated in the same way as social rent properties and that existing lettings arrangements operated by housing authorities and Private Registered Providers will continue to apply. The statutory and regulatory framework for allocations provides scope for local flexibility, and authorities and Private Registered Providers may wish to exercise this discretion in relation to Affordable Rent in order to meet local needs and priorities effectively.

Contracting Out

6.5 The *Local Authorities (Contracting Out of Allocation of Housing and Homelessness Functions) Order 1996* (SI No 3205) – made under s70 of the Deregulation and Contracting Out Act 1994 ('the 1994 Act') – enables housing authorities to contract out certain functions under Part 6. In essence, it allows the contracting out of administrative functions, leaving the responsibility for strategic decisions with the housing authority.

6.6 Schedule 1 to the Order lists allocation functions which may not be contracted out:

- adopting or altering the allocation scheme, including the principles on which the scheme is framed, and consulting Private Registered Providers,
- making the allocation scheme available at the authority's principal office

6.7 The Order therefore provides that the majority of functions under Part 6 may be contracted out. These include:

(i) making enquiries about and deciding a person's eligibility for an allocation
(ii) carrying out reviews of decisions
(iii) securing that advice and information is available free of charge on how to apply for housing
(iv) securing that assistance is available free of charge to people likely to have difficulty in making a housing application without such assistance, and
(v) making individual allocations in accordance with the allocation scheme

6.8 The 1994 Act provides that a contract:

(i) may authorise a contractor to carry out only part of the function concerned
(ii) may specify that the contractor is authorised to carry out functions only in certain cases or areas specified in the contract
(iii) may include conditions relating to the carrying out of the functions, for example prescribing standards of performance
(iv) shall be for a period not exceeding 10 years and may be revoked at any time by the Minister or the housing authority. Any subsisting contract is to be treated as having been repudiated in these circumstances
(v) shall not prevent the authority from exercising the functions to which the contract relates

6.9 The 1994 Act also provides that the authority is responsible for any act or omission of the contractor in exercising functions under the contract, except where:

- the contractor fails to fulfil conditions specified in the contract relating to the exercise of the function
- criminal proceedings are brought in respect of the contractor's act or omission

6.10 Where a housing authority has delegated or contracted out the operation of its allocation functions to an external contractor, the contractor must be made aware of the provisions of Part 6 and advised how the legislation and this guidance apply to them.

6.11 Where there is an arrangement in force under s101 of the Local Government Act 1972 by virtue of which one authority exercises the functions of another, the 1994 Act provides that the authority exercising the function is not allowed to contract it out without the principal authority's consent.

ANNEX 1
Indicators of criteria in reasonable preference categories (c) & (d)

Housing authorities may devise their own indicators of the criteria in the reasonable preference categories. The following list is included for illus-trative purposes and to assist housing authorities in this task. It is by no means comprehensive or exhaustive, and housing authorities may have other, local factors to consider and include as indicators of the categories.

Insanitary, overcrowded and unsatisfactory housing conditions

Lacking bathroom or kitchen
Lacking inside WC
Lacking cold or hot water supplies, electricity, gas, or adequate heating
Lack of access to a garden for young children
Sharing living room, kitchen, bathroom/WC
Property in disrepair
Poor internal or external arrangements
Young children in flats above ground floor

People who need to move on medical or welfare grounds (criteria may apply to any member of the household)

A mental illness or disorder
A physical or learning disability
Chronic or progressive medical conditions (eg MS, HIV/AIDS)
Infirmity due to old age
The need to give or receive care
The need to recover from the effects of violence or threats of violence, or physical, emotional or sexual abuse
Ability to fend for self-restricted for other reasons
Young people at risk
People with behavioural difficulties
Need for adapted housing and/or extra facilities, bedroom or bathroom
Need for improved heating (on medical grounds)
Need for sheltered housing (on medical grounds)
Need for ground floor accommodation (on medical grounds)
Need to be near friends/relatives or medical facility on medical grounds
Need to move following hospitalisation or long term care

ANNEX 2
Rights to reside in the UK derived from EU Law

1. EEA nationals and their family members who have a right to reside in the UK that derives from EU law are not persons subject to immigration control. This means that they will be eligible for an allocation of accommodation under Part 6 unless they fall within one of the categories of persons to be treated as a person from abroad who is ineligible for an allocation of accommodation by virtue of regulation 4 of the Eligibility Regulations.

GENERAL

Nationals of EU countries

2. Nationals of EU countries enjoy a number of different rights to reside in other Member States, including the UK. These rights derive from the EU Treaties, EU secondary legislation (in particular *Directive 2004/38*), and the case law of the European Court of Justice.
3. Whether an individual EU national has a right to reside in the UK will depend on his or her circumstances, particularly his or her economic status (eg whether employed, self-employed, seeking work, a student, or economically inactive etc).

Nationals of Bulgaria and Romania – the A2 accession states

4. A slightly different regime applies to EU nationals who are nationals of Bulgaria and Romania which acceded to the EU on 1 January 2007. Bulgaria and Romania are referred to in this guidance as the A2 accession states.

The Immigration (European Economic Area) Regulations 2006

5. The *Immigration (European Economic Area) Regulations 2006* ('the EEA Regulations' – SI 2006/1003) implement into UK domestic law *Directive 2004/38*. Broadly, the EEA Regulations provide that EU nationals have the right to reside in the UK without the requirement for leave to remain under the Immigration Act 1971 for the first 3 months of their residence, and for longer, if they are a 'qualified person' or they have acquired a permanent right of residence.

Nationals of Iceland, Liechtenstein and Norway, and Switzerland

6. The EEA Regulations extend the same rights to reside in the UK to nationals of Iceland, Liechtenstein and Norway as those afforded to EU nationals. (The EU countries plus Iceland, Liechtenstein and Norway together comprise the EEA.) The EEA Regulations also extend the same rights to reside in the UK to nationals of Switzerland. For the purposes of this guidance, 'EEA nationals' means nationals of any of the EU member states (excluding the UK), and nationals of Iceland, Norway, Liechtenstein and Switzerland.

Initial 3 months' residence

7. Regulation 13 of the EEA Regulations provides that EEA nationals have the right to reside in the UK for a period of up to 3 months without any conditions or formalities other than holding a valid identity card or passport. Therefore, during their first 3 months of residence in the UK, EEA nationals will not be subject to immigration control (unless the right to reside is lost following a decision by an immigration officer in accordance with regulation 13(3) of the EEA Regulations).
8. However, regulations 4(1)(b)(ii) and (c) of the Eligibility Regulations provide that a person who is not subject to immigration control is not eligible for an allocation of accommodation if:
   (i) his or her **only** right to reside in the UK is an initial right to reside for a period not exceeding 3 months under regulation 13 of the EEA Regulations, or
   (ii) his or her **only** right to reside in the Channel Islands, the Isle of Man or the Republic of Ireland (the Common Travel Area) is a right equivalent to the right mentioned in (i) above which is derived from the EU Treaty

Rights of residence for 'qualified persons'

9. Regulation 14 of the EEA Regulations provides that 'qualified persons' have the right to reside in the UK so long as they remain a qualified person. Under regulation 6 of the EEA Regulations, 'qualified person' means:
   (a) a jobseeker
   (b) a worker
   (c) a self-employed person
   (d) a self-sufficient person
   (e) a student

Jobseekers

10. For the purposes of regulation 6(1)(a) of the EEA Regulations, 'jobseeker' means a person who enters the UK in order to seek employment and can provide evidence that he or she is seeking employment and has a genuine chance of being employed.
11. Nationals of Bulgaria and Romania who need to be authorised to work do not have a right to reside in the UK as a jobseeker.[20] However, they may have a right to reside by virtue of another status, eg as a self-sufficient person.
12. Although a person who is a jobseeker is not subject to immigration control, regulation 4 of the Eligibility Regulations provides that a person is not eligible for an allocation of accommodation if:
    (i) his or her **only** right to reside in the UK is derived from his or her status as a jobseeker or the family member of a jobseeker, or
    (ii) his or her **only** right to reside in the Channel Islands, the Common Travel Area is a right equivalent to the right mentioned in (i) above which is derived from the Treaty establishing the European Community

Workers

13. In order to be a worker for the purposes of the EEA Regulations, a person must be employed. That is to say, he or she is obliged to provide services for another person in return for monetary reward and is subject to the control of that other person as regards the way in which the work is to be done.
14. Activity as an employed person may include part time work, seasonal work and cross-border work (ie. where a worker is established in another Member State and travels to work in the UK). However, case law provides that the employment must be effective and genuine economic activity, and not on such a small scale as to be regarded as purely marginal and ancillary.
15. Provided the employment is effective and genuine economic activity, the fact that a person's level of remuneration may be below the level of subsistence or below the national minimum wage, or the fact that a person may be receiving financial assistance from public benefits, would not exclude that person from being a 'worker'.
16. A person who is a worker is not subject to immigration control, and is eligible for an allocation of accommodation whether or not he or she is habitually resident in the Common Travel Area.

20 Regulation 6(2) of the Accession (Immigration and Worker Authorisation) Regulations 2006 SI No 3317.

Retention of worker status

17. A person who is no longer working does not cease to be treated as a 'worker' for the purpose of regulation 6(1)(b) of the EEA Regulations, if he or she:
    (a) is temporarily unable to work as the result of an illness or accident; or
    (b) is recorded as involuntarily unemployed after having being employed in the UK, provided that he or she has registered as a jobseeker with the relevant employment office, and:
        (i) was employed for one year or more before becoming unemployed, or
        (ii) has been unemployed for no more than 6 months, or
        (iii) can provide evidence that he or she is seeking employment in the UK and has a genuine chance of being engaged; or
    (c) is involuntarily unemployed and has embarked on vocational training; or
    (d) has voluntarily ceased working and embarked on vocational training that is related to his or her previous employment.

A2 state workers requiring authorisation who are treated as workers

18. By virtue of the *Accession (Immigration and Worker Authorisation) Regulations 2006* ('the Accession Regulations'), nationals of the A2 states (with certain exceptions) must obtain authorisation to work in the UK until they have accrued a period of 12 months' continuous employment.
19. An A2 national requiring authorisation is only treated as a worker if he or she is actually working and:
    (i) holds an accession worker authorisation document, and
    (ii) is working in accordance with the conditions set out in that document (regulation 9(1) of the Accession Regulations)
20. Authorities may need to contact the employer named in the authorisation document, to confirm that the applicant continues to be employed.

Self-employed persons

21. 'Self-employed person' means a person who establishes himself in the UK in order to pursue activity as a self-employed person in accordance with Article 49 of the Treaty on the Functioning of the European Union.
22. A self-employed person should be able to confirm that he or she is pursuing activity as a self-employed person by providing documents relating to their business. A person who is no longer in self-employment does not cease to be treated as a self-employed person for the purposes of regulation 6(1)(c) of the EEA regulations, if he or she is temporarily unable to pursue his or her activity as a self-employed person as the result of an illness or accident.
23. A2 nationals are not required to be authorised in order to establish themselves in the UK as a self-employed person.
24. A person who is a self-employed is not subject to immigration control and is eligible for an allocation of accommodation whether or not he or she is habitually resident in the Common Travel Area.

Self-sufficient persons

25. Regulation 4(1)(c) of the EEA regulations defines 'self-sufficient person' as a person who has:

(i) sufficient resources not to become a burden on the social assistance system of the UK during his or her period of residence, and
(ii) comprehensive sickness insurance cover in the UK

26. By regulation 4(4) of the EEA Regulations, the resources of a person who is a self-sufficient person (or a student – see below) and, where applicable, any family members, are to be regarded as sufficient if (a) they exceed the maximum level of resources which a UK national and his or her family members may possess if he or she is to become eligible for social assistance under the UK benefit system or, if (a) does not apply, (b) taking into account the personal situation of the person concerned and, where applicable, any family members, it appears to the decision maker that the resources of the person or persons concerned should be regarded as sufficient.
27. Where an EEA national applies for an allocation of accommodation as a self-sufficient person and does not appear to meet the conditions of regulation 4(1)(c) of the EEA regulations, the housing authority will need to consider whether he or she may have some other right to reside in the UK.
28. Where the applicant does not meet the conditions of regulation 4(1)(c) but has previously done so during his or her residence in the UK, the case should be referred to the Home Office for clarification of their status.
29. A person who is a self-sufficient person is not subject to immigration control, but must be habitually resident in the Common Travel Area to be eligible for an allocation of accommodation.

Students

30. Regulation 4(1)(d) of the EEA regulations defines 'student' as a person who : (a) is enrolled at a private or public establishment included on the Register of Education and Training Providers,[21] or is financed from public funds, for the principal purpose of following a course of study, including vocational training, and (b) has comprehensive sickness insurance cover in the UK, and (c) assures the Secretary of State, by means of a declaration or such equivalent means as the person may choose, that he or she (and if applicable his or her family members) has sufficient resources not to become a burden on the social assistance system of the UK during his or her period of residence.
31. A person who is a student is not subject to immigration control but must be habitually resident in the Common Travel Area to be eligible for an allocation of accommodation.

Permanent right of residence

32. Regulation 15 of the EEA Regulations provides that the following persons shall acquire the right to reside in the UK permanently : (a) an EEA national who has resided in the UK in accordance with the EEA regulations for a continuous period of 5 years (b) a non-EEA national who is a family member of an EEA national and who has resided in the UK with the EEA national in accordance with the EEA regulations for a continuous period of 5 years (c) a worker or self-employed person who has ceased activity (see regulation 5 of the EEA Regulations for the definition of worker or self-employed person who has ceased activity) (d) the family member of a worker or self-employed

21 Now known as the Register of Sponsors and held by UKBA.

person who has ceased activity (e) a person who was the family member of a worker or self-employed person who has died, where the family member resided with the worker or self-employed person immediately before the death and the worker or self-employed person had resided continuously in the UK for at least 2 years before the death (or the death was the result of an accident at work or an occupational disease) (f) a person who has resided in the UK in accordance with the EEA regulations for a continuous period of 5 years, and at the end of that period was a family member who has retained the right of residence (see regulation 10 of the EEA Regulations for the definition of a family member who has retained the right of residence). Once acquired, the right of permanent residence can be lost through absence from the UK for a period exceeding two consecutive years.

33. A person with a right to reside permanently in the UK arising from (c), (d) or (e) above is eligible for an allocation of accommodation whether or not he or she is habitually resident in the Common Travel Area. Persons with a permanent right to reside by virtue of (a), (b), or (f) must be habitually resident to be eligible.

RIGHTS OF RESIDENCE FOR CERTAIN FAMILY MEMBERS

The right to reside

34. Regulation 14 of the EEA Regulations provides that the following family members are entitled to reside in the UK:
    (i) a family member of a qualified person residing in the UK
    (ii) a family member of an EEA national with a permanent right of residence under regulation 15
    (iii) a family member who has retained the right of residence (see regulation 10 of the EEA Regulations for the definition)
35. A person who has a right to reside in the UK as the family member of an EEA national under the EEA Regulations will not be subject to immigration control. The eligibility of such a person for an allocation of accommodation should therefore be considered in accordance with regulation 4 of the Eligibility Regulations.
36. When considering the eligibility of a family member, housing authorities should consider whether the person has acquired a right to reside in their own right, for example a permanent right to reside under regulation 15 of the EEA Regulations.

Who is a 'family member'?

37. Regulation 7 of the EEA regulations provides that the following persons are treated as the family members of another person (with certain exceptions for students – see below):
    (a) the spouse of the person
    (b) the civil partner of the person
    (c) a direct descendant of the person, or of the person's spouse or civil partner, who is under the age of 21
    (d) a direct descendant of the person, or of the person's spouse or civil partner, who is over 21 and dependent on the person, or the spouse or civil partner
    (e) an ascendant relative of the person, or of the person's spouse or civil partner, who is dependent on the person or the spouse or civil partner

(f) a person who is an extended family member and is treated as a family member by virtue of regulation 7(3) of the EEA regulations (see below)

Family members of students

38. Regulation 7(2) of the EEA regulations provides that a person who falls within (c), (d) or (e) above shall not be treated as a family member of a student residing in the UK after the period of 3 months beginning on the date the student is admitted to the UK unless:
(i) in the case of paragraph 37(c) and (d) above, the person is the dependant child of the student, or of the spouse or civil partner, or
(ii) the student is also a qualified person (for the purposes of regulation 6(1) of the EEA regulations) other than as a student

Extended family members

39. Broadly, extended family members will be persons who: (a) do not fall within any of the categories (a) to (e) in paragraph 37 above, and (b) are either a relative of an EEA national (or of the EEA national's spouse or civil partner) or the partner of an EEA national, and (c) have been issued with an EEA family permit, a registration certificate or a residence card which is valid and has not been revoked

Family members' eligibility for an allocation of accommodation

Relationship with other rights to reside

40. This section concerns the eligibility of an applicant for an allocation of accommodation whose right to reside is derived from his or her status as the family member of an EEA national with a right to reside. In some cases, a family member will have acquired a right to reside in his or her own right. In particular, a person who arrived in the UK as the family member of an EEA national may have subsequently acquired a permanent right of residence under regulation 15 of the EEA Regulations, as outlined in paragraph 32 (a) – (f) above. The eligibility for an allocation of accommodation of those with a permanent right of residence is discussed at paragraphs 32 and 33.

Family members who must be habitually resident

41. For family members with a right to reside under regulation 14 of the EEA Regulations, the following categories of persons must be habitually resident in the UK, the Channel Islands, the Isle of Man or the Republic of Ireland in order to be eligible for an allocation of accommodation:
(a) a person whose right to reside derives from their status as a family member of an EEA national who is a self-sufficient person for the purposes of regulation 6(1)(d) of the EEA regulations
(b) a person whose right to reside derives from their status as a family member of an EEA national who is a student for the purposes of regulation 6(1)(e) of the EEA regulations
(c) a person whose right to reside is dependent on their status as a family member of an EEA national with a permanent right to reside
(d) a person whose right to reside is dependent on their status as a family member who has retained the right of residence

Family members who are exempt from the habitual residence requirement

42. A person with a right to reside under regulation 14 as a family member of an EEA national who is a worker or a self-employed person for the purposes of regulation 6(1) of the EEA regulations is exempted from the requirement to be habitually resident by regulation 4(2)(d) of the Eligibility Regulations. However, authorities should note that an extended family member (see above) is not counted as a family member for the purposes of regulation 4(2)(d) of the Eligibility Regulations (see regulation 2(3) of the Eligibility Regulations).

Family members of UK nationals exercising rights under the EU Treaty

43. There are some limited cases in which the non-EEA family member of a UK national may have a right to reside under EU law. Under regulation 9 of the EEA Regulations, the family member of a UK national should be treated as an EEA family member where the following conditions are met:
   (i) the UK national is residing in an EEA State as a worker or self-employed person, or was so residing before returning to the UK, and
   (ii) if the family member of the UK national is his spouse or civil partner, the parties are living together in the EEA State, or had entered into a marriage or civil partnership and were living together in that State before the UK national returned to the UK
44. Where the family member of a UK national is to be treated as an EEA family member by virtue of regulation 9 of the EEA Regulations, that person is not subject to immigration control, and his or her eligibility for an allocation of accommodation should therefore be determined in accordance with regulation 4 of the Eligibility Regulations.

ANNEX 3
Worker authorisation scheme

1. Bulgaria and Romania ('the A2') acceded to the European Union on 1 January 2007. A2 nationals have the right to move freely among all EU Member States. However, under the EU Accession Treaty for Bulgaria and Romania existing Member States can impose limitations on the rights of A2 nationals to access their labour markets (and the associated rights of residence) for a transitional period.

The Accession (Immigration and Worker Authorisation) Regulations 2006

2. Under the Accession (Immigration and Worker Authorisation) Regulations 2006 (SI No 3317) ('the Accession Regulations'), nationals of the A2 States (with certain exceptions set out in paragraph 9 below) are required to be authorised to work by the Home Office if they work in the UK during the transitional period. While looking for work (or between jobs) their right to reside will be conditional on them being self-sufficient and not imposing an unreasonable burden on the UK social assistance system. These conditions cease to apply once they have worked in the UK continuously and legally for 12 months.

3. The Accession Regulations also give workers from the A2 states the right to reside in the UK. This means that workers from the A2 states have the same right to equal treatment as other EEA workers while they are working in accordance with work authorisation requirements or are exempt from those requirements.

The worker authorisation scheme

4. Nationals of A2 states who wish to work in the UK (except those who are exempt from the requirement) must have an accession worker authorisation document and must be working in accordance with the conditions set out in that document.
5. Nationals of the A2 states who are self-employed are not required to be authorised if they are working that capacity.
6. The following constitute worker authorisation documents:
   (i) a passport or other travel document endorsed to show that the person was given leave to enter or remain in the UK before 1 January 2007, subject to a condition restricting his or her employment in the UK to a particular employer or category of employment
   If the leave to enter or remain expires before the person qualifies to be exempt from the work authorisation requirements, or they wish to engage in employment other than the job for which the leave was granted, they will need to obtain an accession worker card
   (i) a seasonal agricultural work card issued by the Home Office under the Seasonal Agricultural Workers Scheme. The card is valid for 6 months from the date the person starts work for the agricultural employer specified in the card
   (iii) an accession worker card issued by the Home Office
7. The accession worker card is valid for as long as the person continues to work for the employer specified in the card. If the person changes employer, he or she must apply for a new accession worker card.
8. The worker authorisation scheme is a transitional measure. The Accession Regulations provide for the scheme to operate for up to five years from 1 January 2007 (i.e. until 31 December 2011). However, there is provision for the scheme to be extended for a further two years in the event of a serious disturbance to the labour market. The decision was taken on 23 November 2011 to maintain transitional controls on Romanian and Bulgarian workers until the end of 2013.

A2 nationals exempt from worker authorisation

9. The following are the categories of A2 nationals who are <u>not</u> required to obtain authorisation to work:
   - those who are classified as highly skilled persons and hold a registration certificate allowing them unconditional access to the UK labour market
   - those working legally, and without interruption, in the UK for a period of 12 months or more ending on 31 December 2006 (for example, they may have been already present in the UK as a work permit holder before accession)
   - those who had leave to enter the UK under the Immigration Act 1971 on 31 December 2006 and that leave does not place any restrictions on taking

employment in the United Kingdom (for example, a person may have been given leave to remain as the spouse of a British citizen or as the dependant of a work permit holder)

- those who are providing services in the UK on behalf of an employer established elsewhere in the EEA
- those who are also a national of the UK or another EEA state (other than an A2 state)
- those who are a spouse or civil partner of a national of the UK or a person settled in the UK
- those who are the spouse, civil partner or child under 18 of a person who has limited leave to enter or remain in the UK and that leave allows that person to work in the UK
- those who are a family member (spouse, civil partner or dependant child) of an EEA national who has a right to reside in the UK under the EEA Regulations, including those who are the family member (spouse, civil partner or descendant (under 21 or dependant)) of an A2 national who is working in accordance with worker authorisation requirements
- those who have a permanent right to reside in the UK under regulation 15 of the EEA Regulations
- those who are in the UK as a student and are permitted to work for 20 hours a week, provided they are in possession of a registration certificate confirming that they are exercising a Treaty right as a student

10. In addition, where a person has worked legally in the UK without interruption for a 12-month period falling wholly or partly after 31 December 2006, they will be free from the requirement to seek authorisation. At that stage, they will be able to apply to the Home Office for an EEA residence permit to confirm their right to equal treatment on the same basis as other EEA nationals.

12 months' uninterrupted work

11. In order to establish '12 months' uninterrupted work' an A2 worker must have been working legally in the UK at the beginning and end of the 12-month period. The 12-month period does not have to run continuously. However, any intervening period in which an A2 national is not legally working must not exceed 30 days in total. If more than 30 days between periods of employment occur before a 12-month period of uninterrupted employment is established, a fresh period of 12 months' uninterrupted employment would need to commence from that point.
12. There is no restriction on the number of different authorised jobs (or employers) that a worker can have during a 12-month period of continuous employment.

Highly skilled workers

13. A national of an A2 state is not required to be authorised under the worker authorisation scheme, if he is a highly skilled worker who has been given a registration certificate by the Home Office which includes a statement that he or she has unconditional access to the UK labour market.

ANNEX 4
Habitual residence

1. In practice, when considering housing applications from persons subject to the habitual residence test, it is only necessary to investigate habitual residence if the applicant has arrived or returned to live in the UK during the two year period prior to making the application.

Definition of habitual residence

2. The term 'habitual residence' is not defined in legislation. Housing authorities should always consider the overall circumstances of a case to determine whether someone is habitually resident in the Common Travel Area.

General principles

3. When deciding whether a person is habitually resident, consideration must be given to all the facts of each case in a common sense way. It should be remembered that:
   - the test focuses on the fact and nature of residence
   - a person who is not resident somewhere cannot be habitually resident there
   - residence is a more settled state than mere physical presence in a country. To be resident a person must be seen to be making a home. It need not be the only home or a permanent home but it must be a genuine home for the time being. For example, a short stay visitor or person receiving short term medical treatment is not resident
   - the most important factors for habitual residence are length, continuity and general nature of actual residence rather than intention
   - the practicality of a person's arrangements for residence is a necessary part of determining whether it can be described as settled and habitual
   - established habitual residents who have periods of temporary or occasional absence of long or short duration may still be habitually resident during such absences

Action on receipt of an application

Applicant came to live in the UK during the previous two years

4. If it appears that the applicant came to live in the UK during the previous two years, authorities should make further enquiries to decide if the applicant is habitually resident, or can be treated as such.

Factors to consider

5. The applicant's stated reasons and intentions for coming to the UK will be relevant to the question of whether he or she is habitually resident. If the applicant's stated intention is to live in the UK, and not return to the country from which they came, that intention must be consistent with their actions.
6. To decide whether an applicant is habitually resident in the UK, authorities should consider the factors set out below. However, these do not provide an exhaustive checklist of the questions or factors that need to be considered. Further enquiries may be needed. The circumstances of each case will dictate what information is needed, and all relevant factors should be taken into account.

Why has the applicant come to the UK?

7. If the applicant is returning to the UK after a period spent abroad, and it can be established that the applicant was previously habitually resident in the UK and is returning to resume his or her former period of habitual residence, he or she will be immediately habitually resident.
8. In determining whether an applicant is returning to resume a former period of habitual residence authorities should consider:
   - when the applicant left the UK
   - how long the applicant lived in the UK before leaving
   - why the applicant left the UK
   - how long the applicant intended to remain abroad
   - why the applicant returned
   - whether the applicant's partner and children, if any, also left the UK
   - whether the applicant kept accommodation in the UK
   - if the applicant owned property, whether it was let, and whether the lease was timed to coincide with the applicant's return to the UK
   - what links the applicant kept with the UK
   - whether there have been other brief absences
   - why the applicant has come back to the UK
9. If the applicant has arrived in the UK within the previous two years and is not resuming a period of habitual residence, consideration should be given to his or her reasons for coming to the UK, and in particular to the factors set out below.

Applicant is joining family or friends

10. If the applicant has come to the UK to join or rejoin family or friends, authorities should consider:
    - whether the applicant has sold or given up any property abroad
    - whether the applicant has bought or rented accommodation or is staying with friends
    - whether the move to the UK is intended to be permanent

Applicant's plans

11. Authorities should consider the applicant's plans, eg:
    - if the applicant plans to remain in the UK, whether their stated plan is consistent with their actions
    - whether any arrangements were made for employment and accommodation (even if unsuccessful) before the applicant arrived in the UK
    - whether the applicant bought a one-way ticket
    - whether the applicant brought all their belongings
    - whether there is evidence of links with the UK, eg membership of clubs
12. The fact that a person may intend to live in the UK for the foreseeable future does not, of itself, mean that habitual residence has been established. However, the applicant's intentions along with other factors, for example the disposal of property abroad, may indicate that the applicant is habitually resident in the UK.
13. An applicant who intends to reside in the UK for only a short period, for example for a holiday or to visit friends is unlikely to be habitually resident in the UK.

Length of residence in another country

14. Authorities should consider the length and continuity of an applicant's residence in another country:
    - whether the applicant has any remaining ties with his or her former country of residence
    - whether the applicant stayed in different countries outside the UK
15. It is possible that a person may own a property abroad but still be habitually resident in the UK. A person who has a home or close family in another country would normally retain habitual residence in that country. A person who has previously lived in several different countries but has now moved permanently to the UK may be habitually resident here.

Centre of interest

16. An applicant is likely to be habitually resident in the Common Travel Area despite spending time abroad, if his or her centre of interest is located in one of these places.
17. People who maintain their centre of interest in the Common Travel Area for example a home, a job, friends, membership of clubs, are likely to be habitually resident there. People who have retained their centre of interest in another country and have no particular ties with the Common Travel Area are unlikely to be habitually resident.
18. Authorities should take the following into account when deciding the centre of interest:
    - home
    - family ties
    - club memberships
    - finance accounts
19. If the centre of interest appears to be in the Common Travel Area but the applicant has a home somewhere else, authorities should consider the applicant's intentions regarding the property.
20. It is not uncommon for a person to live in one country but have property abroad that they do not intend to sell. Where such a person has lived in the Common Travel Area for many years, the fact that they have property elsewhere does not necessarily mean that they intend to leave, or that the applicant's centre of interest is elsewhere.

Prevention of homelessness and provision of accommodation for 16 and 17 year old young people who may be homeless and/or require accommodation

Guidance to children's services authorities and local housing authorities about their duties under Part 3 of the Children Act 1989 and Part 7 of the Housing Act 1996 to secure or provide accommodation for homeless 16 and 17 year old young people.

Definitions

For the purposes of this guidance:

(a) 'Homeless' in relation to housing services refers to section 175 of the Housing Act 1996.
(b) 'Requiring accommodation' in relation to children's services refers to section 20 of the Children Act 1989.
(c) 'Main accommodation duty' refers to section 193 of the Housing Act 1996.
(d) 'Threatened with homelessness' means likely to become homeless within 56 days.
(e) 'Young people' refers to 16 and 17 year olds, including those who are pregnant or have children of their own.
(f) 'Housing services' means local housing authority.
(g) 'Children's services' means Local Authority Children's Social Care.
(h) 'The 1989 Act' refers to the Children Act 1989.
(i) 'The 1996 Act' refers to the Housing Act 1996.
(j) An 'Eligible Child' is a child who is aged 16–17 and who has been looked after by a local authority for at least 13 weeks since they were 14, and who continues to be looked after.
(k) A 'Relevant Child' is a child aged 16–17 who is no longer looked after by a local authority, but who was before they ceased to be looked after an eligible child [looked after for at least 13 weeks after the age of 14 and has been looked after for some time while they were aged 16/17].
(l) A 'Qualifying Child' is a child aged 16+ who has been looked after for a period of time amounting to less than 13 weeks since their 14th birthday, and was looked after on or after their 16th birthday.

CHAPTER 1
Introduction

1.1 This joint guidance was first published in April 2010 following a number of judgements handed down by the House of Lords in cases concerning the interrelationship between the duty under section 20 of the Children Act 1989 (the 1989 Act) and duties under Part 7 of the Housing Act 1996 (the 1996 Act) where young people aged 16 or 17 require accommodation. The guidance has been amended to reflect new duties introduced through the Homelessness Reduction Act 2017 (the 2017 Act), and to incorporate other relevant updates.

1.2 Case law has clarified the relationship between the duty under section 20 of the Children Act 1989 (the 1989 Act) and duties under Part 7 of the Housing Act 1996 (the 1996 Act) in the case of 16 or 17 year olds who require accommodation. The House of Lords case *R (G) v Southwark* [2009] UKHL 26 held that, where a 16 or 17 year old is owed duties under section 20 of the 1989 Act, this takes precedence over the duties in the 1996 Act in providing for children in need who require accommodation. Where the specific duty is owed under section 20 of the 1989 Act, a 16 or 17 year old should be accommodated under that provision rather than looking to the general duty owed to children in need and their families under section 17 of the 1989 Act.

1.3 Whilst the section 20 Children Act 1989 duty takes precedence, housing services also have duties towards young people who are homeless or threatened with homelessness. Duties owed by each service will depend on a range of factors, including which service they initially seek help from; the outcomes of any assessments and enquiries; and the wishes and feelings of the young person and their family. **It is therefore essential that children's services and housing services work together to plan and provide services that are centred on young people and their families, and prevent young people from being passed back and forth between services.** For more information on joint working between children's services and housing services see chapter 6.

1.4 16 and 17 year olds who are homeless or threatened with homelessness are likely to be vulnerable and will often be at risk of harm in the absence of intervention. Safeguarding and promoting their welfare should be central to service provision. If there is any concern that a child may be suffering, or likely to suffer, significant harm then local safeguarding procedures must be followed. The statutory guidance '*Working together to Safeguard Children*' sets out what is expected of organisations to safeguard and promote the welfare of children.

1.5 This guidance does not address the wider responsibilities of local authority children's services and their partners to identify and support families where children and young people may be at risk of negative outcomes, including homelessness in the future, by delivering integrated and targeted services in their area. This guidance is solely concerned with the functions of children's services and housing services when young people seek help from, or are referred to, local authorities because of homelessness or being threatened with homelessness.

1.6 This guidance is issued jointly by the Secretary of State for Education and the Secretary of State for Housing, Communities and Local Government under section 7 of the Local Authority Social Services 1970 and section 182 of the Housing Act 1996. Section 7 of the 1970 Act requires local authorities, in exercising their social services functions, to act under the general guidance of the Secretary of State; unless there are exceptional reasons in individual cases authorities are expected to comply with this guidance. Section 182 of the 1996 Act requires housing authorities and social services authorities, in the exercise of their functions relating to homelessness and the prevention of homelessness, to have regard to such guidance as may from time to time be given by the Secretary of State.

CHAPTER 2
Supporting families to stay together

Young people living with their families

2.1 The Secretary of State for Housing, Communities and Local Government and the Secretary of State for Education consider that, generally, it will be in the best interests of most young people to live in the family home, or, where this is not safe or appropriate, with responsible adults in their wider family and friends' network. When a 16 or 17 year old is seeking support because they are homeless or threatened with homelessness, housing services and children's services responses should explicitly recognise this and work pro-actively with young people and their families to identify and resolve the issues which have led to the homelessness crisis. This could involve family support such as family mediation or family group conferences.

2.2 It may be possible to prevent a 16 or 17 year old from having to leave home at all, or it may take much longer to work through significant family tensions and problems. It is therefore important that services are designed to enable this family focus to begin on day one and continue throughout the processes of assessment and, where necessary, the provision of accommodation. Joint working between housing and children's services will support this process.

2.3 Work undertaken by children's services and housing services to prevent a 16 or 17 year old from becoming homeless may be undertaken under both section 17 of the 1989 Act and section 195 of the 1996 Act. Any preventative work should be undertaken alongside the assessment processes outlined in this guidance, and should not delay the provision of accommodation or performance of other statutory duties where these are owed.

2.4 If key issues affecting the young person's welfare and/or the sustainability of their living at home remain unresolved, but they are able to remain or return there, support should be provided to the family through children's services. The needs of the young person should be assessed and, if following assessment determined to be a child in need, set out in their child in need plan.

16 and 17 year olds who may require accommodation with children and/or partners

2.5 By the age of 16 or 17 many young people are forming relationships and a few may themselves be pregnant or have children. Assessment, support and accommodation services should take into account young peoples' relationships as well as any dependent children and, where appropriate, support them to build a positive family life.

2.6 The needs of 16 and 17 year olds' for accommodation should be assessed in the context of their relationship with any 'partner'. In some cases it may be appropriate for a 16 or 17 year old to be accommodated in a situation where they can live with their partner. This must not prevent local authorities from accommodating a 16 or 17 year old under section 20 where the young person is owed a duty under this section. Specific consideration should be given to placement options for young people accommodated under section 20 whilst living with a partner. For example, placement in an alternative arrangement such as a self-contained property with visiting support may be appropriate. It will also be important to have contingency plans in place in case relationships break down.

2.7 Where young parents are provided with accommodation by children's services and become looked after, it does not follow that their child will also be looked after. This is an issue for an entirely separate assessment based on the needs of the child.

CHAPTER 3
Children's services duties towards 16 and 17 year olds who seek help because of homelessness, or being threatened with homelessness

Duties owed to young people who may require accommodation

3.1 Where a 16 or 17 year old seeks help from local authority children's services, or is referred to children's services by some other person or agency as appearing to be homeless or threatened with homelessness, children's services must carry out an assessment of what duties, if any, are owed to them. This applies to all young people, including 17 year olds who are approaching their 18th birthday, and young people who are pregnant or have children in their care. Where the duty in section 20 of the 1989 Act is triggered the local authority are under a duty to accommodate the child.

3.2 If the young person is at risk of becoming homeless in the future, for example because of conflict within the family home, it will be for children's services to determine what support is required depending on the circumstances and the needs of the young person and their family. Where there is no immediate threat of homelessness intervention may be more appropriately led by early help services, whereas if there is an imminent threat of homelessness or if the young person is actually homeless, a child in need assessment must be carried out and the child accommodated under section 20.

3.3 Homeless young people who are unaccompanied asylum seekers without a parent or guardian with responsibility for their care, and other non UK nationals who are not 'eligible' for assistance under homelessness legislation must also be provided with accommodation and support by children's services, but will not require referral to a local housing authority.

3.4 Where a 16 or 17 year old seeks help or is referred, and it appears that they have nowhere safe to stay that night, then children's services must secure suitable emergency accommodation for them under section 20 of the 1989 Act, whilst their needs, including their need for continuing accommodation and support, are further assessed. If the young person is accommodated for a continuous period of more than 24 hours the young person will become looked after (further information on section 20 below)

3.5 Section 17 of the 1989 Act sets out the responsibilities of local authorities to provide services for children in need and their families. It is the general duty of every local authority;

(a) to safeguard and promote the welfare of children within their area who are in need; and

(b) so far as is consistent with that duty, to promote the upbringing of such children by their families

by providing a range and level of services appropriate to those children's needs.

3.6 In addition, under section 47 of the 1989 Act, if a local authority has reasonable cause to suspect that a child living in their area is suffering or likely to suffer significant harm, they are under a duty to investigate. This is to enable them to decide whether they should take any action to safeguard or promote the child's welfare.

3.7 Section 17(10) of the 1989 Act defines a child as being in need if;

(a) they are unlikely to achieve or maintain, or to have the opportunity of achieving or maintaining, a reasonable standard of health or development without the provision for them of services by a local authority under this Part;

(b) their health or development is likely to be significantly impaired, or further impaired, without the provision for them of such services; or

(c) they are disabled

The duties described in section 17 apply to all children in need in the area of the local authority. A child is any person under the age of 18 (see section 105(1) of the 1989 Act).

3.8 Section 20(1) requires that:

(a) every local authority shall provide accommodation for any child in need within their area who appears to them to require accommodation as a result of:

(b) there being no person who has parental responsibility for them;

(c) their being lost or having been abandoned; or

(d) the person who has been caring for them is prevented (whether or not permanently, and for whatever reason) from providing them with suitable accommodation or care.

3.9 In addition, even if the criteria in section 20(1) do not apply, section 20(3) requires that:

Every local authority shall provide accommodation for any child in need within their area who has reached the age of sixteen and whose welfare the authority consider is likely to be seriously prejudiced if they do not provide them with accommodation.

3.10 In addition, section 20 (4), provides that:

(a) A local authority may provide accommodation for any child within their area (even though a person who has parental responsibility for them is able to provide them with accommodation) if they consider that to do so would safeguard or promote the child's welfare.

3.11 Local authority duties for accommodating young people under this section are not simply a matter for local policy. The duty is engaged whenever a child in need in the local authority's area requires accommodation as a result of one of the factors set out in section 20(1)(a) to (c) or in section 20(3).

3.12 Where a young person in need requires accommodation as a result of one of the factors set out in section 20(1) (a) to (c) or section 20(3) then that young person must be provided with accommodation. As a result of being accommodated by children's services for a continuous period of more than 24 hours the young person will become looked after, and the local authority will owe them the duties that are owed to all looked after children, and once they cease to be looked after, the duties that are owed to care leavers under that Act. Whilst accommodated under section 20 the young person will not be eligible for welfare benefits, including housing benefits or housing costs under universal credit. Children's services will have a duty to maintain them, including meeting the cost of accommodation.

3.13 There are only two circumstances in which a local authority might find that a homeless young person should not be accommodated under Section 20, and may instead be owed duties under Housing Act 1996. These are where the young person is:

(b) not a child in need;

(c) a 16 or 17 year old child in need who, having been properly and fully advised of the implications and having the capacity to reach a decision, has decided that they do not want to be accommodated under section 20.

Undertaking Assessments

3.14 Statutory guidance *Working Together to Safeguard Children* sets out the principles, parameters and protocols for assessing children under the Children Act 1989. This guidance should be complied with unless exceptional circumstances arise.

3.15 Identifying the needs of the young person and the best response to these needs will be the function of each assessment. Where this takes place under the 1989 Act, it will be carried out by a social worker who should lead a multi-agency assessment.

3.16 Determining who is in need and the extent of any needs requires professional judgment by social workers, informed by consultation with other professionals familiar with the circumstances of the individual young person and their family. However, where a young person is excluded from home and is, for example, staying with various friends, or sleeping in a car, it is extremely likely that they will be a child in need.

3.17 Where a 16 and 17 year old parent is homeless they are also likely to have significant needs and require accommodation and support as a child in need. Local authorities must also carry out an assessment of need if the young person is a young carer, or the parent carer of a disabled child, as set out in sections 17ZA–17ZD of the 1989 Act.

3.18 A multi-agency assessment should make clear from the outset who is responsible for what actions, within what timescales, and what the possible outcomes of the assessment might be – in line with local protocols for assessment, as required under *Working Together to Safeguard Children.*

3.19 Where a young person seeks help because they are homelessness or threatened with homelessness it is good practice for an assessment of the young person's needs to be conducted jointly by both children's and housing services. Alternatively, any assessment and referral processes should be underpinned by appropriate information sharing so that young people do not have to repeat their stories each time and navigate between agencies. The lead agency will be local authority children's services, given their responsibilities for children in need in their area.

3.20 At the point when the need for an assessment under the 1989 Act is identified for either a young homeless person, or a young person threatened with homelessness, it will be necessary for the social worker leading the assessment to inform the young person and their family of the action to be taken.

3.21 As set out in *Working Together to Safeguard Children*, assessments should be child- centred and must be informed by the views of the young person. It will be essential to establish close contact and rapport with the young person throughout the assessment process, in order to make sure their wishes and feelings are properly understood and to take their views into account. Similarly, it will also be important to maintain contact with the adults who retain parental responsibility for the young person and with any other family members in the young person's network. Undertaking an assessment will involve interviewing the child and family members, and generally it will be expected to be necessary to visit the family home or other accommodation where the young person has been living.

3.22 Young people seeking help because of actual or threatened homelessness are likely to have a range of concurrent needs and these should be assessed fully in accordance with the assessment process set out in *Working Together to Safeguard Children*.

3.23 The most crucial issues to be determined in the first instance will be whether the young person is actually homeless, if the young person is a child in need (section 17) and/or is suffering, or likely to suffer, significant harm (section 47), and/or if the young person requires emergency accommodation. If this is the case, children's services must accommodate them immediately. The welfare of the child is paramount and a 16 or 17 year old must not be placed at risk whilst waiting for the completion of an assessment.

3.24 A high quality assessment will take account of the factors which will promote the welfare of the young person, including the significance of the young person's relationship with their parents, or other adults in their life responsible for their care up until the point that they seek help, or are referred, as homeless or threatened with homelessness. As set out in *Working Together to Safeguard Children*, the assessment should identify the young person's and their family's strengths as well as any difficulties, and should be focussed on outcomes, deciding which services and support to provide so that the young person's needs, including the need for suitable accommodation, are met for the future.

3.25 The majority of young people seeking help because of homelessness or threat of homelessness cite the breakdown of relationships with parents or other carers as the reason for their homelessness. The assessment will need to determine whether or not the young person can return home, with support for them and their family if necessary, or whether this is not a possible or a safe option.

3.26 However, the assessment will also need to be holistic in approach, addressing the young person's wider needs, and, as well as the need for accommodation, it will be necessary to assess what further support the young person needs. For example, a homeless young person not participating in education or training would in the first place need suitable accommodation, but this should be arranged in conjunction with plans to re-engage them with education or training.

3.27 At the conclusion of a multi-agency assessment, local authority children's services should have reached a decision on the young person's needs, and/or the nature and level of any risk and harm being suffered by the young person, and the support that is required to address those needs to improve the young person's outcomes.

3.28 Where a young person seeks help because of homelessness, the assessment must necessarily reach a decision as to whether or not the young person is a child in need and requires accommodation as a result of one the scenarios set out in section 20(1)(a) to (c) or section 20(3).

3.29 In some cases, it may not be necessary for the young person to be accommodated by children's services because the young person's needs can be met by providing other services, for example, support to enable the young person to return to the care of their family or other responsible adults in the young person's network. If children's services conclude that the young person does not require accommodation for this reason, they should consider whether they should provide services for the young person under section 17 of the 1989 Act, as a child in need. Where the local authority decides to provide services, a multi-agency child in need plan should be developed which sets out which agencies will provide which services to the child and family. The plan could include, for example, regular visits from children's services, access to family mediation or family group conferencing, or financial support under section 17(6) to sustain any plan for the young person to live with members of their family.

3.30 If the young person is threatened with homelessness but is not homeless – where a decision reached is that the young person is a child in need, children's services will lead work to prevent the young person being threatened with or becoming homeless in the future. This will be based on the professional judgment of an individual young person's circumstances, whether it is in the young person's best interests to remain with their family and if so, what is needed to support this. Where the young person is a child in need, children's services should use their powers under section 17 of the 1989 Act to provide these services, and set these out within a child in need plan.

Timescales

3.31 The timeliness of an assessment is a critical element of the quality of that assessment and the outcomes for a 16 or 17 year old who is homeless or threatened with homelessness. As set out in *Working Together to Safeguard Children,* the speed with which an assessment is carried out should be determined by the individual young person's circumstances and the nature and level of any risk of harm faced.

3.32 Within one working day of a referral being received, a local authority social worker should make a decision about the type of response that is required and acknowledge receipt to the referrer. Where a young person refers themselves, or is referred by housing services or another agency as appearing to be homeless or threatened with homelessness, children's services should proceed with a child in need assessment.

3.33 Where homelessness is threatened or actual, this should result in a prompt response based on individual circumstances. The maximum timeframe for a statutory assessment to conclude, such that it is possible for the local authority to reach a decision on next steps, should be no longer than 45 working days from the point of referral.

3.34 In the case of a 16 or 17 year old who is threatened with homelessness or is homeless, 45 days is a long period of time, which may involve significant risk and hardship, impacting on their safety, welfare and physical and emotional well-being. Local working arrangements may set out a shorter timescale for completion of the assessment. If an assessment exceeds 45 working days, the social worker should record the reasons for exceeding the time period.

3.35 Where particular needs are identified at any stage of the assessment, social workers should not wait until the assessment reaches a conclusion before commissioning or providing services to support the child and their family, including the provision of accommodation under section 20 of the 1989 Act if necessary.

3.36 Where a housing authority has made the referral of a 16 or 17 year old, social workers should inform the referrer of what action has been or will be taken, setting out in writing the outcome of the assessment and sending this to the housing authority to allow them to record this and take any necessary further action.

3.37 An assessment is not complete until children's services have decided what action is necessary to respond to the young person's needs and this has been communicated to the young person, the adults responsible for their care, housing services and any other relevant agencies.

Young person's wishes and feelings

3.38 Local authority children's services have a duty to ascertain the wishes and feelings of a young person regarding the provision of services to be delivered under section 17 of the Children Act 1989.

3.39 Section 20(6) of the Children Act also requires that:

Before providing accommodation under this section, a local authority shall, as far as is reasonably practicable and consistent with the child's welfare;

(a) ascertain the child's wishes and feelings regarding the provision of accommodation; and

(b) give due consideration (having regard to their age and understanding) to such wishes and feelings of the child as they have been able to ascertain.

3.40 This will include assessing their emotional and behavioural development, and their capacity to make use of wider resources to manage independent living.

3.41 Where a young person says they do not wish to be accommodated, a local authority should reach the conclusion that the young person's wishes are decisive only as part of an overall judgment of their assessed welfare needs and the type and location of accommodation that will meet those needs.

3.42 It will be essential that the young person is fully consulted about and understands the implications of being accommodated by children's services and becoming looked after. The social worker leading the assessment must provide realistic and full information about the package of support that the young person can expect as a looked after child and, subsequently, as a 'former relevant' care leaver (as defined in section 23C (1) of 1989 Act). If they are not looked after for the prescribed period, the young person leaving care would be a 'person qualifying for advice and assistance' as set out in section 24 of the 1989 Act.

3.43 Children's services should also ensure that the young person receives accurate information about what assistance may be available to them if they do not become looked after, including from housing services under Part 7 of the 1996 Act. This will include any entitlement for assistance under Part 7. In particular the considerations a young person needs to be made aware of are:

(a) duties on housing services to undertake an assessment, develop a personalised housing plan and to take steps to help the applicant retain or secure accommodation (sections 195 and section 189B of the 1996 Act),

(b) the requirement on the applicant to cooperate and for applicants to take steps themselves as set out in a personalised plan (section 193B and section 193C of the 1996 Act),

(c) the 'accommodation offer' under the relief duty – suitable accommodation which has a reasonable prospect of being available for occupation for at least 6 months (section 189B and section 195 of the 1996 Act),

(d) the implications of turning down offers of accommodation that are suitable (section 193A of the Housing Act 1996),

(e) the possible risk of being found or becoming homeless intentionally in the future (section 191 of the 1996 Act),

(f) their right to request a review of decisions (section 202 of the 1996 Act).

3.44 This information should be provided in a 'young person friendly' format at the start of the assessment process and be available for the young person to take away for full consideration and to help them seek advice.

3.45 Where there is any doubt about a 16 or 17 year old's capacity to judge what may be in their best interests, e.g. whether they should be accommodated under section 20 of the 1989 Act or seek alternative assistance, there will need to be further discussion involving children's services, housing services, the young person concerned and their family where safe and appropriate, to reach agreement on the way forward.

3.46 Children and young people who have received services under the 1989 Act are able to be supported to make complaints and representation with the help of an independent advocate. Children's services should provide information about access to advocacy services when they explain the assessment process to 16 and 17 year olds seeking help because of homelessness.

3.47 Young people should have access to independent advocacy and support to assist them in weighing up the advantages and disadvantages and coming to a balanced decision and understanding and navigating the housing system. Independent advocacy and support services can play a key role in supporting 16 and 17 year olds who are homeless or threatened with homelessness.

3.48 Some 16 and 17 year olds may decide that they do not wish to be provided with accommodation by children's services under section 20 of the 1989 Act, for example, because they do not wish to be supported as a looked after child. In these circumstances it is important that children's services are clear that the young person's decision is properly informed, and has been reached after careful consideration of all the relevant information. If the young person is subsequently not accommodated by housing services and remains homeless, housing services must inform children's services who may need to take further action.

3.49 Where a 16 or 17 year old child in need wishes to refuse accommodation offered under section 20 of the 1989 Act, children's services must be satisfied that the young person:

(a) has been provided with all relevant information;

(b) is competent to make such a decision; and

(c) that they do not need to take additional safeguarding action.

3.50 Every 16–17 year old assessed as being a child in need but who does not wish to be accommodated under section 20 should have a child in need plan setting out the services that will be provided to meet their needs.

16 and 17 year olds from one local authority area who seek assistance from children's services in another local authority area

3.51 Where a 16 or 17 year old who was living in one local authority area and moves to another local authority area and seeks assistance from children's services in that local authority, the duty to assess falls on the authority area in which the young person is. The authority cannot refuse to consider the young person's immediate needs and expect them to return to the authority in the area presumed to be their 'home' district.

3.52 An initial interview, perhaps combined with enquiries in the area where the young person came from, should be sufficient to establish their connection with the area where they have sought help and their reasons for seeking help there rather than in their 'home' district. These enquiries may be able to establish whether it may be possible for the young person to return to the 'home' district. For example, it might be possible for the authority where the young person seeks help to negotiate with their 'home' authority to take over the assessment of the young person's needs, so that the young person is assessed in a familiar setting close to their family and friends.

3.53 It is essential that disputes about responsibility for the young person in the medium term should not get in the way of the authority that received the young person's request for assistance responding to the young person's immediate needs. The young person concerned must not be passed between local authorities and services whilst a decision is reached about which authority is responsible for assisting them.

Young People in Custody

3.54 Youth offending teams, children's services and (wherever appropriate) housing authorities should work together to ensure effective arrangements are in place to identify young people in custody who may be at risk of homeless on release. Services should cooperate, where appropriate, to ensure that young people can live with parents or guardians, or another appropriate adult, when they leave custody, for example through provision of family mediation, family group conferences or other family support.

3.55 Resettlement planning will begin at the start of a sentence, and continue throughout the young person's time in custody. If at any point it is identified that the young person may require accommodation on release, agencies will need to collaborate to ensure that a suitable accommodation and support placement is arranged in good time.

3.56 Children's services have a duty to accommodate young people who were looked after or relevant children when they entered custody, or have become a relevant child by virtue of having been remanded into local authority care for 13 weeks or more, if they require accommodation on release.

3.57 A young person who is not already a looked after or a relevant child and may require accommodation on release must have a child in need assessment to determine what duties are owed under the 1989 Act, including whether children's services will have a duty to provide accommodation under section 20. If the young person will not be accommodated under section 20, for example because, having been fully informed of the consequences of their decision, they have declined to become looked after, a referral should be made to a housing authority and an assessment made of whether they are a child in need under section 17 of the 1989 Act.

Provision of accommodation under section 17 of the 1989 Act

3.58 Children's services authorities have powers to accommodate children under section 17(6) of the 1989 Act. A young person provided with accommodation under this section would not be looked after and the local authority would not have the corresponding duties set out at in sections 22, 22B, 23, 23ZA–23ZB and 24 of the 1989 Act. However, the provision of accommodation under section 17 will almost always concern children needing to be accommodated with their families.

3.59 The powers of local authorities to provide accommodation under section 17 cannot be used as a substitute for their duty to provide accommodation under section 20(1) of the 1989 Act to homeless 16 and 17 year olds in need. Children's services do not have the option of choosing under which provision they should provide accommodation for homeless 16 and 17 year olds. Section 20 involves an evaluative judgment on some matters but not discretion.[1]

3.60 However, in very limited circumstances the provision of accommodation under section 17 may be appropriate. Where a young person aged 16 or 17 is homeless and requires accommodation, does not wish to be accommodated under section 20 but is subsequently not owed the main accommodation duty by a housing authority, for example because they have refused a suitable offer of accommodation or are found to be intentionally homeless, then the children's services authority should, given the change in circumstances, once again ask them their wishes regarding being accommodated under section 20.

3.61 If the young person still does not wish to be accommodated under section 20 and is judged to have the capacity to make that decision they should be offered accommodation under section 17 with a child in need plan in place, until they no longer require accommodation or they reach the age of 18. In such cases, children's services and housing services will need to work together with the young person to ensure that they are not placed at risk of homelessness as they approach age 18.

The duty to refer to housing services

3.62 Local authority children's services are among the public authorities which are required to notify a housing authority of service users they consider may be homeless or threatened with homelessness (i.e. it is likely they will become

1 *R (G) v Southwark* [2009] UKHL 26 – para 31 http://www.publications.parliament.uk/pa/ld200809/ldjudgmt/jd090520/appg-2.htm

homeless within 56 days) (section 213B of 1996 Act). Before making a referral a public authority must:

(a) have consent to the referral from the individual;

(b) allow the individual to identify the housing authority in England which they would like the notification to be made to; and,

(c) have consent from the individual that their contact details can be supplied so the housing authority can contact them regarding the referral.

3.63 This duty applies where the service user is 16 or 17, as well as to other households. If the young person approaches, or is referred to children's services they must obtain their consent before a referral can be made to the housing authority. This consent should be obtained through an informed conversation with the young person through which they are able to understand the duties owed by children's services and what they should expect to be the outcome of a referral to housing services. Children's services may consider the use of advocacy services appropriate to ensure the young person fully understands the information.

3.64 If a referral is made to a housing authority children's services should include a summary of any initial assessment and provision of support to the young person and what assistance, if any, housing services might provide. When the housing authority receives a referral from children's services the two services should work together to ensure that the needs of the young person are met.

3.65 **The referral does not diminish children's services responsibilities** towards young people as set out in this guidance; rather it should be used to help strengthen communication between children's and housing services, it will not be an alternative to carrying out a child in need or early help assessment. It is recommended that children's and housing services agree how they will use the referral arrangements as part of the process of agreeing joint protocols including what type of information children's services should provide and how housing authorities will respond. Consideration should also be given to how data generated by the referral process can be used to build a shared understanding of youth homelessness in the area. For more information on joint protocols and wider joint working see chapter 6.

CHAPTER 4
Duties placed on housing services when 16 and 17 year olds seek help because of homelessness or being threatened with homelessness

Initial Assessment

4.1 Where a young person approaches housing services for accommodation, or help with obtaining accommodation, housing services should treat this as an application for assistance under Part 7 of the 1996 Act. Under section 184, if housing services have reason to believe the young person may be homeless, or threatened with homelessness, they must make inquiries to determine what duties, if any, are owed to them.

4.2 If the young person is eligible and is (or may be) homeless and, by virtue of being 16–17 years old may have a priority need, the housing authority will have an immediate duty to secure interim accommodation (section 188(1) of the 1996 Act). In considering the suitability of accommodation authorities should bear in mind that 16 and 17 year olds who are homeless and estranged from their family will be particularly vulnerable and in need of support.

Priority need

4.3 The Homelessness (Priority Need for Accommodation) (England) Order 2002 provides that the following have a priority need for accommodation for the purposes of Part 7 of the 1996 Act:

(a) A child aged 16 or 17 who is not a relevant child for the purposes of section 23A of the Children Act 1989 **and** is not owed a duty to provide accommodation under section 20 of that Act (provision of accommodation for children in need).

(b) A person (other than a relevant student) who;

(i) is under twenty-one, and;

(ii) at any time after reaching the age of sixteen, but while still under eighteen, was, but is no longer, looked after, accommodated or fostered.

4.4 Guidance on the assessment of Children Act duties, including whether or not a section 20 duty is owed, are set out in chapter 3. **Housing authorities will be unable to determine whether a 16–17 year old has priority need under the 1996 Act until a child in need assessment has been completed. It is therefore essential that referrals are made and assessments completed in a timely manner.**

Arrangements for Children Act Assessments

4.5 If the outcome of the initial housing authority assessment is a finding that a young person is homeless but not eligible for housing assistance, or is a 'relevant child' owed an accommodation duty under the 1989 Act, immediate arrangements must be made for them to receive assistance from children's services.

4.6 Young people who are eligible for homelessness services should also be referred to children's services during the prevention and/or relief stages as set out below. There will also be circumstances in which a further referral is needed, including for young people who have declined to become looked after, but subsequently lose accommodation or are no longer owed a duty by housing services.

4.7 The fact that a young person may be reluctant to engage with the Children Act assessment process is not in itself a basis for assuming that the young person has rejected any children's services' intervention to provide them with accommodation. Lack of co-operation is no reason for the local authority not to attempt to carry out its duties under the 1989 Act. In these circumstances, the assessment will need to involve careful recording of how the authority has attempted to engage with the young person to assess their needs in order to determine and provide appropriate services. Ultimately, it is not possible to force services on young people who persistently continue to refuse them.

4.8 Where children's services have decided that a section 20 duty is not owed, or the young person does not wish to be accommodated, housing services duties under Part 7 of the 1996 Act will continue.

4.9 In any case, where a housing authority provides accommodation for a child in need, including where the young person has declined to be accommodated under section 20, children's services will need to consider the provision of services under section 17 of the 1989 Act, set out in a child in need plan, and continue to work with housing services to ensure the young person's needs are met.

4.10 Where any safeguarding concerns emerge during their work undertaken with a 16 or 17 year old, the housing authority must make a referral to children's services according to local safeguarding procedures.

Prevention and Relief Duties

4.11 New duties towards people that are homeless or threatened with homelessness were incorporated within Part 7 of the Housing Act 1996 by the Homelessness Reduction Act 2017. These include duties to:

(a) undertake assessments;
(b) develop personalised housing plans; and
(c) take reasonable steps to prevent homelessness (for applicants who are threatened with homelessness) or relieve homelessness (for applicants who are already homeless).

4.12 Young people who are eligible and homeless, or threatened with homelessness, must have an assessment of their needs. This must include:

(a) the circumstances that have caused them to be homeless or threatened with homelessness;
(b) their housing needs, and what accommodation would be suitable for them, their household and anybody who might reasonably be expected to live with them;

and,

(c) the support that would be necessary for them, and anybody who will be living with them, to have and sustain suitable accommodation.

4.13 If a young person who applies or is referred to a housing authority is not homeless, but is threatened with homelessness within 56 days, a prevention duty will be owed irrespective of whether the young person is likely to have a priority need.

4.14 A referral should be made to children's services identifying the threat of homelessness, and services should co-operate together in efforts to prevent the young person from becoming homeless.

4.15 A Personalised Housing Plan must be developed with the young person, setting out the reasonable steps that the housing authority and the young person will take to try and prevent them from becoming homeless. Any steps that the young person is required to take should be proportionate to the age, understanding and assessed capability of the young person to undertake the actions. Other relevant people, for example parents or social workers, may also be requested to take actions as appropriate.

4.16 If a young person is already homeless when they seek help, or they become homeless despite efforts to prevent it, housing services must attempt to relieve their homelessness by ensuring that suitable accommodation is made available to them (section 189B). A Personalised Housing Plan must also be produced, or amended to reflect the changes in housing circumstances. While a Personalised Housing Plan is prepared, emergency accommodation should be provided where necessary. If a child in need assessment has not already been completed one should be commenced immediately. Children's services should conclude the assessment within 45 days. See chapter 3 of this guidance for more information on the child in need assessment process and timescales. The question of which further duties are owed under Part 7 of the 1996 Act will depend in part on the outcome of the assessment by children's services, and whether any duty is owed under section 20 of the 1989 Act.

4.17 **Housing services should seek to work with children's services throughout the process of assessment, planning and attempting to prevent or relieve homelessness so that the child in need assessment and homelessness assessment, and the resulting plans and actions, are co-ordinated. This will enable a focus on working together to meet the needs of the young person and is likely to lead to better and more sustainable outcomes.** See section 6 of this guidance for further information about joint working.

Ending the prevention and relief duties

4.18 The guidance on how the (section 195) prevention and (section 189B) relief duties come to an end is set out in full in chapter 14 of the Homelessness Code of Guidance and include the following:

(a) *The housing authority is satisfied that the applicant has suitable accommodation available for occupation and a reasonable prospect of suitable accommodation being available for at least 6 months from the date of the notice.*
Duties might end in this way if the young person is accommodated under section 20 and/or within a supported housing pathway, and the housing authority is satisfied that suitable accommodation will be available for occupation for at least six months. Where the young person is older than 17 and a half, and children's services duty to accommodate them is likely to end within six months, it is the responsibility of the housing authority to satisfy itself that accommodation will be available for at least six months, for example through being confident that arrangements are in place for the young person to remain in the accommodation beyond their 18th birthday or for a planned transition to other suitable accommodation.

(b) *the housing authority has complied with the prevention or relief duty and 56 days have passed (regardless of whether the applicant is still threatened with homelessness in the case of the prevention duty or whether they have secured accommodation in the case of the relief duty) (sections 195(8)(b) and 189B (7)(b)).*
If the relief duty ends after 56 days without homelessness having been relieved, the housing authority will be required to reach a decision on whether the (section 193(2)) housing duty is owed (see Main Duty paragraphs 4.2–4.27 below).

(c) *The applicant has refused an offer of suitable accommodation and, on the date of refusal, there was a reasonable prospect that suitable accommodation would be available for the minimum prescribed period (sections 195(8)(d) and 189B(7)(c)).*
If a young person refuses suitable accommodation, such as placement within a supported housing pathway, the prevention or relief duty may be brought to an end but without any effect on further duties that might

be owed. Refusal of suitable accommodation within the relief stage will not disapply the young person from the main (section 193(2)) housing duty except where the offer was a 'final offer' of an assured shorthold tenancy or a Part 6 offer.

(d) *the applicant has become homeless intentionally from any accommodation that has been made available to them as a result of reasonable steps taken by the housing authority during the prevention or relief duty, whichever is relevant (sections 195(8)(e) and 189B(7)(d)).*

(e) *the applicant is no longer eligible for assistance (sections 195(8)(f) and 189B(7)(e)).*

(f) *the applicant has deliberately and unreasonably refused to co-operate (sections 195(10) and 189B(9)(b)).*

4.19 If the relief duty ends in any of the ways set out in c- f above, children's services will be required to carry out further assessments of the young person's needs.

Intentional homelessness

4.20 Housing services should take particular care when assessing whether 16–17 year olds are to be considered intentionally homeless from their family home or from accommodation provided for them. For an applicant to be intentionally homeless the actions or omissions that led to their becoming homeless must have been deliberate. Housing authorities will need to be mindful that a homeless 16–17 year old might not have the ability to understand the full consequences of their actions and choices that would be expected of an adult.

4.21 Housing services are reminded that applicants cannot be considered to have become homeless intentionally because of failing to take up an offer of accommodation; homelessness is only capable of being 'intentional' where the applicant has ceased to occupy accommodation that it would have been reasonable for them to continue to occupy. For a young person to be considered intentionally homeless from accommodation provided during the prevention or relief stages (see 4.18 above) the accommodation must have been provided under the reasonable steps provisions and **not** as interim accommodation under Section 188 of the 1996 Act.

4.22 If, for whatever reason, a 16 or 17 year old is found to have become homeless intentionally, housing services should inform children's services immediately (see section on joint protocols in chapter 6 of this guidance). For further guidance about intentional homelessness, authorities should refer to chapter 9 of the Homelessness Code of Guidance.

Deliberate and Unreasonable Refusal to Cooperate

4.23 The prevention and relief duties can be brought to an end under section 193B and section 193C respectively if an applicant deliberately and unreasonably refuses to take any of the steps that they agreed to take, or the housing authority set out for them to take where agreement could not be reached, in their personalised housing plan. In considering whether a young person's actions were both deliberate and unreasonable, housing authorities must take into account their age and maturity, as well as the context in which they are making decisions. This would include considering the impact of homelessness on the young persons mental and emotional health, as well as their ability to understand the consequences of their actions and decisions.

4.24 Housing authorities must have procedures governing the service of notice on applicants who deliberately and unreasonably refuse to cooperate, and might wish to consider how children's services can contribute to these arrangements in respect of homeless 16–17 year olds. More information on non-cooperation is set out in chapter 14 of the Code of Guidance (14.43–14.48).

The Main Housing Duty

4.25 Where a young person who is eligible and unintentionally homeless does not have their homelessness prevented or relieved, housing authorities must assess what further duties (if any) are owed to them. If the young person is not a child in need owed duties under section 20 of the 1989 Act they will have priority need for accommodation and will be owed the main section 193(2) housing duty with the following exceptions:

(a) The relief duty ended due to the young person's unreasonable and deliberate refusal to cooperate, in which case the section 193C(4) duty is owed.

(b) The young person refused a final offer made under section 189B(9)(a) of the 1996 Act, or a Part 6 offer and so is disapplied from the main housing duty. A final offer must be of an assured shorthold tenancy of at least six months duration which is suitable for the young person's needs.

4.26 Authorities should refer to chapter 14 of the Homelessness Code of Guidance for guidance on the ways in which prevention and relief duties end, and chapter 15 for guidance on discharging accommodation duties.

4.27 Where children's services have been providing temporary accommodation and a young person is to be provided with settled accommodation by the housing authority, children's and housing services will need to agree a procedure for children's services to inform housing services that their provision of temporary accommodation will come to an end. This process should aim to minimise anxiety for the young person associated with concerns that they may again find themselves without anywhere to live. Children's services and housing services will need to work together closely to ensure that the young person's ongoing housing needs can be met in the most practical and timely way possible.

Where section 20 and Part 7 duties are not owed

4.28 Where a young person aged 16 or 17 is homeless and requires accommodation, does not wish to be accommodated under section 20 of the 1989 Act but is subsequently not owed an accommodation duty by a housing authority, for example because they have refused a suitable offer of accommodation or are found to be intentionally homeless, then children's services should, given the change in circumstances, once again ask them their wishes regarding being accommodated under section 20.

4.29 If the young person still does not wish to be accommodated and is judged to have the capacity to make that decision, if it is necessary to safeguard and promote the welfare of the young person who is in need, they should be offered accommodation under section 17 of the 1989 Act until they no longer require accommodation or they reach the age of 18. In such cases children's services and housing services will need to work together with the young person to ensure that they are not placed at risk of homelessness as they approach age 18.

Young people from one district who seek assistance from housing services in another district

4.30 Housing services may choose to refer applicants who are homeless and eligible for services to another housing authority under certain circumstances. Referrals can only be made if the person **does not** have a local connection to the area they have applied to; they do have a local connection in the area they are to be referred to; and they would not be at risk of violence or the threat of violence in the area they are referred to.

4.31 In deciding whether or not to refer a young person to another district where they may have a local connection, housing authorities should consider a range of factors, including safeguarding or any risk of significant harm to the young person. In order to ensure that decision making is informed by relevant information, housing services should seek consent to discuss a referral to another authority with relevant children's services, in both the area of housing services and in the area they are minded to make a referral to.

4.32 Further guidance on local connection and referrals to other authorities is available at chapter 10 of the Homelessness Code of Guidance.

4.33 The children's services team undertaking the child in need assessment should be consulted prior to any decision to refer a homeless 16 or 17 year old to another district to ensure that due consideration is given to their safety and welfare.

CHAPTER 5
The provision of suitable accommodation for 16 and 17 year olds.

Placements by children's services

5.1 The Children Act 1989 Guidance and Regulations: Volume 2: care planning, placement and case review provides guidance on the placement of looked after children, and will therefore apply to young people who are accommodated under section 20 of the 1989 Act for a continuous period of more than 24 hours. Placement options include regulated settings such as foster care and children's homes. Sections 22C(6)(d) and 23(2)(f)(i) of the 1989 Act provides that young people may also be placed in 'other arrangements', not regulated under the Care Standards Act 2000, where such a placement best meets their needs. 'Other arrangements' may include supported lodgings, supported housing and independent accommodation where suitable support is provided.

5.2 Some 16 and 17 year olds who require accommodation may be reluctant to take up a placement in foster care or a children's home and the assessment of their emotional and behavioural development may indicate that they do not require the level or kind of supervision and support that foster or children's home care provides. The option to use 'other arrangements' offers scope to provide alternative accommodation and support.

5.3 In accordance with chapter 3 of Part 4 of the Care Planning, Placement and Case Review (England) Regulations 2010 in every case the local authority must establish that the accommodation is suitable. Regulation 27 of schedule 6 to the Care Planning Regulations set out the standards that the authority must be satisfied with in respect of the accommodation and young person.

5.4 Where a young person is placed in other arrangements the local authority must prepare a placement plan. Regulation 9 of the Care Planning Regulations requires a placement plan to be agreed with and signed by the appropriate person. An 'appropriate person' in relation to other arrangements is defined in regulation 2(1) under 22C(6)(d), as the person who will be responsible for the child at the accommodation;

5.5 Any support plan setting out how the supported accommodation service will support the young person should be integral to the placement plan and avoid duplication.

5.6 The placement planning process should involve an exchange of appropriate information included as part of the assessment process which informed the development of the looked after young person's care plan, so that the accommodation provider has a full understanding of the young person's needs and their role in meeting these needs. It will be essential that the provider appreciates the arrangements that the local authority proposes to put in place to make sure that the young person is adequately supported. The placement plan must be explicit about the respective roles and responsibilities of the placement provider and the young person's social worker, their Independent Reviewing Officer and of other staff employed or commissioned by the authority to contribute to the plan for the young person's care.

Placements by housing services

5.7 Accommodation secured by housing authorities under their functions under Part 7 of the 1996 Act must be suitable for the applicant and anyone who normally resides with them or might reasonably be expected to. For further guidance about suitability of accommodation, authorities should refer to chapter 17 of the Homelessness Code of Guidance.

5.8 Consideration of whether accommodation is suitable requires an assessment of all aspects of the accommodation in the light of the relevant needs, requirements and circumstances of the person and their household. Factors to consider when determining suitability include physical standards and safety, whether the landlord is fit and proper, location and affordability.

Considerations for both children's and housing services

5.9 In considering suitability, both children's and housing services should bear in mind that 16 and 17 year olds who are homeless and estranged from their family will be particularly vulnerable and in need of support.

5.10 Children's and housing services are reminded that **bed and breakfast accommodation, including hotels and nightly let accommodation with shared facilities, is not considered suitable for any 16 or 17 year old.**

5.11 Examples of accommodation for use in emergencies include Night stop-type or short- term supported lodgings in the homes of trained and vetted hosts, emergency beds in specialist young peoples' supported accommodation services, other specifically designed crash pad services with on-site support and, for looked after children, emergency foster placements.

5.12 Housing and children's services should be alert to the risks that may be associated with placing vulnerable young people in mixed age hostel settings with people who are considerably older than they are. Young people should **not** be placed in all-ages night shelter provision, even in an emergency.

5.13 Housing and children's services are reminded that 16 and 17 year olds are still children and it will not usually be appropriate for them to be placed in temporary accommodation without on-site support. Accommodation with visiting support may be suitable for some young people; where this is considered authorities should put in place arrangements so that young people can contact support services out of hours.

5.14 Whether accommodation is provided by children's or housing services, arrangements should be in place so that young people have the support that they will need to make a positive transition towards independence. This might include, for example, the provision of supported accommodation or supported lodgings where young people can remain beyond the age of 18 and develop the skills they will need to manage the transition to adulthood.

5.15 This kind of accommodation and support might be jointly commissioned or provided by children's services and housing services and will help children's services to meet their duties to secure sufficient accommodation for looked after children and care leavers in their area.

CHAPTER 6
Joint working to prevent and resolve homelessness among 16 and 17 year olds

6.1 There is a clear legal framework for co-operation between children's services and housing services to meet the needs of children and young people. Section 27 of the 1989 Act empowers a children's services authority to ask other authorities, including any local housing authority, for 'help in the exercise of any of their functions' under Part 3; the requested authority must provide that help if it is compatible with their own statutory or other duties and does not unduly prejudice the discharge of any of their own functions. The Children Act 2004 broadened and strengthened the statutory framework requiring co-operation between relevant statutory services to improve outcomes for children and young people. Core legal requirements are set out in *Working Together to Safeguard* Children, making it clear what individuals and organisations should do and what they can expect of one another.

6.2 The details of local working arrangements regarding 16 or 17 year olds who are threatened with, or who are homeless, are a matter for each area. But when a 16 or 17 year old is threatened with homelessness they are first and foremost a child and therefore children's services have the primary duty to them.

Provision of general advice and information

6.3 In order to help prevent homelessness, children's and housing services may want to consider collaborating to provide relevant information and advice to young people and their families regarding support services available in the area, available housing options for young people, their rights, and how to request further assistance.

6.4 Children's services can provide these services under section 17 of the 1989 Act, which sets out the responsibilities of children's services to provide services for children in need and their families. It is the general duty of every local authority:

(a) to safeguard and promote the welfare of children within their area who are in need; and

(b) so far as is consistent with that duty, to promote the upbringing of such children by their families

by providing a range and level of services appropriate to those children's needs.

6.5 Housing authorities have a duty to provide advisory services to any person in their area and a duty to do so specifically for groups at high risk of homelessness. For further guidance about general advice and information regarding homelessness, authorities should refer to chapter 3 of the Homelessness Code of Guidance.

6.6 The information and advice provided should cover:

(a) preventing homelessness;

(b) securing accommodation when homeless;

(c) the rights of persons who are homeless or threatened with homelessness, and the duties of the authority, under this Part;

(d) any help that is available from the authority or anyone else, whether under this Part or otherwise, for persons in the authority's district who are homeless or may become homeless (whether or not they are threatened with homelessness); and

(e) how to access that help.

Operational joint working – joint protocols

6.7 It is essential that services for 16–17 year olds are underpinned by written joint protocols which set clear and practical arrangements for the provision of services. In formulating a joint protocol, due regard should be given to fact that where duties are owed under section 20 of the 1989 Act they take precedence over the 1996 Act in providing accommodation and support for children in need who require accommodation.

6.8 An effective joint protocol will set out a mutually agreed vision, objectives, systems and processes to ensure effective action to prevent youth homelessness and, where homelessness has occurred and cannot be relieved through a safe return to a family home or to suitable friends, to ensure 16 or 17 year olds have accommodation which meets their needs.

6.9 A joint protocol should also outline that the duties placed on both children's services authorities and housing authorities apply to all 16 and 17 year olds, including those who are pregnant, have children themselves, have an older partner or are in and leaving custody. It should also set out the process for young people referred under 213B of the 2017 Act.

6.10 A joint protocol might cover the following:

(a) Inter-agency arrangements to prevent youth homelessness and provide support to young people to remain living with their families.

(b) Arrangements for assessment and planning for the needs of young people in custody, and the role of Youth Offending Teams within the protocol.

(c) Arrangements for integrated or joint assessment processes between children's services and housing services where 16 and 17 year olds seek help because they are threatened with homelessness or homeless, including information-sharing procedures.

(d) Delivery of the Duty to Refer placed upon children's services to ensure young people who are threatened with homelessness or are homeless are referred, with informed consent, to a local housing authority. This duty, introduced through the 2017 Act should not detract from, and may be used to enhance, performance of other statutory duties or joint working arrangements.

(e) Agreed timescales for assessing whether or not a homeless young person is a child in need and will be provided with accommodation by children's services.

(f) Arrangements for timely assessment and placement provision for young people who require accommodation on release from custody.

(g) Arrangements for access to suitable emergency accommodation when needed.

(h) Arrangements for access to longer term accommodation with support for young people (including looked after children and care leavers) who need this service.

(i) Agreed standards as to how the suitability of accommodation that is not formally regulated or inspected under the Care Standards Act 2000 will be assured.

(j) Arrangements for the provision of accommodation and other services to any 16 and 17 year old who is neither being accommodated by children's services under section 20 nor owed the main accommodation duty. This might happen, for example, where a young person is not eligible under the provisions of the homelessness legislation, or has been found to have become homeless intentionally, and is a child in need who does not wish to be accommodated under section 20.

(k) Integrated monitoring arrangements to provide management information regarding outcomes for young people including through reconciliation with parents or carers.

(l) Processes for resolving any disputes arising between staff from children's services and staff from housing services (for example, where expectations for completing assessments within specified timescales have not been met).

(m) Provision of advice and information to teenagers, including 16 or 17 year olds and their families, in relation to the help available to families with older teenagers, the available housing options for young people within the local area, their rights and how to access help.

(n) Arrangements for identifying longer term risk of homelessness where an assessment finds the young person is not homelessness or threatened with homelessness, and making arrangements to address risk factors and prevent future homelessness.

6.11 The effectiveness and continuing relevance of joint protocols should be reviewed at least annually. Local authorities may find it helpful to establish multi-agency arrangements to monitor the effectiveness of protocols and the performance of local services in responding to young people who are threatened with homelessness or who are homeless. Local authorities will need to consider at the outset what data will be required for monitoring purposes and how the agencies involved will collect and analyse it. These monitoring arrangements will contribute to wider monitoring of the overall effectiveness of local arrangements to safeguard children and young people and promote their welfare.

6.12 It would be good practice for young people who have been provided with services to be consulted about the quality of services and contribute to service reviews.

Operational joint working – integrated youth homelessness services

6.13 One option for service delivery is to establish an integrated 'front door' where children's and housing services work together to provide assessment, homelessness prevention and access to suitable accommodation. Such services may be based with, or otherwise involve other key statutory and third sector services for young people, including education and employment support, advice and support, and health and youth justice services.

6.14 Given that the 1989 Act takes precedence over the 1996 Act, and given their responsibilities for children in need in their areas, children's services should be the lead agency with regard to assessing and meeting the needs of 16 and 17 year olds who seek help because of homelessness.

6.15 An integrated approach can have a number of benefits, for example:

(a) improvement of joint working and information sharing through enhanced communication between children's and housing services;

(b) enabling a joint approach to assessment, minimising the need for separate assessment activity by children's and housing services.

(c) a shared focus on preventing homelessness and co-ordinated approach to doing so;

(d) giving 16 and 17 year olds, and their families, access to information directly from both services regarding the support and, if necessary, accommodation options that may be available both now and in the future;

(e) co-ordinated multi-agency planning and support focussed around the young person and their family, ensuring that they do not have to repeat their stories or risk being passed between authorities.

Strategic joint working

6.16 Children's services should be linked to housing authorities' strategic housing function.

6.17 The anticipated accommodation and support needs of vulnerable young people, including homeless 16 and 17 year olds and care leavers, should be represented in relevant strategies and plans including homelessness strategies, supported housing strategies or commissioning plans, sufficiency strategies, and plans or strategies to coordinate multi-agency working to safeguard children locally and monitor and challenge the effectiveness of local arrangements.

6.18 Consideration should be given to developing collaboration between children's services and commissioners of housing and support services to meet the housing needs of young people in the area including providing suitable accommodation placements for looked after children aged 16 and 17. Services jointly planned and secured might include supported accommodation, floating support, supported lodgings, and more specialist housing provision for particularly vulnerable young people.

ANNEX:
Factors to be considered by children's services when assessing 16–17 year olds who may be children in need

	Dimensions of need	Issues to consider in assessing child's future needs
1	**Accommodation**	Does the child have access to stable accommodation? How far is this suitable to the full range of the child's needs?
2	**Family and social relationships**	Assessment of the child's relationship with their parents and wider family. What is the capacity of the child's family and social network to provide stable and secure accommodation and meet the child's practical, emotional and social needs.
3	**Emotional and behavioural development**	Does the child show self esteem, resilience and confidence? Assessment of their attachments and the quality of their relationships. Does the child show self control and appropriate self awareness?
4	**Education, training and employment**	Information about the child's education experience and background. Assessment as to whether support may be required to enable the child to access education, training or employment.
5	**Financial capability and independent living skills**	Assessment of the child's financial competence and how they will secure financial support in future. Information about the support the child might need to develop self-management and independent living skills.
6	**Health and development**	Assessment of child's physical, emotional and mental health needs.
7	**Identity**	Assessment of the child's needs as a result of their ethnicity, preferred language, cultural background, religion or sexual identity.

Index